Microsoft® ACCESS® 2013

COMPREHENSIVE

ENHANCED EDITION

Microsoft® ACCESS® 2013

COMPREHENSIVE

ENHANCED EDITION

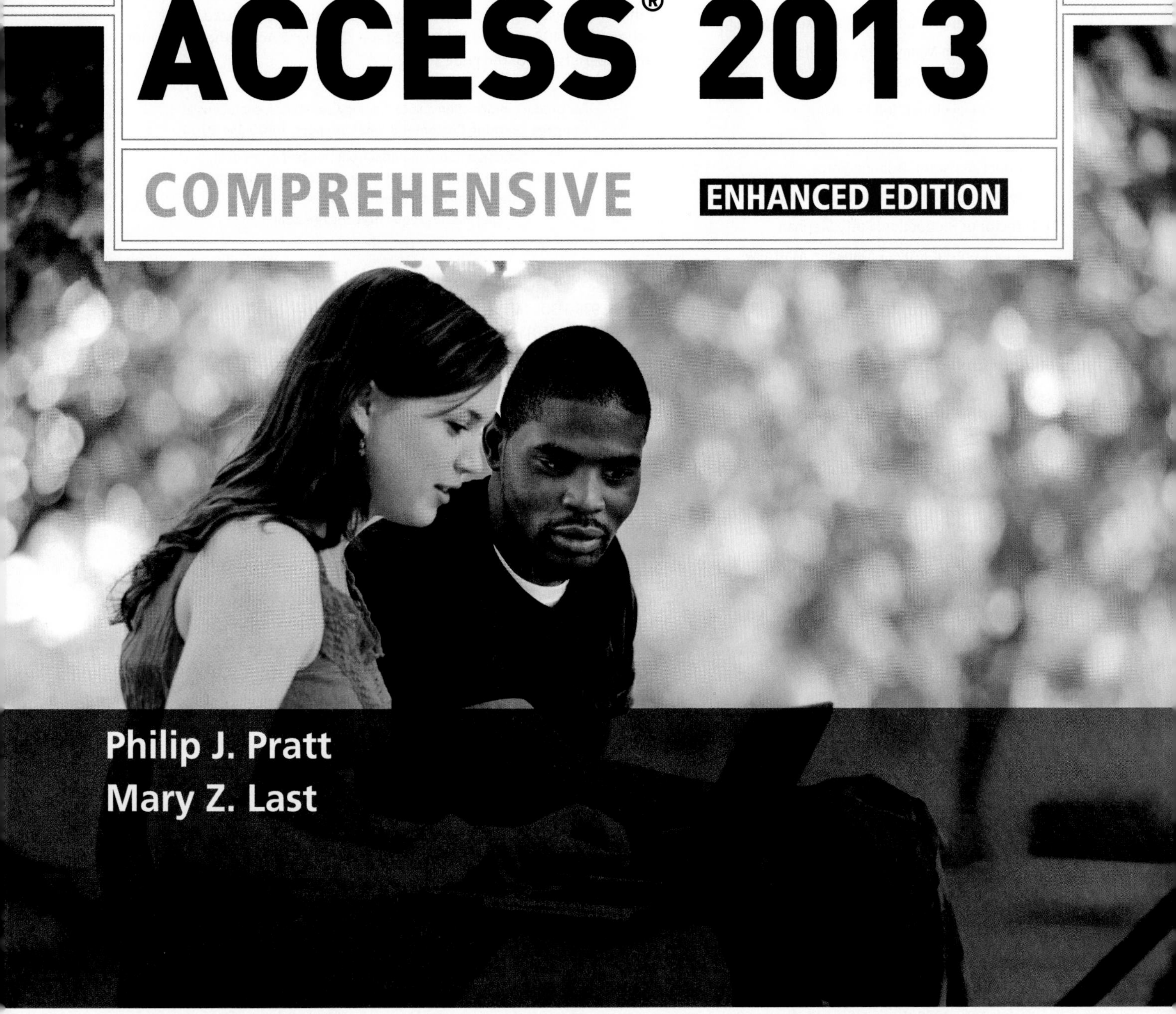

Philip J. Pratt
Mary Z. Last

CENGAGE Learning®

SHELLY CASHMAN SERIES®

Australia • Brazil • Japan • Korea • Mexico • Singapore • Spain • United Kingdom • United States

CENGAGE Learning

Microsoft® Access® 2013: Comprehensive Enhanced Edition
Philip J. Pratt and Mary Z. Last

Product Director: Kathleen McMahon

Senior Director of Development: Marah Bellegarde

Senior Product Team Manager: Lauren Murphy

Product Team Manager: Brian Hyland

Product Development Manager: Leigh Hefferon

Content Developer: Jon Farnham

Associate Content Developer: Crystal Parenteau

Product Assistant: Brianna Vorce

Development Editor: Amanda Brodkin

Director of Production: Patty Stephan

Senior Content Project Manager: Matthew Hutchinson

Marketing Director: Michele McTighe

Marketing Manager: Kristie Clark

Manufacturing Planner: Julio Esperas

QA Manuscript Reviewers: Jeffrey Schwartz, John Freitas, Serge Palladino, Susan Pedicini, Danielle Shaw, Susan Whalen

Composition: Lumina Datamatics, Inc.

Art Director: Marissa Falco

Text Design: Joel Sadagursky

Cover Design: Lisa Kuhn, Curio Press, LCC

Cover Photo: Tom Kates Photography

Proofreader: Lumina Datamatics, Inc.

WCN: 01-100-101

Library of Congress Control Number: 2015934257

ISBN-13: 978-1-305-50115-7
ISBN-10: 1-305-50115-2

Cengage Learning
20 Channel Center Street
Boston, MA 02210
USA

Cengage Learning is a leading provider of customized learning solutions with office locations around the globe, including Singapore, the United Kingdom, Australia, Mexico, Brazil, and Japan. Locate your local office at: **international.cengage.com/region**

Cengage Learning products are represented in Canada by Nelson Education, Ltd.

To learn more about Cengage Learning, visit **www.cengage.com**

Purchase any of our products at your local college bookstore or at our preferred online store at **www.cengagebrain.com**

We dedicate this book to the memory of Thomas J. Cashman (4/29/32 – 1/7/15). As one of the founders of the Shelly Cashman Series, Tom partnered with Gary Shelly to write and publish their first computer education textbook in 1969, revolutionizing the introductory computing course and changing the path of computing course materials. From 1969 through his retirement in 2008, Tom served as educator, author, leader, and inspiration to his fellow authors and Shelly Cashman Series team members. His mark on the series and the introductory computing market is indelible and he will be both remembered and missed.

Printed in the United States of America
1 2 3 4 5 6 7 18 17 16 15

Microsoft® ACCESS® 2013

COMPREHENSIVE **ENHANCED EDITION**

Contents

Microsoft Office 365

Office 365 Essentials

Microsoft Access 2013

CHAPTER ONE

Databases and Database Objects: An Introduction

CHAPTER TWO
Querying a Database

CHAPTER THREE
Maintaining a Database

CHAPTER ELEVEN
Database Design

Preface

The Shelly Cashman Series® offers the finest textbooks in computer education. We are proud that since Mircosoft Office 4.3, our series of Microsoft Office textbooks have been the most widely used books in education. With each new edition of our Office books, we make significant improvements based on the software and comments made by instructors and students. For this Microsoft Access 2013 text, the Shelly Cashman Series development team carefully reviewed our pedagogy and analyzed its effectiveness in teaching today's Office student. Students today read less, but need to retain more. They need not only to be able to perform skills, but to retain those skills and know how to apply them to different settings. Today's students need to be continually engaged and challenged to retain what they're learning.

With this Microsoft Access 2013 text, we continue our commitment to focusing on the users and how they learn best.

Objectives of This Textbook

Microsoft Access 2013: Comprehensive is intended for a ten- to fifteen-week period in a course that teaches Access 2013 as the primary component. No experience with a computer is assumed, and no mathematics beyond the high school freshman level is required. The objectives of this book are:

- To offer a comprehensive presentation of Microsoft Access 2013
- To expose students to practical examples of the computer as a useful tool
- To acquaint students with the proper procedures to create databases suitable for coursework, professional purposes, and personal use
- To help students discover the underlying functionality of Access 2013 so they can become more productive
- To develop an exercise-oriented approach that allows learning by doing

The Shelly Cashman Approach

A Proven Pedagogy with an Emphasis on Project Planning

Each chapter presents a practical problem to be solved within a project planning framework. The project orientation is strengthened by the use of the Roadmap, which provides a visual framework for the project. Step-by-step instructions with supporting screens guide students through the steps. Instructional steps are supported by the Q&A, Experimental Step, and BTW features.

A Visually Engaging Book that Maintains Student Interest

The step-by-step tasks, with supporting figures, provide a rich visual experience for the student. Call-outs on the screens that present both explanatory and navigational information provide students with information they need when they need to know it.

Supporting Reference Materials (Quick Reference)

With the Quick Reference, students can quickly look up information about a single task, such as keyboard shortcuts, and find page references to where in the book the task is illustrated.

Integration of the World Wide Web

The World Wide Web is integrated into the Access 2013 learning experience with (1) BTW annotations; (2) BTW, Q&A, and Quick Reference Summary Web pages; and (3) the Learn Online resources for each chapter.

End-of-Chapter Student Activities

Extensive end-of-chapter activities provide a variety of reinforcement opportunities for students to apply and expand their skills through individual and group work. To complete some of these assignments, you will be required to use the Data Files for Students. Visit www.cengage.com/ct/studentdownload for detailed access instructions or contact your instructor for information about accessing the required files.

New to this Edition

Enhanced Coverage of Critical Thinking Skills

A New Consider This element poses thought-provoking questions throughout each chapter, providing an increased emphasis on critical thinking and problem-solving skills. Also, every task in the project now includes a reason *why* the students are performing the task and *why* the task is necessary.

Enhanced Retention and Transference

A new Roadmap element provides a visual framework for each project, showing students where they are in the process of creating each project, and reinforcing the context of smaller tasks by showing how they fit into the larger project.

Integration of Office with Cloud and Web Technologies

A new Lab focuses entirely on integrating cloud and web technologies with Access 2013, using technologies like SkyDrive and Web Apps.

More Personalization

Each chapter project includes an optional instruction for the student to personalize his or her solution, if required by an instructor, making each student's solution unique.

More Collaboration

A new Research and Collaboration project has been added to the Consider This: Your Turn assignment at the end of each chapter.

Instructor Resources

The Instructor Resources include both teaching and testing aids and can be accessed at www.cengage.com/login.

Instructor's Manual Includes lecture notes summarizing the chapter sections, figures and boxed elements found in every chapter, teacher tips, classroom activities, lab activities, and quick quizzes in Microsoft Word files.

Syllabus Easily customizable sample syllabi that cover policies, assignments, exams, and other course information.

Figure Files Illustrations for every figure in the textbook in electronic form.

Powerpoint Presentations A multimedia lecture presentation system that provides slides for each chapter. Presentations are based on chapter objectives.

Solutions to Exercises Includes solutions for all end-of-chapter and chapter reinforcement exercises.

Test Bank & Test Engine Test banks powered by Cognero include 112 questions for every chapter, featuring objective-based and critical thinking question types, and including page number references and figure references, when appropriate.

Data Files for Students Includes all the files that are required by students to complete the exercises.

Additional Activities for Students Consists of Chapter Reinforcement Exercises, which are true/false, multiple-choice, and short answer questions that help students gain confidence in the material learned.

Learn Online

CengageBrain.com is the premier destination for purchasing or renting Cengage Learning textbooks, eBooks, eChapters, and study tools at a significant discount (eBooks up to 50% off Print). In addition, CengageBrain.com provides direct access to all digital products, including eBooks, eChapters, and digital solutions, such as MindTap and SAM, regardless of where purchased. The following are some examples of what is available for this product on www.cengagebrain.com.

SAM: Skills Assessment Manager Get your students workplace-ready with SAM, the market-leading proficiency-based assessment and training solution for Microsoft Office! SAM's active, hands-on environment helps students master Microsoft Office skills and computer concepts that are essential to academic and career success, delivering the most comprehensive online learning solution for your course!

Through skill-based assessments, interactive trainings, business-centric projects, and comprehensive remediation, SAM engages students in mastering the latest Microsoft Office programs on their own, giving instructors more time to focus on teaching. Computer concepts labs supplement instruction of important technology-related topics and issues through engaging simulations and interactive, auto-graded assessments. With enhancements including streamlined course setup, more robust grading and reporting features, and the integration of fully interactive MindTap Readers containing Cengage Learning's premier textbook content, SAM provides the best teaching and learning solution for your course.

MindLinks MindLinks is a new Cengage Learning Service designed to provide the best possible user experience and facilitate the highest levels of learning retention and outcomes, enabled through a deep integration of Cengage Learning's digital suite into an instructor's Learning Management System (LMS). MindLinks works on any LMS that supports the IMS Basic LTI open standard. Advanced features, including gradebook exchange, are the result of active, enhanced LTI collaborations with industry-leading LMS partners to drive the evolving technology standards forward.

course|notes™
quick reference guide

CourseNotes

Cengage Learning's CourseNotes are six-panel quick reference cards that reinforce the most important and widely used features of a software application in a visual and user-friendly format. CourseNotes serve as a great reference tool during and after the course. CourseNotes are available for software applications, such as Microsoft Office 2013. There are also topic-based CourseNotes available, such as Best Practices in Social Networking, Hot Topics in Technology, and Web 2.0. Visit www.cengagebrain.com to learn more!

Specialist
Certification Prep Tool

Certification Prep Tool

This textbook was developed to instruct on the Microsoft® Office 2013 certification objectives. Microsoft Corporation has developed a set of standardized, performance-based examinations that you can take to demonstrate your overall expertise with Microsoft Office 2013 programs. Microsoft Office 2013 certification provides a number of benefits for you:

- Differentiate yourself in the employment marketplace from those who are not Microsoft Office Specialist or Expert certified.
- Prove skills and expertise when using Microsoft Office 2013.
- Perform at a higher skill level in your job.
- Work at a higher professional level than those who are not certified.
- Broaden your employment opportunities and advance your career more rapidly.

For more information about Microsoft Office 2013 certification, including a complete list of certification objectives, visit the Microsoft website, http://www.microsoft.com/learning. To see which Microsoft Office 2013 certification objectives are addressed by the contents of this text and where each is included in the text, visit the Certification resource on the Student Companion Site located on www.cengagebrain.com. For detailed instructions about accessing available resources, visit www.cengage.com/ct/studentdownload or contact your instructor for information about accessing the required files.

About Our Covers

The Shelly Cashman Series is continually updating our approach and content to reflect the way today's students learn and experience new technology. This focus on student success is reflected on our covers, which feature real students from The University of Rhode Island using the Shelly Cashman Series in their courses, and reflect the varied ages and backgrounds of the students learning with our books. When you use the Shelly Cashman Series, you can be assured that you are learning computer skills using the most effective courseware available.

Textbook Walk-Through

The Shelly Cashman Series Pedagogy: Project-Based — Step-by-Step — Variety of Assessments

Roadmaps provide a visual framework for each project, showing the students where they are in the process of creating each project.

Step-by-step instructions provide a context beyond the point-and-click. Each step provides information on why students are performing each task and what will occur as a result.

Roadmap

In this chapter, you will learn how to create and use the database shown in Figure 1–1 on page AC 3. The following roadmap identifies general activities you will perform as you progress through this chapter:

1. CREATE the FIRST TABLE, Book Rep, using Datasheet view.
2. ADD RECORDS to the Book Rep table.
3. PRINT the CONTENTS of the Book Rep table.
4. IMPORT RECORDS into the second table, Customer.
5. MODIFY the SECOND TABLE using Design view.
6. CREATE a QUERY for the Customer table.
7. CREATE a FORM for the Customer table.
8. CREATE a REPORT for the Customer table.

At the beginning of step instructions throughout the chapter, you will see an abbreviated form of this roadmap. The abbreviated roadmap uses colors to indicate chapter progress: gray means the chapter is beyond that activity, blue means the task being shown is covered in that activity, and black means that activity is yet to be covered. For example, the following abbreviated roadmap indicates the chapter would be showing a task in the 3 PRINT CONTENTS activity.

1 CREATE FIRST TABLE | 2 ADD RECORDS | 3 PRINT CONTENTS | 4 IMPORT RECORDS | 5 MODIFY SECOND TABLE
6 CREATE QUERY | 7 CREATE FORM | 8 CREATE REPORT

Use the abbreviated roadmap as a progress guide while you read or step through ...er.

For an introduction to Windows and instruction about how to perform basic Windows tasks, read the Office and Windows chapter at the beginning of this book, where you can learn how to resize windows, change screen resolution, create folders, move and rename files, use Windows Help, and much more.

...uter to step through the project in this chapter and you ...e figures in this book, you should change your screen's ...information about how to change a computer's resolution, ...ws chap...

To View the Table in Design View

1 CREATE FIRST TABLE | 2 ADD RECORDS | 3 PRINT CONTENTS | 4 IMPORT RECORDS | 5 MODIFY SECOND TABLE
6 CREATE QUERY | 7 CREATE FORM | 8 CREATE REPORT

Even when creating a table in Datasheet view, Design view can be helpful. ***Why?*** *You easily can view the fields, data types, and properties to ensure you have entered them correctly. It is also easier to determine the primary key in Design view.* The following steps display the structure of the Book Rep table in Design view so that you can verify the design is correct.

1

- Tap or click the View arrow (TABLE TOOLS FIELDS tab | Views group) to display the View menu (Figure 1–14).

Q&A Could I just tap or click the View button rather than the arrow?
Yes. Tapping or clicking the button is equivalent to tapping or clicking the command represented by the icon currently appearing on the button. Because the icon on the button in Figure 1–14 is for Design view, tapping or clicking the button would display the table in Design view. If you are uncertain, you can always tap or click the arrow and select from the menu.

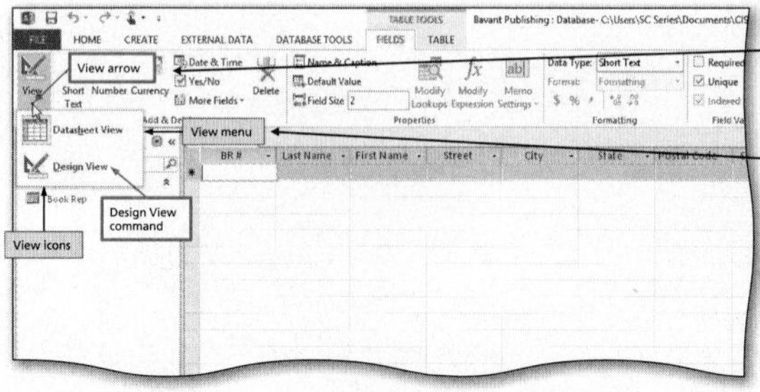

Figure 1–14

Navigational callouts in red show students where to click.

Explanatory callouts summarize what is happening on screen.

2

- Tap or click Design View on the View menu to view the table in Design view (Figure 1–15).

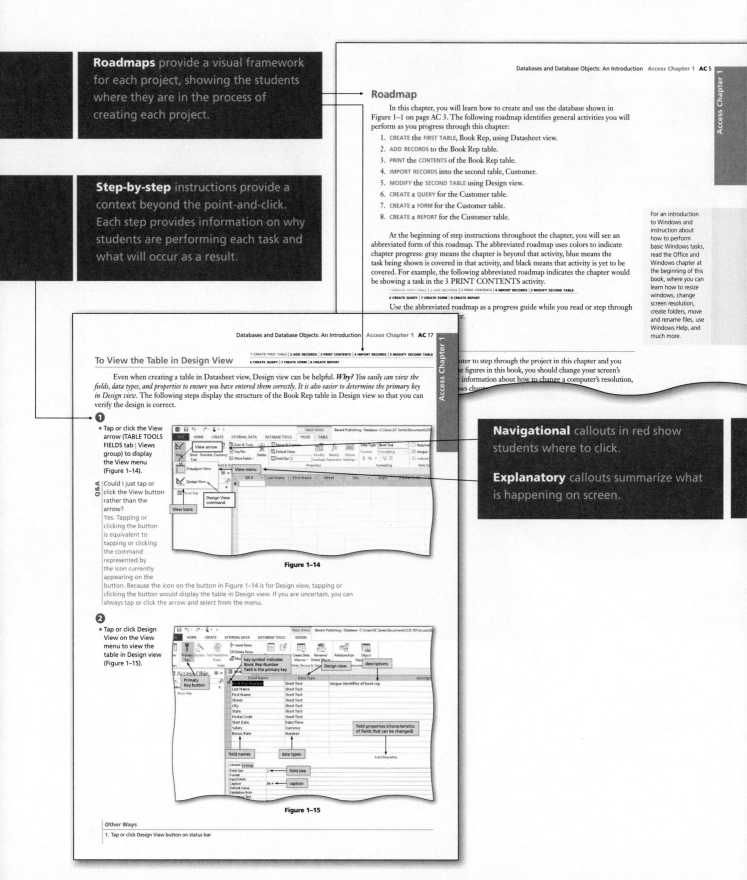

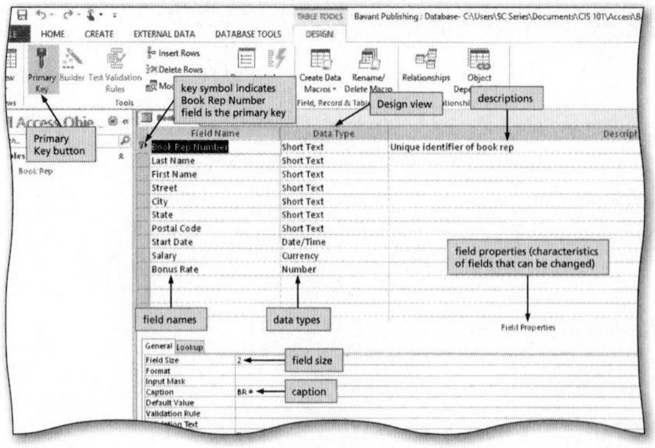

Figure 1–15

Other Ways

1. Tap or click Design View button on status bar

Textbook Walk-Through

The Shelly Cashman Series Pedagogy: Project-Based — Step-by-Step — Variety of Assessments

Q&A boxes anticipate questions students may have when working through the steps and provide additional information about what they are doing right where they need it.

Experiment Steps within the step-by-step instructions encourage students to explore, experiment, and take advantage of the features of the Office 2013 user interface. These steps are not necessary to complete the projects, but are designed to increase confidence with the software and build problem-solving skills.

To Create and View a Parameter Query

The following steps create a parameter query. ***Why?*** *The parameter query will give users at Bavant the ability to enter a different city when they run the query rather than having a specific city as part of the criterion in the query.* The steps also save the query with a new name.

1

- Return to Design view.
- Erase the current criterion in the City column, and then type `[Enter City]` as the new criterion (Figure 2–18).

Q&A What is the purpose of the square brackets?
The square brackets indicate that the text entered is not text that the value in the column must match. Without the brackets, Access would search for records on which the city is Enter City.

What if I typed a field name in the square brackets?
Access would simply use the value in that field. To create a parameter query, you must not use a field name in the square brackets.

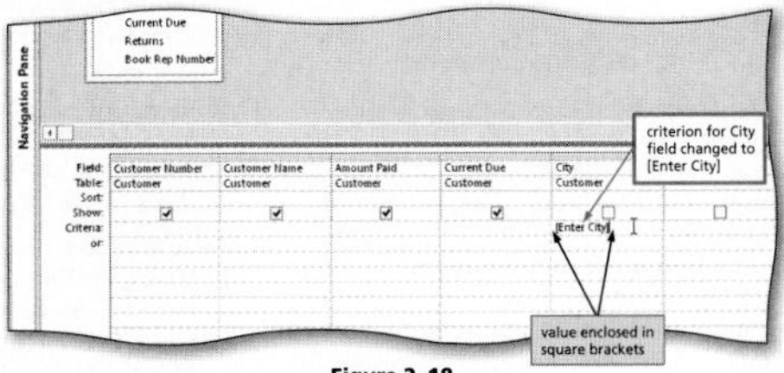

Figure 2–18

2

- Tap or click the Run button (QUERY TOOLS DESIGN tab | Results group) to display the Enter Parameter Value dialog box (Figure 2–19).

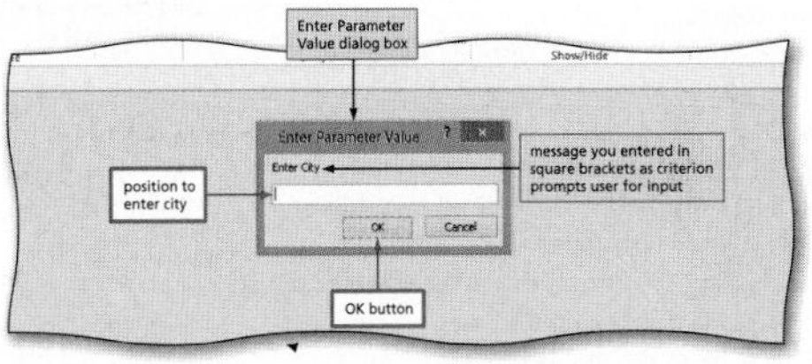

Figure 2–19

3

- Type `Adelphia` as the parameter value in the Enter City text box, and then tap or click the OK button (Enter Parameter Value dialog box) to close the dialog box and view the query (Figure 2–20).

Experiment

- Try using other characters between the square brackets. In each case, run the query. When finished, change the characters between the square brackets back to Enter City.

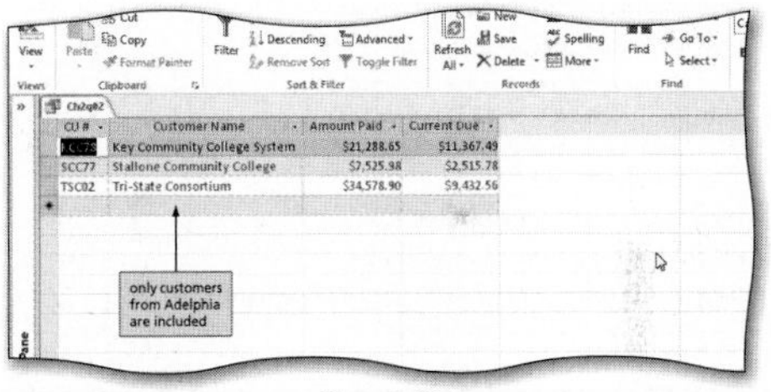

Figure 2–20

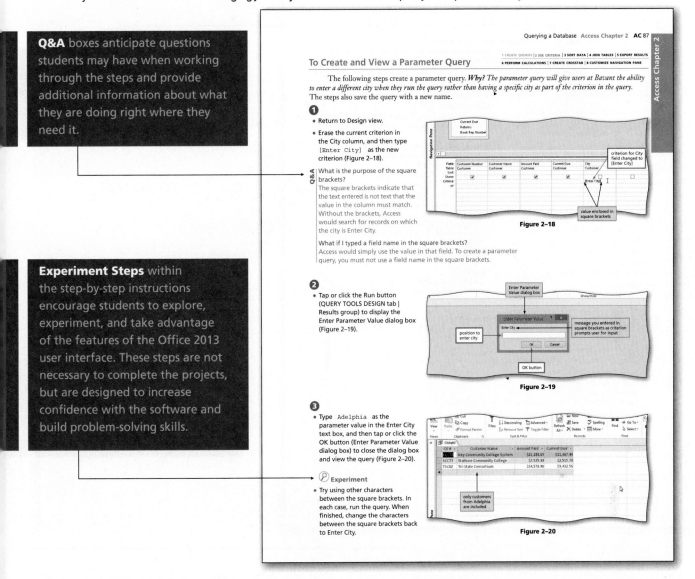

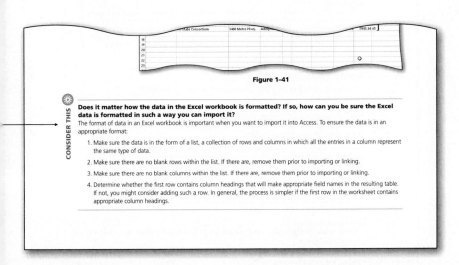

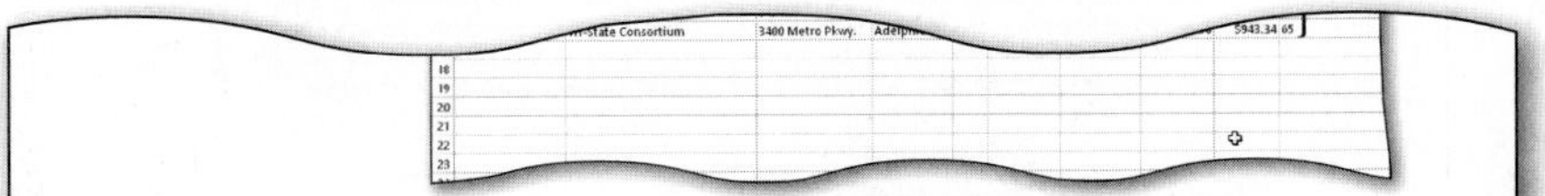

Figure 1–41

CONSIDER THIS

Does it matter how the data in the Excel workbook is formatted? If so, how can you be sure the Excel data is formatted in such a way you can import it?
The format of data in an Excel workbook is important when you want to import it into Access. To ensure the data is in an appropriate format:

1. Make sure the data is in the form of a list, a collection of rows and columns in which all the entries in a column represent the same type of data.
2. Make sure there are no blank rows within the list. If there are, remove them prior to importing or linking.
3. Make sure there are no blank columns within the list. If there are, remove them prior to importing or linking.
4. Determine whether the first row contains column headings that will make appropriate field names in the resulting table. If not, you might consider adding such a row. In general, the process is simpler if the first row in the worksheet contains appropriate column headings.

Consider This boxes pose thought-provoking questions with answers throughout each chapter, promoting critical thought along with immediate feedback.

AC 64 Access Chapter 1 Databases and Database Objects: An Introduction

Chapter Summary

In this chapter you have learned to create an Access database, create tables and add records to a database, print the contents of tables, import data, create queries, create forms, create reports, and change database properties. You also have learned how to design a database. The items listed below include all the new Access skills you have learned in this chapter, with tasks grouped by activity.

Database Object Management
- Delete a Table or Other Object in the Database (AC 58)
- Rename an Object in the Database (AC 58)

Database Properties
- Change Database Properties (AC 55)

File Management
- Run Access (AC 5)
- Create a Database (AC 6)
- Create a Database Using a Template (AC 7)
- Exit Access (AC 24)
- Open a Database from Access (AC 25)
- Back Up a Database (AC 56)
- Compact and Repair a Database (AC 57)
- Close a Database without Exiting Access (AC 57)
- Save a Database with Another Name (AC 57)

Form Creation
- Create a Form (AC 45)

Import Data
- Import an Excel Worksheet (AC 33)

Print Objects
- Preview and Print the Contents of a Table (AC 30)
- Print the Results of a Query (AC 45)
- Print a Report (AC 54)

Query Creation
- Use the Simple Query Wizard to Create a Query (AC 40)
- Use a Criterion in a Query (AC 43)

Report Creation
- Create a Report (AC 48)
- Modify Report Column Headings and Resize Columns (AC 50)
- Add Totals to a Report (AC 53)

Table Creation
- Modify the Primary Key (AC 11)
- Define the Remaining Fields in a Table (AC 14)
- Save a Table (AC 16)
- View the Table in Design View (AC 17)
- Change a Field Size in Design View (AC 18)
- Close the Table (AC 20)
- Resize Columns in a Datasheet (AC 28)
- Modify a Table in Design View (AC 37)

Table Update
- Add Records to a Table (AC 20)
- Add Records to a Table that Contains Data (AC 26)

CONSIDER THIS

What decisions will you need to make when creating your next database?

Use these guidelines as you complete the assignments in this chapter and create your own databases outside of this class.

1. Identify the tables that will be included in the database.
2. Determine the primary keys for each of the tables.
3. Determine the additional fields that should be included in each of the tables.
4. Determine relationships between the tables.
   a) Identify the "one" table.
   b) Identify the "many" table.
   c) Include the primary key of the "one" table as a field in the "many" table.
5. Determine data types for the fields in the tables.
6. Determine additional properties for fields.
   a) Determine if a special caption is warranted.
   b) Determine if a special description is warranted.
   c) Determine field sizes.
   d) Determine formats.
7. Identify and remove any unwanted redundancy.
8. Determine a storage location for the database.
9. Determine the best method for distributing the database objects.

Chapter Summary A listing of the tasks completed within the chapter, grouped into major task categories in an outline format.

Consider This: Plan Ahead box presents a single master planning guide that students can use as they create documents on their own.

Apply Your Knowledge This exercise usually requires students to open and manipulate a file that parallels the activities learned in the chapter.

Databases and Database Objects: An Introduction Access Chapter 1 AC 65

STUDENT ASSIGNMENTS Access Chapter 1

CONSIDER THIS

How should you submit solutions to questions in the assignments identified with a ☼ symbol?

Every assignment in this book contains one or more questions identified with a ☼ symbol. These questions require you to think beyond the assigned database. Present your solutions to the questions in the format required by your instructor. Possible formats may include one or more of these options: write the answer; create a document that contains the answer; present your answer to the class; discuss your answer in a group; record the answer as audio or video using a webcam, smartphone, or portable media player; or post answers on a blog, wiki, or website.

Apply Your Knowledge

Reinforce the skills and apply the concepts you learned in this chapter.

Adding a Caption, Changing a Data Type, Creating a Query, a Form, and a Report

Note: To complete this assignment, you will be required to use the Data Files for Students. Visit www.cengage.com/ct/studentdownload for detailed instructions or contact your instructor for information about accessing the required files.

Instructions: Cosmetics Naturally Inc. manufactures and sells beauty and skin care products made with only natural ingredients. The company's products do not contain any synthetic chemicals, artificial fragrances, or chemical preservatives. Cosmetics Naturally has a database that keeps track of its sales representatives and customers. Each customer is assigned to a single sales rep, but each sales rep may be assigned to many customers. The database has two tables. The Customer table contains data on the customers who purchase Cosmetics Naturally products. The Sales Rep table contains data on the sales reps. You will add a caption, change a data type, create two queries, a form, and a report, as shown in Figure 1–83 on the next page.

Perform the following tasks:

1. Start Access, open the Apply Cosmetics Naturally database from the Data Files for Students, and enable the content.
2. Open the Sales Rep table in Datasheet view, add SR # as the caption for the Sales Rep Number field, and resize all columns to ... the layout of the table and

Textbook Walk-Through

Extend Your Knowledge projects at the end of each chapter allow students to extend and expand on the skills learned within the chapter. Students use critical thinking to experiment with new skills to complete each project.

STUDENT ASSIGNMENTS

Apply Your Knowledge *continued*

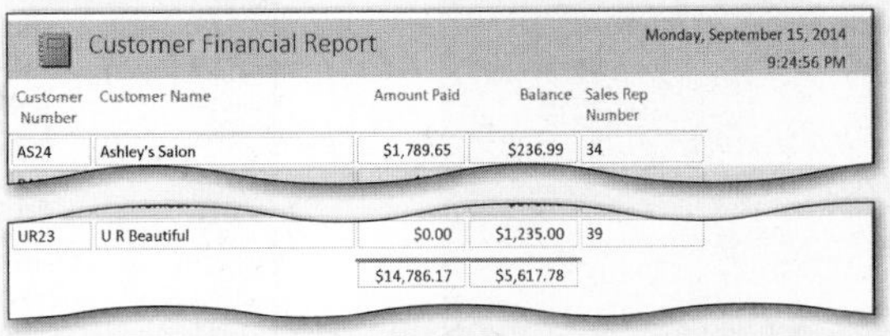

Customer Financial Report
Monday, September 15, 2014
9:24:56 PM
Customer Number
Customer Name
Amount Paid
Balance
Sales Rep Number
AS24
Ashley's Salon
$1,789.65
$236.99
34
UR23
U R Beautiful
$0.00
$1,235.00
39
$14,786.17
$5,617.78

Figure 1–83

Extend Your Knowledge

Extend the skills you learned in this chapter and experiment with new skills. You may need to use Help to complete the assignment.

Using a Database Template to Create a Contacts Database

Note: To complete this assignment, you will be required to use the Data Files for Students. Visit www.cengage.com/ct/studentdownload for detailed instructions or contact your instructor for information about accessing the required files.

Instructions: Access includes both desktop database templates and web-based templates. You can use a template to create a beginning database that can be modified to meet your specific needs. You will use a template to create a Contacts database. The database template includes sample tables, queries, forms, and reports. You will modify the database and create the Contacts Query shown in Figure 1–84.

Perform the following tasks:

1. Start Access.
2. Select the Desktop contacts template in the template gallery and create a new database with the file name Extend Contacts.
3. Enable the content. If requested to do so by your instructor, watch the videos in the Getting Started with Contacts dialog box. Close the Getting Started with Contacts dialog box.
4. Close the Contact List form.
5. Open the Contacts table in Datasheet view and delete the Fax Number field and the Attachments field in the table. The Attachments field has a paperclip as the column heading.
6. Change the data type for the ID field to Short Text, change the field name to Contact ID, and change the field size to 4. Change the column width so that the complete field name is

…cts table and close the table.

…d to create the Contacts Query shown in Figure 1–84. Close the

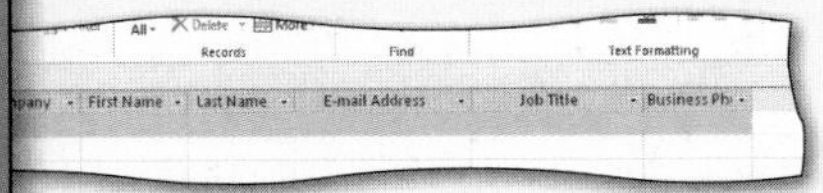

Figure 1–84

STUDENT ASSIGNMENTS Access Chapter 1

9. Open the Phone Book report in Layout view. Delete the control containing the date. Change the title of the report to Contact Phone List.
10. Save the changes to the report.
11. If requested to do so by your instructor, add your first and last names to the end of the title and save the changes to the report.
12. Submit the revised database in the format specified by your instructor.
13. a. Why would you use a template instead of creating a database from scratch with just the fields you need?
    b. The Attachment data type allows you to attach files to a database record. If you were using this database for a job search, what specific documents might you attach to a Contacts record?

Analyze, Correct, Improve

Analyze a database, correct all errors, and improve the design.

Correcting Errors in the Table Structure

Note: To complete this assignment, you will be required to use the Data Files for Students. Visit www.cengage.com/ct/studentdownload for detailed instructions or contact your instructor for information about accessing the required files.

Instructions: Analyze SciFi Movies is a database containing information on classic science fiction movies that your film professor would like to use for teaching. The Movie table shown in Figure 1–85 contains errors to the table structure. Your professor has asked you to correct the errors and make some improvements to the database. Start Access and open the Analyze SciFi Movies database from the Data Files for Students.

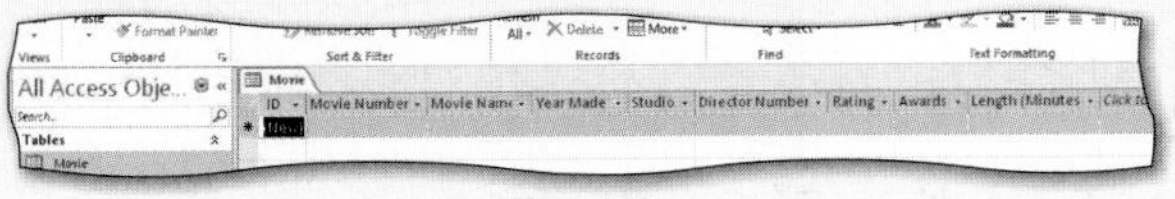

Figure 1–85

1. Correct Movie Number should be the primary key for the Movie table. The ID field should not be a field in the table. The Rating field represents a numerical rating system of one to four to indicate the quality of the movie. Your instructor wants to be able to find the average rating for films directed by a particular director. Only integers should be stored in both the Rating and the Length (Minutes) fields.

2. Improve The default field size for Short Text fields is 255. Changing the field size to more …ately represent the maxim… …ored in a field is one way t…

Analyze, Correct, Improve projects call on the students to analyze a file, discover errors in it, fix the errors, and then improve upon the file using the skills they learned in the chapter.

In the Lab Three in-depth assignments in each chapter that require students to apply the chapter concepts and techniques to solve problems. One Lab is devoted entirely to Cloud and Web 2.0 integration.

STUDENT ASSIGNMENTS

In the Labs

Design, create, modify, and/or use a database following the guidelines, concepts, and skills presented in this chapter. Labs are listed in order of increasing difficulty. Labs 1 and 2, which increase in difficulty, require you to create solutions based on what you learned in the chapter; Lab 3 requires you to create a solution, which uses cloud and web technologies, by learning and investigating on your own from general guidance.

Lab 1: Creating Objects for the Dartt Offsite Services Database

Problem: Dartt Offsite Services is a local company that provides offsite data services and solutions. The company provides remote data backup, disaster recovery planning and services, website backup, and offsite storage of paper documents for small businesses and nonprofit organizations. Service representatives are responsible for communicating data solutions to the client, scheduling backups and other tasks, and resolving any conflicts. The company recently decided to store its client and service rep data in a database. Each client is assigned to a single service rep, but each service rep may be assigned many clients. The database and the Service Rep table have been created, but the Monthly Salary field needs to be added to the table. The records shown in Table 1–6 must be added to the Service Rep table. The company plans to import the Client table from the Excel worksheet shown in Figure 1–86. Dartt would like to finish storing this data in a database and has asked you to help.

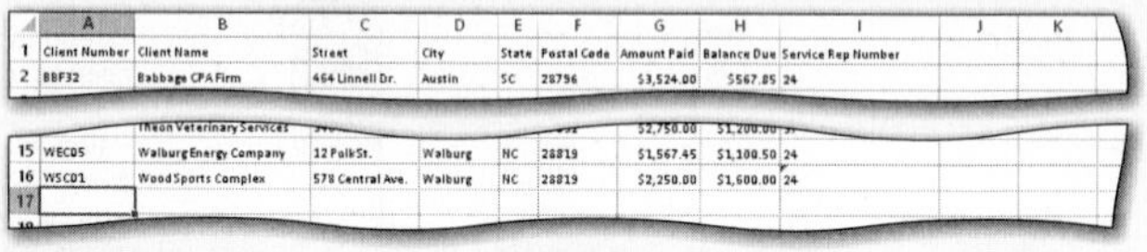

Figure 1–86

Note: To complete this assignment, you will be required to use the Data Files for Students. Visit www.cengage.com/ct/studentdownload for detailed instructions or contact your instructor for information about accessing the required files.

Instructions: Perform the following tasks:

1. Start Access and open the Lab 1 Dartt Offsite Services database from the Data Files for Students.
2. Open the Service Rep table in Datasheet view and add the Monthly Salary field to the end of the table. The field has the Currency data type. Assign the caption SR # to the Service Rep Number field.
3. Add the records shown in Table 1–6.
4. Resize the columns to best fit the data. Save the changes to the layout of the table.

Table 1–6 Data for Service Rep Table

Service Rep Number	Last Name	First Name	Street	City	State	Postal Code	Start Date	Monthly Salary
21	Kelly	Jenna	25 Paint St.	Kyle	SC	28797	5/14/2012	$3,862.45
45	Scott	Josh	1925 Pine Rd.	Byron	SC	28795	4/28/2014	$3,062.08
24	Liu	Mia	265 Marble Dr.	Kyle	SC	28797	1/7/2013	$3,666.67
37	Martinez	Mike	31 Steel St.	Georgetown	SC	28794	5/13/2013	$3,285.00

STUDENT ASSIGNMENTS

Consider This: Your Turn

Apply your creative thinking and problem solving skills to design and implement a solution.

1: Maintaining the Craft Database

Personal/Academic

Instructions: Open the Craft database you used in Chapter 2 on page AC 133. If you did not create this database, contact your instructor for information about accessing the required files.

Part 1: Use the concepts and techniques presented in this chapter to modify the database as follows:

a. The minimum price of any item is $4.00.
b. The Description field should always contain data.
c. Ten oven pulls have been sold. Use an update query to change the on hand value from 25 to 15. Save the update query.
d. Tom Last (student code 4752) has created the items shown in Table 3–4. Use a split form to add these items to the Item table.

Table 3–4 Additional Records for Item table

Item Number	Description	Price	On Hand	Student Code
W128	Child's Stool	$115.00	3	4752
W315	Harmony Stool	$81.00	4	4752
W551	Skittle Pins	$4.00	15	4752

e. A Total Value (On Hand * Price) calculated field should be added to the Item table before the Student Code field. Set the Result Type to Currency and the Decimal Places to 2. (*Hint:* Result Type is a field property for calculated fields.)
f. Specify referential integrity. Cascade the delete but not the update.
g. Add the Total Value field to the Wood Crafts for Sale report created in Chapter 1.
h. All the magazine [illegible] not want to make any m[illegible]

Consider This: Your Turn exercises call on students to apply creative thinking and problem solving skills to design and implement a solution.

Microsoft® ACCESS® 2013

COMPREHENSIVE **ENHANCED EDITION**

Student Success Guide

On the Path to Success

In this Student Success Guide, you explore tools, techniques, and skills essential to your success as a student. In particular, you focus on planning, time management, study tools, critical thinking, and problem solving. As you explore effective practices in these areas, you will also be introduced to Microsoft OneNote 2013, a free-form note-taking application in the Microsoft Office suite that lets you gather, organize, and share digital notes.

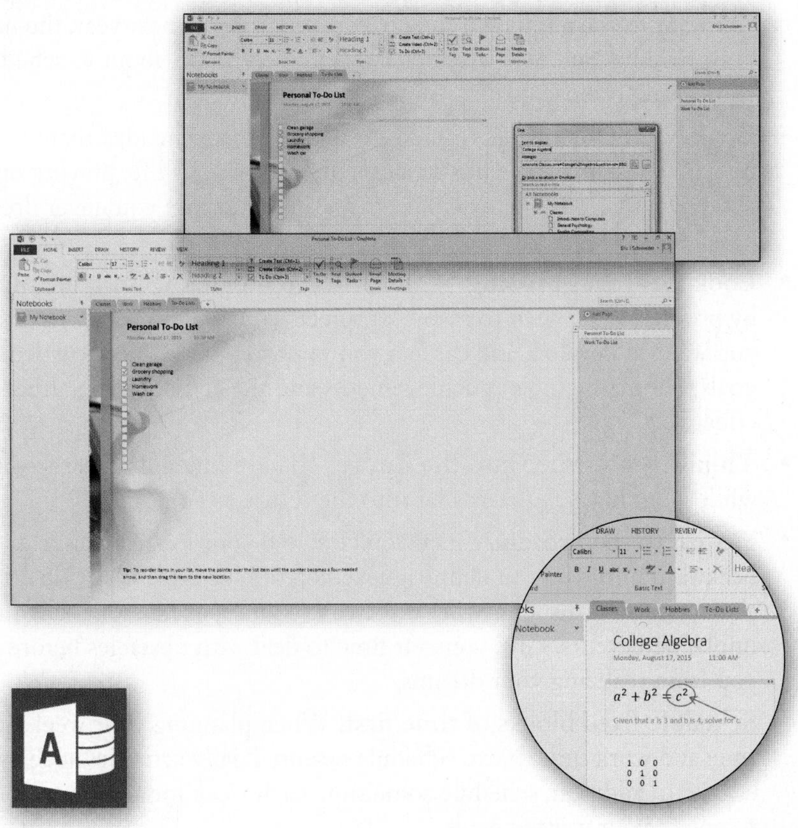

Objectives

You will have mastered the material in this chapter when you can:

- Use Microsoft OneNote to track tasks and organize ideas
- Set and achieve short-term and long-term goals
- Take notes during PowerPoint presentations
- Share OneNote content with others
- Apply critical-thinking strategies to evaluate information
- Follow a four-step process to solve problems

Planning Sets You Free

Benjamin Franklin once said, "If you fail to plan, you are planning to fail." When you set goals and manage time, your life does not just happen by chance. Instead, you design your life. Planning sets you free.

Without planning, you simply dig in and start writing or generating material you might use — but might not. You can actually be less productive and busier at the same time. Planning replaces this haphazard behavior with clearly defined outcomes and action steps.

Planning is a creative venture that continues for a lifetime. Following are planning suggestions that flow directly from this point of view and apply to any type of project or activity, from daily tasks to a multiyear career:

- **Schedule for flexibility and fun.** Be realistic. Expect the unexpected. Set aside time for essential tasks and errands, but don't forget to make room for fun.
- **Back up to view a bigger picture.** Consider your longer-range goals — what you want to accomplish in the next six months, the next year, the next five years, and beyond. Ask whether the activities you're about to schedule actually contribute to those goals.
- **Look boldly for things to change.** Don't accept the idea that you have to put up with substandard results in a certain area of your life. Staying open-minded about what is possible to achieve can lead to a future you never dreamed was possible.
- **Look for what's missing — and what to maintain.** Goals are often fueled by problems you need to resolve, projects you need to complete, relationships you want to develop, and careers you want to pursue. However, consider other goals that maintain your achievements and the activities you already perform effectively.
- **Think even further into the future.** To have fun and unleash your creativity while planning, set goals as far into the future as you can.
- **Return to the present.** Once you've stated your longest-range goals, work backward until you can define a next step to take now. Write down the shorter-term goals along the way. Leave some space in your schedule for unplanned events. Give yourself time to deal with obstacles before they derail you from realizing your dreams.
- **Schedule fixed blocks of time first.** When planning your week, start with class time and work time. Next, schedule essential daily activities such as sleeping and eating. In addition, schedule some time each week for actions that lead directly to one of your written goals.
- **Set clear starting and stopping times.** Set a timer and stick to it. Set aside a specific number of minutes or hours to spend on a certain task. Feeling rushed or sacrificing quality is not the goal here. The point is to push yourself and discover your actual time requirements.
- **Plan for changes in your workload.** To manage your workload over the length of a term or project, plan for a change of pace. Stay on top of your assignments right from the start. Whenever possible, work ahead.
- **Involve others when appropriate.** When you schedule a task that depends on another person's involvement, let that person know — the sooner, the better.

- **Start the day with your Most Important Task.** Review your to-do list and calendar first thing each morning. For an extra level of clarity, condense your to-do list to only one top-priority item — your Most Important Task. Do it as early in the day as possible, impeccably, and with total attention.
- **Plan in a way that works for you.** You can perform the kind of planning that sets you free with any set of tools. What matters above all is clear thinking and specific intentions. You can take any path that leads to your goal.

As you continue through this chapter, you will learn how to use Microsoft OneNote to plan, organize, and maintain the important information and ideas in your life. You will also explore methods for setting and achieving goals, improving study practices, and thinking critically to solve problems.

Quick Tour of Microsoft OneNote

Microsoft OneNote is part of the Microsoft Office suite and provides a single location for storing everything that is important to you, accessible from any device or on the web. Using OneNote, you store information in a **notebook**, a collection of electronic pages with text, graphics, and other content, including sound and video recordings. You organize the pages into tabbed sections as you would a tabbed ring binder. In your school notebook, for example, create a section for each of your courses, and then take notes during class on the pages within each section.

Exploring the OneNote Interface

As part of the Microsoft Office suite, the Microsoft OneNote 2013 desktop application contains a ribbon at the top of the window with seven default tabs: FILE, HOME, INSERT, DRAW, HISTORY, REVIEW, and VIEW. See Figure 1.

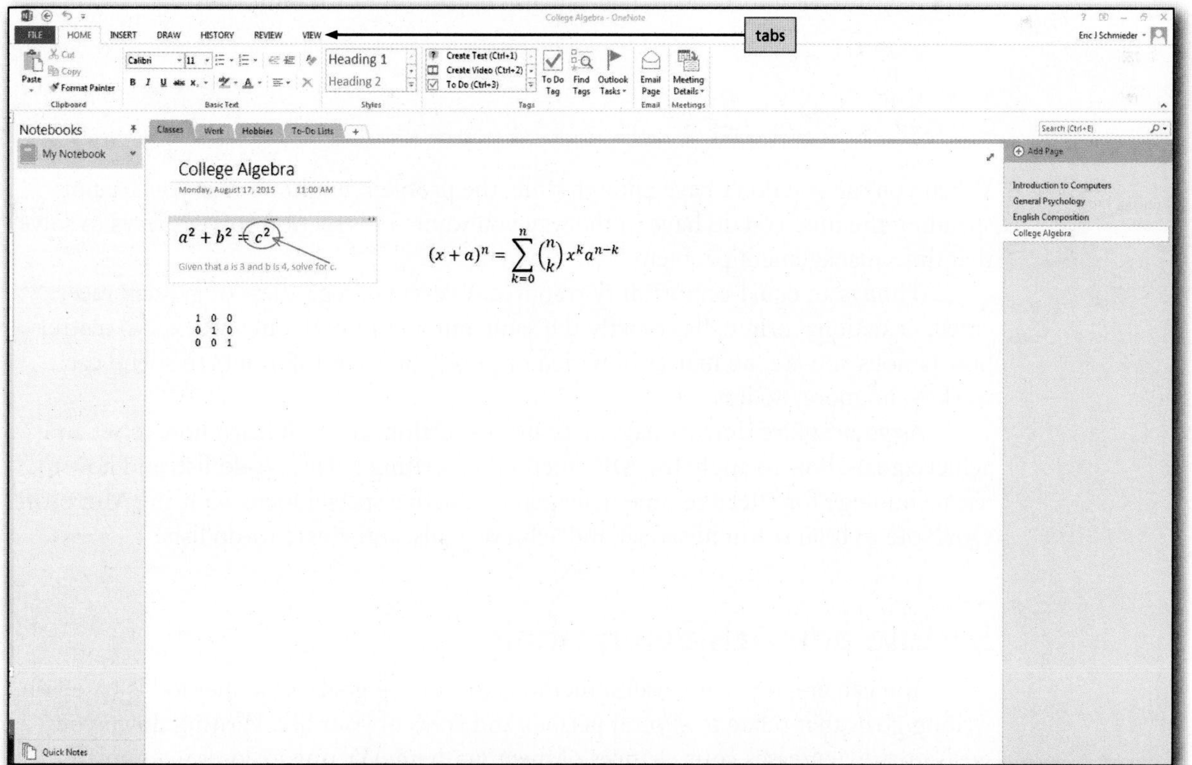

Figure 1 Microsoft OneNote 2013 ribbon

Each tab contains the following types of commands and features:

- **HOME tab**: This tab contains the most commonly used commands and features of Microsoft OneNote, which are divided into six groups: Clipboard, Basic Text, Styles, Tags, Email, and Meetings.
- **INSERT tab**: This tab includes commands for inserting tables, files, images, links, audio and video recordings, date/time stamps, page templates, and symbols.
- **DRAW tab**: This tab includes commands and tools for writing notes on pages, inserting shapes, arranging content, and converting handwritten notes to text or mathematical symbols.
- **HISTORY tab**: This tab includes tools for reviewing unread notes, managing multiple authors in a notebook, and reviewing pages and content in previous versions or pages and content that have been placed in the Notebook Recycle Bin.
- **REVIEW tab**: This tab provides research tools, including a spelling checker and thesaurus, language and translation tools, password-protection options, and links to other notebook sections and pages.
- **VIEW tab**: This tab contains page setup options, zoom tools, and application views, including docking options and the Send to OneNote tool.

Using Page Templates

To get started with OneNote and fill a blank page more quickly and easily, OneNote provides a collection of page templates. A **page template** is a design you apply to new pages in your notebook to provide an appealing background or to create a consistent layout. The OneNote page templates are organized into five categories: Academic, Blank, Business, Decorative, and Planners.

Additional templates are available on Office.com. After you define a standard way of organizing information, you can also create your own templates.

Time Management

When you say you don't have enough time, the problem might be that you are not spending the time you do have in the way you want. This section surveys ways to solve that time-management problem.

Time is an equal-opportunity resource. Everyone, regardless of gender, race, creed, or national origin, has exactly the same number of hours in a week. No matter how famous you are, no matter how rich or poor, you have 168 hours to spend each week — no more, no less.

As you explore time management in this section, you will learn how to set and achieve goals, how to apply the ABC method to writing a daily to-do list, and how to use technology for effective time management, with a special focus on using Microsoft OneNote to brainstorm ideas, set and achieve goals, and create to-do lists.

Setting and Achieving Goals

You can employ many useful methods for setting goals. One method is based on writing goals that relate to several periods and areas of your life. Writing down your goals greatly increases your chances of meeting them. Writing exposes incomplete information, undefined terms, unrealistic deadlines, and other symptoms of fuzzy thinking.

Write Specific Goals

State your written goals as observable actions or measurable results. Think in detail about what will be different when you attain your goals. List the changes in what you'll see, feel, touch, taste, hear, be, do, or have. Specific goals make clear what actions you need to take or what results you can expect. Figure 2 compares vague and specific goals.

Vague Goal	Specific Goal
Get a good education.	Graduate with BS degree in engineering, with honors, by 2017.
Get good grades.	Earn a 3.5 grade point average next semester.
Enhance my spiritual life.	Meditate for 15 minutes daily.
Improve my appearance.	Lose 6 pounds during the next 6 months.
Gain control of my money.	Transfer $100 to my savings account each month.

Figure 2 Vague and specific goals

Write Goals for Several Time Frames

To develop a comprehensive vision of your future, write down the following types of goals:

- **Long-term goals**: Long-term goals represent major targets in your life. They can include goals in education, careers, personal relationships, travel, financial security, and more — whatever is important to you.
- **Midterm goals**: Midterm goals are objectives you can accomplish in one to five years. They include goals such as completing a course of education, paying off a car loan, or achieving a specific career level. These goals usually support your long-term goals.
- **Short-term goals**: Short-term goals are the ones you can accomplish in a year or less. These goals are specific achievements that require action now or in the near future.

Write Goals in Several Areas of Life

People who set goals in only one area of life may find that their personal growth becomes one-sided. They might experience success at work while neglecting their health or relationships with family members and friends.

To avoid this outcome, set goals in a variety of categories, such as education, career, financial life, family life or relationships, social life, contribution (volunteer activities, community services), spiritual life, and level of health. Add goals in other areas as they occur to you.

Reflect on Your Goals

Each week, take a few minutes to think about your goals. You can perform the following spot checks:

- **Check in with your feelings.** Think about how it feels to set your goals. Consider the satisfaction you'll gain in attaining your objectives. If you don't feel a significant emotional connection with a written goal, consider letting it go or filing it away to review later.

- **Check for alignment.** Look for connections among your short-term to midterm goals and your midterm to long-term goals. Look for a fit between all of your goals and your purpose for taking part in higher education as well as your overall purpose in life.
- **Check for obstacles.** Complications can come between you and your goals, such as constraints on time and money. Anticipate obstacles and look for solutions.
- **Check for next steps.** Decide on a series of small, achievable steps you can take to accomplish your short-term goals. Write down these small steps on a daily to-do list. Note your progress and celebrate your successes.

Take Action Immediately

To increase your odds of success, take immediate action. Decrease the gap between stating a goal and starting to achieve it. If you slip and forget about the goal, you can get back on track at any time by *doing* something about it.

Using OneNote to Set Goals

The versatility of Microsoft OneNote allows you to write ideas anywhere on the page, identify notes with a variety of tags, and organize notes into pages and sections, making it a great tool for writing down your goals, organizing your thoughts and ideas, and building connections among them all.

Brainstorm with Quick Notes

Ideas often present themselves without order, structure, or clear fit in the organization of your existing content. Microsoft OneNote provides a feature called Quick Notes for such ideas. A **Quick Note** is a small window you can move anywhere on-screen and use to write reminders and other short notes. Getting the ideas on paper (or in your OneNote notebook) can be the first step in using them to define larger ideas and related goals. Quick Notes are initially unfiled within your notebook, but you can easily move or copy them to other sections. Think of an electronic Quick Note as you would a sticky note on your desk.

Organize Larger Ideas with Sections and Pages

For larger or more defined ideas, establish an organization system in your OneNote notebook so you can easily locate related information. OneNote provides multiple levels of organization within a notebook.

Most OneNote users store content on pages within sections. As your use of OneNote increases, you can organize related sections into groups or increase the detail of pages by creating subpages for better organization. See Figure 3.

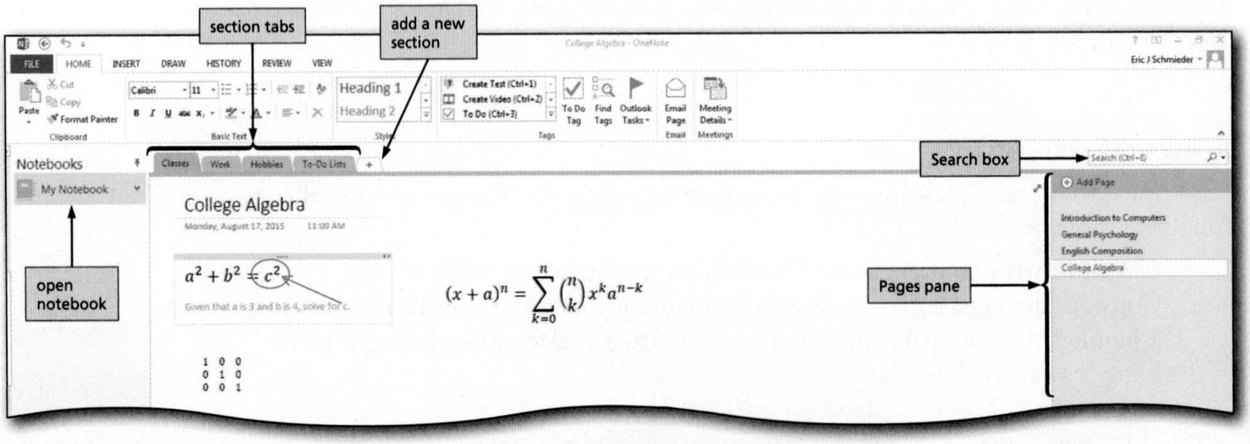

Figure 3 OneNote section tabs and Pages pane

Use Tags to Organize Content in OneNote

OneNote lets you mark notes and other content with tags — keywords that help you find important information — to set reminders, classify information, or set priorities, for example. OneNote provides the following tags by default: To Do, Important, Question, Remember for later, Definition, Highlight, Contact, Address, Phone number, website to visit, Idea, Password, Critical, Project A, Project B, Movie to see, Book to read, Music to listen to, Source for article, Remember for blog, Discuss with <Person A>, Discuss with <Person B>, Discuss with manager, Send in email, Schedule meeting, Call back, To Do priority 1, To Do priority 2, and Client request.

You assign a tag to page content by moving the insertion point to the text you want to tag and then selecting an item from the Tags gallery on the HOME tab of the ribbon. You can create custom tags to meet personal needs for organizing OneNote content in your notebooks.

Creating an ABC Daily To-Do List

One advantage to keeping a daily to-do list is that you don't have to remember what to do next. It's on the list. A typical day in the life of a student is full of separate, often unrelated tasks — reading, attending lectures, reviewing notes, working at a job, writing papers, researching special projects, and running errands. It's easy to forget an important task on a busy day. When that task is written down, you don't have to rely on your memory.

The following steps present the ABC method for creating and using to-do lists. This method involves ranking each item on your list according to three levels of importance: A, B, or C.

Step 1: Brainstorm Tasks

To get started, list all of the tasks you want to complete in a day. Each task will become an item on a to-do list. Don't worry about putting the entries in order or scheduling them yet. Just list everything you want to accomplish.

Step 2: Estimate Time

For each task you wrote down in Step 1, estimate how long it will take to complete the task. Estimating can be tricky. If you allow too little time, you end up feeling rushed. If you allow too much time, you become less productive. For now, use your best guess. If you are unsure, overestimate rather than underestimate how long you need for each task.

Add up the time you estimated to complete all your to-do items. Also add up the number of unscheduled hours in your day. Then compare the two totals. If you have more time assigned to tasks than unscheduled hours in the day, that's a potential problem. To solve it, proceed to Step 3.

Step 3: Rate Each Task by Priority

To prevent overscheduling, decide which to-do items are the most important given the time you have available. One suggestion for making this decision comes from the book *How to Get Control of Your Time and Your Life*, by Alan Lakein — simply label each task A, B, or C:

- The A tasks on your list are the most critical. They include assignments that are coming due or jobs that need to be done immediately.
- The B tasks on your list are important, but less so than the A tasks. They can be postponed, if necessary, for another day.

- The C tasks do not require immediate attention. C tasks are often small, easy jobs with no set deadline. They too can be postponed.

After labeling the items on your to-do list, schedule time for all of the A tasks.

Step 4: Cross off Tasks

Keep your to-do list with you at all times. Cross off, check, or otherwise mark activities when you finish them, and add new tasks when you think of them.

When using the ABC method, you might experience an ailment common to students: C fever. Symptoms include the uncontrollable urge to drop an A task and begin crossing off C items on your to-do list. The reason C fever is so common is that A tasks are usually more difficult or time consuming to achieve and have a higher risk of failure.

Use your to-do list to keep yourself on track, working on your A tasks. Don't panic or berate yourself when you realize that in the last six hours, you have completed nine Cs and not a single A. Just calmly return to the A tasks.

Step 5: Evaluate

At the end of the day, evaluate your performance. Look for A priorities you didn't complete. Look for items that repeatedly turn up as Bs or Cs on your list and never seem to get done. Consider changing them to A tasks or dropping them altogether. Similarly, you might consider lowering the priority of an A task you didn't complete to a B or C task.

When you're finished evaluating, start on tomorrow's to-do list. That way, you can wake up and start working on tasks productively without panicking about what to do.

Creating To-Do Lists in OneNote

The To Do tag in OneNote makes it easy to change any notebook item into a task. When you select an item and then assign the To Do tag to it, a check box appears next to the item. Insert a check mark in the box when you complete the task. You can also use the Planners subcategory of Page Templates in OneNote to generate Simple To Do Lists, Prioritized To Do Lists, and Project To Do Lists quickly and easily — leaving you to merely provide the action items. Figure 4 shows a to-do list based on the Simple To-Do List page template.

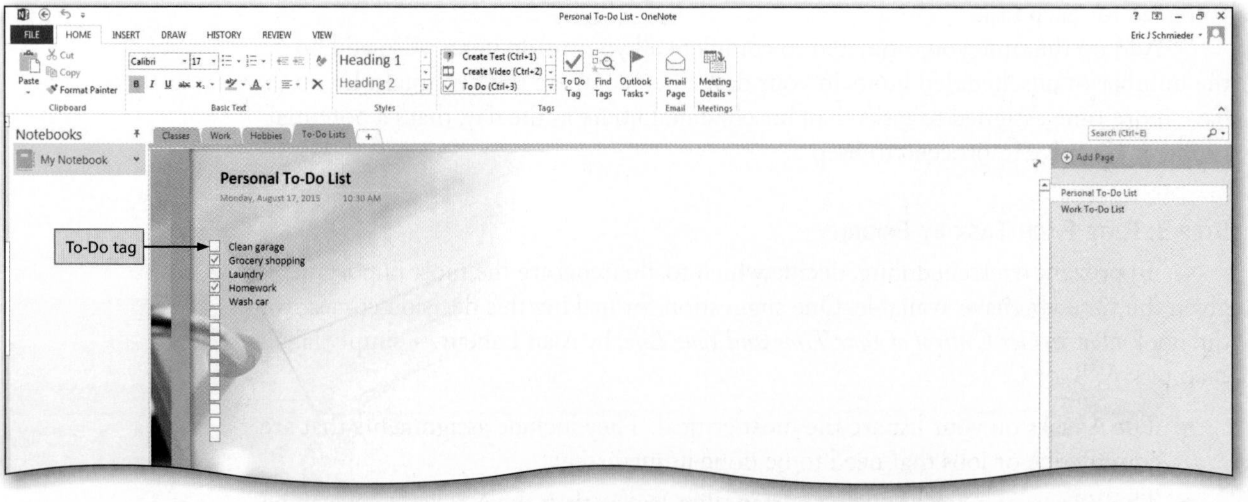

Figure 4 List based on the Simple To-Do List page template

Finding Time

Good news: You have enough time to accomplish the tasks you want to do. All it takes is thinking about the possibilities and making conscious choices.

Everything written about time management can be reduced to three main ideas:

1. Know exactly *what* you want. State your wants as clear, specific goals. Put them in writing.
2. Know *how* to get what you want. Take action to meet your goals. Determine what you'll do *today* to get what you want in the future. Put those actions in writing as well.
3. Strive for balance. When your life lacks balance, you spend most of your time responding to interruptions, last-minute projects, and emergencies. Life feels like a scramble just to survive. You're so busy achieving someone else's goals that you forget about getting what *you* want.

According to Stephen R. Covey, author of *The Seven Habits of Highly Effective People*, the purpose of planning is to carve out space in your life for tasks that are not urgent but are truly important. Examples are exercising regularly, reading, praying or meditating, spending quality time alone or with family members and friends, traveling, and cooking nutritious meals. Each of these tasks contributes directly to your personal goals for the future and to the overall quality of your life in the present.

Think of time management as time *investment*. Spend your most valuable resource in the way you choose.

Study Tools

In this section, you will learn ways to effectively use technology to promote positive study habits and successful results. Specifically, you explore ways to integrate Microsoft OneNote with PowerPoint presentations, web content, and **screen clippings**, also called screenshots, which are images of your screen that you capture using a OneNote tool. You will also learn techniques for interacting with e-books and for collaborating with others through the sharing features of OneNote and Office Online.

Turning PowerPoint Presentations into Powerful Notes

Some students stop taking notes during a PowerPoint presentation. This choice can be hazardous to your academic health for three major reasons:

- **PowerPoint presentations don't include everything.** Instructors and other speakers use PowerPoint to organize their presentations. Topics covered in the slides make up an outline of what your instructor considers important. Speakers create slides to flag the main points and signal transitions between topics. However, speakers usually enhance a presentation with examples and explanations that don't appear on the slides. In addition, slides will not contain any material from class discussion, including any answers that the instructor gives in response to questions.
- **You stop learning.** Taking notes forces you to capture ideas and information in your own words. The act of writing also helps you remember the material. If you stop writing and let your attention drift, you can quickly lose track of the presentation or topic.

- **You end up with major gaps in your notes.** When it's time to review your notes, you'll find that material from PowerPoint presentations is missing. This can be a major problem at exam time.

To create value from PowerPoint presentations, take notes directly on the slides. Continue to observe, record, and review. Use the presentation as a way to *guide* rather than to *replace* your own note taking.

Prepare Before the Presentation

Sometimes instructors make PowerPoint slides available before a lecture. Scan the slides, just as you would preview a reading assignment. Consider printing the slides and bringing them along to class. You can take notes directly on the printed pages.

If you use a laptop for taking notes during class, then you might not want to bother with printing. Open the PowerPoint presentation file and type your notes in the Notes pane, which appears below each slide.

Create OneNote Page Content from PowerPoint Slides

Use the File Printout button on the OneNote INSERT tab in the Files group to print PowerPoint slides directly to OneNote. You can store the slides where you keep your other notes and then take notes on the same page of your notebook as the slide content.

Take Notes During the Presentation

As you take notes during a presentation, be selective in what you write down. Determine what kind of material appears on each slide. Stay alert for new topics, main points, and important details. Taking too many notes makes it hard to keep up with a speaker and separate main points from minor details.

In any case, go *beyond* the slides. Record valuable questions and answers that come up during a discussion, even if they are not a planned part of the presentation.

Use Drawing Objects, Audio, and Video in Your Notes

On touch interface devices, OneNote makes it easy to handwrite your notes or draw symbols and shapes on the notebook pages. For mouse users, the OneNote DRAW tab contains predefined shapes and pen options for creating notes that are more than just text.

On devices that include microphones or webcams, you can use OneNote to capture audio and video recordings in your notebook pages, ensuring that every moment of an important lecture is captured for later review and study.

Review After the Presentation

If you printed out slides before class and took notes on those pages, then find a way to integrate them with the rest of your notes. For example, add references in your notebook to specific slides. Create summary notes that include the major topics and points from readings, class meetings, and PowerPoint presentations.

If you have a copy of the presentation, consider editing it. Cut slides that don't include information you want to remember. Rearrange slides so that the order makes more sense to you. Remember that you can open the original file later to see exactly what your instructor presented.

Add Links to Other Notebook Content

When creating summary note pages in your OneNote notebook, it is good practice to link text or content on the summary page to the detailed notes elsewhere in your notebook. To do so, select the content you want to use as the link, click the Link button in the Links group on the INSERT tab to open the Link dialog box (shown in Figure 5), and then select the location in the OneNote notebook with the detailed content.

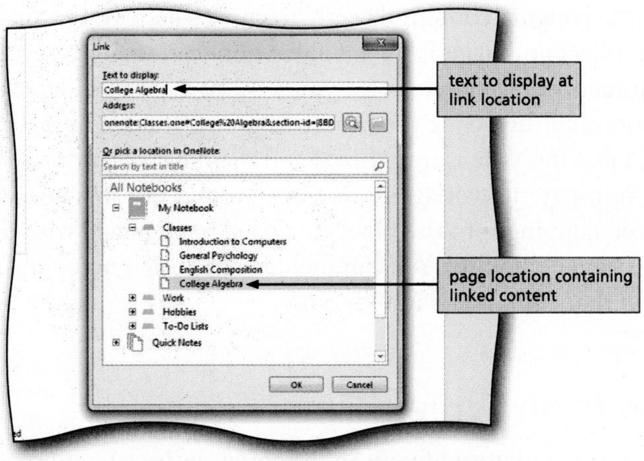

Figure 5 Link dialog box in OneNote 2013

Search Notes and Printouts

You can quickly locate content in your OneNote notebooks using the built-in search features of OneNote 2013. For basic text searches, you can limit the results to content on the current page, current section, current section group, current notebook, or all open notebooks.

After you apply tags to content within the notebook, use the Find Tags button in the Tags group on the HOME tab to locate and filter results based on tags.

Extending Reading to Webpages and E-Books

While reading, skilled readers focus on finding answers to their questions and flagging them in the text. E-books offer features that help with the following steps:

- **Access the table of contents.** For a bigger picture of the text, look for a table of contents that lists chapter headings and subheadings. Click a heading to expand the text for that part of the book.
- **Use navigation tools.** To flip electronic pages, look for Previous and Next buttons or arrows on the right and left borders of each page. Many e-books also offer a Go to Page feature that allows you to enter a specific page number to access the page.
- **Search the text.** Look for a search box that allows you to enter key words and find all the places in the text where those words are mentioned.
- **Follow links to definitions and related information.** Many e-books supply a definition to any word in the text. All you need to do is highlight a word and then click it.
- **Highlight and annotate.** E-books allow you to select words, sentences, or entire paragraphs and highlight them in a bright color. You can also annotate a book by entering your own notes on the pages.

Collect Web Content in OneNote

OneNote makes it easy to collect content with notations and links to the original source. When copying content from an electronic source, OneNote adds a reference to the original location below the pasted content. For web-based resources, OneNote inserts a hyperlink so you can access the source again later.

Insert Screen Clippings

In addition to copying content directly from websites, you can use the Screen Clipping tool to collect an image from any open application. To insert a screen clipping into a notebook, display the item you want to capture in another application, switch to OneNote, and then click the Screen Clipping button in the Images group on the INSERT tab. OneNote is minimized and the most recently used application is displayed with a transparent overlay. Draw a box around the area you want to capture to insert the screen clipping into the OneNote page as an image with details of when you collected the screen clipping. You can include additional notes and annotations using other text and drawing tools in OneNote.

Setting Limits on Screen Time

To get an accurate picture of your involvement in social networking and other online activity, monitor how much time you spend on them for one week. Make conscious choices about how much time you want to spend online and on the phone. Don't let social networking distract you from meeting personal and academic goals.

Using Technology to Collaborate

When planning group projects, look for tools that allow you to create, edit, and share documents, spreadsheets, drawings, presentations, and other files. You can find a growing list of applications for these purposes, including Office Online, which includes an online version of OneNote.

When using collaborative technology, your people skills are as important as your technology skills. Set up a process to make sure that everyone's voice is heard during a virtual meeting. People who are silenced will probably tune out.

Function as a professional whenever you're online. Team members might get to know you mainly through emails and instant messages. Consider the impression you're making with your online presence. Avoid slang, idioms, sarcastic humor, and other expressions that can create misunderstanding. A small dose of civility can make a big difference in the quality of your virtual team experience.

Use Office Online

Office Online is the free, online version of Microsoft Word, Microsoft Excel, Microsoft PowerPoint, and Microsoft OneNote available through Office 365, SharePoint Online, and OneDrive accounts. These tools provide basic functionality from the desktop applications directly in a web browser, giving you the ability to view and edit documents, workbooks, presentations, and notebooks from virtually any device with an Internet connection.

Supported by the cloud storage options associated with Office 365, SharePoint Online, and OneDrive, Office Online makes it easy to do real-time collaborative editing of shared files with classmates, friends, family, and colleagues.

Share Content from OneNote

If you store OneNote notebooks on OneDrive or SharePoint, you can share pages, sections, or entire notebooks with others by using the commands in the Share group on the OneNote FILE tab. You can even share paragraphs of text on pages by right-clicking selected content and then clicking the Copy Link to Paragraph option on the shortcut menu. Export pages, sections, or entire notebooks from OneNote in various formats, including PDF and XPS, for sharing with users who don't have Microsoft OneNote.

Critical Thinking and Problem Solving

It has been said that human beings are rational creatures. Yet no one is born as an effective thinker. Critical thinking — the objective analysis and evaluation of an issue in order to form a judgment — is a learned skill. This is one reason that you study so many subjects in higher education. A broad base of courses helps you develop as a thinker, giving you a foundation for dealing with complex challenges in your career, your relationships, and your community.

Following a Process for Critical Thinking

Learning to think well matters. The rewards are many, and the stakes are high. Major decisions in life — from choosing a major to choosing a spouse — depend on your thinking skills.

Following are strategies that you can use to move freely through six levels of thinking: remembering, understanding, applying, analyzing, evaluating, and creating. The strategies fall into three major categories: check your attitudes, check for logic, and check for evidence.

Check Your Attitudes

The following suggestions help you understand and analyze information free from bias and other filters that cloud clear thinking:

- **Be willing to find various points of view on any issue.** People can have dozens of viewpoints on every important issue. In fact, few problems have any single, permanent solution. Begin seeking alternative views with an open mind. When talking to another person, be willing to walk away with a new point of view — even if it's similar to your original idea, supported with new evidence.
- **Practice tolerance.** One path to critical thinking is tolerance for a wide range of opinions. Taking a position on important issues is natural. Problems emerge, however, when people become so attached to their current viewpoints that they refuse to consider alternatives.
- **Understand before criticizing.** The six levels of thinking build on each other. Before you agree or disagree with an idea, make sure that you *remember* it accurately and truly *understand* it. Polished debaters make a habit of doing this. Often they can sum up their opponent's viewpoint better than anyone else can. This puts them in a much stronger position to *apply*, *analyze*, *evaluate*, and *create* ideas.
- **Watch for hot spots.** Many people have mental "hot spots" — topics that provoke strong opinions and feelings. To become more skilled at examining various points of view, notice your own particular hot spots. In addition, be sensitive to other people's hot spots. Demonstrate tolerance and respect before discussing personal issues.

- **Be willing to be uncertain.** Some of the most profound thinkers have practiced the art of thinking by using a magic sentence: "I'm not sure yet." It is courageous and unusual to take the time to pause, look, examine, be thoughtful, consider many points of view — and be unsure. Uncertainty calls for patience. Give yourself permission to experiment, practice, and learn from mistakes.

Check for Logic

Learning to think logically offers many benefits: When you think logically, you take your reading, writing, speaking, and listening skills to a higher level. You avoid costly mistakes in decision making. You can join discussions and debates with more confidence, cast your votes with a clear head, and become a better-informed citizen.

The following suggestions will help you work with the building blocks of logical thinking — terms, assertions, arguments, and assumptions:

- **Define key terms.** A *term* is a word or phrase that refers to a clearly defined concept. Terms with several different meanings are ambiguous — fuzzy, vague, and unclear. One common goal of critical thinking is to remove ambiguous terms or define them clearly.
- **Look for assertions.** An *assertion* is a complete sentence that contains one or more key terms. The purpose of an assertion is to define a term or to state relationships between terms. These relationships are the essence of what we mean by the term *knowledge*.
- **Look for arguments.** For specialists in logic, an *argument* is a series of related assertions. There are two major types of reasoning used in building arguments — deductive and inductive. *Deductive reasoning* builds arguments by starting with a general assertion and leading to a more specific one. With *inductive reasoning*, the chain of logic proceeds in the opposite direction — from specific to general.
- **Remember the power of assumptions.** Assumptions are beliefs that guide our thinking and behavior. Assumptions can be simple and ordinary. In other cases, assumptions are more complex and have larger effects. Despite the power to influence our speaking and actions, assumptions are often unstated. People can remain unaware of their most basic and far-reaching assumptions — the very ideas that shape their lives. Heated conflict and hard feelings often result when people argue on the level of opinions and forget that the real conflict lies at the level of their assumptions.
- **Look for stated assumptions.** Stated assumptions are literally a thinker's starting points. Critical thinkers produce logical arguments and evidence to support most of their assertions. However, they are also willing to take other assertions as "self-evident" — so obvious or fundamental that they do not need to be proved.
- **Look for unstated assumptions.** In many cases, speakers and writers do not state their assumptions or offer evidence for them. In addition, people often hold many assumptions at the same time, with some of those assumptions contradicting each other. This makes uncovering assumptions a feat worthy of the greatest detective. You can follow a two-step method for testing the validity of any argument. First, state the assumptions. Second, see whether you can find any exceptions to the assumptions. Uncovering assumptions and looking for exceptions can help you detect many errors in logic.

Check for Evidence

In addition to testing arguments with the tools of logic, look carefully at the evidence used to support those arguments. Evidence comes in several forms, including facts, comments from recognized experts in a field, and examples.

Thinking Critically About Information on the Internet

Sources of information on the Internet range from the reputable (such as the Library of Congress) to the flamboyant (such as the *National Enquirer*). People are free to post *anything* on the Internet, including outdated facts as well as intentional misinformation.

Taking a few simple precautions when you surf the Internet can keep you from crashing onto the rocky shore of misinformation.

Distinguish Between Ideas and Information

To think more powerfully about what you find on the Internet, remember the difference between information and ideas. *Information* refers to facts that can be verified by independent observers. *Ideas* are interpretations or opinions based on facts. Several people with the same information might adopt different ideas based on that information.

Don't assume that an idea is more current, reasonable, or accurate just because you find it on the Internet. Apply your critical thinking skills to all published material — print and online.

Look for Overall Quality

Examine the features of a website in general. Notice the effectiveness of the text and visuals as a whole. Also note how well the site is organized and whether you can navigate the site's features with ease. Look for the date that crucial information was posted, and determine how often the site is updated.

Next, get an overview of the site's content. Examine several of the site's pages, and look for consistency of facts, quality of information, and competency with grammar and spelling. Evaluate the site's links to related webpages. Look for links to pages of reputable organizations.

Look at the Source

Find a clear description of the person or organization responsible for the website. If a site asks you to subscribe or become a member, then find out what it does with the personal information that you provide. Look for a way to contact the site's publisher with questions and comments.

Look for Documentation

When you encounter an assertion on a webpage or another Internet resource, note the types and quality of the evidence offered. Look for credible examples, quotations from authorities in the field, documented statistics, or summaries of scientific studies.

Set an Example

In the midst of the Internet's chaotic growth, you can light a path of rationality. Whether you're sending a short email message or building a massive website, bring your own critical thinking skills into play. Every word and image that you send down the wires to the web can display the hallmarks of critical thinking: sound logic, credible evidence, and respect for your audience.

Using OneNote to Enhance Critical Thinking

Using Microsoft OneNote as a tool for collecting your thoughts and ideas into organized sections of information puts your broad base of knowledge in a single searchable location for retrieval, analysis, and connection. During the critical thinking process, you can create a new section or a new page in OneNote and use the techniques discussed earlier in this chapter to link information from multiple areas of your notebook and synthesize those concepts into a final product.

Completing Four Steps to Solve Problems

Think of problem solving as a process with four Ps: Define the *problem*, generate *possibilities*, create a *plan*, and *perform* your plan.

Define the Problem

To define a problem effectively, understand what a problem is: a mismatch between what you want and what you have. Problem solving is all about reducing the gap between these two factors. One simple and powerful strategy for defining problems is simply to put them in writing. When you do this, you might find that potential solutions appear as well.

Generate Possibilities

Now put on your creative thinking hat. Open up. Brainstorm as many possible solutions to the problem as you can. As you generate possibilities, gather relevant facts.

Create a Plan

After rereading your problem definition and list of possible solutions, choose the solution that seems most workable. Think about specific actions that will reduce the gap between what you have and what you want. Visualize the steps you will take to make this solution a reality, and arrange them in chronological order. To make your plan even more powerful, put it in writing.

Perform Your Plan

Ultimately, your skill in solving problems lies in how well you perform your plan. Through the quality of your actions, you become the architect of your own success.

Office 2013 and Windows 8: Essential Concepts and Skills

Objectives

You will have mastered the material in this chapter when you can:

- Use a touch screen
- Perform basic mouse operations
- Start Windows and sign in to an account
- Identify the objects in the Windows 8 desktop
- Identify the apps in and versions of Microsoft Office 2013
- Run an app
- Identify the components of the Microsoft Office ribbon
- Create folders
- Save files
- Change screen resolution
- Perform basic tasks in Microsoft Office apps
- Manage files
- Use Microsoft Office Help and Windows Help

Office 2013 and Windows 8: Essential Concepts and Skills

This introductory chapter uses Access 2013 to cover features and functions common to Office 2013 apps, as well as the basics of Windows 8.

Roadmap

In this chapter, you will learn how to perform basic tasks in Windows and Access. The following roadmap identifies general activities you will perform as you progress through this chapter:

1. SIGN IN to an account
2. USE WINDOWS
3. USE Features in Access that are Common across Office APPS
4. FILE and Folder MANAGEMENT
5. SWITCH between APPS
6. SAVE and Manage FILES
7. CHANGE SCREEN RESOLUTION
8. EXIT APPS
9. USE ADDITIONAL Office APP FEATURES
10. USE Office and Windows HELP

At the beginning of the step instructions throughout the chapter, you will see an abbreviated form of this roadmap. The abbreviated roadmap uses colors to indicate chapter progress: gray means the chapter is beyond that activity, blue means the task being shown is covered in that activity, and black means that activity is yet to be covered. For example, the following abbreviated roadmap indicates the chapter would be showing a task in the 3 USE APPS activity.

1 SIGN IN | 2 USE WINDOWS | 3 USE APPS | 4 FILE MANAGEMENT | 5 SWITCH APPS | 6 SAVE FILES
7 CHANGE SCREEN RESOLUTION | 8 EXIT APPS | 9 USE ADDITIONAL APP FEATURES | 10 USE HELP

Use the abbreviated roadmap as a progress guide while you read or step through the instructions in this chapter.

Introduction to the Windows 8 Operating System

Windows 8 is the newest version of Microsoft Windows, which is a popular and widely used operating system. An **operating system** is a computer program (set of computer instructions) that coordinates all the activities of computer hardware, such as memory, storage devices, and printers, and provides the capability for you to communicate with the computer.

The Windows operating system simplifies the process of working with documents and apps by organizing the manner in which you interact with the computer. Windows is used to run apps. An **app** (short for application) consists of programs designed to make users more productive and/or assist them with personal tasks, such as database management or browsing the web.

The Windows 8 interface begins with the **Start screen**, which shows tiles (Figure 1). A **tile** is a shortcut to an app or other content. The tiles on the Start screen include installed apps that you use regularly. From the Start screen, you can choose which apps to run using a touch screen, mouse, or other input device.

Figure 1

Using a Touch Screen and a Mouse

Windows users who have computers or devices with touch screen capability can interact with the screen using gestures. A **gesture** is a motion you make on a touch screen with the tip of one or more fingers or your hand. Touch screens are convenient because they do not require a separate device for input. Table 1 on the next page presents common ways to interact with a touch screen.

If you are using your finger on a touch screen and are having difficulty completing the steps in this chapter, consider using a stylus. Many people find it easier to be precise with a stylus than with a finger. In addition, with a stylus you see the pointer. If you still are having trouble completing the steps with a stylus, try using a mouse.

Table 1 Touch Screen Gestures

Motion	Description	Common Uses
Tap 	Quickly touch and release one finger one time.	Activate a link (built-in connection) Press a button Run a program or an app
Double-tap 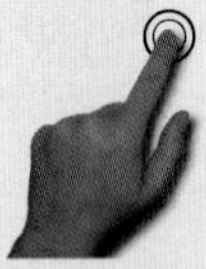	Quickly touch and release one finger two times.	Run a program or an app Zoom in (show a smaller area on the screen, so that contents appear larger) at the location of the double-tap
Press and hold 	Press and hold one finger to cause an action to occur, or until an action occurs.	Display a shortcut menu (immediate access to allowable actions) Activate a mode enabling you to move an item with one finger to a new location
Drag, or slide 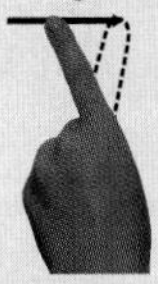	Press and hold one finger on an object and then move the finger to the new location.	Move an item around the screen Scroll
Swipe 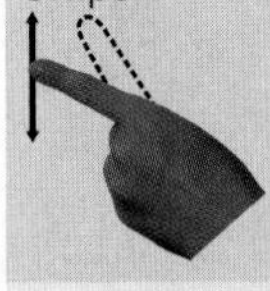	Press and hold one finger and then move the finger horizontally or vertically on the screen.	Select an object Swipe from edge to display a bar such as the Charms bar, Apps bar, and Navigation bar (all discussed later)
Stretch 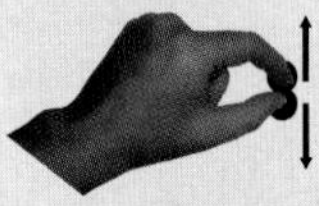	Move two fingers apart.	Zoom in (show a smaller area on the screen, so that contents appear larger)
Pinch 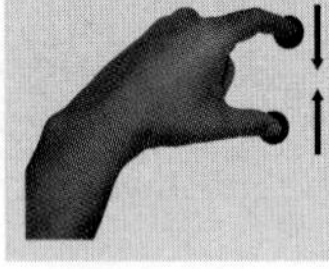	Move two fingers together.	Zoom out (show a larger area on the screen, so that contents appear smaller)

BTW

Problems with Touch

If you are using your finger on a touch screen and are having difficulty completing the steps in this chapter, consider using a stylus. Many people find it easier to be precise with a stylus than with a finger. In addition, with a stylus you see the pointer. If you are still having trouble completing the steps with a stylus, try using a mouse.

BTW

Touch Screen Differences

The Office and Windows interfaces may vary if you are using a touch screen. For this reason, you might notice that the function or appearance of your touch screen differs slightly from this chapter's presentation.

CONSIDER THIS

Will your screen look different if you are using a touch screen?

The Windows and Microsoft Office interface varies slightly if you are using a touch screen. For this reason, you might notice that your Windows or Access screens look slightly different from the screens in this book.

Windows users who do not have touch screen capabilities typically work with a mouse that has at least two buttons. For a right-handed user, the left button usually is the primary mouse button, and the right mouse button is the secondary mouse button. Left-handed people, however, can reverse the function of these buttons.

Table 2 explains how to perform a variety of mouse operations. Some apps also use keys in combination with the mouse to perform certain actions. For example, when you hold down the CTRL key while rolling the mouse wheel, text on the screen may become larger or smaller based on the direction you roll the wheel. The function of the mouse buttons and the wheel varies depending on the app.

BTW

Access and Touch

Access offers limited use of the touch gestures that are more commonly used in the other Office apps.

Table 2 Mouse Operations

Operation	Mouse Action	Example*
Point	Move the mouse until the pointer on the desktop is positioned on the item of choice.	Position the pointer on the screen.
Click	Press and release the primary mouse button, which usually is the left mouse button.	Select or deselect items on the screen or run an app or app feature.
Right-click	Press and release the secondary mouse button, which usually is the right mouse button.	Display a shortcut menu.
Double-click	Quickly press and release the primary mouse button twice without moving the mouse.	Run an app or app feature.
Triple-click	Quickly press and release the primary mouse button three times without moving the mouse.	Select a paragraph.
Drag	Point to an item, hold down the primary mouse button, move the item to the desired location on the screen, and then release the mouse button.	Move an object from one location to another or draw pictures.
Right-drag	Point to an item, hold down the right mouse button, move the item to the desired location on the screen, and then release the right mouse button.	Display a shortcut menu after moving an object from one location to another.
Rotate wheel	Roll the wheel forward or backward.	Scroll vertically (up and down).
Free-spin wheel	Whirl the wheel forward or backward so that it spins freely on its own.	Scroll through many pages in seconds.
Press wheel	Press the wheel button while moving the mouse.	Scroll continuously.
Tilt wheel	Press the wheel toward the right or left.	Scroll horizontally (left and right).
Press thumb button	Press the button on the side of the mouse with your thumb.	Move forward or backward through webpages and/or control media, games, etc.

*Note: The examples presented in this column are discussed as they are demonstrated in this chapter.

Scrolling

A **scroll bar** is a horizontal or vertical bar that appears when the contents of an area may not be visible completely on the screen (Figure 2). A scroll bar contains **scroll arrows** and a **scroll box** that enable you to view areas that currently cannot be seen on the screen. Tapping or clicking the up and down scroll arrows moves the screen content up or down one line. You also can tap or click above or below the scroll box to move up or down a section, or drag the scroll box up or down to move to a specific location.

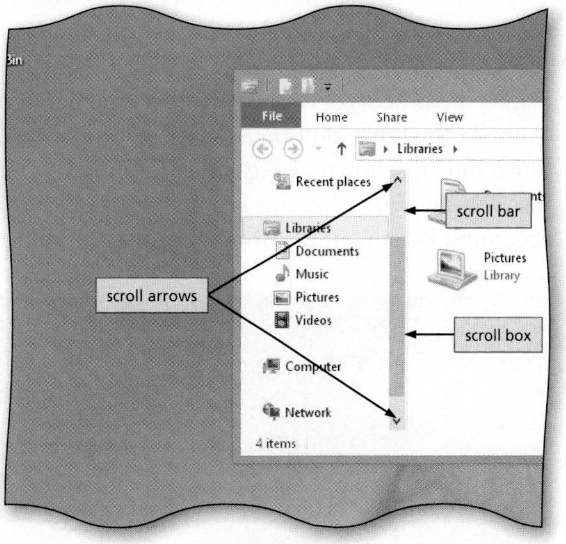

Figure 2

BTW
Pointer
If you are using a touch screen, the pointer may not appear on the screen as you perform touch gestures. The pointer will reappear when you begin using the mouse.

BTW
Minimize Wrist Injury
Computer users frequently switch between the keyboard and the mouse during a database management session; such switching strains the wrist. To help prevent wrist injury, minimize switching. For instance, if your fingers already are on the keyboard, use keyboard keys to scroll. If your hand already is on the mouse, use the mouse to scroll. If your hand is on the touch screen, use touch gestures to scroll.

CONSIDER THIS

What should you do if you are running Windows 7 instead of Windows 8?
Although Windows 8 includes several user interface and feature enhancements, many of the steps in this book work in both Windows 7 and Windows 8. If you have any questions about differences between the two operating systems or how to perform tasks in an earlier version of Windows, contact your instructor.

BTW
BTWs
For a complete list of the BTWs found in the margins of this book, visit the BTW resource on the Student Companion Site located on www.cengagebrain.com. For detailed instructions about accessing available resources, visit www.cengage.com/ct/studentdownload or contact your instructor for information about accessing the required files.

Keyboard Shortcuts

In many cases, you can use the keyboard instead of the mouse to accomplish a task. To perform tasks using the keyboard, you press one or more keyboard keys, sometimes identified as a **keyboard shortcut**. Some keyboard shortcuts consist of a single key, such as the F1 key. For example, to obtain help in many apps, you can press the F1 key. Other keyboard shortcuts consist of multiple keys, in which case a plus sign separates the key names, such as CTRL+ESC. This notation means to press and hold down the first key listed, press one or more additional keys, and then release all keys. For example, to display the Start screen, press CTRL+ESC, that is, hold down the CTRL key, press the ESC key, and then release both keys.

Starting Windows

It is not unusual for multiple people to use the same computer in a work, educational, recreational, or home setting. Windows enables each user to establish a **user account**, which identifies to Windows the resources, such as apps and storage locations, a user can access when working with the computer.

Each user account has a user name and may have a password and an icon, as well. A **user name** is a unique combination of letters or numbers that identifies a specific user to Windows. A **password** is a private combination of letters, numbers, and special characters associated with the user name that allows access to a user's account resources. An icon is a small image that represents an object, thus a **user icon** is a picture associated with a user name.

When you turn on a computer, Windows starts and displays a **lock screen** consisting of the time and date (Figure 3a). To unlock the screen, swipe up or click the lock screen. Depending on your computer's settings, Windows may or may not display a sign-in screen that shows the user names and user icons for users who have accounts on the computer (Figure 3b). This **sign-in screen** enables you to sign in to your user account and makes the computer available for use. Tapping or clicking the user icon begins the process of signing in, also called logging on, to your user account.

At the bottom of the sign-in screen is the 'Ease of access' button and a Shut down button, shown in Figure 4. Tapping or clicking the 'Ease of access' button displays the Ease of access menu, which provides tools to optimize a computer to accommodate the needs of the mobility, hearing, and vision impaired users. Tapping

Figure 3a

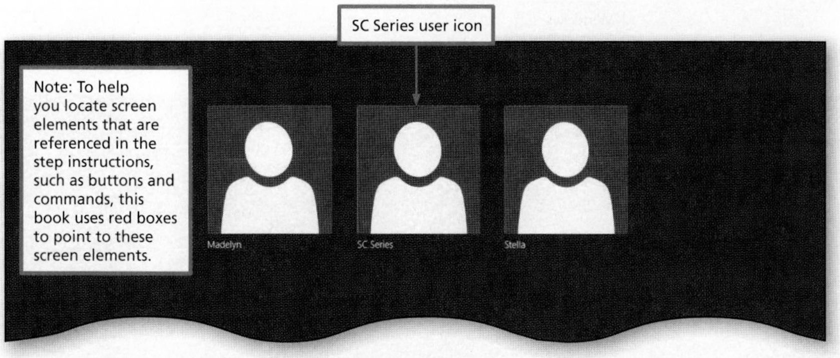

Figure 3b

or clicking the Shut down button displays a menu containing commands related to restarting the computer, putting it in a low-power state, and shutting it down. The commands available on your computer may differ.

- The Sleep command saves your work, turns off the computer fans and hard disk, and places the computer in a lower-power state. To wake the computer from sleep mode, press the power button or lift a laptop's cover, and sign in to your account.
- The Shut down command exits running apps, shuts down Windows, and then turns off the computer.
- The Restart command exits running apps, shuts down Windows, and then restarts Windows.

BTW
Q&As
For a complete list of the Q&As found in many of the step-by-step sequences in this book, visit the Q&A resource on the Student Companion Site located on www.cengagebrain.com. For detailed instructions about accessing available resources, visit www.cengage.com/ct/studentdownload or contact your instructor for information about accessing the required files.

To Sign In to an Account

1 SIGN IN | 2 USE WINDOWS | 3 USE APPS | 4 FILE MANAGEMENT | 5 SWITCH APPS | 6 SAVE FILES
7 CHANGE SCREEN RESOLUTION | 8 EXIT APPS | 9 USE ADDITIONAL APP FEATURES | 10 USE HELP

The following steps, which use SC Series as the user name, sign in to an account based on a typical Windows installation. ***Why?*** *After starting Windows, you might be required to sign in to an account to access the computer's resources.* You may need to ask your instructor how to sign in to your account. If you are using Windows 7, skip these steps and instead perform the steps in the yellow box that immediately follows these Windows 8 steps.

1

- Swipe up or click the lock screen (shown in Figure 3a) to display a sign-in screen (shown in Figure 3b).
- Tap or click the user icon (for SC Series, in this case) on the sign-in screen, which depending on settings, either will display a second sign-in screen that contains a Password text box (Figure 4) or will display the Windows Start screen (shown in Figure 5 on the next page).

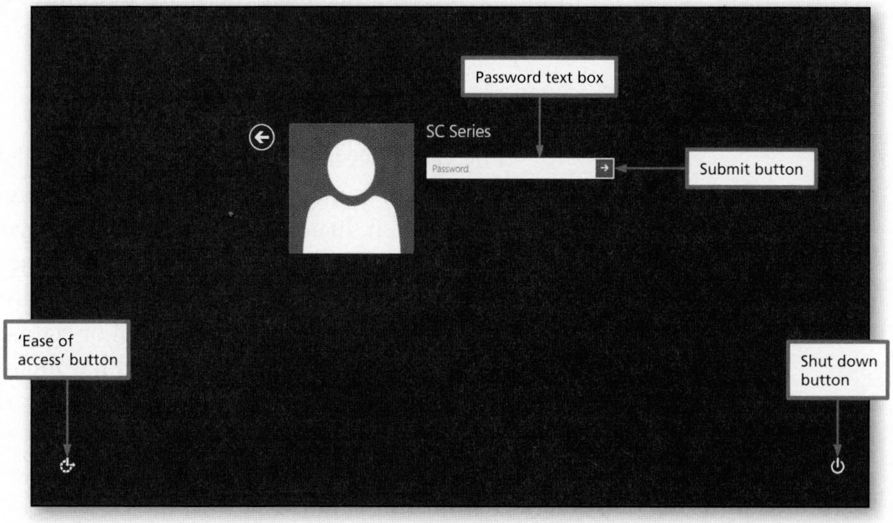

Figure 4

Q&A
Why do I not see a user icon?
Your computer may require you to type a user name instead of tapping or clicking an icon.

What is a text box?
A text box is a rectangular box in which you type text.

Why does my screen not show a Password text box?
Your account does not require a password.

- If Windows displays a sign-in screen with a Password text box, type your password in the text box.

2

- Tap or click the Submit button (shown in Figure 4 on the previous page) to sign in to your account and display the Windows Start screen (Figure 5).

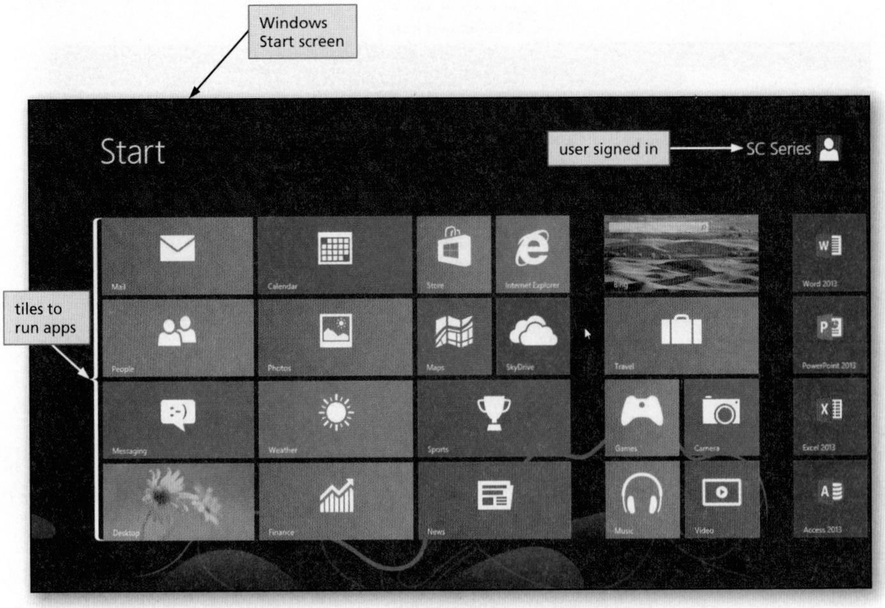

Figure 5

Q&A

Why does my Start screen look different from the one in Figure 5?
The Windows Start screen is customizable, and your school or employer may have modified the screen to meet its needs. Also, your screen resolution, which affects the size of the elements on the screen, may differ from the screen resolution used in this book. Later in this chapter, you learn how to change screen resolution.

How do I type if my tablet has no keyboard?
You can use your fingers to press keys on a keyboard that appears on the screen, called an on-screen keyboard, or you can purchase a separate physical keyboard that attaches to or wirelessly communicates with the tablet.

To Sign In to an Account Using Windows 7

If you are using Windows 7, perform these steps to sign in to an account instead of the previous steps that use Windows 8.

1. Click the user icon on the Welcome screen; depending on settings, this either will display a password text box or will sign in to the account and display the Windows 7 desktop.
2. If Windows 7 displays a password text box, type your password in the text box and then click the arrow button to sign in to the account and display the Windows 7 desktop.

The Windows Start Screen

BTW
Modern UI
The new Windows 8 user interface also is referred to as the Modern UI (user interface).

The Windows Start screen provides a scrollable space for you to access apps that have been pinned to the Start screen (shown in Figure 5). Pinned apps appear as tiles on the Start screen. In addition to running apps, you can perform tasks such as pinning apps (placing tiles) on the Start screen, moving the tiles around the Start screen, and unpinning apps (removing tiles) from the Start screen.

If you swipe up from the bottom of or right-click an open space on the Start screen, the App bar will appear. The **App bar** includes a button that enables you to display all of your apps. When working with tiles, the App bar also provides options for manipulating the tiles, such as resizing them.

CONSIDER THIS

How do you pin apps, move tiles, and unpin apps?

- To pin an app, swipe up from the bottom of the Start screen or right-click an open space on the Start screen to display the App bar, tap or click the All apps button on the App bar to display the Apps list, swipe down on or right-click the app you want to pin, and then tap or click the 'Pin to Start' button on the App bar. One way to return to the Start screen is to swipe up from the bottom or right-click an open space in the Apps list and then tap or click the All apps button again.
- To move a tile, drag the tile to the desired location.
- To unpin an app, swipe down on or right-click the app to display the App bar and then tap or click the 'Unpin from Start' button on the App bar.

Introduction to Microsoft Office 2013

Microsoft Office 2013 is the newest version of Microsoft Office, offering features that provide users with better functionality and easier ways to work with the various files they create. These features include enhanced design tools, such as improved picture formatting tools and new themes, shared notebooks for working in groups, mobile versions of Office apps, broadcast presentations for the web, and a digital notebook for managing and sharing multimedia information.

Microsoft Office 2013 Apps

Microsoft Office 2013 includes a wide variety of apps such as Word, PowerPoint, Excel, Access, Outlook, Publisher, OneNote, InfoPath, SharePoint Workspace, and Lync:

- **Microsoft Word 2013**, or Word, is a full-featured word processing app that allows you to create professional-looking documents and revise them easily.
- **Microsoft PowerPoint 2013**, or PowerPoint, is a complete presentation app that enables you to produce professional-looking presentations and then deliver them to an audience.
- **Microsoft Excel 2013**, or Excel, is a powerful spreadsheet app that allows you to organize data, complete calculations, make decisions, graph data, develop professional-looking reports, publish organized data to the web, and access real-time data from websites.
- **Microsoft Access 2013**, or Access, is a database management system that enables you to create a database; add, change, and delete data in the database; ask questions concerning the data in the database; and create forms and reports using the data in the database.
- **Microsoft Outlook 2013**, or Outlook, is a communications and scheduling app that allows you to manage email accounts, calendars, contacts, and access to other Internet content.
- **Microsoft Publisher 2013**, or Publisher, is a desktop publishing app that helps you create professional-quality publications and marketing materials that can be shared easily.
- **Microsoft OneNote 2013**, or OneNote, is a note taking app that allows you to store and share information in notebooks with other people.
- **Microsoft InfoPath Designer 2013**, or InfoPath, is a form development app that helps you create forms for use on the web and gather data from these forms.
- **Microsoft SharePoint Workspace 2013**, or SharePoint, is a collaboration app that allows you to access and revise files stored on your computer from other locations.
- **Microsoft Lync 2013** is a communications app that allows you to use various modes of communications such as instant messaging, videoconferencing, and sharing files and apps.

Microsoft Office 2013 Suites

A **suite** is a collection of individual apps available together as a unit. Microsoft offers a variety of Office suites, including a stand-alone desktop app (boxed software), Microsoft Office 365, and Microsoft Office Web Apps. **Microsoft Office 365**, or Office 365, provides plans that allow organizations to use Office in a mobile setting while also being able to communicate and share files, depending upon the type of plan selected by the organization. **Microsoft Office Web Apps**, or Web Apps, are apps that allow you to edit and share files on the web using the familiar Office interface. Table 3 on the next page outlines the differences among these Office suites.

Table 3 Office Suites

Apps/ Licenses	Office 365 Home Premium	Office 365 Small Business Premium	Office Home & Student	Office Home & Business	Office Professional
Word	✔	✔	✔	✔	✔
PowerPoint	✔	✔	✔	✔	✔
Excel	✔	✔	✔	✔	✔
Access	✔	✔			✔
Outlook	✔	✔		✔	✔
Publisher	✔	✔			✔
Lync		✔			
OneNote			✔	✔	✔
InfoPath		✔			
Licenses	5	5	1	1	1

During the Office 365 installation, you select a plan, and depending on your plan, you receive different apps and services. Office Web Apps do not require a local installation and are accessed through SkyDrive and your browser. **SkyDrive** is a cloud storage service that provides storage and other services, such as Office Web Apps, to computer users.

CONSIDER THIS

How do you sign up for a SkyDrive account?

- Use your browser to navigate to skydrive.live.com.
- Create a Microsoft account by tapping or clicking the 'Sign up now' link (or a similar link) and then entering your information to create the account.
- Sign in to SkyDrive using your new account.

Apps in a suite, such as Microsoft Office, typically use a similar interface and share features. Once you are comfortable working with the elements and the interface and performing tasks in one app, the similarity can help you apply the knowledge and skills you have learned to another app(s) in the suite. For example, the process for saving a file in Word is the same in PowerPoint, Excel, and the other Office apps. While briefly showing how to use Access, this chapter illustrates some of the common functions across the Office apps and identifies the characteristics unique to Access.

Running and Using an App

To use an app, such as Access, you must instruct the operating system to run the app. Windows provides many different ways to run an app, one of which is presented in this section (other ways to run an app are presented throughout this chapter). After an app is running, you can use it to perform a variety of tasks. The following pages use Access to discuss some elements of the Office interface and to perform tasks that are common to other Office apps.

Access

The term **database** describes a collection of data organized in a manner that allows access, retrieval, and use of that data. **Access** is a database management system. A **database management system** is software that allows you to use a computer to create a database; add, change, and delete data in the database; create queries that allow you to ask questions concerning the data in the database; and create forms and reports using the data in the database.

To Run Access from the Start Screen

The Start screen contains tiles that allow you to run apps, some of which might be stored on your computer. ***Why?*** *When you install an app, for example, tiles are added to the Start screen for the various Office apps included in the suite.*

The following steps, which assume Windows is running, use the Start screen to run Access based on a typical installation. You may need to ask your instructor how to run an Office app on your computer. Although the steps illustrate running the Access app, the steps to run any Office app are similar. If you are using Windows 7, skip these steps and instead perform the steps in the yellow box that immediately follows these Windows 8 steps.

1

- If necessary, scroll to display the Access tile on the Start screen (Figure 6).

Q&A

Why does my Start screen look different?
It might look different because of your computer's configuration. The Start screen may be customized for several reasons, such as usage requirements or security restrictions.

What if the app I want to run is not on the Start screen?
You can display all installed apps by swiping up from the bottom of the Start screen or right-clicking an open space on the Start screen and then tapping or clicking the All apps button on the App bar.

How do I scroll on a touch screen?
Use the slide gesture; that is, press and hold your finger on the screen and then move your finger in the direction you wish to scroll.

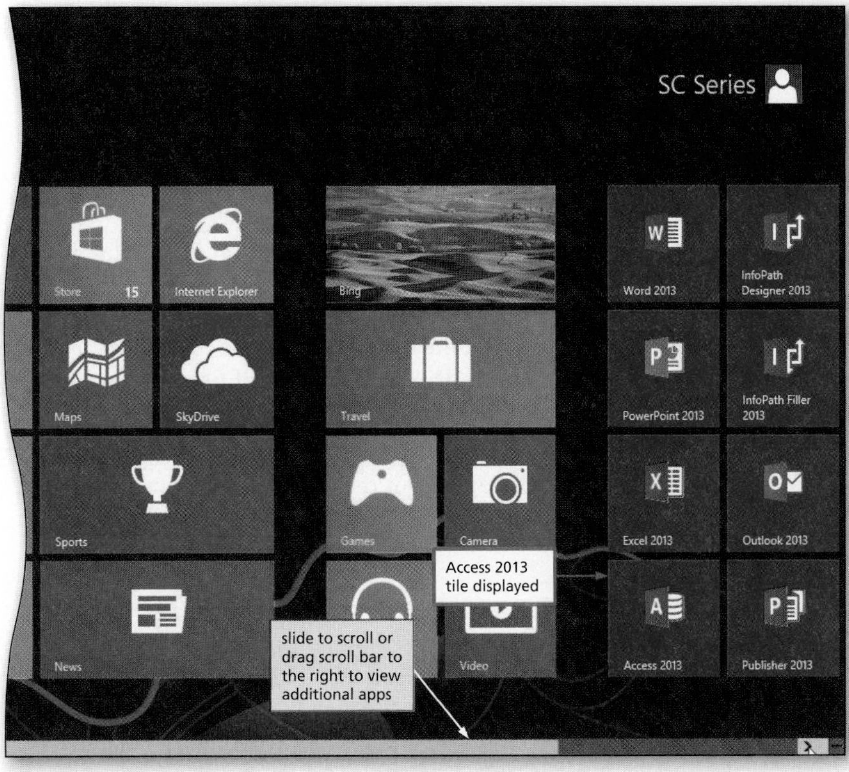

Figure 6

2

- Tap or click the Access 2013 tile to run the Access app (Figure 7).

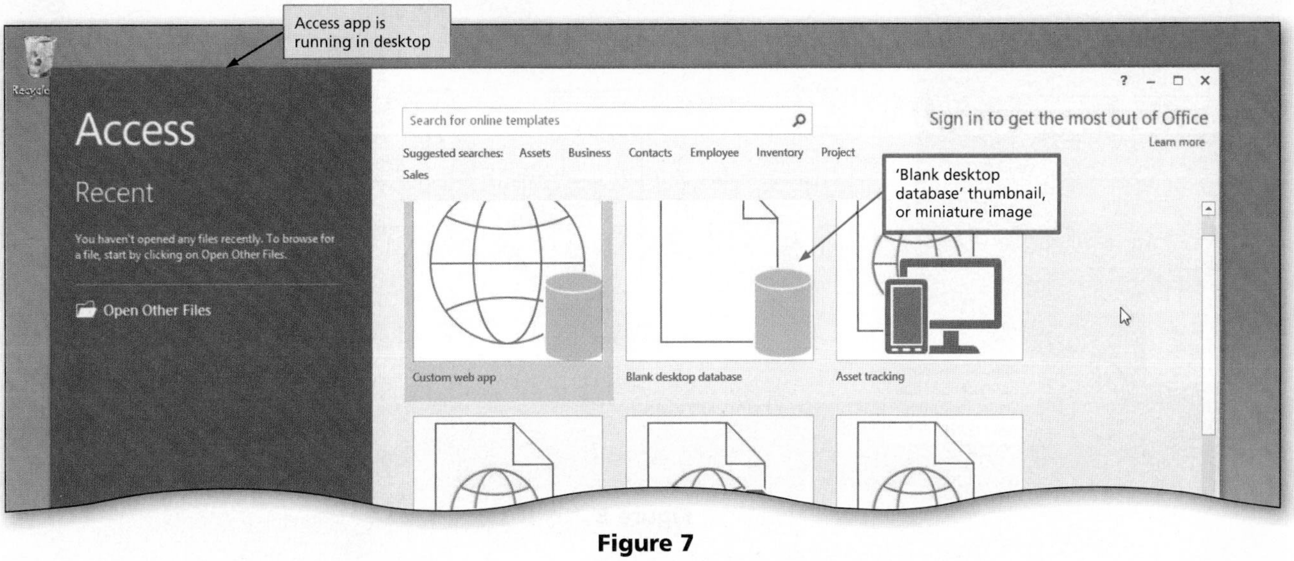

Figure 7

To Run an App Using the Start Menu Using Windows 7

If you are using Windows 7, perform these steps to run an app using the Start menu instead of the previous steps that use Windows 8.

1. Click the Start button on the Windows 7 taskbar to display the Start menu.
2. Click All Programs at the bottom of the left pane on the Start menu to display the All Programs list.
3. If the app you wish to start is located in a folder, click, or scroll to and then click, the folder in the All Programs list to display a list of the folder's contents.
4. Click, or scroll to and then click, the app name in the list to run the selected app.

Windows Desktop

When you run an app in Windows, it may appear in an on-screen work area app, called the **desktop** (shown in Figure 8). You can perform tasks such as placing objects in the desktop, moving the objects around the desktop, and removing items from the desktop.

Some icons also may be displayed in the desktop. For instance, the icon for the **Recycle Bin**, the location of files that have been deleted, appears in the desktop by default. A **file** is a named unit of storage. Files can contain text, images, audio, and video. You can customize your desktop so that icons representing apps and files you use often appear in the desktop.

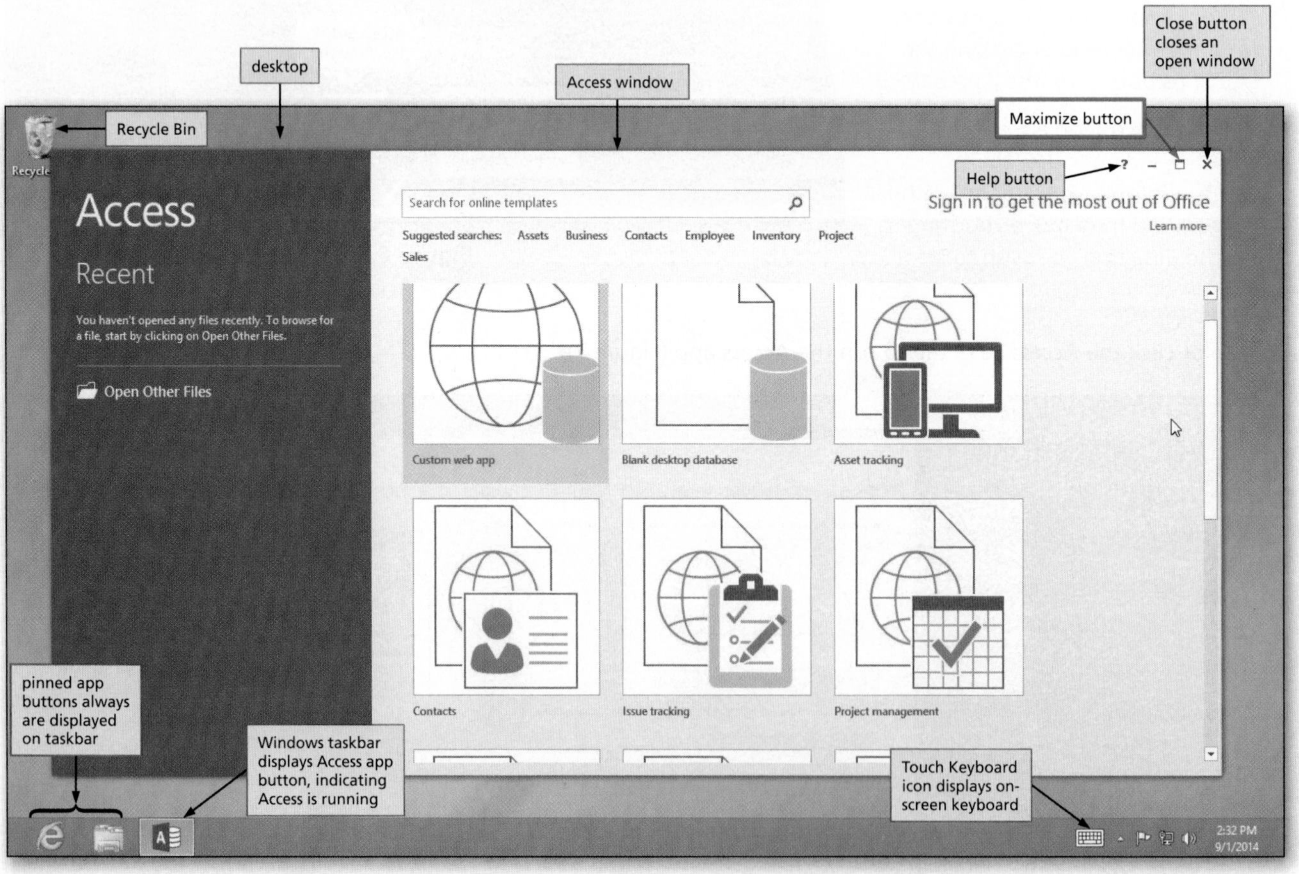

Figure 8

To Switch between an App and the Start Screen

While working with an app such as the Desktop app, you easily can return to the Start screen. The following steps switch from the Desktop app to the Start screen. ***Why?*** *Returning to the Start screen allows you to run any of your other apps.* If you are using Windows 7, read these steps without performing them because Windows 7 does not have a Start screen.

1

- Swipe in from the left edge of the screen, and then back to the left, or point to the lower-left corner of the desktop to display a thumbnail of the Start screen (Figure 9).

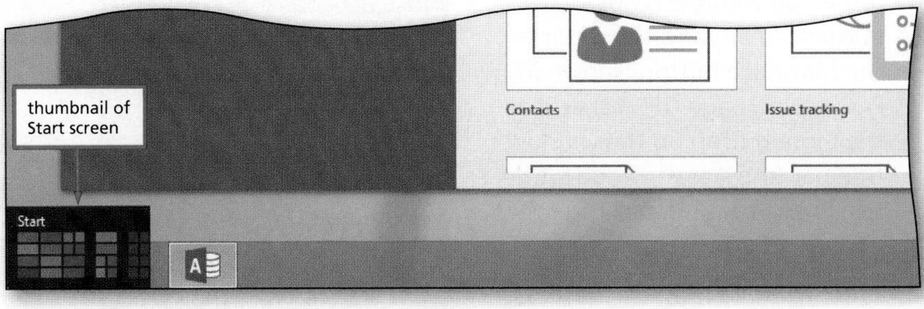

Figure 9

2

- Tap or click the thumbnail of the Start screen to display the Start screen (Figure 10).

3

- Tap or click the Desktop tile to redisplay the Desktop app (shown in Figure 8).

Figure 10

Other Ways

1. Press WINDOWS to display Start screen

To Maximize a Window

1 SIGN IN | 2 USE WINDOWS | 3 USE APPS | 4 FILE MANAGEMENT | 5 SWITCH APPS | 6 SAVE FILES
7 CHANGE SCREEN RESOLUTION | 8 EXIT APPS | 9 USE ADDITIONAL APP | 10 USE HELP

Sometimes content is not visible completely in a window. One method of displaying the entire contents of a window is to **maximize** it, or enlarge the window so that it fills the entire screen. The following step maximizes the Access window; however, any Office app's window can be maximized using this step. ***Why?*** *A maximized window provides the most space available for using the app.*

1

- If the app window is not maximized already, tap or click the Maximize button (shown in Figure 8 on page OFF 12) next to the Close button on the window's title bar (the Access window title bar, in this case) to maximize the window (Figure 11).

Q&A

What happened to the Maximize button?
It changed to a Restore Down button, which you can use to return a window to its size and location before you maximized it.

How do I know whether a window is maximized?
A window is maximized if it fills the entire display area and the Restore Down button is displayed on the title bar.

Figure 11

Other Ways

1. Double-tap or double-click title bar
2. Drag title bar to top of screen

Access Unique Elements

You work on objects such as tables, forms, and reports in the **Access work area**. Figure 12 shows a work area with multiple objects open. **Object tabs** for the open objects appear at the top of the work area. You select an open object by tapping or clicking its tab. In the figure, the Client Form is the selected object. To the left of the work area is the Navigation Pane, which contains a list of all the objects in the database. You use this pane to open an object. You also can customize the way objects are displayed in the Navigation Pane.

Because the Navigation Pane can take up space in the window, you may not have as much open space for working as you would with Word or Excel. You can use the Shutter Bar Open/Close button to minimize the Navigation Pane when you are not using it, which allows more space to work with tables, forms, reports, and other database elements.

BTW
Navigation Pane Style
The onscreen area known as the navigation pane is capitalized when referring to the Access Navigation Pane. When referring to the File Management navigation pane, the term is not capitalized.

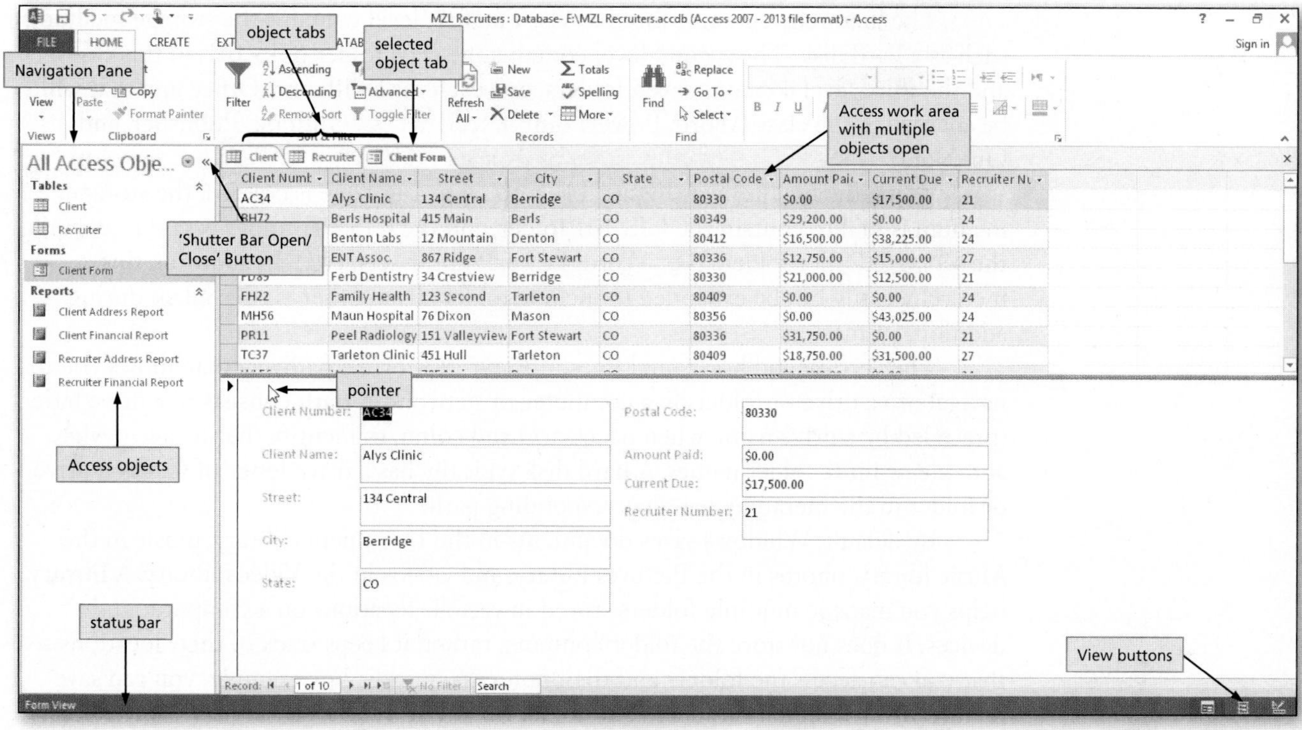

Figure 12

Saving and Organizing Files

Before starting to work in Access, you must either create a new database or open an existing database. When you create a database, the computer places it on a storage medium such as a hard disk, solid state drive (SSD), USB flash drive, or optical disc. The storage medium can be permanent in your computer, may be portable where you remove it from your computer, or may be on a web server you access through a network or the Internet.

A database or other saved document is referred to as a file. A **file name** is the name assigned to a file when it is saved. When saving files, you should organize them so that you easily can find them later. Windows provides tools to help you organize files.

Organizing Files and Folders

You should organize and store databases and other files in folders to help you find the databases or other files quickly.

If you are taking an introductory computer class (CIS 101, for example), you may want to design a series of folders for the different subjects covered in the class. To accomplish this, you can arrange the folders in a hierarchy for the class, as shown in Figure 13.

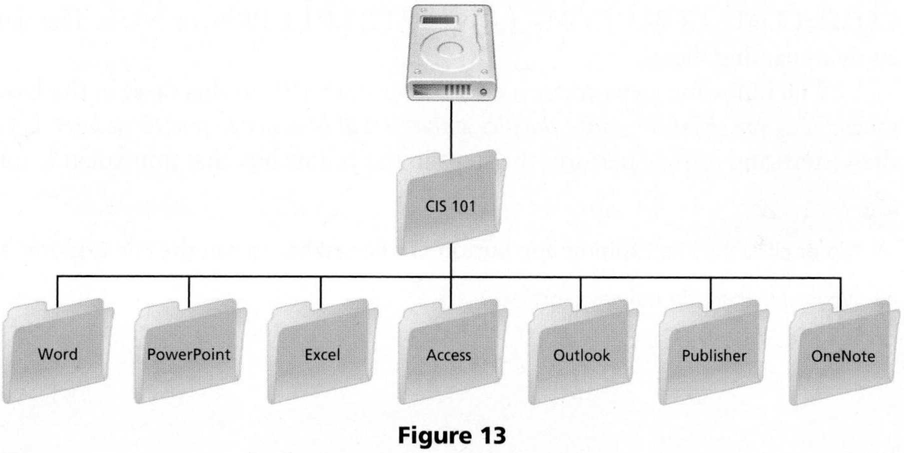

Figure 13

The hierarchy contains three levels. The first level contains the storage medium, such as a hard disk. The second level contains the class folder (CIS 101, in this case), and the third level contains seven folders, one each for a different Office app that will be covered in the class (Word, PowerPoint, Excel, Access, Outlook, Publisher, and OneNote).

When the hierarchy in Figure 13 on the previous page is created, the storage medium is said to contain the CIS 101 folder, and the CIS 101 folder is said to contain the separate Office folders (i.e., Word, PowerPoint, Excel, etc.). In addition, this hierarchy easily can be expanded to include folders from other classes taken during additional semesters.

The vertical and horizontal lines in Figure 13 form a pathway that allows you to navigate to a drive or folder on a computer or network. A **path** consists of a drive letter (preceded by a drive name when necessary) and colon, to identify the storage device, and one or more folder names. A hard disk typically has a drive letter of C. Each drive or folder in the hierarchy has a corresponding path.

By default, Windows saves documents in the Documents library, music in the Music library, photos in the Pictures library, and videos in the Videos library. A **library** helps you manage multiple folders stored in various locations on a computer and devices. It does not store the folder contents; rather, it keeps track of their locations so that you can access the folders and their contents quickly. For example, you can save pictures from a digital camera in any folder on any storage location on a computer. Normally, this would make organizing the different folders difficult. If you add the folders to a library, however, you can access all the pictures from one location regardless of where they are stored.

The following pages illustrate the steps to organize the folders for this class and create a database in one of those folders:

1. Create the folder identifying your class.
2. Create the Access folder in the folder identifying your class.
3. Create the remaining folders in the folder identifying your class.
4. Save a file in the Access folder.
5. Verify the location of the saved file.

To Create a Folder

1 SIGN IN | 2 USE WINDOWS | 3 USE APPS | **4 FILE MANAGEMENT** | **5 SWITCH APPS** | **6 SAVE FILES**
7 CHANGE SCREEN RESOLUTION | **8 EXIT APPS** | **9 USE ADDITIONAL APP** | **10 USE HELP**

When you create a folder, such as the CIS 101 folder shown in Figure 13, you must name the folder. A folder name should describe the folder and its contents. A folder name can contain spaces and any uppercase or lowercase characters, except a backslash (\), slash (/), colon (:), asterisk (*), question mark (?), quotation marks ("), less than symbol (<), greater than symbol (>), or vertical bar (|). Folder names cannot be CON, AUX, COM1, COM2, COM3, COM4, LPT1, LPT2, LPT3, PRN, or NUL. The same rules for naming folders also apply to naming files.

The following steps create a class folder (CIS 101, in this case) in the Documents library. ***Why?*** *When storing files, you should organize the files so that it will be easier to find them later.* If you are using Windows 7, skip these steps and instead perform the steps in the yellow box that immediately follows these Windows 8 steps.

1

- Tap or click the File Explorer app button on the taskbar to run the File Explorer app (Figure 14).

Q&A Why does the title bar say Libraries?
File Explorer, by default, displays the name of the selected library or folder on the title bar.

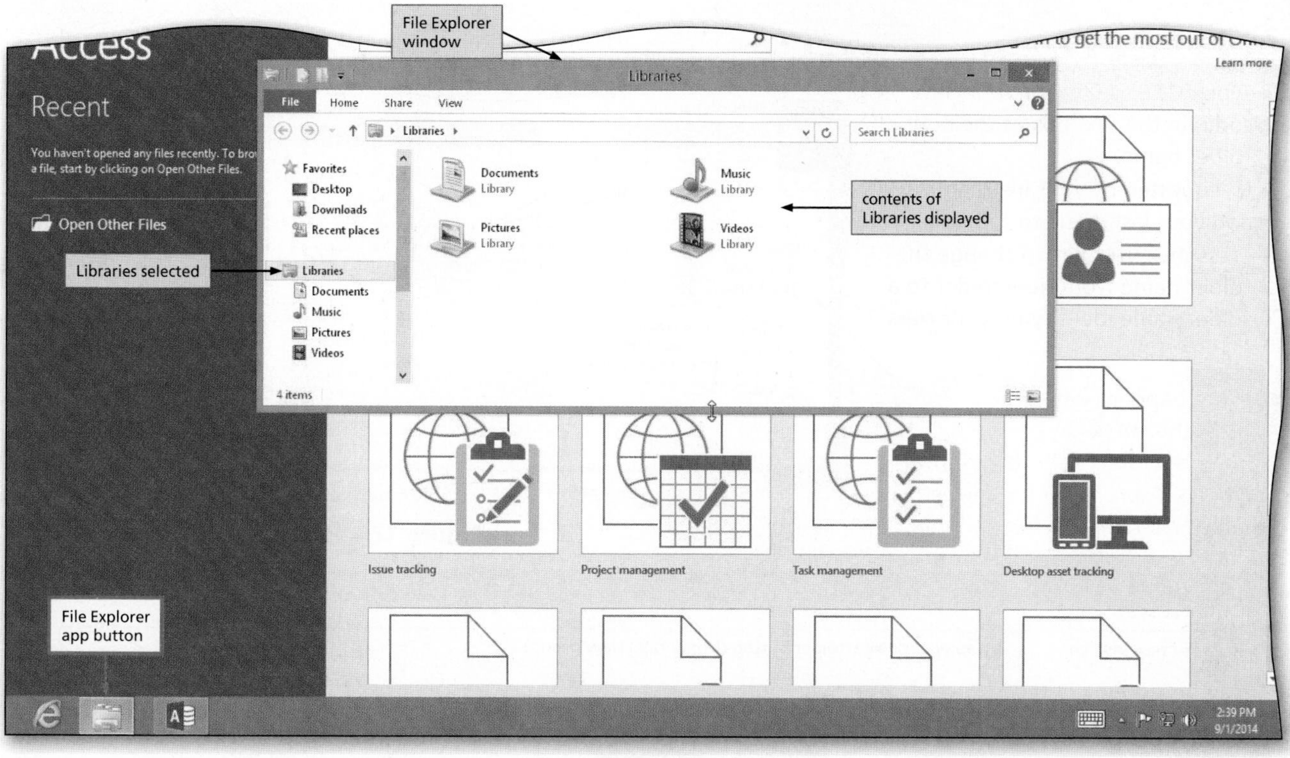

Figure 14

2

- Tap or click the Documents library in the navigation pane to display the contents of the Documents library in the file list (Figure 15).

Q&A What if my screen does not show the Documents, Music, Pictures, and Videos libraries?
Double-tap or double-click Libraries in the navigation pane to expand the list.

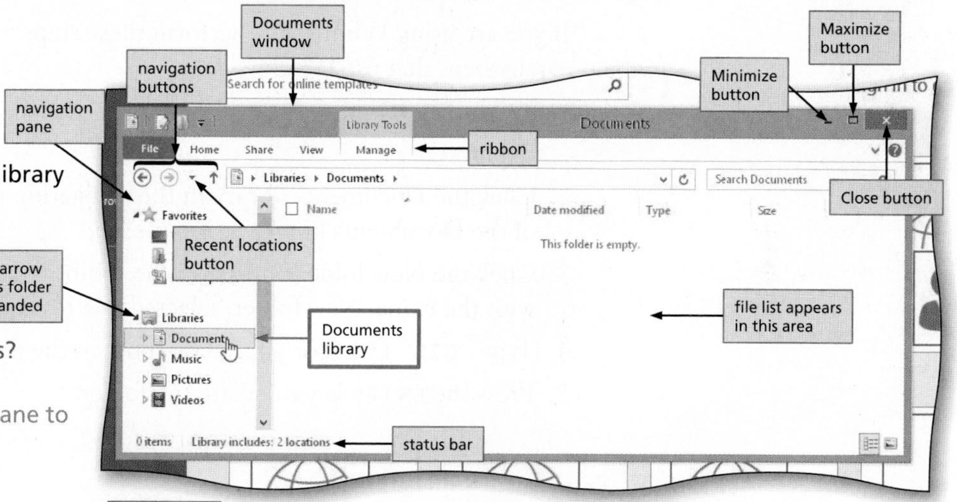

Figure 15

3

- Tap or click the New folder button on the Quick Access Toolbar to create a new folder with the name, New folder, selected in a text box (Figure 16).

Q&A Why is the folder icon displayed differently on my computer?
Windows might be configured to display contents differently on your computer.

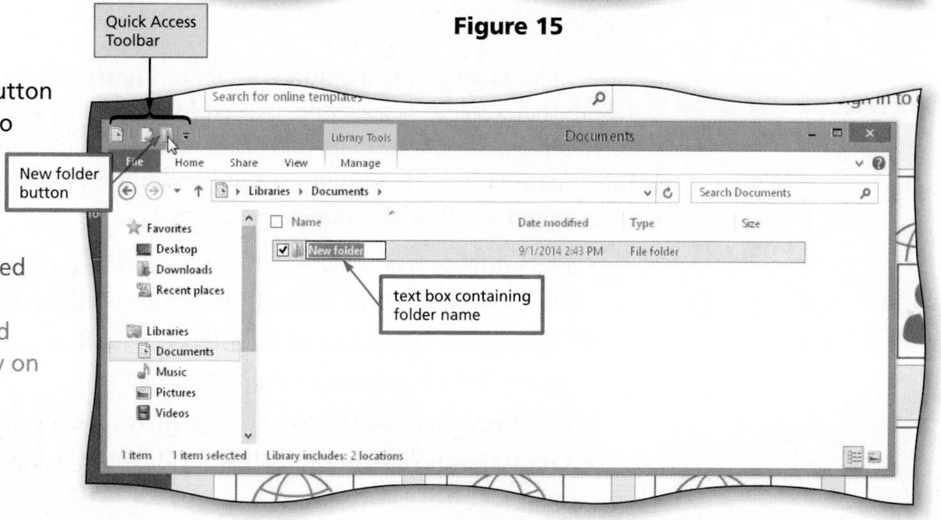

Figure 16

4

- Type **CIS 101** (or your class code) in the text box as the new folder name.
- If requested by your instructor, add your last name to the end.
- Press the ENTER key to change the folder name from New folder to a folder name identifying your class (Figure 17).

Q&A What happens when I press the ENTER key?

The class folder (CIS 101, in this case) is displayed in the file list, which contains the folder name, date modified, type, and size.

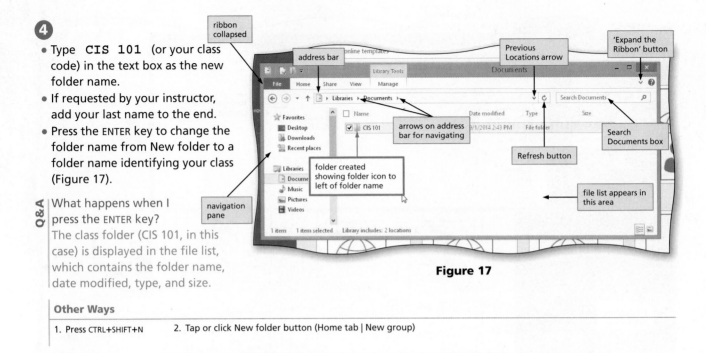

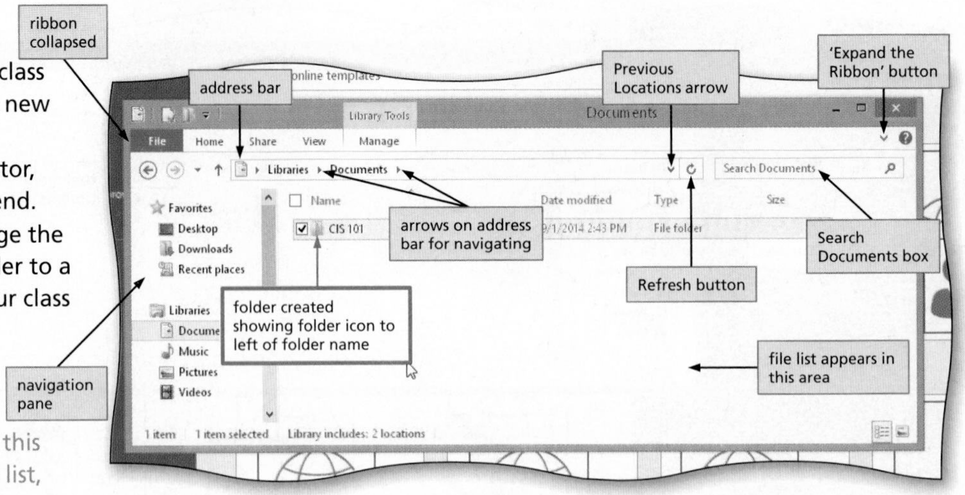

Figure 17

Other Ways

1. Press CTRL+SHIFT+N
2. Tap or click New folder button (Home tab | New group)

To Create a Folder Using Windows 7

If you are using Windows 7, perform these steps to create a folder instead of the previous steps that use Windows 8.

1. Click the Windows Explorer button on the taskbar to run Windows Explorer.
2. Click the Documents library in the navigation pane to display the contents of the Documents library in the file list.
3. Click the New folder button on the toolbar to display a new folder icon with the name, New folder, selected in a text box.
4. Type **CIS 101** (or your class code) in the text box to name the folder.
5. Press the ENTER key to create the folder.

Folder Windows

The Documents window (shown in Figure 17) is called a folder window. Recall that a folder is a specific named location on a storage medium that contains related files. Most users rely on **folder windows** for finding, viewing, and managing information on their computers. Folder windows have common design elements, including the following (shown in Figure 17).

- The **address bar** provides quick navigation options. The arrows on the address bar allow you to visit different locations on the computer.
- The buttons to the left of the address bar allow you to navigate the contents of the navigation pane and view recent pages.
- The **Previous Locations arrow** displays the locations you have visited.
- The **Refresh button** on the right side of the address bar refreshes the contents of the folder list.

- The **search box** contains the dimmed words, Search Documents. You can type a term in the search box for a list of files, folders, shortcuts, and elements containing that term within the location you are searching. A **shortcut** is an icon on the desktop that provides a user with immediate access to an app or file.
- The **ribbon** contains five tabs used to accomplish various tasks on the computer related to organizing and managing the contents of the open window. This ribbon works similarly to the ribbon in the Office apps.
- The **navigation pane** on the left contains the Favorites area, Libraries area, Homegroup area, Computer area, and Network area.
- The **Favorites area** shows your favorite locations. By default, this list contains only links to your Desktop, Downloads, and Recent places.
- The **Libraries area** shows folders included in a library.

To Create a Folder within a Folder

1 SIGN IN | 2 USE WINDOWS | 3 USE APPS | 4 FILE MANAGEMENT | 5 SWITCH APPS | 6 SAVE FILES
7 CHANGE SCREEN RESOLUTION | 8 EXIT APPS | 9 USE ADDITIONAL APP | 10 USE HELP

With the class folder created, you can create folders that will store the files you create using each Office app. The following steps create an Access folder in the CIS 101 folder (or the folder identifying your class). ***Why?*** *To be able to organize your files, you should create a folder structure.* If you are using Windows 7, skip these steps and instead perform the steps in the yellow box that immediately follows these Windows 8 steps.

1

- Double-tap or double-click the icon or folder name for the CIS 101 folder (or the folder identifying your class) in the file list to open the folder (Figure 18).

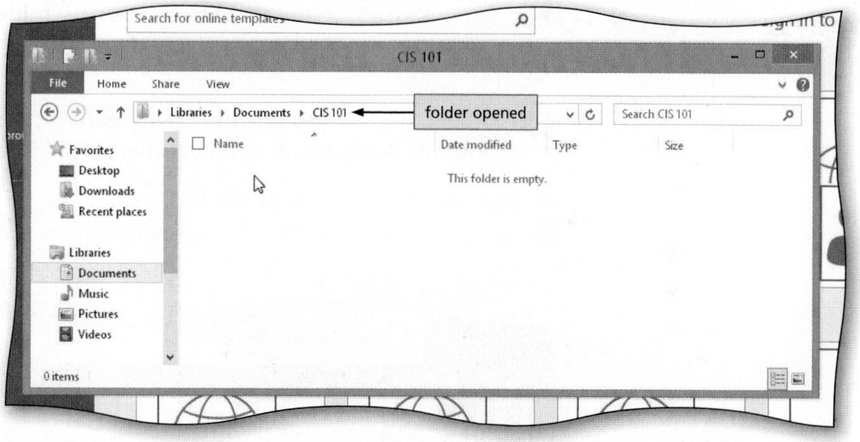

Figure 18

2

- Tap or click the New folder button on the Quick Access Toolbar to create a new folder with the name, New folder, selected in a text box folder.
- Type **Access** in the text box as the new folder name.
- Press the ENTER key to rename the folder (Figure 19).

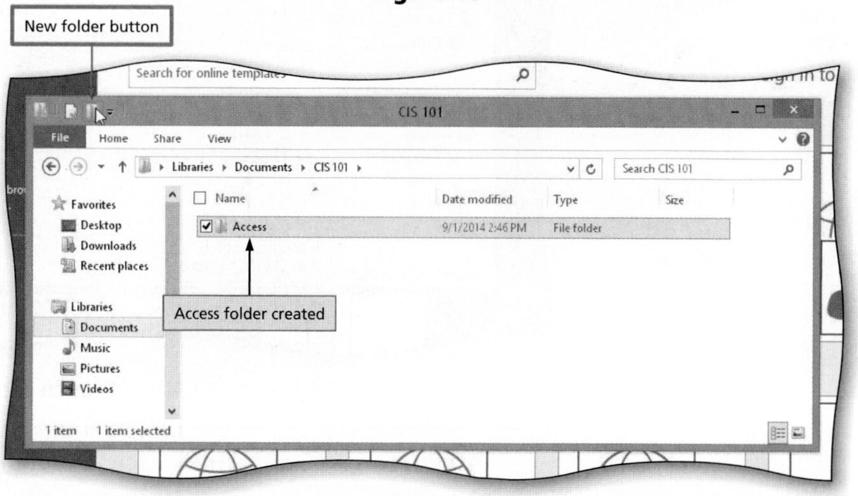

Figure 19

Other Ways

1. Press CTRL+SHIFT+N
2. Tap or click New folder button (Home tab | New group)

To Create a Folder within a Folder Using Windows 7

If you are using Windows 7, perform these steps to create a folder within a folder instead of the previous steps that use Windows 8.

1. Double-click the icon or folder name for the CIS 101 folder (or the folder identifying your class) in the file list to open the folder.
2. Click the New folder button on the toolbar to display a new folder icon and text box for the folder.
3. Type **Access** in the text box to name the folder.
4. Press the ENTER key to create the folder.

To Create the Remaining Folders

Even though you will only use the Access folder in this chapter, for practice you will create some of the remaining folders in the folder identifying your class (in this case, CIS 101). If you are using Windows 7, skip these steps and instead perform the steps in the yellow box that immediately follows these Windows 8 steps.

1. Tap or click the New folder button on the Quick Access Toolbar to create a new folder with the name, New folder, selected in a text box.
2. Type **Excel** in the text box as the new folder name.
3. Press the ENTER key to rename the folder.
4. Repeat Steps 1 through 3 to create each of the remaining folders, using OneNote, Outlook, PowerPoint, and Publisher as the folder names (Figure 20).

Q&A Do I need to create all of the folders?
No, the only one you need to create is the Access folder.

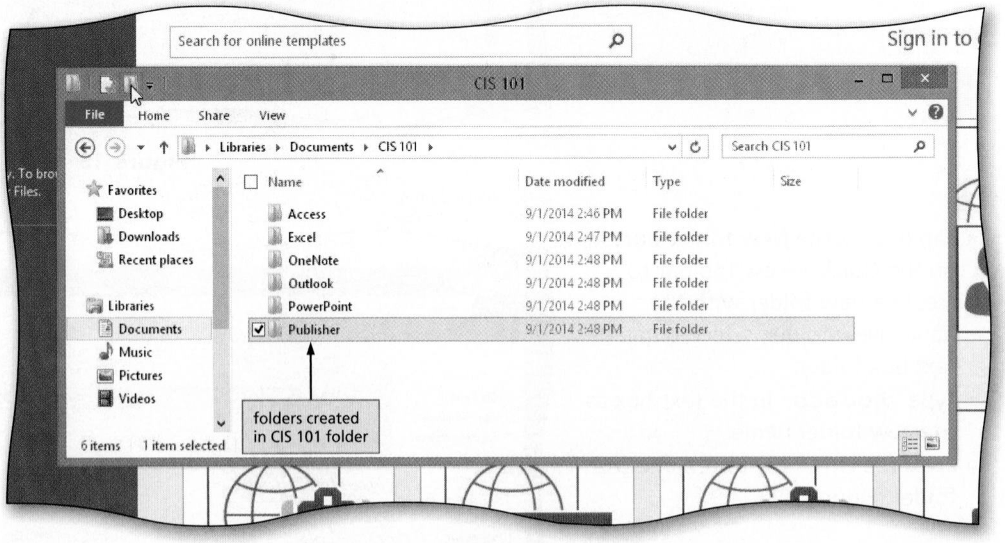

Figure 20

To Create the Remaining Folders Using Windows 7

If you are using Windows 7, perform these steps to create the remaining folders instead of the previous steps that use Windows 8.

1. Click the New folder button on the toolbar to create a new folder with the name, New folder, selected in a text box.
2. Type **Access** in the text box as the new folder name.
3. Press the ENTER key to rename the folder.
4. Repeat Steps 1 through 3 to create each of the remaining folders, using Excel, OneNote, Outlook, PowerPoint, and Publisher as the folder names.

To Expand a Folder, Scroll through Folder Contents, and Collapse a Folder

1 SIGN IN | 2 USE WINDOWS | 3 USE APPS | 4 FILE MANAGEMENT | 5 SWITCH APPS | 6 SAVE FILES | 7 CHANGE SCREEN RESOLUTION | 8 EXIT APPS | 9 USE ADDITIONAL APP | 10 USE HELP

Folder windows display the hierarchy of items and the contents of drives and folders in the file list. You might want to expand a library or folder in the navigation pane to view its contents, slide or scroll through its contents, and collapse it when you are finished viewing its contents. ***Why?*** *When a folder is expanded, you can see all the folders it contains. By contrast, a collapsed folder hides the folders it contains.* The following steps expand, slide or scroll through, and then collapse the folder identifying your class (CIS 101, in this case).

1

- Double-tap or double-click the Documents library in the navigation pane, which expands the library to display its contents and displays a black arrow to the left of the Documents library icon (Figure 21).

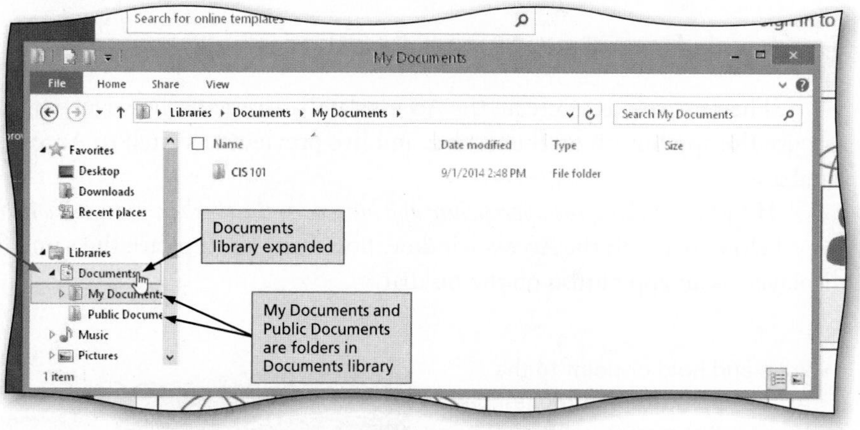

Figure 21

2

- Double-tap or double-click the My Documents folder, which expands the folder to display its contents and displays a black arrow to the left of the My Documents folder icon.

Q&A What is the My Documents folder?
When you save files on your hard disk, the My Documents folder is the default save location.

- Double-tap or double-click the CIS 101 folder, which expands the folder to display its contents and displays a black arrow to the left of the folder icon (Figure 22).

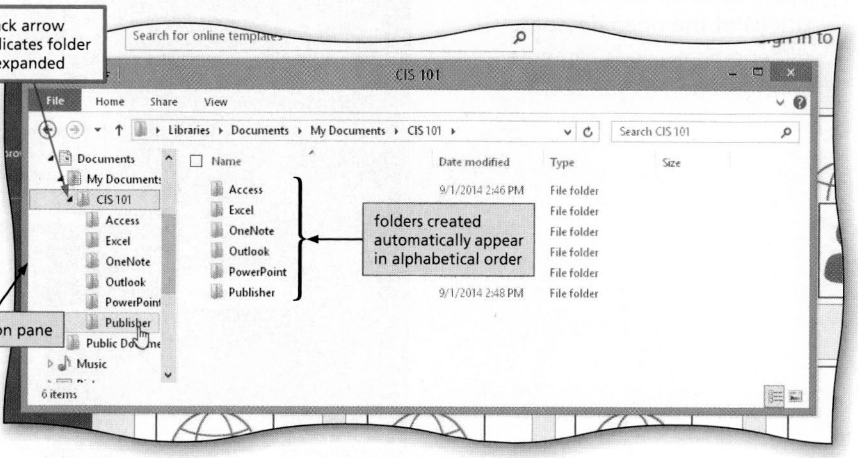

Figure 22

Experiment

- Slide the scroll bar down or click the down scroll arrow on the vertical scroll bar to display additional folders at the bottom of the navigation pane. Slide the scroll bar up or click the scroll bar above the scroll box to move the scroll box to the top of the navigation pane. Drag the scroll box down the scroll bar until the scroll box is halfway down the scroll bar.

3

- Double-tap or double-click the folder identifying your class (CIS 101, in this case) to collapse the folder (Figure 23).

Q&A Why are some folders indented below others? A folder contains the indented folders below it.

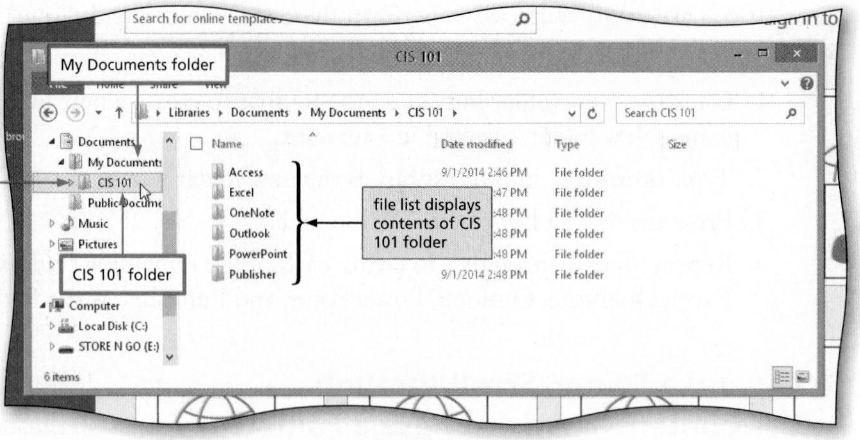

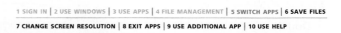

Figure 23

Other Ways

1. Point to display arrows in navigation pane, tap or click white arrow to expand or tap or click black arrow to collapse
2. Select folder to expand or collapse using arrow keys, press RIGHT ARROW to expand; press LEFT ARROW to collapse

To Switch from One App to Another

1 SIGN IN | 2 USE WINDOWS | 3 USE APPS | 4 FILE MANAGEMENT | 5 SWITCH APPS | 6 SAVE FILES
7 CHANGE SCREEN RESOLUTION | 8 EXIT APPS | 9 USE ADDITIONAL APP | 10 USE HELP

The next step is to create the Access database. Access, however, currently is not the active window. You can use the app button on the taskbar and live preview to switch to Access so that you can create the desired database.

***Why?** By clicking the appropriate app button on the taskbar, you can switch to the open app you want to use.* The steps below switch to the Access window; however, the steps are the same for any active Office app currently displayed as an app button on the taskbar.

1

- Press and hold or point to the Access app button on the taskbar to see a live preview of the open database(s) or the window title(s) of the open database(s), depending on your computer's configuration (Figure 24).

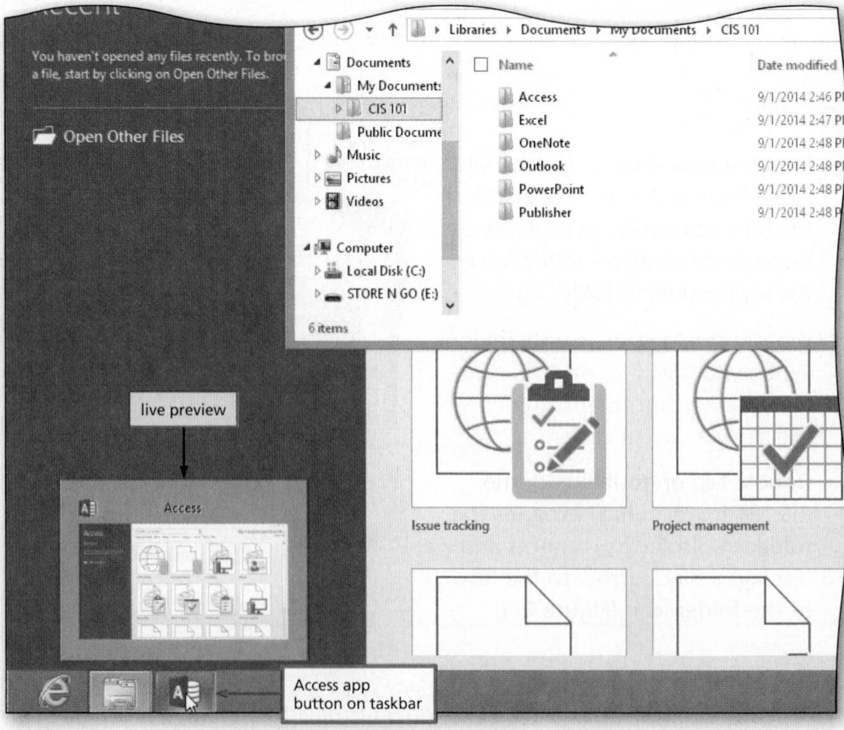

Figure 24

2

- Tap or click the Access app button or the live preview to make the app associated with the app button the active window (Figure 25).

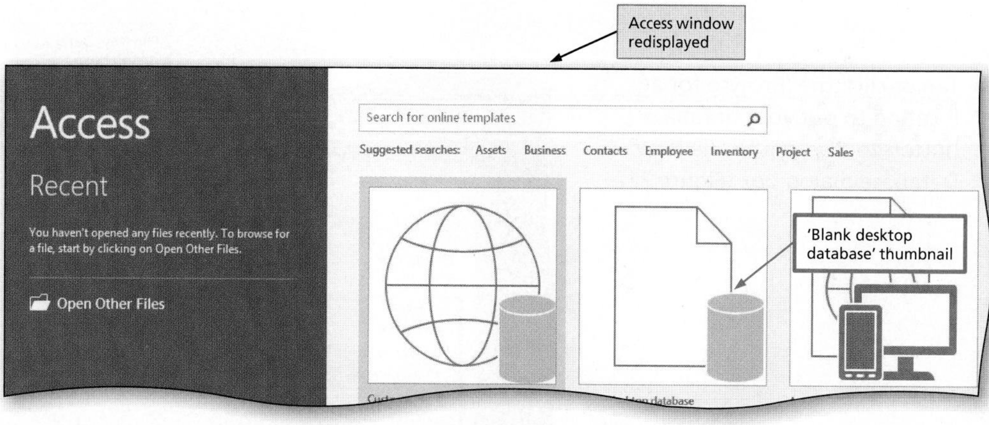

Figure 25

Break Point: If you wish to take a break, this is a good place to do so. To resume at a later time, continue to follow the steps from this location forward.

Creating an Access Database

Unlike the other Office apps, Access saves a database when you first create it. When working in Access, you will add data to an Access database. As you add data to a database, Access automatically saves your changes rather than waiting until you manually save the database or exit Access. In other apps, you first enter data and then save it.

Because Access automatically saves the database as you add and change data, you do not always have to click the Save button on the Quick Access Toolbar. Instead, the Save button in Access is used for saving the objects (including tables, queries, forms, reports, and other database objects) a database contains. You can use either the 'Blank desktop database' option or a template to create a new database. If you already know the organization of your database, you would use the 'Blank desktop database' option. If not, you can use a template. Templates can guide you by suggesting some commonly used database organizations.

To Create a Database in a Folder

1 SIGN IN | 2 USE WINDOWS | 3 USE APPS | 4 FILE MANAGEMENT | 5 SWITCH APPS | 6 SAVE FILES
7 CHANGE SCREEN RESOLUTION | 8 EXIT APPS | 9 USE ADDITIONAL APP | 10 USE HELP

The following steps use the 'Blank desktop database' option to create a database named PJP Marketing in the Access folder in the class folder (CIS 101, in this case) in the Documents library. ***Why?*** *If you want to maintain data for a company, a database is perfect for the job.*

With the folders for storing your files created, you can create the database. The following steps create a database in the Access folder contained in your class folder (CIS 101, in this case) using the file name, PJP Marketing.

1

- Tap or click the 'Blank desktop database' thumbnail (shown in Figure 25) to select the database type.
- Type **PJP Marketing** in the File Name text box to enter the new file name. Do not press the ENTER key after typing the file name because you do not want to create the database yet (Figure 26).

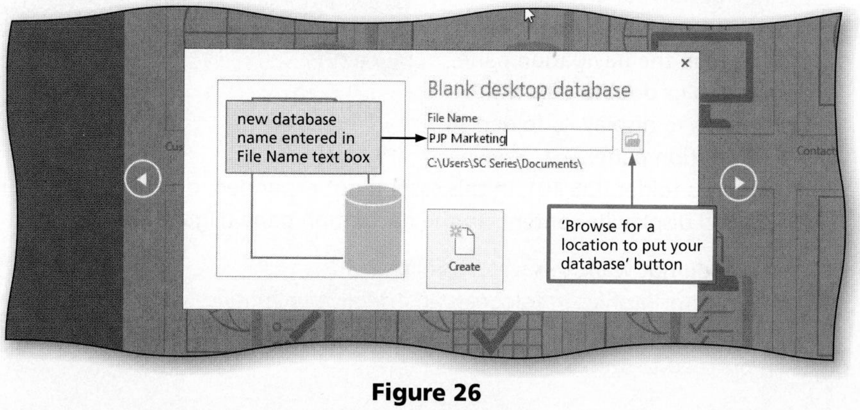

Figure 26

2

- Tap or click the 'Browse for a location to put your database' button to display the File New Database dialog box (Figure 27).

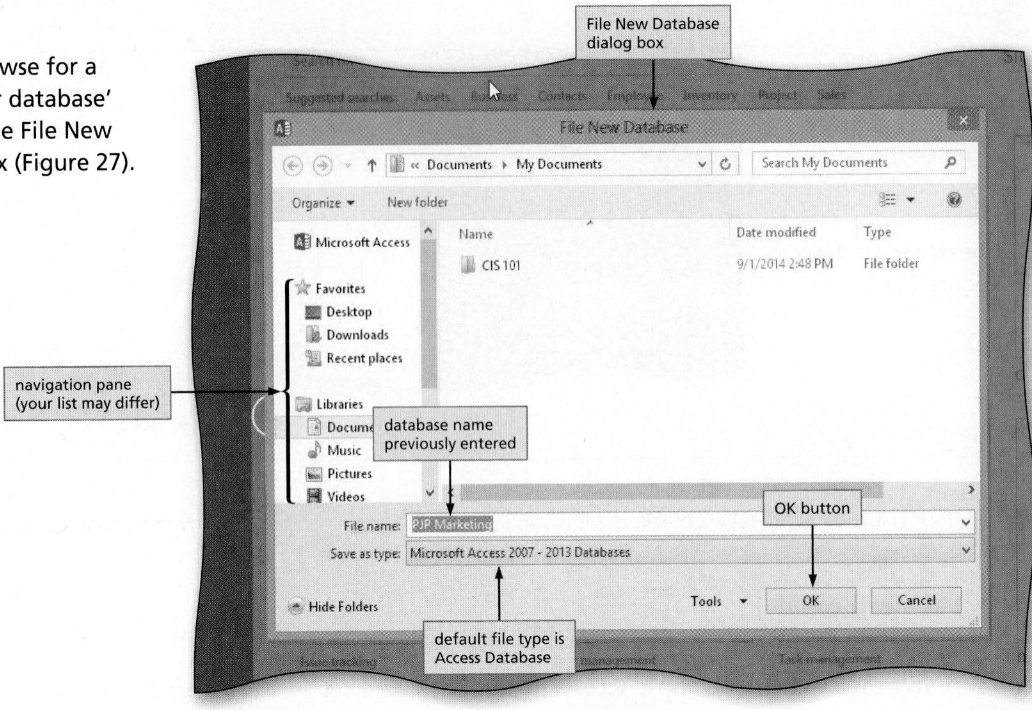

Figure 27

3

- Navigate to the desired save location (in this case, the Access folder in the CIS 101 folder [or your class folder] in the My Documents folder in the Documents library) by performing the tasks in Steps 3a and 3b.

3a

- If the Documents library is not displayed in the navigation pane, slide to scroll or drag the scroll bar in the navigation pane until Documents appears.
- If the Documents library is not expanded in the navigation pane, double-tap or double-click Documents to display its folders in the navigation pane.
- If the My Documents folder is not expanded in the navigation pane, double-tap or double-click My Documents to display its folders in the navigation pane.

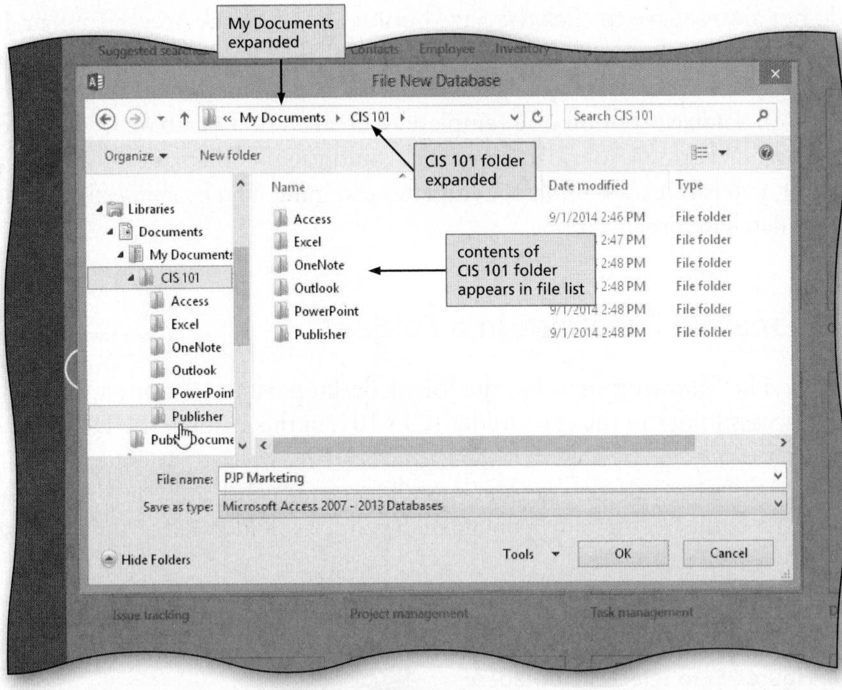

Figure 28

- If your class folder (CIS 101, in this case) is not expanded, double-tap or double-click the CIS 101 folder to select the folder and display its contents in the navigation pane (Figure 28).

Q&A

What if I do not want to save in a folder?

Although storing files in folders is an effective technique for organizing files, some users prefer not to store files in folders. If you prefer not to save this file in a folder, select the storage device on which you wish to save the file and then proceed to Step 5.

3b

- Tap or click the Access folder in the navigation pane to select it as the new save location and display its contents in the file list (Figure 29).

Q&A Why does the 'Save as type' box say Microsoft Access 2007–2013 Databases?

Microsoft Access database formats change with some new versions of Microsoft Access. The most recent format is the Microsoft Access 2007–2013 Databases format.

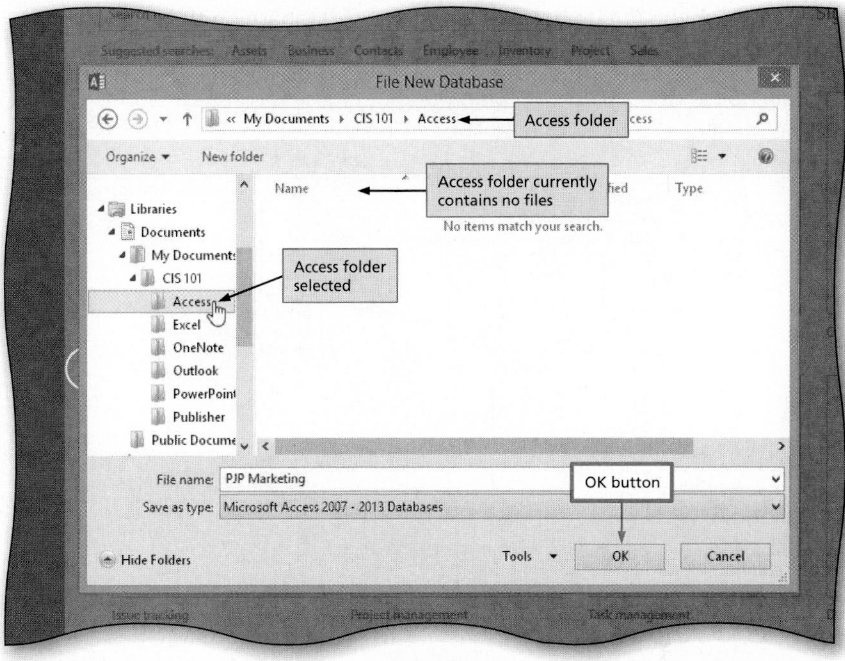

Figure 29

4

- Tap or click the OK button (File New Database dialog box) to select the Access folder as the location for the database and close the dialog box (Figure 30).

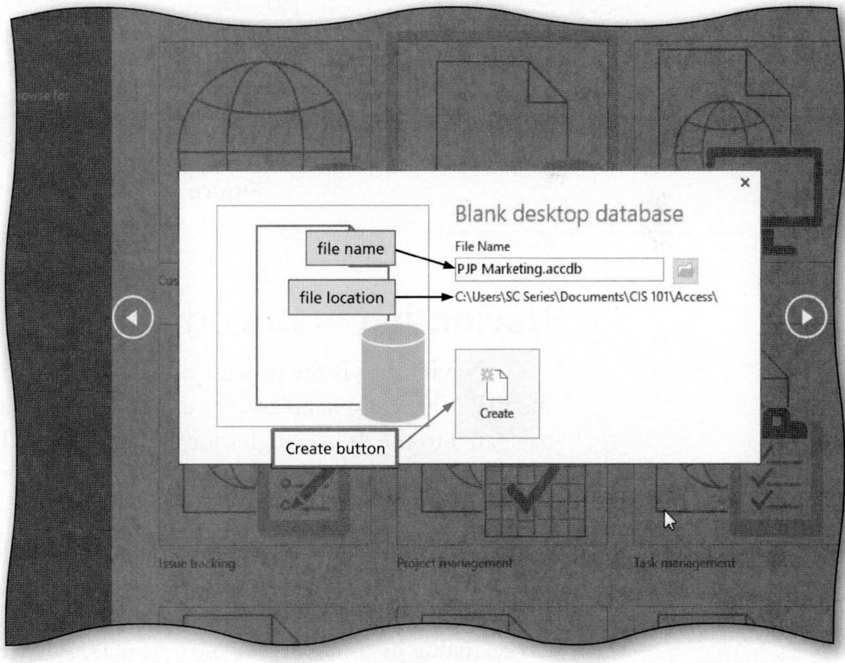

Figure 30

5

- Tap or click the Create button to create the database on the selected drive in the selected folder with the file name, PJP Marketing (Figure 31).

Q&A How do I know that the PJP Marketing database is created?
The file name of the database appears on the title bar.

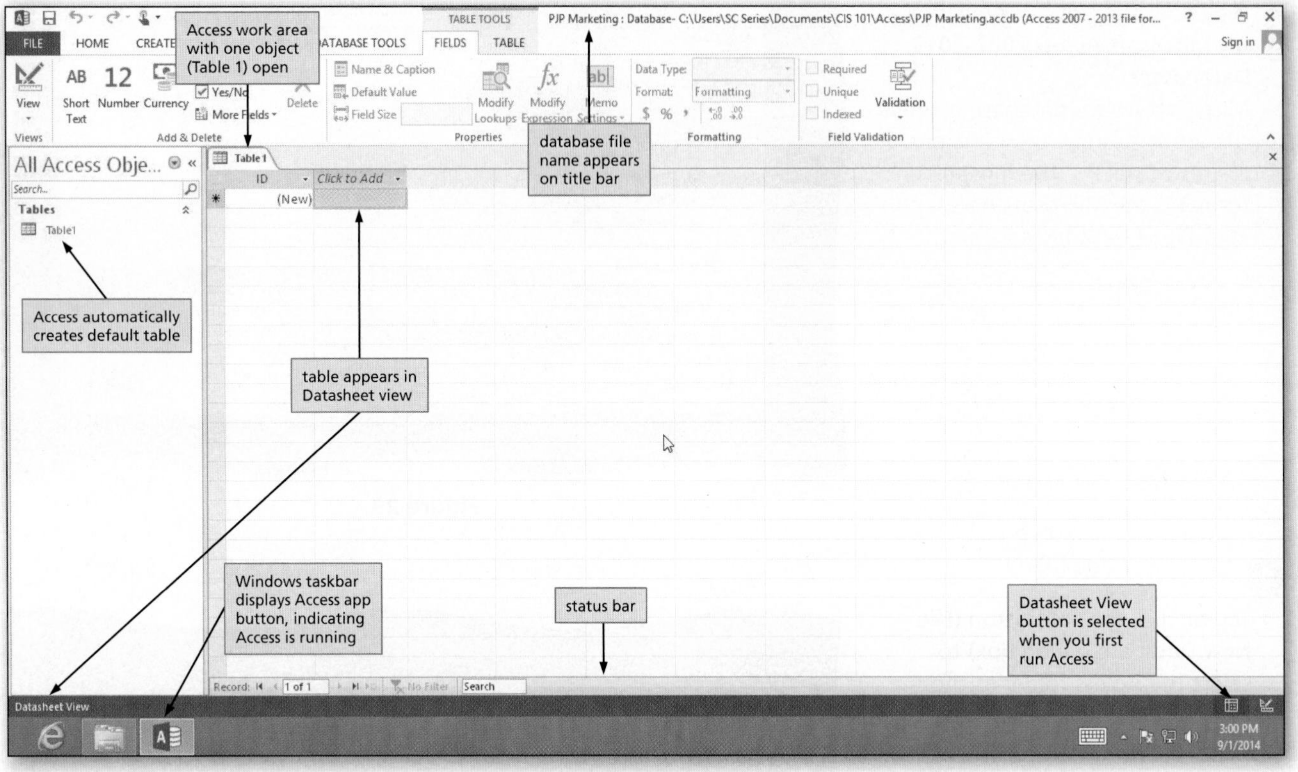

Figure 31

Navigating in Dialog Boxes

Navigating is the process of finding a location on a storage device. While creating the PJP Marketing database, for example, Steps 3a and 3b in the previous set of steps navigated to the Access folder located in the CIS 101 folder in the My Documents folder in the Documents library. When performing certain functions in Windows apps, such as saving a file, opening a file, or inserting a picture in a database object, you most likely will have to navigate to the location where you want to save the file or to the folder containing the file you want to open or insert. Most dialog boxes in Windows apps requiring navigation follow a similar procedure; that is, the way you navigate to a folder in one dialog box, such as the Save As dialog box, is similar to how you might navigate in another dialog box, such as the Open dialog box. If you chose to navigate to a specific location in a dialog box, you would follow the instructions in Steps 3a and 3b.

The Access Window

The Access window consists of a variety of components to make your work more efficient. These include the Navigation Pane, Access work area, ribbon, shortcut menus, and Quick Access Toolbar. Some of these components are common to other Office apps; others are unique to Access.

Navigation Pane and Access Work Area

You work on objects such as tables, forms, and reports in the **Access work area**. In the work area in Figure 31, a single table, Table1, is open in the work area. **Object tabs** for the open objects appear at the top of the work area. If you have multiple objects open at the same time, you can select one of the open objects by tapping or clicking its tab. To the left of the work area is the Navigation Pane. The **Navigation Pane** contains a list of all the objects in the database. You use this pane to open an object. You also can customize the way objects are displayed in the Navigation Pane.

Status Bar The **status bar**, located at the bottom of the Access window, presents information about the database object, the progress of current tasks, and the status of certain commands and keys; it also provides controls for viewing the object. As you enter data or perform certain commands, various indicators may appear on the status bar. The left edge of the status bar in Figure 31 shows that the table object is open in **Datasheet view**. In Datasheet view, the table is represented as a collection of rows and columns called a **datasheet**. Toward the right edge are View buttons, which you can use to change the view that currently appears.

Scroll Bars You use a scroll bar to display different portions of an object. If an object is too long to fit vertically, a vertical scroll bar will appear at the right edge of the work area. If an object is too wide to fit, a horizontal scroll bar also appears at the bottom of the work area. On a scroll bar, the position of the scroll box reflects the location of the portion of the object that is displayed in the work area.

Ribbon The ribbon, located near the top of the window below the title bar, is the control center in Access and other Office apps (Figure 32). The ribbon provides easy, central access to the tasks you perform while creating a database. The ribbon consists of tabs, groups, and commands. Each **tab** contains a collection of groups, and each **group** contains related functions. When you run an Office app, such as Access, it initially displays several main tabs, also called default or top-level tabs. All Office apps have a HOME tab, which contains the more frequently used commands.

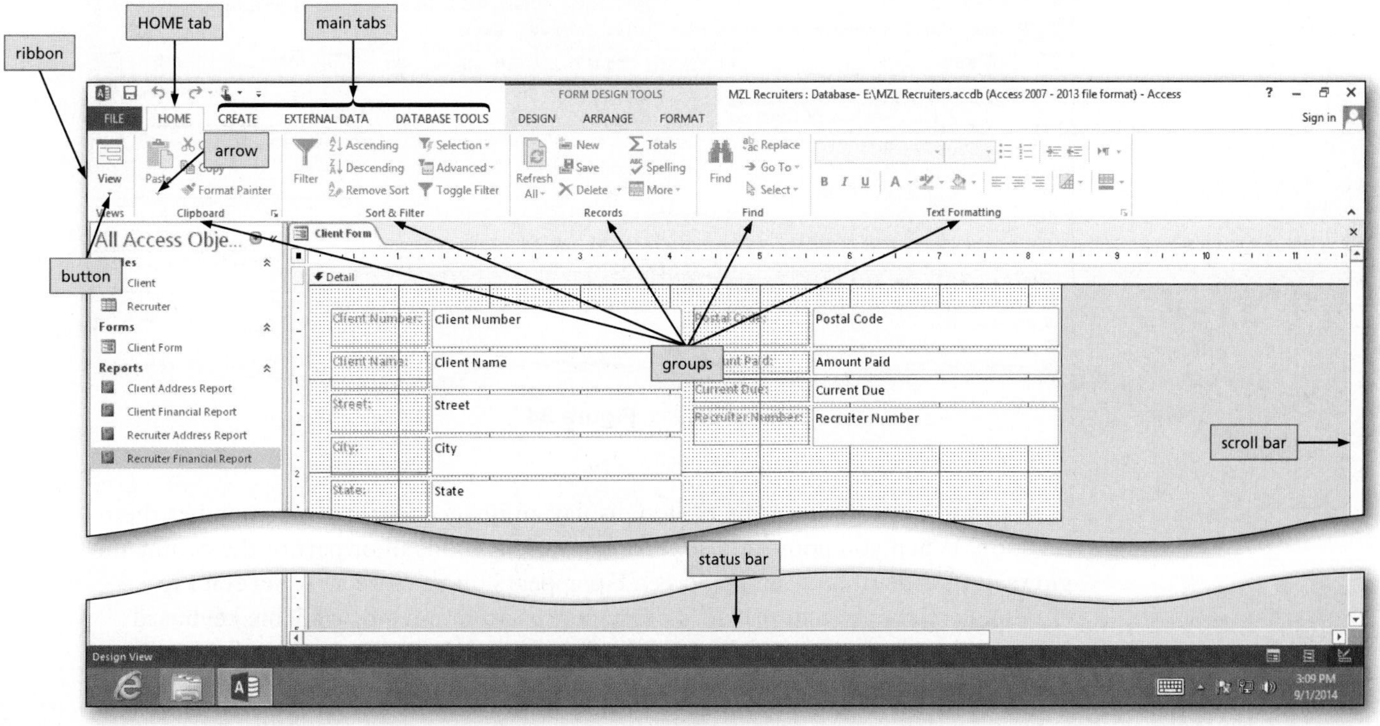

Figure 32

In addition to the main tabs, the Office apps display **tool tabs**, also called contextual tabs (Figure 33), when you perform certain tasks or work with objects such as pictures or tables. If you modify the design of a form, for example, the FORM DESIGN TOOLS tab and its related subordinate DESIGN tab appear, collectively referred to as the FORM DESIGN TOOLS DESIGN tab. When you are finished working with the form, the FORM DESIGN TOOLS DESIGN tab disappears from the ribbon. Access and other Office apps determine when tool tabs should appear and disappear based on tasks you perform.

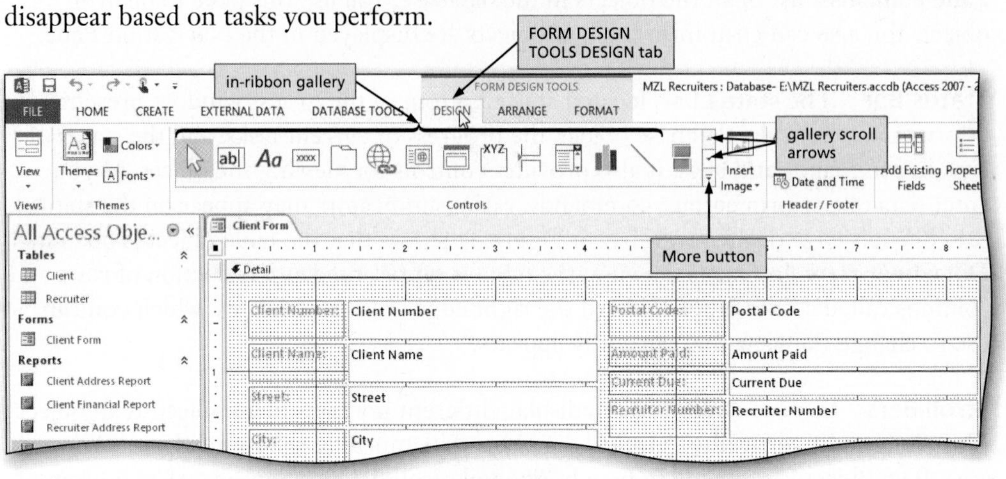

Figure 33

Items on the ribbon include buttons, boxes, and galleries (shown in Figure 32 on the previous page). A **gallery** is a set of choices, often graphical, arranged in a grid or in a list. You can scroll through choices in an in-ribbon gallery by tapping or clicking the gallery's scroll arrows. Or, you can tap or click a gallery's More button to view more gallery options on the screen at a time.

Some buttons and boxes have arrows that, when tapped or clicked, also display a gallery; others always cause a gallery to be displayed when tapped or clicked (Figure 34).

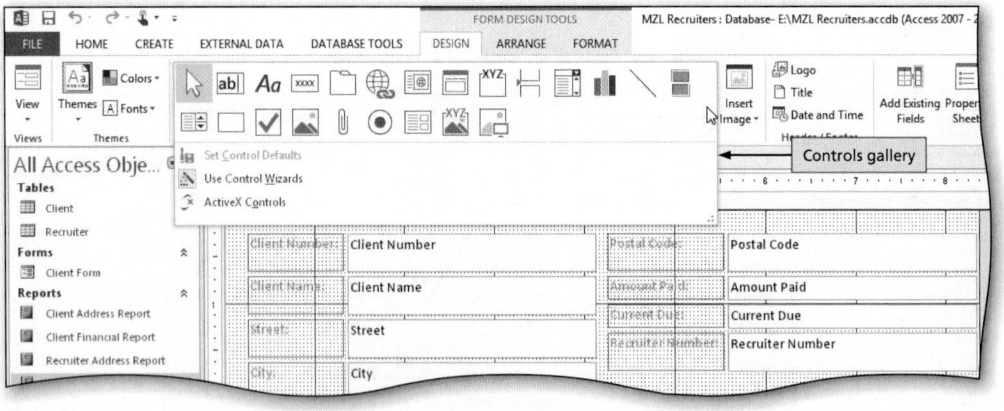

Figure 34

Some commands on the ribbon display an image to help you remember their function. When you point to a command on the ribbon, all or part of the command glows in a shade of blue, and a ScreenTip appears on the screen. A **ScreenTip** is an on-screen note that provides the name of the command, available keyboard shortcut(s), a description of the command, and sometimes instructions for how to obtain help about the command (Figure 35).

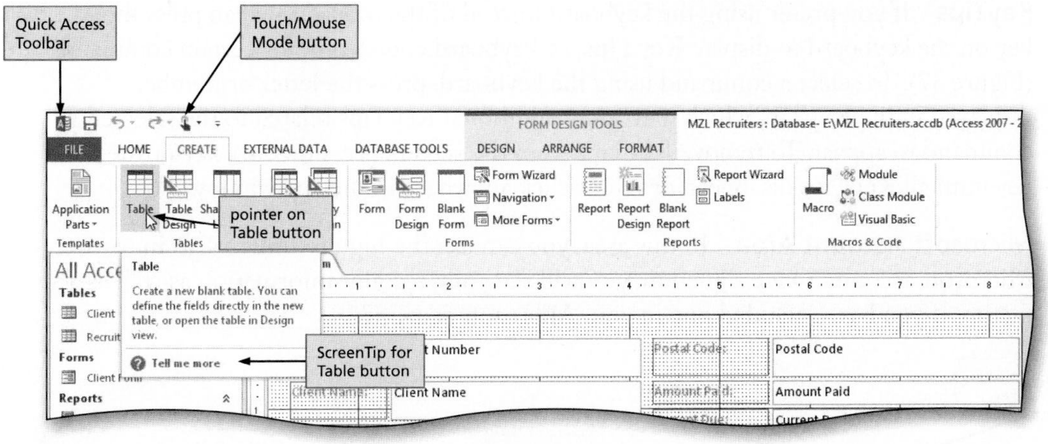

Figure 35

Some groups on the ribbon have a small arrow in the lower-right corner, called a **Dialog Box Launcher**, that when tapped or clicked, displays a dialog box or a task pane with additional options for the group (Figure 36). When presented with a dialog box, you make selections and must close the dialog box before returning to the document. A **task pane**, in contrast to a dialog box, is a window that can remain open and visible while you work in the document.

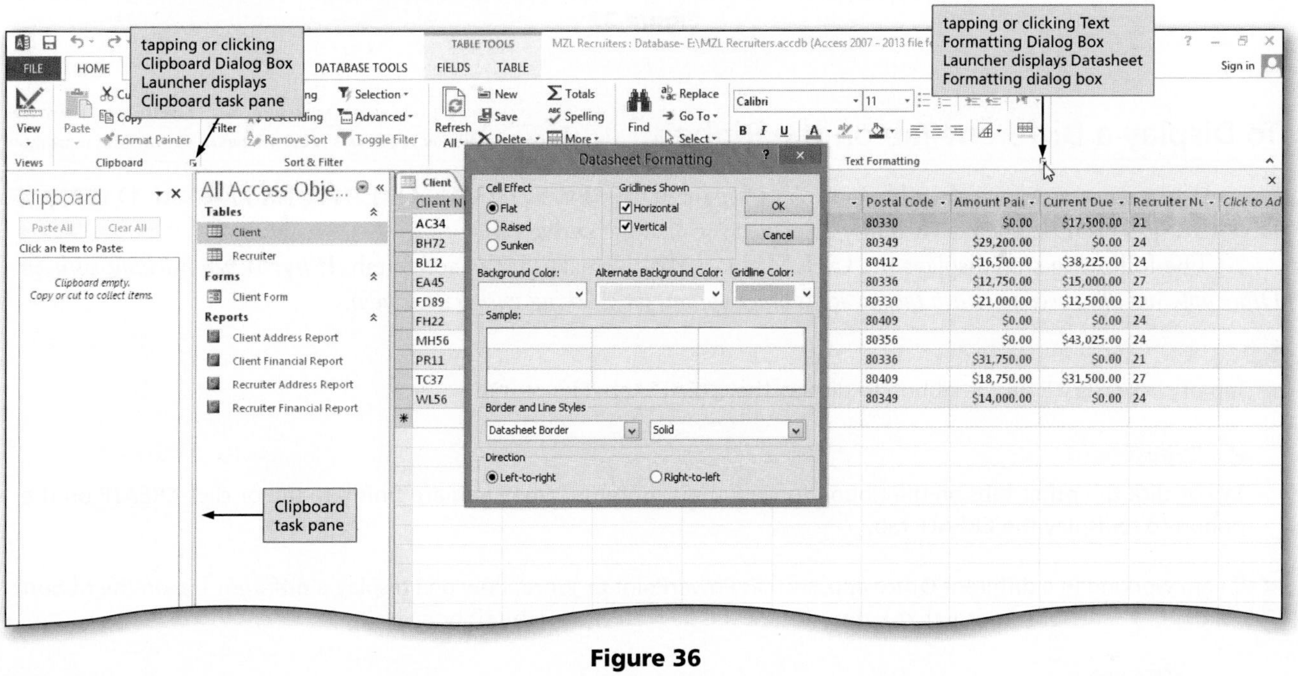

Figure 36

Quick Access Toolbar The **Quick Access Toolbar**, located initially (by default) above the ribbon at the left edge of the title bar, provides convenient, one-tap or one-click access to frequently used commands (shown in Figure 35). The commands on the Quick Access Toolbar always are available, regardless of the task you are performing. The Touch/Mouse Mode button on the Quick Access Toolbar allows you to switch between Touch mode and Mouse mode. If you primarily are using touch gestures, Touch mode will add more space between commands on menus and on the ribbon so that they are easier to tap. While touch gestures are convenient ways to interact with Office apps, not all features are supported when you are using Touch mode. If you are using a mouse, Mouse mode will not add the extra space between buttons and commands. The Quick Access Toolbar is discussed in more depth later in the chapter.

BTW

Touch Mode

The Office and Windows interfaces may vary if you are using Touch mode. For this reason, you might notice that the function or appearance of your touch screen in Access differs slightly from this book's presentation.

KeyTips If you prefer using the keyboard instead of the mouse, you can press the ALT key on the keyboard to display **KeyTips**, or keyboard code icons, for certain commands (Figure 37). To select a command using the keyboard, press the letter or number displayed in the KeyTip, which may cause additional KeyTips related to the selected command to appear. To remove KeyTips from the screen, press the ALT key or the ESC key until all KeyTips disappear, or tap or click anywhere in the app window.

Microsoft Account Area In this area, you can use the Sign in link to sign in to your Microsoft account. Once signed in, you will see your account information as well as a picture if you have included one in your Microsoft account.

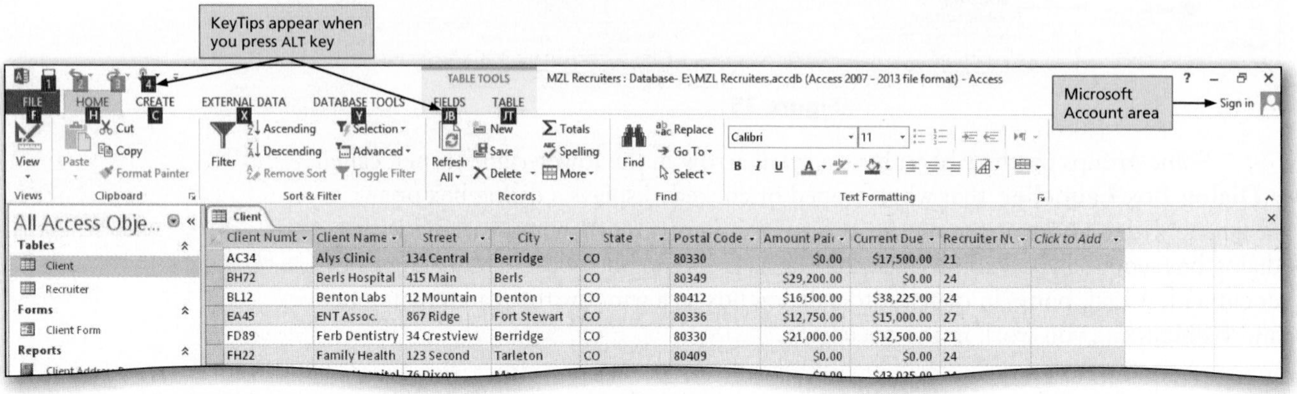

Figure 37

To Display a Different Tab on the Ribbon

1 SIGN IN | 2 USE WINDOWS | 3 USE APPS | 4 FILE MANAGEMENT | 5 SWITCH APPS | 6 SAVE FILES
7 CHANGE SCREEN RESOLUTION | 8 EXIT APPS | 9 USE ADDITIONAL APP FEATURES | 10 USE HELP

When you run Access, the ribbon displays five main tabs: FILE, HOME, CREATE, EXTERNAL DATA, and DATABASE TOOLS. The tab currently displayed is called the **active tab**.

The following step displays the CREATE tab, that is, makes it the active tab. ***Why?*** *When working with an Office app, you may need to switch tabs to access other options for working with a document.*

1

- Tap or click CREATE on the ribbon to display the CREATE tab (Figure 38).

Experiment

- Tap or click the other tabs on the ribbon to view their contents. When you are finished, tap or click CREATE on the ribbon to redisplay the CREATE tab.

Q&A If I am working in a different Office app, such as PowerPoint or Word, how do I display a different tab on the ribbon?
Follow this same procedure; that is, tap or click the desired tab on the ribbon.

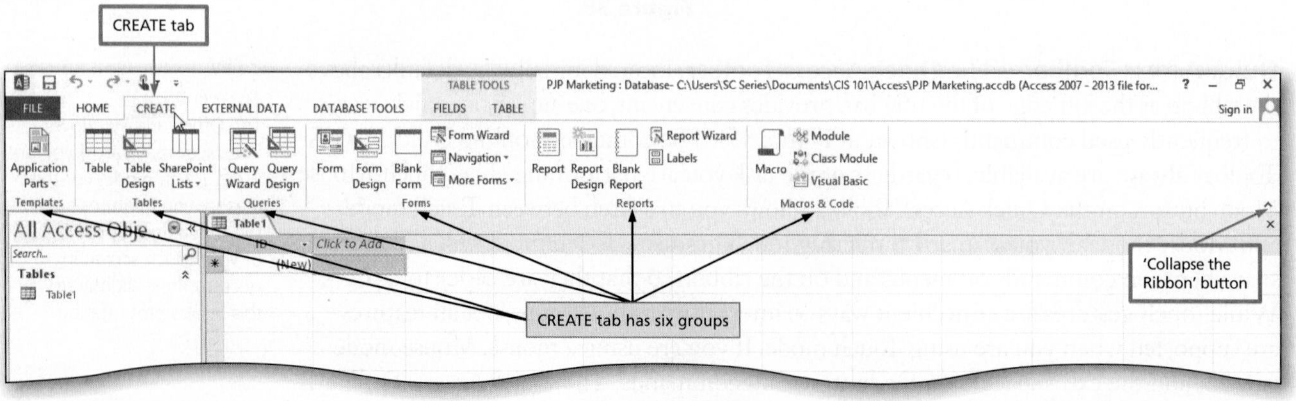

Figure 38

To Collapse and Expand the Ribbon

To display more of a document or other item in the window of an Office app, some users prefer to collapse the ribbon, which hides the groups on the ribbon and displays only the main tabs. Each time you run an Office app, such as Access, the ribbon appears the same way it did the last time you used that Office app. The chapters in this book, however, begin with the ribbon appearing as it did at the initial installation of Office or Access.

The following steps collapse, expand, and restore the ribbon in Access. ***Why?*** *If you need more space on the screen to work with your database, you can collapse the ribbon to gain additional workspace.*

1

- Tap or click the 'Collapse the Ribbon' button on the ribbon (shown in Figure 38) to collapse the ribbon (Figure 39).

Q&A What happened to the groups on the ribbon?
When you collapse the ribbon, the groups disappear so that the ribbon does not take up as much space on the screen.

What happened to the 'Collapse the Ribbon' button?
The 'Pin the ribbon' button replaces the 'Collapse the Ribbon' button when the ribbon is collapsed. You will see the 'Pin the ribbon' button only when you expand a ribbon by tapping or clicking a tab.

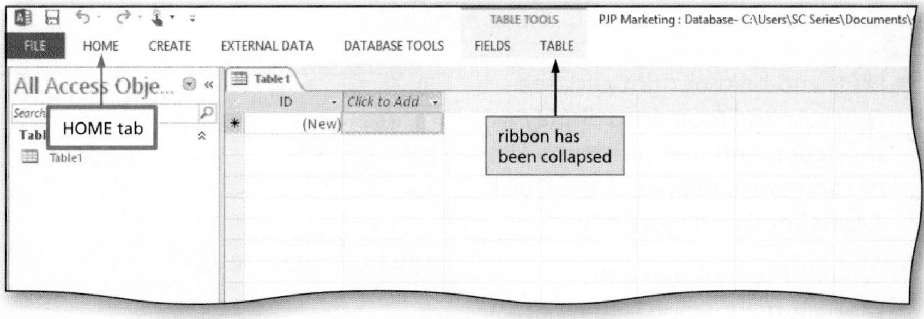

Figure 39

2

- Tap or click HOME on the ribbon to expand the HOME tab (Figure 40).

Q&A Why would I click the HOME tab?
If you want to use a command on a collapsed ribbon, tap or click the main tab to display the groups for that tab. After you select a command on the ribbon, the groups will be collapsed once again. If you decide not to use a command on the ribbon, you can collapse the groups by tapping or clicking the same main tab or tapping or clicking in the app window.

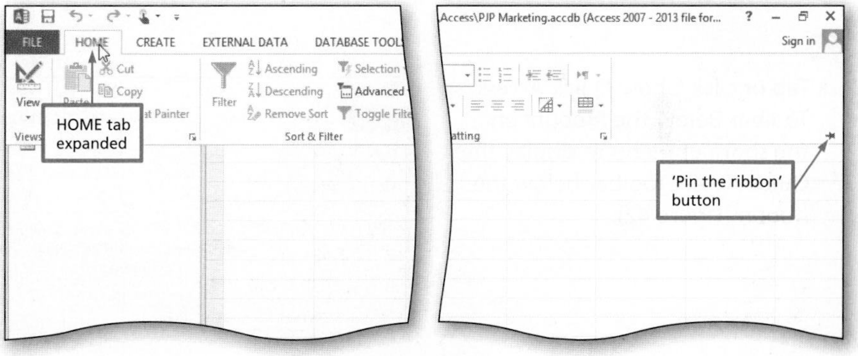

Figure 40

Experiment

- Tap or click HOME on the ribbon to collapse the groups again. Tap or click HOME on the ribbon to expand the HOME tab.

3

- Tap or click the 'Pin the ribbon' button on the expanded HOME tab to restore the ribbon.

Other Ways

1. Double-tap or double-click a main tab on the ribbon
2. Press CTRL+F1

To Use a Shortcut Menu to Relocate the Quick Access Toolbar

1 SIGN IN | 2 USE WINDOWS | 3 USE APPS | **4 FILE MANAGEMENT** | **5 SWITCH APPS** | **6 SAVE FILES**
7 CHANGE SCREEN RESOLUTION | **8 EXIT APPS** | **9 USE ADDITIONAL APP FEATURES** | **10 USE HELP**

When you press and hold or right-click certain areas of the Access and other Office app windows, a shortcut menu will appear. A **shortcut menu** is a list of frequently used commands that relate to an object. ***Why?*** *You can use shortcut menus to access common commands quickly.* When you press and hold or right-click the status bar, for example, a shortcut menu appears with commands related to the status bar. When you press and hold or right-click the Quick Access Toolbar, a shortcut menu appears with commands related to the Quick Access Toolbar. The following steps use a shortcut menu to move the Quick Access Toolbar, which by default is located on the title bar.

1

- Press and hold or right-click the Quick Access Toolbar to display a shortcut menu that presents a list of commands related to the Quick Access Toolbar (Figure 41).

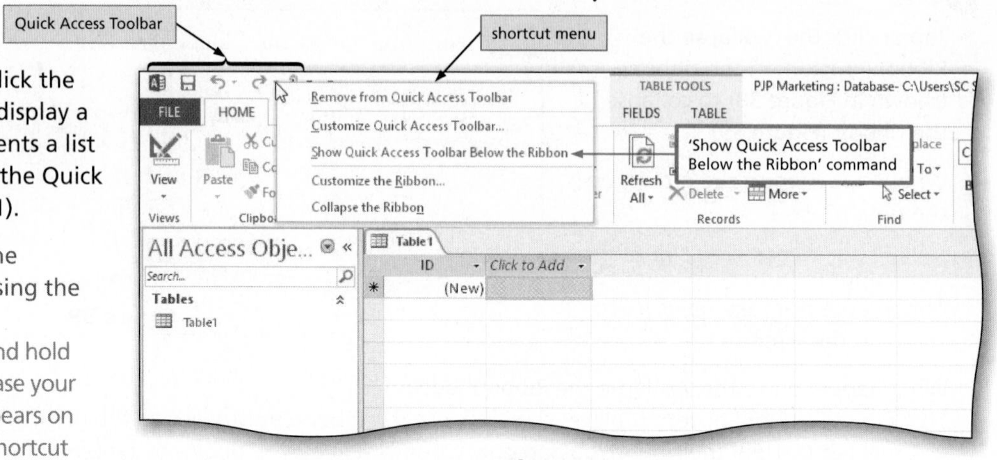

Figure 41

Q&A What if I cannot make the shortcut menu appear using the touch instruction?
When you use the press and hold technique, be sure to release your finger when the circle appears on the screen to display the shortcut menu. If the technique still does not work, you might need to add more space around objects on the screen, making it easier for you to press or tap them. Click the 'Customize Quick Access Toolbar' button and then click 'Touch/Mouse Mode' on the menu. Another option is to use the stylus.

2

- Tap or click 'Show Quick Access Toolbar Below the Ribbon' on the shortcut menu to display the Quick Access Toolbar below the ribbon (Figure 42).

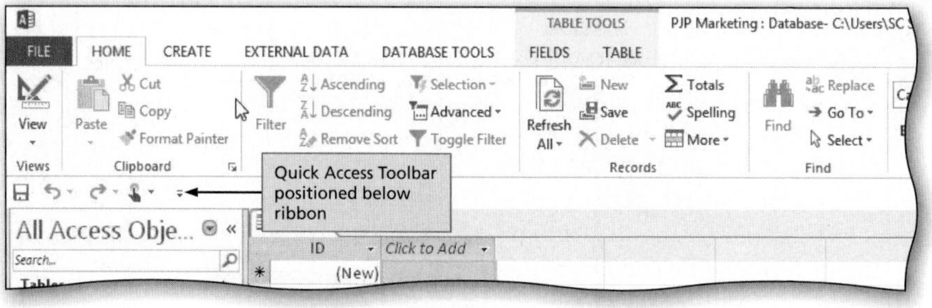

Figure 42

3

- Press and hold or right-click the Quick Access Toolbar to display a shortcut menu (Figure 43).

4

- Tap or click 'Show Quick Access Toolbar Above the Ribbon' on the shortcut menu to return the Quick Access Toolbar to its original position (shown in Figure 41).

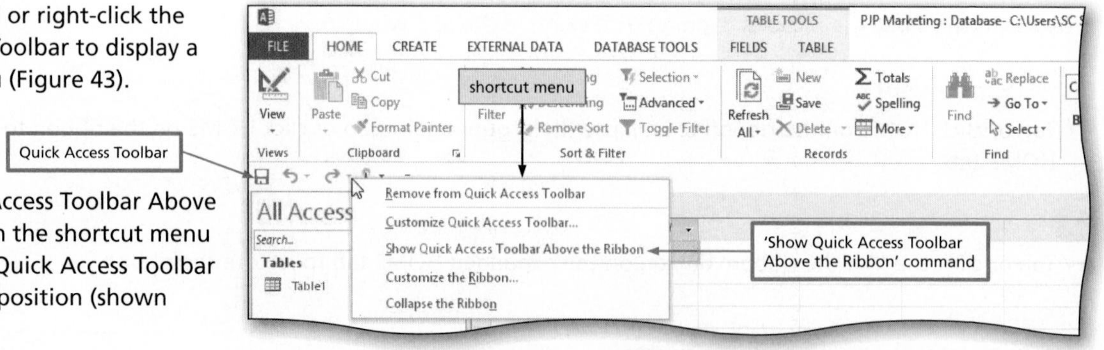

Figure 43

Other Ways

1. Tap or click 'Customize Quick Access Toolbar' button on Quick Access Toolbar, tap or click 'Show Below the Ribbon' or 'Show Above the Ribbon'

To Customize the Quick Access Toolbar

1 SIGN IN | 2 USE WINDOWS | 3 USE APPS | 4 FILE MANAGEMENT | 5 SWITCH APPS | 6 SAVE FILES
7 CHANGE SCREEN RESOLUTION | 8 EXIT APPS | 9 USE ADDITIONAL APP FEATURES | 10 USE HELP

The Quick Access Toolbar provides easy access to some of the more frequently used commands in the Office apps. By default, the Quick Access Toolbar contains buttons for the Save, Undo, and Redo commands. You can customize the Quick Access Toolbar by changing its location in the window, as shown in the previous steps, and by adding more buttons to reflect commands you would like to access easily. The following steps add the Quick Print button to the Quick Access Toolbar in the Access window. ***Why?*** *Adding the Quick Print button to the Quick Access Toolbar speeds up the process of printing.*

1

- Tap or click the 'Customize Quick Access Toolbar' button to display the Customize Quick Access Toolbar menu (Figure 44).

Q&A Which commands are listed on the Customize Quick Access Toolbar menu?
It lists commands that commonly are added to the Quick Access Toolbar.

What do the check marks next to some commands signify?
Check marks appear next to commands that already are on the Quick Access Toolbar. When you add a button to the Quick Access Toolbar, a check mark will be displayed next to its command name.

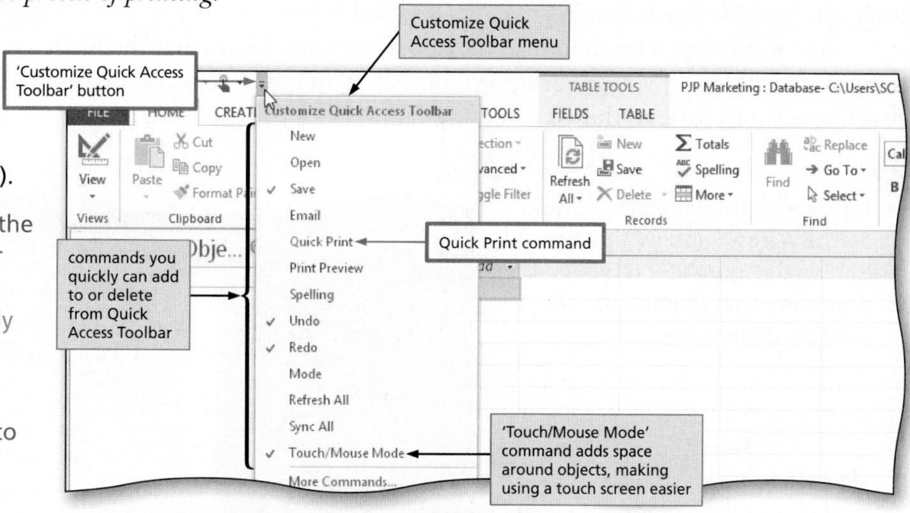

Figure 44

2

- Tap or click Quick Print on the Customize Quick Access Toolbar menu to add the Quick Print button to the Quick Access Toolbar (Figure 45).

Q&A How would I remove a button from the Quick Access Toolbar?
You would press and hold or right-click the button you wish to remove and then tap or click 'Remove from Quick Access Toolbar' on the shortcut menu or tap or click the 'Customize Quick Access Toolbar' button on the Quick Access Toolbar and then click the button name in the Customize Quick Access Toolbar menu to remove the check mark.

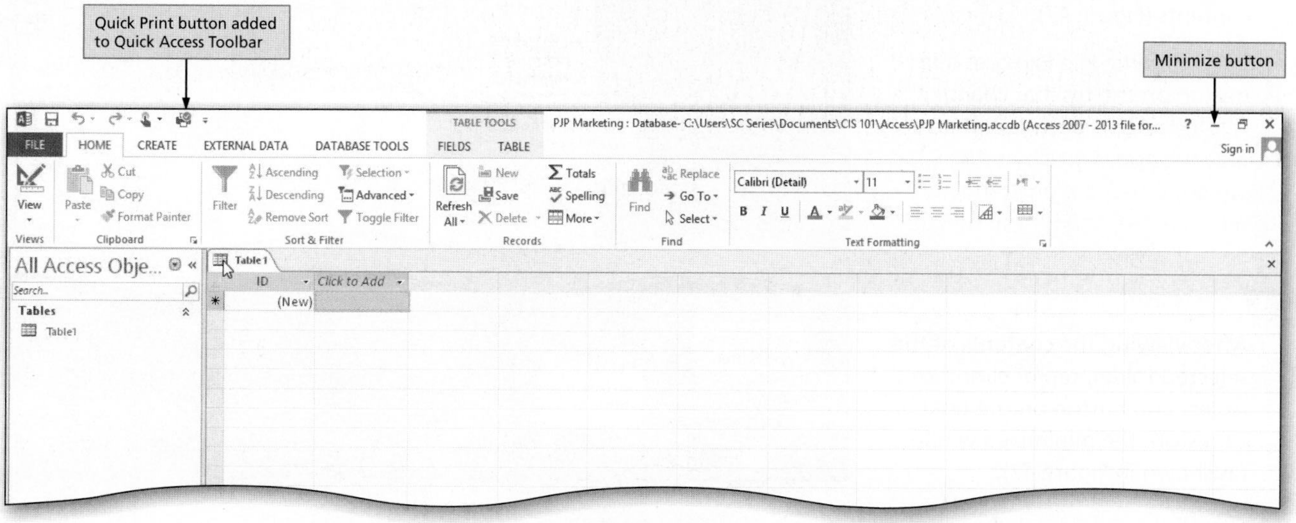

Figure 45

To Minimize and Restore a Window

Before continuing, you can verify that the Access file was saved properly. To do this, you will minimize the Access window and then open the CIS 101 window so that you can verify the file is stored in the CIS 101 folder on the hard disk. A **minimized window** is an open window that is hidden from view but can be displayed quickly by clicking the window's app button on the taskbar.

In the following example, Access is used to illustrate minimizing and restoring windows; however, you would follow the same steps regardless of the Office app you are using. ***Why?*** *Before closing an app, you should make sure your file saved correctly so that you can find it later.*

The following steps minimize the Access window, verify that the file is saved, and then restore the minimized window. If you are using Windows 7, skip these steps and instead perform the steps in the yellow box that immediately follows these Windows 8 steps.

1

- Tap or click the Minimize button on the Access window title bar (shown in Figure 45 on the previous page) to minimize the window (Figure 46).

Q&A Is the minimized window still available?
The minimized window, Access in this case, remains available but no longer is the active window. It is minimized as an app button on the taskbar.

- If the File Explorer window is not open on the screen, tap or click the File Explorer app button on the taskbar to make the File folder window the active window.

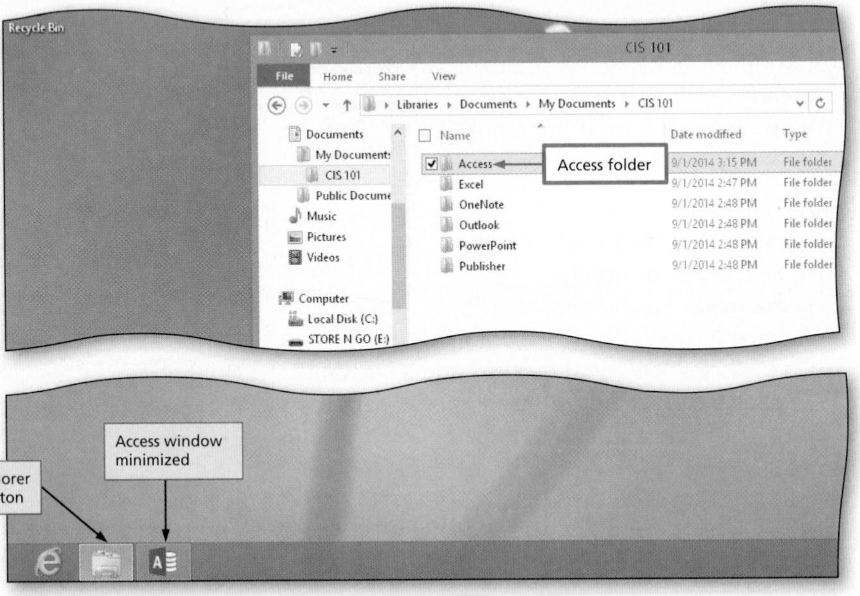

Figure 46

2

- Double-tap or double-click the Access folder in the file list to select the folder and display its contents (Figure 47).

Q&A Why does the File Explorer app button on the taskbar change?
A selected app button indicates that the app is active on the screen. When the button is not selected, the app is running but not active.

3

- After viewing the contents of the selected folder, tap or click the Access app button on the taskbar to restore the minimized window (as shown in Figure 47).

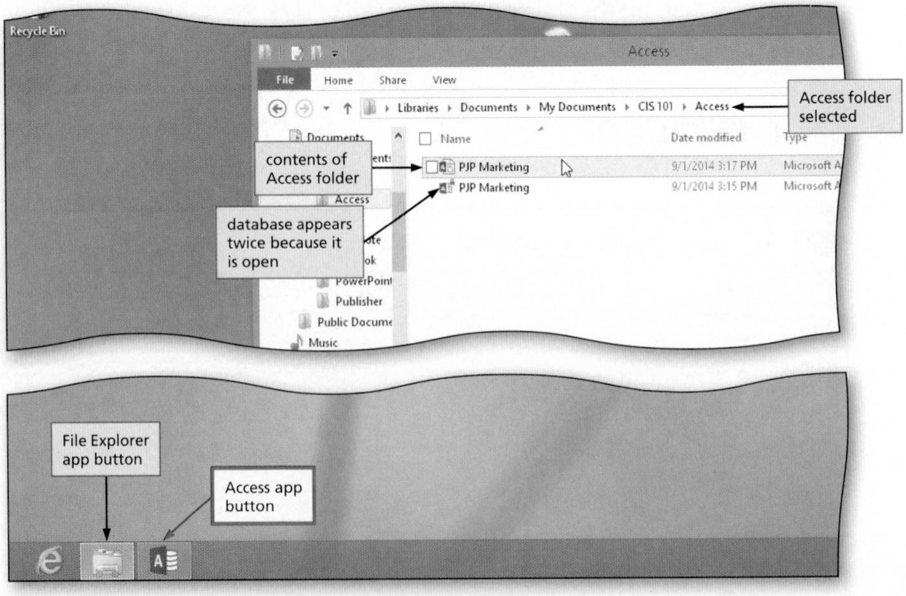

Figure 47

Other Ways

1. Press and hold or right-click title bar, tap or click Minimize on shortcut menu, tap or click taskbar button in taskbar button area
2. Press WINDOWS+M, press WINDOWS+SHIFT+M

To Minimize and Restore a Window Using Windows 7

If you are using Windows 7, perform these steps to minimize and restore a window instead of the previous steps that use Windows 8.

1. Click the Minimize button on the app's title bar to minimize the window.
2. If the Windows Explorer window is not open on the screen, click the Windows Explorer button on the taskbar to make the Windows Explorer window the active window.
3. Double-click the Access folder in the file list to select the folder and display its contents.
4. After viewing the contents of the selected folder, click the Access button on the taskbar to restore the minimized window.

To Sign Out of a Microsoft Account

If you are using a public computer or otherwise wish to sign out of your Microsoft account, you should sign out of the account from the Account gallery in the Backstage view. Signing out of the account is the safest way to make sure that nobody else can access online files or settings stored in your Microsoft account. ***Why?*** *For security reasons, you should sign out of your Microsoft account when you are finished using a public or shared computer. Staying signed in to your Microsoft account might enable others to access your files.*

The following steps sign out of a Microsoft account from Access. You would use the same steps in any Office app. If you do not wish to sign out of your Microsoft account, read these steps without performing them.

1. Tap or click FILE on the ribbon to open the Backstage view.

2. Tap or click the Account tab to display the Account gallery (Figure 48 on the next page).

3. Tap or click the Sign out link, which displays the Remove Account dialog box. If a Can't remove Windows accounts dialog box appears instead of the Remove Account dialog box, tap or click the OK button and skip the remaining steps.

   Q&A: Why does a Can't remove Windows accounts dialog box appear?
   If you signed in to Windows using your Microsoft account, then you also must sign out from Windows, rather than signing out from within Access. When you are finished using Windows, be sure to sign out at that time.

4. Tap or click the Yes button (Remove Account dialog box) to sign out of your Microsoft account on this computer.

   Q&A: Should I sign out of Windows after removing my Microsoft account?
   When you are finished using the computer, you should sign out of Windows for maximum security.

5. Tap or click the Back button in the upper-left corner of the Backstage view to return to the document.

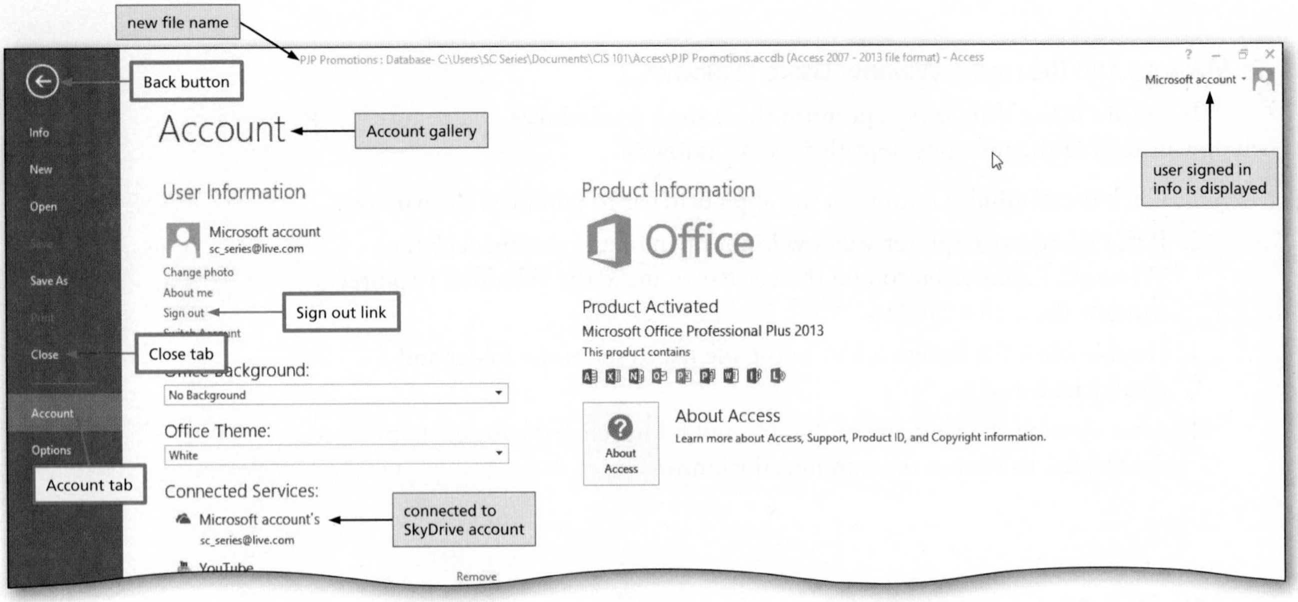

Figure 48

Screen Resolution

Screen resolution indicates the number of pixels (dots) that the computer uses to display the letters, numbers, graphics, and background you see on the screen. When you increase the screen resolution, Windows displays more information on the screen, but the information decreases in size. The reverse also is true: as you decrease the screen resolution, Windows displays less information on the screen, but the information increases in size.

Screen resolution usually is stated as the product of two numbers, such as 1366 × 768 (pronounced "thirteen sixty-six by seven sixty-eight"). A 1366 × 768 screen resolution results in a display of 1366 distinct pixels on each of 768 lines, or about 1,050,624 pixels. Changing the screen resolution affects how the ribbon appears in Office apps and some Windows dialog boxes. Figure 49, for example, shows the Access ribbon at screen resolutions of 1366 × 768 and 1024 × 768. All of the same commands are available regardless of screen resolution. The app (Access, in this case), however, makes changes to the groups and the buttons within the groups to accommodate the various screen resolutions. The result is that certain commands may need to be accessed differently depending on the resolution chosen. A command that is visible on the ribbon and available by tapping or clicking a button at one resolution may not be visible and may need to be accessed using its Dialog Box Launcher at a different resolution.

Comparing the two ribbons in Figure 49, notice the changes in content and layout of the groups and galleries. In some cases, the content of a group is the same in each resolution, but the layout of the group differs. For example, the same gallery and buttons appear in the Text Formatting groups in the two resolutions, but the layouts differ. In other cases, the content and layout are the same across the resolution, but the level of detail differs with the resolution.

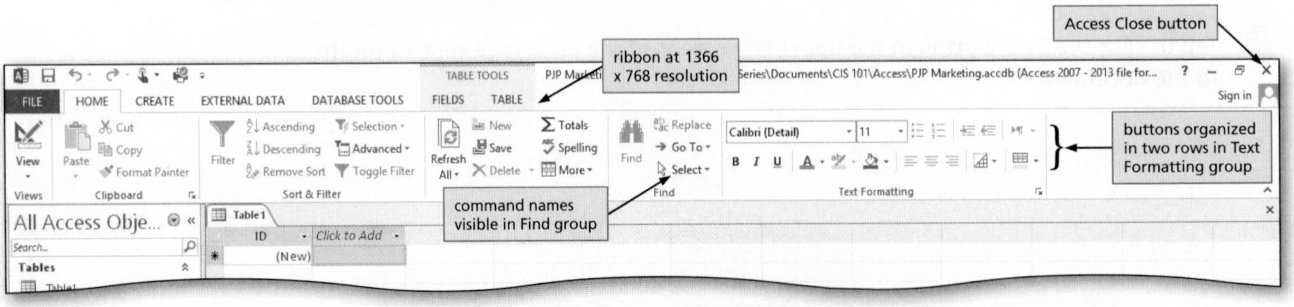

Figure 49 (a) Ribbon at 1366 × 768 Resolution

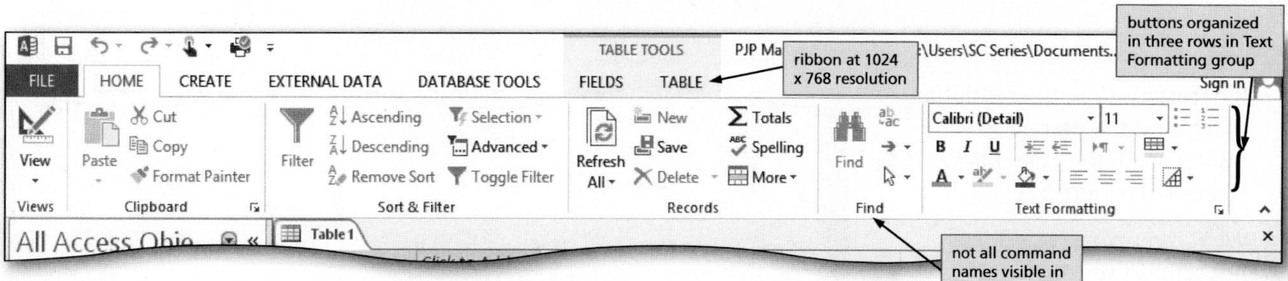

Figure 49 (b) Ribbon at 1024 × 768 Resolution

To Change the Screen Resolution

1 SIGN IN | 2 USE WINDOWS | 3 USE APPS | 4 FILE MANAGEMENT | 5 SWITCH APPS | 6 SAVE FILES
7 CHANGE SCREEN RESOLUTION | 8 EXIT APPS | 9 USE ADDITIONAL APP FEATURES | 10 USE HELP

If you are using a computer to step through the chapters in this book and you want your screen to match the figures, you may need to change your screen's resolution. ***Why?*** *The figures in this book use a screen resolution of 1366 × 768.* The following steps change the screen resolution to 1366 × 768. Your computer already may be set to 1366 × 768. Keep in mind that many computer labs prevent users from changing the screen resolution; in that case, read the following steps for illustration purposes.

1

- Tap or click the Show desktop button, which is located at the far-right edge of the taskbar, to display the Windows desktop.

Q&A I cannot see the Show desktop button. Why not?
When you point to the far-right edge of the taskbar, a small outline appears to mark the Show desktop button.

- Press and hold or right-click an empty area on the Windows desktop to display a shortcut menu that contains a list of commands related to the desktop (Figure 50).

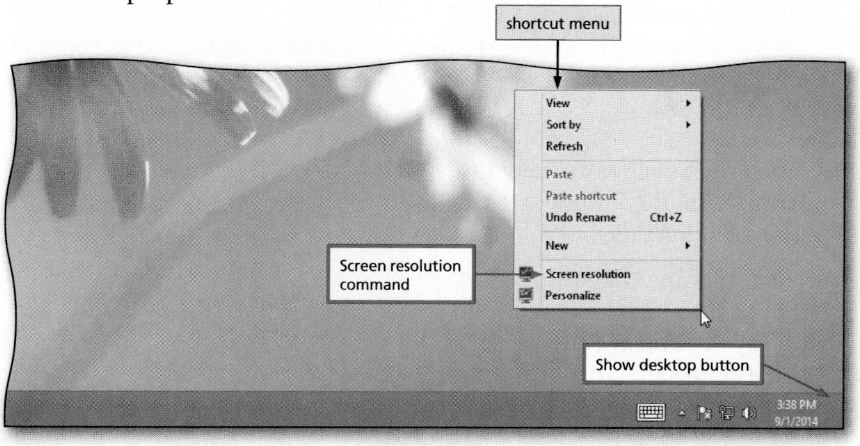

Figure 50

Q&A Why does my shortcut menu display different commands?
Depending on your computer's hardware and configuration, different commands might appear on the shortcut menu.

2

- Tap or click Screen resolution on the shortcut menu to open the Screen Resolution window (Figure 51).

3

- Tap or click the Resolution button in the Screen Resolution window to display the resolution slider.

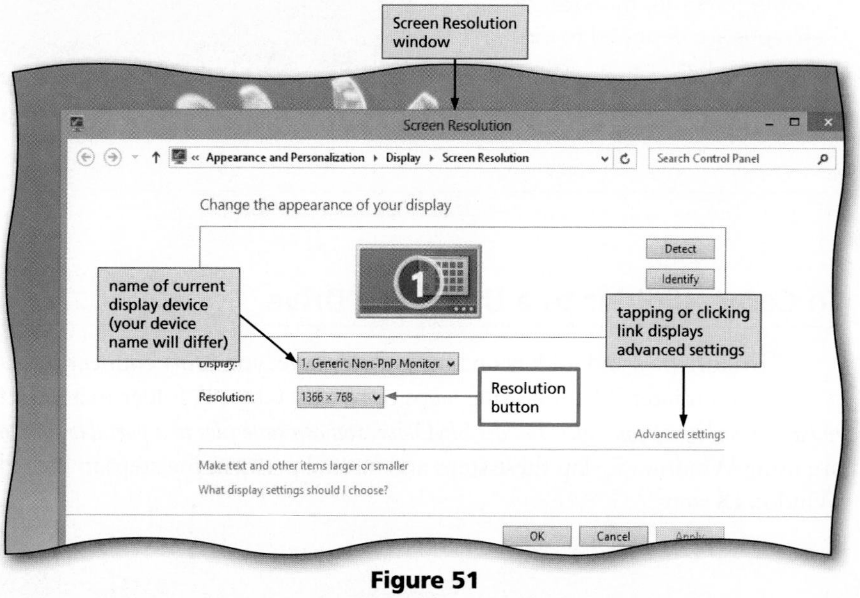

Figure 51

4

- If necessary, drag the resolution slider until the desired screen resolution (in this case, 1366 × 768) is selected (Figure 52).

Q&A What if my computer does not support the 1366 × 768 resolution?
Some computers do not support the 1366 × 768 resolution. In this case, select a resolution that is close to the 1366 × 768 resolution.

What is a slider?
A **slider** is an object that allows users to choose from multiple predetermined options. In most cases, these options represent some type of numeric value. In most cases, one end of the slider (usually the left or bottom) represents the lowest of available values, and the opposite end (usually the right or top) represents the highest available value.

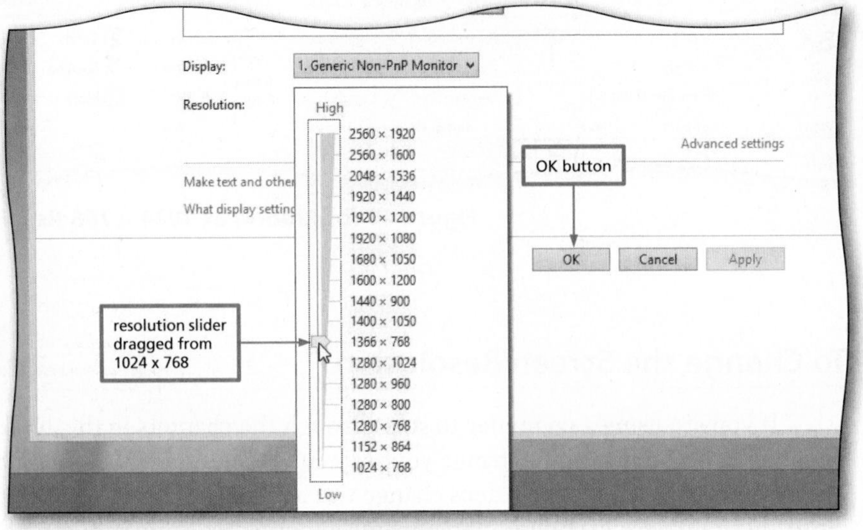

Figure 52

5

- Tap or click an empty area of the Screen Resolution window to close the resolution slider.
- Tap or click the OK button to change the screen resolution and display the Display Settings dialog box (Figure 53).
- Tap or click the Keep changes button (Display Settings dialog box) to accept the new screen resolution.

Q&A Why does a message display stating that the image quality can be improved?
Some computer monitors or screens are designed to display contents better at a certain screen resolution, sometimes referred to as an optimal resolution.

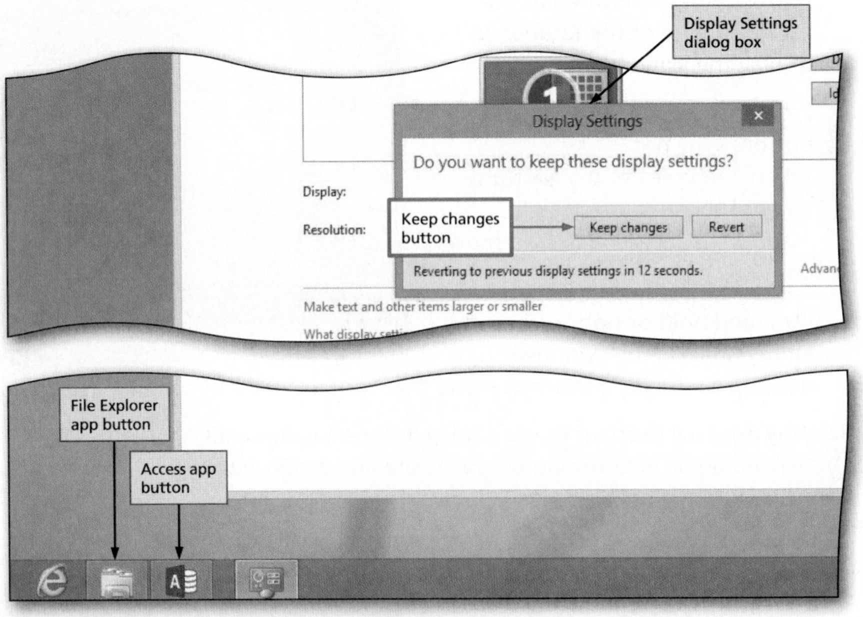

Figure 53

To Copy a Folder to a USB Flash Drive

To store files and folders on a USB flash drive, you must connect the USB flash drive to an available USB port on a computer. The following steps copy your CIS 101 folder to a USB flash drive. ***Why?*** *It often is good practice to have a backup of your files. Besides SkyDrive, you can save files to a portable storage device, such as a USB flash drive.* If you are using Windows 7, skip these steps and instead perform the steps in the yellow box that immediately follows these Windows 8 steps.

1

- Insert a USB flash drive in an available USB port on the computer to connect the USB flash drive.

Q&A How can I ensure the USB flash drive is connected?
In File Explorer, you can use the navigation bar to find the USB flash drive. If it is not showing, then it is not connected properly.

2

- Tap or click the File Explorer app button on the taskbar (shown in Figure 53) to make the folder window the active window.

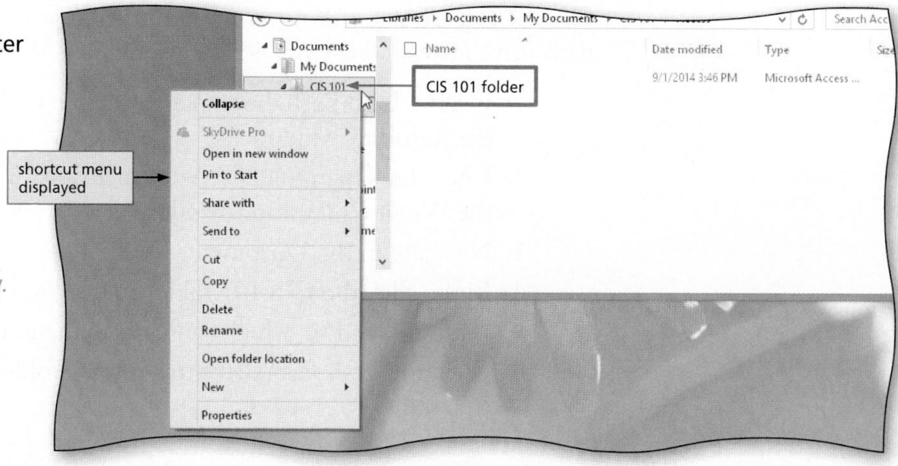

Figure 54

- If necessary, navigate to the CIS 101 folder in the File Explorer window (see Step 3a on page OFF 24 for instructions about navigating to a folder location).
- Press and hold or right-click the CIS 101 folder to display a shortcut menu (Figure 54).

3

- Tap or point to Send to, which displays the Send to submenu (Figure 55).

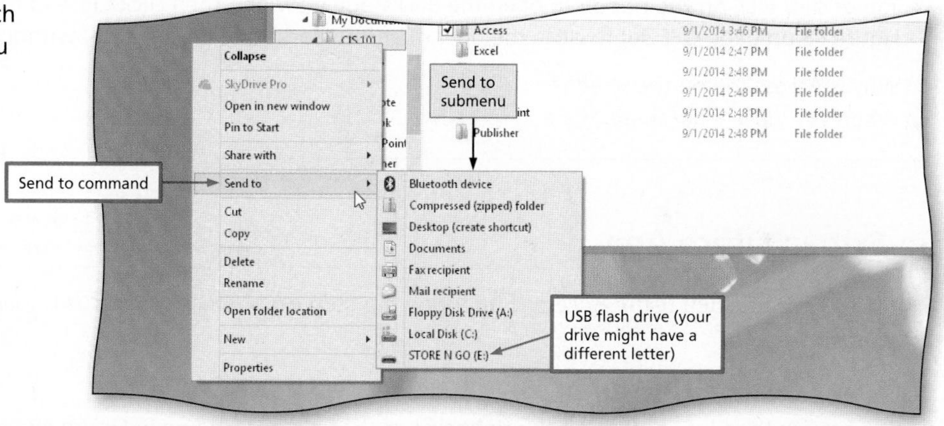

Figure 55

4

- Tap or click the USB flash drive to copy the folder to the USB flash drive (Figure 56).

Q&A Why does the drive letter of my USB flash drive differ?
Windows assigns the next available drive letter to your USB flash drive when you connect it. The next available drive letter may vary by computer, depending on the number of storage devices that currently are connected.

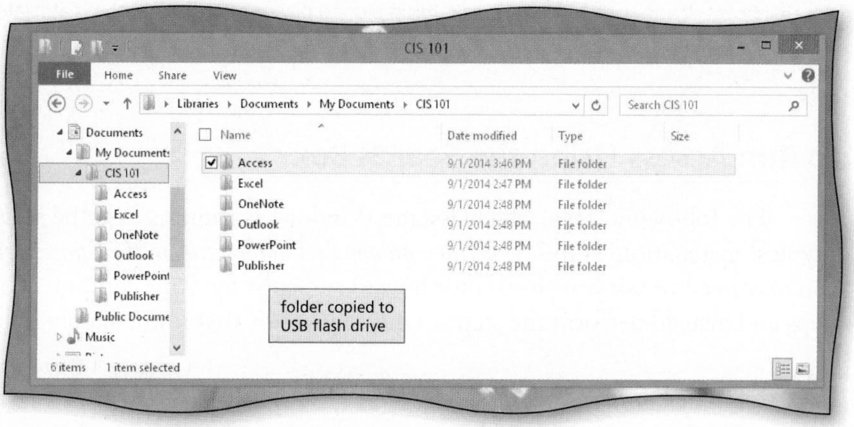

Figure 56

To Copy a Folder to a USB Flash Drive Using Windows 7

If you are using Windows 7, perform these steps to copy a folder to a USB flash drive instead of the previous steps that use Windows 8.

1. Insert a USB flash drive in an available USB port on the computer to open the AutoPlay window.
2. Click the 'Open folder to view files' link in the AutoPlay window to open the Windows Explorer window.
3. Navigate to the Documents library.
4. Right-click the CIS 101 folder to display a shortcut menu.
5. Point to Send to, which causes a submenu to appear.
6. Click the USB flash drive to copy the folder to the USB flash drive.

To Use the Backstage View to Close a Database

1 SIGN IN | 2 USE WINDOWS | 3 USE APPS | 4 FILE MANAGEMENT | 5 SWITCH APPS | 6 SAVE FILES
7 CHANGE SCREEN RESOLUTION | 8 EXIT APPS | 9 USE ADDITIONAL APPS | 10 USE HELP

Assume you need to close the Access database and return to it later. ***Why?*** *You no longer need to work with the PJP Marketing database, so you may close it.* The following step closes an Access database.

1

- Tap or click FILE on the ribbon to open the Backstage view and then click Close in the Backstage view (shown in Figure 48 on page OFF 36) to close the open file (PJP Marketing, in this case) without exiting Access.

Q&A Why is Access still on the screen?
When you close a database, the app remains running.

To Exit an Office App

1 SIGN IN | 2 USE WINDOWS | 3 USE APPS | 4 FILE MANAGEMENT | 5 SWITCH APPS | 6 SAVE FILES
7 CHANGE SCREEN RESOLUTION | 8 EXIT APPS | 9 USE ADDITIONAL APPS | 10 USE HELP

You are finished using Access. The following step exits Access. ***Why?*** *It is good practice to exit an app when you are finished using it.*

1

- Tap or click the Close button on the right side of the title bar (shown in Figure 49a on page OFF 36) to close the file and exit the Office app.

Break Point: If you wish to take a break, this is a good place to do so. To resume at a later time, continue to follow the steps from this location forward.

To Run Access Using the Search Box

The following steps, which assume Windows is running, use the search box to run the Access app based on a typical installation. ***Why?*** *Sometimes an app does not appear on the Start screen, so you can find it quickly by searching.* You may need to ask your instructor how to run apps for your computer. If you are using Windows 7, skip these steps and instead perform the steps in the yellow box that immediately follows these Windows 8 steps.

1

- Swipe in from the right edge of the screen or point to the upper-right corner of the screen to display the Charms bar (Figure 57).

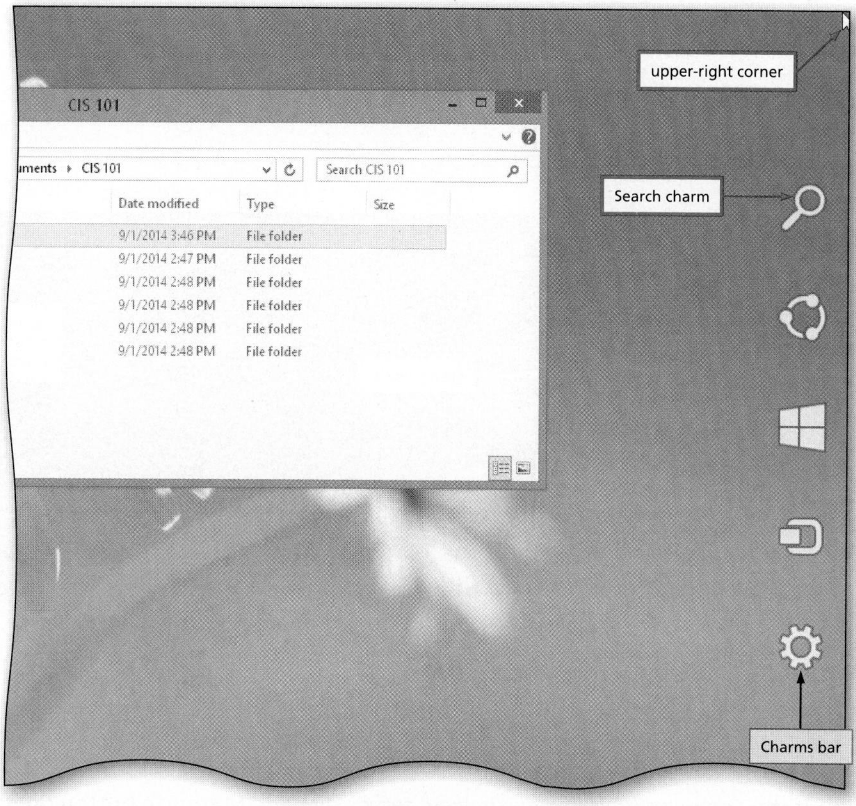

Figure 57

2

- Tap or click the Search charm on the Charms bar to display the Search menu (Figure 58).

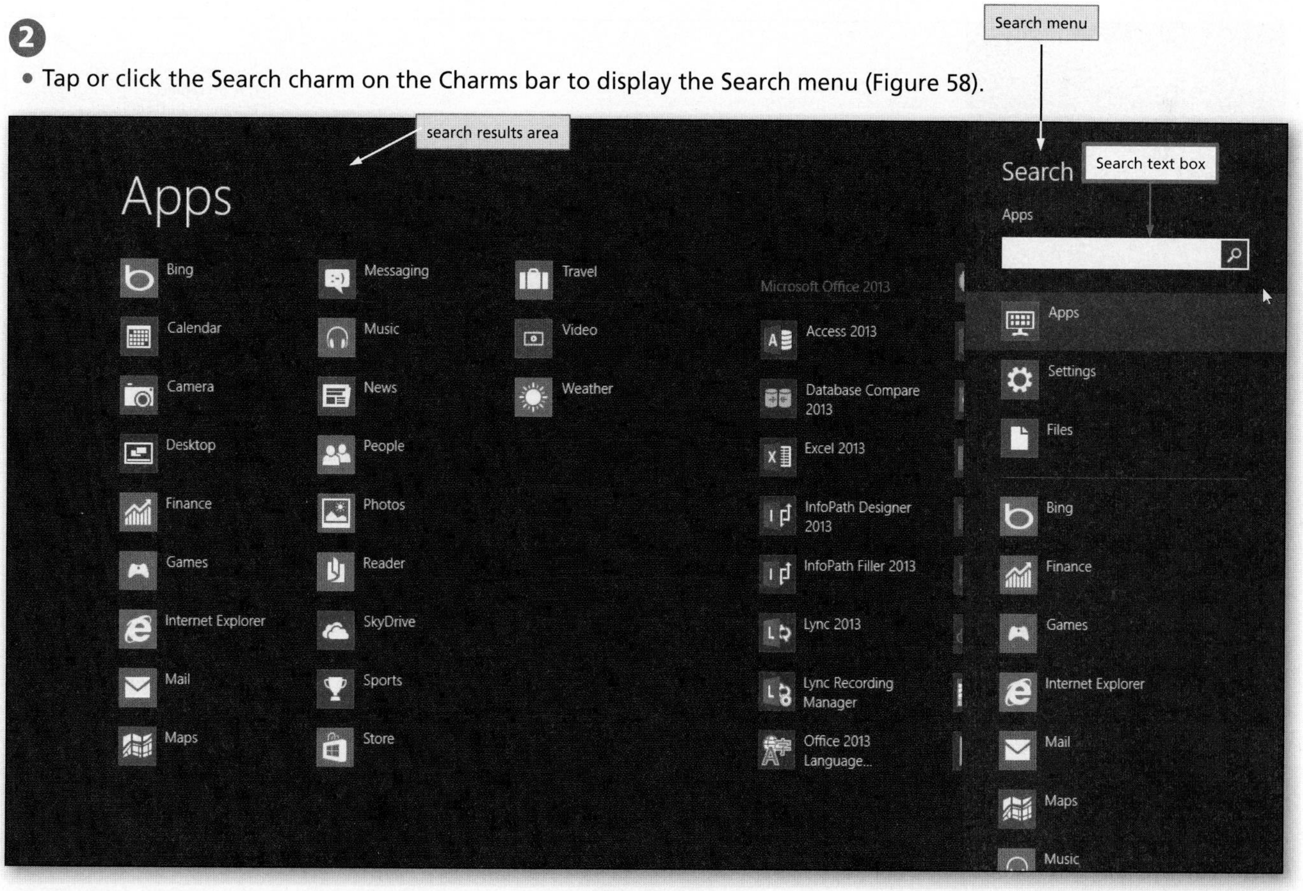

Figure 58

3

- Type **Access 2013** as the search text in the Search text box and watch the search results appear in the Apps list (Figure 59).

Q&A Do I need to type the complete app name or use correct capitalization?
No, you need to type just enough characters of the app name for it to appear in the Apps list. For example, you may be able to type Access or access, instead of Access 2013.

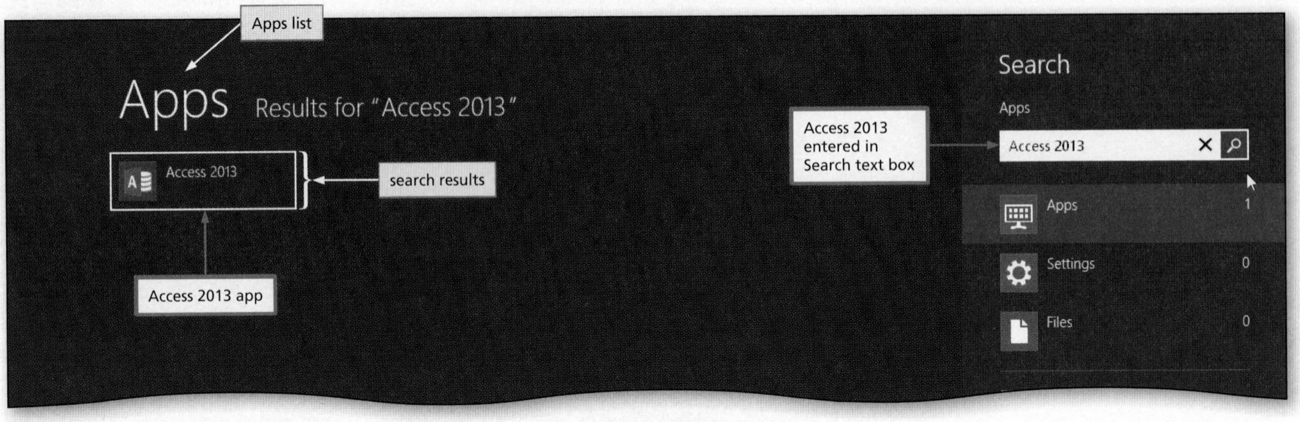

Figure 59

4

- Tap or click the app name, Access 2013 in this case, in the search results to run Access.
- If the app window is not maximized, tap or click the Maximize button on its title bar to maximize the window (Figure 60).

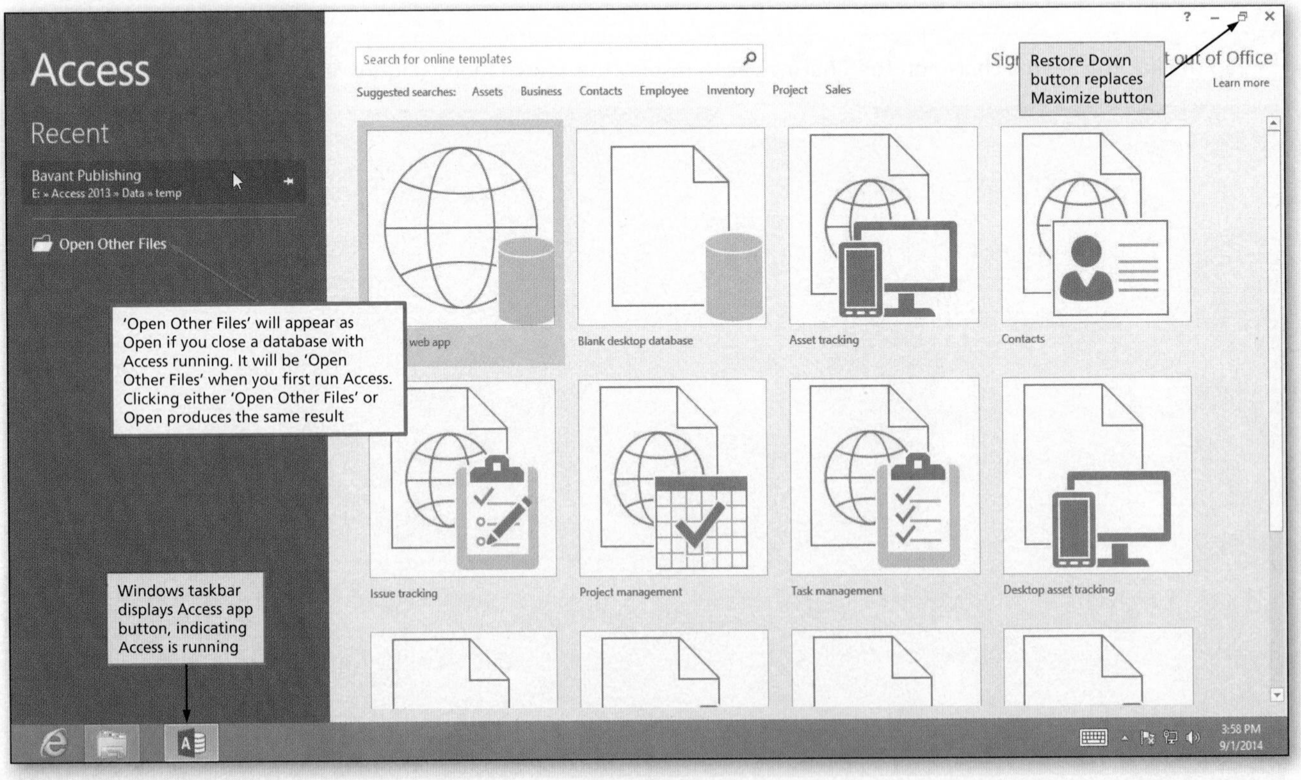

Figure 60

To Run an App Using the Search Box Using Windows 7

If you are using Windows 7, perform these steps to run an app using the search box instead of the previous steps that use Windows 8.

1. Click the Start button on the Windows 7 taskbar to display the Start menu.
2. Type **`Access 2013`** as the search text in the 'Search programs and files' text box and watch the search results appear on the Start menu.
3. Click the app name, Access 2013 in this case, in the search results on the Start menu to run Access.
4. If the app window is not maximized, click the Maximize button on its title bar to maximize the window.

To Open an Existing Database

To work on an existing database, that is, a database you previously created, you must open the database. To do so, you will use the Backstage view. The following step opens an existing database, specifically the PJP Marketing database. ***Why?*** *Because the database has been created already, you just need to open it.*

1

- If you have just run Access, tap or click Open Other Files to display the Open gallery in the Backstage view. If not, tap or click FILE on the ribbon to open the Backstage view and then tap or click Open in the Backstage view to display the Open gallery (Figure 61).

Q&A I see the name of the database I want to open in the Recent list in Backstage view. Can I just tap or click the name to open the file?
Yes. That is an alternative way to open a database, provided the name of the database is included in the Recent list.

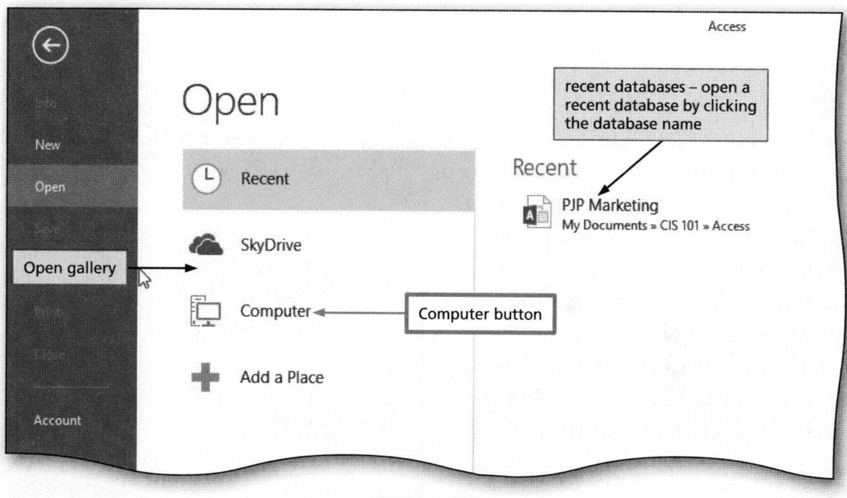

Figure 61

2

- Tap or click Computer to display recent folders accessed on your computer as well as the Browse button (Figure 62).

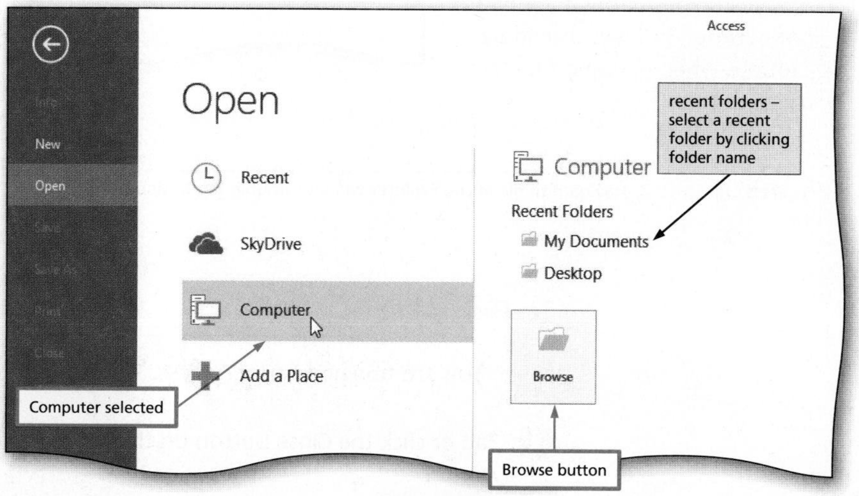

Figure 62

3

- Tap or click the Browse button to display the Open dialog box (Figure 63).

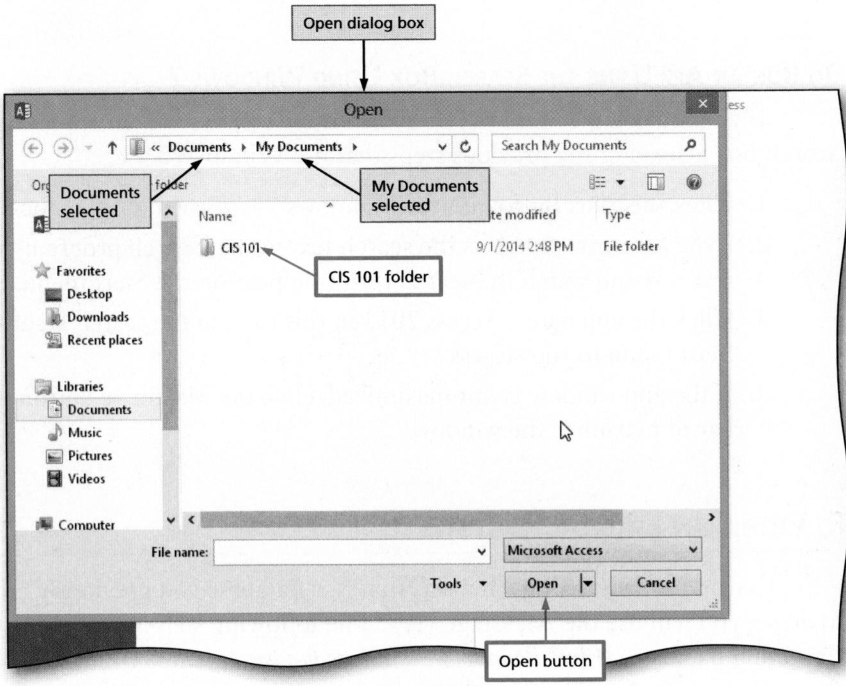

Figure 63

4

- If necessary, navigate to the location of the file to open.
- Tap or click the file to open, PJP Marketing in this case, to select the file.
- Tap or click the Open button (Open dialog box) to open the database (Figure 64). If a security warning appears, tap or click the ENABLE CONTENT button.

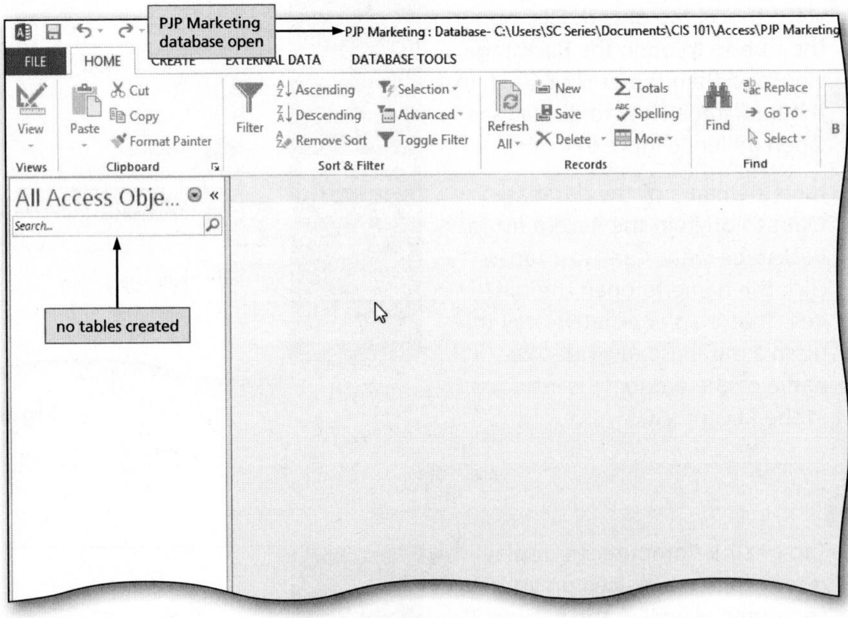

Figure 64

Q&A Why might a Security Warning appear?

A Security Warning appears when you open a database that might contain harmful content. The files you create in this chapter are not harmful, but you should be cautious when opening files from other people.

Other Ways

1. Press CTRL+O 2. Navigate to file in File Explorer window, double-tap or double-click file

To Exit Access

You are finished using Access. The following step exits Access.

1 Tap or click the Close button on the right side of the title bar to close the file and exit Access.

To Create a New Access Database from File Explorer

File Explorer provides a means to create an Access database without running an Office app. The following steps use File Explorer to create an Access database. ***Why?*** *Sometimes you might need to create a database and then return to it later for editing.* If you are using Windows 7, skip these steps and instead perform the steps in the yellow box that immediately follows these Windows 8 steps.

1

- Double-tap or double-click the File Explorer app button on the taskbar to make the folder window the active window.
- If necessary, double-tap or double-click the Documents library in the navigation pane to expand the Documents library.
- If necessary, double-tap or double-click the My Documents folder in the navigation pane to expand the My Documents folder.
- If necessary, double-tap or double-click your class folder (CIS 101, in this case) in the navigation pane to expand the folder.
- Tap or click the Access folder in the navigation pane to display its contents in the file list.
- With the Access folder selected, press and hold or right-click an open area in the file list to display a shortcut menu.
- Tap or point to New on the shortcut menu to display the New submenu (Figure 65).

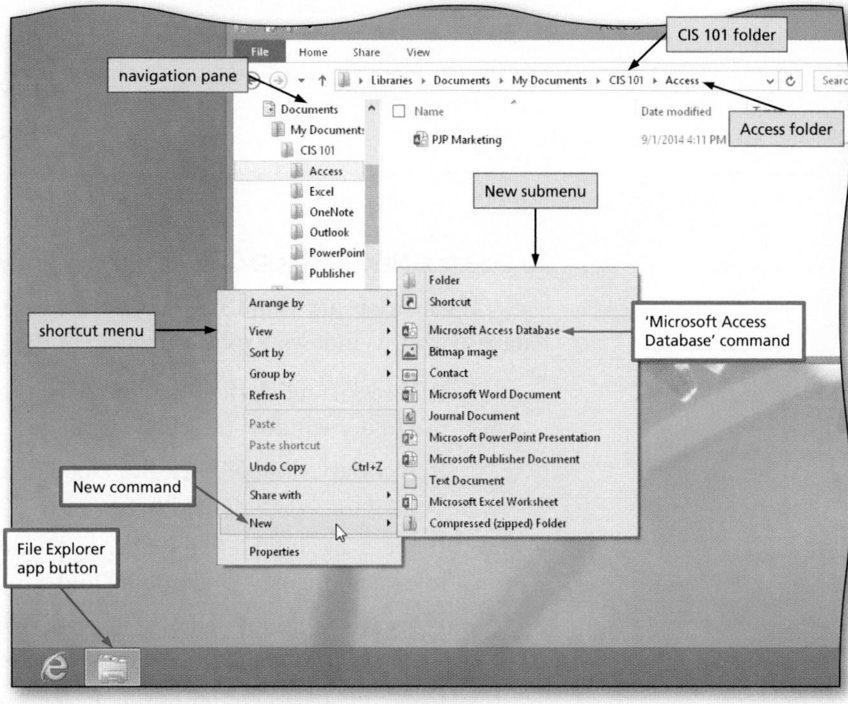

Figure 65

2

- Tap or click 'Microsoft Access Database' on the New submenu to display an icon and text box for a new file in the current folder window with the file name, New Microsoft Access Database, selected (Figure 66).

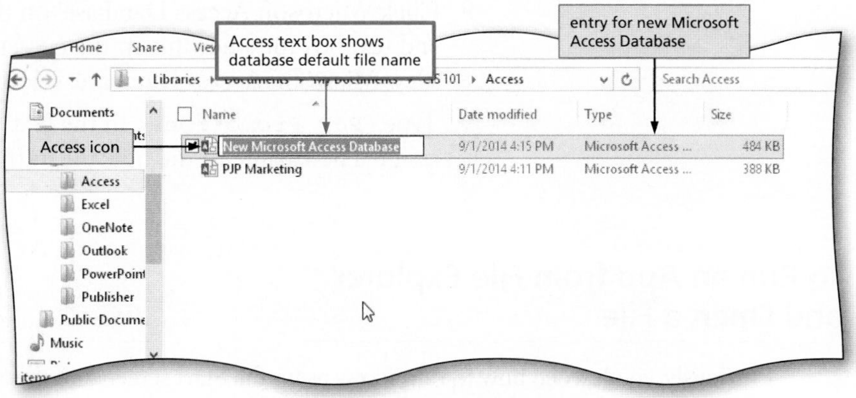

Figure 66

3

- Type **PJP Promotions** in the text box and then press the ENTER key to assign a new name to the new file in the current folder (Figure 67).

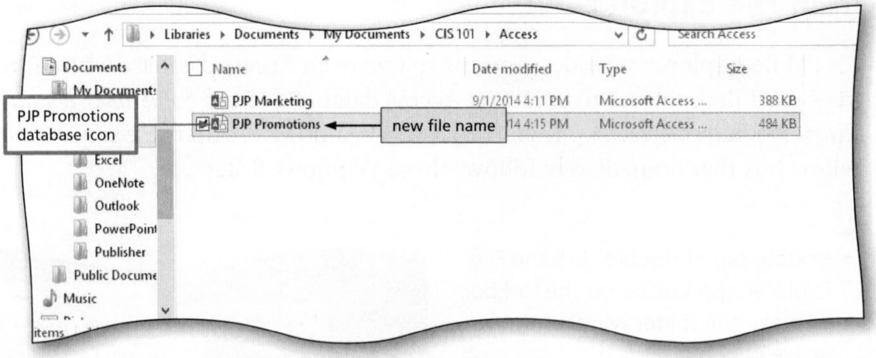

Figure 67

To Create a New Access Database from Windows Explorer Using Windows 7

If you are using Windows 7, perform these steps to create a new Access database from Windows Explorer instead of the previous steps that use Windows 8.

1. If necessary, click the Windows Explorer button on the taskbar to make the folder window the active window.
2. If necessary, double-click the Documents library in the navigation pane to expand the Documents library.
3. If necessary, double-click the My Documents folder in the navigation pane to expand the My Documents folder.
4. If necessary, double-click your class folder (CIS 101, in this case) in the navigation pane to expand the folder.
5. Click the Access folder in the navigation pane to display its contents in the file list.
6. With the Access folder selected, right-click an open area in the file list to display a shortcut menu.
7. Point to New on the shortcut menu to display the New submenu.
8. Click 'Microsoft Access Database' on the New submenu to display an icon and text box for a new file in the current folder window with the name, New Microsoft Access Database, selected.
9. Type **PJP Promotions** in the text box and then press the ENTER key to assign a new name to the new file in the current folder.

To Run an App from File Explorer and Open a File

1 SIGN IN | 2 USE WINDOWS | 3 USE APPS | 4 FILE MANAGEMENT | 5 SWITCH APPS | 6 SAVE FILES
7 CHANGE SCREEN RESOLUTION | 8 EXIT APPS | 9 USE ADDITIONAL APP FEATURES | **10 USE HELP**

Previously, you learned how to run Access using the Start screen and the Search charm. The following steps, which assume Windows is running, use File Explorer to run Access based on a typical installation. ***Why?*** *Another way to run an Office app is to open an existing file from File Explorer, which causes the app in which the file was created to run and then open the selected file.* You may need to ask your instructor how to run Access for your computer. If you are using Windows 7, follow the steps in the yellow box that immediately follows these Windows 8 steps.

1

- If necessary, display the file to open in the folder window in File Explorer (shown in Figure 67).
- Press and hold or right-click the file icon or file name (PJP Promotions, in this case) to display a shortcut menu (Figure 68).

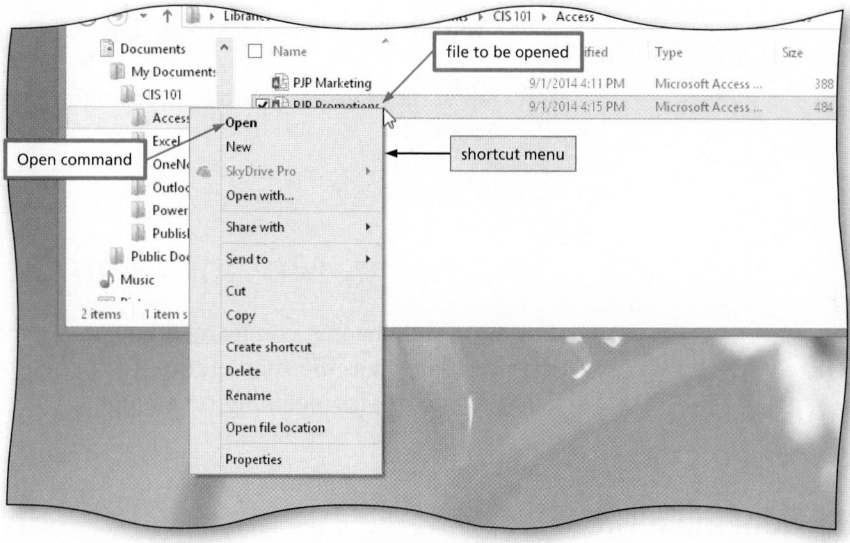

Figure 68

2

- Tap or click Open on the shortcut menu to open the selected file in the app used to create the file, Access in this case (Figure 69). If a security warning appears, tap or click the ENABLE CONTENT button.
- If the Access window is not maximized, tap or click the Maximize button on the title bar to maximize the window.

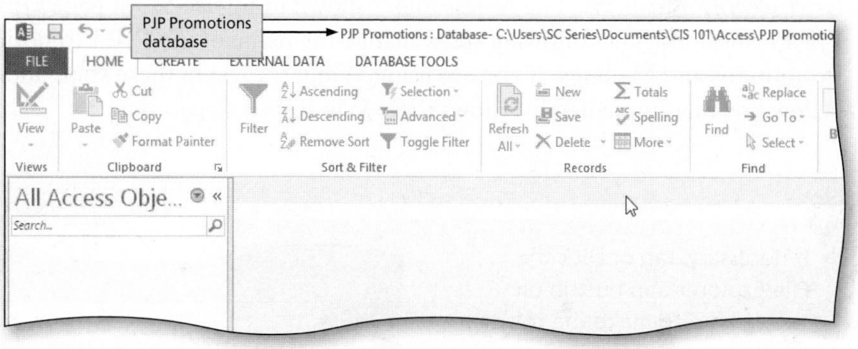

Figure 69

To Run an App from Windows Explorer and Open a File Using Windows 7

If you are using Windows 7, perform these steps to run an app from Windows Explorer and open a file instead of the previous steps that use Windows 8.

1. Display the file to open in the folder window in Windows Explorer.
2. Right-click the file icon or file name (PJP Promotions, in this case) to display a shortcut menu.
3. Click Open on the shortcut menu to open the selected file in the app used to create the file, Access in this case.
4. If the Access window is not maximized, click the Maximize button on the title bar to maximize the window.

To Exit Access

You are finished using Access. The following step exits Access.

1. Tap or click the Close button on the right side of the title bar to close the file and exit Access.

Renaming, Moving, and Deleting Files

Earlier in this chapter, you learned how to organize files in folders, which is part of a process known as **file management**. The following sections cover additional file management topics including renaming, moving, and deleting files.

To Rename a File

1 SIGN IN | 2 USE WINDOWS | 3 USE APPS | **4 FILE MANAGEMENT** | 5 SWITCH APPS | 6 SAVE FILES
7 CHANGE SCREEN RESOLUTION | 8 EXIT APPS | 9 USE ADDITIONAL APP FEATURES | **10 USE HELP**

In some circumstances, you may want to change the name of, or rename, a file or a folder. ***Why?*** *You may want to distinguish a file in one folder or drive from a copy of a similar file, or you may decide to rename a file to better identify its contents.* The Access folder shown in Figure 67 on page OFF 46 contains the Access database, PJP Promotions. The following steps change the name of the PJP Promotions file in the Access folder to PJP Promotions and Mailings. If you are using Windows 7, skip these steps and instead perform the steps in the yellow box that immediately follows these Windows 8 steps.

1

- If necessary, tap or click the File Explorer app button on the taskbar to make the folder window the active window.
- If necessary, navigate to the location of the file to be renamed (in this case, the Access folder in the CIS 101 [or your class folder] folder in the My Documents folder in the Documents library) to display the file(s) it contains in the file list.
- Press and hold or right-click the PJP Promotions icon or file name in the file list to select the PJP Promotions file and display a shortcut menu that presents a list of commands related to files (Figure 70).

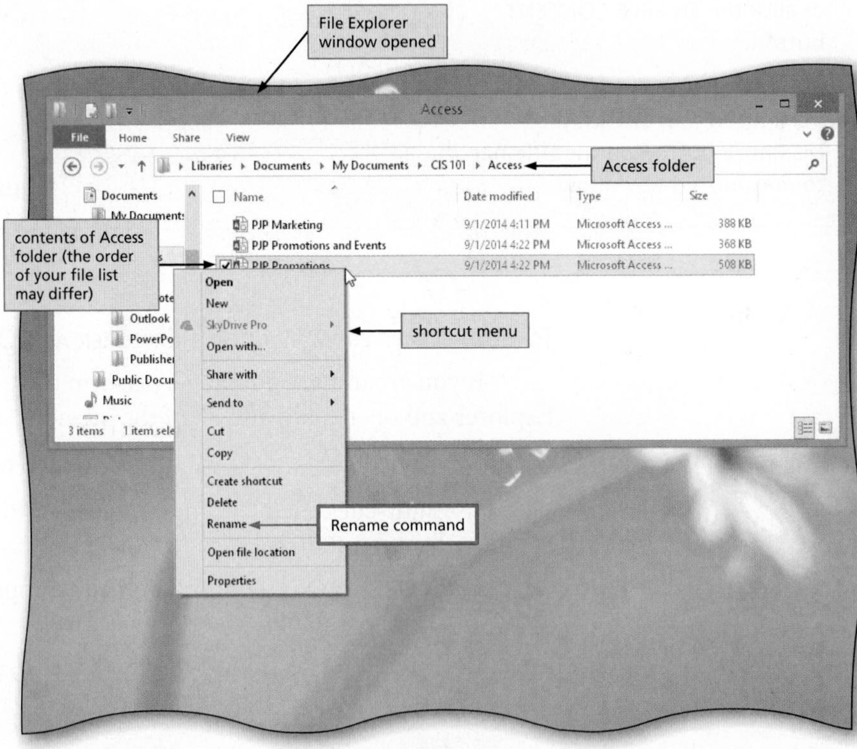

Figure 70

2

- Tap or click Rename on the shortcut menu to place the current file name in a text box.
- Type **PJP Promotions and Mailings** in the text box and then press the ENTER key (Figure 71).

Q&A Are there any risks involved in renaming files that are located on a hard disk?
If you inadvertently rename a file that is associated with certain apps, the apps may not be able to find the file and, therefore, may not run properly. Always use caution when renaming files.

Can I rename a file when it is open?
No, a file must be closed to change the file name.

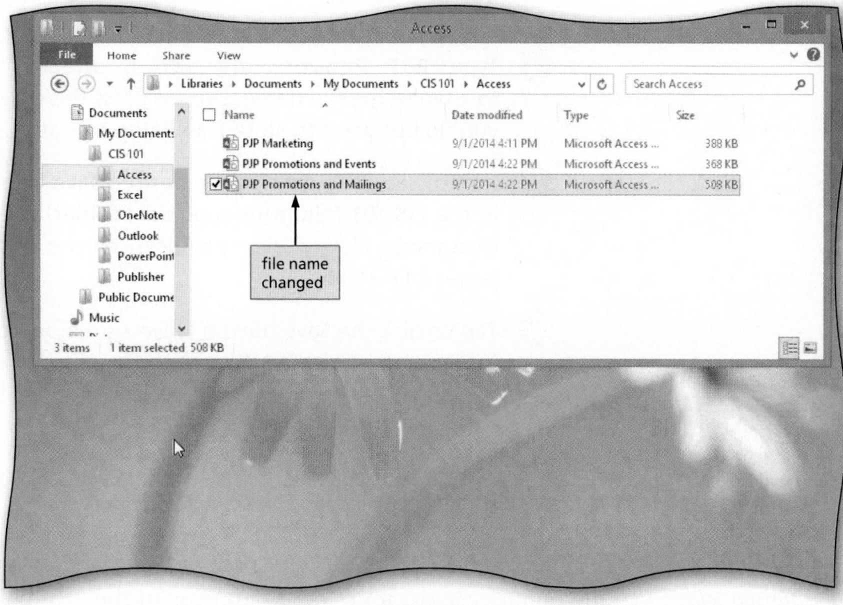

Figure 71

Other Ways

1. Select file, press F2, type new file name, press ENTER 2. Select file, tap or click Rename (Home tab | Organize group), type new file name, press ENTER

To Rename a File Using Windows 7

If you are using Windows 7, perform these steps to rename a file instead of the previous steps that use Windows 8.

1. If necessary, click the Windows Explorer app button on the taskbar to make the folder window the active window.
2. Navigate to the location of the file to be renamed (in this case, the Access folder in the CIS 101 [or your class folder] folder in the My Documents folder in the Documents library) to display the file(s) it contains in the file list.
3. Right-click the PJP Promotions icon or file name in the file list to select the PJP Promotions file and display a shortcut menu that presents a list of commands related to files.
4. Click Rename on the shortcut menu to place the current file name in a text box.
5. Type **PJP Promotions and Mailings** in the text box and then press the ENTER key.

To Save a File with a New File Name

You might want to save a file with a different name or to a different location. For example, you might start a homework assignment with a data file and then save it with a final file name for submission to your instructor, saving it to a location designated by your instructor. The following steps save a file with a different file name.

BTW
New File Names and Renaming
Saving a file with a new name makes a copy of the file with a different name while retaining the original version of the file with its original name. Renaming a file changes its name but does not create a new version of the file.

1 Tap or click the FILE tab to open the Backstage view.

2 Tap or click the Save As tab to display the Save As gallery.

3 With Save Database As and Access Database selected, tap or click the Save As button.

4 Type **PJP Promotions and Events** in the File name box (Save As dialog box) to change the file name. Do not press the ENTER key after typing the file name because you do not want to close the dialog box at this time.

5 If necessary, navigate to the desired save location (in this case, the Access folder in the CIS 101 folder [or your class folder] in the My Documents folder in the Documents library). For specific instructions, perform the tasks in Steps 3a and 3b on pages OFF 24 and 25.

6 Tap or click the Save button (Save As dialog box) to save the document in the selected folder on the selected drive with the entered file name.

To Move a File

1 SIGN IN | 2 USE WINDOWS | 3 USE APPS | 4 FILE MANAGEMENT | 5 SWITCH APPS | 6 SAVE FILES
7 CHANGE SCREEN RESOLUTION | 8 EXIT APPS | 9 USE ADDITIONAL APP FEATURES | 10 USE HELP

Why? *At some time, you may want to move a file from one folder, called the source folder, to another, called the destination folder.* When you move a file, it no longer appears in the original folder. If the destination and the source folders are on the same media, you can move a file by dragging it. If the folders are on different media, then you will need to press and hold and then drag, or right-drag the file, and then click Move here on the shortcut menu. The following step moves the PJP Promotions and Mailings file from the Access folder to the CIS 101 folder. If you are using Windows 7, skip this step and instead perform the steps in the yellow box that immediately follows this Windows 8 step.

1

- In File Explorer, if necessary, navigate to the location of the file to be moved (in this case, the Access folder in the CIS 101 folder [or your class folder] in the Documents library).
- If necessary, tap or click the Access folder in the navigation pane to display the files it contains in the right pane.
- Drag the PJP Promotions and Mailings file in the right pane to the CIS 101 folder in the navigation pane and notice the ScreenTip as you drag the mouse (Figure 72).

Experiment

- Click the CIS 101 folder in the navigation pane to verify that the file was moved.

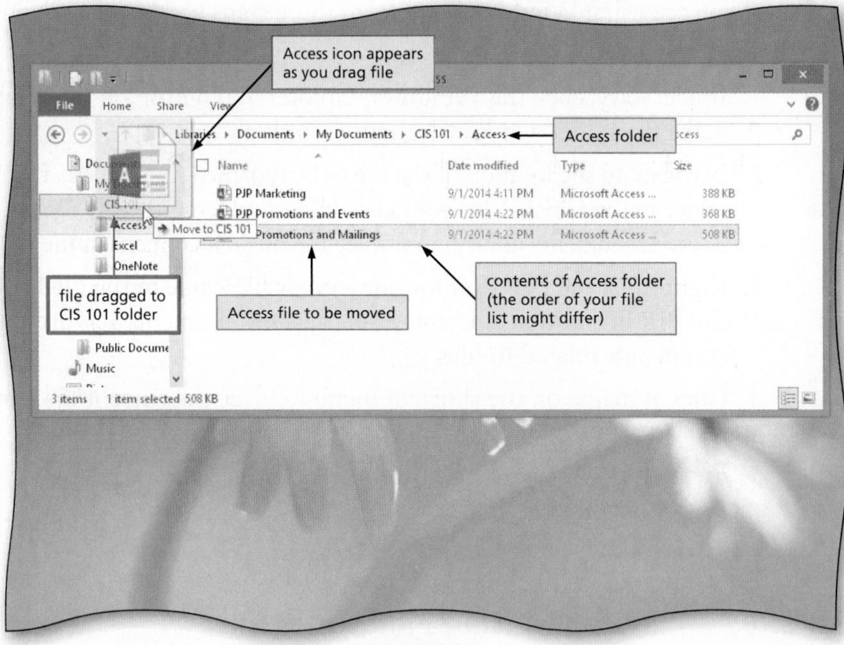

Figure 72

Other Ways

1. Press and hold or right-click file to move, tap or click Cut on shortcut menu, press and hold or right-click destination folder, tap or click Paste on shortcut menu
2. Select file to move, press CTRL+X, select destination folder, press CTRL+V

To Move a File Using Windows 7

If you are using Windows 7, perform these steps to move a file instead of the previous steps that use Windows 8.

1. In Windows Explorer, navigate to the location of the file to be moved (in this case, the Access folder in the CIS 101 folder [or your class folder] in the Documents library).
2. Click the Access folder in the navigation pane to display the files it contains in the right pane.
3. Drag the PJP Promotions and Mailings file in the right pane to the CIS 101 folder in the navigation pane.

To Delete a File

A final task you may want to perform is to delete a file. Exercise extreme caution when deleting a file or files. When you delete a file from a hard disk, the deleted file is stored in the Recycle Bin where you can recover it until you empty the Recycle Bin. If you delete a file from removable media, such as a USB flash drive, the file is deleted permanently. The next steps delete the PJP Promotions and Mailings file from the CIS 101 folder. ***Why?*** *When a file no longer is needed, you can delete it to conserve space in your storage location.* If you are using Windows 7, skip these steps and instead perform the steps in the yellow box that immediately follows these Windows 8 steps.

1

- In File Explorer, navigate to the location of the file to be deleted (in this case, the CIS 101 folder [or your class folder] in the Documents library).
- Press and hold or right-click the PJP Promotions and Mailings icon or file name in the right pane to select the file and display a shortcut menu (Figure 73).

2

- Tap or click Delete on the shortcut menu to delete the file.
- If a dialog box appears, tap or click the Yes button to delete the file.

Q&A Can I use this same technique to delete a folder?
Yes. Right-click the folder and then click Delete on the shortcut menu. When you delete a folder, all of the files and folders contained in the folder you are deleting, together with any files and folders on lower hierarchical levels, are deleted as well.

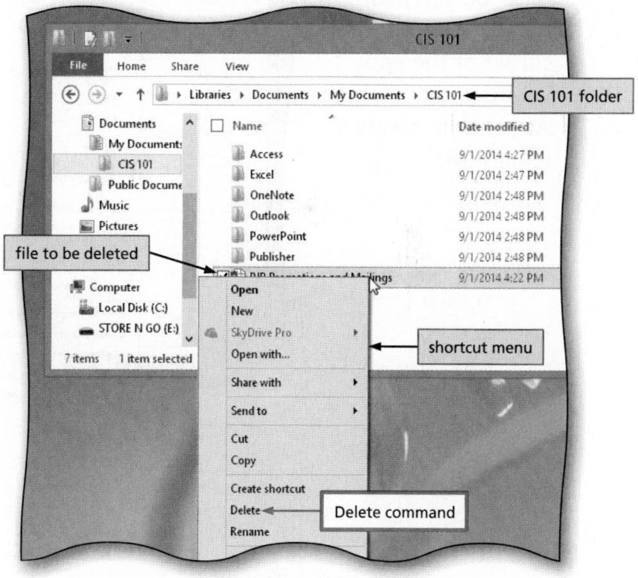

Figure 73

Other Ways

1. Select icon, press DELETE

To Delete a File Using Windows 7

If you are using Windows 7, perform these steps to delete a file instead of the previous steps that use Windows 8.

1. In Windows Explorer, navigate to the location of the file to be deleted (in this case, the CIS 101 folder [or your class folder] in the Documents library).
2. Right-click the PJP Promotions and Mailings icon or file name in the right pane to select the file and display a shortcut menu.
3. Click Delete on the shortcut menu to delete the file.
4. If a dialog box appears, click the Yes button to delete the file.

Microsoft Office and Windows Help

At any time while you are using one of the Office apps, such as Access, you can use Office Help to display information about all topics associated with the app. This section illustrates the use of Access Help. Help in other Office apps operates in a similar fashion.

In Office, Help is presented in a window that has browser-style navigation buttons. Each Office app has its own Help home page, which is the starting Help page that is displayed in the Help window. If your computer is connected to the Internet, the contents of the Help page reflect both the local help files installed on the computer and material from Microsoft's website.

To Open the Help Window in an Office App

1 SIGN IN | 2 USE WINDOWS | 3 USE APPS | 4 FILE MANAGEMENT | 5 SWITCH APPS | 6 SAVE FILES
7 CHANGE SCREEN RESOLUTION | 8 EXIT APPS | 9 USE ADDITIONAL APP FEATURES | **10 USE HELP**

The following step opens the Access Help window. ***Why?*** *You might not understand how certain commands or operations work in Access, so you can obtain the necessary information using help.* The step to open a Help window in other Office programs is similar.

1

- Run Access.
- Tap or click the 'Microsoft Access Help' button near the upper-right corner of the app window to open the Access Help window (Figure 74).

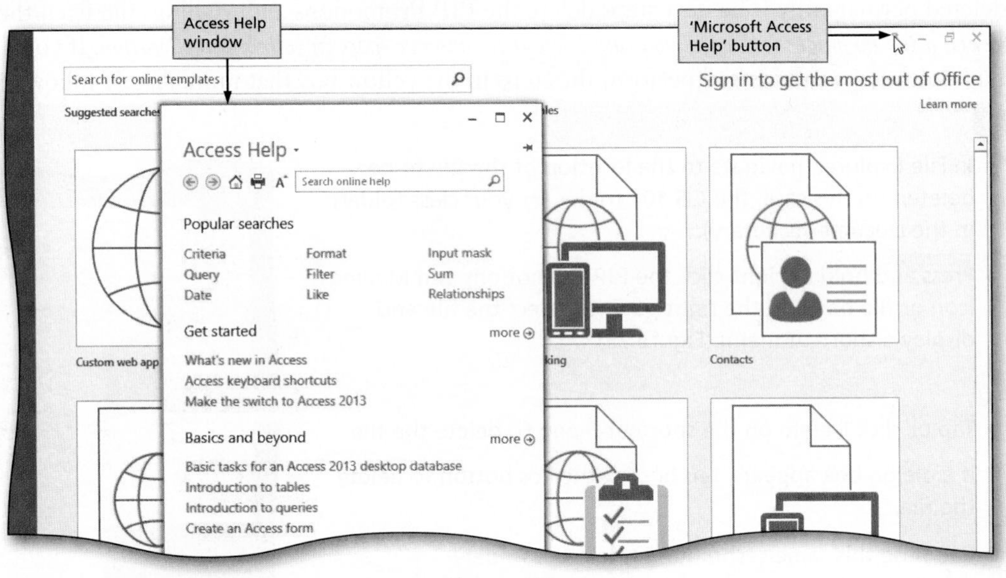

Figure 74

Other Ways

1. Press F1

Moving and Resizing Windows

At times, it is useful, or even necessary, to have more than one window open and visible on the screen at the same time. You can resize and move these open windows so that you can view different areas of and elements in the window. In the case of the Help window, for example, it could be covering database objects in the Access window that you need to see.

To Move a Window by Dragging

1 SIGN IN | 2 USE WINDOWS | 3 USE APPS | 4 FILE MANAGEMENT | 5 SWITCH APPS | 6 SAVE FILES
7 CHANGE SCREEN RESOLUTION | 8 EXIT APPS | 9 USE ADDITIONAL APP FEATURES | **10 USE HELP**

You can move any open window that is not maximized to another location on the desktop by dragging the title bar of the window. ***Why?*** *You might want to have a better view of what is behind the window or just want to move the window so that you can see it better.* The following step drags the Access Help window to the upper-left corner of the desktop.

1

- Drag the window title bar (the Access Help window title bar, in this case) so that the window moves to the upper-left corner of the desktop, as shown in Figure 75.

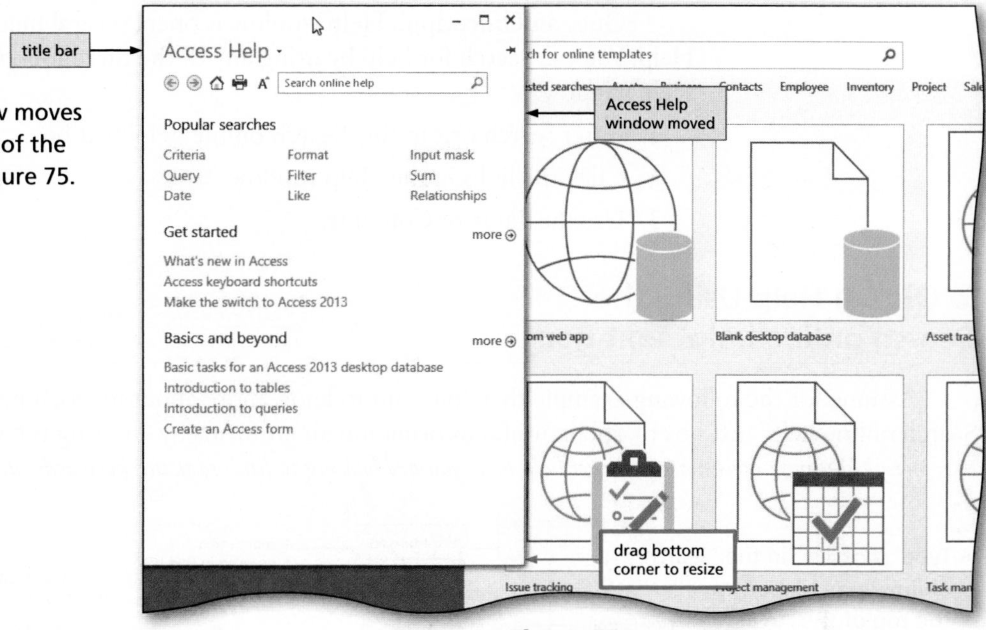

Figure 75

To Resize a Window by Dragging

A method used to change the size of the window is to drag the window borders. The following step changes the size of the Access Help window by dragging its borders. ***Why?*** *Sometimes, information is not visible completely in a window, and you want to increase the size of the window.*

1

- If you are using a mouse, point to the lower-right corner of the window (the Access Help window, in this case) until the pointer changes to a two-headed arrow.
- Drag the bottom border downward to display more of the active window (Figure 76).

Q&A

Can I drag other borders on the window to enlarge or shrink the window?

Yes, you can drag the left, right, and top borders and any window corner to resize a window.

Will Windows remember the new size of the window after I close it?

Yes. When you reopen the window, Windows will display it at the same size it was when you closed it.

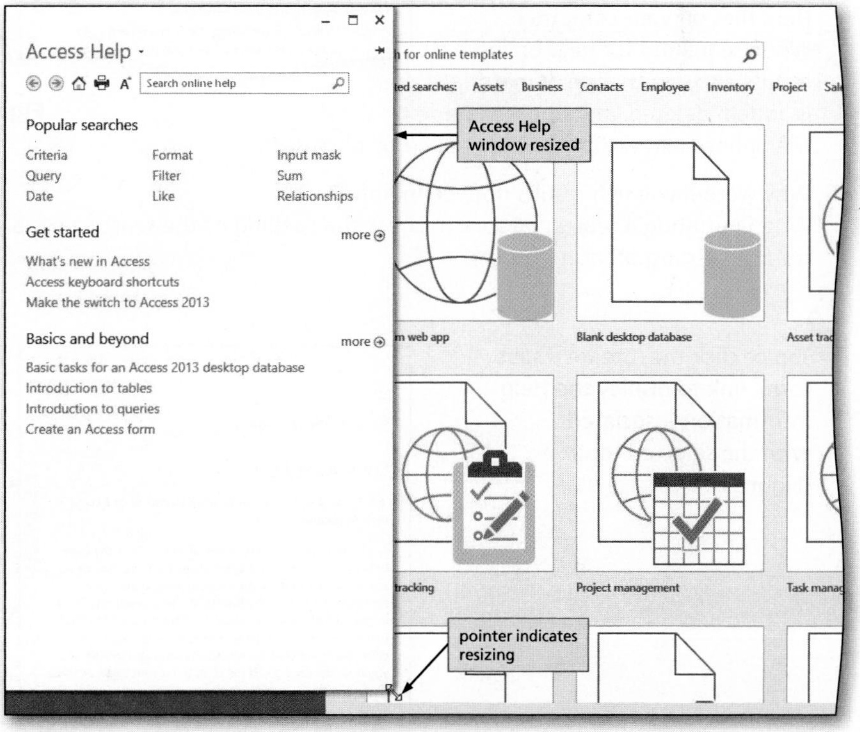

Figure 76

Using Office Help

Once an Office app's Help window is open, several methods exist for navigating Help. You can search for help by using any of the three following methods from the Help window:

1. Enter search text in the 'Search online help' text box.
2. Click the links in the Help window.
3. Use the Table of Contents.

To Obtain Help Using the 'Search online help' Text Box

1 SIGN IN | 2 USE WINDOWS | 3 USE APPS | 4 FILE MANAGEMENT | 5 SWITCH APPS | 6 SAVE FILES
7 CHANGE SCREEN RESOLUTION | 8 EXIT APPS | 9 USE ADDITIONAL APP FEATURES | **10 USE HELP**

Assume for the following example that you want to know more about forms. The following steps use the 'Search online help' text box to obtain useful information about forms by entering the word, forms, as search text. ***Why?** You may not know the exact help topic you are looking to find, so using keywords can help narrow your search.*

1

- Type **`forms`** in the 'Search online help' text box at the top of the Access Help window to enter the search text.
- Tap or click the 'Search online help' button to display the search results (Figure 77).

Q&A

Why do my search results differ?
If you do not have an Internet connection, your results will reflect only the content of the Help files on your computer. When searching for help online, results also can change as material is added, deleted, and updated on the online Help webpages maintained by Microsoft.

Why were my search results not very helpful?
When initiating a search, be sure to check the spelling of the search text; also, keep your search specific to return the most accurate results.

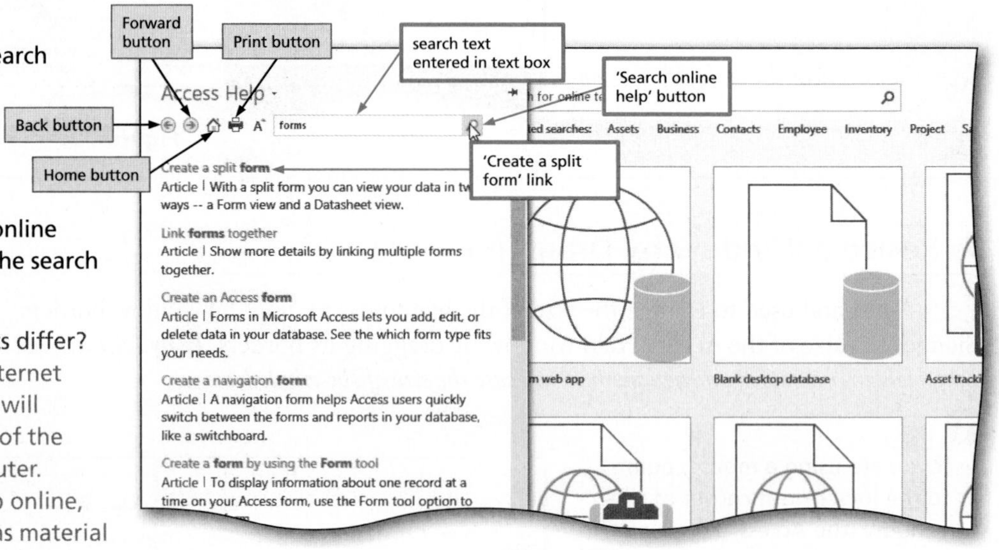

Figure 77

2

- Tap or click the 'Create a split form' link to display the Help information associated with the selected topic (Figure 78).

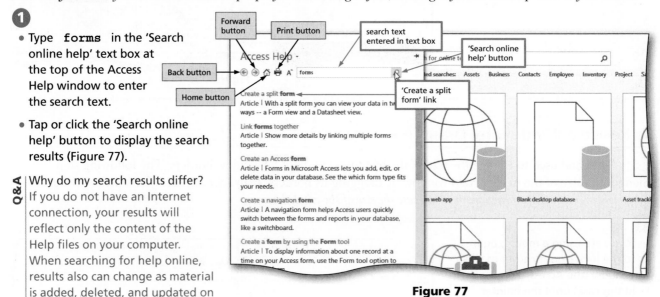

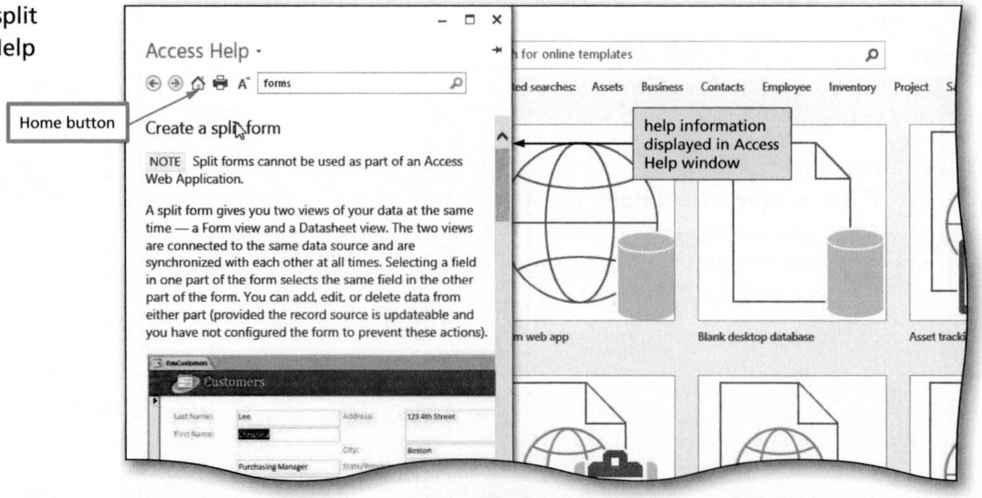

Figure 78

3

- Tap or click the Home button in the Help window to clear the search results and redisplay the Help home page (Figure 79).

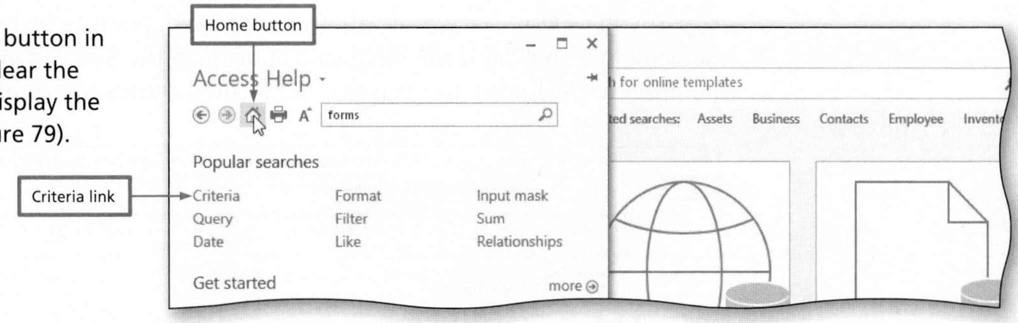

Figure 79

To Obtain Help Using Help Links

1 SIGN IN | 2 USE WINDOWS | 3 USE APPS | 4 FILE MANAGEMENT | 5 SWITCH APPS | 6 SAVE FILES
7 CHANGE SCREEN RESOLUTION | 8 EXIT APPS | 9 USE ADDITIONAL APP FEATURES | 10 USE HELP

If your topic of interest is listed in the Help window, you can click the link to begin browsing the Help categories instead of entering search text. ***Why?*** *You browse Help just as you would browse a website. If you know which category contains your Help information, you can use these links.* The following step finds the Criteria information using the Criteria link from the Access Help home page.

1

- Tap or click the Criteria link on the Help home page (shown in Figure 79) to display the Criteria help links (Figure 80).

2

- After reviewing the page, tap or click the Close button to close the Help window.
- Tap or click Access's Close button to exit Access.

Q&A Why does my Help window display different links?
The content of your Help window might differ because Microsoft continually updates its Help information.

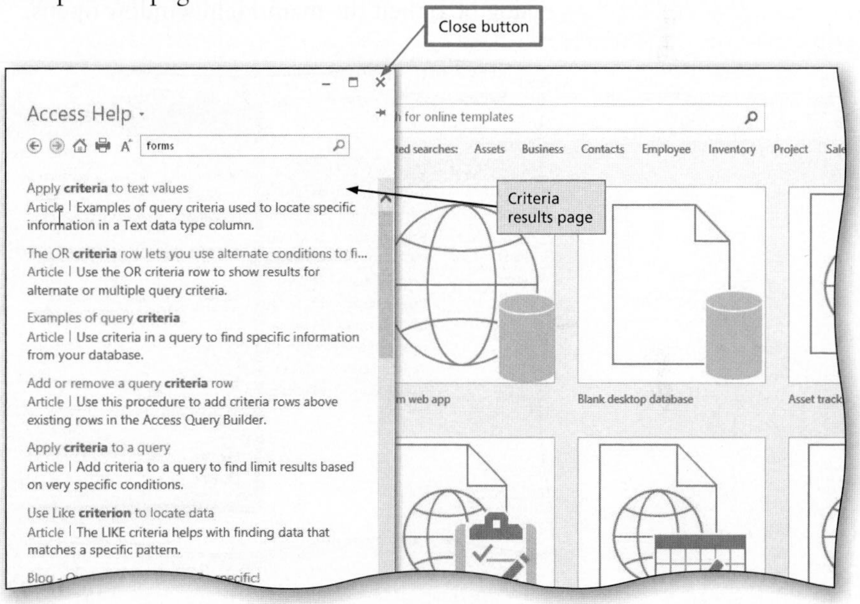

Figure 80

Obtaining Help while Working in an Office App

Help in the Office apps, such as Access, provides you with the ability to obtain help directly, without opening the Help window and initiating a search. For example, you might be unsure about how a particular command works, or you may be presented with a dialog box that you do not know how to use.

Figure 81 shows one option for obtaining help while working in an Office app. If you want to learn more about a command, point to its button and wait for the ScreenTip to appear. If the Help icon appears in the ScreenTip, press the F1 key while pointing to the button to open the Help window associated with that command.

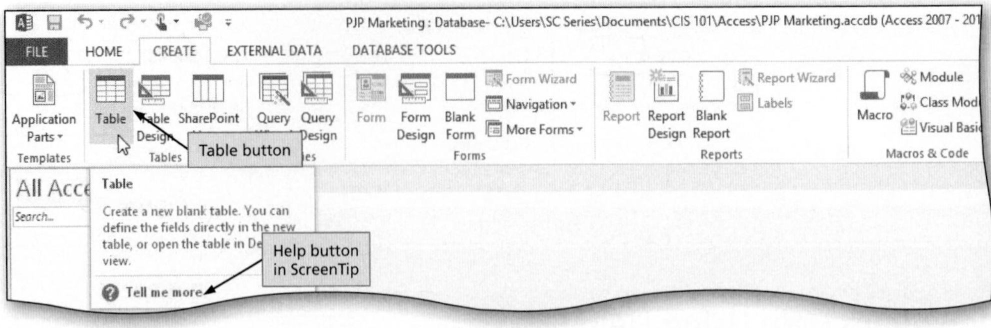

Figure 81

Figure 82 shows a dialog box that contains a Help button. Pressing the F1 key while the dialog box is displayed opens a Help window. The Help window contains help about that dialog box, if available. If no help file is available for that particular dialog box, then the main Help window opens.

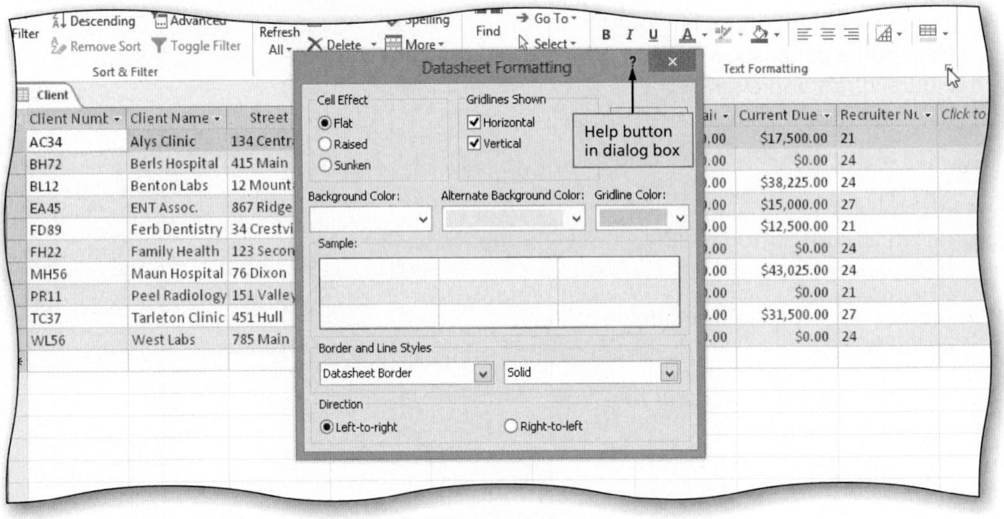

Figure 82

Using Windows Help and Support

One of the more powerful Windows features is Windows Help and Support. **Windows Help and Support** is available when using Windows or when using any Microsoft app running in Windows. The same methods used for searching Microsoft Office Help can be used in Windows Help and Support. The difference is that Windows Help and Support displays help for Windows, instead of for Microsoft Office.

To Use Windows Help and Support

1 SIGN IN | 2 USE WINDOWS | 3 USE APPS | 4 FILE MANAGEMENT | 5 SWITCH APPS | 6 SAVE FILES
7 CHANGE SCREEN RESOLUTION | 8 EXIT APPS | 9 USE ADDITIONAL APP FEATURES | **10 USE HELP**

The following steps use Windows Help and Support and open the Windows Help and Support window, which contains links to more information about Windows. ***Why?*** *This feature is designed to assist you in using Windows or the various apps.* If you are using Windows 7, skip these steps and instead perform the steps in the yellow box that immediately follows these Windows 8 steps.

1

- Swipe in from the right edge of the screen or point to the upper-right corner of the screen to display the Charms bar (Figure 83).

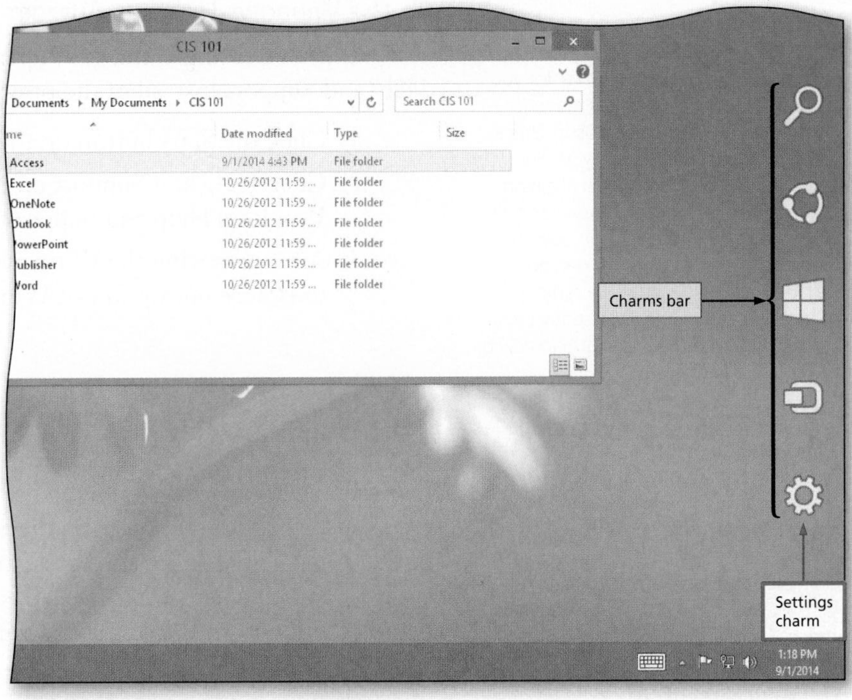

Figure 83

2

- Tap or click the Settings charm on the Charms bar to display the Settings menu (Figure 84).

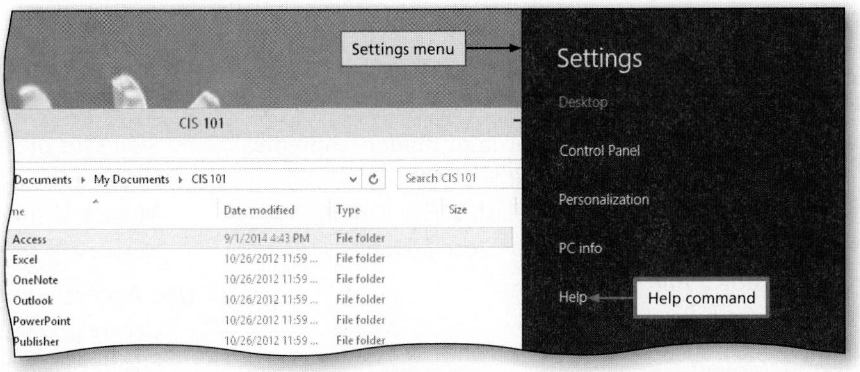

Figure 84

3

- Tap or click Help to open the Windows Help and Support window (Figure 85).

4

- After reviewing the Windows Help and Support window, tap or click the Close button to close the Windows Help and Support window.

Figure 85

Other Ways

1. Press WINDOWS+F1

BTW

Certification

The Microsoft Office Specialist (MOS) program provides an opportunity for you to obtain a valuable industry credential — proof that you have the Microsoft Office 2013 skills required by employers. For more information, visit the Certification resource on the Student Companion Site located on www.cengagebrain.com. For detailed instructions about accessing available resources, visit www.cengage.com/ct/studentdownload or contact your instructor for information about accessing the required files.

BTW

Quick Reference

For a table that lists how to complete the tasks covered in this book using touch gestures, the mouse, ribbon, shortcut menu, and keyboard, see the Quick Reference Summary at the back of this book, or visit the Quick Reference resource on the Student Companion Site located on www.cengagebrain.com. For detailed instructions about accessing available resources, visit www.cengage.com/ct/studentdownload or contact your instructor for information about accessing the required files.

To Use Windows Help and Support with Windows 7

If you are using Windows 7, perform these steps to start Windows Help and Support instead of the previous steps that use Windows 8.

1. Click the Start button on the taskbar to display the Start menu.
2. Click Help and Support on the Start menu to open the Windows Help and Support window.
3. After reviewing the Windows Help and Support window, click the Close button to exit Windows Help and Support.

Chapter Summary

In this chapter, you learned how to use the Windows interface, several touch screen and mouse operations, and file and folder management. You also learned some basic features of Access and discovered the common elements that exist among Microsoft Office apps. The items listed below include all of the new Windows and Access skills you have learned in this chapter, with the tasks grouped by activity.

File Management

Create a Folder (OFF 16)
Create a Folder within a Folder (OFF 19)
Expand a Folder, Scroll through Folder Contents, and Collapse a Folder (OFF 21)
Copy a Folder to a USB Flash Drive (OFF 38)
Use the Backstage View to Close a Database (OFF 40)
Rename a File (OFF 48)
Move a File (OFF 50)
Delete a File (OFF 51)

Use Help

Open the Help Window in an Office App (OFF 52)
Obtain Help Using the 'Search online help' Text Box (OFF 54)
Obtain Help Using Help Links (OFF 55)
Use Windows Help and Support (OFF 56)

Use Windows

Sign In to an Account (OFF 7)
Run Access from the Start Screen (OFF 11)
Switch between an App and the Start Screen (OFF 13)
Maximize a Window (OFF 14)
Switch from One App to Another (OFF 22)
Minimize and Restore a Window (OFF 34)
Sign Out of a Microsoft Account (OFF 35)
Change the Screen Resolution (OFF 37)
Move a Window by Dragging (OFF 52)
Resize a Window by Dragging (OFF 53)

Use Access

Create a Database in a Folder (OFF 23)
Display a Different Tab on the Ribbon (OFF 30)
Collapse and Expand the Ribbon (OFF 31)
Use a Shortcut Menu to Relocate the Quick Access Toolbar (OFF 32)
Customize the Quick Access Toolbar (OFF 33)
Exit an Office App (OFF 40)
Run Access Using the Search Box (OFF 40)
Open an Existing Database (OFF 43)
Create a New Access Database from File Explorer (OFF 45)
Run an App from File Explorer and Open a File (OFF 46)

CONSIDER THIS: PLAN AHEAD

What guidelines should you follow to plan your projects?

The process of communicating specific information is a learned, rational skill. Computers and software, especially Microsoft Office 2013, can help you develop ideas and present detailed information to a particular audience and minimize much of the laborious work of drafting and revising projects. No matter what method you use to plan a project, it is beneficial to follow some specific guidelines from the onset to arrive at a final product that is informative, relevant, and effective. Use some aspects of these guidelines every time you undertake a project, and others as needed in specific instances.

1. Determine the project's purpose.
   a) Clearly define why you are undertaking this assignment.
   b) Begin to draft ideas of how best to communicate information by handwriting ideas on paper; composing directly on a laptop, tablet, or mobile device; or developing a strategy that fits your particular thinking and writing style.
2. Analyze your audience.
   a) Learn about the people who will read, analyze, or view your work.
   b) Determine their interests and needs so that you can present the information they need to know and omit the information they already possess.
   c) Form a mental picture of these people or find photos of people who fit this profile so that you can develop a project with the audience in mind.
3. Gather possible content.
   a) Locate existing information that may reside in spreadsheets, databases, or other files.
   b) Conduct a web search to find relevant websites.
   c) Read pamphlets, magazine and newspaper articles, and books to gain insights of how others have approached your topic.
   d) Conduct personal interviews to obtain perspectives not available by any other means.
   e) Consider video and audio clips as potential sources for material that might complement or support the factual data you uncover.
4. Determine what content to present to your audience.
   a) Write three or four major ideas you want an audience member to remember after reading or viewing your project.
   b) Envision your project's endpoint, the key fact you wish to emphasize, so that all project elements lead to this final element.
   c) Determine relevant time factors, such as the length of time to develop the project, how long readers will spend reviewing your project, or the amount of time allocated for your speaking engagement.
   d) Decide whether a graph, photo, or artistic element can express or enhance a particular concept.
   e) Be mindful of the order in which you plan to present the content, and place the most important material at the top or bottom of the page, because readers and audience members generally remember the first and last pieces of information they see and hear.

CONSIDER THIS

How should you submit solutions to questions in the assignments identified with a ✻ symbol?

Every assignment in this book contains one or more questions identified with a ✻ symbol. These questions require you to think beyond the assigned file. Present your solutions to the questions in the format required by your instructor. Possible formats may include one or more of these options: write the answer; create a document that contains the answer; present your answer to the class; discuss your answer in a group; record the answer as audio or video using a webcam, smartphone, or portable media player; or post answers on a blog, wiki, or website.

Apply Your Knowledge

Reinforce the skills and apply the concepts you learned in this chapter.

Creating a Folder and a Database

Instructions: You will create an Access folder and then create an Access database and save it in the folder.

Perform the following tasks:

1. Open the File Explorer window and then double-tap or double-click to open the Documents library.
2. Tap or click the New folder button on the Quick Access Toolbar to display a new folder icon and text box for the folder name.

Continued >

Apply Your Knowledge *continued*

3. Type `Access` in the text box to name the folder. Press the ENTER key to create the folder in the Documents library.
4. Run Access.
5. Use the 'Blank desktop database' option to create a database with the name Apply 1. Do not press the ENTER key after typing the file name.
6. If requested by your instructor, name the database Apply 1 Lastname where Lastname is your last name.
7. Tap or click the 'Browse for a location to put your database' button and navigate to the Access folder in the Documents library. Tap or click the OK button to select the Access folder as the location for the database and close the dialog box. Tap or click the Create button to create the database.
8. If your Quick Access Toolbar does not show the Quick Print button, add the Quick Print button to the Quick Access Toolbar (Figure 86).

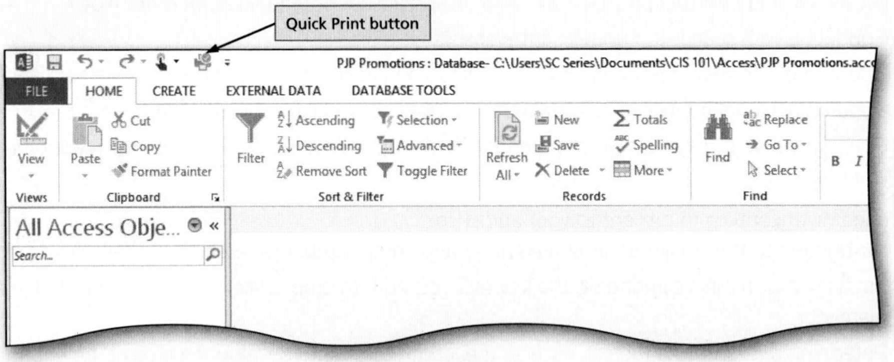

Figure 86

9. Exit Access.
10. Open the File Explorer window, open the Documents library, and then open the Access folder you created in Step 3.
11. Double-tap or double-click the Apply 1 database to start Access and open the Apply 1 database.
12. Remove the Quick Print button from the Quick Access Toolbar. Exit Access.
13. Submit the database in the format specified by your instructor.
14. What other commands might you find useful to include on the Quick Access Toolbar?

Extend Your Knowledge

Extend the skills you learned in this chapter and experiment with new skills. You will use Help to complete the assignment.

Using Help

Instructions: Use Access Help to perform the following tasks.

Perform the following tasks:

1. Run Access.
2. Tap or click the Microsoft Access Help button to open the Access Help window (Figure 87).
3. Search Access Help to answer the following questions.
   a. What shortcut keys are available for finding and replacing text or data?
   b. What type of training courses are available through Help?
   c. What are the steps to add a new group to the ribbon?

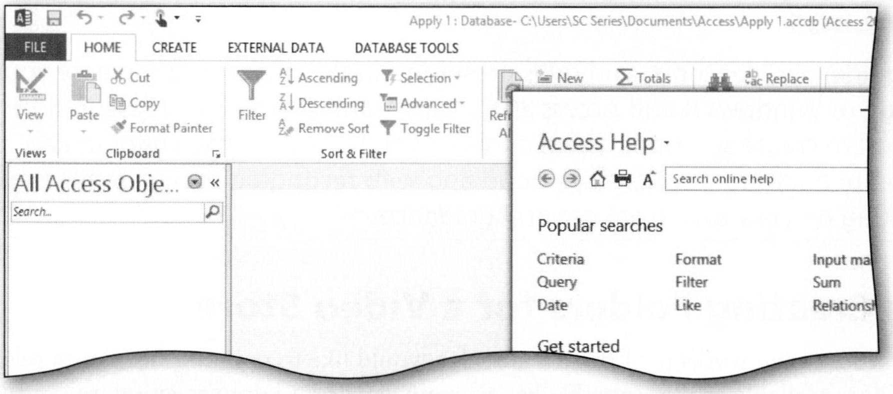

Figure 87

d. What are Quick Parts?
e. What are three features that have been discontinued in Access 2013?
f. What is a template?
g. What is a primary key?
h. How do you back up a database?
i. What is the purpose of compacting and repairing a database?
j. What is the purpose of the Navigation Pane?

4. Type the answers from your searches in a new blank Word document. Save the document with a new file name and then submit it in the format specified by your instructor.
5. If requested by your instructor, enter your name in the Word document.
6. Exit Access and Word.
7. What search text did you use to perform the searches above? Did it take multiple attempts to search and locate the exact information for which you were searching?

Analyze, Correct, Improve

Analyze a file structure, correct all errors, and improve the design.

Organizing Vacation Photos

Note: To complete this assignment, you will be required to use the Data Files for Students. Visit www.cengage.com/ct/studentdownload for detailed instructions or contact your instructor for information about accessing the required files.

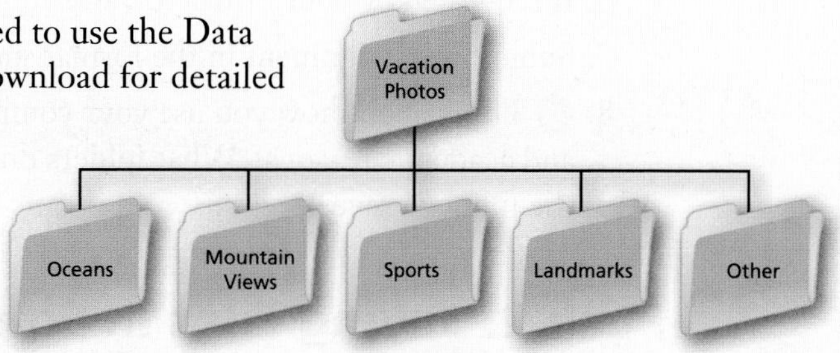

Figure 88

Instructions: Traditionally, you have stored photos from past vacations together in one folder. The photos are becoming difficult to manage, and you now want to store them in appropriate folders. You will create the folder structure shown in Figure 88. You then will move the photos to the folders so that they will be organized properly.

1. Correct Create the folder structure in Figure 88 so that you are able to store the photos in an organized manner. If requested by your instructor, add another folder using your last name as the folder name.

2. Improve View each photo and drag it to the appropriate folder to improve the organization. Submit the assignment in the format specified by your instructor.

3. In which folder did you place each photo? Think about the files you have stored on your computer. What folder hierarchy would be best to manage your files?

In the Labs

Use the guidelines, concepts, and skills presented in this chapter to increase your knowledge of Windows 8 and Access 2013. Labs 1 and 2, which increase in difficulty, require you to create solutions based on what you learned in the chapter; Lab 3 requires you to create a solution, which uses cloud and web technologies, by learning and investigating on your own from general guidance.

Lab 1: Creating Folders for a Video Store

Problem: Your friend works for Ebaird Video. He would like to organize his files in relation to the types of videos available in the store. He has six main categories: drama, action, romance, foreign, biographical, and comedy. You are to create a folder structure similar to Figure 89.

Instructions: Perform the following tasks:

1. Insert a USB flash drive in an available USB port and then open the USB flash drive window.
2. Create the main folder for Ebaird Video.
3. Navigate to the Ebaird Video folder.
4. Within the Ebaird Video folder, create a folder for each of the following: Drama, Action, Romance, Foreign, Biographical, and Comedy.

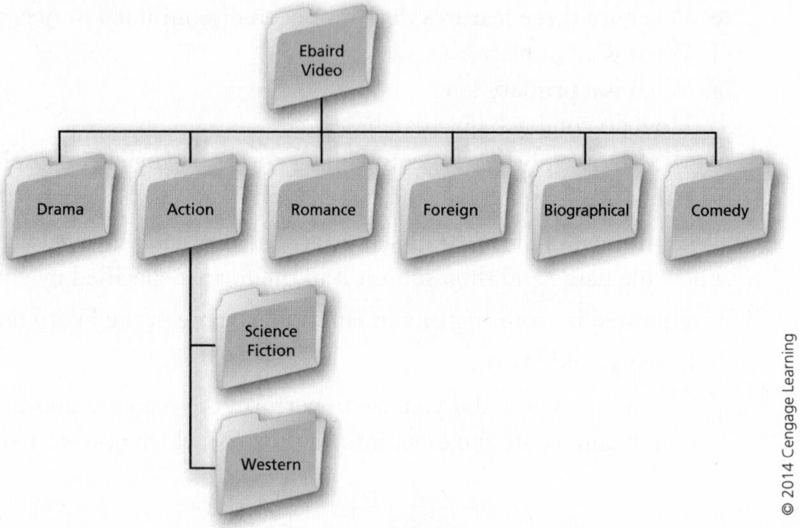

Figure 89

5. Within the Action folder, create two additional folders, one for Science Fiction and the second for Western.
6. If requested by your instructor, add another folder using your last name as the folder name.
7. Submit the assignment in the format specified by your instructor.
8. Think about how you use your computer for various tasks (consider personal, professional, and academic reasons). What folders do you think will be required on your computer to store the files you save?

Lab 2: Saving Files in Folders

Creating Access Databases and Saving Them in Appropriate Folders

Problem: You are taking a class that requires you to complete three Access chapters. You will save the work completed in each chapter in a different folder (Figure 90).

Instructions: Create the folders shown in Figure 90. Then, using Access, create three databases to save in each folder.

1. Create the folder structure shown in Figure 90.
2. Navigate to the Chapter 1 folder.

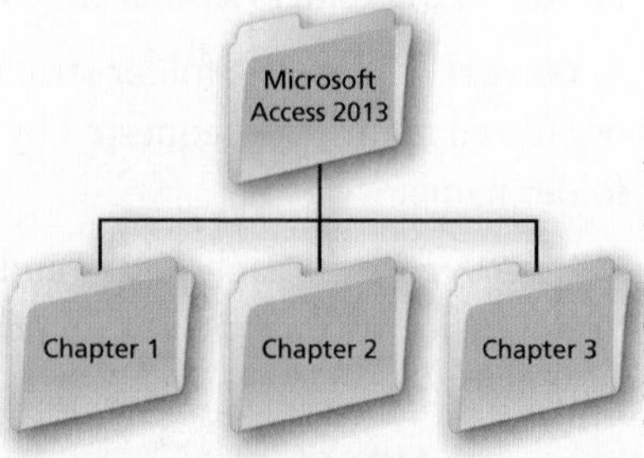

Figure 90

3. Create an Access database named My Chapter 1 Access Database and then save it in the Chapter 1 folder.
4. Navigate to the Chapter 2 folder.
5. Create another Access database named My Chapter 2 Access Database, and then save in the Chapter 2 folder.
6. Navigate to the Chapter 3 folder.
7. Create another Access database named My Chapter 3 Access Database, and then save it in the Chapter 3 folder.
8. If requested by your instructor, add your name to each of the three Access databases using the Rename command.
9. Submit the assignment in the format specified by your instructor.
10. Based on your current knowledge of Windows and Access, how will you organize folders for assignments in this class? Why?

Lab 3: Expand Your World: Cloud and Web Technologies

Creating Folders on SkyDrive and Using the Word Web App

Problem: You are taking a class that requires you to create folders on SkyDrive (Figure 91).

Instructions: Perform the following tasks:

1. Sign in to SkyDrive in your browser.
2. Use the Create button to create the folder structure shown in Figure 91.
3. If requested by your instructor, rename the Notes folder as your name Notes.
4. Submit the assignment in the format specified by your instructor.
5. Based on your current knowledge of SkyDrive, do you think you will use it? Explain why you answered the way you did.

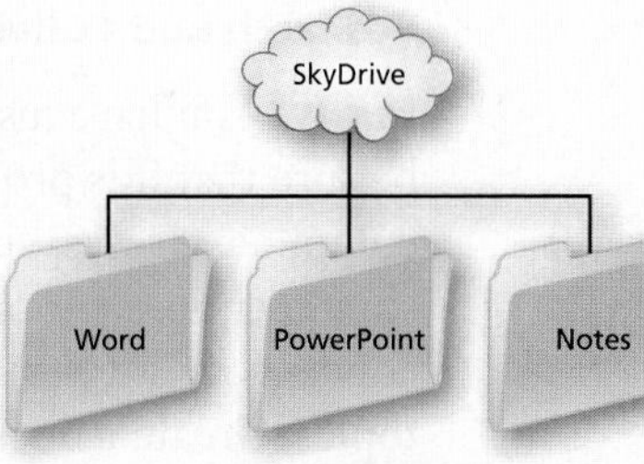

Figure 91

Consider This: Your Turn

Apply your creative thinking and problem solving skills to design and implement a solution.

1: Creating Beginning Files for Classes

Personal/Academic

Part 1: You are taking the following classes: Introduction to Sociology, Chemistry, Calculus, and Marketing. Create folders for each of the classes. Create a folder structure that will store the databases for each of these classes. In the Introduction of Sociology folder, use Access to create a database named Media and Gender. In the Chemistry folder, use Access to create a database named Periodic Table. In the Calculus folder, use Access to create a database with the name of the class. In the Marketing folder, create an Access database named Data Mining Information. If requested by your instructor, add your name to each of the databases. Use the concepts and techniques presented

Continued >

Consider This: Your Turn *continued*

in this chapter to create the folders and files, and store the files in their respective locations. Submit your assignment in the format specified by your instructor.

Part 2: You made several decisions while determining the folder structure in this assignment. What was the rationale behind these decisions? Are there any other decisions that also might have worked?

2: Creating Folders

Professional

Part 1: Your manager at the media store where you work part-time has asked for help with organizing her files. After looking through the files, you decided upon a file structure for her to use, including the following folders: CDs, DVDs, and general merchandise. Within the CDs folder, create folders for music, books, and games. Within the DVDs folder, create folders for movies and television. Within the general merchandise folder, create folders for clothing, portable media players, and cases. If requested by your instructor, add your name to each of the CDs, DVDs, and general merchandise folders. Use the concepts and techniques presented in this chapter to create the folders. Submit your assignment in the format specified by your instructor.

Part 2: You made several decisions while determining the folder structure in this assignment. What was the rationale behind these decisions? Justify why you feel this folder structure will help your manager organize her files.

3: Using Help

Research and Collaboration

Part 1: You have just installed a new computer with the Windows operating system and want to be sure that it is protected from the threat of viruses. You ask two of your friends to help research computer viruses, virus prevention, and virus removal. In a team of three people, each person should choose a topic (computer viruses, virus prevention, and virus removal) to research. Use the concepts and techniques presented in this chapter to use Help to find information regarding these topics. Create a document that contains steps to properly safeguard a computer from viruses, ways to prevent viruses, as well as the different ways to remove a virus should your computer become infected. Submit your assignment in the format specified by your instructor.

Part 2: You made several decisions while searching Windows Help and Support for this assignment. What decisions did you make? What was the rationale behind these decisions? How did you locate the required information about viruses in help?

Learn Online

Reinforce what you learned in this chapter with games, exercises, training, and many other online activities and resources.

Student Companion Site Reinforcement activities and resources are available at no additional cost on www.cengagebrain.com. Visit www.cengage.com/ct/studentdownload for detailed instructions about accessing the resources available at the Student Companion Site.

SAM Put your skills into practice with SAM Projects! If you have a SAM account, go to www.cengage.com/sam2013 to access SAM assignments for this chapter.

Office 365 Essentials

Objectives

You will have mastered the material in this chapter when you can:

- Describe the components of Office 365
- Compare Office 2013 to Office 365 subscription plans
- Understand the productivity tools of Office 365
- Sync multiple devices using Office 365
- Describe how business teams collaborate using SharePoint
- Describe how to use a SharePoint template to design a public website
- Describe how to conduct an online meeting with Lync

Explore Office 365

Introduction to Office 365

Microsoft Office 365 uses the cloud to deliver a subscription-based service offering the newest Office suite and much more. The Microsoft cloud provides Office software and information stored on remote servers all over the world. Your documents are located online or on the cloud, which provides you access to your information anywhere using a PC, Mac, tablet, mobile phone, or other device with an Internet connection. For businesses and students alike, Office 365 offers significant cost savings compared to the traditional cost of purchasing Microsoft Office 2013. In addition to the core desktop Office suite, Office 365 provides access to email, calendars, conferencing, file sharing, and website design, which sync across multiple devices.

Cloud Computing

Cloud computing refers to a collection of computer servers that house resources users access through the Internet (Figure 1). These resources include email messages, schedules, music, photos, videos, games, websites, programs, apps, servers, storage, and more. Instead of accessing these resources on your computer or mobile device, you access them on the cloud.

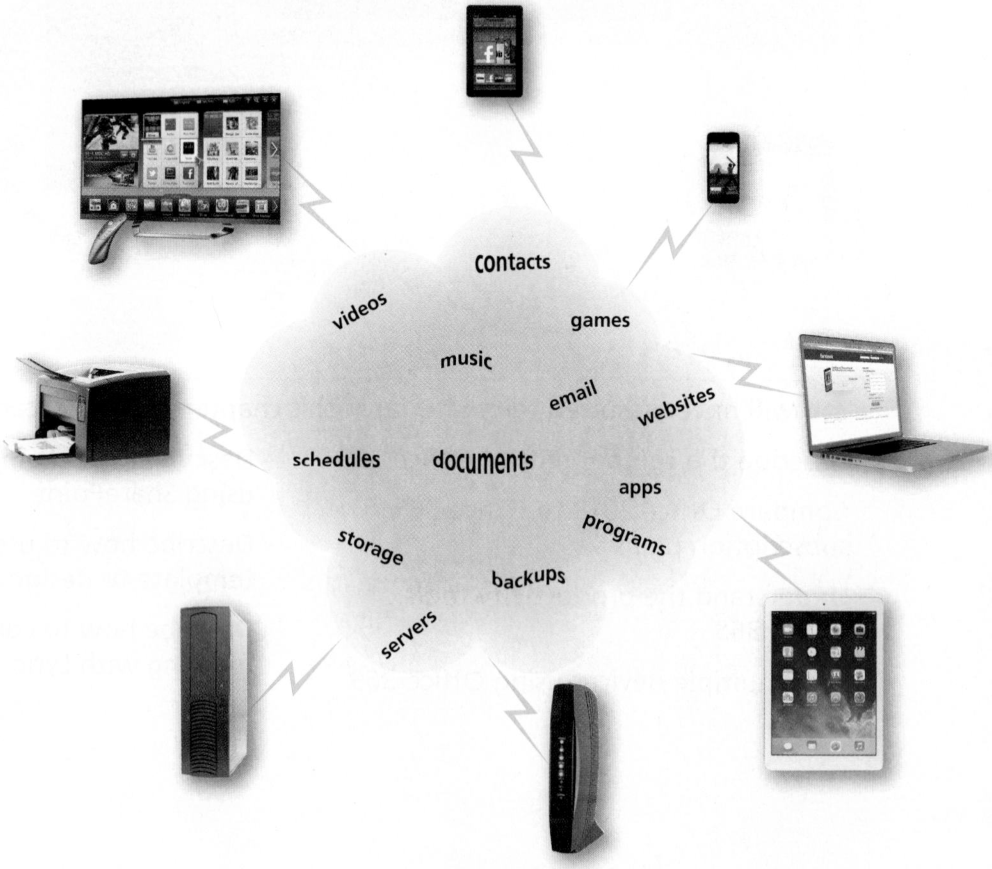

Figure 1

Cloud computing can help businesses be more efficient and save them money by shifting usage and the consumption of resources, such as servers and programs, from a local environment to the Internet. For example, an employee working during the day in California could use computing resources located in an office in London that is closed for the evening. When the company in California uses the computing resources, it pays a fee that is based on the amount of computing time and other resources it consumes, much in the same way that consumers pay utility companies for the amount of electricity they use.

Cloud computing is changing how users access and pay for software applications. Fading fast are the days when software packages were sold in boxes at a physical store location with a one-time purchase software license fee. Instead, the new pricing structure is a subscription-based model, where users pay a monthly or annual fee for the software that you can use on multiple devices. The cloud-based Office 365 offers the Office suite with added features that allow you to communicate and collaborate with others in real time.

CONSIDER THIS

When you create a free Microsoft account, do you get free cloud storage space?
Yes, when you create a free Microsoft account at Outlook.com, you have access to 15 GB of cloud storage for any types of files.

What Is Office 365?

Office 365 is a collection of programs and services, which includes the Microsoft Office suite, file storage, online collaboration, and file synchronization, as shown in Figure 2 on the next page. You can access these services using your computer, tablet (Windows, iPad, or Android), any browser, or supported mobile device. For example, a business has two options for providing Office to their employees. A business could purchase Office 2013 and install the software on company computers and servers; however, this traditional Office 2013 package with perpetual licensing does not include the communication and collaboration tools. Employees could not access the Office software if they were not using their work computers. In contrast, if the business purchases a monthly subscription to Office 365, each employee has access to the Office suite on up to five different computers, whether at home or work; company-wide email; web conferencing; website creation capabilities; unlimited cloud storage; and shared files. An employee can begin a departmental budget on Excel on their office PC, finish the budget on their iPad at home, and review the final budget on their smartphone using Office 365. For a lower price, Office 365 provides many more features. In addition, a business may prefer a subscription plan with predictable monthly costs and no up-front infrastructure costs.

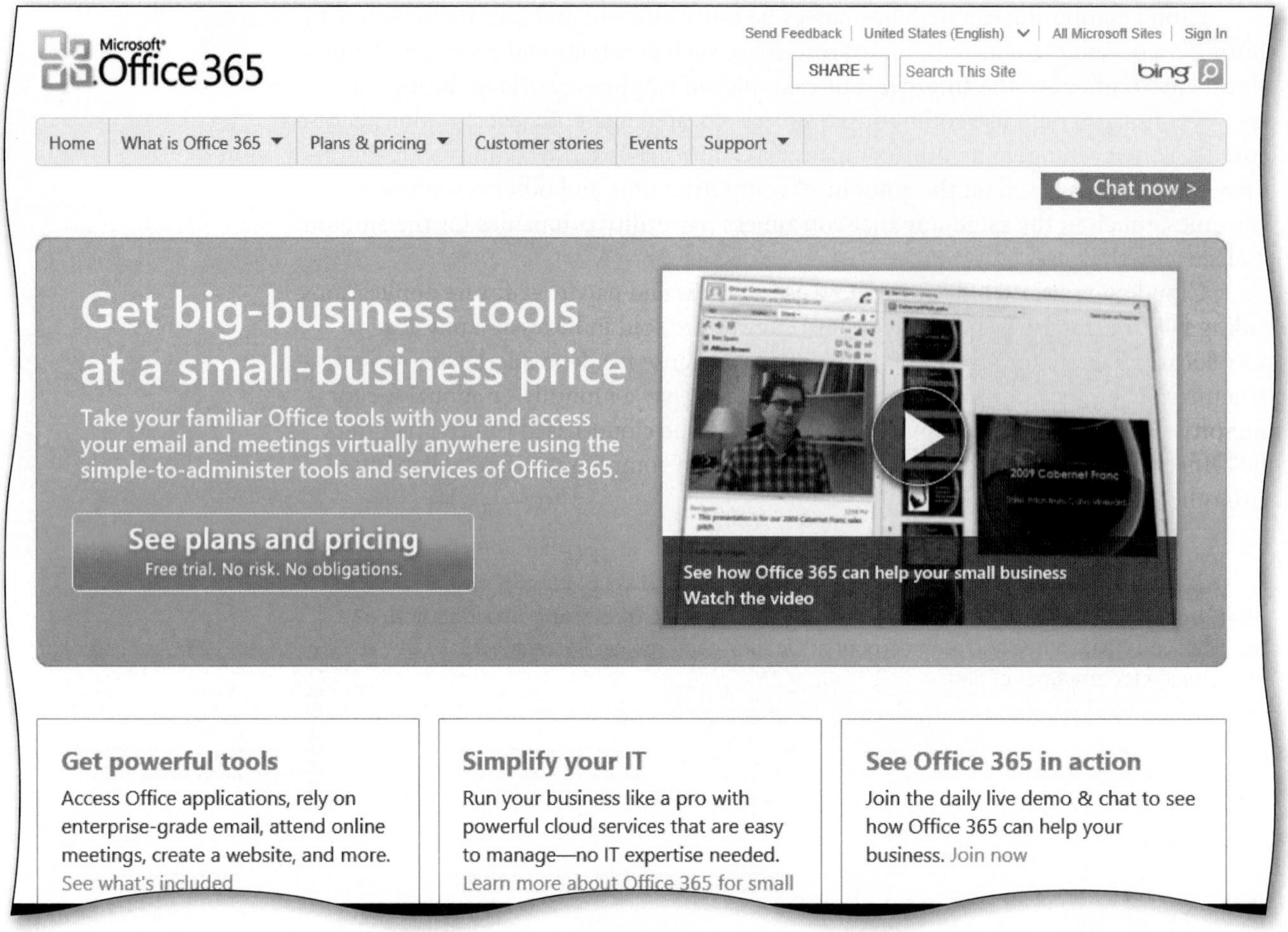

Figure 2

Office 2013 and Office 365 Features Comparison

Office 2013 is the name of the perpetual software package that includes individual applications that can be installed on a single computer. An Office 365 subscription comes with a license to install the software on multiple PCs, Macs, iPad tablets, or smartphones at the same time, giving you more flexibility to use your Office products in your home, school, or workplace, whether on a computer, tablet, or a mobile device. Office 365 provides updated Office 2013 programs as part of a subscription service that includes online storage, sharing, and syncing via Microsoft cloud services as shown in Table 1. A limited version of Office 365 including Word, Excel, PowerPoint, and OneNote can be downloaded from the appropriate app store on mobile devices, such as an iPad or smartphone. Office documents can be created, viewed, and edited using an iPhone, Android, or Windows smartphone. Office applications differ across different platforms and are tailored to work best on each device. The Office applications are available for Mac users and the version numbers may be different from those available for PC users.

Office 365 is available in business, consumer, education, and government editions. Office 365 combines the full version of the Microsoft Office desktop suite with cloud-based versions of Microsoft's communications and collaboration services. The subscription package includes:

- Microsoft Exchange online for shared email and calendars
- Microsoft SharePoint Online for shared file access and public website creation
- Microsoft Office Online for browser viewing
- Microsoft Lync Online for communication services

Table 1 Office 2013 and Office 365 Feature Comparison for PCs and Macs

Office 2013 Professional (Installed on a single device)	Office 365 Subscription (Installed on 2 to 5 devices)
Microsoft Word	Microsoft Word
Microsoft Excel	Microsoft Excel
Microsoft PowerPoint	Microsoft PowerPoint
Microsoft Access (Mac version not available)	Microsoft Access (Mac version not available)
Microsoft Outlook	Microsoft Outlook
Microsoft Publisher	Microsoft Publisher
Microsoft OneNote	Microsoft OneNote
	email and calendars (Exchange Online)
	file sharing (SharePoint Online and Yammer)
	public website design and publishing (SharePoint Online)
	browser-based Office Online
	instant messaging (Lync Online and Yammer)
	audio and video web conferencing (Lync Online)
	screen sharing with shared control (Lync Online)
	technical support

Subscription-Based Office 365 Plans

Microsoft provides various subscription plans for Office 365 with different benefits for each individual or organization. Subscription plans include Office 365 Home Premium for home users, Office 365 ProPlus programs for students and teachers, Office 365 Small Business, Office 365 Small Business Premium, Office 365 Midsize Business, and Office 365 Enterprise and Government. During the Office 365 sign-up process, you create a Microsoft email address and password to use on your multiple devices. A single subscription to an Office 365 Home Premium account can cover an entire household. The Office 365 Home Premium subscription allows up to five concurrent installations by using the same email address and password combination. This means that your mother could be on the main family computer while you use your tablet and smartphone at the same time. You each can sign in with your individual Microsoft accounts using your settings and accessing your own documents using a single Office 365 subscription.

The educational Office 365 ProPlus subscription plan is designed for K12 and higher-education full-time and part-time students, faculty, and staff. By submitting the proper credentials, such as a school email address, students, faculty, and school staff can download Office 365, including full online copies of Word, PowerPoint, Excel, Access, Outlook, Publisher, and OneNote for free if their school has an Office 2013 or 365 site wide license agreement (office.com/getoffice365). In addition, Office 365 ProPlus provides users with unlimited OneDrive cloud storage rather than the free 15 GB provided by a Microsoft account, and 60 Skype world minutes per month for videoconferencing. The Office 365 ProPlus program is limited to five home computers, tablets, or smartphones.

The Microsoft Office 365 Business Plans can provide full support for employees to work from any location, whether they are in their traditional business office, commuting to and from work across the country, or working from a home office. Office 365 Business accommodates up to 300 users. Office 365 Enterprise Plan fits organizations ranging in size from a single employee to 50,000-plus users. Each employee can install Microsoft Office 365 on five different computers.

First Look at Office 365

Microsoft Office 365 subscription plans offer all the same applications that are available in the Microsoft Office Professional 2013 suite in addition to multiple communication and collaboration tools. With Office 365 you can retrieve, edit, and save Office documents on the Office 365 cloud, coauthor documents in real time with others, and quickly initiate computer-based calls, instant messages, and web conferences with others. Microsoft continues to update Office 365 to include new features, so over time expect greater differences between Office 2013 and Office 365.

Productivity Tools

Whether you are inserting audio and video into a Word document to create a high-impact business plan proposal or utilizing the visualization tools in Excel to chart the return on investment of a new mobile marketing program, Office 365 uses a quick-start installation technology, called **Click-to-Run**, that downloads and installs the basics within minutes, so that users are able to start working almost immediately. In effect, the Office 365 subscription provides access to the full Office applications wherever you are working. When you access your Office 365 account management panel, three choices are listed: 32- and 64-bit versions of Office 2013, and Office for Mac. Selecting the third option will initiate a download of an installer that must be run in the standard OS X fashion. When you install Office 365 on a Mac, the most current Mac version of Office is installed.

CONSIDER THIS

Unlike Google, which offers online documents, spreadsheets, and presentations called Google Docs, Microsoft Office 365 installs locally on your computer in addition to being available online.

Email and Calendars

In business, sharing information is essential to meeting the needs of your customers and staff. Office 365 offers shared access to business email, calendars, and contacts using **Exchange Online** from a computer, tablet, phone, and browser. The cloud-based Exchange Online enables business people to access Outlook information from anywhere at any time, while eliminating the cost of purchasing and maintaining servers to store data. If you need to meet with a colleague about a new project, you can compare calendars to view availability, confirm conference room availability, share project contacts, search email messages related to the project, and send email invitations to the project meeting. Exchange Online also allows you to search and access your company's address list.

Online Meetings

When you are working with a team on a project that requires interaction, email and text communications can slow the communications process. Microsoft Lync connects you with others by facilitating real-time, interactive presentations and meetings over the Internet using both video and audio calling. As shown in Figure 3, you can conduct an online meeting with a team member or customer that includes an instant messaging conversation, audio, high-definition video, virtual whiteboards, and screen sharing. If the customer does not have an Office 365 subscription, they still can join the meeting through the invitation link, which runs the Lync Web App.

Skype is another tool in the Office 365 subscription, which enables users to place video calls to computers and smartphones and voice calls to landlines. Skype also supports instant message and file sharing to computers and mobile devices. While Skype may be adequate for simple communication, Lync provides for more robust, comprehensive communications. These robust features include high-definition (HD) videoconferencing capabilities, a whiteboard, and a larger audience. Using Lync, meeting attendees simultaneously can view up to five participants' videos, identify the active speaker, and associate names with faces. Lync supports up to 250 attendees per meeting. Unlike Skype, Lync meetings can be recorded for replaying at a later time. This enables businesses and schools to schedule meetings or organize online classes using Lync capabilities.

In addition to Lync, Microsoft Office 365 Business includes a business social networking tool named Yammer. With Yammer, employees create an online team workspace to discuss projects, deadlines, and share files. By sharing your profile and expertise, coworkers can easily find each other and post messages to keep all team members in the loop.

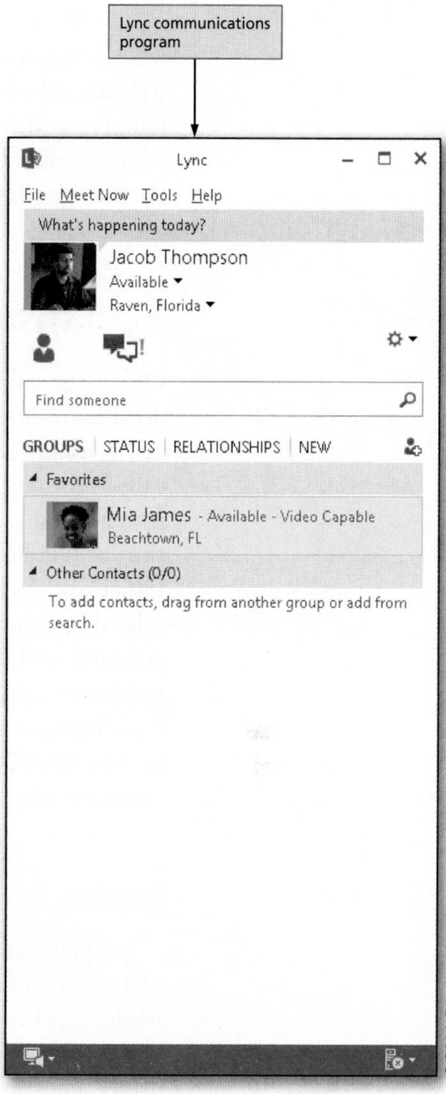

Figure 3

File Sharing

Office 365 includes a team site, which is a password-protected portal that supports sharing of large, difficult-to-email files and provides a single location for the latest versions of documents. In business, for example, colleagues working on common projects can save valuable time by being able to access instantly the latest master copy of each document. Security can be managed through different levels of user access so that users see only what they are supposed to see. Office 365 provides access to shared files using the cloud, making writing, editing, and sharing documents easier. If a construction company creates a commercial bid for a building project, the customers can be invited to view an Excel spreadsheet bid, construction timetable with a shared calendar, and an Access database of all the materials needed using the file sharing feature online.

Website Creation

Office 365 business plan subscriptions include a built-in hosted public website, where customers and clients can find an online storefront of a company. This public website, called the Website, can be customized to market a company by using various templates within the Office 365 cloud. The website creation tools include those for adding a theme, graphics, fonts, maps, directions, blogs, stock tickers, slide shows, PayPal, weather, and videos to interact with the website's visitors.

Synchronization

Office 365 subscription plans provide a central place to store and access your documents and business information. A feature of Office 365 ensures the original and backup computer files in two or more locations are identical through a process called **Active Directory Synchronization**. For example, if you open a PowerPoint presentation on your smartphone while you are riding a city bus and then add a new slide as you head to school, the PowerPoint presentation automatically is synced with Office 365. When you arrive on campus and open the PowerPoint presentation on a school computer, your new slide already is part of the finished slide show. By storing your files in Office 365, you can access your files on another computer if your home computer fails, with no loss of time or important information. When using your mobile phone's data plan, you do not need to search for a Wi-Fi hot spot to connect to the Office 365 cloud. Computer labs in schools can be configured to synchronize automatically all student files to Office 365 online.

Multiple Device Access to Office 365

With a single sign-in process, Office 365 provides access to multiple computers and mobile devices, including Android smartphones and tablets, Apple iPhones and iPads, and Windows phones. After you configure your devices' email settings, you can view your Microsoft account calendar, contacts, and email. Your personalized settings, preferences, and documents can be synchronized among all the different devices included in your Office 365 premium subscription. With the mobility of Office 365, students and employees can work anywhere, accessing information and responding to email requests immediately. If you lose your phone, Office 365 includes a feature that allows you to remotely wipe your phone clean of any data. By wiping your phone's data, you can prevent any unauthorized access to sensitive information, such as your banking information, passwords, and contacts, as well as discourage identity theft. Because your phone contacts and other information are stored on the Microsoft cloud, damaged or lost equipment is never a problem.

CONSIDER THIS

A thief can be quite resourceful if he or she steals your phone. Before you can alert your parents or spouse to the theft, they might receive a text from "you" asking for your ATM or credit card PIN number. Your parents or spouse might then reply with the PIN number. Your bank account could be emptied in minutes.

Teams Using Office 365 in Business

In the business world, rarely does an employee work in isolation. Companies need their employees to collaborate, whether they work in the same office or in locations around the world. Telecommuters working from home can communicate as if they were on-site by using a common team website and conferencing software. SharePoint Online and Lync Online provide seamless communication.

Small business subscription plans as low as $8.25 per user per month allow employees to create and store Word documents, Excel spreadsheets, and PowerPoint presentations online and communicate with one another via email, instant messaging, or video chat as they work on projects together. As shown in Figure 4, a team portal page is shown when you subscribe at https://portal.microsoftonline.com. Larger companies and those requiring more features can take advantage of the Office 365 business premium package, which, in addition to the features listed above, provides access to the Office 365 portal website and eliminates the effort and cost of the users maintaining their own costly computer servers.

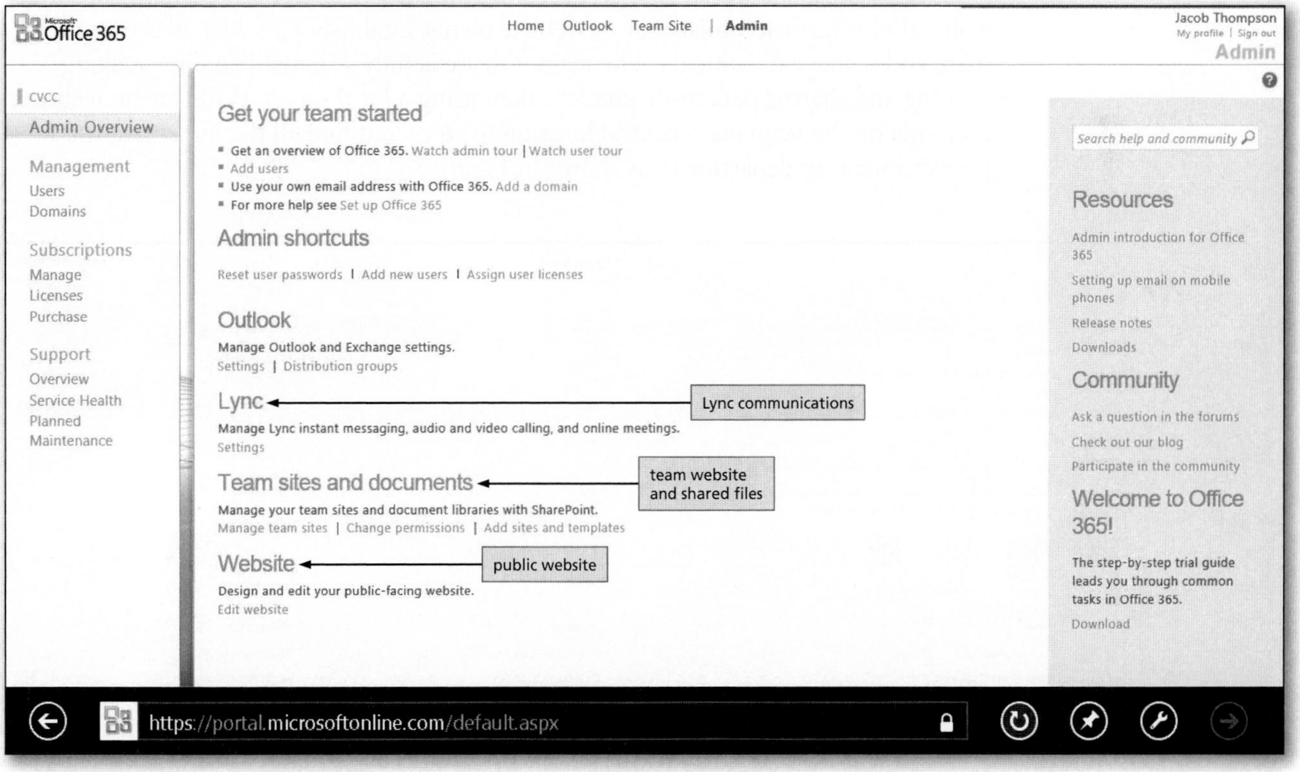

Figure 4

Email Communication Using Exchange

Office 365 includes Exchange Online, an email-based collaborative communications server for business. Exchange enables employees to be more productive by effectively managing email across multiple devices and facilitating teamwork.

Collaboration Using SharePoint

SharePoint Online, a part of Office 365 subscription plans, allows employees to collaborate with one another, share documents, post announcements, and track tasks, as shown in Table 2.

Table 2 Office 365 SharePoint Features

Team Site Feature	Description
Calendar	Track important dates
Shared Document Library	Store related documents according to topic; picture, report, and slide libraries often are included
Task List	Track team tasks according to who is responsible for completion
Team Discussion Board	Discuss the topics at hand in an open forum
Contacts List	Share contact lists of employees, customers, contractors, and suppliers

Office 365 provides the tools to plan meetings. Users can share calendars side by side, view availability, and suggest meeting times from shared calendars. Typically, a SharePoint team administrator or website owner establishes a folder structure to share and manage documents. The team website is fully searchable online, making locating and sharing data more efficient than using a local server. With a team website, everyone on the team has a central location to store and find all the information for a project, client, or department, as shown in Figure 5.

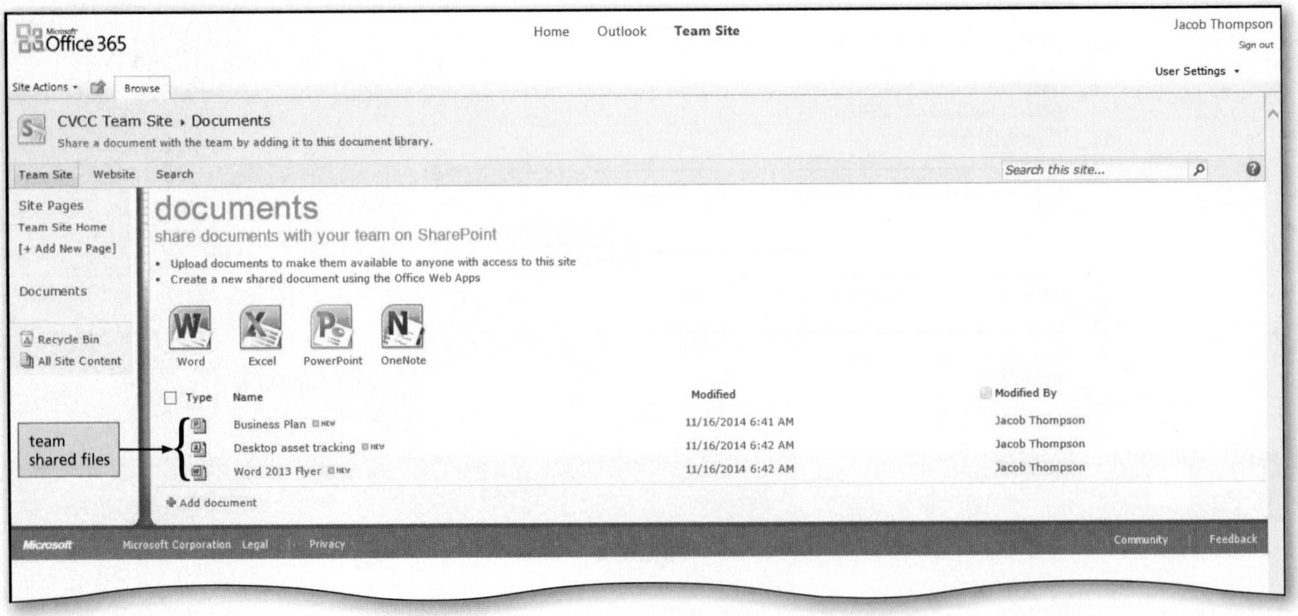

Figure 5

Website Design Using SharePoint

SharePoint provides templates to create a professional looking, public website for an online presence to market your business. As shown in Figure 6, a local pet sitting business is setting up a business website by customizing a SharePoint template. SharePoint Public Website includes features within the Design Manager that you use to customize and design your website by adding your own images, forms, style sheets, maps, themes, and social networking tools. When you finish customizing your business site, you can apply your own domain name to the site. A **domain** is a unique web address that identifies where your website can be found. Office 365 SharePoint hosts your website as part of your subscription. Your customers easily can find your business online and learn about your services.

BTW
Creating SharePoint Intranet Sites
A SharePoint website also can be customized to serve as an internal company website for private communications within the company.

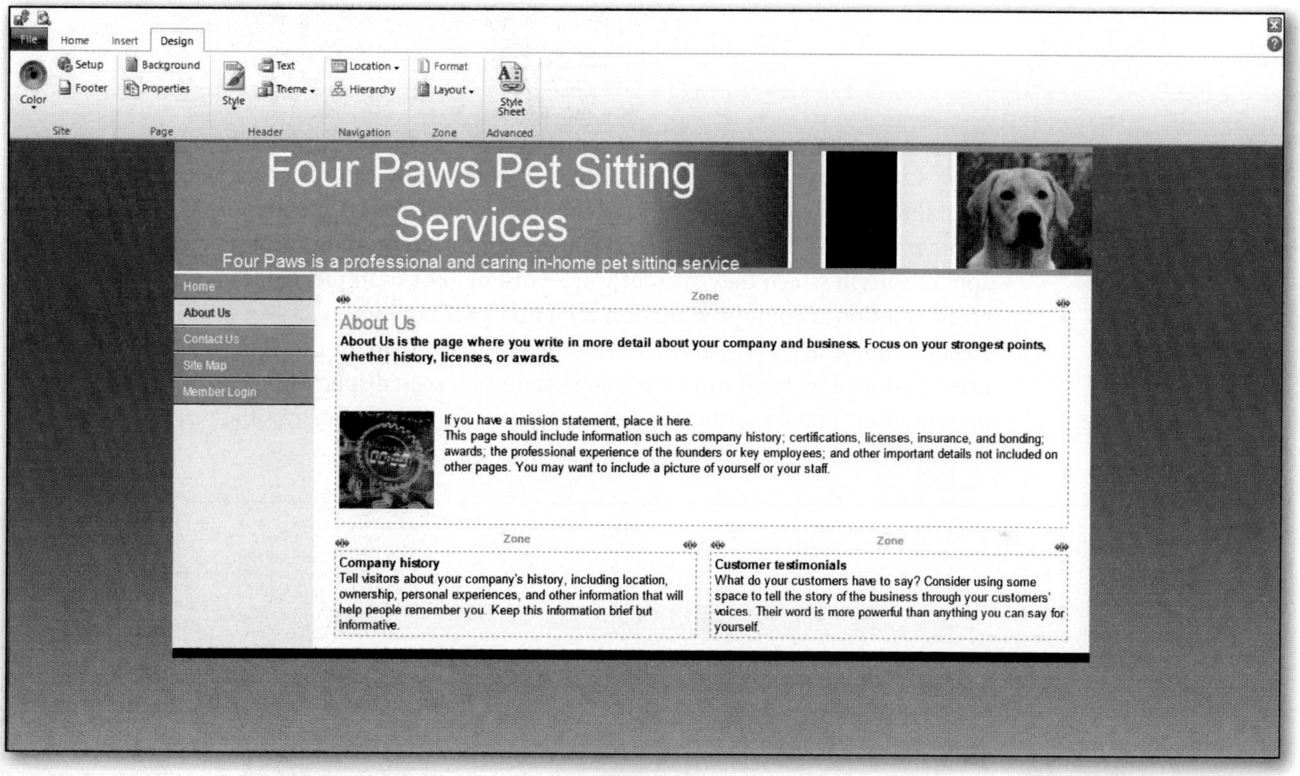

Figure 6

Real-Time Communications Using Lync

Lync Online is Microsoft's server platform for online team communications and comes bundled with Office 365 business subscriptions. As shown in Figure 7, Lync connects in real time to allow instant messaging, videoconferencing, and voice communications; it also integrates with email and Microsoft Office applications.

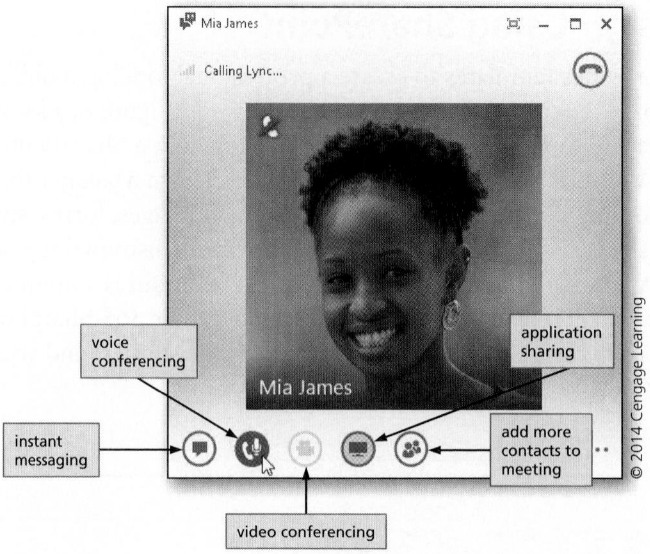

Figure 7

Lync allows you to connect with staff at remote locations using instant messaging capabilities, desktop sharing, videoconferencing, and shared agendas or documents. Lync is integrated into Office 365, which allows staff to start communicating from within the applications in which they currently are working. For example, while an employee is creating a PowerPoint presentation for a new product line, as shown in Figure 8, Lync enables him or her to collaborate with the entire team about the details of the product presentation. The team can view the presenter's screen displaying the PowerPoint presentation. The presenter can share control with any member of the team and can share his or her screen at any time during the Lync meeting.

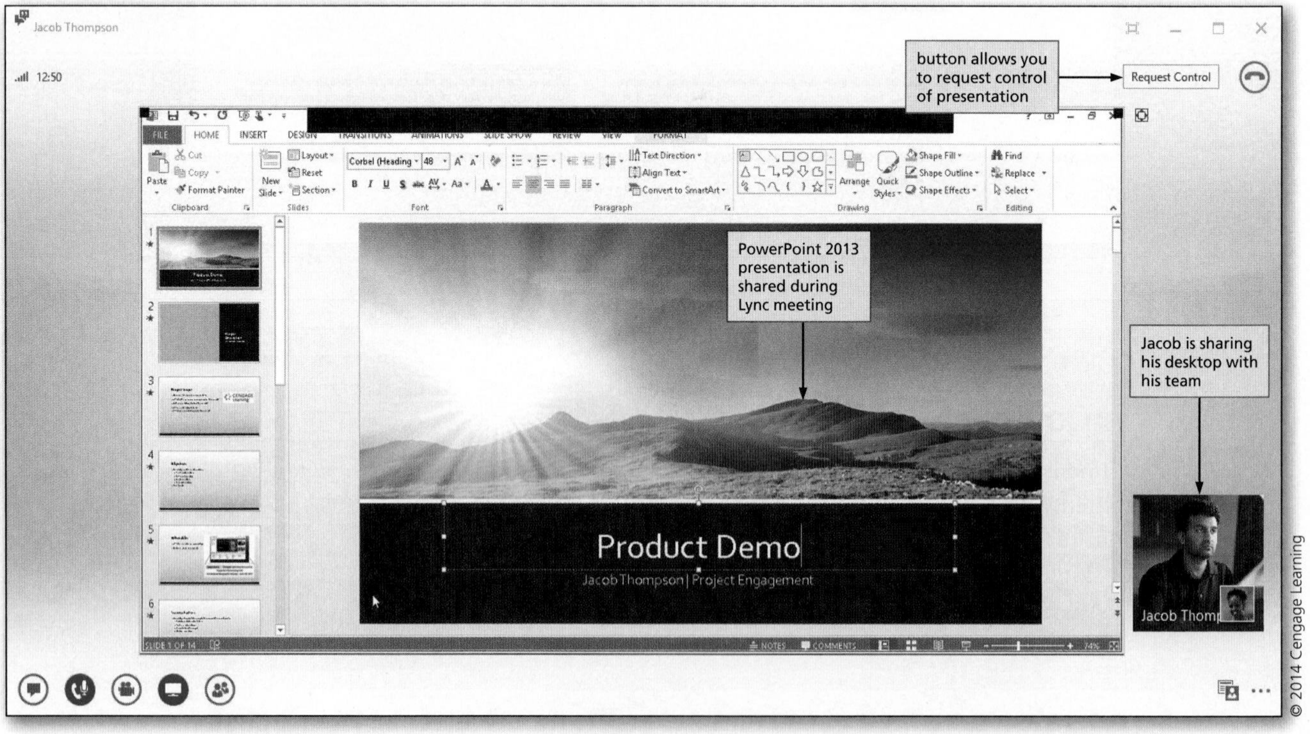

Figure 8

Users can send a Lync meeting request to schedule a team meeting, or an impromptu conversation can be started immediately using the Meet Now feature. Participants receive a Lync meeting request link via an email message, and when they click the meeting request link, Lync automatically connects them to the online conference. If the participant does not have Lync installed, the Lync Web App automatically connects to the Lync meeting through the user's PC or Mac OS X browser. If a participant is away from his or her computer, he or she still can participate using the Lync Mobile apps for Windows Phone, iOS, and Android. As shown in Figure 9, Lync utilizes **instant messaging** (IM), allowing two or more people to share text messages. They can communicate in real time, similar to a voice conversation. In addition to a simple instant message, Lync provides a feature called **persistent chat**, which allows end-users to participate in a working session of instant messages that is persistent or sustained over a specified amount of time in a moderated chat room. Consider having an instant messaging session with a group of colleagues in different parts of your organization, regardless of geographic region, where you all are working on the same project. Over the course of the project, different people post questions and concerns, and others are able to respond to all those who have subscribed to your topic or been admitted to the chat room. Instead of a long trail of email messages, a team can keep information in a controlled environment with a full history of the discussion in one location.

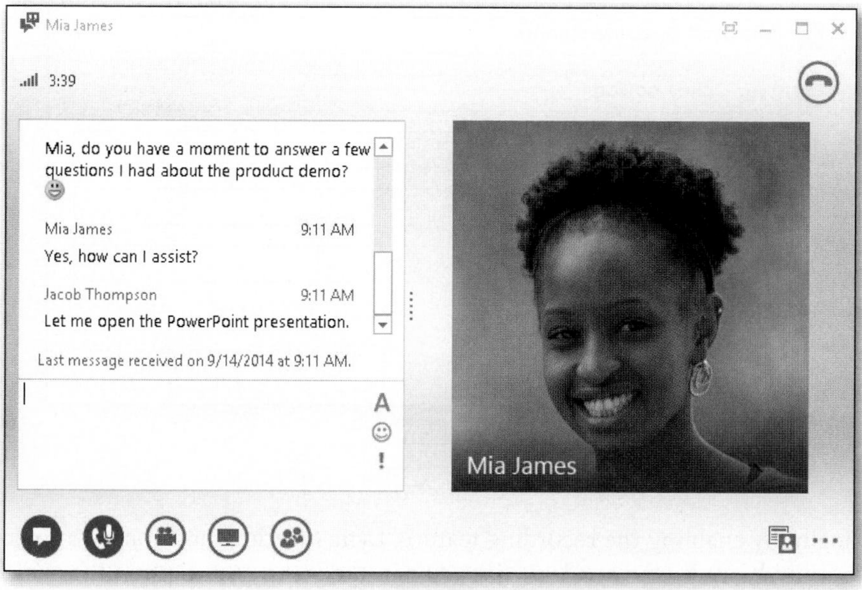

Figure 9

Lync also delivers support for full high-definition (HD) videoconferencing, so that a team can have a clear view of the participants, products, and demos. Before you join the video feed, you can preview your video feed to make sure your video camera is at the correct angle, your image is centered within the video frame, and that your room lighting provides for a clear image. The Lync preview option is important in creating a positive first impression over video. Your audio devices can be tested for clarity to make sure your headset, microphone, and speakers are functioning properly.

Lync provides a polling feature that presenters can use to ask the participants' opinions during a meeting (Figure 10). The poll question can consist of up to seven possible choices. The presenter has the option to view the results privately or share the results with the entire group.

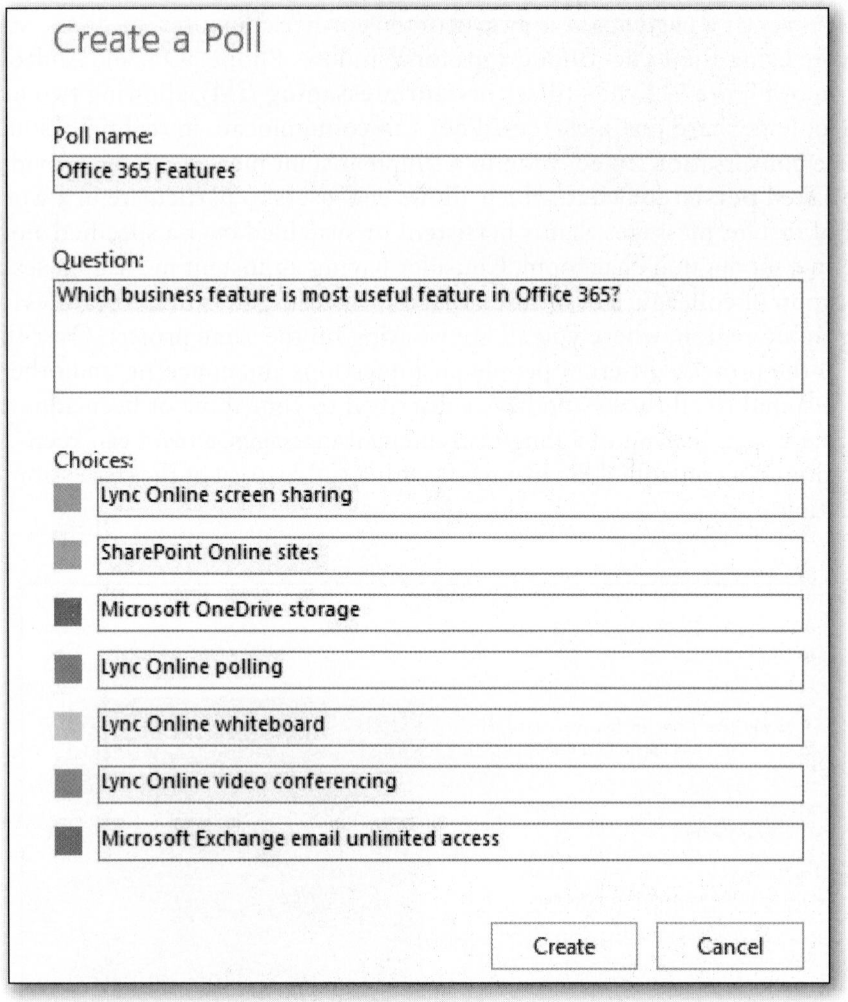

Figure 10

Finally, by enabling the recording feature, Lync meetings and conversations can be captured for viewing at a later time. For instance, you can capture the audio, video, instant messaging (IM), screen sharing, Microsoft PowerPoint presentations, whiteboard, and polling portions of the Lync session and then play them back just as they transpired during the live Lync event. The meeting recordings can be made available to others so that they can view all or part of the Lync event. Instructors can record Lync online class sessions for students who were unable to attend the original presentation. The recording starts in Microsoft Lync; recordings then can be viewed within the Recording Manager feature.

Chapter Summary

In this chapter, you have learned how to subscribe to Office 365, which provides local and online access to Office applications, email, document sharing, web conferencing, and business websites. You also learned how a business can utilize Office 365 features on the cloud to facilitate teamwork. Finally, you learned about the features of SharePoint, Yammer, and Lync, which provide collaboration and communications for business teams using Office 365.

Consider This: Your Turn

Apply your creative thinking and problem solving skills to design and implement a solution.

1: Comparing Office 365 Personal Plans

Personal

Part 1: After graduation, you are considering if it would be a better value to subscribe to Office 365 Personal or Office 365 Home Premium. Write a one-page document comparing the pros and cons of the two subscription plans. Research the different subscriptions in detail at Office365.com. Submit your assignment in the format specified by your instructor.

Part 2: Which type of computer and/or devices would you use with your Office 365 subscription? If you are at a friend's home that does not have Office 365, how could you access your Office files if you do not have your computer or mobile device with you?

2: Upgrading a Local Business to Office 365

Professional

Part 1: You are an employee at Impact Digital Marketing, a small marketing firm with 12 employees. The firm is setting up an Office 365 Business subscription next week, and you need to compose an email message with multiple paragraphs to explain the features of this new subscription plan to the members of your firm. Research the Office 365 Business subscription plan in detail at Office365.com, and compile your findings in an email message. Submit your assignment in the format specified by your instructor.

Part 2: Give three examples of how a marketing firm could use Lync. How could a marketing firm use the SharePoint Websites feature?

3: Conducting a Lync Meeting

Research and Collaboration

* Students need an Office 365 subscription to complete the following assignment.

Part 1: Using your Office 365 subscription, conduct a meeting using Lync. Working with a partner, use your Office 365 subscription to research how to use Lync. Then, conduct a 15-minute Lync meeting, including instant messaging, to discuss the features of Lync. Use the concepts and techniques presented in this chapter to create the Lync meeting. Submit your assignment in the format specified by your instructor.

Part 2: When using Lync in an online class, when would the screen recording feature best be utilized?

1 Databases and Database Objects: An Introduction

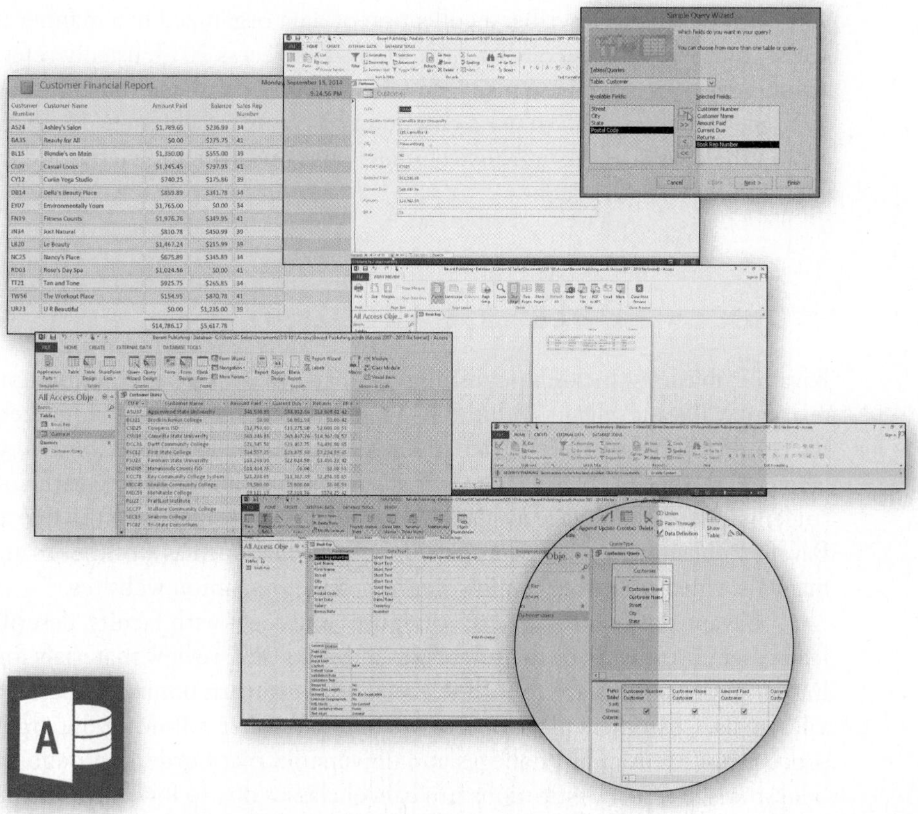

Objectives

You will have mastered the material in this chapter when you can:

- Describe the features of the Access window
- Create a database
- Create tables in Datasheet and Design views
- Add records to a table
- Close a database
- Open a database
- Print the contents of a table
- Create and use a query
- Create and use a form
- Create and print custom reports
- Modify a report in Layout view
- Perform special database operations
- Design a database to satisfy a collection of requirements

1 Databases and Database Objects: An Introduction

Introduction

The term **database** describes a collection of data organized in a manner that allows access, retrieval, and use of that data. Microsoft Access 2013, usually referred to as simply Access, is a database management system. A **database management system** is software that allows you to use a computer to create a database; add, change, and delete data in the database; ask and answer questions concerning the data; and create forms and reports using the data.

Project — Database Creation

Bavant Publishing Inc. is a publishing company that specializes in foreign language textbooks. Bavant sells in both the K-12 and the higher education markets. Recently, Bavant purchased a small, private publisher of Arabic, Russian, Chinese, and Japanese language textbooks. These languages are increasing in popularity with college students. All textbooks are available in hardcover and some are available as e-books. Bavant Publishing also provides ancillary materials, such as workbooks and laboratory manuals, video resources, audio resources, and companion websites.

Bavant representatives visit campuses and meet with faculty, describing the features and strengths of the textbooks and providing review materials for instructors. Bavant pays a base salary to its book reps, who can earn bonus pay based on exceeding sales goals. Customers place orders with the publisher following the organization's procedures; for example, colleges and universities place orders through their bookstores. Because institutions can cancel classes due to low enrollments, customers sometimes return unused books. At the end of an accounting period, these returns are subtracted from the current amount due.

Bavant wants to maintain records on the sales of textbooks from the newly acquired publisher separately from their other foreign language textbooks to better track profitability and market potential. Bavant organizes this data on its customers and book representatives in a database managed by Access. In this way, Bavant keeps its data current and accurate and can analyze it for trends and produce a variety of useful reports.

In a **relational database** such as those maintained by Access, a database consists of a collection of tables, each of which contains information on a specific subject. Figure 1–1 shows the database for Bavant Publishing. It consists of two tables: the Customer table (Figure 1–1a) contains information about Bavant customers, and the Book Rep table (Figure 1–1b) contains information about the book reps to whom these customers are assigned.

caption for Customer Number field

fields

records

CU #	Customer Name	Street	City	State	Postal Code	Amount Paid	Current Due	Returns	BR #	Click to Add
ASU37	Applewood State University	300 University Ave.	Greer	PA	19158	$41,530.98	$38,812.66	$12,008.02	42	
BCJ21	Brodkin Junior College	4806 Park Dr.	Greer	PA	19158	$0.00	$6,081.98	$0.00	42	
CSD25	Cowpens ISD	829 Wooster Ave.	Gossett	PA	19157	$12,750.00	$13,275.00	$2,000.00	53	
CSU10	Camellia State University	725 Camellia St.	Pleasantburg	NJ	07025	$63,246.88	$69,847.76	$14,967.98	53	
DCC34	Dartt Community College	3827 Burgess Dr.	Chambers	NJ	07037	$21,345.50	$23,467.75	$4,496.80	65	
FSC12	First State College	7300 Cedar Rd.	Quaker	DE	19719	$34,557.25	$23,875.98	$7,234.99	65	
FSU23	Farnham State University	1445 Hubert St.	Gaston	DE	19723	$18,268.00	$22,024.50	$3,496.23	42	
HSD05	Hammonds County ISD	446 Lincoln Blvd.	Chesnee	NJ	07053	$18,434.75	$0.00	$0.00	53	
KCC78	Key Community College System	7523 Penn Ave.	Adelphia	PA	19159	$21,288.65	$11,367.49	$2,256.98	65	
MCC45	Mauldin Community College	72 Montrose St.	Chesnee	NJ	07053	$9,500.00	$5,000.00	$0.00	53	
MEC56	Mehitable College	202 College St.	Gaston	DE	19723	$9,111.19	$7,310.76	$574.25	42	
PLI22	PrattLast Institute	236 Ashton Ave.	Pleasantburg	NJ	07025	$17,229.45	$11,769.75	$3,450.50	53	
SCC77	Stallone Community College	1200 Franklin Blvd.	Adelphia	PA	19156	$7,525.98	$2,515.78	$0.00	42	
SEC19	Seaborn College	345 Mather Rd.	Quaker	DE	19719	$9,225.34	$10,496.89	$2,017.67	65	
TSC02	Tri-State Consortium	3400 Metro Pkwy.	Adelphia	PA	19156	$34,578.90	$9,432.56	$943.34	65	
*										

BR # (Book Rep Number) is 42

Figure 1–1 (a) Customer Table

Book Rep

BR #	Last Name	First Name	Street	City	State	Postal Code	Start Date	Salary	Bonus Rate	Click to Add
42	Perez	Melina	261 Porter Dr.	Adelphia	PA	19156	5/14/2012	$31,500.00	0.20	
48	St[illegible]	[illegible]	3135 Simpson Dr.	Pleasantburg	NJ	07025	1/15/2013	$29,000.00	0.20	
53	Ch[illegible]	[illegible]	265 Maxwell St.	Gossett	PA	19157	6/1/2013	$26,250.00	0.19	
65	Ro[illegible]	[illegible]	1827 Maple Ave.	Adelphia	PA	19159	7/1/2014	$7,750.00	0.18	
*								$0.00	0.00	

BR # (Book Rep Number) for Melina Perez is 42

Figure 1–1 (b) Book Rep Table

The rows in the tables are called **records**. A record contains information about a given person, product, or event. A row in the Customer table, for example, contains information about a specific customer, such as the customer's name, address information, and other data.

The columns in the tables are called fields. A **field** contains a specific piece of information within a record. In the Customer table, for example, the fourth field, City, contains the name of the city where the customer is located.

The first field in the Customer table is CU #, which is an abbreviation for Customer Number. Bavant Publishing assigns each customer a number; the Bavant customer numbers consist of three uppercase letters followed by a two-digit number.

The customer numbers are unique; that is, no two customers have the same number. Such a field is a **unique identifier**. A unique identifier, as its name suggests, is a way of uniquely identifying each record in the database. A given customer number will appear only in a single record in the table. Only one record exists, for example, in which the customer number is TSC02. A unique identifier also is called a **primary key**. Thus, the Customer Number field is the primary key for the Customer table.

BTW

BTWs

For a complete list of the BTWs found in the margins of this book, visit the BTW resource on the Student Companion Site located on www.cengagebrain.com. For detailed instructions about accessing available resources, visit www.cengage.com/ct/studentdownload or contact your instructor for information about accessing the required files.

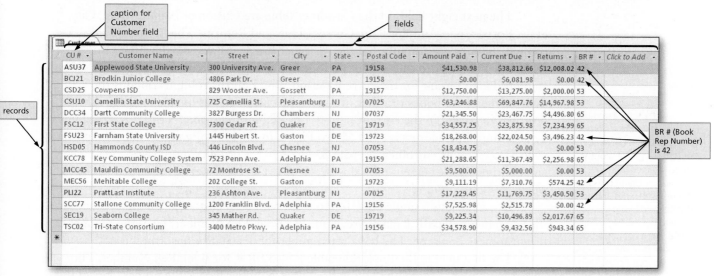

The next eight fields in the Customer table are Customer Name, Street, City, State, Postal Code, Amount Paid, Current Due, and Returns. The Amount Paid column contains the amount that the customer has paid Bavant Publishing year to date (YTD) prior to the current period. The Current Due column contains the amount due to Bavant for the current period. The Returns column contains the dollar value of the books or other products the customer was unable to sell and has returned to Bavant in the current period. For example, customer TSC02 is Tri-State Consortium. The address is 3400 Metro Pkwy., in Adelphia, Pennsylvania. The postal code is 19156. The customer has paid $34,578.90 for products purchased so far. The amount due for the current period is $9,432.56. The customer has returned products worth $943.34.

BTW

Naming Fields

Access 2013 has a number of reserved words, words that have a special meaning to Access. You cannot use these reserved words as field names. For example, Name is a reserved word and could not be used in the Customer table to describe a customer's name. For a complete list of reserved words in Access 2013, consult Access Help.

Bavant assigns a single book rep to work with each customer. The last column in the Customer table, BR # (an abbreviation for Book Rep Number) gives the number of the customer's book rep. The book rep number for Tri-State Consortium is 65.

The first field in the Book Rep table is also BR #, for Book Rep Number. The book rep numbers are unique, so the Book Rep Number field is the primary key of the Book Rep table.

The other fields in the Book Rep table are Last Name, First Name, Street, City, State, Postal Code, Start Date, Salary, and Bonus Rate. The Start Date field gives the date the rep began working for Bavant. The Salary field gives the salary paid to the rep thus far this year. The Bonus Rate gives the potential bonus percentage based on personal performance. The bonus rate applies when the book rep exceeds a predetermined sales goal. For example, book rep 65 is Tracy Rogers. Her address is 1827 Maple Ave., in Adelphia, Pennsylvania. The postal code is 19159. Tracy started working for Bavant on July 1, 2014. So far this year, she has been paid $7,750.00 in salary. Her bonus rate is 0.18 (18%).

The book rep number appears in both the Customer table and the Book Rep table, and relates customers and book reps. Book rep 48, Michael Statnik, recently transferred from another division of the company and has not yet been assigned any customers. His book rep number, therefore, does not appear on any row in the Customer table.

CONSIDER THIS

How would you find the name of the book rep for Tri-State Consortium?

In the Customer table, you see that the book rep number for customer Tri-State Consortium is 65. To find the name of this book rep, look for the row in the Book Rep table that contains 65 in the BR # column. After you have found it, you know that the book rep for Tri-State Consortium is Tracy Rogers.

CONSIDER THIS

How would you find all the customers assigned to Tracy Rogers?

First, look in the Book Rep table to find that her number is 65. You would then look through the Customer table for all the customers that contain 65 in the BR # column. Tracy's customers are DCC34 (Dartt Community College), FSC12 (First State College), KCC78 (Key Community College System), SEC19 (Seaborn College), and TSC02 (Tri-State Consortium).

Roadmap

In this chapter, you will learn how to create and use the database shown in Figure 1–1 on page AC 3. The following roadmap identifies general activities you will perform as you progress through this chapter:

1. CREATE the FIRST TABLE, Book Rep, using Datasheet view.
2. ADD RECORDS to the Book Rep table.
3. PRINT the CONTENTS of the Book Rep table.
4. IMPORT RECORDS into the second table, Customer.
5. MODIFY the SECOND TABLE using Design view.
6. CREATE a QUERY for the Customer table.
7. CREATE a FORM for the Customer table.
8. CREATE a REPORT for the Customer table.

At the beginning of step instructions throughout the chapter, you will see an abbreviated form of this roadmap. The abbreviated roadmap uses colors to indicate chapter progress: gray means the chapter is beyond that activity, blue means the task being shown is covered in that activity, and black means that activity is yet to be covered. For example, the following abbreviated roadmap indicates the chapter would be showing a task in the 3 PRINT CONTENTS activity.

1 CREATE FIRST TABLE | 2 ADD RECORDS | 3 PRINT CONTENTS | 4 IMPORT RECORDS | 5 MODIFY SECOND TABLE
6 CREATE QUERY | 7 CREATE FORM | 8 CREATE REPORT

Use the abbreviated roadmap as a progress guide while you read or step through the instructions in this chapter.

For an introduction to Windows and instruction about how to perform basic Windows tasks, read the Office and Windows chapter at the beginning of this book, where you can learn how to resize windows, change screen resolution, create folders, move and rename files, use Windows Help, and much more.

To Run Access

If you are using a computer to step through the project in this chapter and you want your screens to match the figures in this book, you should change your screen's resolution to 1366 × 768. For information about how to change a computer's resolution, refer to the Office and Windows chapter at the beginning of this book.

The following steps, which assume Windows is running, use the Start screen or the search box to run Access based on a typical installation. You may need to ask your instructor how to run Access on your computer. For a detailed example of the procedure summarized below, refer to the Office and Windows chapter.

1. Scroll the Start screen for an Access 2013 tile. If your Start screen contains an Access 2013 tile, tap or click it to run Access and then proceed to Step 5; if the Start screen does not contain the Access 2013 tile, proceed to the next step to search for the Access app.
2. Swipe in from the right edge of the screen or point to the upper-right corner of the screen to display the Charms bar, and then tap or click the Search charm on the Charms bar to display the Search menu.
3. Type `Access` as the search text in the Search box and watch the search results appear in the Apps list.
4. Tap or click Access 2013 in the search results to run Access.
5. If the Access window is not maximized, tap or click the Maximize button on its title bar to maximize the window.

For an introduction to Office and instruction about how to perform basic tasks in Office apps, read the Office and Windows chapter at the beginning of this book, where you can learn how to run an application, use the ribbon, save a file, open a file, exit an application, use Help, and much more.

Creating a Database

In Access, all the tables, reports, forms, and queries that you create are stored in a single file called a database. Thus, you first must create the database to hold the tables, reports, forms, and queries. You can use either the Blank desktop database option or a template to create a new database. If you already know the tables and fields you want in your database, you would use the Blank desktop database option. If not, you can use a template. Templates can guide you by suggesting some commonly used databases.

One of the few differences between Windows 7 and Windows 8 occurs in the steps to run Access. If you are using Windows 7, click the Start button, type `Access` in the 'Search programs and files' box, click Access 2013, and then, if necessary, maximize the Access window. For detailed steps to run Access in Windows 7, refer to the Office and Windows chapter at the beginning of this book. For a summary of the steps, refer to the Quick Reference located at the back of this book.

To Create a Database

Because you already know the tables and fields you want in the Bavant Publishing database, you would use the Blank desktop database option rather than using a template. The following steps assume you already have created folders for storing your files, for example, a CIS 101 folder (for your class) that contains an Access folder (for your assignments). Thus, these steps save the database in the Access folder in the CIS 101 folder on your desired save location. For a detailed example of the procedure for saving a file in a folder or saving a file on SkyDrive, refer to the Office and Windows chapter at the beginning of this book.

1. Tap or click the 'Blank desktop database' thumbnail to select the database type.
2. Type `Bavant Publishing` in the File Name text box to enter the new file name. Do not press the ENTER key after typing the file name because you do not want to create the database at this time.
3. Tap or click the 'Browse for a location to put your database' button to display the File New Database dialog box.
4. Navigate to the location for the database, for example, the Documents library, the My Documents folder, the folder identifying your class (CIS 101, in this case), and then to the Access folder.
5. Tap or click the OK button (File New Database dialog box) to select the location for the database and close the dialog box.
6. Tap or click the Create button to create the database on the selected drive in the selected folder with the file name, Bavant Publishing (Figure 1–2).

Q&A

The title bar for my Navigation Pane contains All Tables rather than All Access Objects, as in the figure. Is that a problem?
It is not a problem. The title bar indicates how the Navigation Pane is organized. You can carry out the steps in the text with either organization. To make your screens match the ones in the text, tap or click the Navigation Pane arrow and then tap or click Object Type.

I do not have the Search bar that appears on the figure. Is that a problem?
It is not a problem. If your Navigation Pane does not display a Search bar and you want your screens to match the ones in the text, press and hold or right-click the Navigation Pane title bar arrow to display a shortcut menu, and then tap or click Search Bar.

BTW
Organizing Files and Folders
You should organize and store files in folders so that you easily can find the files later. For example, if you are taking an introductory computer class called CIS 101, a good practice would be to save all Access files in an Access folder in a CIS 101 folder. For a discussion of folders and detailed examples of creating folders, refer to the Office and Windows chapter at the beginning of this book.

BTW
Q&As
For a complete list of the Q&As found in many of the step-by-step sequences in this book, visit the Q&A resource on the Student Companion Site located on www.cengagebrain.com. For detailed instructions about accessing available resources, visit www.cengage.com/ct/studentdownload or contact your instructor for information about accessing the required files.

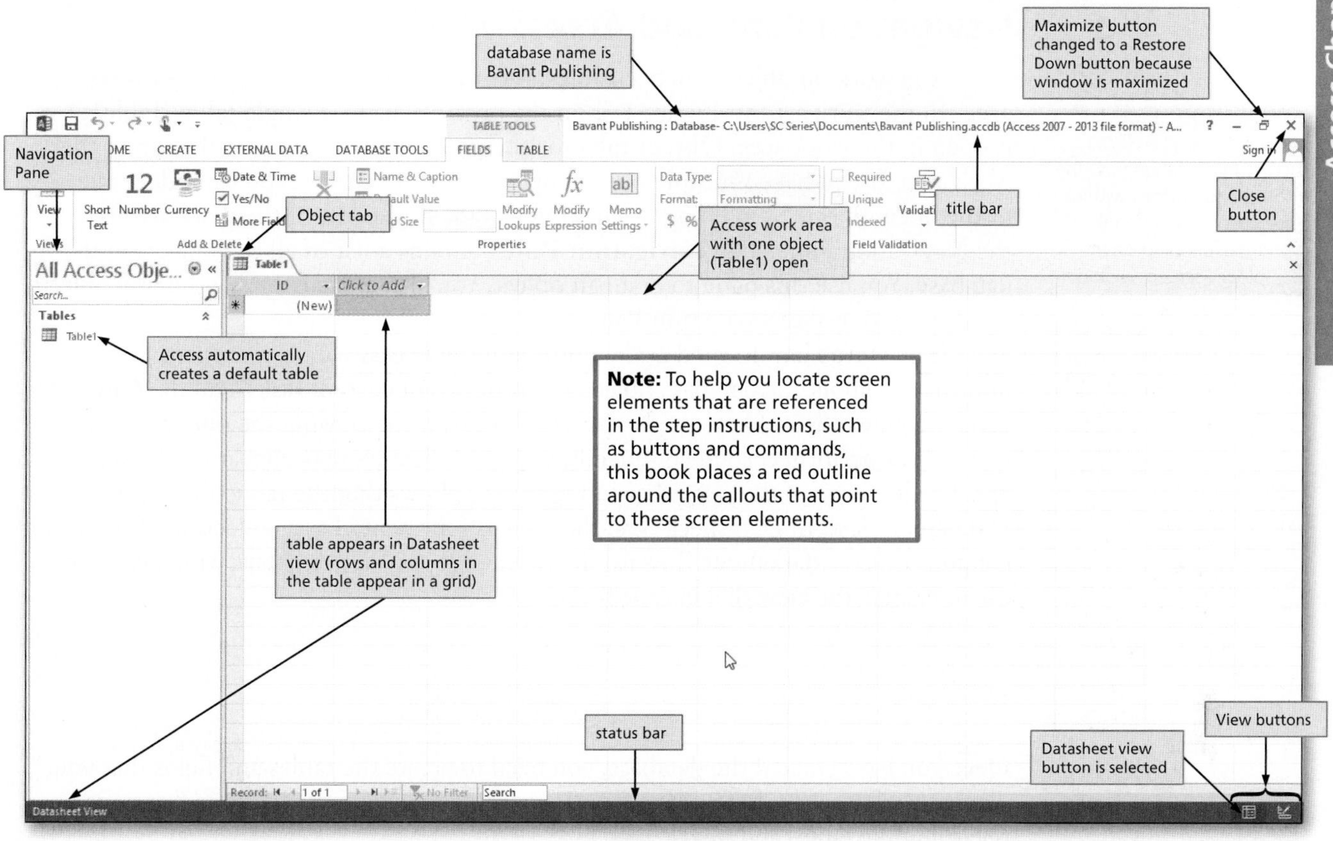

Figure 1–2

To Create a Database Using a Template

Ideally, you will design your own database, create a blank database, and then create the tables you have determined that your database should contain. If you are not sure what database design you will need, you could use a template. Templates can guide you by suggesting some commonly used databases. To create a database using a template, you would use the following steps.

1. If you have another database open, close it without exiting Access by tapping or clicking FILE on the ribbon to open the Backstage view and then tapping or clicking Close.
2. If you do not see a template that you want, you can search Microsoft Office online for additional templates.
3. Tap or click the template you want to use. Be sure you have selected one that indicates it is for a desktop database.
4. Enter a file name and select a location for the database.
5. Tap or click the Create button to create the database.

BTW
Naming Files
The following characters cannot be used in a file name: question mark (?), quotation mark ("), slash (/), backslash (\ ), colon (:), asterisk (*), vertical bar (|), greater than symbol (>), and less than symbol (<).

BTW
Available Templates
The templates gallery includes both desktop and web-based templates. If you are creating an Access database for your own use, select a desktop template. Web-based templates allow you to create databases that you can publish to a SharePoint server.

The Access Window

The Access window consists of a variety of components to make your work more efficient. These include the Navigation Pane, Access work area, ribbon, shortcut menus, and Quick Access Toolbar. Some of these components are common to other Microsoft Office apps; others are unique to Access.

Navigation Pane and Access Work Area

BTW
The Ribbon and Screen Resolution
Access may change how the groups and buttons within the groups appear on the ribbon, depending on the computer's screen resolution. Thus, your ribbon may look different from the ones in this book if you are using a screen resolution other than 1366 × 768.

You work on objects such as tables, forms, and reports in the **Access work area**. In the work area in Figure 1–2 on the previous page, a single table, Table1, is open in the work area. **Object tabs** for the open objects appear at the top of the work area. If you have multiple objects open at the same time, you can select one of the open objects by tapping or clicking its tab. To the left of the work area is the Navigation Pane. The **Navigation Pane** contains a list of all the objects in the database. You use this pane to open an object. You also can customize the way objects are displayed in the Navigation Pane.

The **status bar**, located at the bottom of the Access window, presents information about the database object, the progress of current tasks, and the status of certain commands and keys; it also provides controls for viewing the object. As you type text or perform certain commands, various indicators may appear on the status bar. The left edge of the status bar in Figure 1–2 shows that the table object is open in **Datasheet view**. In Datasheet view, the table is represented as a collection of rows and columns called a **datasheet**. Toward the right edge are View buttons, which you can use to change the view that currently appears.

Determining Tables and Fields

Once you have created the database, you need to create the tables and fields that your database will contain. Before doing so, however, you need to make some decisions regarding the tables and fields.

Naming Tables and Fields

BTW
Naming Tables
Database users typically have their own guidelines for naming tables. Some use the singular version of the object being described while others use the prefix tbl with a table name. This book uses the singular version of the object (Customer, Book Rep).

In creating your database, you must name tables and fields. Before beginning the design process, you must understand the rules Access applies to table and field names. These rules are:

1. Names can be up to 64 characters in length.
2. Names can contain letters, digits, and spaces, as well as most of the punctuation symbols.
3. Names cannot contain periods (.), exclamation points (!), accent graves (`), or square brackets ([ ]).
4. Each field in a table must have a unique name.

BTW
Multiple-Word Names
There are several ways to handle multiple word names. You can omit the space (CustomerNumber) or use an underscore in place of the space (Customer_Number). Another option is to use an underscore in place of a space, but use the same case for all letters (CUSTOMER_NUMBER or customer_number).

The approach to naming tables and fields used in this text is to begin the names with an uppercase letter and to use lowercase for the other letters. In multiple-word names, each word begins with an uppercase letter, and there is a space between words (for example, Customer Number).

Determining the Primary Key

For each table, you need to determine the primary key, the unique identifier. In many cases, you will have obvious choices, such as Customer Number or Book Rep Number. If you do not have an obvious choice, you can use the primary key that Access creates automatically. It is a field called ID. It is an autonumber field, which means that Access will assign the value 1 to the first record, 2 to the second record, and so on.

Determining Data Types for the Fields

For each field in your database, you must determine the field's **data type**, that is, the type of data that can be stored in the field. Four of the most commonly used data types in Access are:

1. **Short Text —** The field can contain any characters. A maximum number of 255 characters is allowed in a field whose data type is Short Text.
2. **Number —** The field can contain only numbers. The numbers can be either positive or negative. Fields assigned this type can be used in arithmetic operations. You usually assign fields that contain numbers but will not be used for arithmetic operations (such as postal codes) a data type of Short Text.
3. **Currency —** The field can contain only monetary data. The values will appear with currency symbols, such as dollar signs, commas, and decimal points, and with two digits following the decimal point. Like numeric fields, you can use currency fields in arithmetic operations. Access assigns a size to currency fields automatically.
4. **Date & Time —** The field can store dates and/or times.

BTW

Text Data Types

Short Text replaces the Text data type in previous editions of Access. Long Text replaces the Memo data type in previous editions.

Table 1–1 shows the other data types that are available in Access.

BTW

Data Types

Different database management systems have different available data types. Even data types that are essentially the same can have different names. The Currency data type in Access, for example, is referred to as Money in SQL Server.

Table 1–1 Additional Data Types

Data Type	Description
Long Text	Field can store a variable amount of text or combinations of text and numbers where the total number of characters may exceed 255.
AutoNumber	Field can store a unique sequential number that Access assigns to a record. Access will increment the number by 1 as each new record is added.
Yes/No	Field can store only one of two values. The choices are Yes/No, True/False, or On/Off.
OLE Object	Field can store an OLE object, which is an object linked to or embedded in the table.
Hyperlink	Field can store text that can be used as a hyperlink address.
Attachment	Field can contain an attached file. Images, spreadsheets, documents, charts, and other elements can be attached to this field in a record in the database. You can view and edit the attached file.
Calculated	Field specified as a calculation based on other fields. The value is not actually stored.

In the Customer table, because the Customer Number, Customer Name, Street, City, and State all can contain letters, their data types should be Short Text. The data type for Postal Code is Short Text instead of Number because you typically do not use postal codes in arithmetic operations; you do not add postal codes or find an average postal code, for example. The Amount Paid, Current Due, and Returns fields contain monetary data, so their data types should be Currency. The Book Rep Number field contains numbers, but you will not use these numbers in arithmetic operations, so its type should be Short Text.

BTW

AutoNumber Fields

AutoNumber fields also are called AutoIncrement fields. In Design view, the New Values field property allows you to increment the field sequentially (Sequential) or randomly (Random). The default is sequential.

Similarly, in the Book Rep table, the data type for the Book Rep Number, Last Name, First Name, Street, City, State, and Postal Code fields all should be Short Text. The Start Date field should be Date & Time. The Salary field contains monetary amounts, so its data type should be Currency. The Bonus Rate field contains numbers that are not dollar amounts, so its data type should be Number.

For fields whose type is Short Text, you can change the field size, that is, the maximum number of characters that can be entered in the field. If you set the field size for the State field to 2, for example, Access will not allow the user to enter more than two characters in the field. On the other hand, fields whose data type is Number often require you to change the field size, which is the storage space assigned to the field by Access. Table 1–2 shows the possible field sizes for Number fields.

Table 1–2 Field Sizes for Number Fields

Field Size	Description
Byte	Integer value in the range of 0 to 255
Integer	Integer value in the range of -32,768 to 32,767
Long Integer	Integer value in the range of -2,147,483,648 to 2,147,483,647
Single	Numeric values with decimal places to seven significant digits — requires 4 bytes of storage
Double	Numeric values with decimal places to more accuracy than Single — requires 8 bytes of storage
Replication ID	Special identifier required for replication
Decimal	Numeric values with decimal places to more accuracy than Single or Double — requires 12 bytes of storage

CONSIDER THIS

What is the appropriate size for the Bonus Rate field?

If the size were Byte, Integer, or Long Integer, only integers could be stored. If you try to store a value that has decimal places, such as 0.18, in fields of these sizes, the portion to the right of the decimal point would be removed, giving a result of 0. To address this problem, the bonus rate should have a size of Single, Double, or Decimal. With such small numbers involved, Single, which requires the least storage of the three, is the appropriate choice.

Creating a Table

BTW

On Screen Keyboard

To display the on-screen touch keyboard, tap the Touch Keyboard button on the Windows taskbar. When finished using the touch keyboard, tap the X button on the touch keyboard to close the keyboard.

To create a table in Access, you must define its structure. That is, you must define all the fields that make up the table and their characteristics. You also must indicate the primary key.

In Access, you can use two different views to create a table: Datasheet view and Design view. In **Datasheet view**, the data in the table is presented in rows and columns, similar to a spreadsheet. Although the main reason to use Datasheet view is to add or update records in a table, you also can use it to create a table or to later modify its structure. The other view, **Design view**, is only used to create a table or to modify the structure of a table.

As you might expect, Design view has more functionality for creating a table than Datasheet view. That is, there are certain actions that only can be performed in Design view. One such action is assigning Single as the field size for the Bonus Rate field. In this chapter, you will create the first table, the Book Rep table, in Datasheet view. Once you have created the table in Datasheet view, you will use Design view to change the field size.

Whichever view you choose to use, before creating the table, you need to know the names and data types of the fields that will make up the table. You also can decide to enter a **description** for a particular field to explain important details about the field. When you select this field, this description will appear on the status bar. You also might choose to assign a **caption** to a particular field. If you assign a caption, Access will display the value you assign, rather than the field name, in datasheets and in forms. If you do not assign a caption, Access will display the field name.

CONSIDER THIS

When would you want to use a caption?

You would use a caption whenever you want something other than the field name displayed. One common example is when the field name is relatively long and the data in the field is relatively short. In the Book Rep table, the name of the first field is Book Rep Number, but the field contains data that is only two characters long. You will change the caption for this field to BR #, which is much shorter than Book Rep Number yet still describes the field. Doing so will enable you to greatly reduce the width of the column.

The results of these decisions for the fields in the Book Rep table are shown in Table 1–3. The table also shows the data types and field sizes of the fields as well as any special properties that need to be changed. The Book Rep Number field has a caption of BR #, enabling the width of the Book Rep Number column to be reduced in the datasheet.

Table 1–3 Structure of Book Rep Table

Field Name	Data Type	Field Size	Notes
Book Rep Number	Short Text	2	Primary Key **Description:** Unique identifier of book rep **Caption:** BR #
Last Name	Short Text	15	
First Name	Short Text	15	
Street	Short Text	20	
City	Short Text	20	
State	Short Text	2	
Postal Code	Short Text	5	
Start Date	Date/Time		(This appears as Date & Time on the menu of available data types)
Salary	Currency		
Bonus Rate	Number	Single	Format: Fixed Decimal Places: 2

If you are using your finger on a touch screen and are having difficulty completing the steps in this chapter, consider using a stylus. Many people find it easier to be precise with a stylus than with a finger. In addition, with a stylus you see the pointer. If you still are having trouble completing the steps with a stylus, try using a mouse.

CONSIDER THIS

How do you determine the field size?

You need to determine the maximum number of characters that can be entered in the field. In some cases, it is obvious. Field sizes of 2 for the State field and 5 for the Postal Code field are certainly the appropriate choices. In other cases, you need to determine how many characters you wish to allow. In the list shown in Table 1–3, Bavant evidently decided allowing 15 characters was sufficient for last names. This field size can be changed later if it proves to be insufficient.

CONSIDER THIS

What is the purpose of the Format and Decimal Places properties?

The format guarantees that bonus rates will be displayed with a fixed number of decimal places. Setting the decimal places property to 2 guarantees that the rates will be displayed with precisely two decimal places. Thus, a bonus rate of 0.2 will be displayed as 0.20.

To Modify the Primary Key

1 CREATE FIRST TABLE | 2 ADD RECORDS | 3 PRINT CONTENTS | 4 IMPORT RECORDS | 5 MODIFY SECOND TABLE
6 CREATE QUERY | 7 CREATE FORM | 8 CREATE REPORT

When you first create your database, Access automatically creates a table for you. You can immediately begin defining the fields. If, for any reason, you do not have this table or inadvertently delete it, you can create the table by tapping or clicking CREATE on the ribbon and then tapping or clicking the Table button (CREATE tab | Tables group). In either case, you are ready to define the fields.

The steps on the next page change the name, data type, and other properties of the first field to match the Book Rep Number field in Table 1–3, which is the primary key. ***Why?*** *Access has already created the first field as the primary key field, which it has named ID. Book Rep Number is a more appropriate choice.*

1

- Press and hold or right-click the column heading for the ID field to display a shortcut menu (Figure 1–3).

Q&A Why does my shortcut menu look different?
You displayed a shortcut menu for the column instead of the column heading. Be sure you press and hold or right-click the column heading.

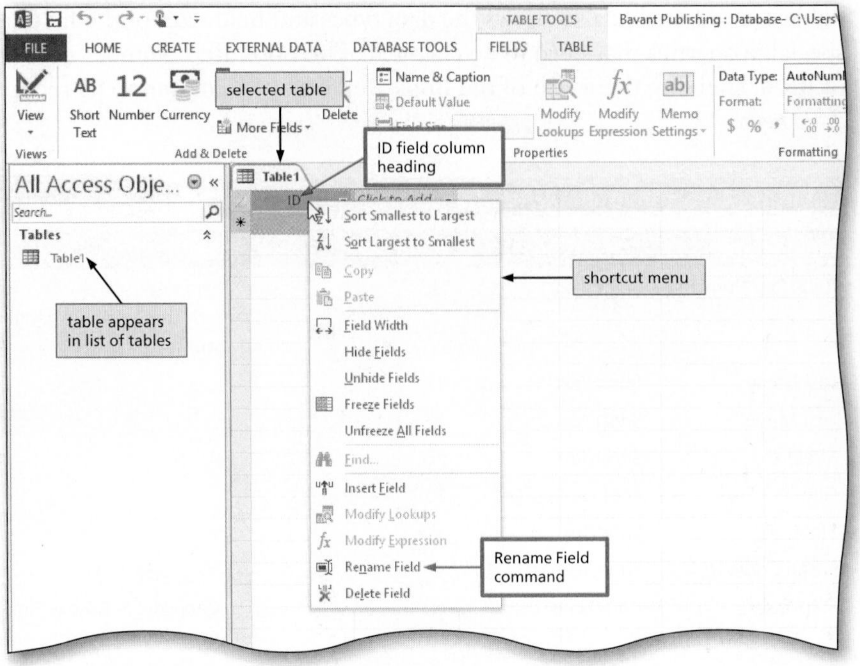

Figure 1–3

2

- Tap or click Rename Field on the shortcut menu to highlight the current name.
- Type `Book Rep Number` to assign a name to the new field.
- Tap or click the white space immediately below the field name to complete the addition of the field (Figure 1–4).

Q&A Why does the full name of the field not appear?
The default column size is not large enough for Book Rep Number to be displayed in its entirety. You will address this issue in later steps.

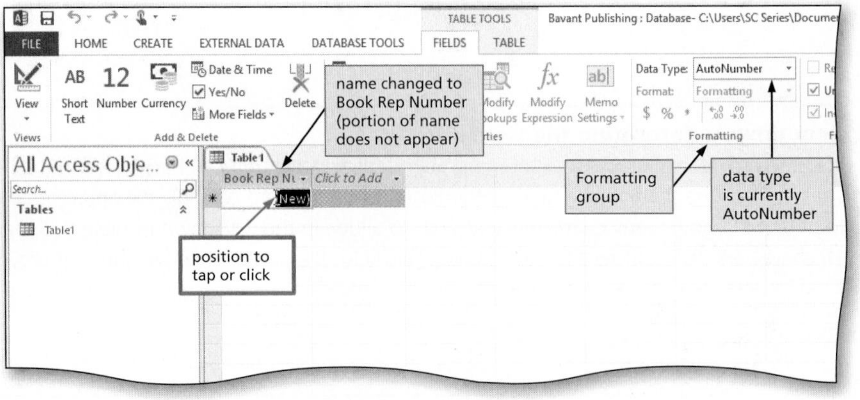

Figure 1–4

3

- Because the data type needs to be changed from AutoNumber to Short Text, tap or click the Data Type arrow (TABLE TOOLS FIELDS tab | Formatting group) to display a menu of available data types (Figure 1–5).

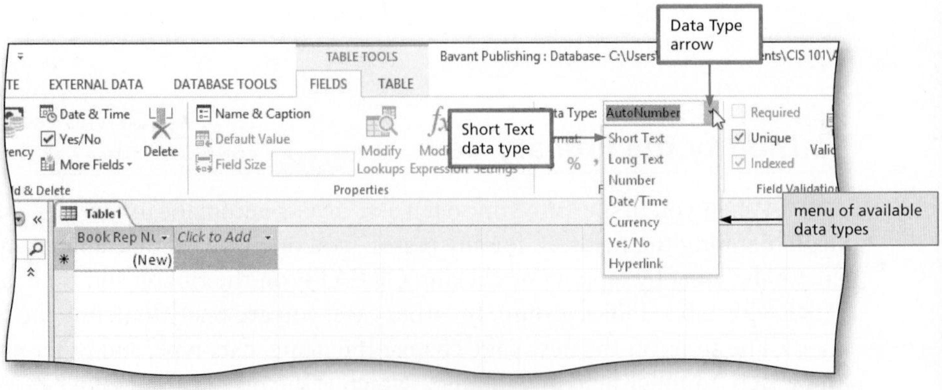

Figure 1–5

4

- Tap or click Short Text to select the data type for the field (Figure 1–6).

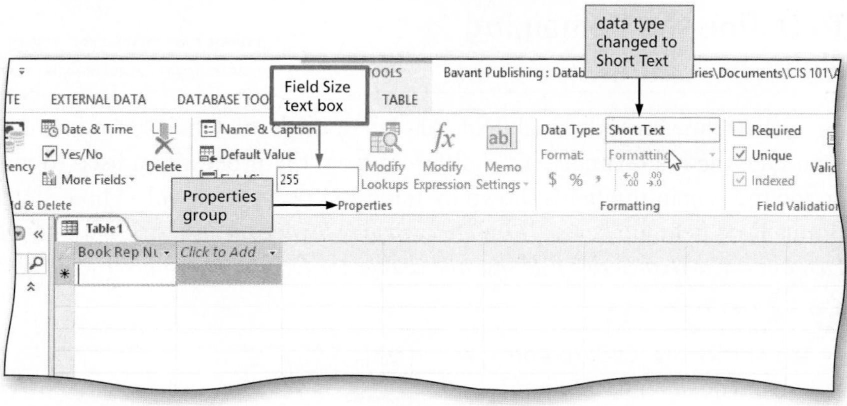

Figure 1–6

5

- Tap or click the Field Size text box (TABLE TOOLS FIELDS tab | Properties group) to select the current field size, use either the DELETE or BACKSPACE keys to erase the current field size, if necessary, and then type `2` as the new field size.
- Tap or click the Name & Caption button (TABLE TOOLS FIELDS tab | Properties group) to display the Enter Field Properties dialog box.
- Tap or click the Caption text box (Enter Field Properties dialog box), and then type `BR #` as the caption.
- Tap or click the Description text box, and then type `Unique identifier of book rep` as the description (Figure 1–7).

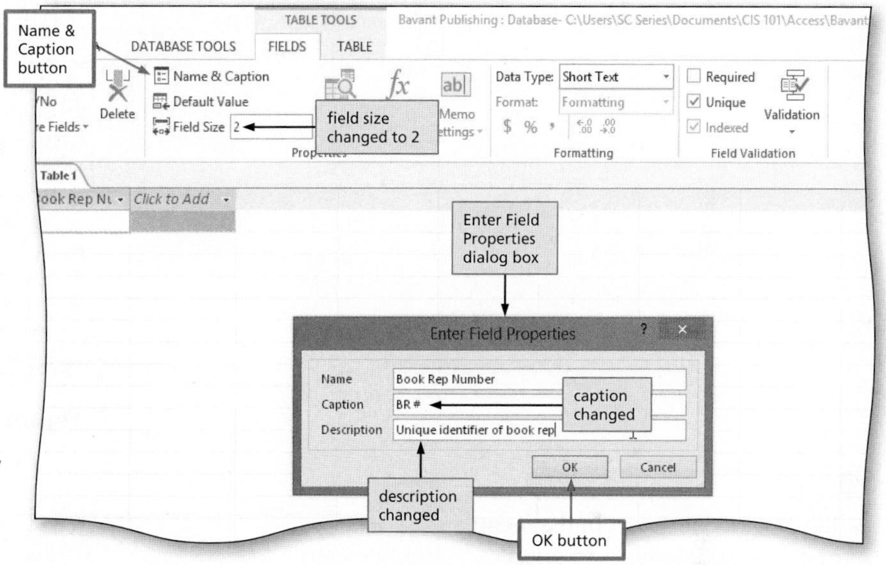

Figure 1–7

6

- Tap or click the OK button (Enter Field Properties dialog box) to change the caption and description (Figure 1–8).

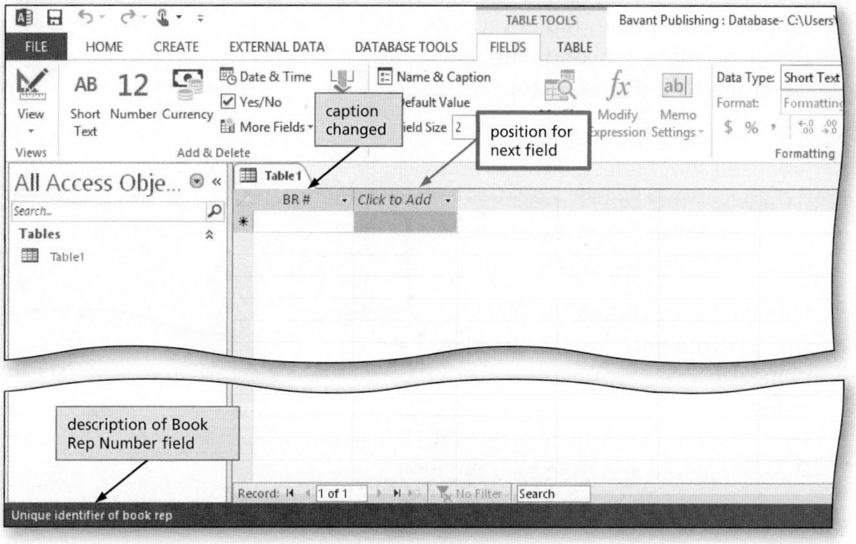

Figure 1–8

To Define the Remaining Fields in a Table

1 CREATE FIRST TABLE | 2 ADD RECORDS | 3 PRINT CONTENTS | 4 IMPORT RECORDS | 5 MODIFY SECOND TABLE
6 CREATE QUERY | 7 CREATE FORM | 8 CREATE REPORT

To define an additional field, you tap or click the Click to Add column heading, select the data type, and then type the field name. This is different from the process you used to modify the ID field. The following steps define the remaining fields shown in Table 1–3 on page AC 11. These steps do not change the field size of the Bonus Rate field, however. ***Why?*** *You can only change the field size of a Number field in Design view. Later, you will use Design view to change this field size and change the format and number of decimal places.*

1

- Tap or click the 'Click to Add' column heading to display a menu of available data types (Figure 1–9).

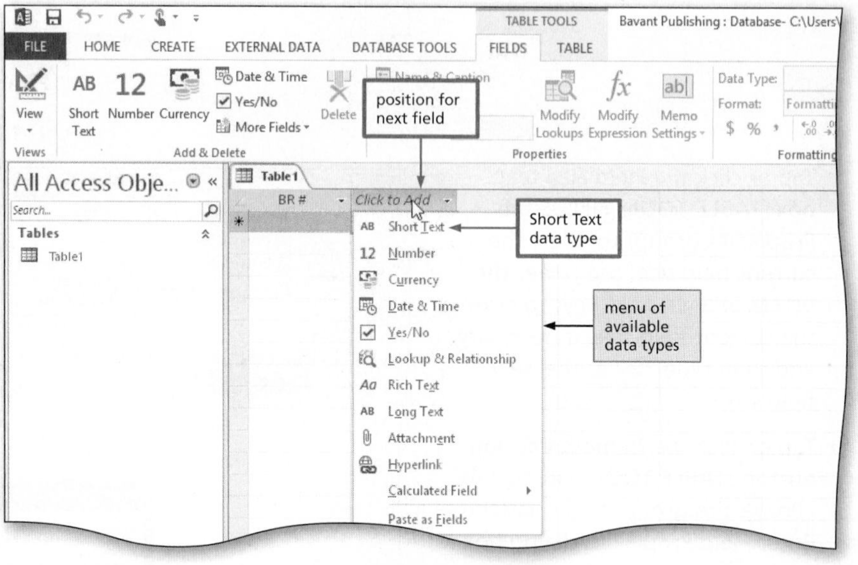

Figure 1–9

2

- Tap or click Short Text in the menu of available data types to select the Short Text data type.
- Type `Last Name` to enter a field name.
- Tap or click the blank space below the field name to complete the change of the name. Tap or click the blank space a second time to select the field (Figure 1–10).

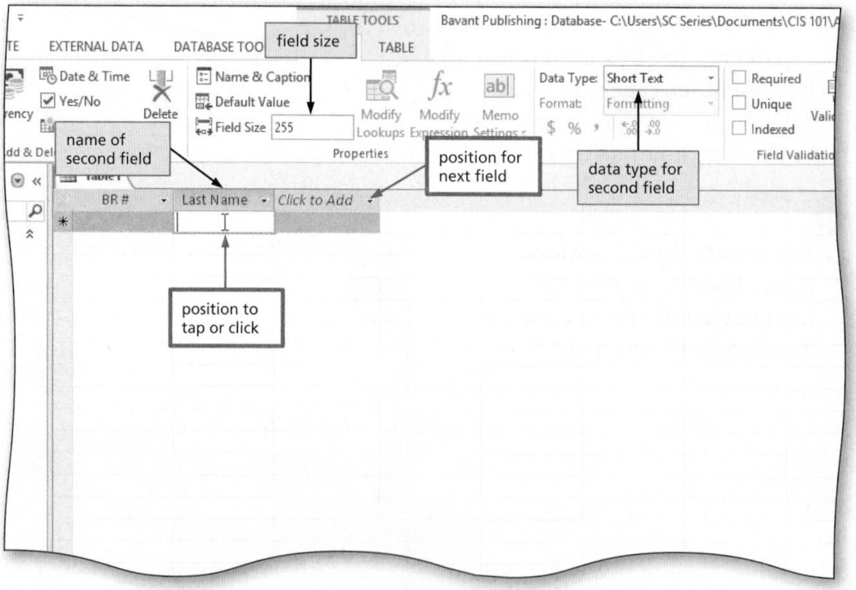

Figure 1–10

Q&A After entering the field name, I realized that I selected the wrong data type. How can I correct it?
Tap or click the Data Type arrow, and then select the correct type.

I inadvertently clicked the blank space before entering the field name. How can I correct the name?
Press and hold or right-click the field name, tap or click Rename Field on the shortcut menu, and then type the new name.

3

- Change the field size to 15 just as you changed the field size of the Book Rep Number field.
- Using the same technique, add the remaining fields in the Book Rep table. For the First Name, Street, City, State, and Postal Code fields, use the Short Text data type, but change the field sizes to match Table 1–3 on page AC 11. For the Start Date field, change the data type to Date & Time. For the Salary field, change the data type to Currency. For the Bonus Rate field, change the data type to Number (Figure 1–11).

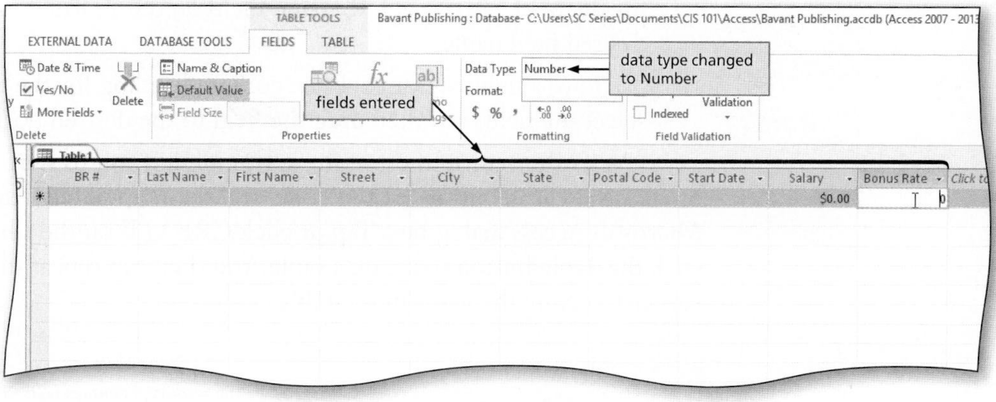

Figure 1–11

Q&A

I have an extra row between the row containing the field names and the row that begins with the asterisk. What happened? Is this a problem? If so, how do I fix it?

You inadvertently added a record to the table by pressing a key. Even pressing the SPACEBAR would add a record. You now have an unwanted record. To fix it, press the ESC key or tap or click the Undo button to undo the action. You may need to do this more than once.

When I try to move on to specify another field, I get an error message indicating that the primary key cannot contain a null value. How do I correct this?

First, tap or click the OK button to remove the error message. Next, press the ESC key or tap or click the Undo button to undo the action. You may need to do this more than once.

BTW

Currency Symbols

To show the symbol for the Euro (€) instead of the dollar sign, change the Format property for the field whose data type is currency. To change the default symbols for currency, change the settings in Windows.

Making Changes to the Structure

When creating a table, check the entries carefully to ensure they are correct. If you discover a mistake while still typing the entry, you can correct the error by repeatedly pressing the BACKSPACE key until the incorrect characters are removed. Then, type the correct characters. If you do not discover a mistake until later, you can use the following techniques to make the necessary changes to the structure:

- To undo your most recent change, tap or click the Undo button on the Quick Access Toolbar. If there is nothing that Access can undo, this button will be dim, and tapping or clicking it will have no effect.
- To delete a field, press and hold or right-click the column heading for the field (the position containing the field name), and then tap or click Delete Field on the shortcut menu.
- To change the name of a field, press and hold or right-click the column heading for the field, tap or click Rename Field on the shortcut menu, and then type the desired field name.
- To insert a field as the last field, tap or click the 'Click to Add' column heading, tap or click the appropriate data type on the menu of available data types, type the desired field name, and, if necessary, change the field size.
- To insert a field between existing fields, press and hold or right-click the column heading for the field that will follow the new field, and then tap or click Insert

BTW

Touch Screen Differences

The Office and Windows interfaces may vary if you are using a touch screen. For this reason, you might notice that the function or appearance of your touch screen differs slightly from this chapter's presentation.

Field on the shortcut menu. Press and hold or right-click the column heading for the field, tap or click Rename Field on the shortcut menu, and then type the desired field name.

- To move a field, tap or click the column heading for the field to be moved to select the field, and then drag the field to the desired position.

As an alternative to these steps, you might want to start over. To do so, tap or click the Close button for the table, and then tap or click the No button in the Microsoft Access dialog box. Tap or click CREATE on the ribbon, and then tap or click the Table button to create a table. You then can repeat the process you used earlier to define the fields in the table.

To Save a Table

1 CREATE FIRST TABLE | 2 ADD RECORDS | 3 PRINT CONTENTS | 4 IMPORT RECORDS | 5 MODIFY SECOND TABLE
6 CREATE QUERY | 7 CREATE FORM | 8 CREATE REPORT

The Book Rep table structure is complete. The final step is to save the table within the database. As part of the process, you will give the table a name. The following steps save the table, giving it the name Book Rep. ***Why?*** *Bavant has decided that Book Rep is an appropriate name for the table.*

1

- Tap or click the Save button on the Quick Access Toolbar to display the Save As dialog box (Figure 1–12).

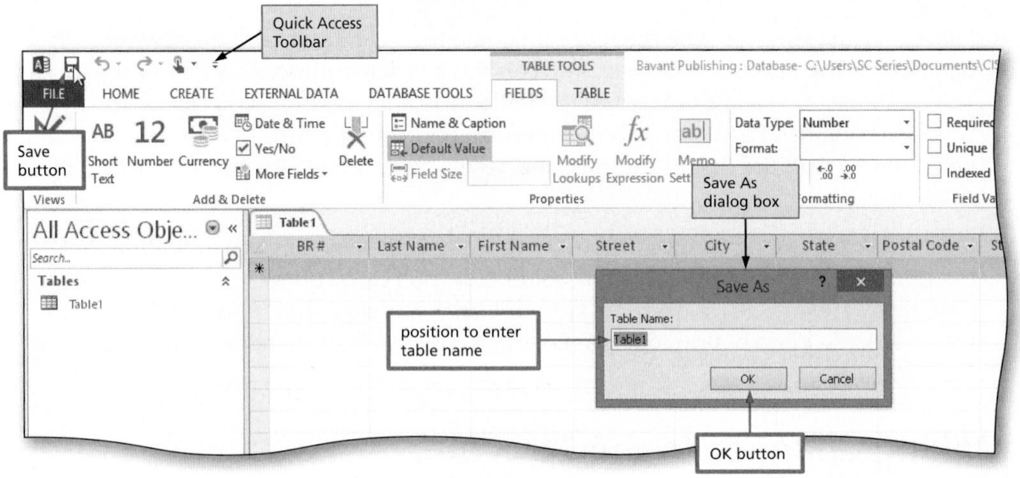

Figure 1–12

2

- Type `Book Rep` to change the name assigned to the table.
- Tap or click the OK button (Save As dialog box) to save the table (Figure 1–13).

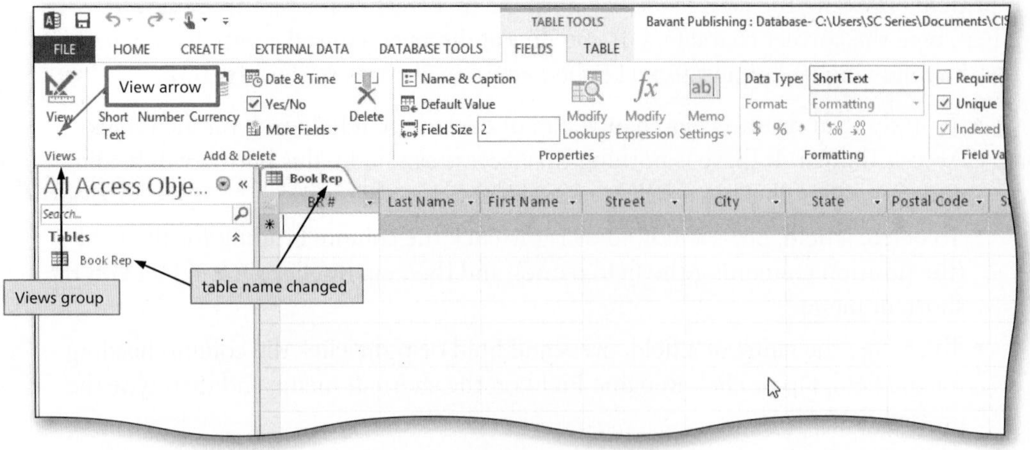

Figure 1–13

Other Ways

1. Tap or click FILE on the ribbon, tap or click Save in the Backstage view
2. Press and hold or right-click tab for table, tap or click Save on shortcut menu
3. Press CTRL+S

To View the Table in Design View

1 CREATE FIRST TABLE | 2 ADD RECORDS | 3 PRINT CONTENTS | 4 IMPORT RECORDS | 5 MODIFY SECOND TABLE
6 CREATE QUERY | 7 CREATE FORM | 8 CREATE REPORT

Even when creating a table in Datasheet view, Design view can be helpful. ***Why?*** *You easily can view the fields, data types, and properties to ensure you have entered them correctly. It is also easier to determine the primary key in Design view.* The following steps display the structure of the Book Rep table in Design view so that you can verify the design is correct.

1

- Tap or click the View arrow (TABLE TOOLS FIELDS tab | Views group) to display the View menu (Figure 1–14).

Q&A Could I just tap or click the View button rather than the arrow?
Yes. Tapping or clicking the button is equivalent to tapping or clicking the command represented by the icon currently appearing on the button. Because the icon on the button in Figure 1–14 is for Design view, tapping or clicking the button would display the table in Design view. If you are uncertain, you can always tap or click the arrow and select from the menu.

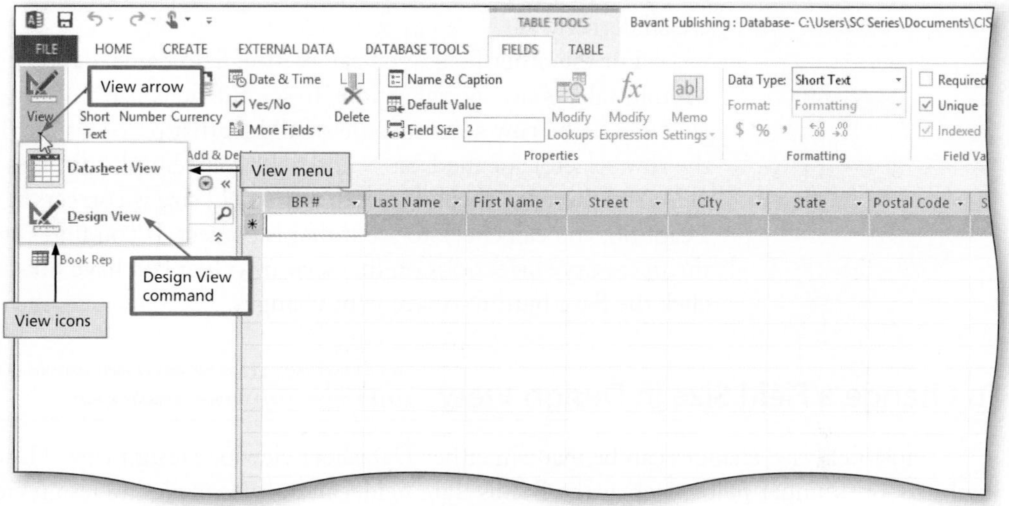

Figure 1–14

2

- Tap or click Design View on the View menu to view the table in Design view (Figure 1–15).

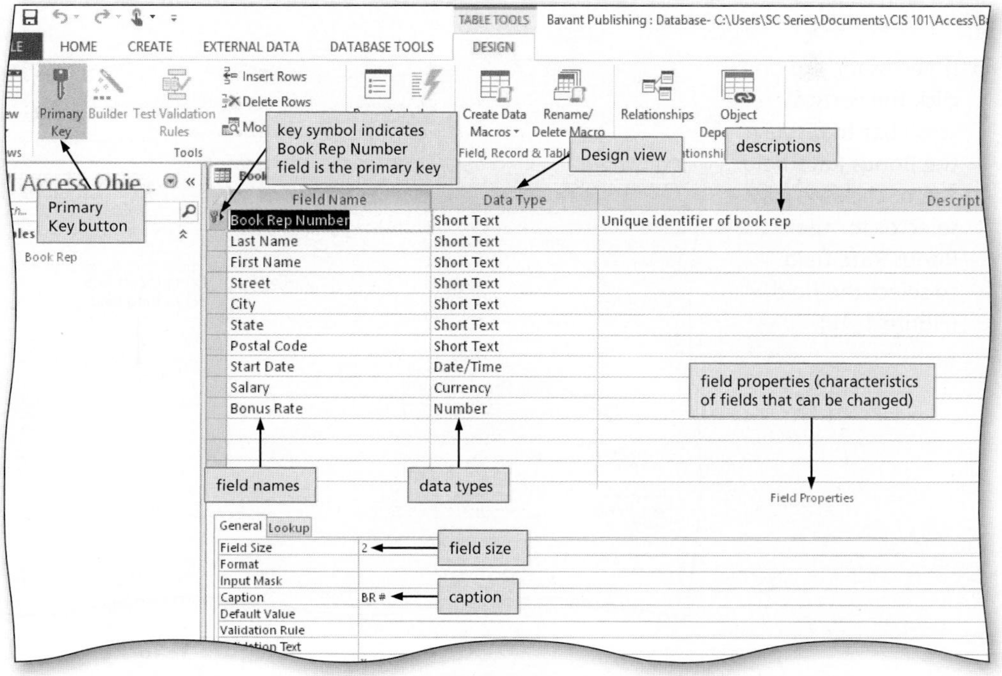

Figure 1–15

Other Ways

1. Tap or click Design View button on status bar

Checking the Structure in Design View

You should use Design view to carefully check the entries you have made. In Figure 1–15 on the previous page, for example, you can see that the Book Rep Number field is the primary key of the Book Rep table by the key symbol in front of the field name. If your table does not have a key symbol, you can tap or click the Primary Key button (TABLE TOOLS DESIGN tab | Tools group) to designate the field as the primary key. You also can check that the data type, description, field size, and caption are all correct.

For the other fields, you can see the field name, data type, and description without taking any special action. To see the field size and/or caption for a field, tap or click the field's **row selector**, the small box that precedes the field. Tapping or clicking the row selector for the Last Name field, for example, displays the properties for the field. You then can check to see that the field size is correct. In addition, if the field has a caption, you can check to see if that is correct. If you find any mistakes, you can make the necessary corrections on this screen. When you have finished, you would tap or click the Save button to save your changes.

To Change a Field Size in Design View

1 CREATE FIRST TABLE | 2 ADD RECORDS | 3 PRINT CONTENTS | 4 IMPORT RECORDS | 5 MODIFY SECOND TABLE
6 CREATE QUERY | 7 CREATE FORM | 8 CREATE REPORT

Most field size changes can be made in either Datasheet view or Design view. However, changing the field size for Number fields, such as the Bonus Rate field, can only be made in Design view. Because the values in the Bonus Rate field have decimal places, only Single, Double, or Decimal would be possible choices for the field size. The difference between these choices concerns the amount of accuracy. Double is more accurate than Single, for example, but requires more storage space. Because the rates are only two decimal places, Single is an acceptable choice.

The following steps change the field size of the Bonus Rate field to Single, the format to Fixed, and the number of decimal places to 2. ***Why change the format and number of decimal places?*** *To ensure that each value will appear with precisely two decimal places.*

1

- If necessary, tap or click the vertical scroll bar to display the Bonus Rate field. Tap or click the row selector for the Bonus Rate field to select the field (Figure 1–16).

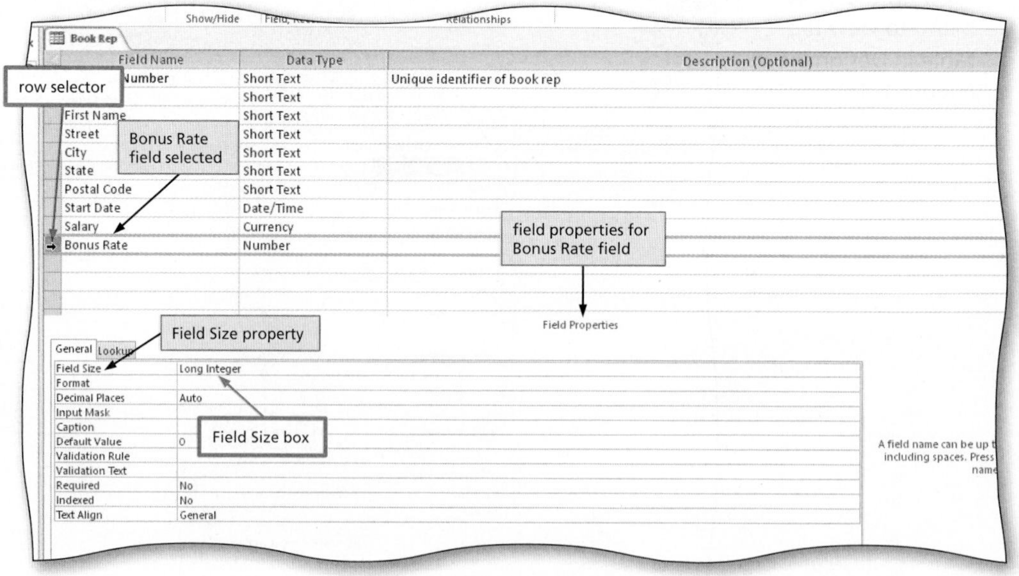

Figure 1–16

2

- Tap or click the Field Size box to display the Field Size arrow.
- Tap or click the Field Size arrow to display the Field Size menu (Figure 1–17).

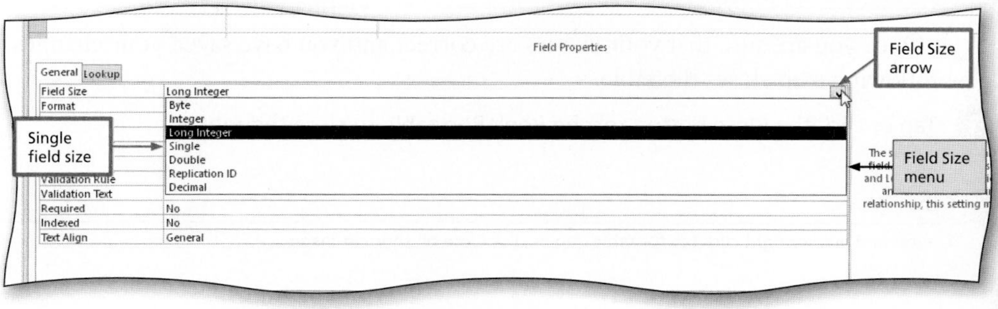

Figure 1–17

Q&A What would happen if I left the field size set to Long Integer?
If the field size is Long Integer, Integer, or Byte, no decimal places can be stored. For example, a value of .10 would be stored as 0. If you enter rates and the values all appear as 0, chances are you did not change the field size property.

3

- Tap or click Single to select single precision as the field size.
- Tap or click the Format box to display the Format arrow.
- Tap or click the Format arrow to open the Format menu (Figure 1–18).

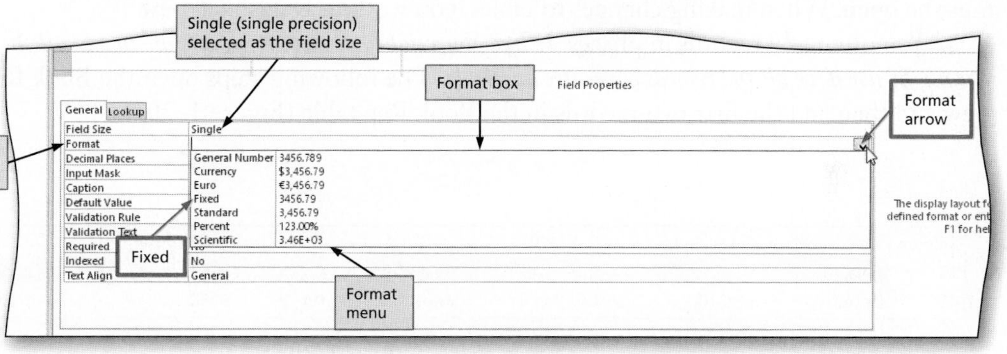

Figure 1–18

4

- Tap or click Fixed to select fixed as the format.
- Tap or click the Decimal Places box to display the Decimal Places arrow.
- Tap or click the Decimal Places arrow to enter the number of decimal places.
- Tap or click 2 to assign the number of decimal places.
- Tap or click the Save button to save your changes (Figure 1–19).

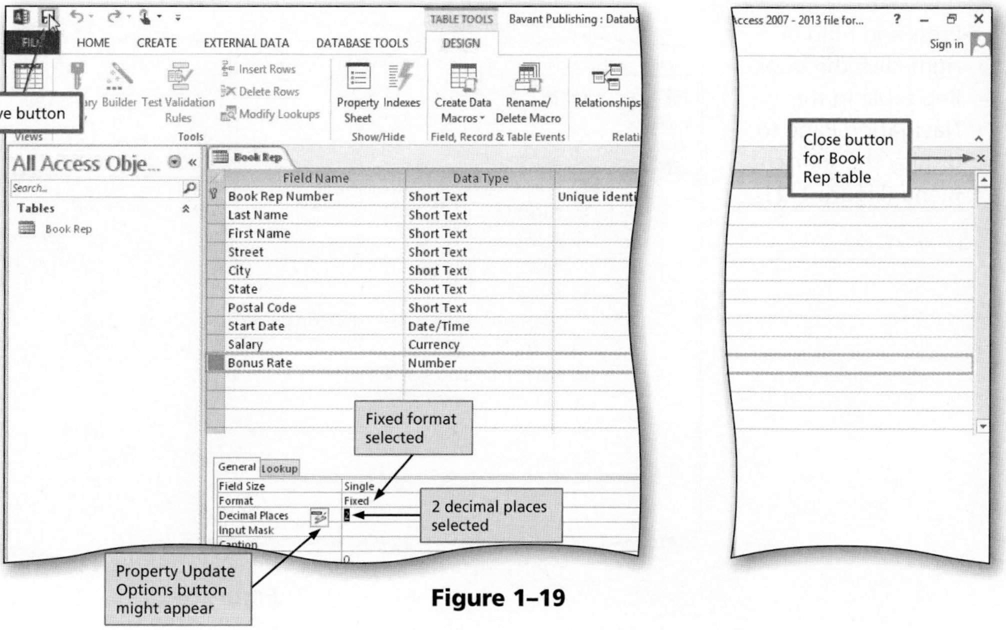

Figure 1–19

Q&A Why did the Property Update Options button appear?
You changed the number of decimal places. The Property Update Options button offers a quick way of making the same change everywhere Bonus Rate appears. So far, you have not added any data or created any forms or reports that use the Bonus Rate field, so no such changes are necessary.

To Close the Table

Once you are sure that your entries are correct and you have saved your changes, you can close the table. The following step closes the table.

1. Tap or click the Close button for the Book Rep table to close the table.

Other Ways

1. Press and hold or right-click tab for table, tap or click Close on shortcut menu

To Add Records to a Table

1 CREATE FIRST TABLE | 2 ADD RECORDS | 3 PRINT CONTENTS | 4 IMPORT RECORDS | 5 MODIFY SECOND TABLE
6 CREATE QUERY | 7 CREATE FORM | 8 CREATE REPORT

Creating a table by building the structure and saving the table is the first step in the two-step process of using a table in a database. The second step is to add records to the table. To add records to a table, the table must be open. When making changes to tables, you work in Datasheet view.

You often add records in phases. ***Why?*** *You might not have enough time to add all the records in one session, or you might not have all the records currently available.* The following steps open the Book Rep table in Datasheet view and then add the first two records in the Book Rep table (Figure 1–20).

BR #	Last Name	First Name	Street	City	State	Postal Code	Start Date	Salary	Bonus Rate
53	Chin	Robert	265 Maxwell St.	Gossett	PA	19157	6/1/2013	$26,250.00	0.19
42	Perez	Melina	261 Porter Dr.	Adelphia	PA	19156	5/14/2012	$31,500.00	0.20

Figure 1–20

1.
- Press and hold or right-click the Book Rep table in the Navigation Pane to display the shortcut menu (Figure 1–21).

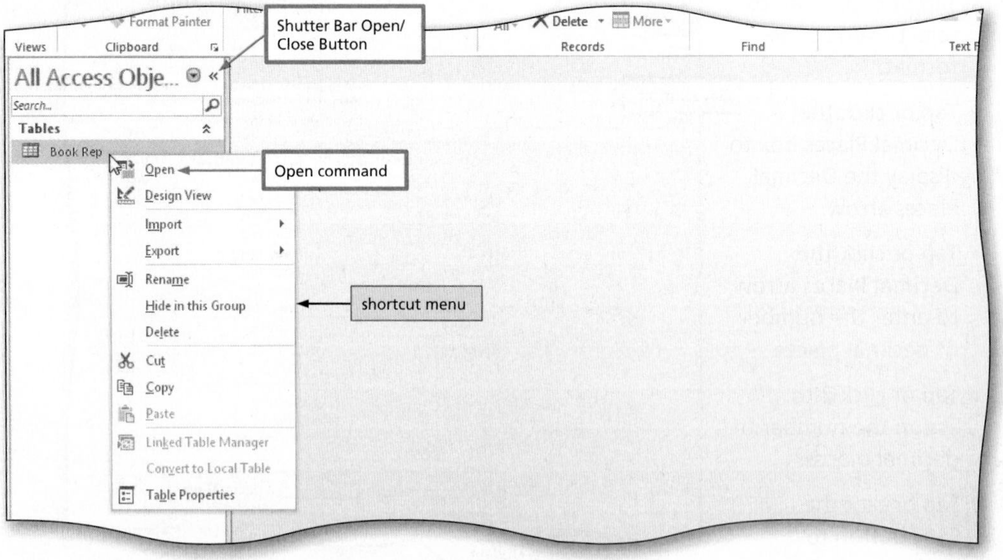

Figure 1–21

2

- Tap or click Open on the shortcut menu to open the table in Datasheet view.
- Tap or click the Shutter Bar Open/Close Button to close the Navigation Pane (Figure 1–22).

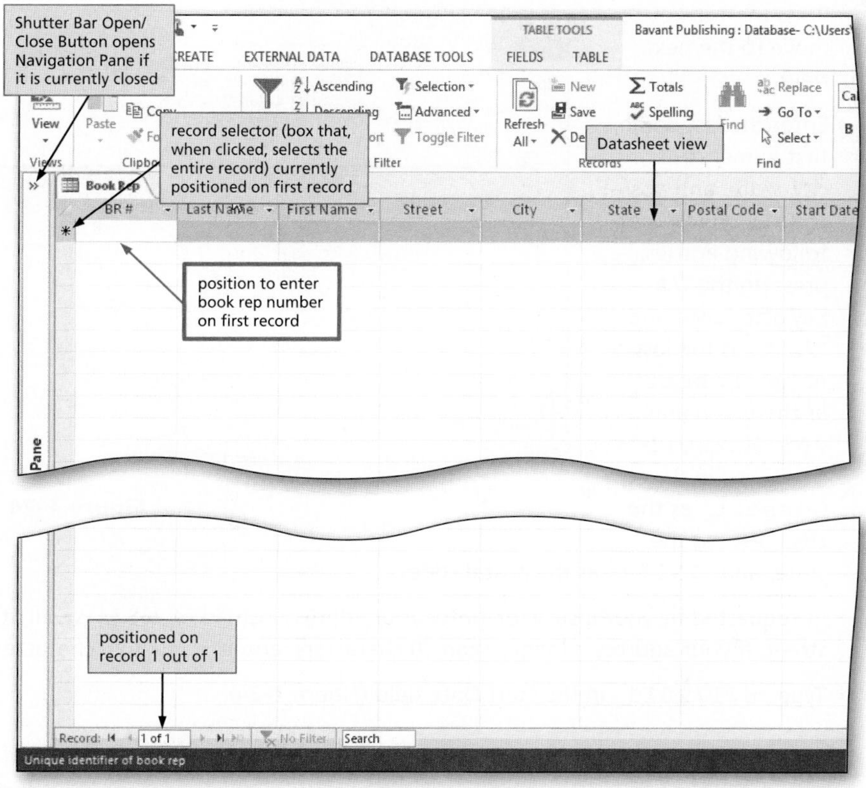

Figure 1–22

3

- Tap or click the first row in the BR # field if necessary to display an insertion point, and type `53` to enter the first book rep number (Figure 1–23).

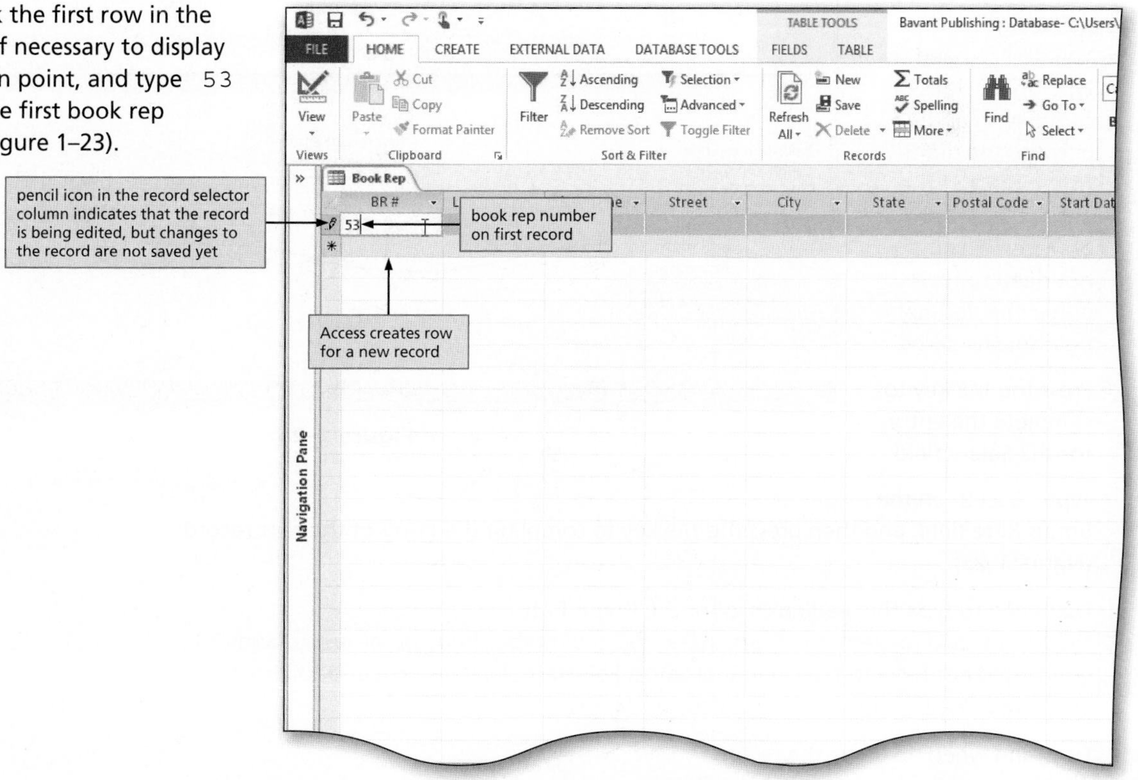

Figure 1–23

4

- Press the TAB key to move to the next field.
- Enter the last name, first name, street, city, state, and postal code by typing the following entries, pressing the TAB key after each one: `Chin` as the last name, `Robert` as the first name, `265 Maxwell St.` as the street, `Gossett` as the city, `PA` as the state, and `19157` as the postal code.
- If requested by your instructor, enter your address instead of 265 Maxwell St. as the street. If your address is longer than 20 characters, enter the first 20 characters.
- Type `6/1/2013` in the Start Date field (Figure 1–24).

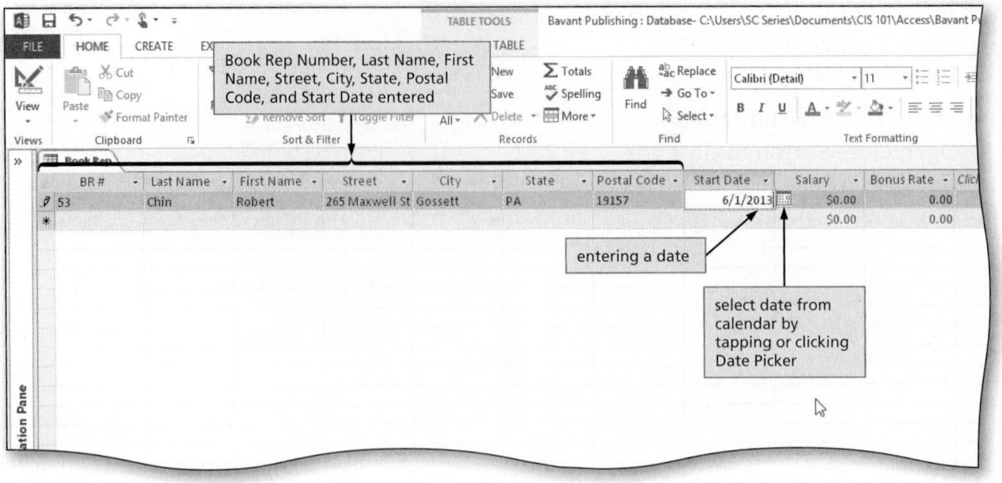

Figure 1–24

5

- Press the TAB key and then type `26250` in the Salary field.

Q&A Do I need to type a dollar sign?
You do not need to type dollar signs or commas. In addition, because the digits to the right of the decimal point are both zeros, you do not need to type either the decimal point or the zeros.

- Press the TAB key to complete the entry for the Salary field.
- Type `0.19` in the Bonus Rate field, and then press the TAB key to complete the entry of the first record (Figure 1–25).

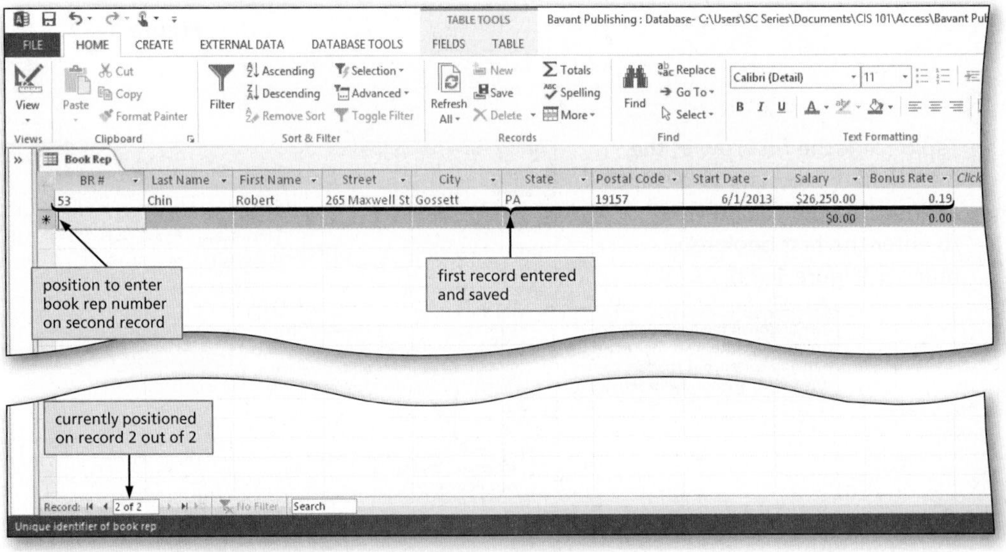

Figure 1–25

Q&A Do I need to type the leading zero for the Bonus Rate?
Typing the leading zero is not necessary. You could type .19 if you prefer. In addition, you would not have to type any final zeros. For example, if you needed to enter 0.20, you could simply type .2 as your entry.

How and when do I save the record?
As soon as you have entered or modified a record and moved to another record, Access saves the original record. This is different from other applications. The rows entered in an Excel worksheet, for example, are not saved until the entire worksheet is saved.

6

- Use the techniques shown in Steps 3 through 5 to enter the data for the second record (Figure 1–26).

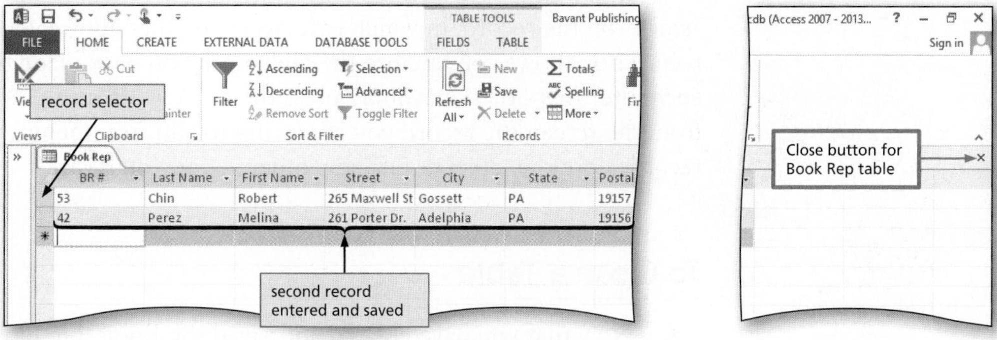

Figure 1–26

Q&A Does it matter that I entered book rep 42 after I entered book rep 53? Should the book rep numbers be in order?

The order in which you enter the records is not important. When you close and later reopen the table, the records will be in book rep number order, because the Book Rep Number field is the primary key.

When I entered the Salary field and changed the data type to Currency, I noticed that the word Currency appeared twice. Why?

The second Currency is the format, which indicates how the data will be displayed. For the Currency data type, Access automatically sets the format to Currency, which is usually what you would want. You could change it to something else, if desired, by tapping or clicking the arrow and selecting the desired format.

Experiment

- Tap or click the Salary field on either of the records. Be sure the TABLE TOOLS FIELDS tab is selected. Tap or click the Format arrow, and then tap or click each of the formats in the Format box menu to see the effect on the values in the Salary field. When finished, tap or click Currency in the Format box menu.

Making Changes to the Data

As you enter data, check your entries carefully to ensure they are correct. If you make a mistake and discover it before you press the TAB key, correct it by pressing the BACKSPACE key until the incorrect characters are removed, and then type the correct characters. If you do not discover a mistake until later, you can use the following techniques to make the necessary corrections to the data:

- To undo your most recent change, tap or click the Undo button on the Quick Access Toolbar. If there is nothing that Access can undo, this button will be dimmed, and tapping or clicking it will have no effect.
- To add a record, tap or click the New (blank) record button, tap or click the position for the Book Rep Number field on the first open record, and then add the record. Do not worry about it being in the correct position in the table. Access will reposition the record based on the primary key, in this case, the Book Rep Number.
- To delete a record, tap or click the record selector, shown in Figure 1–26, for the record to be deleted. Then press the DELETE key to delete the record, and tap or click the Yes button when Access asks you to verify that you want to delete the record.
- To change the contents of one or more fields in a record, the record must be on the screen. If it is not, use any appropriate technique, such as the UP ARROW and DOWN ARROW keys or the vertical scroll bar, to move to the record. If the field you want to correct is not visible on the screen, use the horizontal scroll bar along the bottom of the screen to shift all the fields until the one you want appears. If the value in the field is currently highlighted, you can simply type the new value. If you would rather edit the existing value, you must have an insertion point in the field. You can place the insertion point by tapping or clicking in the field or by pressing the F2 key. You then can use the arrow keys, the DELETE key, and the BACKSPACE key for making the correction. You also can use the INSERT key to switch between Insert and Overtype mode. When you have made the change, press the TAB key to move to the next field.

BTW

AutoCorrect Feature

The AutoCorrect feature of Access corrects common data entry errors. AutoCorrect corrects two capital letters by changing the second letter to lowercase and capitalizes the first letter in the names of days. It also corrects more than 400 commonly misspelled words.

BTW

Other AutoCorrect Options

Using the Office AutoCorrect feature, you can create entries that will replace abbreviations with spelled-out names and phrases automatically. To specify AutoCorrect rules, tap or click FILE on the ribbon to open the Backstage view, tap or click Options, and then tap or click Proofing in the Access Options dialog box.

If you cannot determine how to correct the data, you may find that you are "stuck" on the record, in which case Access neither allows you to move to another record nor allows you to close the table until you have made the correction. If you encounter this situation, simply press the ESC key. Pressing the ESC key will remove from the screen the record you are trying to add. You then can move to any other record, close the table, or take any other action you desire.

To Close a Table

Now that you have created and saved the Book Rep table, you can close it. The following step closes the table.

1. Tap or click the Close button for the Book Rep table, shown in Figure 1–26 on the previous page, to close the table (Figure 1–27).

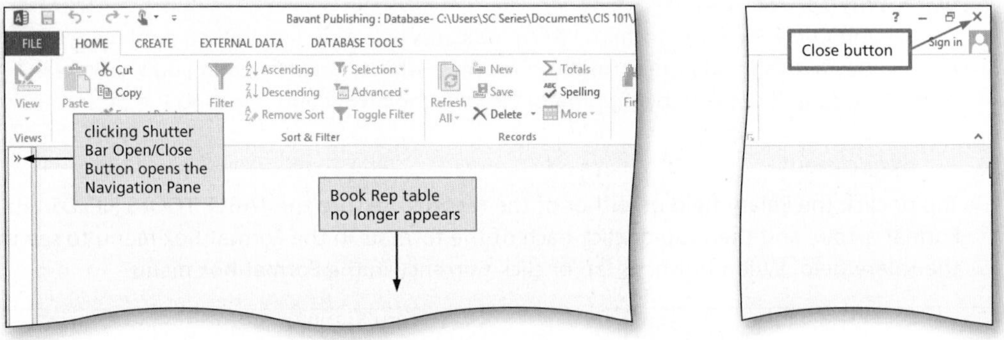

Figure 1–27

To Exit Access

The following steps exit Access. For a detailed example of the procedure summarized below, refer to the Office and Windows chapter at the beginning of this book.

1. Tap or click the Close button on the right side of the title bar to exit Access.
2. If a Microsoft Access dialog box appears, tap or click the Save button to save any changes made to the object since the last save.

Break Point: If you wish to take a break, this is a good place to do so. To resume later, continue following the steps from this location forward.

Starting Access and Opening a Database

Once you have created and later closed a database, you will need to open it in the future in order to use it. Opening a database requires that Access is running on your computer.

To Run Access

1. Scroll the Start screen for an Access 2013 tile. If your Start screen contains an Access 2013 tile, tap or click it to run Access. If the Start screen does not contain the Access 2013 tile, proceed to the next step to search for the Access app.
2. Swipe in from the right edge of the screen or point to the upper-right corner of the screen to display the Charms bar, and then tap or click the Search charm on the Charms bar to display the Search menu.
3. Type `Access` as the search text in the Search text box and watch the search results appear in the Apps list.
4. Tap or click Access 2013 in the search results to run Access.

To Open a Database from Access

Earlier in this chapter, you created the Bavant Publishing database in an appropriate storage location. The following steps open the database from the location you specified when you first created it (for example, the Access folder in the CIS 101 folder). For a detailed example of the procedure summarized below, refer to the Office 2013 and Windows chapter at the beginning of this book.

1. Tap or click FILE on the ribbon to open the Backstage view, if necessary.
2. If the database you want to open is displayed in the Recent list, tap or click the file name to open the database and display the opened database in the Access window; then skip to Step 7. If the database you want to open is not displayed in the Recent list or if the Recent list does not appear, tap or click 'Open Other Files' to display the Open Gallery.
3. If the database you want to open is displayed in the Recent list in the Open gallery, tap or click the file name to open the database and display the opened database in the Access window; then skip to Step 7.
4. Tap or click Computer, SkyDrive, or another location in the left pane and then navigate to the location of the database to be opened (for example, the Access folder in the CIS 101 folder).
5. Tap or click Bavant Publishing to select the database to be opened.
6. Tap or click the Open button (Open dialog box) to open the selected file and display the opened database in the Access window (Figure 1–28).
7. If a Security Warning appears, tap or click the Enable Content button.

BTW

Enabling Content
If the database is one that you created, or if it comes from a trusted source, you can enable the content. You should disable the content of a database if you suspect that your database might contain harmful content or damaging macros.

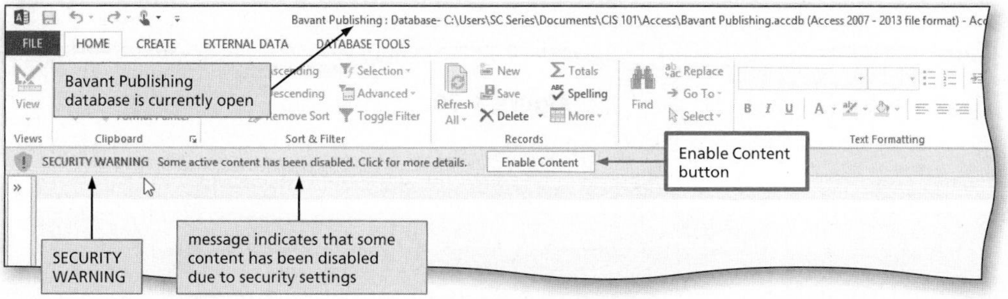

Figure 1–28

To Add Records to a Table that Contains Data

1 CREATE FIRST TABLE | 2 ADD RECORDS | 3 PRINT CONTENTS | 4 IMPORT RECORDS | 5 MODIFY SECOND TABLE
6 CREATE QUERY | 7 CREATE FORM | 8 CREATE REPORT

You can add records to a table that already contains data using a process almost identical to that used to add records to an empty table. The only difference is that you place the insertion point after the last record before you enter the additional data. To position the insertion point after the last record, you can use the **Navigation buttons**, which are buttons used to move within a table, found near the lower-left corner of the screen when a table is open. ***Why not just tap or click the Book Rep Number (BR #) on the first open record?*** *You could do this, but it is a good habit to use the New (blank) record button. Once a table contains more records than will fit on the screen, it is easier to tap or click the New (blank) record button.* The purpose of each Navigation button is described in Table 1–4.

Table 1–4 Navigation Buttons in Datasheet View

Button	Purpose
First record	Moves to the first record in the table
Previous record	Moves to the previous record
Next record	Moves to the next record
Last record	Moves to the last record in the table
New (blank) record	Moves to the end of the table to a position for entering a new record

The following steps add the remaining records (Figure 1–29) to the Book Rep table.

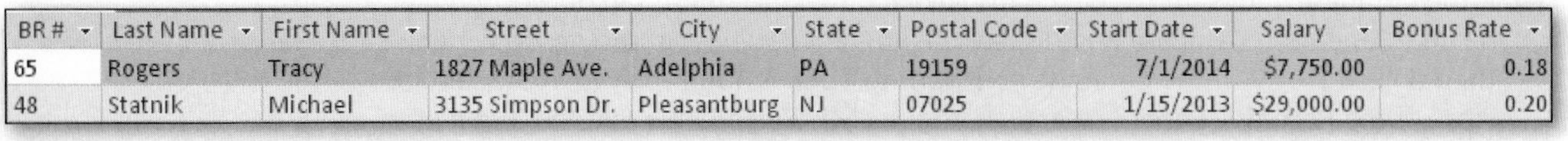

BR #	Last Name	First Name	Street	City	State	Postal Code	Start Date	Salary	Bonus Rate
65	Rogers	Tracy	1827 Maple Ave.	Adelphia	PA	19159	7/1/2014	$7,750.00	0.18
48	Statnik	Michael	3135 Simpson Dr.	Pleasantburg	NJ	07025	1/15/2013	$29,000.00	0.20

Figure 1–29

1

- If the Navigation Pane is closed, tap or click the Shutter Bar Open/Close Button, shown in Figure 1–27 on page AC 24, to open the Navigation Pane (Figure 1–30).

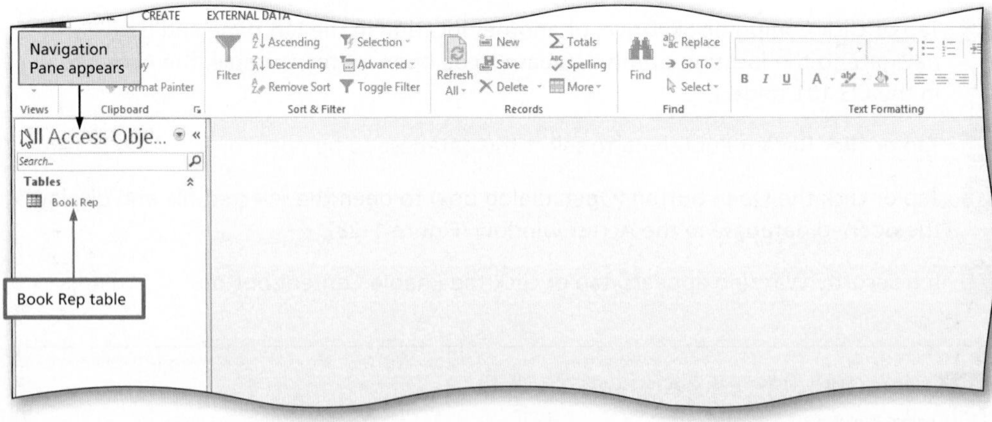

Figure 1–30

2

- Press and hold or right-click the Book Rep table in the Navigation Pane to display a shortcut menu.
- Tap or click Open on the shortcut menu to open the table in Datasheet view.

Q&A Why do the records appear in a different order than the order in which I entered them?
When you open the table, they are sorted in the order of the primary key. In this case, that means they will appear in Book Rep Number order.

- Close the Navigation Pane by tapping or clicking the Shutter Bar Open/Close Button (Figure 1–31).

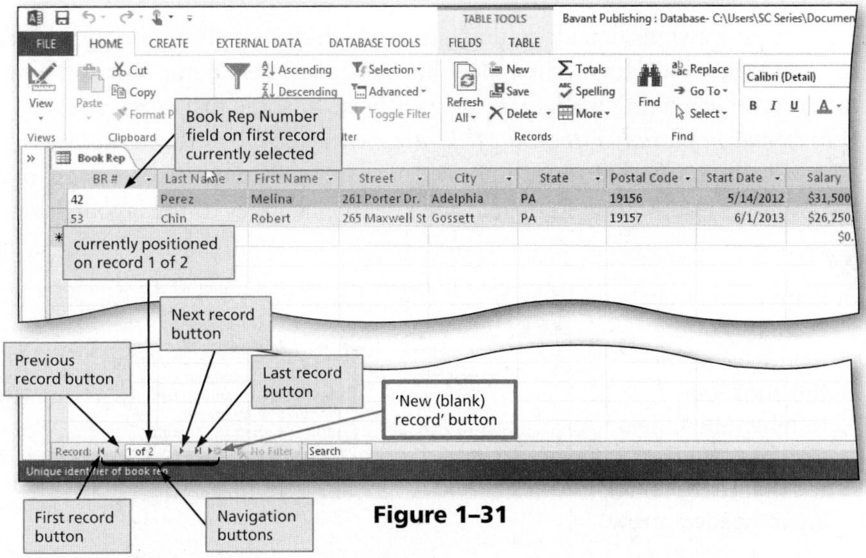

Figure 1–31

3

- Tap or click the 'New (blank) record' button to move to a position to enter a new record (Figure 1–32).

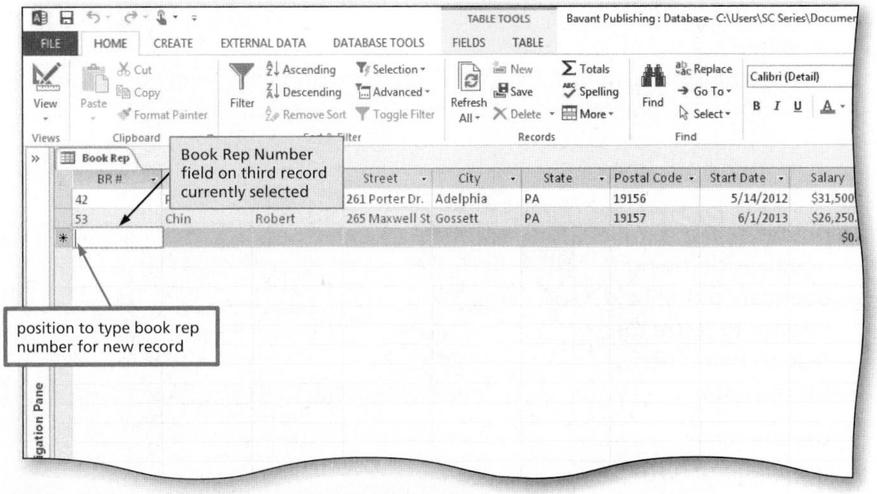

Figure 1–32

4

- Add the records shown in Figure 1–29 using the same techniques you used to add the first two records (Figure 1–33).

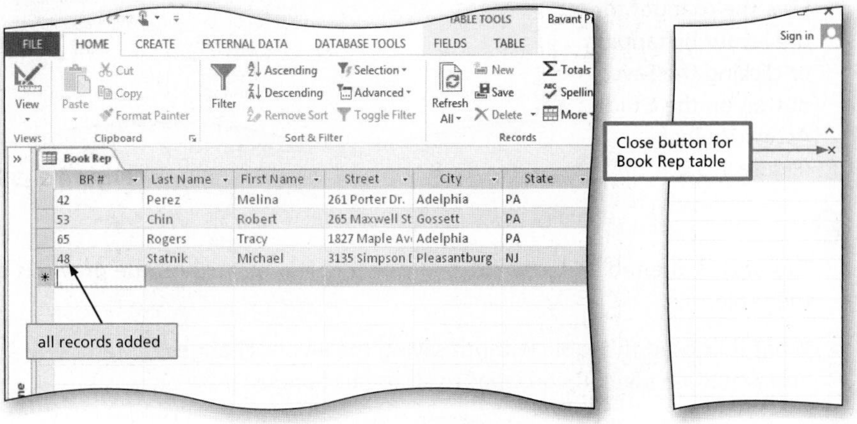

Figure 1–33

Other Ways

1. Tap or click New button (HOME tab | Records group)
2. Press CTRL+PLUS SIGN (+)

To Resize Columns in a Datasheet

1 CREATE FIRST TABLE | 2 ADD RECORDS | 3 PRINT CONTENTS | 4 IMPORT RECORDS | 5 MODIFY SECOND TABLE
6 CREATE QUERY | 7 CREATE FORM | 8 CREATE REPORT

Access assigns default column sizes, which do not always provide space to display all the data in the field. In some cases, the data might appear but the entire field name will not. You can correct this problem by **resizing** the column (changing its size) in the datasheet. In some instances, you may want to reduce the size of a column. ***Why?*** *Some fields, such as the State field, are short enough that they do not require all the space on the screen that is allotted to them.* Changing a column width changes the **layout**, or design, of a table. The following steps resize the columns in the Book Rep table and save the changes to the layout.

1

- Point to the right boundary of the field selector for the Book Rep Number (BR #) field (Figure 1–34) so that the pointer becomes a two-headed arrow.

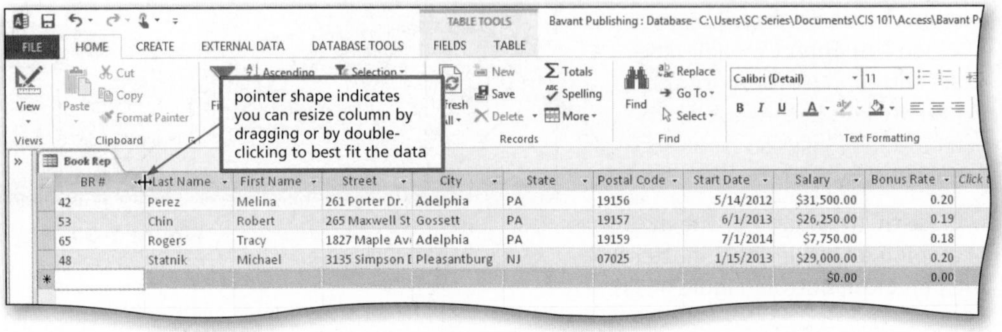

Figure 1–34

Q&A I am using touch and I cannot see the pointer. Is this a problem?
It is not a problem. Remember that if you are using your finger on a touch screen, you will not see the pointer.

2

- Double-tap or double-click the right boundary of the field selector to resize the field so that it best fits the data.
- Use the same technique to resize all the other fields to best fit the data.
- Save the changes to the layout by tapping or clicking the Save button on the Quick Access Toolbar (Figure 1–35).

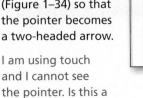

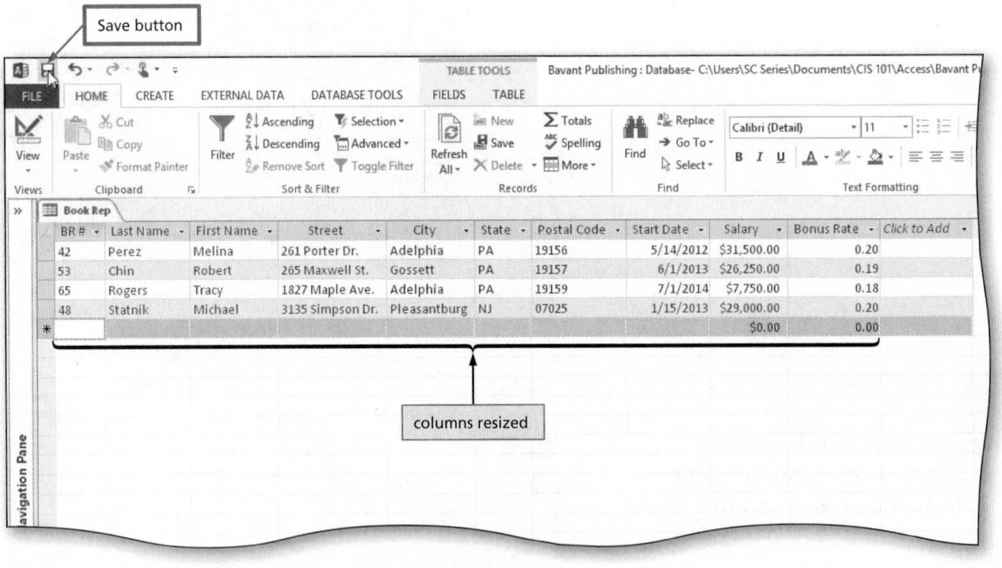

Figure 1–35

3

- Tap or click the table's Close button (shown in Figure 1–33 on the previous page) to close the table.

Q&A What if I closed the table without saving the layout changes?
You would be asked if you want to save the changes.

Other Ways

1. Press and hold or right-click field name, tap or click Field Width

CONSIDER THIS

What is the best method for distributing database objects?

The traditional method of distributing database objects such as tables, reports, and forms uses a printer to produce a hard copy. A **hard copy** or **printout** is information that exists on a physical medium such as paper. Hard copies can be useful for the following reasons:

- Some people prefer proofreading a hard copy of a document rather than viewing it on the screen to check for errors and readability.
- Hard copies can serve as a backup reference if your storage medium is lost or becomes corrupted and you need to recreate the document.

Instead of distributing a hard copy, users can distribute the document as an electronic image that mirrors the original document's appearance. The electronic image of the document can be emailed, posted on a website, or copied to a portable storage medium such as a USB flash drive. Two popular electronic image formats, sometimes called fixed formats, are PDF by Adobe Systems and XPS by Microsoft. In Access, you can create electronic image files through the EXTERNAL DATA tab on the ribbon. Electronic images of documents, such as PDF and XPS, can be useful for the following reasons:

- Users can view electronic images of documents without the software that created the original document (e.g., Access). Specifically, to view a PDF file, you use a program called Adobe Reader, which can be downloaded free from Adobe's website. Similarly, to view an XPS file, you use a program called XPS Viewer, which is included in the latest versions of Windows and Internet Explorer.
- Sending electronic documents saves paper and printer supplies. Society encourages users to contribute to **green computing,** which involves reducing the electricity consumed and environmental waste generated when using computers, mobile devices, and related technologies.

Previewing and Printing the Contents of a Table

When working with a database, you often will need to print a copy of the table contents. Figure 1–36 shows a printed copy of the contents of the Book Rep table. (Yours may look slightly different, depending on your printer.) Because the Book Rep table is substantially wider than the screen, it also will be wider than the normal printed page in portrait orientation. **Portrait orientation** means the printout is across the width of the page. **Landscape orientation** means the printout is across the height of the page. To print the wide database table, you might prefer to use landscape orientation. A convenient way to change to landscape orientation is to preview what the printed copy will look like by using Print Preview. This allows you to determine whether landscape orientation is necessary and, if it is, to change the orientation easily to landscape. In addition, you also can use Print Preview to determine whether any adjustments are necessary to the page margins.

BTW

Changing Printers

To change the default printer that appears in the Print dialog box, tap or click FILE on the ribbon, tap or click the Print tab in the Backstage view, tap or click Print in the Print gallery, then tap or click the Name arrow and select the desired printer.

Book Rep 9/15/2014

BR #	Last Name	First Name	Street	City	State	Postal Code	Start Date	Salary	Bonus Rate
42	Perez	Melina	261 Porter Dr.	Adelphia	PA	19156	5/14/2012	$31,500.00	0.20
48	Statnik	Michael	3135 Simpson Dr.	Pleasantburg	NJ	07025	1/15/2013	$29,000.00	0.20
53	Chin	Robert	265 Maxwell St.	Gossett	PA	19157	6/1/2013	$26,250.00	0.19
65	Rogers	Tracy	1827 Maple Ave.	Adelphia	PA	19159	7/1/2014	$7,750.00	0.18

Figure 1–36

To Preview and Print the Contents of a Table

1 CREATE FIRST TABLE | 2 ADD RECORDS | 3 PRINT CONTENTS | 4 IMPORT RECORDS | 5 MODIFY SECOND TABLE
6 CREATE QUERY | 7 CREATE FORM | 8 CREATE REPORT

The following steps use Print Preview to preview and then print the contents of the Book Rep table. ***Why?*** *By previewing the contents of the table in Print Preview, you can make any necessary adjustments to the orientation or to the margins before printing the contents.*

1

- If the Navigation Pane is closed, open the Navigation Pane by tapping or clicking the Shutter Bar Open/Close Button.
- Be sure the Book Rep table is selected.

Q&A Why do I have to be sure the Book Rep table is selected? It is the only object in the database.
When the database contains only one object, you do not have to worry about selecting the object. Ensuring that the correct object is selected is a good habit to form, however, to make sure that the object you print is the one you want.

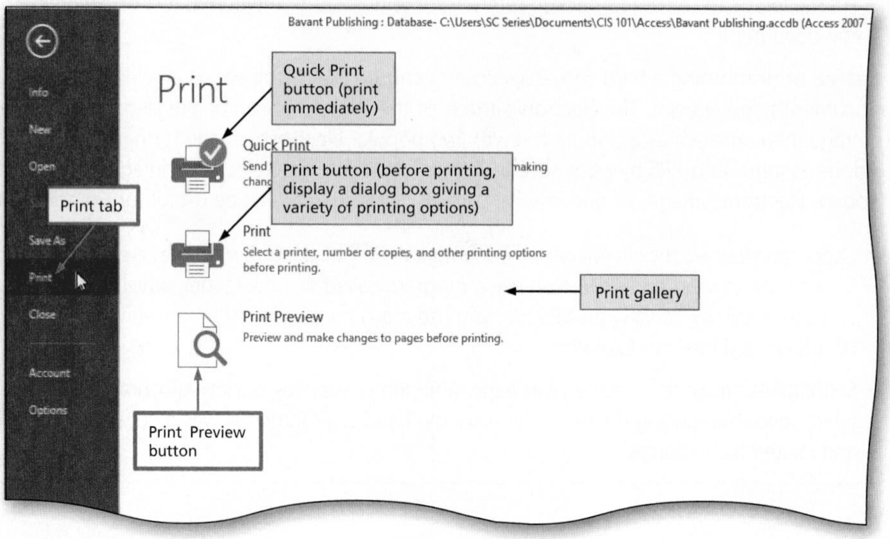

Figure 1–37

- Tap or click FILE on the ribbon to open the Backstage view.
- Tap or click the Print tab in the Backstage view to display the Print gallery (Figure 1–37).

2

- Tap or click the Print Preview button in the Print gallery to display a preview of what the table will look like when printed (Figure 1–38).

Q&A I cannot read the table. Can I magnify a portion of the table?
Yes. Point the pointer, whose shape will change to a magnifying glass, at the portion of the table that you want to magnify, and then tap or click. You can return to the original view of the table by tapping or clicking a second time.

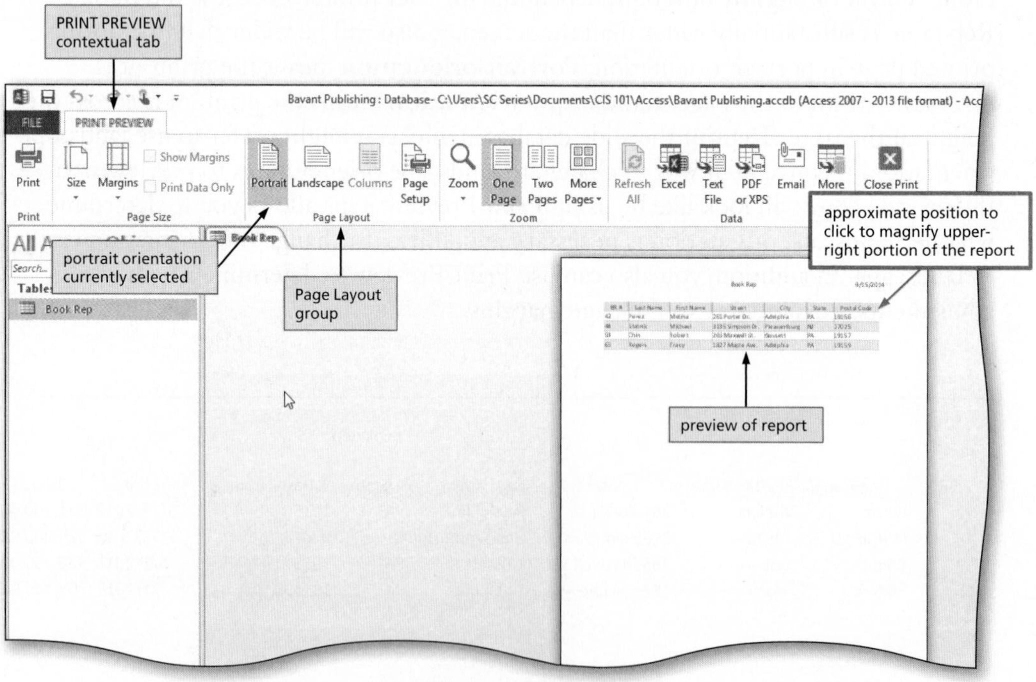

Figure 1–38

3

- Tap or click the pointer in the position shown in Figure 1–38 to magnify the upper-right section of the table (Figure 1–39).

Q&A My table was already magnified in a different area. How can I see the area shown in the figure?
One way is to use the scroll bars to move to the desired portion of the table. You also can tap or click the pointer anywhere in the table to produce a screen like the one shown in Figure 1–38, and then tap or click in the location shown in the figure.

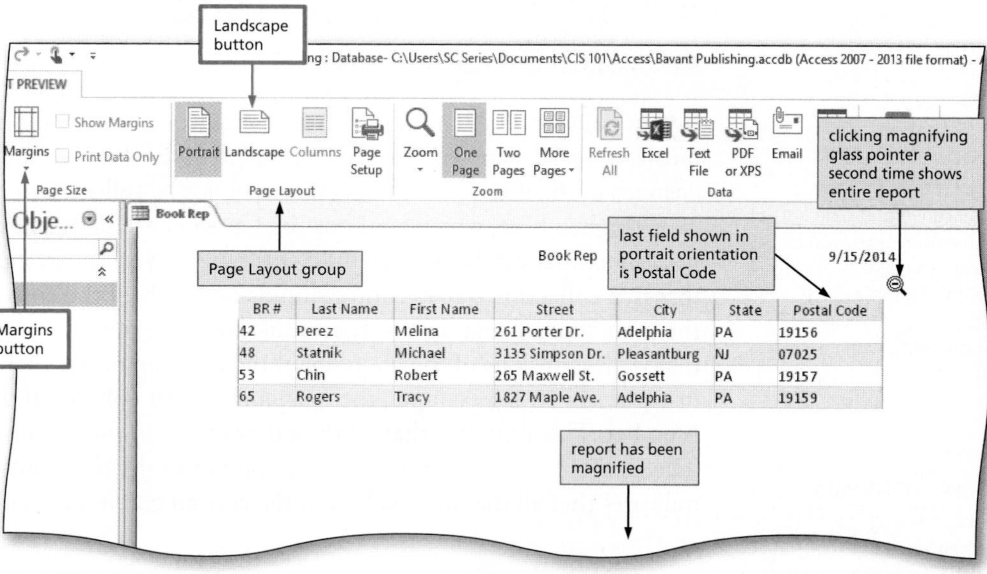

Figure 1–39

4

- Tap or click the Landscape button (PRINT PREVIEW tab | Page Layout group) to change to landscape orientation.
- Tap or click the Margins button (PRINT PREVIEW tab | Page Size group) and then click Normal if necessary to display all the fields (Figure 1–40).

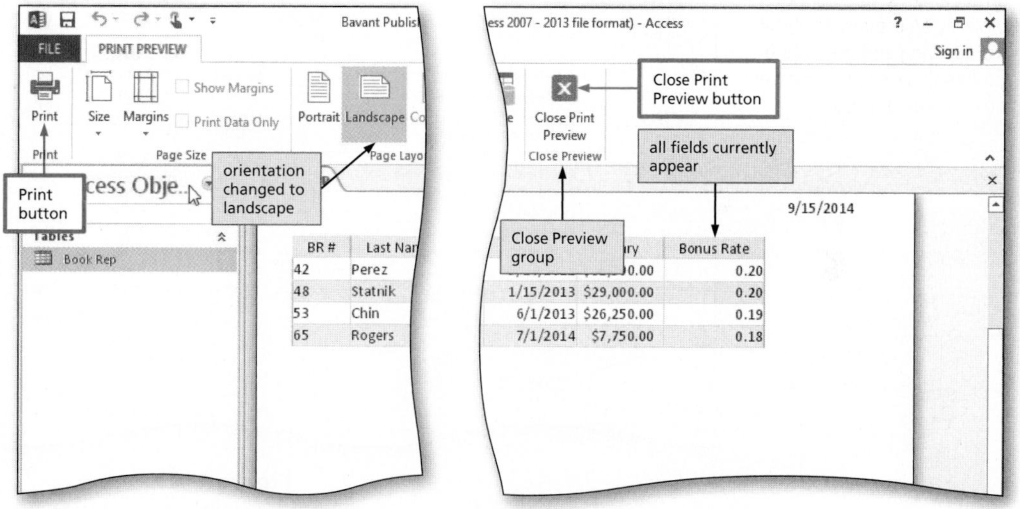

Figure 1–40

5

- Tap or click the Print button (PRINT PREVIEW tab | Print group) to display the Print dialog box.
- Tap or click the OK button (Print dialog box) to print the table.
- When the printer stops, retrieve the hard copy of the Book Rep table.
- Tap or click the Close Print Preview button (PRINT PREVIEW tab | Close Preview group) to close the Print Preview window.

Q&A Do I have to select Print Preview before printing the table?
No. If you wish to print without previewing, you would select either Print or Quick Print rather than Print Preview.

Other Ways

1. Press CTRL+P, tap or click OK button in Print dialog box

Importing or Linking Data from Other Applications to Access

BTW
Importing Data in Other Formats
You can import data into a table from Excel workbooks, Access databases, XML files, ODBC databases such as SQL Server, text files, HTML documents, Outlook folders, and SharePoint lists.

BTW
Linking Versus Importing
When you link to the data in the worksheet, the data appears as a table in the Access database but it is maintained in its original form in Excel. Any changes to the Excel data are reflected when the linked table is viewed in Access. In this arrangement, Access would typically be used as a vehicle for querying and presenting the data, with actual updates being made in Excel.

If your data for a table is stored in an Excel worksheet, you can **import** the data, which means to make a copy of the data as a table in the Access database. In this case, any changes to the data made in Access would not be reflected in the Excel worksheet.

Figure 1–41, which contains the Customer data, is an example of the type of worksheet that can be imported. In this type of worksheet, the data is stored as a **list**, that is, a collection of rows and columns in which all the entries in a column represent the same type of data. In this type of list, the first row contains **column headings**, that is, descriptions of the contents of the column, rather than data. In the worksheet in Figure 1–41, for example, the entry in the first column of the first row is Customer Number. This indicates that all the other values in this column are customer numbers. The fact that the entry in the second column of the first row is Customer Name indicates that all the other values in the second column are customer names.

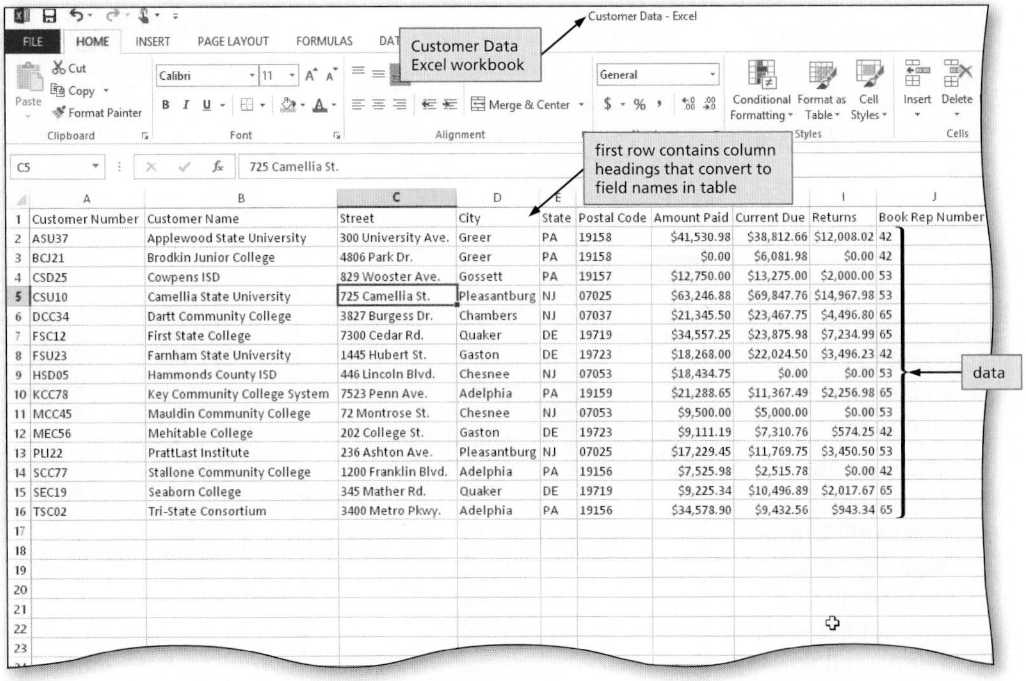

Customer Number	Customer Name	Street	City	State	Postal Code	Amount Paid	Current Due	Returns	Book Rep Number
ASU37	Applewood State University	300 University Ave.	Greer	PA	19158	$41,530.98	$38,812.66	$12,008.02	42
BCJ21	Brodkin Junior College	4806 Park Dr.	Greer	PA	19158	$0.00	$6,081.98	$0.00	42
CSD25	Cowpens ISD	829 Wooster Ave.	Gossett	PA	19157	$12,750.00	$13,275.00	$2,000.00	53
CSU10	Camellia State University	725 Camellia St.	Pleasantburg	NJ	07025	$63,246.88	$69,847.76	$14,967.98	53
DCC34	Dartt Community College	3827 Burgess Dr.	Chambers	NJ	07037	$21,345.50	$23,467.75	$4,496.80	65
FSC12	First State College	7300 Cedar Rd.	Quaker	DE	19719	$34,557.25	$23,875.98	$7,234.99	65
FSU23	Farnham State University	1445 Hubert St.	Gaston	DE	19723	$18,268.00	$22,024.50	$3,496.23	42
HSD05	Hammonds County ISD	446 Lincoln Blvd.	Chesnee	NJ	07053	$18,434.75	$0.00	$0.00	53
KCC78	Key Community College System	7523 Penn Ave.	Adelphia	PA	19159	$21,288.65	$11,367.49	$2,256.98	65
MCC45	Mauldin Community College	72 Montrose St.	Chesnee	NJ	07053	$9,500.00	$5,000.00	$0.00	53
MEC56	Mehitable College	202 College St.	Gaston	DE	19723	$9,111.19	$7,310.76	$574.25	42
PLI22	PrattLast Institute	236 Ashton Ave.	Pleasantburg	NJ	07025	$17,229.45	$11,769.75	$3,450.50	53
SCC77	Stallone Community College	1200 Franklin Blvd.	Adelphia	PA	19156	$7,525.98	$2,515.78	$0.00	42
SEC19	Seaborn College	345 Mather Rd.	Quaker	DE	19719	$9,225.34	$10,496.89	$2,017.67	65
TSC02	Tri-State Consortium	3400 Metro Pkwy.	Adelphia	PA	19156	$34,578.90	$9,432.56	$943.34	65

Figure 1–41

CONSIDER THIS

Does it matter how the data in the Excel workbook is formatted? If so, how can you be sure the Excel data is formatted in such a way you can import it?

The format of data in an Excel workbook is important when you want to import it into Access. To ensure the data is in an appropriate format:

1. Make sure the data is in the form of a list, a collection of rows and columns in which all the entries in a column represent the same type of data.
2. Make sure there are no blank rows within the list. If there are, remove them prior to importing or linking.
3. Make sure there are no blank columns within the list. If there are, remove them prior to importing or linking.
4. Determine whether the first row contains column headings that will make appropriate field names in the resulting table. If not, you might consider adding such a row. In general, the process is simpler if the first row in the worksheet contains appropriate column headings.

The Import process will create a table. In this table, the column headings in the first row of the worksheet become the field names. The rows of the worksheet, other than the first row, become the records in the table. In the process, each field will be assigned the data type that seems the most reasonable, given the data currently in the worksheet. When the Import process is finished, you can use Datasheet or Design view to modify these data types or to make any other changes to the structure you feel are necessary.

To Import an Excel Worksheet

1 CREATE FIRST TABLE | 2 ADD RECORDS | 3 PRINT CONTENTS | 4 IMPORT RECORDS | 5 MODIFY SECOND TABLE
6 CREATE QUERY | 7 CREATE FORM | 8 CREATE REPORT

You import a worksheet by using the Import Spreadsheet Wizard. In the process, you will indicate that the first row in the worksheet contains the column headings. ***Why?*** *You are indicating that Access is to use those column headings as the field names in the Access table.* In addition, you will indicate the primary key for the table. As part of the process, you could, if appropriate, choose not to include all the fields from the worksheet in the resulting table.

The following steps import the Customer worksheet.

1

- Tap or click EXTERNAL DATA on the ribbon to display the EXTERNAL DATA tab (Figure 1–42).

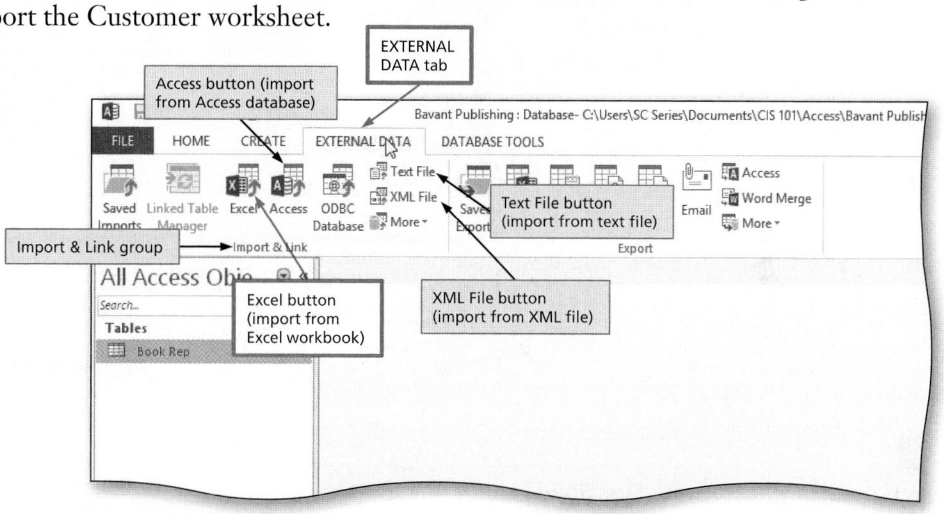

Figure 1–42

2

- Tap or click the Excel button (EXTERNAL DATA tab | Import & Link group) to display the Get External Data - Excel Spreadsheet dialog box.
- Tap or click the Browse button in the Get External Data - Excel Spreadsheet dialog box.
- Navigate to the location containing the workbook (for example, the Access folder in the CIS 101 folder). For a detailed example of this procedure, refer to Steps 4a – 4b in the To Save a File in a Folder section in the Office and Windows chapter at the beginning of this book.
- Tap or click the Customer Data workbook, and then tap or click the Open button to select the workbook (Figure 1–43).

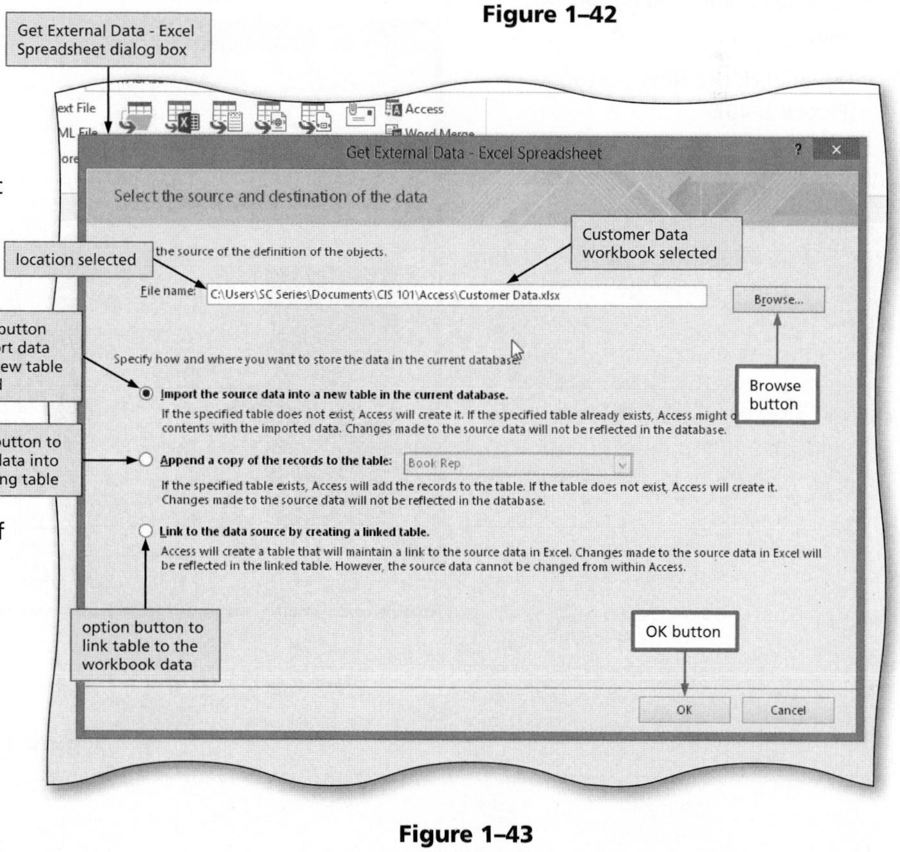

Figure 1–43

3

- With the option button to import the data to a new table selected, tap or click the OK button to display the Import Spreadsheet Wizard dialog box (Figure 1–44).

Q&A What happens if I select the option button to append records to an existing table?

Instead of the records being placed in a new table, they will be added to an existing table that you specify, provided the value in the primary key field does not duplicate that on an existing record.

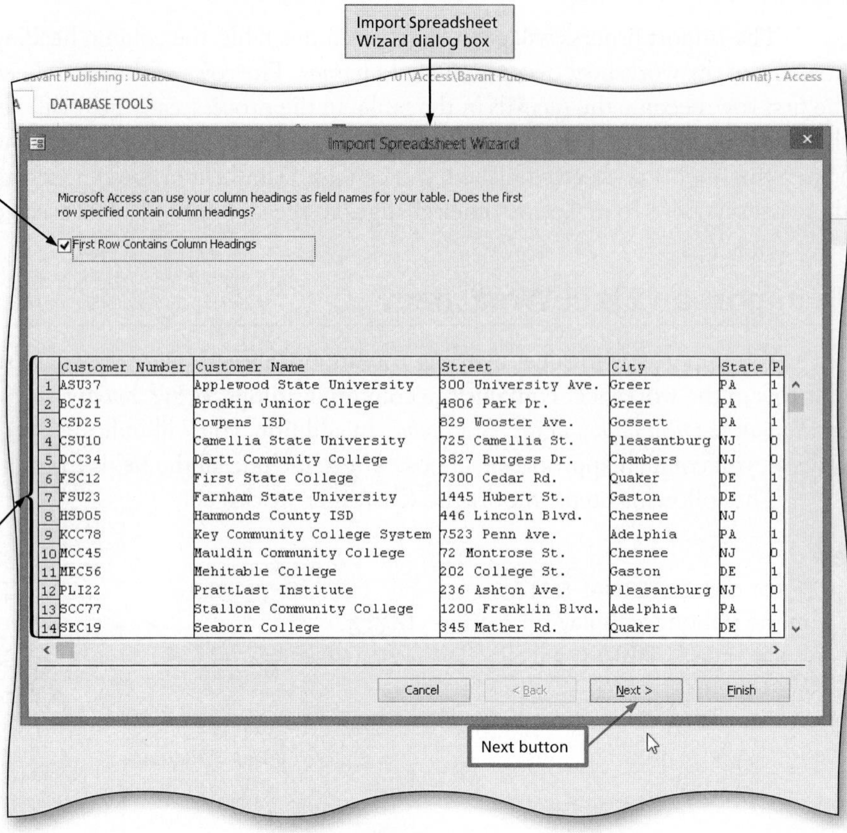

Figure 1–44

4

- If necessary, tap or click First Row Contains Column Headings to select it.
- Tap or click the Next button (Figure 1–45).

Q&A When would I use the Field Options on the Import Spreadsheet Wizard?

You would use these options if you wanted to change properties for one or more fields. You can change the name, the data type, and whether the field is indexed. You also can indicate that some fields should not be imported.

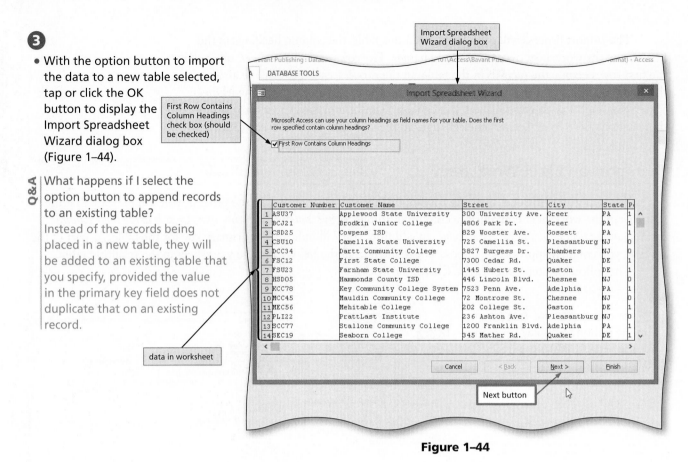

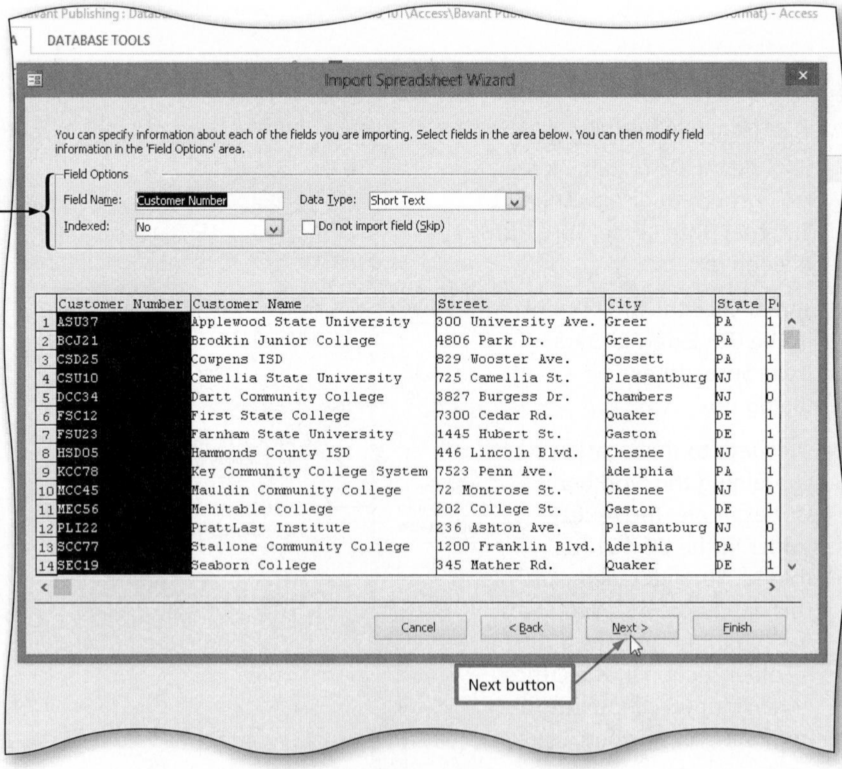

Figure 1–45

5

- Because the Field Options need not be specified, tap or click the Next button (Figure 1–46).

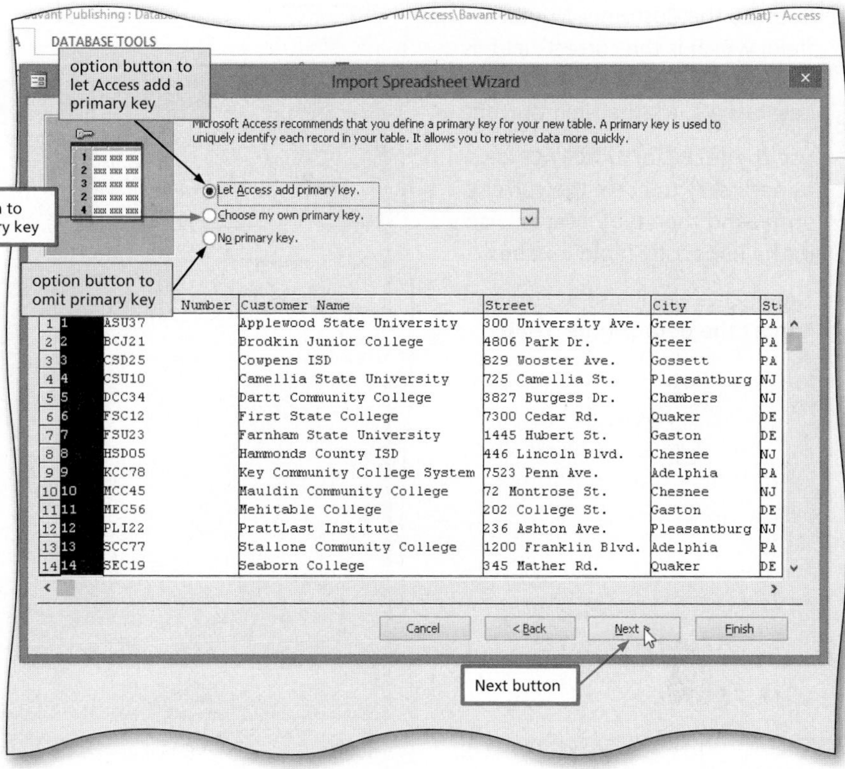

Figure 1–46

6

- Tap or click the 'Choose my own primary key' option button (Figure 1–47).

Q&A How do I decide which option button to select?

If one of the fields is an appropriate primary key, choose your own primary key from the list of fields. If you are sure you do not want a primary key, choose No primary key. Otherwise, let Access add the primary key.

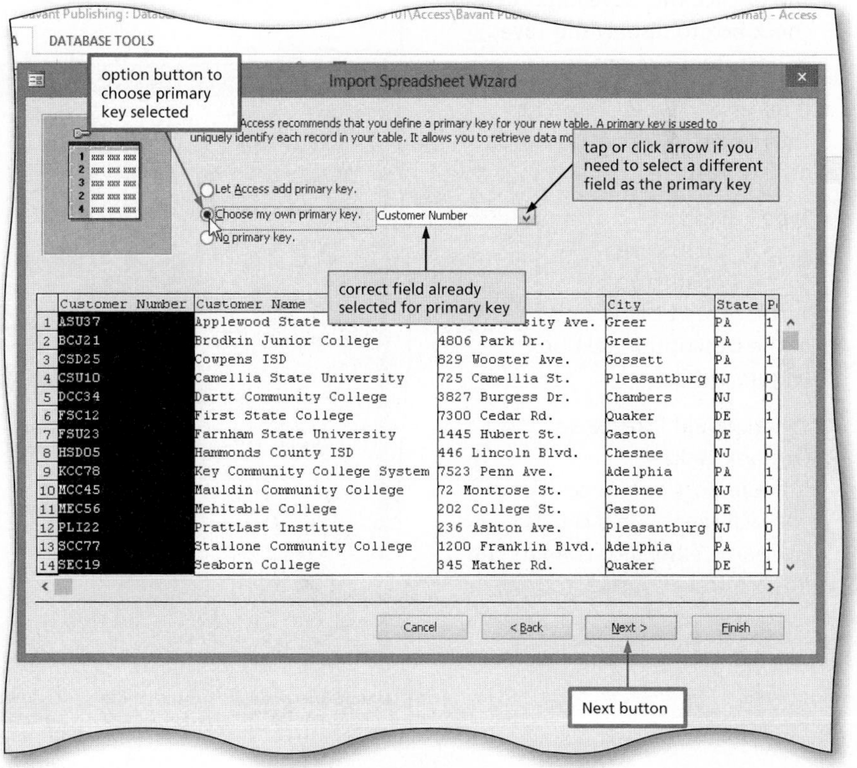

Figure 1–47

7

- Because the Customer Number field, which is the correct field, is already selected as the primary key, tap or click the Next button.
- Use the DELETE or BACKSPACE keys as necessary to erase the current entry, and then type `Customer` in the Import to Table text box.
- Tap or click the Finish button to import the data (Figure 1–48).

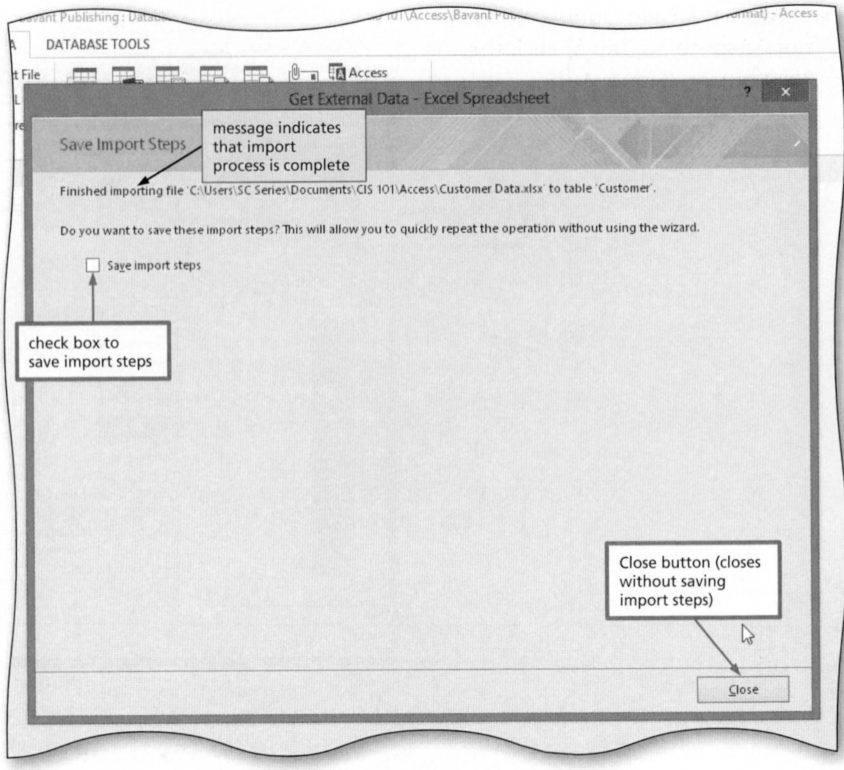

Figure 1–48

8

- Tap or click the 'Save import steps' check box to display the Save import steps options.
- If necessary, type `Import-Customer Data` in the Save as text box.
- Type `Import data from Customer Data workbook into Customer table` in the Description text box (Figure 1–49).

Q&A When would I create an Outlook task?
If the import operation is one you will repeat on a regular basis, you can create and schedule the import process just as you can schedule any other Outlook task.

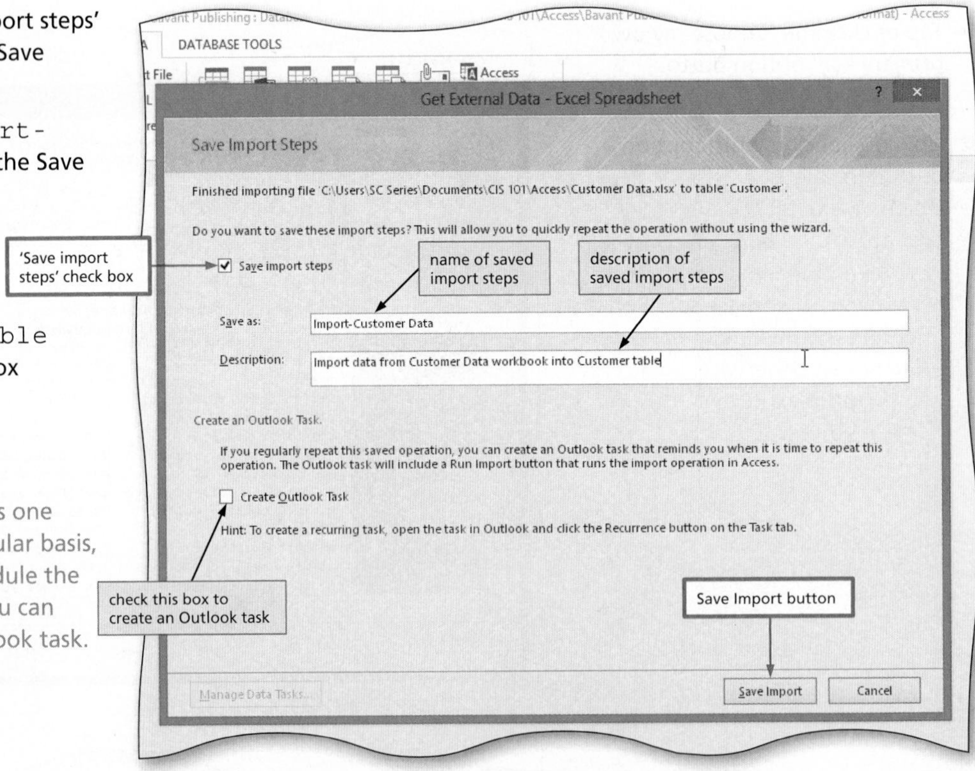

Figure 1–49

9

- Tap or click the Save Import button to save the import steps (Figure 1–50).

Q&A I saved the table as Customer Data. How can I change the name?
Press and hold or right-click the table name in the Navigation Pane. Click Rename on the shortcut menu and change the table name to Customer.

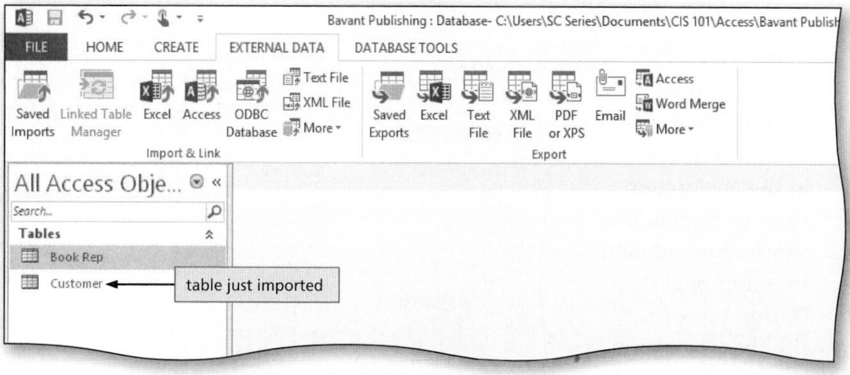

Figure 1–50

Modifying the Table

The import process has created the Customer table. The table has the correct fields and records. There are some details the process cannot handle, however. These include field sizes, descriptions, and captions. You will use Design view to make the necessary changes. The information you need is shown in Table 1–5.

BTW
Creating a Table in Design View
To create a table in Design view, display the CREATE tab, and then tap or click the Table Design button (CREATE tab | Tables group). You will then see the same screen as in Figure 1–51 on the following page, except that there will be no entries. Make all the necessary entries for the fields in your table, save the table, and assign the table a name.

Table 1–5 Structure of Customer Table

Field Name	Data Type	Field Size	Notes
Customer Number	Short Text	5	Primary Key **Description:** Customer Number (three uppercase letters followed by 2-digit number) **Caption:** CU #
Customer Name	Short Text	30	
Street	Short Text	20	
City	Short Text	20	
State	Short Text	2	
Postal Code	Short Text	5	
Amount Paid	Currency		
Current Due	Currency		
Returns	Currency		
Book Rep Number	Short Text	2	**Description:** Book Rep Number (number of book rep for customer) **Caption:** BR #

To Modify a Table in Design View

1 CREATE FIRST TABLE | 2 ADD RECORDS | 3 PRINT CONTENTS | 4 IMPORT RECORDS | 5 MODIFY SECOND TABLE
6 CREATE QUERY | 7 CREATE FORM | 8 CREATE REPORT

You will usually need to modify the design of a table created during the import process. ***Why?*** *Some properties of a table are not specified during the import process, such as descriptions, captions, and field sizes. You also might need to change a data type.* The steps on the next page make the necessary modifications to the design of the Customer table.

1

- Open the Navigation Pane, if necessary.
- Press and hold or right-click the Customer table in the Navigation Pane to display the shortcut menu, and then tap or click Design View on the shortcut menu to open the table in Design view (Figure 1–51).

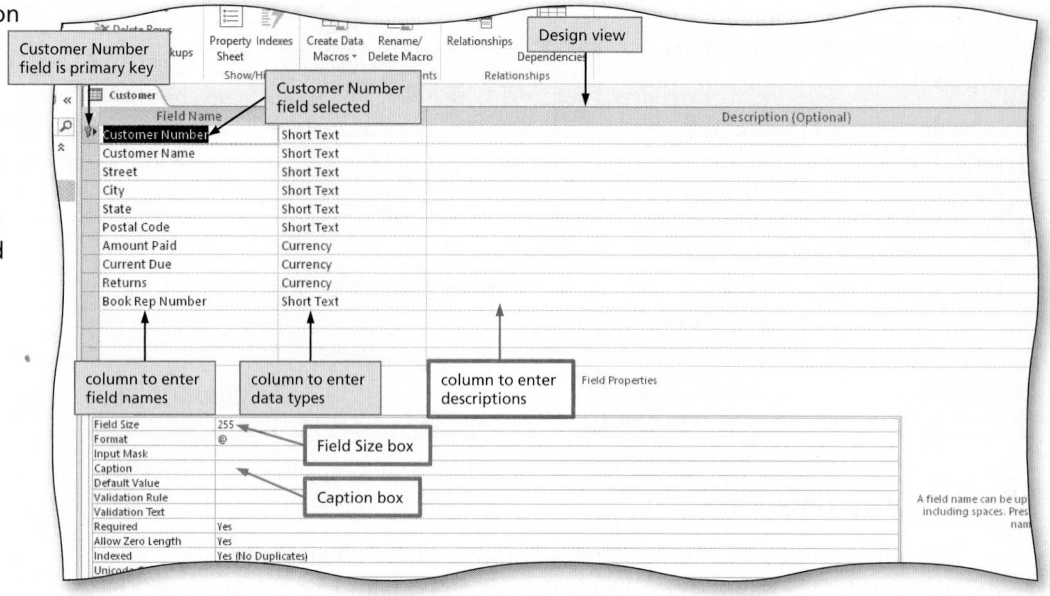

Figure 1–51

2

- Tap or click the Description (Optional) box for the Customer Number field, and then type `Customer Number (three uppercase letters followed by 2-digit number)` as the description.
- With the Customer Number field selected, tap or click the Field Size box, erase the current field size, and type `5` as the new field size.
- Tap or click the Caption box, and type `CU #` as the caption (Figure 1–52).

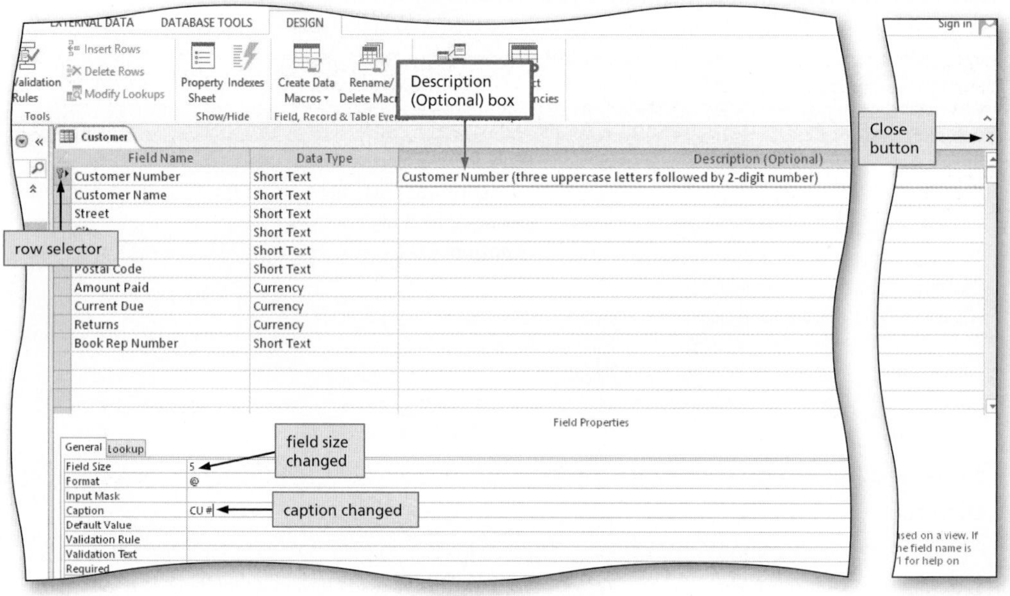

Figure 1–52

3

- Make the other changes shown in Table 1–5 on the previous page. To select a field to be changed, tap or click the field's row selector. For most fields, you only need to change the field size. For the Book Rep Number field, you also need to change the description and caption.
- Tap or click the Save button on the Quick Access Toolbar to save your changes.
- Because you know the data will satisfy the new field sizes, click the Yes button when given a message about the possibility of data loss.

Other Ways

1. Press F6 to move between upper and lower panes in Table Design window

Correcting Errors in the Structure

Whenever you create or modify a table in Design view, you should check the entries carefully to ensure they are correct. If you make a mistake and discover it before you press the TAB key, you can correct the error by repeatedly pressing the BACKSPACE key until the incorrect characters are removed. Then, type the correct characters. If you do not discover a mistake until later, you can tap or click the entry, type the correct value, and then press the ENTER key. You can use the following techniques to make changes to the structure:

- If you accidentally add an extra field to the structure, select the field by tapping or clicking the row selector (the leftmost column on the row that contains the field to be deleted). Once you have selected the field, press the DELETE key. This will remove the field from the structure.
- If you forget to include a field, select the field that will follow the one you want to add by tapping or clicking the row selector, and then press the INSERT key. The remaining fields move down one row, making room for the missing field. Make the entries for the new field in the usual manner.
- If you made the wrong field a primary key field, tap or click the correct primary key entry for the field and then tap or click the Primary Key button (TABLE TOOLS DESIGN tab | Tools group).
- To move a field, tap or click the row selector for the field to be moved to select the field, and then drag the field to the desired position.

As an alternative to these steps, you may want to start over. To do so, tap or click the Close button for the window containing the table, and then tap or click the No button in the Microsoft Access dialog box. You then can repeat the process you used earlier to define the fields in the table.

BTW

Importing Data to an Existing Table

When you create a new table in Design view, you can import data from other sources into the table using the EXTERNAL DATA tab.

To Close the Table

Now that you have completed and saved the Customer table, you can close it. The following step closes the table.

1. Tap or click the Close button for the Customer table (see Figure 1–52) to close the table.

To Resize Columns in a Datasheet

You can resize the columns in the datasheet for the Customer table just as you resized the columns in the datasheet for the Book Rep table. The following steps resize the columns in the Customer table to best fit the data.

1. Open the Customer table in Datasheet view.
2. Double-tap or double-click the right boundary of the field selectors of each of the fields to resize the columns so that they best fit the data.
3. Save the changes to the layout by tapping or clicking the Save button on the Quick Access Toolbar.
4. Close the table.

BTW

Resizing Columns

To resize all columns in a datasheet to best fit simultaneously, select the column heading for the first column, hold down the SHIFT key and select the last column in the datasheet. Then, double-tap or double-click the right boundary of any field selector.

Break Point: If you wish to take a break, this is a good place to do so. You can exit Access now. To resume at a later time, run Access, open the database called Bavant Publishing, and continue following the steps from this location forward.

Additional Database Objects

BTW
Tabbed Documents Versus Overlapping Windows
By default, Access 2013 displays database objects in tabbed documents instead of in overlapping windows. If your database is in overlapping windows mode, tap or click FILE on the ribbon, tap or click Options in the Backstage view, tap or click Current Database in the Access Options dialog box, and select the Display Document Tabs check box and the Tabbed Documents option button.

A database contains many types of objects. Tables are the objects you use to store and manipulate data. Access supports other important types of objects as well; each object has a specific purpose that helps maximize the benefits of a database. Through queries (questions), Access makes it possible to ask complex questions concerning the data in the database and then receive instant answers. Access also allows the user to produce attractive and useful forms for viewing and updating data. Additionally, Access includes report creation tools that make it easy to produce sophisticated reports for presenting data.

Creating Queries

Queries are simply questions, the answers to which are in the database. Access contains a powerful query feature that helps you find the answers to a wide variety of questions. Once you have examined the question you want to ask to determine the fields involved in the question, you can begin creating the query. If the query involves no special sort order, restrictions, or calculations, you can use the Simple Query Wizard.

To Use the Simple Query Wizard to Create a Query

1 CREATE FIRST TABLE | 2 ADD RECORDS | 3 PRINT CONTENTS | 4 IMPORT RECORDS | 5 MODIFY SECOND TABLE
6 CREATE QUERY | 7 CREATE FORM | 8 CREATE REPORT

The following steps use the Simple Query Wizard to create a query that Bavant Publishing might use to obtain financial information on its customers. ***Why?*** *The Simple Query Wizard is the quickest and easiest way to create a query.* This query displays the number, name, amount paid, current due, returns, and book rep number of all customers.

1

- If the Navigation Pane is closed, tap or click the Shutter Bar Open/Close Button to open the Navigation Pane.
- Be sure the Customer table is selected.
- Tap or click CREATE on the ribbon to display the CREATE tab.
- Tap or click the Query Wizard button (CREATE tab | Queries group) to display the New Query dialog box (Figure 1–53).

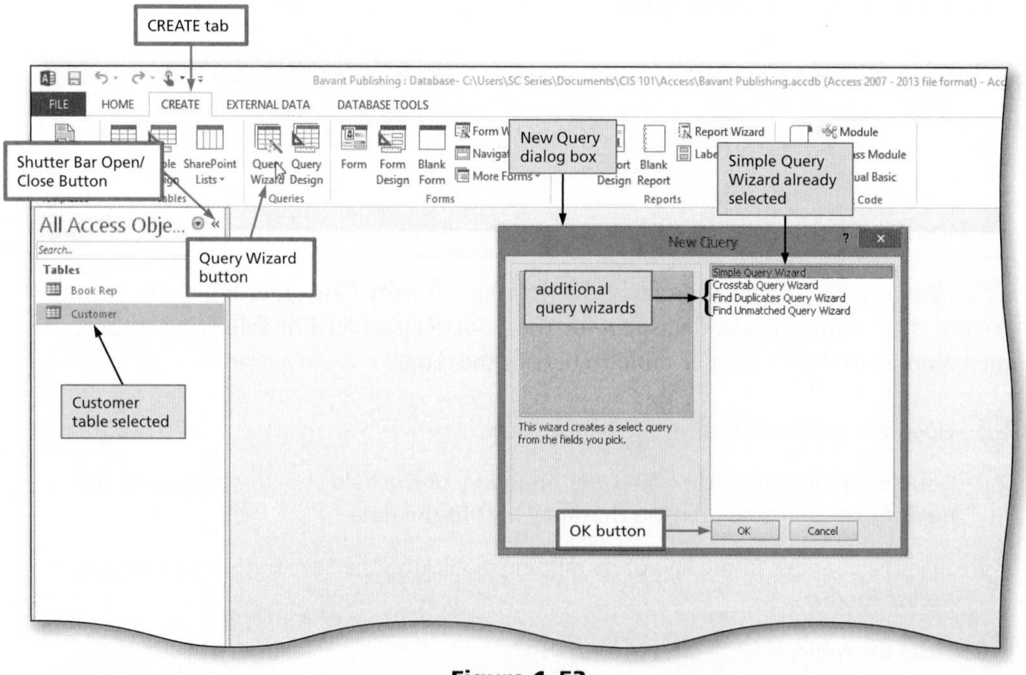

Figure 1–53

2

- Be sure Simple Query Wizard is selected, and then tap or click the OK button (New Query dialog box) to display the Simple Query Wizard dialog box (Figure 1–54).

Q&A What would happen if the Book Rep table were selected instead of the Customer table?
The list of available fields would contain fields from the Book Rep table rather than the Customer table.

If the list contained Book Rep table fields, how could I make it contain Customer table fields?
Tap or click the arrow in the Tables / Queries box, and then tap or click the Customer table in the list that appears.

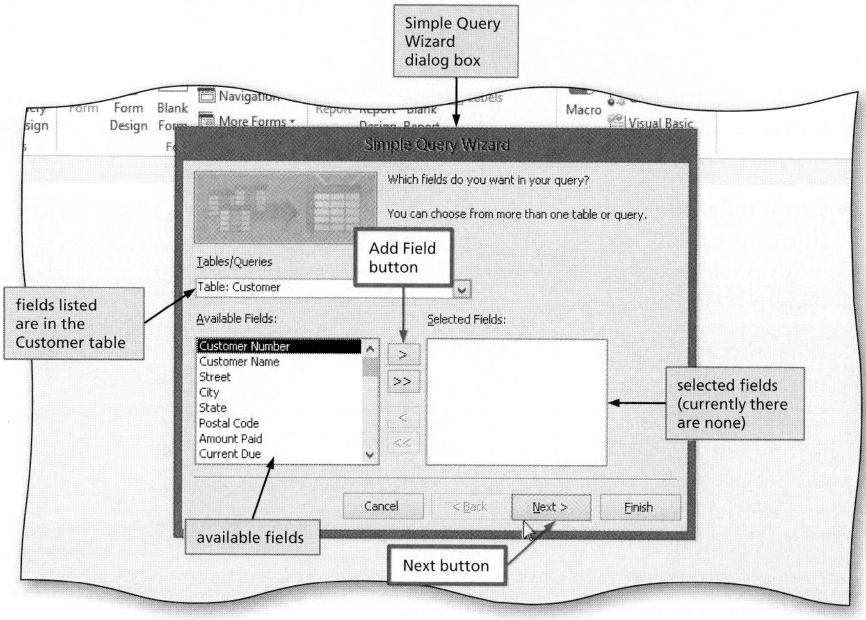

Figure 1–54

3

- With the Customer Number field selected, tap or click the Add Field button to add the field to the query.
- With the Customer Name field selected, tap or click the Add Field button a second time to add the field.
- Tap or click the Amount Paid field, and then tap or click the Add Field button to add the field.
- In a similar fashion, add the Current Due, Returns, and Book Rep Number fields (Figure 1–55).

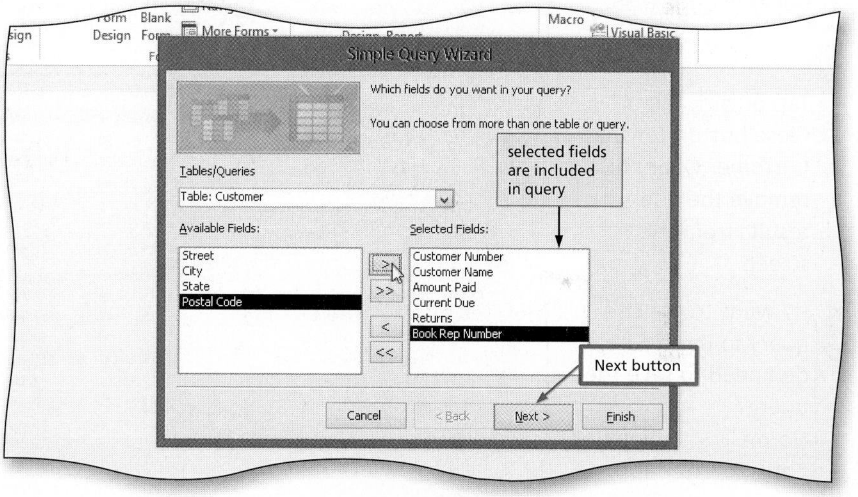

Figure 1–55

4

- Tap or click the Next button to move to the next screen.
- Ensure that the Detail (shows every field of every record) option button is selected (Figure 1–56).

Q&A What is the difference between Detail and Summary?
Detail shows all the records and fields. Summary only shows computations (for example, the total amount paid).

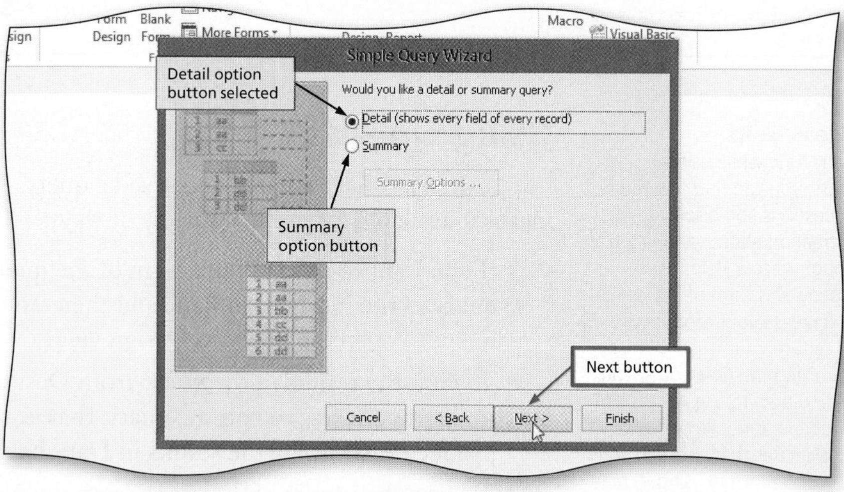

Figure 1–56

5

- Tap or click the Next button to move to the next screen.
- Confirm that the title of the query is Customer Query (Figure 1–57).

Q&A What should I do if the title is incorrect?
Click the box containing the title to produce an insertion point. Erase the current title and then type Customer Query.

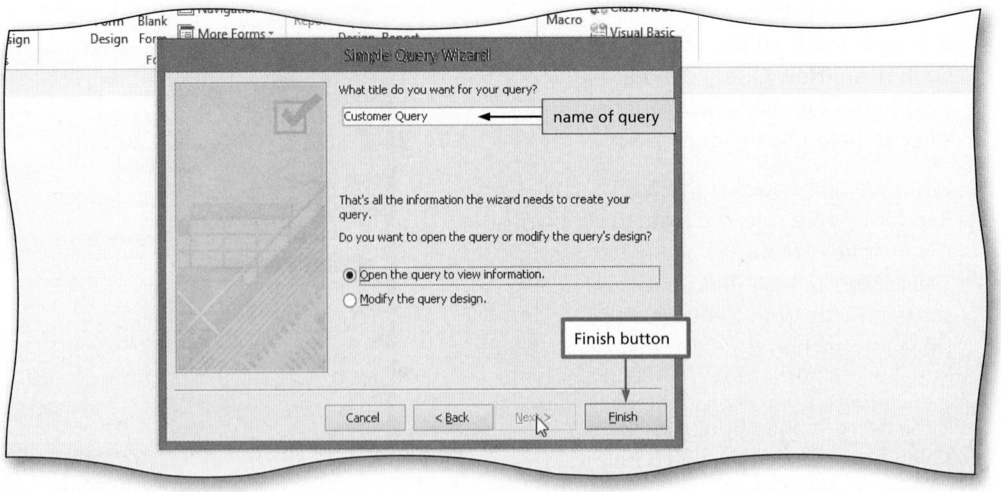

Figure 1–57

6

- Tap or click the Finish button to create the query (Figure 1–58).

7

- Tap or click the Close button for the Customer Query to remove the query results from the screen.

Q&A If I want to use this query in the future, do I need to save the query?
Normally you would. The one exception is a query created by the wizard. The wizard automatically saves the query it creates.

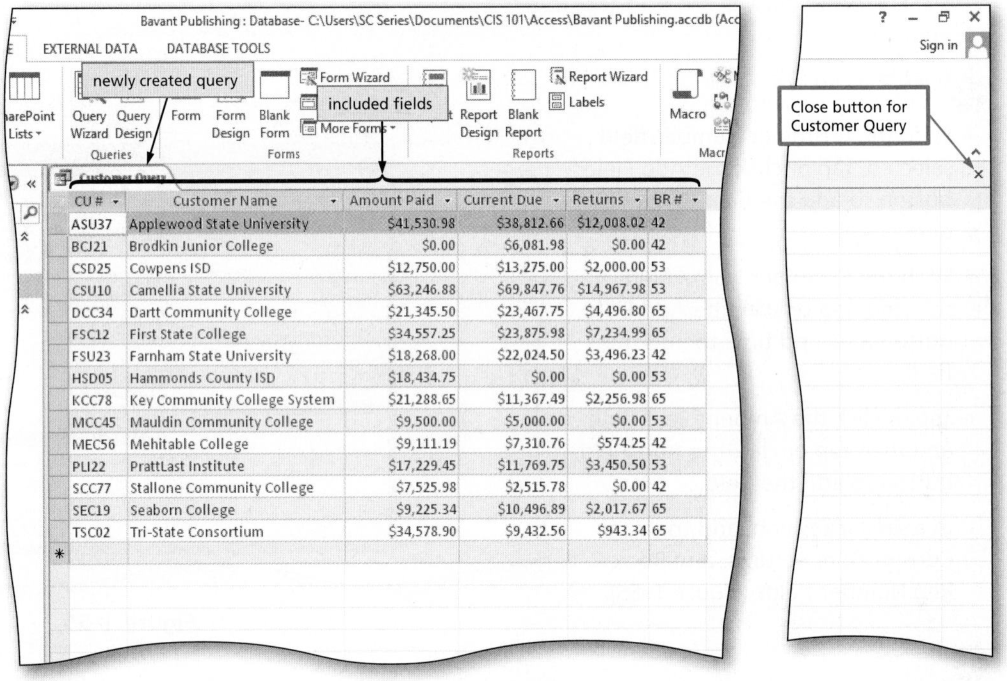

Figure 1–58

BTW
Access Help
At any time while using Access, you can find answers to questions and display information about various topics through Access Help. Used properly, this form of assistance can increase your productivity and reduce your frustrations by minimizing the time you spend learning how to use Access. For instruction about Access Help and exercises that will help you gain confidence in using it, read the Office and Windows chapter at the beginning of this book.

Using Queries

After you have created and saved a query, Access stores it as a database object and makes it available for use in a variety of ways:

- If you want to change the design of the query, press and hold or right-click the query in the Navigation Pane and then tap or click Design View on the shortcut menu to open the query in Design view.
- To view the results of the query from Design view, tap or click the Run button to instruct Access to **run** the query, that is, to perform the necessary actions to produce and display the results in Datasheet view.
- To view the results of the query from the Navigation Pane, open it by pressing and holding or right-clicking the query and tapping or clicking Open on the

shortcut menu. Access automatically runs the query and displays the results in Datasheet view.

- To print the results with the query open in either Design view or Datasheet view, tap or click FILE on the ribbon, tap or click the Print tab, and then tap or click either Print or Quick Print.
- To print the query without first opening it, be sure the query is selected in the Navigation Pane and tap or click FILE on the ribbon, tap or click the Print tab, and then tap or click either Print or Quick Print.

You can switch between views of a query using the View button (HOME tab | Views group). Tapping or clicking the arrow in the bottom of the button produces the View button menu. You then tap or click the desired view in the menu. The two query views you will use in this chapter are Datasheet view (which displays the query results) and Design view (for changing the query design). You also can tap or click the top part of the View button, in which case, you will switch to the view identified by the icon on the button. In the figure, the button contains the icon for Design view, so tapping or clicking the button would change to Design view. For the most part, the icon on the button represents the view you want, so you can usually simply tap or click the button.

BTW
Creating Queries
Although the Simple Query Wizard is a convenient way to create straightforward queries, you will find that many of the queries you create require more control than the wizard provides. In Chapter 2, you will use Design view to create customized queries.

To Use a Criterion in a Query

1 CREATE FIRST TABLE | 2 ADD RECORDS | 3 PRINT CONTENTS | 4 IMPORT RECORDS | 5 MODIFY SECOND TABLE
6 CREATE QUERY | 7 CREATE FORM | 8 CREATE REPORT

After you have determined the fields to be included in a query, you will determine whether you need to further restrict the results of the query. For example, you might want to include only those customers whose book rep number is 53. In such a case, you need to enter the number 53 as a criterion for the book rep field. ***Why?*** *A criterion is a condition that the records must satisfy in order to be included in the query results.* To do so, you will open the query in Design view, enter the criterion below the appropriate field, and then view the results of the query. The following steps enter a criterion to include only the customers of book rep 53 and then view the query results.

1

- Press and hold or right-click the Customer Query in the Navigation Pane to produce a shortcut menu (Figure 1–59).

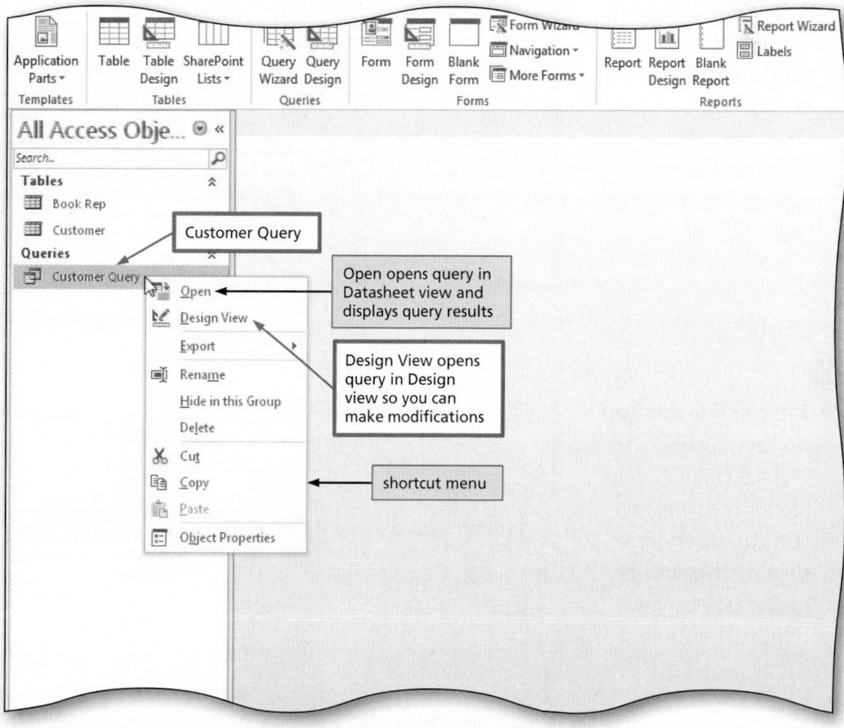

Figure 1–59

2

- Tap or click Design View on the shortcut menu to open the query in Design view (Figure 1–60).

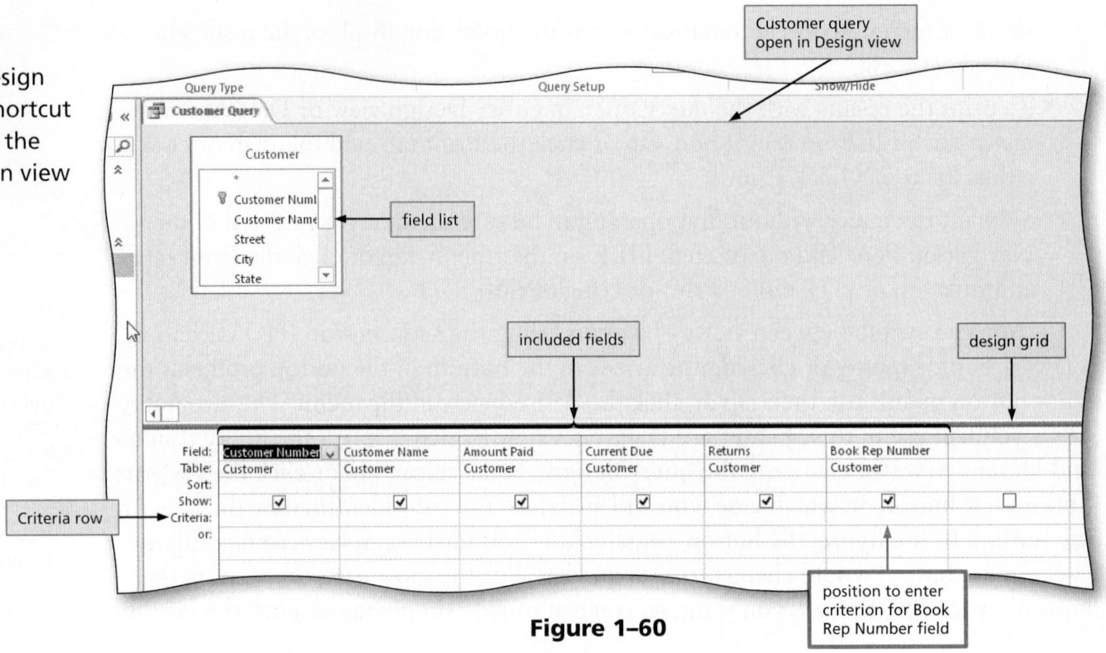

Figure 1–60

3

- Tap or click the Criteria row in the Book Rep Number column of the grid, and then type 53 as the criterion (Figure 1–61).

Q&A The Book Rep Number field is a text field. Do I need to enclose the value for a text field in quotation marks?
You could, but it is not necessary, because Access inserts the quotation marks for you automatically.

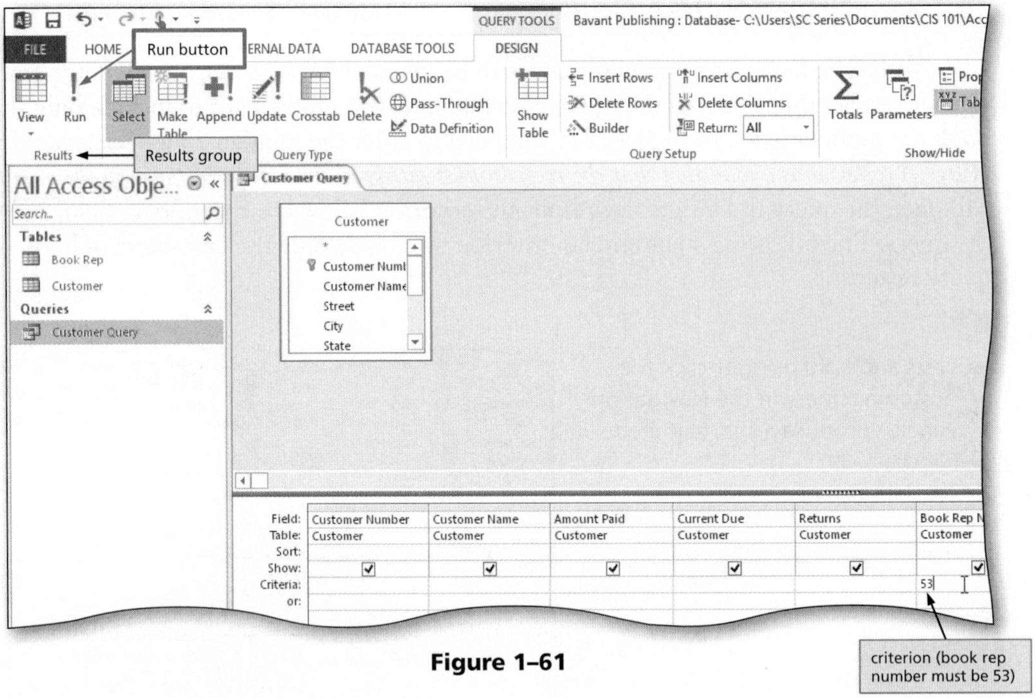

Figure 1–61

4

- Tap or click the Run button (QUERY TOOLS DESIGN tab | Results group) to run the query and display the results in Datasheet view (Figure 1–62).

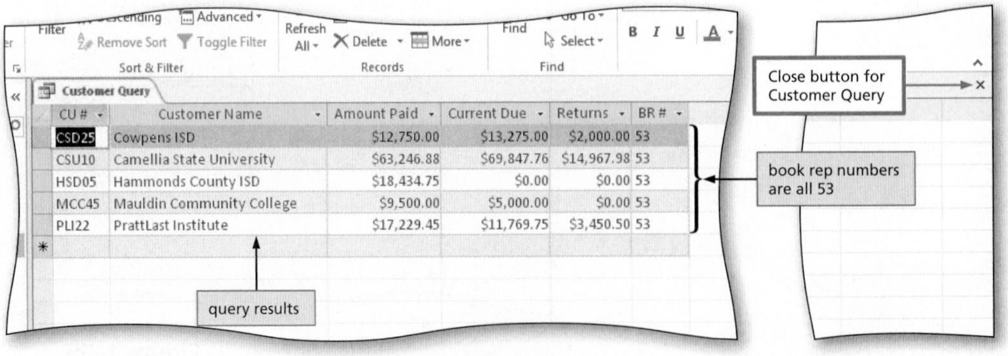

Figure 1–62

5

- Tap or click the Close button for the Customer Query to close the query.
- When asked if you want to save your changes, tap or click the No button.

Q&A If I saved the query, what would happen the next time I ran the query?
You would see only customers of book rep 53.

Could I save a query with another name?
Yes. To save a query with a different name, tap or click FILE on the ribbon, tap or click the Save As tab, tap or click Save Object As, tap or click the Save As button, enter a new file name in the Save As dialog box, and then tap or click the OK button (Save As dialog box).

Other Ways

1. Tap or click View button (QUERY TOOLS DESIGN tab | Results group)
2. Tap or click Datasheet View button on status bar

To Print the Results of a Query

The following steps print the results of a saved query.

1. With the Customer Query selected in the Navigation Pane, tap or click FILE on the ribbon to open the Backstage view.
2. Tap or click the Print tab in the Backstage view to display the Print gallery.
3. Tap or click the Quick Print button to print the query.

Creating and Using Forms

In Datasheet view, you can view many records at once. If there are many fields, however, only some of the fields in each record might be visible at a time. In **Form view**, where data is displayed in a form on the screen, you usually can see all the fields, but only for one record.

To Create a Form

1 CREATE FIRST TABLE | 2 ADD RECORDS | 3 PRINT CONTENTS | 4 IMPORT RECORDS | 5 MODIFY SECOND TABLE
6 CREATE QUERY | **7 CREATE FORM** | **8 CREATE REPORT**

Like a paper form, a **form** in a database is a formatted document with fields that contain data. Forms allow you to view and maintain data. Forms also can be used to print data, but reports are more commonly used for that purpose. The simplest type of form in Access is one that includes all the fields in a table stacked one above the other. The following steps use the Form button to create a form. ***Why?*** *Using the Form button is the simplest way to create this type of form.* The steps then use the form to view records and then save the form.

1

- Select the Customer table in the Navigation Pane.
- If necessary, tap or click CREATE on the ribbon to display the CREATE tab (Figure 1–63).

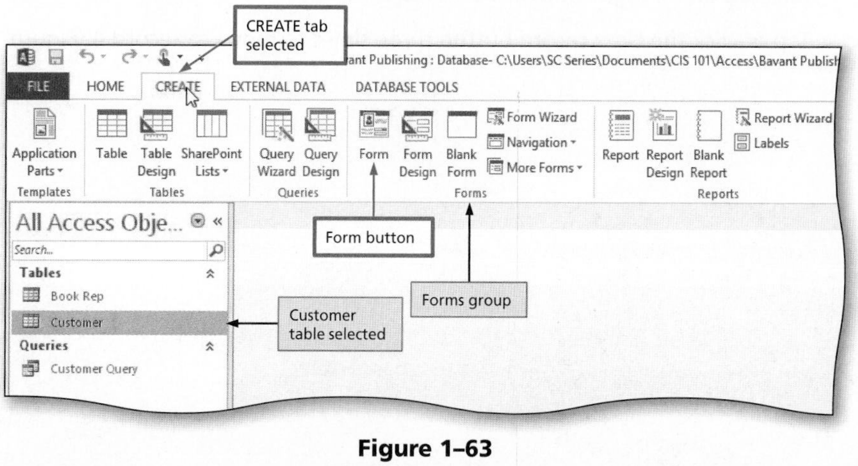

Figure 1–63

2

- Tap or click the Form button (CREATE tab | Forms group) to create a simple form (Figure 1–64).

Q&A A Field list appeared on my screen. What should I do?
Tap or click the Add Existing Fields button (FORM LAYOUT TOOLS DESIGN tab | Tools group) to remove the Field list from the screen.

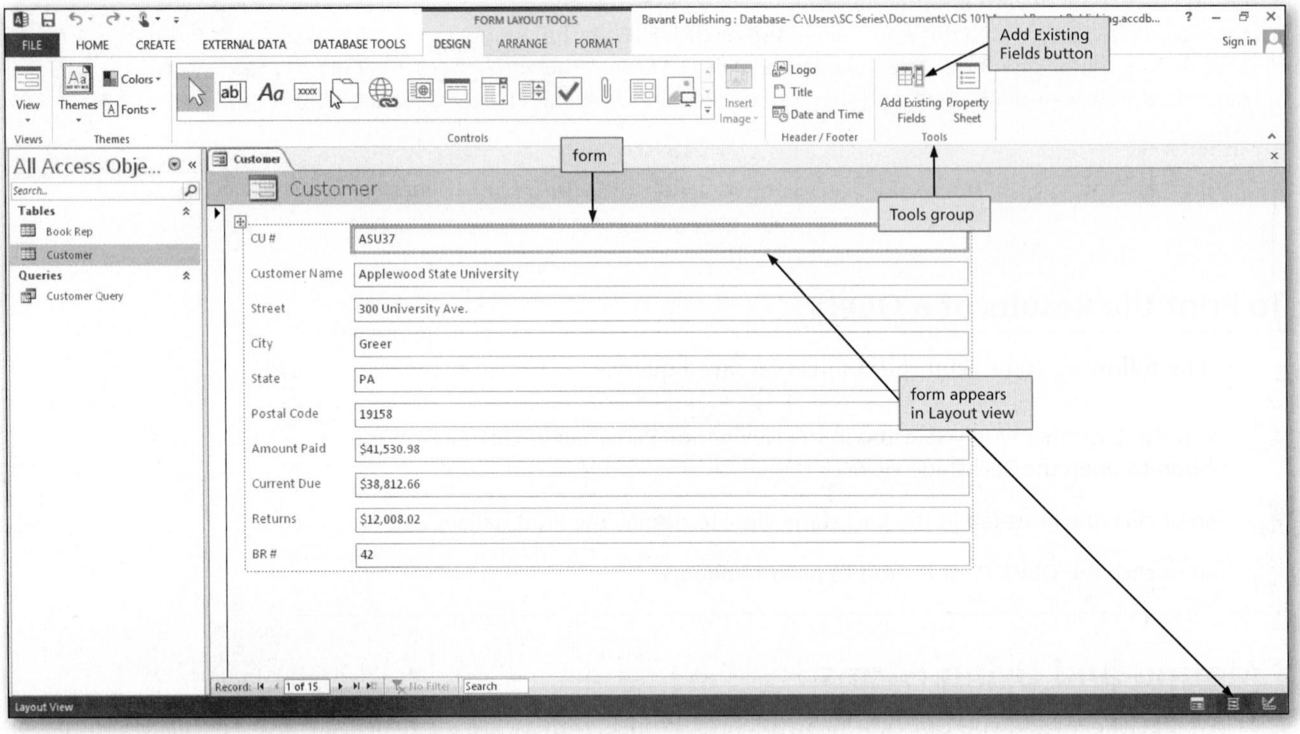

Figure 1–64

3

- Tap or click the Form View button on the Access status bar to display the form in Form view rather than Layout view.

Q&A What is the difference between Layout view and Form view?
Layout view allows you to make changes to the look of the form. Form view is the view you use to examine or make changes to the data.

How can I tell when I am in Layout view?
Access identifies Layout view in three ways. The left side of the status bar will contain the words Layout View; shading will appear around the outside of the selected field in the form; and the Layout View button will be selected on the right side of the status bar.

- Tap or click the Next record button three times to move to record 4 (Figure 1–65).

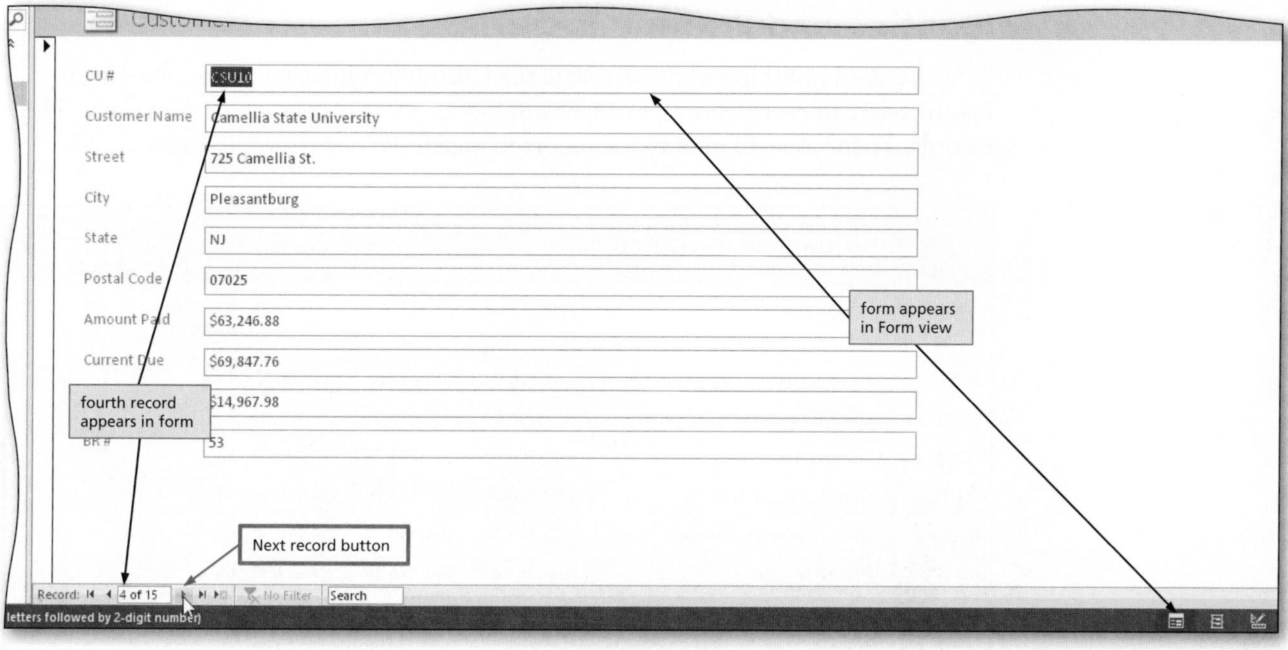

Figure 1–65

4

- Tap or click the Save button on the Quick Access Toolbar to display the Save As dialog box (Figure 1–66).

Q&A Do I have to tap or click the Next record button before saving?

No. The only reason you were asked to tap or click the button was so that you could experience navigation within the form.

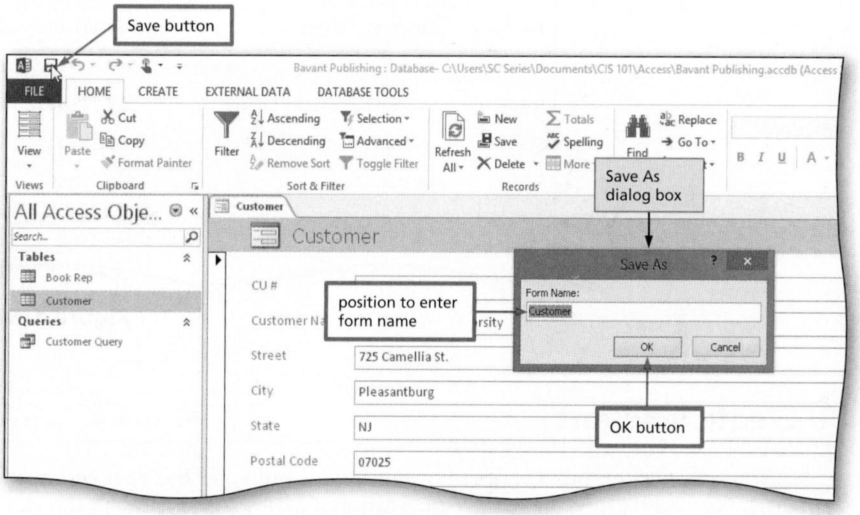

5

- Type `Customer Form` as the form name, and then tap or click the OK button to save the form.

Figure 1–66

- Tap or click the Close button for the form to close the form.

Other Ways

1. Tap or click View button (FORM LAYOUT TOOLS DESIGN tab | Views group)

Using a Form

After you have saved a form, you can use it at any time by pressing and holding or right-clicking the form in the Navigation Pane and then tapping or clicking Open on the shortcut menu. In addition to viewing data in the form, you also can use it to enter or update data, a process that is very similar to updating data using a datasheet. If you plan to use the form to enter or revise data, you must ensure you are viewing the form in Form view.

Break Point: If you wish to take a break, this is a good place to do so. You can exit Access now. To resume at a later time, run Access, open the database called Bavant Publishing, and continue following the steps from this location forward.

Creating and Printing Reports

Bavant Publishing wants to create the Customer Financial Report shown in Figure 1–67. To create this report, you will first create a simple report containing all records. Then, you will modify the report to match the one shown in Figure 1–67.

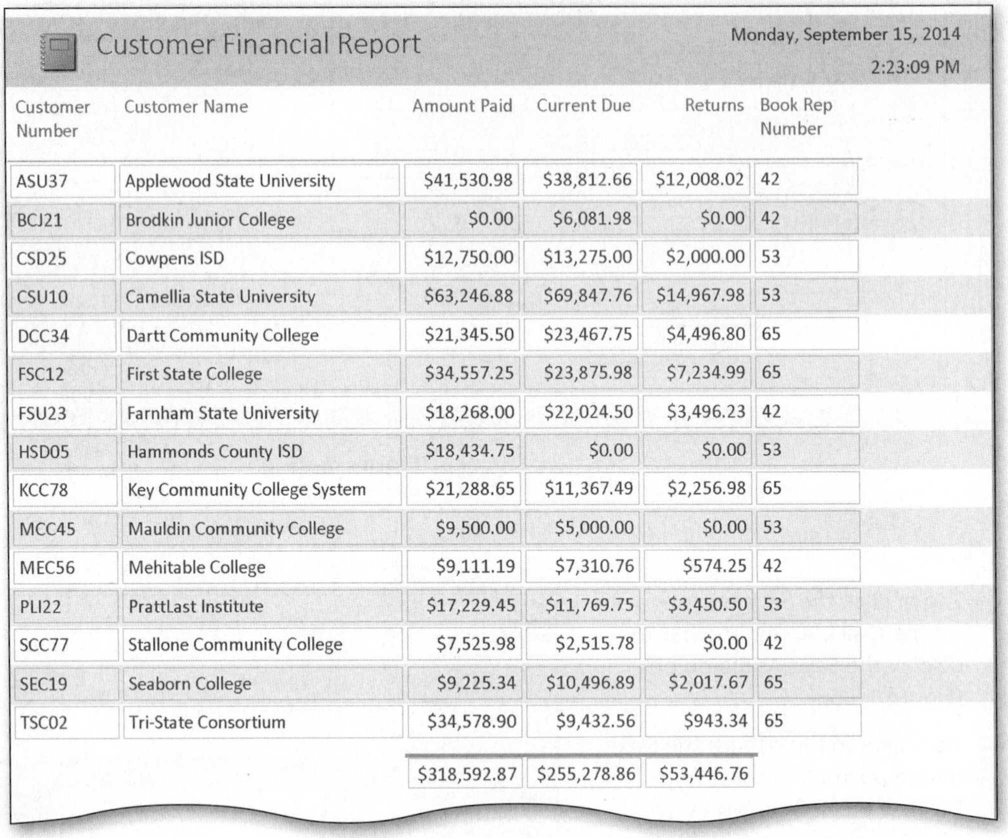

Customer Financial Report

Monday, September 15, 2014
2:23:09 PM

Customer Number	Customer Name	Amount Paid	Current Due	Returns	Book Rep Number
ASU37	Applewood State University	$41,530.98	$38,812.66	$12,008.02	42
BCJ21	Brodkin Junior College	$0.00	$6,081.98	$0.00	42
CSD25	Cowpens ISD	$12,750.00	$13,275.00	$2,000.00	53
CSU10	Camellia State University	$63,246.88	$69,847.76	$14,967.98	53
DCC34	Dartt Community College	$21,345.50	$23,467.75	$4,496.80	65
FSC12	First State College	$34,557.25	$23,875.98	$7,234.99	65
FSU23	Farnham State University	$18,268.00	$22,024.50	$3,496.23	42
HSD05	Hammonds County ISD	$18,434.75	$0.00	$0.00	53
KCC78	Key Community College System	$21,288.65	$11,367.49	$2,256.98	65
MCC45	Mauldin Community College	$9,500.00	$5,000.00	$0.00	53
MEC56	Mehitable College	$9,111.19	$7,310.76	$574.25	42
PLI22	PrattLast Institute	$17,229.45	$11,769.75	$3,450.50	53
SCC77	Stallone Community College	$7,525.98	$2,515.78	$0.00	42
SEC19	Seaborn College	$9,225.34	$10,496.89	$2,017.67	65
TSC02	Tri-State Consortium	$34,578.90	$9,432.56	$943.34	65
		$318,592.87	$255,278.86	$53,446.76	

Figure 1–67

To Create a Report

1 CREATE FIRST TABLE | 2 ADD RECORDS | 3 PRINT CONTENTS | 4 IMPORT RECORDS | 5 MODIFY SECOND TABLE
6 CREATE QUERY | 7 CREATE FORM | **8 CREATE REPORT**

You will first create a report containing all fields. ***Why?*** *It is easiest to create a report with all the fields and then delete the fields you do not want.* The following steps create and save the initial report. They also modify the report title.

1

- Be sure the Customer table is selected in the Navigation Pane.
- Tap or click CREATE on the ribbon to display the CREATE tab (Figure 1–68).

Q&A Do I need to select the Customer table prior to tapping or clicking CREATE on the ribbon?
You do not need to select the table at that point. You do need to select a table prior to tapping or clicking the Report button, because Access will include all the fields in whichever table or query is currently selected.

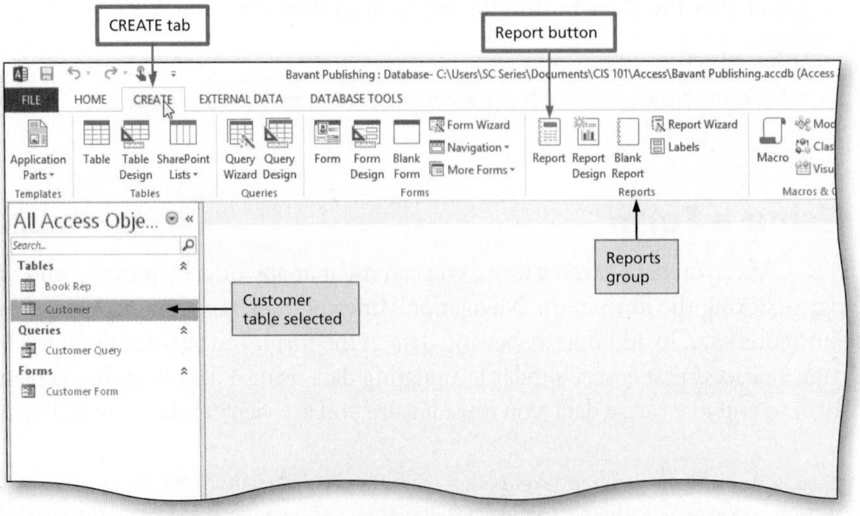

Figure 1–68

2

- Tap or click the Report button (CREATE tab | Reports group) to create the report (Figure 1–69).

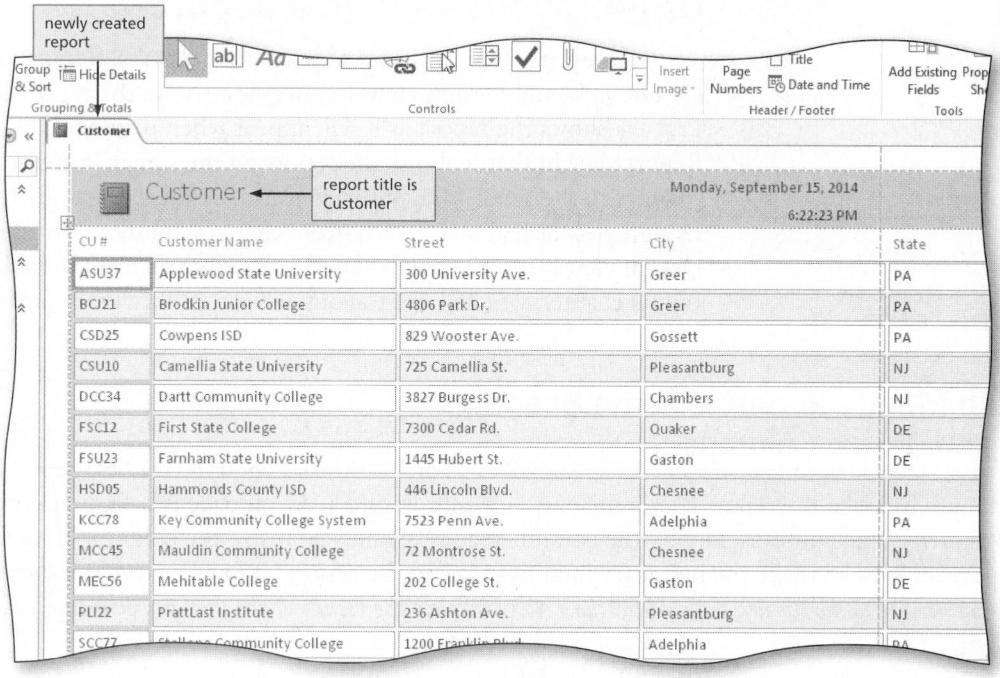

Figure 1–69

Q&A Why is the report title Customer?

Access automatically assigns the name of the table or query as the title of the report. It also automatically includes the date. You can change either of these later.

3

- Tap or click the Save button on the Quick Access Toolbar to display the Save As dialog box, and then type `Customer Financial Report` as the name of the report (Figure 1–70).

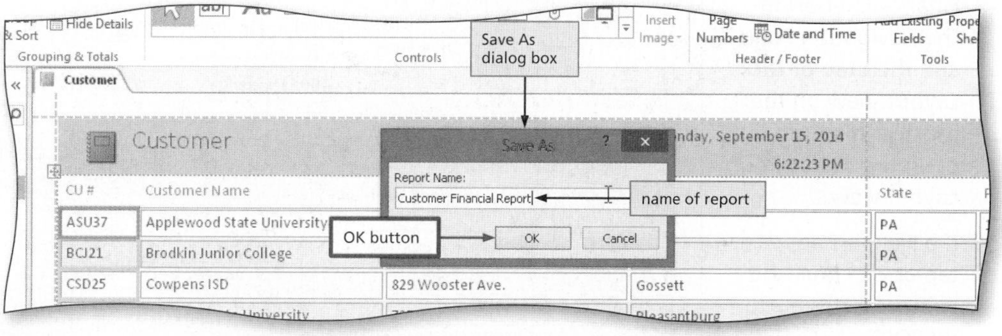

Figure 1–70

4

- Tap or click the OK button (Save As dialog box) to save the report (Figure 1–71).

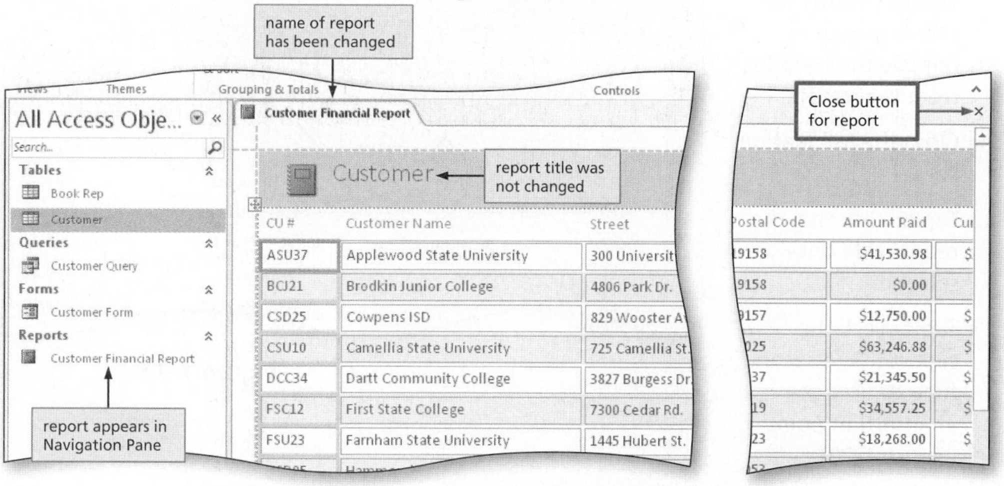

Figure 1–71

Q&A The name of the report changed. Why did the report title not change?

The report title is assigned the same name as the report by default. Changing the name of the report does not change the report title. You can change the title at any time to anything you like.

5

- Close the report by tapping or clicking its Close button.

Using Layout View in a Report

Access has four different ways to view reports: Report view, Print Preview, Layout view, and Design view. Report view shows the report on the screen. Print Preview shows the report as it will appear when printed. Layout view is similar to Report view in that it shows the report on the screen, but also allows you to make changes to the report. Layout view is usually the easiest way to make such changes. Design view also allows you to make changes, but does not show you the actual report. Design view is most useful when the changes you need to make are especially complex. In this chapter, you will use Layout view to modify the report.

To Modify Report Column Headings and Resize Columns

1 CREATE FIRST TABLE | 2 ADD RECORDS | 3 PRINT CONTENTS | 4 IMPORT RECORDS | 5 MODIFY SECOND TABLE
6 CREATE QUERY | 7 CREATE FORM | **8 CREATE REPORT**

To make the report match the one shown in Figure 1–67 on page AC 48, you need to change the title, remove some columns, modify the column headings, and also resize the columns. The following steps use Layout view to make the necessary modifications to the report. ***Why?*** *Working in Layout view gives you all the tools you need to make the desired modifications. You can view the results of the modifications immediately.*

1

- Press and hold or right-click Customer Financial Report in the Navigation Pane, and then tap or click Layout View on the shortcut menu to open the report in Layout view.
- If a Field list appears, tap or click the Add Existing Fields button (REPORT LAYOUT TOOLS DESIGN tab | Tools group) to remove the Field list from the screen.
- Close the Navigation Pane.
- Tap or click the report title once to select it.
- Tap or click the report title a second time to produce an insertion point (Figure 1–72).

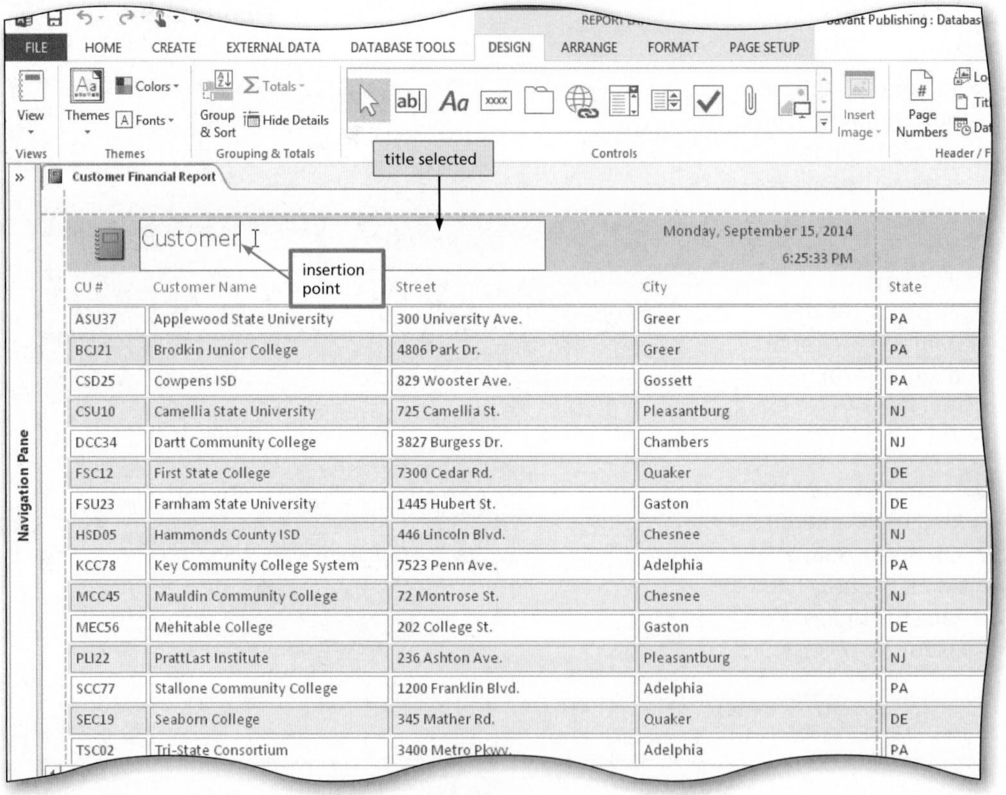

Figure 1–72

Q&A My insertion point is in the middle of Customer. How do I produce an insertion point at the position shown in the figure?

You can use the RIGHT ARROW key to move the insertion point to the position in the figure, or you can tap or click the desired position.

2

- Press the SPACEBAR to insert a space, and then type `Financial Report` to complete the title.
- Tap or click the column heading for the Street field to select it.
- Hold the SHIFT key down and then tap or click the column headings for the City, State, and Postal Code fields to select multiple column headings.

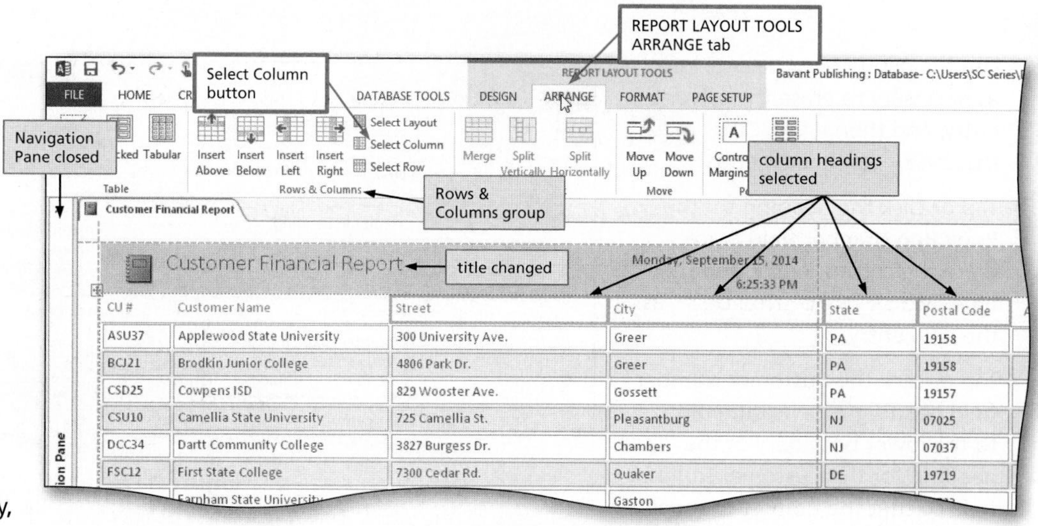

Figure 1–73

Q&A What happens if I do not hold down the SHIFT key?
When you tap or click another column heading, it will be the only one that is selected. To select multiple objects, you need to hold the SHIFT key down for every object after the first selection.

I selected the wrong collection of objects. What should I do?
You can tap or click somewhere else on the report so that the objects you want are not selected, and then begin the process again. Alternatively, you can repeatedly tap or click the Undo button on the Quick Access Toolbar to undo your selections. Once you have done so, you can select the objects you want.

- Tap or click ARRANGE on the ribbon to display the REPORT LAYOUT TOOLS ARRANGE tab (Figure 1–73).

3

- Tap or click the Select Column button (REPORT LAYOUT TOOLS ARRANGE tab | Rows & Columns group) to select the entire columns corresponding to the column headings you selected in the previous step.
- Press the DELETE key to delete the selected columns.
- Tap or click the column heading for the Customer Number field twice, once to select it and the second time to produce an insertion point (Figure 1–74).

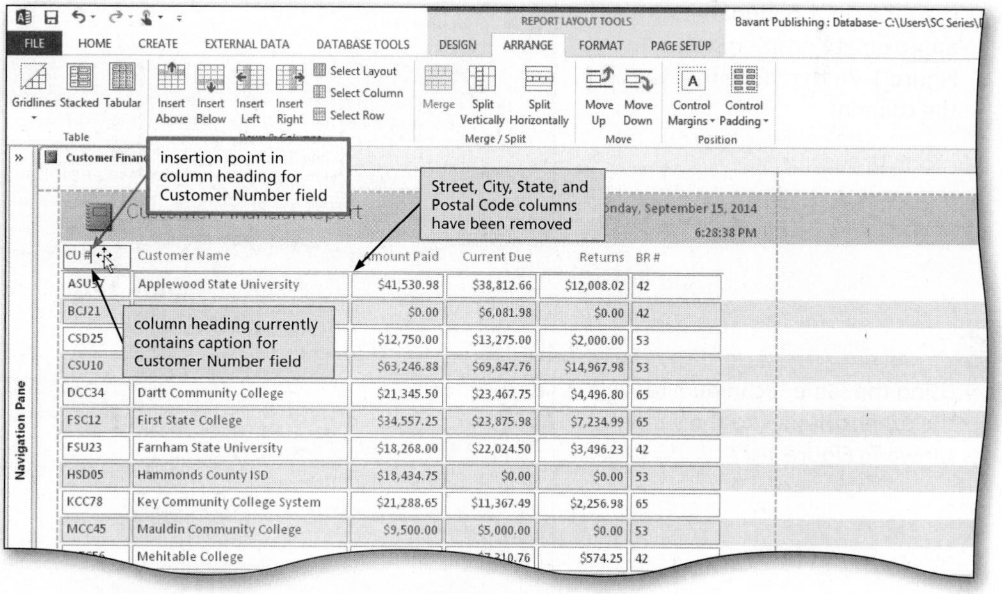

Figure 1–74

Q&A I selected the wrong field. What should I do?
Tap or click somewhere outside the various fields to deselect the one you have selected. Then, tap or click the Customer Number field twice.

4

- Use the DELETE or BACKSPACE keys as necessary to erase the current entry, and then type `Customer Number` as the new entry.
- Tap or click the heading for the Book Rep Number field twice, erase the current entry, and then type `Book Rep Number` as the new entry.
- Tap or click the Customer Number field heading to select it, point to the lower boundary of the heading for the Customer Number field so that the pointer changes to a two-headed arrow, and then drag the lower boundary to the approximate position shown in Figure 1–75 to expand the column headings.

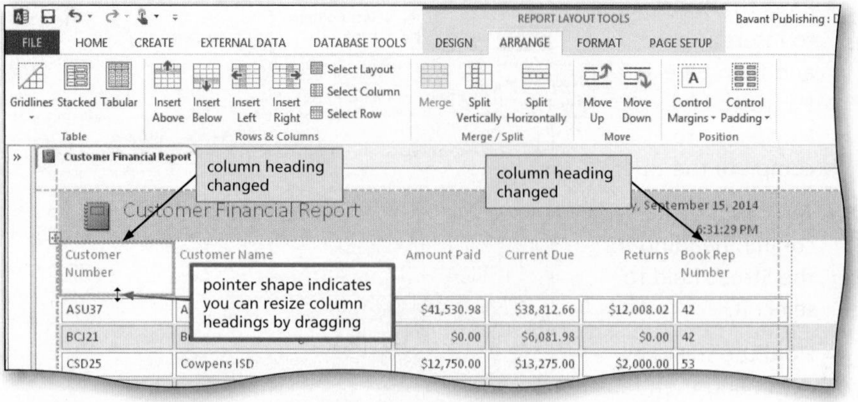

Figure 1–75

Q&A I did something wrong when I dragged and now my report looks strange. What should I do?
Tap or click the Undo button on the Quick Access Toolbar to undo the change. Depending on the specific action you took, you may need to tap or click it more than once.

My screen displays Book Rep Number on one line not two. Is this a problem?
No. You will adjust the column heading in a later step.

5

- Point to the right boundary of the heading for the Customer Number field so that the pointer changes to a two-headed arrow, and then drag the right boundary to the approximate position shown in Figure 1–76 to reduce the width of the column.

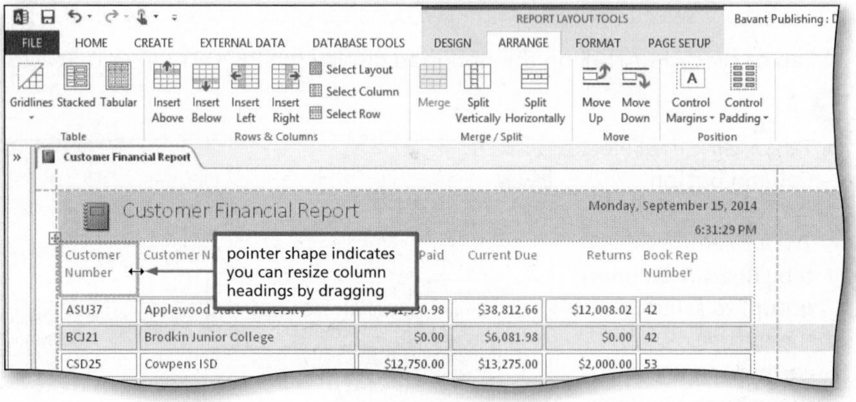

Figure 1–76

6

- Using the same technique, resize the other columns to the sizes shown in Figure 1–77.

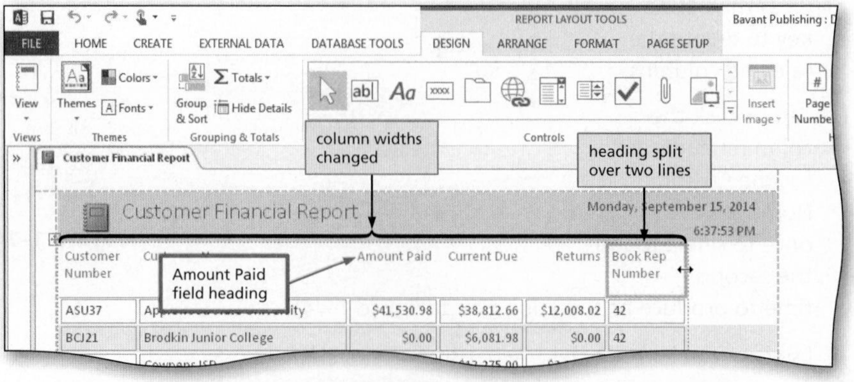

Figure 1–77

To Add Totals to a Report

The report in Figure 1–67 contains totals for the Amount Paid, Current Due, and Returns columns. You can use Layout view to add these totals. The following steps use Layout view to include totals for these three columns. ***Why?*** *In Layout view you can tap or click a single button to add totals. This button sums all the values in the field.*

1

- Tap or click the Amount Paid field heading (shown in Figure 1–77) to select the field.

Q&A Do I have to tap or click the heading? Could I tap or click the field on one of the records?
You do not have to tap or click the heading. You also could tap or click the Amount Paid field on any record.

- Tap or click DESIGN on the ribbon to display the DESIGN tab.
- Tap or click the Totals button (REPORT LAYOUT TOOLS DESIGN tab | Grouping & Totals group) to display the Totals menu containing a list of available calculations (Figure 1–78).

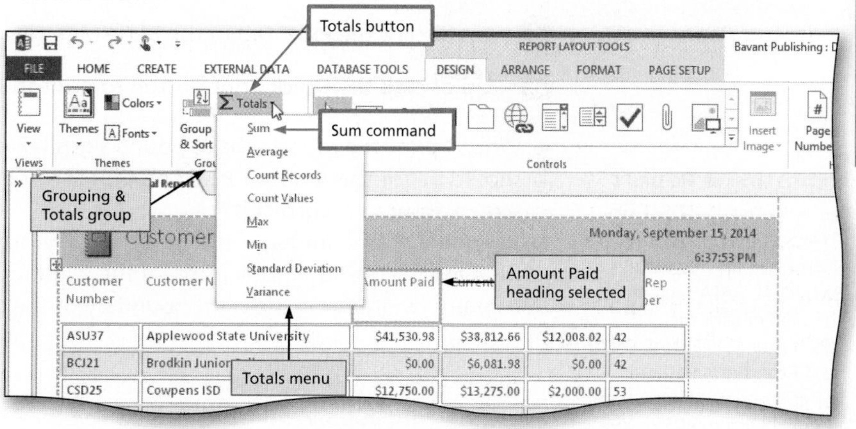

Figure 1–78

2

- Tap or click Sum to calculate the sum of the amount of paid values.
- Using the same technique, add totals for the Current Due and Returns columns.

Q&A When I clicked the Totals button after selecting the Returns field heading, Sum was already checked. Do I still need to tap or click Sum?
No. In fact, if you do tap or click it, you will remove the check mark, which will remove the total from the column.

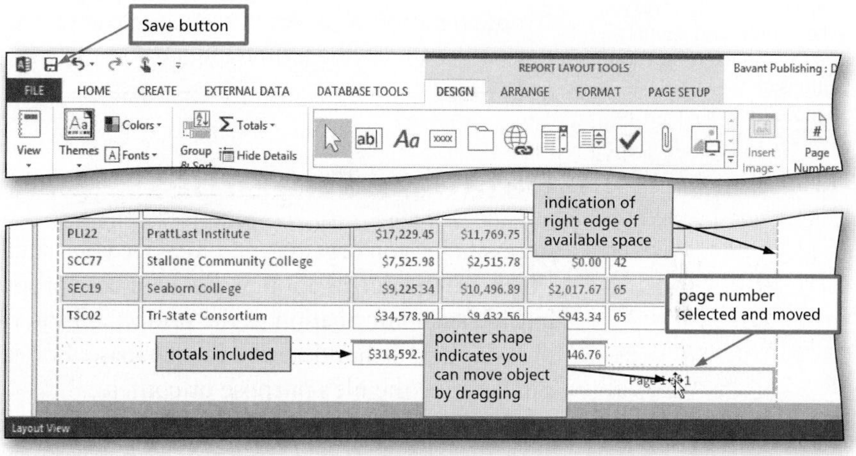

Figure 1–79

- Scroll down to the bottom of the report to verify that the totals are included. If necessary, expand the size of the total controls so they appear completely by dragging the lower boundary of the controls to the approximate position shown in Figure 1–79.
- Tap or click the page number to select it, and then drag it to the approximate position shown in Figure 1–79.

Q&A Why did I need to move the page number?
The dotted line near the right-hand edge of the screen indicates the right-hand border of the available space on the printed page, based on whatever margins and orientation are currently selected. A portion of the page number extends beyond this border. By moving the page number, it no longer extends beyond the border.

3

- Tap or click the Save button on the Quick Access Toolbar to save your changes to the report layout.
- Close the report.

To Print a Report

The following steps print the report.

1. Open the Navigation Pane if necessary, confirm that the Customer Financial Report is selected, and then tap or click FILE on the ribbon to open the Backstage view.
2. Tap or click the Print tab in the Backstage view to display the Print gallery.
3. Tap or click the Quick Print button to print the report.

Q&A When I print the report, I have pound signs (####) rather than numbers where the totals should be for the Amount Paid and Current Due columns. The report looked fine on the screen. How can I correct it?
The columns are not wide enough to display the complete number. Open the report in Layout view and slightly increase the width of the Amount Paid and Current Due columns by dragging the right boundary of the column headings.

How can I print multiple copies of my report?
Tap or click FILE on the ribbon to open the Backstage view. Tap or click the Print tab, tap or click Print in the Print gallery to display the Print dialog box, increase the number in the Number of Copies box, and then tap or click the OK button (Print dialog box).

How can I print a range of pages rather than printing the whole report?
Tap or click FILE on the ribbon to open the Backstage view. Tap or click the Print tab, tap or click Print in the Print gallery to display the Print dialog box, tap or click the Pages option button in the Print Range area, enter the desired page range, and then tap or click the OK button (Print dialog box).

BTW
Exporting a Report as a PDF or XPS File
To export a report as a PDF or XPS file, display the EXTERNAL DATA tab, and then tap or click the PDF or XPS button (EXTERNAL DATA tab | Export group). Enter the appropriate information in the Publish to PDF or XPS dialog box and tap or click the Publish button.

BTW
Report Navigation
When previewing a report, you can use the Navigation buttons on the status bar to move from one page to another.

Database Properties

Access helps you organize and identify your databases by using **database properties,** which are the details about a file. Database properties, also known as **metadata**, can include such information as the project author, title, or subject. **Keywords** are words or phrases that further describe the database. For example, a class name or database topic can describe the file's purpose or content.

Five different types of database properties exist, but the more common ones used in this book are standard and automatically updated properties. **Standard properties** are associated with all Microsoft Office documents and include author, title, and subject. **Automatically updated properties** include file system properties, such as the date you create or change a file, and statistics, such as the file size.

CONSIDER THIS

Why would you want to assign database properties to a database?
Database properties are valuable for a variety of reasons:

- Users can save time locating a particular file because they can view a file's database properties without opening the database.
- By creating consistent properties for files having similar content, users can better organize their databases.
- Some organizations require Access users to add database properties so that other employees can view details about these files.

To Change Database Properties

To change database properties, you would follow these steps.

1. Tap or click FILE on the ribbon to open the Backstage view and then, if necessary, tap or click the Info tab in the Backstage view to display the Info gallery.
2. Click the 'View and edit database properties' link in the right pane of the Info gallery to display the Bavant Publishing Properties dialog box.

Q&A Why are some of the database properties already filled in?
The person who installed Office 2013 on your computer or network might have set or customized the properties.

3. If the property you want to change is displayed in the Properties dialog box, click the text box for the property and make the desired change. Skip the remaining steps.
4. If the property you want to change is not displayed in the Properties dialog box, click the appropriate tab so the property is displayed and then make the desired change.
5. Click the OK button in the Properties dialog box to save your changes and remove the dialog box from the screen.

To Sign Out of a Microsoft Account

If you are signed in to a Microsoft account and are using a public computer or otherwise wish to sign out of your Microsoft account, you should sign out of the account from the Account gallery in the Backstage view before exiting Access. Signing out of the account is the safest way to make sure that nobody else can access SkyDrive files or settings stored in your Microsoft account. The following steps sign out of a Microsoft account from Access. For a detailed example of the procedure summarized below, refer to the Office and Windows chapter at the beginning of this book.

1. If you wish to sign out of your Microsoft account, tap or click FILE on the ribbon to open the Backstage view and then tap or click the Account tab to display the Account gallery.
2. Tap or click the Sign out link, which displays the Remove Account dialog box. If a Can't remove Windows accounts dialog box appears instead of the Remove Account dialog box, click the OK button and skip the remaining steps.

Q&A Why does a Can't remove Windows accounts dialog box appear?
If you signed in to Windows using your Microsoft account, then you also must sign out from Windows, rather than signing out from within Access. When you are finished using Windows, be sure to sign out at that time.

3. Tap or click the Yes button (Remove Account dialog box) to sign out of your Microsoft account on this computer.

Q&A Should I sign out of Windows after signing out of my Microsoft account? [End Q]
When you are finished using the computer, you should sign out of your account for maximum security.

4. Tap or click the Back button in the upper-left corner of the Backstage view to return to the database.

To Exit Access

The following steps exit Access.

1. Tap or click the Close button on the right side of the title bar to close the open database, if there is one, and exit Access.

2. If a Microsoft Access dialog box appears, tap or click the Save button to save any changes made to the database since the last save.

Special Database Operations

Additional operations involved in maintaining a database are backup, recovery, compacting, and repairing.

Backup and Recovery

It is possible to damage or destroy a database. Users can enter data that is incorrect; programs that are updating the database can end abnormally during an update; a hardware problem can occur; and so on. After any such event has occurred, the database may contain invalid data or it might be totally destroyed.

Obviously, you cannot allow a situation in which data has been damaged or destroyed to go uncorrected. You must somehow return the database to a correct state. This process is called recovery; that is, you **recover** the database.

The simplest approach to recovery involves periodically making a copy of the database (called a **backup copy** or a **save copy**). This is referred to as **backing up** the database. If a problem occurs, you correct the problem by overwriting the actual database — often referred to as the **live database** — with the backup copy.

To back up the database that is currently open, you use the Back Up Database command on the Save As tab in the Backstage view. In the process, Access suggests a name that is a combination of the database name and the current date. For example, if you back up the Bavant Publishing database on October 20, 2014, Access will suggest the name, Bavant Publishing_2014-10-20. You can change this name if you desire, although it is a good idea to use this name. By doing so, it will be easy to distinguish between all the backup copies you have made to determine which is the most recent. In addition, if you discover that a critical problem occurred on October 18, 2014, you may want to go back to the most recent backup before October 18. If, for example, the database was not backed up on October 17 but was backed up on October 16, you would use Bavant Publishing_2014-10-16.

To Back Up a Database

You would use the following steps to back up a database to a file on a hard disk or high-capacity removable disk.

1. Open the database to be backed up.
2. Tap or click FILE on the ribbon to open the Backstage view, and then tap or click the Save As tab.
3. With Save Database As selected in the File Types area, tap or click 'Back Up Database' in the Save Database As area, and then tap or click the Save As button.
4. Navigate to the desired location in the Save As box. If you do not want the name Access has suggested, enter the desired name in the File name text box.
5. Tap or click the Save button to back up the database.

Access creates a backup copy with the desired name in the desired location. Should you ever need to recover the database using this backup copy, you can simply copy it over the live version.

Compacting and Repairing a Database

As you add more data to a database, it naturally grows larger. When you delete an object (records, tables, forms, or queries), the space previously occupied by the object does not become available for additional objects. Instead, the additional objects are given new space; that is, space that was not already allocated. To remove this empty space from the database, you must **compact** the database. The same option that compacts the database also repairs problems that might have occurred in the database.

To Compact and Repair a Database

You would use the following steps to compact and repair a database.

1. Open the database to be compacted.
2. Tap or click FILE on the ribbon to open the Backstage view, and then, if necessary, select the Info tab.
3. Tap or click the Compact & Repair Database button in the Info gallery to compact and repair the database.

   The database now is the compacted form of the original.

Additional Operations

Additional special operations include opening another database, closing a database without exiting Access, and saving a database with another name. They also include deleting a table (or other object) as well as renaming an object.

When you open another database, Access will automatically close the database that previously was open. Before deleting or renaming an object, you should ensure that the object has no dependent objects; that is, other objects that depend on the object you want to delete.

To Close a Database without Exiting Access

You would use the following steps to close a database without exiting Access.

1. Tap or click FILE on the ribbon to open the Backstage view.
2. Tap or click Close.

To Save a Database with Another Name

To save a database with another name, you would use the following steps.

1. Tap or click FILE on the ribbon to open the Backstage view, and then select the Save As tab.
2. With Save Database As selected in the Database File Types area and Access Database selected in the Save Database As area, tap or click the Save As button.
3. Enter a name and select a location for the new version.
4. Tap or click the Save button.

CONSIDER THIS

If you want to make a backup, could you just save the database with another name?
You could certainly do that. Using the backup procedure discussed earlier has the advantage that it automatically includes the current database name and the date in the name of the file it creates.

To Delete a Table or Other Object in the Database

You would use the following steps to delete a database object.

1. Press and hold or right-click the object in the Navigation Pane.
2. Tap or click Delete on the shortcut menu.
3. Tap or click the Yes button in the Microsoft Access dialog box.

To Rename an Object in the Database

You would use the following steps to rename a database object.

1. Press and hold or right-click the object in the Navigation Pane.
2. Tap or click Rename on the shortcut menu.
3. Type the new name and press the ENTER key.

Database Design

BTW
Database Design Language (DBDL)
Database Design Language (DBDL) is a commonly accepted shorthand representation for showing the structure of a relational database. You write the name of the table and then within parentheses you list all the columns in the table. If the columns continue beyond one line, indent the subsequent lines.

This section illustrates the **database design** process, that is, the process of determining the tables and fields that make up the database. It does so by showing how you would design the database for Bavant Publishing from a set of requirements. In this section, you will use commonly accepted shorthand to represent the tables and fields that make up the database as well as the primary keys for the tables. For each table, you give the name of the table followed by a set of parentheses. Within the parentheses is a list of the fields in the table separated by commas. You underline the primary key. For example,

Product (<u>Product Code</u>, Description, On Hand, Price) represents a table called Product. The Product table contains four fields: Product Code, Description, On Hand, and Price. The Product Code field is the primary key.

Database Requirements

BTW
Determining Database Requirements
The determination of database requirements is part of a process known as systems analysis. A systems analyst examines existing and proposed documents, and examines organizational policies to determine exactly the type of data needs the database must support.

The Bavant Publishing database must maintain information on both customers and book reps. The business currently keeps this data in two Word tables and two Excel workbooks, as shown in Figure 1–80. They use Word tables for address information and Excel workbooks for financial information.

- For customers, Bavant needs to maintain address data. It currently keeps this data in a Word table (Figure 1–80a).
- Bavant also maintains financial data for each customer. This includes the amount paid, current amount due, and return amount for the customer. It keeps these amounts, along with the customer name and number, in the Excel worksheet shown in Figure 1–80b.
- Bavant keeps book rep address data in a Word table, as shown in Figure 1–80c.
- Just as with customers, it keeps financial data for book reps, including their start date, salary, and bonus rate, in a separate Excel worksheet, as shown in Figure 1–80d.

Customer Number	Customer Name	Street	City	State	Postal Code
ASU37	Applewood State University	300 University Ave.	Greer	PA	19158
BCJ21	Brodkin Junior College	4806 Park Dr.	Greer	PA	19158
CSD25	Cowpens ISD	829 Wooster Ave.	Gossett	PA	19157
CSU10	Camellia State University	725 Camellia St.	Pleasantburg	NJ	07025
DCC34	Dartt Community College	3827 Burgess Dr.	Chambers	NJ	07037
FSC12	First State College	7300 Cedar Rd.	Quaker	DE	19719
FSU23	Farnham State University	1445 Hubert St.	Gaston	DE	19723
HSD05	Hammonds County ISD	446 Lincoln Blvd.	Chesnee	NJ	07053
KCC78	Key Community College System	7523 Penn Ave.	Adelphia	PA	19159
MCC45	Mauldin Community College	72 Montrose St.	Chesnee	NJ	07053
MEC56	Mehitable College	202 College St.	Gaston	DE	19723
PLI22	PrattLast Institute	236 Ashton Ave.	Pleasantburg	NJ	07025
SCC77	Stallone Community College	1200 Franklin Blvd.	Adelphia	PA	19156
SEC19	Seaborn College	345 Mather Rd.	Quaker	DE	19719
TSC02	Tri-State Consortium	3400 Metro Pkwy.	Adelphia	PA	19156

Figure 1–80 (a) Customer Address Information (Word Table)

	A	B	C	D	E	F	G	H
1	Customer Number	Customer Name	Amount Paid	Current Due	Returns			
2	ASU37	Applewood State University	$41,530.98	$38,812.66	$12,008.02			
3	BCJ21	Brodkin Junior College	$0.00	$6,081.98	$0.00			
4	CSD25	Cowpens ISD	$12,750.00	$13,275.00	$2,000.00			
5	CSU10	Camellia State University	$63,246.88	$69,847.76	$14,967.98			
6	DCC34	Dartt Community College	$21,345.50	$23,467.75	$4,496.80			
7	FSC12	First State College	$34,557.25	$23,875.98	$7,234.99			
8	FSU23	Farnham State University	$18,268.00	$22,024.50	$3,496.23			
9	HSD05	Hammonds County ISD	$18,434.75	$0.00	$0.00			
10	KCC78	Key Community College System	$21,288.65	$11,367.49	$2,256.98			
11	MCC45	Mauldin Community College	$9,500.00	$5,000.00	$0.00			
12	MEC56	Mehitable College	$9,111.19	$7,310.76	$574.25			
13	PLI22	PrattLast Institute	$17,229.45	$11,769.75	$3,450.50			
14	SCC77	Stallone Community College	$7,525.98	$2,515.78	$0.00			
15	SEC19	Seaborn College	$9,225.34	$10,496.89	$2,017.67			
16	TSC02	Tri-State Consortium	$34,578.90	$9,432.56	$943.34			

Figure 1–80 (b) Customer Financial Information (Excel Worksheet)

Book Rep Number	Last Name	First Name	Street	City	State	Postal Code
42	Perez	Melina	261 Porter Dr.	Adelphia	PA	19156
48	Statnik	Michael	3135 Simpson Dr.	Pleasantburg	NJ	07025
53	Chin	Robert	265 Maxwell St.	Gossett	PA	19157
65	Rogers	Tracy	1827 Maple Ave.	Adelphia	PA	19159

Figure 1–80 (c) Book Rep Address Information (Word Table)

	A	B	C	D	E	F	G	H	I	J
1	Book Rep Number	Last Name	First Name	Start Date	Salary	Bonus Rate				
2	53	Chin	Robert	6/1/2013	$26,250	0.19				
3	42	Perez	Melina	5/14/2012	$31,500	0.20				
4	65	Rogers	Tracy	7/1/2014	$7,750	0.18				
5	48	Statnik	Michael	1/15/2013	$29,000	0.20				
6										
7										

Figure 1–80 (d) Book Rep Financial Information (Excel Worksheet)

- Finally, Bavant keeps track of which customers are assigned to which book reps. Each customer is assigned to a single book rep, but each book rep might be assigned many customers. Currently, for example, customers ASU37 (Applewood State University), BCJ21 (Brodkin Junior College), FSU23 (Farnham State University), MEC56 (Mehitable College), and SCC77 (Stallone Community College) are assigned to book rep 42 (Melina Perez). Customers CSD25 (Cowpens ISD), CSU10 (Camellia State University), HSD05 (Hammonds County ISD), MCC45 (Mauldin Community College), and PLI22 (PrattLast Institute) are assigned to book rep 53 (Robert Chin). Customers DCC34 (Dartt Community College), FSC12 (First State College), KCC78 (Key Community College System), SEC19 (Seaborn College), and TSC02 (Tri-State Consortium) are assigned to book rep 65 (Tracy Rogers). Bavant has an additional book rep, Michael Statnik, whose number has been assigned as 48, but who has not yet been assigned any customers.

Database Design Process

The database design process involves several steps.

CONSIDER THIS

What is the first step in the process?

Identify the tables. Examine the requirements for the database to identify the main objects that are involved. There will be a table for each object you identify.

In a database for one organization, for example, the main objects might be departments and employees. This would require two tables: one for departments and the other for employees. In the database for another organization, the main objects might be customers and book reps. In this case, there also would be two tables: one for customers and the other for book reps. In still another organization's database, the main objects might be books, publishers, and authors. This database would require three tables: one for books, a second for publishers, and a third for authors.

Identifying the Tables

For the Bavant Publishing database, the main objects are customers and book reps. This leads to two tables, which you must name. Reasonable names for these two tables are:

Customer
Book Rep

CONSIDER THIS

After identifying the tables, what is the second step in the database design process?

Determine the primary keys. Recall that the primary key is the unique identifier for records in the table. For each table, determine the unique identifier. In a Department table, for example, the unique identifier might be the Department Code. For a Book table, the unique identifier might be the ISBN (International Standard Book Number).

Determining the Primary Keys

The next step is to identify the fields that will be the unique identifiers, or primary keys. Customer numbers uniquely identify customers, and book rep numbers uniquely identify book reps. Thus, the primary key for the Customer table is the customer number, and the primary key for the Book Rep table is the book rep number. Reasonable names for these fields would be Customer Number and Book Rep Number, respectively. Adding these primary keys to the tables gives:

Customer (<u>Customer Number</u>)
Book Rep (<u>Book Rep Number</u>)

CONSIDER THIS

What is the third step in the database design process after determining the primary keys?

Determine the additional fields. The primary key will be a field or combination of fields in a table. A table typically will contain many additional fields, each of which contains a type of data. Examine the project requirements to determine these additional fields. For example, in an Employee table, additional fields might include Employee Name, Street Address, City, State, Postal Code, Date Hired, and Salary.

Determining Additional Fields

After identifying the primary keys, you need to determine and name the additional fields. In addition to the customer number, the Customer Address Information shown in Figure 1–80a on page AC 59 contains the customer name, street, city, state, and postal code. These would be fields in the Customer table. The Customer Financial Information shown in Figure 1–80b on page AC 59 also contains the customer number and customer name, which are already included in the Customer table. The financial information also contains the amount paid, current due, and returns. Adding the amount paid, current due, and returns fields to those already identified in the Customer table and assigning reasonable names gives:

Customer (<u>Customer Number</u>, Customer Name, Street, City, State, Postal Code, Amount Paid, Current Due, Returns)

Similarly, examining the Book Rep Address Information in Figure 1–80c on page AC 59 adds the last name, first name, street, city, state, and postal code fields to the Book Rep table. In addition to the book rep number, last name, and first name, the Book Rep Financial Information in Figure 1–80d on page AC 59 would add the start date, salary, and bonus rate. Adding these fields to the Book Rep table and assigning reasonable names gives:

Book Rep (<u>Book Rep Number</u>, Last Name, First Name, Street, City, State, Postal Code, Start Date, Salary, Bonus Rate)

BTW

Additional Data for Bavant Publishing

Bavant could include other types of data in the database. The Customer table could include data on a contact person at each organization, such as, name, telephone number, and email address. The Book Rep table could include the mobile telephone number, email address, and emergency contact information for the book rep.

CONSIDER THIS

What happens as the fourth step, after determining additional fields?

Determine relationships between the tables. A relationship is an association between objects. In a database containing information about departments and employees, there is an association between the departments and the employees. A department is associated with all the employees in the department, and an employee is associated with the department to which he or she is assigned. Technically, you say that a department is related to all the employees in the department, and an employee is related to his or her department.

The relationship between department and employees is an example of a **one-to-many relationship** because one employee is associated with one department, but each department can be associated with many employees. The Department table would be the "one" table in the relationship. The Employee table would be the "many" table in the relationship.

When you have determined that two tables are related, follow these general guidelines:

Identify the "one" table.

Identify the "many" table.

Include the primary key from the "one" table as a field in the "many" table.

BTW
Certification
The Microsoft Office Specialist (MOS) program provides an opportunity for you to obtain a valuable industry credential — proof that you have the Access 2013 skills required by employers. For more information, visit the Certification resource on the Student Companion Site located on www.cengagebrain.com. For detailed instructions about accessing available resources, visit www.cengage.com/ct/studentdownload or contact your instructor for information about accessing the required files.

Determining and Implementing Relationships Between the Tables

According to the requirements, each customer has one book rep, but each book rep can have many customers. Thus, the Book Rep table is the "one" table, and the Customer table is the "many" table. To implement this one-to-many relationship between book reps and customers, add the Book Rep Number field (the primary key of the Book Rep table) to the Customer table. This produces:

Customer (Customer Number, Customer Name, Street, City, State, Postal Code, Amount Paid, Current Due, Returns, Book Rep Number)
Book Rep (Book Rep Number, Last Name, First Name, Street, City, State, Postal Code, Start Date, Salary, Bonus Rate)

CONSIDER THIS

After creating relationships between tables, what is the fifth step in the database design process?
Determine data types for the fields, that is, the type of data that can be stored in the field.

Determining Data Types for the Fields

See Pages AC 9 through AC 10 for a discussion of the available data types and their use in the Bavant Publishing database. That section also discusses other properties that can be assigned, such as captions, field size, and the number of decimal places.

Identifying and Removing Redundancy

BTW
Quick Reference
For a table that lists how to complete the tasks covered in this book using touch gestures, the mouse, ribbon, shortcut menu, and keyboard, see the Quick Reference Summary at the back of this book, or visit the Quick Reference resource on the Student Companion Site located on www.cengagebrain.com. For detailed instructions about accessing available resources, visit www.cengage.com/ct/studentdownload or contact your instructor for information about accessing the required files.

Redundancy means storing the same fact in more than one place. It usually results from placing too many fields in a table — fields that really belong in separate tables — and often causes serious problems. If you had not realized there were two objects, such as customers and book reps, you might have placed all the data in a single Customer table. Figure 1–81 shows an example of a table that includes both customer and book rep information. Notice that the data for a given book rep (number, name, address, and so on) occurs on more than one record. The data for rep 42, Melina Perez, is repeated in the figure. Storing this data on multiple records is an example of redundancy.

name of Book Rep 42 appears more than once

Customer Number	Customer Name	Street	...	Book Rep Number	Last Name	First Name
ASU37	Applewood State University	300 University Ave.	...	42	Perez	Melina
BCJ21	Brodkin Junior College	4806 Park Dr.	...	42	Perez	Melina
CSD25	Cowpens ISD	829 Wooster Ave.	...	53	Chin	Robert
CSU10	Camellia State University	725 Camellia St.	...	53	Chin	Robert
DCC34	Dartt Community College	3827 Burgess Dr.	...	65	Rogers	Tracy
...	...	...	...	...	...	...

Book Rep numbers are 42

Figure 1–81

CONSIDER THIS

What problems does this redundancy cause?

Redundancy results in several problems, including:

1. Wasted storage space. The name of book rep 42, Melina Perez, for example, should be stored only once. Storing this fact several times is wasteful.
2. More complex database updates. If, for example, Melina Perez's name is spelled incorrectly and needs to be changed in the database, her name would need to be changed in several different places.
3. Possible inconsistent data. Nothing prohibits the book rep's last name from being Perez on customer ASU37's record and Perret on customer BCJ21's record. The data would be inconsistent. In both cases, the book rep number is 42, but the last names are different.

CONSIDER THIS

How do you eliminate redundancy?

The solution to the problem is to place the redundant data in a separate table, one in which the data no longer will be redundant. If, for example, you place the data for book reps in a separate table (Figure 1–82), the data for each book rep will appear only once.

Customer Number	Customer Name	Street	...	Book Rep Number
ASU37	Applewood State University	300 University Ave.	...	42
BCJ21	Brodkin Junior College	4806 Park Dr.	...	42
CSD25	Cowpens ISD	829 Wooster Ave.	...	53
CSU10	Camellia State University	725 Camellia St.	...	53
DCC34	Dartt Community College	3827 Burgess Dr.	...	65

Book Rep numbers are 42

Book Rep Number	Last Name	First Name	...
42	Perez	Melina	...
48	Statnik	Michael	...
53	Chin	Robert	...
65	Rogers	Tracy	...

name of Book Rep 42 appears only once

Figure 1–82

Notice that you need to have the book rep number in both tables. Without it, there would be no way to tell which book rep is associated with which customer. The remaining book rep data, however, was removed from the Customer table and placed in the Book Rep table. This new arrangement corrects the problems of redundancy in the following ways:

1. Because the data for each book rep is stored only once, space is not wasted.
2. Changing the name of a book rep is easy. You need to change only one row in the Book Rep table.
3. Because the data for a book rep is stored only once, inconsistent data cannot occur.

Designing to omit redundancy will help you to produce good and valid database designs. You should always examine your design to see if it contains redundancy. If it does, you should decide whether you need to remove the redundancy by creating a separate table.

If you examine your design, you will see that there is one area of redundancy (see the data in Figure 1–1 on page AC 3). Cities and states are both repeated. Every customer whose postal code is 19158, for example, has Greer as the city and PA as the state. To remove this redundancy, you would create a table with the primary key Postal Code and City and State as additional fields. City and State would be removed from the Customer table. Having City, State, and Postal Code in a table is very common, however, and usually you would not take such action. No other redundancy exists in your tables.

BTW

Postal Codes

Some organizations with customers throughout the country have a separate table of postal codes, cities, and states. When placing an order, you typically are asked for your postal code (or ZIP code), rather than city, state, and postal code. You then are asked to confirm that the city and state correspond to that postal code.

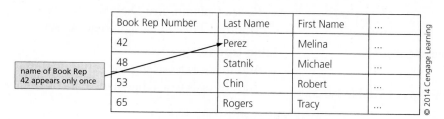

Chapter Summary

In this chapter you have learned to create an Access database, create tables and add records to a database, print the contents of tables, import data, create queries, create forms, create reports, and change database properties. You also have learned how to design a database. The items listed below include all the new Access skills you have learned in this chapter, with tasks grouped by activity.

Database Object Management
- Delete a Table or Other Object in the Database (AC 58)
- Rename an Object in the Database (AC 58)

Database Properties
- Change Database Properties (AC 55)

File Management
- Run Access (AC 5)
- Create a Database (AC 6)
- Create a Database Using a Template (AC 7)
- Exit Access (AC 24)
- Open a Database from Access (AC 25)
- Back Up a Database (AC 56)
- Compact and Repair a Database (AC 57)
- Close a Database without Exiting Access (AC 57)
- Save a Database with Another Name (AC 57)

Form Creation
- Create a Form (AC 45)

Import Data
- Import an Excel Worksheet (AC 33)

Print Objects
- Preview and Print the Contents of a Table (AC 30)
- Print the Results of a Query (AC 45)
- Print a Report (AC 54)

Query Creation
- Use the Simple Query Wizard to Create a Query (AC 40)
- Use a Criterion in a Query (AC 43)

Report Creation
- Create a Report (AC 48)
- Modify Report Column Headings and Resize Columns (AC 50)
- Add Totals to a Report (AC 53)

Table Creation
- Modify the Primary Key (AC 11)
- Define the Remaining Fields in a Table (AC 14)
- Save a Table (AC 16)
- View the Table in Design View (AC 17)
- Change a Field Size in Design View (AC 18)
- Close the Table (AC 20)
- Resize Columns in a Datasheet (AC 28)
- Modify a Table in Design View (AC 37)

Table Update
- Add Records to a Table (AC 20)
- Add Records to a Table that Contains Data (AC 26)

CONSIDER THIS

What decisions will you need to make when creating your next database?

Use these guidelines as you complete the assignments in this chapter and create your own databases outside of this class.

1. Identify the tables that will be included in the database.
2. Determine the primary keys for each of the tables.
3. Determine the additional fields that should be included in each of the tables.
4. Determine relationships between the tables.
   a) Identify the "one" table.
   b) Identify the "many" table.
   c) Include the primary key of the "one" table as a field in the "many" table.
5. Determine data types for the fields in the tables.
6. Determine additional properties for fields.
   a) Determine if a special caption is warranted.
   b) Determine if a special description is warranted.
   c) Determine field sizes.
   d) Determine formats.
7. Identify and remove any unwanted redundancy.
8. Determine a storage location for the database.
9. Determine the best method for distributing the database objects.

CONSIDER THIS

How should you submit solutions to questions in the assignments identified with a ✻ symbol?

Every assignment in this book contains one or more questions identified with a ✻ symbol. These questions require you to think beyond the assigned database. Present your solutions to the questions in the format required by your instructor. Possible formats may include one or more of these options: write the answer; create a document that contains the answer; present your answer to the class; discuss your answer in a group; record the answer as audio or video using a webcam, smartphone, or portable media player; or post answers on a blog, wiki, or website.

Apply Your Knowledge

Reinforce the skills and apply the concepts you learned in this chapter.

Adding a Caption, Changing a Data Type, Creating a Query, a Form, and a Report

Note: To complete this assignment, you will be required to use the Data Files for Students. Visit www.cengage.com/ct/studentdownload for detailed instructions or contact your instructor for information about accessing the required files.

Instructions: Cosmetics Naturally Inc. manufactures and sells beauty and skin care products made with only natural ingredients. The company's products do not contain any synthetic chemicals, artificial fragrances, or chemical preservatives. Cosmetics Naturally has a database that keeps track of its sales representatives and customers. Each customer is assigned to a single sales rep, but each sales rep may be assigned to many customers. The database has two tables. The Customer table contains data on the customers who purchase Cosmetics Naturally products. The Sales Rep table contains data on the sales reps. You will add a caption, change a data type, create two queries, a form, and a report, as shown in Figure 1–83 on the next page.

Perform the following tasks:

1. Start Access, open the Apply Cosmetics Naturally database from the Data Files for Students, and enable the content.
2. Open the Sales Rep table in Datasheet view, add SR # as the caption for the Sales Rep Number field, and resize all columns to best fit the data. Save the changes to the layout of the table and close the table.
3. Open the Customer table in Design view and change the data type for the Postal Code field to Short Text. Change the field size for the field to 5. Save the changes to the table and close the table.
4. Use the Simple Query Wizard to create a query for the Customer table that contains the Customer Number, Customer Name, Amount Paid, Balance, and Sales Rep Number. The query is a detail query. Use the name Customer Query for the query and close the query.
5. Create a simple form for the Sales Rep table. Save the form and use the name Sales Rep for the form. Close the form.
6. Create the report shown in Figure 1–83 for the Customer table. The report includes totals for both the Amount Paid and Balance fields. Be sure the totals appear completely. You might need to expand the size of the total controls. Move the page number so that it is within the margins. Save the report as Customer Financial Report.
7. If requested by your instructor, add your last name to the title of the report, that is, change the title to Customer Financial Report LastName where LastName is your actual last name.
8. Compact and repair the database.
9. Submit the revised database in the format specified by your instructor.
10. ✻ How would you change the field name of the Balance field in the Customer table to Current Balance?

Continued >

Apply Your Knowledge *continued*

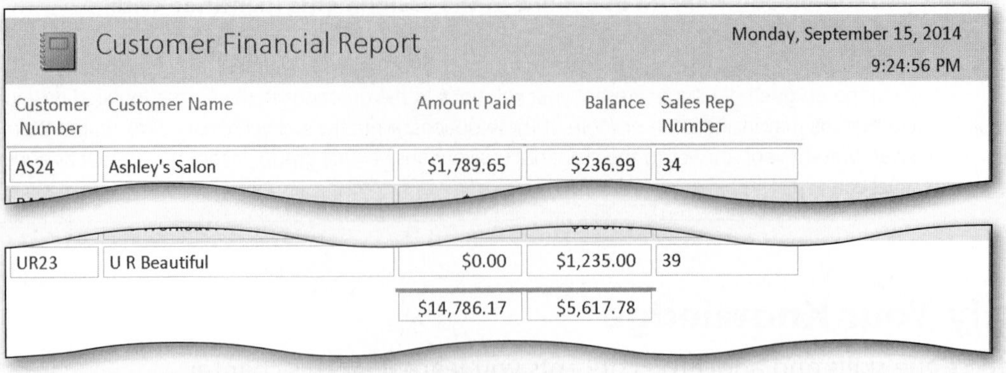

Figure 1–83

Extend Your Knowledge

Extend the skills you learned in this chapter and experiment with new skills. You may need to use Help to complete the assignment.

Using a Database Template to Create a Contacts Database

Note: To complete this assignment, you will be required to use the Data Files for Students. Visit www.cengage.com/ct/studentdownload for detailed instructions or contact your instructor for information about accessing the required files.

Instructions: Access includes both desktop database templates and web-based templates. You can use a template to create a beginning database that can be modified to meet your specific needs. You will use a template to create a Contacts database. The database template includes sample tables, queries, forms, and reports. You will modify the database and create the Contacts Query shown in Figure 1–84.

Perform the following tasks:

1. Start Access.
2. Select the Desktop contacts template in the template gallery and create a new database with the file name Extend Contacts.
3. Enable the content. If requested to do so by your instructor, watch the videos in the Getting Started with Contacts dialog box. Close the Getting Started with Contacts dialog box.
4. Close the Contact List form.
5. Open the Contacts table in Datasheet view and delete the Fax Number field and the Attachments field in the table. The Attachments field has a paperclip as the column heading.
6. Change the data type for the ID field to Short Text, change the field name to Contact ID, and change the field size to 4. Change the column width so that the complete field name is displayed.
7. Save the changes to the Contacts table and close the table.
8. Use the Simple Query Wizard to create the Contacts Query shown in Figure 1–84. Close the query.

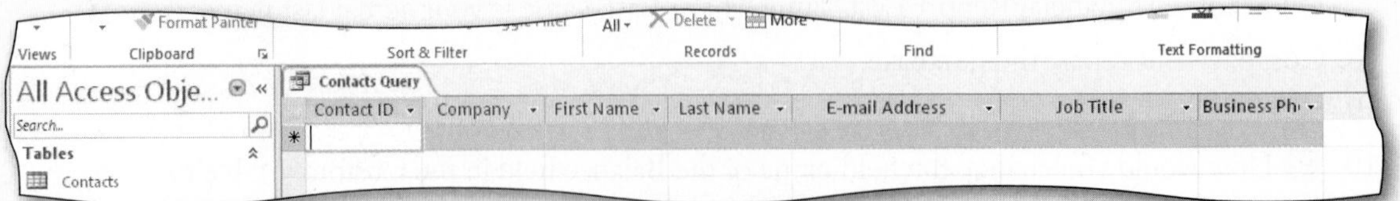

Figure 1–84

9. Open the Phone Book report in Layout view. Delete the control containing the date. Change the title of the report to Contact Phone List.
10. Save the changes to the report.
11. If requested to do so by your instructor, add your first and last names to the end of the title and save the changes to the report.
12. Submit the revised database in the format specified by your instructor.
13. a. Why would you use a template instead of creating a database from scratch with just the fields you need?
    b. The Attachment data type allows you to attach files to a database record. If you were using this database for a job search, what specific documents might you attach to a Contacts record?

Analyze, Correct, Improve

Analyze a database, correct all errors, and improve the design.

Correcting Errors in the Table Structure

Note: To complete this assignment, you will be required to use the Data Files for Students. Visit www.cengage.com/ct/studentdownload for detailed instructions or contact your instructor for information about accessing the required files.

Instructions: Analyze SciFi Movies is a database containing information on classic science fiction movies that your film professor would like to use for teaching. The Movie table shown in Figure 1–85 contains errors to the table structure. Your professor has asked you to correct the errors and make some improvements to the database. Start Access and open the Analyze SciFi Movies database from the Data Files for Students.

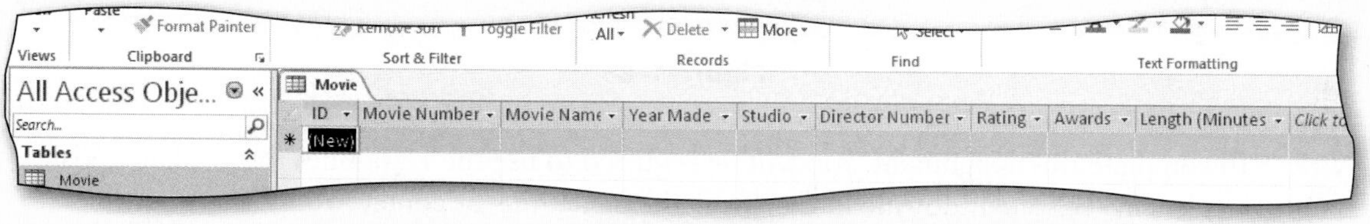

Figure 1–85

1. Correct Movie Number should be the primary key for the Movie table. The ID field should not be a field in the table. The Rating field represents a numerical rating system of one to four to indicate the quality of the movie. Your instructor wants to be able to find the average rating for films directed by a particular director. Only integers should be stored in both the Rating and the Length (Minutes) fields.

2. Improve The default field size for Short Text fields is 255. Changing the field size to more accurately represent the maximum number of characters that can be stored in a field is one way to improve the accuracy of the data. The Movie Number, Director Number, and Awards fields should have a maximum size of 3 characters. The Year Made field should have a maximum field size of 4. The Movie Name and Studio fields should have a maximum field size of 50. If instructed to do so by your instructor, rename the Movie table as Movie Last Name where Last Name is your last name. Submit the revised database in the format specified by your instructor.

3. The Awards field currently has a data type of Short Text, but the only values that will be stored in that field are Yes and No to indicate whether the movie won any awards. What would be a more appropriate data type for this field?

In the Labs

Design, create, modify, and/or use a database following the guidelines, concepts, and skills presented in this chapter. Labs are listed in order of increasing difficulty. Labs 1 and 2, which increase in difficulty, require you to create solutions based on what you learned in the chapter; Lab 3 requires you to create a solution, which uses cloud and web technologies, by learning and investigating on your own from general guidance.

Lab 1: Creating Objects for the Dartt Offsite Services Database

Problem: Dartt Offsite Services is a local company that provides offsite data services and solutions. The company provides remote data backup, disaster recovery planning and services, website backup, and offsite storage of paper documents for small businesses and nonprofit organizations. Service representatives are responsible for communicating data solutions to the client, scheduling backups and other tasks, and resolving any conflicts. The company recently decided to store its client and service rep data in a database. Each client is assigned to a single service rep, but each service rep may be assigned many clients. The database and the Service Rep table have been created, but the Monthly Salary field needs to be added to the table. The records shown in Table 1–6 must be added to the Service Rep table. The company plans to import the Client table from the Excel worksheet shown in Figure 1–86. Dartt would like to finish storing this data in a database and has asked you to help.

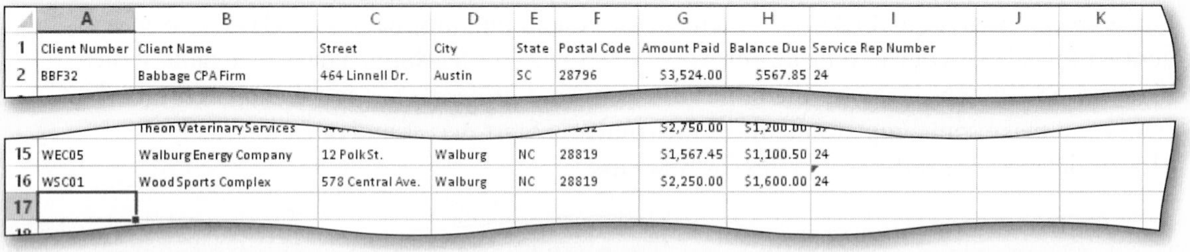

A B C D E F G H I J K
Client Number | Client Name | Street | City | State | Postal Code | Amount Paid | Balance Due | Service Rep Number
BBF32 | Babbage CPA Firm | 464 Linnell Dr. | Austin | SC | 28796 | $3,524.00 | $567.85 | 24
Theon Veterinary Services | $2,750.00
WEC05 | Walburg Energy Company | 12 Polk St. | Walburg | NC | 28819 | $1,567.45 | $1,100.50 | 24
WSC01 | Wood Sports Complex | 578 Central Ave. | Walburg | NC | 28819 | $2,250.00 | $1,600.00 | 24

Figure 1–86

Note: To complete this assignment, you will be required to use the Data Files for Students. Visit www.cengage.com/ct/studentdownload for detailed instructions or contact your instructor for information about accessing the required files.

Instructions: Perform the following tasks:

1. Start Access and open the Lab 1 Dartt Offsite Services database from the Data Files for Students.
2. Open the Service Rep table in Datasheet view and add the Monthly Salary field to the end of the table. The field has the Currency data type. Assign the caption SR # to the Service Rep Number field.
3. Add the records shown in Table 1–6.
4. Resize the columns to best fit the data. Save the changes to the layout of the table.

Table 1–6 Data for Service Rep Table

Service Rep Number	Last Name	First Name	Street	City	State	Postal Code	Start Date	Monthly Salary
21	Kelly	Jenna	25 Paint St.	Kyle	SC	28797	5/14/2012	$3,862.45
45	Scott	Josh	1925 Pine Rd.	Byron	SC	28795	4/28/2014	$3,062.08
24	Liu	Mia	265 Marble Dr.	Kyle	SC	28797	1/7/2013	$3,666.67
37	Martinez	Mike	31 Steel St.	Georgetown	SC	28794	5/13/2013	$3,285.00

5. Import the Lab 1–1 Client Data workbook shown in Figure 1–86 into the database. The first row of the workbook contains the column headings. Client Number is the primary key for the new table. Assign the name Client to the table. Save the Import steps, and assign the name Import-Client Data to the steps. Assign Import Client Data as the description.
6. Open the Client table in Design view and make the following changes:
   a. Change the field size for the Client Number field to 5. Change the field size for the Client Name field to 30. Change the field size for the Street and City fields to 20. Change the field size for the State field to 2 and the field size for the Postal Code field to 5. Change the field size for the Service Rep Number field to 2.
   b. Add the caption CL # to the Client Number field.
   c. Add the caption SR # to the Service Rep Number field.
7. Save the changes to the Client table. If a Microsoft Access dialog box appears with the 'Some data may be lost' message, click the Yes button.
8. Open the Client table in Datasheet view and resize all columns to best fit the data. Save the changes to the layout of the table.
9. Create a query using the Simple Query Wizard for the Client table that displays the Client Number, Client Name, Amount Paid, Balance Due, and Service Rep Number. Save the query as Client Query.
10. Create the report shown in Figure 1–87 for the Client table. The report should include the Client Number, Client Name, Amount Paid, Balance Due, and Service Rep Number fields. Include totals for the Amount Paid and Balance Due fields. Be sure to change the column headings to those shown in Figure 1–87. Save the report as Client Financial Report.
11. If requested to do so by your instructor, change the address for Jenna Kelly in the Service Rep table to your address. If your address is longer than 20 characters, simply enter as much as you can.
12. Submit the revised database in the format specified by your instructor.
13. You entered the records for the Service Rep table in the order shown in Table 1–6 on the previous page, that is service reps 21, 45, 24, 37. What order will the records be in after you close and reopen the Service Rep table? Why?

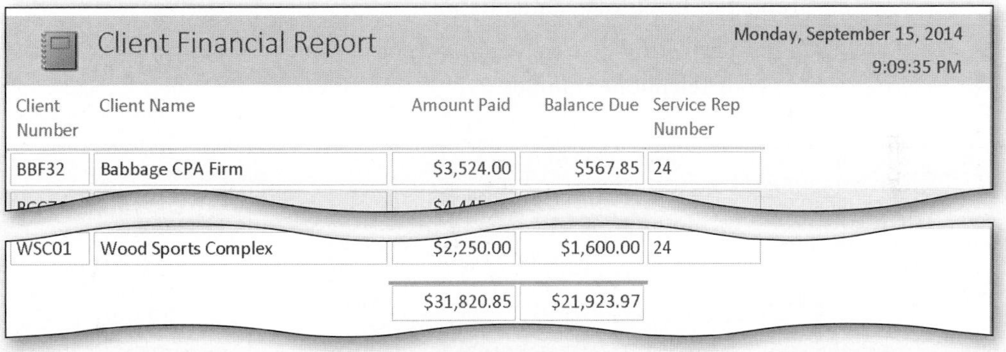
Client Financial Report — Monday, September 15, 2014 — 9:09:35 PM

Client Number	Client Name	Amount Paid	Balance Due	Service Rep Number
BBF32	Babbage CPA Firm	$3,524.00	$567.85	24
WSC01	Wood Sports Complex	$2,250.00	$1,600.00	24
		$31,820.85	$21,923.97	

Figure 1–87

Lab 2: Creating the Tennis Logos Database

Problem: Tennis Logos supplies customized tennis clothing and accessories for clubs and tournaments. The company purchases these items from suppliers at wholesale prices and adds the customer's logo. The final item price is determined by marking up the wholesale price and adding a fee that is based on the complexity of the logo. Tennis Logos also does graphic design work for customers. Currently, the information about the items and the suppliers is stored in two Excel workbooks. Each item is assigned to a single supplier, but each supplier may be assigned many items. You are to create a database that will store the item and supplier information. You already have determined that you need two tables, a Supplier table and an Item table, in which to store the information.

Note: To complete this assignment, you will be required to use the Data Files for Students. Visit www.cengage.com/ct/studentdownload for detailed instructions or contact your instructor for information about accessing the required files.

Continued >

In the Labs *continued*

Instructions: Perform the following tasks:

1. Use the Blank desktop database option to create a new database in which to store all objects related to the items for sale. Call the database Lab 2 Tennis Logos.
2. Import the Lab 1–2 Supplier Data Excel workbook into the database. The first row of the workbook contains the column headings. Supplier Code is the primary key for the new table. Assign the name Supplier to the table. Do not save the Import steps.
3. Open the Supplier table in Datasheet view. Change the field size for the Supplier Code field to 2; the field size for the Supplier Name field to 30; and the field size for the Telephone Number field to 12.
4. Import the Lab 1–2 Item Data Excel workbook into the database. The first row of the workbook contains the column headings. Item Number is the primary key for this table. Assign the name Item to the table. Save the Import steps, and assign the name Import-Item Data to the steps. You do not need a description.
5. Open the Item table in Design view. Change the field size for the Item Number field to 4. Change the field size for the Description field to 30. Add the caption Wholesale for the Wholesale Price field. The On Hand field should be an Integer field. Be sure that the field size for the Supplier Code in the Item table is identical to the field size for the Supplier Code in the Supplier table. Save the changes to the table and close the table.
6. Open the Item table in Datasheet view and resize the columns to best fit the data. Save the changes to the layout of the table and close the table.
7. Create a query for the Item table. Include the Item Number, Description, Wholesale Price, Base Cost, and Supplier Code. Save the query as Item Query.
8. Create a simple form for the Item table. Use the name Item for the form.
9. Create the report shown in Figure 1–88 for the Item table. Do not add any totals. Save the report as Inventory Status Report.
10. If requested to do so by your instructor, change the telephone number for Last Merchandisers to your telephone number.
11. Submit the database in the format specified by your instructor.
12. If you had designed this database, could you have used the field name, Name, for the Supplier Name? If not, why not?

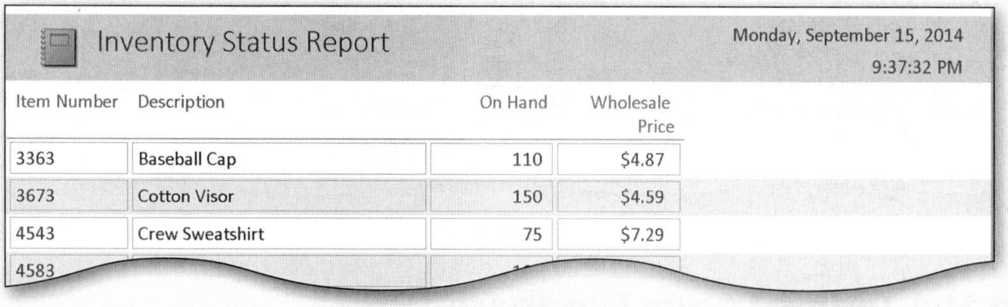

Inventory Status Report
Monday, September 15, 2014
9:37:32 PM
Item Number
Description
On Hand
Wholesale Price
3363
Baseball Cap
110
$4.87
3673
Cotton Visor
150
$4.59
4543
Crew Sweatshirt
75
$7.29
4583

Figure 1–88

Lab 3: Expand Your World: Cloud and Web Technologies Exporting Query Results and Reports

Problem: You and two of your friends have started a pet sitting business. You want to be able to share query results and reports, so you have decided to store the items on the SkyDrive. You are still learning Access, so you are going to create a sample query and the report shown in Figure 1–89, export the results, and save to the SkyDrive.

Note: To complete this assignment, you will be required to use the Data Files for Students. Visit www.cengage.com/ct/studentdownload for detailed instructions or contact your instructor for information about accessing the required files.

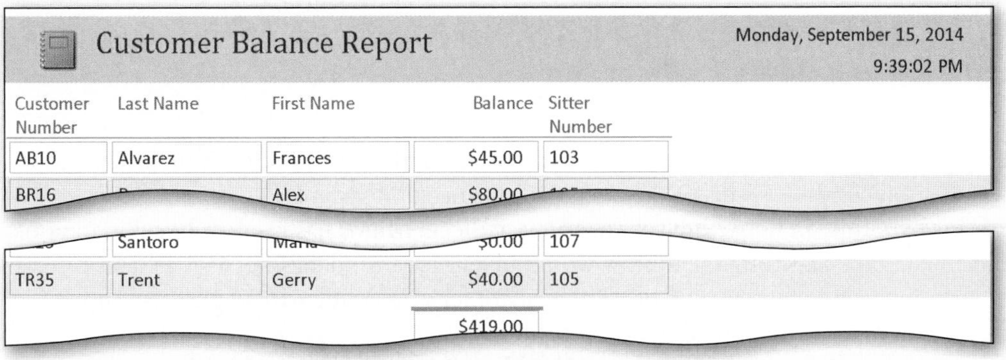

Customer Balance Report
Monday, September 15, 2014
9:39:02 PM
Customer Number
Last Name
First Name
Balance
Sitter Number
AB10
Alvarez
Frances
$45.00
103
BR16
Alex
Santoro
107
TR35
Trent
Gerry
$40.00
105
$419.00

Figure 1–89

Instructions:

1. Open the Lab 3 Pet Sitters database from the Data Files for Students.
2. Use the Simple Query Wizard to create a query that includes the Customer Number, First Name, Last Name, Balance, and Sitter Number. Save the query as Customer Query.
3. Export the Customer Query as an XPS document to your SkyDrive in the Access folder.
4. Create the report shown in Figure 1–89. Save the report as Customer Balance Report.
5. Export the Customer Balance Report as a PDF document to your Sky Drive in the Access folder. For information about how to use the Sky Drive, refer to the Office and Windows chapter at the beginning of this book.
6. If requested to do so by your instructor, open the Sitter table and change the last name and first name for sitter 103 to your last name and your first name.
7. Submit the assignment in the format specified by your instructor.
8. Based on your current knowledge of XPS and PDF documents, which one do you think you would use most frequently? Why?

Consider This: Your Turn

Apply your creative thinking and problem solving skills to design and implement a solution.

1. Creating the Craft Database

Note: To complete this assignment, you will be required to use the Data Files for Students. Visit www.cengage.com/ct/studentdownload for detailed instructions or contact your instructor for information about accessing the required files.

Personal/Academic

Part 1: You attend a college that is renowned for its school of arts and crafts. Students who major in arts and crafts can sell their designs online through the college bookstore. The bookstore has used an Excel workbook to store data on wood-crafted items as well as the students who created the items. Because you are a major in computer science and also are studying woodworking, your senior project is to create a database of these wood-crafted items. The database must keep track of the wood-crafted items for sale and maintain data on the students who created the items. Each item is created by a single student, but each student may have created several items.

Based on the information in the Your Turn 1–1 Craft workbook, use the concepts and techniques presented in this chapter to design and create a database to store the craft data. Create a Wood Crafts for Sale report that lists the item number, description, price, and student code. Submit your assignment in the format specified by your instructor.

Part 2: You made several decisions while determining the table structures and adding data to the tables in this assignment. What method did you use to add the data to each table? Are there any other methods that also would have worked?

Continued >

Consider This: Your Turn *continued*

2. Creating the Mums Landscaping Database

Professional

Part 1: Mums Landscaping is a local company that provides landscaping and lawn maintenance services to commercial customers, such as businesses, housing subdivisions, and schools. You worked for Mums part-time in both high school and in college. Mums has used an Excel workbook to store financial data on its customers but now would like to create a database that includes information on its customers and crew supervisors. Each customer is assigned to a single crew supervisor, but each supervisor may be assigned many customers.

Based on the information in the Your Turn 1–2 Mums Landscaping workbook, use the concepts and techniques presented in this chapter to design and create a database to store the data that Mums needs. Submit your assignment in the format specified by your instructor.

Part 2: You made several decisions while creating the Mums Landscaping database in this assignment. What did you decide to use as the primary key for each table? Why?

3. Creating an Electronic Assets Database

Research and Collaboration

Part 1: In today's world, most college students will own at least one electronic device, such as a cell phone. Many students have multiple electronic devices. Microsoft Access includes a desktop Asset tracking template that you can modify to keep track of your electronic devices, such as cell phone, MP3 player, and computer. Get together with your group and make a list of the electronic devices that each of you own. Use the desktop Asset tracking template to create an Electronic Assets database. Watch the video to learn how the database works. As a team, review the fields in the Assets table and decide which fields to include in the database. Delete any unwanted fields. Decide how you will describe each device, for example, will you use the term cell phone, smartphone, or mobile phone? Have each team member enter at least two devices. Create a query to find one type of device, such as cell phone. Submit your assignment in the format specified by your instructor.

Part 2: You made several decisions while creating the Electronic Assets database. Which fields did you decide to delete from the Assets table? What terms did you use to describe each device? What was the rationale for these decisions?

Learn Online

Reinforce what you learned in this chapter with games, exercises, training, and many other online activities and resources.

Student Companion Site Reinforcement activities and resources are available at no additional cost on www.cengagebrain.com. Visit www.cengage.com/ct/studentdownload for detailed instructions about accessing the resources available at the Student Companion Site.

SAM Put your skills into practice with SAM! If you have a SAM account, go to www.cengage.com/sam2013 to access SAM assignments for this chapter.

2 Querying a Database

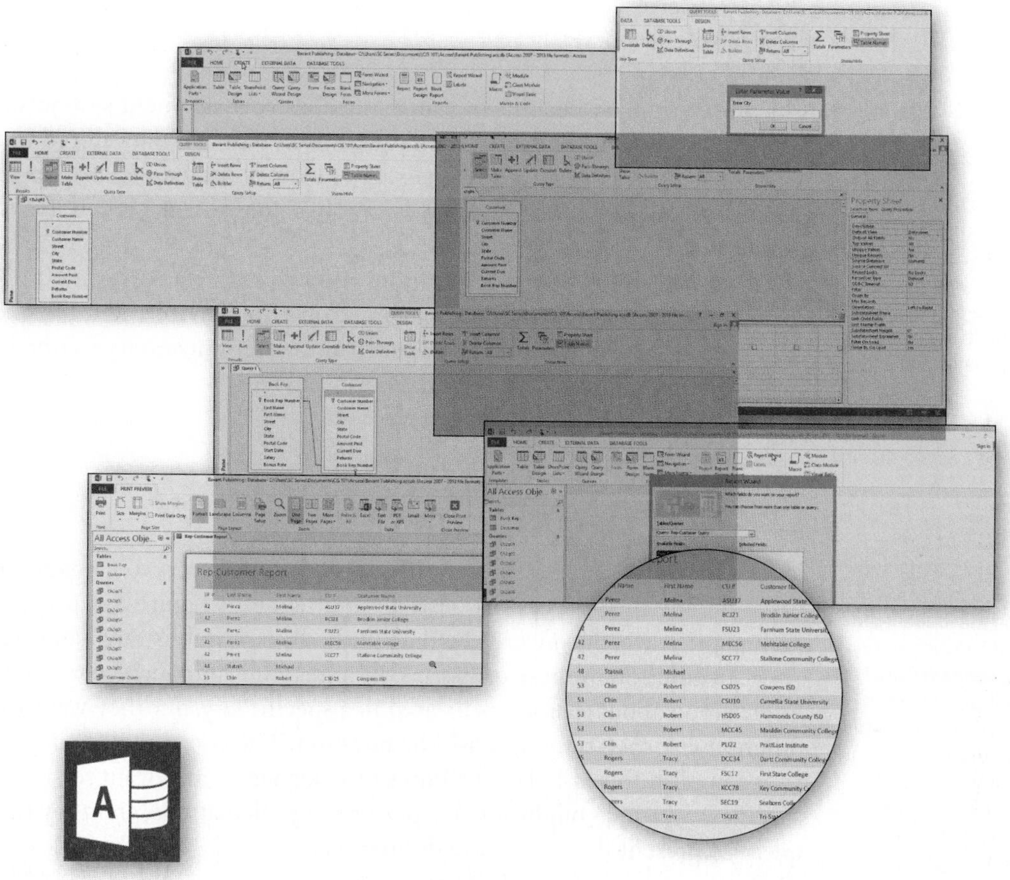

Objectives

You will have mastered the material in this chapter when you can:

- Create queries using Design view
- Include fields in the design grid
- Use text and numeric data in criteria
- Save a query and use the saved query
- Create and use parameter queries
- Use compound criteria in queries
- Sort data in queries
- Join tables in queries
- Create a report and a form from a query
- Export data from a query to another application
- Perform calculations and calculate statistics in queries
- Create crosstab queries
- Customize the Navigation Pane

2 Querying a Database

Introduction

One of the primary benefits of using a database management system such as Access is having the ability to find answers to questions related to data stored in the database. When you pose a question to Access, or any other database management system, the question is called a query. A **query** is simply a question presented in a way that Access can process.

To find the answer to a question, you first create a corresponding query using the techniques illustrated in this chapter. After you have created the query, you instruct Access to run the query, that is, to perform the steps necessary to obtain the answer. Access then displays the answer in Datasheet view.

BTW
Select Queries
The queries you create in this chapter are select queries. In a select query, you retrieve data from one or more tables using criteria that you specify and display the data in a datasheet.

BTW
BTWs
For a complete list of the BTWs found in the margins of this book, visit the BTW resource on the Student Companion Site located on www.cengagebrain.com. For detailed instructions about accessing available resources, visit www.cengage.com/ct/studentdownload or contact your instructor for information about accessing the required files.

Project — Querying a Database

One of the most important benefits of using Access to manage a database is easily finding the answers to questions and requests. Figure 2–1 presents examples of such queries, which concern the data in the Bavant Publishing database.

In addition to these questions, Bavant Publishing managers need to find information about customers located in a specific city, but they want to enter a different city each time they ask the question. The company can use a parameter query to accomplish this task. Bavant Publishing managers also want to summarize data in a specific way, which might involve performing calculations, and they can use a crosstab query to present the data in the desired form.

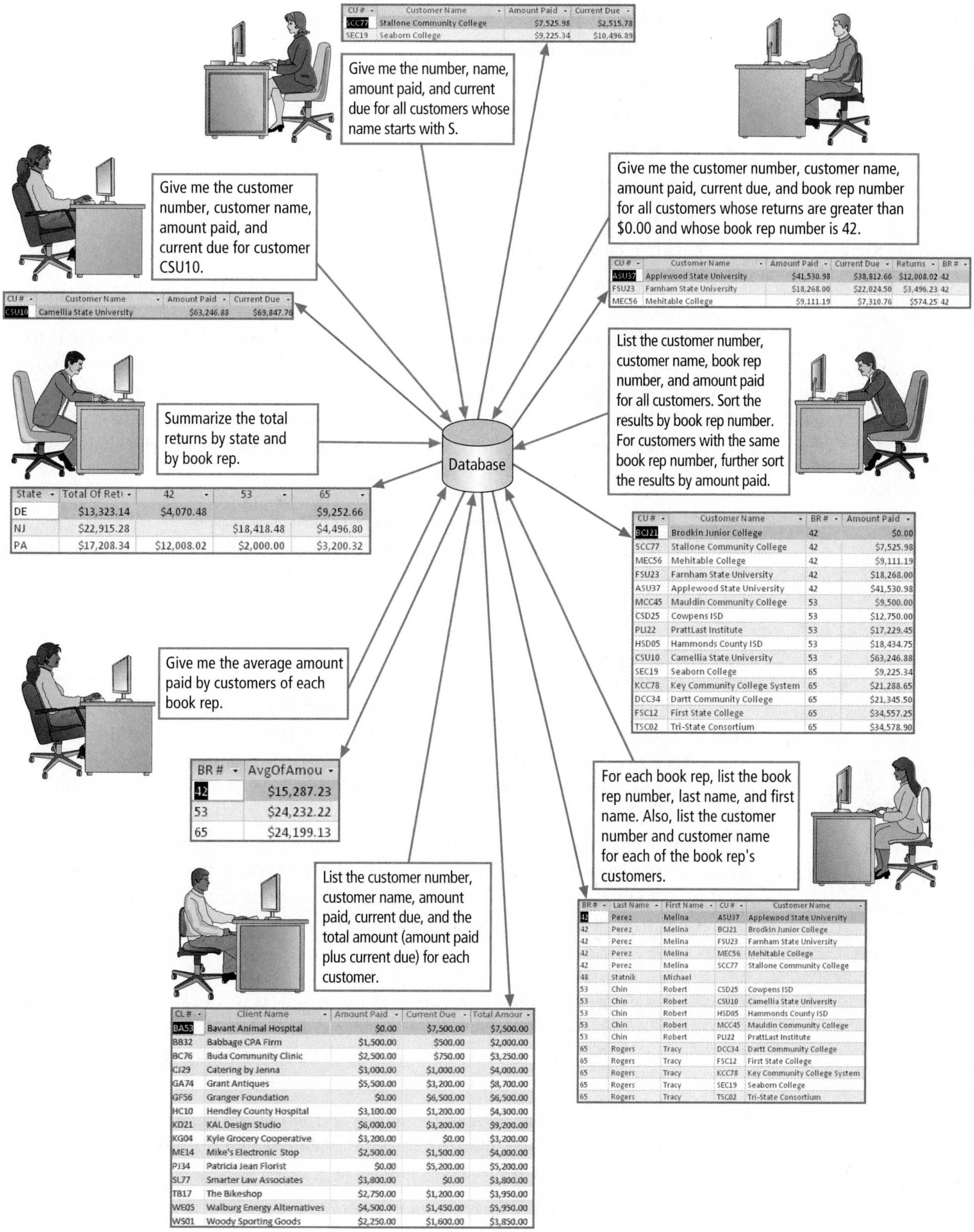

CU #	Customer Name	Amount Paid	Current Due
SCC77	Stallone Community College	$7,525.98	$2,515.78
SEC19	Seaborn College	$9,225.34	$10,496.89

CU #	Customer Name	Amount Paid	Current Due	Returns	BR #
ASU37	Applewood State University	$41,530.98	$38,812.66	$12,008.02	42
FSU23	Farnham State University	$18,268.00	$22,024.50	$3,496.23	42
MEC56	Mehitable College	$9,111.19	$7,310.76	$574.25	42

CU #	Customer Name	Amount Paid	Current Due
CSU10	Camellia State University	$63,246.88	$69,847.76

State	Total Of Ret	42	53	65
DE	$13,323.14	$4,070.48		$9,252.66
NJ	$22,915.28		$18,418.48	$4,496.80
PA	$17,208.34	$12,008.02	$2,000.00	$3,200.32

CU #	Customer Name	BR #	Amount Paid
BCJ21	Brodkin Junior College	42	$0.00
SCC77	Stallone Community College	42	$7,525.98
MEC56	Mehitable College	42	$9,111.19
FSU23	Farnham State University	42	$18,268.00
ASU37	Applewood State University	42	$41,530.98
MCC45	Mauldin Community College	53	$9,500.00
CSD25	Cowpens ISD	53	$12,750.00
PLI22	PrattLast Institute	53	$17,229.45
HSD05	Hammonds County ISD	53	$18,434.75
CSU10	Camellia State University	53	$63,246.88
SEC19	Seaborn College	65	$9,225.34
KCC78	Key Community College System	65	$21,288.65
DCC34	Dartt Community College	65	$21,345.50
FSC12	First State College	65	$34,557.25
TSC02	Tri-State Consortium	65	$34,578.90

BR #	AvgOfAmou
42	$15,287.23
53	$24,232.22
65	$24,199.13

BR #	Last Name	First Name	CU #	Customer Name
42	Perez	Melina	ASU37	Applewood State University
42	Perez	Melina	BCJ21	Brodkin Junior College
42	Perez	Melina	FSU23	Farnham State University
42	Perez	Melina	MEC56	Mehitable College
42	Perez	Melina	SCC77	Stallone Community College
48	Statnik	Michael		
53	Chin	Robert	CSD25	Cowpens ISD
53	Chin	Robert	CSU10	Camellia State University
53	Chin	Robert	HSD05	Hammonds County ISD
53	Chin	Robert	MCC45	Mauldin Community College
53	Chin	Robert	PLI22	PrattLast Institute
65	Rogers	Tracy	DCC34	Dartt Community College
65	Rogers	Tracy	FSC12	First State College
65	Rogers	Tracy	KCC78	Key Community College System
65	Rogers	Tracy	SEC19	Seaborn College
65	Rogers	Tracy	TSC02	Tri-State Consortium

CL #	Client Name	Amount Paid	Current Due	Total Amour
BA53	Bavant Animal Hospital	$0.00	$7,500.00	$7,500.00
BB32	Babbage CPA Firm	$1,500.00	$500.00	$2,000.00
BC76	Buda Community Clinic	$2,500.00	$750.00	$3,250.00
CJ29	Catering by Jenna	$3,000.00	$1,000.00	$4,000.00
GA74	Grant Antiques	$5,500.00	$3,200.00	$8,700.00
GF56	Granger Foundation	$0.00	$6,500.00	$6,500.00
HC10	Hendley County Hospital	$3,100.00	$1,200.00	$4,300.00
KD21	KAL Design Studio	$6,000.00	$3,200.00	$9,200.00
KG04	Kyle Grocery Cooperative	$3,200.00	$0.00	$3,200.00
ME14	Mike's Electronic Stop	$2,500.00	$1,500.00	$4,000.00
PJ34	Patricia Jean Florist	$0.00	$5,200.00	$5,200.00
SL77	Smarter Law Associates	$3,800.00	$0.00	$3,800.00
TB17	The Bikeshop	$2,750.00	$1,200.00	$3,950.00
WE05	Walburg Energy Alternatives	$4,500.00	$1,450.00	$5,950.00
WS01	Woody Sporting Goods	$2,250.00	$1,600.00	$3,850.00

Figure 2–1

Roadmap

In this chapter, you will learn how to create and use the queries shown in Figure 2–1 on the previous page. The following roadmap identifies general activities you will perform as you progress through this chapter:

1. CREATE QUERIES in Design view.
2. USE CRITERIA in queries.
3. SORT DATA in queries.
4. JOIN TABLES in queries.
5. EXPORT query RESULTS.
6. PERFORM CALCULATIONS in queries.
7. CREATE a CROSSTAB query.
8. CUSTOMIZE the NAVIGATION PANE.

For an introduction to Windows and instruction about how to perform basic Windows tasks, read the Office and Windows chapter at the beginning of this book, where you can learn how to resize windows, change screen resolution, create folders, move and rename files, use Windows Help, and much more.

At the beginning of the step instructions throughout the chapter, you will see an abbreviated form of this roadmap. The abbreviated roadmap uses colors to indicate chapter progress: gray means the chapter is beyond that activity, blue means the task being shown is covered in that activity, and black means that activity is yet to be covered. For example, the following abbreviated roadmap indicates the chapter would be showing a task in the 3 SORT DATA activity.

1 CREATE QUERIES | 2 USE CRITERIA | 3 SORT DATA | 4 JOIN TABLES | 5 EXPORT RESULTS
6 PERFORM CALCULATIONS | 7 CREATE CROSSTAB | 8 CUSTOMIZE NAVIGATION PANE

Use the abbreviated roadmap as a progress guide while you read or step through the instructions in this chapter.

To Run Access

If you are using a computer to step through the project in this chapter and you want your screens to match the figures in this book, you should change your screen's resolution to 1366 × 768. For information about how to change a computer's resolution, refer to the Office and Windows chapter at the beginning of this book.

The following steps, which assume Windows is running, use the Start screen or the search box to run Access based on a typical installation. You may need to ask your instructor how to run Access on your computer. For a detailed example of the procedure summarized below, refer to the Office and Windows chapter.

For an introduction to Office and instruction about how to perform basic tasks in Office programs, read the Office and Windows chapter at the beginning of this book, where you can learn how to run an app, use the ribbon, save a file, open a file, exit an app, use Help, and much more.

1. Scroll the Start screen for an Access 2013 tile. If your Start screen contains an Access 2013 tile, tap or click it to run Access and then proceed to Step 5; if the Start screen does not contain the Access 2013 tile, proceed to the next step to search for the Access app.
2. Swipe in from the right edge of the screen or point to the upper-right corner of the screen to display the Charms bar, and then tap or click the Search charm on the Charms bar to display the Search menu.
3. Type `Access` as the search text in the Search text box and watch the search results appear in the Apps list.

4. Tap or click Access 2013 in the search results to run Access.
5. If the Access window is not maximized, tap or click the Maximize button on its title bar to maximize the window.

To Open a Database from Access

In the previous chapter, you created the Bavant Publishing database in an appropriate storage location. The following steps open the database from the location you specified when you first created it (for example, the Access folder in the CIS 101 folder). For a detailed example of the procedure summarized below, refer to the Office and Windows chapter at the beginning of this book.

1. Tap or click FILE on the ribbon to open the Backstage view, if necessary.
2. If the database you want to open is displayed in the Recent list, tap or click the file name to open the database and display the opened database in the Access window; then skip to Step 7. If the database you want to open is not displayed in the Recent list or if the Recent list does not appear, tap or click 'Open Other Files' to display the Open Gallery.
3. If the database you want to open is displayed in the Recent list in the Open gallery, tap or click the file name to open the database and display the opened database in the Access window; then skip to Step 7.
4. Tap or click Computer, SkyDrive, or another location in the left pane and then navigate to the location of the database to be opened (for example, the Access folder in the CIS 101 folder).
5. Tap or click Bavant Publishing to select the database to be opened.
6. Tap or click the Open button (Open dialog box) to open the selected file and display the opened database in the Access window.
7. If a Security Warning appears, tap or click the Enable Content button.

One of the few differences between Windows 7 and Windows 8 occurs in the steps to run Access. If you are using Windows 7, click the Start button, type `Access` in the 'Search programs and files' box, click Access 2013, and then, if necessary, maximize the Access window. For detailed steps to run Access in Windows 7, refer to the Office and Windows chapter at the beginning of this book. For a summary of the steps, refer to the Quick Reference located at the back of this book.

Creating Queries

As you learned in Chapter 1, you can use queries in Access to find answers to questions about the data contained in the database. *Note:* In this chapter, you will save each query example. When you use a query for another task, such as to create a form or report, you will assign a specific name to a query, for example, Rep-Customer Query. In situations in which you will not use the query again, you will assign a name using a convention that includes the chapter number and a query number, for example, Ch2q01. Queries are numbered consecutively.

To Create a Query in Design View

1 CREATE QUERIES | 2 USE CRITERIA | 3 SORT DATA | 4 JOIN TABLES | 5 EXPORT RESULTS
6 PERFORM CALCULATIONS | 7 CREATE CROSSTAB | 8 CUSTOMIZE NAVIGATION PANE

In Chapter 1, you used the Simple Query Wizard to create a query. Most of the time, however, you will use Design view, which is the primary option for creating queries. ***Why?*** *Once you have created a new query in Design view, you have more options than with the wizard and can specify fields, criteria, sorting, calculations, and so on.* The following steps create a new query in Design view.

1

- Tap or click the 'Shutter Bar Open/Close Button' to close the Navigation Pane.
- Tap or click CREATE on the ribbon to display the CREATE tab (Figure 2–2).

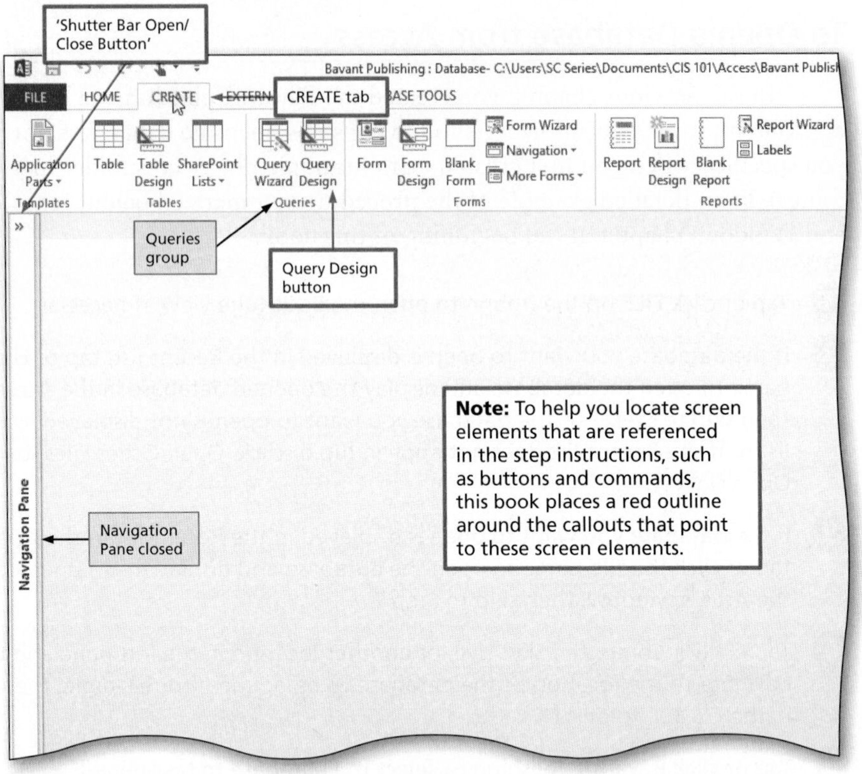

Figure 2–2

2

- Tap or click the Query Design button (CREATE tab | Queries group) to create a new query (Figure 2–3).

Q&A Is it necessary to close the Navigation Pane?
No. Closing the pane gives you more room for the query, however, so it is usually a good practice.

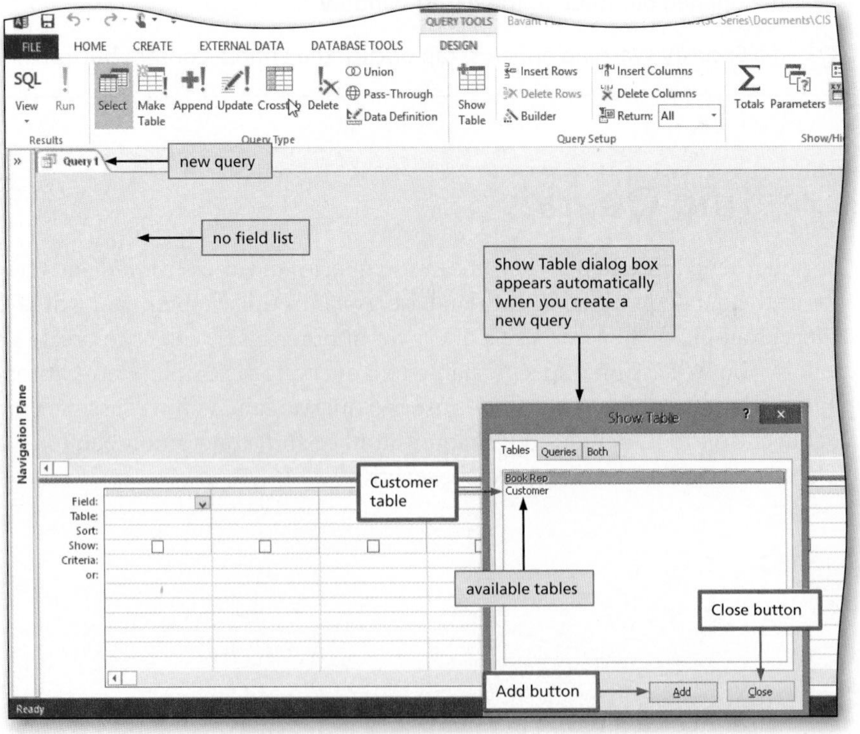

Figure 2–3

3

- Tap or click the Customer table (Show Table dialog box) to select the table.
- Tap or click the Add button to add the selected table to the query.
- Tap or click the Close button to remove the dialog box from the screen.

Q&A What if I inadvertently add the wrong table?
Press and hold or right-click the table that you added in error and tap or click Remove Table on the shortcut menu. You also can just close the query, indicate that you do not want to save it, and then start over.

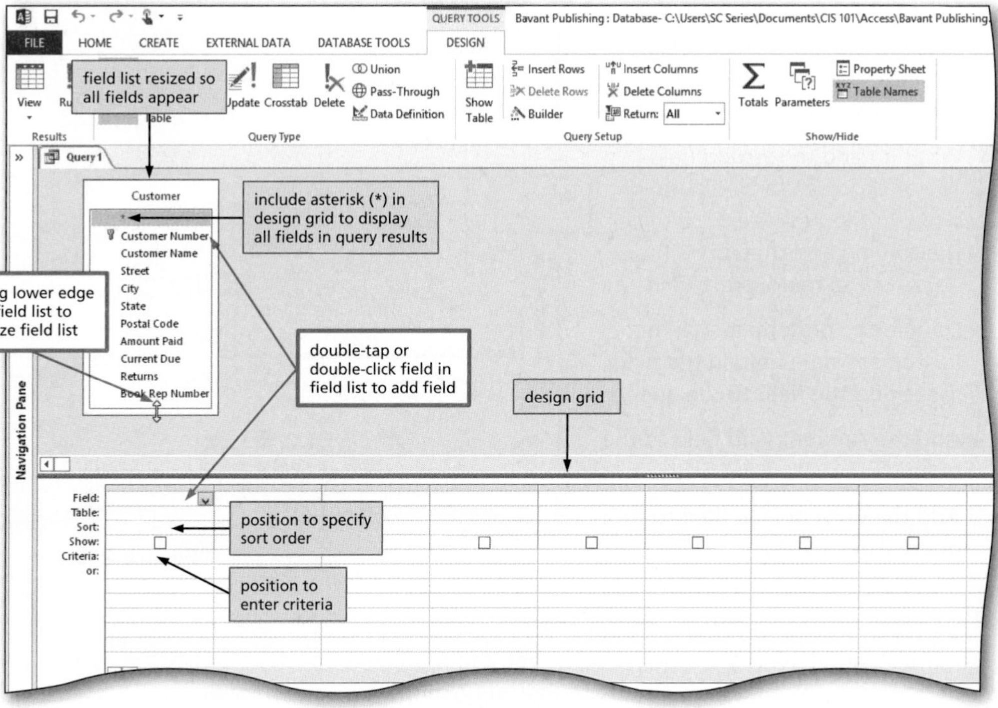

Figure 2–4

- Drag the lower edge of the field list down far enough so all fields in the table appear (Figure 2–4).

Q&A Is it essential that I resize the field list?
No. You can always scroll through the list of fields using the scroll bar. Resizing the field list so that all fields appear is usually more convenient.

To Add Fields to the Design Grid

1 CREATE QUERIES | 2 USE CRITERIA | 3 SORT DATA | 4 JOIN TABLES | 5 EXPORT RESULTS
6 PERFORM CALCULATIONS | 7 CREATE CROSSTAB | 8 CUSTOMIZE NAVIGATION PANE

Once you have a new query displayed in Design view, you are ready to make entries in the **design grid**, the portion of the window where you specify fields and criteria for the query. The design grid is located in the lower pane of the window. You add the fields you want included in the query to the Field row in the grid. ***Why add fields to the grid?*** *Only the fields that appear in the design grid will be included in the query results.* The following step begins creating a query that Bavant Publishing might use to obtain the customer number, customer name, amount paid, and current due for a particular customer.

1

- Double-tap or double-click the Customer Number field in the field list to add the field to the query.

Q&A What if I add the wrong field?
Tap or click just above the field name in the design grid to select the column and then press the DELETE key to remove the field.

- Double-tap or double-click the Customer Name field in the field list to add the field to the query.
- Add the Amount Paid field to the query.
- Add the Current Due field to the query (Figure 2–5).

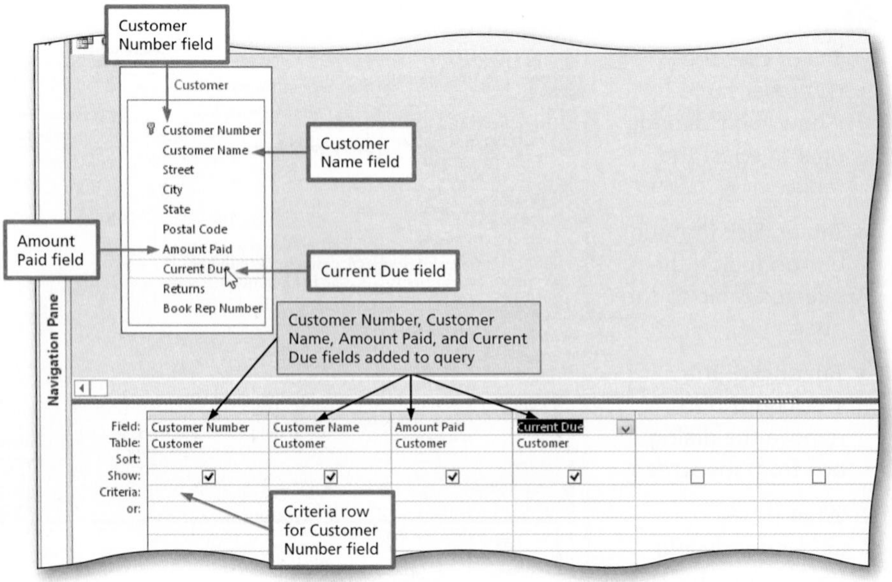

Figure 2–5

Q&A What if I want to include all fields? Do I have to add each field individually?
No. Instead of adding individual fields, you can double-tap or double-click the asterisk (*) to add the asterisk to the design grid. The asterisk is a shortcut indicating all fields are to be included.

If you are using your finger on a touch screen and are having difficulty completing the steps in this chapter, consider using a stylus. Many people find it easier to be precise with a stylus than with a finger. In addition, with a stylus you see the pointer. If you still are having trouble completing the steps with a stylus, try using a mouse.

Determining Criteria

When you use queries, usually you are looking for those records that satisfy some criterion. In the simple query you created in the previous chapter, for example, you entered a criterion to restrict the records to those with the book rep number 53. In another query, you might want the name, amount paid, and current due amounts for the customer whose number is CSU10, for example, or for those customers whose names start with the letters, Gr. You enter criteria in the Criteria row in the design grid below the field name to which the criterion applies. For example, to indicate that the customer number must be CSU10, you first must add the Customer Number field to the design grid. You then would type CSU10 in the Criteria row below the Customer Number field.

Running the Query

After adding the appropriate fields and defining the query's criteria, you must run the query to get the results. To view the results of the query from Design view, tap or click the Run button to instruct Access to run the query, that is, to perform the necessary actions to produce and display the results in Datasheet view.

BTW
Touch Screen Differences
The Office and Windows interfaces may vary if you are using a touch screen. For this reason, you might notice that the function or appearance of your touch screen differs slightly from this chapter's presentation.

To Use Text Data in a Criterion

To use **text data** (data in a field whose data type is Short Text) in criteria, simply type the text in the Criteria row below the corresponding field name, just as you did in Chapter 1. In Access, you do not need to enclose text data in quotation marks as you do in many other database management systems. ***Why?*** *Access will enter the quotation marks automatically, so you can simply type the desired text.* The following steps finish creating a query that Bavant Publishing might use to obtain the customer number, customer name, amount paid, and current due amount of customer CSU10. These steps add the appropriate criterion so that only the desired customer will appear in the results. The steps also save the query.

1

- Tap or click the Criteria row for the Customer Number field to produce an insertion point.
- Type `CSU10` as the criterion (Figure 2–6).

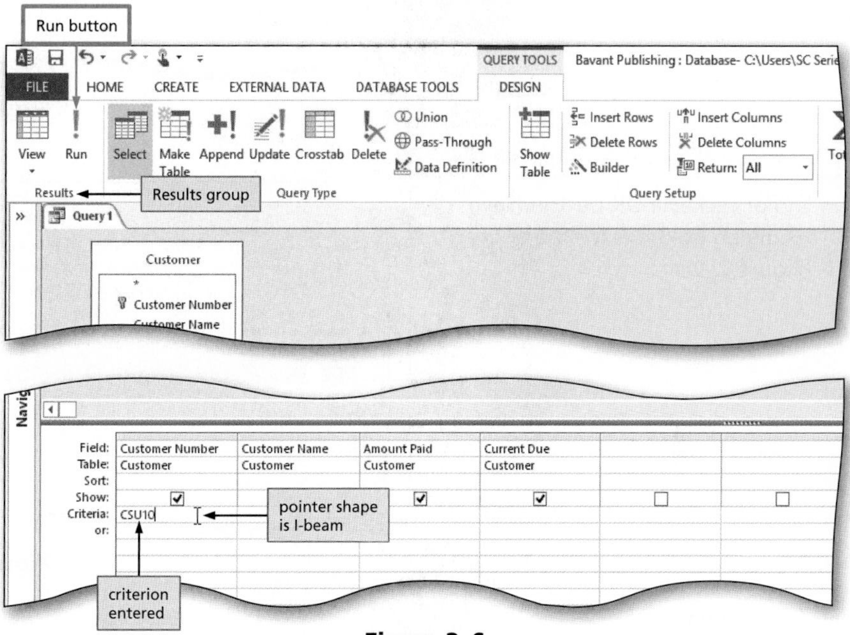

Figure 2–6

2

- Tap or click the Run button (QUERY TOOLS DESIGN tab | Results group) to run the query (Figure 2–7).

Q&A Can I also use the View button in the Results group to run the query?

Yes. You can tap or click the View button to view the query results in Datasheet view.

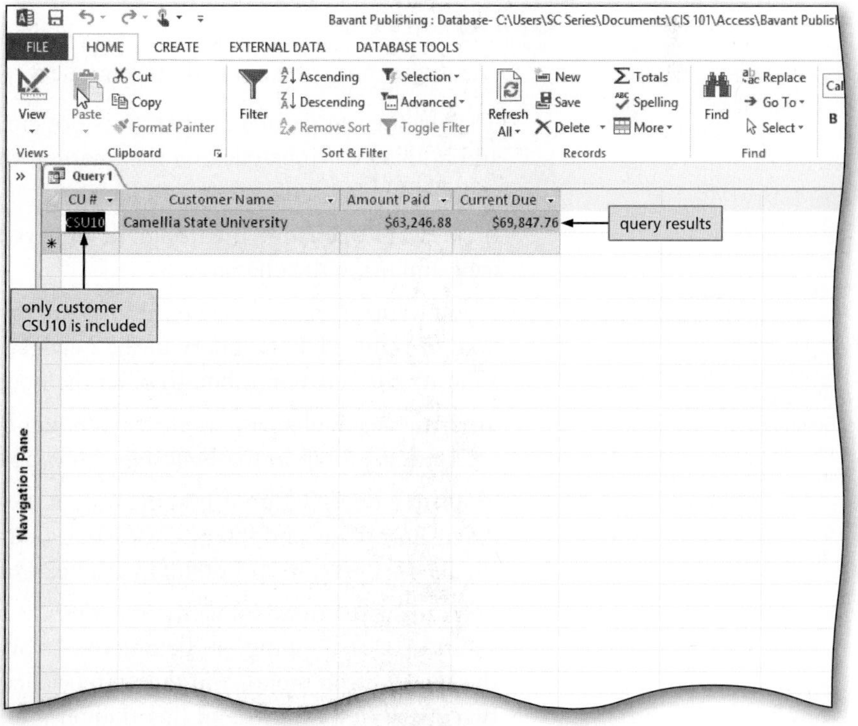

Figure 2–7

3

- Tap or click the Save button on the Quick Access Toolbar to display the Save As dialog box.
- Type `Ch2q01` as the name of the query (Figure 2–8).

Q&A Can I also save from Design view?
Yes. You can save the query when you view it in Design view just as you can save it when you view query results in Datasheet view.

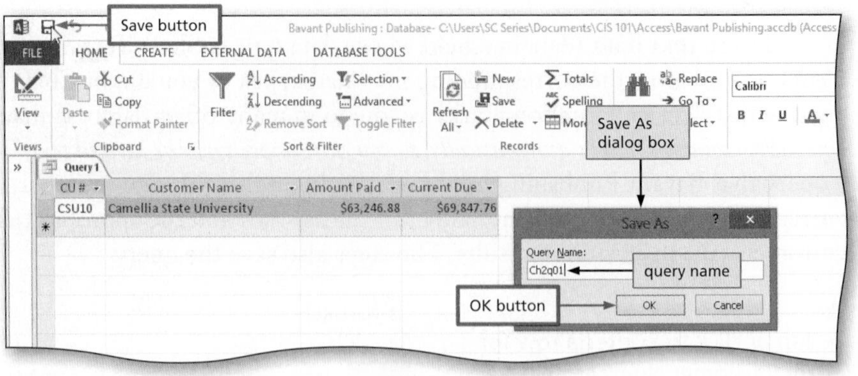

Figure 2–8

4

- Tap or click the OK button (Save As dialog box) to save the query (Figure 2–9).

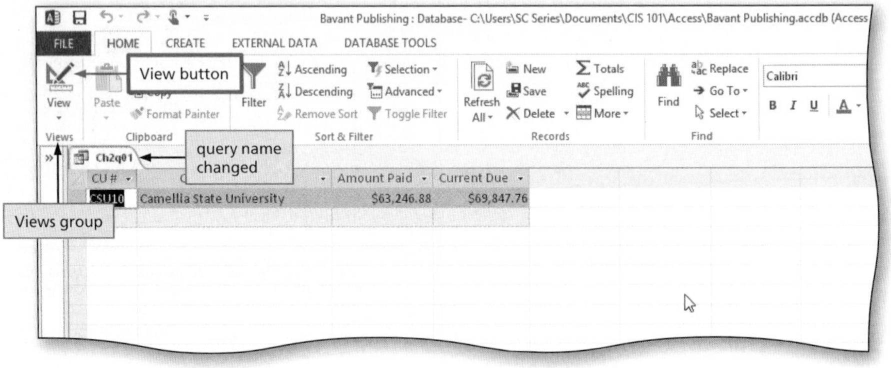

Figure 2–9

Other Ways

1. Press and hold or right-click query tab, tap or click Save on shortcut menu
2. Press CTRL + S

BTW
Touch and Pointers
Remember that if you are using your finger on a touch screen, you will not see the pointer.

BTW
The Ribbon and Screen Resolution
Access may change how the groups and buttons within the groups appear on the ribbon, depending on the computer's screen resolution. Thus, your ribbon may look different from the ones in this book if you are using a screen resolution other than 1366 × 768.

Using Saved Queries

After you have created and saved a query, you can use it in a variety of ways:

- To view the results of a query that is not currently open, open it by pressing and holding or right-clicking the query in the Navigation Pane and tapping or clicking Open on the shortcut menu.
- If you want to change the design of a query that is already open, return to Design view and make the changes.
- If you want to change the design of a query that is not currently open, press and hold or right-click the query in the Navigation Pane and then tap or click Design View on the shortcut menu to open the query in Design view.
- To print the results with a query open, tap or click FILE on the ribbon, tap or click the Print tab in the Backstage view, and then tap or click Quick Print.
- To print a query without first opening it, be sure the query is selected in the Navigation Pane and tap or click FILE on the ribbon, tap or click the Print tab in the Backstage view, and then tap or click Quick Print.
- You can switch between views of a query using the View button (HOME tab | Views group). Tapping or clicking the arrow at the bottom of the button produces the View button menu. You then tap or click the desired view in the menu. The two query views you use in this chapter are Datasheet view (to see the results) and Design view (to change the design). You can tap or click the top part of the

View button, in which case you will switch to the view identified by the icon on the button. In Figure 2–9, the View button displays the icon for Design view, so tapping or clicking the button would change to Design view. For the most part, the icon on the button represents the view you want, so you can usually simply tap or click the button.

BTW

On Screen Keyboard

To display the on-screen touch keyboard, tap the Touch Keyboard button on the Windows taskbar. When finished using the touch keyboard, tap the X button on the touch keyboard to close the keyboard

Wildcards

Microsoft Access supports wildcards. **Wildcards** are symbols that represent any character or combination of characters. One common wildcard, the **asterisk** (*), represents any collection of characters. Another wildcard symbol is the **question mark (?)**, which represents any individual character.

CONSIDER THIS

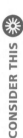

What does S* represent? What does T?m represent?

S* represents the letter, S, followed by any collection of characters. T?m represents the letter, T, followed by any single character, followed by the letter, m. A search for T?m might return the names Tim or Tom.

To Use a Wildcard

1 CREATE QUERIES | 2 USE CRITERIA | 3 SORT DATA | 4 JOIN TABLES | 5 EXPORT RESULTS
6 PERFORM CALCULATIONS | 7 CREATE CROSSTAB | 8 CUSTOMIZE NAVIGATION PANE

The following steps modify the previous query to use the asterisk wildcard so that Bavant Publishing can select only those customers whose names begin with S. ***Why?** Because you do not know how many characters will follow the S, the asterisk wildcard symbol is appropriate.* The steps also save the query with a new name using the Save As command.

1

- Tap or click the View button (HOME tab | Views group), shown in Figure 2–9 on page AC 82, to return to Design view.
- If necessary, tap or click the Criteria row below the Customer Number field to produce an insertion point.

Q&A The text I entered now has quotation marks surrounding it. What happened?
Criteria for text data needs to be enclosed in quotation marks. You do not have to type the quotation marks; Access adds them automatically.

- Use the DELETE or BACKSPACE key as necessary to delete the current entry.
- Tap or click the Criteria row below the Customer Name field to produce an insertion point.
- Type `S*` as the criterion (Figure 2–10).

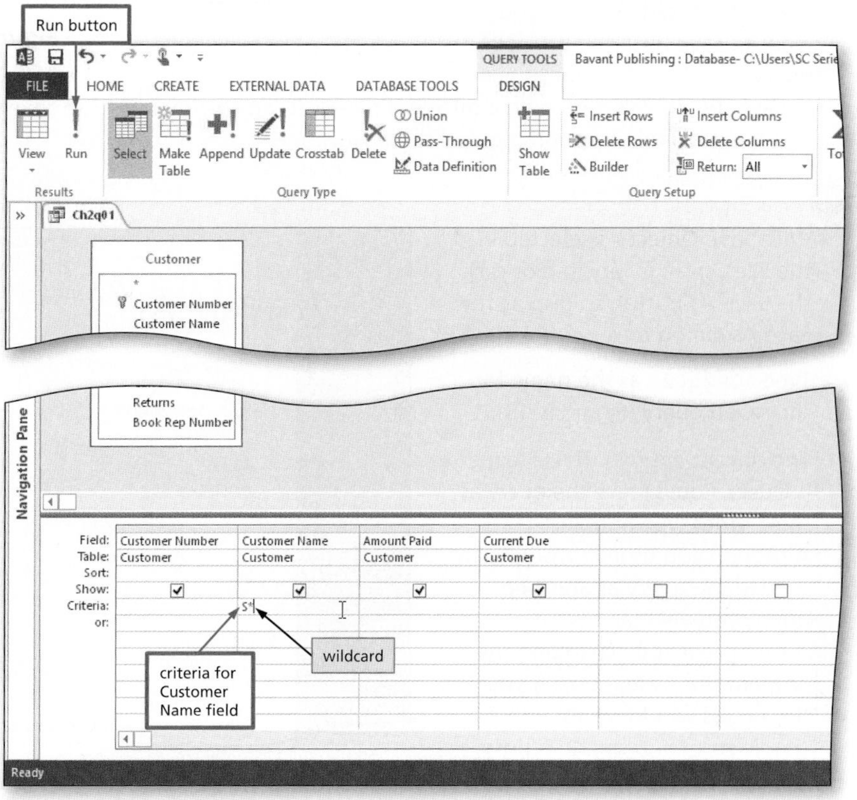

Figure 2–10

2

- Run the query by tapping or clicking the Run button (QUERY TOOLS DESIGN tab | Results group) (Figure 2–11).

Experiment

- Change the letter S to lowercase in the criteria and run the query to determine whether case makes a difference when entering a wildcard.

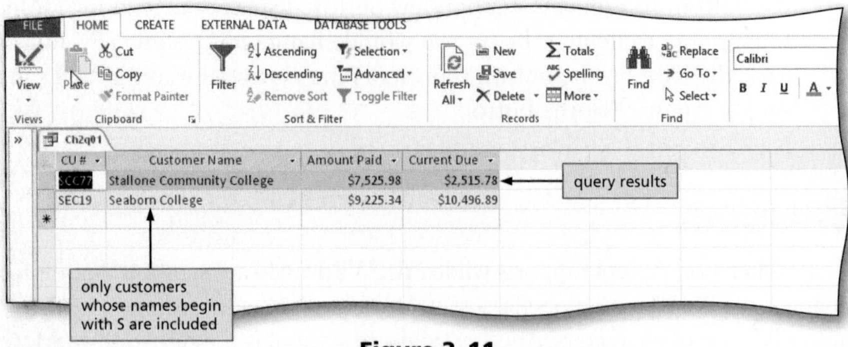

Figure 2–11

3

- Tap or click FILE on the ribbon to open the Backstage view.
- Tap or click the Save As tab in the Backstage view to display the Save As gallery.
- Tap or click Save Object As in the File Types area (Figure 2–12).

Q&A Can I just tap or click the Save button on the Quick Access Toolbar as I did when saving the previous query?

If you tapped or clicked the Save button, you would replace the previous query with the version you just created. Because you want to save both the previous query and the new one, you need to save the new version with a different name. To do so, you must use Save Object As, which is available through the Backstage view.

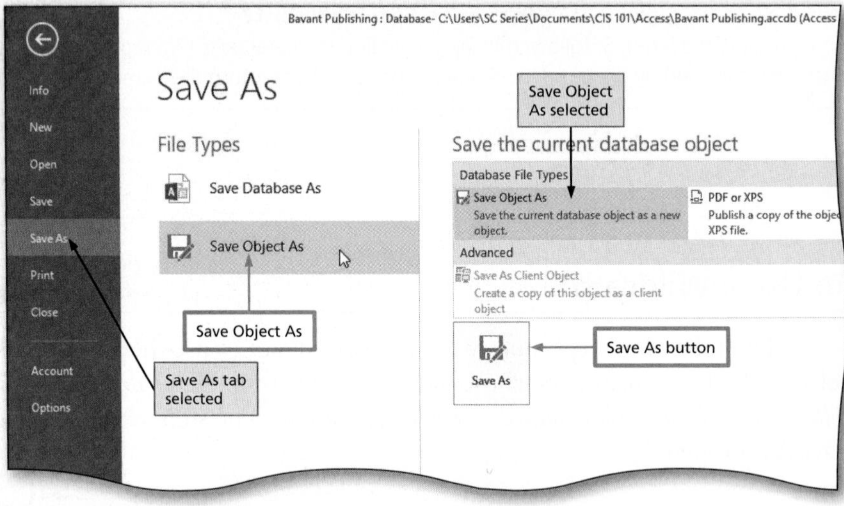

Figure 2–12

4

- With Save Object As selected in the File Types gallery, tap or click the Save As button to display the Save As dialog box.
- Type `Ch2q02` as the name for the saved query (Figure 2–13).

Q&A The current entry in the As text box is Query. Could I save the query as some other type of object?

Although you usually would want to save the query as another query, you also can save it as a form or report by changing the entry in the As text box. If you do, Access would create either a simple form or a simple report for the query.

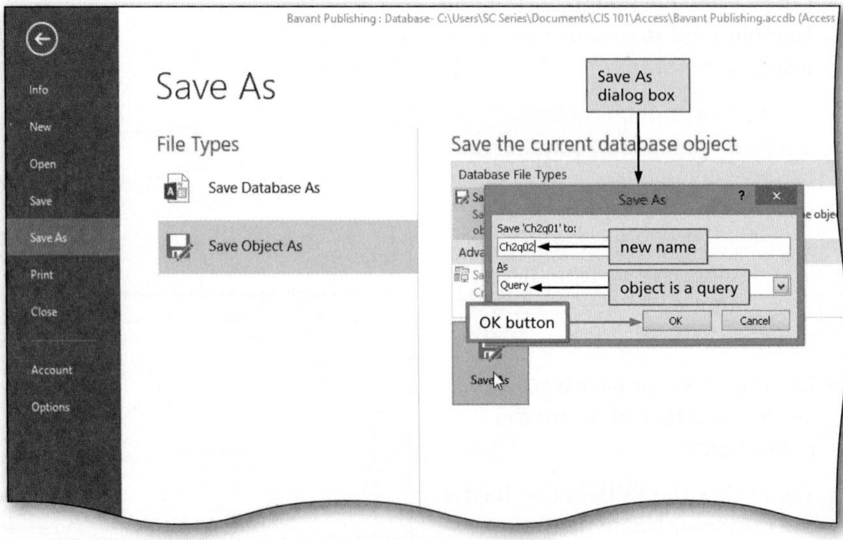

Figure 2–13

5

- Tap or click the OK button (Save As dialog box) to save the query with the new name and close the Backstage view (Figure 2–14).

Q&A How can I tell that the query was saved with the new name?
The new name will appear on the tab.

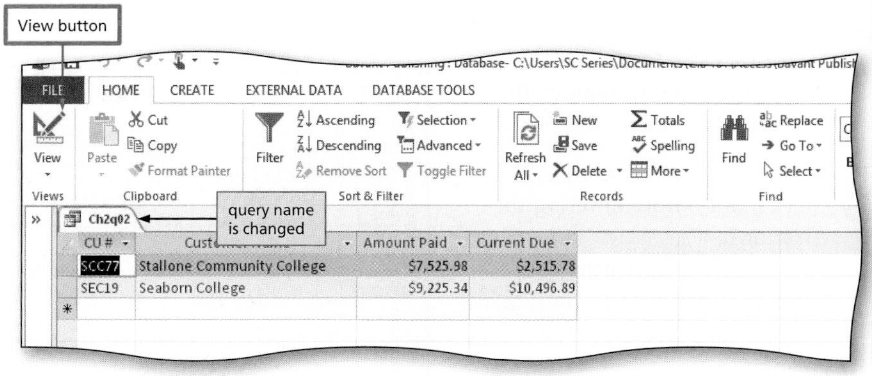

Figure 2–14

Other Ways

1. Tap or click Design View button on status bar

To Use Criteria for a Field Not Included in the Results

1 CREATE QUERIES | 2 USE CRITERIA | 3 SORT DATA | 4 JOIN TABLES | 5 EXPORT RESULTS
6 PERFORM CALCULATIONS | 7 CREATE CROSSTAB | 8 CUSTOMIZE NAVIGATION PANE

In some cases, you might require criteria for a particular field that should not appear in the results of the query. For example, you may want to see the customer number, customer name, address, and amount paid for all customers located in Gaston. The criteria involve the City field, but you do not want to include the City field in the results.

To enter a criterion for the City field, it must be included in the design grid. Normally, it would then appear in the results. To prevent this from happening, remove the check mark from its Show check box in the Show row of the grid. ***Why?*** *A check mark in the Show Check box instructs Access to show the field in the result. If you remove the check mark, you can use the field in the query but not display it in the query results.*

The following steps modify the previous query so that Bavant Publishing can select only those customers located in Gaston. Bavant does not want the city to appear in the results, however. The steps also save the query with a new name.

1

- Tap or click the View button (HOME tab | Views group), shown in Figure 2–14, to return to Design view.

Q&A The text I entered is now preceded by the word, Like. What happened?
Criteria including wildcards need to be preceded by the word, Like. However, you do not have to type it; Access adds the word automatically to any criterion involving a wildcard.

- Erase the criterion in the Criteria row of the Customer Name field.
- Add the City field to the query.
- Type `Gaston` as the criterion for the City field (Figure 2–15).

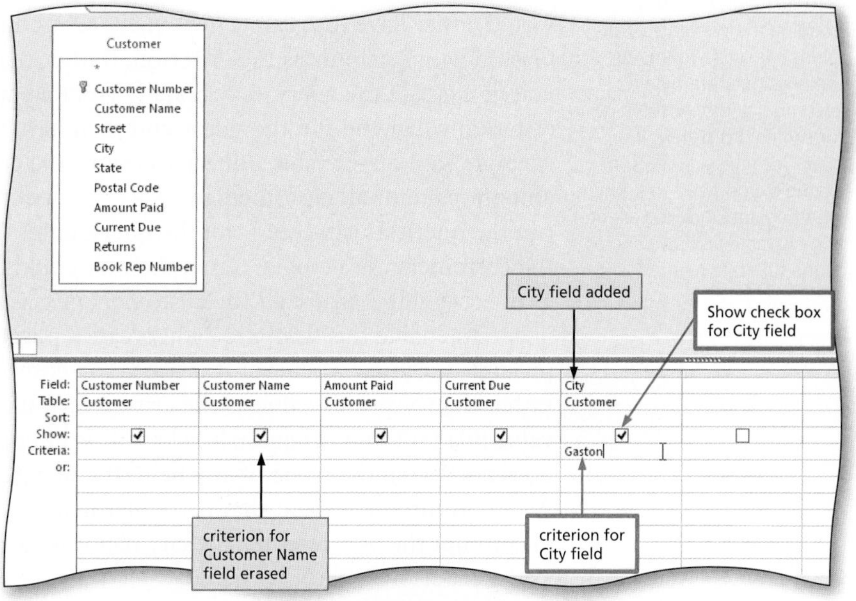

Figure 2–15

2

- Tap or click the Show check box for the City field to remove the check mark (Figure 2–16).

Q&A Could I have removed the check mark before entering the criterion?

Yes. The order in which you perform the two operations does not matter.

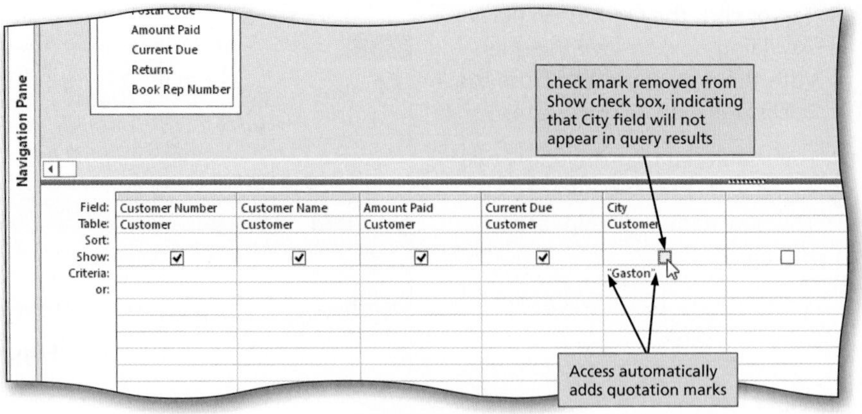

Figure 2–16

3

- Run the query (Figure 2–17).

Experiment

- Tap or click the View button to return to Design view, enter a different city name as the criterion, and run the query. Repeat this process with additional city names, including at least one city name that is not in the database. When finished, change the criterion back to Gaston.

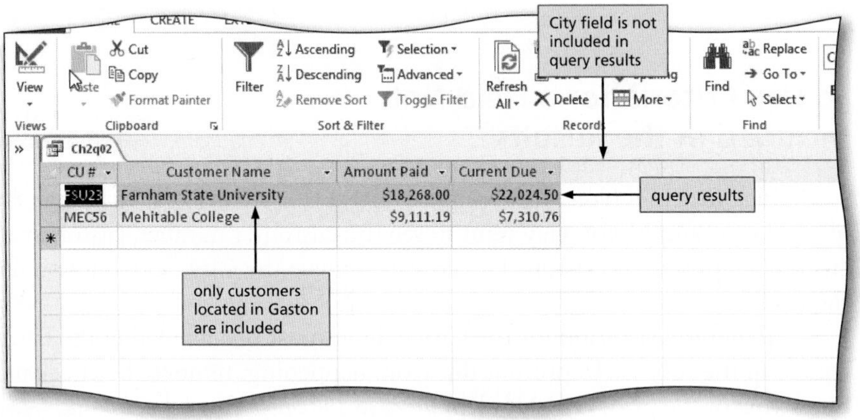

Figure 2–17

BTW

Designing Queries

Before creating queries, examine the contents of the tables involved. You need to know the data type for each field and how the data for the field is stored. If a query includes a state, for example, you need to know whether state is stored as the two-character abbreviation or as the full state name.

Creating a Parameter Query

If you wanted to find customers located in Adelphia instead of Gaston, you would either have to create a new query or modify the existing query by replacing Gaston with Adelphia as the criterion. Rather than giving a specific criterion when you first create the query, occasionally you may want to be able to enter part of the criterion when you run the query and then have the appropriate results appear. For example, you might want a query to return the customer number, customer name, and amount paid for all customers in a specific city, specifying a different city each time you run the query. A user could run the query, enter Adelphia as the city, and then see all the customers in Adelphia. Later, the user could use the same query but enter Gaston as the city, and then see all the customers in Gaston.

To enable this flexibility, you create a **parameter query**, which is a query that prompts for input whenever it is used. You enter a parameter (the prompt for the user), rather than a specific value as the criterion. You create the parameter by enclosing a value in a criterion in square brackets. It is important that the value in the brackets does not match the name of any field. If you enter a field name in square brackets, Access assumes you want that particular field and does not prompt the user for input. To prompt the user to enter the city name as the input, you could place [Enter City] as the criterion in the City field.

To Create and View a Parameter Query

The following steps create a parameter query. ***Why?*** *The parameter query will give users at Bavant the ability to enter a different city when they run the query rather than having a specific city as part of the criterion in the query.* The steps also save the query with a new name.

1

- Return to Design view.
- Erase the current criterion in the City column, and then type `[Enter City]` as the new criterion (Figure 2–18).

Q&A What is the purpose of the square brackets?
The square brackets indicate that the text entered is not text that the value in the column must match. Without the brackets, Access would search for records on which the city is Enter City.

What if I typed a field name in the square brackets?
Access would simply use the value in that field. To create a parameter query, you must not use a field name in the square brackets.

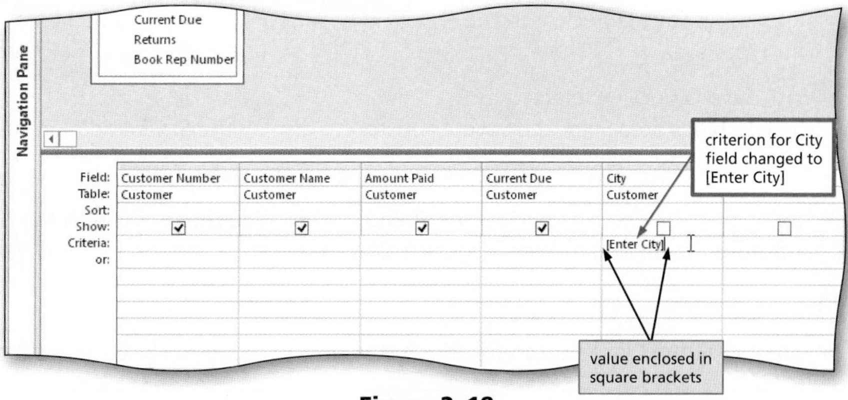

Figure 2–18

2

- Tap or click the Run button (QUERY TOOLS DESIGN tab | Results group) to display the Enter Parameter Value dialog box (Figure 2–19).

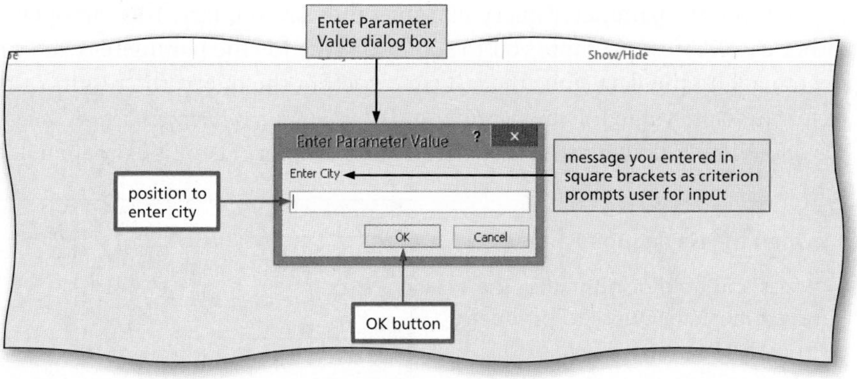

Figure 2–19

3

- Type `Adelphia` as the parameter value in the Enter City text box, and then tap or click the OK button (Enter Parameter Value dialog box) to close the dialog box and view the query (Figure 2–20).

Experiment

- Try using other characters between the square brackets. In each case, run the query. When finished, change the characters between the square brackets back to Enter City.

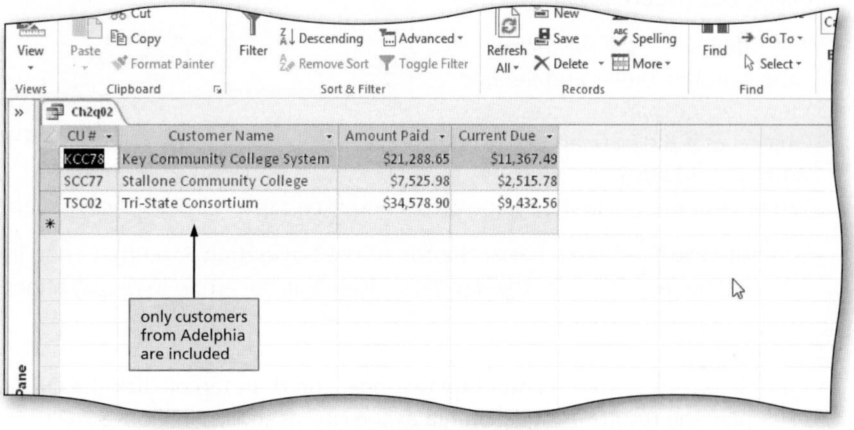

Figure 2–20

4

- Tap or click FILE on the ribbon to open the Backstage view.
- Tap or click the Save As tab in the Backstage view to display the Save As gallery.
- Tap or click Save Object As in the File Types area.
- With Save Object As selected in the File Types area, click the Save As button to display the Save As dialog box.
- Type `Customer-City Query` as the name for the saved query.
- Tap or click the OK button (Save As dialog box) to save the query with the new name and close the Backstage view (Figure 2–21).

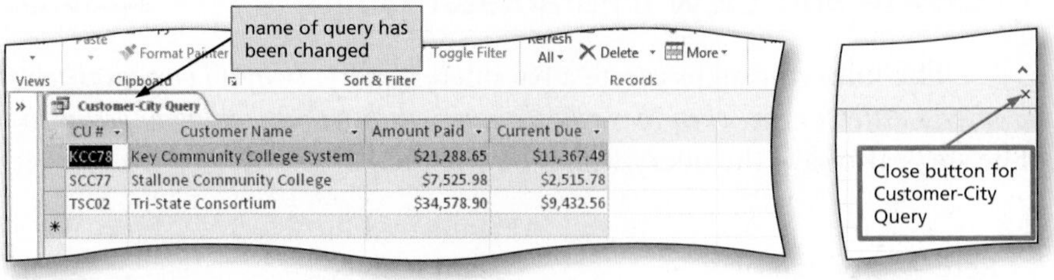

Figure 2–21

5

- Tap or click the Close button for the Customer-City query to close the query.

Break Point: If you wish to take a break, this is a good place to do so. You can exit Access now. To resume later, run Access, open the database called Bavant Publishing, and continue following the steps from this location forward.

To Use a Parameter Query

1 CREATE QUERIES | 2 USE CRITERIA | 3 SORT DATA | 4 JOIN TABLES | 5 EXPORT RESULTS
6 PERFORM CALCULATIONS | 7 CREATE CROSSTAB | 8 CUSTOMIZE NAVIGATION PANE

You use a parameter query like any other saved query. You can open it or you can print the query results. In either case, Access prompts you to supply a value for the parameter each time you use the query. If changes have been made to the data since the last time you ran the query, the results of the query may be different, even if you enter the same value for the parameter. ***Why?*** *As with other queries, the query always uses the data that is currently in the table.* The following steps use the parameter query named Customer-City Query.

1

- Open the Navigation Pane.
- Press and hold or right-click the Customer-City Query to produce a shortcut menu.
- Tap or click Open on the shortcut menu to open the query and display the Enter Parameter Value dialog box (Figure 2–22).

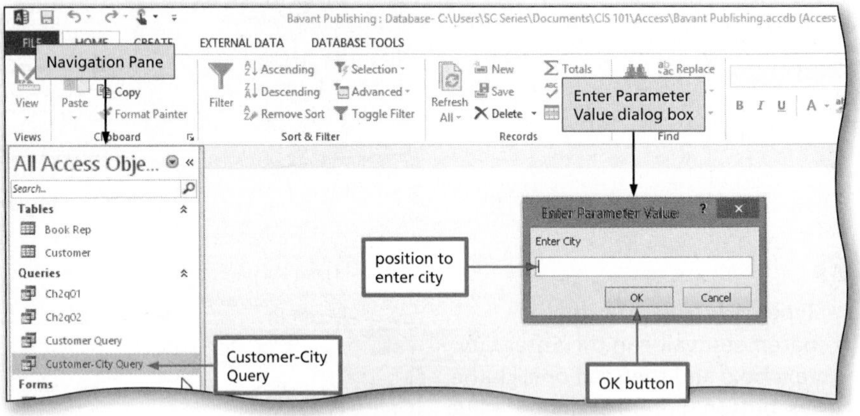

Figure 2–22

Q&A The title bar for my Navigation Pane contains Tables and Related Views rather than All Access Objects as it did in Chapter 1. What should I do?
Tap or click the Navigation Pane arrow and then tap or click All Access Objects.

I do not have the Search bar at the top of the Navigation Pane that I had in Chapter 1. What should I do?
Press and hold or right-click the Navigation Pane title bar arrow to display a shortcut menu, and then tap or click Search Bar.

2

- Type `Adelphia` in the Enter City text box, and then tap or click the OK button (Enter Parameter Value dialog box) to display the results using Adelphia as the city, as shown in Figure 2–21.
- Close the query.

To Use a Number in a Criterion

To enter a number in a criterion, type the number without any dollar signs or commas. ***Why?*** *If you enter a dollar sign, Access assumes you are entering text. If you enter a comma, Access considers the criterion invalid.* The following steps create a query that Bavant Publishing might use to display all customers whose current due amount is $0. The steps also save the query with a new name.

1

- Close the Navigation Pane.
- Tap or click CREATE on the ribbon to display the CREATE tab.
- Tap or click the Query Design button (CREATE tab | Queries group) to create a new query.
- Tap or click the Customer table (Show Table dialog box) to select the table.

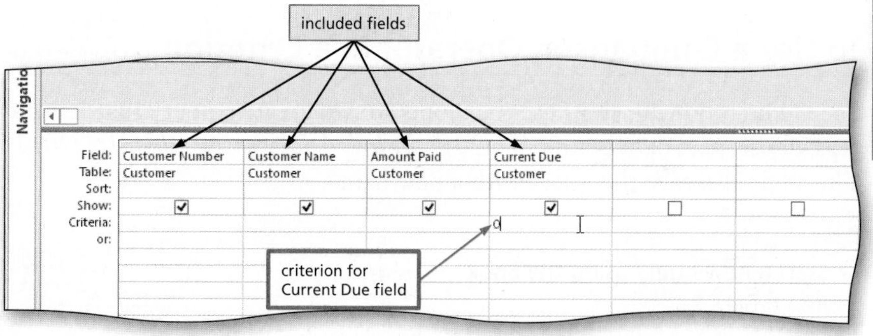

Figure 2–23

- Tap or click the Add button to add the selected table to the query.
- Tap or click the Close button to remove the dialog box from the screen.
- Drag the lower edge of the field list down far enough so all fields in the list are displayed.
- Include the Customer Number, Customer Name, Amount Paid, and Current Due fields in the query.
- Type `0` as the criterion for the Current Due field (Figure 2–23).

Q&A Do I need to enter a dollar sign and decimal point?
No. Access will interpret 0 as $0 because the data type for the Current Due field is currency.

2

- Run the query (Figure 2–24).

Q&A Why did Access display the results as $0.00 when I only entered 0?
Access uses the format for the field to determine how to display the result. In this case, the format indicated that Access should include the dollar sign, decimal point, and two decimal places.

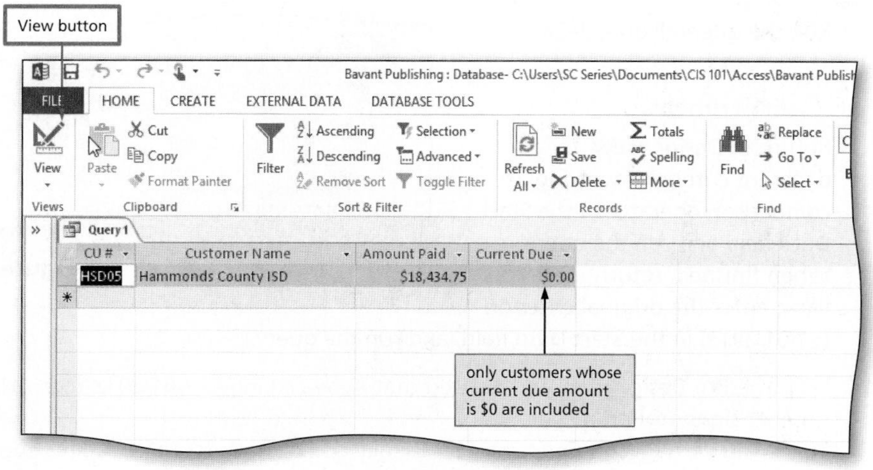

Figure 2–24

3

- Save the query as Ch2q03.

Q&A How do I know when to use the Save button to save a query or use the Backstage view to perform a Save As?
If you are saving a new query, the simplest way is to use the Save button on the Quick Access Toolbar. If you are saving changes to a previously saved query but do not want to change the name, use the Save button. If you want to save a previously saved query with a new name, you must use the Backstage view and perform a Save Object As.

- Close the query.

Comparison Operators

Unless you specify otherwise, Access assumes that the criteria you enter involve equality (exact matches). In the last query, for example, you were requesting those customers whose current due amount is equal to 0 (zero). In other situations, you might want to find a range of results; for example, you could request customers whose current due is greater than $1,000.00. If you want a query to return something other than an exact match, you must enter the appropriate **comparison operator**. The comparison operators are > (greater than), < (less than), >= (greater than or equal to), <= (less than or equal to), and NOT (not equal to).

To Use a Comparison Operator in a Criterion

1 CREATE QUERIES | 2 USE CRITERIA | 3 SORT DATA | 4 JOIN TABLES | 5 EXPORT RESULTS
6 PERFORM CALCULATIONS | 7 CREATE CROSSTAB | 8 CUSTOMIZE NAVIGATION PANE

The following steps use the > operator to create a query that Bavant Publishing might use to find all book reps whose start date is after 1/1/2013. ***Why?*** *A date greater than 1/1/2013 means the date comes after 1/1/2013.* The steps also save the query with a new name.

1

- Start a new query using the Book Rep table.
- Include the Book Rep Number, Last Name, First Name, and Start Date fields.
- Type `>1/01/2013` as the criterion for the Start Date field (Figure 2–25).

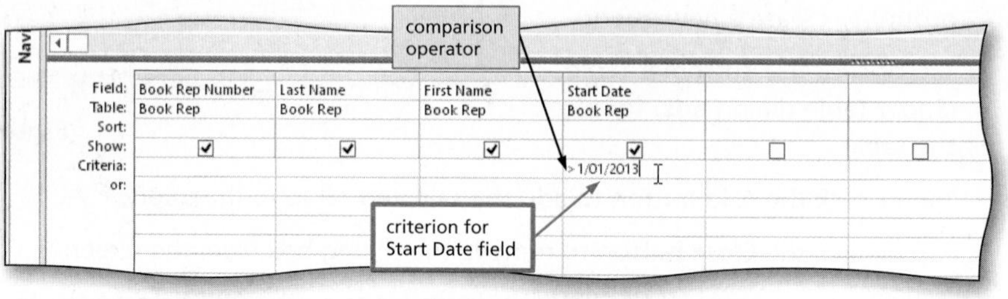

Figure 2–25

Q&A Did I have to type the leading zero in the Day portion of the date?
No. You could have typed 1/1/2013. Some people often type the day using two digits, such as 1/01/2013. You also could have typed a leading zero in the month, 01/01/2013.

2

- Run the query (Figure 2–26).

Experiment

- Return to Design view. Try a different criterion involving a comparison operator in the Start Date field and run the query. When finished, return to Design view, enter the original criterion (>1/01/2013) in the Start Date field, and run the query.

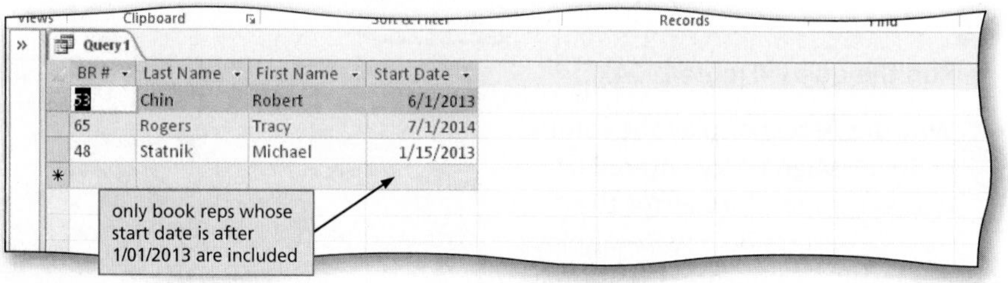

Figure 2–26

Q&A I returned to Design view and noticed that Access changed 1/01/2013 to #1/01/2013#. Why does the date now have number signs around it?
This is the date format in Access. You usually do not have to enter the number signs because in most cases Access will insert them automatically.

My records are in a different order. Is this a problem?
No. The important thing is which records are included in the results. You will see later in this chapter how you can specify the specific order you want for cases when the order is important.

Can I use the same comparison operators with text data?
Yes. Comparison operators function the same whether you use them with number fields, currency fields, date fields, or text fields.

3

- Save the query as Ch2q04.
- Close the query.

Using Compound Criteria

Often your search data must satisfy more than one criterion. This type of criterion is called a **compound criterion** and is created using the words AND or OR.

In an **AND criterion**, each individual criterion must be true in order for the compound criterion to be true. For example, an AND criterion would allow you to find customers that have returns greater than $0.00 and whose book rep is book rep 42.

An **OR criterion** is true if either individual criterion is true. An OR criterion would allow you to find customers that have returns greater than $0.00 as well as customers whose book rep is book rep 42. In this case, any customer who has returns greater than $0.00 would be included in the answer, regardless of whether the customer's book rep is book rep 42. Likewise, any customer whose book rep is book rep 42 would be included, regardless of whether the customer has returns greater than $0.00.

BTW
Queries: Query-by-Example
Query-By-Example, often referred to as QBE, was a query language first proposed in the mid-1970s. In this approach, users asked questions by filling in a table on the screen. The Access approach to queries is based on Query-By-Example.

To Use a Compound Criterion Involving AND

1 CREATE QUERIES | 2 USE CRITERIA | 3 SORT DATA | 4 JOIN TABLES | 5 EXPORT RESULTS
6 PERFORM CALCULATIONS | 7 CREATE CROSSTAB | 8 CUSTOMIZE NAVIGATION PANE

To combine criteria with AND, place the criteria on the same row of the design grid. ***Why?*** *Placing the criteria in the same row indicates that both criteria must be true in Access.* The following steps use an AND criterion to enable Bavant to find those customers who have returns greater than $0.00 and whose book rep is rep 42. The steps also save the query.

1

- Start a new query using the Customer table.
- Include the Customer Number, Customer Name, Amount Paid, Current Due, Returns, and Book Rep Number fields.
- Type `>0` as the criterion for the Returns field.
- Type `42` as the criterion for the Book Rep Number field (Figure 2–27).

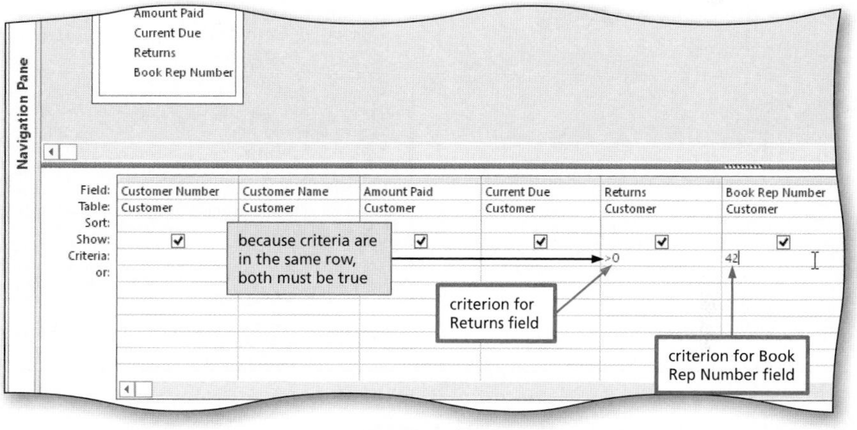

Figure 2–27

2

- Run the query (Figure 2–28).

3

- Save the query as Ch2q05.

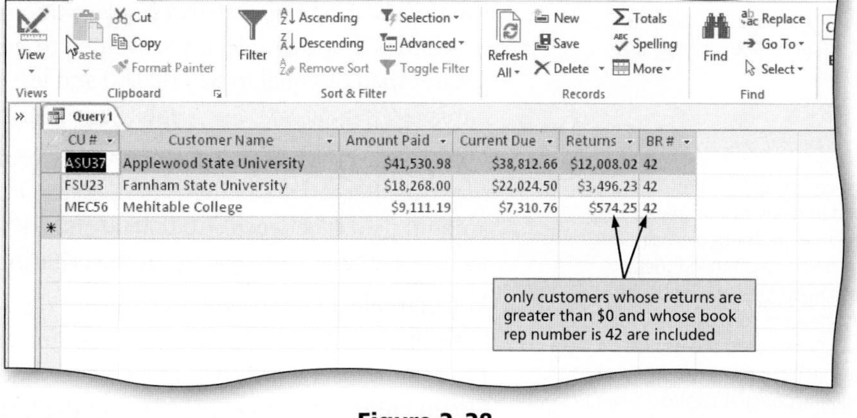

Figure 2–28

To Use a Compound Criterion Involving OR

1 CREATE QUERIES | 2 USE CRITERIA | 3 SORT DATA | 4 JOIN TABLES | 5 EXPORT RESULTS
6 PERFORM CALCULATIONS | 7 CREATE CROSSTAB | 8 CUSTOMIZE NAVIGATION PANE

To combine criteria with OR, each criterion must go on separate rows in the Criteria area of the grid. ***Why?*** *Placing criteria on separate rows indicates at least one criterion must be true in Access.* The following steps use an OR criterion to enable Bavant to find those customers who have returns greater than $0.00 or whose book rep is rep 42 (or both). The steps also save the query with a new name.

1

- Return to Design view.
- If necessary, tap or click the Criteria entry for the Book Rep Number field and then use the BACKSPACE key or the DELETE key to erase the entry ("42").
- Tap or click the or row (the row below the Criteria row) for the Book Rep Number field, and then type `42` as the entry (Figure 2–29).

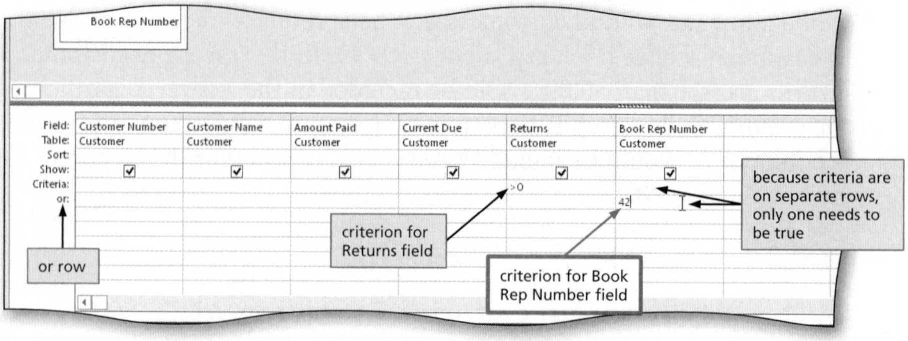

Figure 2–29

2

- Run the query (Figure 2–30).

3

- Save the query as Ch2q06.

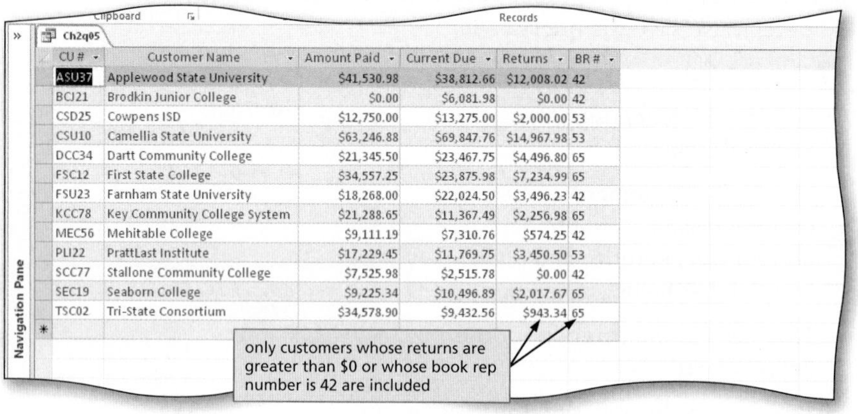

Figure 2–30

BTW
Rearranging Fields in a Query
To move a field in the design grid, tap or click the column selector for the field to select the field and drag it to the appropriate location.

BTW
Q&As
For a complete list of the Q&As found in many of the step-by-step sequences in this book, visit the Q&A resource on the Student Companion Site located on www.cengagebrain.com. For detailed instructions about accessing available resources, visit www.cengage.com/ct/studentdownload or contact your instructor for information about accessing the required files.

Special Criteria

You can use three special criteria in queries:

1. If you want to create a criterion involving a range of values in a single field, you can use the **AND operator**. You place the word AND between the individual conditions. For example, if you wanted to find all customers whose amount paid is greater than or equal to $20,000.00 and less than or equal to $40,000.00, you would enter `>= 20000 AND <= 40000` as the criterion in the Amount Paid column.
2. You can select values in a given range by using the **BETWEEN operator**. This is often an alternative to the AND operator. For example, to find all customers whose amount paid is between $20,000.00 and $40,000.00, inclusive, you would enter `BETWEEN 20000 AND 40000` as the criterion in the Amount Paid column.
3. You can select a list of values by using the **IN operator**. You follow the word IN with the list of values in parentheses. For example, to find customers whose book rep number is 42 and customers whose book rep is 65 using the IN operator, you would enter `IN ("42","65")` on the Criteria row in the Book Rep Number column. Unlike when you enter a simple criterion, you must enclose text values in quotation marks.

CONSIDER THIS

How would you find customers whose book rep number is 42 or 65 without using the IN operator?
Place the number 42 in the Criteria row of the Book Rep Number column. Place the number 65 in the or row of the Book Rep Number column.

Sorting

In some queries, the order in which the records appear is irrelevant. All you need to be concerned about are the records that appear in the results. It does not matter which one is first or which one is last.

In other queries, however, the order can be very important. You may want to see the cities in which customers are located and would like them arranged alphabetically. Perhaps you want to see the customers listed by book rep number. Further, within all the customers of any given book rep, you might want them to be listed by amount paid from largest amount to smallest.

To order the records in a query result in a particular way, you **sort** the records. The field or fields on which the records are sorted is called the **sort key**. If you are sorting on more than one field (such as sorting by amount paid within book rep number), the more important field (Book Rep Number) is called the **major key** (also called the **primary sort key**) and the less important field (Amount Paid) is called the **minor key** (also called the **secondary sort key**).

To sort in Microsoft Access, specify the sort order in the Sort row of the design grid below the field that is the sort key. If you specify more than one sort key, the sort key on the left will be the major sort key, and the one on the right will be the minor key.

BTW
Sorting Data in a Query
When sorting data in a query, the records in the underlying tables (the tables on which the query is based) are not actually rearranged. Instead, the DBMS determines the most efficient method of simply displaying the records in the requested order. The records in the underlying tables remain in their original order.

BTW
Clearing the Design Grid
You also can clear the design grid using the ribbon. To do so, tap or click the HOME tab, tap or click the Advanced button to display the Advanced menu, and then tap or click Clear Grid on the Advanced menu.

To Clear the Design Grid

1 CREATE QUERIES | 2 USE CRITERIA | 3 SORT DATA | 4 JOIN TABLES | 5 EXPORT RESULTS
6 PERFORM CALCULATIONS | 7 CREATE CROSSTAB | 8 CUSTOMIZE NAVIGATION PANE

Why? *If the fields you want to include in the next query are different from those in the previous query, it is usually simpler to start with a clear grid, that is, one with no fields already in the design grid.* You always can clear the entries in the design grid by closing the query and then starting over. A simpler approach to clearing the entries is to select all the entries and then press the DELETE key. The following steps return to Design view and clear the design grid.

1

- Return to Design view.
- Tap or click just above the Customer Number column heading in the grid to select the column.

Q&A I clicked above the column heading, but the column is not selected. What should I do?
You did not point to the correct location. Be sure the pointer changes into a down-pointing arrow and then tap or click again.

- Hold the SHIFT key down and tap or click just above the Book Rep Number column heading to select all the columns (Figure 2–31).

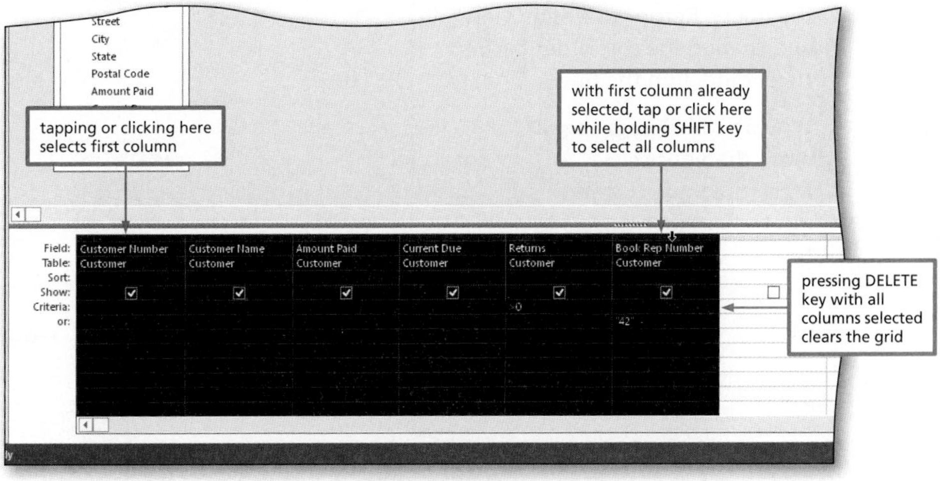

Figure 2–31

2

- Press the DELETE key to clear the design grid.

To Sort Data in a Query

1 CREATE QUERIES | 2 USE CRITERIA | 3 SORT DATA | 4 JOIN TABLES | 5 EXPORT RESULTS
6 PERFORM CALCULATIONS | 7 CREATE CROSSTAB | 8 CUSTOMIZE NAVIGATION PANE

If you determine that the query results should be sorted, you will need to specify the sort key. The following steps sort the cities in the Customer table by indicating that the City field is to be sorted. The steps specify Ascending sort order. ***Why?*** *When sorting text data, Ascending sort order arranges the results in alphabetical order.*

1

- Include the City field in the design grid.
- Tap or click the Sort row below the City field, and then tap or click the Sort arrow to display a menu of possible sort orders (Figure 2–32).

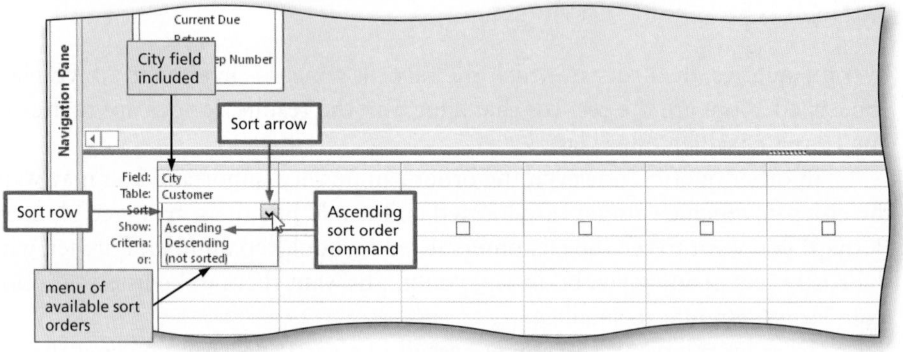

Figure 2–32

2

- Tap or click Ascending to select the sort order (Figure 2–33).

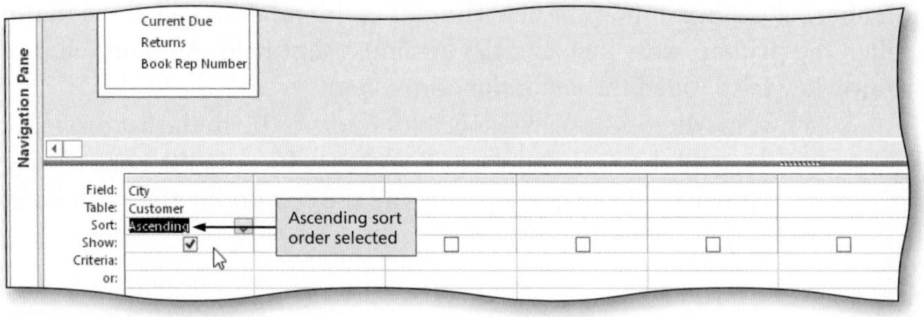

Figure 2–33

3

- Run the query (Figure 2–34).

Experiment

- Return to Design view and change the sort order to Descending. Run the query. Return to Design view and change the sort order back to Ascending. Run the query.

Q&A Why do some cities appear more than once?

More than one customer is located in those cities.

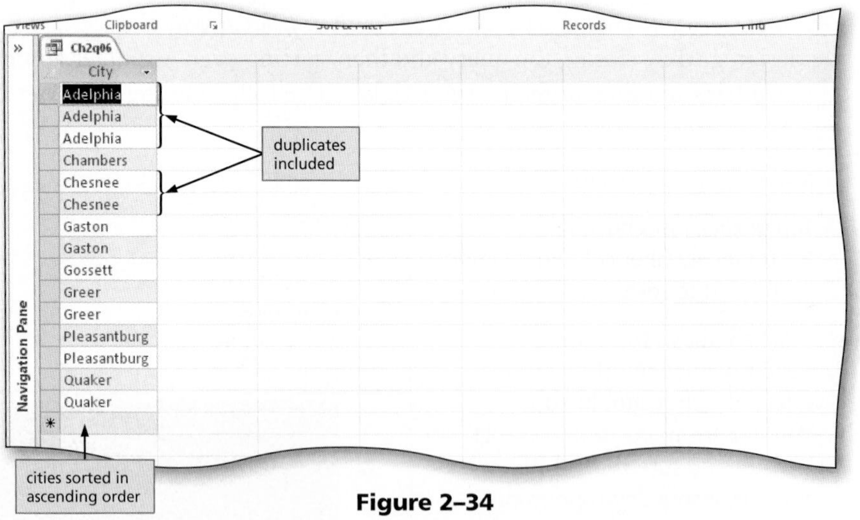

Figure 2–34

To Omit Duplicates

1 CREATE QUERIES | 2 USE CRITERIA | 3 SORT DATA | 4 JOIN TABLES | 5 EXPORT RESULTS
6 PERFORM CALCULATIONS | 7 CREATE CROSSTAB | 8 CUSTOMIZE NAVIGATION PANE

When you sort data, duplicates normally are included. In the query shown in Figure 2–34, for example, Adelphia appears three times. Several other cities appear twice. You eliminate duplicates using the query's property sheet. A **property sheet** is a window containing the various properties of the object. To omit duplicates, you will use the property sheet to change the Unique Values property from No to Yes.

The following steps create a query that Bavant Publishing might use to obtain a sorted list of the cities in the Customer table in which each city is listed only once. ***Why?*** *Unless you wanted to know how many customers were located in each city, the duplicates typically do not add any value.* The steps also save the query with a new name.

1

- Return to Design view.
- Tap or click the second field (the empty field to the right of City) in the design grid to produce an insertion point.
- If necessary, tap or click DESIGN on the ribbon to display the DESIGN tab.
- Tap or click the Property Sheet button (QUERY TOOLS DESIGN tab | Show/Hide group) to display the property sheet (Figure 2–35).

Q&A My property sheet looks different. What should I do?
If your sheet looks different, close the property sheet and repeat this step.

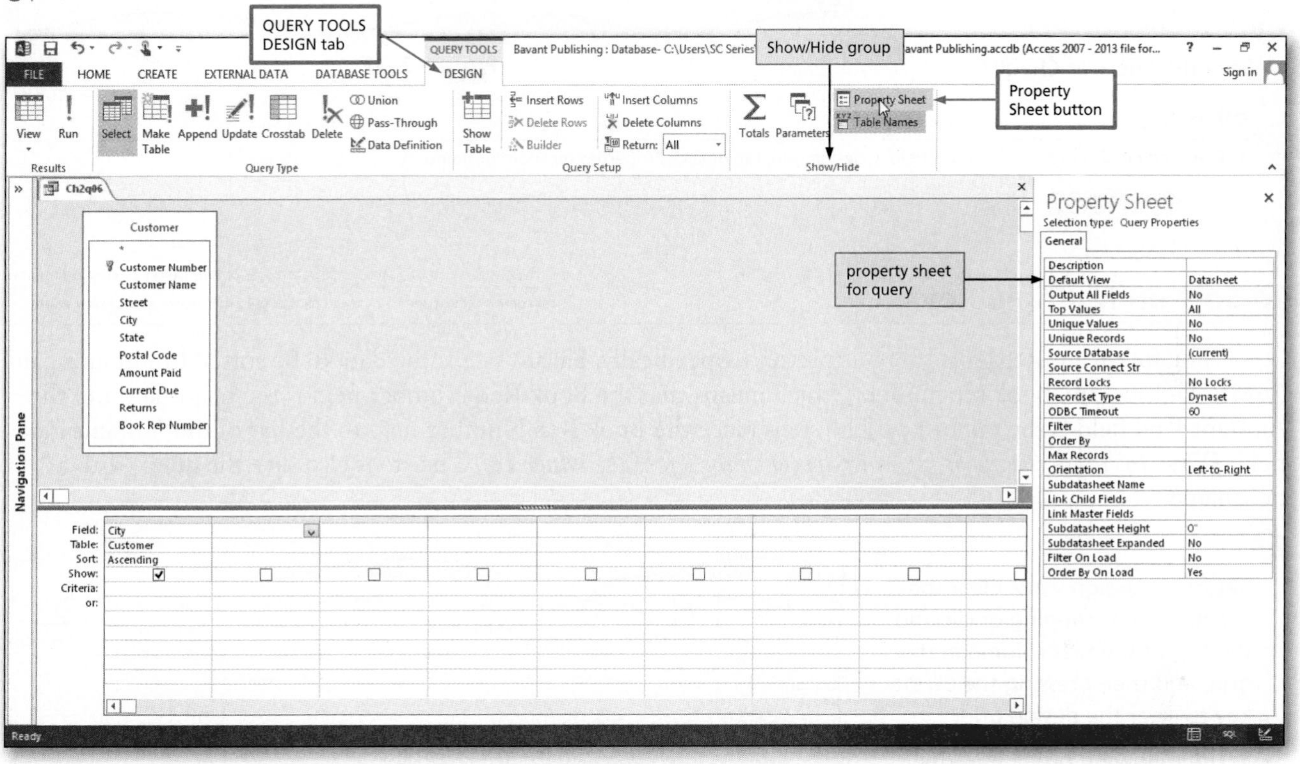

Figure 2–35

2

- Tap or click the Unique Values property box, and then tap or click the arrow that appears to display a list of available choices (Figure 2–36).

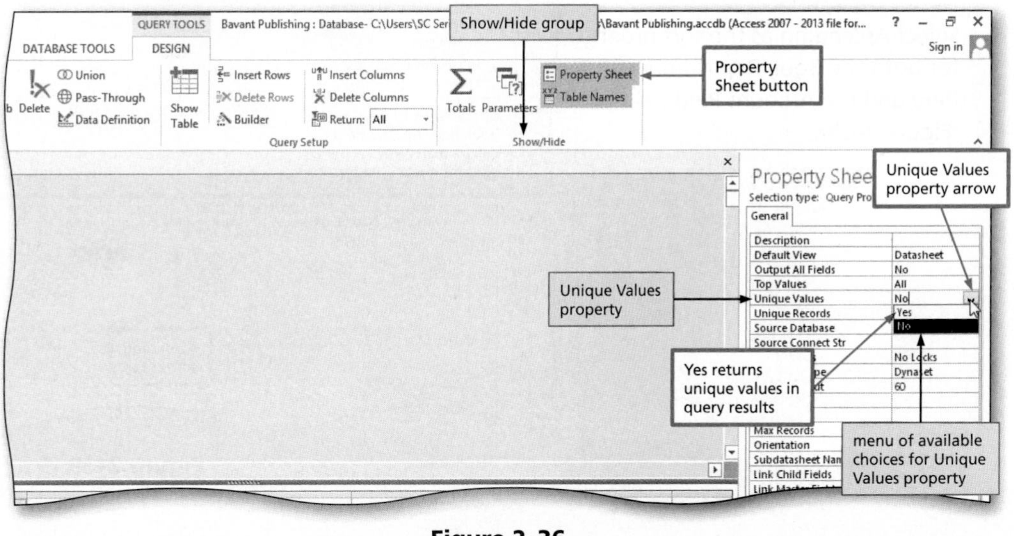

Figure 2–36

3

- Tap or click Yes to indicate that the query will return unique values, which means that each value will appear only once in the query results.
- Close the Query Properties property sheet by tapping or clicking the Property Sheet button (QUERY TOOLS DESIGN tab | Show/Hide group) a second time.
- Run the query (Figure 2–37).

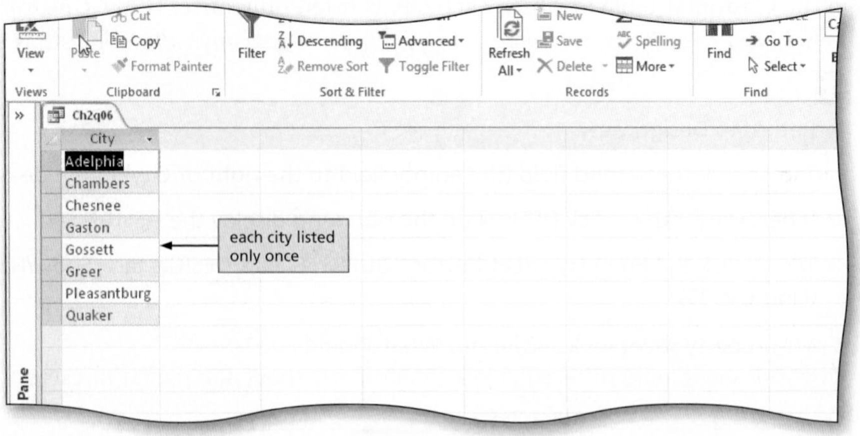

Figure 2–37

4

- Save the query as Ch2q07.

Other Ways

1. Press and hold or right-click second field in design grid, tap or click Properties on shortcut menu

To Sort on Multiple Keys

1 CREATE QUERIES | 2 USE CRITERIA | 3 SORT DATA | 4 JOIN TABLES | 5 EXPORT RESULTS
6 PERFORM CALCULATIONS | 7 CREATE CROSSTAB | 8 CUSTOMIZE NAVIGATION PANE

The following steps sort on multiple keys. Specifically, Bavant needs the data to be sorted by amount paid (low to high) within book rep number, which means that the Book Rep Number field is the major key and the Amount Paid field is the minor key. The steps place the Book Rep Number field to the left of the Amount Paid field. ***Why?*** *In Access, the major key must appear to the left of the minor key.* The steps also save the query with a new name.

1

- Return to Design view. Clear the design grid by tapping or clicking the top of the first column in the grid, and then pressing the DELETE key to clear the design grid.
- In the following order, include the Customer Number, Customer Name, Book Rep Number, and Amount Paid fields in the query.
- Select Ascending as the sort order for both the Book Rep Number field and the Amount Paid field (Figure 2–38).

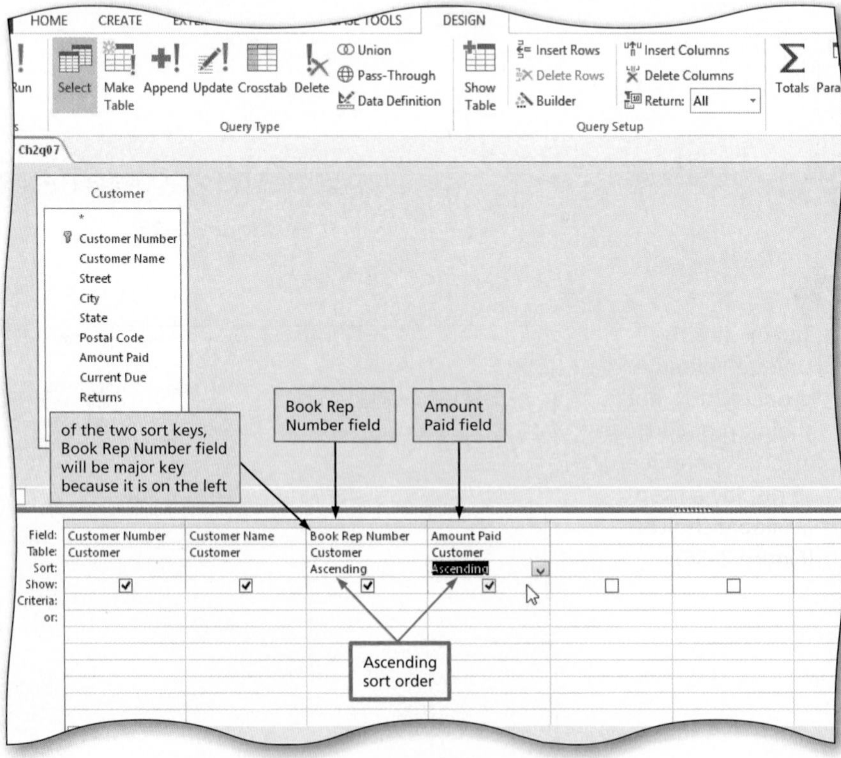

Figure 2–38

2

- Run the query (Figure 2–39).

Experiment

- Return to Design view and try other sort combinations for the Book Rep Number and Amount Paid fields, such as Ascending for Book Rep Number and Descending for Amount Paid. In each case, run the query to see the effect of the changes. When finished, select Ascending as the sort order for both fields.

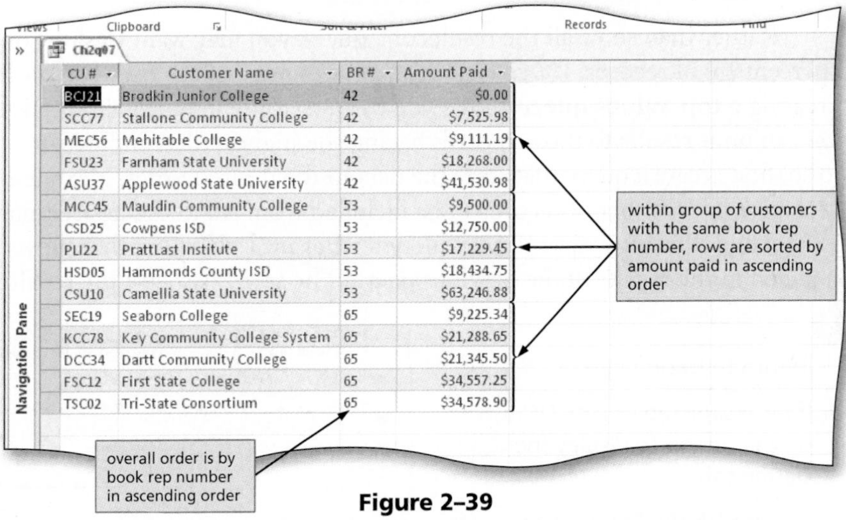

Figure 2–39

Q&A What if the Amount Paid field is to the left of the Book Rep Number field?

It is important to remember that the major sort key must appear to the left of the minor sort key in the design grid. If you attempted to sort by amount paid within book rep number, but placed the Amount Paid field to the left of the Book Rep Number field, your results would be incorrect.

3

- Save the query as Ch2q08.

CONSIDER THIS

Is there any way to sort the records in this same order, but have the Amount Paid field appear to the left of the Book Rep Number field in the query results?

Yes. Remove the check mark from the Book Rep Number field, and then add an additional Book Rep Number field at the end of the query. The first Book Rep Number field will be used for sorting but will not appear in the results. The second will appear in the results, but will not be involved in the sorting process.

CONSIDER THIS

How do you approach the creation of a query that might involve sorting?

Examine the query or request to see if it contains words such as *order* or *sort*. Such words imply that the order of the query results is important. If so, you need to sort the query.

If sorting is required, identify the field or fields on which the results are to be sorted. In the request, look for language such as *ordered by* or *sort the results by*, both of which would indicate that the specified field is a sort key.

If using multiple sort keys, determine the major and minor keys. If you are using two sort keys, determine which one is the more important, or the major key. Look for language such as *sort by amount paid within book rep number*, which implies that the overall order is by book rep number. In this case, the Book Rep Number field would be the major sort key and the Amount Paid field would be the minor sort key.

Determine sort order. Words such as *increasing*, *ascending*, or *low-to-high* imply Ascending order. Words such as *decreasing*, *descending*, or *high-to-low* imply Descending order. Sorting in *alphabetical order* implies Ascending order. If there were no words to imply a particular order, you would typically use Ascending.

Examine the query or request to see if there are any special restrictions. One common restriction is to exclude duplicates. Another common restriction is to list only a certain number of records, such as the first five records.

To Create a Top-Values Query

Rather than show all the results of a query, you may want to show only a specified number of records or a percentage of records. ***Why?*** *You might not need to see all the records, just enough to get a general idea of the results.* Creating a **top-values query** allows you to restrict the number of records that appear. When you sort records, you can limit results to those records having the highest (descending sort) or lowest (ascending sort) values. To do so, first create a query that sorts the data in the desired order. Next, use the Return box on the DESIGN tab to change the number of records to be included from All to the desired number or percentage.

The following steps create a query for Bavant Publishing that shows only the first five records that were included in the results of the previous query. The steps also save the resulting query with a new name.

1

- Return to Design view.
- If necessary, tap or click DESIGN on the ribbon to display the Design tab.
- Tap or click the Return arrow (QUERY TOOLS DESIGN tab | Query Setup group) to display the Return menu (Figure 2–40).

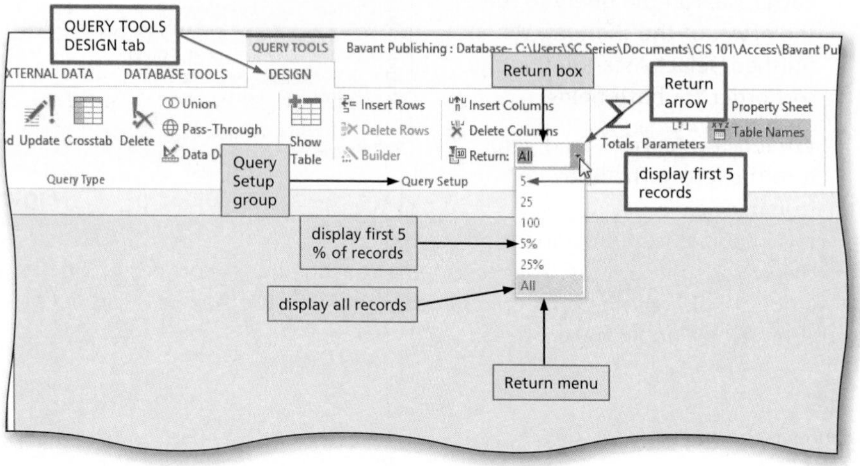

Figure 2–40

2

- Tap or click 5 in the Return menu to specify that the query results should contain the first five rows.

Q&A Could I have typed the 5? What about other numbers that do not appear in the list?

Yes, you could have typed the 5. For numbers not appearing in the list, you must type the number.

- Run the query (Figure 2–41).

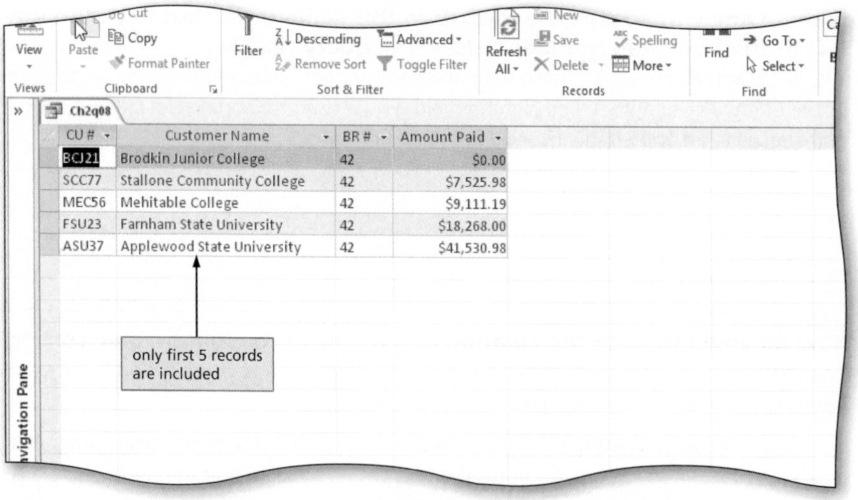

Figure 2–41

3

- Save the query as Ch2q09.
- Close the query.

Q&A Do I need to close the query before creating my next query?

Not necessarily. When you use a top-values query, however, it is important to change the value in the Return box back to All. If you do not change the Return value back to All, the previous value will remain in effect. Consequently, you might not get all the records you should in the next query. A good practice whenever you use a top-values query is to close the query as soon as you are done. That way, you will begin your next query from scratch, which guarantees that the value is reset to All.

Break Point: If you wish to take a break, this is a good place to do so. You can exit Access now. To resume later, run Access, open the database called Bavant Publishing, and continue following the steps from this location forward.

Joining Tables

In designing a query, you need to determine whether more than one table is required. For example, if the question being asked involves data from both the Customer and Book Rep tables, then both tables are required for the query. A query might require listing the number and name of each customer (from the Customer table) along with the number and name of the customer's book rep (from the Book Rep table). Both the Customer and Book Rep tables are required for this query. You need to **join** the tables to find records in the two tables that have identical values in matching fields (Figure 2–42). In this example, you need to find records in the Customer table and the Book Rep table that have the same value in the Book Rep Number fields.

BTW

Ad Hoc Relationships

When you join tables in a query, you are creating an ad hoc relationship, that is, a relationship between tables created for a specific purpose. In Chapter 3, you will create general-purpose relationships using the Relationships window.

Give me the number and name of each customer along with the number and name of the customer's book rep.

Customer Table

CU #	Customer Name	...	BR #
ASU37	Applewood State University	...	42
BCJ21	Brodkin Junior College	...	42
CSD25	Cowpens ISD	...	53
CSU10	Camellia State University	...	53
DCC34	Dartt Community College	...	65
FSC12	First State College	...	65
FSU23	Farnham State University	...	42
HSD05	Hammonds County ISD	...	53
KCC78	Key Community College System	...	65
MCC45	Mauldin Community College	...	53
MEC56	Mehitable College	...	42
PLI22	PrattLast Institute	...	53
SCC77	Stallone Community College	...	42
SEC19	Seaborn College	...	65
TSC02	Tri-State Consortium	...	65

Book Rep Table

BR #	Last Name	First Name	...
42	Perez	Melina	...
48	Statnik	Michael	...
53	Chin	Robert	...
65	Rogers	Tracy	...

Customer Table

CU #	Customer Name	...	BR #	Last Name	First Name	...
ASU37	Applewood State University	...	42	Perez	Melina	...
BCJ21	Brodkin Junior College	...	42	Perez	Melina	...
CSD25	Cowpens ISD	...	53	Chin	Robert	...
CSU10	Camellia State University	...	53	Chin	Robert	...
DCC34	Dartt Community College	...	65	Rogers	Tracy	...
FSC12	First State College	...	65	Rogers	Tracy	...
FSU23	Farnham State University	...	42	Perez	Melina	...
HSD05	Hammonds County ISD	...	53	Chin	Robert	...
KCC78	Key Community College System	...	65	Rogers	Tracy	...
MCC45	Mauldin Community College	...	53	Chin	Robert	...
MEC56	Mehitable College	...	42	Perez	Melina	...
PLI22	PrattLast Institute	...	53	Chin	Robert	...
SCC77	Stallone Community College	...	42	Perez	Melina	...
SEC19	Seaborn College	...	65	Rogers	Tracy	...
TSC02	Tri-State Consortium	...	65	Rogers	Tracy	...

Figure 2–42

BTW

Join Line

If you do not get a join line automatically, there may be a problem with one of your table designs. Open each table in Design view and make sure that the data types are the same for the matching field in both tables and that one of the matching fields is the primary key in a table. Correct these errors and create the query again.

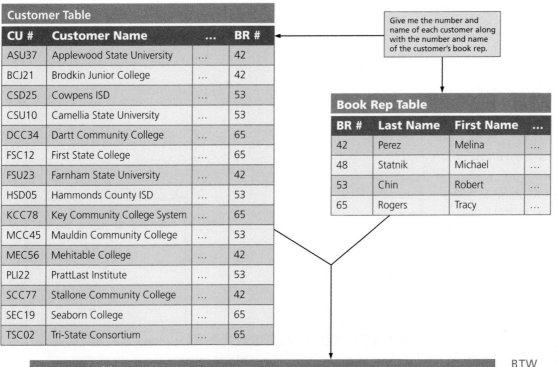

To Join Tables

If you have determined that you need to join tables, you first will bring field lists for both tables to the upper pane of the Query window while working in Design view. Access will draw a line, called a **join line**, between matching fields in the two tables, indicating that the tables are related. You then can select fields from either table. Access joins the tables automatically.

The first step is to create a new query and add the Book Rep table to the query. Then, add the Customer table to the query. A join line should appear, connecting the Book Rep Number fields in the two field lists. ***Why might the join line not appear?*** *If the names of the matching fields differ from one table to the other, Access will not insert the line. You can insert it manually, however, by tapping or clicking one of the two matching fields and dragging the pointer to the other matching field.*

The following steps create a query to display information from both the Customer table and the Book Rep table.

1

- Tap or click CREATE on the ribbon to display the CREATE tab.
- Tap or click the Query Design button (CREATE tab | Queries group) to create a new query.
- If necessary, tap or click the Book Rep table (Show Table dialog box) to select the table.
- Tap or click the Add button (Show Table dialog box) to add a field list for the Book Rep Table to the query (Figure 2–43).

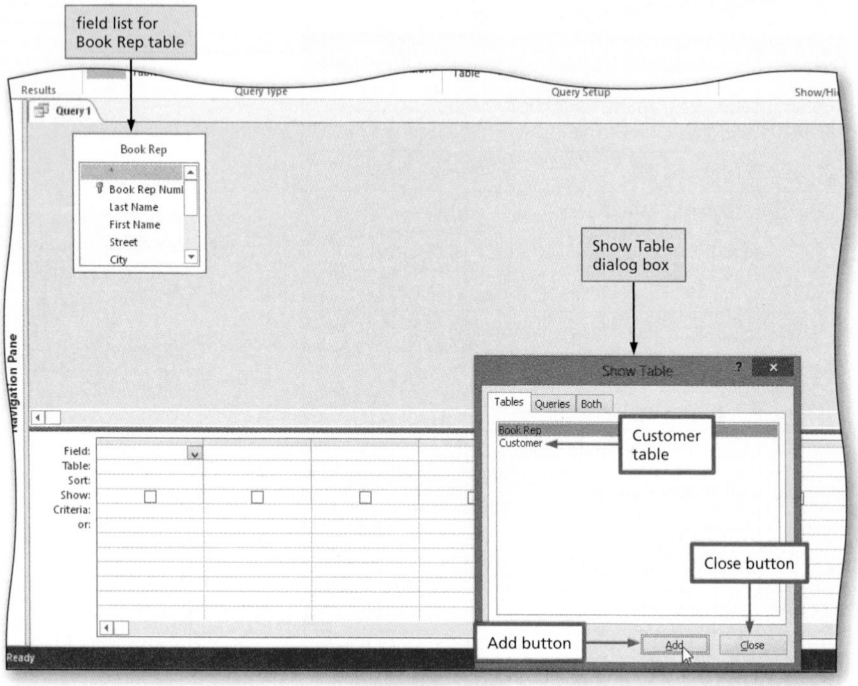

Figure 2–43

2

- Tap or click the Customer table (Show Table dialog box).
- Tap or click the Add button (Show Table dialog box) to add a field list for the Customer table.
- Close the Show Table dialog box by tapping or clicking the Close button.
- Expand the size of the two field lists so all the fields in the Book Rep and Customer tables appear (Figure 2–44).

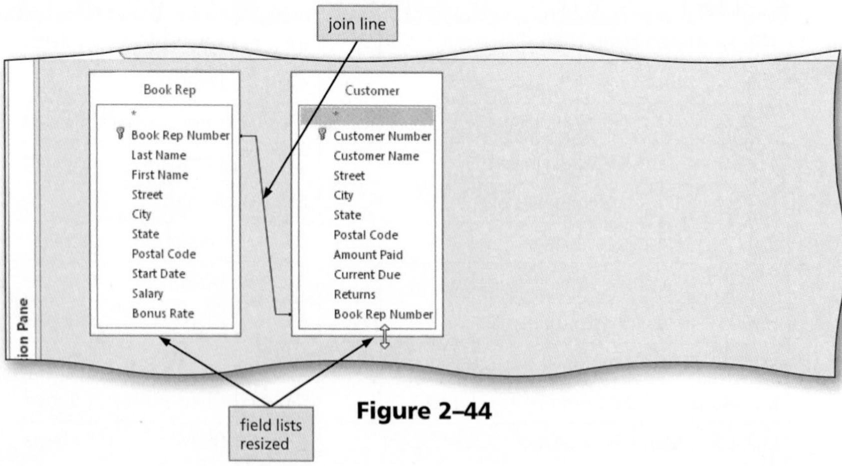

Figure 2–44

Q&A I did not get a join line. What should I do?

Ensure that the names of the matching fields are the same, the data types are the same, and the matching field is the primary key in one of the two tables. If all of these factors are true and you still do not have a join line, you can produce one by pointing to a matching field and dragging to the other matching field.

3

- In the design grid, include the Book Rep Number, Last Name, and First Name fields from the Book Rep Table as well as the Customer Number and Customer Name fields from the Customer table.
- Select Ascending as the sort order for both the Book Rep Number field and the Customer Number field (Figure 2–45).

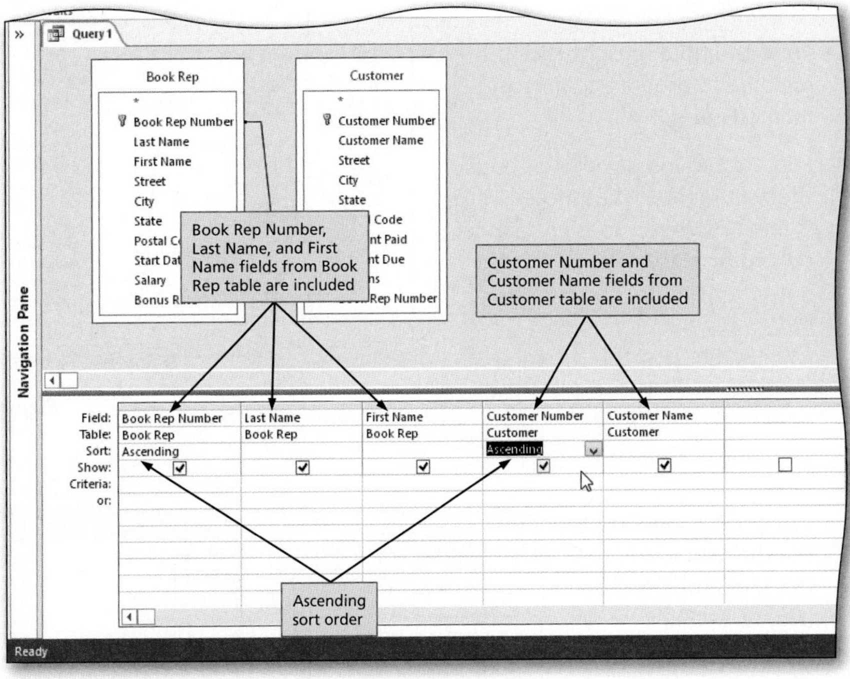

Figure 2–45

4

- Run the query (Figure 2–46).

5

- Tap or click the Save button on the Quick Access Toolbar to display the Save As dialog box.
- Type `Rep-Customer Query` as the query name.

6

- Tap or click the OK button (Save As dialog box) to save the query.

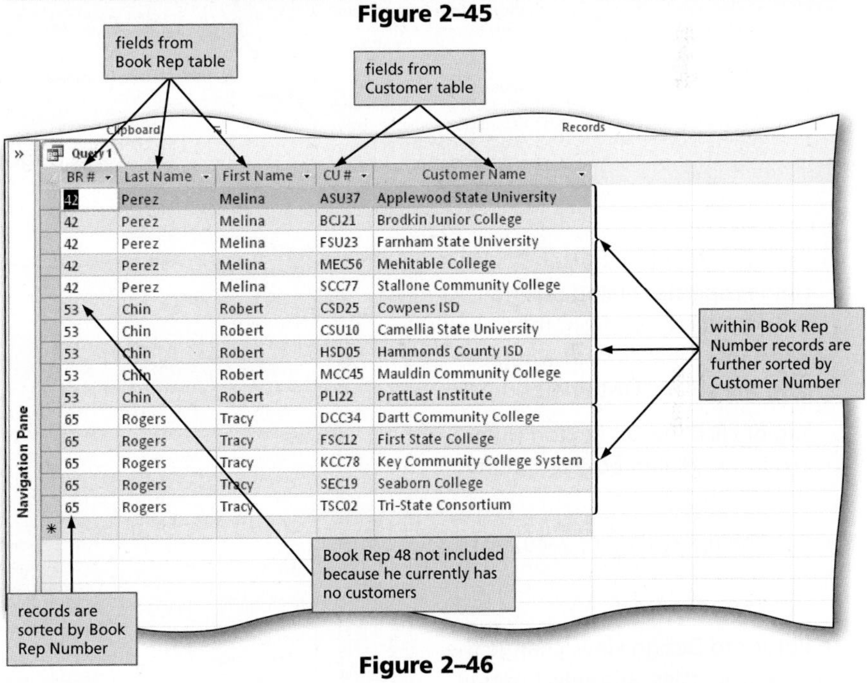

Figure 2–46

To Change Join Properties

1 CREATE QUERIES | 2 USE CRITERIA | 3 SORT DATA | 4 JOIN TABLES | **5 EXPORT RESULTS**
6 PERFORM CALCULATIONS | 7 CREATE CROSSTAB | 8 CUSTOMIZE NAVIGATION PANE

Normally, records that do not match do not appear in the results of a join query. For example, the book rep named Michael Statnik does not appear in the results. ***Why?*** *He currently does not have any customers.* To cause such a record to be displayed, you need to change the **join properties**, which are the properties that indicate which records appear in a join. The following steps change the join properties of the Rep-Customer Query so that Bavant can include all book reps in the results, rather than only those reps who have already been assigned customers.

1

- Return to Design view.
- Press and hold or right-click the join line to produce a shortcut menu (Figure 2–47).

Q&A I do not see Join Properties on my shortcut menu. What should I do?
If Join Properties does not appear on your shortcut menu, you did not point to the appropriate portion of the join line. You will need to point to the correct (middle) portion and press and hold or right-click again.

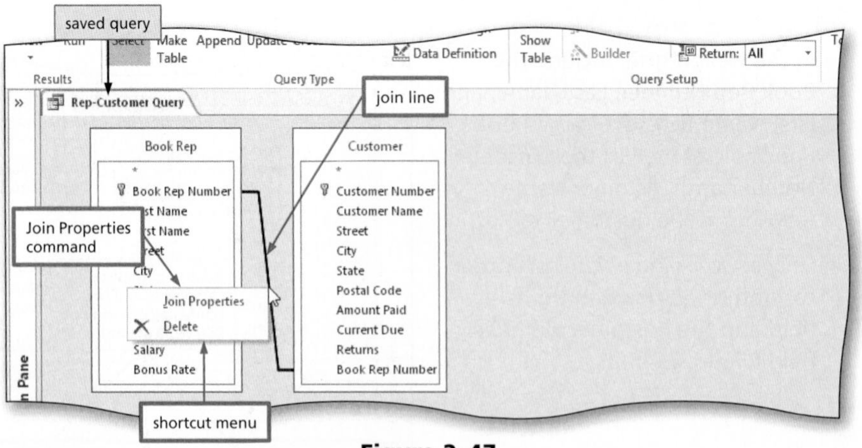

Figure 2–47

2

- Tap or click Join Properties on the shortcut menu to display the Join Properties dialog box (Figure 2–48).

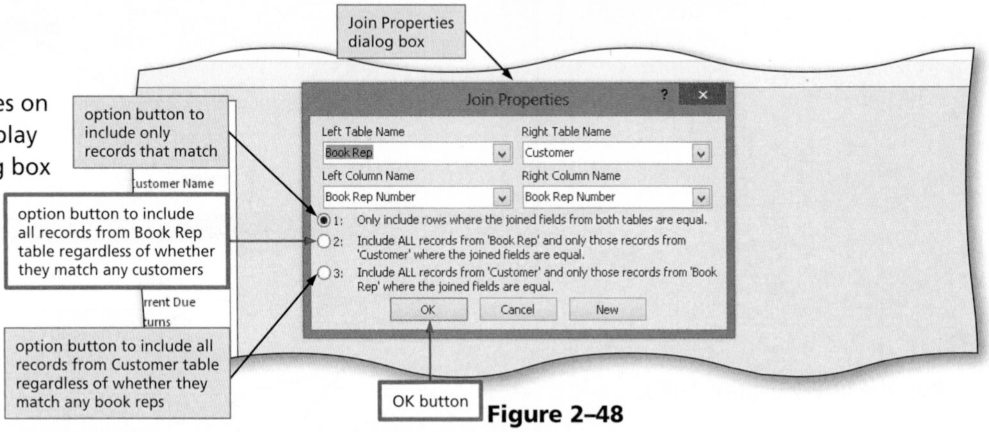

Figure 2–48

3

- Tap or click option button 2 (Join Properties dialog box) to include all records from the Book Rep Table regardless of whether they match any customers.
- Tap or click the OK button (Join Properties dialog box) to modify the join properties.
- Run the query (Figure 2–49).

Experiment

- Return to Design view, change the Join properties, and select option button 3. Run the query to see the effect of this option. When done, return to Design view, change the join properties, and once again select option button 2.

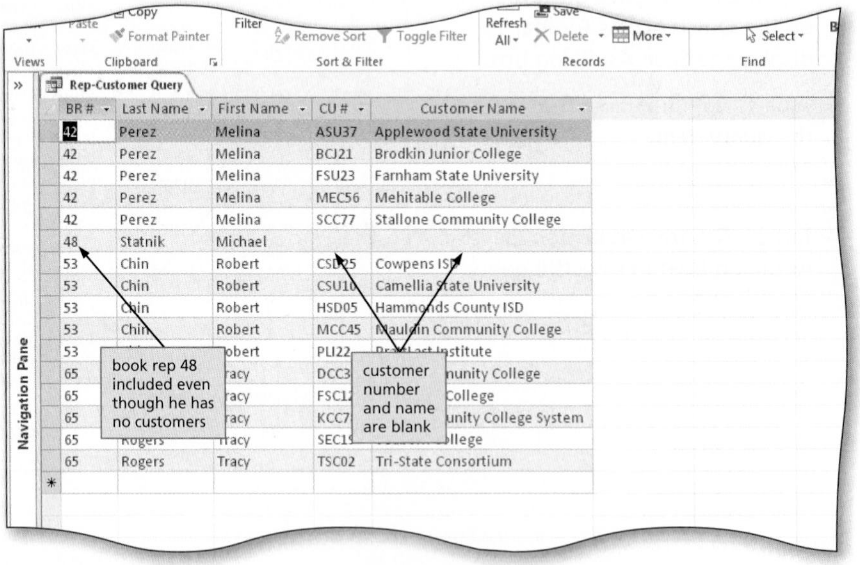

Figure 2–49

4

- Tap or click the Save button on the Quick Access Toolbar to save the changes to the query.
- Close the Rep-Customer Query.

Q&A I see a dialog box that asks if I want to save the query. What should I do?
Tap or click the OK button to save the query.

To Create a Report from a Query

You can use queries in the creation of reports. The report in Figure 2–50 involves data from more than one table. ***Why?*** *The Last Name and First Name fields are in the Book Rep table. The Customer Number and Customer Name fields are in the Customer table. The Book Rep Number field is in both tables.* The easiest way to create such a report is to base it on a query that joins the two tables. The following steps use the Report Wizard and the Rep-Customer Query to create the report.

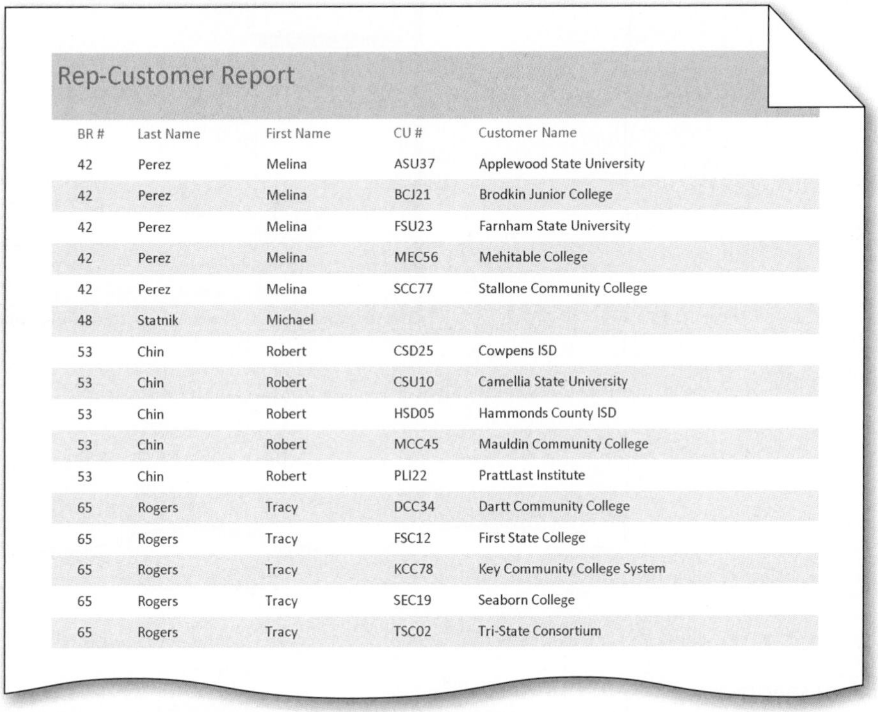
Rep-Customer Report

BR #	Last Name	First Name	CU #	Customer Name
42	Perez	Melina	ASU37	Applewood State University
42	Perez	Melina	BCJ21	Brodkin Junior College
42	Perez	Melina	FSU23	Farnham State University
42	Perez	Melina	MEC56	Mehitable College
42	Perez	Melina	SCC77	Stallone Community College
48	Statnik	Michael		
53	Chin	Robert	CSD25	Cowpens ISD
53	Chin	Robert	CSU10	Camellia State University
53	Chin	Robert	HSD05	Hammonds County ISD
53	Chin	Robert	MCC45	Mauldin Community College
53	Chin	Robert	PLI22	PrattLast Institute
65	Rogers	Tracy	DCC34	Dartt Community College
65	Rogers	Tracy	FSC12	First State College
65	Rogers	Tracy	KCC78	Key Community College System
65	Rogers	Tracy	SEC19	Seaborn College
65	Rogers	Tracy	TSC02	Tri-State Consortium

Figure 2–50

1

- Open the Navigation Pane, and then select the Rep-Customer Query in the Navigation Pane.
- Tap or click CREATE on the ribbon to display the CREATE tab.
- Tap or click the Report Wizard button (CREATE tab | Reports group) to display the Report Wizard dialog box (Figure 2–51).

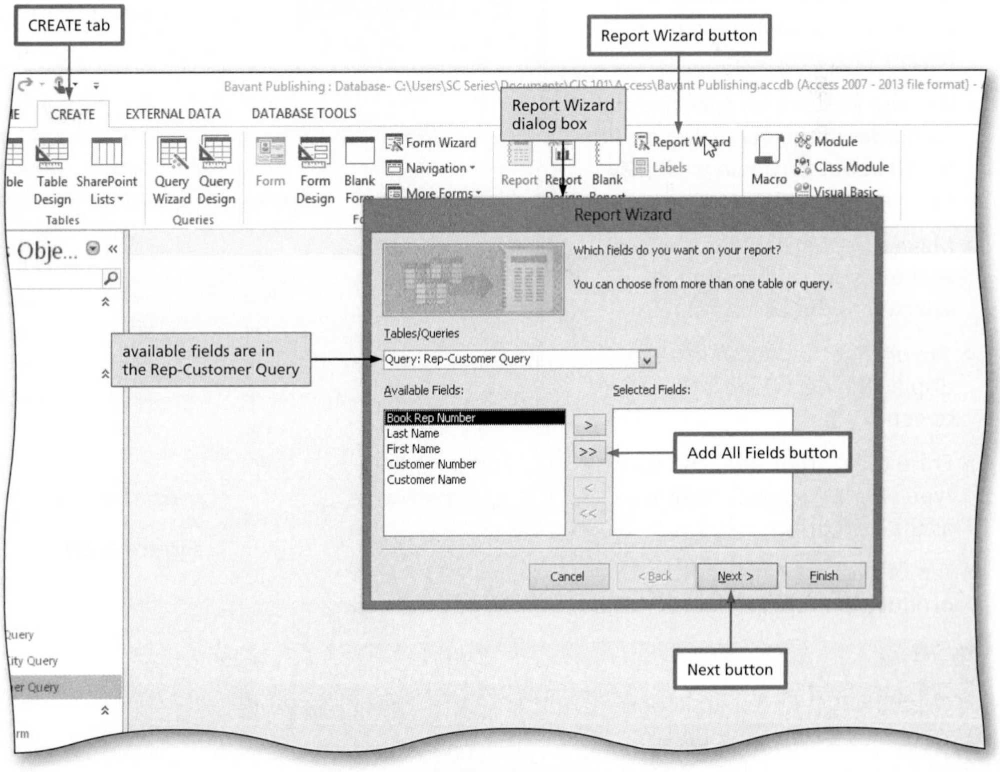

Figure 2–51

2

- Tap or click the Add All Fields button (Report Wizard dialog box) to add all the fields in the Rep-Customer Query.
- Tap or click the Next button to display the next Report Wizard screen (Figure 2–52).

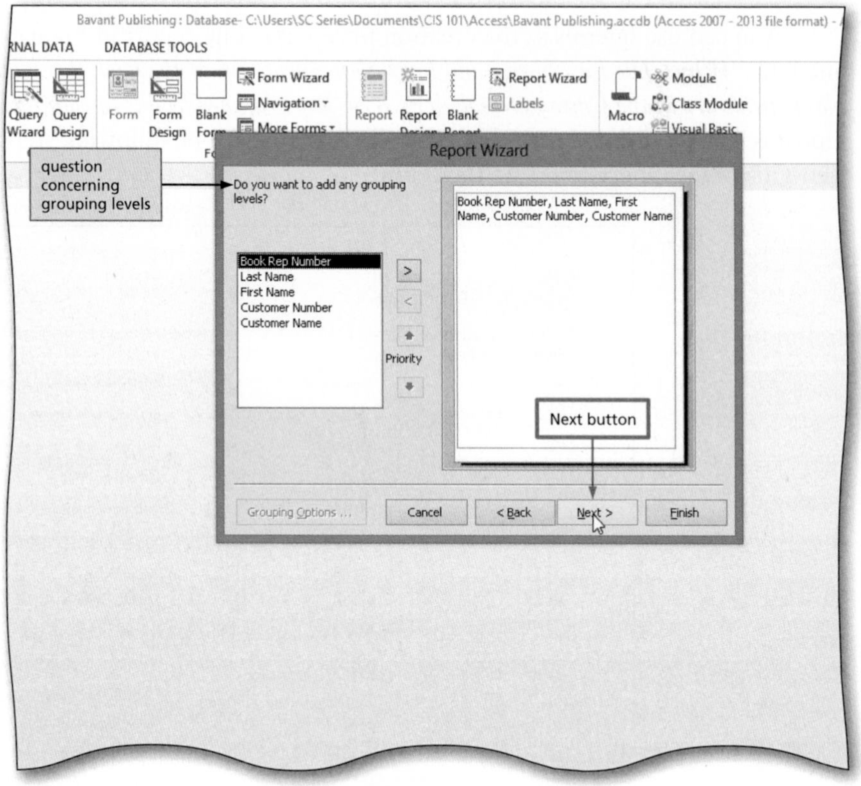

Figure 2–52

3

- Because you will not specify any grouping, tap or click the Next button in the Report Wizard dialog box to display the next Report Wizard screen.
- Because you already specified the sort order in the query, tap or click the Next button again to display the next Report Wizard screen.
- Make sure that Tabular is selected as the Layout and Portrait is selected as the Orientation.
- Tap or click the Next button to display the next Report Wizard screen.
- Erase the current title, and then type `Rep-Customer Report` as the new title.
- Tap or click the Finish button to produce the report (Figure 2–53).

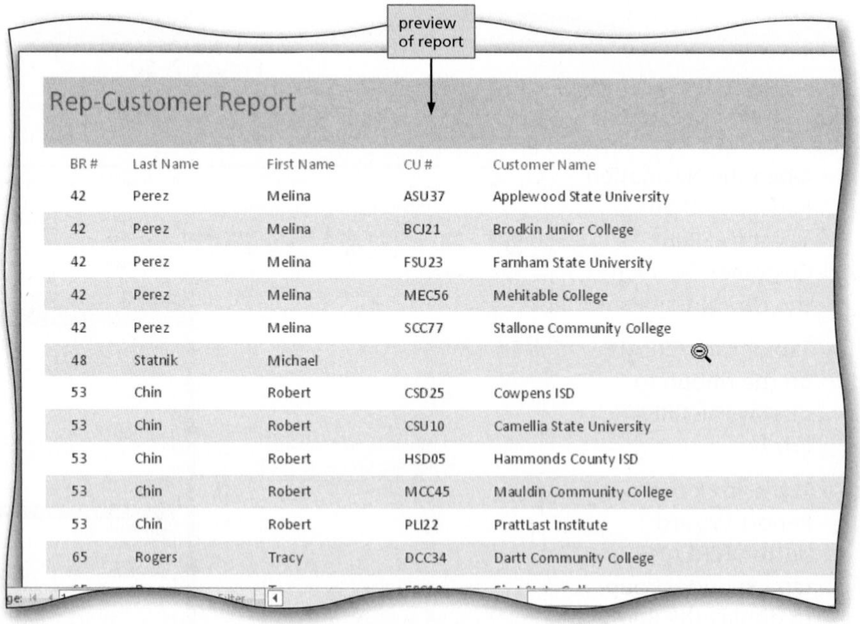

Figure 2–53

4

- Close the Rep-Customer Report.

To Print a Report

The following steps print a hard copy of the report.

1. With the Rep-Customer Report selected in the Navigation Pane, tap or click FILE on the ribbon to open the Backstage view.
2. Tap or click the Print tab in the Backstage view to display the Print gallery.
3. Tap or click the Quick Print button to print the report.

CONSIDER THIS

How would you approach the creation of a query that might involve multiple tables?

Examine the request to see if all the fields involved in the request are in one table. If the fields are in two (or more) tables, you need to join the tables.

If joining is required, identify the matching fields in the two tables that have identical values. Look for the same column name in the two tables or for column names that are similar.

Determine whether sorting is required. Queries that join tables often are used as the basis for a report. If this is the case, it may be necessary to sort the results. For example, the Rep-Customer Report is based on a query that joins the Book Rep and Customer tables. The query is sorted by book rep number and customer number.

Examine the request to see if there are any special restrictions. For example, the user only may want customers whose current due amount is $0.00.

Examine the request to see if you only want records from both tables that have identical values in matching fields. If you want to see records in one of the tables that do not have identical values, then you need to change the join properties.

Creating a Form for a Query

In the previous chapter, you created a form for the Customer table. You also can create a form for a query. Recall that a form in a database is a formatted document with fields that contain data. Forms allow you to view and maintain data.

To Create a Form for a Query

1 CREATE QUERIES | 2 USE CRITERIA | 3 SORT DATA | **4 JOIN TABLES** | **5 EXPORT RESULTS**
6 PERFORM CALCULATIONS | **7 CREATE CROSSTAB** | **8 CUSTOMIZE NAVIGATION PANE**

The following steps create a form, then save the form. ***Why?*** *The form will be available for future use in viewing the data in the query.*

1

- If necessary, select the Rep-Customer Query in the Navigation Pane.
- Tap or click CREATE on the ribbon to display the CREATE tab (Figure 2–54).

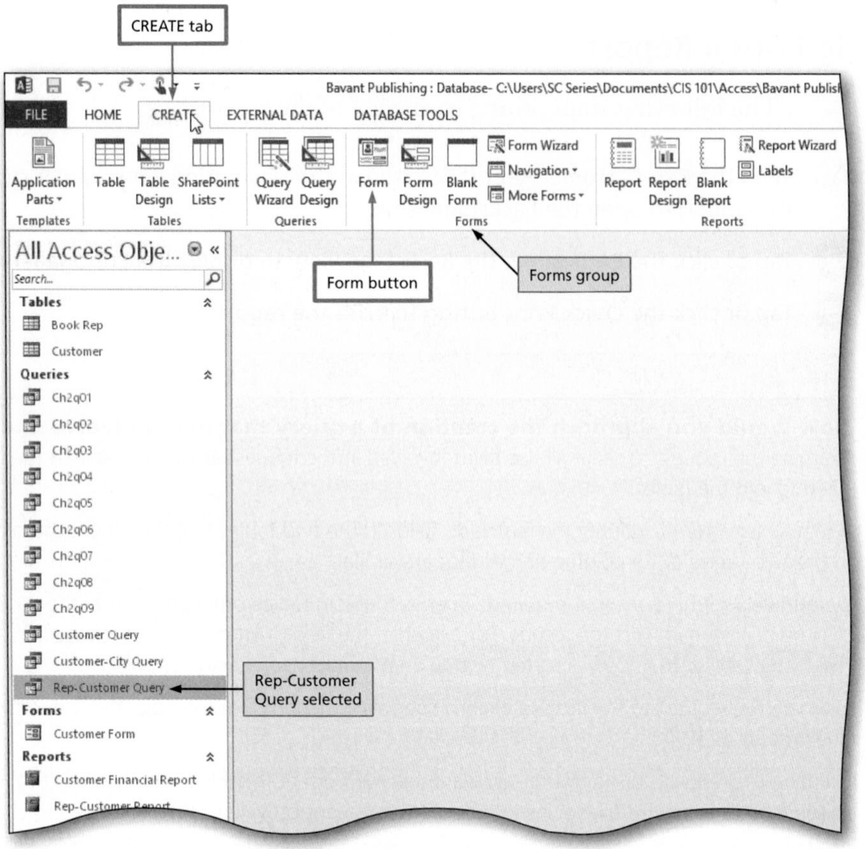

Figure 2–54

2

- Tap or click the Form button (CREATE tab | Forms group) to create a simple form (Figure 2–55).

Q&A I see a field list also. What should I do?

Tap or click the Close button for the Field List.

3

- Tap or click the Save button on the Quick Access Toolbar to display the Save As dialog box.
- Type `Rep-Customer Form` as the form name.

4

- Tap or click the OK button to save the form.
- Tap or click the Close button for the form to close the form.

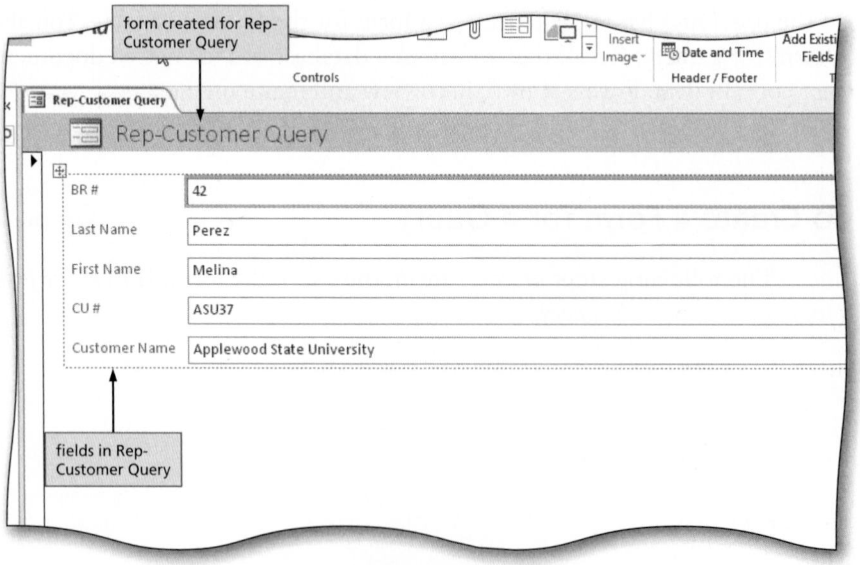

Figure 2–55

Using a Form

After you have saved a form, you can use it at any time by pressing and holding or right-clicking the form in the Navigation Pane and then tapping or clicking Open on the shortcut menu. If you plan to use the form to enter data, you must ensure you are viewing the form in Form view.

Exporting Data from Access to Other Applications

You can **export**, or copy, tables or queries from an Access database so that another application (for example, Excel or Word) can use the data. The application that will receive the data determines the export process to be used. You can export to text files in a variety of formats. For applications to which you cannot directly export data, you often can export an appropriately formatted text file that the other application can import. Figure 2–56 shows the workbook produced by exporting the Rep-Customer Query to Excel. The columns in the workbook have been resized to best fit the data.

BTW
Distributing a Document
Instead of printing and distributing a hard copy of a document, you can distribute the document electronically. Options include sending the document via email; posting it on cloud storage (such as SkyDrive) and sharing the file with others; posting it on a social networking site, blog, or other website; and sharing a link associated with an online location of the document. You also can create and share a PDF or XPS image of the document, so that users can view the file in Acrobat Reader or XPS Viewer instead of in Access.

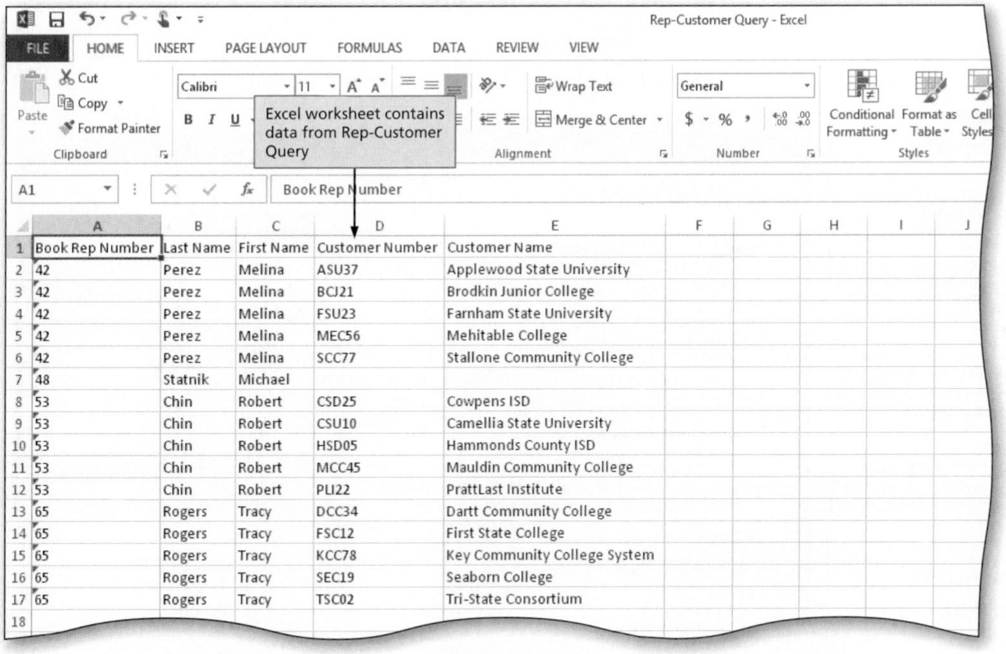

Figure 2–56

1 CREATE QUERIES | 2 USE CRITERIA | 3 SORT DATA | 4 JOIN TABLES | **5 EXPORT RESULTS**
6 PERFORM CALCULATIONS | 7 CREATE CROSSTAB | 8 CUSTOMIZE NAVIGATION PANE

To Export Data to Excel

For Bavant Publishing to make the Rep-Customer Query available to Excel users, it needs to export the data. To export data to Excel, select the table or query to be exported and then tap or click the Excel button in the Export group on the EXTERNAL DATA tab. The steps on the next page export the Rep-Customer Query to Excel and save the export steps. ***Why save the export steps?*** *By saving the export steps, you could easily repeat the export process whenever you like without going through all the steps.* You would use the saved steps to export data in the future by tapping or clicking the Saved Exports button (EXTERNAL DATA tab | Export group) and then selecting the steps you saved.

1

- If necessary, tap or click the Rep-Customer Query in the Navigation Pane to select it.
- Tap or click EXTERNAL DATA on the ribbon to display the EXTERNAL DATA tab (Figure 2–57).

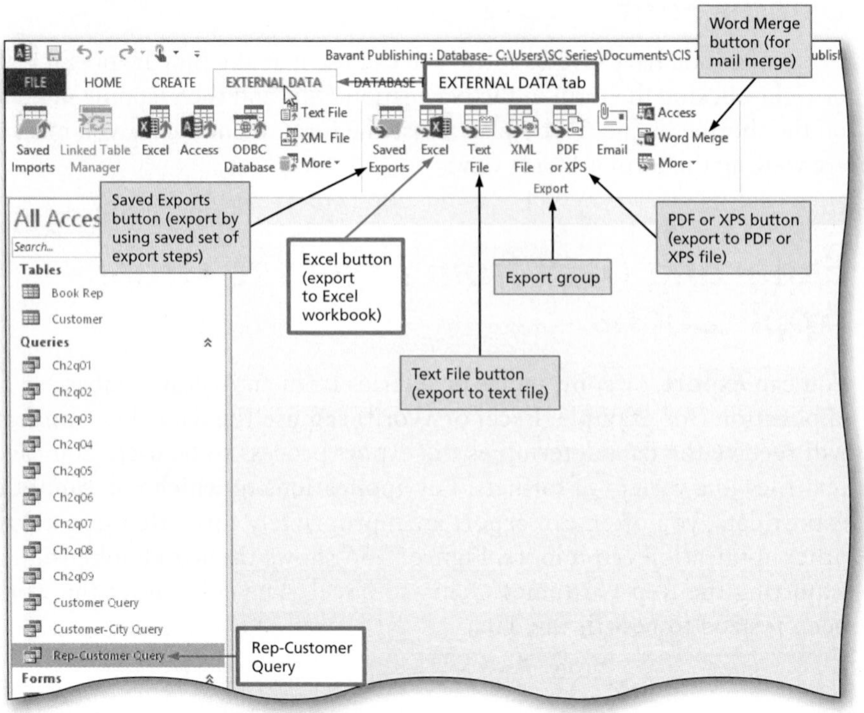

Figure 2–57

2

- Tap or click the Excel button (EXTERNAL DATA tab | Export group) to display the Export-Excel Spreadsheet dialog box.
- Tap or click the Browse button (Export-Excel Spreadsheet dialog box), and then navigate to the location where you wish to export the query (for example, the Access folder in the CIS 101 folder).
- Be sure the file name is Rep-Customer Query and then tap or click the Save button (File Save dialog box) to select the file name and location (Figure 2–58).

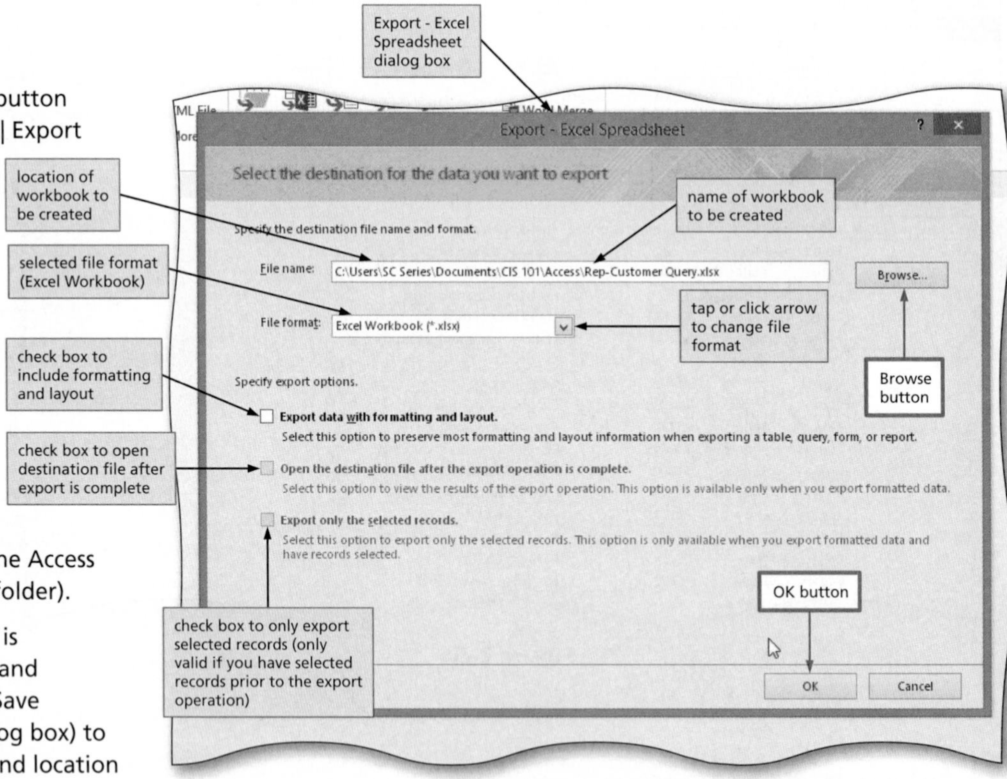

Figure 2–58

Q&A

Did I need to browse?
No. You could type the appropriate file location.

Could I change the name of the file?
You could change it. Simply replace the current file name with the one you want.

What if the file I want to export already exists?
Access will indicate that the file already exists and ask if you want to replace it. If you tap or click the Yes button, the file you export will replace the old file. If you tap or click the No button, you must either change the name of the export file or cancel the process.

3

- Tap or click the OK button (Export-Excel Spreadsheet dialog box) to export the data (Figure 2–59).

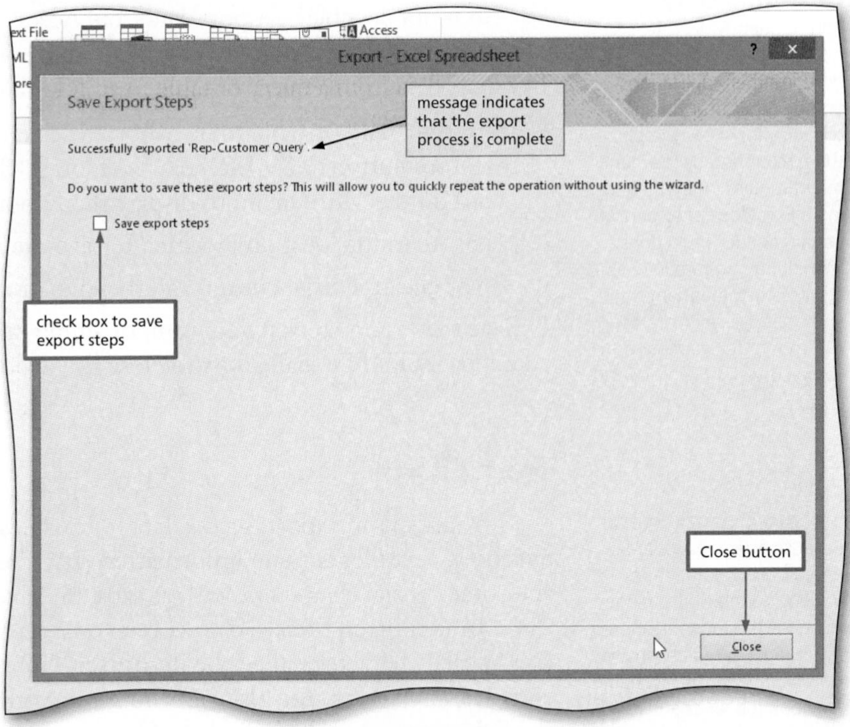

Figure 2–59

4

- Tap or click the 'Save export steps' check box (Export-Excel Spreadsheet dialog box) to display the Save Export Steps options.
- If necessary, type `Export-Rep-Customer Query` in the Save as text box.
- Type `Export the Rep-Customer Query without formatting` in the Description text box (Figure 2–60).

Q&A How could I re-use the export steps?

You can use these steps to export data in the future by tapping or clicking the Saved Exports button (EXTERNAL DATA tab | Export group) and then selecting the steps you saved.

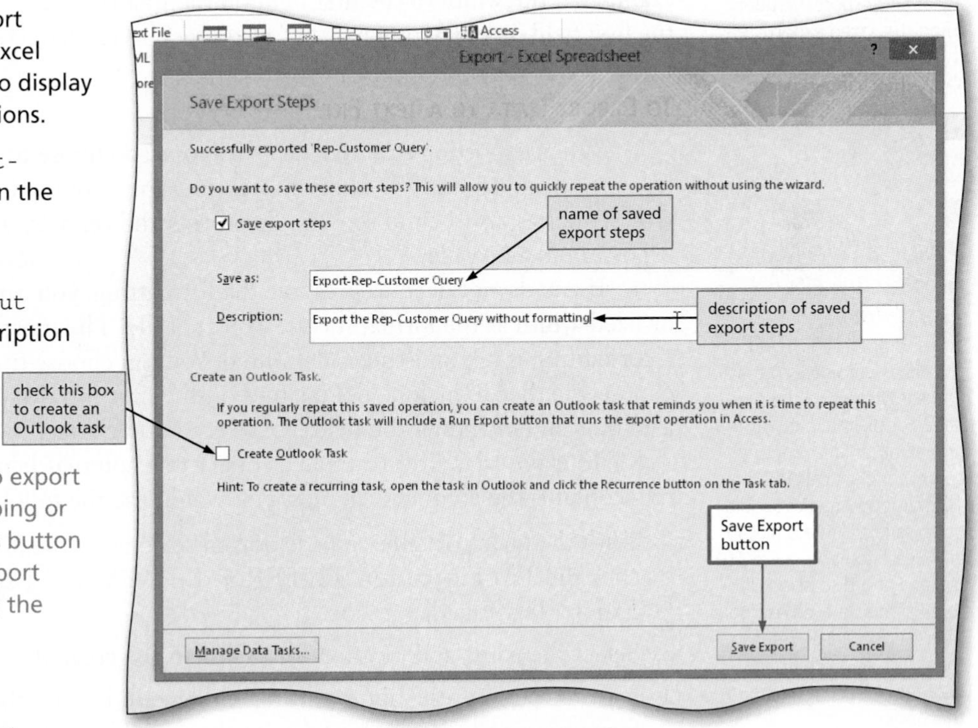

Figure 2–60

5

- Tap or click the Save Export button (Export-Excel Spreadsheet dialog box) to save the export steps.

Other Ways

1. Press and hold or right-click database object in Navigation Pane, tap or click Export

BTW
Exporting Data
You frequently need to export data so that it can be used in other applications and by other users in an organization. For example, the Accounting department might require financial data in an Excel format to perform certain financial functions. Marketing might require a list of customer names and addresses in Word or RTF format for marketing campaigns.

To Export Data to Word

It is not possible to export data from Access to the standard Word format. It is possible, however, to export the data as a rich text format (RTF) file, which Word can use. To export data from a query or table to an RTF file, you would use the following steps.

1. With the query or table to be exported selected in the Navigation Pane, tap or click the More button (EXTERNAL DATA tab | Export group) and then tap or click Word on the More menu to display the Export-RTF File dialog box.
2. Navigate to the location in which to save the file and assign a file name.
3. Tap or click the Save button, and then tap or click the OK button to export the data.
4. Save the export steps if you want, or simply tap or click the Close button in the Export-RTF File dialog box to close the dialog box without saving the export steps.

BTW
Saving Export Steps
Because query results are based on the data in the underlying tables, a change to an underlying table would result in a new query answer. For example, if the last name for book rep 42 changed from Perez to Smith, the change would be made in the Book Rep table. If you run the Rep-Customer Query again and export the query using the saved export steps, the Excel workbook would show the changed name.

Text Files

You also can export Access data to text files, which can be used for a variety of purposes. Text files contain unformatted characters, including alphanumeric characters, and some special characters, such as tabs, carriage returns, and line feeds.

In **delimited files**, each record is on a separate line and the fields are separated by a special character, called the **delimiter**. Common delimiters are tabs, semicolons, commas, and spaces. You also can choose any other value that does not appear within the field contents as the delimiter. The comma-separated values (CSV) file often used in Excel is an example of a delimited file.

In **fixed-width files**, the width of any field is the same on every record. For example, if the width of the first field on the first record is 12 characters, the width of the first field on every other record also must be 12 characters.

To Export Data to a Text File

When exporting data to a text file, you can choose to export the data with formatting and layout. This option preserves much of the formatting and layout in tables, queries, forms, and reports. For forms and reports, this is the only option for exporting to a text file.

If you do not need to preserve the formatting, you can choose either delimited or fixed-width as the format for the exported file. The most common option, especially if formatting is not an issue, is delimited. You can choose the delimiter. You also can choose whether to include field names on the first row. In many cases, delimiting with a comma and including the field names is a good choice.

To export data from a table or query to a comma-delimited file in which the first row contains the column headings, you would use the following steps.

BTW
Organizing Files and Folders
You should organize and store files in folders so that you easily can find the files later. For example, if you are taking an introductory computer class called CIS 101, a good practice would be to save all Access files in an Access folder in a CIS 101 folder. For a discussion of folders and detailed examples of creating folders, refer to the Office and Windows chapter at the beginning of this book.

1. With the query or table to be exported selected in the Navigation Pane, tap or click the Text File button (EXTERNAL DATA tab | Export group) to display the Export-Text File dialog box.
2. Select the name and location for the file to be created.
3. If you need to preserve formatting and layout, be sure the 'Export data with formatting and layout' check box is checked. If you do not need to preserve formatting and layout, make sure the check box is not checked. Once you have made your selection, tap or click the OK button in the Export-Text File dialog box.
4. To create a delimited file, be sure the Delimited option button is selected in the Export Text Wizard dialog box. To create a fixed-width file, be sure the Fixed Width option button is selected. Once you have made your selection, tap or click the Next button.

5. a. If you are exporting to a delimited file, choose the delimiter that you want to separate your fields, such as a comma. Decide whether to include field names on the first row and, if so, tap or click the 'Include Field Names on First Row' check box. If you want to select a text qualifier, select it in the Text Qualifier list. When you have made your selections, tap or click the Next button.
   b. If you are exporting to a fixed-width file, review the position of the vertical lines that separate your fields. If any lines are not positioned correctly, follow the directions on the screen to reposition them. When you have finished, tap or click the Next button.
6. Tap or click the Finish button to export the data.
7. Save the export steps if you want, or simply tap or click the Close button in the Export-Text File dialog box to close the dialog box without saving the export steps.

BTW

Join Types

The type of join that finds records from both tables that have identical values in matching fields is called an inner join. An inner join is the default join in Access. Outer joins are used to show all the records in one table as well as the common records; that is, the records that share the same value in the join field. In a left outer join, all rows from the table on the left are included. In a right outer join, all rows from the table on the right are included.

Adding Criteria to a Join Query

Sometimes you will want to join tables, but you will not want to include all possible records. For example, you would like to create a report showing only those customers whose amount paid is greater than $20,000.00. In this case, you would relate the tables and include fields just as you did before. You also will include criteria. To include only those customers whose amount paid is more than $20,000.00, you will include >20000 as a criterion for the Amount Paid field.

To Restrict the Records in a Join

1 CREATE QUERIES | 2 USE CRITERIA | 3 SORT DATA | 4 JOIN TABLES | 5 EXPORT RESULTS
6 PERFORM CALCULATIONS | 7 CREATE CROSSTAB | 8 CUSTOMIZE NAVIGATION PANE

The following steps modify the Rep-Customer Query so that the results for Bavant Publishing include a criterion. ***Why?*** *Bavant wants to include only those customers whose amount paid is more than $20,000.00.*

1

- Open the Navigation Pane, if necessary, and then press and hold or right-click the Rep-Customer Query to produce a shortcut menu.
- Tap or click Design View on the shortcut menu to open the Rep-Customer Query in Design view.
- Close the Navigation Pane.
- Add the Amount Paid field to the query.
- Type `>20000` as the criterion for the Amount Paid field (Figure 2–61).

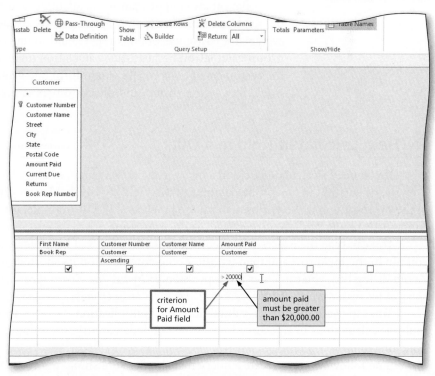

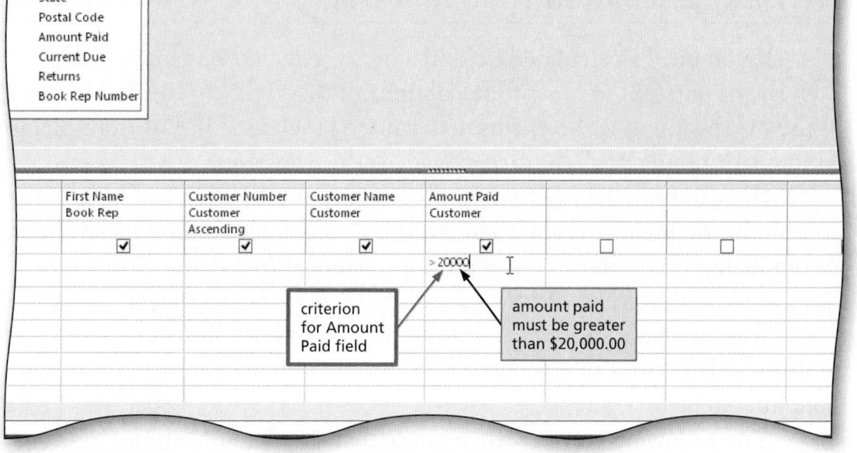

Figure 2–61

2

- Run the query (Figure 2–62).

3

- Close the query.
- When asked if you want to save your changes, tap or click the No button.

Q&A What would happen if I saved the changes?

The next time you used this query, you would only see customers whose amount paid is more than $20,000.00.

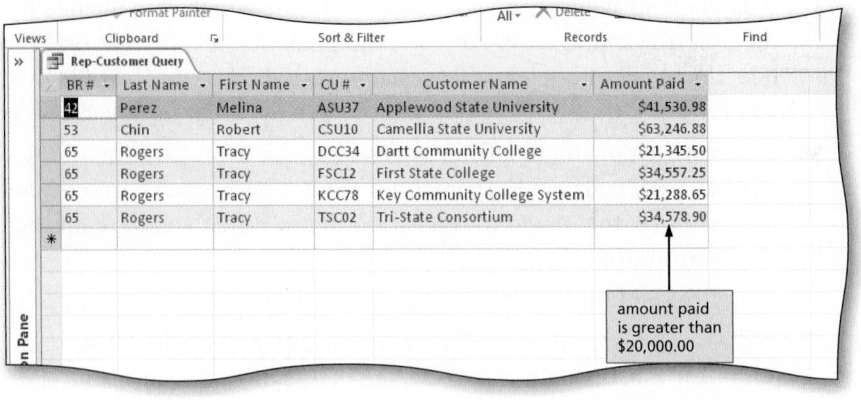

Figure 2–62

BTW

Expression Builder

Access includes a tool to help you create complex expressions. If you click Build on the shortcut menu (see Figure 2–63), Access displays the Expression Builder dialog box, which includes an expression box, operator buttons, and expression elements. You can type parts of the expression directly and paste operator buttons and expression elements into the box. You also can use functions in expressions.

Calculations

If a special calculation is required for a query, you need to determine whether the calculation is **an individual record calculation** (for example, adding the values in two fields) or a **group calculation** (for example, finding the total of the values in a particular field on all the records).

Bavant Publishing might want to know the total amount (amount paid and current due) from each customer. This would seem to pose a problem because the Customer table does not include a field for total amount. You can calculate it, however, because the total amount is equal to the amount paid plus the current due. A field that can be computed from other fields is called a **calculated field** or a **computed field.** A calculated field is an individual record calculation because each calculation only involves fields in a single record.

Bavant also might want to calculate the average amount paid for the customers of each book rep. That is, they may want the average for customers of book rep 42, the average for customers of book rep 53, and so on. This type of calculation is called a **group calculation** because each calculation involves groups of records. In this example, the customers of book rep 42 would form one group, the customers of book rep 53 would be a second group, and the customers of book rep 65 would form a third group.

To Use a Calculated Field in a Query

1 CREATE QUERIES | 2 USE CRITERIA | 3 SORT DATA | 4 JOIN TABLES | 5 EXPORT RESULTS
6 PERFORM CALCULATIONS | 7 CREATE CROSSTAB | 8 CUSTOMIZE NAVIGATION PANE

If you need a calculated field in a query, you enter a name, or alias, for the calculated field, a colon, and then the calculation in one of the columns in the Field row of the design grid for the query. Any fields included in the expression must be enclosed in square brackets ([ ]). For example, for the total amount, you will type Total Amount:[Amount Paid]+[Current Due] as the expression.

You can type the expression directly into the Field row. The preferred method, however, is to select the column in the Field row and then use the Zoom command on its shortcut menu. When Access displays the Zoom dialog box, you can enter the expression. ***Why use the Zoom command?*** *You will not be able to see the entire entry in the Field row, because the space available is not large enough.*

You can use addition (+), subtraction (−), multiplication (*), or division (/) in calculations. If you have multiple calculations in an expression, you can include parentheses to indicate which calculations should be done first.

The following steps create a query that Bavant Publishing might use to obtain financial information on its customers, including the total amount (amount paid + current due), which is a calculated field.

1

- Create a query with a field list for the Customer table.
- Add the Customer Number, Customer Name, Amount Paid, and Current Due fields to the query.
- Press and hold or right-click the Field row in the first open column in the design grid to display a shortcut menu (Figure 2–63).

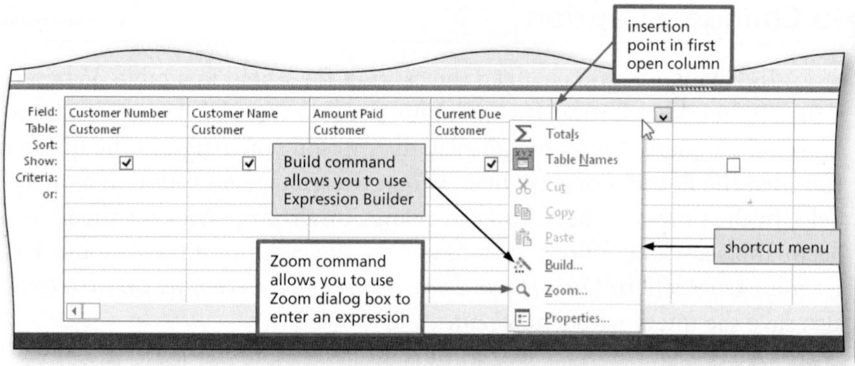

Figure 2–63

2

- Tap or click Zoom on the shortcut menu to display the Zoom dialog box.
- Type `Total Amount:[Amount Paid]+[Current Due]` in the Zoom dialog box (Figure 2–64).

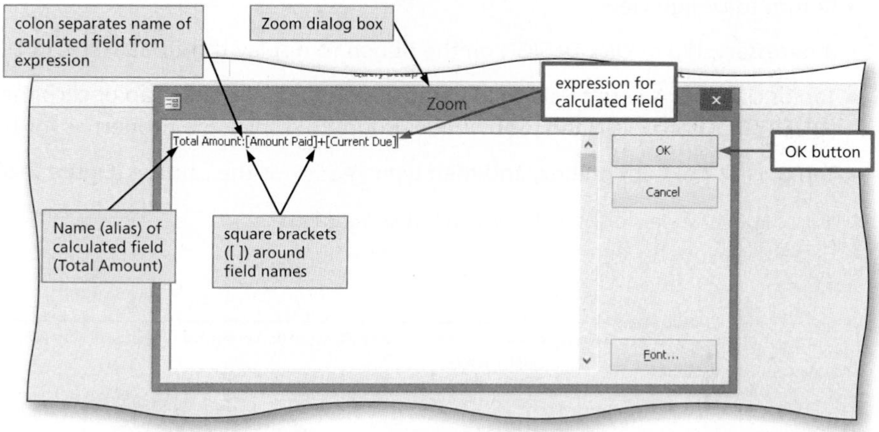

Figure 2–64

Q&A Do I always need to put square brackets around field names?

If the field name does not contain spaces, square brackets are technically not required. It is a good practice, however, to get in the habit of using the brackets in field calculations.

3

- Tap or click the OK button (Zoom dialog box) to enter the expression (Figure 2–65).

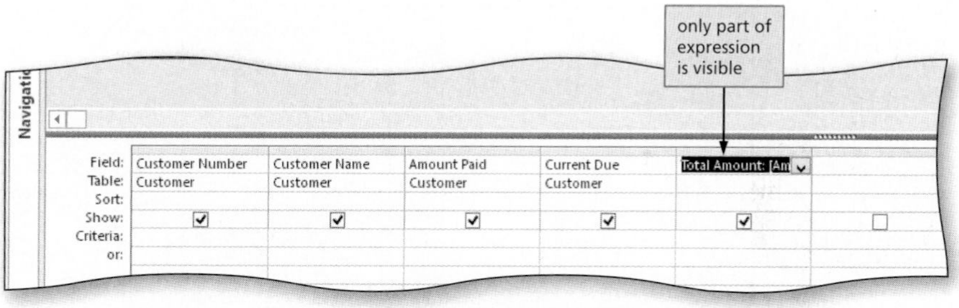

Figure 2–65

4

- Run the query (Figure 2–66).

Experiment

- Return to Design view and try other expressions. In at least one case, omit the Total Amount and the colon. In at least one case, intentionally misspell a field name. In each case, run the query to see the effect of your changes. When finished, reenter the original expression.

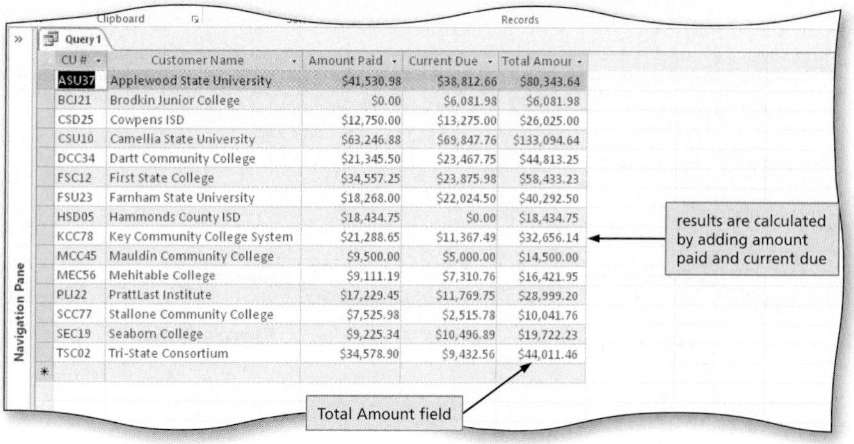

Figure 2–66

Other Ways

1. Press SHIFT+F2

To Change a Caption

In Chapter 1, you changed the caption for a field in a table. When you assigned a caption, Access displayed it in datasheets and forms. If you did not assign a caption, Access displayed the field name. You also can change a caption in a query. Access will display the caption you assign in the query results. When you omitted duplicates, you used the query property sheet. When you change a caption in a query, you use the property sheet for the field. In the property sheet, you can change other properties for the field, such as the format and number of decimal places. The following steps change the caption of the Amount Paid field to Paid and the caption of the Current Due field to Due. ***Why?*** *These changes give shorter, yet very readable, column headings for the fields.* The steps also save the query with a new name.

1

- Return to Design view.
- If necessary, tap or click DESIGN on the ribbon to display the QUERY TOOLS DESIGN tab.
- Tap or click the Amount Paid field in the design grid, and then tap or click the Property Sheet button (QUERY TOOLS DESIGN tab | Show/Hide group) to display the properties for the Amount Paid field.
- Tap or click the Caption box, and then type `Paid` as the caption (Figure 2–67).

Q&A My property sheet looks different. What should I do?
Close the property sheet and repeat this step.

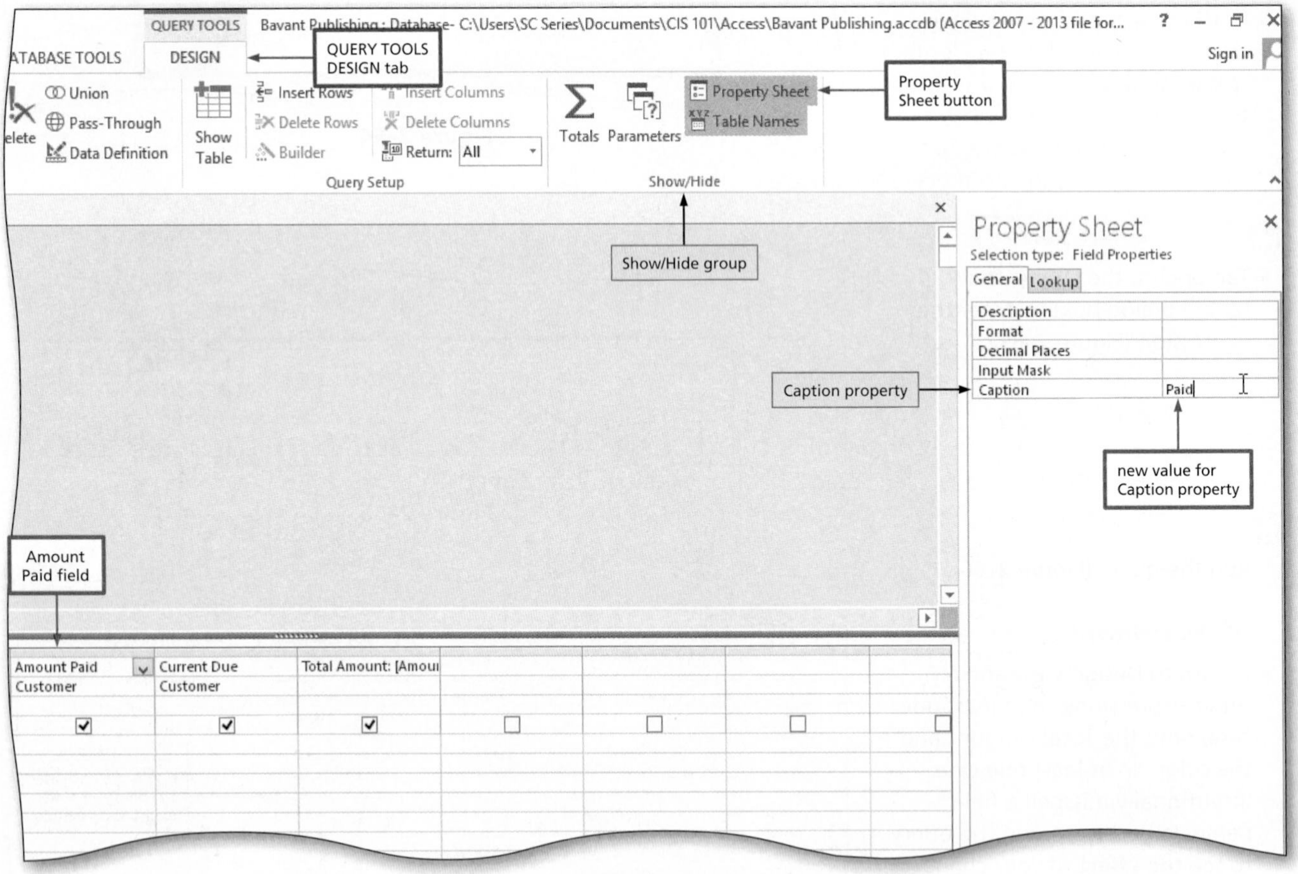

Figure 2–67

2

- Close the property sheet by tapping or clicking the Property Sheet button a second time.
- Tap or click the Current Due field in the design grid, and then tap or click the Property Sheet button (QUERY TOOLS DESIGN tab | Show/Hide group).
- Tap or click the Caption box, and then type `Due` as the caption.
- Close the Property Sheet by tapping or clicking the Property Sheet button a second time.
- Run the query (Figure 2–68).

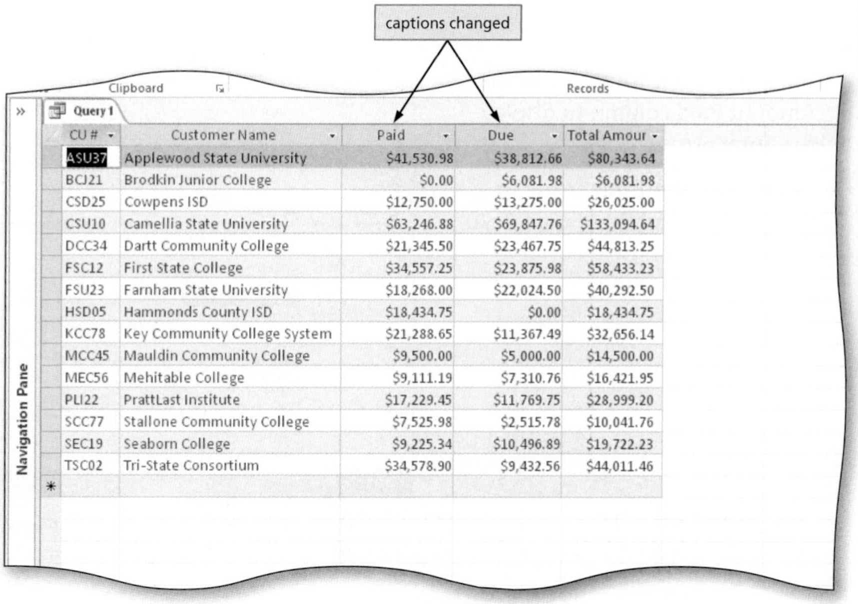

Figure 2–68

3

- Save the query as Ch2q10.
- Close the query.

Other Ways

1. Press and hold or right-click field in design grid, tap or click Properties on shortcut menu

To Calculate Statistics

1 CREATE QUERIES | 2 USE CRITERIA | 3 SORT DATA | 4 JOIN TABLES | 5 EXPORT RESULTS
6 PERFORM CALCULATIONS | 7 CREATE CROSSTAB | 8 CUSTOMIZE NAVIGATION PANE

For group calculations, Microsoft Access supports several built-in statistics: COUNT (count of the number of records), SUM (total), AVG (average), MAX (largest value), MIN (smallest value), STDEV (standard deviation), VAR (variance), FIRST (first value), and LAST (last value). These statistics are called aggregate functions. An **aggregate function** is a function that performs some mathematical function against a group of records. To use an aggregate function in a query, you include it in the Total row in the design grid. In order to do so, you must first include the Total row by tapping or clicking the Totals button on the DESIGN tab. ***Why?*** *The Total row usually does not appear in the grid.*

The following steps create a new query for the Customer table. The steps include the Total row in the design grid, and then calculate the average amount paid for all customers.

1

- Create a new query with a field list for the Customer table.
- Tap or click the Totals button (QUERY TOOLS DESIGN tab | Show/Hide group) to include the Total row in the design grid.
- Add the Amount Paid field to the query (Figure 2–69).

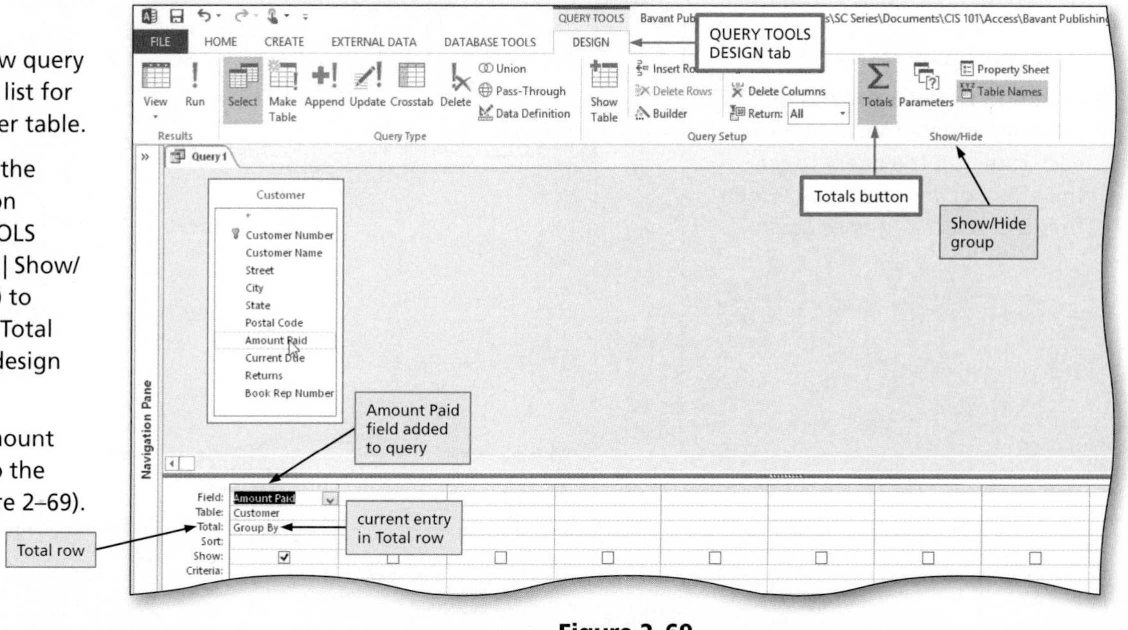

Figure 2–69

2

- Tap or click the Total row in the Amount Paid column to display the Total arrow.
- Tap or click the Total arrow to display the Total list (Figure 2–70).

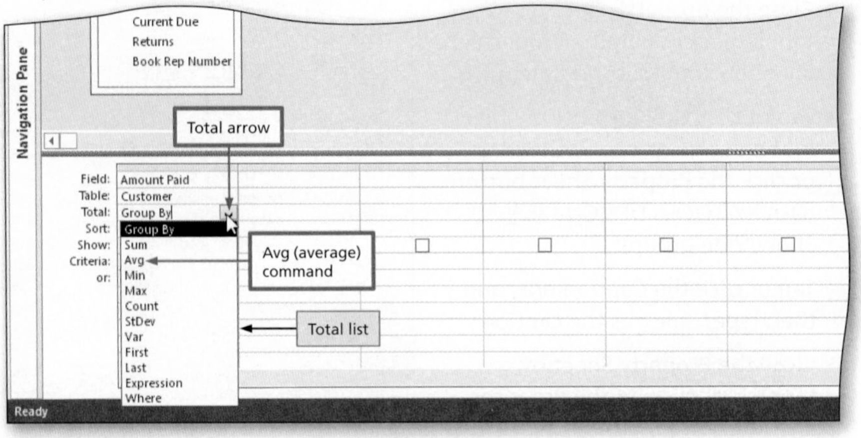

Figure 2–70

3

- Tap or click Avg to select the calculation that Access is to perform (Figure 2–71).

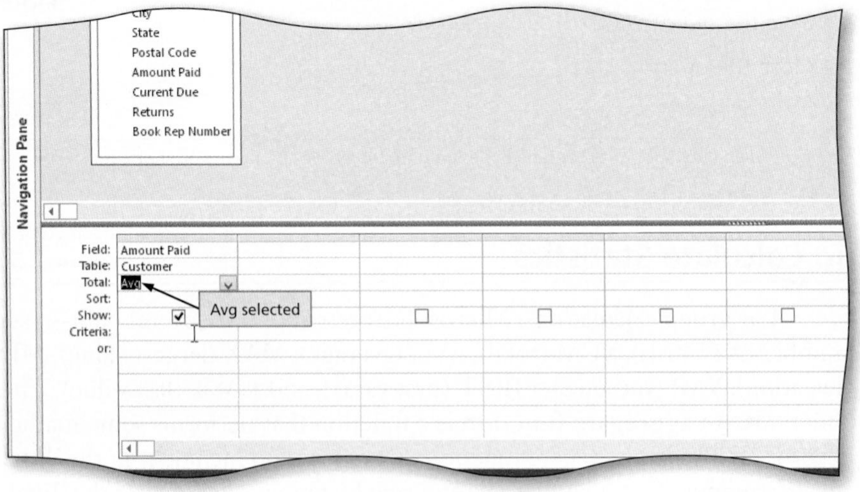

Figure 2–71

4

- Run the query (Figure 2–72).

Experiment

- Return to Design view and try other aggregate functions. In each case, run the query to see the effect of your selection. When finished, select Avg once again.

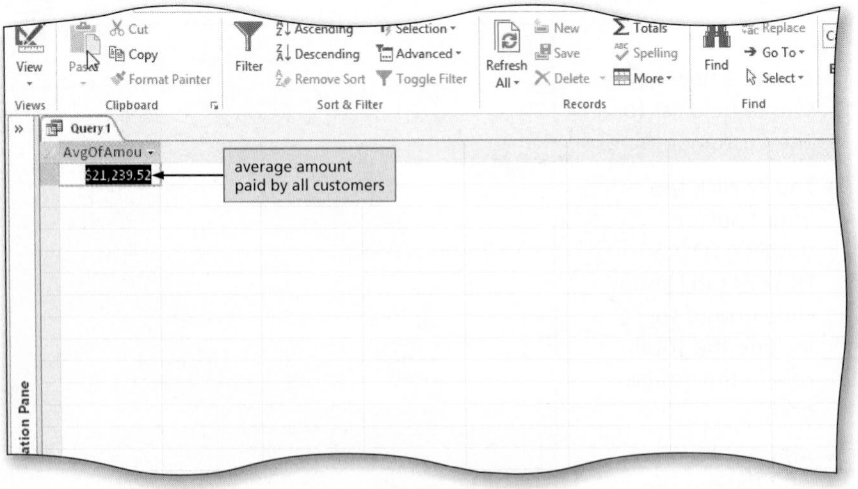

Figure 2–72

To Use Criteria in Calculating Statistics

Why? *Sometimes calculating statistics for all the records in the table is appropriate. In other cases, however, you will need to calculate the statistics for only those records that satisfy certain criteria.* To enter a criterion in a field, first you select Where as the entry in the Total row for the field, and then enter the criterion in the Criteria row. Access uses the word, Where, to indicate that you will enter a criterion. The following steps use this technique to calculate the average amount paid for customers of book rep 42. The steps also save the query with a new name.

1

- Return to Design view.
- Include the Book Rep Number field in the design grid.
- Tap or click the Total row in the Book Rep Number column.
- Tap or click the Total arrow in the Book Rep Number column to produce a Total list (Figure 2–73).

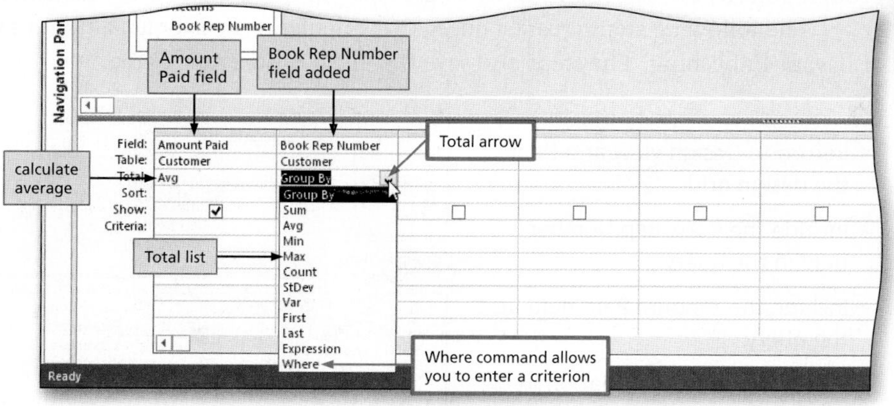

Figure 2–73

2

- Tap or click Where to be able to enter a criterion.
- Type `42` as the criterion for the Book Rep Number field (Figure 2–74).

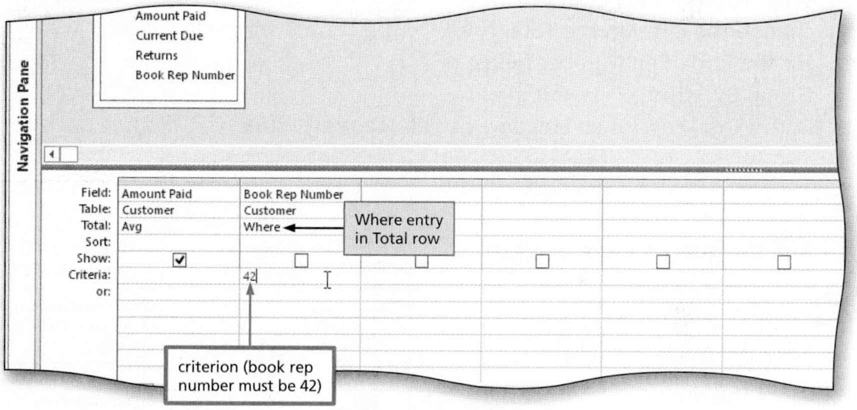

Figure 2–74

3

- Run the query (Figure 2–75).

4

- Save the query as Ch2q11.

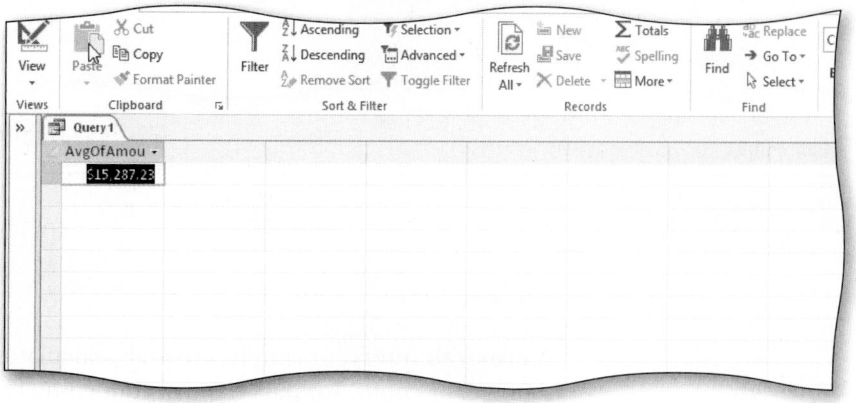

Figure 2–75

To Use Grouping

Why? *Statistics often are used in combination with grouping; that is, statistics are calculated for groups of records. For example, Bavant could calculate the average amount paid for the customers of each book rep, which would require the average for the customers of book rep 42, the average for customers of book rep 53, and so on.* **Grouping** means creating groups of records that share some common characteristic. In grouping by Book Rep Number, for example, the customers of book rep 42 would form one group, the customers of book rep 53 would form a second, and the customers of book rep 65 would form a third group. The calculations then are made for each group. To indicate grouping in Access, select Group By as the entry in the Total row for the field to be used for grouping.

The following steps create a query that calculates the average amount paid for customers of each book rep at Bavant Publishing. The steps also save the query with a new name.

1

- Return to Design view and clear the design grid.
- Include the Book Rep Number field in the query.
- Include the Amount Paid field in the query.
- Select Avg as the calculation in the Total row for the Amount Paid field (Figure 2–76).

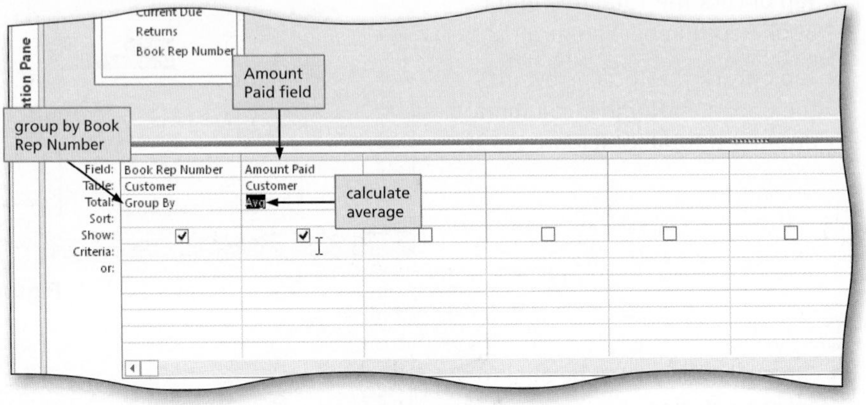

Figure 2–76

Q&A Why was it not necessary to change the entry in the Total row for the Book Rep Number field?
Group By, which is the initial entry in the Total row when you add a field, is correct. Thus, you did not need to change the entry.

2

- Run the query (Figure 2–77).

3

- Save the query as Ch2q12.
- Close the query.

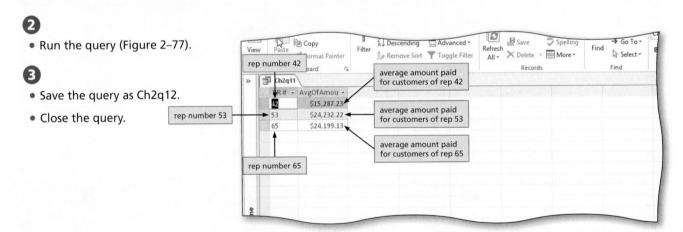

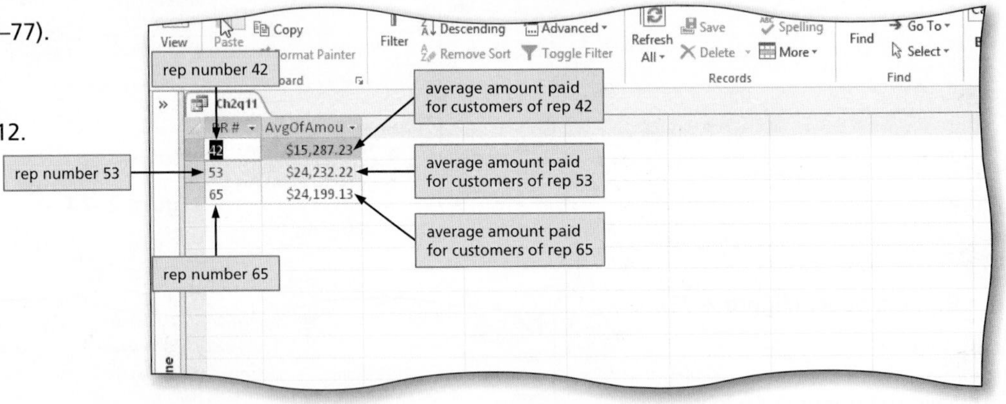

Figure 2–77

Crosstab Queries

A **crosstab query**, or simply, crosstab, calculates a statistic (for example, sum, average, or count) for data that is grouped by two different types of information. One of the types will appear down the side of the resulting datasheet, and the other will appear across the top. Crosstab queries are useful for summarizing data by category or group.

For example, if a query must summarize the sum of the returns grouped by both state and book rep number, you could have states as the row headings, that is, down the side. You could have book rep numbers as the column headings, that is, across the top. The entries within the datasheet represent the total of the returns. Figure 2–78 shows a crosstab in which the total of returns is grouped by both state and book rep number, with states down the left side and book rep numbers across the top. For example, the entry in the row labeled DE and in the column labeled 42 represents the total of the returns by all customers of book rep 42 who are located in Delaware.

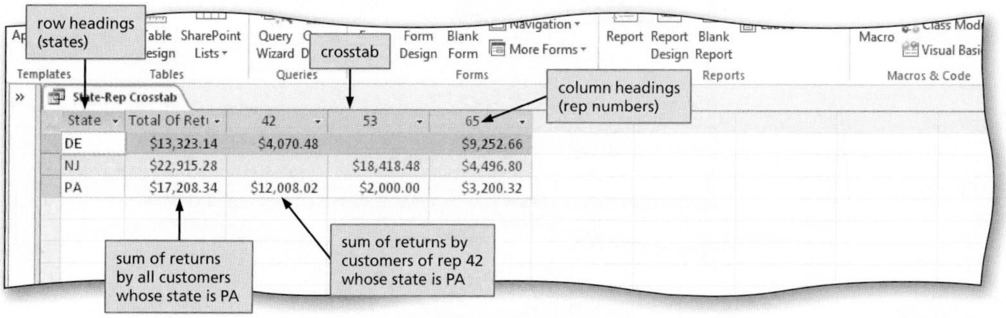

Figure 2–78

CONSIDER THIS

How do you know when to use a crosstab query?

If data is to be grouped by two different types of information, you can use a crosstab query. You will need to identify the two types of information. One of the types will form the row headings and the other will form the column headings in the query results.

To Create a Crosstab Query

1 CREATE QUERIES | 2 USE CRITERIA | 3 SORT DATA | 4 JOIN TABLES | 5 EXPORT RESULTS
6 PERFORM CALCULATIONS | 7 CREATE CROSSTAB | 8 CUSTOMIZE NAVIGATION PANE

The following steps use the Crosstab Query Wizard to create a crosstab query. ***Why?*** *Bavant Publishing wants to group data on returns by two types of information: state and book rep.*

1

- Tap or click CREATE on the ribbon to display the CREATE tab.
- Tap or click the Query Wizard button (CREATE tab | Queries group) to display the New Query dialog box (Figure 2–79).

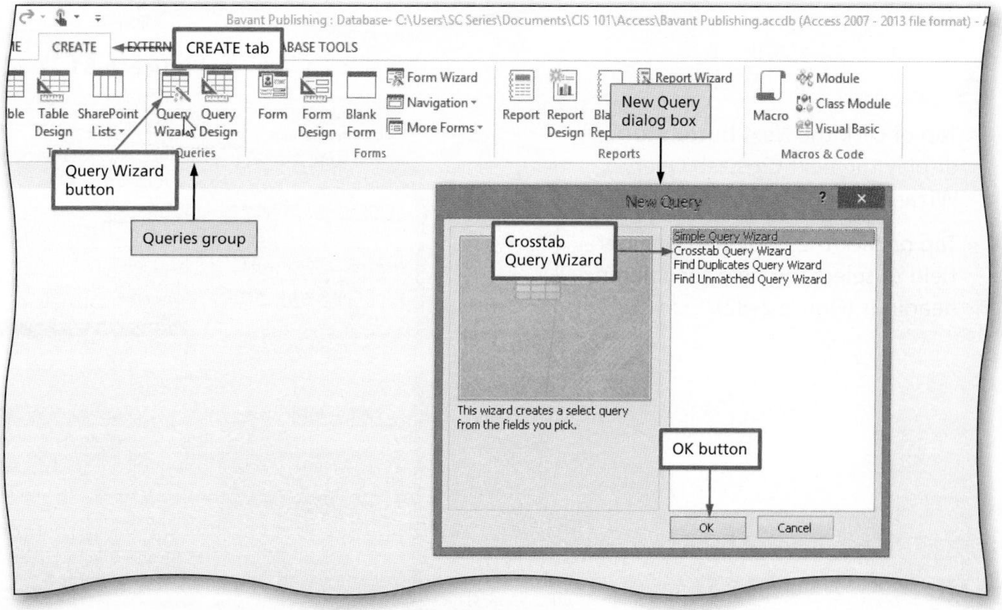

Figure 2–79

2

- Tap or click Crosstab Query Wizard (New Query dialog box).
- Tap or click the OK button to display the Crosstab Query Wizard dialog box (Figure 2–80).

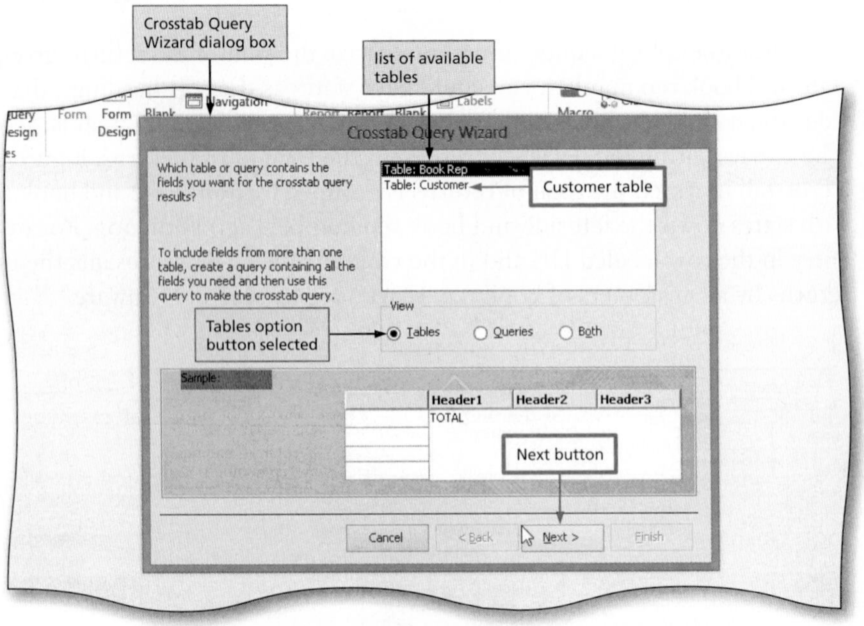

Figure 2–80

3

- With the Tables option button selected, tap or click Table: Customer to select the Customer table, and then tap or click the Next button to display the next Crosstab Query Wizard screen.
- Tap or click the State field, and then tap or click the Add Field button to select the State field for row headings (Figure 2–81).

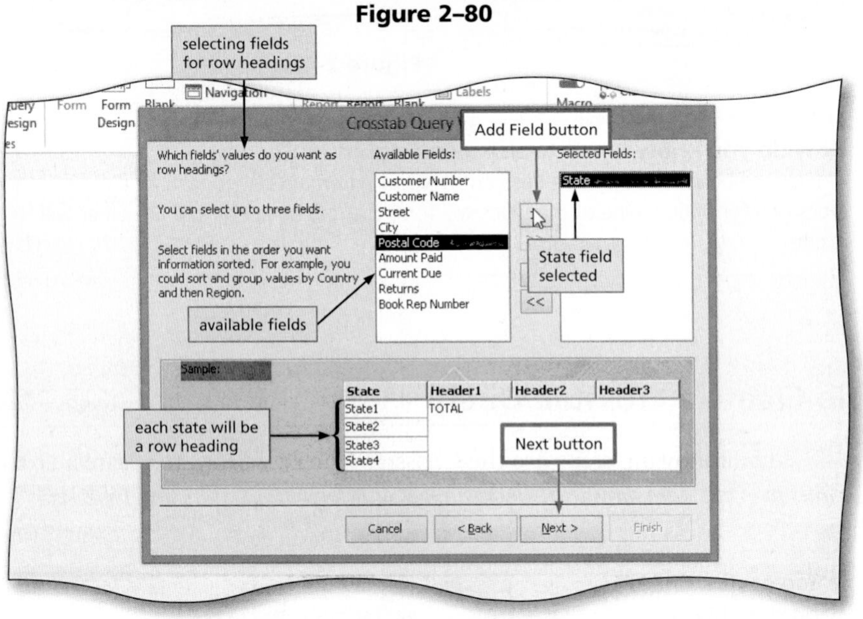

Figure 2–81

4

- Tap or click the Next button to display the next Crosstab Query Wizard screen.
- Tap or click the Book Rep Number field to select the field for column headings (Figure 2–82).

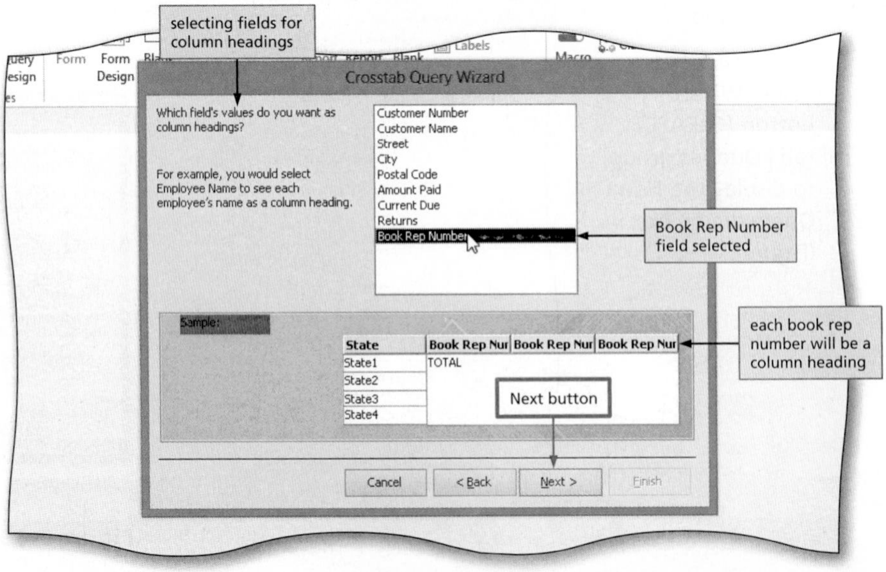

Figure 2–82

5

- Tap or click the Next button to display the next Crosstab Query Wizard screen.
- Tap or click the Returns field to select the field for calculations.

Experiment

- Tap or click other fields. For each field, examine the list of calculations that are available. When finished, tap or click the Returns field again.
- Tap or click Sum to select the calculation to be performed (Figure 2–83).

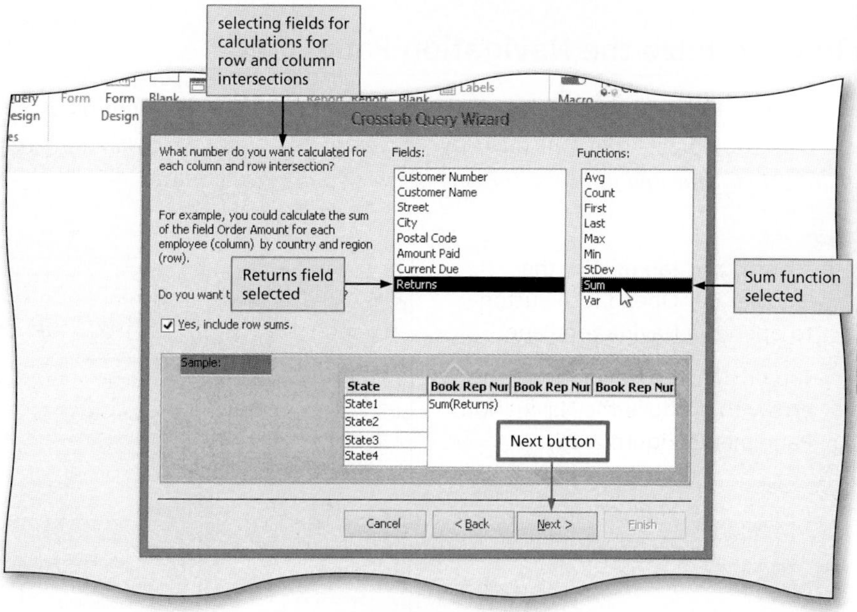

Figure 2–83

Q&A My list of functions is different. What did I do wrong?

Either you clicked the wrong field, or the Returns field has the wrong data type. For example, if you mistakenly assigned it the Short Text data type, you would not see Sum in the list of available calculations.

6

- Tap or click the Next button to display the next Crosstab Query Wizard screen.
- Erase the text in the name text box and type `State-Rep Crosstab` as the name of the query (Figure 2–84).

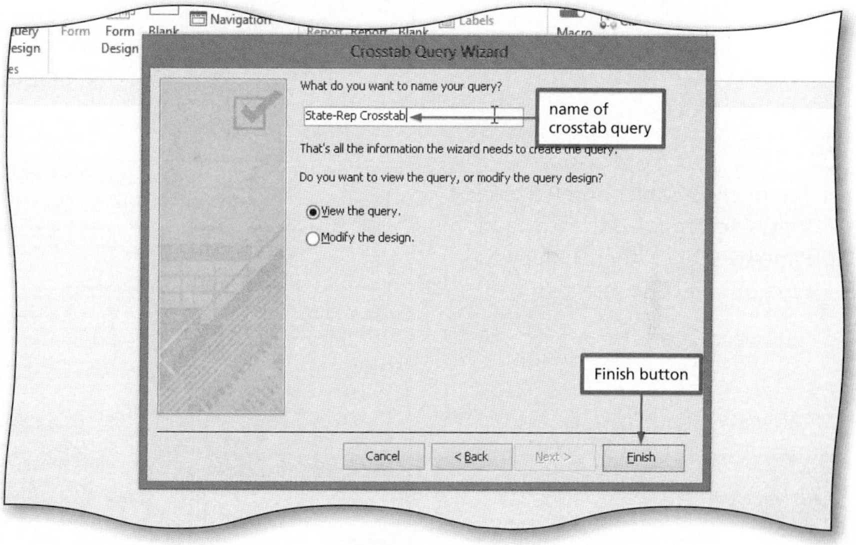

Figure 2–84

7

- If requested to do so by your instructor, name the crosstab query as FirstName LastName Crosstab where FirstName and LastName are your first and last names.
- Tap or click the Finish button to produce the crosstab shown in Figure 2–78 on page AC 119.
- Close the query.

Customizing the Navigation Pane

Currently, the entries in the Navigation Pane are organized by object type. That is, all the tables are together, all the queries are together, and so on. You might want to change the way the information is organized. For example, you might want to have the Navigation Pane organized by table, with all the queries, forms, and reports associated with a particular table appearing after the name of the table. You also can use the Search bar to restrict the objects that appear to only those that have a certain collection of characters in their name. For example, if you entered the letters, Cu, only those objects containing Cu somewhere within the name will be included.

BTW

Access Help

At any time while using Access, you can find answers to questions and display information about various topics through Access Help. Used properly, this form of assistance can increase your productivity and reduce your frustrations by minimizing the time you spend learning how to use Access. For instruction about Access Help and exercises that will help you gain confidence in using it, read the Office and Windows chapter at the beginning of this book.

To Customize the Navigation Pane

The following steps change the organization of the Navigation Pane. They also use the Search bar to restrict the objects that appear. ***Why?*** *Using the Search bar, you can reduce the number of objects that appear in the Navigation Pane and just show the ones in which you are interested.*

1

- If necessary, tap or click the 'Shutter Bar Open/Close Button' to open the Navigation Pane.
- Tap or click the Navigation Pane arrow to produce the Navigation Pane menu (Figure 2–85).

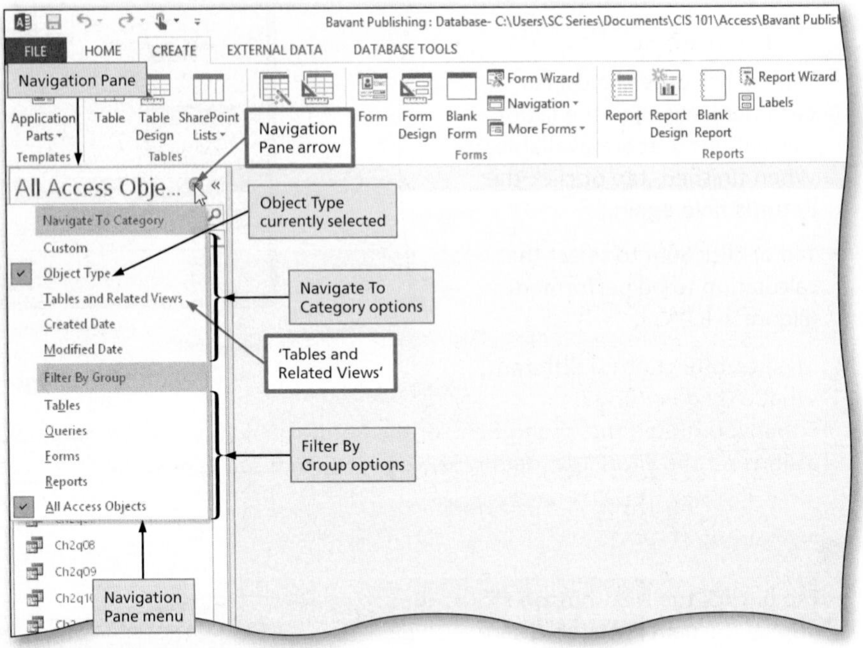

Figure 2–85

2

- Tap or click 'Tables and Related Views' to organize the Navigation Pane by table rather than by the type of object (Figure 2–86).

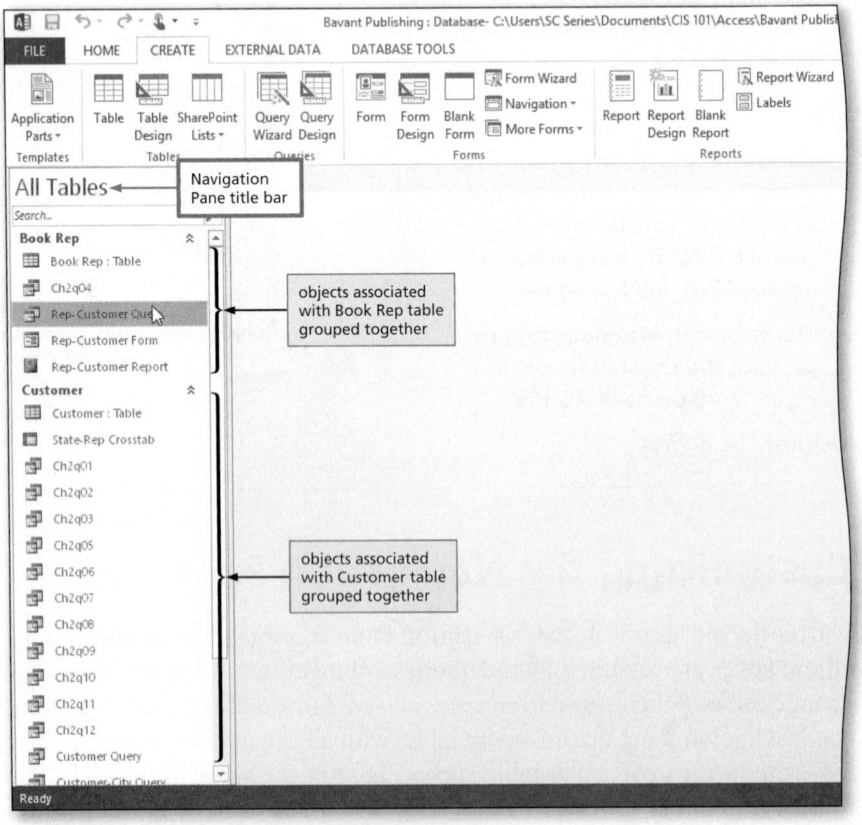

Figure 2–86

3

- Tap or click the Navigation Pane arrow to produce the Navigation Pane menu.
- Tap or click Object Type to once again organize the Navigation Pane by object type.

Experiment

- Select different Navigate To Category options to see the effect of the option. With each option you select, select different Filter By Group options to see the effect of the filtering. When you have finished experimenting, select the 'Object Type Navigate To Category' option and the 'All Access Objects Filter By Group' option.

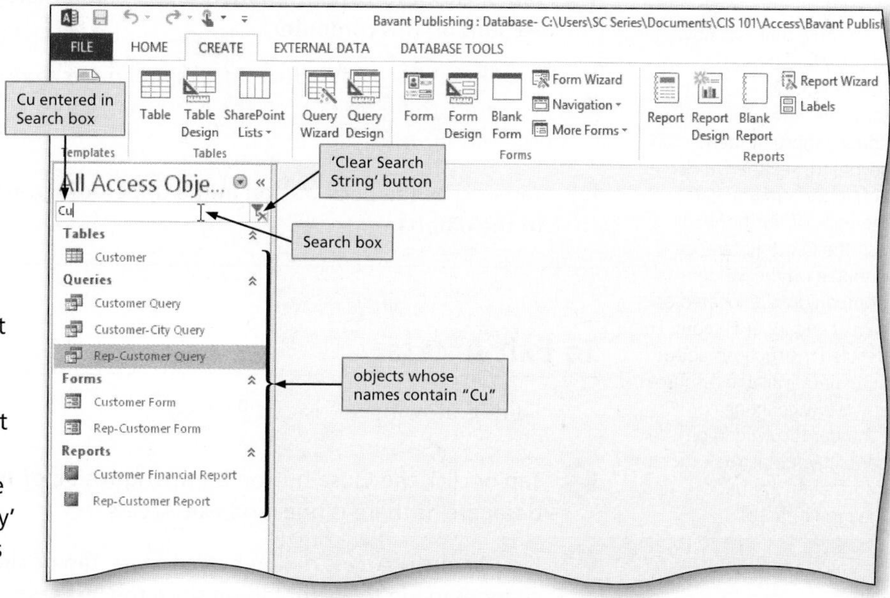

Figure 2–87

4

- If the Search bar does not appear, press and hold or right-click the Navigation Pane and tap or click Search Bar on the shortcut menu.
- Tap or click in the Search box to produce an insertion point.
- Type `Cu` as the search string to restrict the objects displayed to only those containing the desired string (Figure 2–87).

5

- Tap or click the 'Clear Search String' button to remove the search string and redisplay all objects.

Q&A Did I have to tap or click the button to redisplay all objects? Could I simply have erased the current string to achieve the same result?
You did not have to tap or click the button. You could have used the DELETE or BACKSPACE keys to erase the current search string.

To Sign Out of a Microsoft Account

If you are signed in to a Microsoft account and are using a public computer or otherwise wish to sign out of your Microsoft account, you should sign out of the account from the Account gallery in the Backstage view before exiting Access. Signing out of the account is the safest way to make sure that nobody else can access SkyDrive files or settings stored in your Microsoft account. The following steps sign out of a Microsoft account from Access. For a detailed example of the procedure summarized below, refer to the Office and Windows chapter at the beginning of this book.

BTW
Certification
The Microsoft Office Specialist (MOS) program provides an opportunity for you to obtain a valuable industry credential — proof that you have the Access 2013 skills required by employers. For more information, visit the Certification resource on the Student Companion Site located on www.cengagebrain.com. For detailed instructions about accessing available resources, visit www.cengage.com/ct/studentdownload or contact your instructor for information about accessing the required files.

1. If you wish to sign out of your Microsoft account, tap or click FILE on the ribbon to open the Backstage view and then tap or click the Account tab to display the Account gallery.
2. Tap or click the Sign out link, which displays the Remove Account dialog box. If a Can't remove Windows accounts dialog box appears instead of the Remove Account dialog box, click the OK button and skip the remaining steps.

Q&A Why does a Can't remove Windows accounts dialog box appear?
If you signed in to Windows using your Microsoft account, then you also must sign out from Windows, rather than signing out from within Access. When you are finished using Windows, be sure to sign out at that time.

BTW
Quick Reference
For a table that lists how to complete the tasks covered in this book using touch gestures, the mouse, ribbon, shortcut menu, and keyboard, see the Quick Reference Summary at the back of this book, or visit the Quick Reference resource on the Student Companion Site located on www.cengagebrain.com. For detailed instructions about accessing available resources, visit www.cengage.com/ct/studentdownload or contact your instructor for information about accessing the required files.

3. Tap or click the Yes button (Remove Account dialog box) to sign out of your Microsoft account on this computer.

Q&A Should I sign out of Windows after signing out of my Microsoft account?
When you are finished using the computer, you should sign out of your account for maximum security.

4. Tap or click the Back button in the upper-left corner of the Backstage view to return to the database.

To Exit Access

The following steps exit Access.

1. Tap or click the Close button on the right side of the title bar to close the open database, if there is one, and exit Access.
2. If a Microsoft Access dialog box appears, tap or click the Save button to save any changes made to the database since the last save.

Chapter Summary

In this chapter you have learned to create queries, enter fields, enter criteria, use text and numeric data in queries, use wildcards, use compound criteria, create parameter queries, sort data in queries, join tables in queries, perform calculations in queries, and create crosstab queries. You also learned to create a report and a form that used a query, to export a query, and to customize the Navigation Pane. The items listed below include all the new Access skills you have learned in this chapter, with tasks grouped by activity.

Calculations in Queries
- Use a Calculated Field in a Query (AC 112)
- Calculate Statistics (AC 115)
- Use Criteria in Calculating Statistics (AC 117)
- Use Grouping (AC 118)

Crosstab Query
- Create a Crosstab Query (AC 119)

Criteria in Queries
- Use Text Data in a Criterion (AC 81)
- Use a Wildcard (AC 83)
- Use Criteria for a Field Not Included in the Results (AC 85)
- Use a Number in a Criterion (AC 89)
- Use a Comparison Operator in a Criterion (AC 90)
- Use a Compound Criterion Involving AND (AC 91)
- Use a Compound Criterion Involving OR (AC 92)

Design Grid
- Clear the Design Grid (AC 93)

Export Data
- Export Data to Excel (AC 107)
- Export Data to Word (AC 110)
- Export Data to a Text File (AC 110)

Form Creation
- Create a Form for a Query (AC 105)

Join Queries
- Join Tables (AC 100)
- Change Join Properties (AC 101)
- Restrict the Records in a Join (AC 111)

Navigation Pane
- Customize the Navigation Pane (AC 122)

Parameter Query
- Create and View a Parameter Query (AC 87)
- Use a Parameter Query (AC 88)

Query Creation
- Create a Query in Design View (AC 78)
- Add Fields to the Design Grid (AC 79)
- Change a Caption (AC 114)

Report Creation
- Create a Report from a Query (AC 103)

Sort in Queries
- Sort Data in a Query (AC 94)
- Omit Duplicates (AC 94)
- Sort on Multiple Keys (AC 96)
- Create a Top-Values Query (AC 98)

CONSIDER THIS

What decisions will you need to make when creating queries?
Use these guidelines as you complete the assignments in this chapter and create your own queries outside of this class.

1. Identify the fields by examining the question or request to determine which fields from the tables in the database are involved.
2. Identify restrictions or the conditions that records must satisfy to be included in the results.
3. Determine whether special order is required.
   a) Determine the sort key(s).
   b) If using two sort keys, determine the major and minor key.
   c) Determine sort order. If there are no words to imply a particular order, you would typically use Ascending.
   d) Determine restrictions, such as excluding duplicates.
4. Determine whether more than one table is required.
   a) Determine which tables to include.
   b) Determine the matching fields.
   c) Determine whether sorting is required.
   d) Determine restrictions.
   e) Determine join properties.
5. Determine whether calculations are required.
   a) For individual record calculations, determine the calculation and a name for the calculated field.
   b) For group calculations, determine the calculation as well as the field to be used for grouping.
6. If data is to be summarized and the data is to be grouped by two different types of information, create a crosstab query.

CONSIDER THIS

How should you submit solutions to questions in the assignments identified with a ✱ symbol?
Every assignment in this book contains one or more questions identified with a ✱ symbol. These questions require you to think beyond the assigned database. Present your solutions to the questions in the format required by your instructor. Possible formats may include one or more of these options: write the answer; create a document that contains the answer; present your answer to the class; discuss your answer in a group; record the answer as audio or video using a webcam, smartphone, or portable media player; or post answers on a blog, wiki, or website.

Apply Your Knowledge

Reinforce the skills and apply the concepts you learned in this chapter.

Using Wildcards in a Query, Creating a Parameter Query, Joining Tables, and Creating a Report

Instructions: Start Access. Open the Apply Cosmetics Naturally database that you modified in Apply Your Knowledge in Chapter 1 on page AC 65. (If you did not complete the exercise, see your instructor for a copy of the modified database.)

Perform the following tasks:

1. Create a query for the Customer table and add the Customer Number, Customer Name, Amount Paid, and Balance fields to the design grid. Add a criterion to find all customers whose names start with the letter C. Run the query and then save it as Apply 2 Step 1 Query.
2. Create a query for the Customer table and add the Customer Number, Customer Name, Amount Paid, and Sales Rep Number fields to the design grid. Sort the records in descending order by Amount Paid. Add a criterion for the Sales Rep Number field that allows the user to enter a different sales rep each time the query is run. Run the query and enter 41 as the sales rep number to test the query. Save the query as Apply 2 Step 2 Query.

Continued >

Apply Your Knowledge *continued*

3. Create a query that joins the Sales Rep and Customer tables. Add the Sales Rep Number, Last Name, and First Name fields from the Sales Rep table and the Customer Number and Customer Name fields from the Customer table to the design grid. Sort the records in ascending order by Customer Number within Sales Rep Number. All sales reps should appear in the result, even if they currently have no customers. Run the query and save it as Rep-Customer Query.
4. Create the report shown in Figure 2–88. The report uses the Rep-Customer Query.

Rep-Customer Report

SR #	Last Name	First Name	CU #	Customer Name
34	Johnson	Bobbi	AS24	Ashley's Salon
34	Johnson	Bobbi	DB14	Della's Beauty Place
34	Johnson	Bobbi	EY07	Environmentally Yours
34	Johnson	Bobbi	NC25	Nancy's Place
34	Johnson	Bobbi	TT21	Tan and Tone
39	Gutaz	Nicholas	BL15	Blondie's on Main
39	Gutaz	Nicholas	CY12	Curlin Yoga Studio
39	Gutaz	Nicholas	JN34	Just Natural
39	Gutaz	Nicholas	LB20	Le Beauty
39	Gutaz	Nicholas	UR23	U R Beautiful
41	Orlon	Jake	BA35	Beauty for All
41	Orlon	Jake	CL09	Casual Looks
41	Orlon	Jake	FN19	Fitness Counts
41	Orlon	Jake	RD03	Rose's Day Spa
41	Orlon	Jake	TW56	The Workout Place
55	Sinson	Terry		

Figure 2–88

5. If requested to do so by your instructor, rename the Rep-Customer Report in the Navigation Pane as LastName-Customer Report where LastName is your last name.
6. Submit the revised database in the format specified by your instructor.
7. What criteria would you enter in the Customer Name field if you wanted to find all customers who had the word Beauty somewhere in their name?

Extend Your Knowledge

Extend the skills you learned in this chapter and experiment with new skills. You may need to use Help to complete the assignment.

Creating Crosstab Queries Using Criteria, and Exporting a Query

Note: To complete this assignment, you will be required to use the Data Files for Students. Visit www.cengage.com/ct/studentdownload for detailed instructions or contact your instructor for information about accessing the required files.

Instructions: Start Access. Open the Extend Janitorial Services database. Janitorial Services is a small business that provides janitorial services to commercial businesses. The owner has created an Access database in which to store information about the customers she serves and the cleaning staff she employs. You will create the crosstab query shown in Figure 2–89. You also will query the database using specified criteria, and export a query.

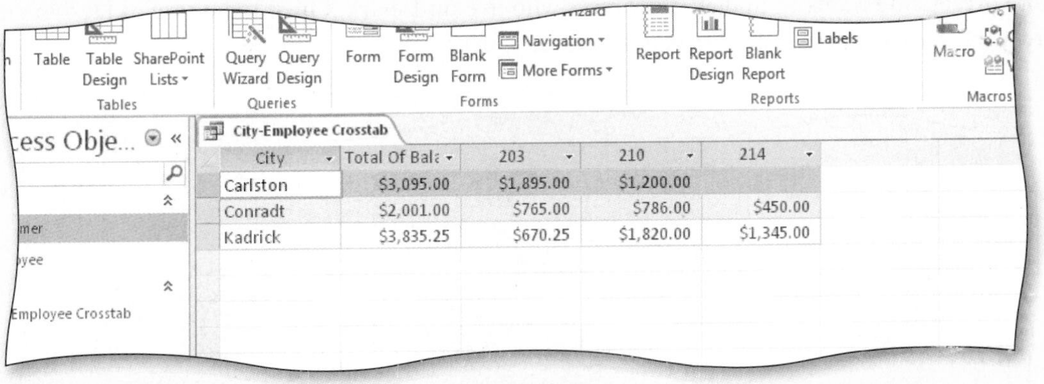

Figure 2–89

Perform the following tasks:

1. Create the crosstab query shown in Figure 2–89. The crosstab groups the total of customers' balance by city and employee number.
2. Create a query to find all customers who are not located in Kadrick. Include the Customer Number, Customer Name, and Balance fields in the query results. Save the query as Extend 2 Step 2 Query.
3. Create a query to find all employees whose first name is either Timmy or Tammy. Include the Employee Number, First Name, and Last Name in the query results. Save the query as Extend 2 Step 3 Query.
4. Create a query to find all customers where the employee number is either 210 or 214 and the balance is greater than $1,000.00. Include the Customer Number, Customer Name, Balance, and Employee Number fields in the design grid. Use the IN operator in your query design. Save the query as Extend 2 Step 4 Query.
5. Export the City-Employee Crosstab as a Word file with the name City-Employee Crosstab.rtf and save the export steps.
6. Open the Customer table and change the balance for customer AT23 to $755.
7. If requested to do so by your instructor, change the customer name of customer AT23 from Atlas Repair to Last Name Repair where Last Name is your last name.
8. Use the saved export steps to export the City-Employee Crosstab again. When asked if you want to replace the existing file, click Yes.
9. Submit the revised database and the exported RTF file in the format specified by your instructor.
10. How would you create the query in Step 4 without using the IN operator?

Analyze, Correct, Improve

Analyze a database, correct all errors, and improve the design.

Correcting Errors in the Table Structure

Note: To complete this assignment, you will be required to use the Data Files for Students. Visit www.cengage.com/ct/studentdownload for detailed instructions or contact your instructor for information about accessing the required files.

Instructions: Analyze Fitness is a database maintained by the Sports Science department at your university. Graduate students work with local residents as personal trainers to earn the necessary hours required for certification. The department chair has asked you to correct and improve two of the queries she created. Start Access and open the Analyze Fitness database from the Data Files for Students.

1. Correct The query shown in Figure 2–90 returns 0 results, and the department chair knows that is not correct. She wants to find all customers who live on Levick. Open the query in Design view, correct the errors, and save as Corrected Criteria Query.

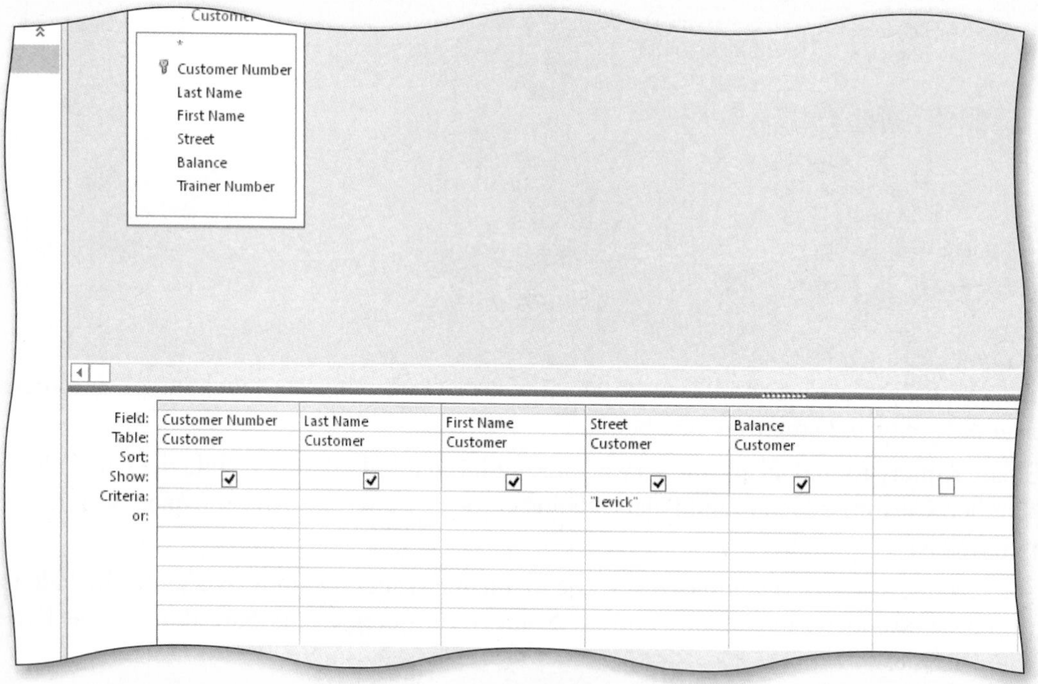

Figure 2–90

2. Improve The department chair also created the query shown in Figure 2–91. The query is sorted correctly, but she wanted Trainer Number to appear as the last field in the query result. She also would like to change the caption for the Balance field to Due. Improve the query to display the results in the desired order. Save the query as Improved Sort Query. Submit the revised database in the format specified by your instructor.

3. Why does the query shown in Figure 2–90 return 0 results?

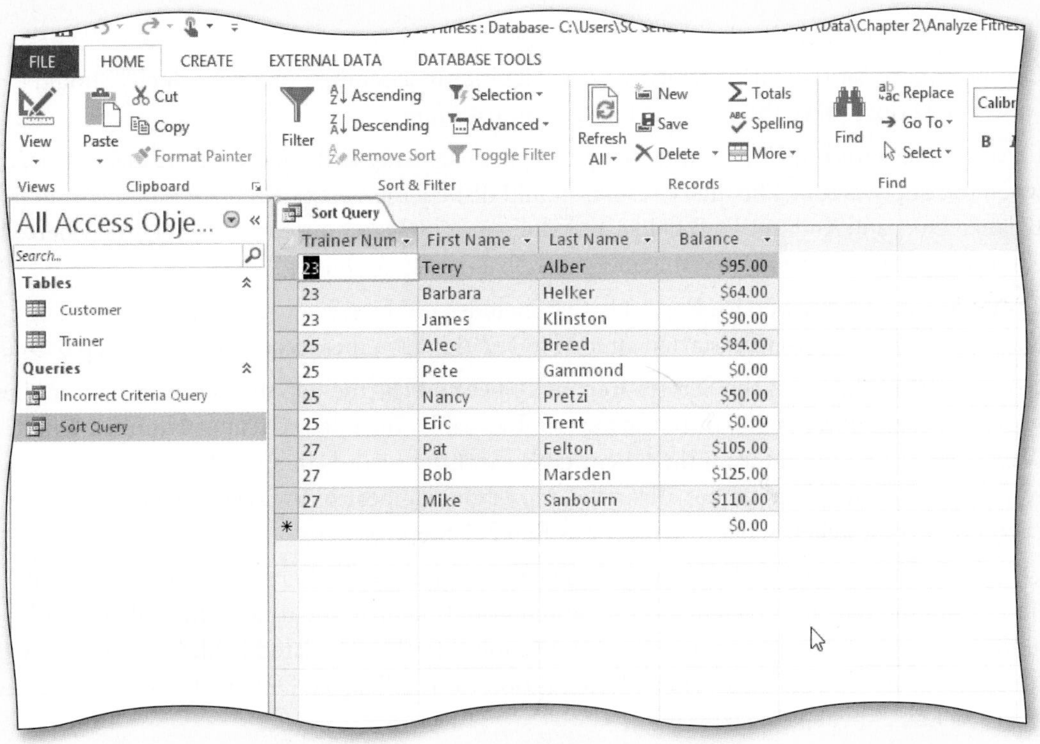

Figure 2–91

In the Labs

Design, create, modify, and/or use a database following the guidelines, concepts, and skills presented in this chapter. Labs are listed in order of increasing difficulty. Labs 1 and 2, which increase in difficulty, require you to create solutions based on what you learned in the chapter; Lab 3 requires you to create a solution, which uses cloud and web technologies, by learning and investigating on your own from general guidance.

Lab 1: Querying the Dartt Offsite Services Database

Problem: The management of Dartt Offsite Services has determined a number of questions it wants the database management system to answer. You must obtain the answers to these questions.

Note: Use the database modified in Lab 1 of Chapter 1 on page AC 68 for this assignment, or see your instructor for information on accessing the required files.

Instructions: Perform the following tasks:

1. Start Access. Open the Lab 1 Dartt Offsite Services database and create a new query for the Client table. Add the Client Number, Client Name, Amount Paid, Balance Due, and Service Rep Number fields to the design grid, and restrict the query results to only those clients where the service rep number is 37. Save the query as Lab 2-1 Step 1 Query.
2. Create a query for the Client table that includes the Client Number, Client Name, and Balance Due fields for all clients located in North Carolina (NC) with a balance due less than $1,000.00. Save the query as Lab 2-1 Step 2 Query.
3. Create a query for the Client table that includes the Client Number, Client Name, Street, City, and State field for all clients whose names begin with Ba. Save the query as Lab 2-1 Step 3 Query.

Continued >

In the Labs *continued*

4. Create a query for the Client table that lists all cities in ascending order. Each city should appear only once. Save the query as Lab 2-1 Step 4 Query.
5. Create a query for the Client table that allows the user to type the name of the desired city when the query is run. The query results should display the Client Number, Client Name, Balance Due, and Amount Paid fields. Test the query by searching for those records where the client is located in Austin. Save the query as Lab 2-1 Step 5 Query.
6. Create a query for the Service Rep table that includes the First Name, Last Name, and Start Date for all service reps who started after May 1, 2013. Save the query as Lab 2-1 Step 6 Query.
7. Create a query that joins the Service Rep and Client tables. Include the Service Rep Number, Last Name, and First Name from the Service Rep table. Include the Client Number, Client Name, and Amount Paid from the Client table. Sort the records in ascending order by service rep's last name and client name. All service reps should appear in the result even if they currently have no clients. Save the query as Lab 2-1 Step 7 Query.
8. Open the Lab 2-1 Step 7 Query in Design view and remove the Service Rep table from the query. Add the Balance Due field to the design grid. Calculate the total of the balance and amount paid amounts. Assign the alias Total Amount to the calculated field. Change the caption for the Amount Paid field to Paid and the caption for the Balance Due field to Owe. Save the query as Lab 2-1 Step 8 Query.
9. Create a query for the Client table to display the total amount paid amount for service rep 24. Save the query as Lab 2-1 Step 9 Query.
10. Create a query for the Client table to display the average balance amount for each service rep. Save the query as Lab 2-1 Step 10 Query.
11. Create the crosstab query shown in Figure 2–92. The crosstab groups the average of clients' amount paid amounts by state and service rep number. Save the crosstab as State-Service Rep Crosstab.

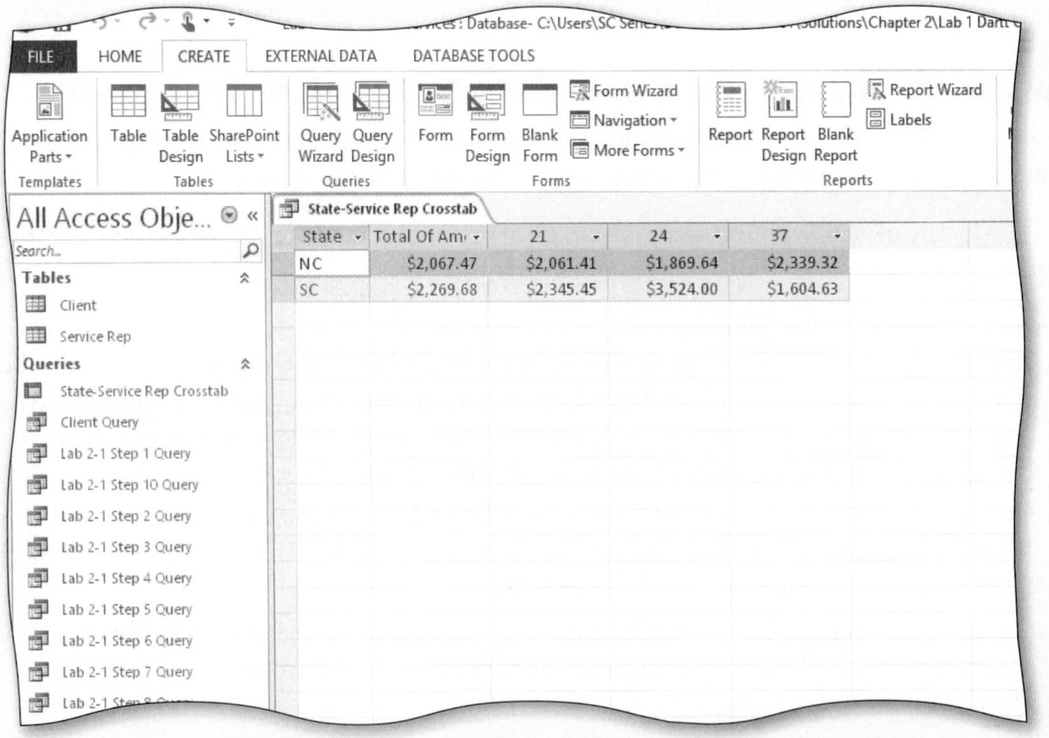

Figure 2–92

12. If requested to do so by your instructor, open the Lab 2-1 Step 1 query and change the caption for the Service Rep Number field to your last name.
13. Submit the revised database in the format specified by your instructor.
14. How would you modify the query in Step 7 to include only service reps that currently have clients?

Lab 2: Querying the Tennis Logos Database

Problem: The manager of Tennis Logos has determined a number of questions he wants the database management system to answer. You must obtain answers to these questions.

Note: Use the database created in Lab 2 of Chapter 1 on page AC 69 for this assignment or see your instructor for information on accessing the required files.

Instructions: Perform the following tasks:

1. Start Access. Open the Lab 2 Tennis Logos database and create a query for the Item table that includes all fields and all records in the Item table. Name the query Lab 2-2 Step 1 Query.
2. Create a query for the Item table that includes the Item Number, Description, Wholesale Price, and Supplier Code fields for all records where the supplier code is SD. Save the query as Lab 2-2 Step 2 Query.
3. Create a query for the Item table that includes the Item Number and Description fields for all items where the description starts with C. Save the query as Lab 2-2 Step 3 Query.
4. Create a query for the Item table that includes the Item Number and Description for all items with a Base Cost greater than $10.00. Save the query as Lab 2-2 Step 4 Query.
5. Create a query for the Item table that includes the Item Number, Description, and Wholesale Price fields for all items with a Wholesale Price between $1.00 and $4.00. Save the query as Lab 2-2 Step 5 Query.
6. Create a query for the Item table that includes the Item Number, Description, On Hand, and Wholesale Price fields for all items where the number on hand is less than 100 and the wholesale price is less than $3.00. Save the query as Lab 2-2 Step 6 Query.
7. Create a query for the Item table that includes the Item Number, Description, Wholesale Price, and Supplier Code for all items that have a Wholesale Price greater than $10.00 or a Supplier Code of LM. Save the query as Lab 2-2 Step 7 Query.
8. Create a query that joins the Supplier and the Item tables. Include the Supplier Code and Supplier Name from the Supplier table and the Item Number, Description, Wholesale Price, and Base Cost fields from the Item table. Sort the query in ascending order by Supplier Code and Description. Save the query as Supplier-Item Query.
9. Create a form for the Supplier-Item Query. Save the form as Supplier-Item Form.
10. If requested to do so by your instructor, rename the form in the Navigation Pane as LastName-Item Form where LastName is your last name.
11. Create the report shown in Figure 2–93. The report uses the Supplier-Item Query but does not use all the fields in the query.
12. Create a query for the Item table that includes the Item Number, Description, Base Cost, and Wholesale Price. Calculate the difference between Base Cost and Wholesale Price (Base Cost – Wholesale Price). Assign the alias Cost Difference to the calculated field. Save the query as Lab 2-2 Step 12 Query.

Continued >

In the Labs *continued*

Supplier-Item Report

Supplier Name	Description	Wholesale	Base Cost
Last Merchandisers	Baseball Cap	$4.87	$6.10
Last Merchandisers	Cotton Visor	$4.59	$5.74
Last Merchandisers	Foam Visor	$0.79	$1.00
Last Merchandisers	V-Neck Pullover	$13.60	$15.75
Last Merchandisers	V-Neck Vest	$20.85	$25.02
Pratt Clothing	Crew Sweatshirt	$7.29	$8.75
Pratt Clothing	Crew T-Shirt	$2.81	$3.38
Pratt Clothing	Fleece Vest	$28.80	$34.50
Pratt Clothing	Golf Shirt	$10.06	$12.35
Pratt Clothing	Windbreaker	$15.17	$18.20
Pratt Clothing	Zip Hoodie	$16.67	$20.04
Scryps Distributors	Drink Holder	$0.82	$1.07
Scryps Distributors	Sports Bottle	$1.04	$1.35
Scryps Distributors	Tote Bag	$1.26	$1.75
Scryps Distributors	Travel Mug	$2.47	$3.50

Figure 2–93

13. Create a query for the Item table that displays the average Wholesale Price and the average Base Cost of all items. Save the query as Lab 2-2 Step 13 Query.
14. Submit the revised database in the format specified by your instructor.
15. There are two ways to create the query in step 1. What are they? Which one did you use?

Lab 3: Expand Your World: Cloud and Web Technologies Creating Queries, Customizing the Navigation Pane, and Using the Excel Web App

Problem: Shopper is a small business that does personal shopping for clients. You will create two queries for the owner, customize the Navigation Pane, export a query in CSV format, open the exported file, and then modify the file using the Excel Web app.

Note: To complete this assignment, you will be required to use the Data Files for Students. Visit www.cengage.com/ct/studentdownload for detailed instructions or contact your instructor for information about accessing the required files.

Instructions: Perform the following tasks:

1. Open the Lab 3 Shopper database. Create and save a query that joins the Shopper and Client tables. Include the Last Name and First Name from the Shopper table and the Client Number, Last Name, First Name, and Balance fields from the Client table. Sort the query by shopper Last Name and Client Number.

2. Create and save a query for the Client table. The query result should display the Last Name, First Name, Amount Paid, Balance, and Shopper Number in that order. Sort the query by Last Name within Shopper Number.
3. Change the organization of the Navigation Pane so that all objects associated with the Client table are grouped together and all objects associated with the Shopper table are grouped together.
4. Export the query you created in Step 2 above as a CSV file. Do not save the export steps.
5. Upload the CSV file to your SkyDrive and open the file in the Excel Web app.
6. Delete the Shopper Number column and resize the remaining columns.
7. If requested to do so by your instructor, change the last name and first name of the first client to your last name and first name.
8. Save and close the Excel workbook.
9. Submit the revised database and Excel workbook in the format specified by your instructor.
10. Study the query result from Step 2 above. What do you notice about the first name and last name field headings? Why do they appear as they do?

Consider This: Your Turn

Apply your creative thinking and problem solving skills to design and implement a solution.

1: Querying the Craft Database

Personal/Academic

Instructions: Open the Craft database you created in Chapter 1 on page AC 73. If you did not create this database, contact your instructor for information about accessing the required files.

Part 1: Use the concepts and techniques presented in this chapter to create queries for the following. Save each query.

a. Find the item number and description of all items that contain the word, Rack.
b. Find the item number and description of all items made by students with a student code of 3962 or 7568.
c. Find the item number, description, and price of all items that have a price between $20.00 and $40.00.
d. Find the total price (price * on hand) of each item available for sale. Show the item number, description, price, on hand, and total price in the result. Change the caption for the On Hand field to Quantity.
e. Find the seller of each item. Show the student's last name and first name as well as the item number, description, price, and on hand. Sort the results by description within student last name.
f. Create a form based on the query you created in Step e.
g. Determine the average price of items grouped by student code.
h. Determine the two most expensive items for sale. Show the description and price.

Submit your assignment in the format specified by your instructor.

Part 2: You made several decisions while creating the queries in this assignment, including the query in Step b. What was the rationale behind your decisions? There are two ways to create the query in Step b. What are they? Which one did you use?

Continued >

Consider This: Your Turn *continued*

2: Querying the Mums Landscaping Database

Professional

Instructions: Open the Mums Landscaping database you created in Chapter 1 on page AC 73. If you did not create this database, contact your instructor for information about accessing the required files.

Part 1: Use the concepts and techniques presented in this chapter to create queries for the following. Save each query.

a. Find all supervisors who started prior to January 1, 2013. Show the supervisor's first name, last name, and hourly rate.
b. Find the customer name and address of all customers located on Cantor.
c. Find the customer number, customer name, amount paid, and balance for all customers whose amount paid is $0.00 or whose balance is $0.00.
d. Create a parameter query for the Customer table that will allow the user to enter a different postal code each time the query is run. The user should see all fields in the query result.
e. Create a crosstab query that groups the total of customer's balance amounts by postal code and supervisor number.
f. Find the supervisor for each customer. List the supervisor number, last name, first name, customer number, customer name, and balance. Sort the results by customer number within supervisor number.
g. Open the query you created in Step f above and restrict retrieval to only those customers whose balance is greater than $500.00.
h. Estimate the weekly pay for each supervisor by multiplying the hourly rate by 40. Show the supervisor's first name, last name, hourly rate, and weekly pay.

Submit your assignment in the format specified by your instructor.

Part 2: You made several decisions while creating the queries in this assignment, including the calculation in Step h above. What was the rationale behind your decisions, and how could you modify the query in Step h if the Supervisor table included a field called Hours Worked in which the actual hours worked was stored?

3: Creating Queries to Analyze Data

Research and Collaboration

Part 1: Examine a website that contains weather data, such as weather.com or Bing weather, and, as a team, select 30 cities of interest in your state or province. Create a database that contains one table and has the following fields: City, State or Province, High Temp, Low Temp, and Conditions. Use standard weather terms for the Conditions field, such as rainy, snowy, cloudy, clear, and so on. Create queries that do the following:

a. Display the five cities with the highest high temperature.
b. Display the five cities with the lowest low temperature.
c. Display the average high and low temperatures for all cities.
d. Display the average high and low temperatures for all cities where the conditions were clear.
e. Calculate the difference between the high and low temperatures for each city.
f. Display the high and low temperatures for each city in both Fahrenheit and Celsius.

Submit your assignment in the format specified by your instructor.

Part 2: You made several decisions while creating the queries in this assignment, including the grouping in Steps c and d and the calculations in Steps e and f. What was the rationale behind your decisions? How would you modify the query in Step d above to show the average high and low temperatures in cities grouped by Condition?

Learn Online

Reinforce what you learned in this chapter with games, exercises, training, and many other online activities and resources.

Student Companion Site Reinforcement activities and resources are available at no additional cost on www.cengagebrain.com. Visit www.cengage.com/ct/studentdownload for detailed instructions about accessing the resources available at the Student Companion Site.

SAM Put your skills into practice with SAM! If you have a SAM account, go to www.cengage.com/sam2013 to access SAM assignments for this chapter.

3 Maintaining a Database

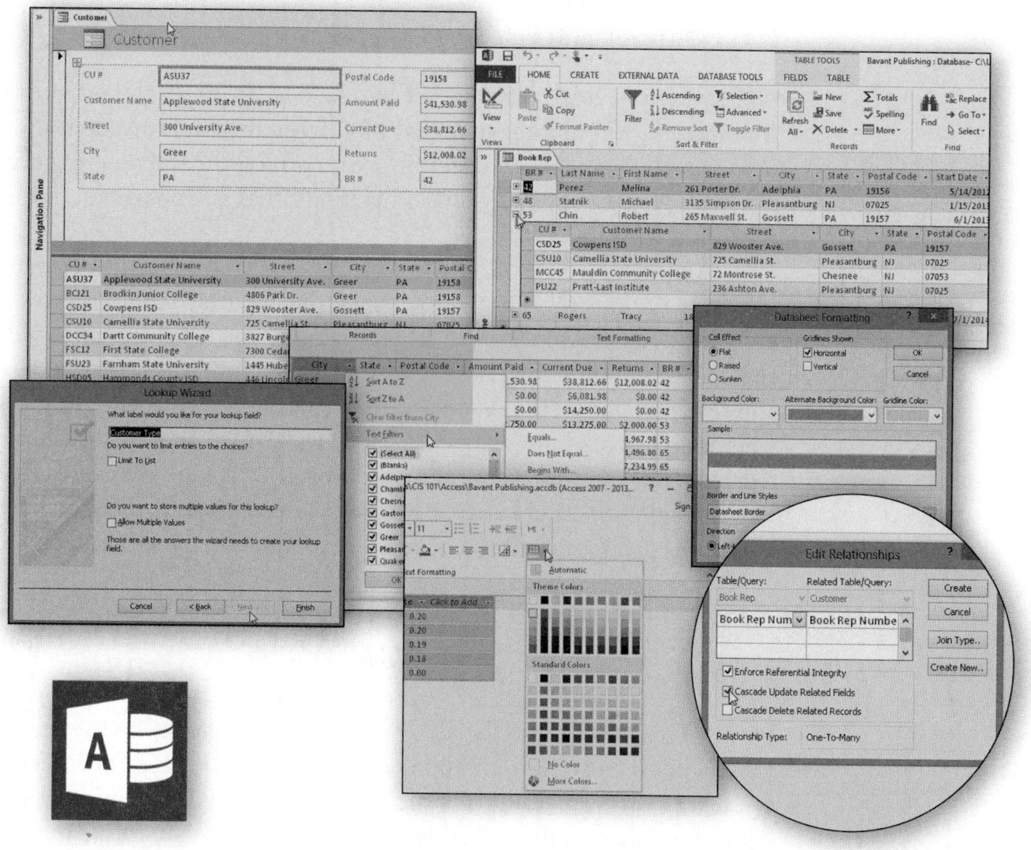

Objectives

You will have mastered the material in this chapter when you can:

- Add, change, and delete records
- Search for records
- Filter records
- Update a table design
- Use action queries to update records
- Use delete queries to delete records
- Specify validation rules, default values, and formats
- Create and use single-valued lookup fields
- Create and use multivalued lookup fields
- Add new fields to an existing report
- Format a datasheet
- Specify referential integrity
- Use a subdatasheet
- Sort records

3 | Maintaining a Database

Introduction

BTW
BTWs
For a complete list of the BTWs found in the margins of this book, visit the BTW resource on the Student Companion Site located on www.cengagebrain.com. For detailed instructions about accessing available resources, visit www.cengage.com/ct/studentdownload or contact your instructor for information about accessing the required files.

Once you have created a database and loaded it with data, you must maintain it. **Maintaining the database** means modifying the data to keep it up to date by adding new records, changing the data for existing records, and deleting records. Updating can include mass updates or mass deletions, that is, updates to, or deletions of, many records at the same time.

Maintenance of a database also can involve the need to **restructure the database** periodically, that is, to change the database structure. Restructuring can include adding new fields to a table, changing the characteristics of existing fields, and removing existing fields. Restructuring also includes the creation of validation rules and referential integrity. Validation rules ensure the validity of the data in the database, whereas referential integrity ensures the validity of the relationships. Maintaining a database also can include filtering records, a process that ensures that only the records that satisfy some criterion appear when viewing and updating the data in a table. Changing the appearance of a datasheet is a maintenance activity.

Project — Maintaining a Database

BTW
Q&As
For a complete list of the Q&As found in many of the step-by-step sequences in this book, visit the Q&A resource on the Student Companion Site located on www.cengagebrain.com. For detailed instructions about accessing available resources, visit www.cengage.com/ct/studentdownload or contact your instructor for information about accessing the required files.

Bavant Publishing faces the task of keeping its database up to date. As the company takes on new customers and book reps, it will need to add new records, make changes to existing records, and delete records. Bavant believes that it can serve its customers better by changing the structure of the database to categorize the customers by type. The company will do this by adding a Customer Type field to the Customer table. Book reps believe they can maintain better customer relationships if the database includes the list of resources that are of interest to each customer. The company will do so by adding a Resources Needed field to the Customer table. Because customers may need more than one resource, this field will be a multivalued field, which is a field that can store multiple values or entries. Along with these changes, Bavant staff wants to change the appearance of a datasheet when displaying data.

Bavant would like the ability to make mass updates, that is, to update or delete many records in a single operation. It wants rules that make sure users can enter only valid, or appropriate, data into the database. Bavant also wants to ensure that the database cannot contain the name of a customer who is not associated with a specific book rep.

Figure 3–1 summarizes some of the various types of activities involved in maintaining the Bavant Publishing database.

Figure 3–1

Roadmap

In this chapter, you will learn how to maintain a database by performing the tasks shown in Figure 3–1. The following roadmap identifies general activities you will perform as you progress through this chapter:

1. UPDATE RECORDS using a form.
2. FILTER RECORDS using various filtering options.
3. CHANGE the STRUCTURE of a table.
4. Make MASS CHANGES to a table.
5. Create VALIDATION RULES.
6. CHANGE the APPEARANCE of a datasheet.
7. Specify REFERENTIAL INTEGRITY.
8. ORDER RECORDS in a datasheet.

At the beginning of step instructions throughout the chapter, you will see an abbreviated form of this roadmap. The abbreviated roadmap uses colors to indicate chapter progress: gray means the chapter is beyond that activity; blue means the task being shown is covered in that activity, and black means that activity is yet to be covered. For example, the following abbreviated roadmap indicates the chapter would be showing a task in the 3 CHANGE STRUCTURE activity.

1 UPDATE RECORDS | 2 FILTER RECORDS | 3 CHANGE STRUCTURE | 4 MASS CHANGES | 5 VALIDATION RULES
6 CHANGE APPEARANCE | 7 REFERENTIAL INTEGRITY | 8 ORDER RECORDS

Use the abbreviated roadmap as a progress guide while you read or step through the instructions in this chapter.

For an introduction to Windows and instruction about how to perform basic Windows tasks, read the Office and Windows chapter at the beginning of this book, where you can learn how to resize windows, change screen resolution, create folders, move and rename files, use Windows Help, and much more.

For an introduction to Office and instruction about how to perform basic tasks in Office apps, read the Office and Windows chapter at the beginning of this book, where you can learn how to run an application, use the ribbon, save a file, open a file, exit an application, use Help, and much more.

To Run Access

If you are using a computer to step through the project in this chapter and you want your screens to match the figures in this book, you should change your screen's resolution to 1366 × 768. For information about how to change a computer's resolution, refer to the Office and Windows chapter at the beginning of this book.

The following steps, which assume Windows 8 is running, use the Start screen or the search box to run Access based on a typical installation. You may need to ask your instructor how to run Access on your computer. For a detailed example of the procedure summarized below, refer to the Office and Windows chapter.

1. Scroll the Start screen for an Access 2013 tile. If your Start screen contains an Access 2013 tile, tap or click it to run Access and then proceed to Step 5; if the Start screen does not contain the Access 2013 tile, proceed to the next step to search for the Access app.
2. Swipe in from the right edge of the screen or point to the upper-right corner of the screen to display the Charms bar, and then tap or click the Search charm on the Charms bar to display the Search menu.
3. Type `Access` as the search text in the Search text box and watch the search results appear in the Apps list.
4. Tap or click Access 2013 in the search results to run Access.
5. If the Access window is not maximized, tap or click the Maximize button on its title bar to maximize the window.

To Open a Database from Access

The following steps open the Bavant Publishing database from the location you specified when you first created it (for example, the Access folder in the CIS 101 folder). For a detailed example of the procedure summarized below, refer to the Office and Windows chapter at the beginning of this book.

One of the few differences between Windows 7 and Windows 8 occurs in the steps to run Access. If you are using Windows 7, click the Start button, type `Access` in the 'Search programs and files' box, click Access 2013, and then, if necessary, maximize the Access window. For detailed steps to run Access in Windows 7, refer to the Office and Windows chapter at the beginning of this book. For a summary of the steps, refer to the Quick Reference located at the back of this book.

1. Tap or click FILE on the ribbon to open the Backstage view, if necessary.
2. If the database you want to open is displayed in the Recent list, tap or click the file name to open the database and display the opened database in the Access window; then skip to Step 7. If the database you want to open is not displayed in the Recent list or if the Recent list does not appear, tap or click 'Open Other Files' to display the Open Gallery.
3. If the database you want to open is displayed in the Recent list in the Open gallery, tap or click the file name to open the database and display the opened database in the Access window; then skip to Step 7.
4. Tap or click Computer, SkyDrive, or another location in the left pane and then navigate to the location of the database to be opened (for example, the Access folder in the CIS 101 folder).
5. Tap or click Bavant Publishing to select the database to be opened.
6. Tap or click the Open button (Open dialog box) to open the selected file and display the opened database in the Access window.
7. If a SECURITY WARNING appears, tap or click the Enable Content button.

Updating Records

Keeping the data in a database up to date requires updating records in three ways: adding new records, changing the data in existing records, and deleting existing records. In Chapter 1, you added records to a database using Datasheet view; that is, as you added records, the records appeared on the screen in a datasheet. The data looked like a table. When you need to add additional records, you can use the same techniques.

In Chapter 1, you used a simple form to view records. You also can use a **split form**, a form that allows you to simultaneously view both simple form and datasheet views of the data. You can use either portion of a split form to add or update records. To add new records, change existing records, or delete records, you use the same techniques you used in Datasheet view.

BTW

The Ribbon and Screen Resolution

Access may change how the groups and buttons within the groups appear on the ribbon, depending on the computer's screen resolution. Thus, your ribbon may look different from the ones in this book if you are using a screen resolution other than 1366 × 768.

To Create a Split Form

1 UPDATE RECORDS | 2 FILTER RECORDS | 3 CHANGE STRUCTURE | 4 MASS CHANGES | 5 VALIDATION RULES
6 CHANGE APPEARANCE | 7 REFERENTIAL INTEGRITY | 8 ORDER RECORDS

The following steps create a split form. ***Why?*** *With a split form, you have the advantage of seeing a single record in a form, while simultaneously viewing several records in a datasheet.*

1

- Open the Navigation Pane if it is currently closed.
- If necessary, tap or click the Customer table in the Navigation Pane to select it.
- Tap or click CREATE on the ribbon to display the CREATE tab.
- Tap or click the More Forms button (CREATE tab | Forms group) to display the More Forms menu (Figure 3–2).

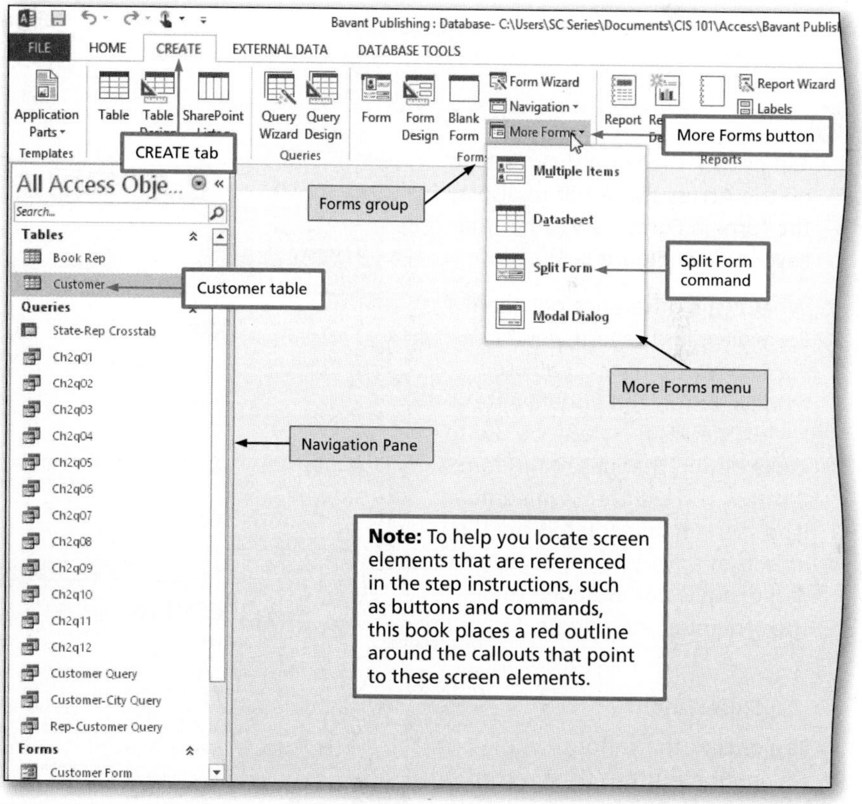

Figure 3–2

2

- Tap or click Split Form to create a split form based on the Customer table.
- Close the Navigation Pane (Figure 3–3).

Q&A Is the form automatically saved?
No. You will take specific actions later to save the form.

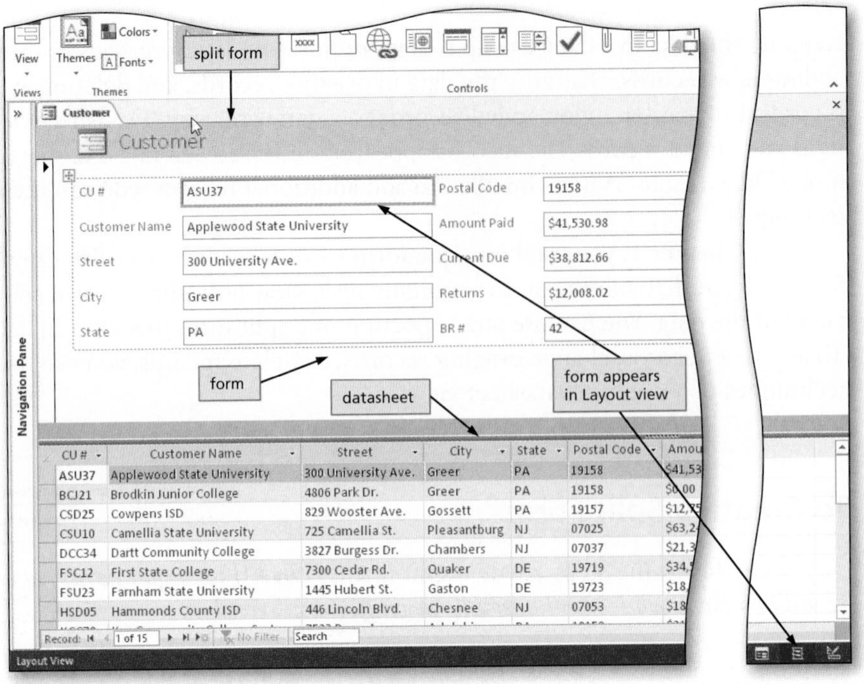

Figure 3–3

3

- Tap or click the Form View button on the Access status bar to display the form in Form view rather than Layout view (Figure 3–4).

Q&A What is the difference between Form view and Layout view?
Form view is the view you use to view, enter, and update data. Layout view is the view you use to make design changes to the form. It shows you the form with data in it so you can immediately see the effects of any design changes you make, but is not intended to be used to enter and update data.

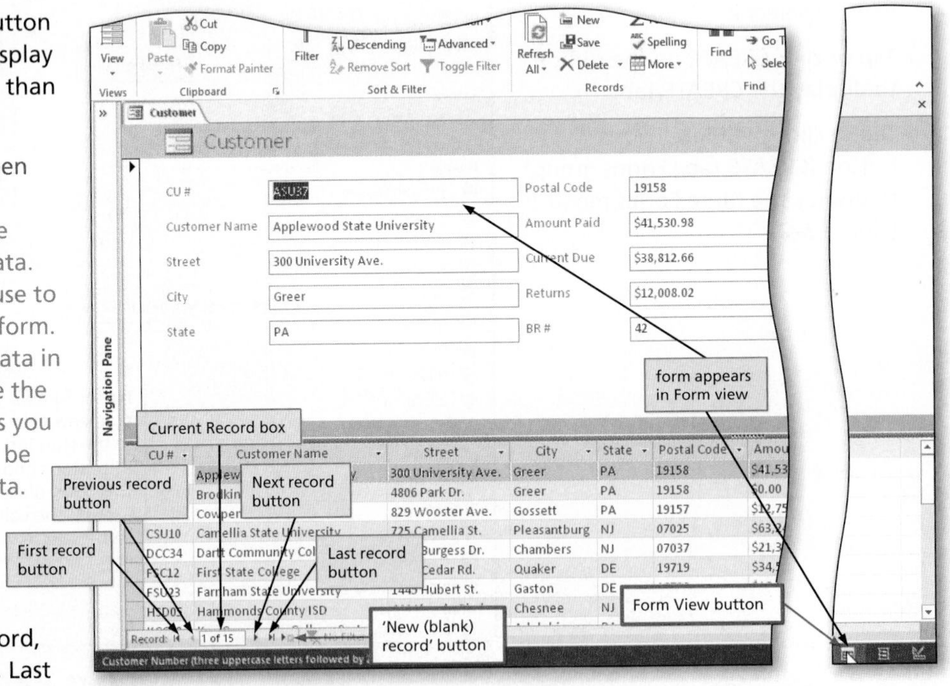

Figure 3–4

Experiment

- Tap or click the various Navigation buttons (First record, Next record, Previous record, Last record, and, 'New (blank) record') to see each button's effect. Tap or click the Current Record box, change the record number, and press the ENTER key to see how to move to a specific record.

4

- Tap or click the Save button on the Quick Access Toolbar to display the Save As dialog box.
- Type `Customer Split Form` as the form name (Figure 3–5).

5

- Tap or click the OK button (Save As dialog box) to save the form.

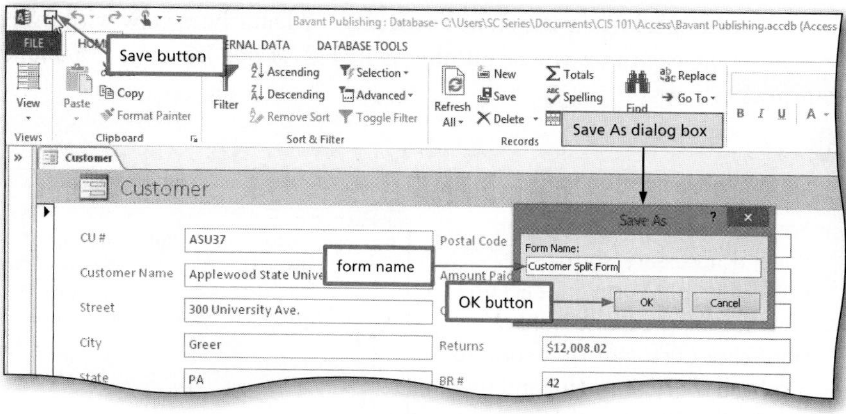

Figure 3–5

Other Ways

1. Press and hold or right-click tab for form, tap or click Form View on shortcut menu

To Use a Form to Add Records

1 UPDATE RECORDS | 2 FILTER RECORDS | 3 CHANGE STRUCTURE | 4 MASS CHANGES | 5 VALIDATION RULES
6 CHANGE APPEARANCE | 7 REFERENTIAL INTEGRITY | 8 ORDER RECORDS

Once a form or split form is open in Form view, you can add records using the same techniques you used to add records in Datasheet view. In a split form, the changes you make on the form are automatically made on the datasheet. You do not need to take any special action. The following steps use the split form that you just created to add records. ***Why?*** *With a split form, as you add a record, you can immediately see the effect of the addition on the datasheet.*

1

- Tap or click the 'New (blank) record' button on the Navigation bar to enter a new record, and then type the data for the new record, as shown in Figure 3–6. Press the TAB key after typing the data in each field, except after typing the data for the final field (Book Rep Number).

2

- Press the TAB key to complete the entry of the record.
- Close the form.

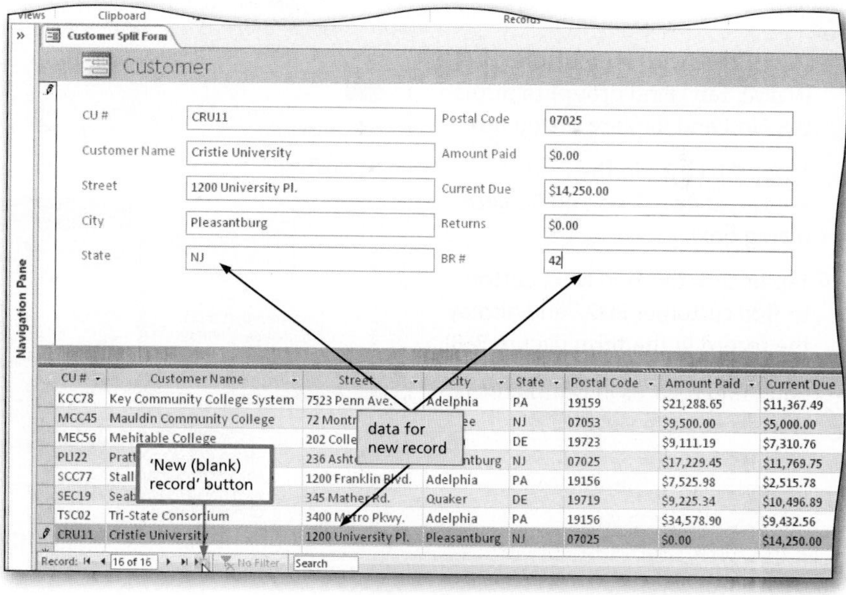

Figure 3–6

Other Ways

1. Tap or click New button (HOME tab | Records group)
2. Press CTRL+PLUS SIGN (+)

To Search for a Record

1 UPDATE RECORDS | 2 FILTER RECORDS | 3 CHANGE STRUCTURE | 4 MASS CHANGES | 5 VALIDATION RULES
6 CHANGE APPEARANCE | 7 REFERENTIAL INTEGRITY | 8 ORDER RECORDS

In the database environment, **searching** means looking for records that satisfy some criteria. Looking for the customer whose number is PLI22 is an example of searching. The queries in Chapter 2 also were examples of searching. Access had to locate those records that satisfied the criteria.

You can perform a search in Form view or Datasheet view without creating a query. The following steps search for the customer whose number is PLI22. ***Why?*** *You want to locate the record quickly so you can update this customer's record.*

1

- Open the Navigation Pane.
- Scroll down in the Navigation Pane, if necessary, so that Customer Split Form appears on your screen, press and hold or right-click Customer Split Form to display a shortcut menu, and then tap or click Open on the shortcut menu to open the form in Form view.

Q&A Which command on the shortcut menu gives me Form view? I see both Layout View and Design View, but no option for Form View.

The Open command opens the form in Form view.

- Close the Navigation Pane (Figure 3–7).

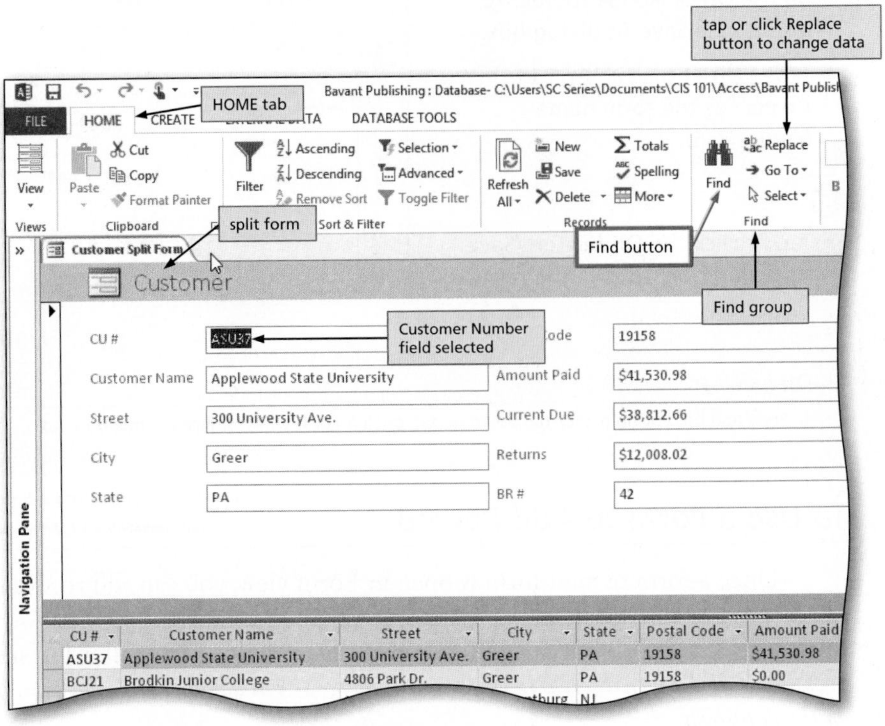

Figure 3–7

2

- Tap or click the Find button (HOME tab | Find group) to display the Find and Replace dialog box.
- Type `PLI22` in the Find What text box (Find and Replace dialog box).
- Tap or click the Find Next button to find customer PLI22 and display the record in the form (Figure 3–8).

Q&A Can I find records in Datasheet view or in Form view?

Yes. You use the same process to find records whether you are viewing the data with a split form, in Datasheet view, or in Form view.

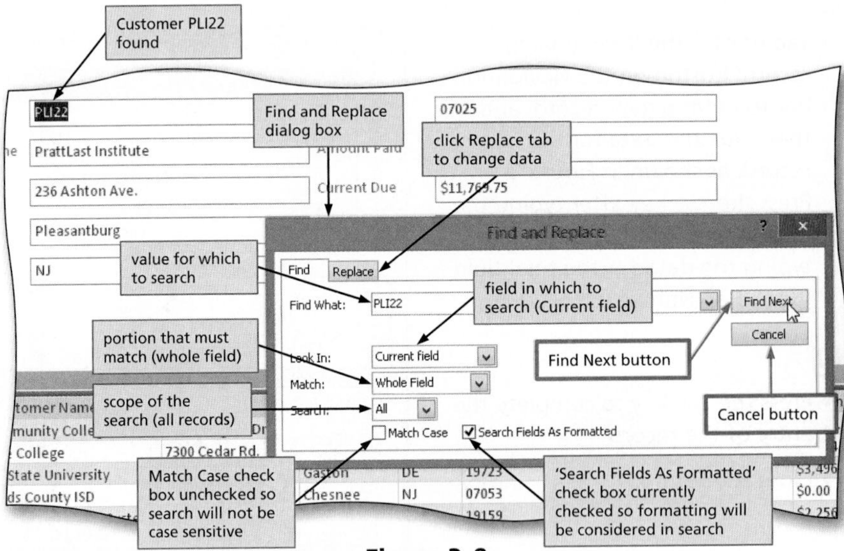

Figure 3–8

3

- Tap or click the Cancel button (Find and Replace dialog box) to remove the dialog box from the screen.

Q&A Why does the button in the dialog box read, Find Next, rather than simply Find?

In some cases, after locating a record that satisfies a criterion, you might need to find the next record that satisfies the same criterion. For example, if you just found the first customer whose book rep number is 42, you then may want to find the second such customer, then the third, and so on. To do so, tap or click the Find Next button. You will not need to retype the value each time.

Other Ways

1. Press CTRL+F

CONSIDER THIS

Can you replace one value with another using the Find and Replace dialog box?
Yes. Either tap or click the Replace button (HOME tab | Find group) or tap or click the Replace tab in the Find and Replace dialog box. You then can enter both the value to find and the new value.

To Update the Contents of a Record

1 UPDATE RECORDS | 2 FILTER RECORDS | 3 CHANGE STRUCTURE | 4 MASS CHANGES | 5 VALIDATION RULES
6 CHANGE APPEARANCE | 7 REFERENTIAL INTEGRITY | 8 ORDER RECORDS

The following step uses Form view to change the name of customer PLI22 from PrattLast Institute to Pratt-Last Institute. ***Why?*** *Bavant determined that this customer's name was missing the hyphen.* After locating the record to be changed, select the field to be changed by clicking the field. You also can press the TAB key repeatedly until the desired field is selected. Then make the appropriate changes. (Clicking the field automatically produces an insertion point. If you use the TAB key, you will need to press F2 to produce an insertion point.)

1

- Tap or click in the Customer Name field in the form for customer PLI22 immediately to the left of the L in the word, PrattLast.
- Type a hyphen (-) before Last.
- Press the TAB key to complete the change and move to the next field (Figure 3–9).

Q&A

Could I have changed the contents of the field in the datasheet portion of the split form?
Yes. You will first need to ensure the record to be changed appears in the datasheet. You then can change the value just as in the form.

Do I need to save my change?
No. Once you move to another record or close this form, the change to the name will become permanent.

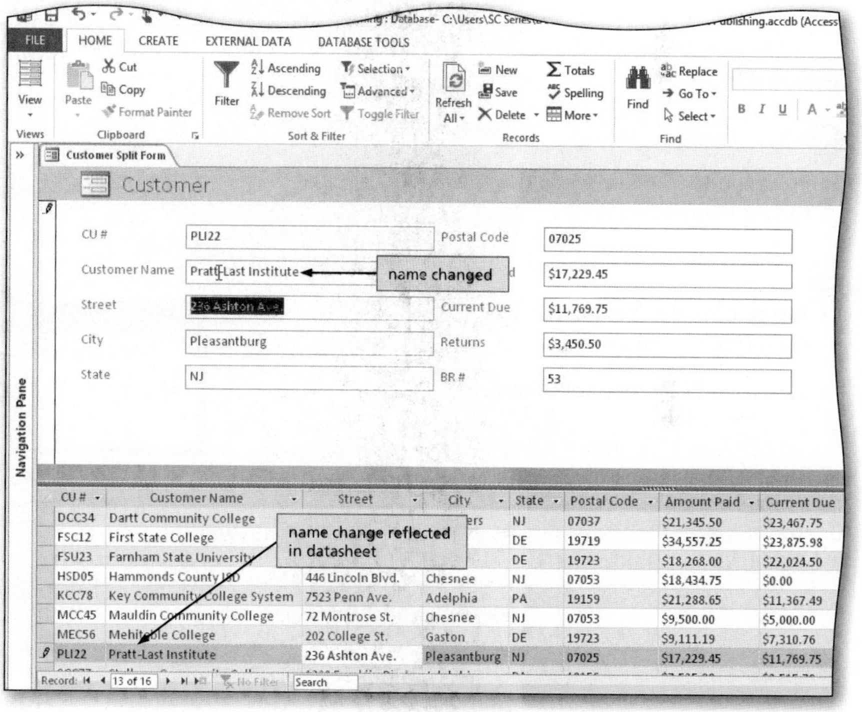

Figure 3–9

To Delete a Record

1 UPDATE RECORDS | 2 FILTER RECORDS | 3 CHANGE STRUCTURE | 4 MASS CHANGES | 5 VALIDATION RULES
6 CHANGE APPEARANCE | 7 REFERENTIAL INTEGRITY | 8 ORDER RECORDS

When records no longer are needed, you should delete the records (remove them) from the table. The steps on the next page delete customer HSD05. ***Why?*** *Customer HSD05 no longer is served by Bavant Publishing and its final payment has been received, so the record can be deleted.*

1

- With the Customer Split Form open, tap or click the record selector in the datasheet for customer HSD05 to select the record (Figure 3–10).

Q&A That technique works in the datasheet portion. How do I select the record in the form portion?

With the desired record appearing in the form, tap or click the record selector (the triangle in front of the record) to select the entire record.

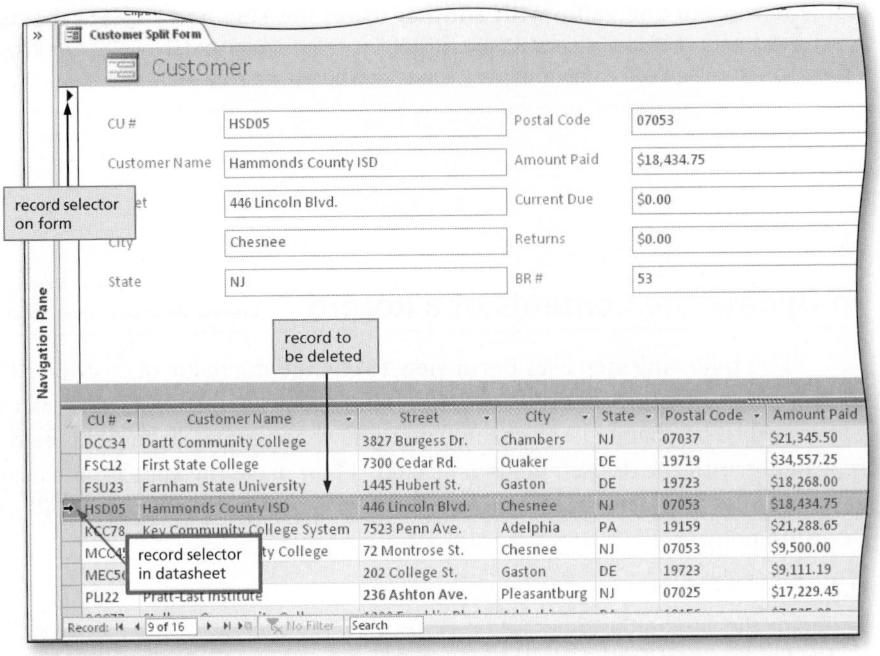

Figure 3–10

2

- Press the DELETE key to delete the record (Figure 3–11).

3

- Tap or click the Yes button to complete the deletion.
- Close the Customer Split Form.

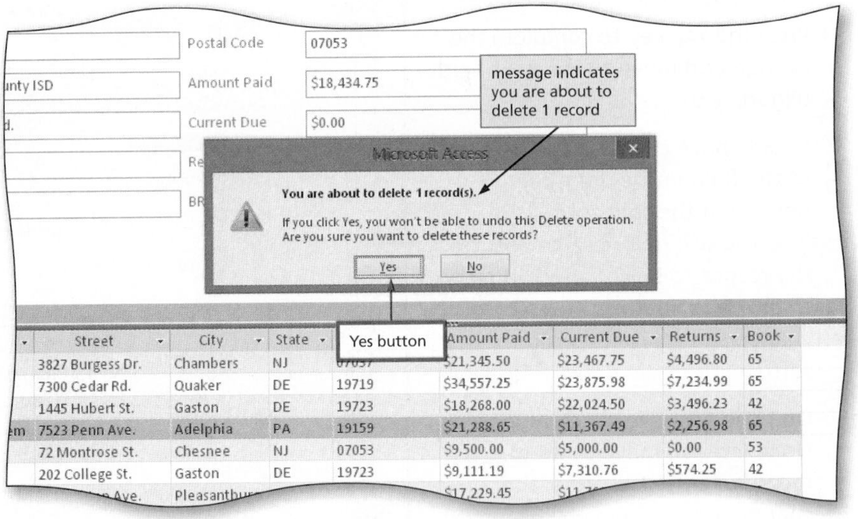

Figure 3–11

Other Ways

1. Tap or click Delete arrow (HOME tab | Records group), tap or click Delete Record on Delete menu

Filtering Records

BTW
Using the Find button
You can use the Find button (HOME tab | Find group) to search for records in datasheets, forms, query results, and reports.

You can use the Find button in either Datasheet view or Form view to locate a record quickly that satisfies some criterion (for example, the customer number is PLI22). All records appear, however, not just the record or records that satisfy the criterion. To have only the record or records that satisfy the criterion appear, use a **filter**. Four types of filters are available: Filter By Selection, Common Filters, Filter By Form, and Advanced Filter/Sort. You can use a filter in either Datasheet view or Form view.

To Use Filter By Selection

1 UPDATE RECORDS | 2 FILTER RECORDS | 3 CHANGE STRUCTURE | 4 MASS CHANGES | 5 VALIDATION RULES
6 CHANGE APPEARANCE | 7 REFERENTIAL INTEGRITY | 8 ORDER RECORDS

To use Filter By Selection, you give Access an example of the data you want by selecting the data within the table. You then choose the option you want on the Selection menu. The following steps use Filter By Selection in Datasheet view to display only the records for customers in Greer. ***Why?*** *Filter by Selection is appropriate for displaying these records and is the simplest type of filter.*

1

- Open the Navigation Pane.
- Open the Customer table, and close the Navigation Pane.
- Tap or click the City field on the first record to specify Greer as the city (Figure 3–12).

Q&A Could I have selected the City field on another record where the city is also Greer to select the same city?
Yes. It does not matter which record you select as long as the city is Greer.

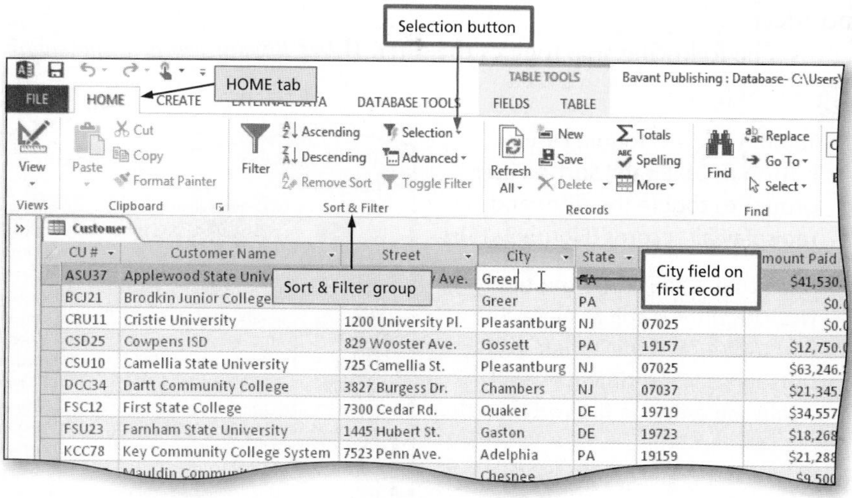

Figure 3–12

2

- Tap or click the Selection button (HOME tab | Sort & Filter group) to display the Selection menu (Figure 3–13).

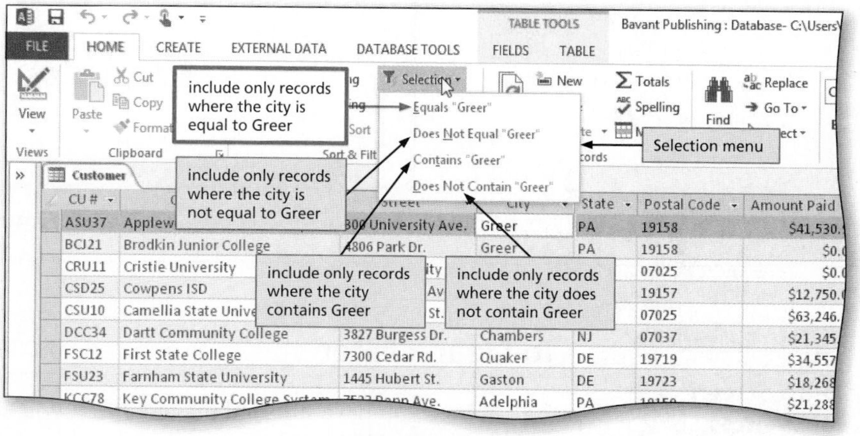

Figure 3–13

3

- Tap or click Equals "Greer" to select only those customers whose city is Greer (Figure 3–14).

Q&A Can I also filter in Form view?
Yes. Filtering works the same whether you are viewing the data with a split form, in Datasheet view, or in Form view.

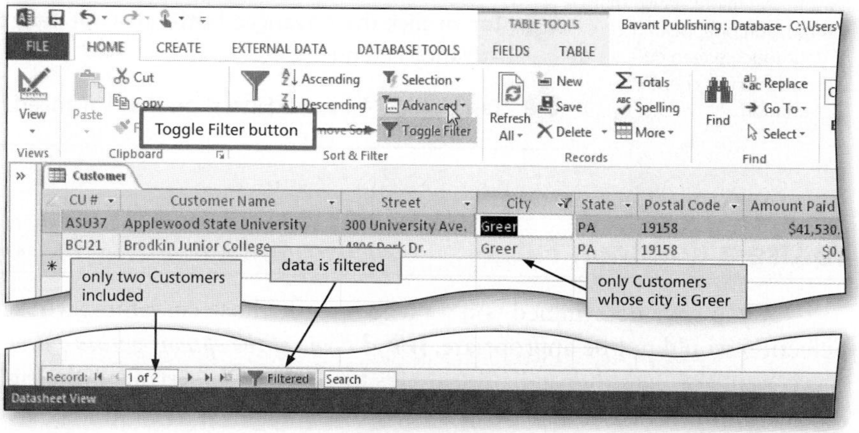

Figure 3–14

To Toggle a Filter

1 UPDATE RECORDS | 2 FILTER RECORDS | 3 CHANGE STRUCTURE | 4 MASS CHANGES | 5 VALIDATION RULES
6 CHANGE APPEARANCE | 7 REFERENTIAL INTEGRITY | 8 ORDER RECORDS

The Toggle Filter button toggles between filtered and unfiltered displays of the records in the table. That is, if only filtered records currently appear, clicking the Toggle Filter button will redisplay all records. If all records are currently displayed and there is a filter that is in effect, clicking the Toggle Filter button will display only the filtered records. If no filter is active, the Toggle Filter button will be dimmed, so clicking it would have no effect.

The following step toggles the filter. ***Why?*** *Bavant wants to once again view all the records.*

1

- Tap or click the Toggle Filter button (HOME tab | Sort & Filter group) to toggle the filter and redisplay all records (Figure 3–15).

Q&A Does that action clear the filter?

No. The filter is still in place. If you tap or click the Toggle Filter button a second time, you will again see only the filtered records.

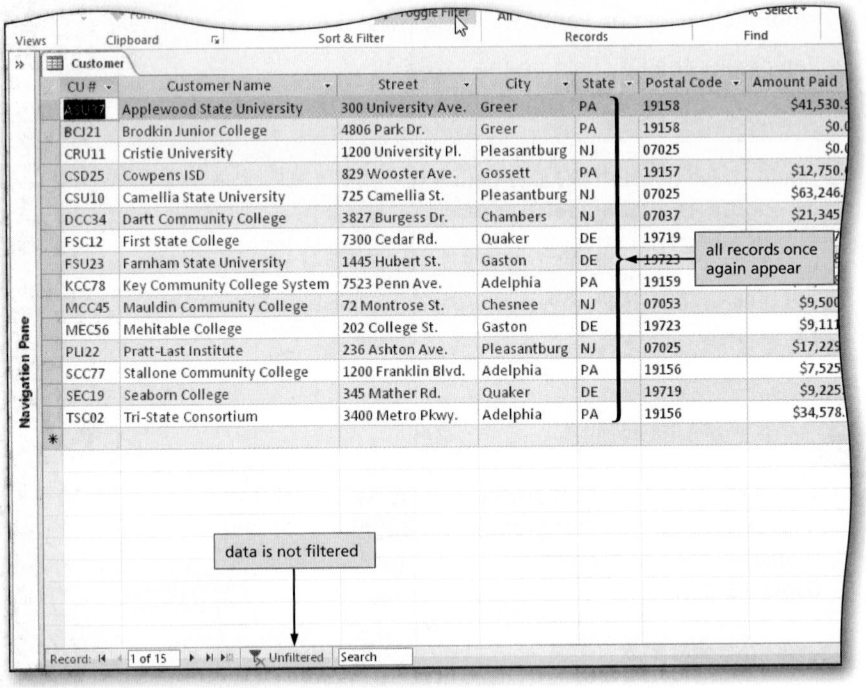

Figure 3–15

To Clear a Filter

> **BTW**
> **Touch Screen Differences**
> The Office and Windows interfaces may vary if you are using a touch screen. For this reason, you might notice that the function or appearance of your touch screen differs slightly from this chapter's presentation.

Once you have finished using a filter, you can clear the filter. After doing so, you no longer will be able to use the filter by clicking the Toggle Filter button. The following steps clear the filter.

1. Tap or click the Advanced button (HOME tab | Sort & Filter group) to display the Advanced menu.
2. Tap or click 'Clear All Filters' on the Advanced menu.

To Use a Common Filter

1 UPDATE RECORDS | 2 FILTER RECORDS | 3 CHANGE STRUCTURE | 4 MASS CHANGES | 5 VALIDATION RULES
6 CHANGE APPEARANCE | 7 REFERENTIAL INTEGRITY | 8 ORDER RECORDS

If you have determined you want to include those customers whose city begins with G, Filter By Selection would not be appropriate. ***Why?*** *None of the options within Filter by Selection would support this type of criterion.* You can filter individual fields by clicking the arrow to the right of the field name and using one of the **common filters** that are available for the field. You can modify a common filter by customizing it for the specific field. The following steps customize a common filter to include only those customers whose city begins with G.

1

- Tap or click the City arrow to display the common filter menu.
- Point to the Text Filters command to display the custom text filters (Figure 3–16).

Q&A I selected the City field and then clicked the Filter button on the HOME tab | Sort & Filter group. My screen looks the same. Is this right?

Yes. That is another way to display the common filter menu.

If I wanted certain cities included, could I use the check boxes?

Yes. Be sure the cities you want are the only ones checked.

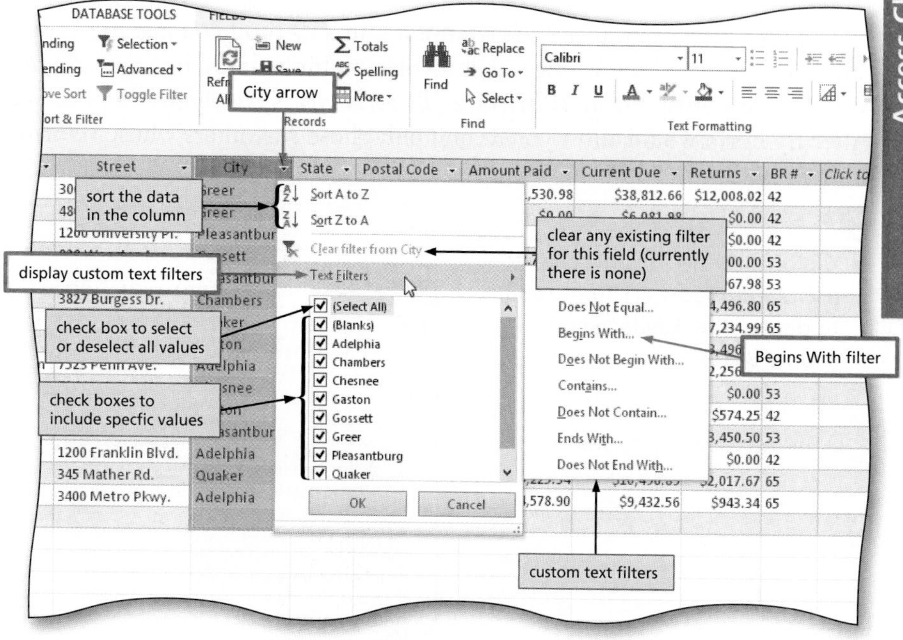

Figure 3–16

2

- Tap or click Begins With to display the Custom Filter dialog box.
- Type G as the 'City begins with' value (Figure 3–17).

Experiment

- Try other options in the common filter menu to see their effects. When done, once again select those customers whose city begins with G.

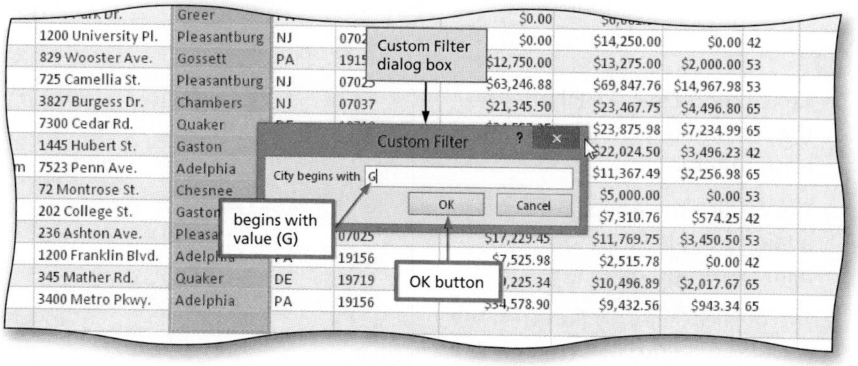

Figure 3–17

3

- Tap or click the OK button to filter the records (Figure 3–18).

Q&A Can I use the same technique in Form view?

In Form view, you would need to tap or click the field and then tap or click the Filter button to display the Common Filter menu. The rest of the process would be the same.

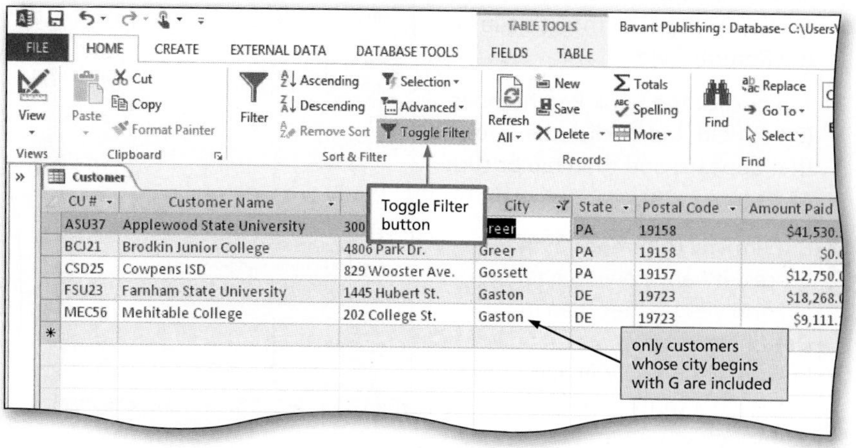

Figure 3–18

4

- Tap or click the Toggle Filter button (HOME tab | Sort & Filter group) to toggle the filter and redisplay all records.

Other Ways

1. Press and hold or right-click field, tap or click Text Filters on shortcut menu

To Use Filter By Form

Filter By Selection and the common filters method you just used are quick and easy ways to filter by the value in a single field. For filters that involve multiple fields, however, these methods are not appropriate, so you would use Filter By Form. ***Why?*** *Filter By Form allows you to filter based on multiple fields and criteria.* For example, Filter By Form would allow you to find only those customers whose returns are $0.00 and whose book rep number is 42. The following steps use Filter By Form to restrict the records that appear.

1

- Tap or click the Advanced button (HOME tab | Sort & Filter group) to display the Advanced menu (Figure 3–19).

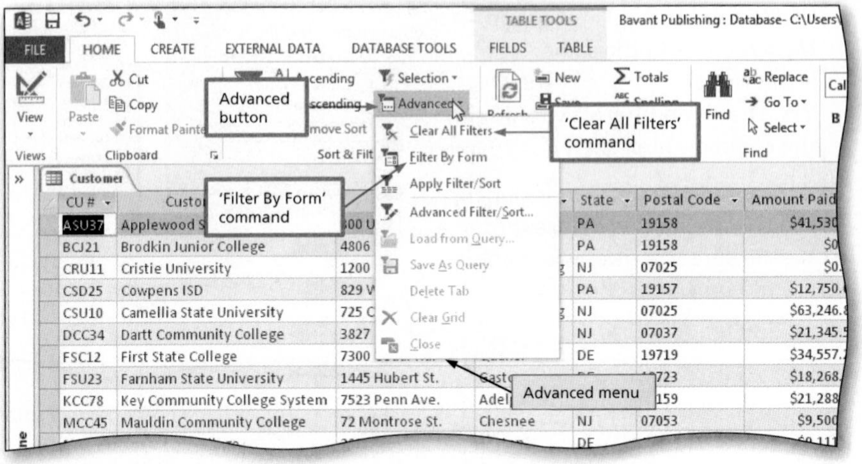

Figure 3–19

2

- Tap or click 'Clear All Filters' on the Advanced menu to clear the existing filter.
- Tap or click the Advanced button again to display the Advanced menu a second time.
- Tap or click 'Filter By Form' on the Advanced menu.
- Tap or click the blank row in the Returns field, tap or click the arrow that appears, and then tap or click 0 to specify the value in the Returns field.
- Tap or click the Book Rep Number (BR #) field, tap or click the arrow that appears, and then tap or click 42 (Figure 3–20).

Q&A Is there any difference in the process if I am viewing a table in Form view rather than in Datasheet view?

In Form view, you will make your entries in a form rather than a datasheet. Otherwise, the process is the same.

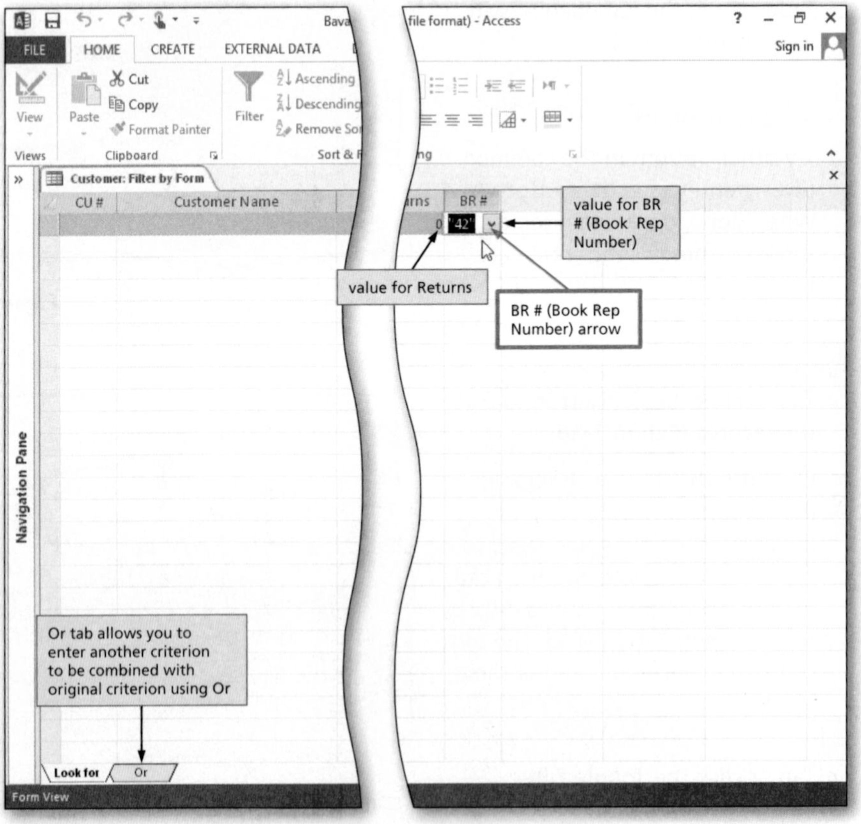

Figure 3–20

3

- Tap or click the Toggle Filter button (HOME tab | Sort & Filter group) to apply the filter (Figure 3–21).

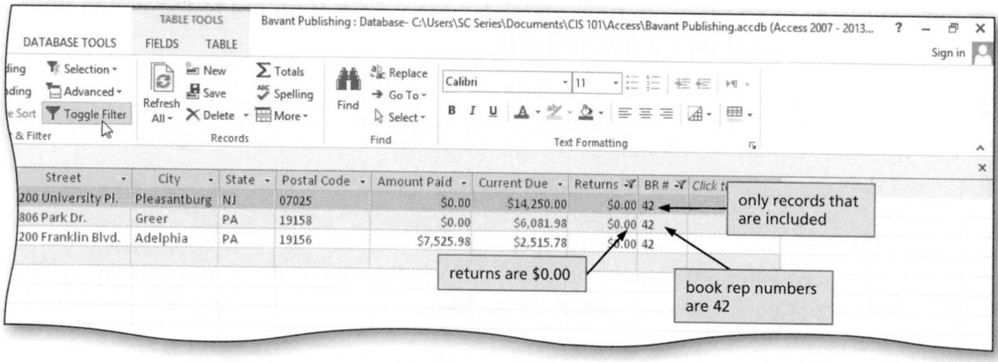

Figure 3–21

Experiment

- Select 'Filter by Form' again and enter different criteria. In each case, toggle the filter to see the effect of your selection. When done, once again select those customers whose returns are 0 and whose book rep number is 42.

Other Ways

1. Tap or click the Advanced button (HOME tab | Sort & Filter group), tap or click Apply Filter/Sort on Advanced menu

To Use Advanced Filter/Sort

1 UPDATE RECORDS | 2 FILTER RECORDS | 3 CHANGE STRUCTURE | 4 MASS CHANGES | 5 VALIDATION RULES
6 CHANGE APPEARANCE | 7 REFERENTIAL INTEGRITY | 8 ORDER RECORDS

In some cases, your criteria will be too complex even for Filter By Form. You might decide you want to include any customer whose returns are 0 and whose book rep number is 42. Additionally, you might want to include any customer whose returns are greater than $4,000, no matter who the customer's book rep is. Further, you might want to have the results sorted by name. The following steps use Advanced Filter/Sort to accomplish this task. ***Why?*** *Advanced Filter/Sort supports complex criteria as well as the ability to sort the results.*

1

- Tap or click the Advanced button (HOME tab | Sort & Filter group) to display the Advanced menu, and then tap or click 'Clear All Filters' on the Advanced menu to clear the existing filter.
- Tap or click the Advanced button to display the Advanced menu a second time.
- Tap or click 'Advanced Filter/Sort' on the Advanced menu.
- Expand the size of the field list so all the fields in the Customer table appear.
- Include the Customer Name field and select Ascending as the sort order to specify the order in which the filtered records will appear.
- Include the Book Rep Number field and enter **42** as the criterion.
- Include the Returns field and enter **0** as the criterion in the Criteria row and **>4000** as the criterion in the or row (Figure 3–22).

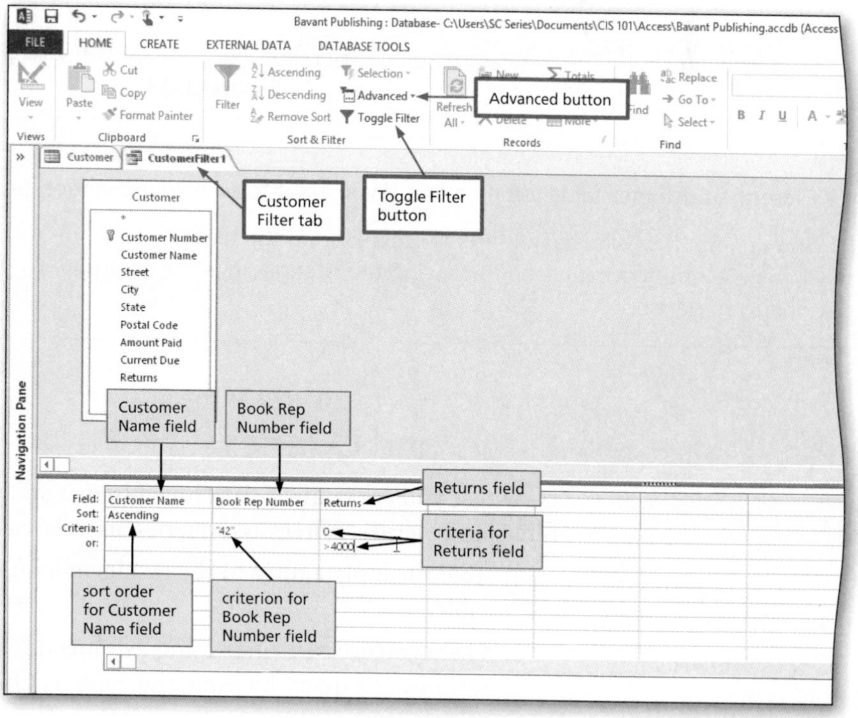

Figure 3–22

2

- Tap or click the Toggle Filter button (HOME tab | Sort & Filter group) to toggle the filter so that only records that satisfy the criteria will appear (Figure 3–23).

Q&A Why are those particular records included?
The second, fourth, and seventh records are included because the book rep number is 42 and the returns are $0.00. The other records are included because the returns are over $4,000.

Experiment

- Select Advanced Filter/Sort again and enter different sorting options and criteria. In each case, toggle the filter to see the effect of your selection. When done, change back to the sorting options and criteria you entered in Step 1.

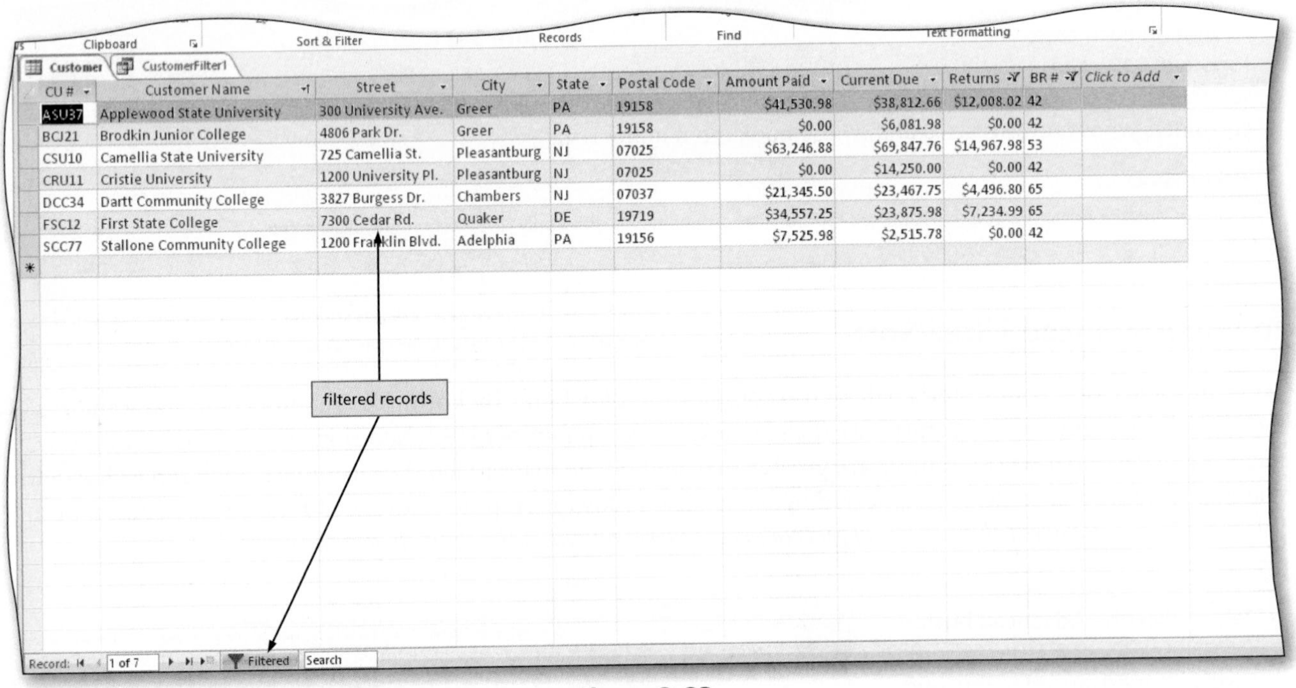

Figure 3–23

3

- Close the Customer table. When asked if you want to save your changes, tap or click the No button.

Q&A Should I not have cleared all filters before closing the table?
If you are closing a table and not saving the changes, it is not necessary to clear the filter. No filter will be active when you next open the table.

Filters and Queries

Now that you are familiar with how filters work, you might notice similarities between filters and queries. Filters and queries are related in three ways.

1. You can apply a filter to the results of a query just as you can apply a filter to a table.
2. Once you create a filter using Advanced Filter/Sort, you can save the filter settings as a query by using the 'Save as Query' command on the Advanced menu.
3. You can restore filter settings that you previously saved in a query by using the 'Load from Query' command on the Advanced menu.

BTW
Using Wildcards in Filters
Both the question mark(?) and the asterisk (*) wildcards can be used in filters created using Advanced Filter/Sort.

CONSIDER THIS

How do you determine whether to use a query or a filter?
The following guidelines apply to this decision.

If you think that you will frequently want to display records that satisfy this exact criterion, you should consider creating a query whose results only contain the records that satisfy the criterion. To display those records in the future, simply open the query.

If you are viewing data in a datasheet or form and decide you want to restrict the records to be included, it is easier to create a filter than a query. You can create and use the filter while you are viewing the data.

If you have created a filter that you would like to be able to use again, you can save the filter as a query.

CONSIDER THIS

Once you have decided to use a filter, how do you determine which type of filter to use?
If your criterion for filtering is that the value in a particular field matches or does not match a certain specific value, you can use Filter By Selection.

If your criterion only involves a single field but is more complex (for example, the criterion specifies that the value in the field begins with a certain collection of letters) you can use a common filter.

If your criterion involves more than one field, use Filter By Form.

If your criterion involves more than a single And or Or, or if it involves sorting, you will probably find it simpler to use Advanced Filter/Sort.

Break Point: If you wish to take a break, this is a good place to do so. You can quit Access now. To resume at a later time, start Access, open the database called Bavant Publishing, and continue following the steps from this location forward.

Changing the Database Structure

When you initially create a database, you define its **structure**; that is, you assign names and types to all the fields. In many cases, the structure you first define will not continue to be appropriate as you use the database.

Perhaps a field currently in the table no longer is necessary. If no one ever uses a particular field, it is not needed in the table. Because it is occupying space and serving no useful purpose, you should remove it from the table. You also would need to delete the field from any forms, reports, or queries that include it.

More commonly, an organization will find that it needs to maintain additional information that was not anticipated at the time the database was first designed. The organization's own requirements may have changed. In addition, outside regulations that the organization must satisfy may change as well. Either case requires the addition of fields to an existing table.

Although you can make some changes to the database structure in Datasheet view, it is usually easier and better to make these changes in Design view.

BTW
Changing Data Types
It is possible to change the data type for a field that already contains data. Before doing so, you should consider the effect on other database objects, such as forms, queries, and reports. For example, you could convert a Short Text field to a Long Text field if you find that you do not have enough space to store the data that you need. You also could convert a Number field to a Currency field or vice versa.

BTW
Organizing Files and Folders
You should organize and store files in folders so that you easily can find the files later. For example, if you are taking an introductory computer class called CIS 101, a good practice would be to save all Access files in an Access folder in a CIS 101 folder. For a discussion of folders and detailed examples of creating folders, refer to the Office and Windows chapter at the beginning of this book.

To Delete a Field

If a field in one of your tables no longer is needed, you should delete the field; for example, it may serve no useful purpose, or it may have been included by mistake. To delete a field, you would use the following steps.

1. Open the table in Design view.
2. Tap or click the row selector for the field to be deleted.
3. Press the DELETE key.
4. When Access displays the dialog box requesting confirmation that you want to delete the field, tap or click the Yes button.

BTW
Database Backup
If you are doing mass changes to a database, be sure to back up the database prior to doing the updates.

To Move a Field

If you decide you would rather have a field in one of your tables in a different position, you can move it. To move a field, you would use the following steps.

1. Open the table in Design view.
2. Tap or click the row selector for the field to be deleted.
3. Drag the field to the desired position.
4. Release the mouse button or lift your finger to place the field in the new position.

To Add a New Field

1 UPDATE RECORDS | 2 FILTER RECORDS | 3 CHANGE STRUCTURE | 4 MASS CHANGES | 5 VALIDATION RULES
6 CHANGE APPEARANCE | 7 REFERENTIAL INTEGRITY | 8 ORDER RECORDS

You can add fields to a table in a database. The following steps add the Customer Type field to the Customer table immediately after the Postal Code field. ***Why?*** *Bavant Publishing has decided that it needs to categorize its customers by adding an additional field, Customer Type. The possible values for Customer Type are HS (which indicates the customer is a high school or an intermediate school district), COM (which indicates the customer is a community college), or UNI (which indicates the customer is a university or four-year college).*

1

- If necessary, open the Navigation Pane, open the Customer table in Design view, and then close the Navigation Pane.
- Tap or click the row selector for the Amount Paid field, and then press the INSERT key to insert a blank row above the selected field (Figure 3–24).

2

- Tap or click the Field Name column for the new field to produce an insertion point.
- Type `Customer Type` as the field name and then press the TAB key.

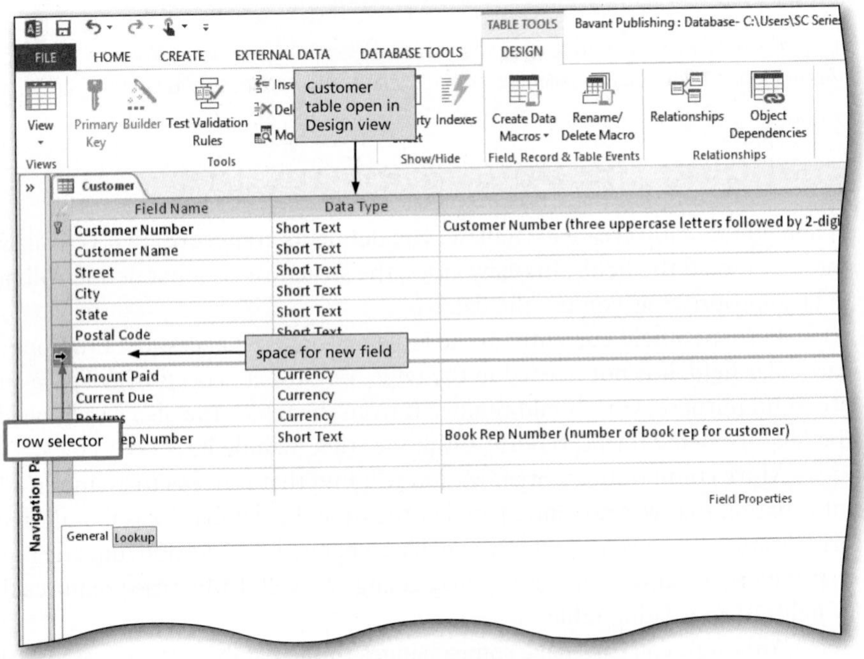

Figure 3–24

Other Ways

1. Tap or click Insert Rows button (TABLE TOOLS Design tab | Tools group)

To Create a Lookup Field

1 UPDATE RECORDS | 2 FILTER RECORDS | 3 CHANGE STRUCTURE | 4 MASS CHANGES | 5 VALIDATION RULES
6 CHANGE APPEARANCE | 7 REFERENTIAL INTEGRITY | 8 ORDER RECORDS

A **lookup field** allows the user to select from a list of values when updating the contents of the field. The following steps make the Customer Type field a lookup field. ***Why?*** *The Customer Type field has only three possible values, making it an appropriate lookup field.*

1

- If necessary, tap or click the Data Type column for the Customer Type field, and then tap or click the Data Type arrow to display the menu of available data types (Figure 3–25).

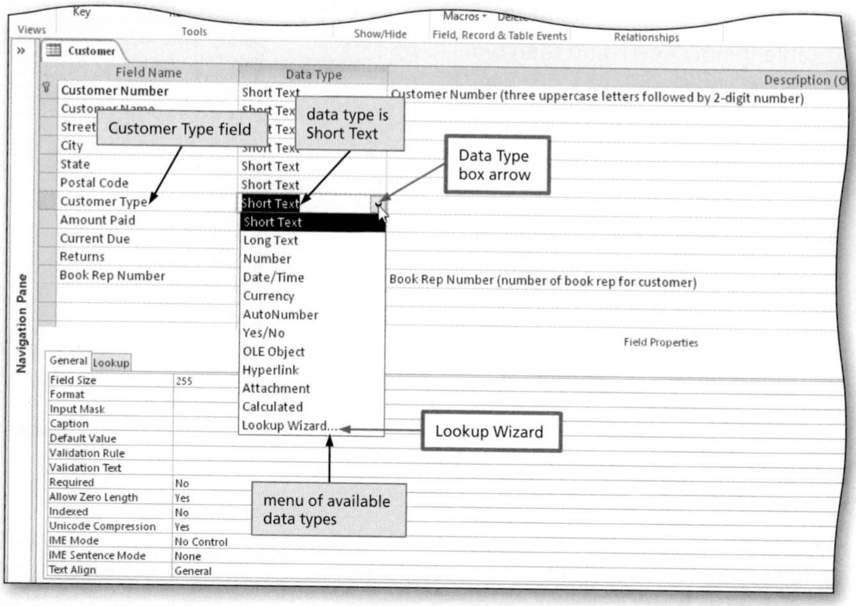

Figure 3–25

2

- Tap or click Lookup Wizard, and then tap or click the 'I will type in the values that I want.' option button (Lookup Wizard dialog box) to indicate that you will type in the values (Figure 3–26).

Q&A When would I use the other option button?

You would use the other option button if the data to be entered in this field were found in another table or query.

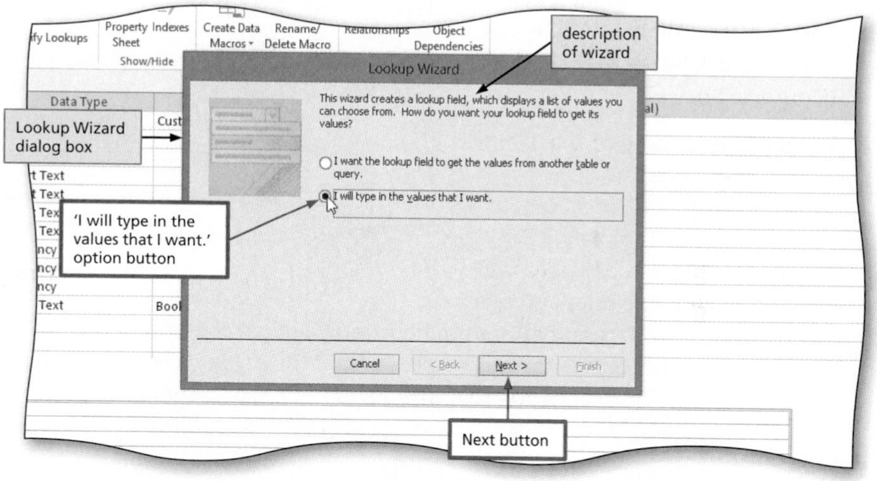

Figure 3–26

3

- Tap or click the Next button to display the next Lookup Wizard screen (Figure 3–27).

Q&A Why did I not change the field size for the Customer Type field?

You could have changed the field size to 3, but it is not necessary. When you create a lookup field and indicate specific values for the field, you automatically restrict the field size.

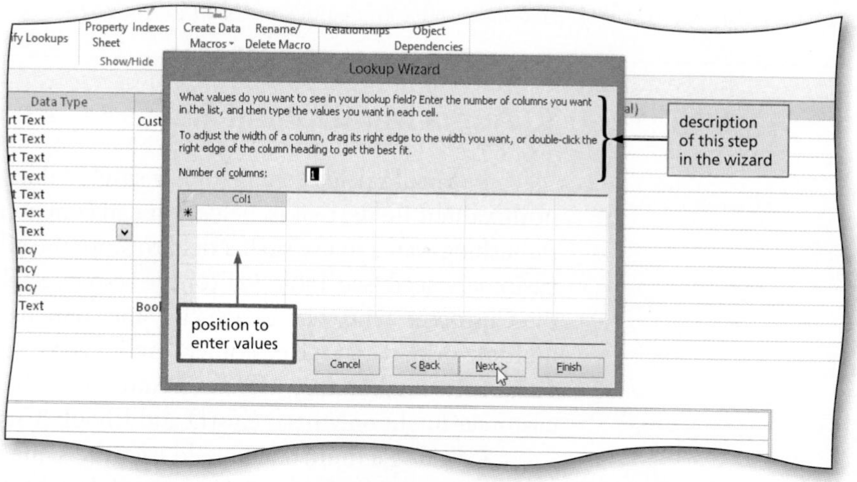

Figure 3–27

4

- Tap or click the first row of the table (below Col1), and then type **HS** as the value in the first row.
- Press the DOWN ARROW key, and then type **COM** as the value in the second row.
- Press the DOWN ARROW key, and then type **UNI** as the value in the third row (Figure 3–28).

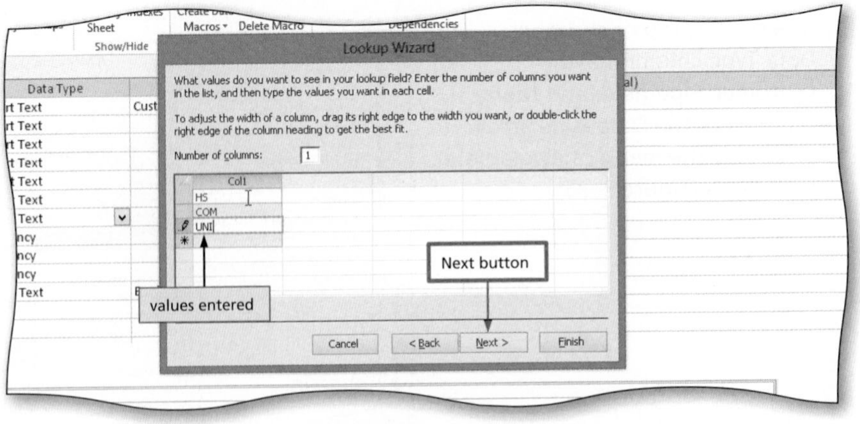

Figure 3–28

5

- Tap or click the Next button to display the next Lookup Wizard screen.
- Ensure Customer Type is entered as the label for the lookup field and that the 'Allow Multiple Values' check box is NOT checked (Figure 3–29).

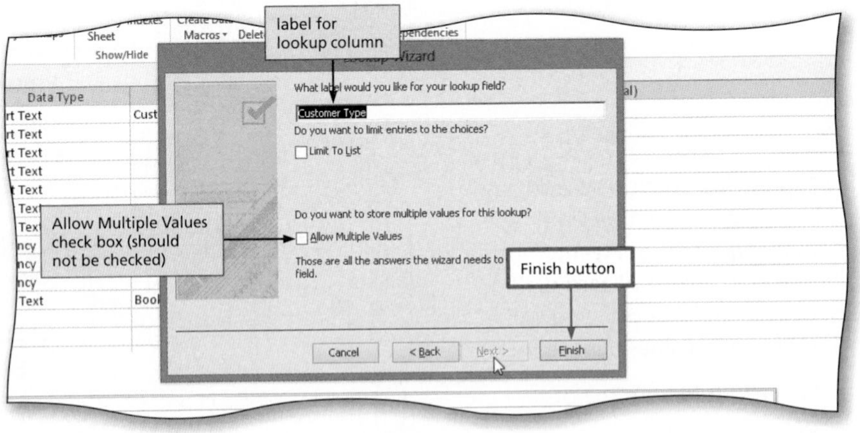

Figure 3–29

Q&A What is the purpose of the 'Limit To List' check box?
With a lookup field, users can select from the list of values, in which case they can only select items in the list. They can also type their entry, in which case they are not necessarily limited to items in the list. If you check the 'Limit To List' check box, users would be limited to items in the list, even if they type their entry. You will accomplish this same restriction later in this chapter with a validation rule, so you do not need to check this box.

6

- Tap or click the Finish button to complete the definition of the lookup field.

Q&A Why does the data type for the Customer Type field still show Short Text?
The data type is still Short Text because the values entered in the wizard were entered as text.

To Add a Multivalued Field

Normally, fields contain only a single value. In Access, it is possible to have **multivalued fields**, that is, fields that can contain more than one value. Bavant Publishing wants to use such a field to store the abbreviations of the various resources its customers need (see Table 3–1 for the resource abbreviations and descriptions). Unlike the Customer Type, where each customer only had one type, customers can require multiple resources. One customer might need Audio, PrMan, PrWrk, and Txt (Audio CD, Printed Laboratory Manual, Printed Workbook, and Printed Textbook). Another customer might only need CustD and Ebook (Custom Digital and Electronic Textbook).

Creating a multivalued field uses the same process as creating a lookup field, with the exception that you check the 'Allow Multiple Values' check box. The following steps create a multivalued field.

Table 3–1 Resource Abbreviations and Descriptions

Resource Abbreviation	Description
Audio	Audio CD
CDVD	Culture DVD
CustD	Custom Digital
CustP	Custom Print
Ebook	Electronic Textbook
OlMan	Online Laboratory Manual
OlWrk	Online Workbook
PrMan	Printed Laboratory Manual
PrWrk	Printed Workbook
SDVD	Sitcom DVD
Txt	Printed Textbook

1. Tap or click the row selector for the Amount Paid field, and then press the INSERT key to insert a blank row.
2. Tap or click the Field Name column for the new field, type `Resources Needed` as the field name, and then press the TAB key.
3. Tap or click the Data Type arrow to display the menu of available data types for the Resources Needed field, and then tap or click Lookup Wizard in the menu of available data types to start the Lookup Wizard.
4. Tap or click the 'I will type in the values that I want.' option button to indicate that you will type in the values.
5. Tap or click the Next button to display the next Lookup Wizard screen.
6. Tap or click the first row of the table (below Col1), and then type `Audio` as the value in the first row.
7. Enter the remaining values from the first column in Table 3–1. Before typing each value, press the DOWN ARROW key to move to a new row.
8. Tap or click the Next button to display the next Lookup Wizard screen.
9. Ensure that Resources Needed is entered as the label for the lookup field.
10. Tap or click the 'Allow Multiple Values' check box to allow the user to enter multiple values.
11. Tap or click the Finish button to complete the definition of the Lookup Wizard field.

BTW

Modifying Table Properties

You can change the properties of a table by opening the table in Design view and then clicking the Property Sheet button. To display the records in a table in an order other than primary key (the default sort order), use the Order By property. For example, to display the Customer table automatically in Customer Name order, change the Order By property setting to Customer. Customer Name in the property box, close the property sheet, and save the change to the table design. When you open the Customer table in Datasheet view, the records will be sorted in Customer Name order.

BTW

Multivalued Fields

Do not use multivalued fields if you plan to move your data to another relational database management system, such as SQL Server at a later date. SQL Server and other relational DMBSs do not support multivalued fields.

To Modify Single or Multivalued Lookup Fields

At some point you might want to change the list of choices in a lookup field. If you need to modify a single or multivalued lookup field, you would use the following steps.

1. Open the table in Design view and select the field to be modified.
2. Tap or click the Lookup tab in the Field Properties pane.
3. Change the list in the Row Source property to the desired list of values.

To Add a Calculated Field

A field that can be computed from other fields is called a **calculated field** or a **computed field**. In Chapter 2, you created a calculated field in a query that provided total amount data. In Access 2013, it is also possible to include a calculated field in a table. Users will not be able to update this field. ***Why?*** *Access will automatically perform the necessary calculation and display the appropriate value whenever you display or use this field in any way.* The following steps add to the Customer table a field that calculates the sum of the Amount Paid and Current Due fields.

1

- Tap or click the row selector for the Returns field, and then press the INSERT key to insert a blank row above the selected field.
- Tap or click the Field Name column for the new field.
- Type `Total Amount` as the field name, and then press the TAB key.
- Tap or click the Data Type arrow to display the menu of available data types (Figure 3–30).

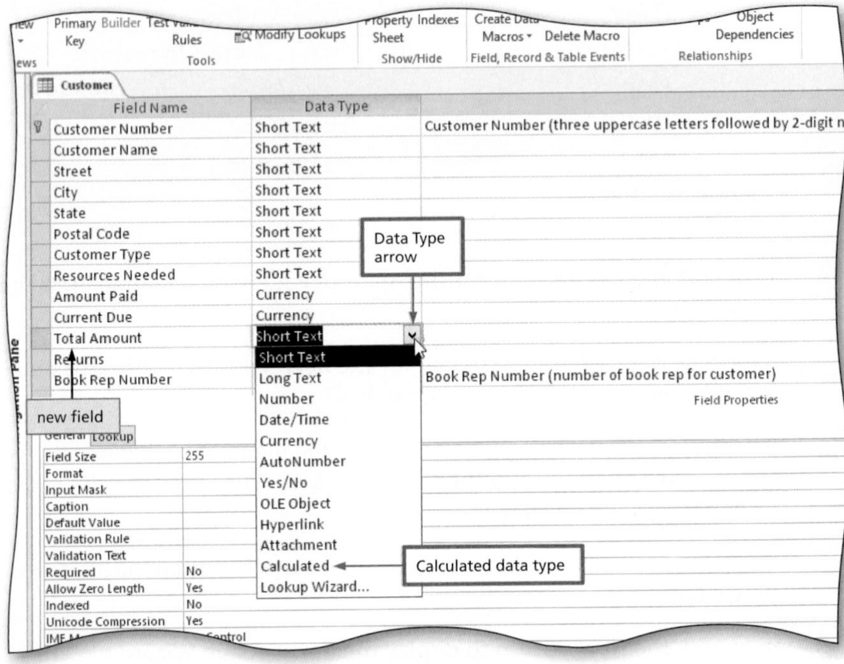

Figure 3–30

2

- Tap or click Calculated to select the Calculated data type and display the Expression Builder dialog box (Figure 3–31).

Q&A I do not have the list of fields in the Expression Categories area. What should I do?

Tap or click Customer in the Expression Elements area.

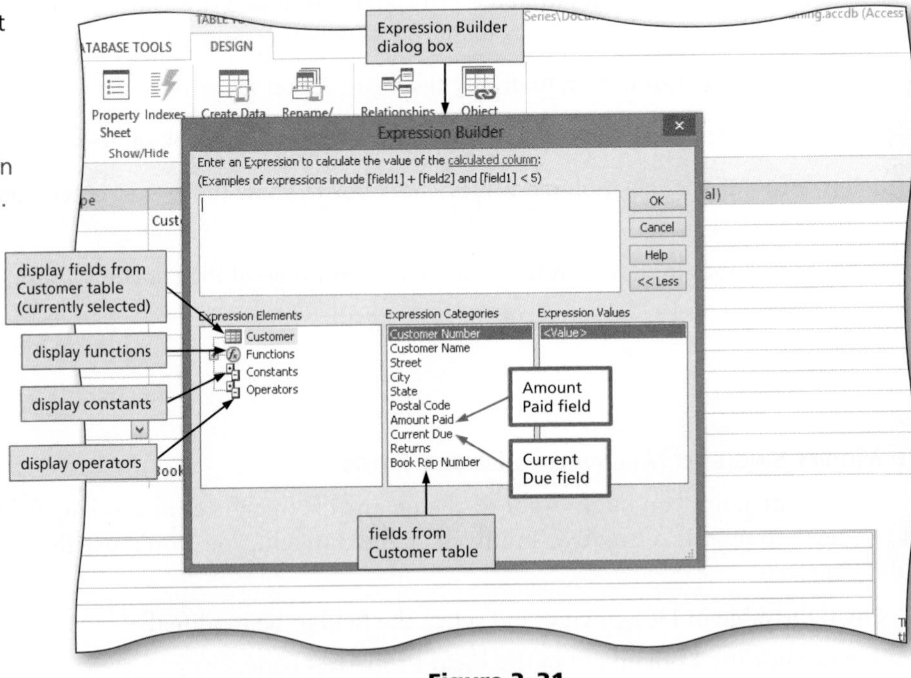

Figure 3–31

3

- Double-tap or double-click the Amount Paid field in the Expression Categories area (Expression Builder dialog box) to add the field to the expression.
- Type a plus sign (+).

Q&A Could I select the plus sign from a list rather than typing it?
Yes. Tap or click Operators in the Expression Elements area to display available operators, and then double-tap or double-click the plus sign.

- Double-tap or double-click the Current Due field in the Expression Categories area (Expression Builder dialog box) to add the field to the expression (Figure 3–32).

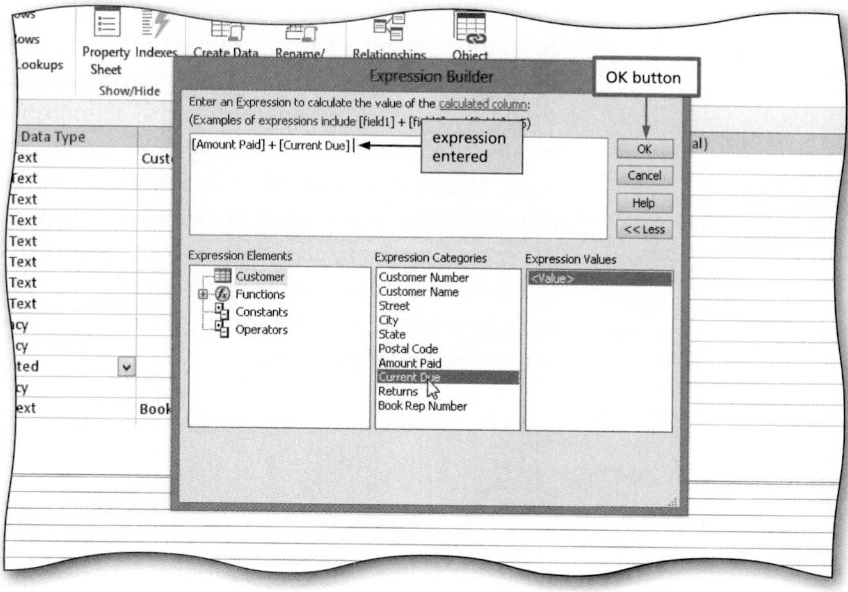

Figure 3–32

4

- Tap or click the OK button (Expression Builder dialog box) to enter the expression in the Expression property of the Total Amount (Figure 3–33).

Q&A Could I have typed the expression in the Expression Builder dialog box rather than selecting the fields from a list?
Yes. You can use whichever technique you find more convenient.

When I entered a calculated field in a query, I typed the expression in the Zoom dialog box. Could I have used the Expression Builder instead?
Yes. To do so, you would tap or click Build rather than Zoom on the shortcut menu.

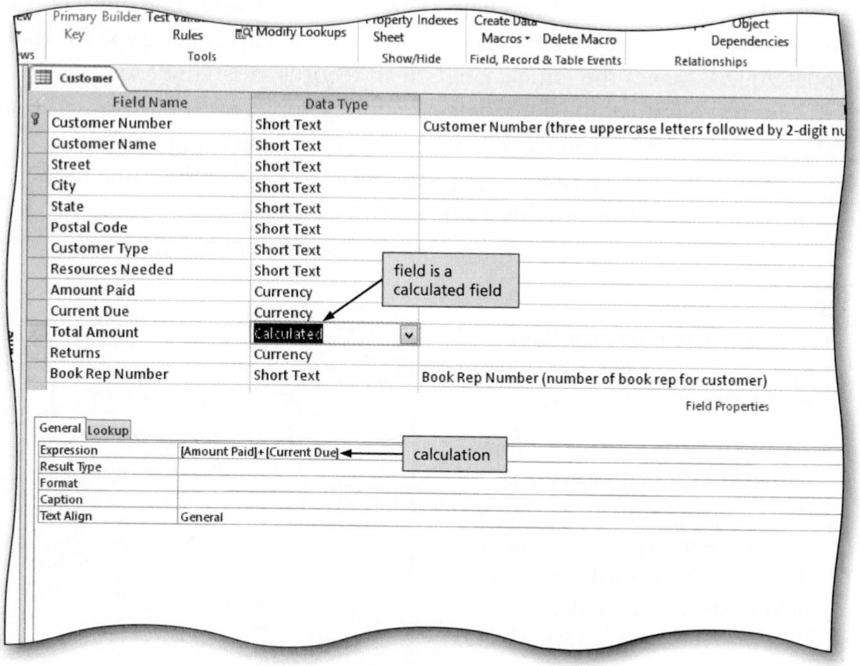

Figure 3–33

To Save the Changes and Close the Table

The following steps save the changes; that is, they save the addition of the new fields and close the table.

1. Tap or click the Save button on the Quick Access Toolbar to save the changes.
2. Close the Customer table.

BTW
Calculated Fields
You can use the the Result Type field property to format the calculated field values.

BTW
Viewing Records Before Updating
You can view records affected by an update query before running the query. To do so, use the Select button to convert the query to a select query, add any additional fields that would help you identify the records, and then view the results. Make any necessary corrections to the query in Design view. When you are satisfied, use the Update button to once again convert the query to an update query.

Mass Changes

In some cases, rather than making individual changes to records, you will want to make mass changes. That is, you will want to add, change, or delete many records in a single operation. You can do this with action queries. Unlike the select queries that you created in Chapter 2, which simply presented data in specific ways, an **action query** adds, deletes, or changes data in a table. An **update query** allows you to make the same change to all records satisfying some criterion. If you omit the criterion, you will make the same changes to all records in the table. A **delete query** allows you to delete all the records satisfying some criterion. You can add the results of a query to an existing table by using an **append query**. You also can add the query results to a new table by using a **make-table query**.

To Use an Update Query

1 UPDATE RECORDS | 2 FILTER RECORDS | 3 CHANGE STRUCTURE | **4 MASS CHANGES** | **5 VALIDATION RULES**
6 CHANGE APPEARANCE | **7 REFERENTIAL INTEGRITY** | **8 ORDER RECORDS**

The new Customer Type field is blank on every record in the Customer table. One approach to entering the information for the field would be to step through the entire table, assigning each record its appropriate value. If most of the customers have the same type, it would be more convenient to use an update query to assign a single value to all customers and then update the Customer Type for those customers whose type differs. An update query makes the same change to all records satisfying a criterion.

In the Bavant Publishing database, for example, most customers are type UNI. Initially, you can set all the values to UNI. Later, you can change the type for community colleges and high schools.

The following steps use an update query to change the value in the Customer Type field to UNI for all the records. Because all records are to be updated, criteria are not required. ***Why?*** *If there is a criterion, the update only takes place on those records that satisfy the criterion. Without a criterion, the update applies to all records.*

1

- Create a new query for the Customer table, and ensure the Navigation Pane is closed.
- Tap or click the Update button (QUERY TOOLS DESIGN tab | Query Type group) to specify an update query, double-tap or double-click the Customer Type field to select the field, tap or click the Update To row in the first column of the design grid, and then type `UNI` as the new value (Figure 3–34).

Q&A If I change my mind and do not want an update query, how can I change the query back to a select query?
Tap or click the Select button (QUERY TOOLS DESIGN tab | Query Type group).

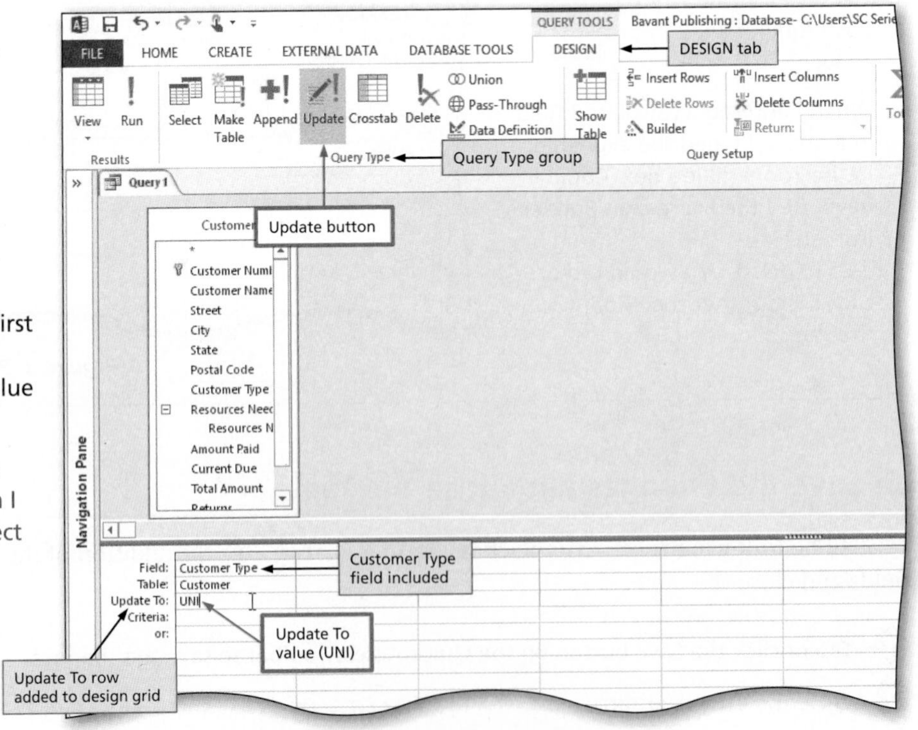

Figure 3–34

2

- Tap or click the Run button (QUERY TOOLS DESIGN tab | Results group) to run the query and update the records (Figure 3–35).

Q&A The dialog box did not appear on my screen when I ran the query. What happened?
If the dialog box did not appear, it means that you did not tap or click the Enable Content button when you first opened the database. Close the database, open it again, and enable the content. Then, create and run the query again.

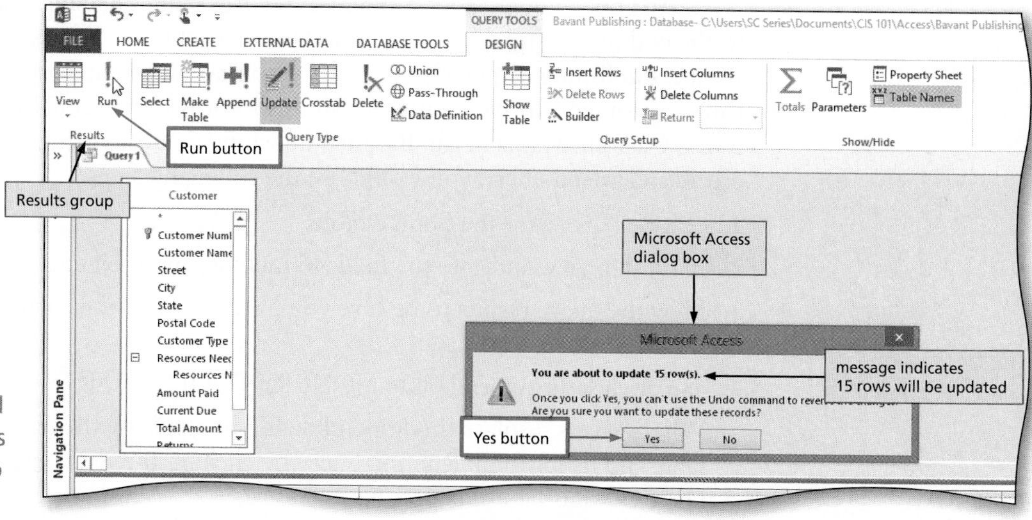

Figure 3–35

3

- Tap or click the Yes button to make the changes.

Experiment

- Create an update query to change the customer type to COM. Enter a criterion to restrict the records to be updated, and then run the query. Open the table to view your changes. When finished, create and run an update query to change the customer type to UNI on all records.

- Close the query. Because you do not need to use this update query again, do not save the query.

Other Ways

1. Press and hold or right-click any open area in upper pane, point to Query Type on shortcut menu, tap or click Update Query on Query Type submenu

To Use a Delete Query

In some cases, you might need to delete several records at a time. If, for example, all high school customers are to be serviced by another publisher, the customers with this customer type can be deleted from the Bavant Publishing database. Instead of deleting these customers individually, which could be very time-consuming in a large database, you can delete them in one operation by using a delete query, which is a query that deletes all the records satisfying the criteria entered in the query. To create a delete query, you would use the following steps.

> BTW
> **Delete Queries**
> If you do not specify any criteria in a delete query, Access will delete all the records in the table.

1. Create a query for the table containing the records to be deleted.
2. In Design view, indicate the fields and criteria that will specify the records to delete.
3. Tap or click the Delete button (QUERY TOOLS DESIGN tab | Query Type group).
4. Run the query by clicking the Run button (QUERY TOOLS DESIGN tab | Results group).
5. When Access indicates the number of records to be deleted, tap or click the Yes button.

To Use an Append Query

An append query adds a group of records from one table, called the Source table, to the end of another table, called the Destination table. For example, suppose that Bavant Publishing acquires some new customers and a database containing a table with those customers. To avoid entering all this information manually, you can append it to the Customer table in the Bavant Publishing database using the append query. To create an append query, you would use the following steps.

1. Create a query for the Source table.
2. In Design view, indicate the fields to include, and then enter any necessary criteria.
3. View the query results to be sure you have specified the correct data, and then return to Design view.
4. Tap or click the Append button (QUERY TOOLS DESIGN tab | Query Type group).
5. When Access displays the Append dialog box, specify the name of the Destination table and its location. Run the query by clicking the Run button (QUERY TOOLS DESIGN tab | Results group).
6. When Access indicates the number of records to be appended, tap or click the OK button.

BTW
Archive Tables
You can use a make table query to create an archive table. An archive table is a table that contains data that is no longer used in operations but that might still be needed by the organization.

To Use a Make-Table Query

In some cases, you might want to create a new table that contains only records copied from an existing table. If so, use a make-table query to add the records to a new table. To create a make-table query, you would use the following steps.

1. Create a query for the Source table.
2. In Design view, indicate the fields to include, and then enter any necessary criteria.
3. View the query results to be sure you have specified the correct data, and then return to Design view.
4. Tap or click the Make Table button (QUERY TOOLS DESIGN tab | Query Type group).
5. When Access displays the Make Table dialog box, specify the name of the Destination table and its location. Run the query by clicking the Run button (QUERY TOOLS DESIGN tab | Results group).
6. When Access indicates the number of records to be inserted, tap or click the OK button.

Break Point: If you wish to take a break, this is a good place to do so. You can quit Access now. To resume at a later time, start Access, open the database called Bavant Publishing, and continue following the steps from this location forward.

Validation Rules

You now have created, loaded, queried, and updated a database. Nothing you have done so far, however, restricts users to entering only valid data, that is, data that follows the rules established for data in the database. An example of such a rule would be that customer types can only be HS, COM, or UNI. To ensure the entry of valid data, you create **validation rules**, that is, rules that a user must follow when entering the data. As you will see, Access will prevent users from entering data that does not follow the rules. The steps also specify **validation text**, which is the message that will appear if a user attempts to violate the validation rule.

BTW
Database Design: Validation
In most organizations, decisions about what is valid and what is invalid data are made during the requirements gathering process and the database design process.

Validation rules can indicate a **required field**, a field in which the user *must* enter data; failing to enter data into a required field generates an error. Validation rules can restrict a user's entry to a certain **range of values**; for example, the values in the Returns field must be between $0 and $30,000. They can specify a **default value**, that is, a value that Access will display on the screen in a particular field before the user begins adding a record. To make data entry of customer numbers more convenient, you also can have lowercase letters appear automatically as uppercase letters. Finally, validation rules can specify a collection of acceptable values.

To Change a Field Size

The Field Size property for text fields represents the maximum number of characters a user can enter in the field. Because the field size for the Customer Number field is five, for example, a user would not be able to enter a sixth character in the field. Occasionally, you will find that the field size that seemed appropriate when you first created a table is no longer appropriate. In the Customer table, there is a street name that needs to be longer than 20 characters. To allow this name in the table, you need to change the field size for the Street field to a number that is large enough to accommodate the new name. The following step changes the field size for the Street field from 20 to 25.

BTW

Using Wildcards in Validation Rules

You can include wildcards in validation rules. For example, if you enter the expression, like T?, in the Validation Rule for the State field, the only valid entries for the field will be TN or TX.

1. Open the Customer table in Design view and close the Navigation Pane.
2. Select the Street field by clicking its row selector.
3. Tap or click the Field Size property to select it, delete the current entry (20), and then type **25** as the new field size.

To Specify a Required Field

1 UPDATE RECORDS | 2 FILTER RECORDS | 3 CHANGE STRUCTURE | 4 MASS CHANGES | **5 VALIDATION RULES**
6 CHANGE APPEARANCE | **7 REFERENTIAL INTEGRITY** | **8 ORDER RECORDS**

To specify that a field is to be required, change the value for the Required property from No to Yes. The following step specifies that the Customer Name field is to be a required field. ***Why?*** *Users will not be able to leave the Customer Name field blank when entering or editing records.*

1

- Select the Customer Name field by clicking its row selector.
- Tap or click the Required property box in the Field Properties pane, and then tap or click the down arrow that appears.
- Tap or click Yes in the list to make Customer Name a required field (Figure 3–36).

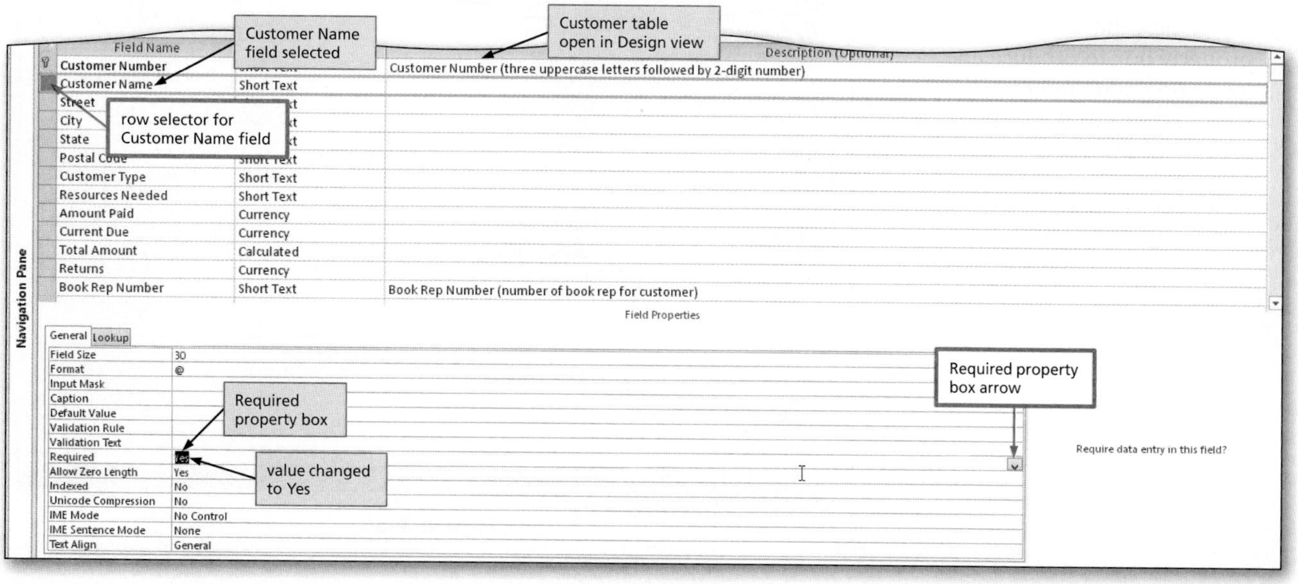

Figure 3–36

To Specify a Range

The following step specifies that entries in the Returns field must be between $0 and $30,000. To indicate this range, the criterion specifies that the returns amount must be both >= 0 (greater than or equal to 0) and <= 30000 (less than or equal to 30,000). ***Why?*** *Combining these two criteria with the word, and, is logically equivalent to being between $0.00 and $30,000.00.*

1

- Select the Returns field by clicking its row selector, tap or click the Validation Rule property box to produce an insertion point, and then type `>=0 and <=30000` as the rule.
- Tap or click the Validation Text property box to produce an insertion point, and then type `Must be at least $0.00 and at most $30,000.00` as the text (Figure 3–37).

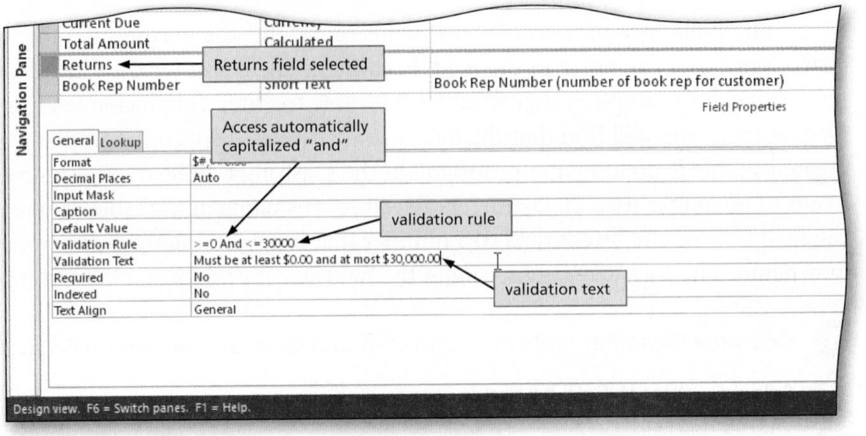

Figure 3–37

Q&A What is the effect of this change?
Users now will be prohibited from entering a returns amount that is either less than $0.00 or greater than $30,000.00 when they add records or change the value in the Returns field.

To Specify a Default Value

To specify a default value, enter the value in the Default Value property box. The following step specifies UNI as the default value for the Customer Type field. ***Why?*** *More customers at Bavant have type UNI than either of the other types. By making it the default value, if users do not enter a customer type, the type will be UNI.*

1

- Select the Customer Type field, tap or click the Default Value property box to produce an insertion point, and then type `=UNI` as the value (Figure 3–38).

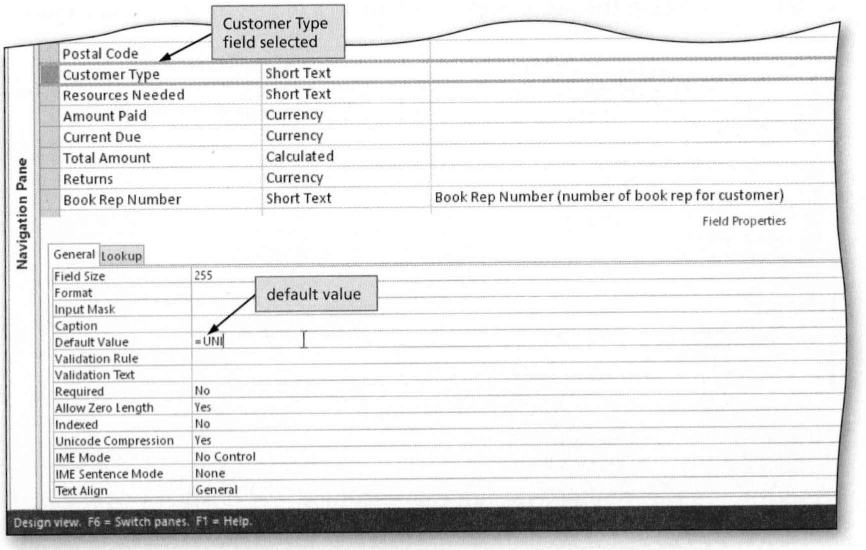

Figure 3–38

Q&A Do I need to type the equal (=) sign?
No. You could enter UNI as the default value.

To Specify a Collection of Legal Values

1 UPDATE RECORDS | 2 FILTER RECORDS | 3 CHANGE STRUCTURE | 4 MASS CHANGES | 5 VALIDATION RULES
6 CHANGE APPEARANCE | 7 REFERENTIAL INTEGRITY | 8 ORDER RECORDS

The only **legal values**, or **allowable values**, for the Customer Type field are HS, COM, and UNI. The following step creates a validation rule to specify these as the only legal values for the Customer Type field. ***Why?*** *The validation rule prohibits users from entering any other value in the Customer Type field.*

1

- With the Customer Type field selected, tap or click the Validation Rule property box to produce an insertion point and then type `=HS or =COM or =UNI` as the validation rule.
- Tap or click the Validation Text property box, and then type `Must be HS, COM, or UNI` as the validation text (Figure 3–39).

Q&A What is the effect of this change?
Users now will be allowed to enter only HS, COM, or UNI in the Customer Type field when they add records or make changes to this field.

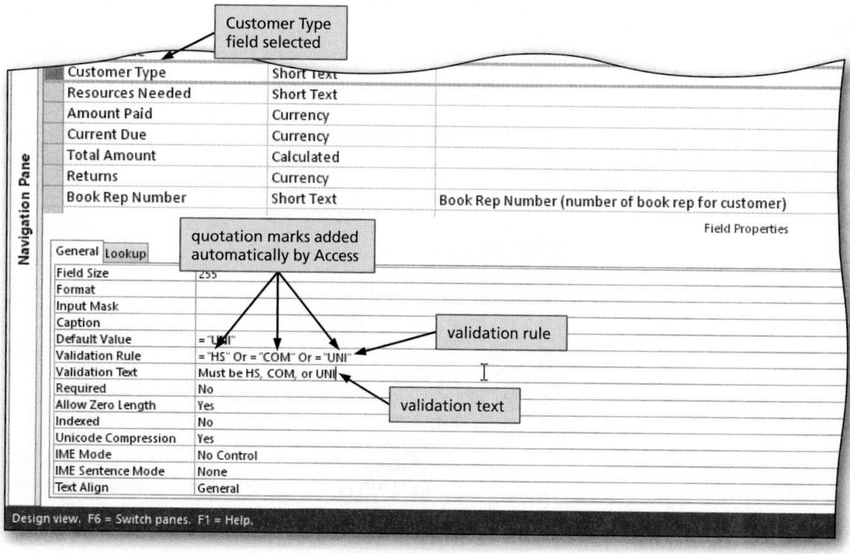

Figure 3–39

To Specify a Format

1 UPDATE RECORDS | 2 FILTER RECORDS | 3 CHANGE STRUCTURE | 4 MASS CHANGES | 5 VALIDATION RULES
6 CHANGE APPEARANCE | 7 REFERENTIAL INTEGRITY | 8 ORDER RECORDS

To affect the way data appears in a field, you can use a **format**. To use a format with a Short Text field, you enter a special symbol, called a **format symbol**, in the field's Format property box. The Format property uses different settings for different data types. The following step specifies a format for the Customer Number field using the > symbol. ***Why?*** *The > format symbol causes Access to display lowercase letters automatically as uppercase letters, which is appropriate for the Customer Number field.* There is another symbol, the < symbol, which causes Access to display uppercase letters automatically as lowercase letters.

1

- Select the Customer Number field.
- Tap or click the Format property box, erase the current format (@), if it appears on your screen, and then type > (Figure 3–40).

Q&A Where did the current format (@) come from and what does it mean?
Access added this format when you created the table by importing data from an Excel workbook. It simply means any character or a space. It is not needed here.

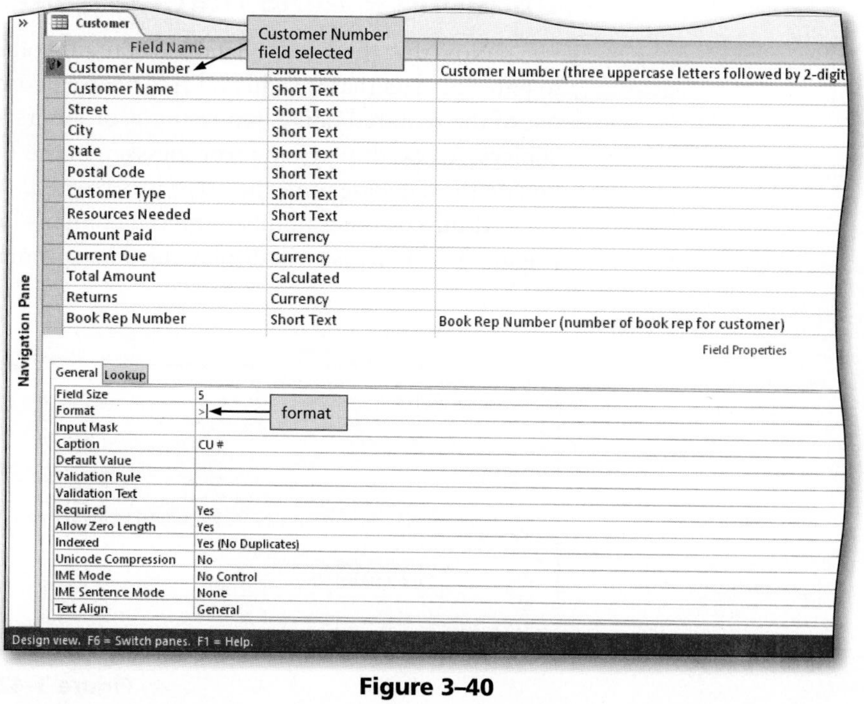

Figure 3–40

To Save the Validation Rules, Default Values, and Formats

BTW
Using the BETWEEN Operator in Validation Rules
You can use the BETWEEN operator to specify a range of values. For example, to specify that entries in the Returns field must be between $0 and $30,000, type BETWEEN 0 and 30000 as the rule.

The following steps save the validation rules, default values, and formats.

1. Tap or click the Save button on the Quick Access Toolbar to save the changes (Figure 3–41).
2. If a Microsoft Access dialog box appears, tap or click the No button to save the changes without testing current data.

Q&A When would you want to test current data?
If you have any doubts about the validity of the current data, you should be sure to test the current data.

3. Close the Customer table.

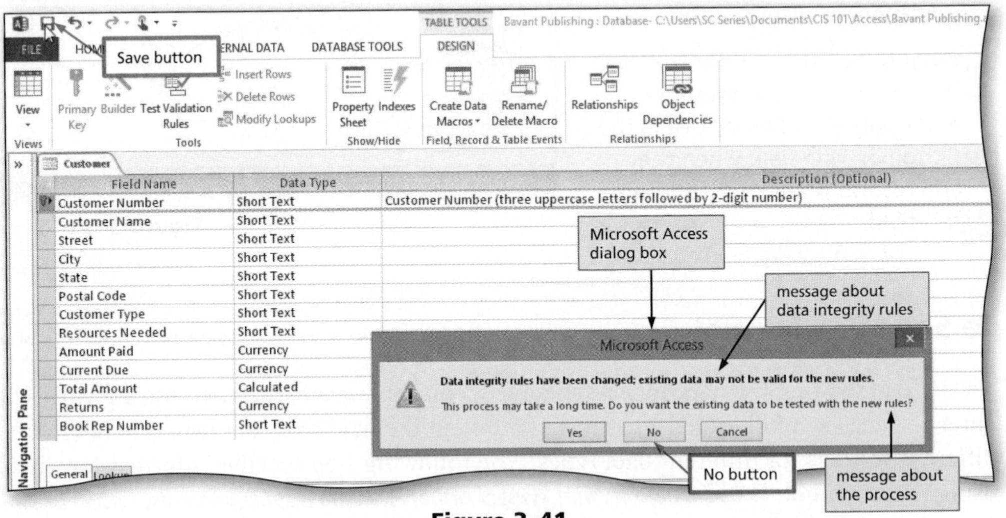

Figure 3–41

Updating a Table that Contains Validation Rules

Now that the Bavant database contains validation rules, Access restricts the user to entering data that is valid and is formatted correctly. If a user enters a number that is out of the required range, for example, or enters a value that is not one of the possible choices, Access displays an error message in the form of a dialog box. The user cannot update the database until the error is corrected.

If the customer number entered contains lowercase letters, such as wip22 (Figure 3–42), Access will display the data automatically as WIP22 (Figure 3–43).

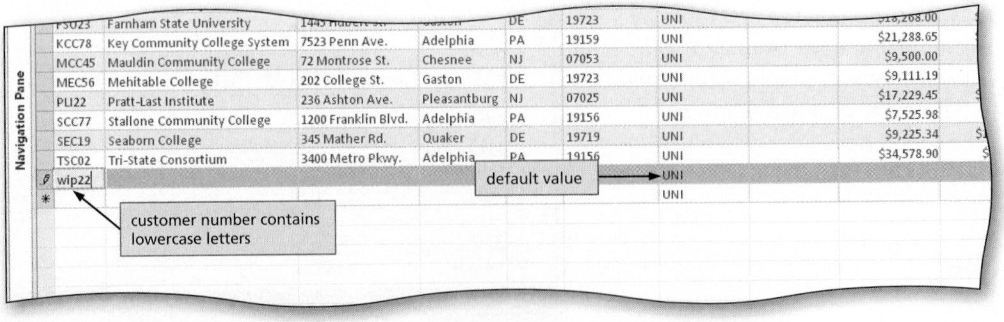

Figure 3–42

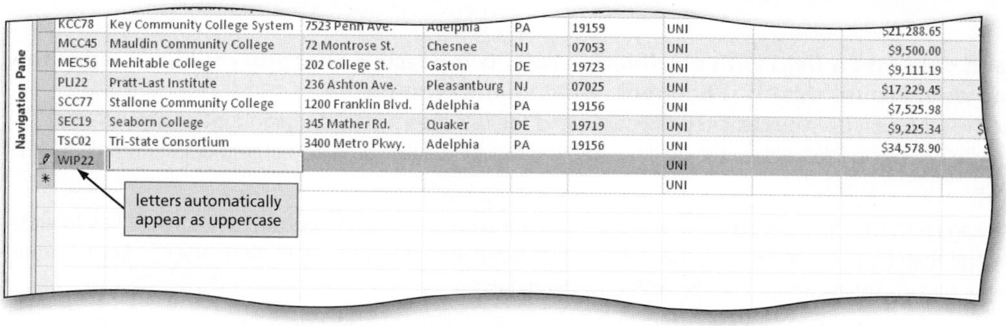

Figure 3–43

If the customer type is not valid, such as xxx, Access will display the text message you specified (Figure 3–44) and prevent the data from entering the database.

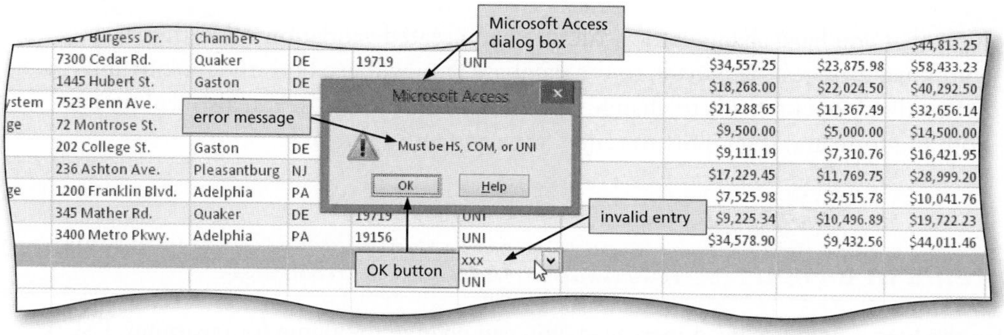

Figure 3–44

If the returns amount is not valid, such as 40000, which is too large, Access also displays the appropriate message (Figure 3–45) and refuses to accept the data.

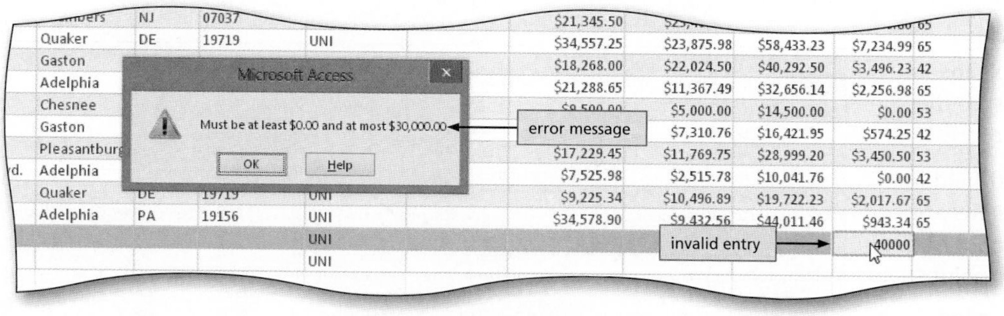

Figure 3–45

If a required field contains no data, Access indicates this by displaying an error message as soon as you attempt to leave the record (Figure 3–46). The field must contain a valid entry before Access will move to a different record.

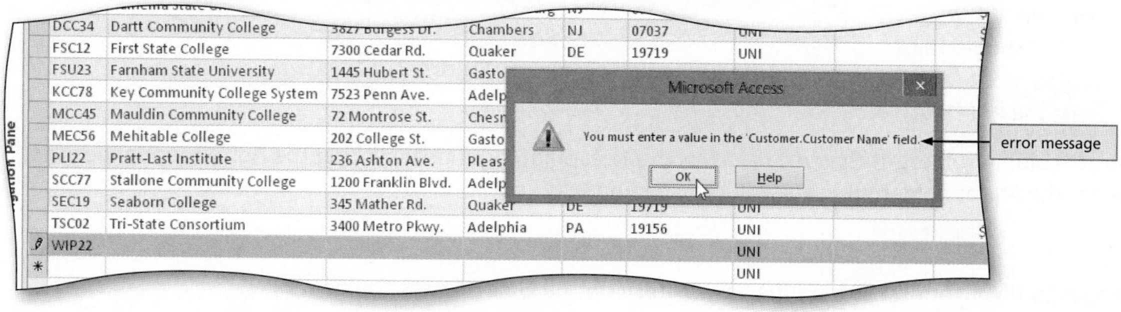

Figure 3–46

CONSIDER THIS

When entering invalid data into a field with a validation rule, is it possible that you could not enter the data correctly? What would cause this? If it happens, what should you do?

If you cannot remember the validation rule you created or if you created the rule incorrectly, you might not be able to enter the data. In such a case, you will be unable to leave the field or close the table because you have entered data into a field that violates the validation rule.

If this happens, first try again to type an acceptable entry. If this does not work, repeatedly press the BACKSPACE key to erase the contents of the field and then try to leave the field. If you are unsuccessful using this procedure, press the ESC key until the record is removed from the screen. The record will not be added to the database.

Should the need arise to take this drastic action, you probably have a faulty validation rule. Use the techniques of the previous sections to correct the existing validation rules for the field.

Making Additional Changes to the Database

Now that you have changed the structure and created validation rules, there are additional changes to be made to the database. You will use both the lookup and multivalued lookup fields to change the contents of the fields. You also will update both the form and the report to reflect the changes in the table.

To Change the Contents of a Field

1 UPDATE RECORDS | 2 FILTER RECORDS | 3 CHANGE STRUCTURE | 4 MASS CHANGES | **5 VALIDATION RULES**
6 CHANGE APPEARANCE | **7 REFERENTIAL INTEGRITY** | **8 ORDER RECORDS**

Now that the size for the Street field has been increased, you can change the name for customer TSC02 from 3400 Metro Pkwy. to 3400 Metropolitan Pkwy. and then resize the column, just as you resized columns in Chapter 1 on page AC 28. ***Why?*** *Changing the field size for the field does not automatically increase the width of the corresponding column in the datasheet.* The following steps change the Street name and resize the column in the datasheet to accommodate the new name.

1

- Open the Customer table in Datasheet view and ensure the Navigation Pane is closed.
- Tap or click in the Street field for customer TSC02 immediately to the right of the letter, o, of Metro to produce an insertion point.
- Change the street from 3400 Metro Pkwy. to 3400 Metropolitan Pkwy. by typing `politan` and pressing the TAB key.

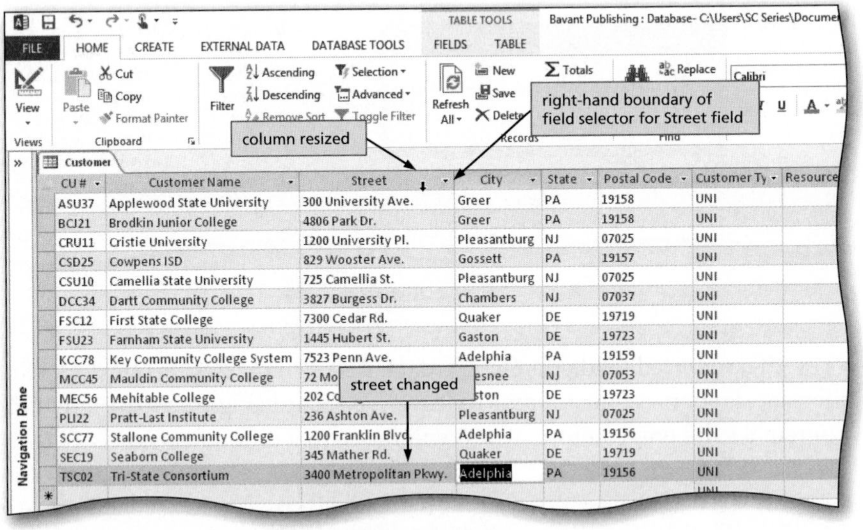

Figure 3–47

Q&A I cannot add the extra characters. Whatever I type replaces what is currently in the cell. What happened and what should I do?

You are in Overtype mode, not Insert mode. Press the INSERT key and correct the entry.

- Resize the Street column to best fit the new data by double-tapping or double-clicking the right boundary of the field selector for the Street field, that is, the column heading (Figure 3–47).

2

- Save the changes to the layout by clicking the Save button on the Quick Access Toolbar.
- Close the Customer table.

To Use a Lookup Field

Earlier, you changed all the entries in the Customer Type field to UNI. You have created a rule that will ensure that only legitimate values (HS, COM, or UNI) can be entered in the field. You also made Customer Type a lookup field. ***Why?*** *You can make changes to a lookup field for individual records by simply clicking the field to be changed, clicking the arrow that appears in the field, and then selecting the desired value from the list.* The following steps change the incorrect Customer Type values to the correct values.

1

- Open the Customer table in Datasheet view and ensure the Navigation Pane is closed.
- Tap or click in the Customer Type field on the second record to display an arrow.
- Tap or click the arrow to display the drop-down list of available choices for the Customer Type field (Figure 3–48).

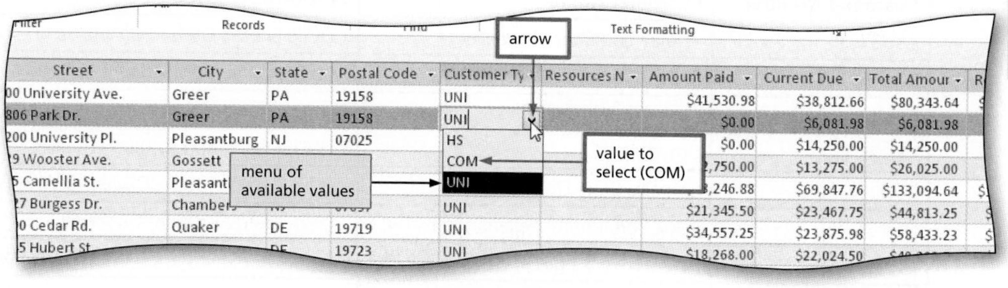

Figure 3–48

Q&A

I got the drop-down list as soon as I clicked. I did not need to tap or click the arrow. What happened?
If you tap or click in the position where the arrow would appear, you will get the drop-down list. If you tap or click anywhere else, you would need to tap or click the arrow.

Could I type the value instead of selecting it from the list?
Yes. Once you have either deleted the previous value or selected the entire previous value, you can begin typing. You do not have to type the full entry. When you begin with the letter, C, for example, Access will automatically add the OM.

2

- Tap or click COM to change the value.
- In a similar fashion, change the values on the other records to match those shown in Figure 3–49.

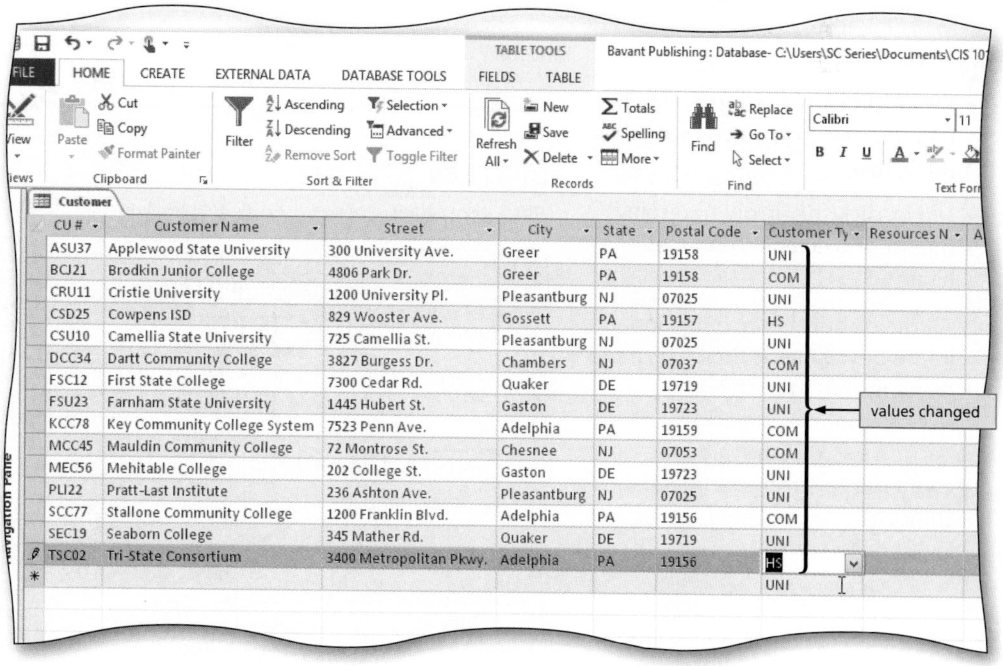

Figure 3–49

To Use a Multivalued Lookup Field

Using a multivalued lookup field is similar to using a regular lookup field. The difference is that when you drop down the list, the entries all will be preceded by check boxes. ***Why?*** *Having the check boxes allows you to make multiple selections. You check all the entries that you want.* The appropriate entries are shown in Figure 3–50. As indicated in the figure, the resources needed for customer ASU37 are CDVD, Ebook, OlMan, OlWrk, SDVD, and Txt.

Customer Number	Customer Name	Resources Needed
ASU37	Applewood State University	CDVD, Ebook, OlMan, OlWrk, SDVD, Txt
BCJ21	Brodkin Junior College	Audio, PrMan, PrWrk, Txt
CRU11	Cristie University	CustD, Ebook
CSD25	Cowpens ISD	CDVD, PrWrk, SDVD, Txt
CSU10	Camellia State University	Audio, CDVD, Ebook, OlMan, OlWrk, PrMan, PrWrk, SDVD, Txt
DCC34	Dartt Community College	CDVD, Ebook, OlMan, OlWrk, SDVD
FSC12	First State College	Audio, CDVD, PrMan, PrWrk, SDVD, Txt
FSU23	Farnham State University	CDVD, CustD, CustP, Ebook, OlMan, OlWrk, SDVD
KCC78	Key Community College System	Audio, CDVD, Ebook, OlMan, OlWrk, PrMan, PrWrk, SDVD, Txt
MCC45	Mauldin Community College	Audio, PrMan, PrWrk, Txt
MEC56	Mehitable College	Audio, CDVD, PrMan, PrWrk, SDVD, Txt
PLI22	Pratt-Last Institute	CDVD, CustD, CustP, Ebook, OlMan, OlWrk, SDVD
SCC77	Stallone Community College	Audio, PrMan, PrWrk, Txt
SEC19	Seaborn College	CDVD, CustD, CustP, SDVD
TSC02	Tri-State Consortium	Audio, CDVD, Ebook, OlMan, OlWrk, PrMan, PrWrk, SDVD, Txt

Figure 3–50

The following steps make the appropriate entries for the Resources Needed field.

1

- Tap or click the Resources Needed field on the first record to display the arrow.
- Tap or click the arrow to display the list of available resources (Figure 3–51).

Q&A All the resources currently appear in the box. What if there were too many resources to fit?

Access would automatically include a scroll bar that you could use to scroll through all the choices.

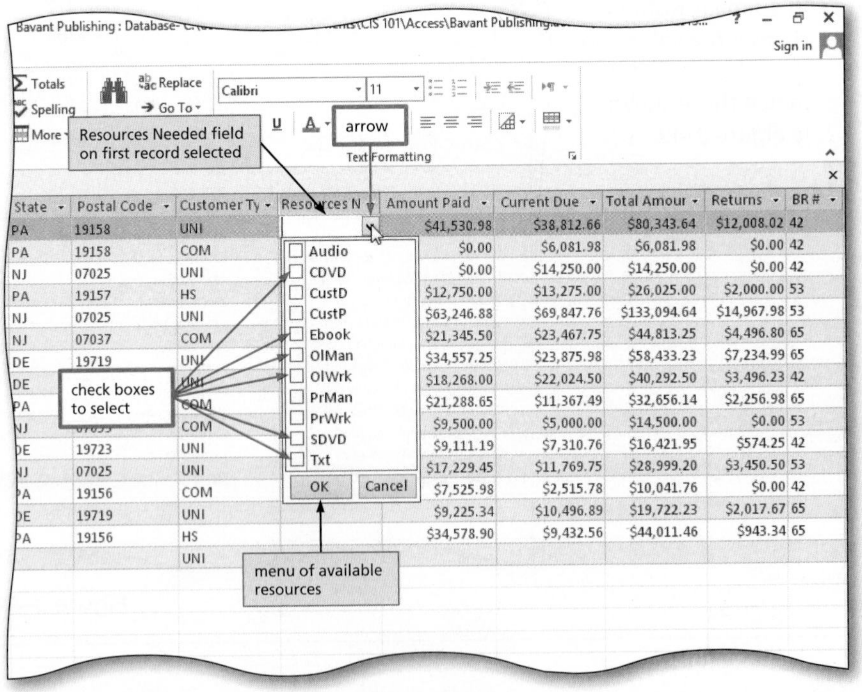

Figure 3–51

2

- Tap or click the CDVD, Ebook, OlMan, OlWrk, SDVD, and Txt check boxes to select the resources for the first customer (Figure 3–52).

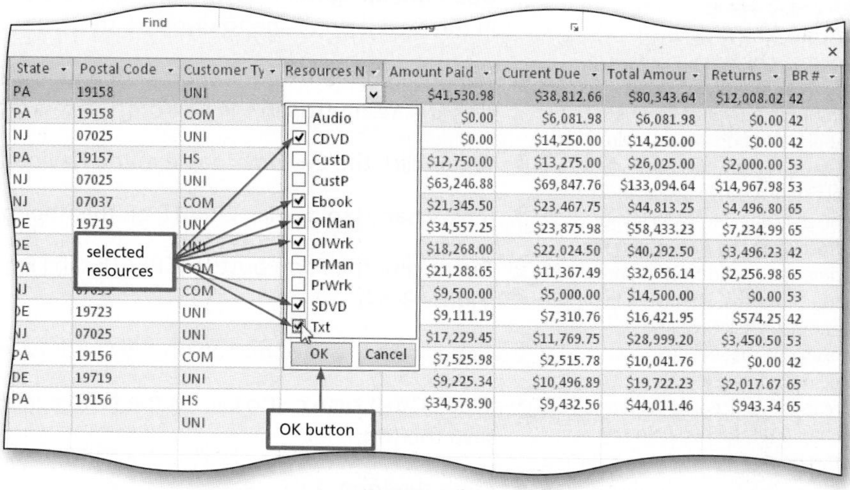

Figure 3–52

3

- Tap or click the OK button to complete the selection.
- Using the same technique, enter the resources given in Figure 3–50 for the remaining customers.
- Double-tap or double-click the right boundary of the field selector for the Resources Needed field to resize the field so that it best fits the data (Figure 3–53).

4

- Save the changes to the layout by clicking the Save button on the Quick Access Toolbar.
- Close the Customer table.

Q&A What if I closed the table without saving the layout changes?

You would be asked if you want to save the changes.

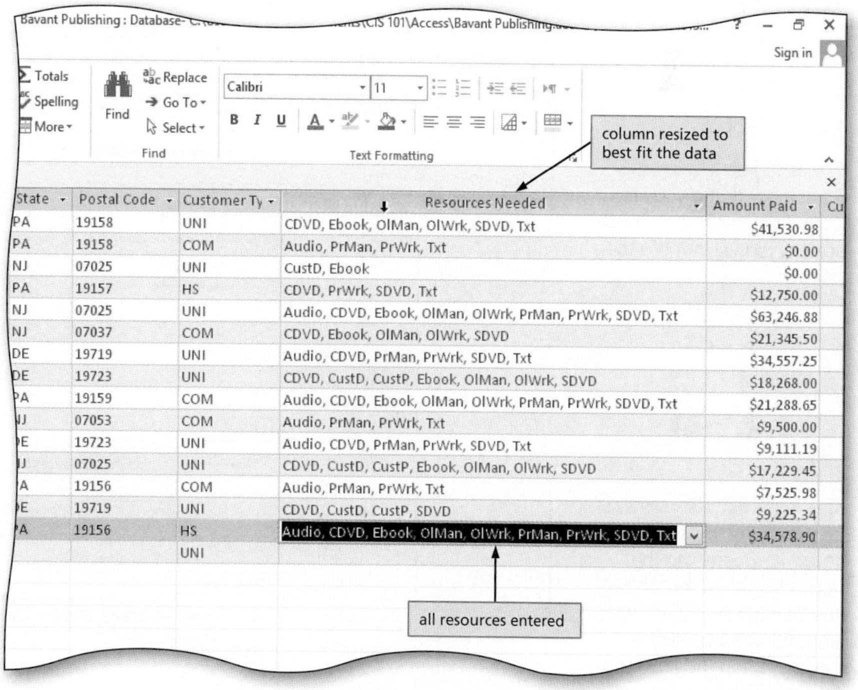

Figure 3–53

To Update a Form to Reflect the Changes in the Table

In the first chapter, on page AC 46, you clicked the Form button (CREATE tab | Forms group) to create a simple form that contained all the fields in the Customer table. Now that you have added fields, the form you created, Customer Form, no longer contains all the fields in the table. The steps on the next page delete the Customer Form and then create it a second time.

BTW
Access Help
At any time while using Access, you can find answers to questions and display information about various topics through Access Help. Used properly, this form of assistance can increase your productivity and reduce your frustrations by minimizing the time you spend learning how to use Access. For instruction about Access Help and exercises that will help you gain confidence in using it, read the Office and Windows chapter at the beginning of this book.

1. Open the Navigation Pane, and then press and hold or right-click the Customer Form in the Navigation Pane to display a shortcut menu.
2. Tap or click Delete on the shortcut menu to delete the selected form, and then tap or click the Yes button in the Microsoft Access dialog box to confirm the deletion.
3. Tap or click the Customer table in the Navigation Pane to select the table.
4. If necessary, tap or click CREATE on the ribbon to display the CREATE tab.
5. Tap or click the Form button (CREATE tab | Forms group) to create a simple form (Figure 3–54).
6. Tap or click the Save button on the Quick Access Toolbar to save the form.
7. Type `Customer Form` as the form name, and then tap or click the OK button to save the form.
8. Close the form.

BTW
Touch and Pointers
Remember that if you are using your finger on a touch screen, you will not see the pointer.

BTW
On Screen Keyboard
To display the on-screen touch keyboard, tap the Touch Keyboard button on the Windows taskbar. When finished using the touch keyboard, tap the X button on the touch keyboard to close the keyboard.

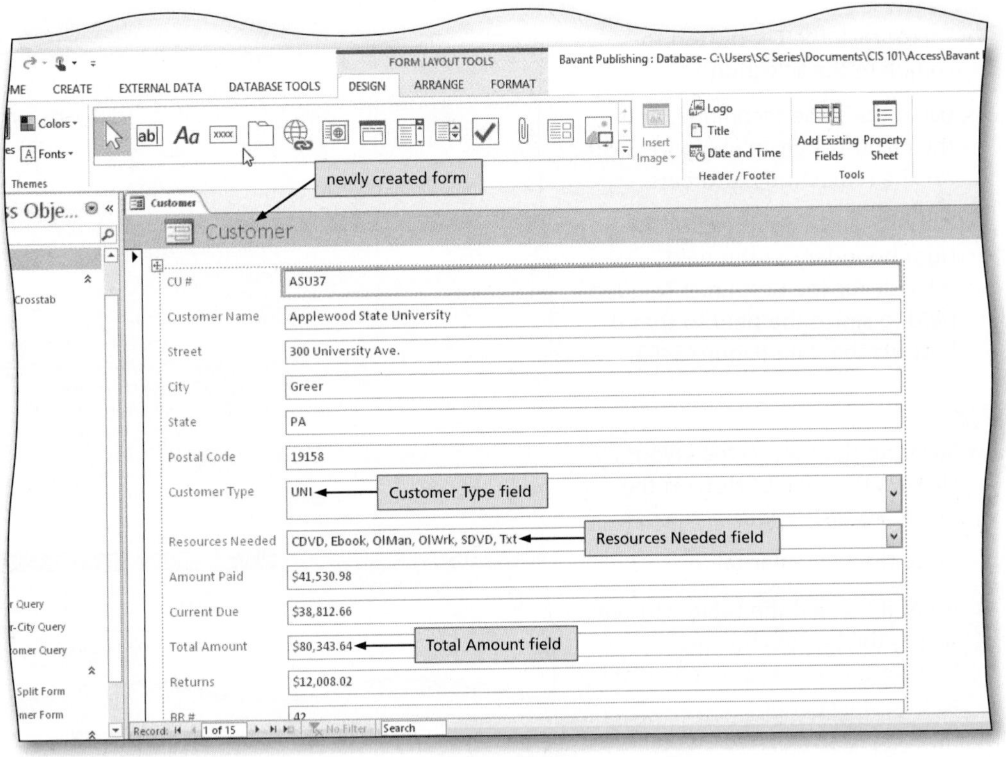

Figure 3–54

To Update a Report to Reflect the Changes in the Table

1 UPDATE RECORDS | 2 FILTER RECORDS | 3 CHANGE STRUCTURE | 4 MASS CHANGES | **5 VALIDATION RULES**
6 CHANGE APPEARANCE | 7 REFERENTIAL INTEGRITY | 8 ORDER RECORDS

You also may want to include the new fields in the Customer Financial Report you created earlier. Just as you did with the form, you could delete the current version of the report and then create it all over again. It would be better, however, to modify the report in Layout view. ***Why?*** *There are several steps involved in creating the Customer Financial report, so it is more complicated than the process of re-creating the form.* In Layout view, you easily can add new fields. The following steps modify the Customer Financial Report by adding the Customer Type and Total Amount fields. To accommodate the extra fields, the steps also change the orientation of the report from Portrait to Landscape.

1

- Open the Navigation Pane, if necessary, and then press and hold or right-click the Customer Financial Report in the Navigation Pane to display a shortcut menu.
- Tap or click Layout View on the shortcut menu to open the report in Layout view.
- Close the Navigation Pane.
- Tap or click the 'Add Existing Fields' button (REPORT LAYOUT TOOLS DESIGN tab | Tools group) to display a field list (Figure 3–55).

Q&A Why are there two Resources Needed fields in the list?

They serve different purposes. If you were to select Resources Needed, you would get all the resources for a given customer on one line. If you were to select Resources Needed.Value, each resource would be on a separate line. You are not selecting either one for this report.

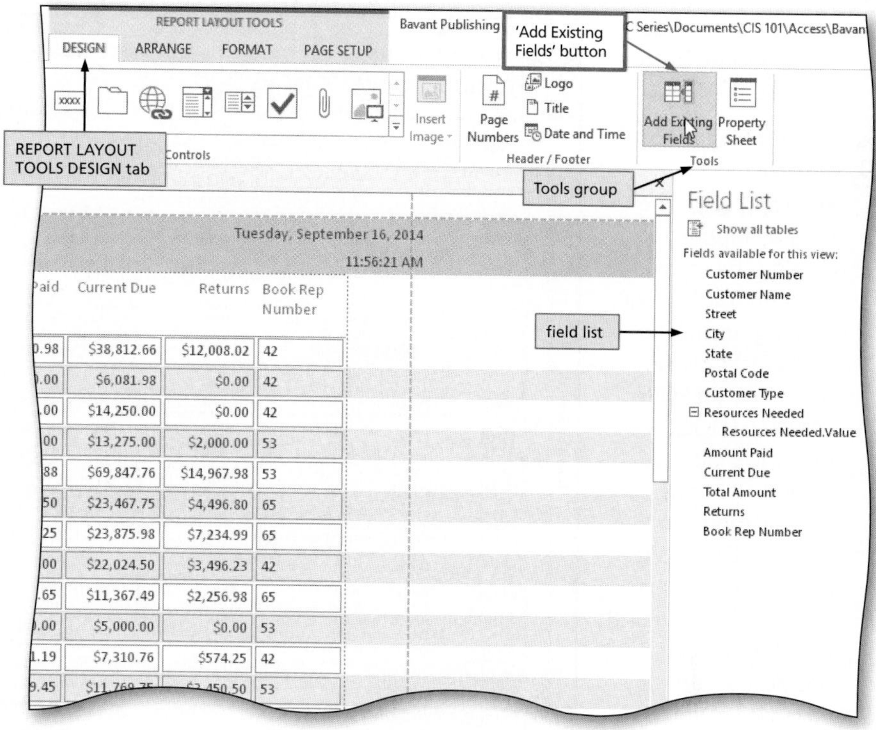

Figure 3–55

2

- Drag the Customer Type field in the field list until the line to the left of the pointer is between the Customer Name and Amount Paid fields (Figure 3–56).

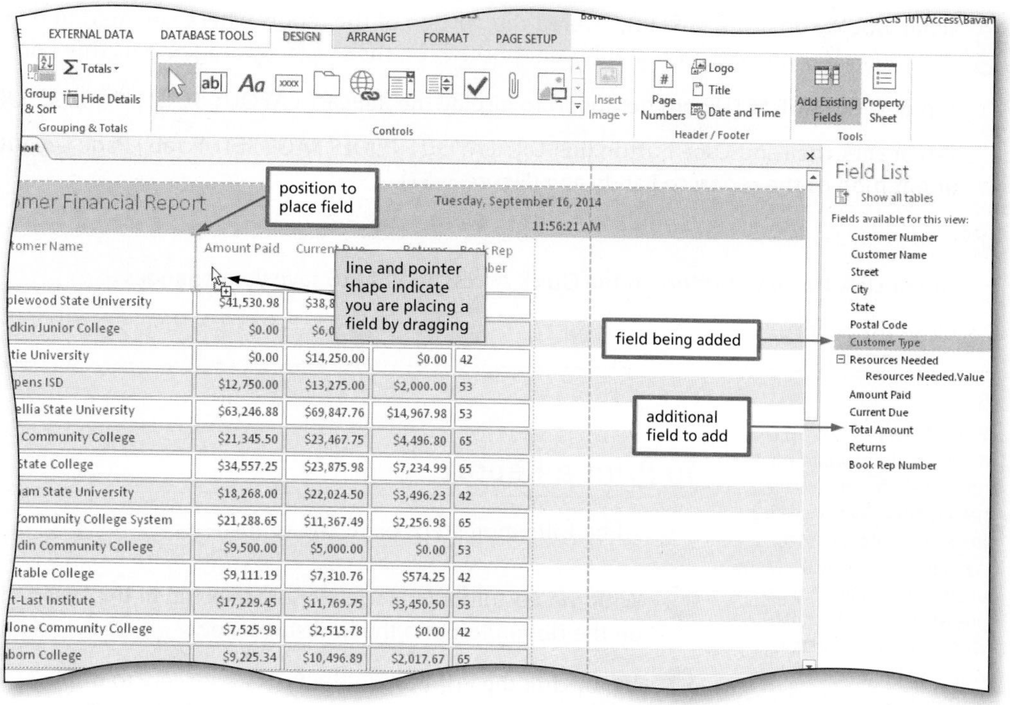

Figure 3–56

3

- Release your finger or the mouse button to place the field.

Q&A What if I make a mistake?
You can delete the field by tapping or clicking the column heading for the field, tapping or clicking the Select Column command (REPORT LAYOUT TOOLS ARRANGE tab | Rows & Columns group) and then pressing the DELETE key. You can move the field by dragging it to the correct position. As an alternative, you can close the report without saving it and then open it again in Layout view.

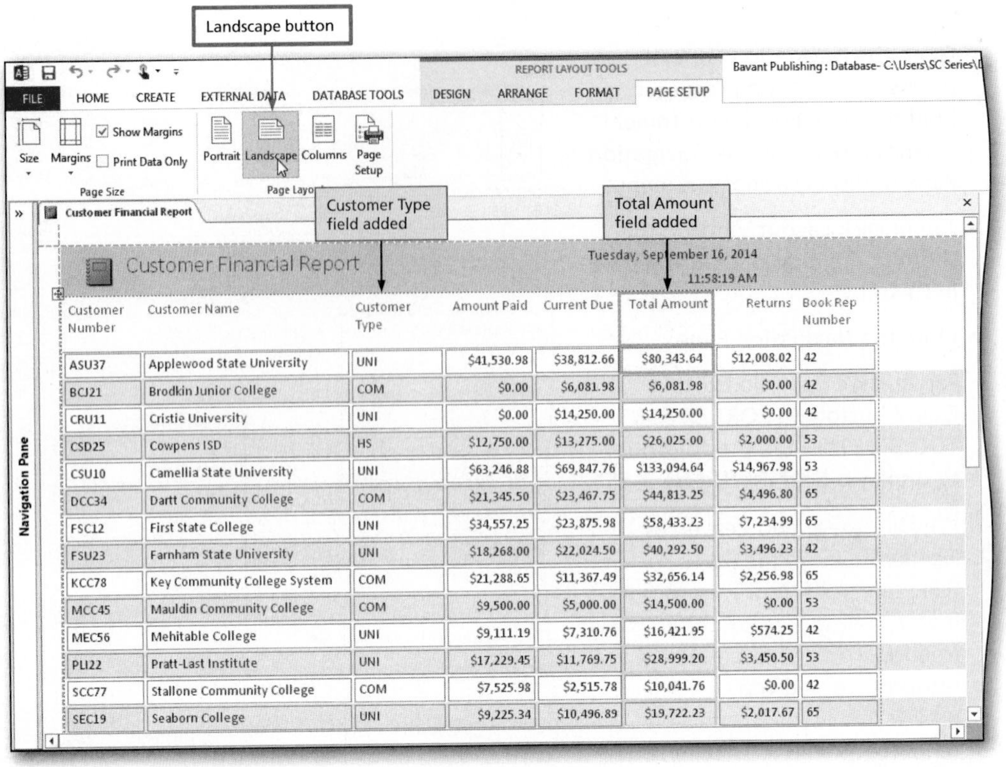

Figure 3–57

- Using the same technique, add the Total Amount field between the Current Due and Returns fields.
- Tap or click the 'Add Existing Fields' button (REPORT LAYOUT TOOLS DESIGN tab | Tools group) to remove the field list from the screen.

Q&A What would I do if the field list covered the portion of the report where I wanted to insert a new field?
You can move the field list to a different position on the screen by dragging its title bar.

- Tap or click PAGE SETUP on the ribbon to display the REPORT LAYOUT TOOLS PAGE SETUP tab.
- Tap or click the Landscape button (REPORT LAYOUT TOOLS PAGE SETUP tab | Page Layout group) to change the orientation of the report to Landscape (Figure 3–57).

4

- Tap or click the Save button on the Quick Access Toolbar to save your changes.
- Close the report.

BTW
Problems with Touch
If you are using your finger on a touch screen and are having difficulty completing the steps in this chapter, consider using a stylus. Many people find it easier to be precise with a stylus than with a finger. In addition, with a stylus you see the pointer. If you are still having trouble completing the steps with a stylus, try using a mouse.

To Print a Report

The following steps print the report.

1. With the Customer Financial Report selected in the Navigation Pane, tap or click FILE on the ribbon to open the Backstage view.
2. Tap or click the Print tab in the Backstage view to display the Print gallery.
3. Tap or click the Quick Print button to print the report.

Changing the Appearance of a Datasheet

You can change the appearance of a datasheet in a variety of ways. You can include totals in the datasheet. You can also change the appearance of gridlines. You can change the text colors and font.

To Include Totals in a Datasheet

1 UPDATE RECORDS | 2 FILTER RECORDS | 3 CHANGE STRUCTURE | 4 MASS CHANGES | 5 VALIDATION RULES
6 CHANGE APPEARANCE | 7 REFERENTIAL INTEGRITY | 8 ORDER RECORDS

The following steps first include an extra row, called the Total row, in the datasheet for the Book Rep table. ***Why?*** *It is possible to include totals and other statistics at the bottom of a datasheet in the Total row.* The steps then display the total of the salary for all the book reps.

1

- Open the Book Rep table in Datasheet view and close the Navigation Pane.
- Tap or click the Totals button (HOME tab | Records group) to include the Total row in the datasheet.
- Tap or click the Total row in the Salary column to display an arrow.
- Tap or click the arrow to display a menu of available calculations (Figure 3–58).

Q&A Will I always get the same list?
No. You will only get the items that are applicable to the type of data in the column. You cannot calculate the sum of text data, for example.

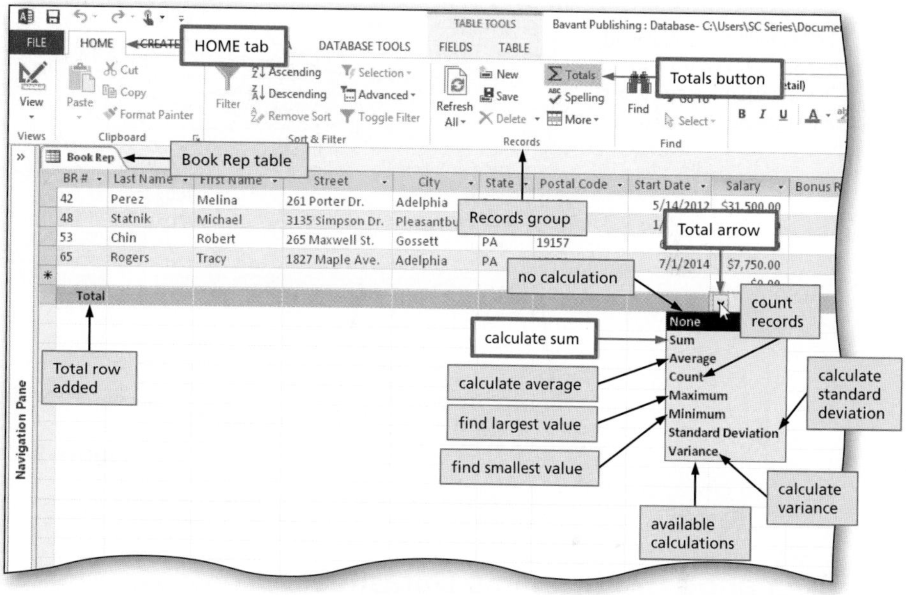

Figure 3–58

2

- Tap or click Sum to calculate the total of the salary amounts (Figure 3–59).

Experiment

- Experiment with other statistics. When finished, once again select the sum.

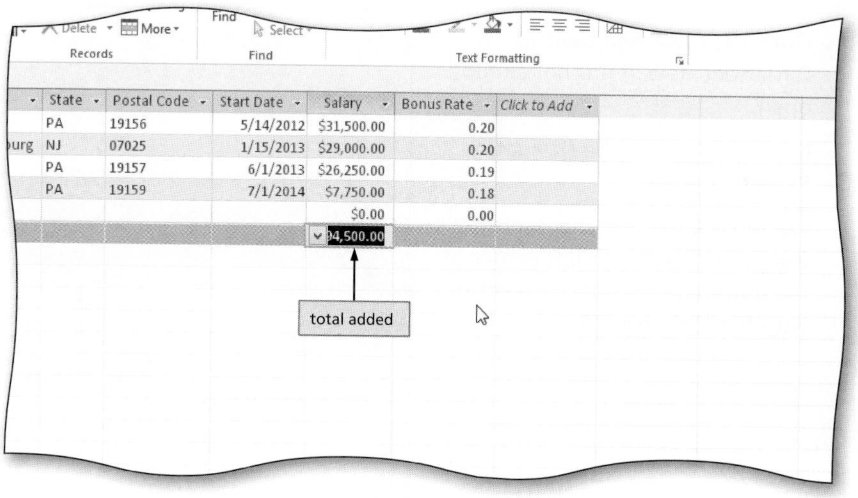

Figure 3–59

To Remove Totals from a Datasheet

If you no longer want the totals to appear as part of the datasheet, you can remove the Total row. The following step removes the Total row.

1. Tap or click the Totals button (HOME tab | Records group), which is shown in Figure 3–58 on the previous page, to remove the Total row from the datasheet.

Figure 3–60 shows the various buttons, found in the Text Formatting group on the HOME tab, that are available to change the datasheet appearance. The changes to the datasheet will be reflected not only on the screen, but also when you print or preview the datasheet.

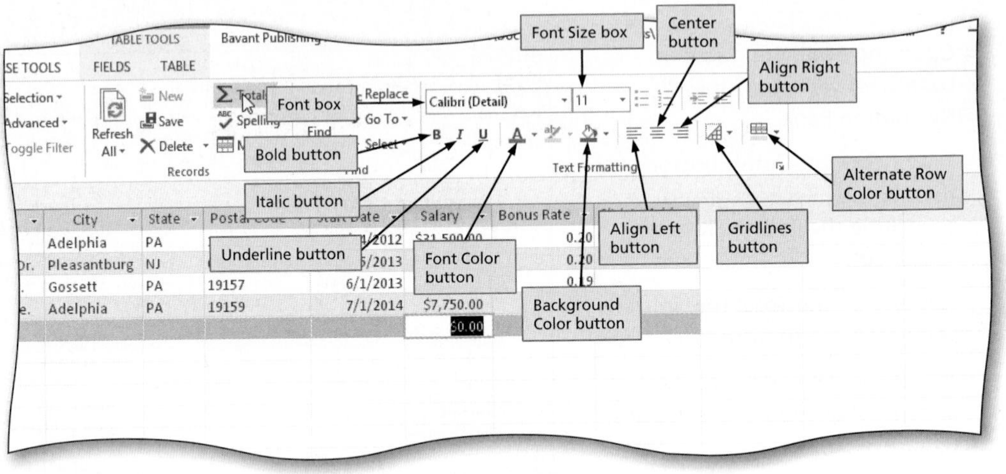

Figure 3–60

BTW
Distributing a Document
Instead of printing and distributing a hard copy of a document, you can distribute the document electronically. Options include sending the document via email; posting it on cloud storage (such as SkyDrive) and sharing the file with others; posting it on a social networking site, blog, or other website; and sharing a link associated with an online location of the document. You also can create and share a PDF or XPS image of the document, so that users can view the file in Acrobat Reader or XPS Viewer instead of in Access.

To Change Gridlines in a Datasheet

1 UPDATE RECORDS | 2 FILTER RECORDS | 3 CHANGE STRUCTURE | 4 MASS CHANGES | 5 VALIDATION RULES
6 CHANGE APPEARANCE | **7 REFERENTIAL INTEGRITY** | **8 ORDER RECORDS**

The following steps change the datasheet so that only horizontal gridlines are included. ***Why?*** *You might prefer the appearance of the datasheet with only horizontal gridlines.*

1

- Open the Book Rep table in Datasheet view, if it is not already open.
- If necessary, close the Navigation Pane.
- Tap or click the datasheet selector, the box in the upper-left corner of the datasheet, to select the entire datasheet (Figure 3–61).

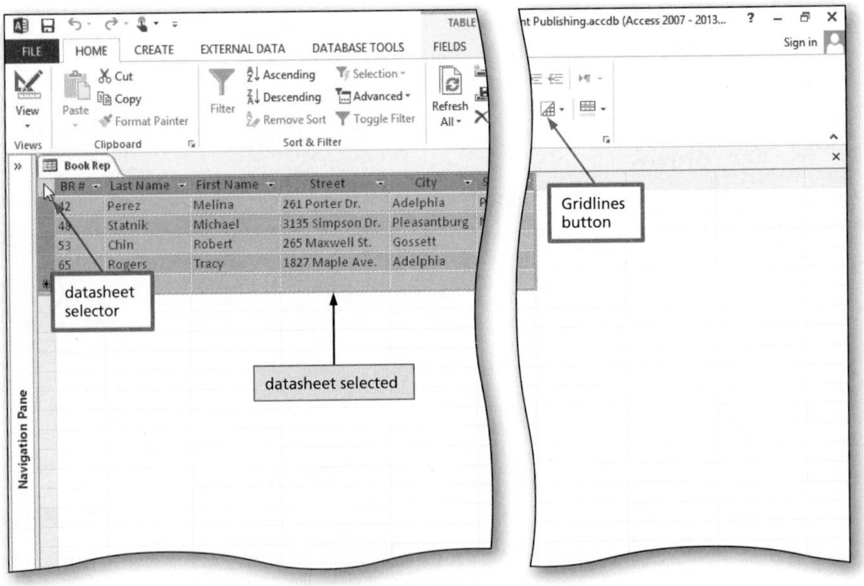

Figure 3–61

2

- Tap or click the Gridlines button (HOME tab | Text Formatting group) to display the Gridlines gallery (Figure 3–62).

Q&A Does it matter whether I tap or click the button or the arrow?
In this case, it does not matter. Either action will display the gallery.

3

- Tap or click Gridlines: Horizontal in the Gridlines gallery to include only horizontal gridlines.

Experiment

- Experiment with other gridline options. When finished, once again select horizontal gridlines.

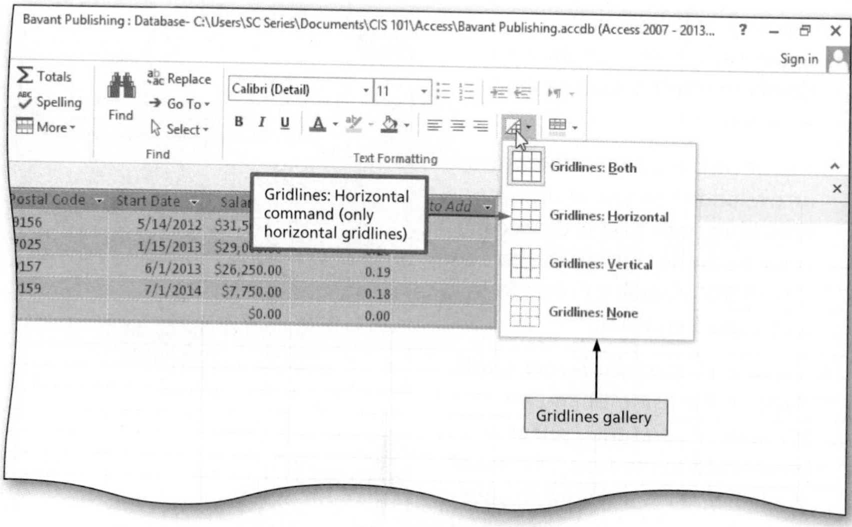

Figure 3–62

To Change the Colors and Font in a Datasheet

1 UPDATE RECORDS | 2 FILTER RECORDS | 3 CHANGE STRUCTURE | 4 MASS CHANGES | 5 VALIDATION RULES
6 CHANGE APPEARANCE | 7 REFERENTIAL INTEGRITY | 8 ORDER RECORDS

You also can modify the appearance of the datasheet by changing the colors and the font. The following steps change the Alternate Fill color, a color that appears on every other row in the datasheet. ***Why?*** *Having rows appear in alternate colors is an attractive way to visually separate the rows.* The steps also change the font color, the font, and the font size.

1

- With the datasheet for the Book Rep table selected, tap or click the Alternate Row Color button arrow (HOME tab | Text Formatting group) to display the color palette (Figure 3–63).

Q&A Does it matter whether I tap or click the button or the arrow?
Yes. Clicking the arrow produces a color palette. Clicking the button applies the currently selected color. When in doubt, you should tap or click the arrow.

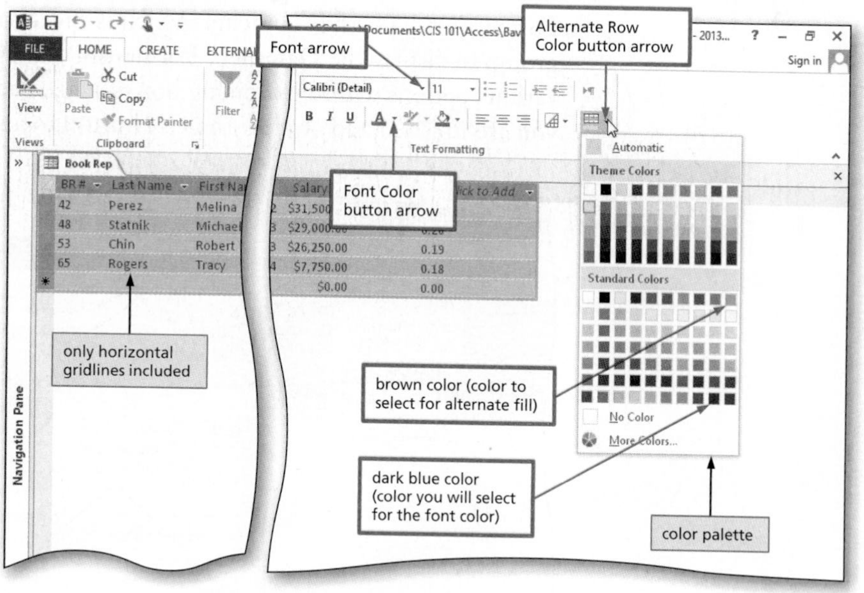

Figure 3–63

2

- Tap or click Brown in the upper-right corner of Standard Colors to select brown as the alternate color.
- Tap or click the Font Color button arrow, and then tap or click the dark blue color that is the second color from the right in the bottom row in the Standard Colors to select the font color.
- Tap or click the Font arrow, scroll down in the list until Bodoni MT appears, and then select Bodoni MT as the font. (If it is not available, select any font of your choice.)
- Tap or click the Font Size arrow and select 10 as the font size (Figure 3–64).

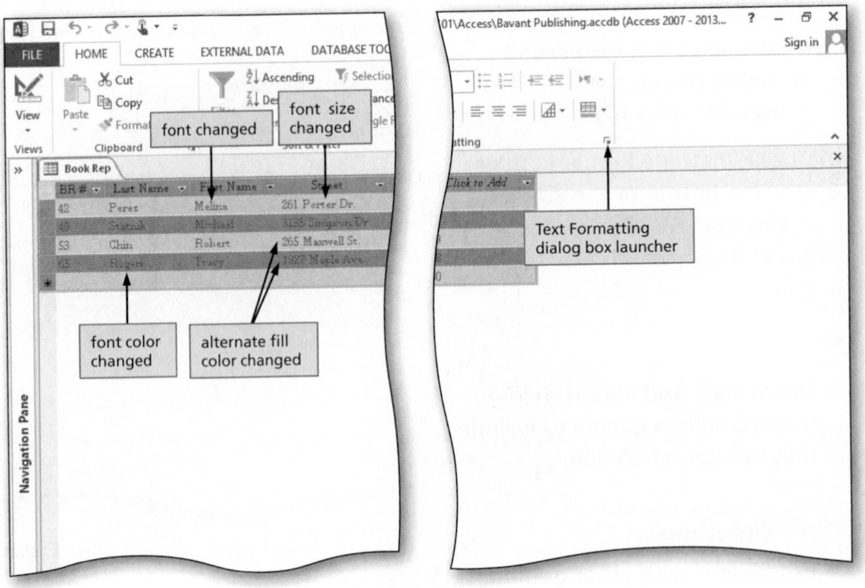

Figure 3–64

Q&A Does the order in which I make these selections make a difference?
No. You could have made these selections in any order.

Experiment

- Experiment with other colors, fonts, and font sizes. When finished, return to the options selected in this step.

Using the Datasheet Formatting Dialog Box

As an alternative to using the individual buttons, you can tap or click the Datasheet Formatting dialog box launcher, which is the arrow at the right of the Text Formatting group, to display the Datasheet Formatting dialog box (Figure 3–65). You can use the various options within the dialog box to make changes to the datasheet format. Once you are finished, tap or click the OK button to apply your changes.

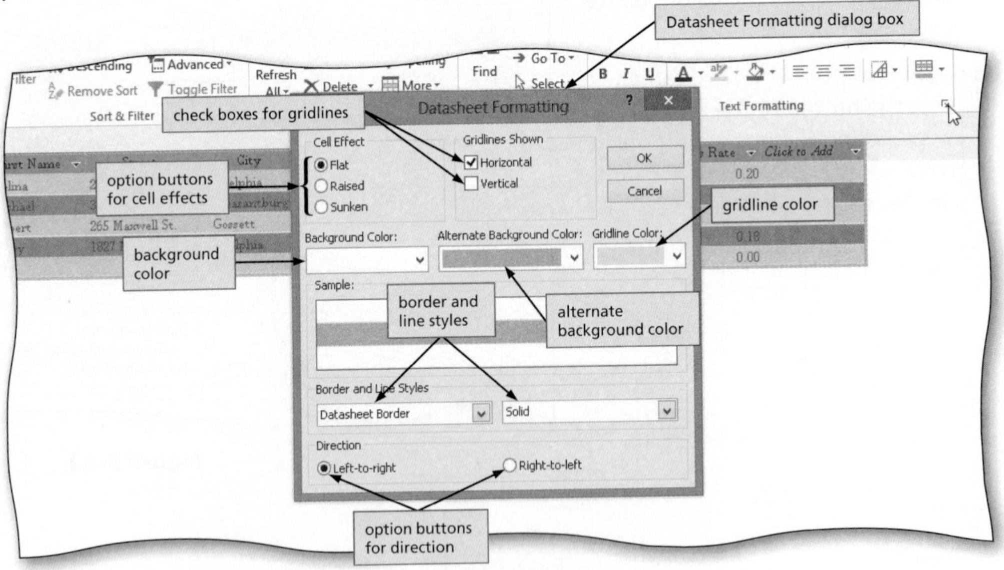

Figure 3–65

To Close the Datasheet without Saving the Format Changes

The following steps close the datasheet without saving the changes to the format. Because the changes are not saved, the next time you open the Book Rep table in Datasheet view, it will appear in the original format. If you had saved the changes, the changes would be reflected in its appearance.

1. Close the Book Rep table.
2. Tap or click the No button in the Microsoft Access dialog box when asked if you want to save your changes.

CONSIDER THIS

What kind of decisions should I make in determining whether to change the format of a datasheet?

- Would totals or other calculations be useful in the datasheet? If so, include the Total row and select the appropriate computations.
- Would another gridline style make the datasheet more useful? If so, change to the desired gridlines.
- Would alternating colors in the rows make them easier to read? If so, change the alternate fill color.
- Would a different font and/or font color make the text stand out better? If so, change the font color and/or the font.
- Is the font size appropriate? Can you see enough data at one time on the screen and yet have the data be readable? If not, change the font size to an appropriate value.
- Is the column spacing appropriate? Are some columns wider than they need to be? Do some columns not display all the data? Change the column sizes as necessary.

As a general guideline, once you have decided on a particular look for a datasheet, all datasheets in the database should have the same look, unless there is a compelling reason for a datasheet to differ.

Multivalued Fields in Queries

You can use multivalued fields in queries in the same way you use other fields in queries. You can choose to display the multiple values either on a single row or on multiple rows in the query results.

BTW
Using Criteria with Multivalued Fields
To enter criteria in a multivalued field, simply enter the criteria in the Criteria row. For example, to find all customers who need audio, enter Audio in the Criteria row.

To Include Multiple Values on One Row of a Query

1 UPDATE RECORDS | 2 FILTER RECORDS | 3 CHANGE STRUCTURE | 4 MASS CHANGES | 5 VALIDATION RULES
6 CHANGE APPEARANCE | **7 REFERENTIAL INTEGRITY** | **8 ORDER RECORDS**

To include a multivalued field in the results of a query, place the field in the query design grid just like any other field. ***Why?*** *When you treat the multivalued field like any other field, the results will list all of the values for the multivalued field on a single row.* The following steps create a query to display the customer number, customer name, customer type, and resources needed for all customers.

1

- Create a query for the Customer table and close the Navigation Pane.
- Include the Customer Number, Customer Name, Customer Type, and Resources Needed fields (Figure 3–66).

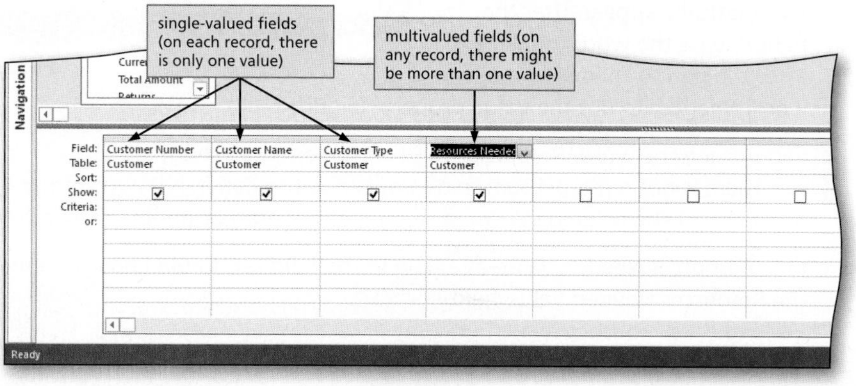

Figure 3–66

2

- Run the query and view the results (Figure 3–67).

Q&A Can I include criteria for the multivalued field?
Yes. You can include criteria for the multivalued field.

3

- Save the query as Ch3q01.

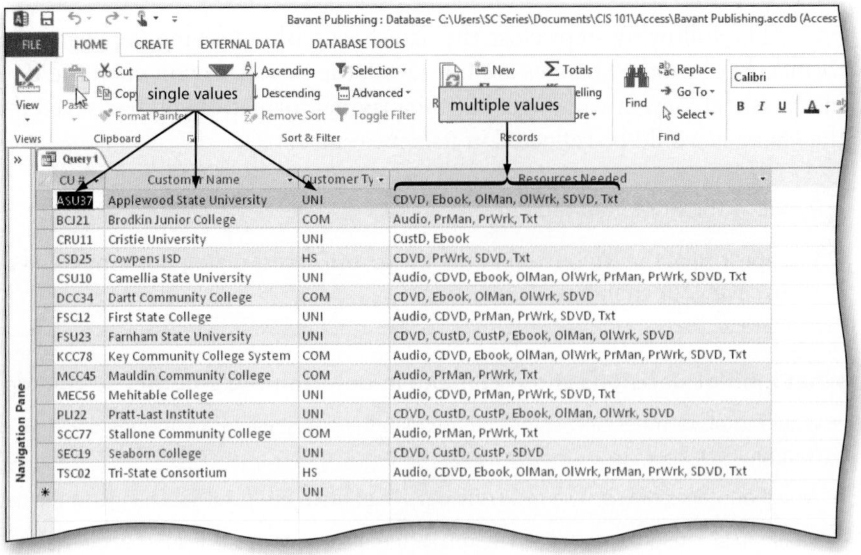

Figure 3–67

To Include Multiple Values on Multiple Rows of a Query

1 UPDATE RECORDS | 2 FILTER RECORDS | 3 CHANGE STRUCTURE | 4 MASS CHANGES | 5 VALIDATION RULES
6 CHANGE APPEARANCE | **7 REFERENTIAL INTEGRITY** | **8 ORDER RECORDS**

You may want to see the multiple resources needed for a customer on separate rows rather than a single row. ***Why?*** *Each row in the results will focus on one specific resource that is needed.* To do so, you need to use the Value property of the Resources Needed field, by following the name of the field with a period and then the word, Value. The following steps use the Value property to display each resource on a separate row.

1

- Return to Design view and ensure that the Customer Number, Customer Name, Customer Type, and Resources Needed fields are included in the design grid.
- Tap or click the Resources Needed field to produce an insertion point, press the RIGHT ARROW key as necessary to move the insertion point to the end of the field name, and then type a period.
- If the word, Value, did not automatically appear after the period, type the word **value** after the period following the word, Needed, to use the Value property (Figure 3–68).

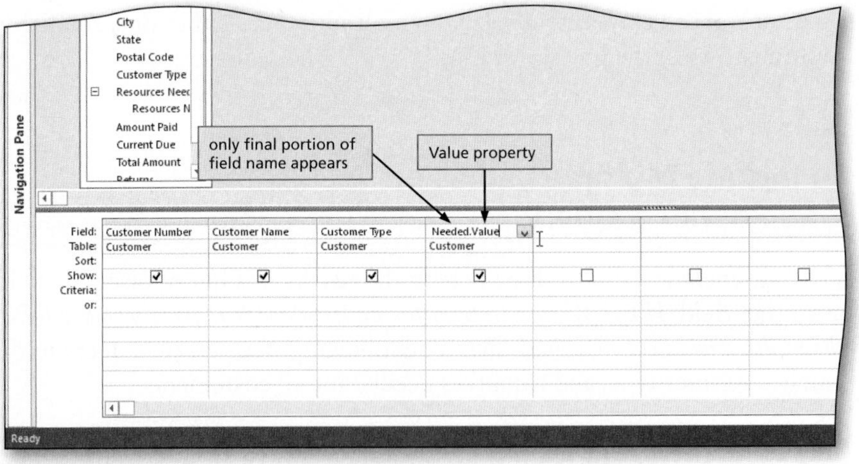

Figure 3–68

Q&A I do not see the word, Resources. Did I do something wrong?
No. There is not enough room to display the entire name. If you wanted to see it, you could point to the right boundary of the column selector and then either drag or double-tap or double-click.

I see Resources Needed.Value as a field in the field list. Could I have deleted the Resources Needed field and added the Resources Needed.Value field?
Yes. Either approach is fine.

2

- Run the query and view the results (Figure 3–69).

Q&A Can I now include criteria for the multivalued field?

Yes. You could enter a criterion just like in any other query.

3

- Save the query as a new object in the database named Ch3q02.
- Close the query.

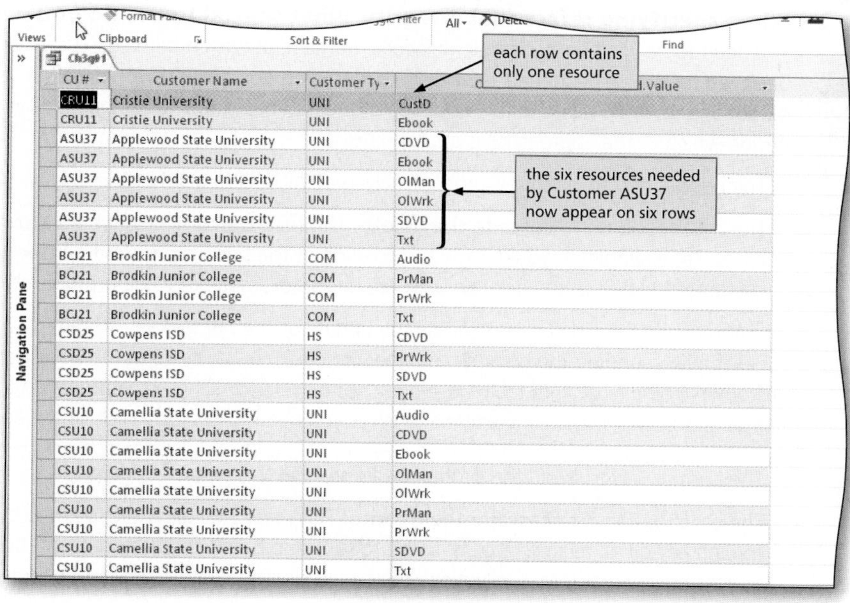

Figure 3–69

Break Point: If you wish to take a break, this is a good place to do so. You can quit Access now. To resume at a later time, start Access, open the database called Bavant Publishing, and continue following the steps from this location forward.

Referential Integrity

When you have two related tables in a database, it is essential that the data in the common fields match. There should not be a customer in the Customer table whose book rep number is 42, for example, unless there is a record in the Book Rep table whose number is 42. This restriction is enforced through **referential integrity**, which is the property that ensures that the value in a foreign key must match that of another table's primary key.

A **foreign key** is a field in one table whose values are required to match the *primary key* of another table. In the Customer table, the Book Rep Number field is a foreign key that must match the primary key of the Book Rep table; that is, the book rep number for any customer must be a book rep currently in the Book Rep table. A customer whose book rep number is 92, for example, should not be stored because no such book rep exists.

In Access, to specify referential integrity, you must explicitly define a relationship between the tables by using the Relationships button. As part of the process of defining a relationship, you indicate that Access is to enforce referential integrity. Access then prohibits any updates to the database that would violate the referential integrity.

The type of relationship between two tables specified by the Relationships command is referred to as a **one-to-many relationship**. This means that *one* record in the first table is related to, or matches, *many* records in the second table, but each record in the second table is related to only *one* record in the first. In the Bavant Publishing database, for example, a one-to-many relationship exists between the Book Rep table and the Customer table. *One* book rep is associated with *many* customers, but each customer is associated with only a single book rep. In general, the table containing the foreign key will be the *many* part of the relationship.

BTW

Relationships

You also can use the Relationships window to specify a one-to-one relationship. In a one-to-one relationship, the matching fields are both primary keys. If Bavant Publishing maintained a company car for each book rep, the data concerning the cars might be kept in a Car table, in which the primary key is Book Rep Number — the same primary key as the Book Rep table. Thus, there would be a one-to-one relationship between book reps and cars.

CONSIDER THIS

When specifying referential integrity, what special issues do you need to address?

You need to decide how to handle deletions. In the relationship between customers and book reps, for example, deletion of a book rep for whom customers exist, such as book rep number 42, would violate referential integrity. Customers for book rep 42 no longer would relate to any book rep in the database. You can handle this in two ways. For each relationship, you need to decide which of the approaches is appropriate.

- The normal way to avoid this problem is to prohibit such a deletion.
- The other option is to **cascade the delete.** This means that Access would allow the deletion but then delete all related records. For example, it would allow the deletion of the book rep from the Book Rep table but then automatically delete any customers related to the deleted book rep. In this example, cascading the delete would obviously not be appropriate.

You also need to decide how to handle the update of the primary key. In the relationship between book reps and customers, for example, changing the book rep number for book rep 42 to 43 in the Book Rep table would cause a problem because some customers in the Customer table have book rep number 42. These customers no longer would relate to any book rep. You can handle this in two ways. For each relationship, you need to decide which of the approaches is appropriate.

- The normal way to avoid this problem is to prohibit this type of update.
- The other option is to **cascade the update.** This means to allow the change, but make the corresponding change in the foreign key on all related records. In the relationship between customers and book reps, for example, Access would allow the update but then automatically make the corresponding change for any customer whose book rep number was 42. It now will be 43.

To Specify Referential Integrity

1 UPDATE RECORDS | 2 FILTER RECORDS | 3 CHANGE STRUCTURE | 4 MASS CHANGES | 5 VALIDATION RULES
6 CHANGE APPEARANCE | **7 REFERENTIAL INTEGRITY** | **8 ORDER RECORDS**

The following steps use the Relationships button on the DATABASE TOOLS tab to specify referential integrity by explicitly indicating a relationship between the Book Rep and Customer tables. The steps also ensure that updates will cascade, but that deletes will not. ***Why?*** *By specifying that updates will cascade, it will be possible to change the Book Rep Number for a book rep, and the same change will automatically be made for all customers of that book rep. By not specifying that deletes will cascade, it will not be possible to delete a book rep who has related customers.*

1

- Tap or click DATABASE TOOLS on the ribbon to display the DATABASE TOOLS tab. (Figure 3–70).

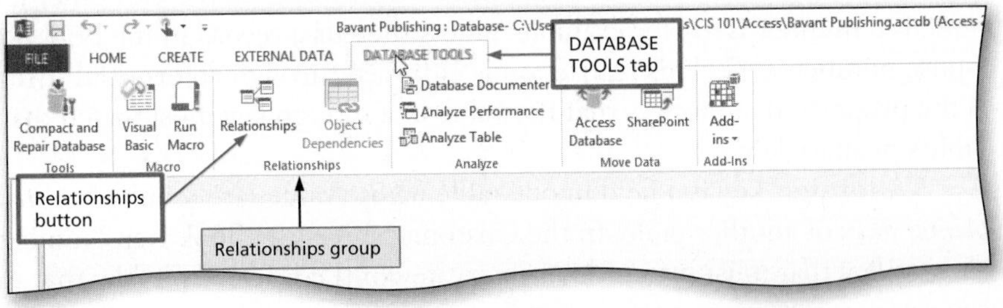

Figure 3–70

2

- Tap or click the Relationships button (DATABASE TOOLS tab | Relationships group) to open the Relationships window and display the Show Table dialog box (Figure 3–71).

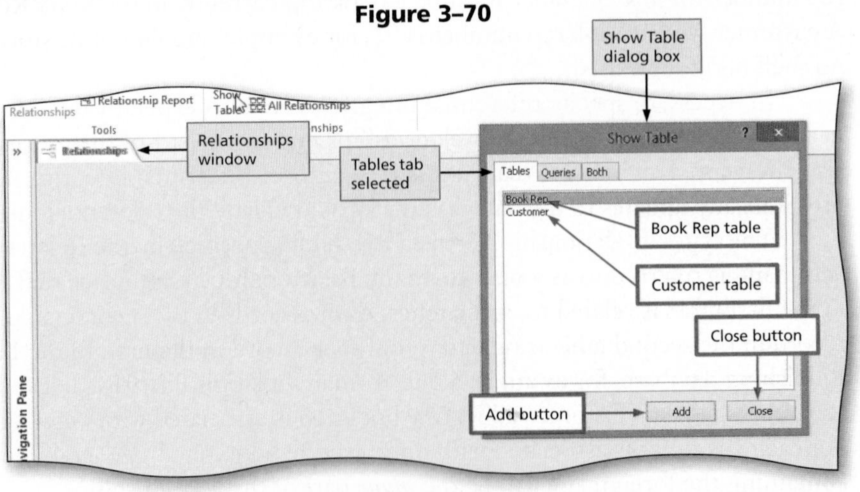

Figure 3–71

3

- If necessary, tap or click the Book Rep table (Show Table dialog box), and then tap or click the Add button to add a field list for the Book Rep table to the Relationships window.
- Tap or click the Customer table (Show Table dialog box), and then tap or click the Add button to add a field list for the Customer table to the Relationships window.
- Tap or click the Close button (Show Table dialog box) to close the dialog box.
- Resize the field lists that appear so all fields are visible (Figure 3–72).

Q&A Do I need to resize the field lists?
No. You can use the scroll bars to view the fields. Before completing the next step, however, you would need to make sure the Book Rep Number fields in both tables appear on the screen.

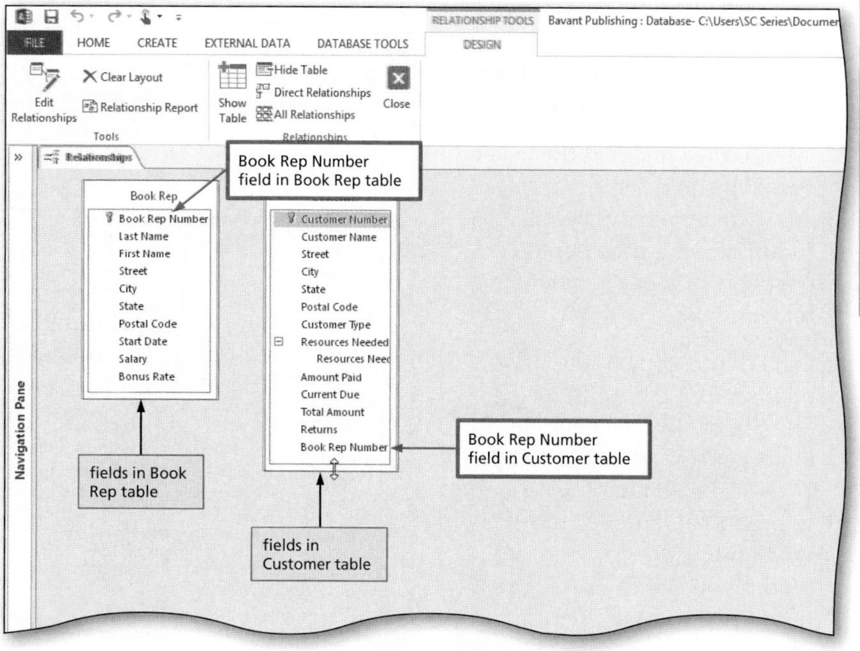

Figure 3–72

4

- Drag the Book Rep Number field in the Book Rep table field list to the Book Rep Number field in the Customer table field list to display the Edit Relationships dialog box to create a relationship.

Q&A Do I actually move the field from the Book Rep table to the Customer table?
No. The pointer will change shape to indicate you are in the process of dragging, but the field does not move.

- Tap or click the 'Enforce Referential Integrity' check box (Edit Relationships dialog box).
- Tap or click the 'Cascade Update Related Fields' check box (Figure 3–73).

Q&A The Cascade check boxes were dim until I clicked the 'Enforce Referential Integrity' check box. Is that correct?
Yes. Until you have chosen to enforce referential integrity, the cascade options are not applicable.

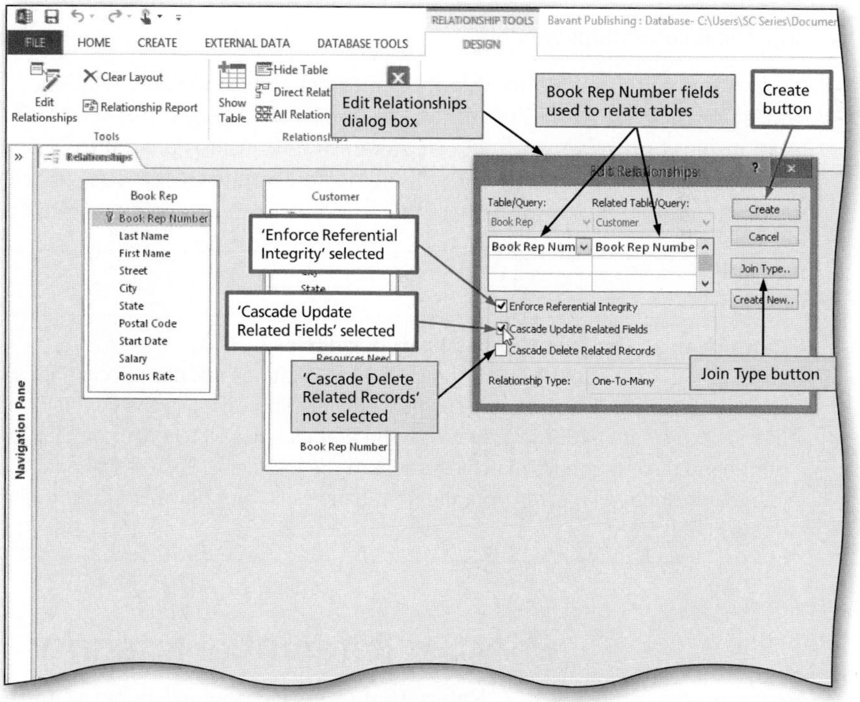

Figure 3–73

5

- Tap or click the Create button (Edit Relationships dialog box) to complete the creation of the relationship (Figure 3–74).

Q&A What is the symbol at the lower end of the join line?
It is the mathematical symbol for infinity. It is used here to denote the "many" end of the relationship.

Can I print a copy of the relationship?
Yes. Tap or click the Relationship Report button (RELATIONSHIP TOOLS DESIGN tab | Tools group) to produce a report of the relationship. You can print the report. You also can save it as a report in the database for future use. If you do not want to save it, close the report after you have printed it and do not save the changes.

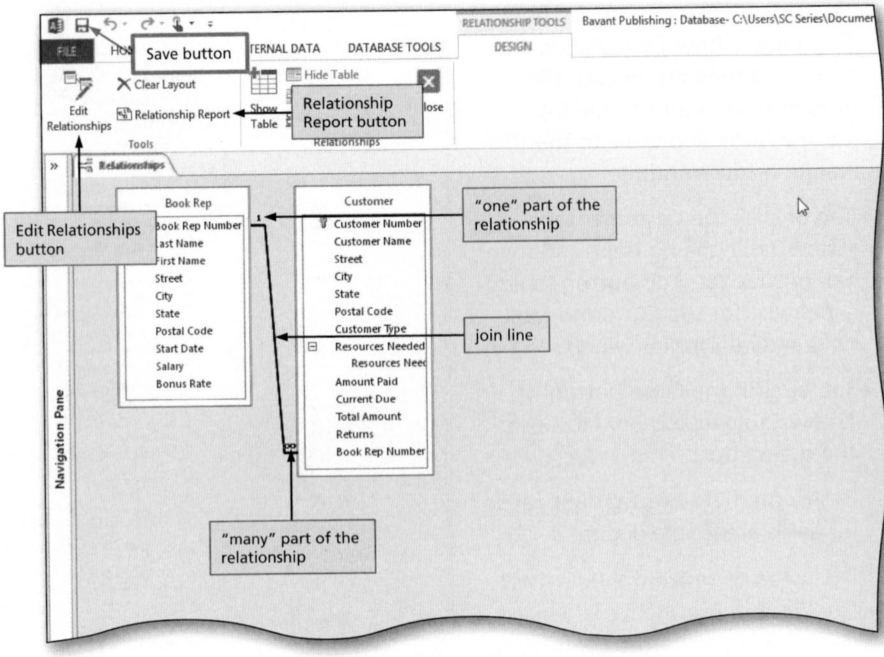

Figure 3–74

6

- Tap or click the Save button on the Quick Access Toolbar to save the relationship you created.
- Close the Relationships window.

Q&A Can I later modify the relationship if I want to change it in some way?
Yes. Tap or click DATABASE TOOLS on the ribbon to display the DATABASE TOOLS tab, and then tap or click the Relationships button (DATABASE TOOLS tab | Relationships group) to open the Relationships window. To add another table, tap or click the Show Table button on the Design tab. To remove a table, tap or click the Hide Table button. To edit a relationship, select the relationship and tap or click the Edit Relationships button.

CONSIDER THIS

Can I change the join type as I can in queries?
Yes. Tap or click the Join Type button in the Edit Relationships dialog box. Tap or click option button 1 to create an INNER join, that is, a join in which only records with matching values in the join fields appear in the result. Tap or click option button 2 to create a LEFT join, that is, a join that includes all records from the left-hand table, but only records from the right-hand table that have matching values in the join fields. Tap or click option button 3 to create a RIGHT join, that is, a join that includes all records from the right-hand table, but only records from the left-hand table that have matching values in the join fields.

BTW
Exporting a Relationship Report
You also can export a relationship report. To export a report as a PDF or XPS file, press and hold or right-click the report in the Navigation Pane, tap or click Export on the shortcut menu, and then tap or click PDF or XPS as the file type.

Effect of Referential Integrity

Referential integrity now exists between the Book Rep and Customer tables. Access now will reject any number in the Book Rep Number field in the Customer table that does not match a book rep number in the Book Rep table. Attempting to change the book rep number for a customer to one that does not match any book rep in the Book Rep table would result in the error message shown in Figure 3–75. Similarly, attempting to add a customer whose book rep number does not match would produce the same error message.

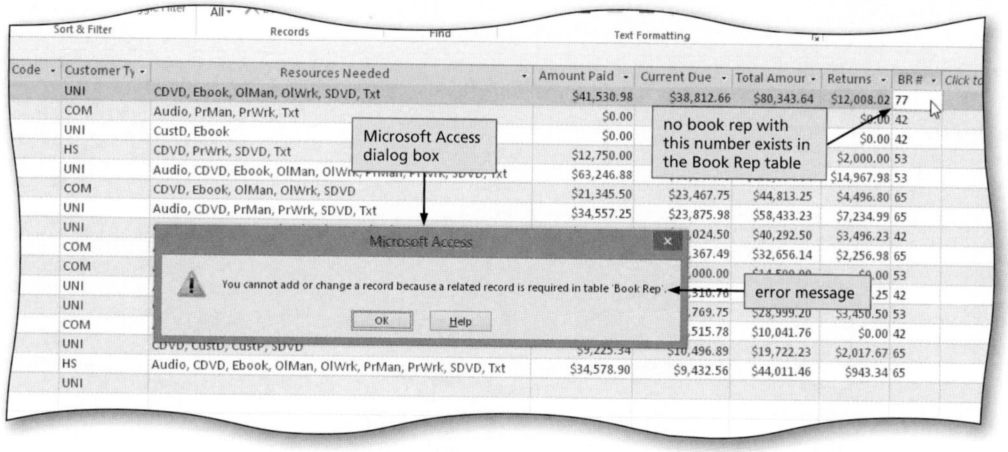

Figure 3–75

Access also will reject the deletion of a book rep for whom related customers exist. Attempting to delete book rep 42 from the Book Rep table, for example, would result in the message shown in Figure 3–76.

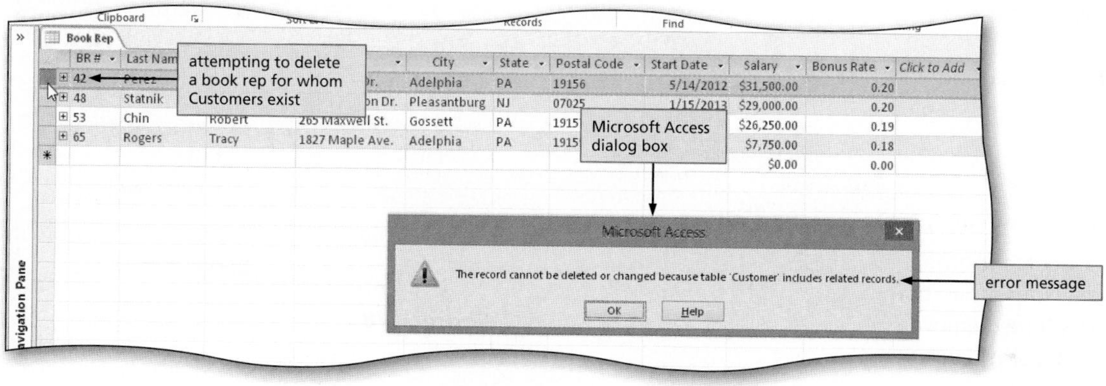

Figure 3–76

Access would, however, allow the change of a book rep number in the Book Rep table. Then it automatically makes the corresponding change to the book rep number for all the book rep's customers. For example, if you changed the book rep number of book rep 42 to 24, the same 24 would appear in the book rep number field for customers whose book rep number had been 42.

To Use a Subdatasheet

1 UPDATE RECORDS | 2 FILTER RECORDS | 3 CHANGE STRUCTURE | 4 MASS CHANGES | 5 VALIDATION RULES
6 CHANGE APPEARANCE | 7 REFERENTIAL INTEGRITY | **8 ORDER RECORDS**

It is possible to view the customers of a given book rep when you are viewing the datasheet for the Book Rep table. ***Why is data from one table visible when viewing the other table?*** *The Book Rep table is now explicitly related to the Customer table.* One consequence of the tables being explicitly related is that the customers for a book rep can appear below the book rep in a **subdatasheet**. The availability of such a subdatasheet is indicated by a plus sign that appears in front of the rows in the Book Rep table. The steps on the next page display the subdatasheet for book rep 53.

1

- Open the Book Rep table in Datasheet view and close the Navigation Pane (Figure 3–77).

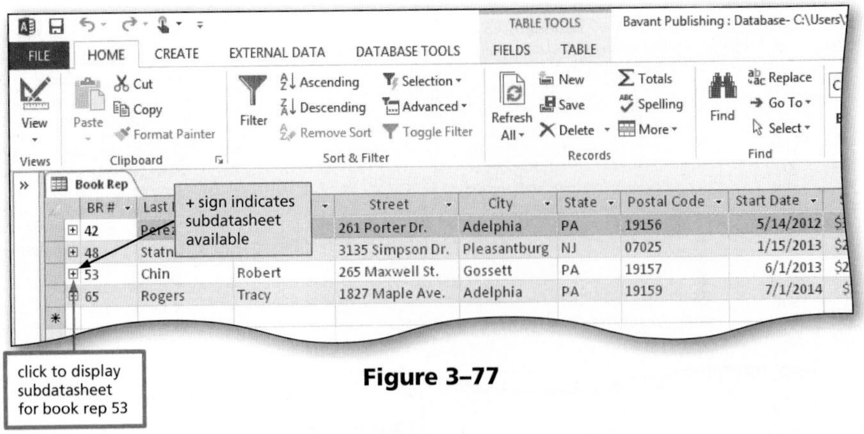

Figure 3–77

2

- Tap or click the plus sign in front of the row for book rep 53 to display the subdatasheet (Figure 3–78).

Q&A How do I hide the subdatasheet when I no longer want it to appear?
When you clicked the plus sign, it changed to a minus sign. Tap or click the minus sign.

Experiment

- Display subdatasheets for other book reps. Display more than one subdatasheet at a time. Remove the subdatasheets from the screen.

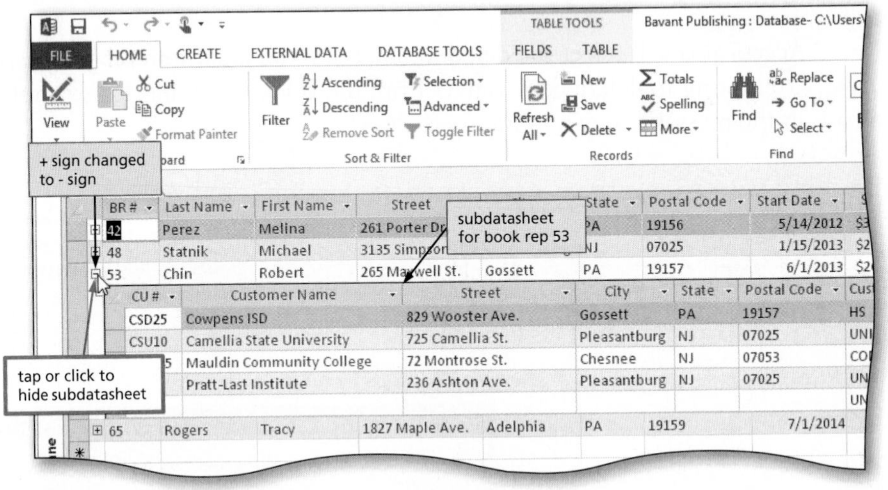

Figure 3–78

3

- If requested by your instructor, replace the city and state for book rep 53 with your city and state.
- Close the datasheet for the Book Rep table.

Handling Data Inconsistency

In many organizations, databases evolve and change over time. One department may create a database for its own internal use. Employees in another department may decide they need their own database containing much of the same information. For example, the Purchasing department of an organization may create a database of products that it buys and the Receiving department may create a database of products that it receives. Each department is keeping track of the same products. When the organization eventually merges the databases, they may find inconsistencies and duplication. The Find Duplicates Query Wizard and the Find Unmatched Query Wizard can assist in clearing the resulting database of duplication and errors.

To Find Duplicate Records

One reason to include a primary key for a table is to eliminate duplicate records. A possibility still exists, however, that duplicate records can get into your database. You would use the following steps to find duplicate records using the Find Duplicates Query Wizard.

1. Tap or click CREATE on the ribbon, and then tap or click the Query Wizard button (CREATE tab | Queries group).
2. When Access displays the New Query dialog box, tap or click the Find Duplicates Query Wizard and then tap or click the OK button.
3. Identify the table and field or fields that might contain duplicate information.
4. Indicate any other fields you want displayed.
5. Finish the wizard to see any duplicate records.

To Find Unmatched Records

Occasionally, you might need to find records in one table that have no matching records in another table. For example, you may want to determine which book reps currently have no customers. You would use the following steps to find unmatched records using the Find Unmatched Query Wizard.

1. Tap or click CREATE on the ribbon, and then tap or click the Query Wizard button (CREATE tab | Queries group).
2. When Access displays the New Query dialog box, tap or click the Find Unmatched Query Wizard and then tap or click the OK button.
3. Identify the table that might contain unmatched records, and then identify the related table.
4. Indicate the fields you want displayed.
5. Finish the wizard to see any unmatched records.

Ordering Records

Normally, Access sequences the records in the Customer table by customer number whenever listing them because the Customer Number field is the primary key. You can change this order, if desired.

To Use the Ascending Button to Order Records

1 UPDATE RECORDS | 2 FILTER RECORDS | 3 CHANGE STRUCTURE | 4 MASS CHANGES | 5 VALIDATION RULES
6 CHANGE APPEARANCE | 7 REFERENTIAL INTEGRITY | **8 ORDER RECORDS**

To change the order in which records appear, use the Ascending or Descending buttons. Either button reorders the records based on the field in which the insertion point is located.

The steps on the next page order the records by city using the Ascending button. ***Why?*** *Using the Ascending button is the quickest and easiest way to order records.*

1

- Open the Customer table in Datasheet view and close the Navigation Pane.
- Tap or click the City field on the first record to select the field (Figure 3–79).

Q&A Did I have to tap or click the field on the first record?
No. Any other record would have worked as well.

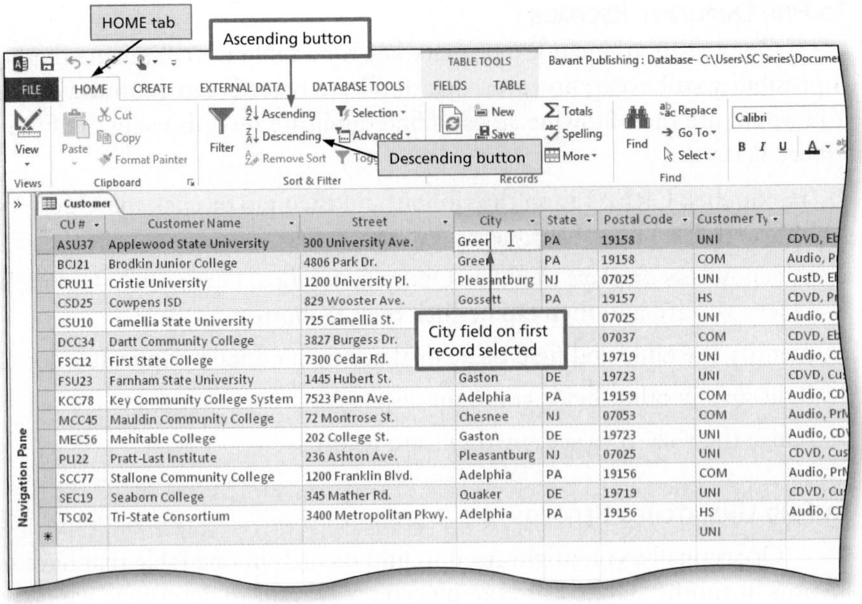

Figure 3–79

2

- Tap or click the Ascending button (HOME tab | Sort & Filter group) to sort the records by City (Figure 3–80).

3

- Close the Customer table.
- Tap or click the No button (Microsoft Access dialog box) when asked if you want to save your changes.

Q&A What if I saved the changes?
The next time you open the table the records will be sorted by city.

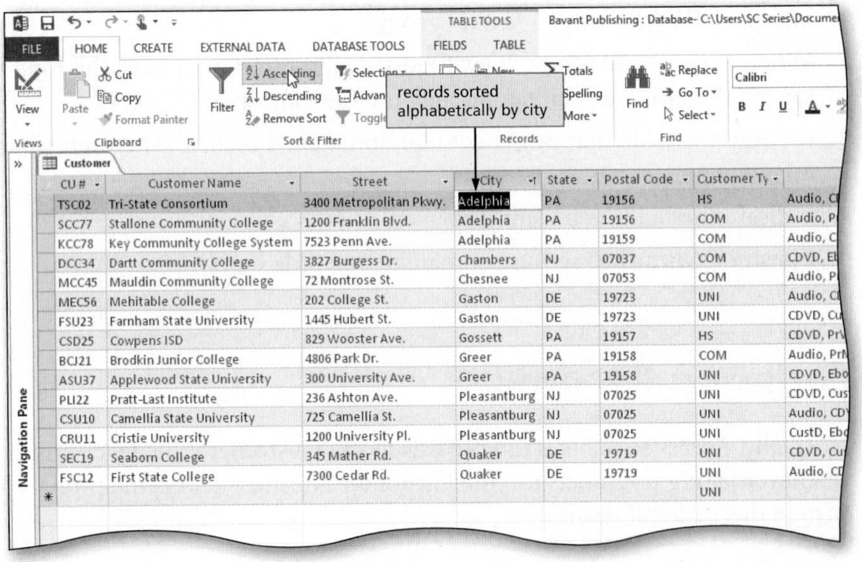

Figure 3–80

Other Ways

1. Press and hold or right-click field name, tap or click Sort A to Z (for ascending) or Sort Z to A (for descending)

To Use the Ascending Button to Order Records on Multiple Fields

Just as you are able to sort the answer to a query on multiple fields, you also can sort the data that appears in a datasheet on multiple fields. To do so, the major and minor keys must be next to each other in the datasheet with the major key on the left. (If this is not the case, you can drag the columns into the correct position. Instead of dragging, however, usually it will be easier to use a query that has the data sorted in the desired order.)

To sort on a combination of fields where the major key is just to the left of the minor key, you would use the following steps.

1. Tap or click the field selector at the top of the major key column to select the entire column.
2. Hold down the SHIFT key and then tap or click the field selector for the minor key column to select both columns.
3. Tap or click the Ascending button to sort the records.

To Sign Out of a Microsoft Account

If you are signed in to a Microsoft account and are using a public computer or otherwise wish to sign out of your Microsoft account, you should sign out of the account from the Account gallery in the Backstage view before exiting Access. Signing out of the account is the safest way to make sure that nobody else can access SkyDrive files or settings stored in your Microsoft account. The following steps sign out of a Microsoft account from Access. For a detailed example of the procedure summarized below, refer to the Office and Windows chapter at the beginning of this book.

1. If you wish to sign out of your Microsoft account, tap or click FILE on the ribbon to open the Backstage view and then tap or click the Account tab to display the Account gallery.
2. Tap or click the Sign out link, which displays the Remove Account dialog box. If a Can't remove Windows accounts dialog box appears instead of the Remove Account dialog box, click the OK button and skip the remaining steps.

Q&A Why does a Can't remove Windows accounts dialog box appear?
If you signed in to Windows using your Microsoft account, then you also must sign out from Windows, rather than signing out from within Access. When you are finished using Windows, be sure to sign out at that time.

3. Tap or click the Yes button (Remove Account dialog box) to sign out of your Microsoft account on this computer.

Q&A Should I sign out of Windows after signing out of my Microsoft account?
When you are finished using the computer, you should sign out of your account for maximum security.

4. Tap or click the Back button in the upper-left corner of the Backstage view to return to the database.

BTW
Certification
The Microsoft Office Specialist (MOS) program provides an opportunity for you to obtain a valuable industry credential — proof that you have the Access 2013 skills required by employers. For more information, visit the Certification resource on the Student Companion Site located on www.cengagebrain.com. For detailed instructions about accessing available resources, visit www.cengage.com/ct/studentdownload or contact your instructor for information about accessing the required files.

BTW
Quick Reference
For a table that lists how to complete the tasks covered in this book using touch gestures, the mouse, ribbon, shortcut menu, and keyboard, see the Quick Reference Summary at the back of this book, or visit the Quick Reference resource on the Student Companion Site located on www.cengagebrain.com. For detailed instructions about accessing available resources, visit www.cengage.com/ct/studentdownload or contact your instructor for information about accessing the required files.

To Exit Access

This project now is complete. The following steps exit Access.

1. Tap or click the Close button on the right side of the title bar to exit Access.
2. If a Microsoft Access dialog box appears, tap or click the Save button to save any changes made to the object since the last save.

Chapter Summary

In this chapter you have learned how to use a form to add records to a table, search for records, delete records, filter records, create and use lookup fields, create calculated fields, create and use multivalued fields, make mass changes, create validation rules, change the appearance of a datasheet, specify referential integrity, and use subdatasheets. The items listed below include all the new Access skills you have learned in this chapter, with tasks grouped by activity.

Data Inconsistency
- Find Duplicate Records (AC 187)
- Find Unmatched Records (AC 187)

Datasheet Appearance
- Include Totals in a Datasheet (AC 175)
- Change Gridlines in a Datasheet (AC 176)
- Change the Colors and Font in a Datasheet (AC 177)

Filter Records
- Use Filter By Selection (AC 147)
- Toggle a Filter (AC 148)
- Use a Common Filter (AC 148)
- Use Filter By Form (AC 150)
- Use Advanced Filter/Sort (AC 151)

Form Creation and Use
- Create a Split Form (AC 141)
- Use a Form to Add Records (AC 143)

Lookup Field Use
- Use a Lookup Field (AC 169)
- Use a Multivalued Lookup Field (AC 170)

Mass Changes
- Use an Update Query (AC 160)
- Use a Delete Query (AC 161)
- Use an Append Query (AC 162)
- Use a Make-Table Query (AC 162)

Multivalued Fields
- Include Multiple Values on One Row of a Query (AC 179)
- Include Multiple Values on Multiple Rows of a Query (AC 180)

Referential Integrity
- Specify Referential Integrity (AC 182)
- Use a Subdatasheet (AC 185)

Sort Records
- Use the Ascending Button to Order Records (AC 187)
- Use the Ascending Button to Order Records on Multiple Fields (AC 188)

Structure Change
- Delete a Field (AC 153)
- Move a Field (AC 154)
- Add a New Field (AC 154)
- Create a Lookup Field (AC 154)
- Modify Single or Multivalued Lookup Fields (AC 157)
- Add a Calculated Field (AC 158)
- Update a Report to Reflect the Changes in the Table (AC 172)

Table Update
- Search for a Record (AC 143)
- Update the Contents of a Record (AC 145)
- Delete a Record (AC 145)
- Change the Contents of a Field (AC 168)

Validation Rules
- Specify a Required Field (AC 163)
- Specify a Range (AC 164)
- Specify a Default Value (AC 164)
- Specify a Collection of Legal Values (AC 165)
- Specify a Format (AC 165)

CONSIDER THIS

What decisions will you need to make when maintaining your own databases?

Use these guidelines as you complete the assignments in this chapter and maintain your own databases outside of this class.

1. Determine when it is necessary to add, change, or delete records in a database.
2. Determine whether you should filter records.
   a) If your criterion for filtering is that the value in a particular field matches or does not match a certain specific value, use Filter By Selection.
   b) If your criterion only involves a single field but is more complex, use a common filter.
   c) If your criterion involves more than one field, use Filter By Form.
   d) If your criterion involves more than a single And or Or, or if it involves sorting, use Advanced Filter/Sort.
3. Determine whether additional fields are necessary or whether existing fields should be deleted.
4. Determine whether validation rules, default values, and formats are necessary.
   a) Can you improve the accuracy of the data entry process by enforcing data validation?
   b) What values are allowed for a particular field?
   c) Are there some fields in which one particular value is used more than another?
   d) Are there some fields for which special formats would be appropriate?
5. Determine whether changes to the format of a datasheet are desirable.
   a) Would totals or other calculations be useful in the datasheet?
   b) Would different gridlines make the datasheet more useful?
   c) Would alternating colors in the rows make them easier to read?
   d) Would a different font and/or font color make the text stand out better?
   e) Is the font size appropriate?
   f) Is the column spacing appropriate?
6. Identify related tables in order to implement relationships between the tables.
   a) Is there a one-to-many relationship between the tables?
   b) If so, which table is the one table?
   c) Which table is the many table?
7. When specifying referential integrity, address deletion and update policies.
   a) Decide how to handle deletions. Should deletion be prohibited or should the delete cascade?
   b) Decide how to handle the update of the primary key. Should the update be prohibited or should the update cascade?

CONSIDER THIS

How should you submit solutions to questions in the assignments identified with a symbol?

Every assignment in this book contains one or more questions identified with a symbol. These questions require you to think beyond the assigned database. Present your solutions to the questions in the format required by your instructor. Possible formats may include one or more of these options: write the answer; create a document that contains the answer; present your answer to the class; discuss your answer in a group; record the answer as audio or video using a webcam, smartphone, or portable media player; or post answers on a blog, wiki, or website.

Apply Your Knowledge

Reinforce the skills and apply the concepts you learned in this chapter.

Adding Lookup Fields, Specifying Validation Rules, Updating Records, Updating Reports, and Creating Relationships

Instructions: Start Access. Open the Apply Cosmetics Naturally database that you modified in Apply Your Knowledge in Chapter 2 on page AC 125. (If you did not complete the exercise, see your instructor for a copy of the modified database.)

Continued >

Apply Your Knowledge *continued*

Perform the following tasks:

1. Open the Customer table in Design view.
2. Add a Lookup field called Customer Type to the Customer table. The field should appear after the Postal Code field. The field will contain data on the type of customer. The customer types are FIT (Fitness Centers, Exercise Studios), RET (retail stores), and SAL (salons, spas). Save the changes to the Customer table.
3. Create the following validation rules for the Customer table.
   a. Specify the legal values FIT, RET, and SAL for the Customer Type field. Enter `Must be FIT, RET, or SAL` as the validation text.
   b. Format the Customer Number field to ensure that any letters entered in the field appear as uppercase.
   c. Make the Customer Name field a required field.
4. Save the changes and close the table. You do not need to test the current data.
5. Create an update query for the Customer table. Change all the entries in the Customer Type field to SAL. Save the query as Customer Type Update Query.
6. Open the Customer table in Datasheet view, update the following records, and then close the table:
   a. Change the customer type for customers CY12, FN19, TT21, and TW56 to FIT.
   b. Change the customer type for customers BL15, EY07, and JN34 to RET.
7. Open the Customer Financial Report in Layout view and add the Customer Type field to the report as shown in Figure 3–81. Save the report.

Customer Financial Report

Tuesday, September 30, 2014
1:39:09 PM

Customer Number	Customer Name	Customer Type	Amount Paid	Balance	Sales Rep Number
AS24	Ashley's Salon	SAL	$1,789.65	$236.99	34
BA35	Beauty for All	SAL	$0.00	$275.75	41
BL15	Blondie's on Main	RET	$1,350.00	$555.00	39
CL09	Casual Looks	SAL	$1,245.45	$297.95	41
CY12	Curlin Yoga Studio	FIT	$740.25	$175.86	39
DB14	Della's Beauty Place	SAL	$859.89	$341.78	34
EY07	Environmentally Yours	RET	$1,765.00	$0.00	34
FN19	Fitness Counts	FIT	$1,976.76	$349.95	41
JN34	Just Natural	RET	$810.78	$450.99	39
LB20	Le Beauty	SAL	$1,467.24	$215.99	39
NC25	Nancy's Place	SAL	$675.89	$345.89	34
RD03	Rose's Day Spa	SAL	$1,024.56	$0.00	41
TT21	Tan and Tone	FIT	$925.75	$265.85	34
TW56	The Workout Place	FIT	$154.95	$870.78	41
UR23	U R Beautiful	SAL	$0.00	$1,235.00	39
			$14,786.17	$5,617.78	

Figure 3–81

8. Establish referential integrity between the Sales Rep table (the one table) and the Customer table (the many table). Cascade the update but not the delete. Save the relationship.
9. Create a relationship report for the relationship, save the report, and close the report. (*Hint:* See the Q&A on page AC 184 for directions on creating a relationship report.)
10. If requested to do so by your instructor, rename the relationship report as Relationships for First Name Last Name where First Name Last Name is your name.
11. Submit the revised database in the format specified by your instructor.
12. The Customer Type field currently has three possible values. How would you add the value GRO to the Customer Type list?

Extend Your Knowledge

Extend the skills you learned in this chapter and experiment with new skills. You may need to use Help to complete the assignment.

Creating Action Queries and Adding Totals to a Datasheet

Note: To complete this assignment, you will be required to use the Data Files for Students. Visit www.cengage.com/ct/studentdownload for detailed instructions or contact your instructor for information about accessing the required files.

Instructions: Surplus is a small business that purchases merchandise closeouts and resells to the public. The owner has created an Access database in which to store information about the items he sells. He recently acquired some new inventory. The inventory is currently stored in the Additional Surplus database.

Perform the following tasks:

1. Start Access and open the Additional Surplus database from the Data Files for Students.
2. Create and run an append query to append the data in the Surplus table to the Item table in the Extend Surplus database. The result of the append query will be the Item table shown in Figure 3–82.

Item Code	Description	On Hand	Selling Price	Click to Add
3663	Air Deflector	8	$5.99	
3673	Energy Booklet	25	$2.99	
4553	Energy Saving Kit	7	$43.25	
4573	Faucet Aerator	20	$0.99	
4583	Fluorescent Light Bulb	18	$4.75	
5923	Low Flow Shower Head	11	$8.99	
6185	Luminescent Night Light	12	$4.50	
6234	Programmable Thermostat	3	$36.99	
6345	Rain Gauge	16	$3.15	
7123	Retractable Clothesline	10	$13.99	
7934	Shower Timer	15	$2.99	
8136	Smoke Detector	10	$6.50	
8344	Toilet Tank Water Saver	18	$3.50	
8590	Water Conservation Kit	8	$13.99	
9458	Windows Insulator Kit	10	$5.25	
BA35	Bat House	14	$30.99	
BL06	Bug Mister	9	$8.99	
GF12	Globe Feeder	12	$7.50	
LM05	Leaf Mister	5	$18.00	
SF03	Suet Feeder	8	$3.79	
WF10	Window Feeder	11	$8.49	
*				

Figure 3–82

3. Open the Item table in the Extend Surplus database and sort the datasheet in ascending order by Description.
4. Add a totals row to the datasheet and display the sum of the items on hand and the average selling price. Save the changes to the table layout and close the table.
5. Create and run a make-table query for the Item table to create a new table, Discount Items, in the Extend Surplus database. Only items where the number on hand is fewer than 10 should be included in the Discount Items table.
6. If requested to do so by your instructor, change the description for BA35 in the Item table to First Name Last Name House where First Name and Last Name are your first and last names.
7. Submit the revised database in the format specified by your instructor.
8. If the additional surplus items were in an Excel workbook, how would you add them to the Item table?

Analyze, Correct, Improve

Analyze a database, correct all errors, and improve the design.

Correcting the Database Structure and Improving the Appearance of a Datasheet

Note: To complete this assignment, you will be required to use the Data Files for Students. Visit www.cengage.com/ct/studentdownload for detailed instructions or contact your instructor for information about accessing the required files.

Instructions: Analyze Travel is a database maintained by the International Studies department at your university. The department keeps a database of students interested in Study Abroad programs. The Student table shown in Figure 3–83 contains errors that must be corrected. Some improvements to the table's appearance would make it easier for student workers to use. Start Access and open the Analyze Travel database from the Data Files for Students.

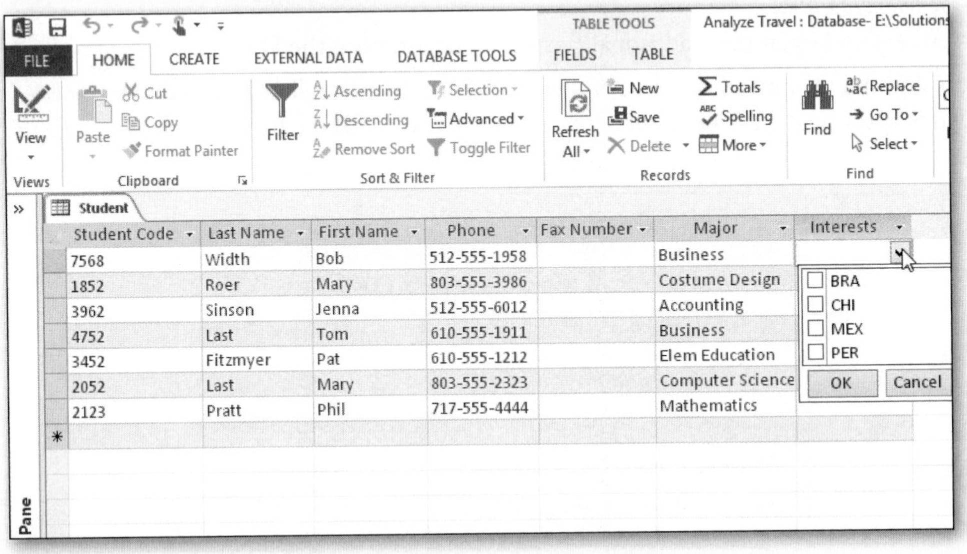

Figure 3–83

1. Correct Interests is a multi-valued field to indicate trips of interest. A trip to Belize (BEL) was omitted from the list and needs to be added. The Fax Number field was added by mistake and must be deleted.

2. Improve Different individuals update this database. Some have complained that the small font combined with the fluorescent lighting makes it difficult to view the table. Change the appearance of the table by changing the font to Arial, the font size to 12, and the alternate fill color to White, Background 1, Darker 15%. Bold the datasheet and sort the table by student last name and first name in ascending order. If instructed to do so by your instructor, change the first name and last name of student 3452 to your first and last name. Save the changes to the layout of the table.

3. What other reasons would a user have for changing the appearance of a datasheet?

In the Labs

Design, create, modify, and/or use a database following the guidelines, concepts, and skills presented in this chapter. Labs are listed in order of increasing difficulty. Labs 1 and 2, which increase in difficulty, require you to create solutions based on what you learned in the chapter; Lab 3 requires you to create a solution, which uses cloud and web technologies, by learning and investigating on your own from general guidance.

Lab 1: Maintaining the Dartt Offsite Services Database

Problem: Dartt Offsite Services is expanding rapidly and needs to make some database changes to handle the expansion. The company needs to know more about its customers, such as services needed. It also needs to add validation rules, and update records in the database.

Note: Use the database modified in Lab 1 of Chapter 2 for this assignment, or see your instructor for information on accessing the files required for this book.

Instructions: Perform the following tasks:

1. Open the Lab 1 Dartt Offsite Services database and open the Client table in Design view.
2. Add a multivalued lookup field, Services Needed, to the Client table. The field should appear after the Postal Code field. Table 3–2 lists the services abbreviations and descriptions that management would like in the multivalued field. Save the change to the table.

Table 3–2 Services Abbreviations and Descriptions

Services Abbreviation	Description
Arch	Archival Storage
Data	Data Backup
Drec	Disaster Recovery
Net	Network Backup
Shrd	Shred Documents
Web	Website Backup

3. Add a calculated field named Total Amount (Amount Paid + Balance Due) to the Client table. The field should follow the Balance Due field. Save the change to the table.
4. Create the following rules for the Client table and save the changes:
   a. Ensure that any letters entered in the Client Number field appear as uppercase.
   b. Make Client Name a required field.
   c. Ensure that only the values SC and NC can be entered in the State field. Include validation text.
   d. Assign a default value of NC to the State field.
5. Use Filter By Form to find all records where the city is Kyle and the balance due is $0.00. Delete the record(s). Do not save the filter.
6. Open the Client table in Datasheet view and add the data shown in Figure 3–84 to the Services Needed field. Resize the field to best fit and save the changes to the layout of the table.

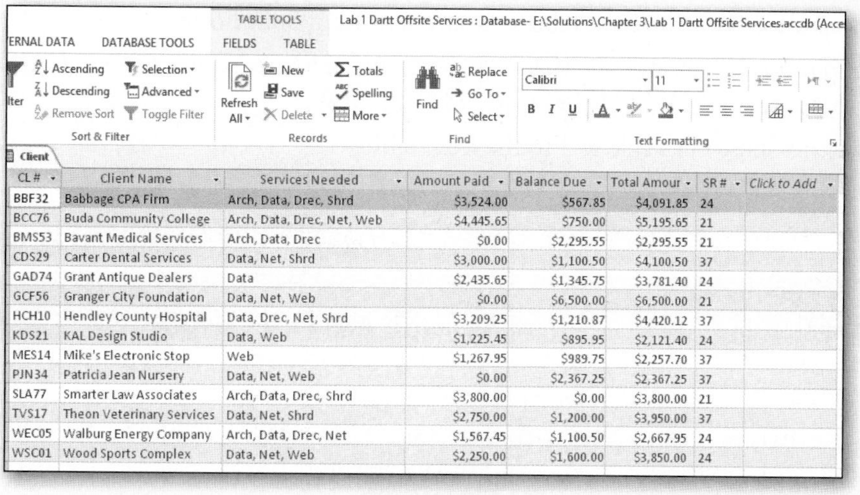

CL #	Client Name	Services Needed	Amount Paid	Balance Due	Total Amour	SR #	Click to Add
BBF32	Babbage CPA Firm	Arch, Data, Drec, Shrd	$3,524.00	$567.85	$4,091.85	24	
BCC76	Buda Community College	Arch, Data, Drec, Net, Web	$4,445.65	$750.00	$5,195.65	21	
BMS53	Bavant Medical Services	Arch, Data, Drec	$0.00	$2,295.55	$2,295.55	21	
CDS29	Carter Dental Services	Data, Net, Shrd	$3,000.00	$1,100.50	$4,100.50	37	
GAD74	Grant Antique Dealers	Data	$2,435.65	$1,345.75	$3,781.40	24	
GCF56	Granger City Foundation	Data, Net, Web	$0.00	$6,500.00	$6,500.00	21	
HCH10	Hendley County Hospital	Data, Drec, Net, Shrd	$3,209.25	$1,210.87	$4,420.12	37	
KDS21	KAL Design Studio	Data, Web	$1,225.45	$895.95	$2,121.40	24	
MES14	Mike's Electronic Stop	Web	$1,267.95	$989.75	$2,257.70	37	
PJN34	Patricia Jean Nursery	Data, Net, Web	$0.00	$2,367.25	$2,367.25	37	
SLA77	Smarter Law Associates	Arch, Data, Drec, Shrd	$3,800.00	$0.00	$3,800.00	21	
TVS17	Theon Veterinary Services	Data, Net, Shrd	$2,750.00	$1,200.00	$3,950.00	37	
WEC05	Walburg Energy Company	Arch, Data, Drec, Net	$1,567.45	$1,100.50	$2,667.95	24	
WSC01	Wood Sports Complex	Data, Net, Web	$2,250.00	$1,600.00	$3,850.00	24	

Figure 3–84

Continued >

In the Labs *continued*

7. Open the Service Rep table in Design view and change the field size for the Last Name field to 20. Save the changes and close the table.
8. Open the Service Rep table in Datasheet view, find the record for service rep 21, and change the last name to Kelly-Williamson. Resize the column to best fit.
9. If requested to do so by your instructor, change the last name for service rep 45 to your last name. If your last name is longer than 20 characters, simply enter as much as you can.
10. Save the changes to the layout of the table and close the Service Rep table.
11. Establish referential integrity between the Service Rep table (the one table) and the Client table (the many table). Cascade the update but not the delete.
12. Submit the revised database in the format specified by your instructor.
13. What would the validation rule be if the only allowable values in the State field were NC, SC, or TN?

Lab 2: Maintaining the Tennis Logos Database

Problem: The manager of Tennis Logos needs to change the database structure, add validation rules, and update records.

Note: Use the database modified in Lab 2 of Chapter 2 on page AC 131 for this assignment or see your instructor for information on accessing the files required for this book.

Instructions: Perform the following tasks:

1. Open the Tennis Logos database, and then open the Item table in Design view.
2. Add a lookup field, Item Type, to the Item table. The field should appear after the Description field. The field will contain data on the type of item for sale. The item types are CAP (caps, hats, visors), CLO (clothing), and NOV (novelties).
3. Add the following validation rules to the Item table and save the changes:
   a. Make Description a required field.
   b. Specify the legal values CAP, CLO, and NOV for the Item Type field. Include validation text.
   c. Assign CLO as the default value for the Item Type field.
   d. Specify that number on hand must be between 0 and 250. Include validation text.
4. Using a query, assign the value CLO to the Item Type field for all records. Save the query as Update Query.
5. Create a split form for the Item table and save it as Item Split Form.
6. Use the split form to change the item type for items 3363, 3673, and 6234 to CAP. Change the item type for items 5923, 7123, 7934, and 8136 to NOV.
7. Add the items shown in Table 3–3 to the Item table.

Table 3–3 Additional Records for Item table

Item Number	Description	Item Type	On Hand	Wholesale Price	Base Cost	Supplier Code
6523	Mouse Pad	NOV	100	$1.29	$1.59	SD
6974	Pen	NOV	225	$0.49	$0.79	SD
8206	Turtleneck	CLO	55	$11.29	$11.59	PC

8. Create an advanced filter for the Item table. Filter the table to find all items with fewer than 75 items on hand. Sort the filter by Item Type and Description. Save the filter settings as a query and name the filter Reorder Filter.
9. Using a query, delete all records in the Item table where the description starts with the letter Z. Save the query as Delete Query.
10. If requested to do so by your instructor, right-click the Item table in the Navigation Pane, click Table Properties, and add a description for the Item table that includes your first and last name and the date you completed this assignment. Save the change to the table property.
11. Specify referential integrity between the Supplier table (the one table) and the Item table (the many table). Cascade the update but not the delete.
12. Add the Item Type field to the Inventory Status Report. It should follow the Description field.
13. Submit the revised database in the format specified by your instructor.
14. There are two ways to enter the validation rule in Step 3d. What are they? Which one did you use?

Lab 3: Expand Your World: Cloud and Web Technologies

Filtering Records, Editing Relationships, and Exporting Relationship Reports

Problem: As a way to earn money for college, you and a few friends have started a dog walking business. You use Access to manage your business and are still learning how to create and edit relationships. You want to be able to export a relationship report to share your knowledge with your friends.

Note: To complete this assignment, you will be required to use the Data Files for Students. Visit www.cengage.com/ct/studentdownload for detailed instructions or contact your instructor for information about accessing the required files.

Instructions: Perform the following tasks:

1. Open the Lab 3 Dog Walkers database from the Data Files for Students.
2. In the Relationships window, edit the relationship to cascade the update.
3. Create a relationship report for the relationship and save the report with the name Relationship Report for First Name Last Name where first and last name are your first and last name.
4. Change the Walker Number for Alice Kerdy to 101.
5. In the Walker table, move the First Name field so that it appears before the Last Name field.
6. Export the relationship report as a PDF file and upload to your SkyDrive.
7. Share the PDF file with your instructor.
8. Submit the revised database in the format specified by your instructor.
9. What happened in the Customer table when you changed the Walker Number to 101?

Consider This: Your Turn

Apply your creative thinking and problem solving skills to design and implement a solution.

1: Maintaining the Craft Database

Personal/Academic

Instructions: Open the Craft database you used in Chapter 2 on page AC 133. If you did not create this database, contact your instructor for information about accessing the required files.

Part 1: Use the concepts and techniques presented in this chapter to modify the database as follows:

a. The minimum price of any item is $4.00.
b. The Description field should always contain data.
c. Ten oven pulls have been sold. Use an update query to change the on hand value from 25 to 15. Save the update query.
d. Tom Last (student code 4752) has created the items shown in Table 3–4. Use a split form to add these items to the Item table.

Table 3–4 Additional Records for Item table

Item Number	Description	Price	On Hand	Student Code
W128	Child's Stool	$115.00	3	4752
W315	Harmony Stool	$81.00	4	4752
W551	Skittle Pins	$4.00	15	4752

e. A Total Value (On Hand * Price) calculated field should be added to the Item table before the Student Code field. Set the Result Type to Currency and the Decimal Places to 2. (*Hint:* Result Type is a field property for calculated fields.)
f. Specify referential integrity. Cascade the delete but not the update.
g. Add the Total Value field to the Wood Crafts for Sale report created in Chapter 1.
h. All the magazine racks have been sold and Tom Last does not want to make any more. Use a delete query to remove the item. Save the delete query.

Submit your assignment in the format specified by your instructor.

Part 2: You made several decisions while completing this assignment, including specifying referential integrity. What was the rationale behind your decisions? What would happen if you deleted the record for Tom Last (student code 4752) from the Student table?

2: Maintaining the Mums Landscaping Database

Professional

Instructions: Open the Mums Landscaping database you used in Chapter 2 on page AC 134. If you did not create this database, contact your instructor for information about accessing the required files.

Part 1: Use the concepts and techniques presented in this chapter to modify the database according to the following requirements:

a. Mums could better serve its customers by adding a field that would list the type of services each customer needs. Table 3–5 lists the service abbreviations and descriptions that should appear in the field.

Table 3–5 Services Abbreviations and Descriptions

Services Abbreviation	Description
IRR	Irrigation
LND	Landscaping
LWN	Lawn Care
PLT	Plant Maintenance
TRE	Tree Pruning

b. A Total Amount field that summed the Amount Paid and Balance fields would be beneficial for the reports that Mums needs.

c. Hill Accessories is no longer a customer of Mums. Use Find or Filter By Selection to delete this record.

d. Add the data for the services needed multivalued field as shown in Figure 3–85.

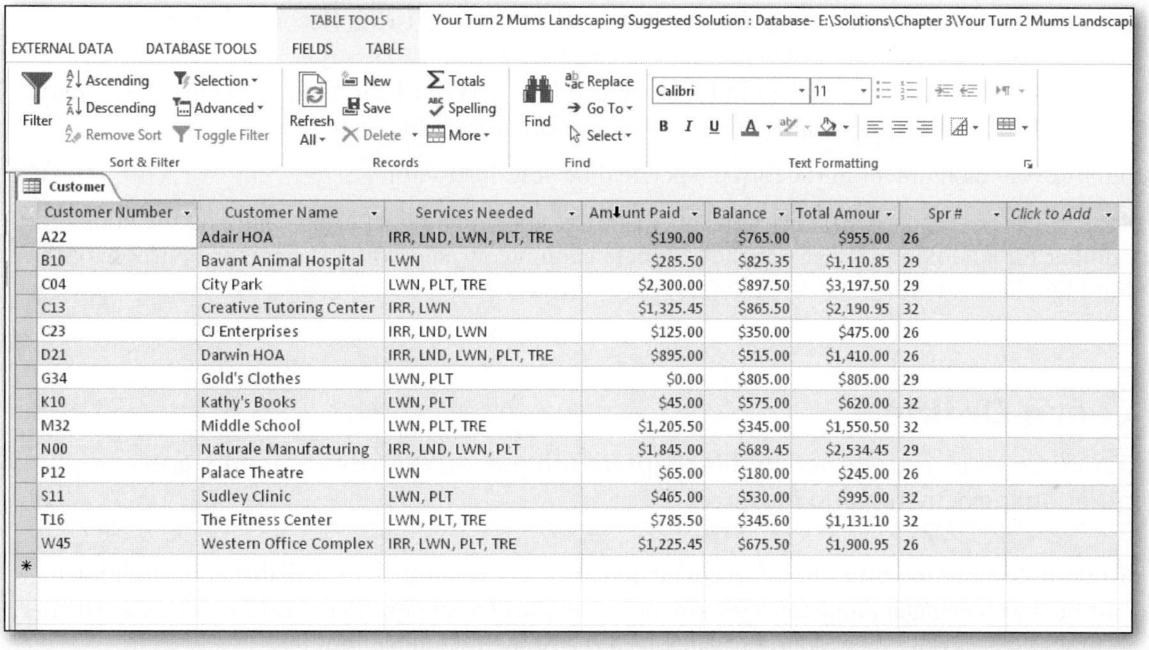

Customer Number	Customer Name	Services Needed	Amount Paid	Balance	Total Amour	Spr #	Click to Add
A22	Adair HOA	IRR, LND, LWN, PLT, TRE	$190.00	$765.00	$955.00	26	
B10	Bavant Animal Hospital	LWN	$285.50	$825.35	$1,110.85	29	
C04	City Park	LWN, PLT, TRE	$2,300.00	$897.50	$3,197.50	29	
C13	Creative Tutoring Center	IRR, LWN	$1,325.45	$865.50	$2,190.95	32	
C23	CJ Enterprises	IRR, LND, LWN	$125.00	$350.00	$475.00	26	
D21	Darwin HOA	IRR, LND, LWN, PLT, TRE	$895.00	$515.00	$1,410.00	26	
G34	Gold's Clothes	LWN, PLT	$0.00	$805.00	$805.00	29	
K10	Kathy's Books	LWN, PLT	$45.00	$575.00	$620.00	32	
M32	Middle School	LWN, PLT, TRE	$1,205.50	$345.00	$1,550.50	32	
N00	Naturale Manufacturing	IRR, LND, LWN, PLT	$1,845.00	$689.45	$2,534.45	29	
P12	Palace Theatre	LWN	$65.00	$180.00	$245.00	26	
S11	Sudley Clinic	LWN, PLT	$465.00	$530.00	$995.00	32	
T16	The Fitness Center	LWN, PLT, TRE	$785.50	$345.60	$1,131.10	32	
W45	Western Office Complex	IRR, LWN, PLT, TRE	$1,225.45	$675.50	$1,900.95	26	

Figure 3–85

e. Add the Total Amount field to the Customer Financial Report.

f. An entry should always appear in the Customer Name field. Any letters in the Customer Number field should appear in uppercase.

g. A customer's balance should never equal or exceed $1,000.00.

h. Specify referential integrity. Cascade the update but not the delete.

Submit your assignment in the format specified by your instructor.

Part 2: You made several decisions while including adding a calculated field, Total Amount, to the database. What was the rationale behind your decisions? Does the calculated field actually exist in the database? Are there any issues that you need to consider when you create a calculated field?

Continued >

Consider This: Your Turn *continued*

3: Understanding Database Maintenance

Research and Collaboration

Part 1: Before you begin this assignment, you and your teammates need to decide on a team name. Once you have agreed on a name, save the Bavant Publishing database as Team Name Publishing where Team Name is the name of your team. Use this database for this assignment. As your group completes the assignment, complete the following tasks, keeping track of problems you encounter, the solutions you apply, and any other observations. Create a blog, a Google document, or a Word document on the SkyDrive on which to store the team's observations.

a. For every member in the team, add a record to the Book Rep table. Use your own names but fictitious data for the remaining fields. Record in the team document or blog what happened when you added the records. For example, was someone's name too long to fit within the allotted field size?
b. Based on the records currently in the Book Rep table, change the field size for any field that was too short to store a value. In the team document, identify the fields you changed.
c. Change the book rep number for Robert Chin from 53 to 56. Record in your team document the result of making this change.
d. Create queries using the Find Unmatched Query Wizard and the Find Duplicates Query Wizard. Record the query results in your team document.

Submit your assignment in the format specified by your instructor.

Part 2: You made several decisions while in this assignment, including changing the book rep number for a book rep. What was the rationale behind your decisions? What is the purpose of the Find Duplicates Wizard?

Learn Online

Reinforce what you learned in this chapter with games, exercises, training, and many other online activities and resources.

Student Companion Site Reinforcement activities and resources are available at no additional cost on www.cengagebrain.com. Visit www.cengage.com/ct/studentdownload for detailed instructions about accessing the resources available at the Student Companion Site.

SAM Put your skills into practice with SAM! If you have a SAM account, go to www.cengage.com/sam2013 to access SAM assignments for this chapter.

4 Creating Reports and Forms

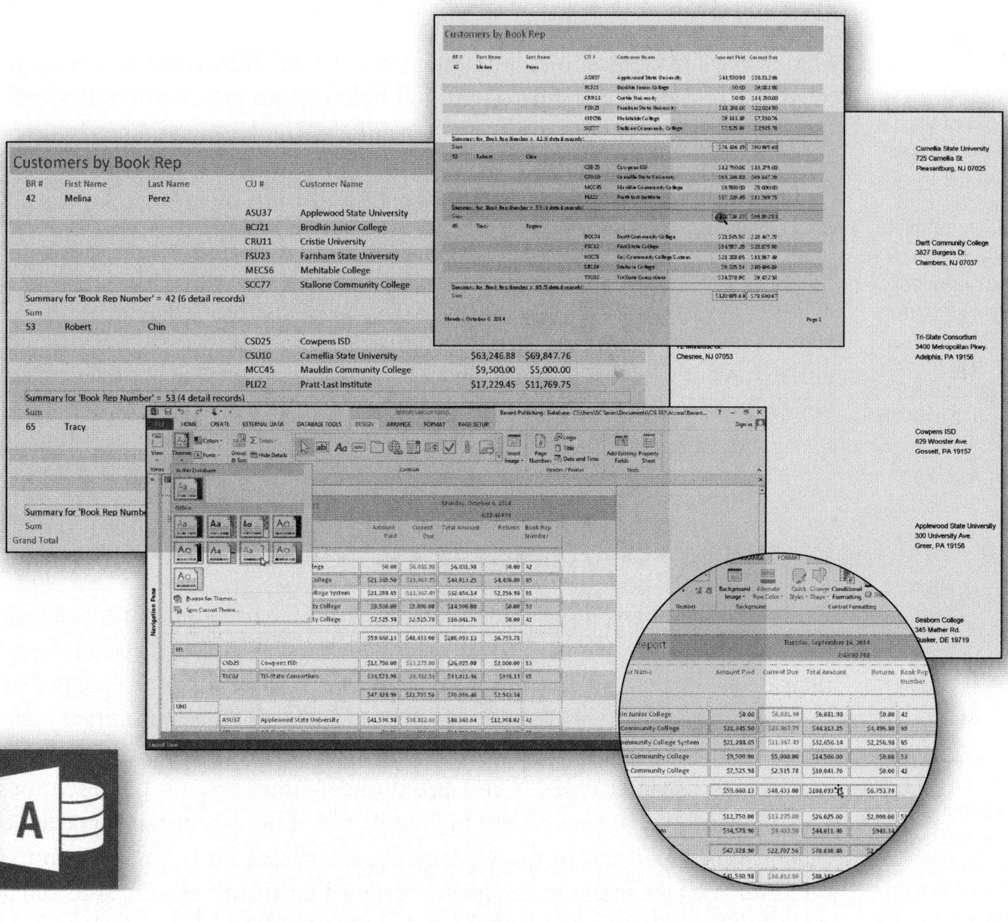

Objectives

You will have mastered the material in this chapter when you can:

- Create reports and forms using wizards
- Modify reports and forms in Layout view
- Group and sort data in a report
- Add totals and subtotals to a report
- Conditionally format controls
- Resize columns
- Filter records in reports and forms
- Print reports and forms
- Apply themes
- Add a field to a report or form
- Add a date
- Change the format of a control
- Move controls
- Create and print mailing labels

4 Creating Reports and Forms

Introduction

BTW
BTWs
For a complete list of the BTWs found in the margins of this book, visit the BTW resource on the Student Companion Site located on www.cengagebrain.com. For detailed instructions about accessing available resources, visit www.cengage.com/ct/studentdownload or contact your instructor for information about accessing the required files.

One of the advantages to maintaining data in a database is the ability to present the data in attractive reports and forms that highlight certain information. Reports present data in an organized format that is usually printed. The data can come from one or more tables. On the other hand, you usually view forms on the screen, although you can print them. In addition to viewing data, you can also use forms to update data. That is, you can use forms to add records, delete records, or change records. Like reports, the data in the form can come from one or more tables. This chapter shows how to create reports and forms by creating two reports and a form. There are several ways to create both reports and forms. One approach is to use the Report or Form Wizard. You also can use either Layout view or Design view to create or modify a report or form. In this chapter, you will use Layout view for this purpose. In later chapters, you will learn how to use Design view. You also will use the Label Wizard to produce mailing labels.

Project — Reports and Forms

BTW
Q&As
For a complete list of the Q&As found in many of the step-by-step sequences in this book, visit the Q&A resource on the Student Companion Site located on www.cengagebrain.com. For detailed instructions about accessing available resources, visit www.cengage.com/ct/studentdownload or contact your instructor for information about accessing the required files.

Bavant Publishing is now able to better keep track of its sales information and to target customer needs by using the database of customers and reps. Bavant hopes to improve their decision-making capability further by using two custom reports that meet their specific needs. Figure 4–1 shows the first report, which is a modified version of an existing report. The report features grouping. The report shown in Figure 4–1 groups records by customer types. There are three separate groups, one each for the three possible customer types: COM, HS, and UNI. The appropriate type appears before each group. The totals of the Amount Paid, Current Due, Total Amount, and Returns fields for the customers in the group (called a **subtotal**) appear after the group. At the end of the report are grand totals of the same fields.

Figure 4–2 on page AC 204 shows the second report. This report encompasses data from both the Book Rep table and the Customer table. Like the report in Figure 4–1, the data is grouped, although this time it is grouped by book rep number. Not only does the rep number appear before each group, but the first name and last name of the rep appear as well. Like the first report, this report contains subtotals.

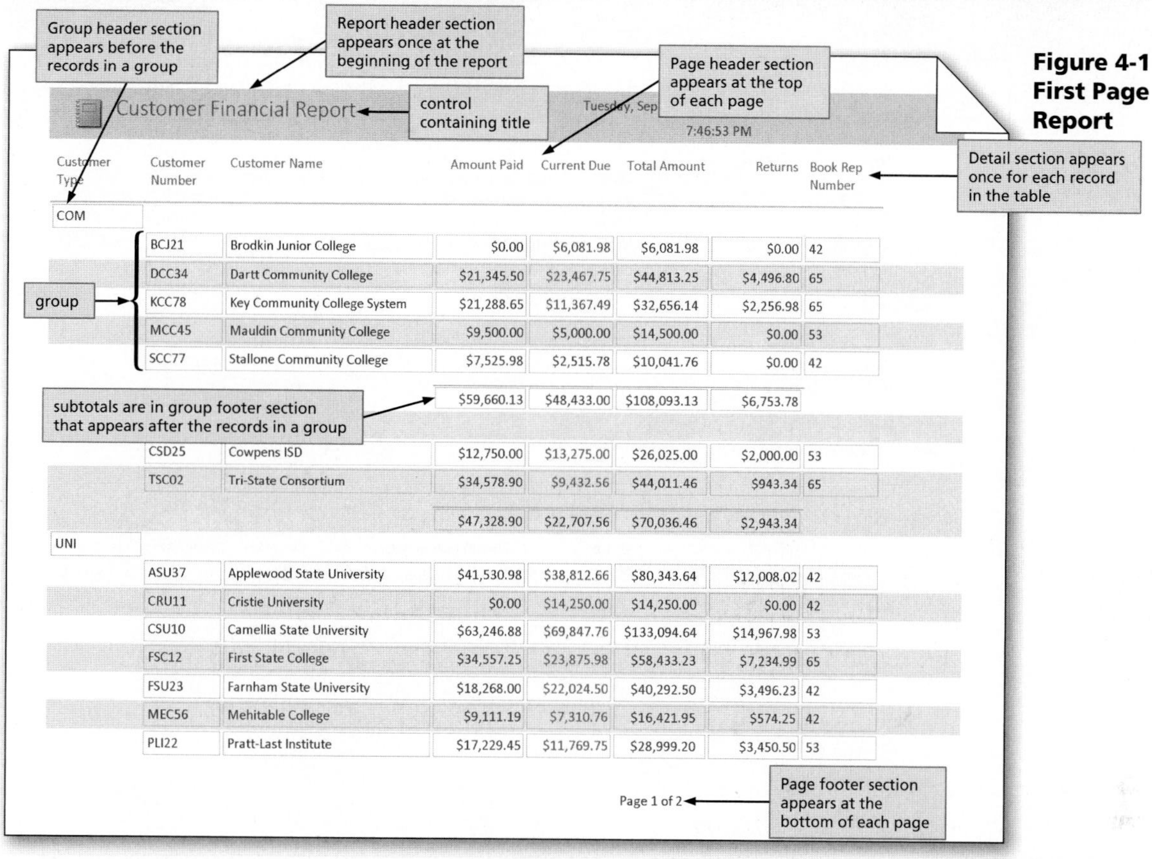

Figure 4-1 (a) First Page of Report

Figure 4-1 (b) Second Page of Report

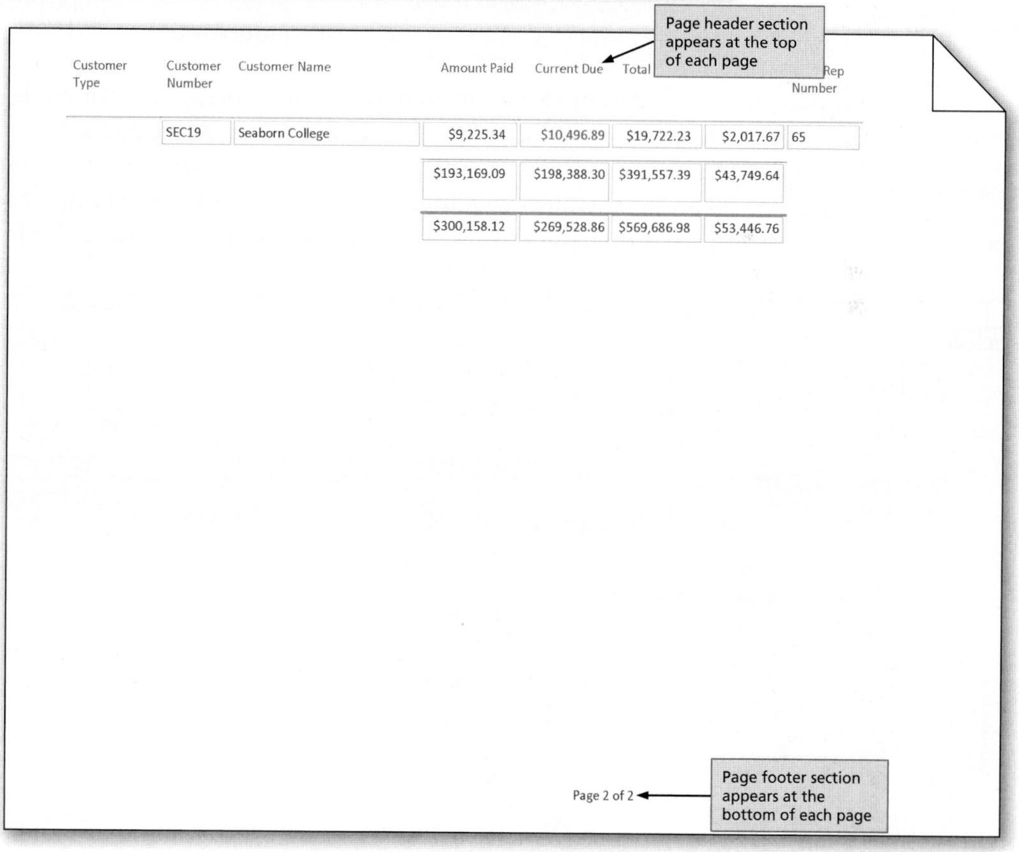

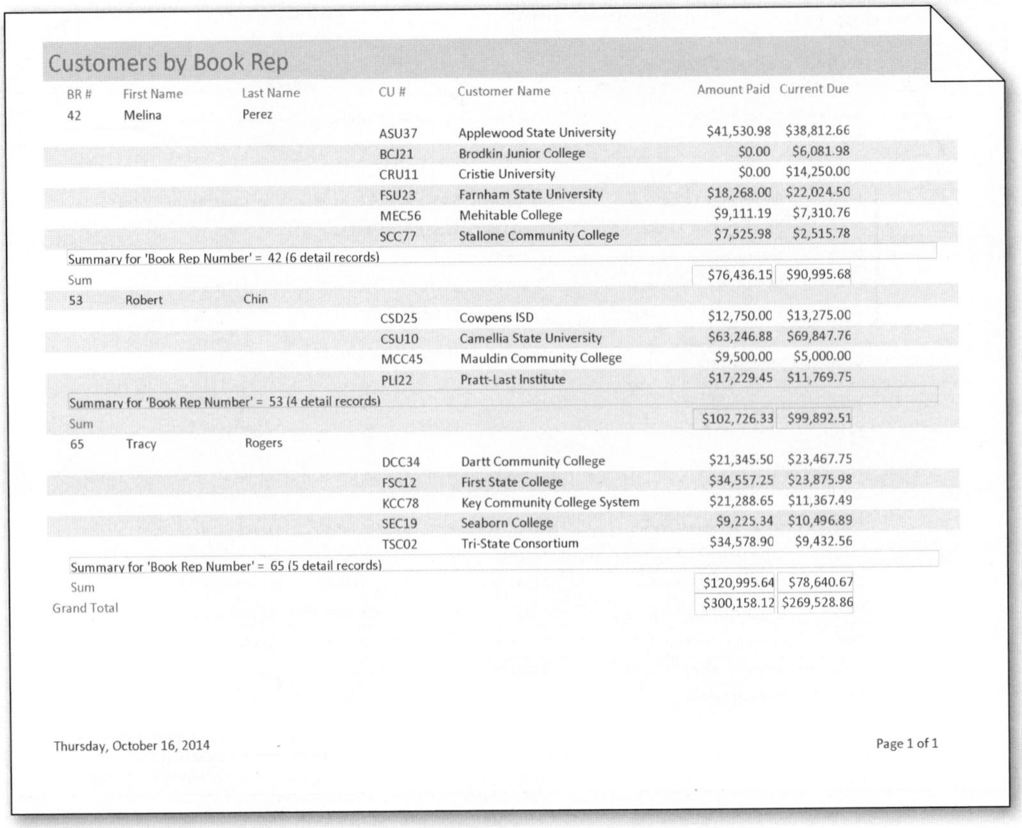

Customers by Book Rep

BR #	First Name	Last Name	CU #	Customer Name	Amount Paid	Current Due
42	Melina	Perez				
			ASU37	Applewood State University	$41,530.98	$38,812.66
			BCJ21	Brodkin Junior College	$0.00	$6,081.98
			CRU11	Cristie University	$0.00	$14,250.00
			FSU23	Farnham State University	$18,268.00	$22,024.50
			MEC56	Mehitable College	$9,111.19	$7,310.76
			SCC77	Stallone Community College	$7,525.98	$2,515.78
Summary for 'Book Rep Number' = 42 (6 detail records)						
Sum					$76,436.15	$90,995.68
53	Robert	Chin				
			CSD25	Cowpens ISD	$12,750.00	$13,275.00
			CSU10	Camellia State University	$63,246.88	$69,847.76
			MCC45	Mauldin Community College	$9,500.00	$5,000.00
			PLI22	Pratt-Last Institute	$17,229.45	$11,769.75
Summary for 'Book Rep Number' = 53 (4 detail records)						
Sum					$102,726.33	$99,892.51
65	Tracy	Rogers				
			DCC34	Dartt Community College	$21,345.50	$23,467.75
			FSC12	First State College	$34,557.25	$23,875.98
			KCC78	Key Community College System	$21,288.65	$11,367.49
			SEC19	Seaborn College	$9,225.34	$10,496.89
			TSC02	Tri-State Consortium	$34,578.90	$9,432.56
Summary for 'Book Rep Number' = 65 (5 detail records)						
Sum					$120,995.64	$78,640.67
Grand Total					$300,158.12	$269,528.86

Thursday, October 16, 2014 Page 1 of 1

Figure 4–2

BTW

Consider Your Audience

Always design reports and forms with your audience in mind. Make your reports and forms accessible to individuals who may have problems with color blindness or reduced vision.

Bavant also wants to improve the process of updating data by using a custom form, as shown in Figure 4–3. The form has a title and a date. Unlike the form you can create by clicking the Form button, this form does not contain all the fields in the Customer table. In addition, the fields are in a different order than in the table. For this form, Bavant likes the appearance of including the fields in a stacked layout.

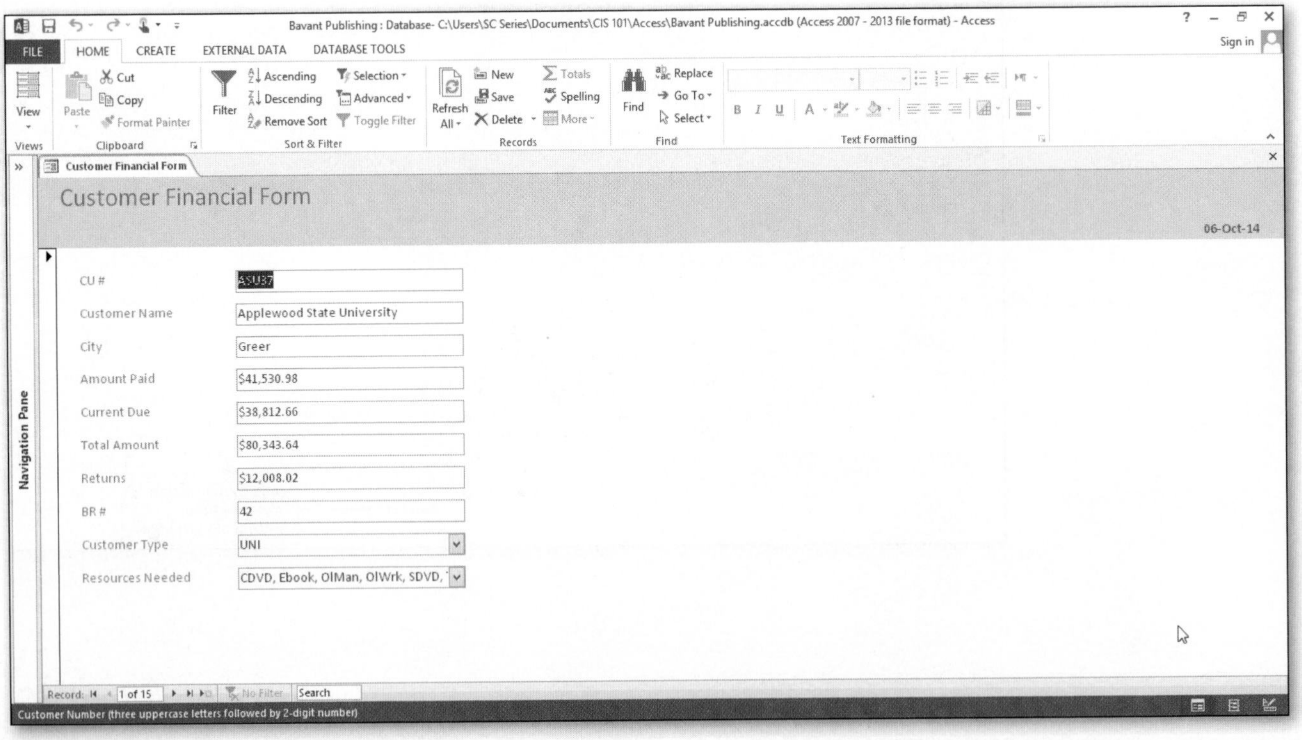

Figure 4–3

Bavant also wants to be able to produce mailing labels for its customers. These labels must align correctly with the particular labels Bavant uses and must be sorted by postal code (Figure 4–4).

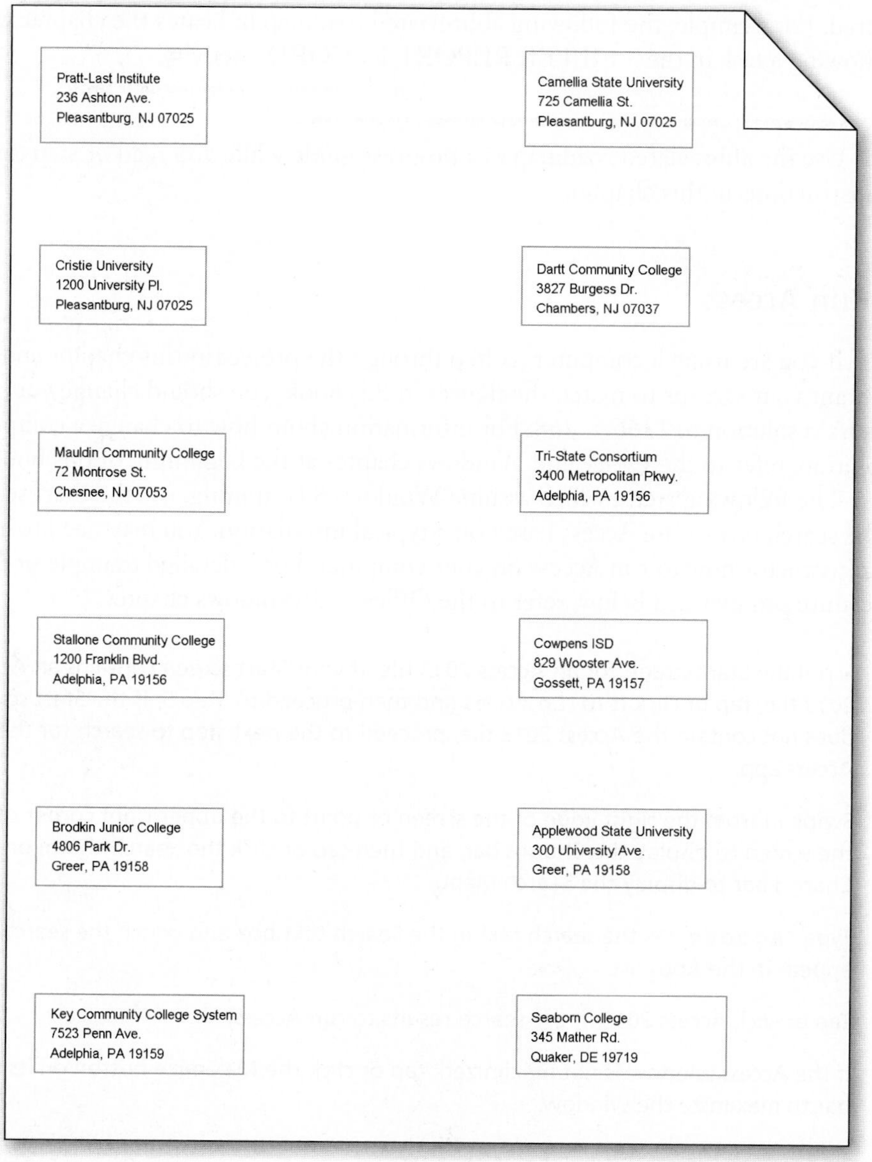

Figure 4–4

Roadmap

In this chapter, you will learn how to create the reports, forms, and labels shown in Figure 4–1 on page AC 203 through Figure 4–4. The following roadmap identifies general activities you will perform as you progress through this chapter:

1. GROUP, SORT, and TOTAL in a report.
2. CONDITIONALLY FORMAT CONTROLS in a report.
3. FILTER REPORT RECORDS.
4. Create a MULTIPLE-TABLE REPORT.
5. Create a form using the FORM WIZARD.
6. MODIFY CONTROLS in a control layout on a form.
7. FILTER FORM RECORDS.
8. Create MAILING LABELS.

BTW
The Ribbon and Screen Resolution
Access may change how the groups and buttons within the groups appear on the ribbon, depending on the computer's screen resolution. Thus, your ribbon may look different from the ones in this book if you are using a screen resolution other than 1366 x 768.

At the beginning of step instructions throughout the chapter, you will see an abbreviated form of this roadmap. The abbreviated roadmap uses colors to indicate chapter progress: gray means the chapter is beyond that activity; blue means the task being shown is covered in that activity, and black means that activity is yet to be covered. For example, the following abbreviated roadmap indicates the chapter would be showing a task in the 3 FILTER REPORT RECORDS activity.

1 GROUP, SORT, & TOTAL | 2 CONDITIONALLY FORMAT CONTROLS | 3 FILTER REPORT RECORDS | 4 MULTIPLE-TABLE REPORT
5 FORM WIZARD | 6 MODIFY CONTROLS | 7 FILTER FORM RECORDS | 8 MAILING LABELS

Use the abbreviated roadmap as a progress guide while you read or step through the instructions in this chapter.

To Run Access

If you are using a computer to step through the project in this chapter and you want your screens to match the figures in this book, you should change your screen's resolution to 1366 × 768. For information about how to change a computer's resolution, refer to the Office and Windows chapter at the beginning of this book.

The following steps, which assume Windows 8 is running, use the Start screen or the search box to run Access based on a typical installation. You may need to ask your instructor how to run Access on your computer. For a detailed example of the procedure summarized below, refer to the Office and Windows chapter.

BTW
Touch Screen Differences
The Office and Windows interfaces may vary if you are using a touch screen. For this reason, you might notice that the function or appearance of your touch screen differs slightly from this chapter's presentation.

1. Scroll the Start screen for an Access 2013 tile. If your Start screen contains an Access 2013 tile, tap or click it to run Access and then proceed to Step 5; if the Start screen does not contain the Access 2013 tile, proceed to the next step to search for the Access app.
2. Swipe in from the right edge of the screen or point to the upper-right corner of the screen to display the Charms bar, and then tap or click the Search charm on the Charms bar to display the Search menu.
3. Type `Access` as the search text in the Search text box and watch the search results appear in the Apps list.
4. Tap or click Access 2013 in the search results to run Access.
5. If the Access window is not maximized, tap or click the Maximize button on its title bar to maximize the window.

One of the few differences between Windows 7 and Windows 8 occurs in the steps to run Access. If you are using Windows 7, click the Start button, type `Access` in the 'Search programs and files' box, click Access 2013, and then, if necessary, maximize the Access window. For detailed steps to run Access in Windows 7, refer to the Office and Windows chapter at the beginning of this book. For a summary of the steps, refer to the Quick Reference located at the back of this book.

To Open a Database from Access

The following steps open the Bavant Publishing database from the location you specified when you first created it (for example, the Access folder in the CIS 101 folder). For a detailed example of the procedure summarized below, refer to the Office and Windows chapter at the beginning of this book.

1. Tap or click FILE on the ribbon to open the Backstage view, if necessary.
2. If the database you want to open is displayed in the Recent list, tap or click the file name to open the database and display the opened database in the Access window; then skip to Step 7. If the database you want to open is not displayed in the Recent list or if the Recent list does not appear, tap or click 'Open Other Files' to display the Open Gallery.

3. If the database you want to open is displayed in the Recent list in the Open gallery, tap or click the file name to open the database and display the opened database in the Access window; then skip to Step 7.
4. Tap or click Computer, SkyDrive, or another location in the left pane, and then navigate to the location of the database to be opened (for example, the Access folder in the CIS 101 folder).
5. Tap or click Bavant Publishing to select the database to be opened.
6. Tap or click the Open button (Open dialog box) to open the selected file and display the opened database in the Access window.
7. If a Security Warning appears, tap or click the Enable Content button.

Report Creation

When working with a report in Access, there are four different ways to view the report: Report view, Print Preview, Layout view, and Design view. Report view shows the report on the screen. Print Preview shows the report as it will appear when printed. Layout view is similar to Report view in that it shows the report on the screen, but it also allows you to make changes to the report. Using Layout view is usually the easiest way to make such changes. Design view also allows you to make changes, but it does not show you the actual report. It is most useful when the changes you need to make are complex. In this chapter, you will use Layout view to modify the report.

If you are using your finger on a touch screen and are having difficulty completing the steps in this chapter, consider using a stylus. Many people find it easier to be precise with a stylus than with a finger. In addition, with a stylus you see the pointer. If you still are having trouble completing the steps with a stylus, try using a mouse.

Report Sections

A report is divided into various sections to help clarify the presentation of data. A typical report consists of a Report Header section, Page Header section, Detail section, Page Footer section, and Report Footer section (see Figure 4–1 on page AC 203). In Design view, which you will use in later chapters, you can see the names for each section on the screen. Even though the names of the sections are not visible in Layout view, it is still useful to understand the purpose of the various sections.

The contents of the Report Header section appear once at the beginning of the report. In the Customer Financial Report, the report title is in the Report Header section. The contents of the Report Footer section appear once at the end of the report. In the Customer Financial Report, the Report Footer section contains the grand totals of Amount Paid, Current Due, Total Amount, and Returns. The contents of the Page Header section appear once at the top of each page and typically contain the column headers. The contents of the Page Footer section appear once at the bottom of each page and often contain a date and a page number. The contents of the Detail section appear once for each record in the table; for example, once for Brodkin Junior College, once for Dartt Community College, and so on. In this report, the detail records contain the customer number, customer name, amount paid, current due, total amount, returns, and book rep number.

When the data in a report is grouped, there are two additional sections. The contents of the Group Header section are printed before the records in a particular group, and the contents of the Group Footer section are printed after the group. In the Customer Financial Report, the Group Header section contains the Customer Type, and the Group Footer section contains subtotals of Amount Paid, Current Due, Total Amount, and Returns.

BTW
Report Design Considerations
The purpose of any report is to present specific information. Make sure that the meaning of the row and column headings is clear. You can use different fonts and sizes by changing the appropriate properties, but do not overuse them. Finally, be consistent when creating reports. Once you decide on a general report style or theme, stick with it throughout your database.

To Group and Sort in a Report

1 GROUP, SORT, & TOTAL | 2 CONDITIONALLY FORMAT CONTROLS | 3 FILTER REPORT RECORDS | 4 MULTIPLE-TABLE REPORT
5 FORM WIZARD | 6 MODIFY CONTROLS | 7 FILTER FORM RECORDS | 8 MAILING LABELS

In Layout view of the report, you can specify both grouping and sorting by using the Group & Sort button on the DESIGN tab. The following steps open the Customer Financial Report in Layout view and then specify both grouping and sorting in the report. ***Why?*** *Bavant has determined that the records in the report should be grouped by customer type. That is, all the customers of a given type should appear together immediately after the type. Within the customers in a given type, they have determined that customers are to be ordered by customer number.*

1

- Press and hold or right-click the Customer Financial Report in the Navigation Pane to produce a shortcut menu.
- Tap or click Layout View on the shortcut menu to open the report in Layout view.
- Close the Navigation Pane.
- If a field list appears, close the field list by tapping or clicking the 'Add Existing Fields' button (REPORT LAYOUT TOOLS DESIGN tab | Tools group).
- Tap or click the Group & Sort button (REPORT LAYOUT TOOLS DESIGN tab | Grouping & Totals group) to display the Group, Sort, and Total pane (Figure 4–5).

Q&A My report is in a different order. Do I need to change it?
No. You will change the order of the records in the following steps.

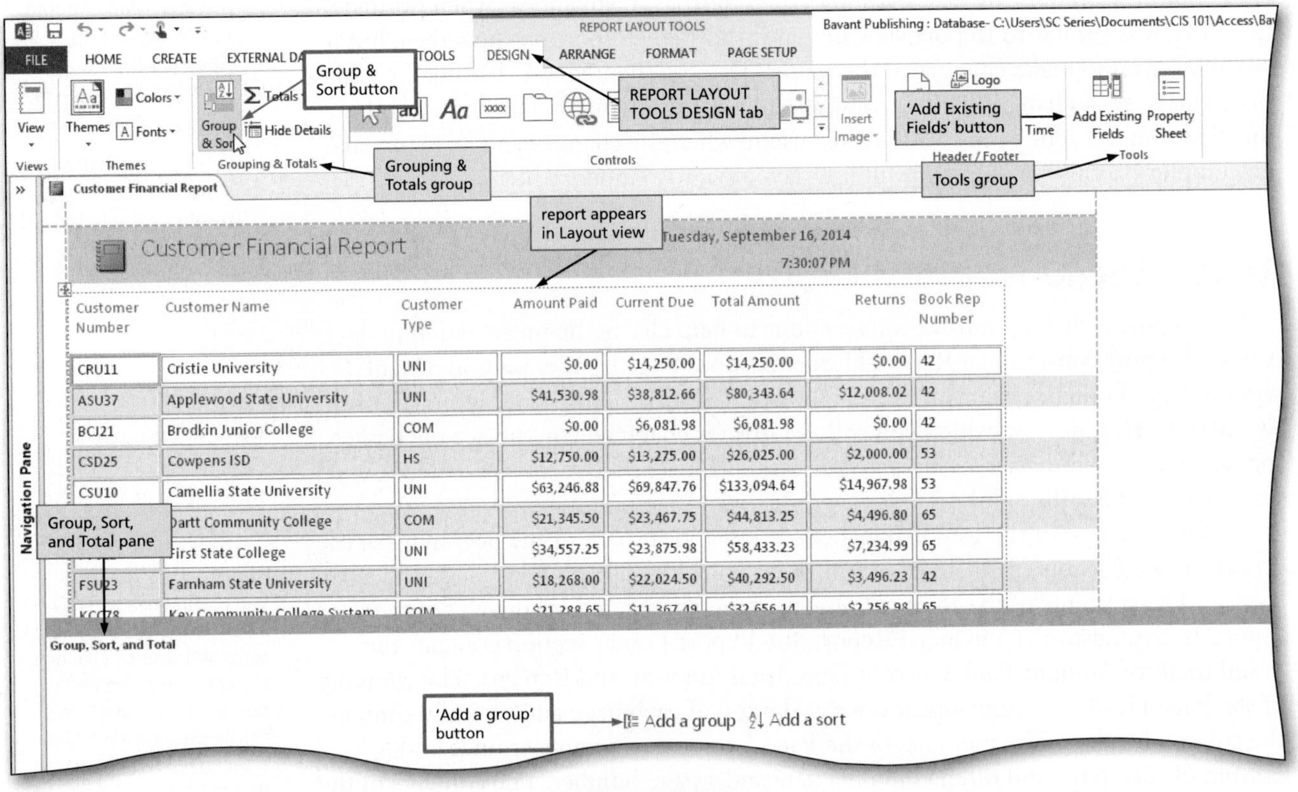

Figure 4–5

2

- Tap or click the 'Add a group' button to add a group (Figure 4–6).

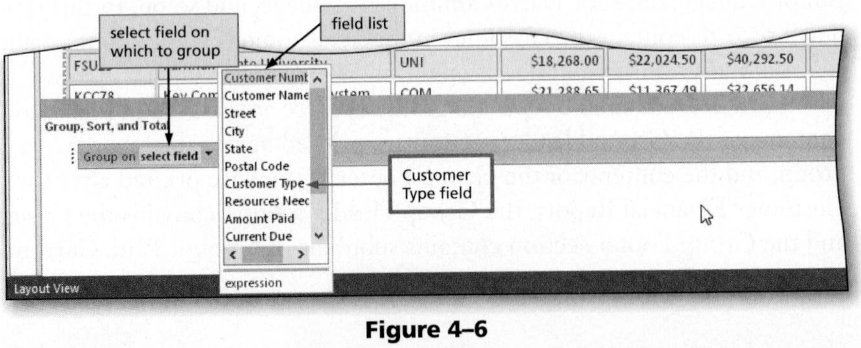

Figure 4–6

3

- Tap or click the Customer Type field in the field list to select a field for grouping and group the records on the selected field (Figure 4–7).

Q&A Does the field on which I group have to be the first field?

No. If you select a field other than the first field, Access will move the field you select into the first position.

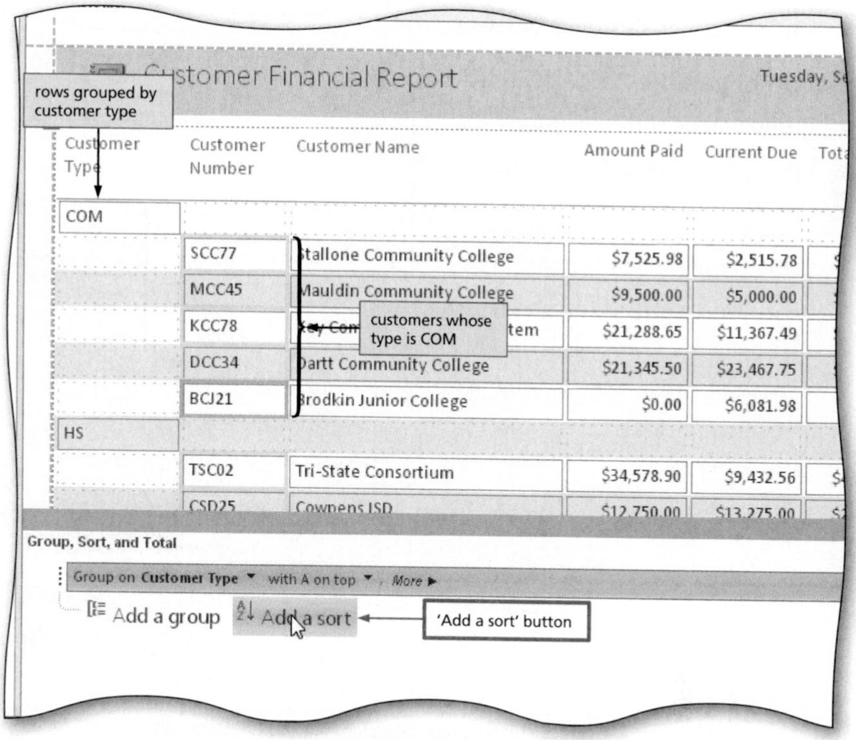

Figure 4–7

4

- Tap or click the 'Add a sort' button to add a sort (Figure 4–8).

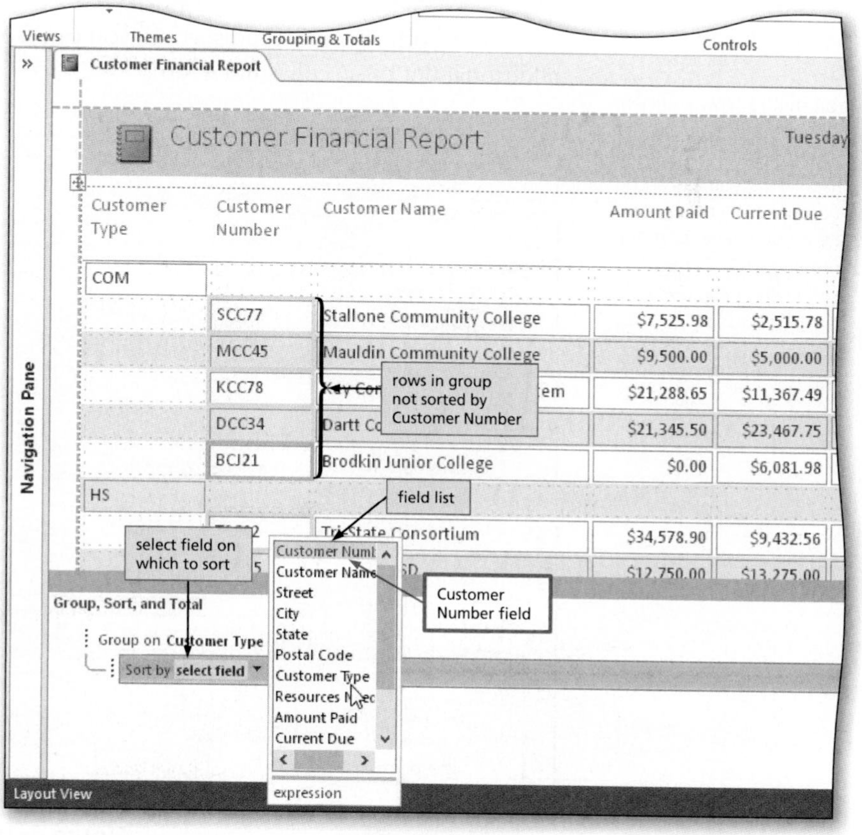

Figure 4–8

5

- Tap or click the Customer Number field in the field list to specify the field on which the records in each group will be sorted (Figure 4–9).

Q&A I thought the report would be sorted by Customer Type, because I chose to group on that field. What is the effect of choosing to sort by Customer Number?
This sort takes place within groups. You are specifying that within the list of customers of the same type, the customers will be ordered by customer number.

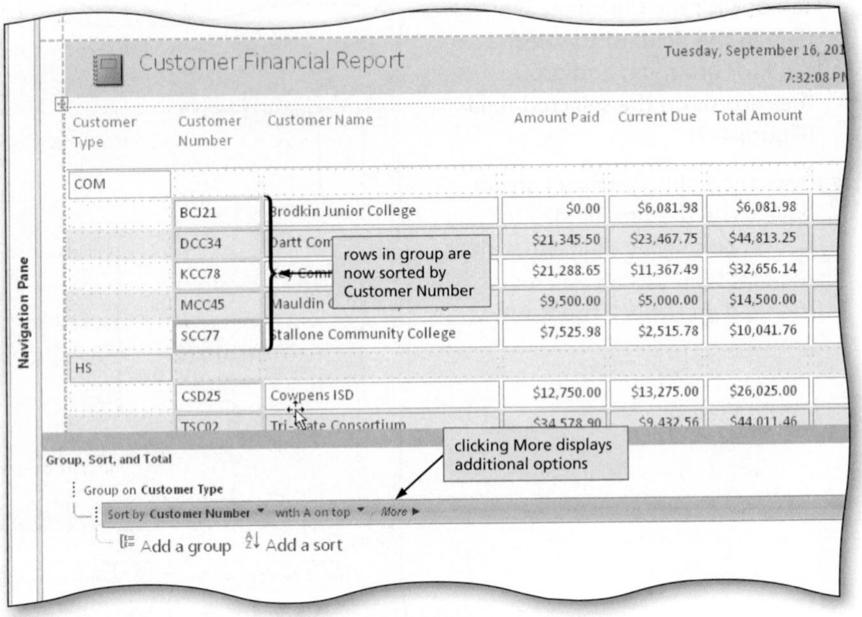

Figure 4–9

Other Ways

1. Press and hold or right-click column header for field on which to group, tap or click Group On (field name)

Grouping and Sorting Options

BTW
Grouping
You should allow sufficient white space between groups. If you feel the amount is insufficient, you can add more space by enlarging the group header or group footer.

For both grouping and sorting, you can tap or click the More button to specify additional options (see Figure 4–10).

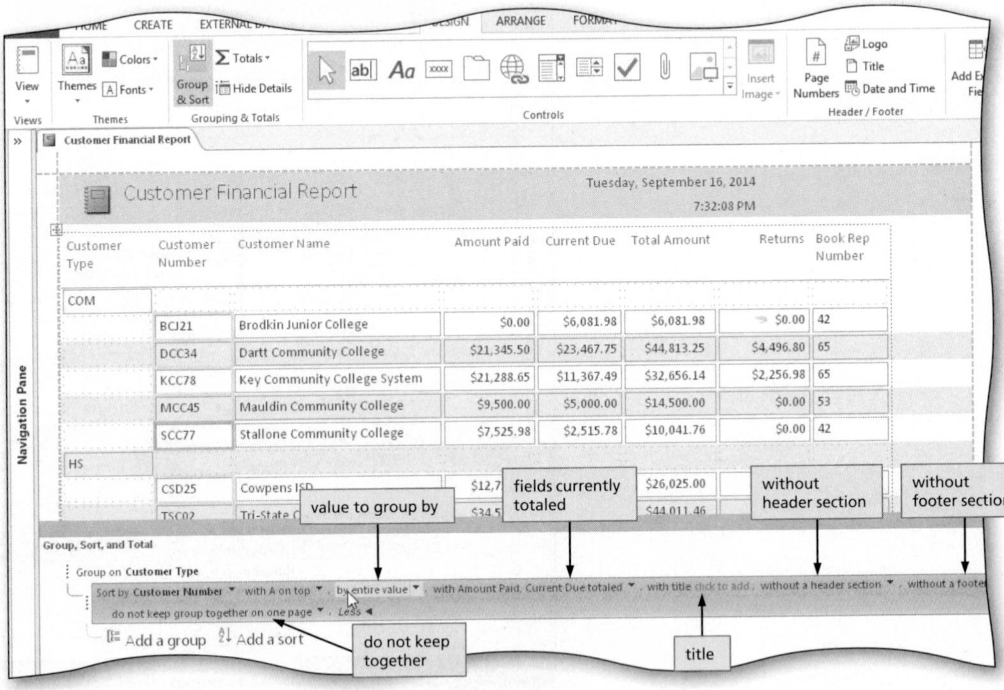

Figure 4–10

CONSIDER THIS

What is the purpose of the additional options?

- **Value.** You can choose the number of characters of the value on which to group. Typically, you would group by the entire value, for example, the entire city name. You could choose, however, to only group on the first character, in which case all customers in cities that begin with the same letter would be considered a group. You also could group by the first two characters or by a custom number of characters.
- **Totals.** You can choose the values to be totaled. You can specify whether the totals are to appear in the group header or in the group footer and whether to include a grand total. You also can choose whether to show group totals as a percentage of the grand total.
- **Title.** You can customize the group title.
- **Header section.** You can include or omit a header section for the group.
- **Footer section.** You can include or omit a footer section for the group.
- **Keep together.** You can indicate whether Access should attempt to keep portions of a group together on the same page. The default setting does not keep portions of a group together, but you can specify that Access should keep a whole group together on one page, when possible. If the group will not fit on the remainder of the page, Access will move the group header and the records in a group to the next page. Finally, you can choose to have Access keep the header and the first record together on one page. If the header would fit at the bottom of a page, but there would not be room for the first record, Access will move the header to the next page.

Report Controls

The various objects on a report are called **controls**. You can manipulate these controls to modify their location and appearance. The report title, column headers, contents of various fields, subtotals, and so on are all contained in controls. When working in Layout view, as you will do in this chapter, Access handles details concerning placement, sizing, and format of these controls for you automatically. When working in Design view, you will see and manipulate the controls. Even when working in Layout view, however, it is useful to understand the concepts of controls.

The report shown in Figure 4–1 on page AC 203 has a control containing the title, Customer Financial Report. The report also includes a control containing each column header (Customer Type, Customer Number, Customer Name, Amount Paid, Current Due, Total Amount, Returns, and Book Rep Number). A control in the Group Header section displays the customer type. There are four controls in the Group Footer section: One control displays the subtotal of Amount Paid, a second displays the subtotal of Current Due, a third displays the subtotal of Total Amount, and the fourth displays the subtotal of Returns. The Detail section has controls containing the customer number, customer name, amount paid, current due, total amount, returns, and book rep number.

Access has three types of controls: bound controls, unbound controls, and calculated controls. **Bound controls** are used to display data that comes from the database, such as the customer number and name. **Unbound controls** are not associated with data from the database and are used to display such things as the report's title. Finally, **calculated controls** are used to display data that is calculated from other data, such as a total.

BTW

Touch and Pointers

Remember that if you are using your finger on a touch screen, you will not see the pointer.

BTW

On-Screen Keyboard

To display the on-screen touch keyboard, tap the Touch Keyboard button on the Windows taskbar. When finished using the touch keyboard, tap the X button on the touch keyboard to close the keyboard.

To Add Totals and Subtotals

1 GROUP, SORT, & TOTAL | 2 CONDITIONALLY FORMAT CONTROLS | 3 FILTER REPORT RECORDS | 4 MULTIPLE-TABLE REPORT
5 FORM WIZARD | 6 MODIFY CONTROLS | 7 FILTER FORM RECORDS | 8 MAILING LABELS

To add totals or other statistics, use the Totals button on the DESIGN tab. You then select from a menu of aggregate functions, which are functions that perform some mathematical function against a group of records. The available aggregate functions, or calculations, are Sum (total), Average, Count Records, Count Values, Max (largest value), Min (smallest value), Standard Deviation, and Variance. Because the report is grouped, each group will have a **subtotal**, that is, a total for just the records in the group. At the end of the report, there will be a **grand total**, that is, a total for all records.

The following steps specify totals for several of the fields. ***Why?*** *Along with determining to group data in this report, Bavant also has determined that subtotals and grand totals of the Amount Paid, Current Due, Total Amount, and Returns fields should be included.* Even though you previously specified totals for the Amount Paid, Current Due, and Returns fields, you need to do so again because of the grouping.

1

- Tap or click the Amount Paid column header to select the field.

Q&A Does it have to be the column header?
No, you could tap or click the Amount Paid field on any record.

- Tap or click the Totals button (REPORT LAYOUT TOOLS DESIGN tab | Grouping & Totals group) to display the list of available calculations (Figure 4–11).

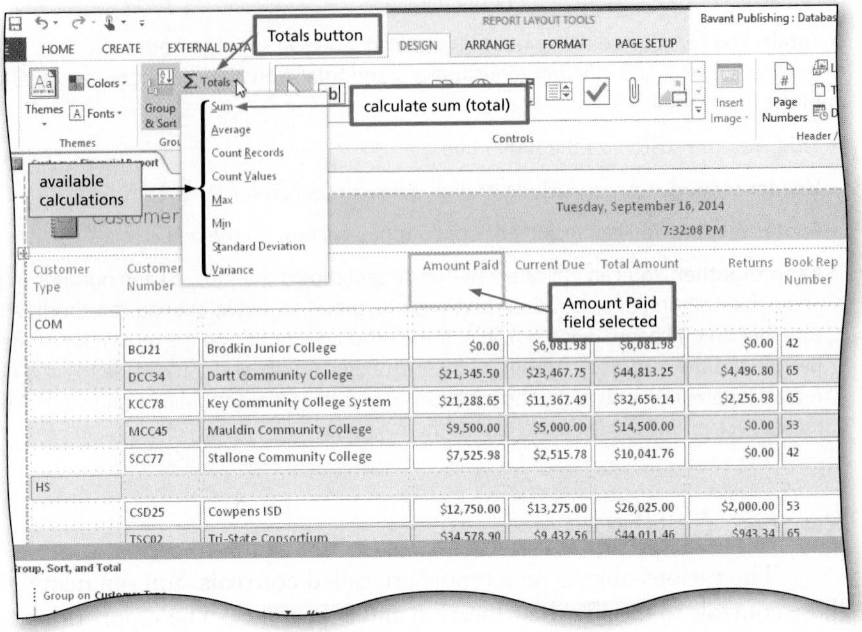

Figure 4–11

2

- Tap or click Sum to calculate the sum of the Amount Paid values.
- If the subtotal does not appear completely, drag the lower boundary of the control for the subtotal to the approximate position shown in Figure 4–12.

Q&A I moved the control rather than resizing it. What did I do wrong?
You dragged the control rather than dragging its lower boundary. Click the Undo button on the Quick Access Toolbar to undo your change and then drag again, making sure you are pointing to the lower boundary.

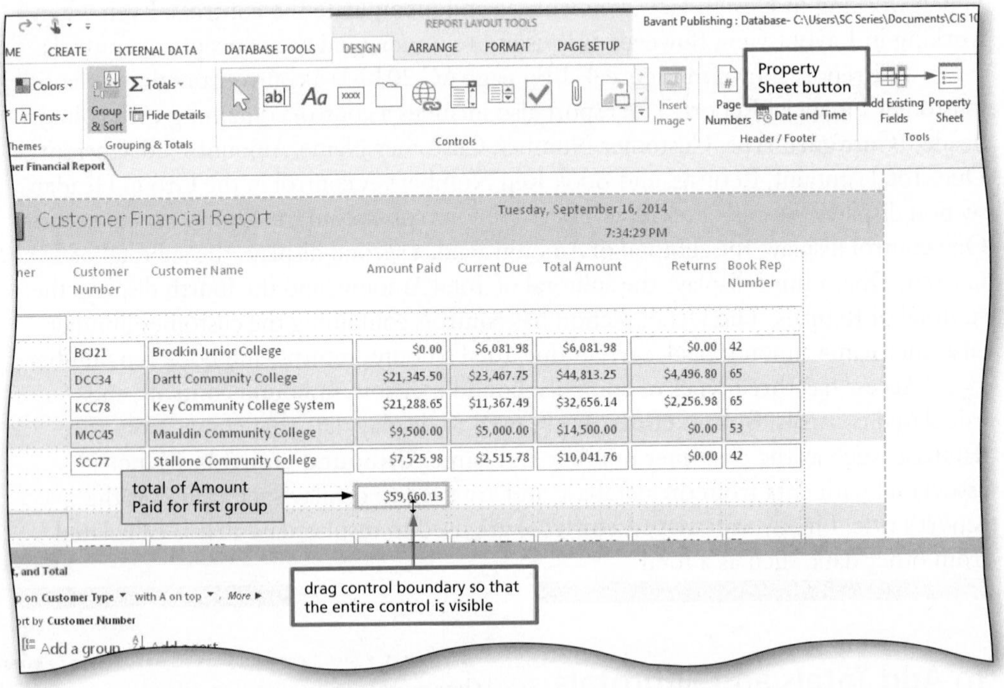

Figure 4–12

3

- Using the same technique as in Steps 1 and 2, add subtotals for the Current Due, Total Amount, and Returns fields.
- Tap or click the subtotal of the Total Amount field to select it.
- Tap or click the Property Sheet button (REPORT LAYOUT TOOLS DESIGN tab | Tools group) to display the property sheet for the subtotal control.
- Tap or click the Format box to produce an arrow, and then tap or click the Format arrow.
- Tap or click Currency.
- Tap or click the Property Sheet button (REPORT LAYOUT TOOLS DESIGN tab | Tools group) to close the property sheet (Figure 4–13).

4

- Scroll to the bottom of the report and use the same technique to change the format for the grand total of Total Amount to Currency.
- If necessary, drag the lower boundaries of the controls for the grand totals so that the numbers appear completely.

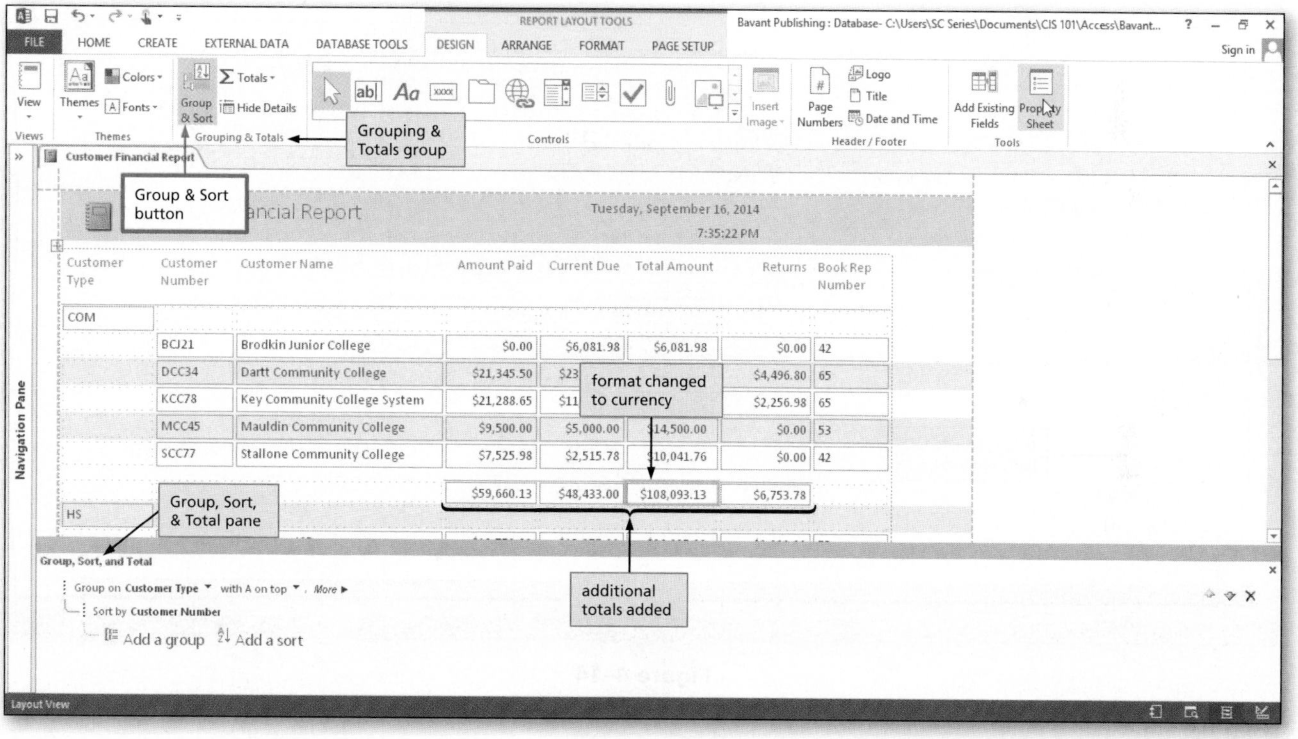

Figure 4–13

Other Ways

1. Press and hold or right-click column header for field, tap or click Total (field name)

To Remove the Group, Sort, and Total Pane

1 GROUP, SORT, & TOTAL | 2 CONDITIONALLY FORMAT CONTROLS | 3 FILTER REPORT RECORDS | 4 MULTIPLE-TABLE REPORT
5 FORM WIZARD | 6 MODIFY CONTROLS | 7 FILTER FORM RECORDS | 8 MAILING LABELS

The following step removes the Group, Sort, and Total pane from the screen. ***Why?*** *Because you have specified the required grouping and sorting for the report, you no longer need to use the Group, Sort, and Total pane.*

1

- Tap or click the Group & Sort button (REPORT LAYOUT TOOLS DESIGN tab | Grouping & Totals group) to remove the Group, Sort, and Total pane (Figure 4–14).

Q&A Do I need to remove the Group, Sort, and Total pane?

No. Doing so provides more room on the screen for the report, however. You can easily display the pane whenever you need it by tapping or clicking the Group & Sort button again.

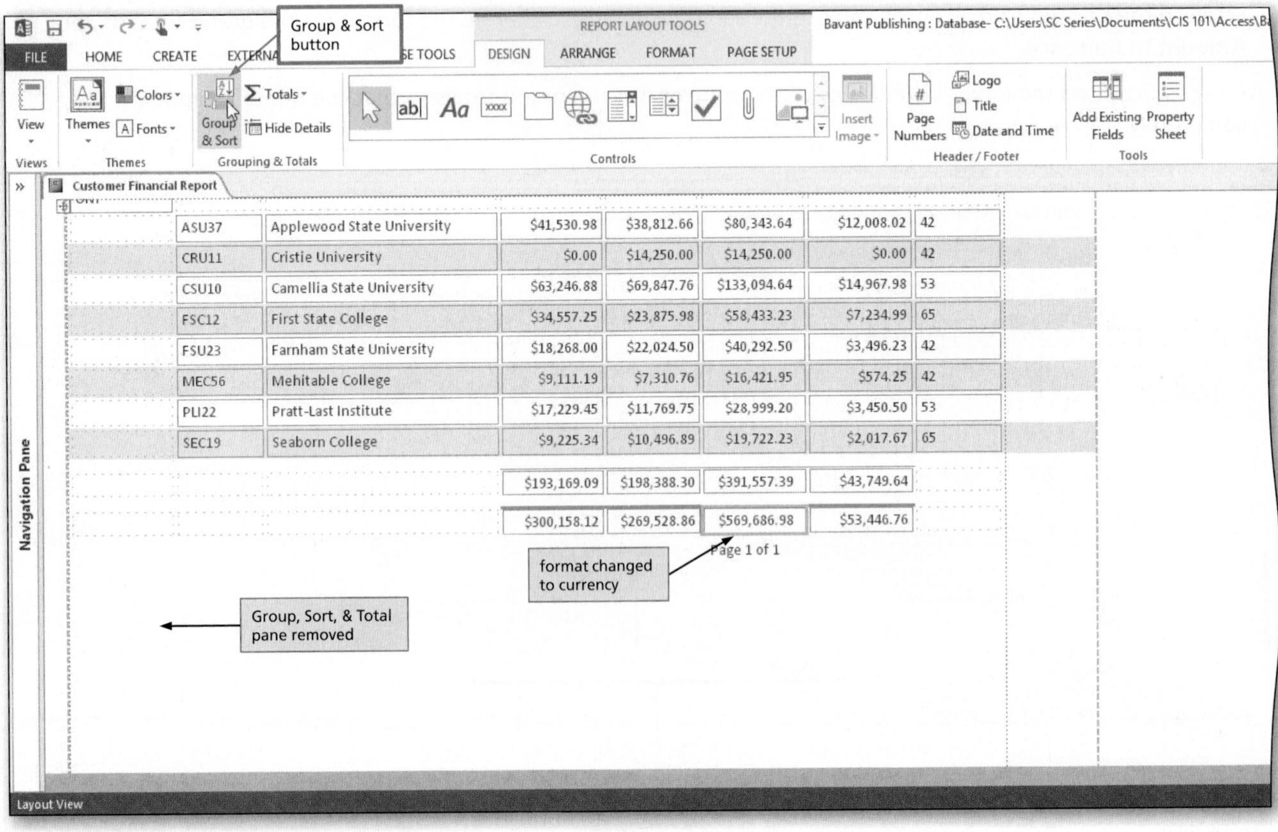

Figure 4–14

Other Ways

1. Tap or click 'Close Grouping Dialog Box' button

CONSIDER THIS

How do you determine the organization of the report or form?

Determine various details concerning how the data in your report or form is to be organized.

Determine sort order. Is there a special order in which the records should appear?

Determine grouping. Should the records be grouped in some fashion? If so, what should appear before the records in a group? If, for example, customers are grouped by city, the name of the city should probably appear before the group. What should appear after the group? For example, does the report include some fields for which subtotals should be calculated? If so, the subtotals would come after the group. Determine whether you need multiple levels of grouping.

To Conditionally Format Controls

1 GROUP, SORT, & TOTAL | 2 CONDITIONALLY FORMAT CONTROLS | 3 FILTER REPORT RECORDS | 4 MULTIPLE-TABLE REPORT
5 FORM WIZARD | 6 MODIFY CONTROLS | 7 FILTER FORM RECORDS | 8 MAILING LABELS

Conditional formatting is special formatting that is applied to values that satisfy some criterion. Bavant management has decided to apply conditional formatting to the Current Due field. ***Why?*** *They would like to emphasize values in the Current Due field that are greater than or equal to $6,000 by changing the font color to red.* The following steps conditionally format the Current Due field by specifying a **rule** that states that if the values in the field are greater than or equal to $6,000, such values will be formatted in red.

1

- Scroll to the top of the report.
- Tap or click FORMAT on the ribbon to display the REPORT LAYOUT TOOLS FORMAT tab.
- Tap or click the Current Due field on the first record to select the field (Figure 4–15).

Q&A Does it have to be the first record?
No. You could tap or click the field on any record.

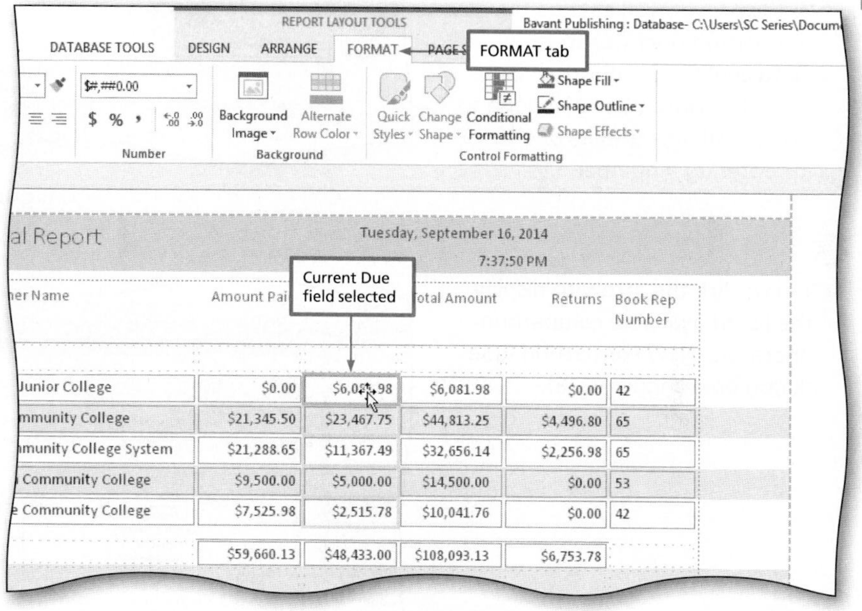

Figure 4–15

2

- Tap or click the Conditional Formatting button (REPORT LAYOUT TOOLS FORMAT tab | Control Formatting group) to display the Conditional Formatting Rules Manager dialog box (Figure 4–16).

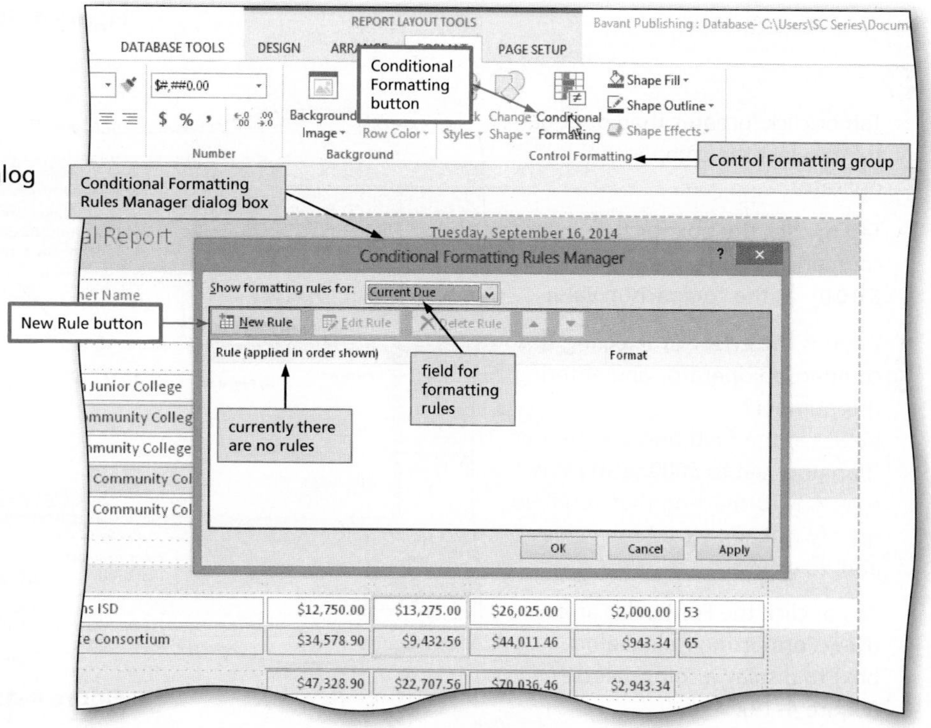

Figure 4–16

3

- Tap or click the New Rule button (Conditional Formatting Rules Manager dialog box) to display the New Formatting Rule dialog box (Figure 4–17).

Q&A I see that there are two boxes to enter numbers. I only have one number to enter, 6000. Am I on the right screen?

Yes. Next, you will change the comparison operator from 'between' to 'greater than or equal to.' Once you have done so, Access will only display one box for entering a number.

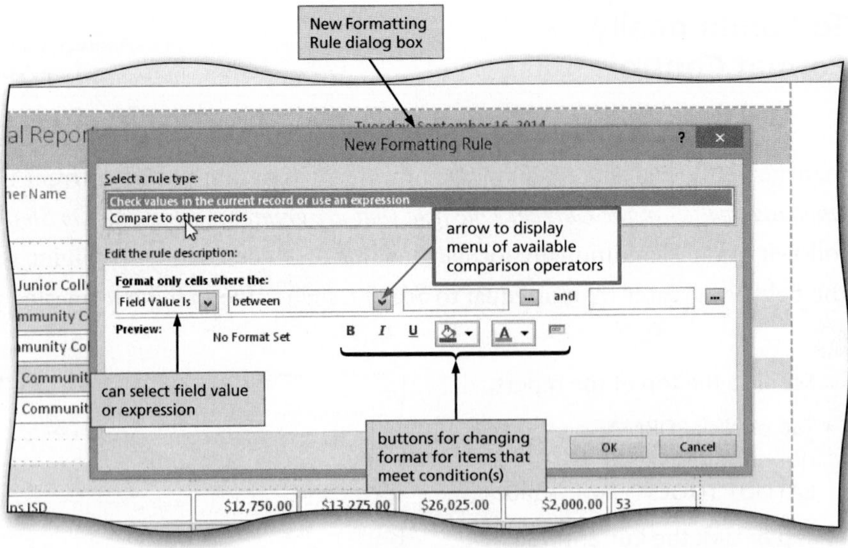

Figure 4–17

4

- Tap or click the arrow to display the list of available comparison operators (New Formatting Rule dialog box) (Figure 4–18).

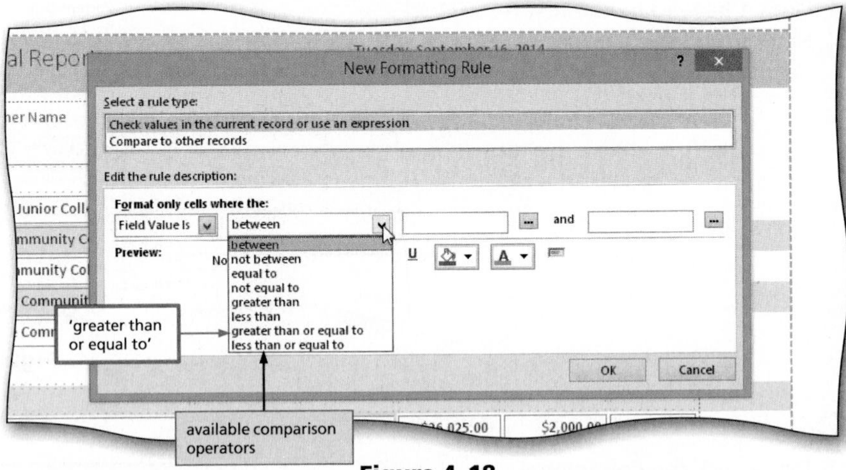

Figure 4–18

5

- Tap or click 'greater than or equal to' to select the comparison operator.
- Tap or click the box for the comparison value, and then type 6000 as the comparison value.

Q&A What is the effect of selecting this comparison operator and entering this number?

Values in the field that are greater than or equal to 6000 satisfy this rule. Any formatting that you now specify will apply to those values and no others.

- Tap or click the Font color arrow (New Formatting Rule dialog box) to display a color palette (Figure 4–19).

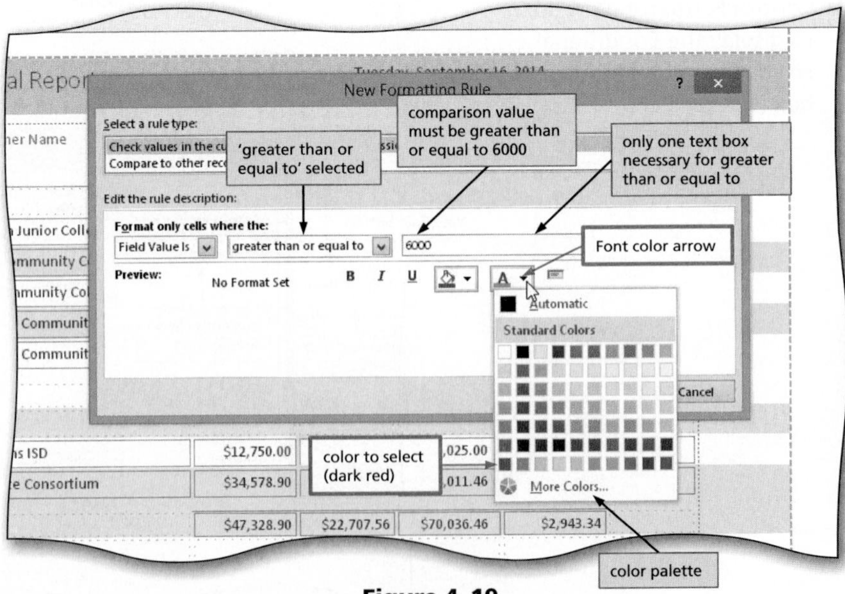

Figure 4–19

6

- Tap or click the dark red color in the lower-left corner of the color palette to select the color (Figure 4–20).

Q&A What other changes could I specify for those values that satisfy the rule?
You could specify that the value is bold, italic, and/or underlined. You could also specify a background color.

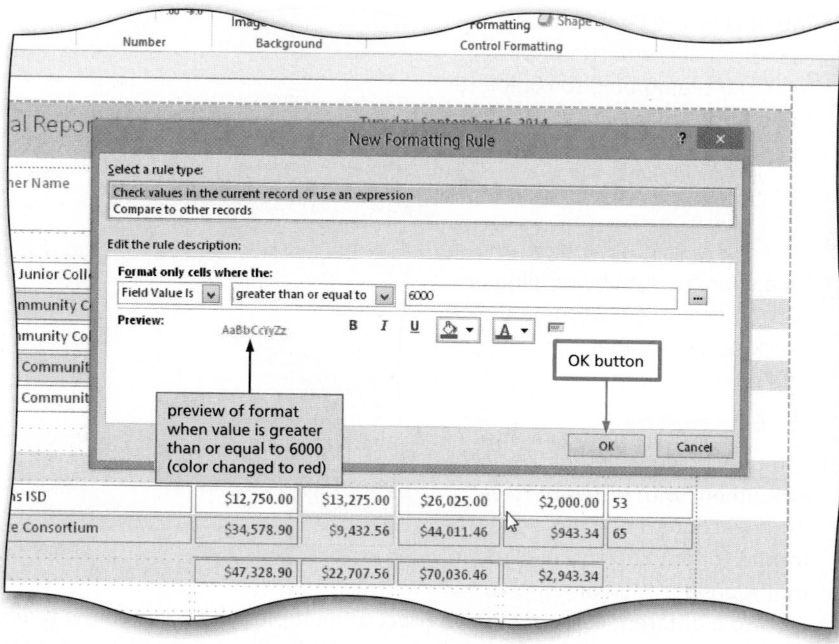

Figure 4–20

7

- Tap or click the OK button (New Formatting Rule dialog box) to enter the rule (Figure 4–21).

Q&A What if I have more than one rule?
The rules are applied in the order in which they appear in the dialog box. If a value satisfies the first rule, the specified formatting will apply, and no further rules will be tested. If not, the value will be tested against the second rule. If it satisfies the rule, the formatting for the second rule would apply. If not, the value would be tested against the third rule, and so on.

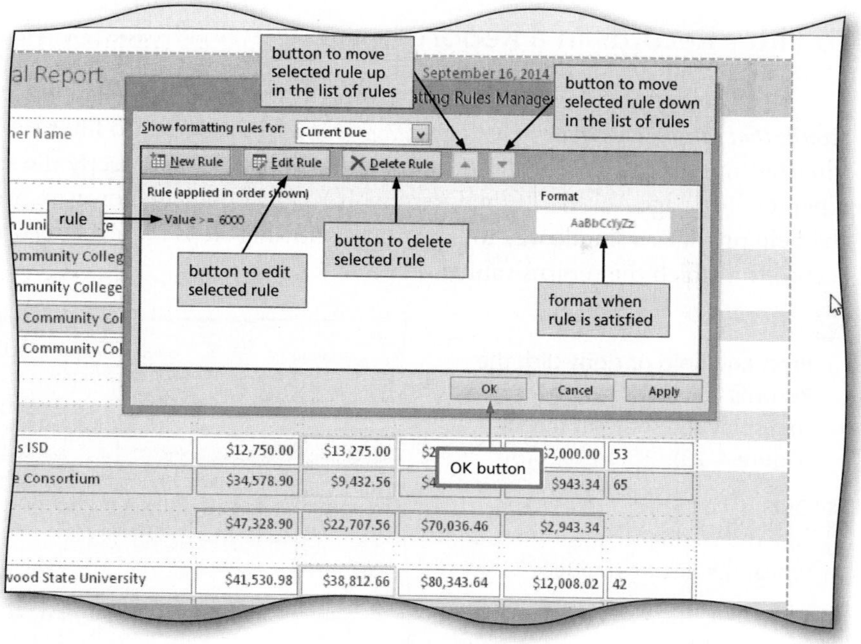

Figure 4–21

Q&A Can I change this conditional formatting later?
Yes. Select the field for which you had applied conditional formatting on any record, tap or click the Conditional Formatting button (REPORT LAYOUT TOOLS FORMAT tab | Control Formatting group), tap or click the rule you want to change, tap or click the Edit Rule button, and then make the necessary changes. You also can delete the selected rule by tapping or clicking the Delete Rule button, or move the selected rule by tapping or clicking the up or down arrows.

8

- Tap or click the OK button (Conditional Formatting Rules Manager dialog box) to complete the entry of the conditional formatting rules and apply the rule (Figure 4–22).

9

- Save your changes by tapping or clicking the Save button on the Quick Access Toolbar.

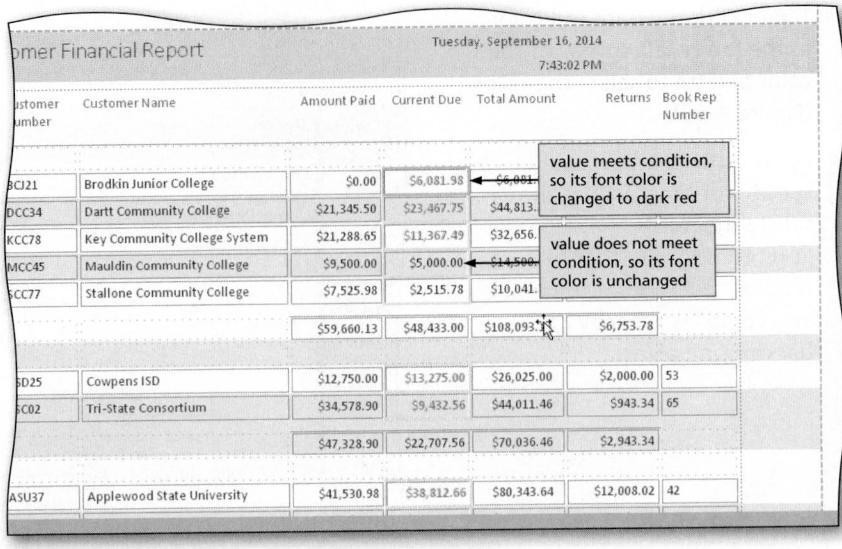

Figure 4–22

Experiment

- After saving your changes, experiment with different rules. Add a second rule that changes the format for any current due amount that is greater than or equal to $500 to a different color to see the effect of multiple rules. Change the order of rules to see the effect of a different order. When you have finished, delete any additional rules you have added so that the report contains only the one rule that you created earlier.

To Filter Records in a Report

1 GROUP, SORT, & TOTAL | 2 CONDITIONALLY FORMAT CONTROLS | 3 FILTER REPORT RECORDS | 4 MULTIPLE-TABLE REPORT
5 FORM WIZARD | 6 MODIFY CONTROLS | 7 FILTER FORM RECORDS | 8 MAILING LABELS

You sometimes might want to filter records in a report. ***Why?** You may want to include in a report only those records that satisfy some criterion and to change that criterion easily.* To filter records in a report, you can use the filter buttons in the Sort & Filter group on the HOME tab in exactly the same way you did on a datasheet in Chapter 3 on page AC 147. If the filter involves only one field, however, pressing and holding or right-clicking the field provides a simple way to filter. The following steps filter the records in the report to include only those records on which the returns value is not $0.00.

1

- Press and hold or right-click the Returns field on the first record to display the shortcut menu (Figure 4–23).

Q&A Did I have to pick the first record?
No. You could pick any record on which the Returns value is $0.00.

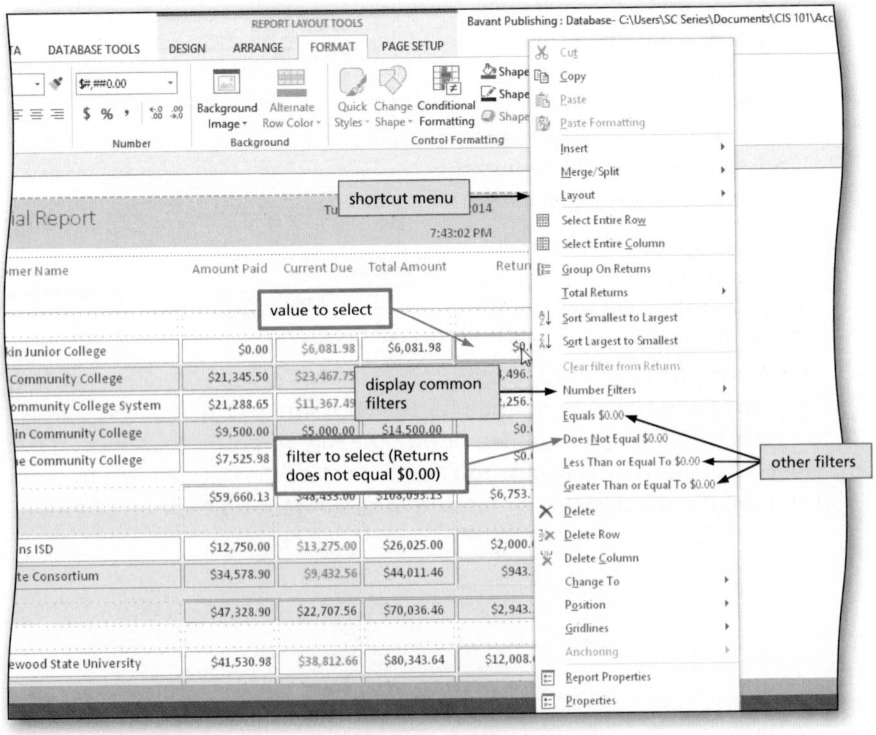

Figure 4–23

2

- Tap or click 'Does Not Equal $0.00' on the shortcut menu to restrict the records to those on which the Returns value is not $0.00 (Figure 4–24).

Q&A When would you use Number Filters?
You would use Number Filters if you need filters that are not on the main shortcut menu or if you need the ability to enter specific values other than the ones shown on the shortcut menu. If those filters are insufficient for your needs, you can use Advanced Filter/Sort, which is accessible through the Advanced button (HOME tab | Sort & Filter group).

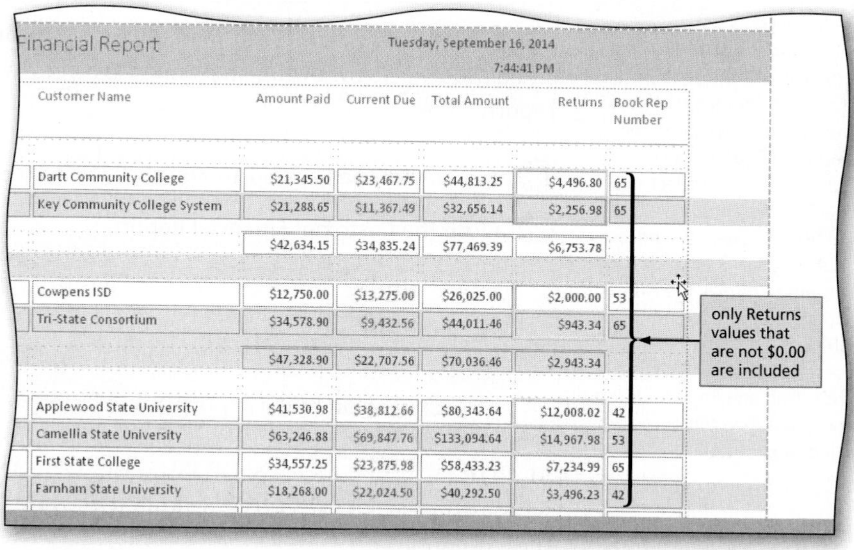

Figure 4–24

Other Ways

1. Tap or click Selection button (HOME tab | Sort & Filter group)

To Clear a Report Filter

1 GROUP, SORT, & TOTAL | 2 CONDITIONALLY FORMAT CONTROLS | **3 FILTER REPORT RECORDS** | 4 MULTIPLE-TABLE REPORT
5 FORM WIZARD | 6 MODIFY CONTROLS | 7 FILTER FORM RECORDS | 8 MAILING LABELS

The following steps clear the filter on the Returns field. ***Why?*** *When you no longer want the records to be filtered, you clear the filter, so that all records are again included.*

1

- Press and hold or right-click the Returns field on the second record to display the shortcut menu (Figure 4–25).

Q&A Did I have to pick the second record?
No. You could pick the Returns field on any record.

2

- Tap or click 'Clear filter from Returns' on the shortcut menu to clear the filter and redisplay all records.

Experiment

- Try other filters on the shortcut menu for the Returns field to see their effect. When you are done with each, clear the filter.

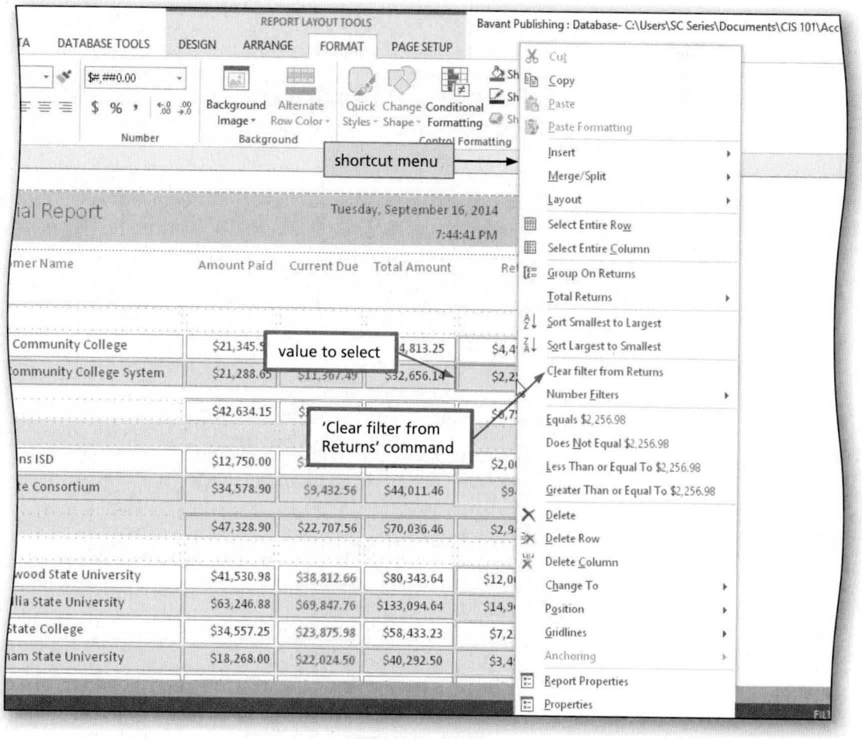

Figure 4–25

Other Ways

1. Tap or click Advanced button (HOME tab | Sort & Filter group), tap or click Clear All Filters on Advanced menu

BTW
Searching for Records in a Report
You can use the Find button to search for records in a report. To do so, open the report in Report view or Layout view and select the field in the report on which to search. Click the Find button (HOME tab | Find group) to display the Find and Replace dialog box. Type the desired value on which to search in the Find What text box (Find and Replace dialog box) and then tap or click the Find Next button.

To Save and Close a Report

Now that you have completed work on your report, you should save the report and close it. The following steps first save your work on the report and then close the report.

1. Tap or click the Save button on the Quick Access Toolbar to save your work.
2. Close the Customer Financial Report.

The Arrange and Page Setup Tabs

When working on a report in Layout view, you can make additional layout changes by using the REPORT LAYOUT TOOLS ARRANGE and/or PAGE SETUP tabs. The ARRANGE tab is shown in Figure 4–26. Table 4–1 shows the buttons on the ARRANGE tab along with the Enhanced ScreenTips that describe their function.

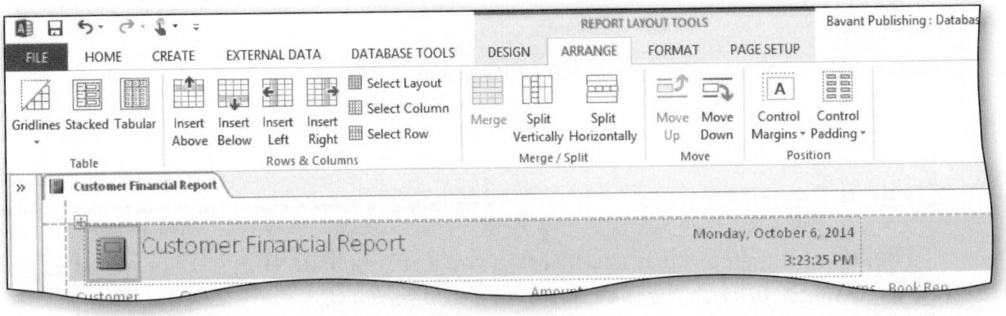

Figure 4–26

BTW
Using the ARRANGE Tab
Because the commands located on the ARRANGE tab are actions associated with previously selected controls, be sure to select the desired control or controls first.

Table 4–1 ARRANGE Tab

Button	Enhanced ScreenTip
Gridlines	Gridlines.
Stacked	Create a layout similar to a paper form, with labels to the left of each field.
Tabular	Create a layout similar to a spreadsheet, with labels across the top and data in columns below the labels.
Insert Above	Insert above.
Insert Below	Insert below.
Insert Left	Insert left.
Insert Right	Insert right.
Select Layout	Select layout.
Select Column	Select column.
Select Row	Select row.
Merge	Merge cells.
Split Vertically	Split the selected layout into two rows.
Split Horizontally	Split the selected layout into two columns.
Move Up	Move up.
Move Down	Move down.
Control Margins	Specify the location of information displayed within the control.
Control Padding	Set the amount of spacing between controls and the gridlines of a layout.

The REPORT LAYOUT TOOLS PAGE SETUP tab is shown in Figure 4–27. Table 4–2 shows the buttons on the PAGE SETUP tab along with the Enhanced ScreenTips that describe their function.

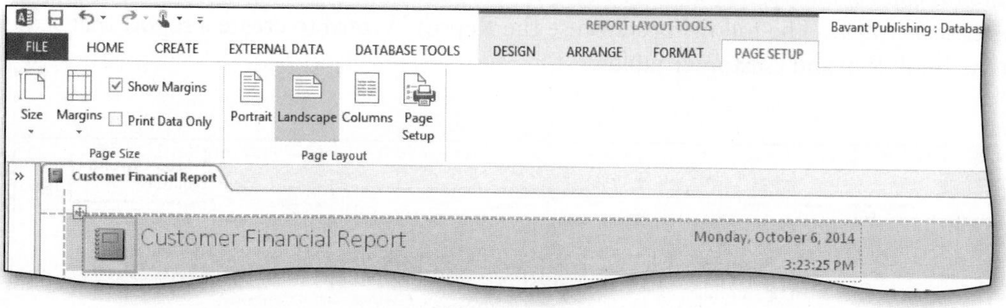

Figure 4–27

Table 4–2 PAGE SETUP Tab

Button	Enhanced ScreenTip
Size	Choose a paper size for the current section.
Margins	Select the margin sizes for the entire document or the current section.
Show Margins	Show margins.
Print Data Only	Print data only.
Portrait	Change to portrait orientation.
Landscape	Change to landscape orientation.
Columns	Columns.
Page Setup	Show the Page Setup dialog box.

To Print a Report

The following steps print the report.

1. With the Customer Financial Report selected in the Navigation Pane, tap or click FILE on the ribbon to open the Backstage view.
2. Tap or click the Print tab in the Backstage view to display the Print gallery.
3. Tap or click the Quick Print button to print the report.

Q&A How can I print multiple copies of my report?
Tap or click FILE on the ribbon to open the Backstage view. Tap or click the Print tab, tap or click Print in the Print gallery to display the Print dialog box, increase the number in the Number of Copies box, and then tap or click the OK button (Print dialog box).

BTW
Distributing a Document
Instead of printing and distributing a hard copy of a document, you can distribute the document electronically. Options include sending the document via email; posting it on cloud storage (such as SkyDrive) and sharing the file with others; posting it on a social networking site, blog, or other website; and sharing a link associated with an online location of the document. You also can create and share a PDF or XPS image of the document, so that users can view the file in Acrobat Reader or XPS Viewer instead of in Access.

Multiple-Table Reports

Sometimes you will create reports that require data from more than one table. You can use the Report Wizard to create a report based on multiple tables just as you can use it to create reports based on single tables or queries.

To Create a Report that Involves Multiple Tables

1 GROUP, SORT, & TOTAL | 2 CONDITIONALLY FORMAT CONTROLS | 3 FILTER REPORT RECORDS | **4 MULTIPLE-TABLE REPORT**
5 FORM WIZARD | 6 MODIFY CONTROLS | 7 FILTER FORM RECORDS | 8 MAILING LABELS

***Why?** Bavant needs a report that includes the Book Rep Number, First Name, and Last Name fields from the Book Rep table. In addition, for each customer of the rep, they need the Customer Number, Customer Name, Amount Paid, and Current Due fields from the Customer table.* The following steps use the Report Wizard to create a report that includes fields from both the Book Rep and Customer tables.

1

- Open the Navigation Pane if it is currently closed.
- Tap or click the Book Rep table in the Navigation Pane to select it.
- Tap or click CREATE on the ribbon to display the CREATE tab.
- Tap or click the Report Wizard button (CREATE tab | Reports group) to start the Report Wizard (Figure 4–28).

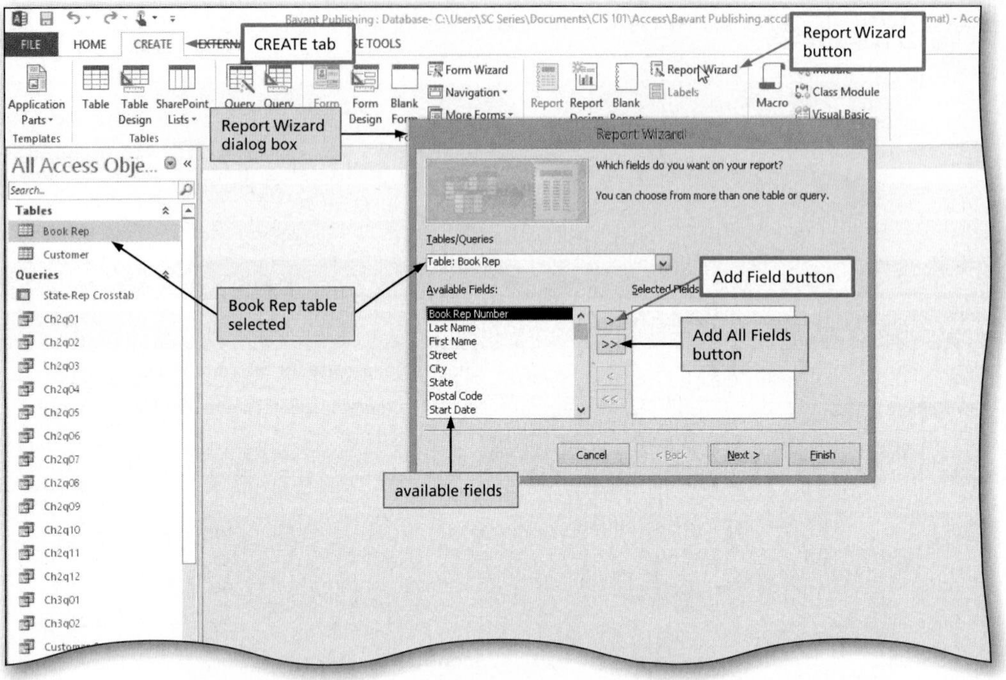

Figure 4–28

Q&A My Navigation Pane does not look like the one in this screen. Is that a problem? How do I change it?

No, this is not a problem, but you should change the Navigation Pane so it matches the screens in this chapter. To do so, tap or click the Navigation Pane arrow and then tap or click Object Type.

2

- Tap or click the Add Field button to add the Book Rep Number field to the report.
- Add the First Name field by tapping or clicking it and then tapping or clicking the Add Field button.
- Add the Last Name field in the same manner.
- Tap or click the Tables/Queries arrow, and then tap or click Table: Customer in the Tables/Queries list box (Figure 4–29).

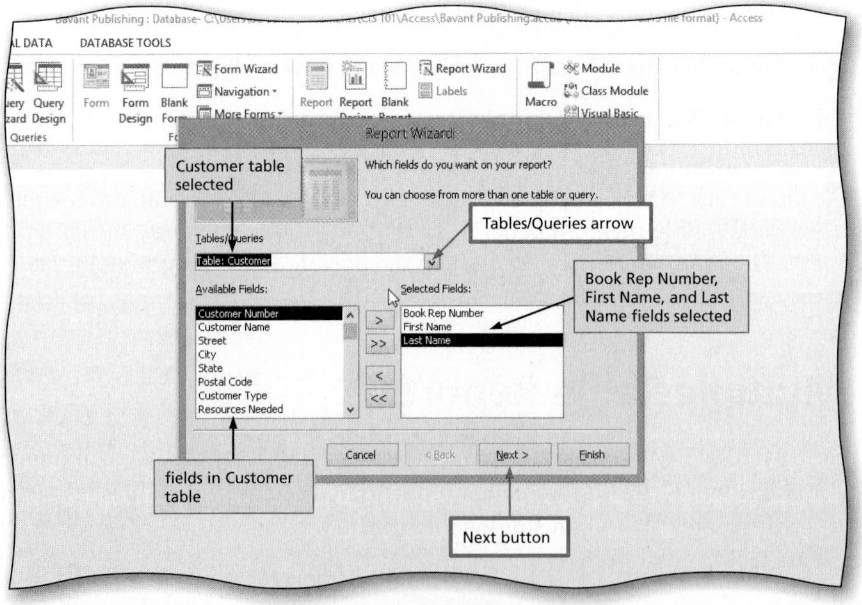

Figure 4–29

3

- Add the Customer Number, Customer Name, Amount Paid, and Current Due fields by tapping or clicking the field and then tapping or clicking the Add Field button.
- Tap or click the Next button (Figure 4–30).

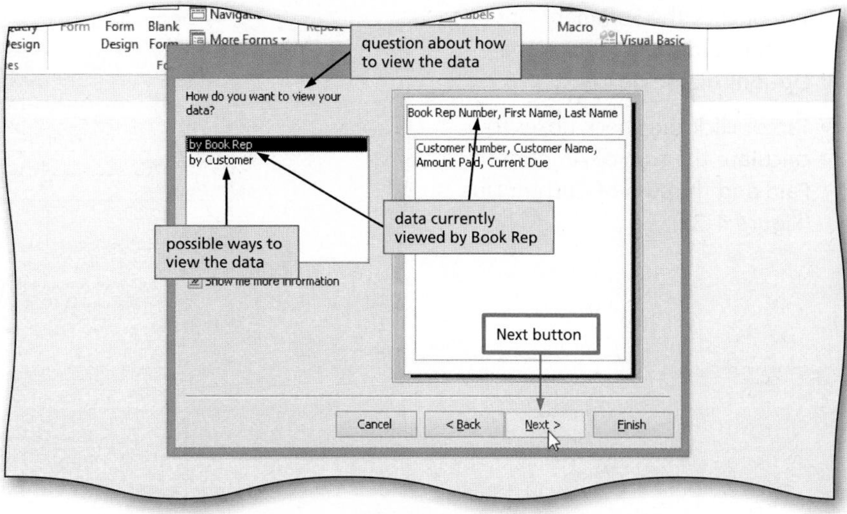

Figure 4–30

4

- Because the report is to be viewed by Book Rep table, and by Book Rep table already is selected, tap or click the Next button (Figure 4–31).

Q&A I did not get this screen. Instead, I got an error message that said something about the tables not being related.

In Chapter 3, you create a relationship between the tables. That relationship must exist for the Report Wizard to be able to create the report. Return to Chapter 3, complete the steps on pages AC 182 through 184, and then begin these steps again.

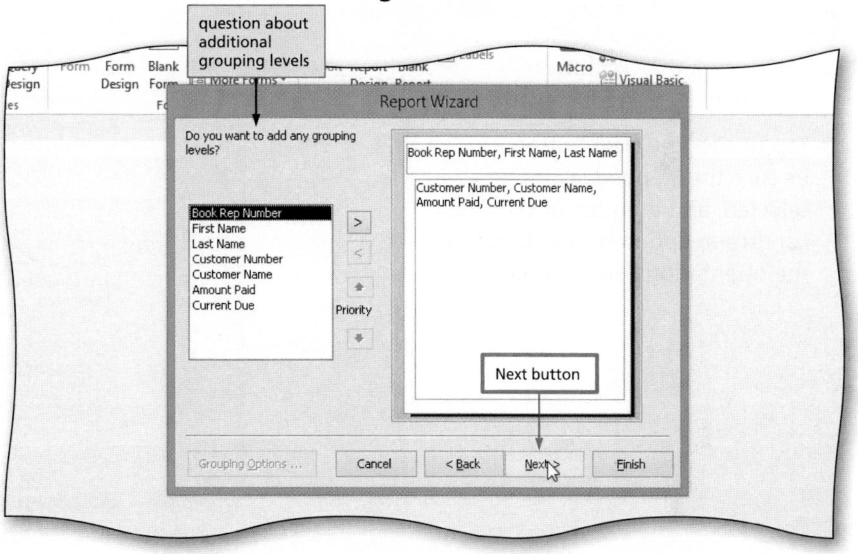

Figure 4–31

5

- Tap or click the Next button to move to the next Report Wizard screen.
- Tap or click the arrow in the text box labeled 1, and then tap or click the Customer Number field in the list to select the sort order (Figure 4–32).

Q&A When would I use the Summary Options button?

You would use the Summary Options button if you want to specify subtotals or other calculations for the report while using the wizard. You also can use it to produce a summary report by selecting Summary Only, which will omit all detail records from the report.

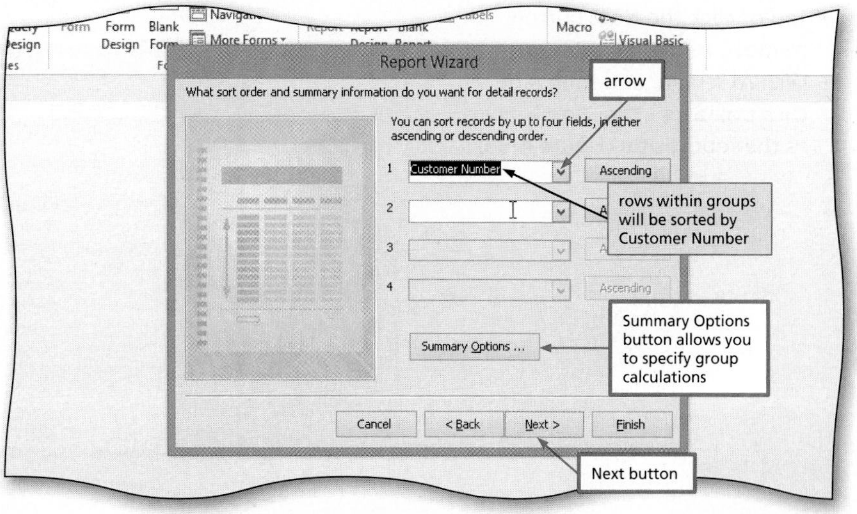

Figure 4–32

6

- Tap or click the Summary Options button to display the Summary Options dialog box.
- Tap or click the check boxes to calculate the sum of Amount Paid and the sum of Current Due (Figure 4–33)

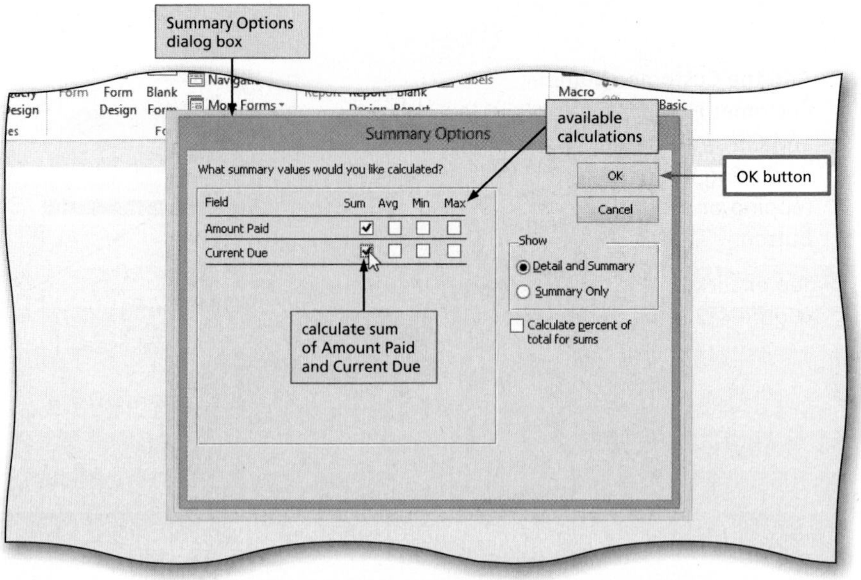

Figure 4–33

7

- Tap or click the OK button (Summary Options dialog box).
- Tap or click the Next button, be sure the Stepped layout is selected, and then tap or click the Landscape option button to select the orientation (Figure 4–34).

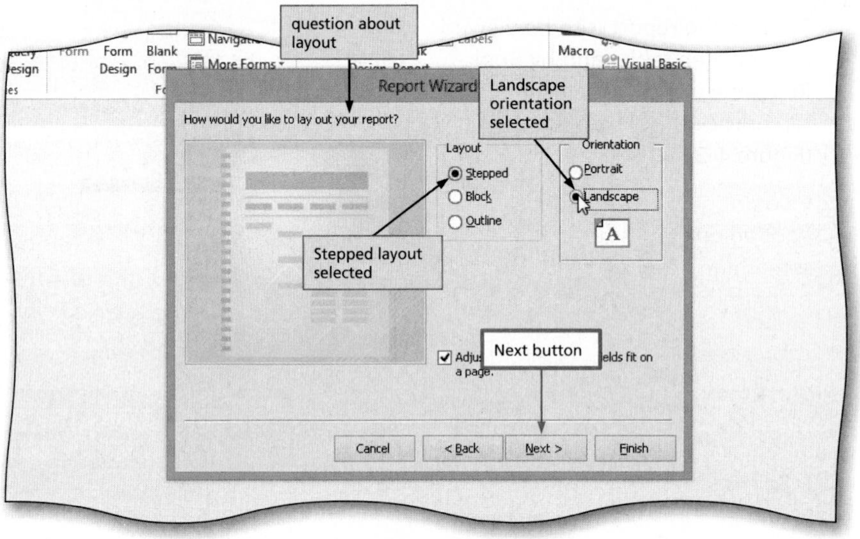

Figure 4–34

8

- Tap or click the Next button to move to the next Report Wizard screen, and then type `Customers by Book Rep` as the report title (Figure 4–35).

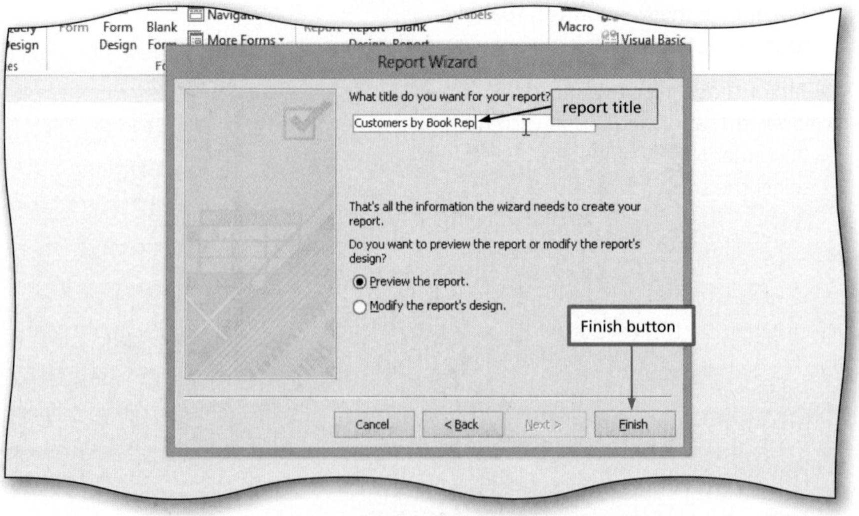

Figure 4–35

9

- Tap or click the Finish button to produce the report (Figure 4–36).

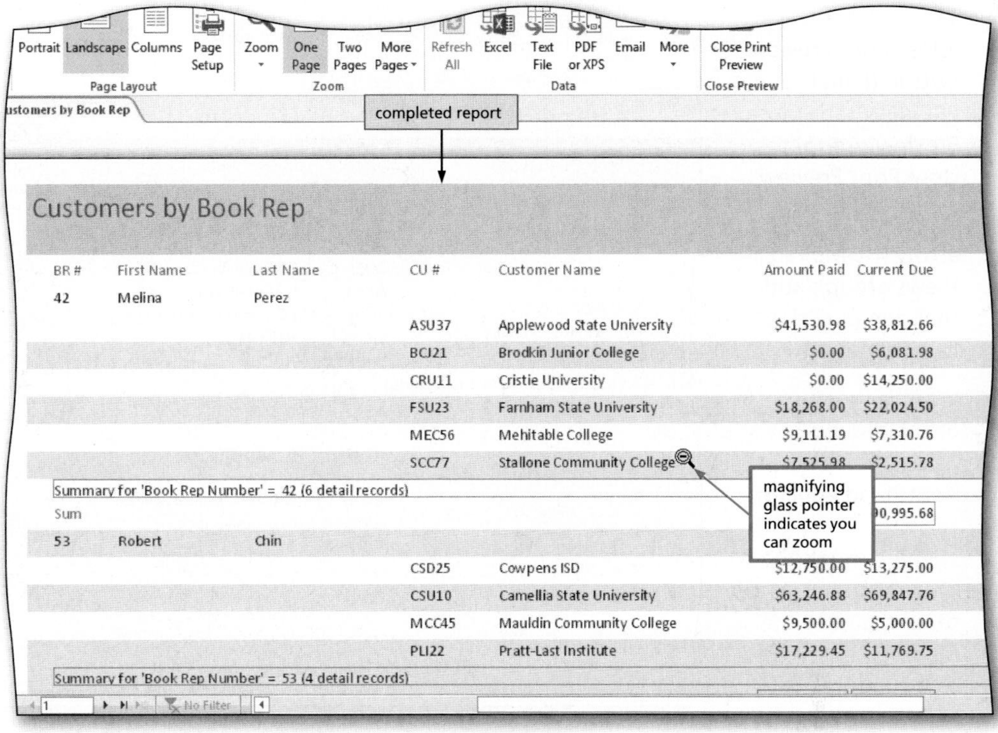

Figure 4–36

10

- Tap or click the magnifying glass pointer somewhere within the report to view more of the report (Figure 4–37).

Experiment

- Zoom in on various positions within the report. When finished, view a complete page of the report.

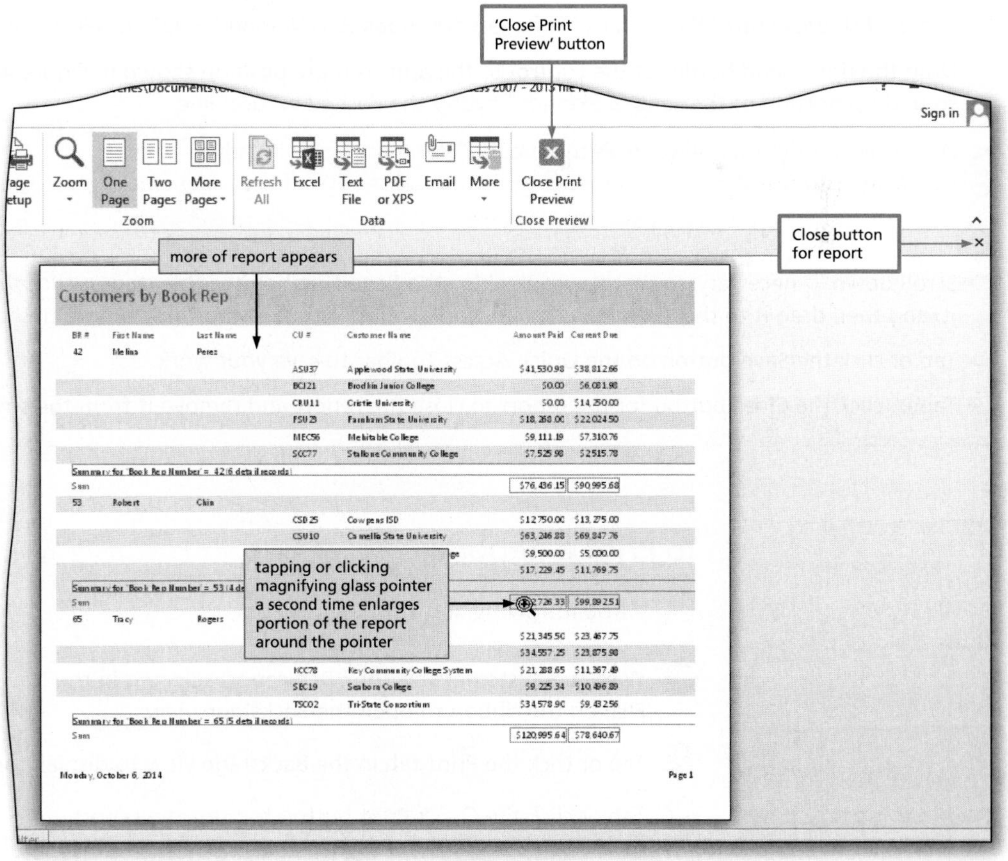

Figure 4–37

11

- Tap or click the 'Close Print Preview' button (PRINT PREVIEW tab | Close Preview group) to close Print Preview.
- Tap or click the View arrow (HOME tab | Views group), and then tap or click Layout View.

Q&A What is the purpose of the dashed vertical line near the right-hand edge of the screen?
The line shows the right-hand border of the amount of the report that will print on one page. If any portion of the report extends beyond the line, the report may not print correctly.

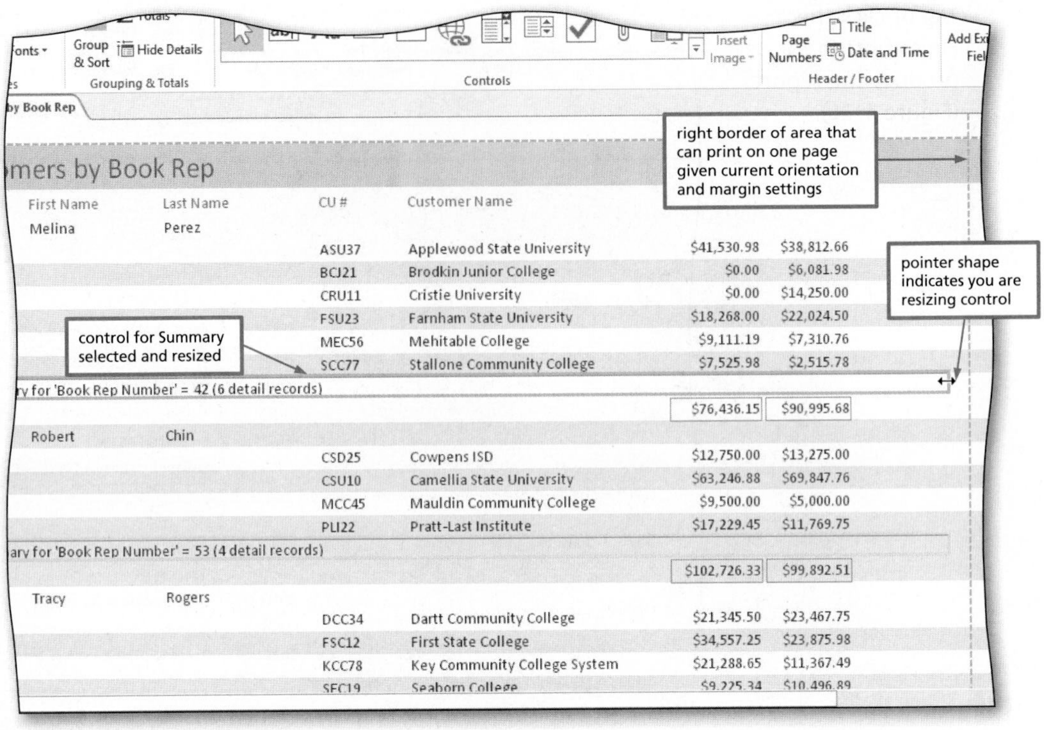

Figure 4–38

- Tap or click the control that begins "Summary for 'Book Rep Number' = 42" to select the control.
- Drag the right-hand border of the control to the approximate position shown in Figure 4–38 to resize the control so that no portion of the control extends beyond the dashed vertical line.

Q&A Do I have to resize all the controls that begin "Summary" individually?
No. When you resize one of them, the others will all be resized the same amount automatically.

12

- Scroll down, if necessary, so that the control for the Page Number is visible, tap or click the Page number to select it, and then drag it to the left so that no portion of the control extends beyond the dashed line.
- Tap or click the Save button on the Quick Access Toolbar to save your work.
- Tap or click the Close button for the report to close the report and remove it from the screen.

To Print a Report

BTW
Summary Reports
You can create a summary report in either Layout view or Design view.

The following steps print the report.

1. With the Customers by Book Rep report selected in the Navigation Pane, tap or click FILE on the ribbon to open the Backstage view.
2. Tap or click the Print tab in the Backstage view to display the Print gallery.
3. Tap or click the Quick Print button to print the report.

CONSIDER THIS

How do you determine the tables and fields that contain the data needed for the report?

First you need to know the requirements for the report. Precisely what data is the report intended to convey? Once you understand those requirements, follow these guidelines:

Examine the requirements for the report to determine the tables. Do the requirements only relate to data in a single table, or does the data come from multiple tables? What is the relationship between the tables?

Examine the requirements for the report to determine the fields necessary. Look for all the data items specified for the report. Each should correspond to a field in a table or be able to be computed from fields in a table. This information gives you the list of fields to include.

Determine the order of the fields. Examine the requirements to determine the order in which the fields should appear. Be logical and consistent in your ordering. For example, in an address, the city should come before the state and the state should come before the postal code, unless there is some compelling reason for another order.

Creating a Report in Layout View

In Chapter 1, you used the Report button initially to create a report containing all the fields in a table. You then deleted the unwanted fields so that the resulting report contained only the desired fields. At that point you used Layout view to modify the report and produce the report you wanted.

You also can use Layout view to create single- or multiple-table reports from scratch. To do so, you would first create a blank report and display a field list for the table containing the first fields you want to include on the report (Figure 4–39).

BTW

Multicolumn Reports

There are times when you may want to create a report that has multiple columns. For example, a telephone list with employee name and phone number could print in multiple columns. To do so, create the report using Layout view or Design view and then tap or click the PAGE SETUP tab, tap or click the Columns button, enter the number of columns, select the desired column layout, and then tap or click the OK button.

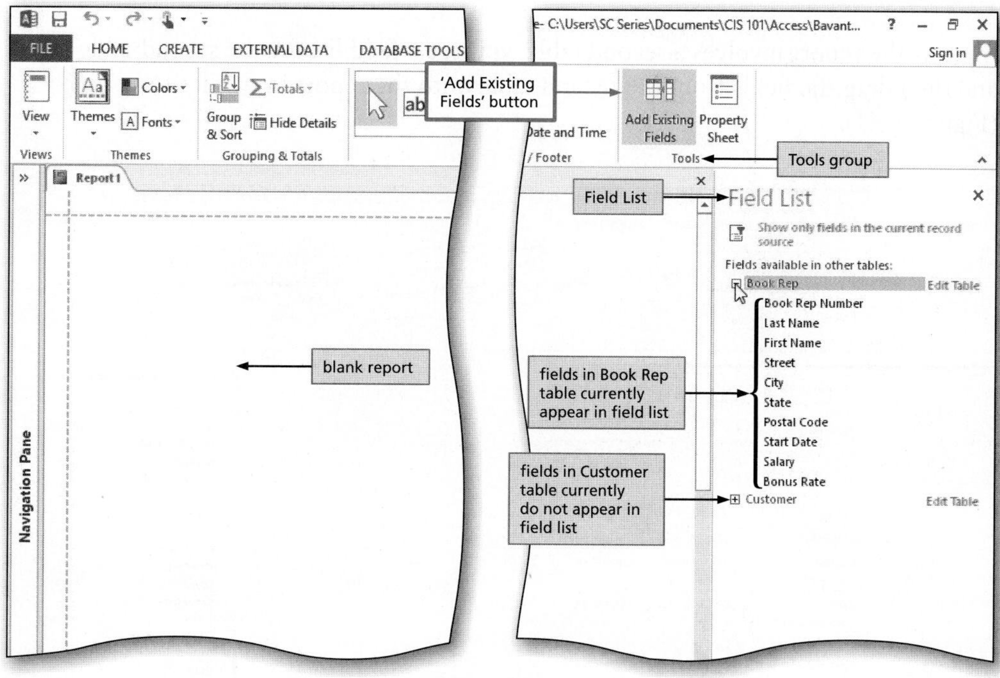

Figure 4–39

You then would drag any fields you want from the table onto the report in the order you want them to appear (Figure 4–40).

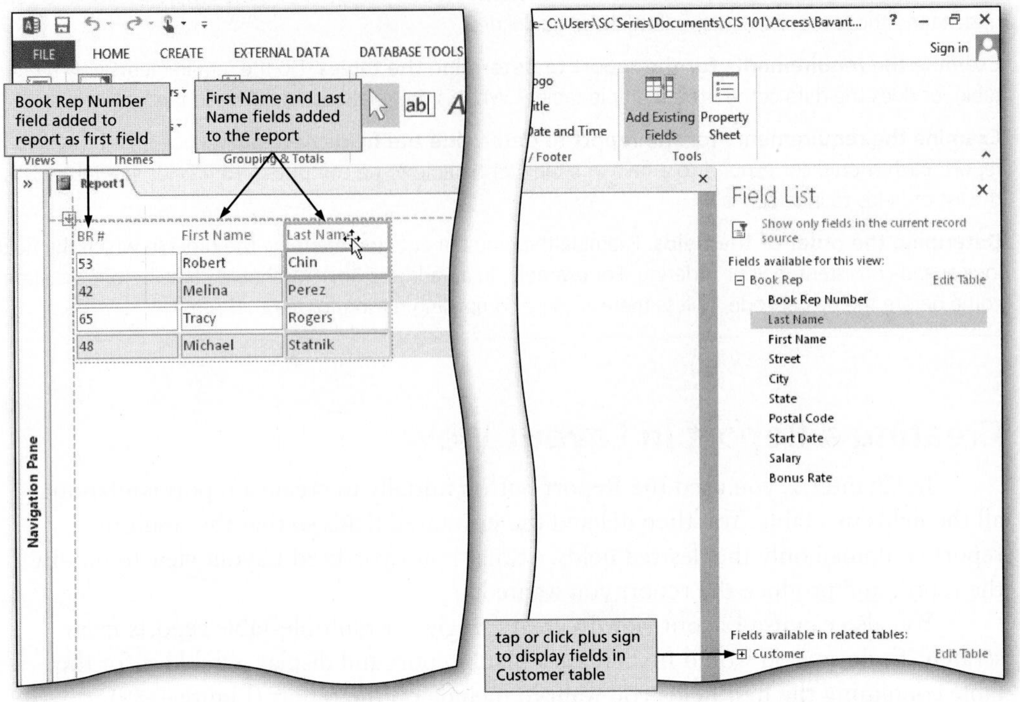

Figure 4–40

If the report involves a second table, you use a field list for the second table and then drag the fields from the second table onto the report in the desired order (Figure 4–41).

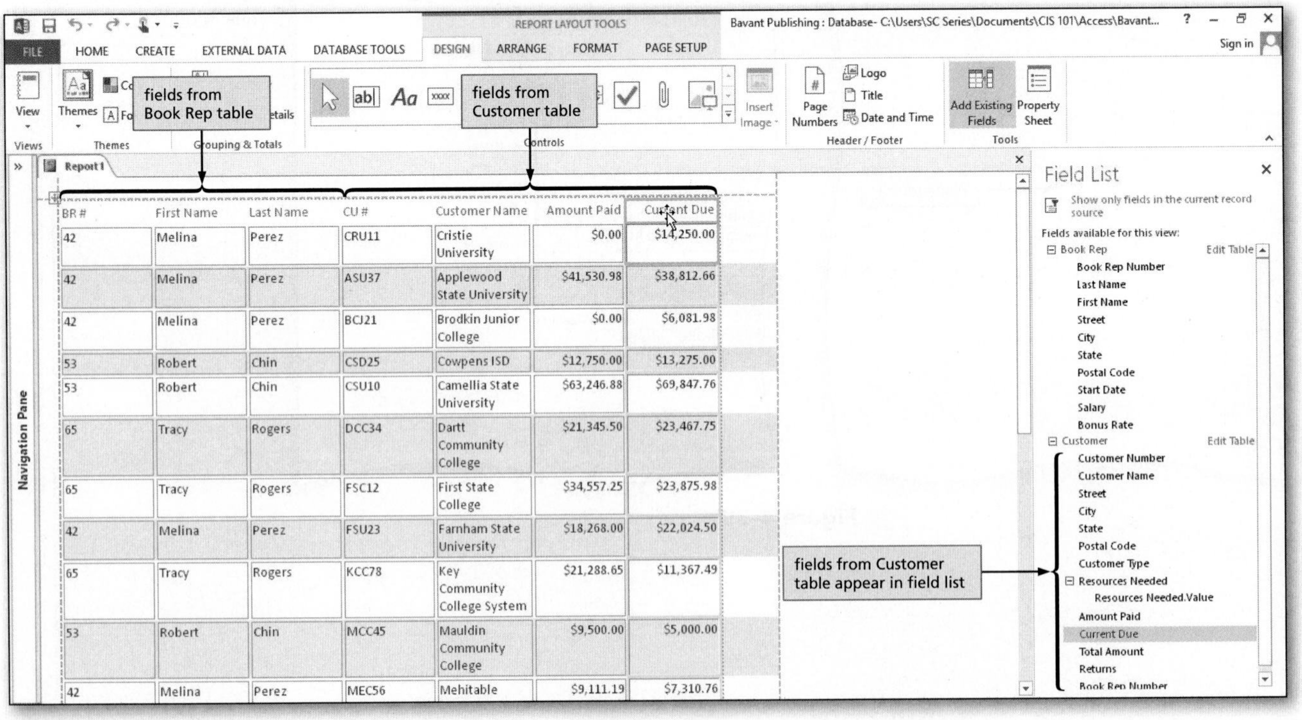

Figure 4–41

When you create a report in Layout view, the report does not automatically contain a title, but you can add one by tapping or clicking the Title button (REPORT LAYOUT TOOLS DESIGN tab | Header/Footer group) (Figure 4–42).

Once you have added the title, you can type whatever title you want for the report.

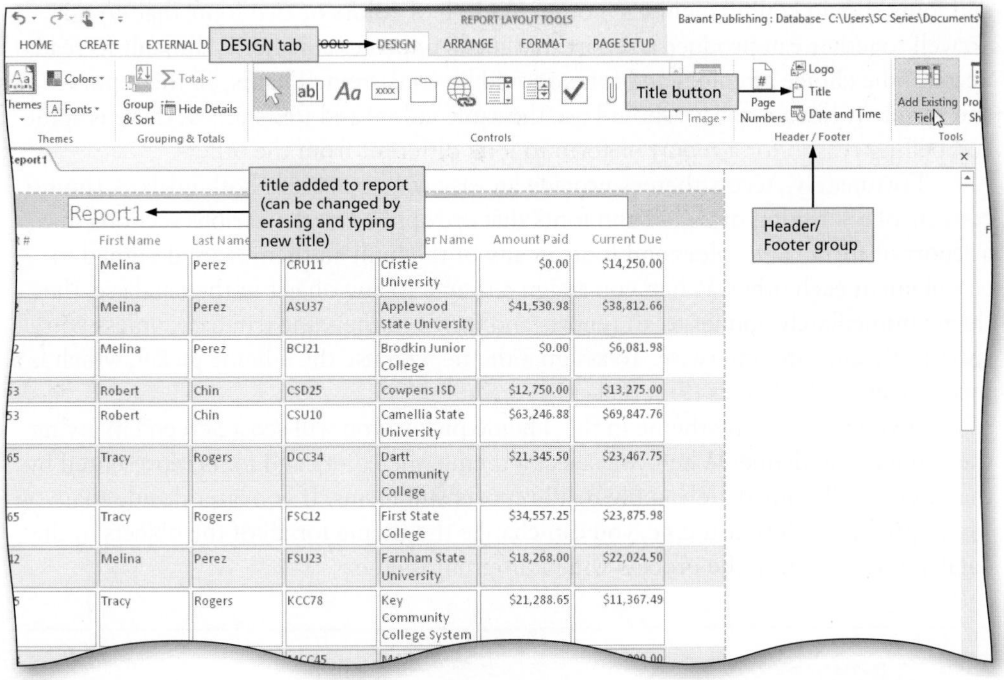

Figure 4–42

To Create a Report in Layout View by Creating a Blank Report

If you want to create a report in Layout view, you would use the following steps.

1. Tap or click CREATE on the ribbon to display the CREATE tab.
2. Tap or click the Blank Report button (CREATE tab | Reports group) to create a blank report.
3. If a field list does not appear, display a field list by tapping or clicking the 'Add Existing Fields' button (REPORT LAYOUT TOOLS DESIGN tab | Tools group).
4. If the tables do not appear in the field list, tap or click Show All Tables.
5. If the fields in a table do not appear, tap or click the plus sign in front of the name of the table.
6. Drag the fields from the field list onto the report in the desired order.
7. If the report involves a second table, be sure the fields in the second table appear, and then drag the fields from the second table onto the report in the desired order. (If the field list covers the portion of the report where you want to drag the fields, move the field list to a different position by dragging its title bar.)
8. To add a title to the report, tap or click the Title button (REPORT LAYOUT TOOLS DESIGN tab | Header/Footer group) and then type the desired title.

Using Themes

The most important characteristic of a report or form is that it contains the desired data presented in a useful arrangement. Another important characteristic, however, is the general appearance of the form. The colors and fonts that you use in the various sections of a report or form contribute to this look. You should keep in mind two important goals when assigning colors and fonts. First, the various colors and fonts should complement each other. A clash of colors or two fonts that do not go well together can produce a report that looks unprofessional or is difficult to read. Second, the choice of colors and fonts should be consistent. That is, all the reports and forms within a database should use the same colors and fonts unless there is some compelling reason for a report or form to look different from the others.

Fortunately, Access themes provide an easy way to achieve both goals. A **theme** consists of a selection of colors and fonts that are applied to the various sections in a report or form. The colors and fonts in any of the built-in themes are designed to complement each other. When you assign a theme to any object in the database, the theme immediately applies to all reports and forms in the same database, unless you specifically indicate otherwise. To assign a theme, you use the Theme picker, which is a menu of available themes (Figure 4–43).

If you point to any theme in the Theme picker, you will see a ScreenTip giving the name of the theme. When you select a theme, the colors and fonts represented by that theme will immediately apply to all reports and forms. If you later decide that you would prefer a different theme, you can change the theme for all of the objects in the database by repeating the process with a different theme.

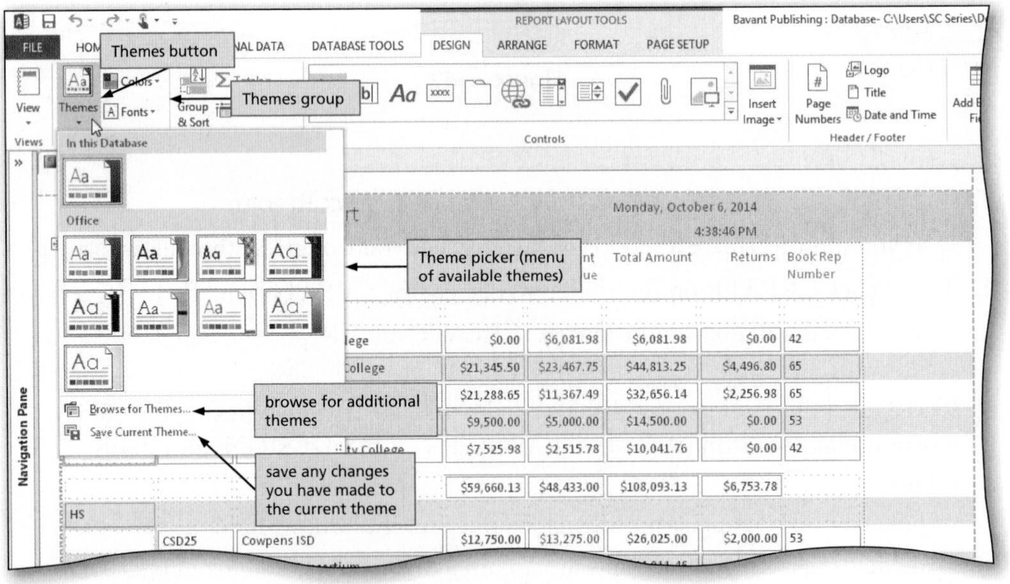

Figure 4–43

You can also use the Browse for Themes command to browse for themes that are not listed as part of a standard Access installation, but are available for download. You can also create your own customized theme by specifying a combination of fonts and colors and using the Save Current Theme command to save your combination. If, after selecting a theme using the Themes button, you do not like the colors in the current theme, you can change the theme's colors. Tap or click the Colors button (REPORT LAYOUT TOOLS DESIGN tab | Themes group) (Figure 4–44), and then select an alternative color scheme.

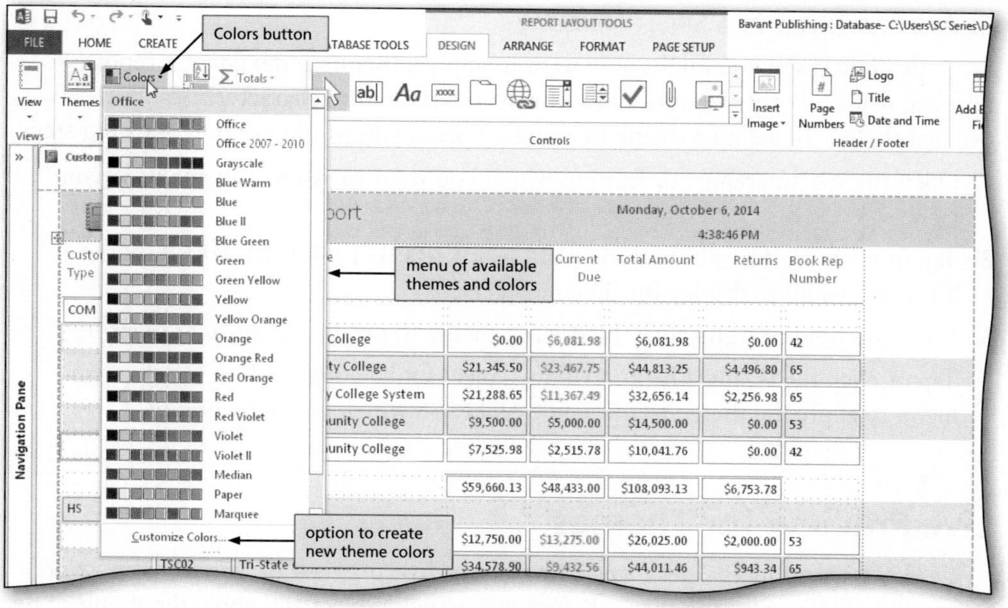

Figure 4–44

Similarly, if you do not like the fonts in the current theme, you can tap or click the Fonts button (REPORT LAYOUT TOOLS DESIGN tab | Themes group) (Figure 4–45). You then can select an alternative font.

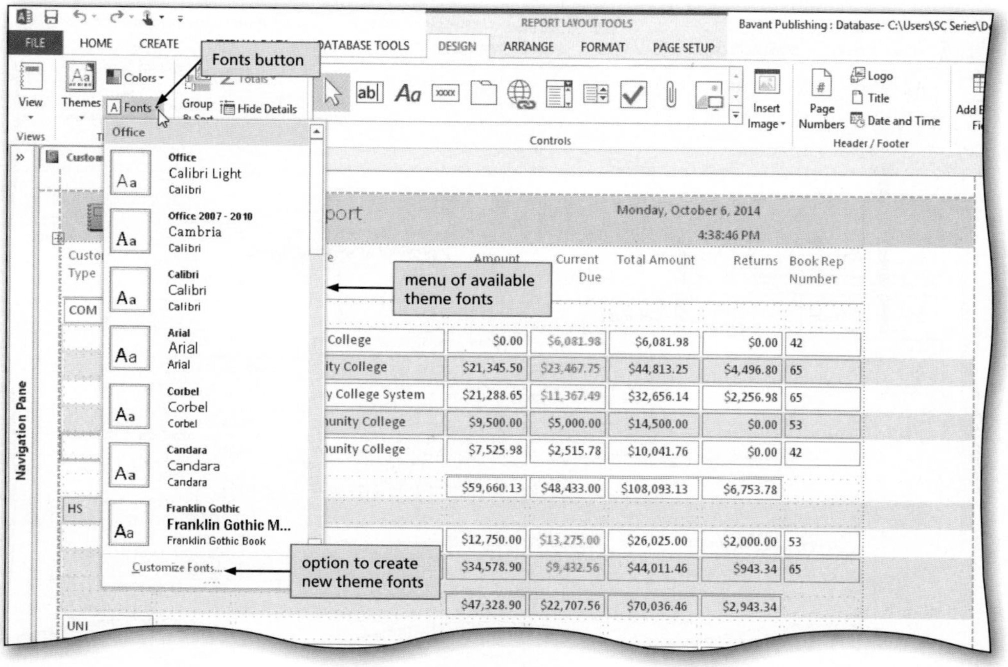

Figure 4–45

To Assign a Theme to All Objects

To assign a theme, it is easiest to use Layout view. You can use Design view as well, but it is easier to see the result of picking a theme when you are viewing the report or form in Layout view. To assign a theme to all reports and forms, you would use the following steps.

1. Open any report or form in Layout view.
2. Tap or click the Themes button (REPORT LAYOUT TOOLS DESIGN tab | Themes group) to display the Theme picker.
3. Tap or click the desired theme.

To Assign a Theme to a Single Object

In some cases, you might only want to apply a theme to the current report or form, while all other reports and forms would retain the characteristics from the original theme. To assign a theme to a single object, you would use the following steps.

1. Open the specific report or form to which you want to assign a theme in Layout view.
2. Tap or click the Themes button (REPORT LAYOUT TOOLS DESIGN tab | Themes group) to display the Theme picker.
3. Press and hold or right-click the desired theme to produce a shortcut menu.
4. Tap or click the 'Apply Theme to This Object Only' command on the shortcut menu to apply the theme to the single object on which you are working.

Live Preview for Themes

When selecting themes, Access furnishes a **live preview** of what the report or form will look like with the theme before you actually select and apply the theme. The report or form will appear as it would in the theme to which you are currently pointing (Figure 4–46). If you like that theme, you then can select the theme by tapping or clicking the left mouse button.

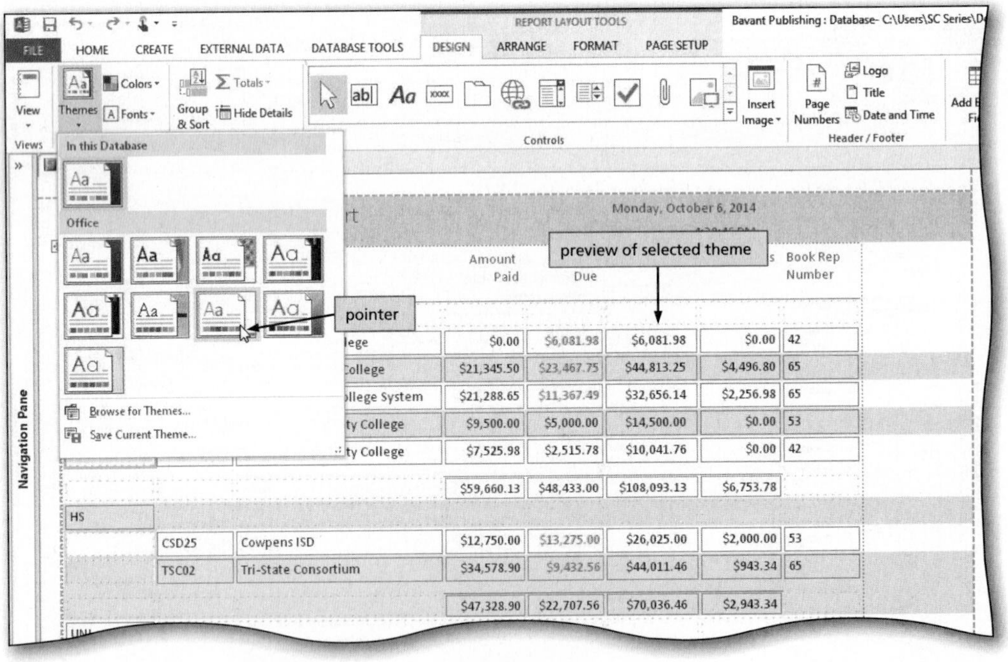

Figure 4–46

To Create a Summary Report

1 GROUP, SORT, & TOTAL | 2 CONDITIONALLY FORMAT CONTROLS | 3 FILTER REPORT RECORDS | 4 MULTIPLE-TABLE REPORT
5 FORM WIZARD | 6 MODIFY CONTROLS | 7 FILTER FORM RECORDS | 8 MAILING LABELS

A report that includes the group calculations such as subtotals, but does not include the individual detail lines, is called a **summary report**. ***Why?*** *You might need a report that only shows the overall group calculations, but not all the records.* The following steps hide the detail lines in the Customer Financial Report, thus creating a summary report.

1

- Open the Customer Financial Report in Layout view and close the Navigation Pane.

2

- Tap or click the Hide Details button (REPORT LAYOUT TOOLS DESIGN tab | Grouping & Totals group) to hide the details in the report (Figure 4–47).

Q&A How can I see the details once I have hidden them?
Tap or click the Hide Details button a second time.

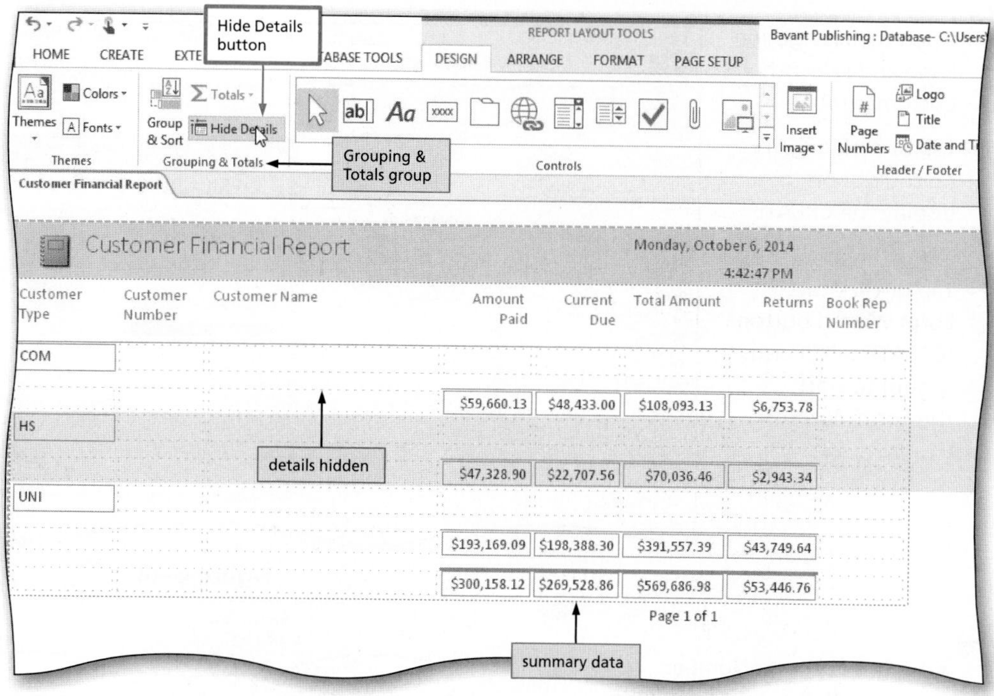

Figure 4–47

Q&A There seems to be a lot of space before the Amount Paid and Current Due fields. Is that a problem?
The extra space is the space that would be occupied by the customer number and name if you had not hidden the details. It is not a problem. If you wanted a report that was strictly a summary report, you would not have included those fields. If the fields were not included, hiding the details would not have produced this space.

3

- Close the report without saving your changes.

Q&A What would happen if I saved the report?
The next time you view the report, the details would still be hidden. If that happened and you wanted to show all the details, just tap or click the Hide Details button a second time.

Break Point: If you wish to take a break, this is a good place to do so. You can quit Access now. To resume at a later time, start Access, open the database called Bavant Publishing, and continue following the steps from this location forward.

Form Creation

In Chapter 1, you created a simple form consisting of all the fields in the Customer table. To create more customized forms, you can use the Access Form Wizard. Once you have used the Form Wizard to create a form, you can modify that form in either Layout view or Design view.

To Use the Form Wizard to Create a Form

1 GROUP, SORT, & TOTAL | 2 CONDITIONALLY FORMAT CONTROLS | 3 FILTER REPORT RECORDS | 4 MULTIPLE-TABLE REPORT
5 FORM WIZARD | **6 MODIFY CONTROLS** | **7 FILTER FORM RECORDS** | **8 MAILING LABELS**

The steps on the next page use the Form Wizard to create an initial version of the Customer Financial Form. ***Why?*** *Using the Form Wizard is the easiest way to create this form.* The initial version will contain the Customer Number, Customer Name, Customer Type, Resources Needed, Amount Paid, Current Due, Total Amount, Returns, and Book Rep Number fields.

1

- Open the Navigation Pane and select the Customer table.
- Tap or click CREATE on the ribbon to display the CREATE tab.
- Tap or click the Form Wizard button (CREATE tab | Forms group) to start the Form Wizard (Figure 4–48).

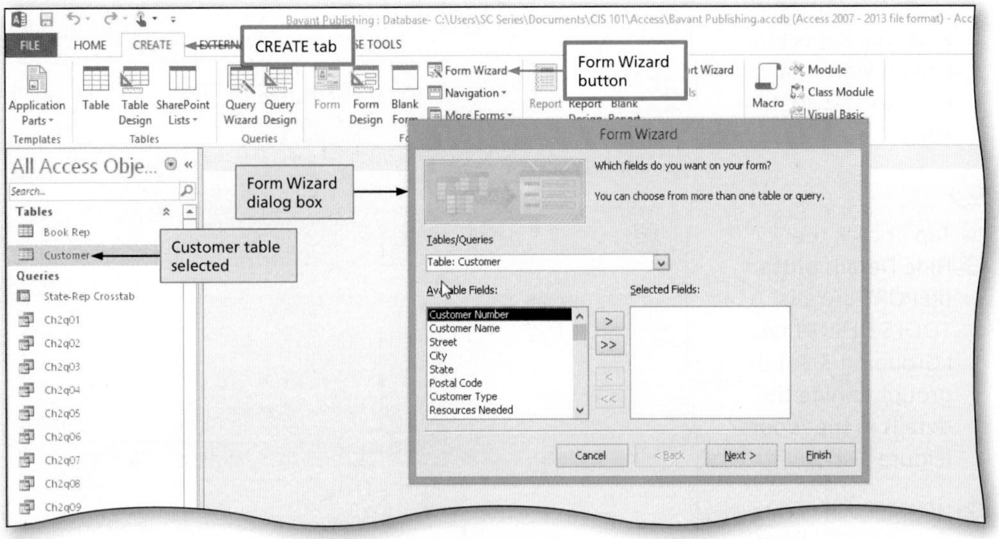

Figure 4–48

2

- Add the Customer Number, Customer Name, Customer Type, Resources Needed, Amount Paid, Current Due, Total Amount, Returns, and Book Rep Number fields to the form (Figure 4–49).

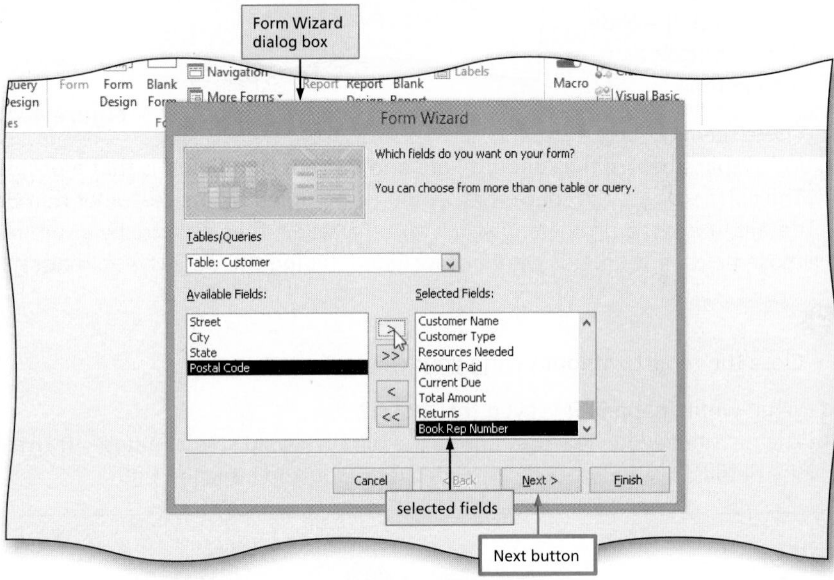

Figure 4–49

3

- Tap or click the Next button to display the next Form Wizard screen (Figure 4–50).

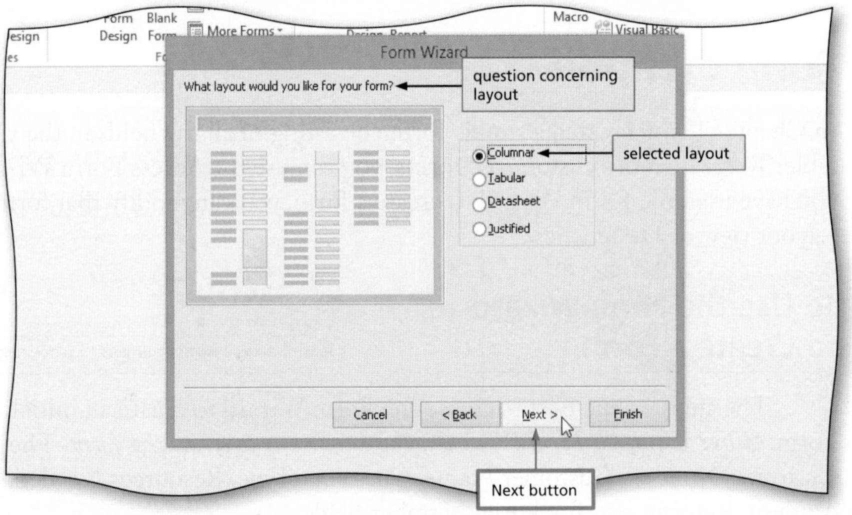

Figure 4–50

4

- Be sure the Columnar layout is selected, tap or click the Next button to display the next Form Wizard screen, and then type `Customer Financial Form` as the title for the form (Figure 4–51).

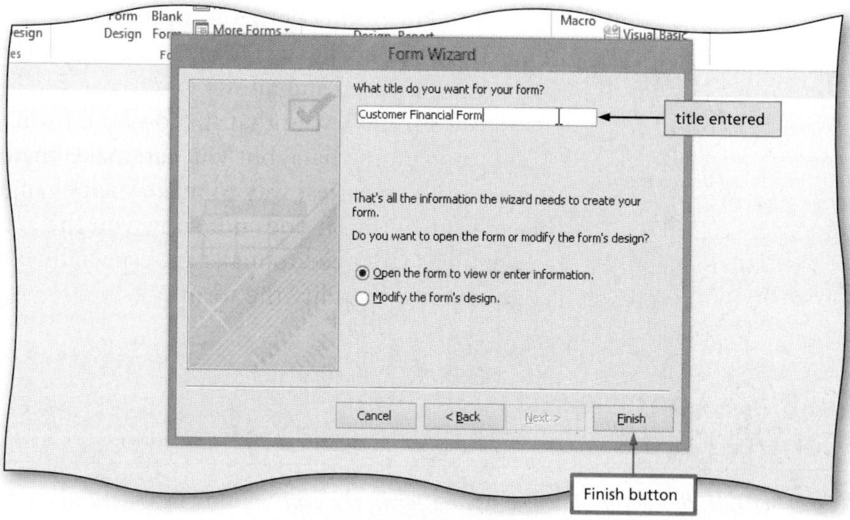

Figure 4–51

5

- Tap or click the Finish button to complete and display the form (Figure 4–52).

6

- Tap or click the Close button for the Customer Financial Form to close the form.

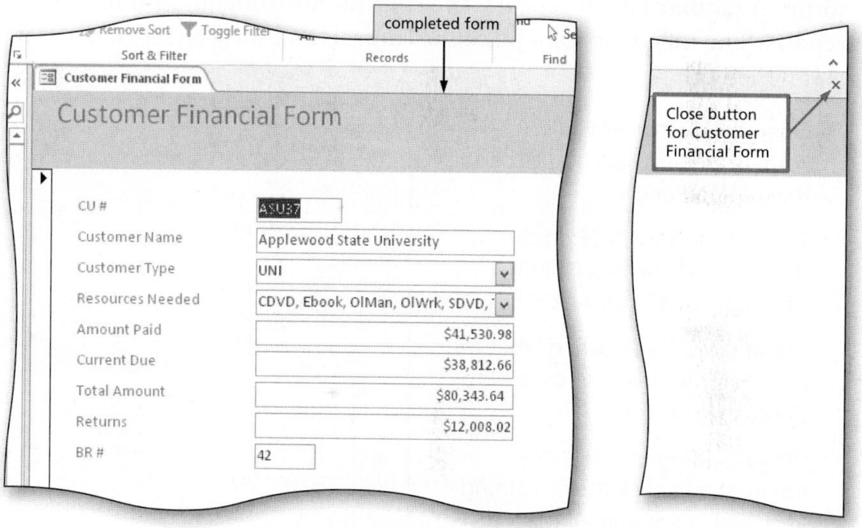

Figure 4–52

Form Sections

A form typically has only three sections. The Form Header section appears at the top of the form and usually contains the form title. It also may contain a logo and/or a date. The body of the form is in the Detail section. The Form Footer section appears at the bottom of the form and is often empty.

Form Controls

Just as with reports, the various items on a form are called controls. Forms include the same three types of controls: bound controls, unbound controls, and calculated controls. Bound controls have attached labels that typically display the name of the field that supplies the data for the control. The **attached label** for the Customer Number field, for example, is the portion of the screen immediately to the left of the field. It contains the words, Customer Number.

BTW

Form Design Considerations

Forms should be appealing visually and present data logically and clearly. Properly designed forms improve both the speed and accuracy of data entry. Forms that are too cluttered or contain too many different effects can be hard on the eyes. Some colors are more difficult than others for individuals to see. Be consistent when creating forms. Once you decide on a general style or theme for forms, stick with it throughout your database.

Views Available for Forms

When working with a form in Access, there are three different ways to view the form: Form view, Layout view, and Design view. Form view shows the form on the screen and allows you to use the form to update data. Layout view is similar to Form view in that it shows the form on the screen. In Layout view, you cannot update the data, but you can make changes to the layout of the form, and it is usually the easiest way to make such changes. Design view also allows you to make changes, but it does not show you the actual form. It is most useful when the changes you need to make are especially complex. In this chapter, you will use Layout view to modify the form.

To Place Controls in a Control Layout

1 GROUP, SORT, & TOTAL | 2 CONDITIONALLY FORMAT CONTROLS | 3 FILTER REPORT RECORDS | 4 MULTIPLE-TABLE REPORT
5 FORM WIZARD | 6 MODIFY CONTROLS | **7 FILTER FORM RECORDS** | **8 MAILING LABELS**

Why? *To use Layout view with a form, the controls must be placed in a control layout.* A **control layout** is a guide that aligns the controls to give the form or report a uniform appearance. Access has two types of control layouts. A **stacked layout** arranges the controls vertically with labels to the left of the control and is commonly used in forms. A **tabular layout** arranges the controls horizontally with the labels across the top and is typically used in reports. The following steps place the controls and their attached labels in a stacked control layout.

1

- Open the Customer Financial Form in Layout view and close the Navigation Pane.
- Tap or click ARRANGE on the ribbon to display the FORM LAYOUT TOOLS ARRANGE tab.
- Tap or click the attached label for the Customer Number control to select the control.
- While holding the SHIFT key down, tap or click the remaining attached labels and all the controls (Figure 4–53).

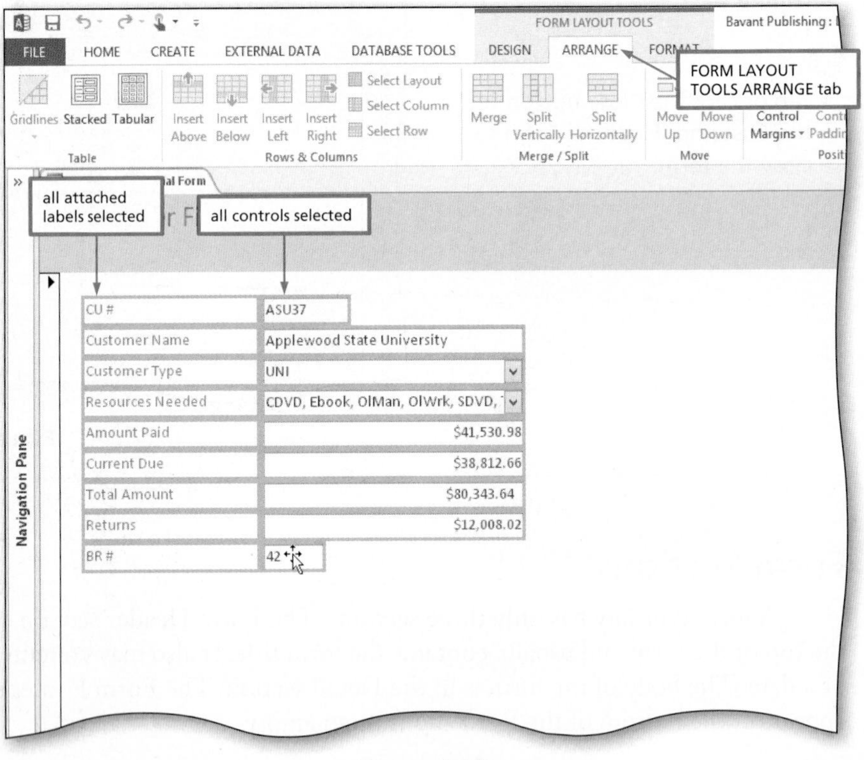

Figure 4–53

Q&A Did I have to select the attached labels and controls in that order?
No. As long as you select all of them, the order in which you selected them does not matter.

Q&A When I clicked some of the controls, they moved so they are no longer aligned as well as they are in the figure. What should I do?
You do not have to worry about it. Once you complete the next step, they once again will be aligned properly.

2

- Tap or click the Stacked button (FORM LAYOUT TOOLS ARRANGE tab | Table group) to place the controls in a stacked layout (Figure 4–54).

Q&A How can I tell whether the controls are in a control layout?
Look for the Control Layout indicator in the upper-left corner of the control layout.

Q&A What is the difference between stacked layout and tabular layout?
In a stacked layout, which more often is used in forms, the controls are placed vertically with the labels to the left of the controls. In a tabular layout, which more often is used in reports, the controls are placed horizontally with the labels above the controls.

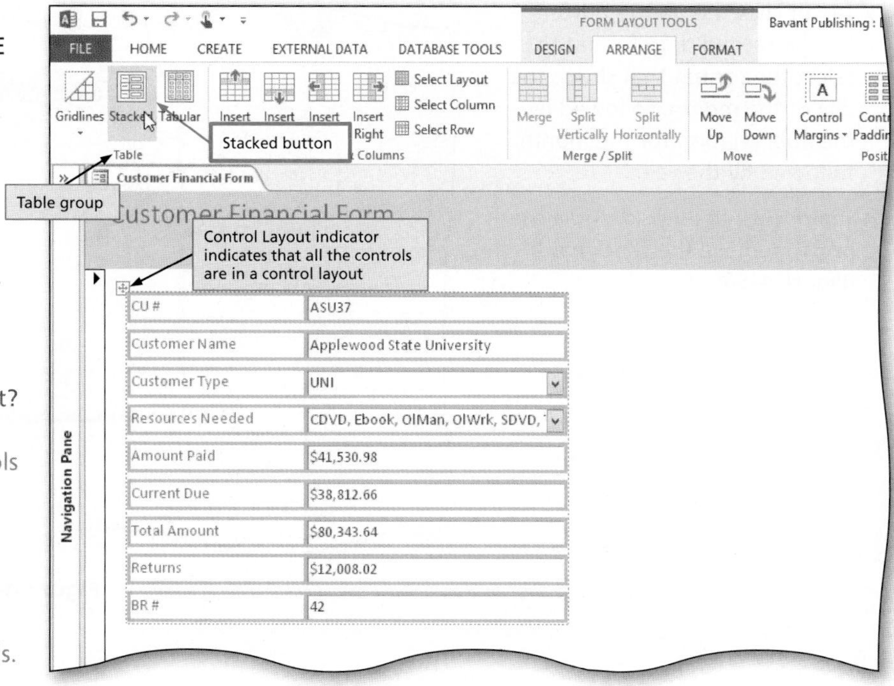

Figure 4–54

To Enhance a Form by Adding a Date

1 GROUP, SORT, & TOTAL | 2 CONDITIONALLY FORMAT CONTROLS | 3 FILTER REPORT RECORDS | 4 MULTIPLE-TABLE REPORT
5 FORM WIZARD | 6 MODIFY CONTROLS | 7 FILTER FORM RECORDS | 8 MAILING LABELS

Why? *To enhance the look of a report or form, you can add special items, such as a logo or title. You also can add the date and/or the time. In the case of reports, you can add a page number as well.* To add any of these items, you use the appropriate button in the Header/Footer group of the DESIGN tab. The following steps use the Date and Time button to add a date to the Customer Financial Form.

1

- Tap or click DESIGN on the ribbon to display the FORM LAYOUT TOOLS DESIGN tab.
- Tap or click the 'Date and Time' button (FORM LAYOUT TOOLS DESIGN tab | Header/Footer group) to display the Date and Time dialog box (Figure 4–55).

Q&A What is the purpose of the various check boxes and option buttons?
If the Include Date check box is checked, you must pick a date format from the three option buttons underneath the check box. If it is not checked, the option buttons will be dimmed. If the Include Time check box is checked, you must pick a time format from the three option buttons underneath the check box. If it is not checked, the option buttons will be dimmed.

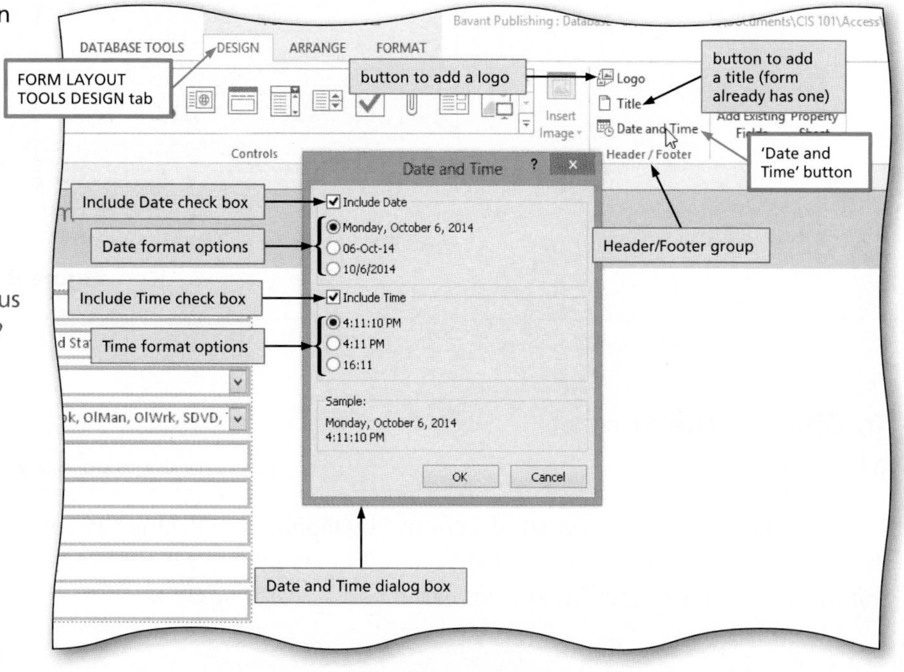

Figure 4–55

2

- Tap or click the option button for the second date format to select the format that shows the day of the month, followed by the abbreviation for the month, followed by the year.
- Tap or click the Include Time check box to remove the check mark (Figure 4–56).

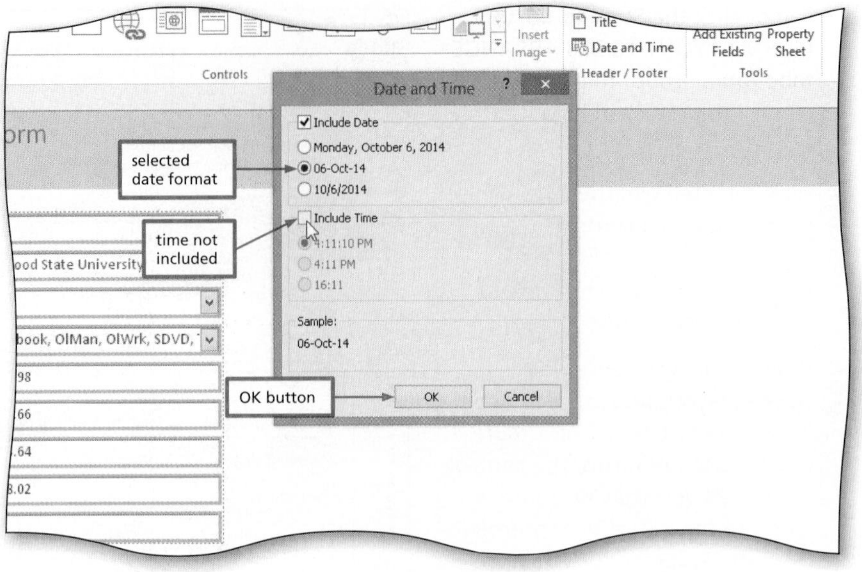

Figure 4–56

3

- Tap or click the OK button (Date and Time dialog box) to add the date to the form (Figure 4–57).

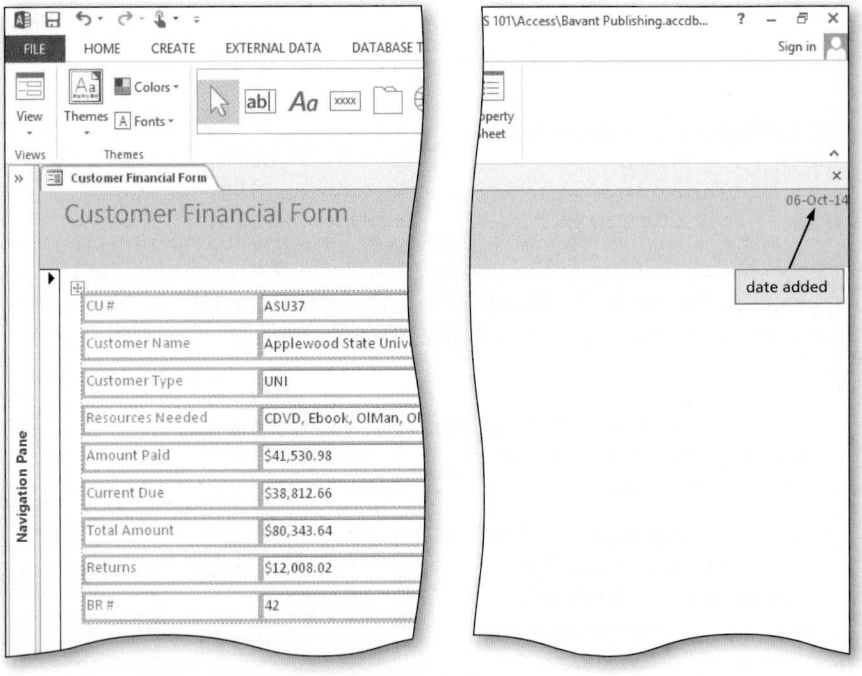

Figure 4–57

To Change the Format of a Control

1 GROUP, SORT, & TOTAL | 2 CONDITIONALLY FORMAT CONTROLS | 3 FILTER REPORT RECORDS | 4 MULTIPLE-TABLE REPORT
5 FORM WIZARD | **6 MODIFY CONTROLS** | **7 FILTER FORM RECORDS** | **8 MAILING LABELS**

You can change the format of a control by tapping or clicking the control and then tapping or clicking the appropriate button on the FORMAT tab. The following step uses this technique to bold the date. ***Why?*** *The requirements for the form specify that the date is bold so that it stands out.*

1

- Tap or click the Date control to select it.
- Tap or click FORMAT on the ribbon to display the FORM LAYOUT TOOLS FORMAT tab.
- Tap or click the Bold button (FORM LAYOUT TOOLS FORMAT tab | Font group) to bold the date (Figure 4–58).

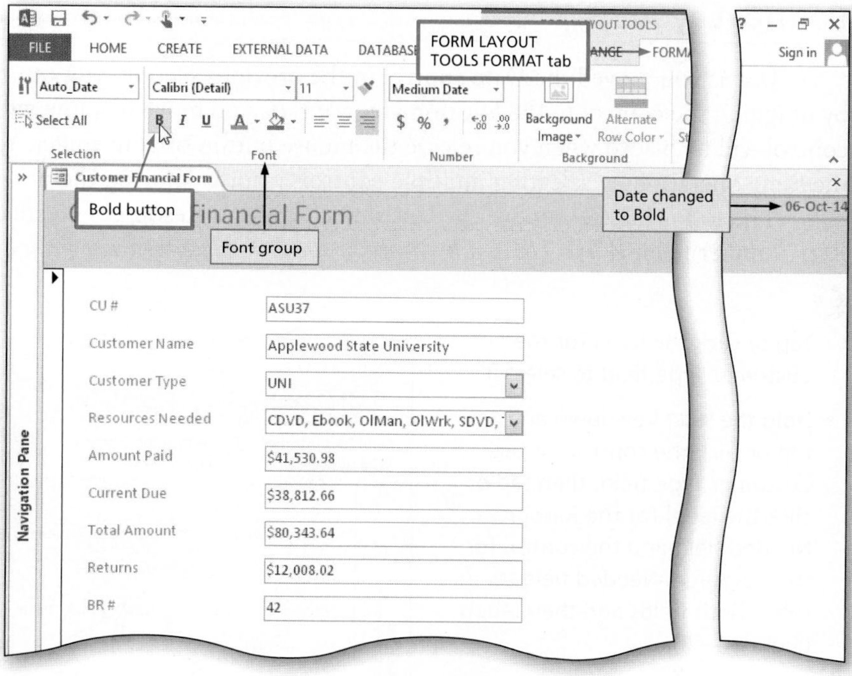

Figure 4–58

To Move a Control

1 GROUP, SORT, & TOTAL | 2 CONDITIONALLY FORMAT CONTROLS | 3 FILTER REPORT RECORDS | 4 MULTIPLE-TABLE REPORT
5 FORM WIZARD | 6 MODIFY CONTROLS | 7 FILTER FORM RECORDS | 8 MAILING LABELS

You can move a control by dragging the control. The following step moves the Date control to the lower edge of the form header. ***Why?*** *The requirements for the form specify this location for the date.*

1

- Point to the Date control so that the pointer changes to a four-headed arrow, and then drag the Date control to the lower boundary of the form header in the approximate position shown in Figure 4–59.

Q&A I moved my pointer a little bit and it became a two-headed arrow. Can I still drag the pointer?

If you drag when the pointer is a two-headed arrow, you will resize the control. To move the control, it must be a four-headed arrow.

Q&A Could I drag other objects as well? For example, could I drag the title to the center of the form header?

Yes. Just be sure you are pointing at the object and the pointer is a four-headed arrow. You can then drag the object to the desired location.

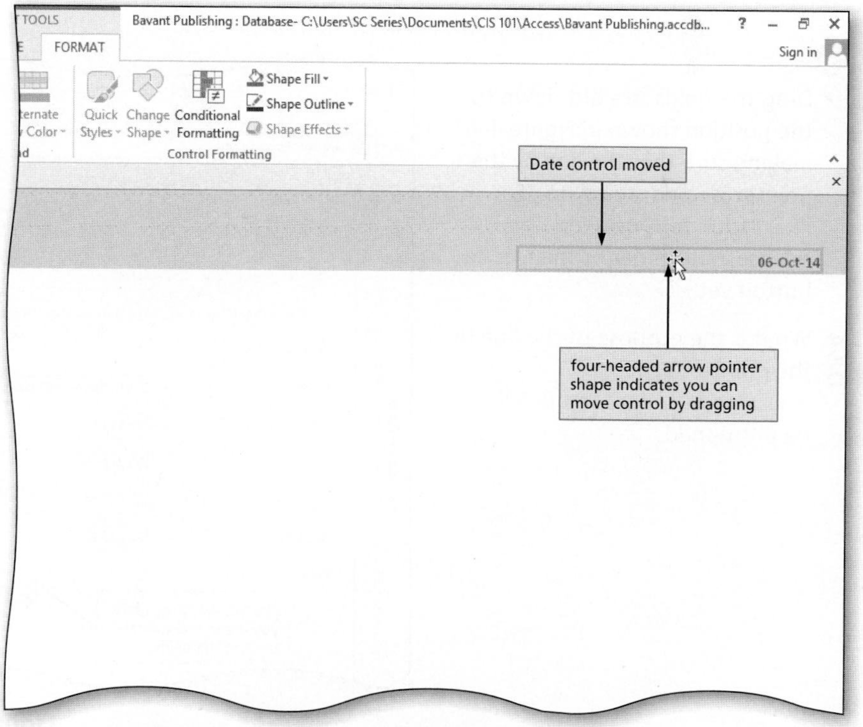

Figure 4–59

To Move Controls in a Control Layout

1 GROUP, SORT, & TOTAL | 2 CONDITIONALLY FORMAT CONTROLS | 3 FILTER REPORT RECORDS | 4 MULTIPLE-TABLE REPORT
5 FORM WIZARD | 6 MODIFY CONTROLS | 7 FILTER FORM RECORDS | 8 MAILING LABELS

Just as you moved the Date control in the previous section, you can move a control within a control layout by dragging the control to the location you want. As you move it, a line will indicate the position where the control will be placed when you release the mouse button or your finger. You can move more than one control in the same operation by selecting multiple controls prior to moving them.

The following steps move the Customer Type and Resources Needed fields so that they follow the Book Rep Number field. ***Why?*** *The requirements for the form place these two fields after the Book Rep Number field.*

1

- Tap or click the label for the Customer Type field to select it.
- Hold the SHIFT key down and tap or click the control for the Customer Type field, then tap or click the label for the Resources Needed field and the control for the Resources Needed field to select both fields and their labels (Figure 4–60).

Q&A Why did I have to hold the SHIFT key down when I clicked the remaining controls?

If you did not hold the SHIFT key down, you would only select the control for the Resources Needed field (the last control selected). The other controls no longer would be selected.

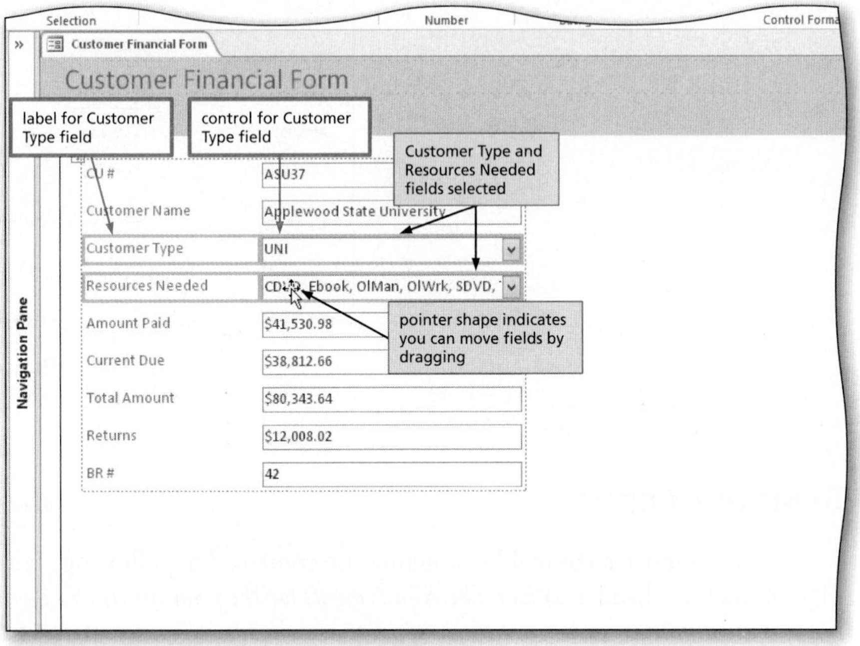

Figure 4–60

2

- Drag the fields straight down to the position shown in Figure 4–61, making sure that the line by the pointer is under the data. (For illustration purposes, do not release your finger or the mouse button yet.)

Q&A What is the purpose of the line by the pointer?

It shows you where the fields will be positioned.

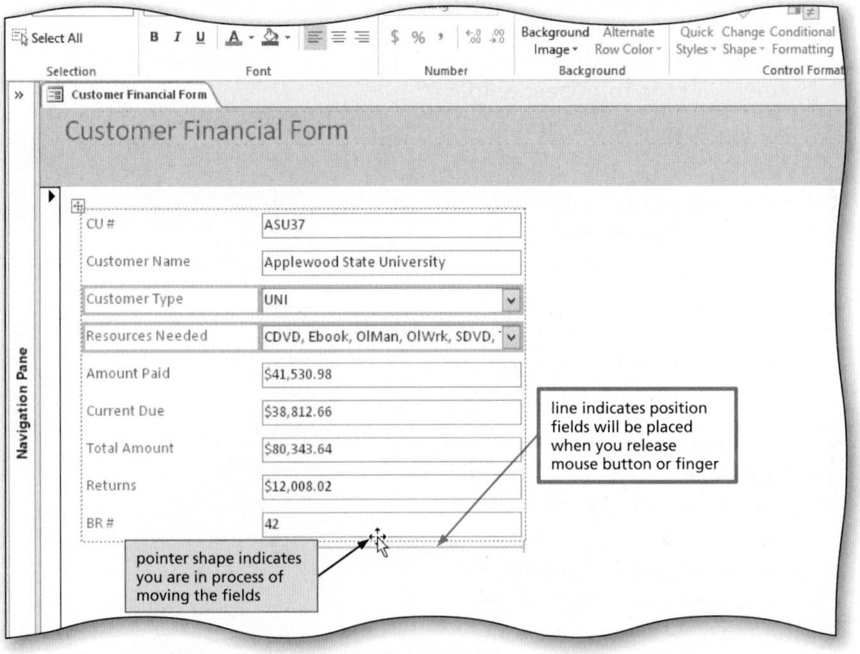

Figure 4–61

3

- Release your finger or the mouse button to complete the movement of the fields (Figure 4–62).

Q&A I inadvertently had the line under the label rather than the data when I released the mouse button. The data that I moved is now under the field names. How do I fix this?
You can try to move it back where it was, but that can be tricky. The easiest way is to use the Undo button on the Quick Access Toolbar to undo your change.

Q&A I inadvertently moved my pointer so that the line became vertical and was located between a label and the corresponding data when I released the mouse button. It seemed to split the form. The data I moved appears right where the line was. It is between a label and the corresponding data. How do I fix this?
Use the Undo button on the Quick Access Toolbar to undo your change.

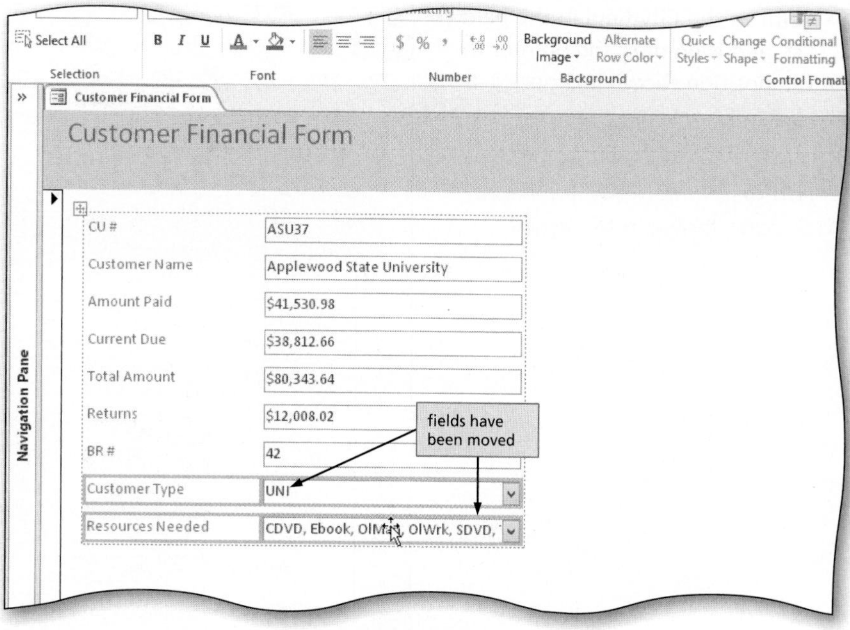

Figure 4–62

To Add a Field

1 GROUP, SORT, & TOTAL | 2 CONDITIONALLY FORMAT CONTROLS | 3 FILTER REPORT RECORDS | 4 MULTIPLE-TABLE REPORT
5 FORM WIZARD | 6 MODIFY CONTROLS | **7 FILTER FORM RECORDS** | **8 MAILING LABELS**

Why? *Just as with a report, once you have created an initial form, you might decide that the form should contain an additional field.* The following steps use a field list to add the City field to the Customer Financial Form.

1

- Tap or click DESIGN on the ribbon to display the FORM LAYOUT TOOLS DESIGN tab.
- Tap or click the 'Add Existing Fields' button (FORM LAYOUT TOOLS DESIGN tab | Tools group) to display a field list (Figure 4–63).

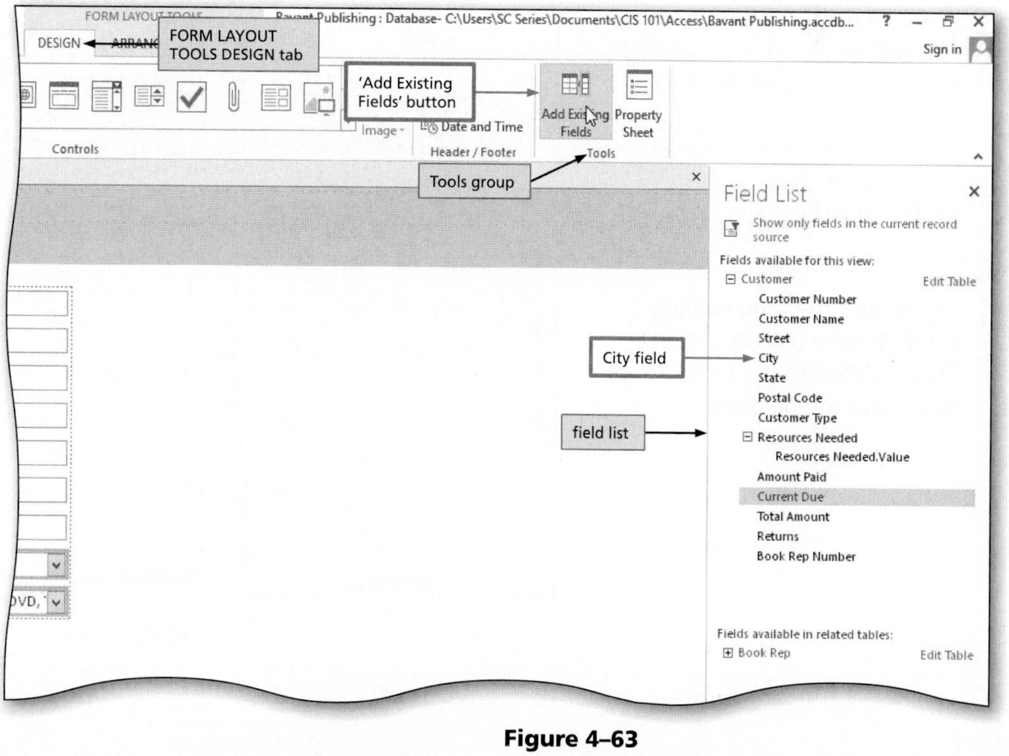

Figure 4–63

2

- Point to the City field in the field list, and then drag the pointer to the position shown in Figure 4–64.

Q&A Does it have to be exact?
The exact pointer position is not critical as long as the line is in the position shown in the figure.

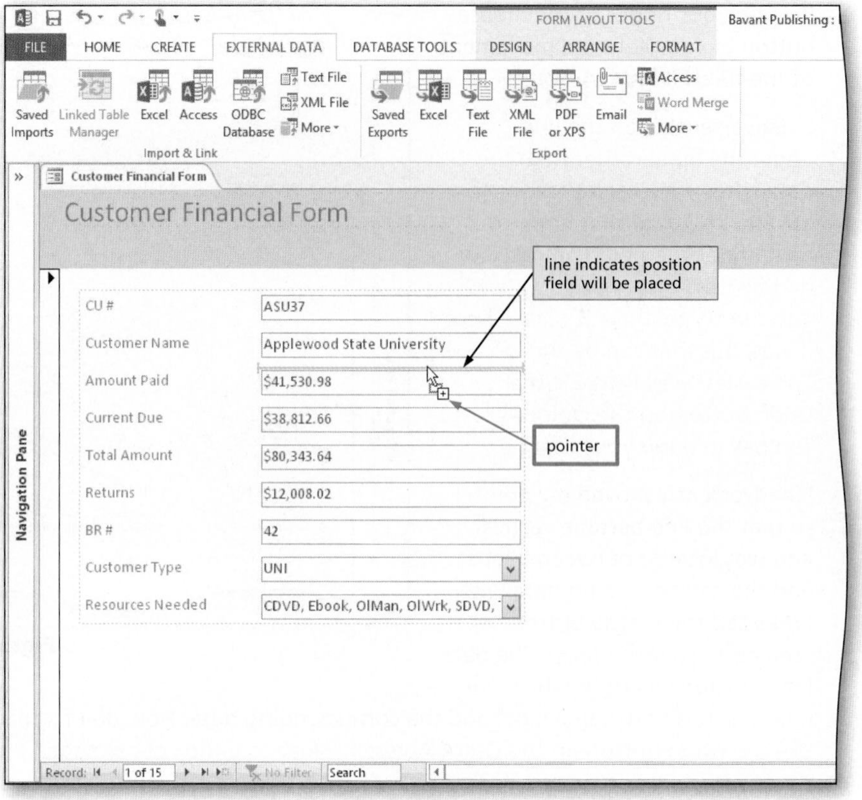

Figure 4–64

3

- Release your finger or the mouse button to place the field (Figure 4–65).

Q&A What if I make a mistake?
Just as when you are modifying a report, you can delete the field by tapping or clicking the field and then pressing the DELETE key. You can move the field by dragging it to the correct position.

4

- Tap or click the 'Add Existing Fields' button (FORM LAYOUT TOOLS DESIGN tab | Tools group) to remove the field list.

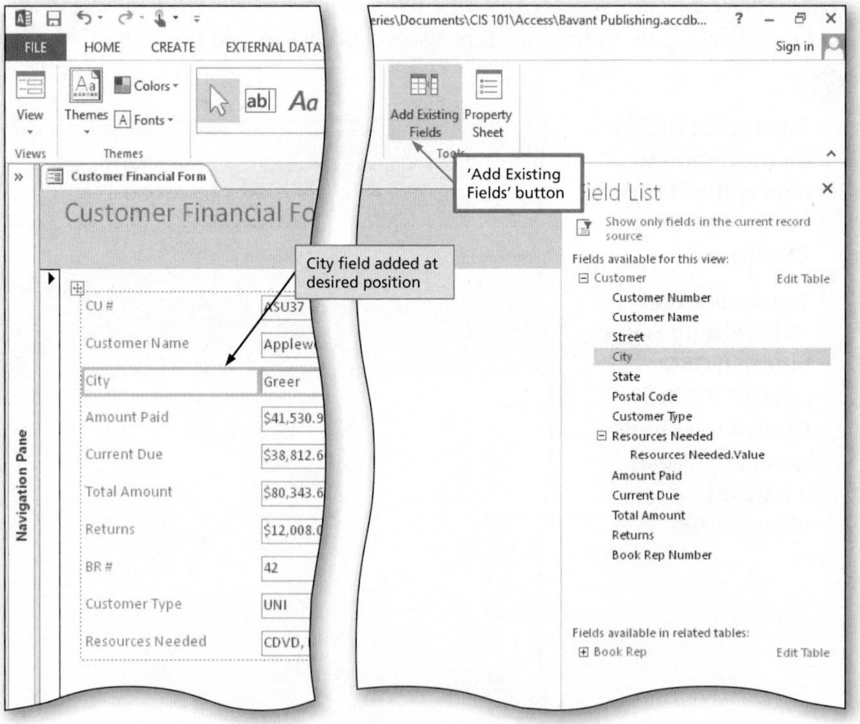

Figure 4–65

To Filter and Sort Using a Form

1 GROUP, SORT, & TOTAL | 2 CONDITIONALLY FORMAT CONTROLS | 3 FILTER REPORT RECORDS | 4 MULTIPLE-TABLE REPORT
5 FORM WIZARD | 6 MODIFY CONTROLS | 7 FILTER FORM RECORDS | 8 MAILING LABELS

***Why?** Just as in a datasheet, you often need to filter and sort data when using a form.* You can do so using Advanced Filter/Sort, which is a command on the Advanced menu. The following steps use Advanced Filter/Sort to filter the records to those records whose city begins with the letter, G. They also sort the records by customer name. The effect of this filter and sort is that as you use the form to move through customers, you will only encounter those customers whose cities begin with G. In addition, you will encounter those customers in customer name order.

1

- Tap or click HOME on the ribbon to display the HOME tab.
- Tap or click the Advanced button (HOME tab | Sort & Filter group) to display the Advanced menu (Figure 4–66).

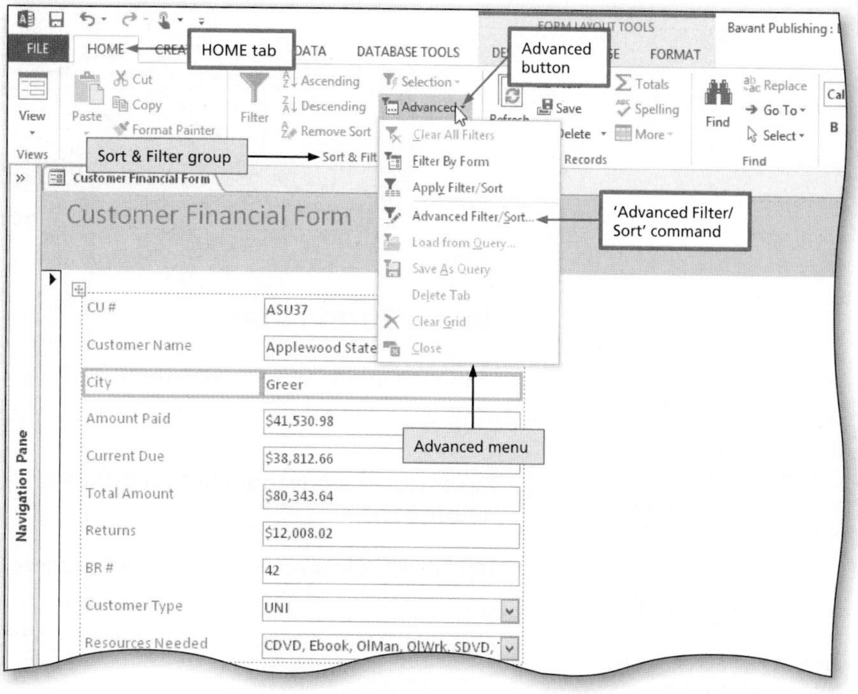

Figure 4–66

2

- Tap or click 'Advanced Filter/Sort' on the Advanced menu.
- If necessary, resize the field list so that the Customer Name and City fields appear.
- Add the Customer Name field to the design grid and select Ascending sort order.
- Add the City field and type **G*** as the criterion for the City field (Figure 4–67).

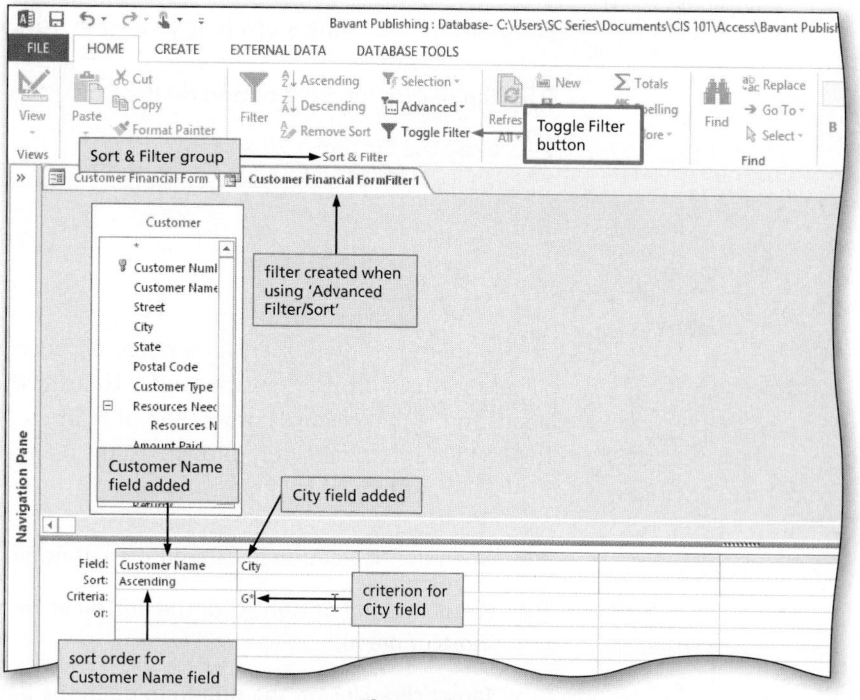

Figure 4–67

3

- Tap or click the Toggle Filter button (HOME tab | Sort & Filter group) to filter the records (Figure 4–68).

Q&A I can only see one record at a time in the form. How can I see which records are included?
You would have to scroll through the records. For example, you could repeatedly tap or click the Next record button.

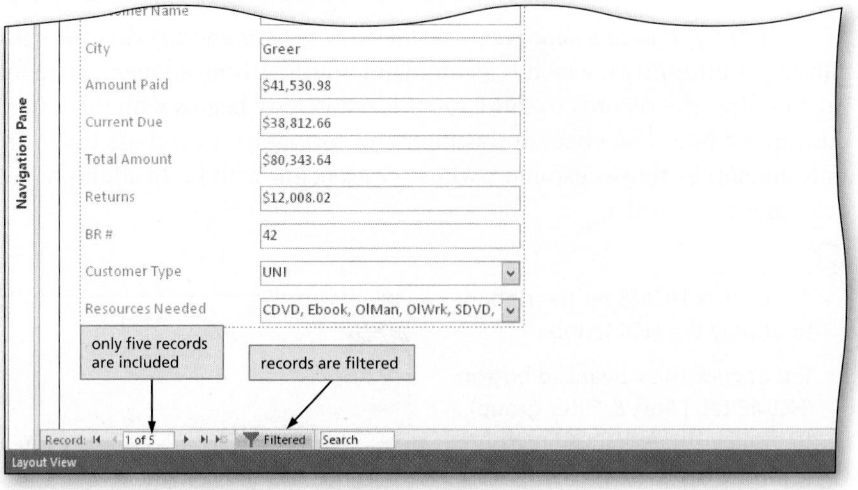

Figure 4–68

To Clear a Form Filter

When you no longer want the records to be filtered, you clear the filter. The following steps clear the current filter for the Customer Financial Form.

1. Tap or click the Advanced button (HOME tab | Sort & Filter group) to display the Advanced menu.
2. Tap or click 'Clear All Filters' on the Advanced menu to clear the filter.

BTW
Conditional Formatting
Conditional formatting is available for forms as well as reports. To conditionally format controls on a form, open the Form in Layout view or Design view, select the control to format, tap or click the Conditional Formatting button, and then follow the steps on pages AC 215 through AC 218.

To Save and Close a Form

Now that you have completed work on your form, you should save the form and close it. The following steps first save your work on the form and then close the form.

1. Tap or click the Save button on the Quick Access Toolbar to save your work.
2. Close the Customer Financial Form.

To Print a Form

You can print all records, a range of records, or a selected record of a form by selecting the appropriate print range. To print the selected record, the form must be open. To print all records or a range of records, you can simply highlight the form in the Navigation Pane. The following steps open the Customer Financial Form and then print the first record in the form, which is the selected record.

BTW
Printing Forms
To change the page setup and page layout options, such as adjusting margins and changing the orientation, for a form, use the Print Preview window. To open the Print Preview window for a form, tap or click FILE on the ribbon, tap or click Print, and then tap or click Print Preview.

1. Open the Navigation Pane, and then, if necessary, select the Customer Financial Form.
2. Press and hold or right-click the Customer Financial Form and tap or click Open on the shortcut menu.
3. Tap or click FILE on the ribbon to open the Backstage view.

4. Tap or click the Print tab in the Backstage view to display the Print gallery.
5. Tap or click the Print button to display the Print dialog box.
6. Tap or click the Selected Record(s) option button in the Print Range section, and then tap or click the OK button.
7. Close the Customer Financial Form.

The Arrange Tab

Forms, like reports, have an ARRANGE tab that you can use to modify the form's layout. However, the PAGE SETUP tab is not available for forms. The buttons on the ARRANGE tab and the functions of those buttons are just like the ones described in Table 4–1 on page AC 220.

BTW
Customizing Mailing Labels
Once you create mailing labels, you can customize them just as you can customize other reports. In Design view, you can add a picture to the label, change the font size, adjust the spacing between controls, or make any other desired changes.

Mailing Labels

Organizations need to send all kinds of correspondence — such as invoices, letters, reports, and surveys — to customers and other business partners on a regular basis. Using preprinted mailing labels eliminates much of the manual labor involved in preparing mailings. In Access, mailing labels are a special type of report. When this report prints, the data appears on the mailing labels aligned correctly and in the order you specify.

To Create Labels

1 GROUP, SORT, & TOTAL | 2 CONDITIONALLY FORMAT CONTROLS | 3 FILTER REPORT RECORDS | 4 MULTIPLE-TABLE REPORT
5 FORM WIZARD | 6 MODIFY CONTROLS | 7 FILTER FORM RECORDS | 8 MAILING LABELS

To create labels, you will typically use the Label wizard. ***Why?*** *Using the wizard, you can specify the type and dimensions, the font, and the content of the label.* The following steps create the labels.

1

- If necessary, open the Navigation Pane and select the Customer table.
- Tap or click CREATE on the ribbon to display the CREATE tab.
- Tap or click the Labels button (CREATE tab | Reports group) to display the Label Wizard dialog box.
- Ensure that English is selected as the Unit of Measure and that Avery is selected in the 'Filter by manufacturer' box.
- Scroll through the product numbers until C2163 appears, and then tap or click C2163 in the Product number list to select the specific type of labels (Figure 4–69).

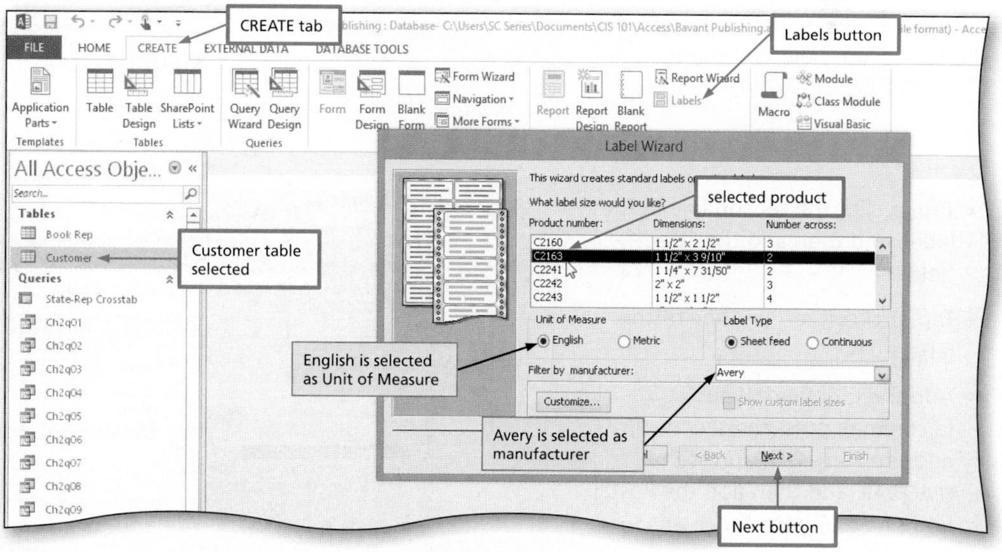

Figure 4–69

2

- Tap or click the Next button (Figure 4–70).

Q&A What font characteristics could I change with this screen?
You could change the font, the font size, the font weight, and/or the font color. You could also specify italic or underlining.

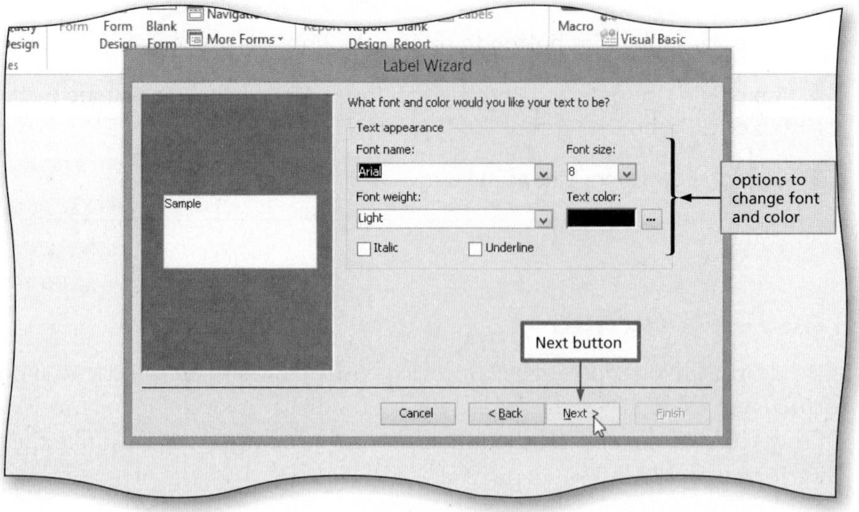

Figure 4–70

3

- Tap or click the Next button to accept the default font and color settings.
- Tap or click the Customer Name field, and then tap or click the Add Field button (Figure 4–71).

Q&A What should I do if I make a mistake?
You can erase the contents of any line in the label by tapping or clicking in the line to produce an insertion point and then using the DELETE or BACKSPACE key to erase the current contents. You then can add the correct field by tapping or clicking the field and then tapping or clicking the Add Field button.

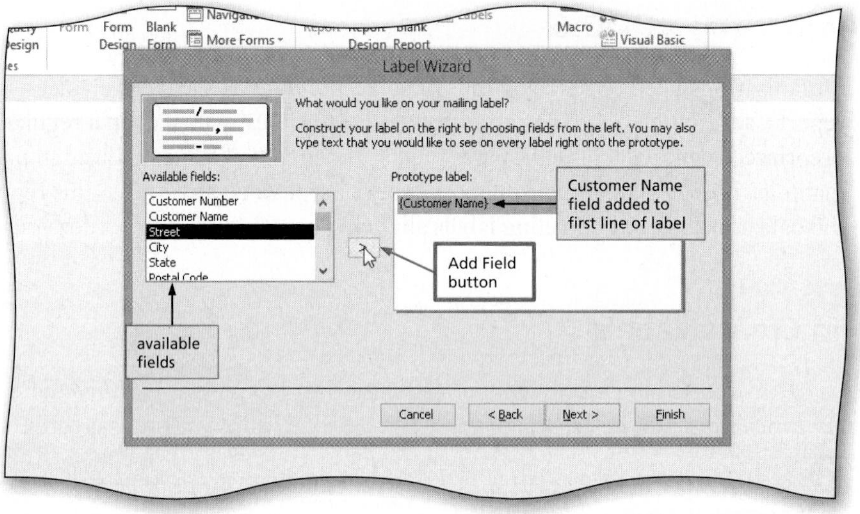

Figure 4–71

4

- Tap or click the second line in the label, and then add the Street field.
- Tap or click the third line of the label.
- Add the City field, type , (a comma), press the SPACEBAR, add the State field, press the SPACEBAR, and then add the Postal Code field (Figure 4–72).

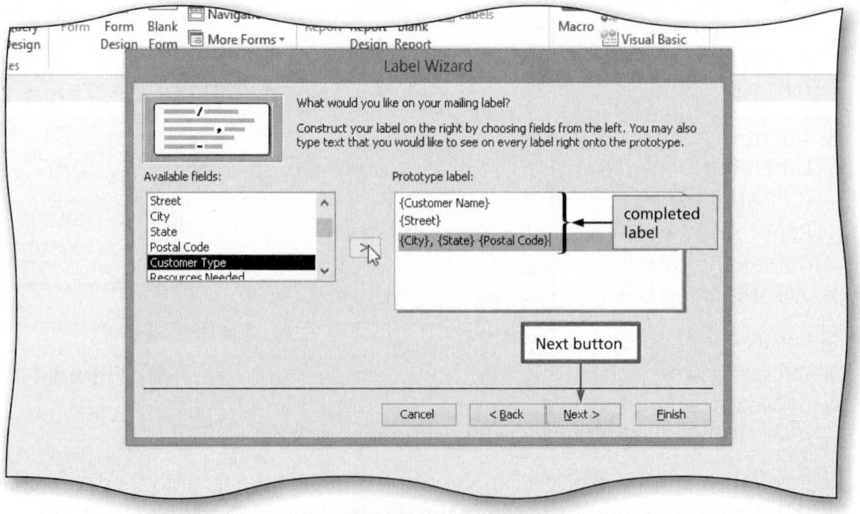

Figure 4–72

5

- Because you have now added all the necessary fields to the label, tap or click the Next button.
- Select the Postal Code field as the field to sort by, and then tap or click the Add Field button (Figure 4–73).

Q&A Why am I sorting by postal code?
When you need to do a bulk mailing, that is, send a large number of items using a special postage rate, mail organizations often require that the mail be sorted in postal code order.

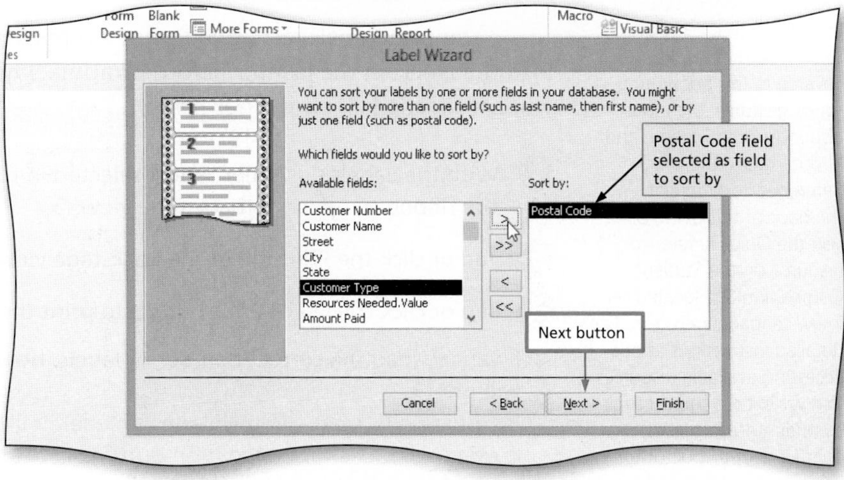

Figure 4–73

6

- Tap or click the Next button.
- Ensure the name for the report (that is, the labels) is Labels Customer (Figure 4–74).
- If requested to do so by your instructor, name the labels report as Labels FirstName LastName where FirstName and LastName are your first and last names.

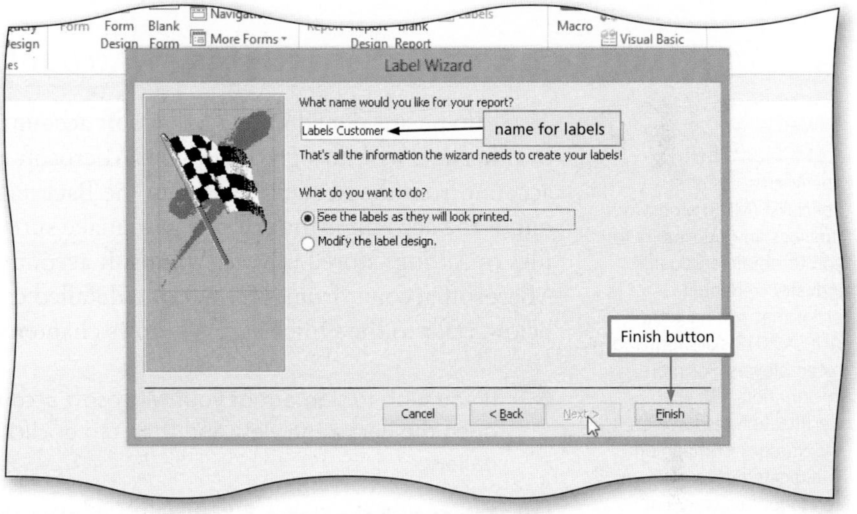

Figure 4–74

7

- Tap or click the Finish button to complete the labels (Figure 4–75).

8

- Close the Labels Customer report.

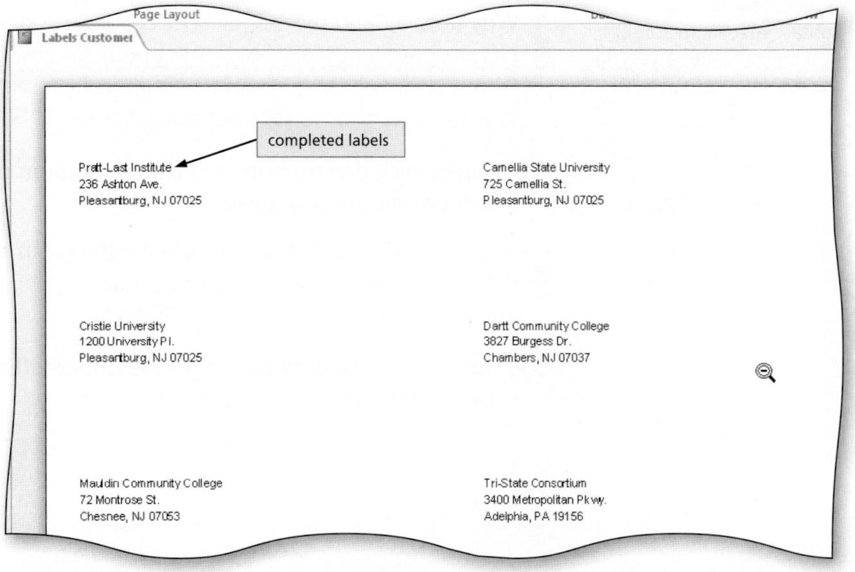

Figure 4–75

BTW
Quick Reference
For a table that lists how to complete the tasks covered in this book using touch gestures, the mouse, ribbon, shortcut menu, and keyboard, see the Quick Reference Summary at the back of this book, or visit the Quick Reference resource on the Student Companion Site located on www.cengagebrain.com. For detailed instructions about accessing available resources, visit www.cengage.com/ct/studentdownload or contact your instructor for information about accessing the required files.

To Print Labels

You print labels just as you print a report. The only difference is that you must load the labels in the printer before printing. The following steps print the labels once you have loaded labels in your printer.

1. With the Labels Customer report selected in the Navigation Pane, tap or click FILE on the ribbon to open the Backstage view.
2. Tap or click the Print tab in the Backstage view to display the Print gallery.
3. Tap or click the Quick Print button to print the report.

Q&A I want to load the correct number of labels. How do I know how many pages of labels will print?
If you are unsure how many pages of labels will print, open the label report in Print Preview first. Use the Navigation buttons in the status bar of the Print Preview window to determine how many pages of labels will print.

BTW
Certification
The Microsoft Office Specialist (MOS) program provides an opportunity for you to obtain a valuable industry credential — proof that you have the Access 2013 skills required by employers. For more information, visit the Certification resource on the Student Companion Site located on www.cengagebrain.com. For detailed instructions about accessing available resources, visit www.cengage.com/ct/studentdownload or contact your instructor for information about accessing the required files.

To Sign Out of a Microsoft Account

If you are signed in to a Microsoft account and are using a public computer or otherwise wish to sign out of your Microsoft account, you should sign out of the account from the Account gallery in the Backstage view before exiting Access. Signing out of the account is the safest way to make sure that nobody else can access SkyDrive files or settings stored in your Microsoft account. The following steps sign out of a Microsoft account from Access. For a detailed example of the procedure summarized below, refer to the Office and Windows chapter at the beginning of this book.

1. If you wish to sign out of your Microsoft account, tap or click FILE on the ribbon to open the Backstage view and then tap or click the Account tab to display the Account gallery.
2. Tap or click the Sign out link, which displays the Remove Account dialog box. If a Can't remove Windows accounts dialog box appears instead of the Remove Account dialog box, click the OK button and skip the remaining steps.

Q&A Why does a Can't remove Windows accounts dialog box appear?
If you signed in to Windows using your Microsoft account, then you also must sign out from Windows, rather than signing out from within Access. When you are finished using Windows, be sure to sign out at that time.

3. Tap or click the Yes button (Remove Account dialog box) to sign out of your Microsoft account on this computer.

Q&A Should I sign out of Windows after signing out of my Microsoft account?
When you are finished using the computer, you should sign out of your account for maximum security.

4. Tap or click the Back button in the upper-left corner of the Backstage view to return to the database.

To Exit Access

The following steps exit Access.

1. Tap or click the Close button on the right side of the title bar to exit Access.
2. If a Microsoft Access dialog box appears, tap or click the Save button to save any changes made to the object since the last save.

Chapter Summary

In this chapter you have learned to use wizards to create reports and forms, modify the layout of reports and forms using Layout view, group and sort in a report, add totals to a report, conditionally format controls, filter records in reports and forms, resize and move controls, add fields to reports and forms, create a stacked layout for a form, add a date, move controls in a control layout, apply themes, and create mailing labels. The items listed below include all the new Access skills you have learned in this chapter.

Conditional Formatting

Conditionally Format Controls (AC 215)

Controls

Place Controls in a Control Layout (AC 236)
Change the Format of a Control (AC 238)
Move a Control (AC 239)
Move Controls in a Control Layout (AC 240)

Filtering

Filter Records in a Report (AC 218)
Clear a Report Filter (AC 219)
Filter and Sort Using a Form (AC 243)

Form Creation

Use the Form Wizard to Create a Form (AC 233)
Enhance a Form by Adding a Date (AC 237)
Add a Field (AC 241)

Grouping

Group and Sort in a Report (AC 208)
Add Totals and Subtotals (AC 211)
Remove the Group, Sort, and Total Pane (AC 214)

Mailing Labels

Create Labels (AC 245)

Report Creation

Create a Report that Involves Multiple Tables (AC 222)
Create a Report in Layout View by Creating a Blank Report (AC 229)
Create a Summary Report (AC 232)

Themes

Assign a Theme to All Objects (AC 231)
Assign a Theme to a Single Object (AC 232)

CONSIDER THIS

What decisions will you need to make when creating your own reports and forms?

Use these guidelines as you complete the assignments in this chapter and create your own reports and forms outside of this class.

1. Determine whether the data should be presented in a report or a form.
   a. Do you intend to print the data? If so, a report would be the appropriate choice.
   b. Do you intend to view the data on the screen, or will the user update data? If so, a form would be the appropriate choice.
2. Determine the intended audience for the report or form.
   a. Who will use the report or form?
   b. Will the report or form be used by individuals external to the organization? For example, many government agencies require reports from organizations. If so, government regulations will dictate the report requirements. If the report is for internal use, the user will have specific requirements based on the intended use.
   c. Adding unnecessary data to a report or form can make the form or report unreadable. Include only data necessary for the intended use.
   d. What level of detail should the report or form contain? Reports used in day-to-day operations need more detail than weekly or monthly reports requested by management.
3. Determine the tables that contain the data needed for the report or form.
   a. Is all the data found in a single table?
   b. Does the data come from multiple related tables?
4. Determine the fields that should appear on the report or form.
5. Determine the organization of the report or form.
   a. In what order should the fields appear?
   b. How should they be arranged?
   c. Should the records in a report be grouped in some way?
   d. Are any calculations required?
6. Determine the format of the report or form.
   a. What information should be in the report or form header?
   b. Do you want a title and date?
   c. Do you want a logo?
   d. What information should be in the body of the report or form?
   e. Is any conditional formatting required?
   f. What style should be applied to the report or form? In other words, determine the visual characteristics that the various portions of the report or form should have.
   g. Is it appropriate to apply a theme to the reports, forms, and other objects in the database?
7. Review the report or form after it has been in operation to determine whether any changes are necessary.
   a. Is the order of the fields still appropriate?
   b. Are any additional fields required?
8. For mailing labels, determine the contents, order, and type of label.
   a. What fields should appear on the label?
   b. How should the fields be arranged?
   c. Is there a certain order (for example, by postal code) in which the labels should be printed?
   d. Who is the manufacturer of the labels and what is the style number for the labels?
   e. What are the dimensions for each label?
   f. How many labels print across a page?

CONSIDER THIS

How should you submit solutions to questions in the assignments identified with a symbol?

Every assignment in this book contains one or more questions identified with a symbol. These questions require you to think beyond the assigned database. Present your solutions to the questions in the format required by your instructor. Possible formats may include one or more of these options: write the answer; create a document that contains the answer; present your answer to the class; discuss your answer in a group; record the answer as audio or video using a webcam, smartphone, or portable media player; or post answers on a blog, wiki, or website.

Apply Your Knowledge

Reinforce the skills and apply the concepts you learned in this chapter.

Creating Two Reports and a Form

Note: To complete this assignment, you will be required to use the Data Files for Students. Visit www.cengage.com/ct/studentdownload for detailed instructions or contact your instructor for information about accessing the required files.

Instructions: Start Access. Open the database, Apply Beauty Organically, from the Data Files for Students, and enable the content.

The Beauty Organically Company distributes beauty and skin care products made from natural ingredients. The company employs sales representatives to sell to retail stores, fitness centers, and salons. You will create two reports and a form for the company's sales manager.

Perform the following tasks:

1. Open the Customer Financial Report in Layout view and modify the report to create the report shown in Figure 4–76. The report is grouped by Customer Type and sorted by Customer Number. Include subtotals and grand totals for the Amount Paid, Balance, and Total Amount fields. Apply conditional formatting to the Balance field by changing the font color to dark red for all records where the Balance is greater than or equal to $300.00. Save the changes to the report.

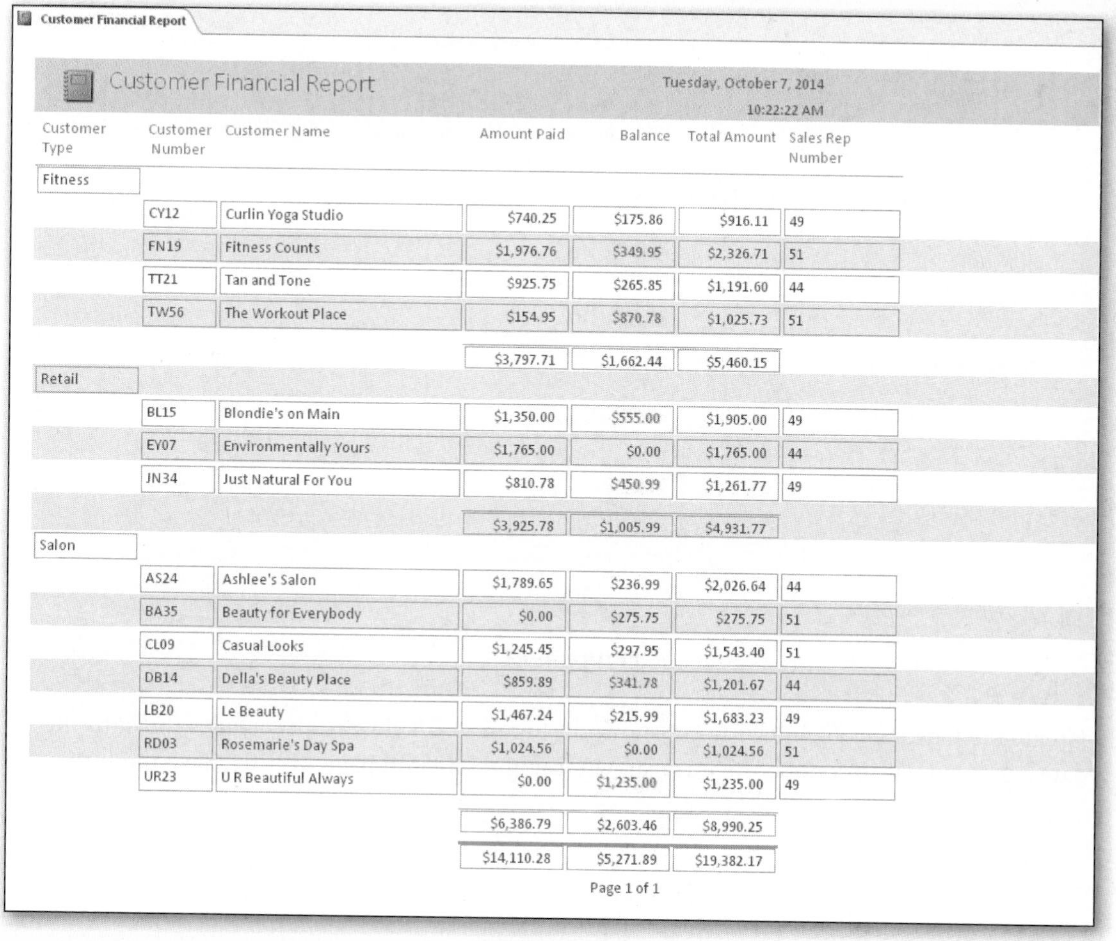

Customer Financial Report

Customer Financial Report — Tuesday, October 7, 2014 10:22:22 AM

Customer Type	Customer Number	Customer Name	Amount Paid	Balance	Total Amount	Sales Rep Number
Fitness						
	CY12	Curlin Yoga Studio	$740.25	$175.86	$916.11	49
	FN19	Fitness Counts	$1,976.76	$349.95	$2,326.71	51
	TT21	Tan and Tone	$925.75	$265.85	$1,191.60	44
	TW56	The Workout Place	$154.95	$870.78	$1,025.73	51
			$3,797.71	$1,662.44	$5,460.15	
Retail						
	BL15	Blondie's on Main	$1,350.00	$555.00	$1,905.00	49
	EY07	Environmentally Yours	$1,765.00	$0.00	$1,765.00	44
	JN34	Just Natural For You	$810.78	$450.99	$1,261.77	49
			$3,925.78	$1,005.99	$4,931.77	
Salon						
	AS24	Ashlee's Salon	$1,789.65	$236.99	$2,026.64	44
	BA35	Beauty for Everybody	$0.00	$275.75	$275.75	51
	CL09	Casual Looks	$1,245.45	$297.95	$1,543.40	51
	DB14	Della's Beauty Place	$859.89	$341.78	$1,201.67	44
	LB20	Le Beauty	$1,467.24	$215.99	$1,683.23	49
	RD03	Rosemarie's Day Spa	$1,024.56	$0.00	$1,024.56	51
	UR23	U R Beautiful Always	$0.00	$1,235.00	$1,235.00	49
			$6,386.79	$2,603.46	$8,990.25	
			$14,110.28	$5,271.89	$19,382.17	

Page 1 of 1

Figure 4–76

Continued >

Apply Your Knowledge *continued*

2. Create the Customers by Sales Rep report shown in Figure 4–77. Include a total for the Total Amount field. Save the report.

Customers by Sales Rep

SR #	First Name	Last Name	CU #	Customer Name	Total Amount
44	Bobbi	Johnson			
			AS24	Ashlee's Salon	$2,026.64
			DB14	Della's Beauty Place	$1,201.67
			EY07	Environmentally Yours	$1,765.00
			TT21	Tan and Tone	$1,191.60
Summary for 'Sales Rep Number' = 44 (4 detail records)					
Sum					$6,184.91
49	Nicholas	Gutaz			
			BL15	Blondie's on Main	$1,905.00
			CY12	Curlin Yoga Studio	$916.11
			JN34	Just Natural For You	$1,261.77
			LB20	Le Beauty	$1,683.23
			UR23	U R Beautiful Always	$1,235.00
Summary for 'Sales Rep Number' = 49 (5 detail records)					
Sum					$7,001.11
51	Jake	Orlon			
			BA35	Beauty for Everybody	$275.75
			CL09	Casual Looks	$1,543.40
			FN19	Fitness Counts	$2,326.71
			RD03	Rosemarie's Day Spa	$1,024.56
			TW56	The Workout Place	$1,025.73
Summary for 'Sales Rep Number' = 51 (5 detail records)					
Sum					$6,196.15
Grand Total					$19,382.17

Tuesday, October 7, 2014 Page 1 of 1

Figure 4–77

3. Create the Customer Financial Form shown in Figure 4–78. The form includes the current date and is similar in style to the form shown in Figure 4–3 on page AC 204. Save the form.

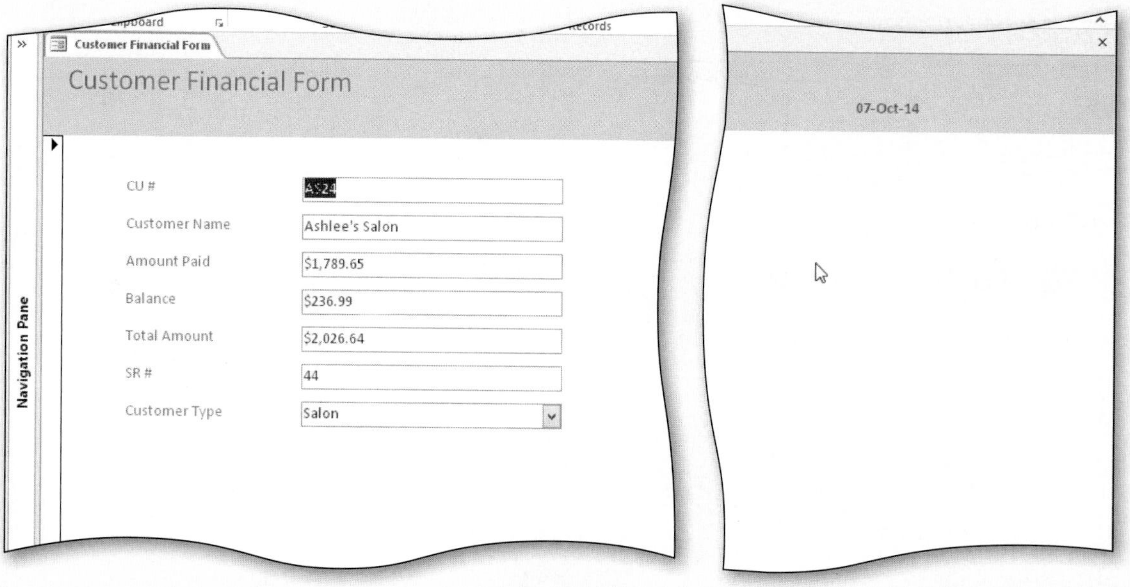

Figure 4–78

4. If requested to do so by your instructor, rename the Customers by Sales Rep report as Customers by LastName where LastName is your last name.
5. Submit the revised database in the format specified by your instructor.
6. How would you add the City field to the Customer Financial Form?

Extend Your Knowledge

Extend the skills you learned in this chapter and experiment with new skills. You may need to use Help to complete the assignment.

Creating a Summary Report and Assigning Themes to Reports and Forms

Note: To complete this assignment, you will be required to use the Data Files for Students. Visit www.cengage.com/ct/studentdownload for detailed instructions or contact your instructor for information about accessing the required files.

Instructions: Start Access. Open the Extend MothersHelpers database from the Data Files for Students. MothersHelpers is a company that provides college-age workers to do small household jobs. You will create a summary report for the MothersHelpers database, assign a theme to an existing report, and create a form.

Perform the following tasks:

1. Use the Report Wizard to create the summary report shown in Figure 4–79 on the next page. Name the report Customers by Helper Summary. Group the report by Helper ID and sort by customer number within Helper ID. Include a grand total for the Amount Owed field. Change the orientation to landscape.
2. Open the Customer Financial Report in Layout view. Change the theme for the report to Organic and the Theme Colors to Violet II. Save your changes to the report. *Note*: This theme also will apply to the Customers by Helper Summary report.

Continued >

Extend Your Knowledge *continued*

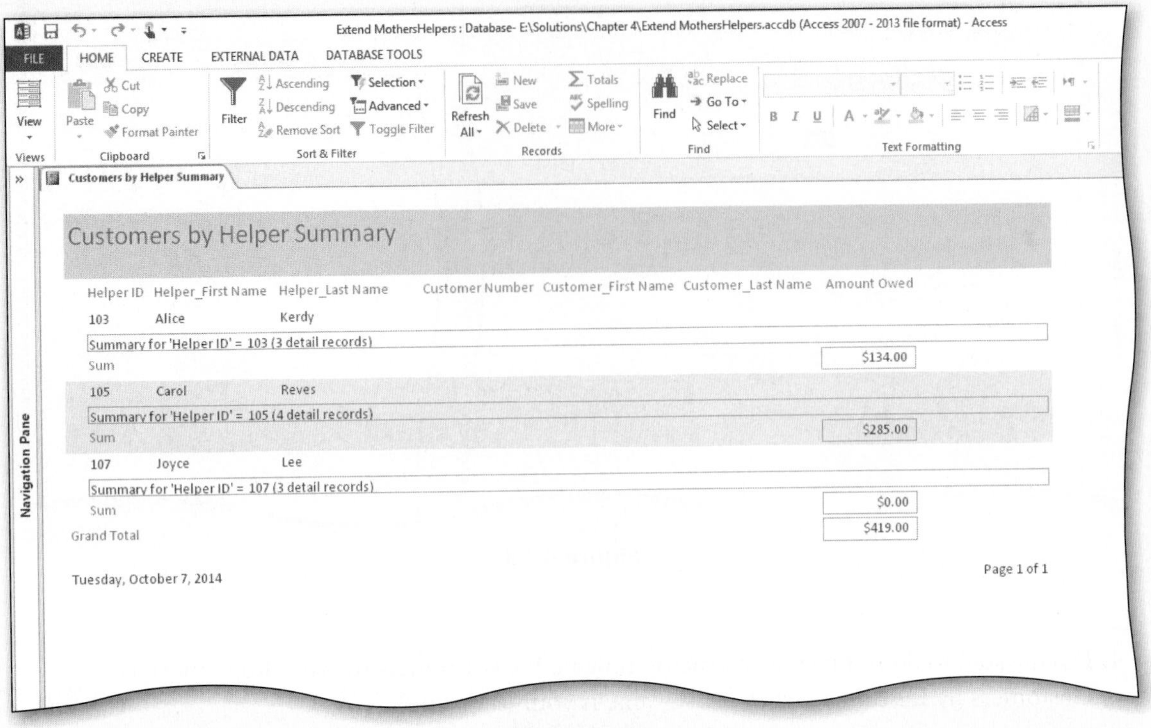

Figure 4–79

3. Create the Customer Financial Form shown in Figure 4–80. The form has a stacked control layout. Apply the Integral theme to this form only. Save the changes to the form.

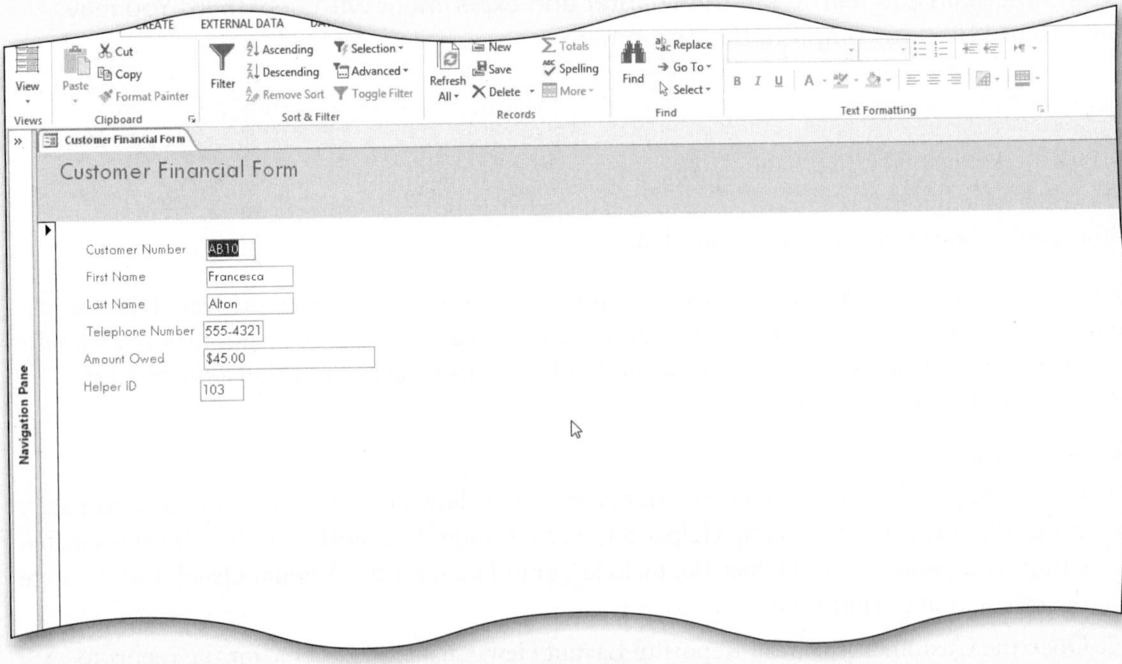

Figure 4–80

4. If requested to do so by your instructor, open the Customer Financial Form in Form view and change the first name and last name for Customer AB10 to your first and last names.
5. Submit the revised database in the format specified by your instructor.
6. How would you change the theme font for the Customer Financial Form to Arial?

Analyze, Correct, Improve

Analyze a database, correct all errors, and improve the design.

Correcting Form Design Errors and Improving a Report

Note: To complete this assignment, you will be required to use the Data Files for Students. Visit www.cengage.com/ct/studentdownload for detailed instructions or contact your instructor for information about accessing the required files.

Instructions: Start Access. Open the Analyze PestControl database from the Data Files for Students. The owner of this local pest control company has asked you to look at the database she created and make some changes to the form and report.

1. Correct The form shown in Figure 4–81 is missing the Telephone Number. The field should appear before the Balance field. Also, the customer first name should appear before the customer last name. The form is missing the current date. The date should be in the format day-month-year. Place the date in the bottom of the form header section and bold the date.

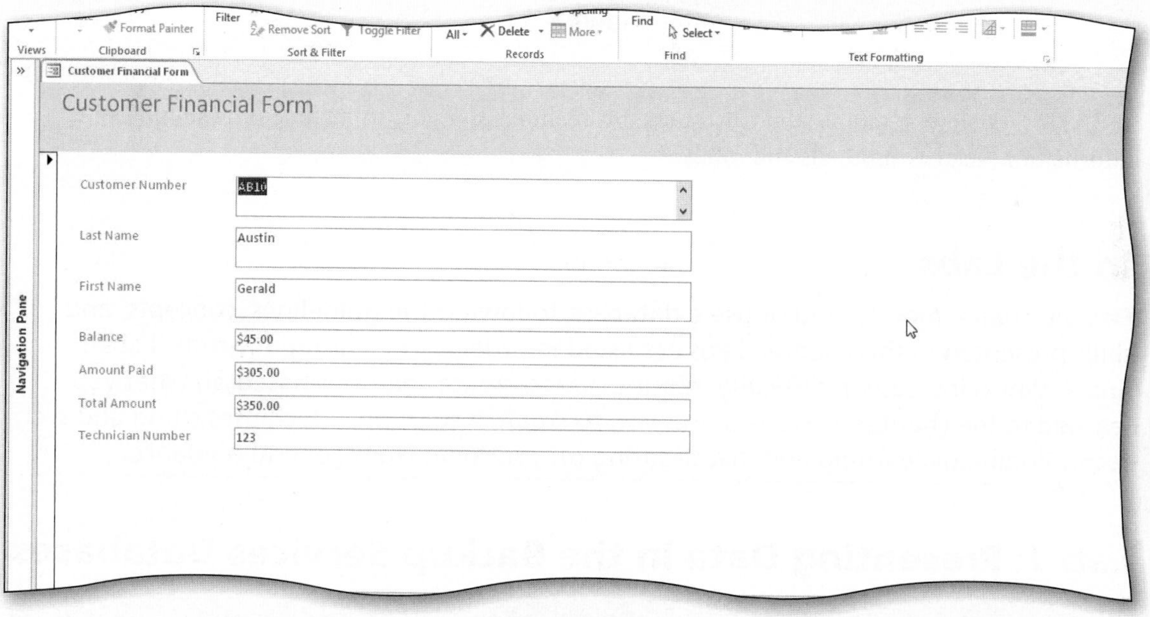

Figure 4–81

2. Improve The report shown in Figure 4–82 on the next page would be easier to read if the customers were listed within the groups alphabetically by customer last name. Adding totals for the Balance, Amount Paid, and Total Amount fields would provide more financial detail. To find customers who have not paid anything on their account, it would be beneficial to highlight those customers whose amount paid value is $0.00 by making the amount appear with a yellow background. Make these changes to improve the appearance of the report. If instructed to do so by your instructor, change the first and last names for technician 123 to your first and last names.

Continued >

Analyze, Correct, Improve *continued*

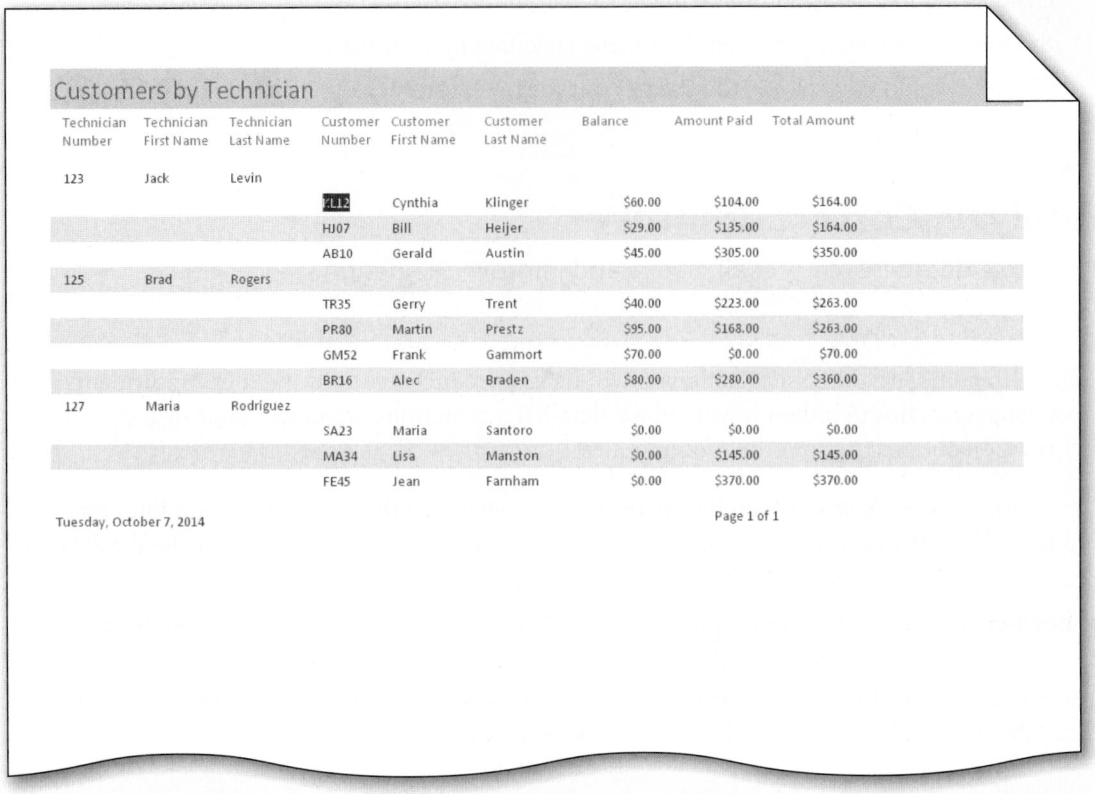

Customers by Technician

Technician Number	Technician First Name	Technician Last Name	Customer Number	Customer First Name	Customer Last Name	Balance	Amount Paid	Total Amount
123	Jack	Levin						
			KL12	Cynthia	Klinger	$60.00	$104.00	$164.00
			HJ07	Bill	Heijer	$29.00	$135.00	$164.00
			AB10	Gerald	Austin	$45.00	$305.00	$350.00
125	Brad	Rogers						
			TR35	Gerry	Trent	$40.00	$223.00	$263.00
			PR80	Martin	Prestz	$95.00	$168.00	$263.00
			GM52	Frank	Gammort	$70.00	$0.00	$70.00
			BR16	Alec	Braden	$80.00	$280.00	$360.00
127	Maria	Rodriguez						
			SA23	Maria	Santoro	$0.00	$0.00	$0.00
			MA34	Lisa	Manston	$0.00	$145.00	$145.00
			FE45	Jean	Farnham	$0.00	$370.00	$370.00

Tuesday, October 7, 2014 Page 1 of 1

Figure 4–82

3. How could you modify the Customers by Technician report to include only summary information, such as subtotals and totals?

In the Labs

Design, create, modify, and/or use a database following the guidelines, concepts, and skills presented in this chapter. Labs are listed in order of increasing difficulty. Labs 1 and 2, which increase in difficulty, require you to create solutions based on what you learned in the chapter; Lab 3 requires you to create a solution, which uses cloud and web technologies, by learning and investigating on your own from general guidance.

Lab 1: Presenting Data in the Backup Services Databases

Problem: Backup Services provides offsite data services and solutions for small businesses and nonprofit organizations. Service representatives work with clients to plan for needed services, schedule backups, and resolve conflicts. Management needs your help in preparing reports and forms to present data for decision making.

Note: To complete this assignment, you will be required to use the Data Files for Students. Visit www.cengage.com/ct/studentdownload for detailed instructions or contact your instructor for information about accessing the required files.

Instructions: Perform the following tasks:

1. Run Access and open the Lab 1 Backup Services database from the Data Files for Students.
2. Open the Client Financial Report in Layout view and modify the report to create the report shown in Figure 4–83. Add the Total Amount field to the report. Group the report by City, and sort by Client Number within City. Include totals for the Amount Paid, Balance Due, and Total Amount fields. Change the orientation to landscape. Make sure the total controls are displayed completely and that the Total Amount subtotals and grand total have the currency format.

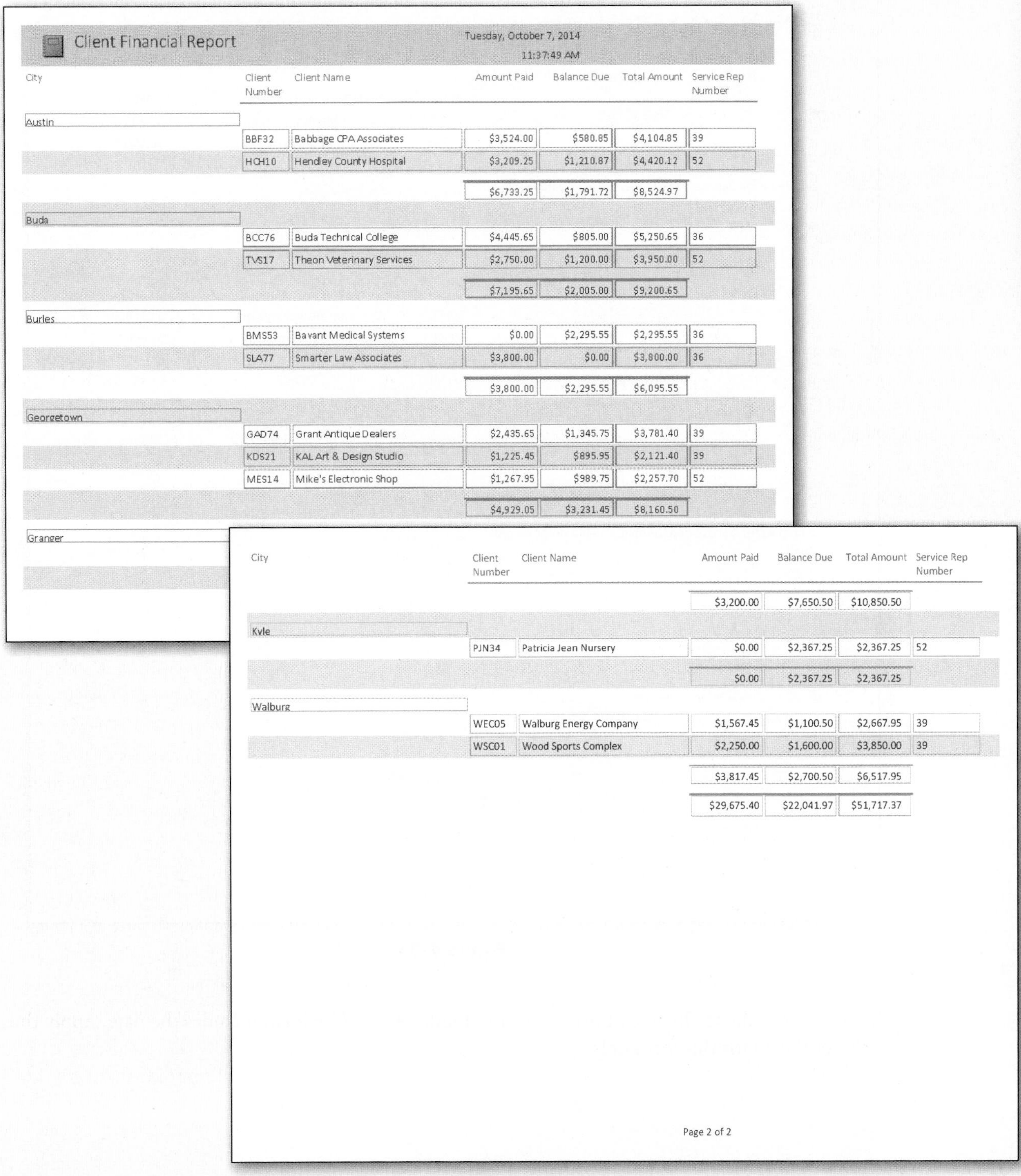

Client Financial Report

Tuesday, October 7, 2014
11:37:49 AM

City	Client Number	Client Name	Amount Paid	Balance Due	Total Amount	Service Rep Number
Austin						
	BBF32	Babbage CPA Associates	$3,524.00	$580.85	$4,104.85	39
	HCH10	Hendley County Hospital	$3,209.25	$1,210.87	$4,420.12	52
			$6,733.25	$1,791.72	$8,524.97	
Buda						
	BCC76	Buda Technical College	$4,445.65	$805.00	$5,250.65	36
	TVS17	Theon Veterinary Services	$2,750.00	$1,200.00	$3,950.00	52
			$7,195.65	$2,005.00	$9,200.65	
Burles						
	BMS53	Bavant Medical Systems	$0.00	$2,295.55	$2,295.55	36
	SLA77	Smarter Law Associates	$3,800.00	$0.00	$3,800.00	36
			$3,800.00	$2,295.55	$6,095.55	
Georgetown						
	GAD74	Grant Antique Dealers	$2,435.65	$1,345.75	$3,781.40	39
	KDS21	KAL Art & Design Studio	$1,225.45	$895.95	$2,121.40	39
	MES14	Mike's Electronic Shop	$1,267.95	$989.75	$2,257.70	52
			$4,929.05	$3,231.45	$8,160.50	
Granger						

City	Client Number	Client Name	Amount Paid	Balance Due	Total Amount	Service Rep Number
			$3,200.00	$7,650.50	$10,850.50	
Kyle						
	PJN34	Patricia Jean Nursery	$0.00	$2,367.25	$2,367.25	52
			$0.00	$2,367.25	$2,367.25	
Walburg						
	WEC05	Walburg Energy Company	$1,567.45	$1,100.50	$2,667.95	39
	WSC01	Wood Sports Complex	$2,250.00	$1,600.00	$3,850.00	39
			$3,817.45	$2,700.50	$6,517.95	
			$29,675.40	$22,041.97	$51,717.37	

Page 2 of 2

Figure 4–83

Continued >

In the Labs *continued*

3. Create the Clients by Service Rep report shown in Figure 4–84. Sort by Client Number and include the average for the Balance Due field. Change the orientation to landscape. If the Balance Due field does not appear completely, open the report in Layout view and increase the size of the field.

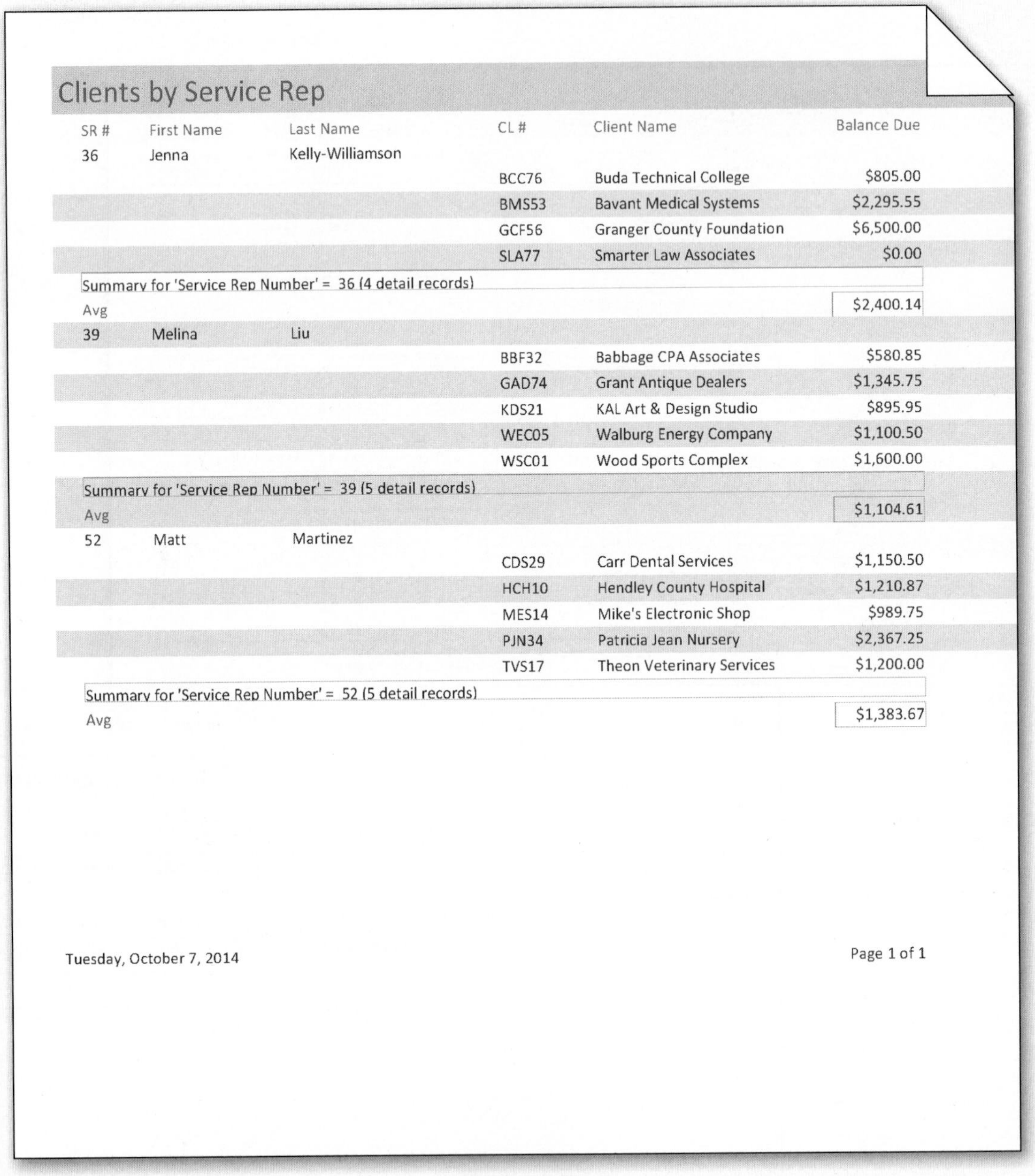

Clients by Service Rep

SR #	First Name	Last Name	CL #	Client Name	Balance Due
36	Jenna	Kelly-Williamson			
			BCC76	Buda Technical College	$805.00
			BMS53	Bavant Medical Systems	$2,295.55
			GCF56	Granger County Foundation	$6,500.00
			SLA77	Smarter Law Associates	$0.00
Summary for 'Service Rep Number' = 36 (4 detail records)					
Avg					$2,400.14
39	Melina	Liu			
			BBF32	Babbage CPA Associates	$580.85
			GAD74	Grant Antique Dealers	$1,345.75
			KDS21	KAL Art & Design Studio	$895.95
			WEC05	Walburg Energy Company	$1,100.50
			WSC01	Wood Sports Complex	$1,600.00
Summary for 'Service Rep Number' = 39 (5 detail records)					
Avg					$1,104.61
52	Matt	Martinez			
			CDS29	Carr Dental Services	$1,150.50
			HCH10	Hendley County Hospital	$1,210.87
			MES14	Mike's Electronic Shop	$989.75
			PJN34	Patricia Jean Nursery	$2,367.25
			TVS17	Theon Veterinary Services	$1,200.00
Summary for 'Service Rep Number' = 52 (5 detail records)					
Avg					$1,383.67

Tuesday, October 7, 2014

Page 1 of 1

Figure 4–84

4. Create the Client Financial Form shown in Figure 4–85. The form includes the date. Apply the Facet theme for this form only.

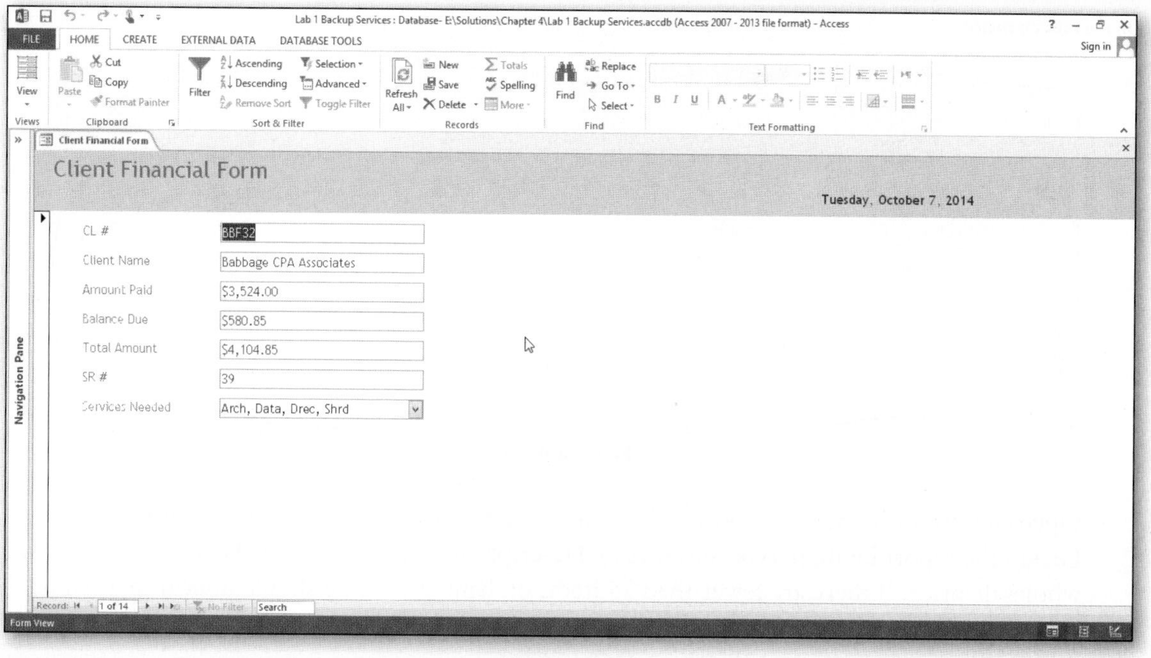

Figure 4–85

5. Create mailing labels for the Client table. Use Avery labels C2163 and format the labels with client name on the first line, street on the second line, and city, state, and postal code on the third line. Include a comma and a space after the city and a space between state and postal code. Sort the labels by postal code.
6. If requested to do so by your instructor, rename the mailing labels as Labels First Name Last Name where First Name and Last Name are your first and last names.
7. Submit the revised database in the format specified by your instructor.
8. How could you display only the records of service rep 39 in the Client Financial Form?

Lab 2: Presenting Data in the Sports Logo Database

Problem: Sports Logo supplies customized clothing and accessories for sporting events. The company purchases these items from suppliers at wholesale prices and adds the customer's logo. The final item price is determined by marking up the wholesale price and adding a fee that is based on the complexity of the logo. The sales department would like to prepare reports and forms for the database.

Note: To complete this assignment, you will be required to use the Data Files for Students. Visit www.cengage.com/ct/studentdownload for detailed instructions or contact your instructor for information about accessing the required files.

Instructions: Perform the following tasks:

1. Run Access and open the Lab 2 Sports Logo database from the Data Files for Students.
2. Open the Item Status Form in Layout view and create the form shown in Figure 4–86 on the next page. Be sure to place the controls in a control layout. If there are fewer than 100 items on hand, the on hand value should appear in a red bold font. Save the changes to the form.

Continued >

In the Labs *continued*

Figure 4–86

3. Open the Inventory Status Report in Layout view and create the report shown in Figure 4–87. Group the report by Item Type and sort by Description within item type. Display the average wholesale price. If there are fewer than 75 items on hand, the value should appear in a red bold font. Save the changes to the report.

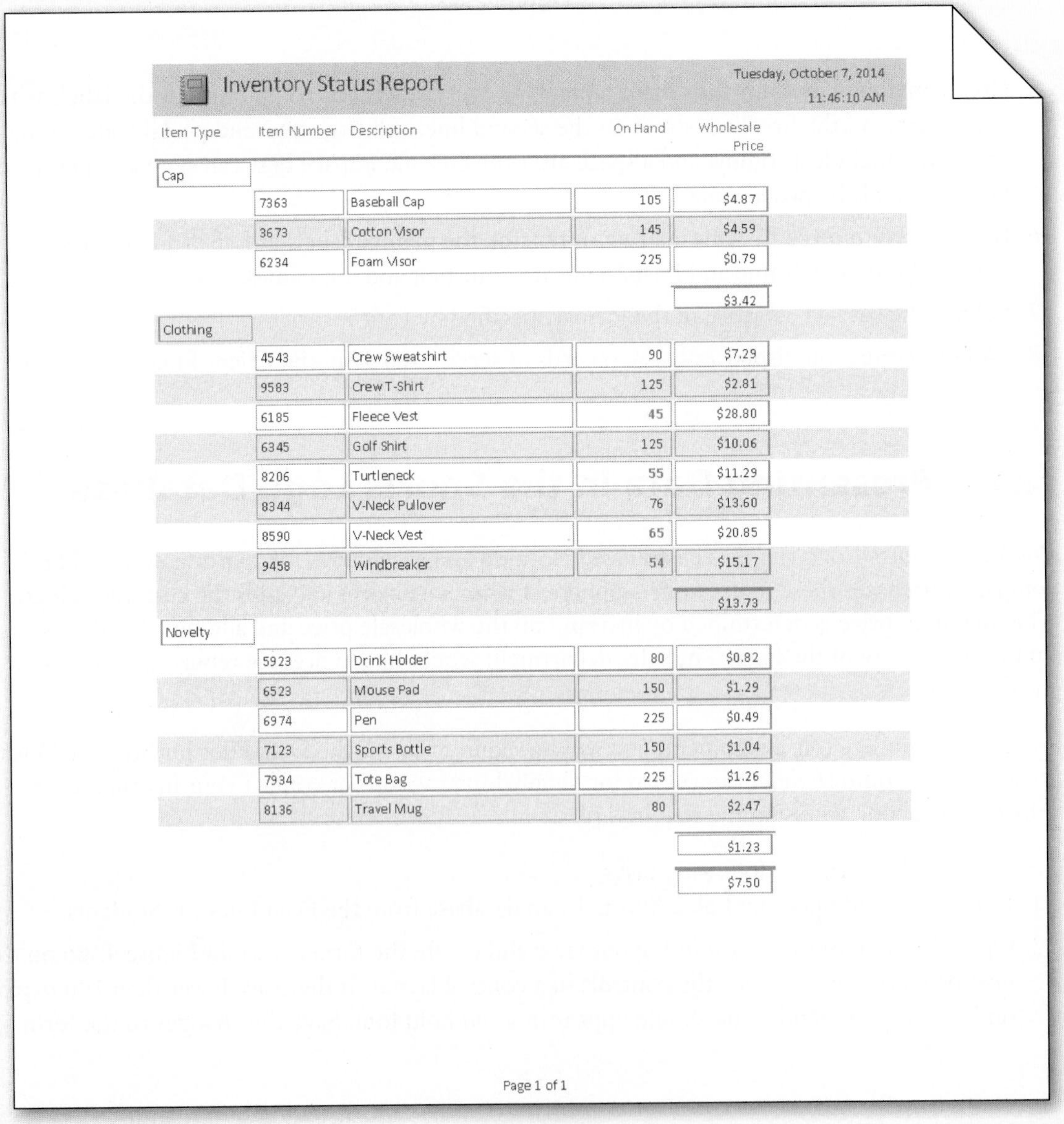

Figure 4–87

4. Filter the report for all items where the number on hand is 60 or fewer. Save the filtered report as Filtered Inventory Status Report.
5. Use the Report Wizard to create the Items by Supplier report shown in Figure 4–88. The report is grouped by Supplier Name and sorted by Description within Supplier Name. Change to landscape orientation.

Items by Supplier

Supplier Name	Description	Item Number	Wholesale
Last Merchants			
	Baseball Cap	7363	$4.87
	Cotton Visor	3673	$4.59
	Foam Visor	6234	$0.79
	V-Neck Pullover	8344	$13.60
	V-Neck Vest	8590	$20.85
PJPratt Clothing			
	Crew Sweatshirt	4543	$7.29
	Crew T-Shirt	9583	$2.81
	Fleece Vest	6185	$28.80
	Golf Shirt	6345	$10.06
	Turtleneck	8206	$11.29
	Windbreaker	9458	$15.17
Scrypt Distributors			
	Drink Holder	5923	$0.82
	Mouse Pad	6523	$1.29
	Pen	6974	$0.49
	Sports Bottle	7123	$1.04
	Tote Bag	7934	$1.26
	Travel Mug	8136	$2.47

Tuesday, October 7, 2014 Page 1 of 1

Figure 4–88

6. If requested to do so by your instructor, rename the Items by Supplier report as Items by First Name Last Name where First Name and Last Name are your first and last names.
7. Submit the revised database in the format specified by your instructor.
8. You used the Report Wizard to create the Items by Supplier report. How could you modify this report to display the average wholesale price?

Lab 3: Expand Your World: Cloud and Web Technologies Using Conditional Formatting and Exporting Reports

Problem: You are the manager of the energy saving device section of the local hardware store. You keep track of your inventory using an Access database. You want to be able to quickly locate items that need to be reordered. You also want to export reports in a format that you can share with vendors.

Continued >

In the Labs *continued*

Note: To complete this assignment, you will be required to use the Data Files for Students. Visit www.cengage.com/ct/studentdownload for detailed instructions or contact your instructor for information about accessing the required files.

Instructions: Perform the following tasks:

1. Open the Lab 3 Energy Saving database from the Data Files for Students.
2. Open the Inventory Status Report in Layout view and create a rule to format the On Hand field with a yellow background and bold red font when the On Hand value is fewer than 10. Change the title for the report to Reorder Report, and then save the report as Reorder Report.
3. Export the Inventory Status Report as a Word/RTF file.
4. Export the Reorder Report as a PDF file.
5. Upload both reports to your SkyDrive.
6. Open the RTF file in the Word Web app and add your name to the report title. Delete the current date and time. Save the file.
7. Submit the revised database, the Word document, and the PDF file in the format specified by your instructor.
8. What happened to the Inventory Status Report when you opened it as a Word document?

Consider This: Your Turn

Apply your creative thinking and problem solving skills to design and implement a solution.

1: Presenting Data in the Artisan Crafts Database

Personal/Academic

Note: To complete this assignment, you will be required to use the Data Files for Students. Visit www.cengage.com/ct/studentdownload for detailed instructions or contact your instructor for information about accessing the required files.

Part 1: You attend a university that is renowned for its school of arts and crafts. Students who major in arts and crafts can sell their work through the university. For your senior project, you created a database in which to store the craft items for sale and the students who created the items. You now need to create reports and forms for the database.

Open the Your Turn 1 Artisan Crafts database from the Data Files for Students. Then, use the concepts and techniques presented in this chapter to perform each of the following tasks:

a. Create a report that includes data from both the Student and the Item table. Include the Student Code, First Name, and Last Name fields from the Student table. Include the Item Number and Description from the Item table. Group the report by student code and sort by item number. Change to landscape orientation.

b. Modify the Crafts For Sale report so that the report is grouped by student code. Within student code, the records should be sorted by Item Number. Include the average of the Price field and the sum of the Total Value field for each group. Use conditional formatting to emphasize any values in the Price field that are greater than $25.00.

c. Create labels for the Item table. These labels will be used to tag items. Include the student code on the first line, the item number and description on the second line, and the price on the third line. Use a label size, font size, and weight that will make it easy for individuals to read the label.

Submit your assignment in the format specified by your instructor.

Part 2: You made several decisions while creating the reports and forms for this assignment, including creating labels. What was the rationale behind your decisions? What other issues do you need to consider when you create labels? Would you add any additional identifying information to the label?

2: Presenting Data in the Carel Landscaping Database

Professional

Note: To complete this assignment, you will be required to use the Data Files for Students. Visit www.cengage.com/ct/studentdownload for detailed instructions or contact your instructor for information about accessing the required files.

Part 1: Carel Landscaping is a local company that provides landscaping and lawn maintenance services to commercial customers, such as businesses, homeowners' associations, and schools. You work part-time for Carel and the owner has asked you to create two reports and a form.

Open the Your Turn 2 Carel Landscaping database from the Data Files for Students. Then, use the concepts and techniques presented in this chapter to perform each of the following tasks:

a. Modify the Customer Financial Report so that the report is grouped by supervisor number. Sort the report by customer number within supervisor number. Use conditional formatting to highlight any values in the Balance field that are greater than $800.00.

b. Create a report that includes data from both the Supervisor table and the Customer table. Include the Supervisor Number, First Name, and Last Name from the Supervisor table. Include the Customer Number, Customer Name, Amount Paid, and Balance fields from the Customer table. Group the report by supervisor number and sort by customer number. Include subtotals for the two currency fields. Change the orientation to landscape.

c. Create a form for the Customer table. Include the Customer Number, Customer Name, Balance, Amount Paid, Total Amount, Supervisor Number, and Services Requested fields on the form.

d. Filter the form you created in Step c for all customers where the Amount Paid is greater than $1,000.00 and sort the results in descending order by amount paid. Save the form as Filtered Form.

Submit your assignment in the format specified by your instructor.

Part 2: You made several decisions while creating these reports and forms, including conditionally formatting values. What was the rationale behind your decisions? Which formatting option did you choose for the conditional formatting? Why? What other options are available?

3: Understanding Report and Form Themes

Research and Collaboration

Part 1: Before you begin this assignment, each team member should save the Bavant Publishing database as Team Member Name Publishing where Team Member Name is the name of the member. For example, if there are three members in your team each member should rename the database with their name. Use the database for this assignment. Create a blog, a Google document, or a Word document on the SkyDrive on which to store the team's research findings and observations for this assignment.

a. Each team member should pick a different theme, theme colors, and theme fonts and modify the Customer Financial Report and the Customer Financial Form with the theme. Compare the themes and as a team vote on which theme you prefer. Record your vote and your reason in your blog or other shared document.

Continued >

Consider This: Your Turn *continued*

b. Use a web search engine to research form design guidelines; for example, there are certain fonts that you should not use for a title and certain colors that are harder for individuals to see. Document your research and cite your references in your blog or shared document. (*Hint:* A shared OneNote notebook would be ideal for this assignment.)

c. Then, as a group, create a form that illustrates poor design features. In your blog or document, explain what design principles were violated.

Submit your assignment in the format specified by your instructor.

Part 2: You made several decisions while in this assignment, including changing themes for reports and forms. What was the rationale behind your decisions? Would your decisions be different if the form and reports were going to be used by individuals external to Bavant Publishing? Why or why not?

Learn Online

Reinforce what you learned in this chapter with games, exercises, training, and many other online activities and resources.

Student Companion Site Reinforcement activities and resources are available at no additional cost on www.cengagebrain.com. Visit www.cengage.com/ct/studentdownload for detailed instructions about accessing the resources available at the Student Companion Site.

SAM Put your skills into practice with SAM! If you have a SAM account, go to www.cengage.com/sam2013 to access SAM assignments for this chapter.

5 Multiple-Table Forms

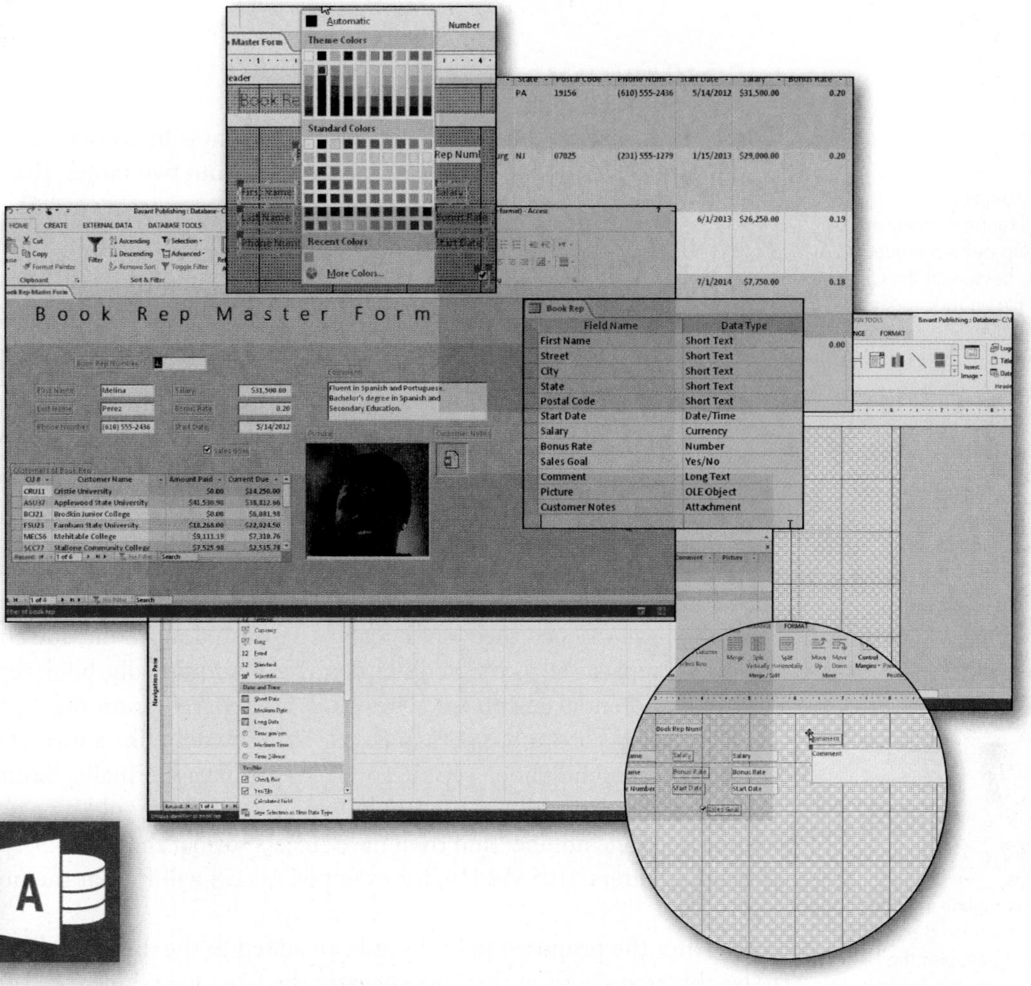

Objectives

You will have mastered the material in this project when you can:

- Add Yes/No, Long Text, OLE Object, and Attachment fields
- Use the Input Mask Wizard
- Update fields and enter data
- Change row and column size
- Create a form with a subform in Design view
- Modify a subform and form design
- Enhance the form title
- Change tab stops and tab order
- Use the form to view data and attachments
- View object dependencies
- Use Date/Time, Long Text, and Yes/No fields in a query
- Create a form with a datasheet

5 | Multiple-Table Forms

Introduction

BTW
Q&As
For a complete list of the Q&As found in many of the step-by-step sequences in this book, visit the Q&A resource on the Student Companion Site located on www.cengagebrain.com. For detailed instructions about accessing available resources, visit www.cengage.com/ct/studentdownload or contact your instructor for information about accessing the required files.

This chapter adds to the Bavant database several new fields that require special data types. It then creates a form incorporating data from two tables. Recall that the two tables, Book Rep and Customer, are related in a one-to-many relationship, with one book rep being related to many customers, but each customer being related to only one book rep. The form will show one book rep at a time, but also will include the many customers of that book rep. This chapter also creates queries that use the added fields.

Project — Multiple-Table Forms

Bavant Publishing uses its database to keep records about customers and book reps. After using the database for several months, however, Bavant has found that it needs to maintain additional data on its book reps. The company wants to identify those book reps who have reached their sales goals. They also want to include comments about each book rep as well as the book rep's picture. Additionally, book reps now maintain files about potential customers. These files are separate from the database; some are maintained in Word and others in Excel. Bavant would like a way to attach these files to the corresponding book rep's record in the database. Finally, Bavant wants to add the Phone Number field to the Book Rep table. Users should type only the digits in the telephone number and then have Access format the number appropriately. If the user enters 6105552436, for example, Access will format the number as (610) 555–2436.

BTW
BTWs
For a complete list of the BTWs found in the margins of this book, visit the BTW resource on the Student Companion Site located on www.cengagebrain.com. For detailed instructions about accessing available resources, visit www.cengage.com/ct/studentdownload or contact your instructor for information about accessing the required files.

After the proposed fields have been added to the database, Bavant wants users to be able to use a form that incorporates the Customer and Book Rep tables and that includes the newly added fields as well as some of the existing fields in the Book Rep table. The form also should include the customer number, name, amount paid, and current due amount for the customers of each book rep. Bavant would like to see multiple customers on the screen at the same time (Figure 5–1). The database should allow users to scroll through all the customers of a book rep and to open any of the attachments concerning the book rep's customer notes. Finally, Bavant requires queries that use the Sales Goal, Start Date, and Comment fields.

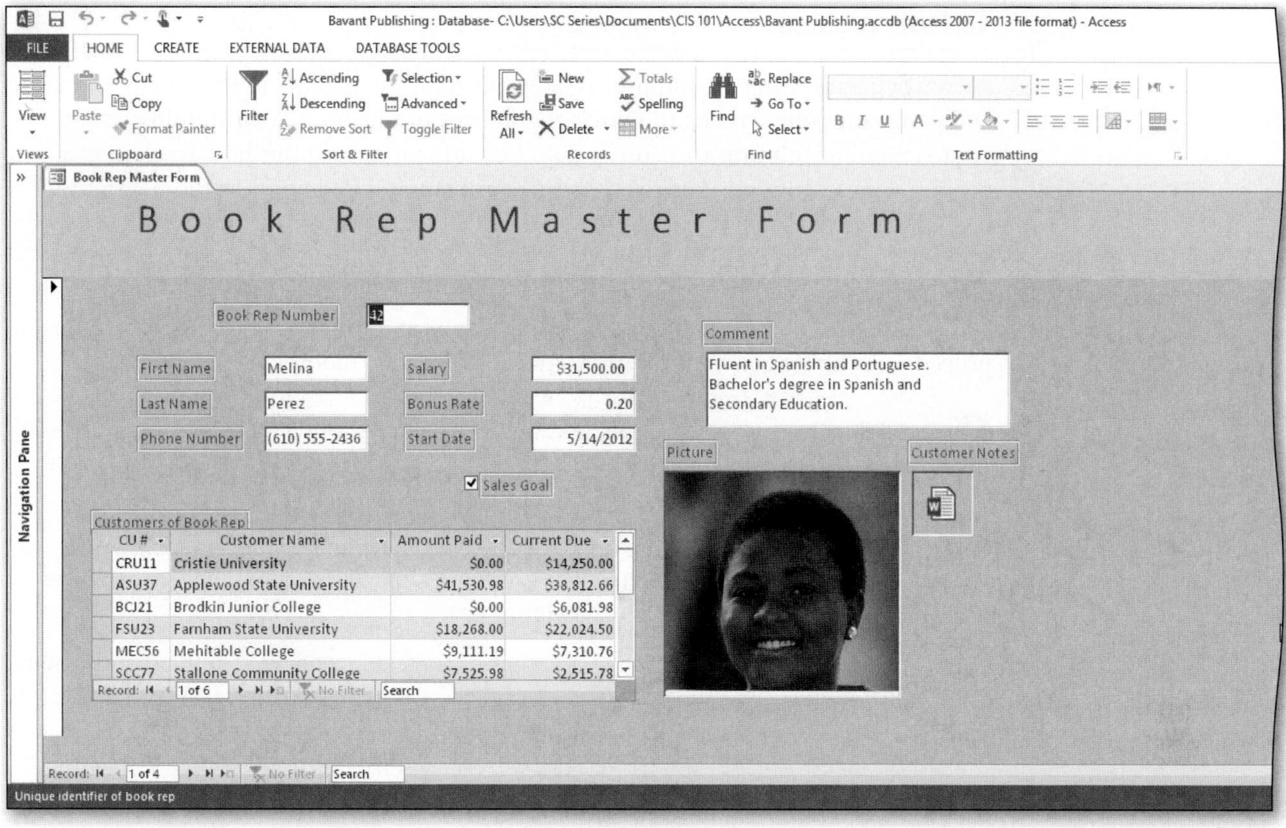

Figure 5–1

Roadmap

In this chapter, you will learn how to create and use the form shown in Figure 5–1. The following roadmap identifies general activities you will perform as you progress through this chapter:

1. ADD FIELDS to the Book Rep table
2. ENTER DATA into the new fields
3. CREATE a FORM for the Book Rep table
4. ADD CONTROLS to the form
5. ADD a SUBFORM to the form
6. MODIFY the SUBFORM
7. ENHANCE the FORM
8. CREATE QUERIES with the new fields

At the beginning of step instructions throughout the chapter, you will see an abbreviated form of this roadmap. The abbreviated roadmap uses colors to indicate chapter progress: gray means the chapter is beyond that activity, blue means the task being shown is covered in that activity, and black means that activity is yet to be covered. For example, the following abbreviated roadmap indicates the chapter would be showing a task in the 3 CREATE FORM activity.

1 ADD FIELDS | 2 ENTER DATA | 3 CREATE FORM | 4 ADD CONTROLS | 5 ADD SUBFORM

6 MODIFY SUBFORM | 7 ENHANCE FORM | 8 CREATE QUERIES

Use the abbreviated roadmap as a progress guide while you read or step through the instructions in this chapter.

To Run Access

BTW
The Ribbon and Screen Resolution
Access may change how the groups and buttons within the groups appear on the ribbon, depending on the computer's screen resolution. Thus, your ribbon may look different from the ones in this book if you are using a screen resolution other than 1366 × 768.

If you are using a computer to step through the project in this chapter and you want your screens to match the figures in this book, you should change your screen's resolution to 1366 × 768. For information about how to change a computer's resolution, refer to the Office and Windows chapter at the beginning of this book.

The following steps, which assume Windows is running, use the Start screen or the search box to run Access based on a typical installation. You may need to ask your instructor how to run Access on your computer. For a detailed example of the procedure summarized below, refer to the Office and Windows chapter.

1. Scroll the Start screen for an Access 2013 tile. If your Start screen contains an Access 2013 tile, tap or click it to run Access; if the Start screen does not contain the Access 2013 tile, proceed to the next step to search for the Access app.
2. Swipe in from the right edge of the screen or point to the upper-right corner of the screen to display the Charms bar, and then tap or click the Search charm on the Charms bar to display the Search menu.
3. Type `Access` as the search text in the Search text box and watch the search results appear in the Apps list.
4. Tap or click Access 2013 in the search results to run Access.

To Open a Database from Access

BTW
Touch Screen Differences
The Office and Windows interfaces may vary if you are using a touch screen. For this reason, you might notice that the function or appearance of your touch screen differs slightly from this chapter's presentation.

BTW
On-Screen Keyboard
To display the on-screen touch keyboard, tap the Touch Keyboard button on the Windows taskbar. When finished using the touch keyboard, tap the X button on the touch keyboard to close the keyboard.

The following steps open the Bavant Publishing database from the location you specified when you first created it (for example, the Access folder in the CIS 101 folder). For a detailed example of the procedure summarized below, refer to the Office and Windows chapter at the beginning of this book.

1. Tap or click FILE on the ribbon to open the Backstage view, if necessary.
2. If the database you want to open is displayed in the Recent list, tap or click the file name to open the database and display the opened database in the Access window; then skip to Step 7. If the database you want to open is not displayed in the Recent list or if the Recent list does not appear, tap or click 'Open Other Files' to display the Open Gallery.
3. If the database you want to open is displayed in the Recent list in the Open gallery, tap or click the file name to open the database and display the opened database in the Access window; then skip to Step 7.
4. Tap or click Computer, SkyDrive, or another location in the left pane, and then navigate to the location of the database to be opened (for example, the Access folder in the CIS 101 folder).
5. Tap or click Bavant Publishing to select the database to be opened.
6. Tap or click the Open button (Open dialog box) to open the selected file and display the opened database in the Access window.
7. If a Security Warning appears, tap or click the Enable Content button.

Adding Special Fields

Having analyzed its requirements, the management of Bavant has identified a need for some new fields for the Book Rep table. They need a Phone Number field and they want to assist users in entering the correct format for a phone number, so the field will use an input mask. An **input mask** specifies how data is to be entered and how it will appear. For example, an input mask can indicate that a phone number has parentheses around the first three digits and a hyphen between the sixth and seventh digits. Bavant also needs a Sales Goal field, which uses a value of Yes or No to indicate whether a rep has met his or her goal; this field's data type will be Yes/No. They need a Comment field, which will be a Long Text field. The Customer Notes field, which must be able to contain multiple attachments for each book rep, will be an Attachment field. The Picture field is the only field whose data type is uncertain — it could be either OLE Object, which can contain objects created by a variety of applications, or Attachment.

Certainly, OLE Object is an appropriate data type for a picture, because when you store an image as an OLE object, the image stays with the database. On the other hand, if an Attachment field contains a picture, the field will display the picture. Other types of attachments, such as Word documents and Excel workbooks, appear in the Attachment field as an icon representing the type of attachment. Bavant Publishing has decided to use OLE Object as the Picture field data type for two reasons. First, the form shown in Figure 5–1 on page AC 267 contains another field that must be an Attachment field, the Customer Notes field. In Datasheet view, an Attachment field appears as a paper clip rather than the field name. Thus, if the Picture field were also an Attachment field, the form would display two paper clips, leading to potential confusion. A second potential problem with using an Attachment field for pictures occurs when you have multiple attachments to a record. Only the first attachment routinely appears in the field on either a datasheet or form. Thus, if the picture were not the first attachment, it would not appear.

BTW

OLE Object Fields

OLE Object Fields can store video clips, sound, and other objects from Windows-based apps.

BTW

Long Text Fields

Long Text fields can store up to a gigabyte of text. If you need to keep a historical record of changes to a Long Text field, set the value for the Append Only property to Yes. To use formatting such as bold and underline in a Long Text field, set the value for the Text Format property to Rich Text.

To Add Fields with New Data Types to a Table

1 ADD FIELDS | 2 ENTER DATA | 3 CREATE FORM | 4 ADD CONTROLS | 5 ADD SUBFORM
6 MODIFY SUBFORM | 7 ENHANCE FORM | 8 CREATE QUERIES

You add the new fields to the Book Rep table by modifying the design of the table and inserting the fields at the appropriate position in the table structure. The following steps add the Sales Goal, Comment, Picture, and Customer Notes fields to the Book Rep table. ***Why?*** *Bavant has determined that they need these fields added to the table.*

1

- If necessary, open the Navigation Pane.
- Press and hold or right-click the Book Rep table to display a shortcut menu (Figure 5–2).

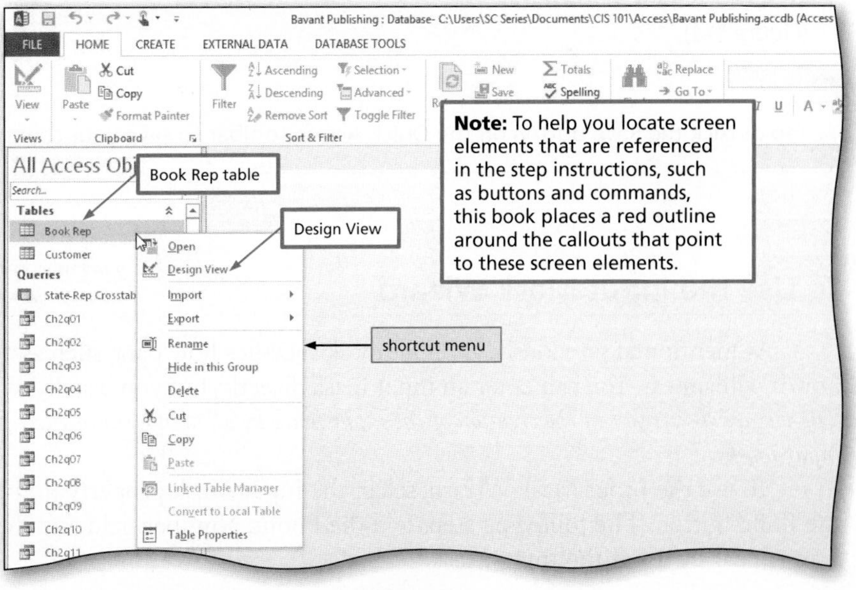

Figure 5–2

2

- Tap or click Design View on the shortcut menu to open the table in Design view (Figure 5–3).

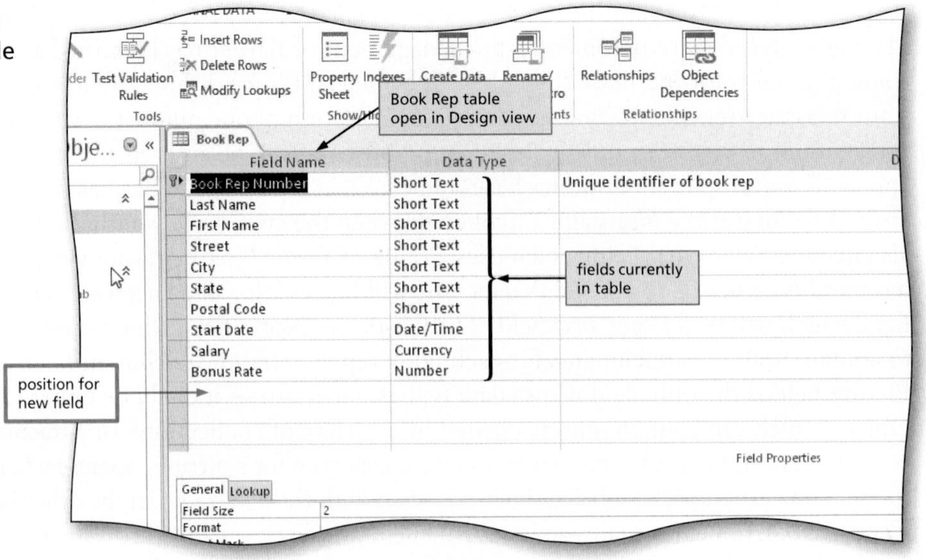

Figure 5–3

3

- Tap or click the first open field to select the position for the first additional field.
- Type **Sales Goal** as the field name, press the TAB key, tap or click the Data Type arrow, select Yes/No as the data type, and then press the TAB key twice to move to the next field.
- Use the same technique to add a field with Comment as the field name and Long Text as the data type, a field with Picture as the field name and OLE Object as the data type, and a field with Customer Notes as the field name and Attachment as the data type (Figure 5–4).

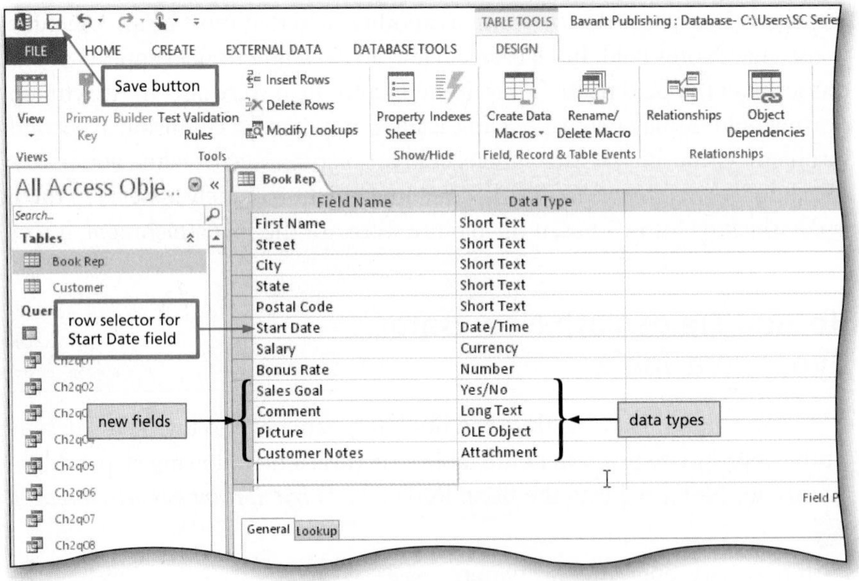

Figure 5–4

4

- Tap or click the Save button on the Quick Access Toolbar to save your changes.

To Use the Input Mask Wizard

1 ADD FIELDS | 2 ENTER DATA | 3 CREATE FORM | 4 ADD CONTROLS | 5 ADD SUBFORM
6 MODIFY SUBFORM | 7 ENHANCE FORM | 8 CREATE QUERIES

As mentioned previously, an input mask specifies how data, such as a phone number, is to be entered and how it will appear. You can enter an input mask directly, but you usually will use the Input Mask Wizard. ***Why?*** *The wizard assists you in the creation of the input mask by allowing you to select from a list of the most frequently used input masks.*

To use the Input Mask Wizard, select the Input Mask property in the field's property sheet and then select the Build button. The following steps add the Phone Number field and then specify how the telephone number is to appear by using the Input Mask Wizard.

1

- Tap or click the row selector for the Start Date field (shown in Figure 5–4), and then press the INSERT key to insert a blank row above Start Date.
- Tap or click the Field Name column for the new field.
- Type **`Phone Number`** as the field name, and then press the TAB key to enter the field.
- Tap or click the Input Mask property box (Figure 5–5).

Q&A Do I need to change the data type?
No. Short Text is the appropriate data type for the Phone Number field.

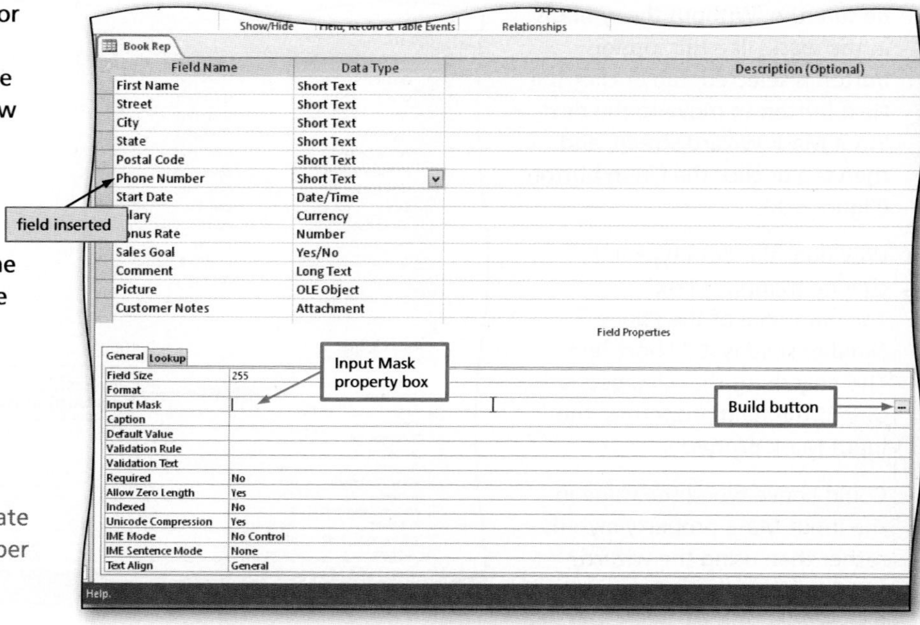

Figure 5–5

2

- Tap or click the Build button to use a wizard to enter the input mask.
- If a dialog box appears asking you to save the table, tap or click the Yes button. (If a dialog box displays a message that the Input Mask Wizard is not installed, check with your instructor before proceeding with the following steps.)
- Ensure that Phone Number is selected (Figure 5–6).

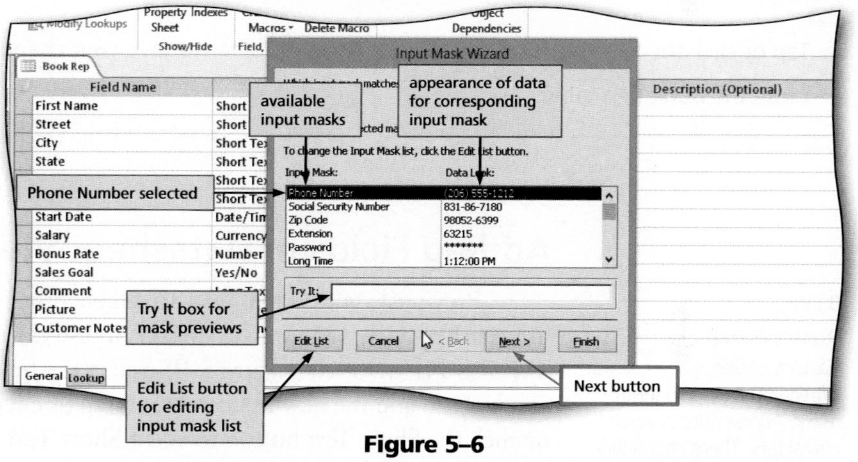

Figure 5–6

Experiment

- Tap or click different input masks and enter data in the Try It text box to see the effect of the input mask. When you are done, tap or click the Phone Number input mask.

3

- Tap or click the Next button to move to the next Input Mask Wizard screen, where you then are given the opportunity to change the input mask.
- Because you do not need to change the mask, tap or click the Next button a second time (Figure 5–7).

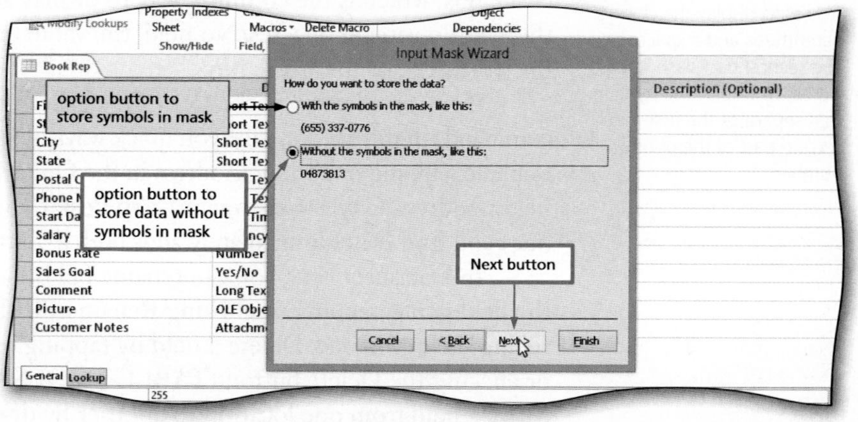

Figure 5–7

4

- **Be sure the 'Without the symbols in the mask, like this' option button is selected, tap or click the Next button to move to the next Input Mask Wizard screen, and then tap or click the Finish button (Figure 5–8).**

Q&A

Why does the data type not change to Input Mask?
The data type of the Phone Number field is still Short Text. The only thing that changed is one of the field properties, the Input Mask property.

Could I have typed the value in the Input Mask property myself, rather than using the wizard?
Yes. Input masks can be complex, however, so it is usually easier and safer to use the wizard.

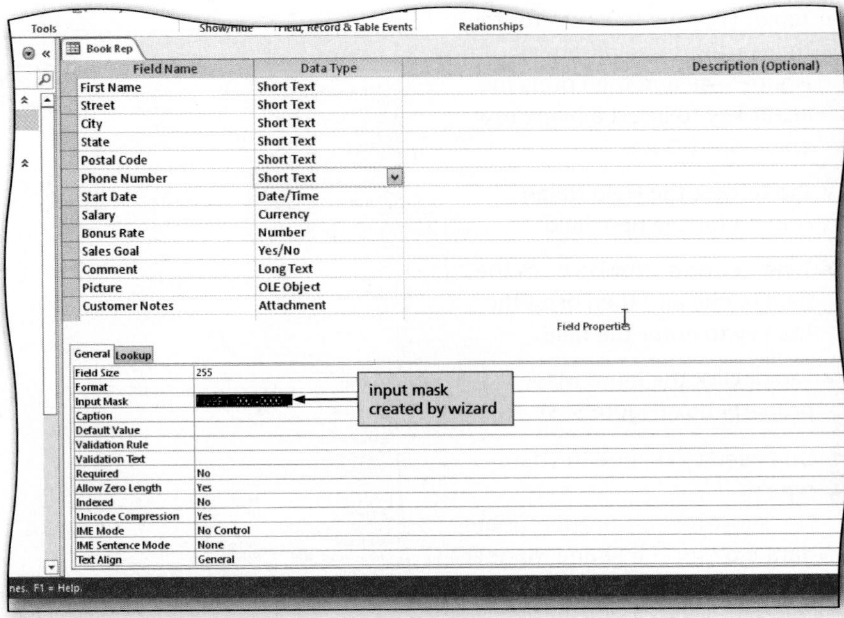

Figure 5–8

5

- **Tap or click the Save button on the Quick Access Toolbar to save your changes.**
- **Close the Book Rep table.**

Adding Fields in Datasheet View

BTW
Input Mask Characters
When you create an input mask, Access adds several characters. These characters control the literal values that appear when you enter data. For example, the first backslash in the input mask in Figure 5–8 displays the opening parenthesis. The double quotes force Access to display the closing parenthesis and a space. The second backslash forces Access to display the hyphen that separates the first and second part of the phone number.

Previously you added fields to a table using Design view. You also can add fields in Datasheet view. One way to do so is to use the Add & Delete group on the TABLE TOOLS FIELDS tab (Figure 5–9). Select the field that precedes the position where you want to add the new field and then tap or click the appropriate button. You can tap or click the Short Text button to add a Short Text field, the Number button to add a Number field, the Currency button to add a Currency field, and so on. Alternatively, you can tap or click the More Fields button as shown in the figure to display the Data Type gallery. You then can tap or click a data type in the gallery to add a field with that type.

The gallery gives some additional control on the data type. For example, if you tap or click the Check Box version of a Yes/No field, the field will be displayed as a check box, which is the common way to display such a field. If instead you tap or click the Yes/No version of a Yes/No field, the value in the field will be displayed as either the word, Yes, or the word, No.

If you scroll down in the Data Type gallery, you will find a Quick Start section. The commands in this section give you quick ways of adding some common types of fields. For example, tapping or clicking Address in the Quick Start section immediately adds several fields: Address, City, State Province, Zip Postal, and Country Region. Tapping or clicking Start and End Dates immediately adds both a Start Date field and an End Date field.

In Datasheet view, you can rename fields by pressing and holding or right-clicking the field name, tapping or clicking Rename Field on the shortcut menu, and then typing the new name. Delete a field by tapping or clicking the field and then tapping or clicking the Delete button (TABLE TOOLS FIELDS tab | Add & Delete group). Move a field from one location to another by dragging the field.

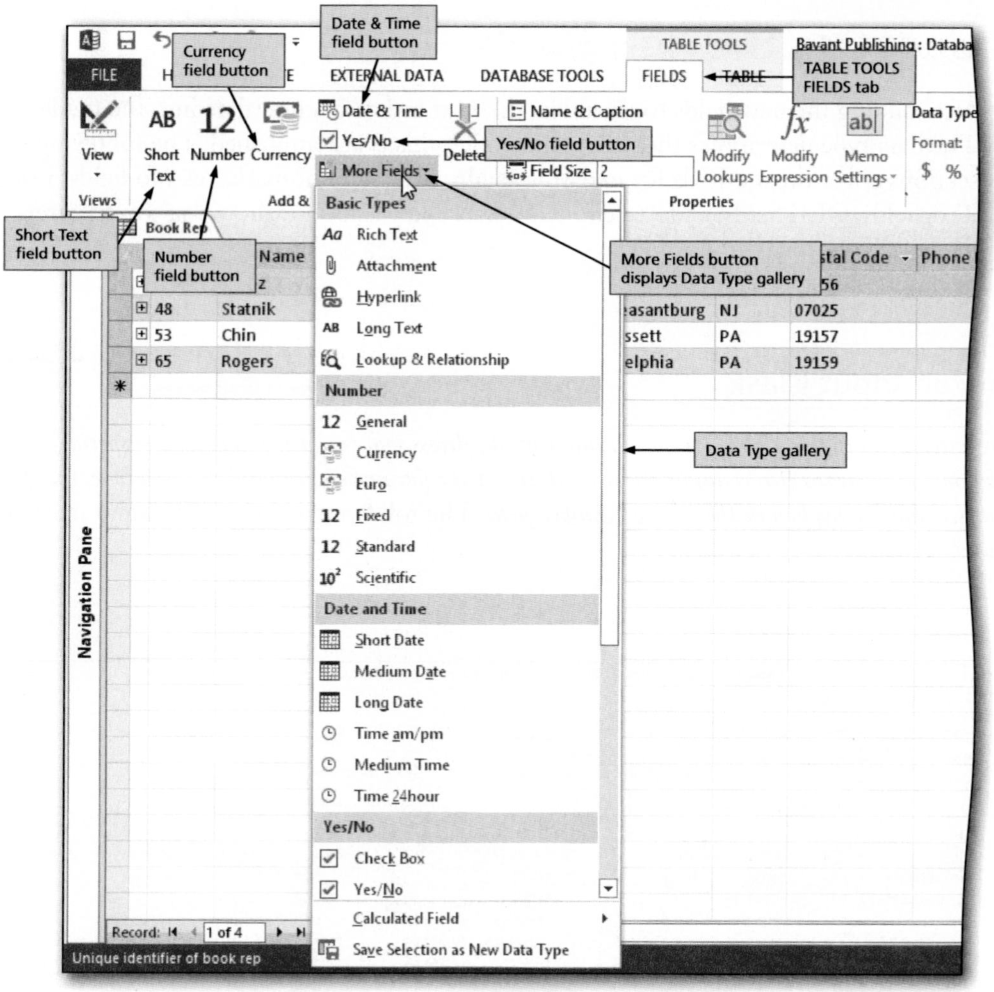

Figure 5–9

How do you determine if fields need special data types or an input mask?

Determine whether an input mask is appropriate. Sometimes the data in the field should be displayed in a special way, for example, with parentheses and a hyphen like a phone number, or separated into three groups of digits like a Social Security number. If so, should Access assist the user in entering the data in the right format? For example, by including an input mask in a field, Access can automatically insert the parentheses and a hyphen when a user enters a phone number.

Determine whether the Yes/No data type is appropriate. A field is a good candidate for the Yes/No data type if the only possible field values are Yes or No, True or False, or On or Off.

Determine whether the Long Text data type is appropriate. A field that contains text that is variable in length and potentially very long is an appropriate use of the Long Text data type. If you want to use special text effects, such as bold and italic, you can assign the field the Long Text data type and change the value of the field's Text Format property from Plain Text to Rich Text. You also can collect history on the changes to a Long Text field by changing the value of the field's Append Only property from No to Yes. If you do so, when you right-click the field and click Show Column History on the shortcut menu, you will see a record of all changes made to the field.

Determine whether the OLE Object data type is appropriate. Does the field contain a picture? Does it contain an object created by other applications that support **OLE (Object Linking and Embedding)**?

Determine whether the Attachment data type is appropriate. Will the field contain one or more attachments that were created in other applications? If so, the Attachment data type is appropriate. It allows you to store multiple attachments on each record. You can view and manipulate these attachments in their original application.

Determine whether the Hyperlink data type is appropriate. A field with the hyperlink data type contains a hyperlink, that is a link to another location, such as a web page or a file. Will the field contain an email address, links to other Office documents, or links to webpages? If so, Hyperlink is appropriate.

Updating the New Fields

After adding the new fields to the table, the next task is to enter data into the fields. The data type determines the manner in which this is accomplished. The following sections cover the methods for updating fields with an input mask, Yes/No fields, Long Text fields, OLE fields, and Attachment fields. They also show how you would enter data in Hyperlink fields.

To Enter Data Using an Input Mask

1 ADD FIELDS | 2 ENTER DATA | **3 CREATE FORM** | **4 ADD CONTROLS** | **5 ADD SUBFORM**
6 MODIFY SUBFORM | **7 ENHANCE FORM** | **8 CREATE QUERIES**

Why? *When you are entering data in a field that has an input mask, Access will insert the appropriate special characters in the proper positions. This means Access automatically will insert the parentheses around the area code, the space following the second parenthesis, and the hyphen in the Phone Number field.* The following steps use the input mask to add the telephone numbers.

1

- Open the Book Rep table and close the Navigation Pane.
- Tap or click at the beginning of the Phone Number field on the first record to display an insertion point in the field (Figure 5–10).

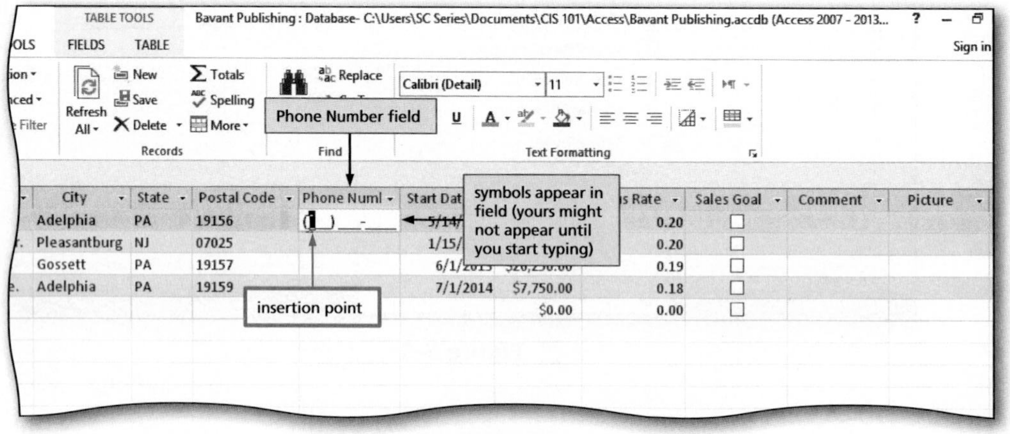

Figure 5–10

Q&A I do not see the parentheses and hyphen as shown in the figure. Did I do something wrong?

Depending on exactly where you tap or click, you might not see the symbols. Regardless, as soon as you start typing in the field, the symbols should appear.

2

- Type `6105552436` as the telephone number (Figure 5–11).

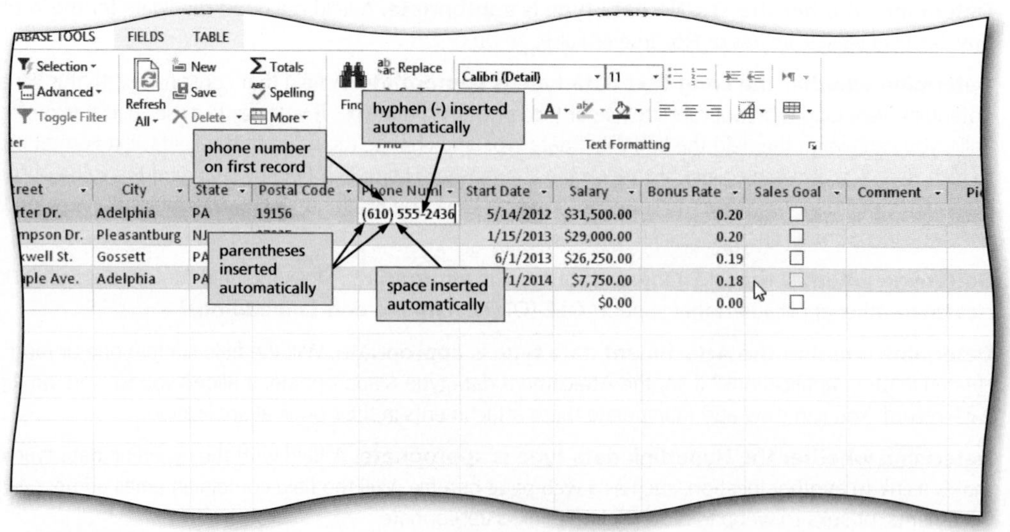

Figure 5–11

3

- Use the same technique to enter the remaining telephone numbers, as shown in Figure 5–12.
- If requested to do so by your instructor, change the phone number for book rep 42 to your phone number.

Q&A Do I need to click at the beginning of the field?

Yes. If you do not, the data will not be entered correctly.

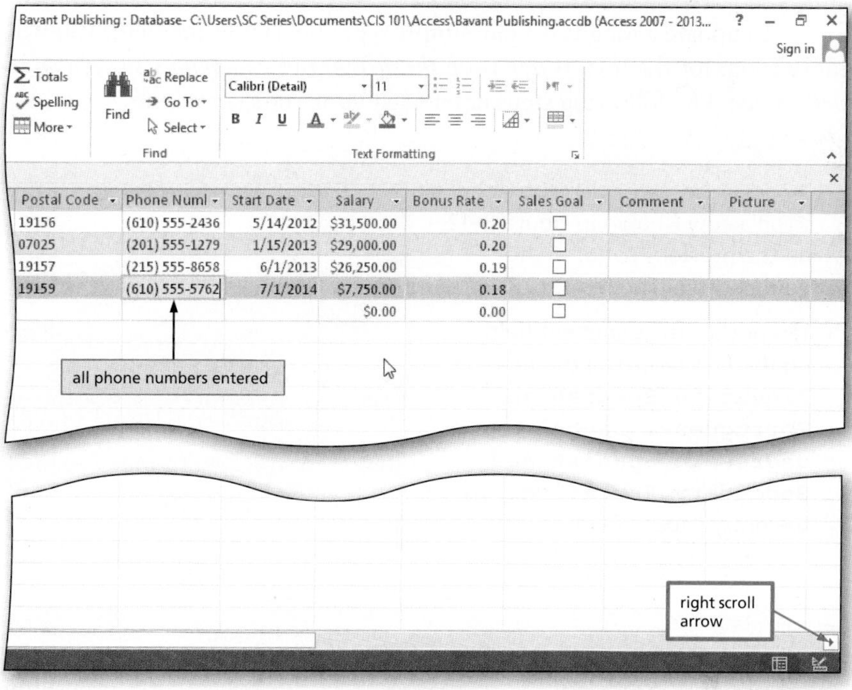

Figure 5–12

To Enter Data in Yes/No Fields

1 ADD FIELDS | 2 ENTER DATA | 3 CREATE FORM | 4 ADD CONTROLS | 5 ADD SUBFORM
6 MODIFY SUBFORM | 7 ENHANCE FORM | 8 CREATE QUERIES

Fields that are Yes/No fields contain check boxes. To set the value to Yes, place a check mark in the check box. ***Why?*** *A check mark indicates the value is Yes or True.* To set a value to No, leave the check box blank. The following step sets the value of the Sales Goal field, a Yes/No field, to Yes for the first record.

1

- If necessary, tap or click the right scroll arrow (shown in Figure 5–12) until the new fields appear.
- Tap or click the check box in the Sales Goal field on the first record to place a check mark in the box (Figure 5–13).

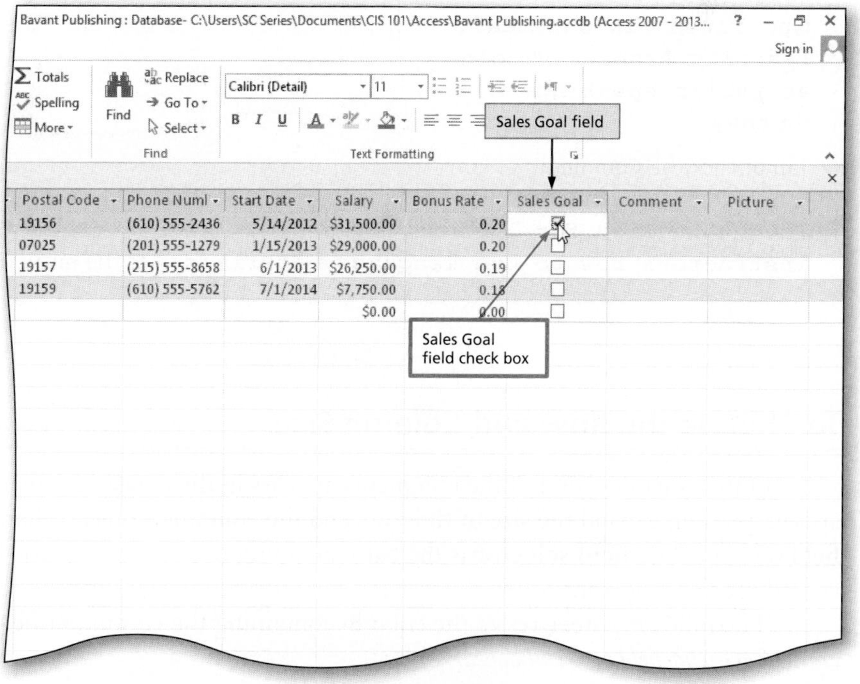

Figure 5–13

To Enter Data in Long Text Fields

1 ADD FIELDS | 2 ENTER DATA | 3 CREATE FORM | 4 ADD CONTROLS | 5 ADD SUBFORM
6 MODIFY SUBFORM | 7 ENHANCE FORM | 8 CREATE QUERIES

To update a long text field, simply type the data in the field. You will later change the spacing to allow more room for the text. ***Why?*** *With the current row and column spacing on the screen, only a small portion of the text will appear.* The following steps enter each book rep's comment.

1

- If necessary, tap or click the right scroll arrow (shown in Figure 5–12 on the previous page) so the Comment field appears.
- Tap or click the Comment field on the first record, and then type **`Fluent in Spanish and Portuguese. Bachelor's degree in Spanish and Secondary Education.`** as the entry (Figure 5–14).

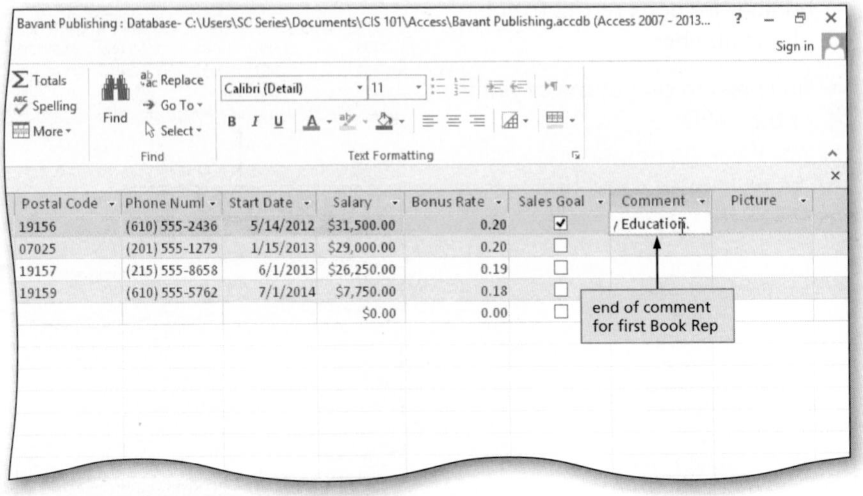

Figure 5–14

2

- Tap or click the Comment field on the second record, and then type **`Senior sales representative. Transferred to new division to mentor other book reps.`** as the entry.
- Tap or click the Comment field on the third record, and then type **`Fluent in Japanese. Learning Arabic. Excels at public speaking.`** as the entry.
- Tap or click the Comment field on the fourth record, and then type **`Taught English for 2 years in Russia. Expert at teaching instructors how to use language materials.`** as the entry (Figure 5–15).

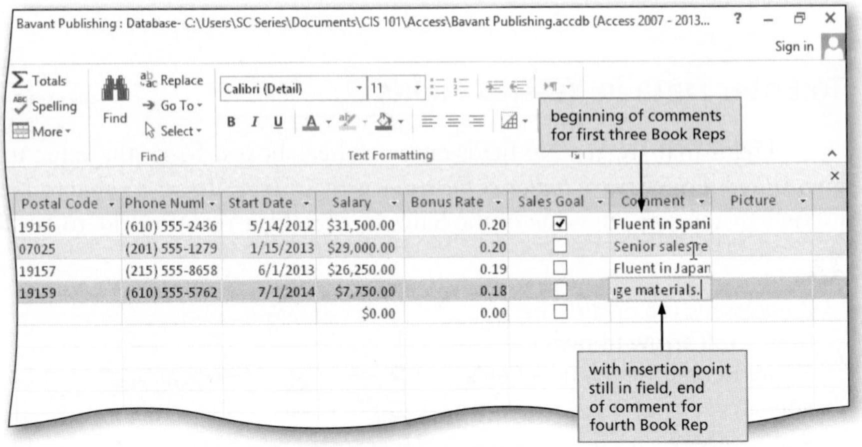

Figure 5–15

To Change the Row and Column Size

1 ADD FIELDS | 2 ENTER DATA | 3 CREATE FORM | 4 ADD CONTROLS | 5 ADD SUBFORM
6 MODIFY SUBFORM | 7 ENHANCE FORM | 8 CREATE QUERIES

Only a small portion of the comments appears in the datasheet. To allow more of the information to appear, you can expand the size of the rows and the columns. You can change the size of a column by using the field selector. The **field selector** is the bar containing the field name. To change the size of a row, you use a record's record selector.

The following steps resize the column containing the Comment field and the rows of the table. ***Why?*** *The entire Comment field text will appear.*

1

- Drag the right edge of the field selector for the Comment field to the right to resize the Comment column to the approximate size shown in Figure 5–16.

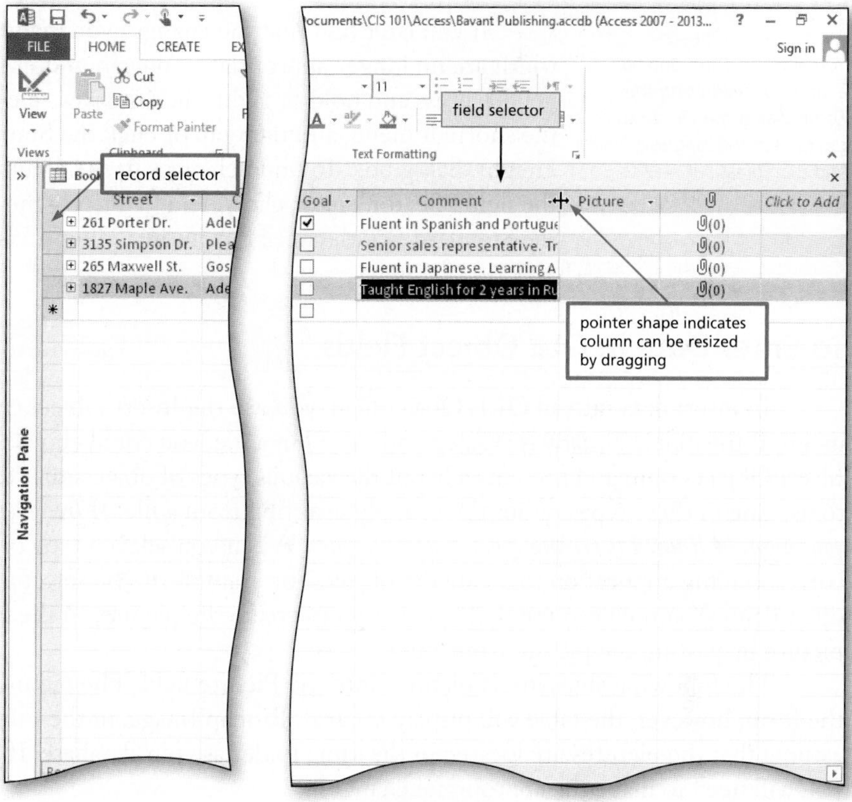

Figure 5–16

2

- Drag the lower edge of the record selector to approximately the position shown in Figure 5–17.

Q&A Can rows be different sizes?
No. All rows must be the same size.

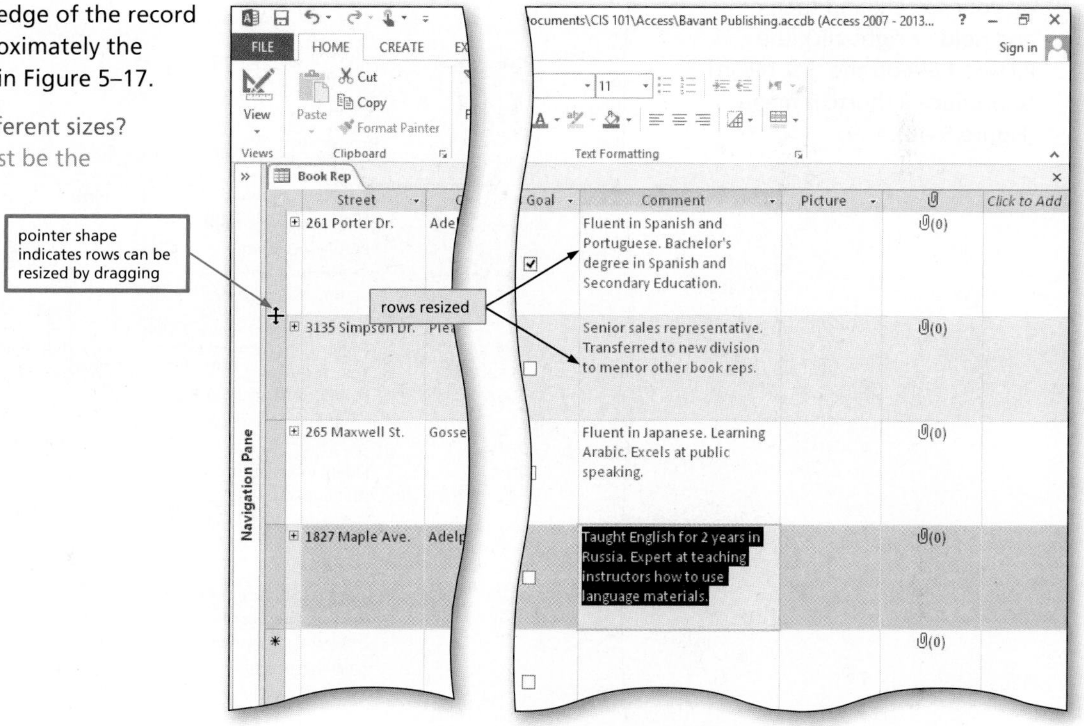

Figure 5–17

Other Ways

1. Press and hold or right-click record selector, tap or click Row Height to change row spacing
2. Press and hold or right-click field selector, tap or click Field Width to change column size

BTW
Entering Data in Long Text Fields
You also can enter data in a long text field using the Zoom dialog box. To do so, tap or click the long text field and then press SHIFT+F2 to open the Zoom dialog box.

Undoing Changes to Row Height and Column Width

If you later find that the changes you made to the row height or the column width are no longer appropriate, you can undo them. To undo changes to the row height, press and hold or right-click the row selector, tap or click Row Height on the shortcut menu, and then tap or click the Standard Height check box in the Row Height dialog box. To undo changes to the column width, press and hold or right-click the field selector, tap or click Field Width on the shortcut menu, and then tap or click the Standard Width check box in the Column Width dialog box.

To Enter Data in OLE Object Fields

1 ADD FIELDS | 2 ENTER DATA | 3 CREATE FORM | 4 ADD CONTROLS | 5 ADD SUBFORM
6 MODIFY SUBFORM | 7 ENHANCE FORM | 8 CREATE QUERIES

To insert data into an OLE Object field, you use the Insert Object command on the OLE field's shortcut menu. If the object already is created and stored in a file, you could choose to insert it directly from the file. The Insert Object command presents a list of the various types of objects that can be inserted, and it often is better to use one of these types rather than simply inserting from a file. ***Why?*** *Depending on your installation of Access, you might be limited to certain types of graphics files.* When you select a type of object to insert, Access will open the corresponding application to create the object. For example, if you select a Bitmap Image object type, Access will open Paint. You then can use that application to create the picture. In the case of Paint, you easily can create the picture by pasting the picture from a file.

The following steps insert pictures into the Picture field. The pictures will be visible as photographs in the form; however, the table will display the text, Bitmap Image, in the Picture field in the datasheet. The steps assume that the pictures are located in the same folder as your database. If your pictures are located elsewhere, you will need to make the appropriate changes.

1

- Ensure the Picture field appears on your screen, and then press and hold or right-click the Picture field on the first record to produce a shortcut menu (Figure 5–18).

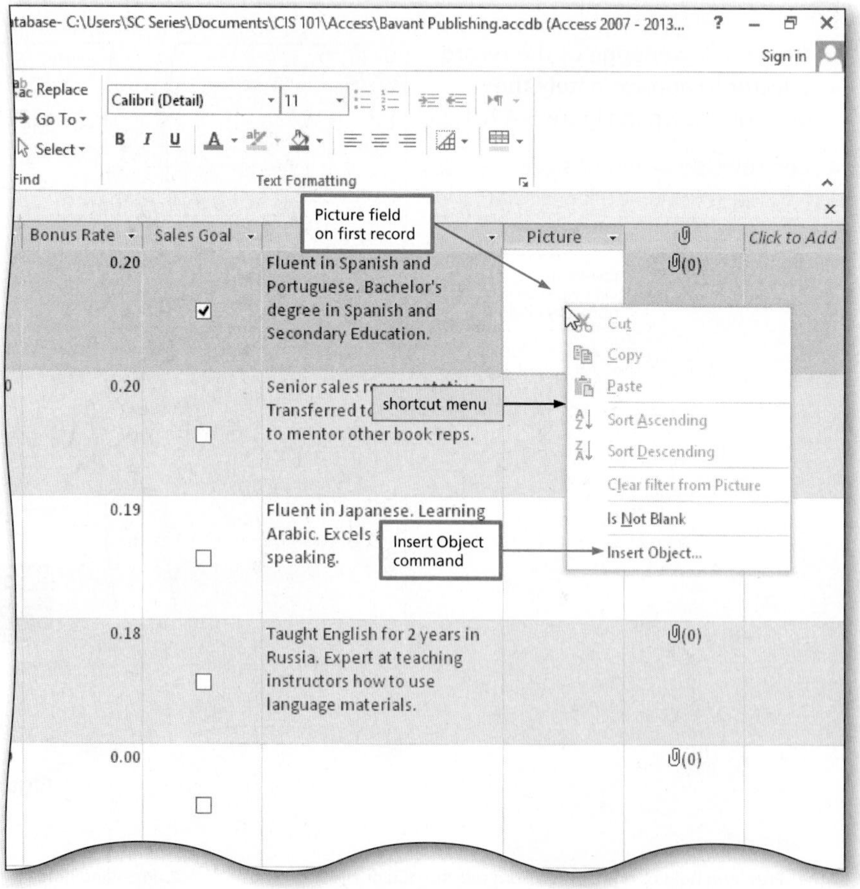

Figure 5–18

2

- Tap or click Insert Object on the shortcut menu to display the Microsoft Access dialog box (Figure 5–19).

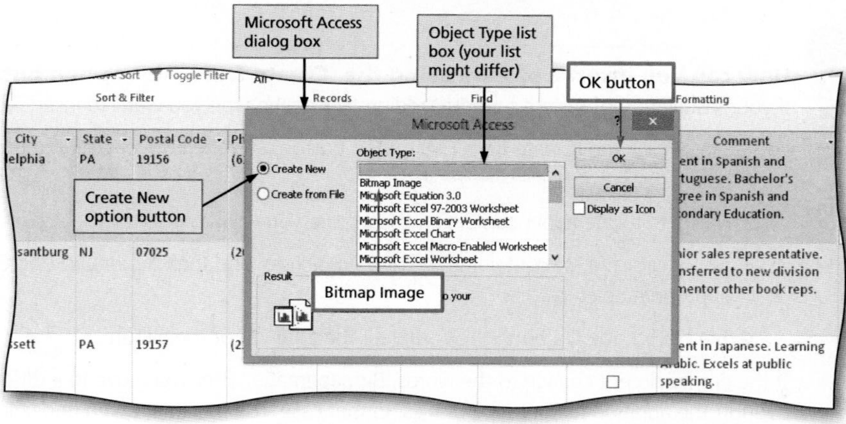

Figure 5–19

3

- Select the Bitmap Image object type from the Object Type list.
- Tap or click the OK button to open the Paint application.
- Tap or click the Paste button arrow (Home tab | Clipboard group) in the Paint application to display the Paste menu (Figure 5–20).

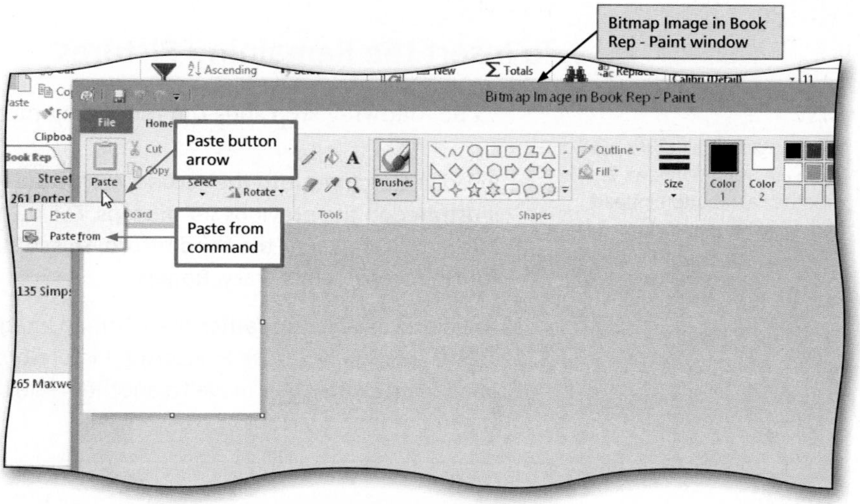

Figure 5–20

4

- Tap or click the Paste from command to paste a picture.
- Navigate to the location for the jpg file named Melina_Perez, select the file, and then tap or click the Open button.
- Tap or click the File tab in the Paint application (Figure 5–21).

5

- Tap or click the 'Exit and return to document' command to return to Access and the Book Rep table and insert the picture.

Q&A I do not see the picture. I just see the words, Bitmap Image. Is that correct?

Yes. You will see the actual picture when you use this field in a form.

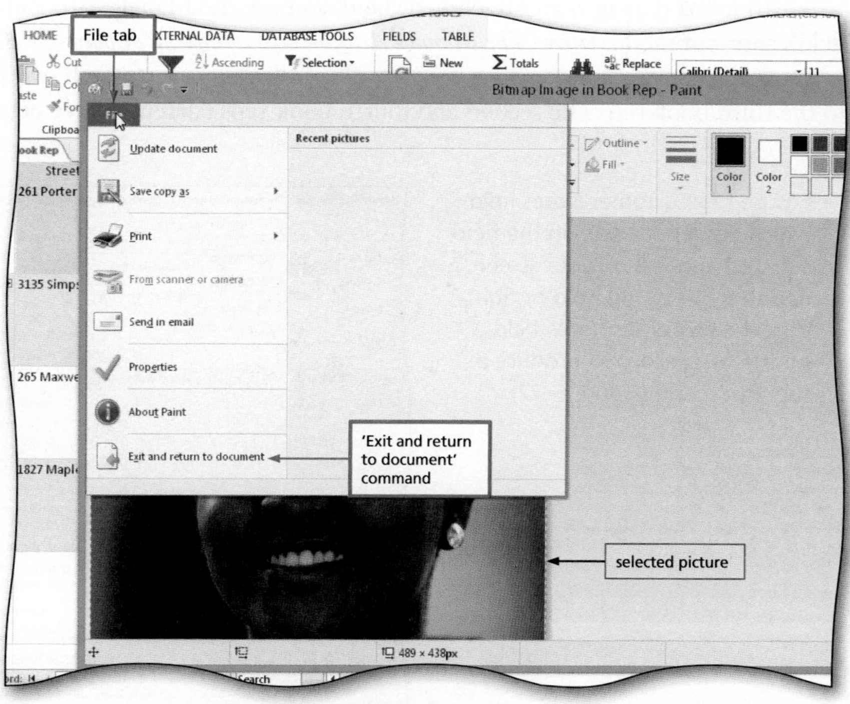

Figure 5–21

CONSIDER THIS

How can you insert a picture using the 'Create from File' option button?

If your installation of Access supports adding files of the type you want to insert, you would use the following steps:

1. Tap or click the 'Create from File' option button, and then tap or click the Browse button to display the Browse dialog box.
2. Navigate to the folder containing the picture you wish to insert.
3. Tap or click the file containing the desired picture, and then tap or click the OK button (Browse dialog box) to select the appropriate picture.
4. Tap or click the OK button to complete the addition of the picture.

If the entries do not change to the words, Bitmap Image, after you move to a different record, your installation does not support the addition of your type of files. In that case, use the steps given under To Enter Data in OLE Object Fields.

To Insert the Remaining Pictures

BTW
Windows 7 and Paint
If you are using Windows 7, click the Paint button instead of the File tab.

The following step adds the remaining pictures.

1 **Insert the pictures into the second, third, and fourth records using the techniques illustrated in the previous set of steps. For the second record, select the picture named Michael_Statnik. For the third record, select the picture named Robert_Chin. For the fourth record, select Tracy_Rogers.**

Q&A I see Paintbrush Picture rather than Bitmap Image. Did I do something wrong?
The entries initially will be Paintbrush Picture but they should change to the words, Bitmap Image, after you move to another record. They also should change after you close and reopen the table.

To Enter Data in Attachment Fields

1 ADD FIELDS | 2 ENTER DATA | 3 CREATE FORM | 4 ADD CONTROLS | 5 ADD SUBFORM
6 MODIFY SUBFORM | 7 ENHANCE FORM | 8 CREATE QUERIES

To insert data into an Attachment field, you use the Manage Attachments command on the Attachment field's shortcut menu. ***Why?*** *The Manage Attachments command displays the Attachments dialog box, which you can use to attach as many files as necessary to the field.* The following steps attach two files to the first book rep and one file to the third book rep. The second and fourth book reps currently have no attachments.

1

- Ensure the Customer Notes field, which has a paper clip in the field selector, appears on your screen, and then press and hold or right-click the Customer Notes field on the first record to produce a shortcut menu (Figure 5–22).

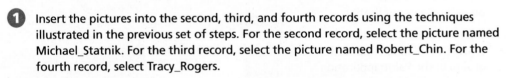

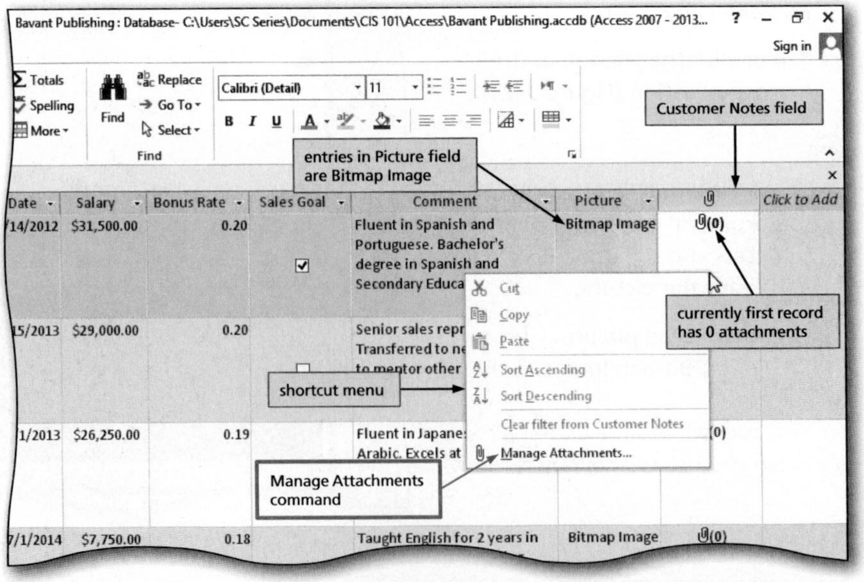

Figure 5–22

2

- Tap or click Manage Attachments on the shortcut menu to display the Attachments dialog box (Figure 5–23).

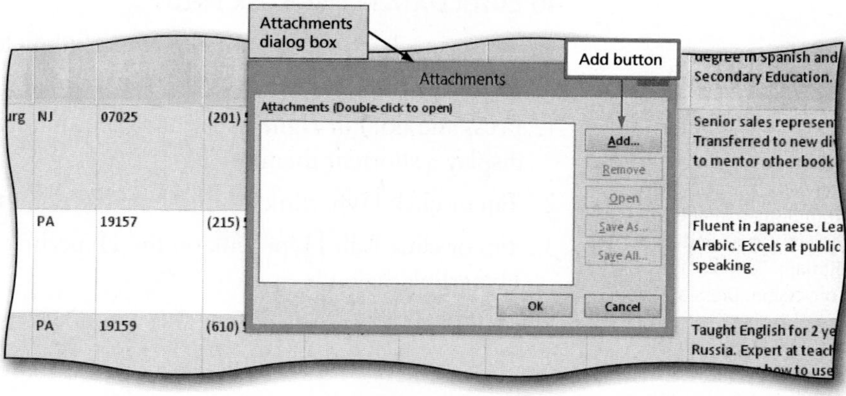

Figure 5–23

3

- Tap or click the Add button (Attachments dialog box) to display the Choose File dialog box, where you can add an attachment.
- Navigate to the folder containing your attachment files. (If your attachments are located elsewhere, navigate to the folder where they are located instead.)
- Tap or click Melina Perez Customers, a Word file, and then tap or click the Open button (Choose File dialog box) to attach the file.
- Tap or click the Add button (Attachments dialog box).
- Tap or click Melina Perez Potential Customers, an Excel file, and then tap or click the Open button to attach the file (Figure 5–24).

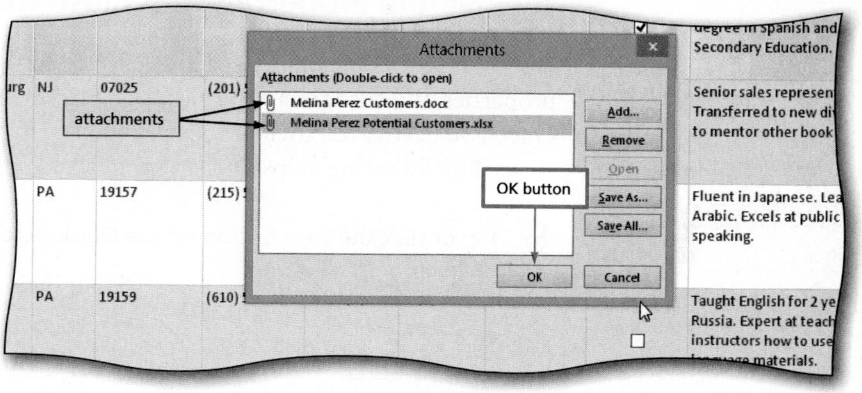

Figure 5–24

4

- Tap or click the OK button (Attachments dialog box) to close the Attachments dialog box.
- Using the same technique, attach the Robert Chin Potential Customers file to the third record (Figure 5–25). (The second and fourth records have no attachments.)

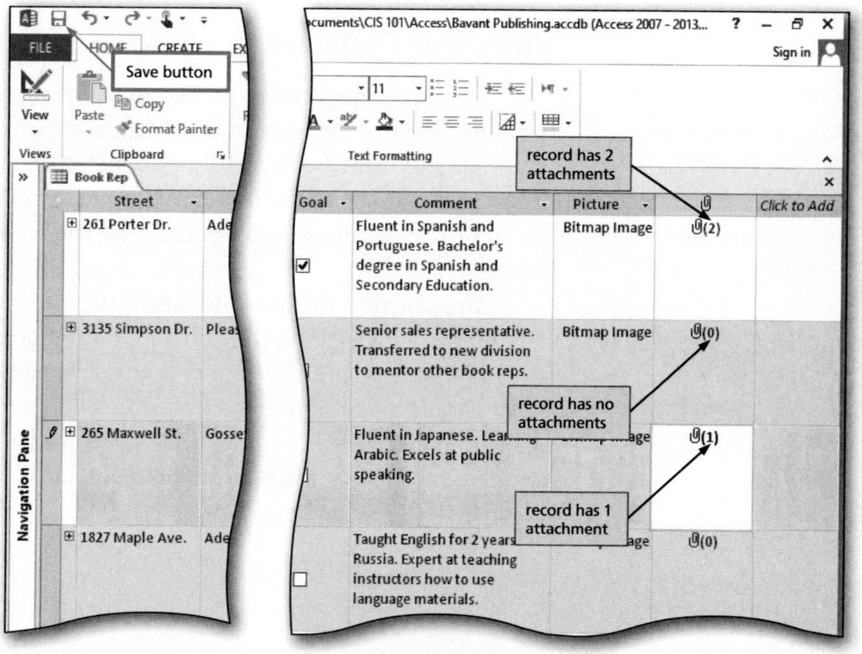

Figure 5–25

BTW
OLE Object Fields
OLE Object fields can occupy a great deal of space. To save space in your database, you can convert a picture from Bitmap Image to Picture (Device Independent Bitmap). To make the conversion, press and hold or right-click the field, tap or click Bitmap Image Object, tap or click Convert, and then select Picture (Device Independent Bitmap) in the Convert dialog box.

BTW
Hyperlink Fields
You can store email addresses in Hyperlink fields.

To Enter Data in Hyperlink Fields

If your database contained a Hyperlink field, you would insert data by using the following steps.

1. Press and hold or right-click the Hyperlink field in which you want to enter data to display a shortcut menu.
2. Tap or click Hyperlink on the shortcut menu to display the Hyperlink submenu.
3. Tap or click Edit Hyperlink on the Hyperlink submenu to display the Insert Hyperlink dialog box.
4. Type the desired web address in the Address text box.
5. Tap or click the OK button (Insert Hyperlink dialog box).

To Save the Properties and Close the Table

The row and column spacing are table properties. When changing any table properties, the changes apply only as long as the table is active *unless they are saved.* Once you have saved them, they will apply every time you open the table.

The following steps first save the properties and then close the table.

1. **Tap or click the Save button on the Quick Access Toolbar to save the changes to the table properties.**
2. **Close the table.**

Break Point: If you wish to stop working through the chapter at this point, you can resume the project at a later time by starting Access, opening the database called Bavant Publishing, and continuing to follow the steps from this location forward.

BTW
Attachment Fields
To view attachments, you must have the application that created the attachment file installed on your computer.

Viewing Pictures and Attachments in Datasheet View

Although the pictures do not appear on the screen, you can view them within the table. To view the picture of a particular book rep, press and hold or right-click the Picture field for the book rep. Tap or click Bitmap Image Object on the shortcut menu, and then tap or click Open. The picture will appear. Once you have finished viewing the picture, close the window containing the picture by tapping or clicking its Close button.

You can view the attachments in the Customer Notes field by pressing and holding or right-clicking the field and then tapping or clicking Manage Attachments on the shortcut menu. The attachments then appear in the Attachments dialog box. To view an attachment, tap or click the attachment and then tap or click the Open button (Attachments dialog box). The attachment will appear in its original application. After you have finished viewing the attachment, close the original application and close the dialog box.

Multiple-Table Form Techniques

With the additional fields in place, Bavant Publishing management is ready to incorporate data from both the Book Rep and Customer tables in a single form. The form will display data concerning one book rep at a time. It also will display data concerning the many customers assigned to the book rep. The relationship between book reps and customers is a one-to-many relationship in which the Book Rep table is the "one" table and the Customer table is the "many" table.

To include the data for the many customers of a book rep on the form, the customer data will appear in a **subform**, which is a form that is contained within another form. The form in which the subform is contained is called the **main form**. Thus, the main form will contain book rep data, and the subform will contain customer data.

BTW

Touch and Pointers

Remember that if you are using your finger on a touch screen, you will not see the pointer.

CONSIDER THIS

When a form includes data from multiple tables, how do you relate the tables?

Once you determine that you need data from more than one table, you need to determine the main table and its relationship to any other table.

Determine the main table the form is intended to view and/or update. You need to identify the purpose of the form and the table it is really intended to show, which is the *main* table.

Determine how the additional table should fit into the form. If the additional table is the "many" part of the relationship, the data probably should be in a subform or datasheet. If the additional table is the "one" part of the relationship, the data probably should appear simply as fields on the form.

To Create a Form in Design View

1 ADD FIELDS | 2 ENTER DATA | 3 CREATE FORM | 4 ADD CONTROLS | 5 ADD SUBFORM
6 MODIFY SUBFORM | 7 ENHANCE FORM | 8 CREATE QUERIES

You can create a form in Design view. ***Why?*** *Design view gives you increased flexibility in laying out a form by using a blank design on which you place objects in the precise locations you want.* The following steps create a form in Design view.

1

- If necessary, open the Navigation Pane and be sure the Book Rep table is selected.
- Tap or click CREATE on the ribbon to display the CREATE tab (Figure 5–26).

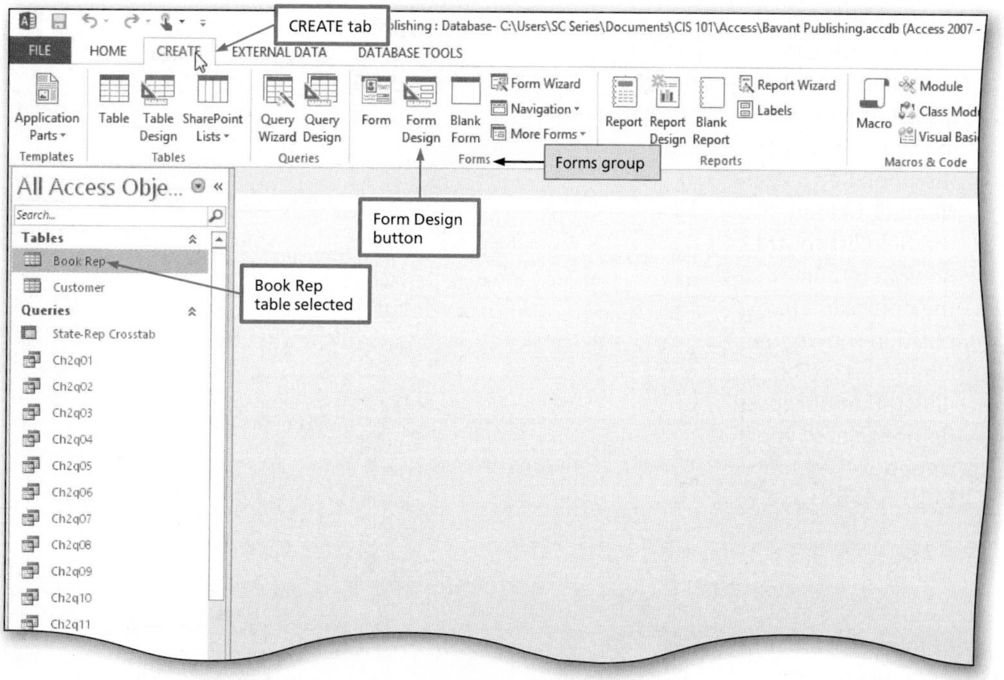

Figure 5–26

2

- Tap or click the Form Design button (CREATE tab | Forms group) to create a new form in Design view.
- Close the Navigation Pane.
- If a field list does not appear, tap or click the 'Add Existing Fields' button (FORM DESIGN TOOLS DESIGN tab | Tools group) to display a field list (Figure 5–27). If you do not see the tables listed, tap or click, 'Show all tables'. (Your list might show all fields in the Customer table.)

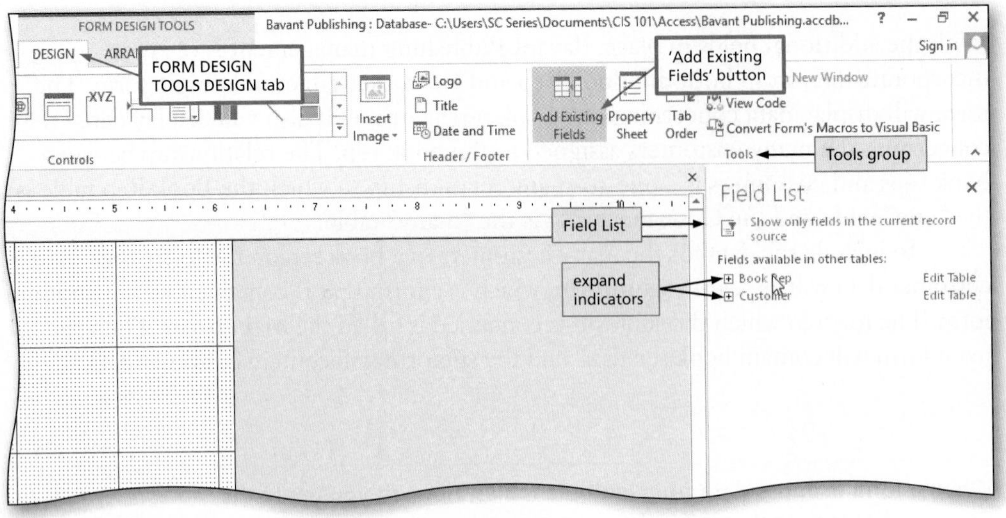

Figure 5–27

Q&A How do I display the fields in the Book Rep table?
Tap or click the expand indicator (+) in front of the Book Rep table to display the fields.

To Add a Control for a Field to the Form

1 ADD FIELDS | 2 ENTER DATA | 3 CREATE FORM | 4 ADD CONTROLS | **5 ADD SUBFORM**
6 MODIFY SUBFORM | **7 ENHANCE FORM** | **8 CREATE QUERIES**

To place a control for a field on a form, drag the field from the field list to the desired position. The following steps place the Book Rep Number field on the form. ***Why?*** *The Book Rep Number field is the first field on the form.*

1

- If necessary, tap or click the expand indicator for the Book Rep table to display the fields in the table. Drag the Book Rep Number field in the field list for the Book Rep table to the approximate position shown in Figure 5–28. (For illustration purposes, do not release your finger or the mouse button yet.)

Q&A Do I have to be exact?
No. Just be sure you are in the same general location.

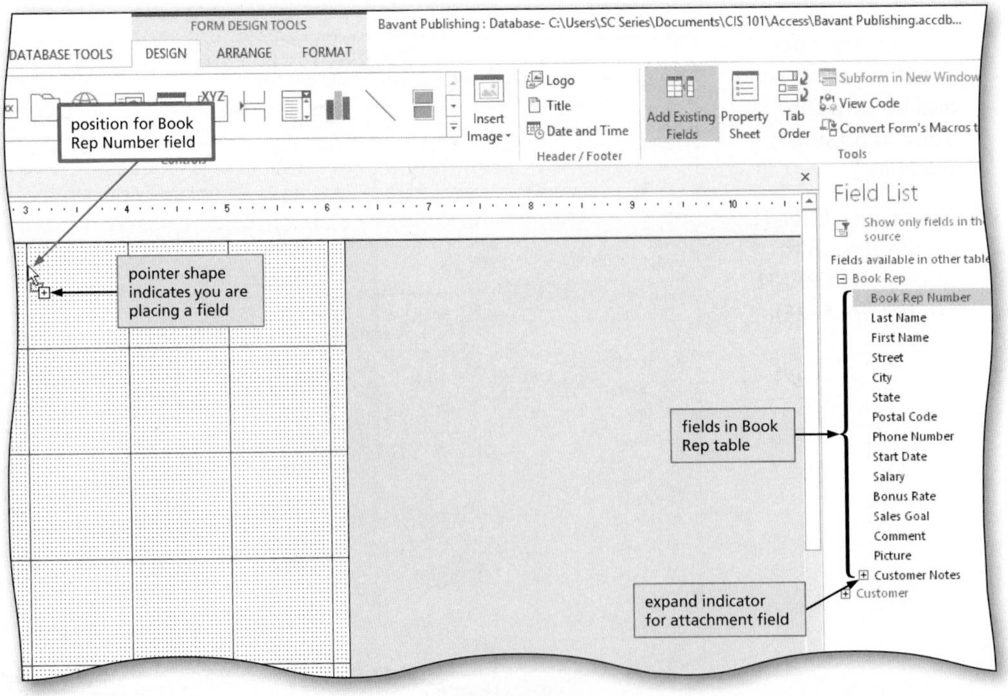

Figure 5–28

2

- Release your finger or the mouse button to place a control for the field (Figure 5–29).

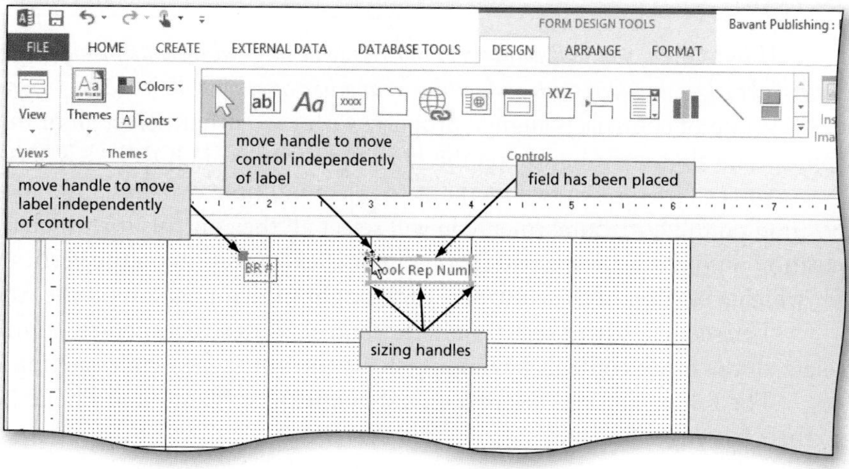

Figure 5–29

To Save the Form

Before continuing with the form creation, it is a good idea to save the form. The following steps save the form and assign it the name Book Rep Master Form.

1. Tap or click the Save button on the Quick Access Toolbar.
2. Type **`Book Rep Master Form`** as the name of the form.
3. Tap or click the OK button to save the form.

To Add Controls for Additional Fields

1 ADD FIELDS | 2 ENTER DATA | 3 CREATE FORM | 4 ADD CONTROLS | 5 ADD SUBFORM
6 MODIFY SUBFORM | 7 ENHANCE FORM | 8 CREATE QUERIES

The following step places controls for the First Name, Last Name, Phone Number, Salary, Bonus Rate, Start Date, and Sales Goal fields on the form by dragging the fields from the field list. ***Why?*** *These fields all need to be included in the form.*

1

- Drag the First Name, Last Name, Phone Number, Salary, Bonus Rate, Start Date, and Sales Goal fields and their labels to the approximate positions shown in Figure 5–30.

Q&A Do I have to align them precisely?
You can, but you do not need to. In the next steps, you will instruct Access to align the fields properly.

What if I drag the wrong field from the field list? Can I undo my action?
Yes. Tap or click the Undo button.

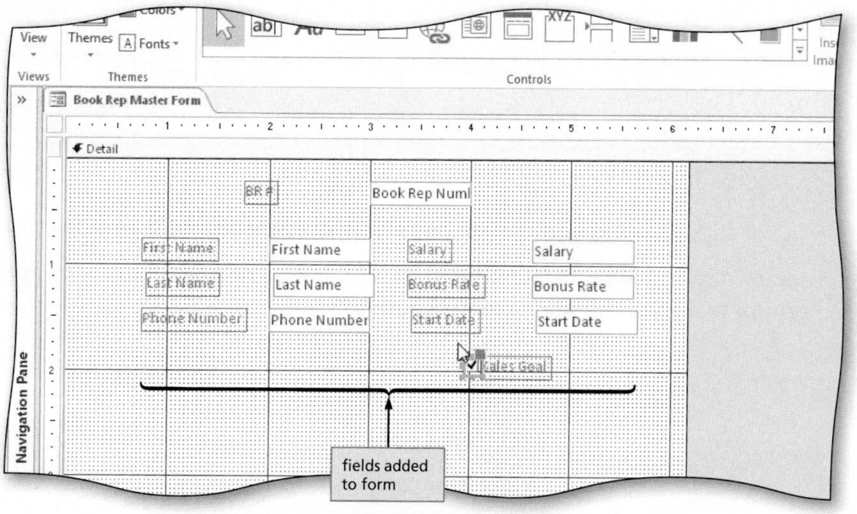

Figure 5–30

To Align Controls on the Left

Why? *Often, you will want form controls to be aligned in some fashion. For example, the controls might be aligned so their right edges are even with each other. In another case, controls might be aligned so their top edges are even.* To ensure that a group of controls is aligned properly with each other, select all of the affected controls, and then use the appropriate alignment button on the FORM DESIGN TOOLS ARRANGE tab.

You can use one of two methods to select multiple controls. One way is to use a ruler. If you tap or click a position on the horizontal ruler, you will select all the controls for which a portion of the control is under that position on the ruler. Similarly, if you tap or click a position on the vertical ruler, you will select all the controls for which a portion of the control is to the right of that position on the ruler.

The second way to select multiple controls is to select the first control by tapping or clicking it. Then, select all the other controls by holding down the SHIFT key while tapping or clicking the control.

The following steps select the First Name, Last Name, and Phone Number controls and then align them so their left edges line up.

1

- Tap or click the First Name control (the white space, not the label) to select the control.
- Hold the SHIFT key down and tap or click the Last Name control to select an additional control. Do not release the SHIFT key.
- Tap or click the Phone Number control to select a third control, and then release the SHIFT key.

Q&A I selected the wrong collection of fields. How can I start over?
Simply begin the process again, making sure you do not hold the SHIFT key down when you select the first field.

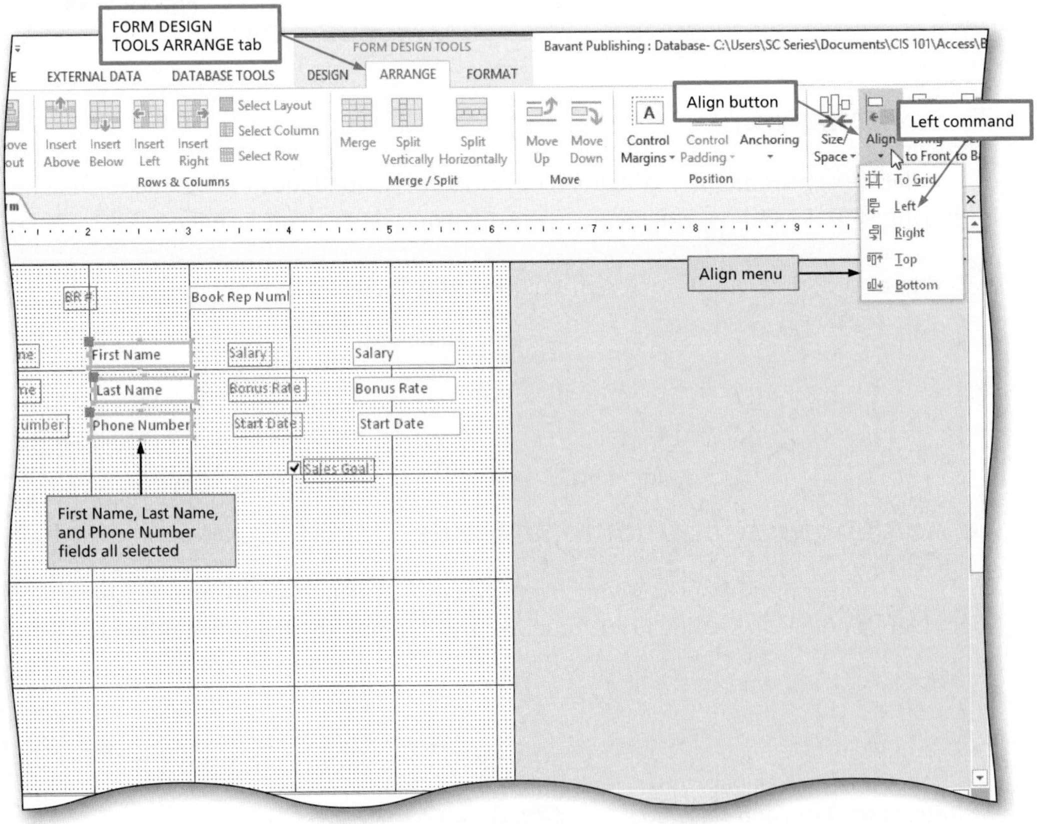

Figure 5–31

- Tap or click ARRANGE on the ribbon to display the FORM DESIGN TOOLS ARRANGE tab.
- Tap or click the Align button (FORM DESIGN TOOLS ARRANGE tab | Sizing & Ordering group) to display the Align menu (Figure 5–31).

2

- Tap or click the Left command on the Align menu to align the controls on the left (Figure 5–32).

3

- Tap or click outside any of the selected controls to deselect the controls.
- Using the same technique, align the labels for the First Name, Last Name, and Phone Number fields on the left.
- Using the same technique, align the Salary, Bonus Rate, and Start Date fields on the left.
- If necessary, align the labels for the Salary, Bonus Rate, and Start Date fields on the left.

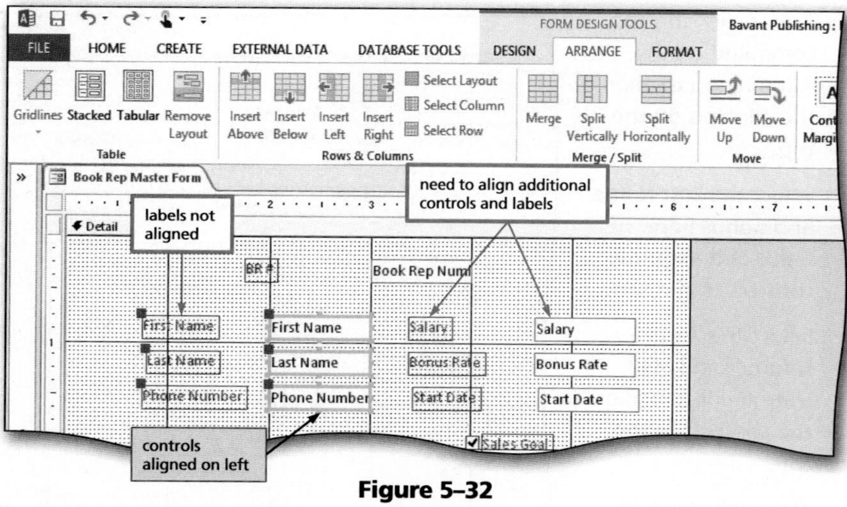

Figure 5–32

Other Ways

1. Press and hold or right-click selected controls, tap or click Align

To Align Controls on the Top and Adjust Vertical Spacing

1 ADD FIELDS | 2 ENTER DATA | 3 CREATE FORM | 4 ADD CONTROLS | **5 ADD SUBFORM**
6 MODIFY SUBFORM | **7 ENHANCE FORM** | **8 CREATE QUERIES**

Why? *Aligning the top edges of controls improves the neatness and appearance of a form. In addition, you might want the vertical spacing between controls to be the same.* The following steps align the First Name and Salary controls so that they are aligned on the top. Once these controls are aligned, you adjust the vertical spacing so that the same amount of space separates each row of controls.

1

- Select the label for the First Name control, the First Name control, the label for the Salary control, and the Salary control.
- Tap or click the Align button (FORM DESIGN TOOLS ARRANGE tab | Sizing & Ordering group) to display the Align menu (Figure 5–33).

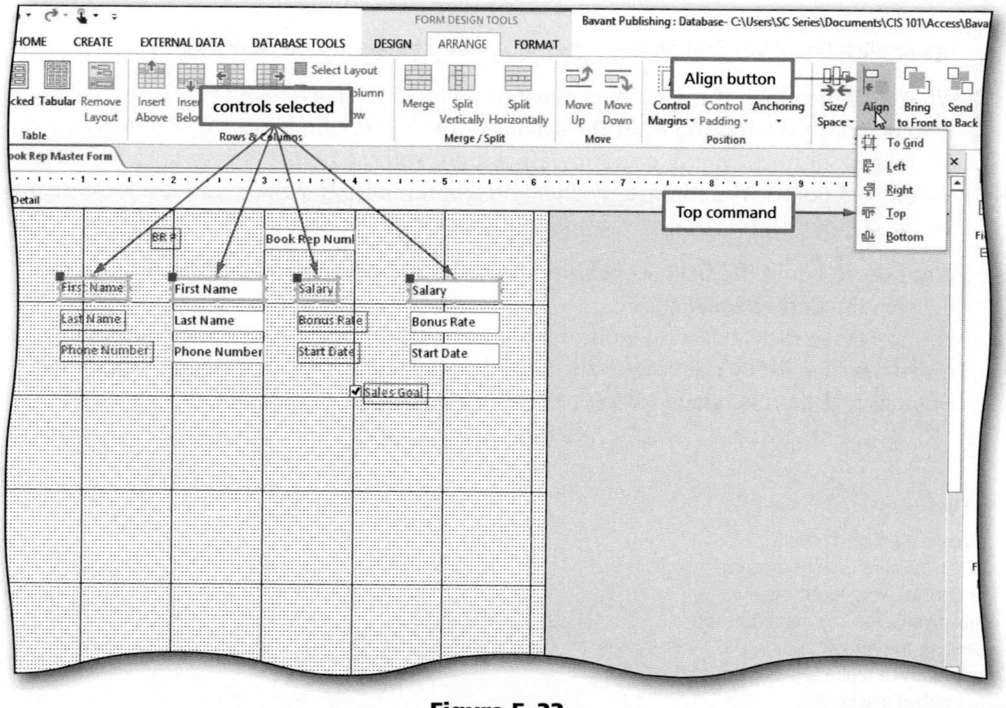

Figure 5–33

2

- Tap or click the Top command on the Align menu to align the controls on the top.
- Select the Last Name and Bonus Rate fields and align the controls to the top.
- Select the Phone Number and Start Date fields and align the controls to the top.
- Tap or click outside any of the selected controls to deselect the controls.
- Select the First Name, Last Name, Phone Number, Salary, Bonus Rate, and Start Date fields.
- Tap or click the Size/Space button (FORM DESIGN TOOLS ARRANGE tab | Sizing & Ordering group) to display the Size/Space menu (Figure 5–34).

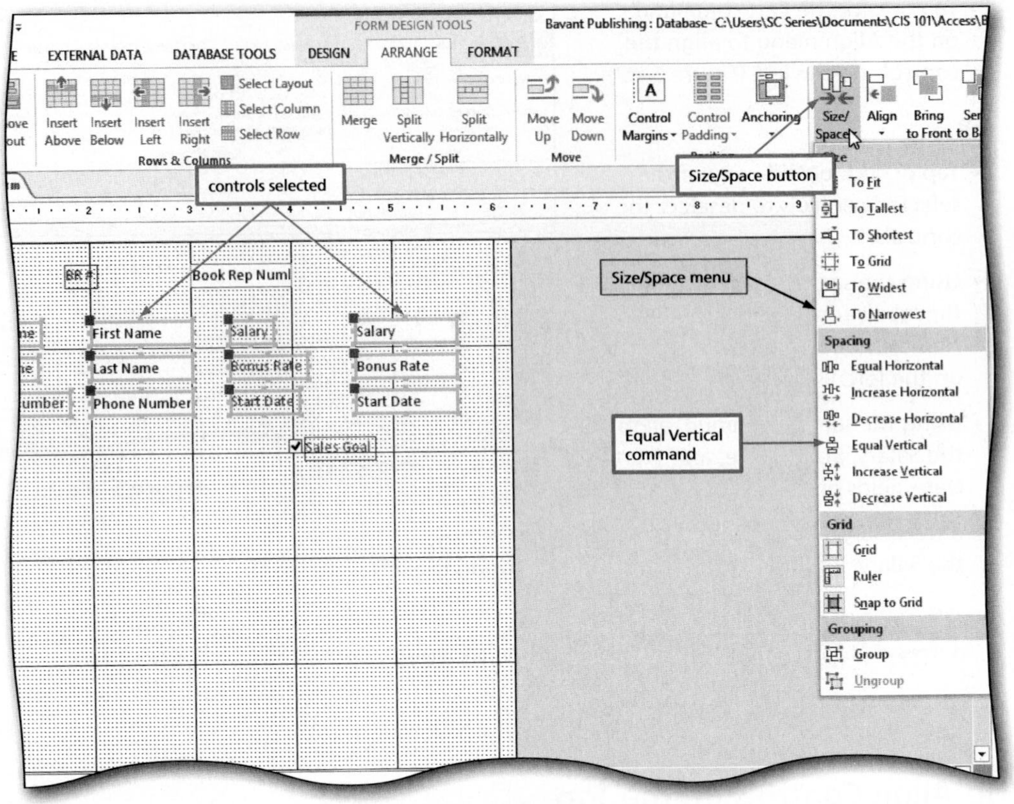

Figure 5–34

Q&A Do I need to select the labels too?
No. If you select the control, its label also is selected.

3

- Tap or click Equal Vertical on the Size/Space menu to specify the spacing.

Q&A What is the purpose of the other commands on the Size/Space menu?
You can adjust the spacing to fit the available space. You can adjust the space to match the tallest, shortest, widest, or narrowest section. You can adjust the space to match the closest grid points. You can specify equal horizontal spacing. Finally, you can increase or decrease either the vertical or the horizontal spacing.

What do you do if the field list obscures part of the form, making it difficult to place fields in the desired locations?
You can move the field list to a different location by dragging its title bar. You can also resize the field list by pointing to the border of the field list so that the mouse pointer changes to a double-headed arrow. You then can drag to adjust the size.

BTW
Moving Controls
When you are dragging a label or control, you might need to make very small movements. You can use the arrow keys on the keyboard to make fine adjustments to control placement.

To Add Controls for the Remaining Fields

1 ADD FIELDS | 2 ENTER DATA | 3 CREATE FORM | 4 ADD CONTROLS | **5 ADD SUBFORM**
6 MODIFY SUBFORM | 7 ENHANCE FORM | 8 CREATE QUERIES

The following steps place controls for the Comment, Picture, and Customer Notes fields and also move their attached labels to the desired position. ***Why?*** *Controls for these fields are to be included in the completed form.*

1

- Drag the control for the Comment field from the field list to the approximate position shown in Figure 5–35.

Q&A Is there enough space on the form to add the Comment field?

Yes. The size of the form will expand as you drag the field to the form.

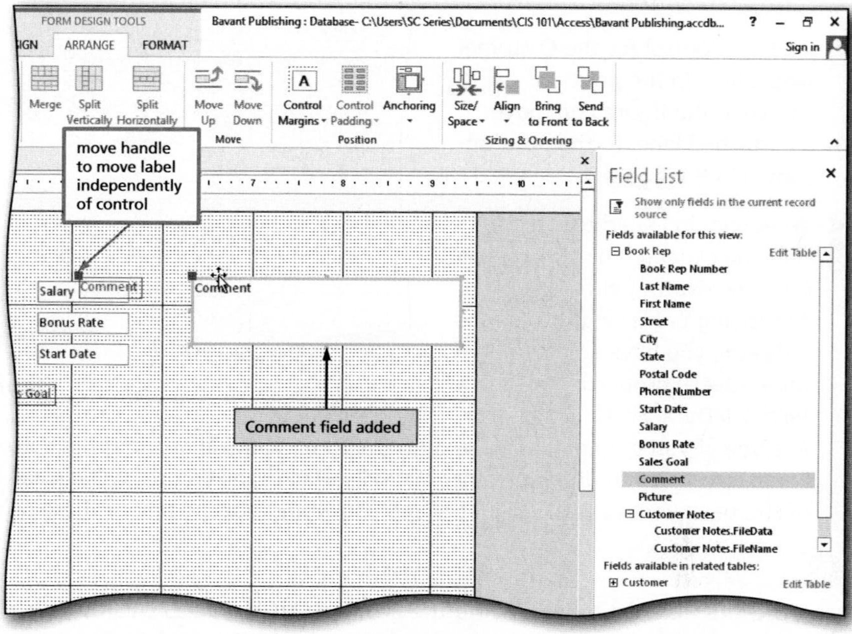

Figure 5–35

2

- Move the label for the Comment field to the position shown in Figure 5–36 by dragging its move handle.

Q&A I started to move the label and the control moved along with it. What did I do?

You were not pointing at the handle to move the label independently of the control. Make sure you are pointing to the little box in the upper-left corner of the label.

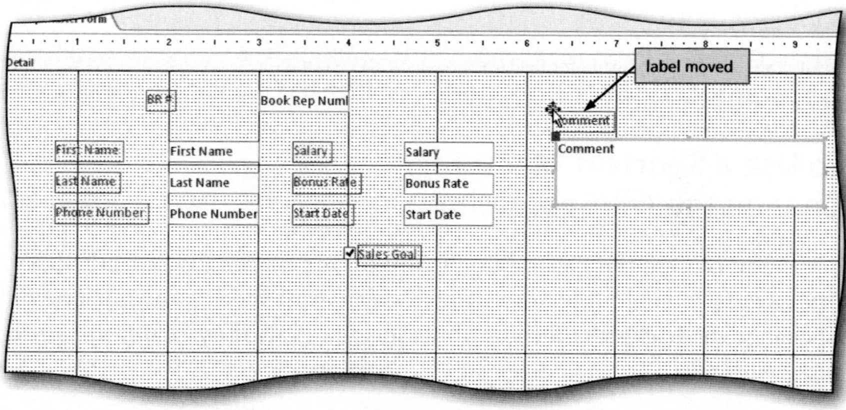

Figure 5–36

3

- Using the same techniques, move the control for the Picture field to the approximate position shown in Figure 5–37 and move its label to the position shown in the figure.

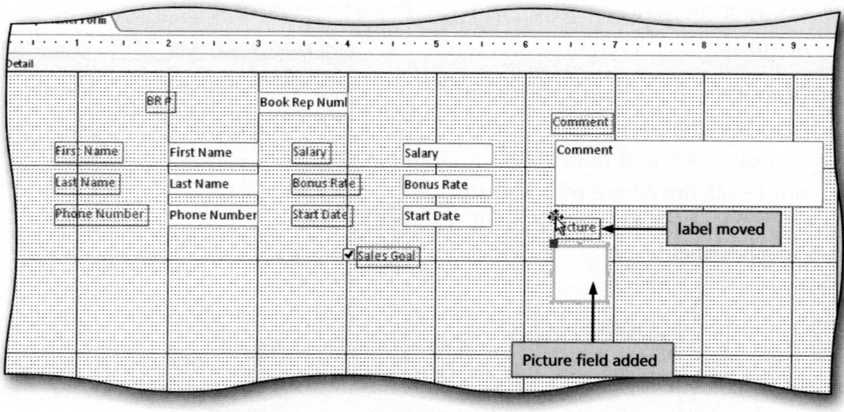

Figure 5–37

4

- Tap or click the control for the Picture field and drag the lower-right corner to the approximate position shown in Figure 5–38 to resize the control.
- Add the control for the Customer Notes field in the position shown in the figure and move its attached label to the position shown in the figure.

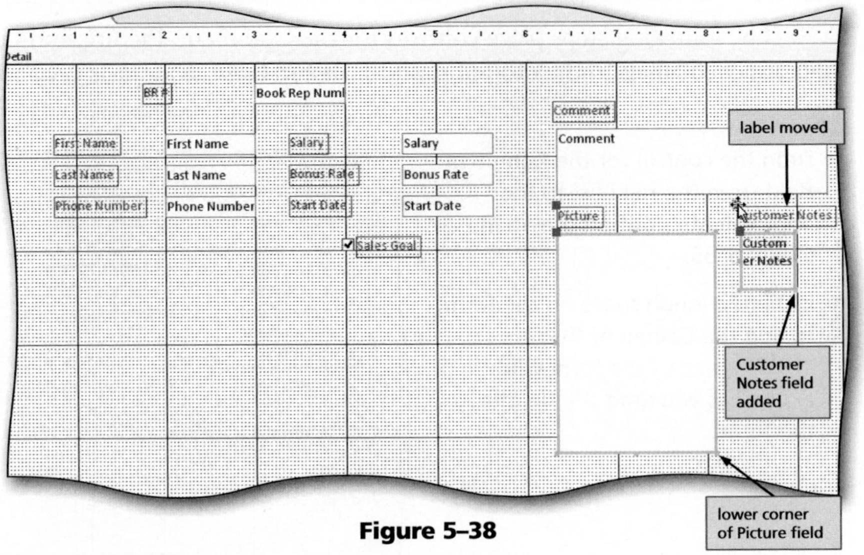

Figure 5–38

Q&A When would I need to tap or click the expand indicator for the Customer Notes field?

By tapping or clicking the expand indicator, you have access to three special properties of the field: FileData, FileName, and FileType. If you drag one of these onto the form, you will only get the corresponding information in the control. For example, if you drag Customer Notes.FileName, the control will display the file name for the attachment. Most of the time, you want the field itself, so you would not use any of these properties.

5

- Close the field list by displaying the FORM DESIGN TOOLS DESIGN tab and then tapping or clicking the 'Add Existing Fields' button (FORM DESIGN TOOLS DESIGN tab | Tools group), which is shown in Figure 5–27 on page AC 284.

Other Ways

1. Tap or click Close button for field list

To Use a Shortcut Menu to Change the Fill/Back Color

1 ADD FIELDS | 2 ENTER DATA | 3 CREATE FORM | 4 ADD CONTROLS | **5 ADD SUBFORM**
6 MODIFY SUBFORM | **7 ENHANCE FORM** | **8 CREATE QUERIES**

You can use the Background Color button on the FORM DESIGN TOOLS FORMAT tab to change the background color of a form. You also can use a shortcut menu. The following steps use a shortcut menu to change the background color of the form to gray. ***Why?*** *Using a shortcut menu is a simple way to change the background color.*

1

- Press and hold or right-click in the approximate position shown in Figure 5–39 to produce a shortcut menu.

Q&A Does it matter where I press and hold or right-click?

You can press and hold or right-click anywhere on the form as long as you are outside of all the controls.

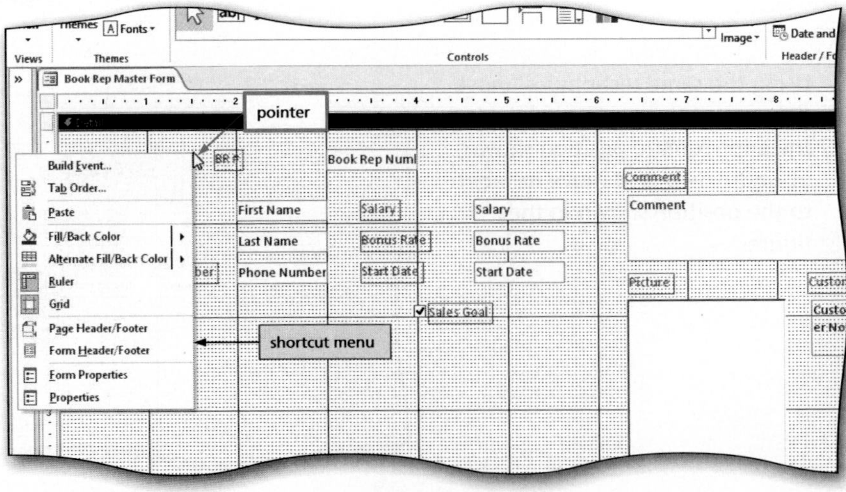

Figure 5–39

2

- Point to the 'Fill/Back Color' arrow on the shortcut menu to display a color palette (Figure 5–40).

3

- Tap or click the gray color (row 3, column 1) shown in Figure 5–40 to change the fill/back color to gray.

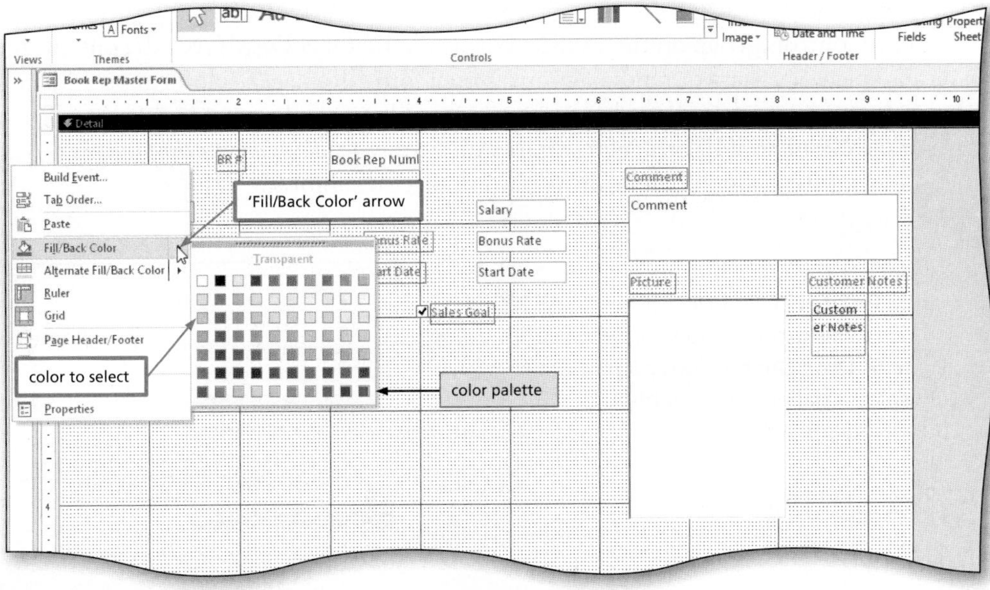

Figure 5–40

To Add a Title

1 ADD FIELDS | 2 ENTER DATA | 3 CREATE FORM | 4 ADD CONTROLS | **5 ADD SUBFORM**
6 MODIFY SUBFORM | 7 ENHANCE FORM | 8 CREATE QUERIES

A form should have a descriptive title. ***Why?*** *The title gives a concise visual description of the purpose of the form.* The following step adds a title to the form.

1

- Be sure the FORM DESIGN TOOLS DESIGN tab is selected.
- Tap or click the Title button (FORM DESIGN TOOLS DESIGN tab | Header/Footer group) to add a title to the form (Figure 5–41).

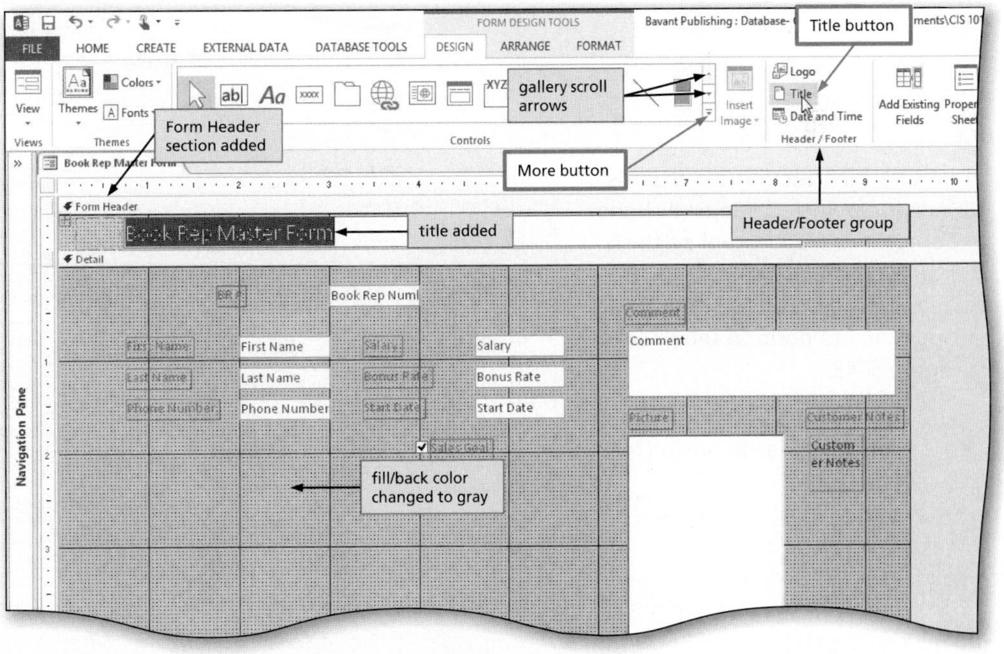

Figure 5–41

Q&A Why is there a new section?
The form title belongs in the Form Header section. When you tapped or clicked the Title button, Access added the Form Header section automatically and placed the title in it.

Could I add a Form Header section without having to tap or click the Title button?
Yes. Press and hold or right-click anywhere on the form background and tap or click Form Header/Footer on the shortcut menu.

To Place a Subform

The Controls group on the FORM DESIGN TOOLS DESIGN tab contains buttons called tools that you use to place a variety of types of controls on a form. To place a subform on a form, you use the Subform/Subreport tool. Before doing so, however, you should ensure that the 'Use Control Wizards' button is selected. ***Why?*** *If the Use Control Wizards button is selected, a wizard will guide you through the process of adding the subform.* The following steps use the Subform Wizard to place a subform.

1

- Tap or click the More button (FORM DESIGN TOOLS DESIGN tab | Controls group) (shown in Figure 5–41 on the previous page) to display a gallery of available tools (Figure 5–42).

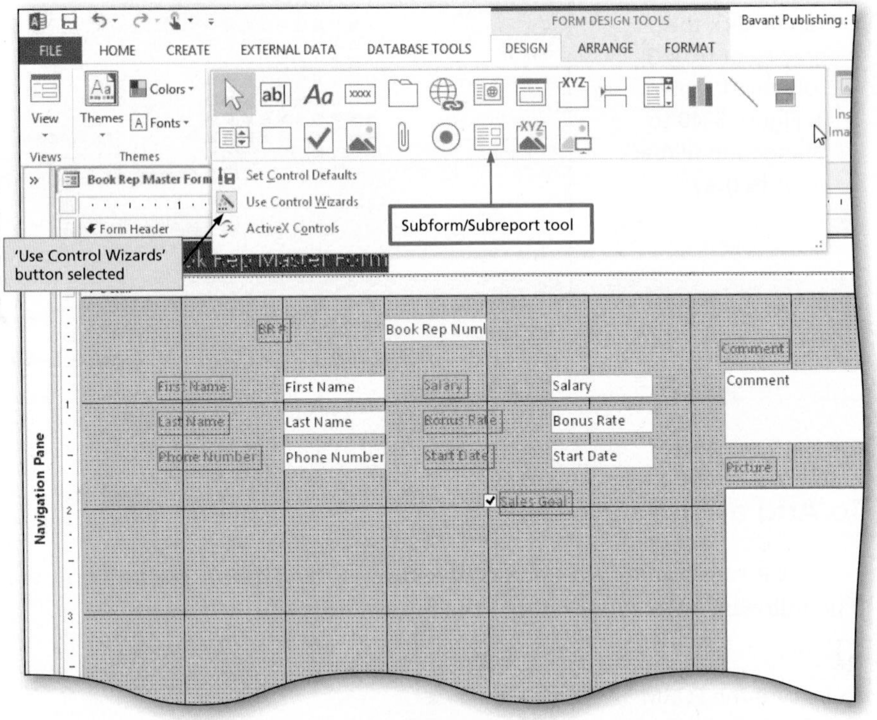

Figure 5–42

2

- Be sure the 'Use Control Wizards' button is selected, tap or click the Subform/Subreport tool on the FORM DESIGN TOOLS DESIGN tab, and then move the pointer to the approximate position shown in Figure 5–43.

Q&A How can I tell whether the 'Use Control Wizards' button is selected?

The icon for the 'Use Control Wizards' button will be highlighted, as shown in Figure 5–42. If it is not, tap or click the 'Use Control Wizards' button to select it, tap or click the More button, and then tap or click the Subform/Subreport tool.

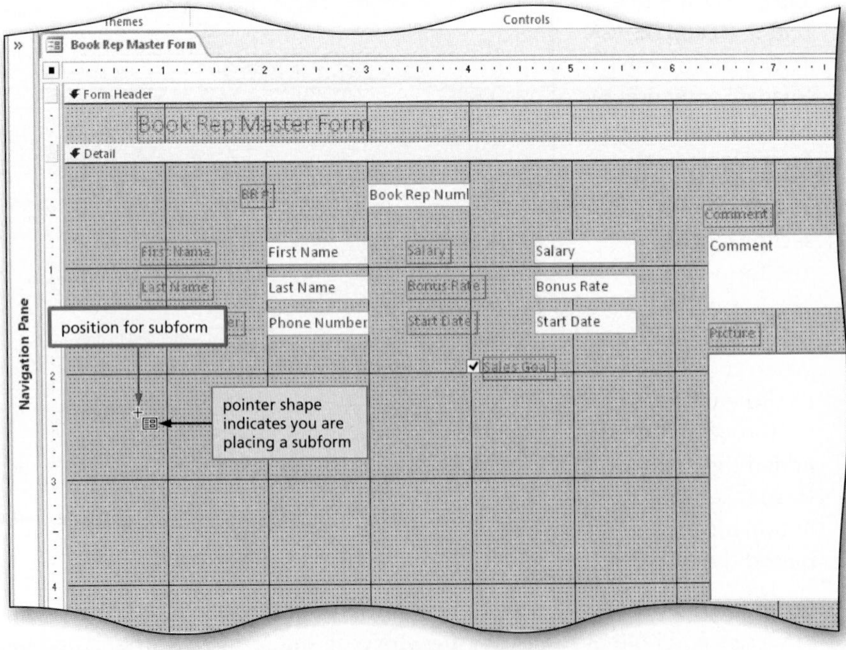

Figure 5–43

3

- Tap or click the position shown in Figure 5–43 and then ensure the 'Use existing Tables and Queries' option button is selected (SubForm Wizard dialog box) (Figure 5–44).

Q&A My control is placed on the screen, but no wizard appeared. What should I do?
Press the DELETE key to delete the control you placed. Ensure that the 'Use Control Wizards' button is selected, as described previously.

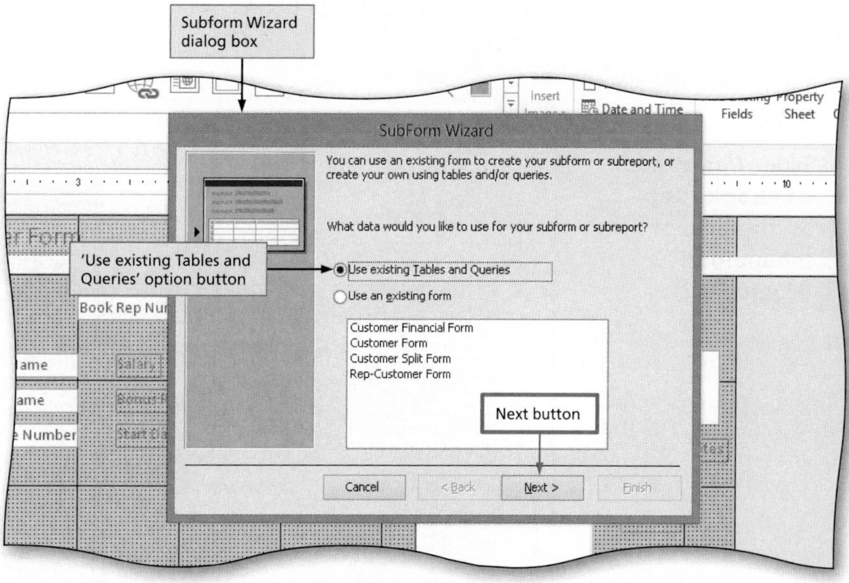

Figure 5–44

4

- Tap or click the Next button.
- Tap or click the Tables/Queries arrow, and then tap or click the Customer table to select the table that contains the fields for the subform.
- Add the Customer Number, Customer Name, Amount Paid, and Current Due fields by tapping or clicking the field, and then tapping or clicking the Add Field button (SubForm Wizard dialog box) (Figure 5–45).

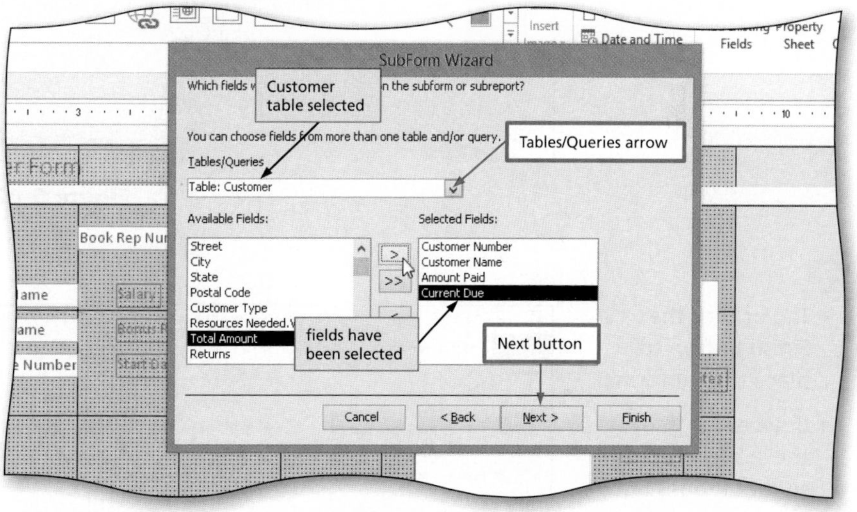

Figure 5–45

5

- Tap or click the Next button to move to the next SubForm Wizard dialog box.
- Be sure the 'Choose from a list.' option button is selected (Figure 5–46).

Q&A Why do I use this option?
Most of the time, Access will have determined the appropriate fields to link the subform and the main form and placed an entry specifying those fields in the list. By choosing from the list, you can take advantage of the information that Access has created for you. The other option is to define your own, in which case you would need to specify the appropriate fields.

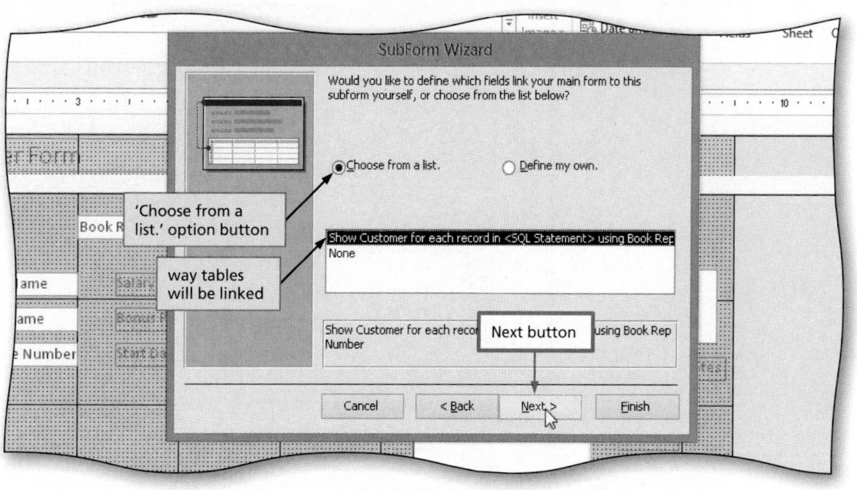

Figure 5–46

6

- Tap or click the Next button.
- Type **Customers of Book Rep** as the name of the subform (Figure 5–47).

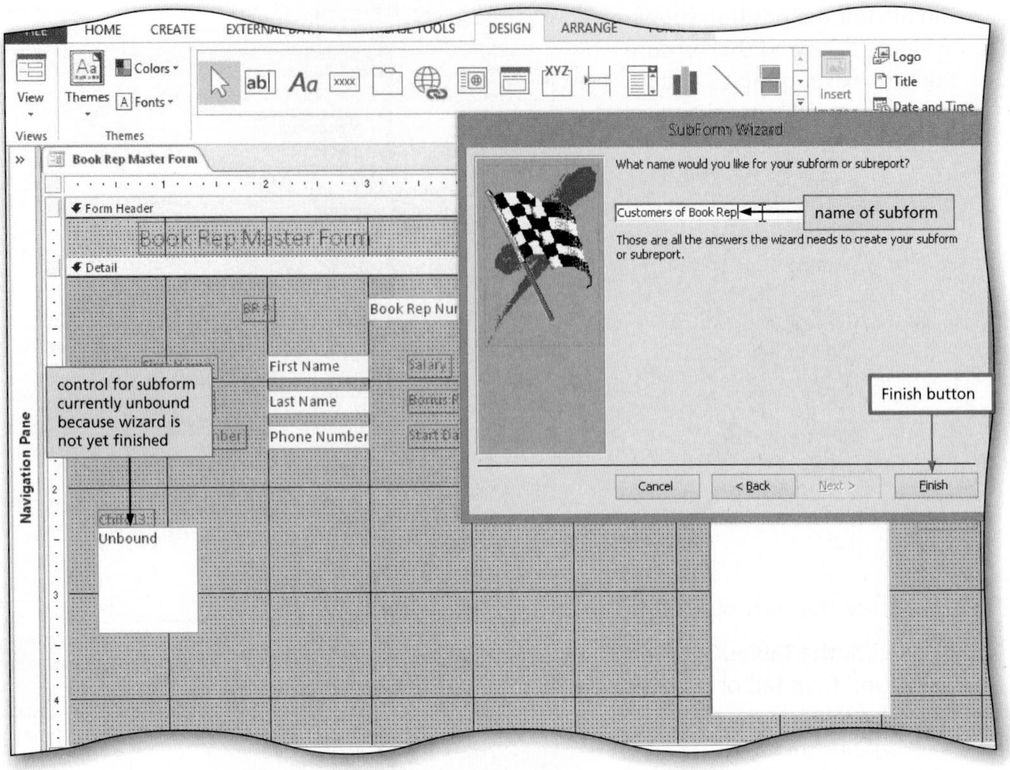

Figure 5–47

7

- Tap or click the Finish button to place the subform.
- If necessary, move the subform control so that it does not overlap any other controls on the form (Figure 5–48).

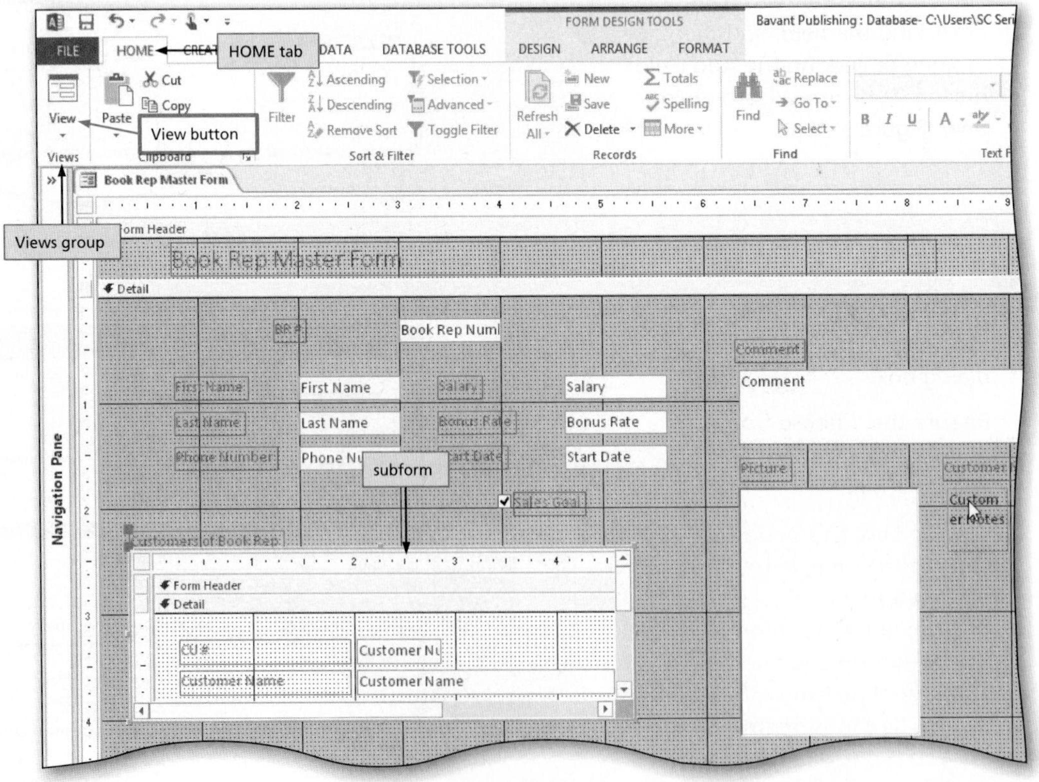

Figure 5–48

To View the Form

The following step views the form in Form view.

1. Tap or click the View button (HOME tab | Views group) to view the form in Form view (Figure 5–49).

Q&A Everything looks good except the subform. I do not see all the fields I should see. What should I do?

You need to modify the subform, which you will do in the upcoming steps.

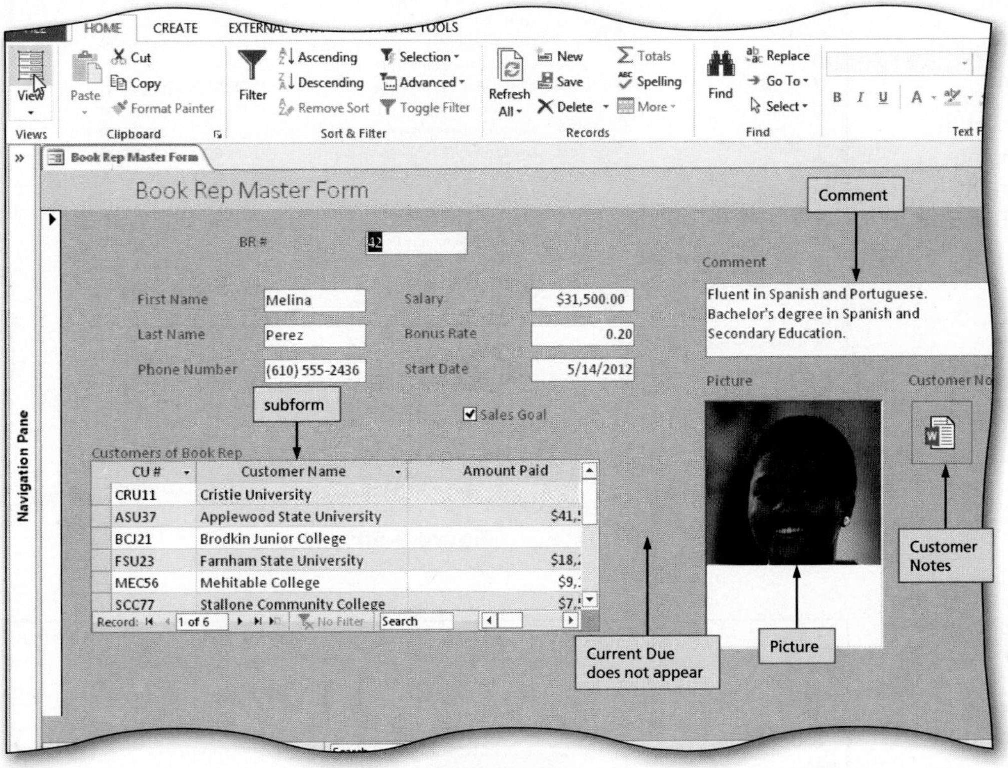

Figure 5–49

To Close and Save a Form

The following steps first save and then close the Book Rep Master Form.

1. Tap or click the Save button on the Quick Access Toolbar to save the form.
2. Close the Book Rep Master Form by tapping or clicking the Close button for the form.

Break Point: If you wish to stop working through the chapter at this point, you can resume the project at a later time by starting Access, opening the database called Bavant Publishing, and continuing to follow the steps from this location forward.

To Modify a Subform and Move the Picture

1 ADD FIELDS | 2 ENTER DATA | 3 CREATE FORM | 4 ADD CONTROLS | 5 ADD SUBFORM
6 MODIFY SUBFORM | **7 ENHANCE FORM** | **8 CREATE QUERIES**

The next task is to resize the columns in the subform, which appears on the form in Datasheet view. The subform exists as a separate object in the database; it is stored independently of the main form. The following steps open the subform and then resize the columns. ***Why?*** *The column sizes need to be adjusted so that the data is displayed correctly.* The steps then view the form and finally move and resize the picture.

1

- Open the Navigation Pane.
- Press and hold or right-click the Customers of Book Rep form to produce a shortcut menu.
- Tap or click Open on the shortcut menu to open the form.
- Resize the columns to best fit the data by double-tapping or double-clicking the right boundaries of the field selectors (Figure 5–50).

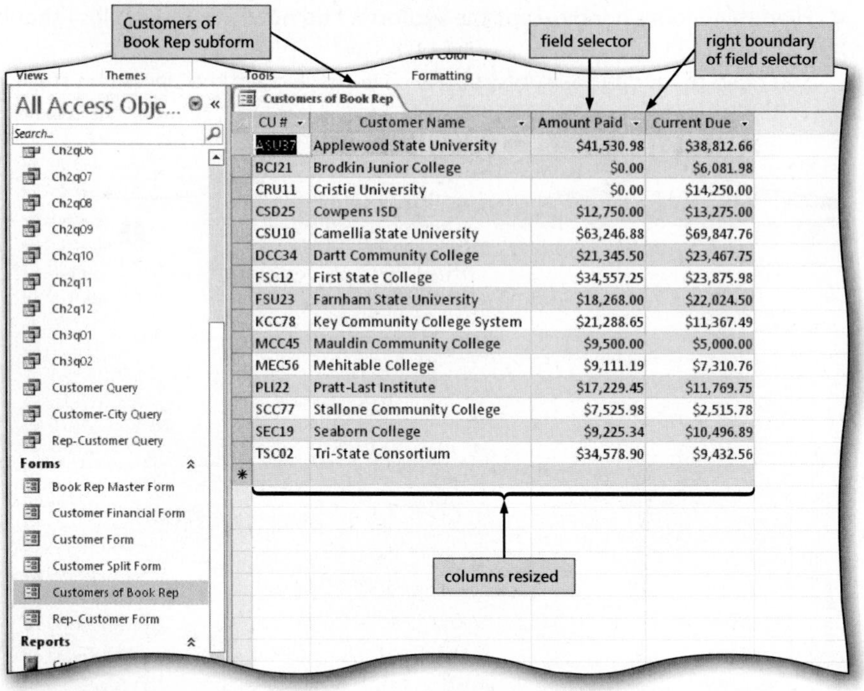

Figure 5–50

2

- Save your changes, and then close the subform.
- Open the Book Rep Master Form in Design view, and then close the Navigation Pane.
- Tap or click the boundary of the subform to select it.
- Adjust the approximate size and position of the subform to match the one shown in Figure 5–51.

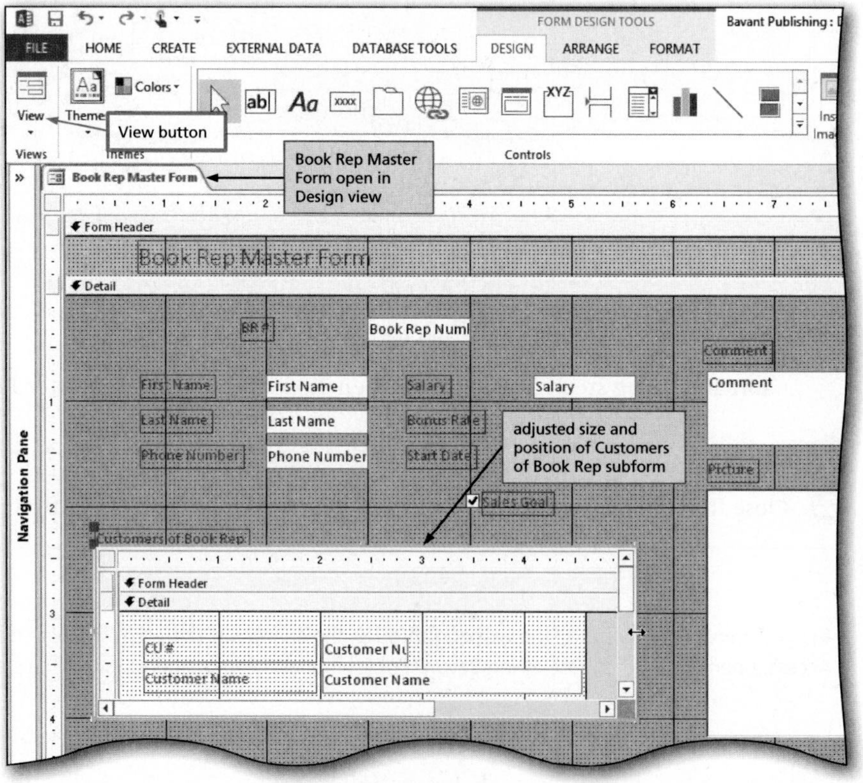

Figure 5–51

6

- Close the property sheet by tapping or clicking the Property Sheet button (FORM DESIGN TOOLS DESIGN tab | Tools group).
- Tap or click the View button to view the form in Form view (Figure 5–61).

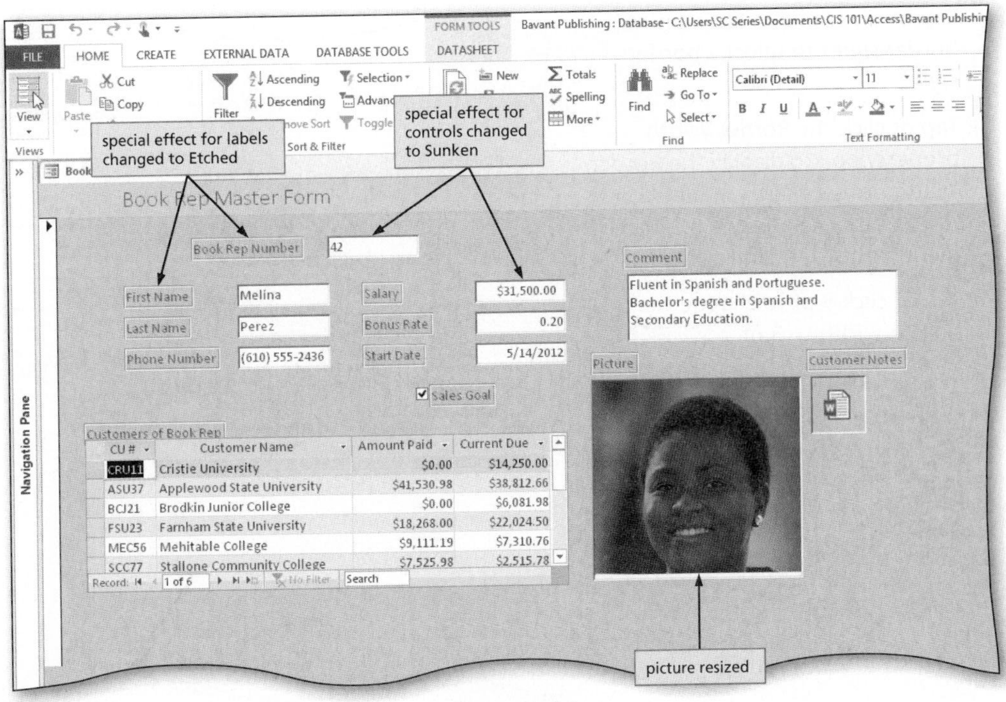

Figure 5–61

To Modify the Appearance of a Form Title

1 ADD FIELDS | 2 ENTER DATA | 3 CREATE FORM | 4 ADD CONTROLS | 5 ADD SUBFORM
6 MODIFY SUBFORM | 7 ENHANCE FORM | 8 CREATE QUERIES

Why? You can enhance the title in a variety of ways by changing its appearance. These options include moving it, resizing it, changing the font size, changing the font weight, and changing the alignment. The following steps enhance the form title.

1

- Return to Design view.
- Resize the Form Header section by dragging down the lower boundary of the section to the approximate position shown in Figure 5–62.

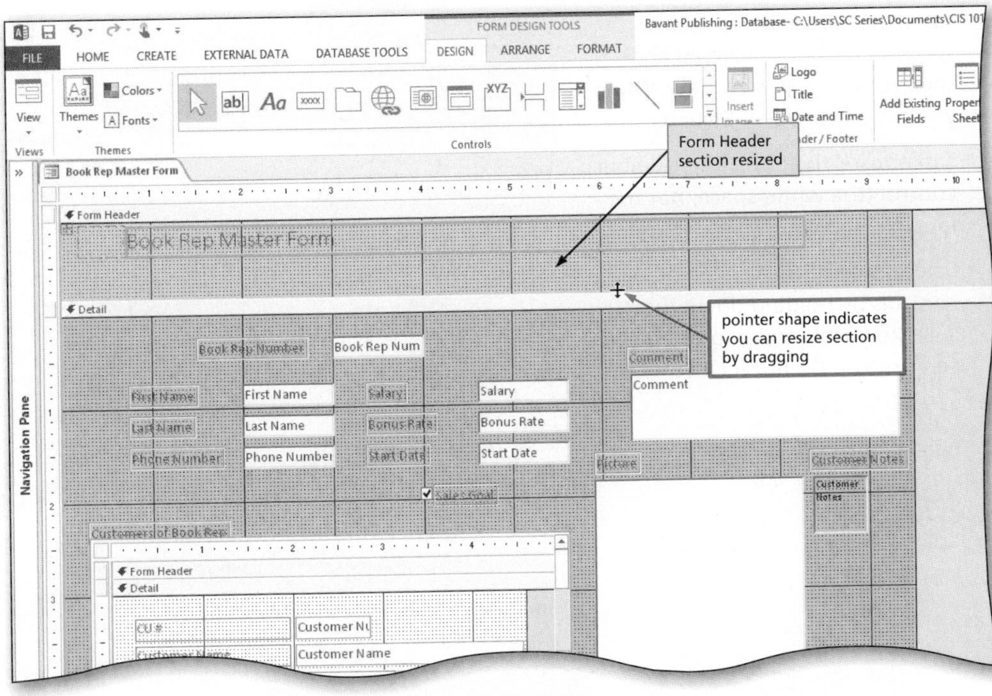

Figure 5–62

4

- Tap or click Solid in the menu of border styles to select a border style.
- Tap or click the Border Width property box to display the Border Width property arrow, and then tap or click the arrow to display a menu of border widths.
- Tap or click 3 pt to change the border width to 3 pt.
- Tap or click the Special Effect property box to display the Special Effect property arrow, and then tap or click the arrow to display a menu of special effects (Figure 5–59).

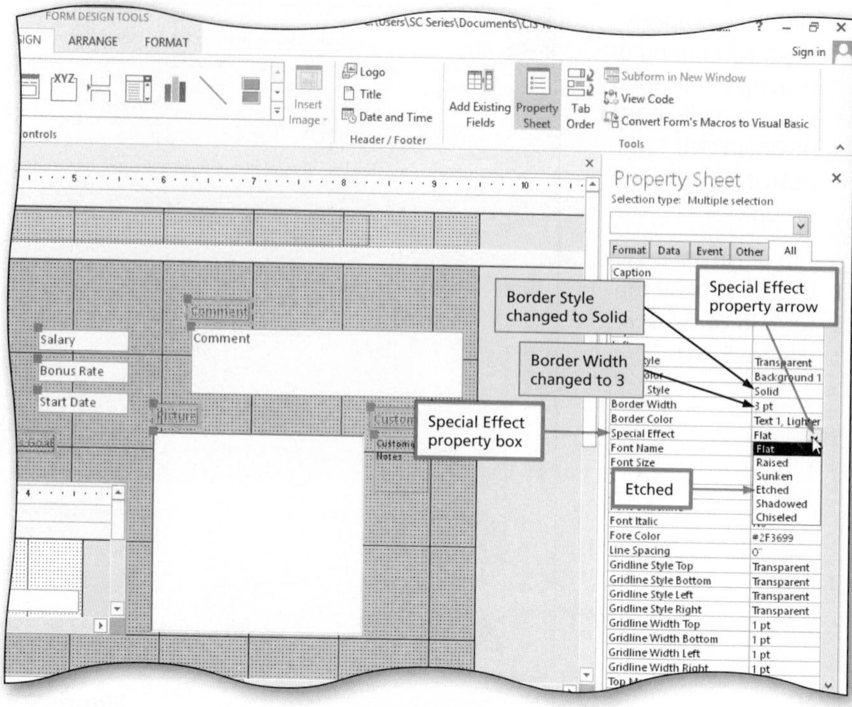

Figure 5–59

5

- Tap or click Etched in the menu of special effects to select a special effect.

Experiment

- Try other special effects. In each case, view the form to see the special effect you selected and then return to Design view. When you are done, select Etched.
- Tap or click the Book Rep Number control (the white space, not the label) to select it.
- Select each of the remaining controls by holding down the SHIFT key while tapping or clicking the control. Do not include the subform.
- Select Sunken for the special effect (Figure 5–60).

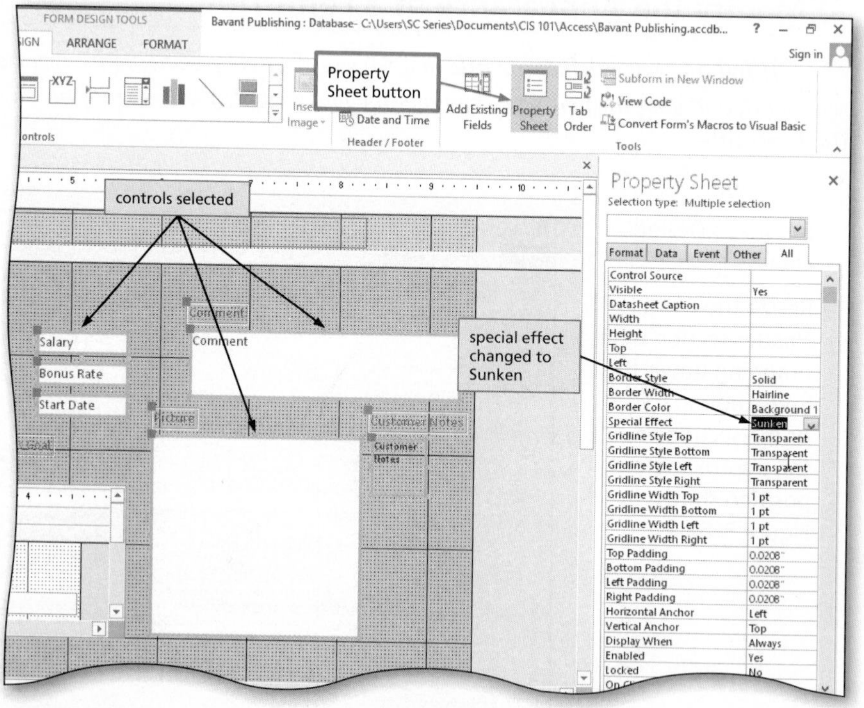

Figure 5–60

2

- Display the FORM DESIGN TOOLS FORMAT tab.
- Tap or click the Font Color arrow (FORM DESIGN TOOLS FORMAT tab | Font group) to display a color palette (Figure 5–57).

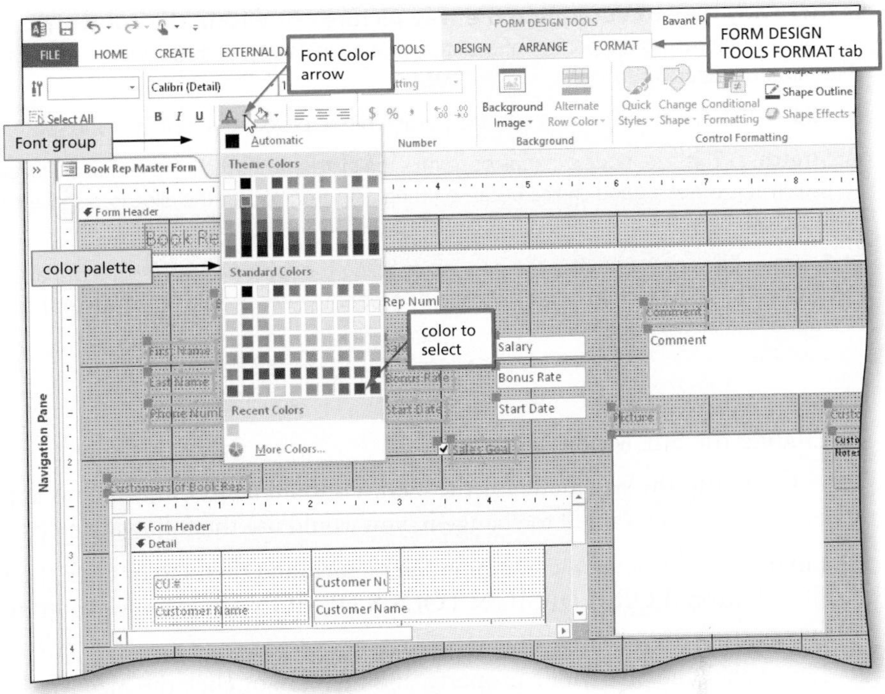

Figure 5–57

3

- Tap or click the blue color in the second position from the right in the bottom row of Standard Colors to change the font color for the labels.

Experiment

- Try other colors by tapping or clicking the Font Color arrow and then tapping or clicking the other color to see which colors you think would be good choices for the font. View the form to see the effect of your choice, and then return to Design view. When done, select the blue color.
- Display the FORM DESIGN TOOLS DESIGN tab.
- Tap or click the Property Sheet button (FORM DESIGN TOOLS DESIGN tab | Tools group) to produce the property sheet for the selected labels. If your property sheet appears on the left side of the screen, drag it to the right. Make sure the All tab is selected.
- Tap or click the Border Style property box to display the Border Style property arrow, and then tap or click the arrow to display a menu of border styles (Figure 5–58).

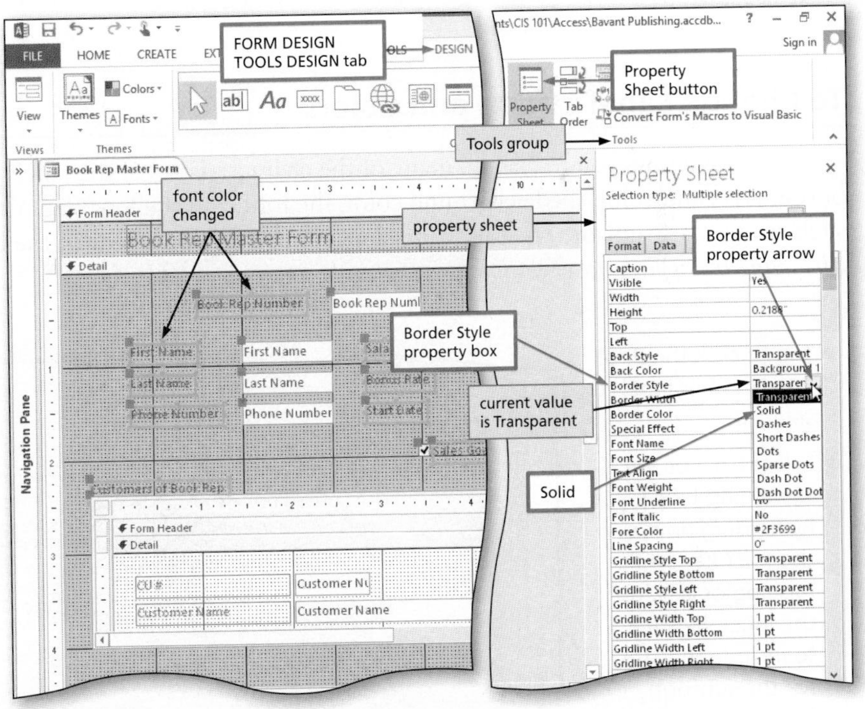

Figure 5–58

Q&A The property sheet is too small to display the property arrow. Can I change the size of the property sheet?

Yes. Point to the border of the property sheet so that the pointer changes to a two-headed arrow. You then can drag to adjust the size.

CONSIDER THIS

Is there any way to determine the way pictures fit within the control?

Yes. Access determines the portion of a picture that appears as well as the way it appears using the **size mode** property. The three size modes are as follows:

Clip — This size mode displays only the portion of the picture that will fit in the space allocated to it.

Stretch — This size mode expands or shrinks the picture to fit the precise space allocated on the screen. For photographs, usually this is not a good choice because fitting a photograph to the allocated space can distort the picture, giving it a stretched appearance.

Zoom — This size mode does the best job of fitting the picture to the allocated space without changing the look of the picture. The entire picture will appear and be proportioned correctly. Some white space may be visible either above or to the right of the picture, however.

To Change the Size Mode

Currently, the size mode for the picture should be Zoom, which is appropriate. If it were not and you wanted to change it, you would use the following steps.

1. Tap or click the control containing the picture, and then tap or click the Property Sheet button (FORM DESIGN TOOLS DESIGN tab | Tools group) to display the control's property sheet.
2. Tap or click the Size Mode property, and then tap or click the Size Mode property arrow.
3. Tap or click Zoom, and then close the property sheet by tapping or clicking its Close button.

To Change Label Effects and Colors

1 ADD FIELDS | 2 ENTER DATA | 3 CREATE FORM | 4 ADD CONTROLS | 5 ADD SUBFORM
6 MODIFY SUBFORM | 7 ENHANCE FORM | **8 CREATE QUERIES**

Access allows you to change many of the characteristics of the labels in the form. You can change the border style and color, the background color, the font, and the font size. You also can apply special label effects, such as raised or sunken. The following steps change the font color of the labels and add special effects. ***Why?*** *Modifying the appearance of the labels improves the appearance of the form.*

1

- Tap or click the Book Rep Number label to select it.
- Select each of the remaining labels by holding down the SHIFT key while tapping or clicking the label. Be sure to include the label for the subform (Figure 5–56).

Q&A Does the order in which I select the labels make a difference?

No. The only thing that is important is that they are all selected when you are done.

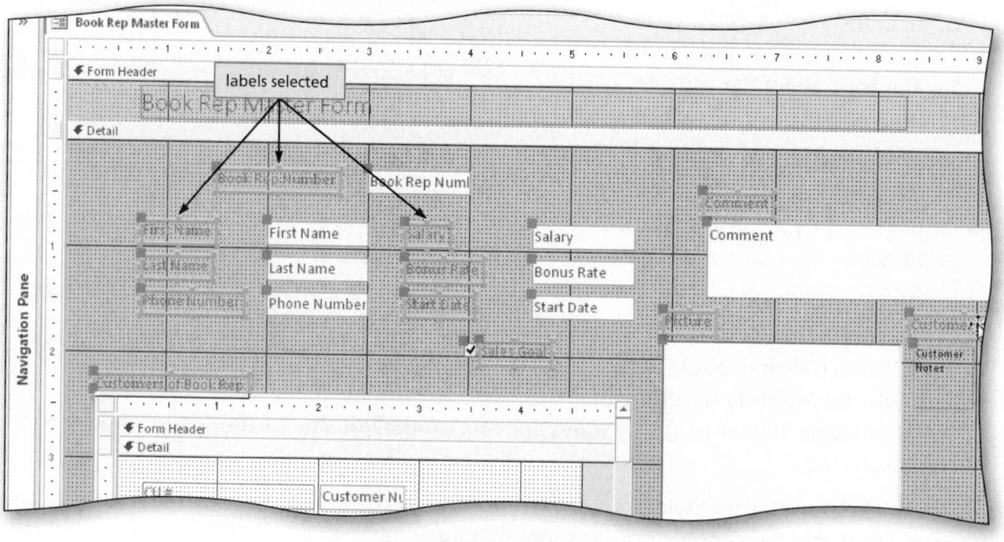

Figure 5–56

2

- Tap or click the control containing the form title to select the control.
- Drag the lower-right sizing handle to resize the control to the approximate size shown in Figure 5–63.

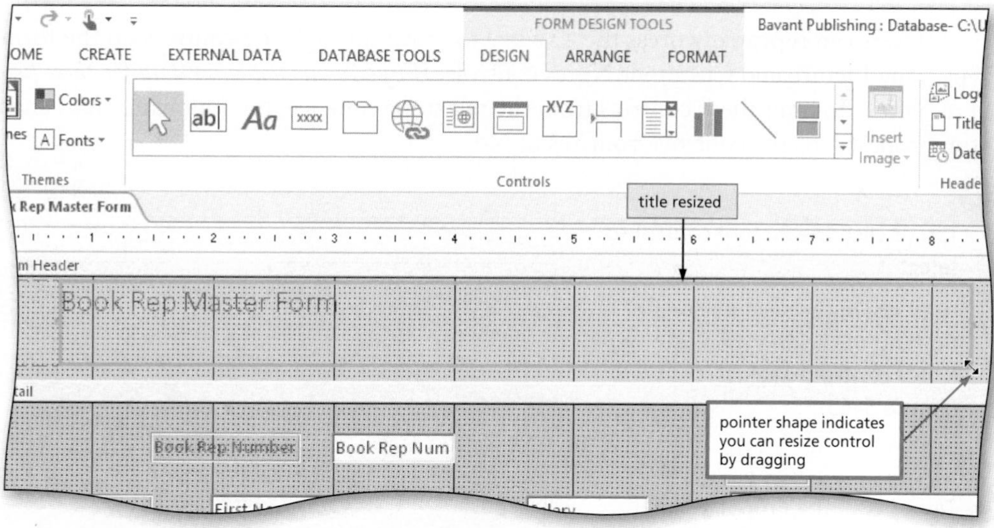

Figure 5–63

3

- Tap or click the Property Sheet button (FORM DESIGN TOOLS DESIGN tab | Tools group) to display the control's property sheet.
- Tap or click the Font Size property box, tap or click the Font Size property arrow, and then tap or click 28 to change the font size.
- In a similar fashion, change the Text Align property value to Distribute and the Font Weight property value to Semi-bold (Figure 5–64).

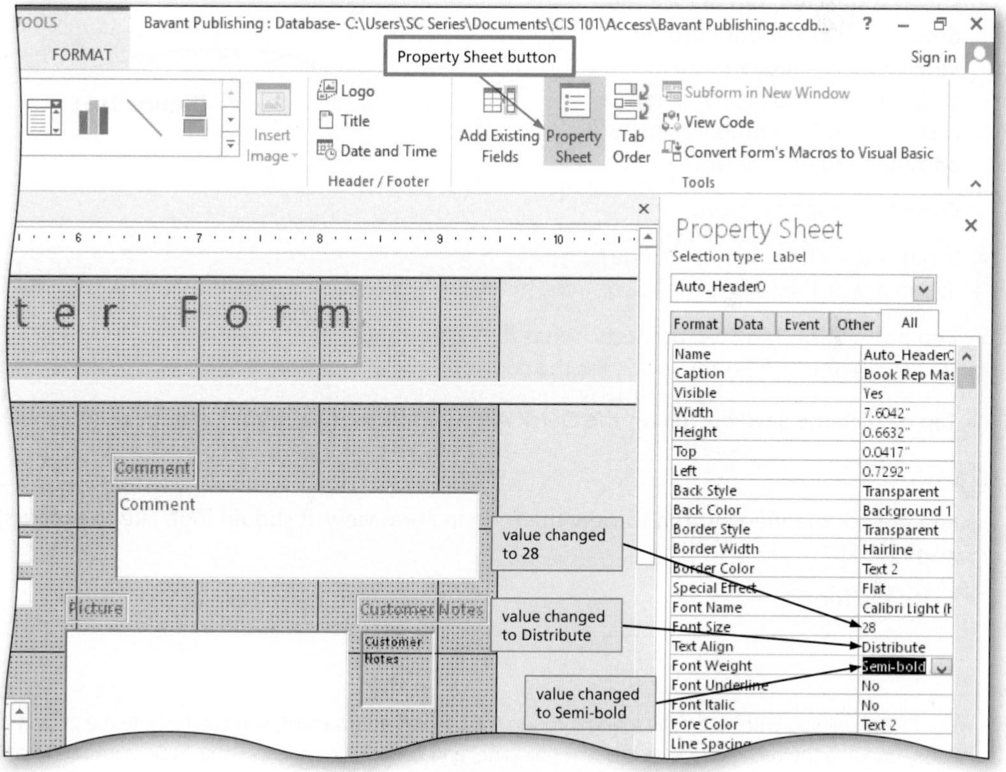

Figure 5–64

4

- Close the property sheet by tapping or clicking the Property Sheet button (FORM DESIGN TOOLS DESIGN tab | Tools group).

Other Ways

1. Enter font size value in Font Size box

To Change a Tab Stop

1 ADD FIELDS | 2 ENTER DATA | 3 CREATE FORM | 4 ADD CONTROLS | 5 ADD SUBFORM
6 MODIFY SUBFORM | 7 ENHANCE FORM | **8 CREATE QUERIES**

Users can repeatedly press the TAB key to move through the controls on the form; however, they should bypass the Picture and Customer Notes controls. ***Why?*** *You do not enter data for these fields as you do the other fields on the form.* To omit these controls from the tab stop sequence, the following steps change the value of the Tab Stop property for the controls from Yes to No.

1

- Tap or click the Picture control to select it.
- Hold down the SHIFT key while tapping or clicking the Customer Notes control to select it as well (Figure 5–65).

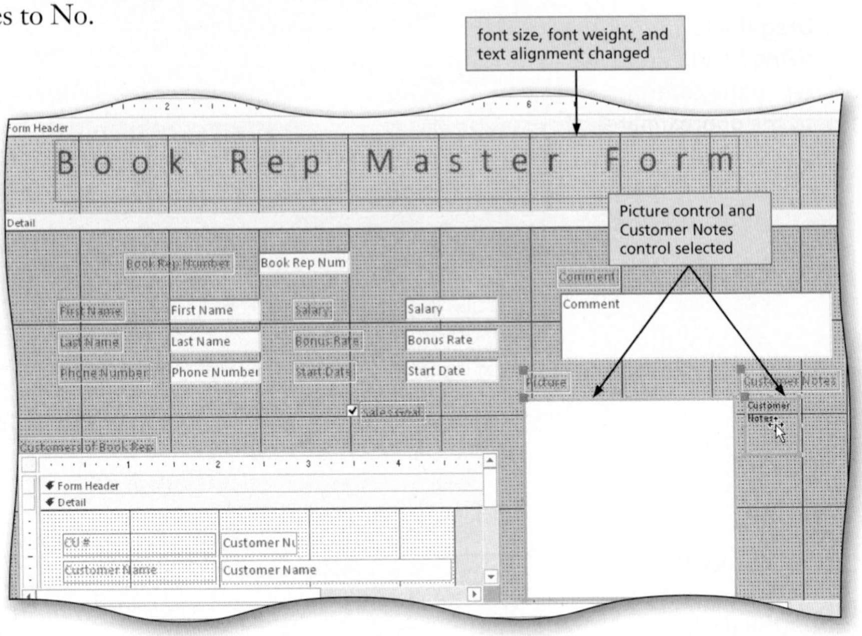

Figure 5–65

2

- Tap or click the Property Sheet button (FORM DESIGN TOOLS DESIGN tab | Tools group) to display the property sheet.
- Make sure the All tab (Property Sheet) is selected, tap or click the down scroll arrow until the Tab Stop property appears, tap or click the Tab Stop property, tap or click the Tab Stop property arrow, and then tap or click No.
- Close the property sheet.

Q&A What is the effect of this change?
When a user tabs through the controls, he or she will bypass the Picture control and the Customer Notes control.

I do not see the Tab Stop property. What did I do wrong?
You tapped or clicked the labels for the controls, not the controls.

- Tap or click the Save button on the Quick Access Toolbar to save your changes.

3

- Tap or click the View button to view the form in Form view. It should look like the form shown in Figure 5–1 on page AC 267.
- Close the form.

Break Point: If you wish to stop working through the chapter at this point, you can resume the project at a later time by starting Access, opening the database called Bavant Publishing, and continuing to follow the steps from this location forward.

Changing the Tab Order

BTW
Auto Order Button
If you tap or click the Auto Order button in the Tab Order dialog box, Access will create a top-to-bottom and left-to-right tab order.

Users can repeatedly press the TAB key to move through the fields on a form. Access determines the order in which the fields are encountered in this process. If you prefer a different order, you can change the order by tapping or clicking the Tab Order button (FORM DESIGN TOOLS DESIGN tab | Tools group). You then can use the Tab Order dialog box (Figure 5–66) to change the order by dragging rows to their desired position as indicated in the dialog box.

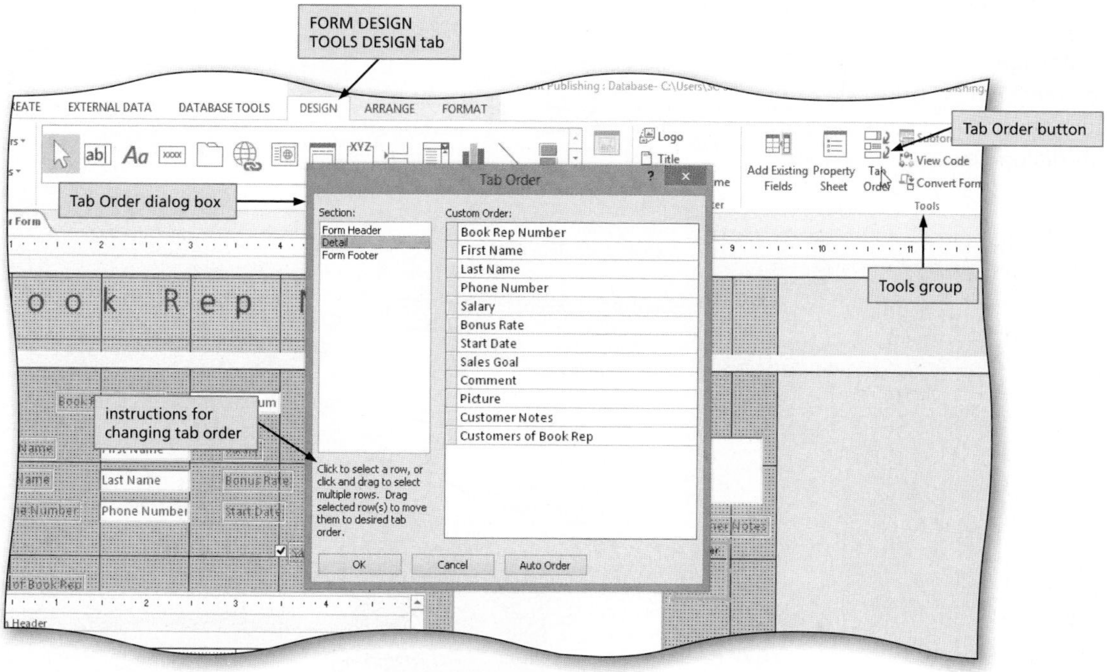

Figure 5–66

To Use the Form

1 ADD FIELDS | 2 ENTER DATA | 3 CREATE FORM | 4 ADD CONTROLS | 5 ADD SUBFORM
6 MODIFY SUBFORM | 7 ENHANCE FORM | **8 CREATE QUERIES**

The form gives you flexibility in selecting both book reps and the customers of the book rep. ***Why?*** *You can use the Navigation buttons at the bottom of the screen to move among book reps. You can use the Navigation buttons in the subform to move among the customers of the book rep currently shown on the screen.* The following steps use the form to display desired data.

1

- Open the Navigation Pane if it is currently closed.
- Press and hold or right-click the Book Rep Master Form, and then tap or click Open on the shortcut menu.
- Close the Navigation Pane.
- Press and hold or right-click the Customer Notes field to display a shortcut menu (Figure 5–67).

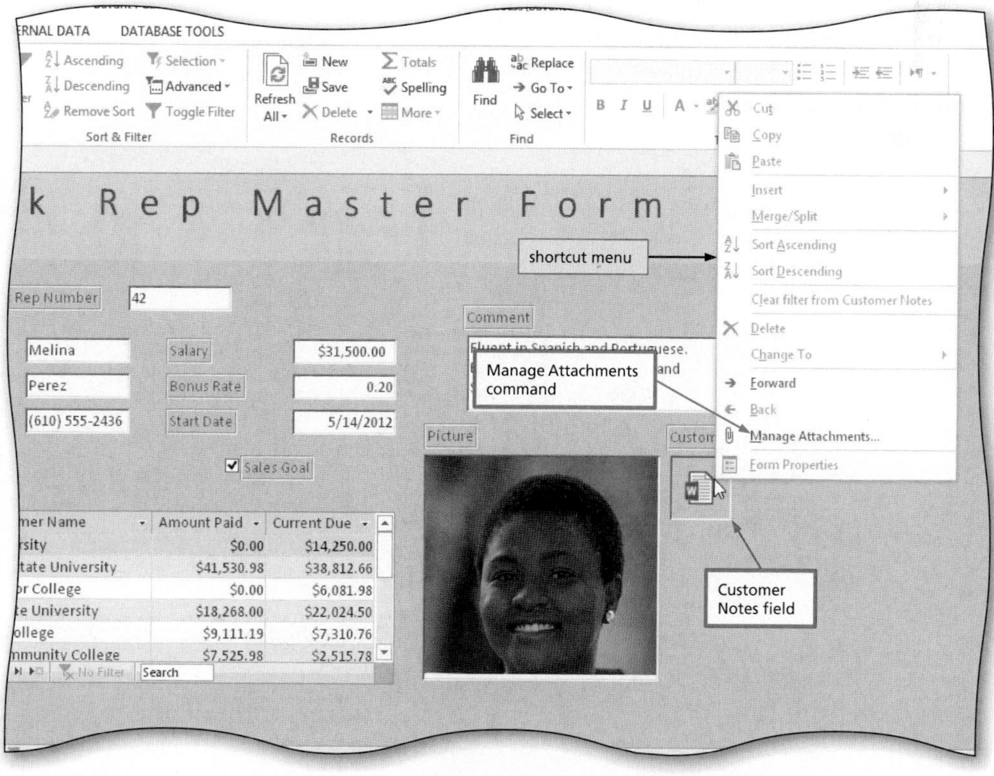

Figure 5–67

2

- Tap or click the Manage Attachments command on the shortcut menu to display the Attachments dialog box (Figure 5–68).

Q&A How do I use this dialog box? Select an attachment and tap or click the Open button to view the attachment in its original application. Tap or click the Add button to add a new attachment or the Remove button to remove the selected attachment. By tapping or clicking the Save button, you can save the selected attachment as a file in whatever location you specify. You can save all attachments at once by tapping or clicking the Save All button.

Experiment

- Open both attachments to see how they look in the original applications. When finished, close each original application.

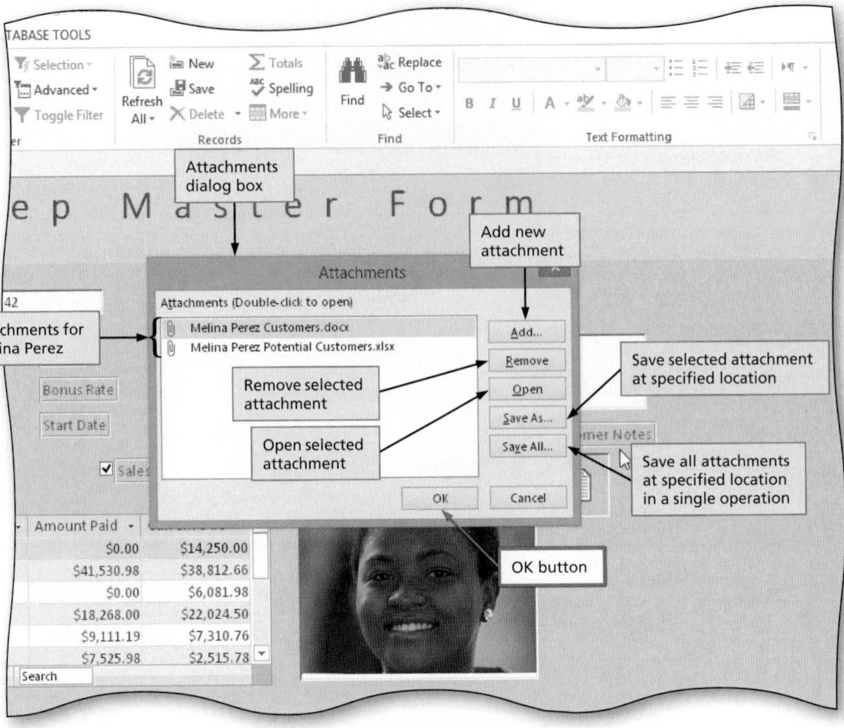

Figure 5–68

3

- Tap or click the OK button to close the Attachments dialog box.
- Tap or click the form's Next record button three times to display the data for book rep 65 (Figure 5–69).

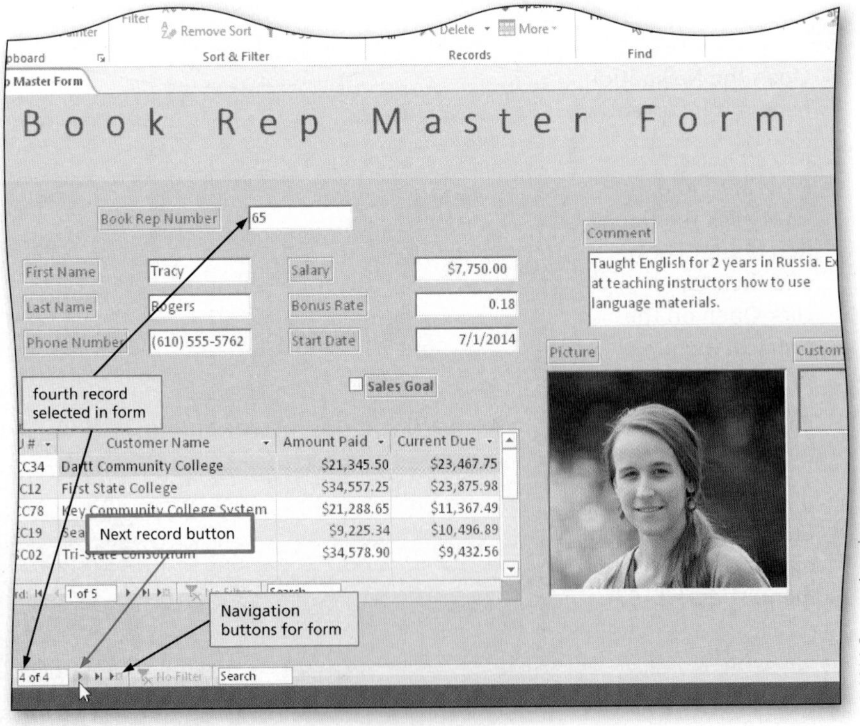

Figure 5–69

4

- Tap or click the subform's Next record button twice to highlight the third customer of book rep 65 (Figure 5–70).

5

- Close the form.

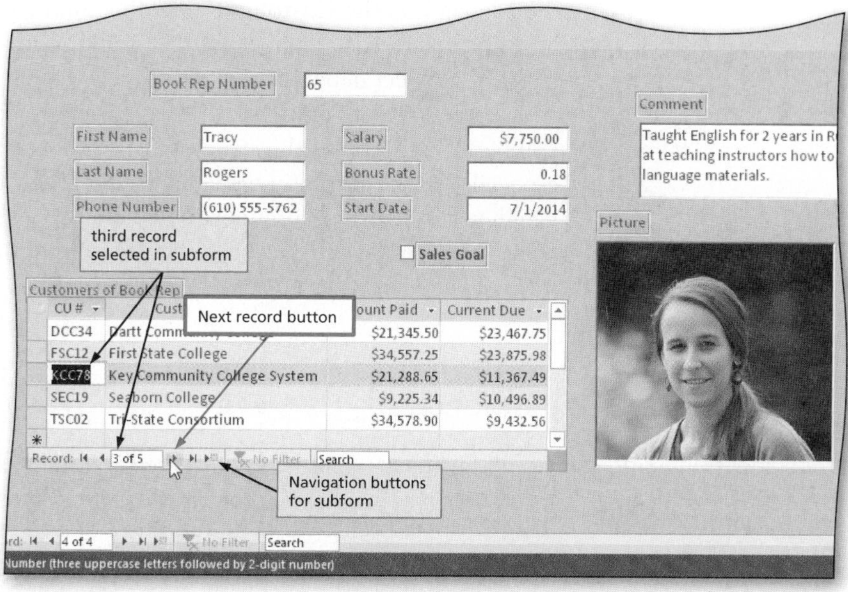

Figure 5–70

Other Ways

1. Double-tap or double-click Attachments control

Navigation in the Form

The previous steps illustrated the way you work with a main form and subform. Tapping or clicking the Navigation buttons for the main form moves to a different book rep. Tapping or clicking the Navigation buttons for the subform moves to a different customer of the book rep who appears in the main form. The following are other actions you can take within the form:

1. To move from the last field in the main form to the first field in the subform, press the TAB key. To move back to the last field in the main form, press CTRL+SHIFT+TAB.
2. To move from the last field in the subform to the first field in the next record's main form, press CTRL+TAB.
3. To switch from the main form to the subform using touch or the mouse, tap or click anywhere in the subform. To switch back to the main form, tap or click any control in the main form. Tapping or clicking the background of the main form will not cause the switch to occur.

BTW
Navigation
To go to a specific record in the main form, enter the record number in the Current Record box for the main form. To go to a specific record in the subform, enter the record number in the Current Record box for the subform.

BTW
Distributing a Document
Instead of printing and distributing a hard copy of a document, you can distribute the document electronically. Options include sending the document via email; posting it on cloud storage (such as SkyDrive) and sharing the file with others; posting it on a social networking site, blog, or other website; and sharing a link associated with an online location of the document. You also can create and share a PDF or XPS image of the document, so that users can view the file in Acrobat Reader or XPS Viewer instead of in Access.

Object Dependencies

In Access, objects can depend on other objects. For example, a report depends on the table or query on which it is based. A change to the structure of the table or query could affect the report. For example, if you delete a field from a table, any report based on that table that uses the deleted field would no longer be valid.

You can view information on dependencies between database objects. Viewing a list of objects that use a specific object helps in the maintenance of a database and avoids errors when changes are made to the objects involved in the dependency. For example, many items, such as queries and forms, use data from the Customer table and thus depend on the Customer table. By tapping or clicking the Object Dependencies button, you can see what items are based on the object. You also can see the items on which the object depends.

If you are unfamiliar with a database, viewing object dependencies can help you better understand the structure of the database. Viewing object dependencies is especially useful after you have made changes to the structure of tables. If you know which reports, forms, and queries depend on a table, you will be better able to make changes to a table without negatively affecting the related database objects.

To View Object Dependencies

1 ADD FIELDS | 2 ENTER DATA | 3 CREATE FORM | 4 ADD CONTROLS | 5 ADD SUBFORM
6 MODIFY SUBFORM | 7 ENHANCE FORM | **8 CREATE QUERIES**

The following steps view the objects that depend on the Customer table. ***Why?*** *The objects that depend on the Customer table are the ones that might be affected by any change you make to the table.*

1

- Open the Navigation Pane and tap or click the Customer table.
- Display the DATABASE TOOLS tab.
- Tap or click the Object Dependencies button (DATABASE TOOLS tab | Relationships group) to display the Object Dependencies pane.
- If necessary, tap or click the 'Objects that depend on me' option button to select it (Figure 5–71).

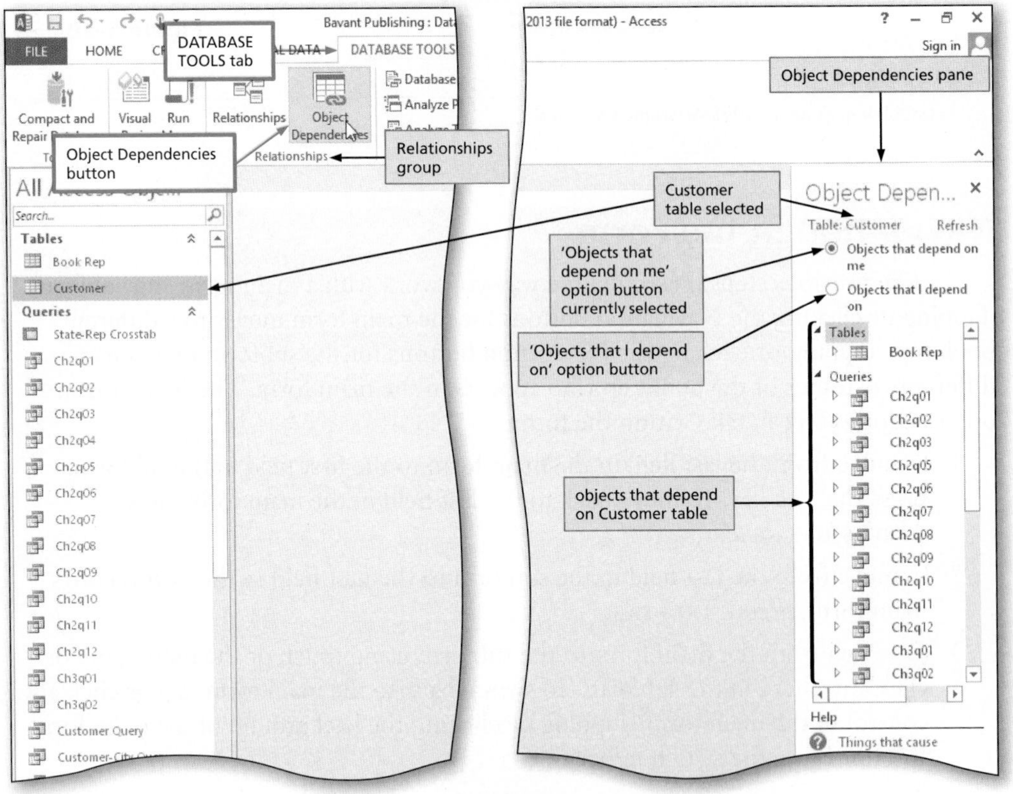

Figure 5–71

Experiment

- Tap or click the 'Objects that I depend on' option button to see the objects on which the Customer table depends. Then try both options for other objects in the database.

2

- Close the Object Dependencies pane by tapping or clicking the Object Dependencies button (DATABASE TOOLS tab | Relationships group) a second time.

Date/Time, Long Text, and Yes/No Fields in Queries

By specifying book rep start dates using Date/Time fields, Bavant Publishing can run queries to find book reps hired before or after a certain date. Another use of the date field might be calculating a rep's length of service by subtracting the start date from the current date. Similarly, management can search for book reps with specific qualifications by adding Long Text and Yes/No fields.

To use Date/Time fields in queries, you simply type the dates, including the slashes. To search for records with a specific date, you must type the date. You also can use comparison operators. To find all the book reps whose start date is after May 15, 2013, for example, you type >5/15/2013 as the criterion.

You also can use Long Text fields in queries by searching for records that contain a specific word or phrase in the Long Text field. To do so, you use wildcards. For example, to find all the book reps who have the word, Fluent, somewhere in the Comment field, you type *Fluent* as the criterion. The asterisk at the beginning indicates that any characters can appear before the word, Fluent. The asterisk at the end indicates that any characters can appear after the word, Fluent.

To use Yes/No fields in queries, type the word, Yes, or the word, No, as the criterion. The following steps create and run queries that use Date/Time, Long Text, and Yes/No fields.

BTW

Long Text Fields in Queries

When you query long text fields, consider alternative spellings and phrases. For example, Computer Science also can be referenced as CS.

BTW

Date Fields in Queries

To test for the current date in a query, type Date() in the Criteria row of the appropriate column. Typing <Date() in the Criteria row for the Start Date, for example, finds those book reps who started anytime before the date on which you run the query.

To Use Date/Time, Long Text, and Yes/No Fields in a Query

1 ADD FIELDS | 2 ENTER DATA | 3 CREATE FORM | 4 ADD CONTROLS | 5 ADD SUBFORM
6 MODIFY SUBFORM | 7 ENHANCE FORM | **8 CREATE QUERIES**

The following steps use Date/Time, Long Text, and Yes/No fields in queries to search for book reps who meet specific criteria. ***Why?*** *Bavant wants to find book reps who started after May 15, 2013 and who have the word, Fluent, in their comment field. They also want to find reps who have met their sales goal.*

1

- Create a query for the Book Rep table and include the Book Rep Number, Last Name, First Name, Start Date, Comment, and Sales Goal fields in the query (Figure 5–72).

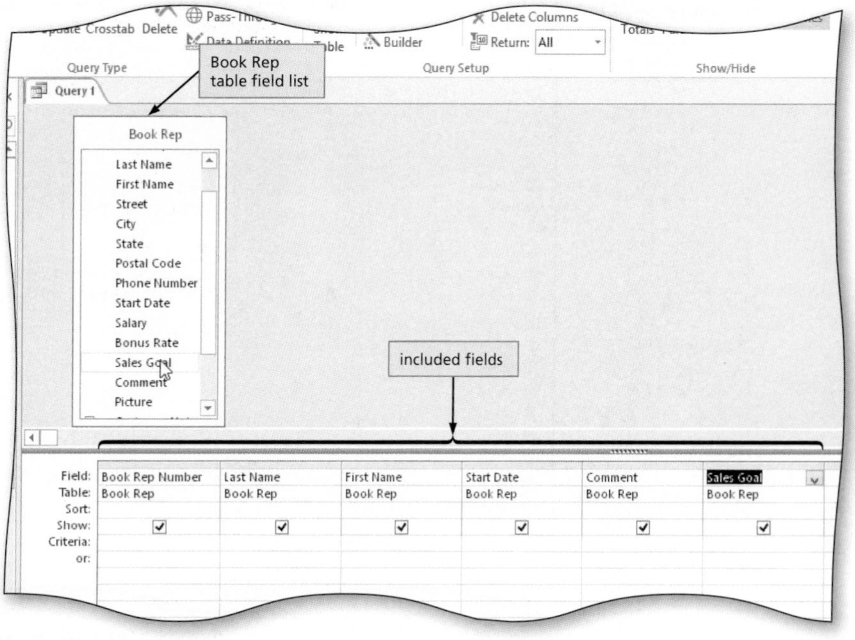

Figure 5–72

2

- Tap or click the Criteria row under the Start Date field, and then type **>5/15/2013** as the criterion.
- Tap or click the Criteria row under the Comment field, and then type ***Fluent*** as the criterion (Figure 5–73).

Q&A Why does the date have number signs (#) around it?
This is the date format in Access. Access reformatted the date appropriately as soon as you selected the Criteria row for the Comment field.

Are wild card searches in comment fields case-sensitive?
No.

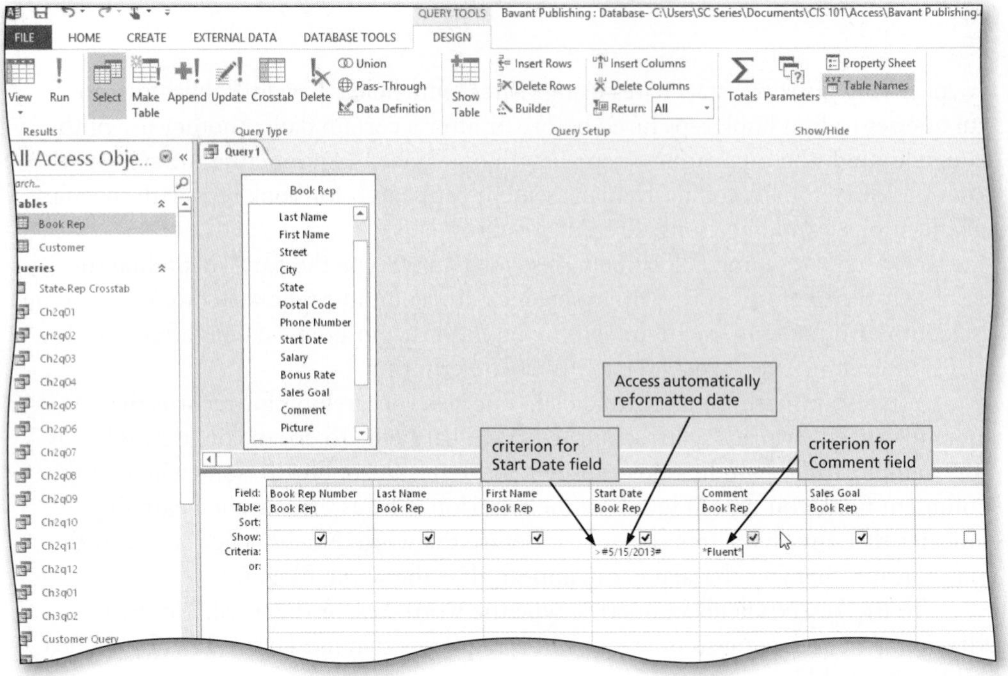

Figure 5–73

3

- Tap or click the View button to view the results (Figure 5–74).

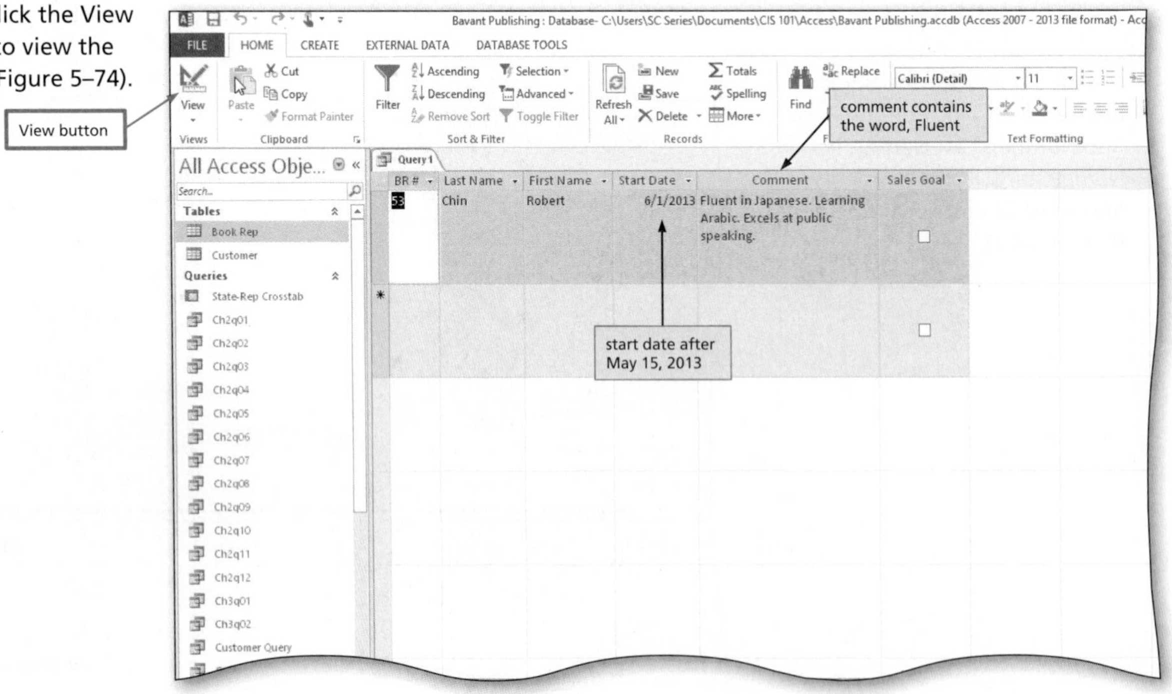

Figure 5–74

4

- Tap or click the View button to return to Design view (Figure 5–75).

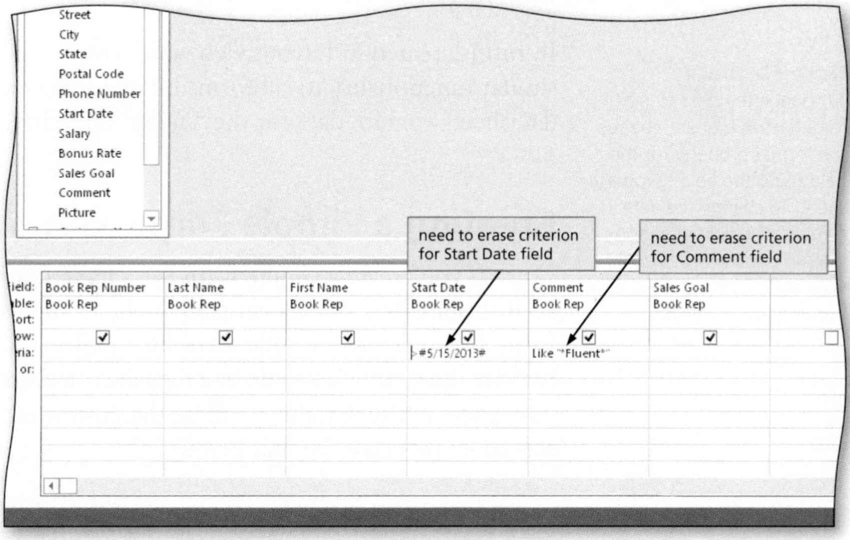

Figure 5–75

5

- Erase the criteria in the Start Date and Comment fields.
- Tap or click the Criteria row under the Sales Goal field, and then type **`Yes`** as the criterion (Figure 5–76).

Q&A Do I have to type Yes?
You also could type True.

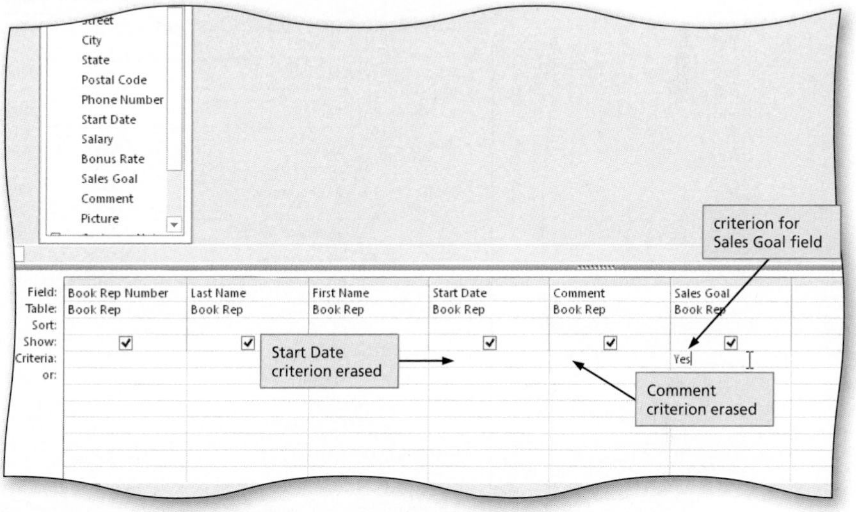

Figure 5–76

6

- Tap or click the View button to view the results (Figure 5–77).

Experiment

- Try other combinations of values in the Start Date field, the Comment field, and/or the Sales Goal field. In each case, view the results.

7

- Close the query without saving the results.

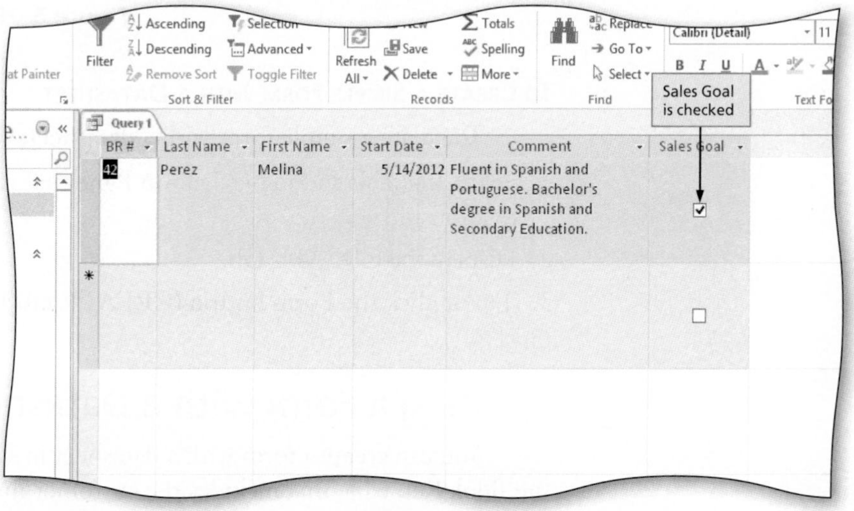

Figure 5–77

Datasheets in Forms

BTW
Date Formats
To change the date format for a date in a query, change the format property for the field using the field's property sheet. To change the date format for a field in a table, open the table in Design view and change the format property for the field.

In forms created in Layout view, subforms are not available, but you can achieve similar functionality to subforms by including datasheets. Like subforms, the datasheets contain data for the "many" table in the relationship.

Creating a Simple Form with a Datasheet

If you create a simple form for a table that is the "one" table in a one-to-many relationship, Access automatically includes the "many" table in a datasheet within the form. If you create a simple form for the Book Rep table, for example, Access will include the Customer table in a datasheet within the form, as in Figure 5–78. The customers in the datasheet will be the customers of the book rep currently on the screen, in this case, Melina Perez.

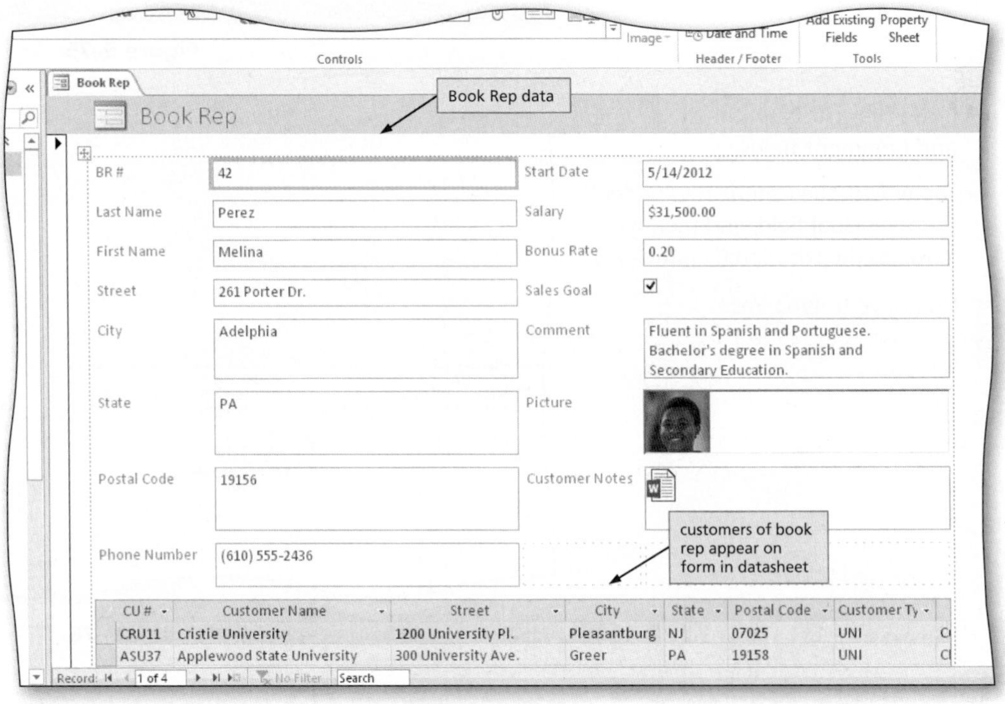

Figure 5–78

To Create a Simple Form with a Datasheet

To create a simple form with a datasheet, you would use the following steps.

1. Select the table in the Navigation Pane that is the "one" part of a one-to-many relationship.
2. Display the CREATE tab.
3. Tap or click the Form button (CREATE tab | Forms group).

Creating a Form with a Datasheet in Layout View

You can create a form with a datasheet in Layout view. To create a form based on the Book Rep table that includes the customer number, which is stored in the Customer table, you would first use the field list to add the required fields from the "one" table. In Figure 5–79, fields from the Book Rep table have been added to the form.

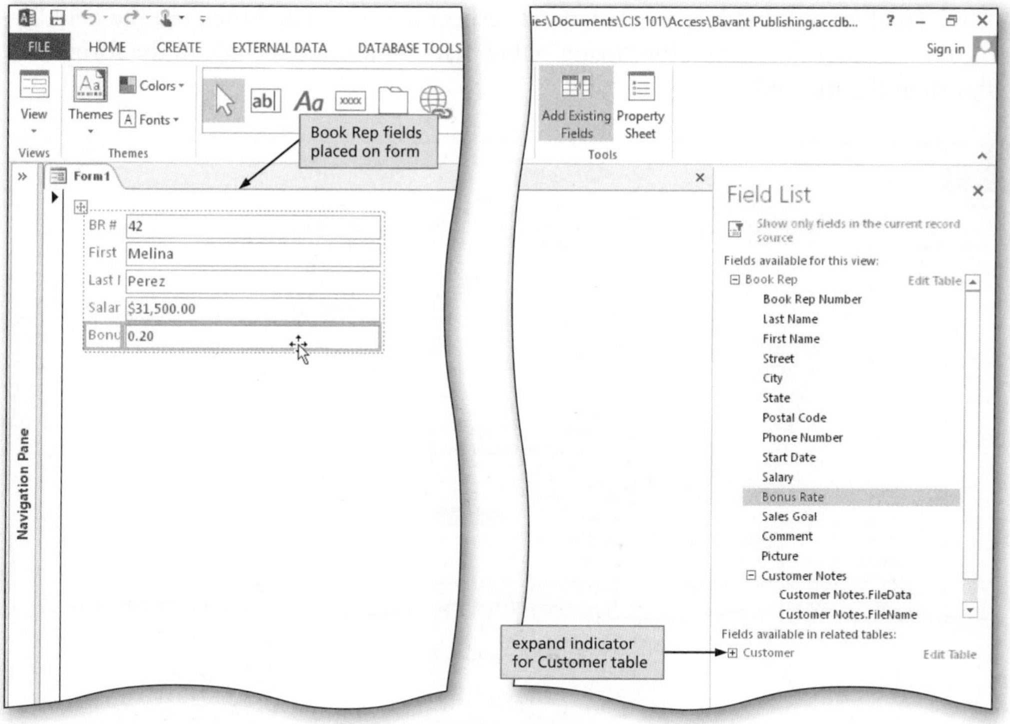

Figure 5–79

Next, you would use the field list to add a single field from the "many" table, as shown in Figure 5–80, in which the Customer Number field has been added. Access will automatically create a datasheet containing this field.

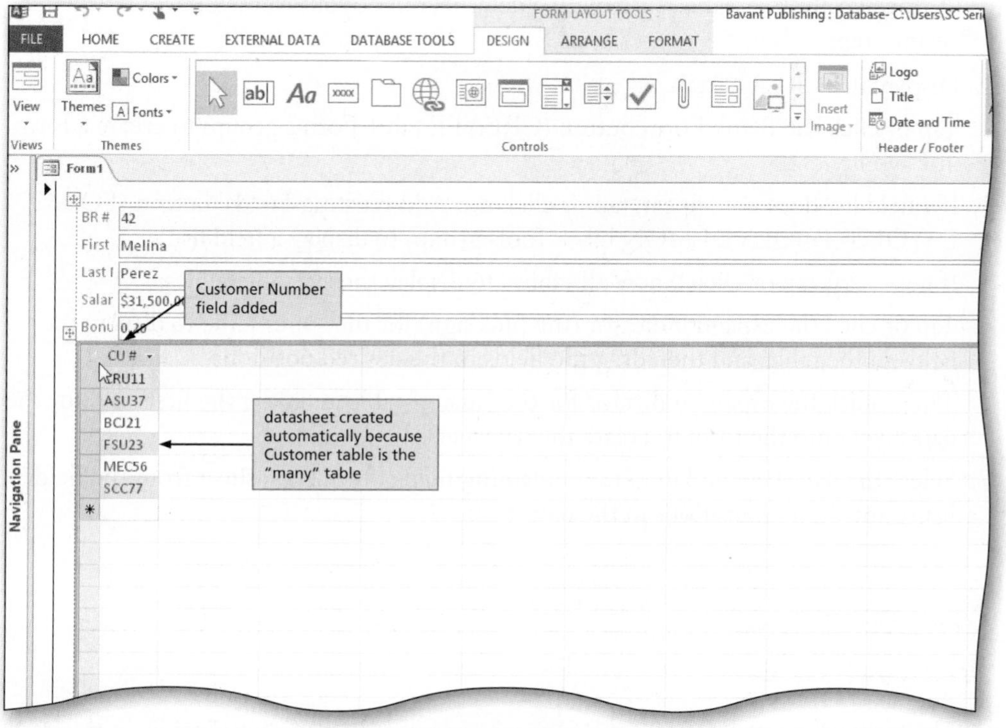

Figure 5–80

Finally, you would tap or click the datasheet to select it and then use the field list to add the other fields from the "many" table that you want to include in the form, as shown in Figure 5–81.

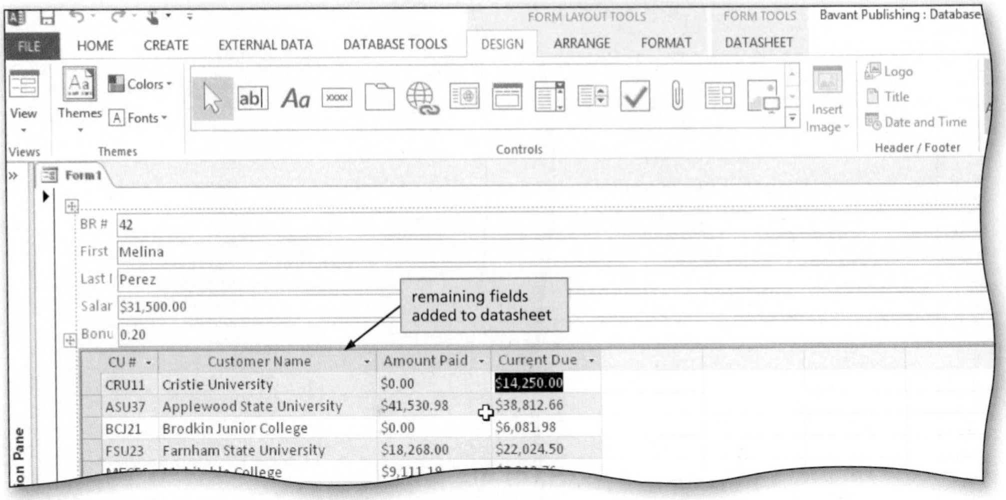

Figure 5–81

CONSIDER THIS

Can you modify the form so that the complete labels for the book rep fields appear?

Yes. Tap or click any of the labels for the book rep fields to select the label, and then tap or click the Select Column button (ARRANGE tab | Rows & Columns group) to select all the labels. You can then drag the right boundary of any of the labels to resize all the labels simultaneously.

To Create a Form with a Datasheet in Layout View

Specifically, to create a form with a datasheet in Layout view, you would use the following steps.

1. Display the CREATE tab.
2. Tap or click the Blank Form button (CREATE tab | Forms group) to create a form in Layout view.
3. If a field list does not appear, tap or click the 'Add Existing Fields' button (FORM LAYOUT TOOLS DESIGN tab | Tools group) to display a field list.
4. If necessary, tap or click 'Show all tables' to display the available tables.
5. Tap or click the expand indicator (the plus sign) for the "one" table to display the fields in the table, and then drag the fields to the desired positions.
6. Tap or click the expand indicator for the "many" table and drag the first field for the datasheet onto the form to create the datasheet.
7. Select the datasheet and drag the remaining fields for the datasheet from the field list to the desired locations in the datasheet.

BTW

Placing Fields on a Datasheet

Be sure to select the datasheet before adding additional fields to the datasheet. When dragging a field from the field list to the datasheet, drag the field to the right boundary of the previous field. The pointer will change to show that you are placing a control and you will see a vertical line.

Creating a Multiple-Table Form Based on the Many Table

All the forms discussed so far in this chapter were based on the "one" table, in this case, the Book Rep table. The records from the "one" table were included in a subform. You can also create a multiple-table form based on the "many" table, in this case, the Customer table. Such a form is shown in Figure 5–82.

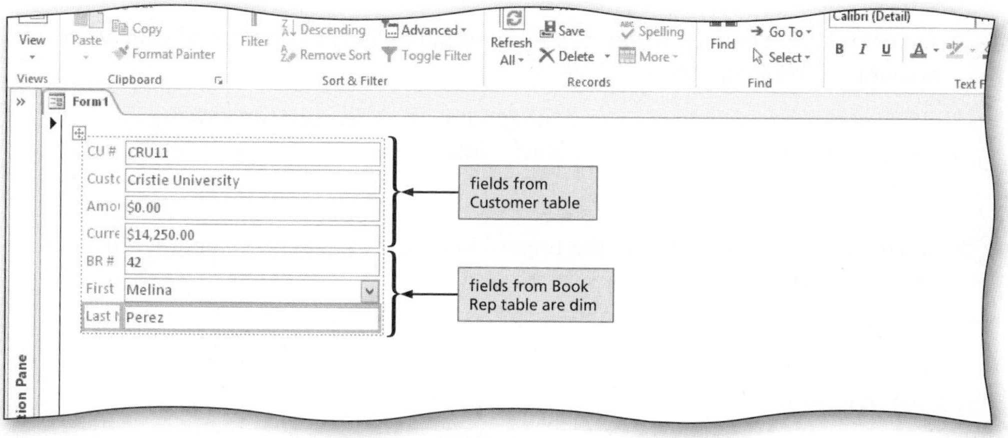

Figure 5–82

In this form, the Customer Number, Customer Name, Amount Paid, Current Due, and Book Rep Number fields are in the Customer table. The First Name and Last Name fields are found in the Book Rep table and are included in the form to help to identify the book rep whose number appears in the Book Rep Number field.

To Create a Multiple-Table Form Based on the Many Table

To create a multiple-table form based on the "many" table, you would use the following steps.

1. Tap or click the Blank Form button (CREATE tab | Forms group) to create a form in Layout view.
2. If a field list does not appear, tap or click the 'Add Existing Fields' button on the DESIGN tab to display a field list.
3. Drag the fields for the "many" table to the desired positions.
4. Drag the fields for the "one" table to the desired positions.

To Sign Out of a Microsoft Account

If you are signed in to a Microsoft account and are using a public computer or otherwise wish to sign out of your Microsoft account, you should sign out of the account from the Account gallery in the Backstage view before exiting Access. Signing out of the account is the safest way to make sure that nobody else can access SkyDrive files or settings stored in your Microsoft account. The following steps sign out of a Microsoft account from Access. For a detailed example of the procedure summarized below, refer to the Office and Windows chapter at the beginning of this book.

BTW
Quick Reference
For a table that lists how to complete the tasks covered in this book using touch gestures, the mouse, ribbon, shortcut menu, and keyboard, see the Quick Reference Summary at the back of this book, or visit the Quick Reference resource on the Student Companion Site located on www.cengagebrain.com. For detailed instructions about accessing available resources, visit www.cengage.com/ct/studentdownload or contact your instructor for information about accessing the required files.

1. If you wish to sign out of your Microsoft account, tap or click FILE on the ribbon to open the Backstage view and then tap or click the Account tab to display the Account gallery.

2. Tap or click the Sign out link, which displays the Remove Account dialog box. If a Can't remove Windows accounts dialog box appears instead of the Remove Account dialog box, click the OK button and skip the remaining steps.

Q&A
Why does a Can't remove Windows accounts dialog box appear?
If you signed in to Windows using your Microsoft account, then you also must sign out from Windows, rather than signing out from within Access. When you are finished using Windows, be sure to sign out at that time.

BTW
Certification
The Microsoft Office Specialist (MOS) program provides an opportunity for you to obtain a valuable industry credential — proof that you have the Access 2013 skills required by employers. For more information, visit the Certification resource on the Student Companion Site located on www.cengagebrain.com. For detailed instructions about accessing available resources, visit www.cengage.com/ct/studentdownload or contact your instructor for information about accessing the required files.

3. Tap or click the Yes button (Remove Account dialog box) to sign out of your Microsoft account on this computer.

Q&A Should I sign out of Windows after signing out of my Microsoft account?
When you are finished using the computer, you should sign out of your account for maximum security.

4. Tap or click the Back button in the upper-left corner of the Backstage view to return to the database.

To Exit Access

The following steps exit Access.

1. Tap or click the Close button on the right side of the title bar to exit Access.
2. If a Microsoft Access dialog box appears, tap or click the Yes button to save any changes made to the object since the last save.

Chapter Summary

In this chapter you have learned to use Yes/No, Long Text, OLE Object, and Attachment data types; create and use an input mask; create a form and add a subform; enhance the look of the controls on a form; use a form with a subform; create queries involving Yes/No, Date/Time, and Long Text fields; view object dependencies; and create forms containing datasheets in Layout view. The items listed below include all the new Access skills you have learned in this chapter.

CONSIDER THIS

What decisions will you need to make when creating your own forms?

Use these guidelines as you complete the assignments in this chapter and create your own forms outside of this class.

1. Determine the purpose of the fields to see if they need special data types.
   a. If the field only contains values such as Yes and No or True and False, it should have Yes/No as the data type.
   b. If the field contains an extended comment, it should have Long Text as the data type.
   c. If the field contains a picture or other special object, its data type should be OLE object.
   d. If the field contains attachments, its data type should be Attachment.
2. Determine whether the form requires data from more than one table.
3. If the form requires data from more than one table, determine the relationship between the tables.
   a. Identify one-to-many relationships.
   b. For each relationship, identify the "one" table and the "many" table.
4. If the form requires data from more than one table, determine on which of the tables the form is to be based.
   a. Which table contains data that is the focus of the form, that is, which table is the main table?
5. Determine the fields from each table that need to be on the form.
   a. Decide exactly how the form will be used, and identify the fields that are necessary to support this use.
   b. Determine whether there are any additional fields that, while not strictly necessary, would make the form more functional.
6. When changing the structure of a table or query, examine object dependencies to see if any report or form might be impacted by the change.
7. Determine the tab order for form controls.
   a. Change the tab order if the form requires a certain progression from one control to the next.
   b. Remove tab stops for those controls for which form navigation is not required.

CONSIDER THIS

How should you submit solutions to questions in the assignments identified with a ✲ symbol?

Every assignment in this book contains one or more questions identified with a ✲ symbol. These questions require you to think beyond the assigned database. Present your solutions to the questions in the format required by your instructor. Possible formats may include one or more of these options: write the answer; create a document that contains the answer; present your answer to the class; discuss your answer in a group; record the answer as audio or video using a webcam, smartphone, or portable media player; or post answers on a blog, wiki, or website.

Apply Your Knowledge

Reinforce the skills and apply the concepts you learned in this chapter.

Adding Phone Number, Yes/No, Long Text, and OLE Object Fields, Using an Input Mask Wizard, and Querying Long Text Fields

Note: To complete this assignment, you will be required to use the Data Files for Students. Visit www.cengage.com/ct/studentdownload for detailed instructions or contact your instructor for information about accessing the required files.

Instructions: Start Access, and then open the Apply Beauty Organically database that you used in Chapter 4. If you did not create this database, see your instructor about accessing the required files.

Perform the following tasks:

1. Open the Sales Rep table in Design view.
2. Add the Phone Number, Eligibility, Comment, and Picture fields to the Sales Rep table structure, as shown in Figure 5–83. Be sure the Phone Number field appears after the Postal Code field and create an input mask for the field. Store the phone number data without symbols. Eligibility is a field that indicates whether a sales rep is eligible for the company's sales award.

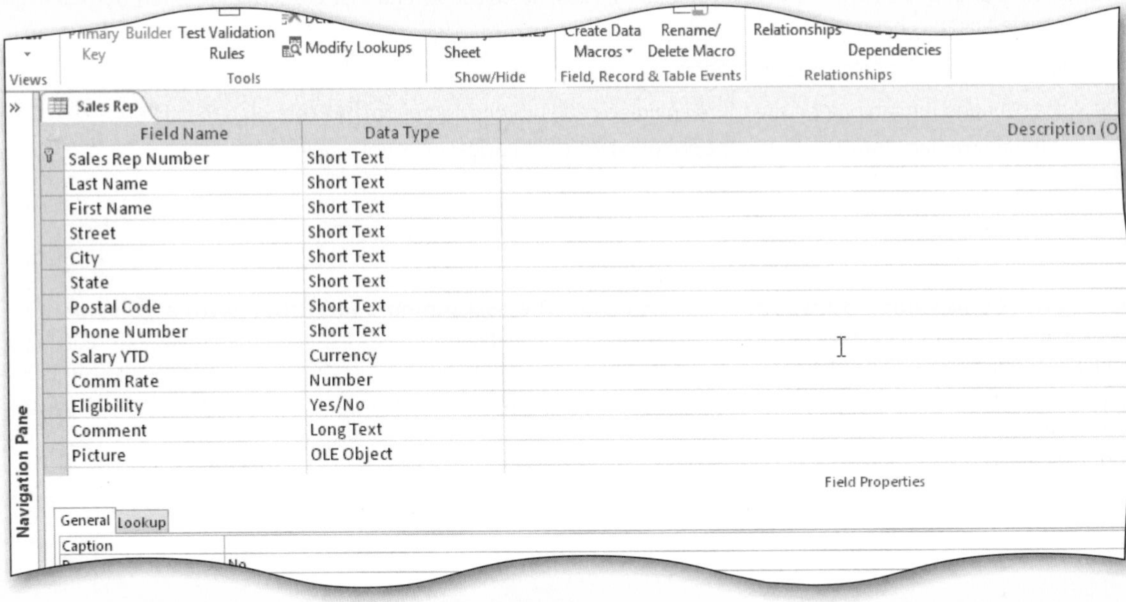

Figure 5–83

3. Add the data shown in Table 5–1 to the Sales Rep table. Adjust the row and column spacing to best fit the data. Save the changes to the layout of the table.

Table 5–1 Data for Sales Rep Table

Sales Rep Number	Phone Number	Eligibility	Comment	Picture
44	615-555-2222	Yes	Has a BA in Marketing. Helps to train new employees.	Pict1.jpg
49	704-555-4433	No	Has a BA in Economics. Working on MBA.	Pict2.jpg
51	804-555-8877	Yes	Certified Personal Trainer. Enjoys working with fitness centers.	Pict3.jpg
65	704-555-5498	No	Has a BA in Marketing. Excellent computer skills.	Pict4.jpg

4. If requested to do so by your instructor, change the phone number for sales rep number 44 to your phone number.
5. Query the Sales Rep table to find all sales reps with degrees in Marketing. Include the Sales Rep Number, Last Name, First Name, and Phone Number fields in the query. Save the query as Apply 5 Step 5 Query.
6. Query the Sales Rep table to find all sales reps with degrees in Marketing and who are eligible for a sales award. Include the Sales Rep Number, Last Name, First Name, and Comment fields in the query. Save the query as Apply 5 Step 6 Query.
7. Submit the revised database in the format specified by your instructor.
8. What value did you enter in the criteria row for the Eligibility field in the query in Step 6 above? Could you have entered the criteria differently? If yes, then how would you enter the criteria?

Extend Your Knowledge

Extend the skills you learned in this chapter and experiment with new skills. You may need to use Help to complete the assignment.

Adding Hyperlink Fields and Creating Multiple-Table Forms Using Layout View

Note: To complete this assignment, you will be required to use the Data Files for Students. Visit www.cengage.com/ct/studentdownload for detailed instructions or contact your instructor for information about accessing the required files.

Instructions: Start Access. Open the Extend Human Resources database from the Data Files for Students. Extend Human Resources is a recruiting company that recruits employees for positions in the Health Sciences fields. You will add a Hyperlink field to the Client table. You also will create the form shown in Figure 5–84.

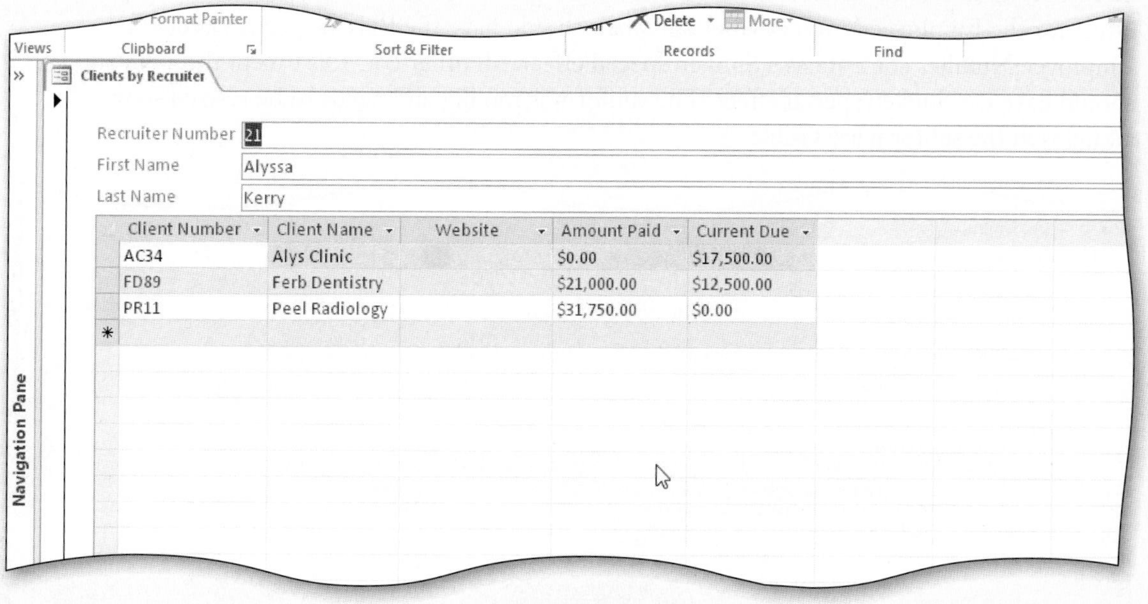

Figure 5–84

Continued >

Extend Your Knowledge *continued*

Perform the following tasks:

1. Open the Client table in Design view and add a field with the Hyperlink data type. Insert the field after the Postal Code field. Use Website as the name of the field.
2. Open the Client table in Datasheet view and add data for the Website field to the first record. Use your school website as the URL. If necessary, resize the column so the complete URL is displayed.
3. If requested to do so by your instructor, enter your name as a hyperlink in the second record of the Client table.
4. Use Layout view to create the multiple-table form shown in Figure 5–84 on the previous page. The Client table appears as a subform in the form. The Recruiter table is the "one" table in the form. Use Clients by Recruiter as the form name. Change the orientation of the form to Landscape.
5. Submit the revised database in the format specified by your instructor.
6. How would you add a field for an email address to the Recruiter table?

Analyze, Correct, Improve

Analyze a database, correct all errors, and improve the design.

Correcting Form Design Error and Improving a Report

Note: To complete this assignment, you will be required to use the Data Files for Students. Visit www.cengage.com/ct/studentdownload for detailed instructions or contact your instructor for information about accessing the required files.

Instructions: Start Access. Open the Analyze Maintenance database from the Data Files for Students. Maintenance is a company that does household maintenance for customers in several planned communities. The owner of this company has asked you to correct some errors in a form he created and to improve the form design.

1. Correct The Employee Master Form shown in Figure 5–85 currently has the Raised special effect for the Employee Number label. All labels should have the Raised special effect. The Employee Number control has a Sunken special effect. All other controls except the subform should have the Sunken special effect. The subform is too big and needs to be resized so that all fields in the subform are visible.

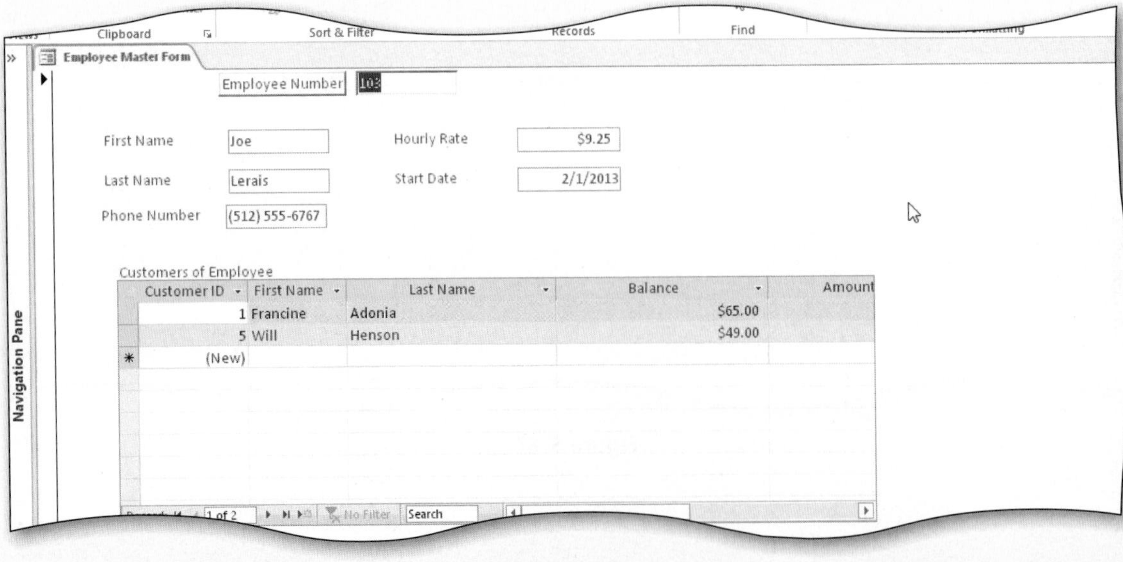

Figure 5–85

2. Improve The form shown in Figure 5–85 would be more visually appealing with a background color. Change the color of the form background to light gray (row 2, column 1). Also, the purpose of the form would be easier to discern with a title. Add the title, Employee Master Form, to the form. The title should have a Raised appearance, a text alignment of Distribute with a font size of 24, and font weight of bold. If instructed to do so by your instructor, change the first and last names for employee number 103 to your first and last name.

3. The font color for the title is currently blue. How could you change the font color to Dark Red?

In the Labs

Design, create, modify, and/or use a database following the guidelines, concepts, and skills presented in this chapter. Labs are listed in order of increasing difficulty. Labs 1 and 2, which increase in difficulty, require you to create solutions based on what you learned in the chapter; Lab 3 requires you to create a solution, which uses cloud and web technologies, by learning and investigating on your own from general guidance.

Lab 1: Adding Fields and Creating Multiple-Table Forms for the Backup Services Databases

Problem: Backup Services needs to maintain additional data on service reps. Management needs to store notes about each service rep, indicate whether the service rep has MOS certification, and display a picture of the service rep. They also need to store the phone number of each service rep. Management wants a form that displays service rep information and the clients for whom they are responsible.

Note: To complete this assignment, you will be required to use the Data Files for Students. Visit www.cengage.com/ct/studentdownload for detailed instructions or contact your instructor for information about accessing the required files.

Instructions: Perform the following tasks:

1. Run Access and open the Lab 1 Backup Services database you used in Chapter 4. If you did not create this database, see your instructor about accessing the required files.
2. Add the Certification, Comment, and Picture fields to the end of the Service Rep table. Insert the Phone Number field after the Postal Code field and create the input mask shown in Figure 5–86 on the next page for the Phone Number field. Save the changes to the structure of the table.
3. Add the data shown in Table 5–2 to the Service Rep table. Adjust the row and column spacing to best fit the data. Save the changes to the layout of the table.

Table 5–2 Data for Service Rep Table

Sales Rep Number	Phone Number	Certification	Comment	Picture
36	803-555-2212	Yes	Has previous military experience. Has a BS in Computer Science.	Pict1.jpg
39	803-555-4343	Yes	Specialist in cybersecurity.	Pict4.jpg
52	803-555-8787	No	Has a BS in Information Systems.	Pict2.jpg
60	803-555-9854	No	Working on an MIS degree.	Pict3.jpg

Continued >

In the Labs *continued*

4. If requested to do so by your instructor, change the phone number for service rep 36 to your phone number.
5. Create the form shown in Figure 5–86. Use Service Rep Master Form as the name of the form, and Clients of Service Rep as the name of the subform. Users should not be able to tab through the Picture control. The title is centered with a font weight of bold and a font size of 24.

Figure 5–86

6. Query the Service Rep table to find all service reps who started before January 1, 2013 and who have MOS certification. Include the Service Rep Number, Last Name, and First Name in the query results. Save the query as Lab 5–1 Step 6 Query.
7. Submit the revised database in the format specified by your instructor.
8. The Service Rep table includes a Start Date field in the format, mm/dd/yyyy. How could you add an input mask for the Start Date field?

Lab 2: Adding Fields and Creating Multiple-Table Forms for the Sports Logo Database

Problem: The management of Sports Logo has found that they need to maintain additional data on suppliers. Management needs to keep track of whether the supplier accepts returns, and whether the supplier allows online ordering. Management also would like to attach to each supplier's record Excel files that contain historical cost data. Sports Logo requires a form that displays information about the supplier as well as the items that are purchased from suppliers.

Note: To complete this assignment, you will be required to use the Data Files for Students. Visit www.cengage.com/ct/studentdownload for detailed instructions or contact your instructor for information about accessing the required files.

Instructions: Perform the following tasks:

1. Run Access and open the Lab 2 Sports Logo database you used in Chapter 4. If you did not create this database, see your instructor about accessing the required files.
2. Add the Returns, Online Ordering, and Cost History fields to the end of the Supplier table structure.
3. Add the data shown in Table 5–3 to the Supplier table.

Table 5–3 Data for Supplier Table

Supplier Code	Returns	Online Ordering	Cost History
LM	Yes	No	LM_History.xlsx
PC	No	Yes	PC_History.xlsx
SD	Yes	Yes	SD_History.xlsx

4. Create the form shown in Figure 5–87. Use Supplier Master Form as the name of the form and Items of Supplier as the name of the subform. The title is shadowed and centered with a font size of 24 and a Dark Red font color. The labels are chiseled with a Dark Red font color and the controls, except the subform control, are sunken. Be sure the entire title appears and that the entire Supplier Name is visible.

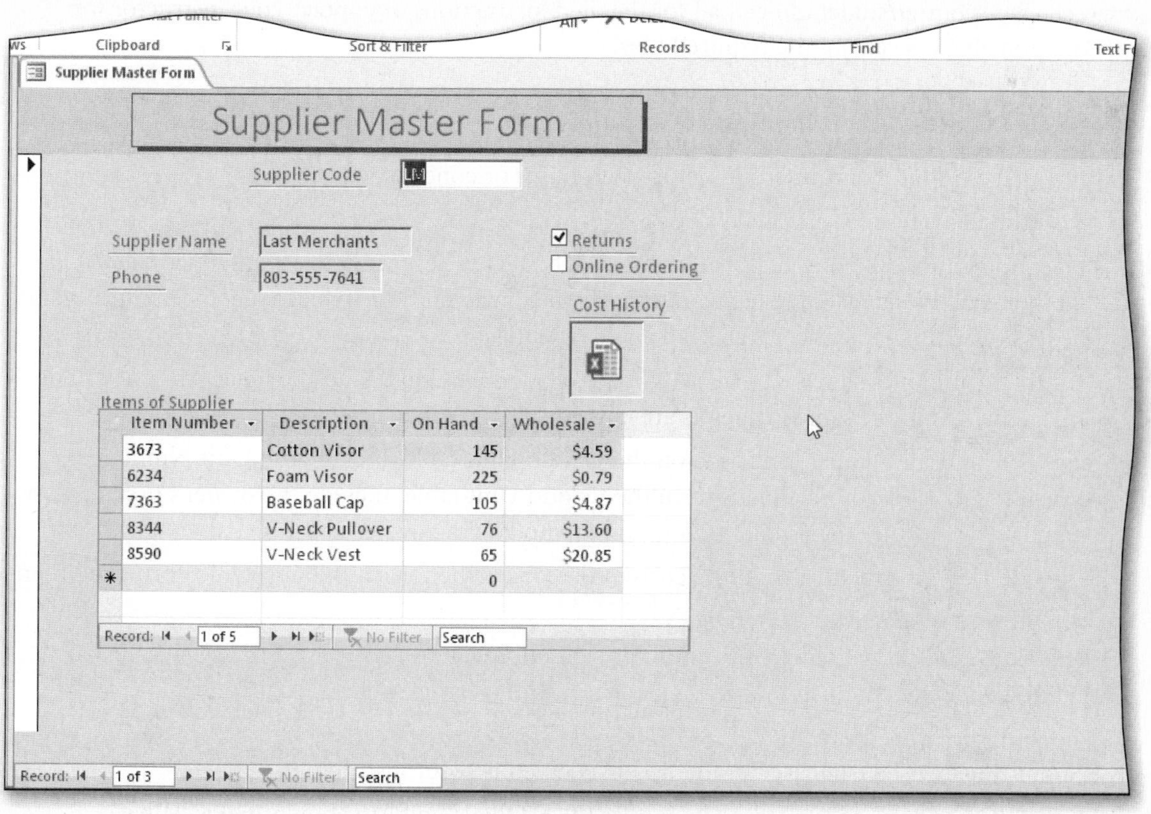

Figure 5–87

Continued >

In the Labs *continued*

5. If requested to do so by your instructor, change the name for Supplier Code LM to your first and last name.
6. Open the Supplier Master Form and then open the cost history for PJ Pratt Clothing. Change the previous cost for item 6185 to $27.50. Save the change to the workbook.
7. Query the Supplier table to find all suppliers that accept returns and allow online ordering. Include the Supplier Code and Supplier Name in the query results. Save the query as Lab 5–2 Step 7 Query.
8. Submit the revised database in the format specified by your instructor.
9. What additional field(s) would you add to the Supplier table to assist with online ordering?

Lab 3: Expand Your World: Cloud and Web Technologies

Adding Picture and Attachment Fields and Creating Multiple-Table Forms

Problem: Condo Rentals is a database of condos for rent. To understand the difference between Attachment and OLE Object data types, you will add those fields to the Condo table. Then, you will insert images that you download from the Internet. Finally, you will create a multiple-table form for the database.

Note: To complete this assignment, you will be required to use the Data Files for Students. Visit www.cengage.com/ct/studentdownload for detailed instructions or contact your instructor for information about accessing the required files.

Instructions: Perform the following tasks:

1. Access the office.com website or any other website containing royalty-free images and search the images to find four different pictures of houses or condos.
2. Save these images to your data disk or SkyDrive.
3. Open the Lab 3 Condo Rentals database from the Data Files for Students and open the Condo Unit table in Design view. Add a Condo Image field with an OLE Object data type. Add a Picture field with an Attachment data type. The fields should appear before the Owner Code field.
4. Use the techniques shown on pages AC 278 through AC 280 to add the images to the Condo Image field. Add the same images as attachments to the Picture field.
5. Create a multiple-table form based on the Condo Unit table. Include the Unit Number, Weekly Rate, and For Sale fields from the Condo Unit table. Include the owner's first and last name on the form. Users should not be able to update the owner name fields.
6. Include a title for the form and the current date. Save the form as Condo Unit Form, and then open the form in Design view.
7. Add the Condo Image field and the Picture field to the form. If necessary, use the size mode property to adjust your images in the Condo Image field so that they appear appropriately.
8. Submit the revised database in the format specified by your instructor.
9. In this assignment you stored images as OLE Object and Attachment fields. What differences did you notice on the form? Which storage method do you prefer and why?

Consider This: Your Turn

Apply your creative thinking and problem solving skills to design and implement a solution.

Note: To complete this assignment, you will be required to use the Data Files for Students. Visit www.cengage.com/ct/studentdownload for detailed instructions or contact your instructor for information about accessing the required files.

1: Adding Fields and Creating Multiple-Table Forms for the Artisan Crafts Database

Personal/Academic

Instructions: Open the Your Turn 1 Artisan Crafts database you used in Chapter 4. If you did not create this database, see your instructor about accessing the required files.

Part 1: You need to add some additional data to the Student table. You also need to create a form for the Student table that shows items made by each student. Use the concepts and techniques presented in this chapter to perform each of the following tasks:

a. Add a Picture field and a Biography field to the Student table. The Picture field will store a picture of the student and the Biography field will store a Word document that contains a brief biography of the student.

b. Add the data for these fields to the Student table. For the pictures, select pictures from the Data File for Students or use your own photos. For the biographies, create a brief biography of each student in Word and attach the Word files.

c. Create a Student Master Form for the Student table that is similar in design to the form shown in Figure 5–1 on page AC 267. Include the Student Code, First Name, Last Name, Phone, Picture, and Biography fields from the Student table on the form. The subform should display the Item Number, Description, Price, and On Hand fields from the Item table. Customize the form by adding special effects to controls and labels and by changing the background color of the form. Add a title and the current date to the form header.

Submit your assignment in the format specified by your instructor.

Part 2: You made several decisions while adding the fields and creating the form for this assignment. What was the rationale behind your decisions? Would you add any additional files to the Attachments field? Would you add any additional fields to the Student table?

2: Adding Fields and Creating Multiple-Table Forms for the Carel Landscaping Database

Professional

Instructions: Open the Your Turn 2 Carel Landscaping database that you used in Chapter 4. If you did not create this database, see your instructor about accessing the required files.

Part 1: The owner of Carel Landscaping would like you to add some fields to the Supervisor table. He also would like to create a form for the Supervisor table that shows the customers of each supervisor. Use the concepts and techniques presented in this chapter to perform each of the following tasks:

a. Add a phone number field, a picture field, and a notes field to the Supervisor table. The phone number field should have an input mask.

b. Add the data for these fields to the Supervisor table. Create phone numbers to store in the phone number field. For the pictures, select pictures from the Data File for Students or use your own photos. For the Notes field, add the notes shown in Table 5–4 on the next page. Make sure all data appears in the datasheet.

Continued >

Consider This: Your Turn *continued*

Table 5–4 Data for Supplier Table

Supervisor Number	Notes
39	Has an AA degree in Horticulture. Working on a BS in Biology.
41	Has an AA degree in Landscaping.
52	Has a BA in Spanish.

c. Create a Supervisor Master Form for the Supervisor table that is similar in design to the form shown in Figure 5–1 on page AC 267. Include the Supervisor Number, First Name, Last Name, Phone Number, Hourly Rate, Start Date, Picture, and Notes fields from the Supervisor table on the form. The subform should display the Customer Number, Customer Name, Amount Paid, and Balance fields from the Customer table. Customize the form by adding special effects to controls and labels and by changing the background color of the form. Add a title and the current date to the form header.

d. Create a query that finds all supervisors who started after January 1, 2013 and have a degree in landscaping.

Submit your assignment in the format specified by your instructor.

Part 2: You made several decisions while adding the fields and creating the form for this assignment. What was the rationale behind your decisions? Would you add any additional fields to the Supervisor table?

3: Understanding Fields, Multiple-Table Forms, and Object Dependencies

Research and Collaboration

Part 1: Before you begin this assignment, the team should save the Bavant Publishing database as your team name database. For example, if your team is the Fab Five, then name the database Fab Five.

a. As a team, decide if there are any fields that could be added to the Customer table. For example, it might be useful to have a hyperlink field that contains the website for the customer and another hyperlink field that contains an email address for the customer. Also, a field that contains additional notes about each customer may be appropriate. Modify the Customer table design to accommodate these new fields. Then, add data to the fields. You can use existing websites for various schools in your area.

b. Create a Multiple-Table form based on the Customer table and include the book rep's first and last name on the form. Users should not be able to update the book rep name fields. Experiment with resizing the form. Change the tab order of the fields.

c. Determine the object dependencies for each table in the database. Create a blog, a Google document, or a Word document on the SkyDrive on which to store a short report that explains the importance of understanding object dependencies.

Submit your assignment in the format specified by your instructor.

Part 2: You made several decisions while adding these fields and creating the forms for this assignment. What was the rationale behind your decisions?

Learn Online

Reinforce what you learned in this chapter with games, exercises, training, and many other online activities and resources.

Student Companion Site Reinforcement activities and resources are available at no additional cost on www.cengagebrain.com. Visit www.cengage.com/ct/studentdownload for detailed instructions about accessing the resources available at the Student Companion Site.

SAM Put your skills into practice with SAM! If you have a SAM account, go to www.cengage.com/sam2013 to access SAM assignments for this chapter.

6 Advanced Report Techniques

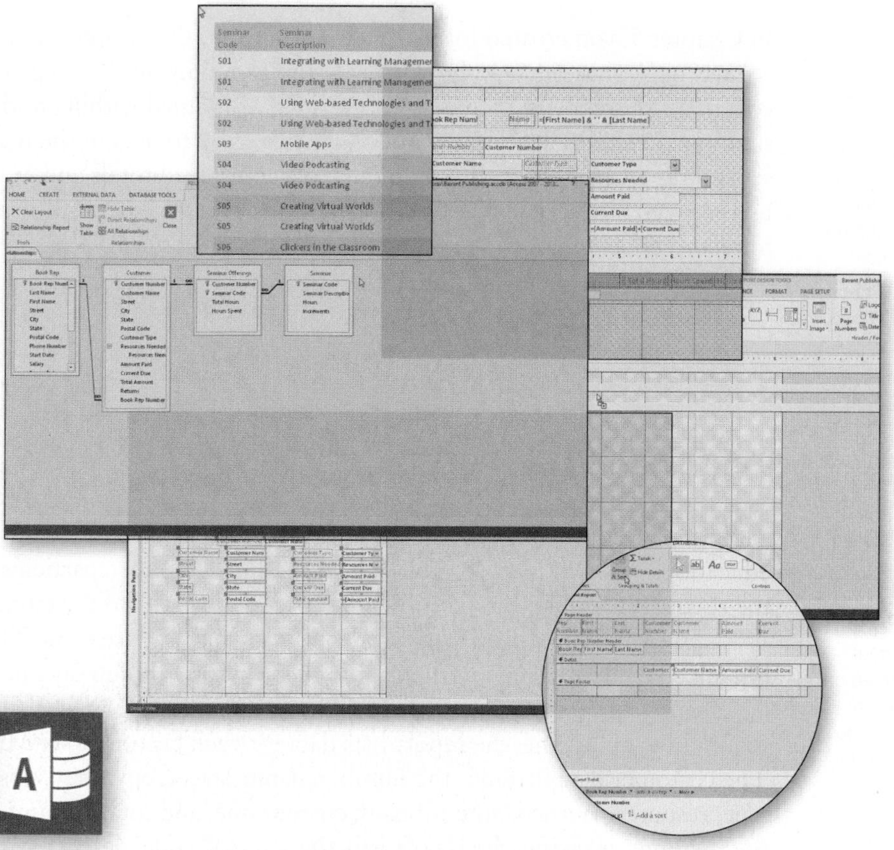

Objectives

You will have mastered the material in this project when you can:

- Create and relate additional tables
- Create queries for reports
- Create reports in Design view
- Add fields and text boxes to a report
- Format report controls
- Group and ungroup report controls
- Update multiple report controls
- Add and modify a subreport
- Modify section properties
- Add a title, page number, and date to a report
- Preview, print, and publish a report
- Add totals and subtotals to a report
- Include a conditional value in a report

6 | Advanced Report Techniques

Introduction

BTW
Q&As
For a complete list of the Q&As found in many of the step-by-step sequences in this book, visit the Q&A resource on the Student Companion Site located on www.cengagebrain.com. For detailed instructions about accessing available resources, visit www.cengage.com/ct/studentdownload or contact your instructor for information about accessing the required files.

In Chapter 5, you created forms in Design view. In this chapter, you will create two reports in Design view. Both reports feature grouping and sorting. The first report contains a subreport, which is a report that is contained within another report. The subreport contains data from a query and is related to data in the main report. The second report uses aggregate functions to calculate subtotals and grand totals. It also uses a function to calculate a value where the actual calculation will vary from record to record depending on whether a given criterion is true.

Project — Creating Detailed Reports

BTW
BTWs
For a complete list of the BTWs found in the margins of this book, visit the BTW resource on the Student Companion Site located on www.cengagebrain.com. For detailed instructions about accessing available resources, visit www.cengage.com/ct/studentdownload or contact your instructor for information about accessing the required files.

Bavant Publishing wants a master list of book reps. This list should be available as an Access report and will have the name, Book Rep Master List. For each book rep, the report will include full details for all the customers assigned to the book rep. In addition, Bavant offers seminars designed to help customers understand the various educational tools available to them. For customers who are participating in seminars, the report should list the specific seminars being offered to the customer.

The Book Rep Master List report is shown in Figure 6–1a. The report is organized by book rep, with the data for each rep beginning on a new page. For each book rep, the report lists the number, first name, and last name. Following the book rep number and name, the report lists data for each customer served by that book rep. The customer data includes the number, name, street, city, state, postal code, customer type, resources needed, amount paid, current due, and total amount. For each seminar the customer is taking, the report lists the seminar code, description, total hours the seminar requires, hours already spent, and hours remaining.

To attract new customers and reward current customers, many publishers offer discounts. Bavant is considering the effect of offering a discount on the current due amount to its current customers. The exact amount of the discount depends on how much the customer already has paid. If the amount paid is more than \$20,000, the discount will be 4 percent of the current due amount. If the amount paid is \$20,000 or less, then the discount will be 2 percent of the current due amount. To assist in determining the discount, Bavant needs a report like the one shown in Figure 6–1b on page AC 332. The report groups customers by book rep. It includes subtotals of both the Amount Paid and Current Due fields. In addition, although not visible in the figure, it includes grand totals of both fields at the end of the report. Finally, it shows the discount amount, which is calculated by multiplying the current due amount by .04 (4 percent) for those customers for whom the amount paid is more than \$20,000.00 and by .02 (2 percent) for all others.

Roadmap

In this chapter, you will learn how to create the reports shown in Figure 6–1. The following roadmap identifies general activities you will perform as you progress through this chapter:

1. CREATE and relate additional TABLES.
2. CREATE QUERIES for a report.
3. CREATE a REPORT.
4. SPECIFY GROUPING AND SORTING.
5. Add fields and TEXT BOXES to the report.
6. ADD a SUBREPORT to the report.
7. ADD a TITLE, PAGE NUMBER, AND DATE to the report.
8. CREATE a SECOND REPORT.

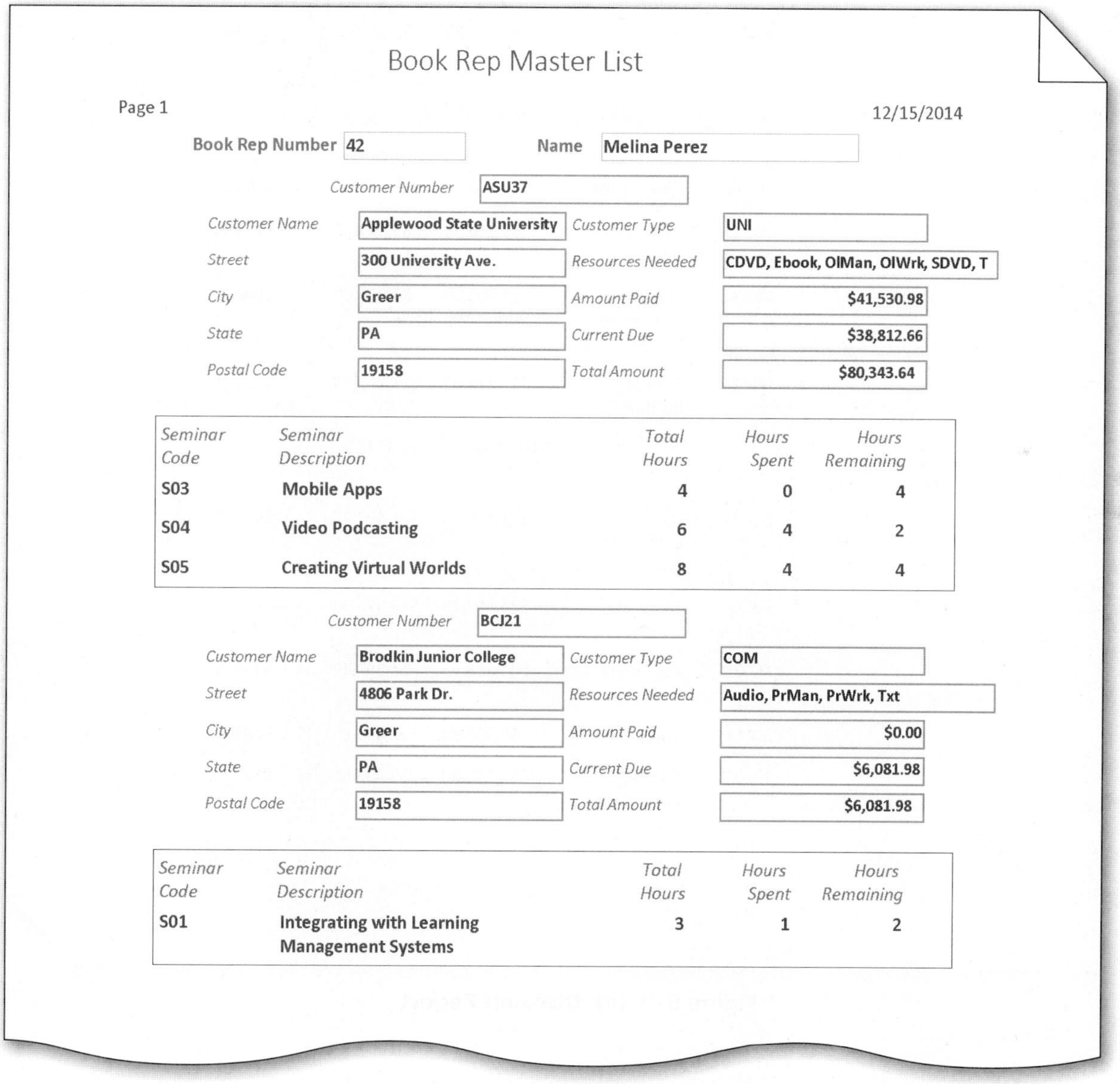

Figure 6–1 (a) Book Rep Master List

Discount Report

Rep Number	First Name	Last Name	Customer Number	Customer Name	Amount Paid	Current Due	Discount
42	Melina	Perez					
			ASU37	Applewood State University	$41,530.98	$38,812.66	$1,552.51
			BCJ21	Brodkin Junior College	$0.00	$6,081.98	$121.64
			CRU11	Cristie University	$0.00	$14,250.00	$285.00
			FSU23	Farnham State University	$18,268.00	$22,024.50	$440.49
			MEC56	Mehitable College	$9,111.19	$7,310.76	$146.22
			SCC77	Stallone Community College	$7,525.98	$2,515.78	$50.32
				Subtotals	$76,436.15	$90,995.68	
53	Robert	Chin					
			CSD25	Cowpens ISD	$12,750.00	$13,275.00	$265.50
			CSU10	Camellia State University	$63,246.88	$69,847.76	$2,793.91
			MCC45	Mauldin Community College	$9,500.00	$5,000.00	$100.00
			PLI22	Pratt-Last Institute	$17,229.45	$11,769.75	$235.40
				Subtotals	$102,726.33	$99,892.51	
65	Tracy	Rogers					
			DCC34	Dartt Community College	$21,345.50	$23,467.75	$938.71
			FSC12	First State College	$34,557.25	$23,875.98	$955.04
			KCC78	Key Community College System	$21,288.65	$11,367.49	$454.70
			SEC19	Seaborn College	$9,225.34	$10,496.89	$209.94
			TSC02	Tri-State Consortium	$34,578.90	$9,432.56	$377.30

Page 1 12/15/2014

Figure 6–1 (b) Discount Report

At the beginning of step instructions throughout the chapter, you will see an abbreviated form of this roadmap. The abbreviated roadmap uses colors to indicate chapter progress: gray means the chapter is beyond that activity; blue means the task being shown is covered in that activity; and black means that activity is yet to be covered. For example, the following abbreviated roadmap indicates the chapter would be showing a task in the 3 CREATE REPORT activity.

1 CREATE TABLES | 2 CREATE QUERIES | 3 CREATE REPORT | 4 SPECIFY GROUPING & SORTING | 5 ADD FIELDS
6 ADD SUBREPORT | 7 ADD TITLE, PAGE NUMBER, & DATE | 8 CREATE SECOND REPORT

Use the abbreviated roadmap as a progress guide while you read or step through the instructions in this chapter.

To Run Access

If you are using a computer to step through the project in this chapter and you want your screens to match the figures in this book, you should change your screen's resolution to 1366 × 768. For information about how to change a computer's resolution, refer to the Office and Windows chapter at the beginning of this book.

The following steps, which assume Windows is running, use the Start screen or the search box to run Access based on a typical installation. You may need to ask your instructor how to run Access on your computer. For a detailed example of the procedure summarized below, refer to the Office and Windows chapter.

BTW
The Ribbon and Screen Resolution
Access may change how the groups and buttons within the groups appear on the ribbon, depending on the computer's screen resolution. Thus, your ribbon may look different from the ones in this book if you are using a screen resolution other than 1366 × 768.

1. Scroll the Start screen for an Access 2013 tile. If your Start screen contains an Access 2013 tile, tap or click it to run Access; if the Start screen does not contain the Access 2013 tile, proceed to the next step to search for the Access app.
2. Swipe in from the right edge of the screen or point to the upper-right corner of the screen to display the Charms bar, and then tap or click the Search charm on the Charms bar to display the Search menu.
3. Type `Access` as the search text in the Search text box and watch the search results appear in the Apps list.
4. Tap or click Access 2013 in the search results to run Access.

To Open a Database from Access

The following steps open the Bavant Publishing database from the location you specified when you first created it (for example, the Access folder in the CIS 101 folder). For a detailed example of the procedure summarized below, refer to the Office and Windows chapter at the beginning of this book.

1. Tap or click FILE on the ribbon to open the Backstage view, if necessary.
2. If the database you want to open is displayed in the Recent list, tap or click the file name to open the database and display the opened database in the Access window; then skip to Step 7. If the database you want to open is not displayed in the Recent list or if the Recent list does not appear, tap or click Open Other Files to display the Open Gallery.
3. If the database you want to open is displayed in the Recent list in the Open gallery, tap or click the file name to open the database and display the opened database in the Access window; then skip to Step 7.

4. Tap or click Computer, SkyDrive, or another location in the left pane and then navigate to the location of the database to be opened (for example, the Access folder in the CIS 101 folder).
5. Tap or click Bavant Publishing to select the database to be opened.
6. Tap or click the Open button (Open dialog box) to open the selected file and display the opened database in the Access window.
7. If a Security Warning appears, tap or click the Enable Content button.

Additional Tables

BTW
Touch Screen Differences
The Office and Windows interfaces may vary if you are using a touch screen. For this reason, you might notice that the function or appearance of your touch screen differs slightly from this chapter's presentation.

Because the book reps at Bavant work collaboratively with customers as learning consultants, they are frequently asked to present seminars on education technologies and techniques for integrating educational resources into the classroom. Bavant would like to incorporate this data in the Bavant Publishing database.

Before creating the reports, you need to create two additional tables for the Bavant Publishing database. The first table, Seminar, is shown in Tables 6–1a and 6–1b. As described in Table 6–1a, each seminar has a number and a description. The table also includes the total hours for which the seminar usually is offered and its increments; that is, the standard time blocks in which the seminar usually is offered. Table 6–1b contains the specific seminars that the book reps at Bavant Publishing offer to their customers. The first row, for example, indicates that seminar S01 is called Integrating with Learning Management Systems. It typically is offered in one-hour increments for a total of three hours.

BTW
AutoNumber Field as Primary Key
When you create a table in Datasheet view, Access automatically creates an ID field with the AutoNumber data type as the primary key field. As you add records to the table, Access increments the ID field so that each record will have a unique value in the field. AutoNumber fields are useful when there is no data field in a table that is a suitable primary key.

Table 6–1a Structure of Seminar Table

Field Name	Data Type	Field Size	Comments
Seminar Code	Short Text	3	Primary Key
Seminar Description	Short Text	50	
Hours	Number	Integer	
Increments	Number	Integer	

Table 6–1b Seminar Table

Seminar Code	Seminar Description	Hours	Increments
S01	Integrating with Learning Management Systems	3	1
S02	Using Web-based Technologies and Tools	2	1
S03	Mobile Apps	4	2
S04	Video Podcasting	6	2
S05	Creating Virtual Worlds	8	2
S06	Clickers in the Classroom	2	1
S07	Online Course Strategies	3	1
S08	Using Social Networking	4	2

The second table, Seminar Offerings, is described in Table 6–2a and contains a customer number, a seminar code, the total number of hours that the seminar is scheduled for the customer, and the number of hours already spent in the seminar. The primary key of the Seminar Offerings table is a combination of the Customer Number and Seminar Code fields.

Table 6–2b gives the data for the Seminar Offerings table. For example, the first record shows that customer number ASU37 currently has scheduled seminar S03 (Mobile Apps). The seminar is scheduled for four hours, and they have not yet spent any hours in class.

If you examine the data in Table 6–2b, you see that the Customer Number field cannot be the primary key for the Seminar Offerings table. The first and second records, for example, both have a customer number of ASU37. The Seminar Code field also cannot be the primary key. The second and ninth records, for example, both have seminar code S04. Rather, the primary key is the combination of both Customer Number and Seminar Code.

BTW

Copy the Structure of a Table

If you want to create a table that has a structure similar to an existing table, you can copy the structure of the table only. Select the table in the Navigation Pane and tap or click Copy, then tap or click Paste. In the Paste Table As dialog box, type the new table name and tap or click the Structure Only option button. Then, tap or click the OK button. To modify the new table, open it in Design view.

Table 6–2a Structure of Seminar Offerings Table

Field Name	Data Type	Field Size	Comments
Customer Number	Short Text	5	Part of Primary Key
Seminar Code	Short Text	3	Part of Primary Key
Total Hours	Number	Integer	
Hours Spent	Number	Integer	

BTW

Many-to-Many Relationships

There is a many-to-many relationship between the Customer table and the Seminar table. To implement a many-to-many relationship in a relational database management system such as Access, you create a third table, often called a junction or intersection table, that has as its primary key the combination of the primary keys of each of the tables involved in the many-to-many relationship. The primary key of the Seminar Offerings table is the combination of the Customer Number and the Seminar Code fields.

Table 6–2b Seminar Offerings Table

Customer Number	Seminar Code	Total Hours	Hours Spent
ASU37	S03	4	0
ASU37	S04	6	4
ASU37	S05	8	4
BCJ21	S01	3	1
CRU11	S06	2	0
CSD25	S07	3	2
CSU10	S02	2	1
CSU10	S08	4	2
FSC12	S04	6	2
FSC12	S06	2	1
KCC78	S05	8	2
MCC45	S01	3	2
MEC56	S07	3	0
SEC19	S02	2	1
SEC19	S07	3	1

To Create the New Tables

1 CREATE TABLES | 2 CREATE QUERIES | 3 CREATE REPORT | 4 SPECIFY GROUPING & SORTING | 5 ADD FIELDS
6 ADD SUBREPORT | 7 ADD TITLE, PAGE NUMBER, & DATE | 8 CREATE SECOND REPORT

You will use Design view to create the new tables. The steps to create the new tables are similar to the steps you used previously to add fields to an existing table and to define primary keys. The only difference is the way you specify a primary key. ***Why?*** *In the Seminar Offerings table, the primary key consists of more than one field.*

To specify a primary key containing more than one field, you must select both fields that make up the primary key by tapping or clicking the row selector for the first field, and then hold down the SHIFT key while tapping or clicking the row selector for the second field. Once the fields are selected, you can use the Primary Key button to indicate that the primary key consists of both fields.

The following steps create the tables in Design view.

1

- If necessary, close the Navigation Pane.
- Display the CREATE tab (Figure 6–2).

2

- Tap or click the Table Design button (CREATE tab | Tables group) to create a table in Design view.
- Enter the information for the fields in the Seminar table as indicated in Table 6–1a on page AC 334, selecting Seminar Code as the primary key, and selecting the indicated field sizes.
- Save the table using the name `Seminar` and close the table.

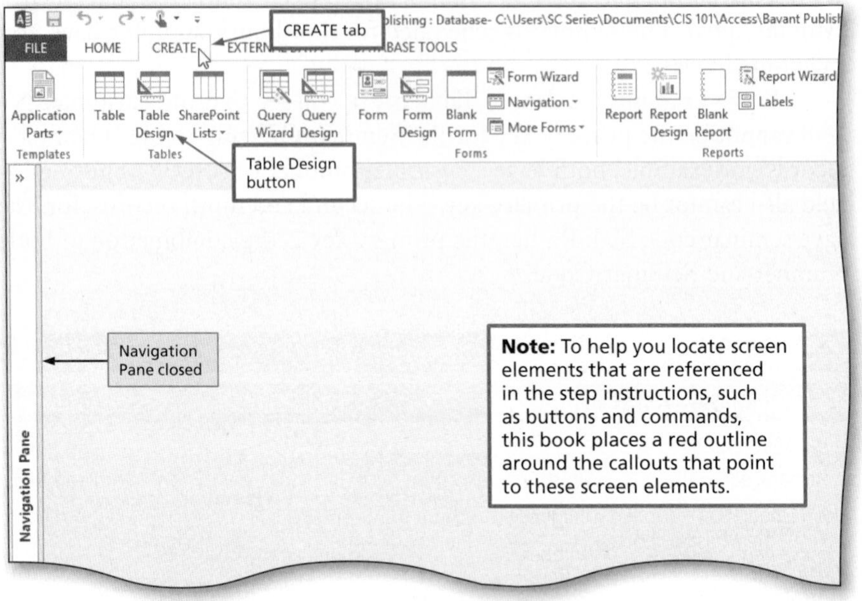

Figure 6–2

3

- Display the CREATE tab and then tap or click the Table Design button (CREATE tab | Tables group) to create a second table in Design view.
- Enter the information for the fields in the Seminar Offerings table as indicated in Table 6–2a on the previous page.
- Tap or click the row selector for the Customer Number field.
- Hold down the SHIFT key and then tap or click the row selector for the Seminar Code field so both fields are selected.
- Tap or click the Primary Key button (TABLE TOOLS DESIGN tab | Tools group) to select the combination of the two fields as the primary key (Figure 6–3).

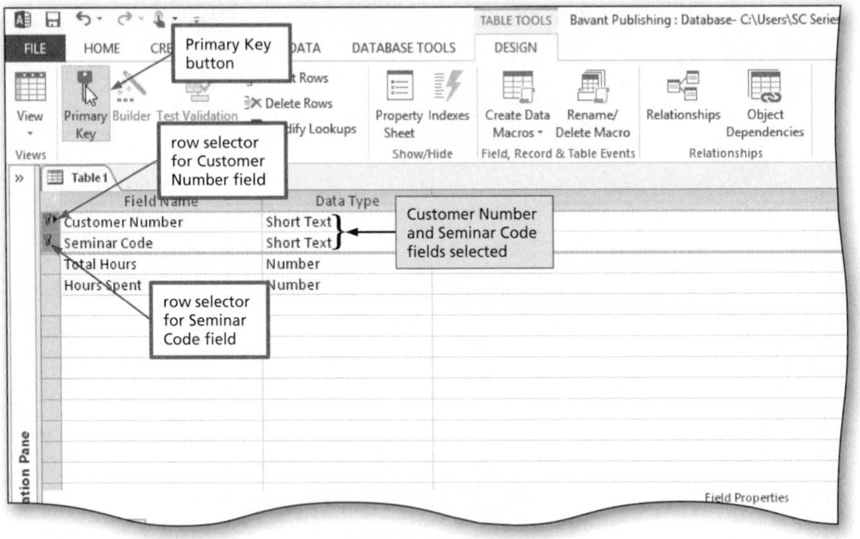

Figure 6–3

4

- Save the table using the name Seminar Offerings and close the table.

Q&A I realized I designated the wrong fields as the primary key. How can I correct the primary key?

Click any field that participates in the primary key, and click the Primary Key button to remove the primary key. You then can specify the correct primary key.

To Import the Data

Now that the tables have been created, you need to add data to them. You could enter the data manually, or if the data is already in electronic form, you could import the data. The data for the Seminar and Seminar Offerings tables is included in the Data Files for Students. The files are text files formatted as delimited files. The Seminar data is in a tab-delimited text (.txt) file, and the Seminar Offerings data is in a comma-separated values (.csv) file, which is also a delimited text file. The following steps import the data.

1. With the Bavant Publishing database open, display the EXTERNAL DATA tab and then tap or click the Text File button (EXTERNAL DATA tab | Import & Link group) to display the Get External Data - Text File dialog box.
2. Tap or click the Browse button (Get External Data - Text File dialog box) and then navigate to the location containing the text file (for example, the Access folder in the CIS 101 folder). For a detailed example of this procedure, refer to Steps 3a – 3b in the To Save a File in a Folder section in the Office and Windows chapter at the beginning of this book.
3. Select the Seminar file and tap or click the Open button.
4. Select the 'Append a copy of the records to the table' option button, select the Seminar table from the drop-down list, and then tap or click the OK button. With the Delimited option button selected, tap or click the Next button.
5. With the Tab option button selected, tap or click the 'First Row Contains Field Names' check box, tap or click the Next button, and then tap or click the Finish button.
6. Tap or click the Close button to close the Get External Data - Text Box dialog box without saving the import steps.
7. Use the technique shown in Steps 1 through 6 to import the Seminar Offerings.csv file into the Seminar Offerings table. Be sure the Comma option button is selected and there is a check mark in the 'First Row Contains Field Names' check box.

Q&A

I got an error message after I tapped or clicked the Finish button that indicated there were errors. The data was not imported. What should I do?

First, tap or click the Cancel button to terminate the process. Then, review the structure of the table in Design view to ensure that the field names are all spelled correctly and that the data types are correct. Correct any errors you find, save your work, and then redo the steps to import the data.

Linking versus Importing

When an external table or worksheet is imported into an Access database, a copy of the data is placed in a table in the database. The original data still exists, just as it did before, but no further connection exists between it and the data in the database. Changes to the original data do not affect the data in the database. Likewise, changes in the database do not affect the original data.

It also is possible to link data stored in a variety of formats to Access databases. To do so, you would select the 'Link to the data source by creating a linked table' option button when importing data, rather than the 'Import the source data into a new table in the current database' or 'Append a copy of the records to the table' option buttons. With linking, the connection is maintained; changes made to the data in the external table or worksheet affect the Access table.

BTW

Linking

Two of the primary reasons to link data from another program to Access are to use the query and report features of Access. When you link an Access database to data in another program, all changes to the data must be made in the source program. For example, if you link an Excel workbook to an Access database, you cannot edit the linked table in Access. You must make all changes to the data in Excel.

To identify that a table is linked to other data, Access displays an arrow in front of the table in the Navigation Pane. In addition, an icon is displayed in front of the name that indicates the type of file to which the data is linked. For example, an Excel icon in front of the name indicates that the table is linked to an Excel worksheet.

To Modify Linked Tables

After you link tables between a worksheet and a database or between two databases, you can modify many of the linked table's features. To rename the linked table, set view properties, and set links between tables in queries, you would use the following steps.

1. Tap or click the 'Linked Table Manager' button (EXTERNAL DATA tab | Import & Link group) to update the links.
2. Select the linked table for which you want to update the links.
3. Tap or click the OK button.

To Relate the New Tables

1 CREATE TABLES | 2 CREATE QUERIES | 3 CREATE REPORT | 4 SPECIFY GROUPING & SORTING | 5 ADD FIELDS
6 ADD SUBREPORT | 7 ADD TITLE, PAGE NUMBER, & DATE | 8 CREATE SECOND REPORT

The following steps relate the tables. ***Why?*** *The new tables need to be related to the existing tables in the Bavant Publishing database. The Customer and Seminar Offerings tables are related through the Customer Number field that exists in both tables. The Seminar and Seminar Offerings tables are related through the Seminar Code fields in both tables.*

1

- If necessary, close any open datasheet on the screen by tapping or clicking its Close button, and then display the DATABASE TOOLS tab.
- Tap or click the Relationships button (DATABASE TOOLS tab | Relationships group) to open the Relationships window (Figure 6–4).

Q&A I only see one table, did I do something wrong?
Tap or click the All Relationships button to display all the tables in relationships.

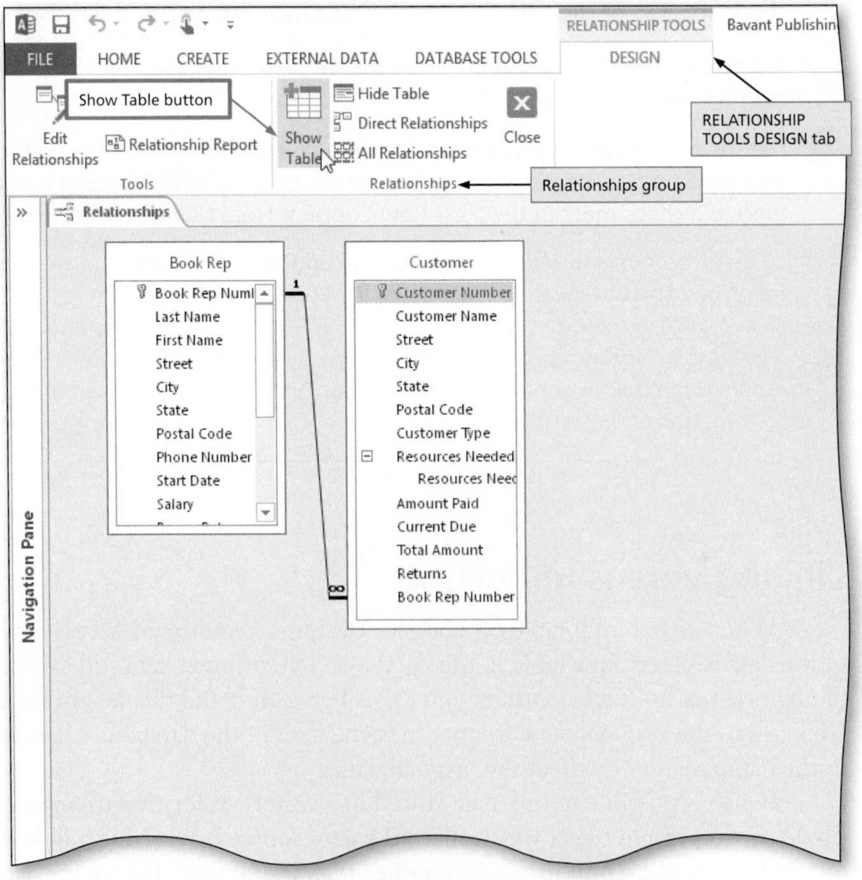

Figure 6–4

2

- Tap or click the Show Table button (RELATIONSHIP TOOLS DESIGN tab | Relationships group) to display the Show Table dialog box (Figure 6–5).

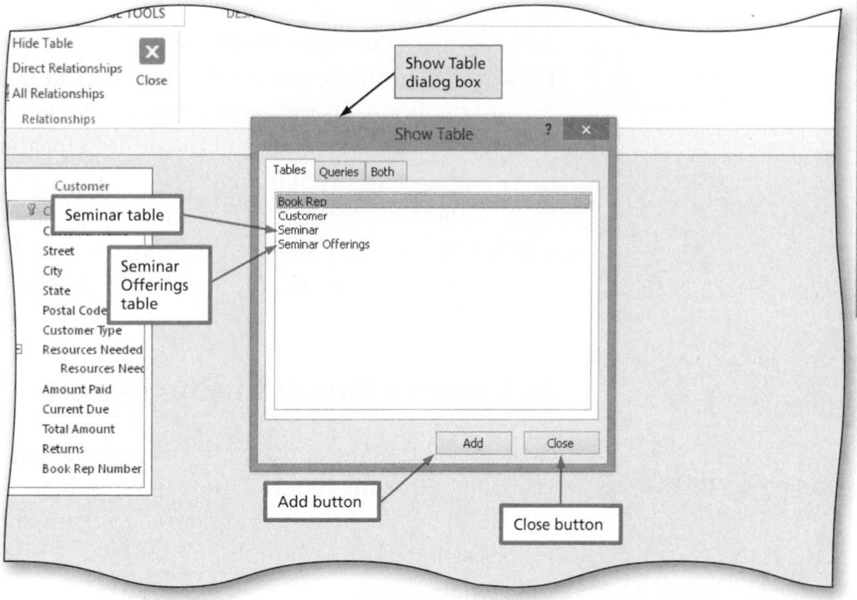

Figure 6–5

3

- Tap or click the Seminar Offerings table, tap or click the Add button (Show Table dialog box), tap or click the Seminar table, tap or click the Add button again, and then tap or click the Close button to add the tables to the Relationships window.

Q&A I cannot see the Seminar Offerings table. Should I repeat the step?
If you cannot see the table, it is behind the dialog box. You do not need to repeat the step.

- Drag the Customer Number field in the Customer table to the Customer Number field in the Seminar Offerings table to display the Edit Relationships dialog box. Tap or click the 'Enforce Referential Integrity' check box (Edit Relationships dialog box) and then tap or click the Create button to create the relationship.

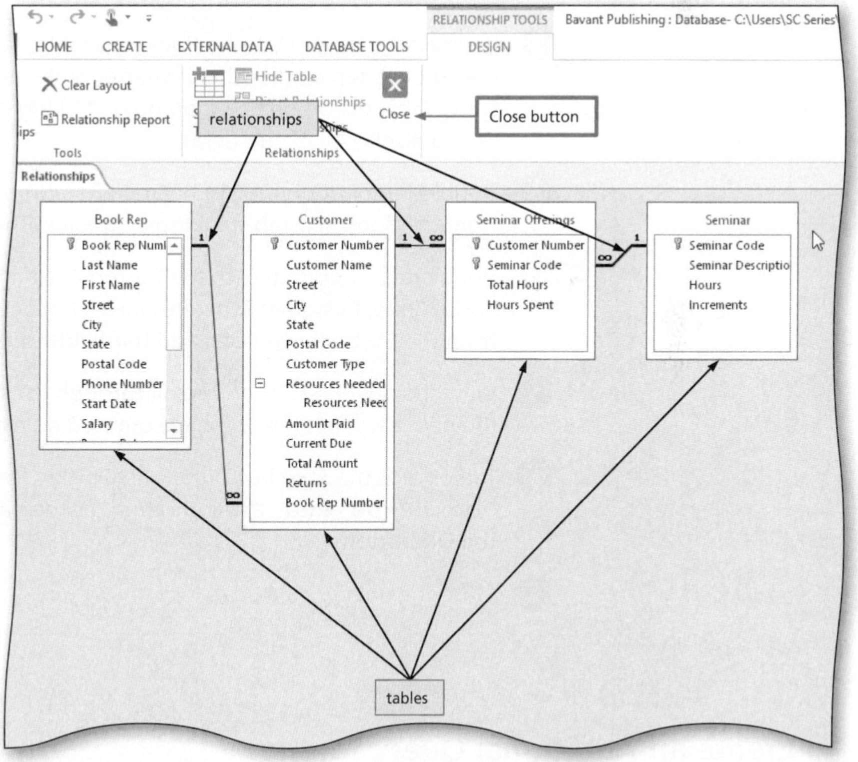

Figure 6–6

- Drag the Seminar Code field from the Seminar table to the Seminar Code field in the Seminar Offerings table. Tap or click the 'Enforce Referential Integrity' check box (Edit Relationships dialog box) and then tap or click the Create button to create the relationship (Figure 6–6).

4

- Tap or click the Save button on the Quick Access Toolbar to save the changes and then tap or click the Close button (RELATIONSHIP TOOLS DESIGN tab | Relationships group).

Creating Reports in Design View

BTW
Touch and Pointers
Remember that if you are using your finger on a touch screen, you will not see the pointer.

Previously, you have used both Layout view and the Report Wizard to create reports. However, you simply can create the report in Design view. You also can use Design view to modify a report you previously created. If you create a report in Design view, you must place all the fields in the desired locations. You also must specify any sorting or grouping that is required.

Whether you use the wizard or simply use Design view, you must determine on which table or query to base the report. If you decide to base the report on a query, you first must create the query, unless it already exists.

To Create a Query for the Report

BTW
On-Screen Keyboard
To display the on-screen touch keyboard, tap the Touch Keyboard button on the Windows taskbar. When finished using the touch keyboard, tap the X button on the touch keyboard to close the keyboard.

Bavant's requirements for the reports specify that it would be convenient to use two queries for the report. These queries do not yet exist. You will need to create the two queries. The first query relates book reps and customers, and the second query relates seminars and seminar offerings. The following steps create the Book Reps and Customers query.

1. If necessary, close the Navigation Pane, display the CREATE tab, and then tap or click the Query Design button (CREATE tab | Queries group) to create a new query.
2. If necessary, tap or click the Book Rep table, tap or click the Add button (Show Table dialog box), tap or click the Customer table, tap or click the Add button, close the Show Table dialog box by tapping or clicking its Close button, and then resize the field lists to display all of the fields.
3. Double-tap or double-click the Book Rep Number, First Name, and Last Name fields from the Book Rep table to display them in the design grid.
4. Double-tap or double-click the Customer Number, Customer Name, Street, City, State, Postal Code, Customer Type, Resources Needed, Amount Paid, and Current Due fields from the Customer table to add the fields to the design grid.
5. View the query results and scroll through the fields to make sure you have included all the necessary fields. If you have omitted a field, return to Design view and add it.
6. Tap or click the Save button on the Quick Access Toolbar to save the query, type `Book Reps and Customers` as the name of the query, and then tap or click the OK button.
7. Close the query.

To Create an Additional Query for the Report Using Expression Builder

1 CREATE TABLES | 2 CREATE QUERIES | 3 CREATE REPORT | 4 SPECIFY GROUPING & SORTING | 5 ADD FIELDS
6 ADD SUBREPORT | 7 ADD TITLE, PAGE NUMBER, & DATE | 8 CREATE SECOND REPORT

The following steps create the Seminar Offerings and Seminars query that includes a calculated field for hours remaining, that is, the total number of hours minus the hours spent. ***Why?*** *Bavant Publishing needs to include in the Book Rep Master List the number of hours that remain in a seminar offering.*

1

- Display the CREATE tab and then tap or click the Query Design button (CREATE tab | Queries group) to create a new query.
- Tap or click the Seminar table, tap or click the Add button (Show Table dialog box), tap or click the Seminar Offerings table, tap or click the Add button, and then tap or click the Close button to close the Show Table dialog box.
- Double-tap or double-click the Customer Number and Seminar Code fields from the Seminar Offerings table to add the fields to the design grid.
- Double-tap or double-click the Seminar Description field from the Seminar table.
- Double-tap or double-click the Total Hours and Hours Spent fields from the Seminar Offerings table to add the fields to the design grid.
- Tap or click the Field row in the first open column in the design grid to select it.
- Tap or click the Builder button (QUERY TOOLS DESIGN tab | Query Setup group) to display the Expression Builder dialog box (Figure 6–7).

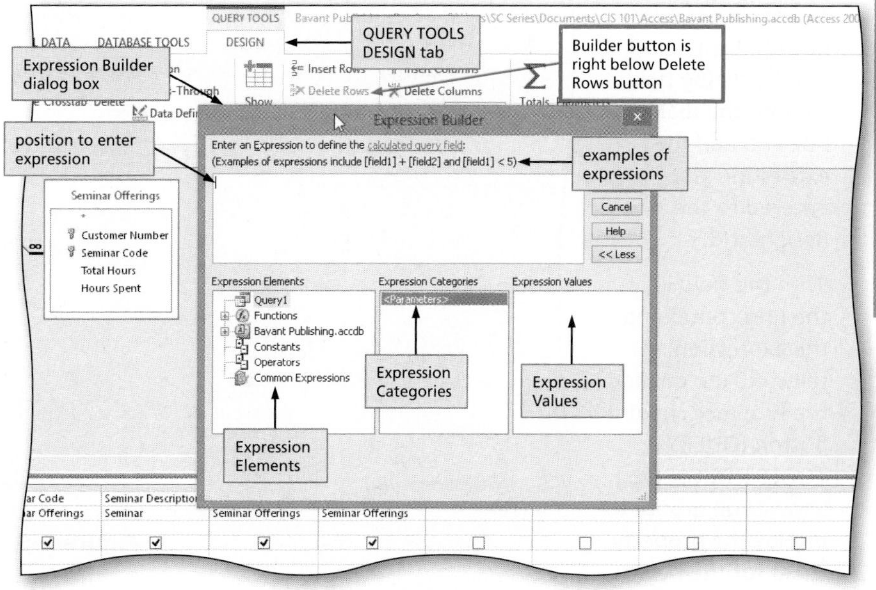

Figure 6–7

2

- Double-tap or double-click Bavant Publishing in the Expression Elements section to display the categories of objects within the Bavant Publishing database, and then double-tap or double-click Tables to display a list of tables.
- Tap or click the Seminar Offerings table to select it.
- Double-tap or double-click the Total Hours field to add it to the expression.
- Type a minus sign (-) to add it to the expression.
- Double-tap or double-click the Hours Spent field to add it to the expression (Figure 6–8).

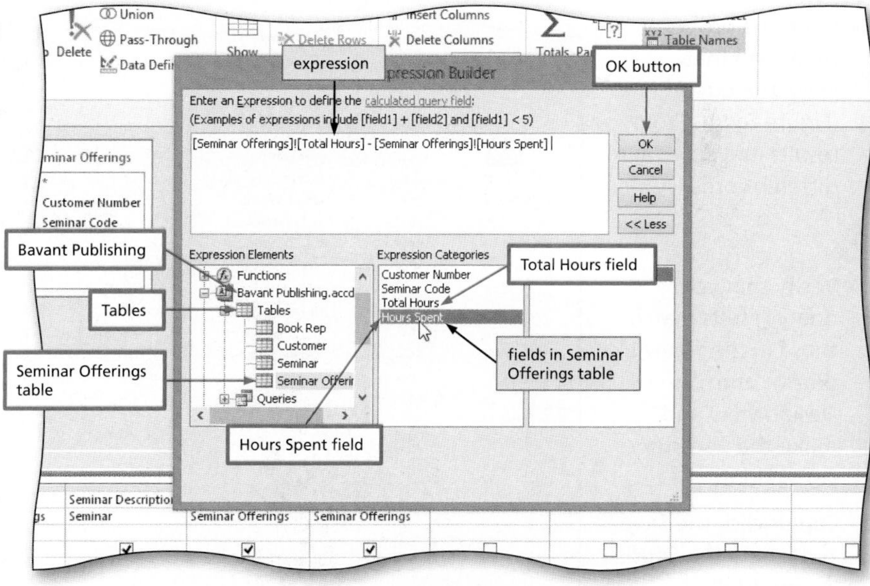

Figure 6–8

Q&A

Why are the fields preceded by a table name and an exclamation point?

This notation qualifies the field; that is, it indicates to which table the field belongs.

Could I type the expression instead of using the Expression Builder?

Yes. You could type it directly into the design grid. You also could press and hold or right-click the column and tap or click Zoom to allow you to type the expression in the Zoom dialog box. Finally, you could use the Expression Builder, but simply type the expression rather than tapping or clicking any buttons. Use whichever method you find most convenient.

3

- Tap or click the OK button (Expression Builder dialog box) to close the dialog box and add the expression you entered to the design grid.
- With the field in the grid containing the expression selected, tap or click the Property Sheet button (QUERY TOOLS DESIGN tab | Show/Hide group) to display the property sheet for the new field.

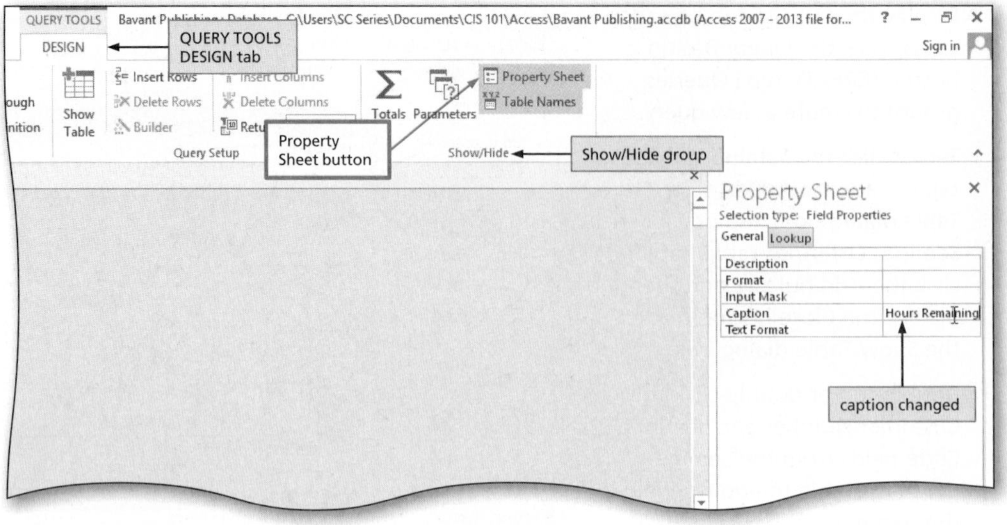

Figure 6–9

- Ensure that the General tab is selected, tap or click the Caption property box and type `Hours Remaining` as the caption (Figure 6–9).

Q&A I do not have a Caption property in my property sheet. What went wrong? What should I do?
You either inadvertently tapped or clicked a different location in the grid, or you have not yet completed entering the expression. The easiest way to ensure you have done both is to tap or click any other column in the grid and then tap or click the column with the expression.

4

- Close the property sheet and then view the query (Figure 6–10). (Your results might be in a different order.)

5

- Verify that your query results match those in the figure. If not, return to Design view and make the necessary corrections.
- Tap or click the Save button on the Quick Access Toolbar, type `Seminar Offerings and Seminars` as the name of the query, and then tap or click the OK button to save the query.
- Close the query.

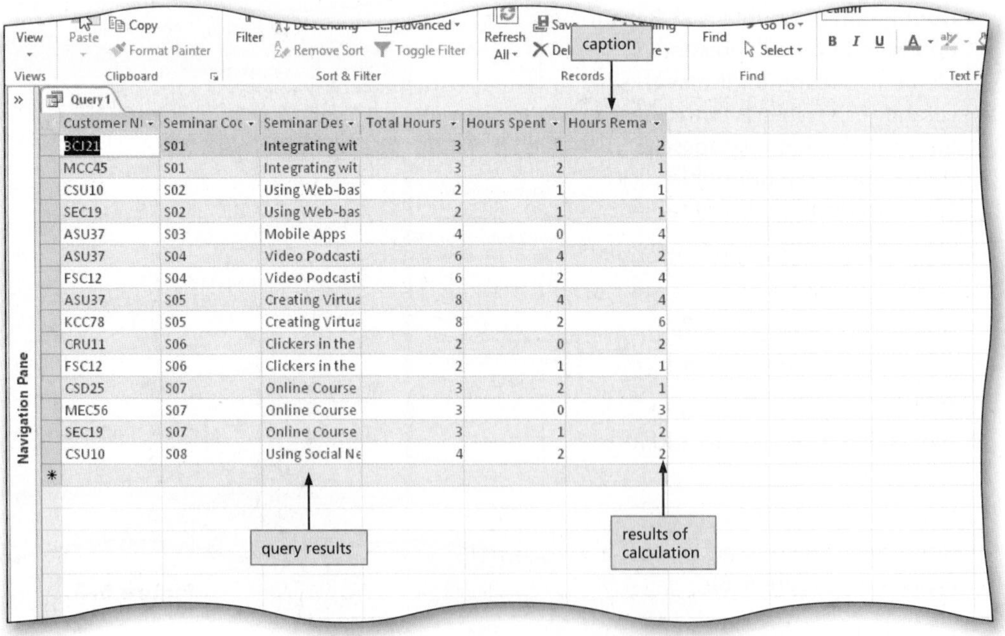

Figure 6–10

Other Ways

1. Press and hold or right-click field in grid, tap or click Build

CONSIDER THIS

How do you determine the tables and fields for the report?
If you determine that data should be presented as a report, you then need to determine what tables and fields contain the data for the report.

Examine the requirements for the report in general to determine the tables. Do the requirements only relate to data in a single table, or does the data come from multiple tables? Is the data in a query, or could you create a query that contains some or all of the fields necessary for the report?

Examine the specific requirements for the report to determine the fields necessary. Look for all the data items that are specified for the report. Each item should correspond to a field in a table, or it should be able to be computed from a field in a table. This information gives you the list of fields to include in the query.

Determine the order of the fields. Examine the requirements to determine the order in which the fields should appear. Be logical and consistent in your ordering. For example, in an address, the city should come before the state, and the state should come before the postal code, unless there is some compelling reason for another order.

CONSIDER THIS

What decisions do you make in determining the organization of the report?
Determine sort order. Is there a special order in which the records should appear?

Determine grouping. Should the records be grouped in some fashion? If so, what information should appear before the records in a group? If, for example, customers are grouped by book rep number, the number of the book rep should probably appear before the group. Should the book rep name also appear? What should appear after the group? For example, are there some fields for which subtotals should be calculated? If so, the subtotals would come after the group.

Determine whether to include a subreport. Rather than use grouping, you can include a subreport, as shown in the Book Rep Master List shown in Figure 6–1a on page AC 331. The data concerning seminar offerings for the customer could have been presented by grouping the seminar offerings' data by customer number. The headings currently in the subreport would have appeared in the group header. Instead, it is presented in a subreport. Subreports, which are reports in their own right, offer more flexibility in formatting than group headers and footers. More important, in the Book Rep Master List, some customers do not have any seminar offerings. If this information were presented using grouping, the group header will still appear for these customers. With a subreport, customers who have no seminar offerings do not appear.

To Create an Initial Report in Design View

1 CREATE TABLES | 2 CREATE QUERIES | 3 CREATE REPORT | 4 SPECIFY GROUPING & SORTING | 5 ADD FIELDS
6 ADD SUBREPORT | 7 ADD TITLE, PAGE NUMBER, & DATE | 8 CREATE SECOND REPORT

Creating the report shown in Figure 6–1a on page AC 331 from scratch involves creating the initial report in Design view, adding the subreport, modifying the subreport separately from the main report, and then making the final modifications to the main report.

When you want to create a report from scratch, you use Design view rather than the Report Wizard. ***Why?*** *The Report Wizard is suitable for simple, customized reports. With Report Design, you can make advanced design changes, such as adding subreports.*

The following steps create the initial version of the Book Rep Master List and select the **record source** for the report; that is, the table or query that will furnish the data for the report. The steps then specify sorting and grouping for the report.

1

- Display the CREATE tab.
- Tap or click the Report Design button (CREATE tab | Reports group) to create a report in Design view.
- Ensure the selector for the entire report, the box in the upper-left corner of the report, contains a small black square, which indicates it is selected.
- Tap or click the Property Sheet button (REPORT DESIGN TOOLS DESIGN tab | Tools group) to display a property sheet.

Q&A Can I make the property sheet box wider so I can see more of the items in the Record Source list?
Yes, you can make the property sheet wider by dragging its left or right border.

- Drag the left border, if necessary to increase the width of the property sheet.

- With the All tab (Property Sheet) selected, tap or click the Record Source property box arrow to display the list of available tables and queries (Figure 6–11).

Q&A Can I move the property sheet?
Yes, you can move the property sheet by dragging its title bar.

2

- Tap or click the Book Reps and Customers query to select the query as the record source for the report.
- Close the property sheet by tapping or clicking the Property Sheet button (REPORT DESIGN TOOLS DESIGN tab | Tools group).

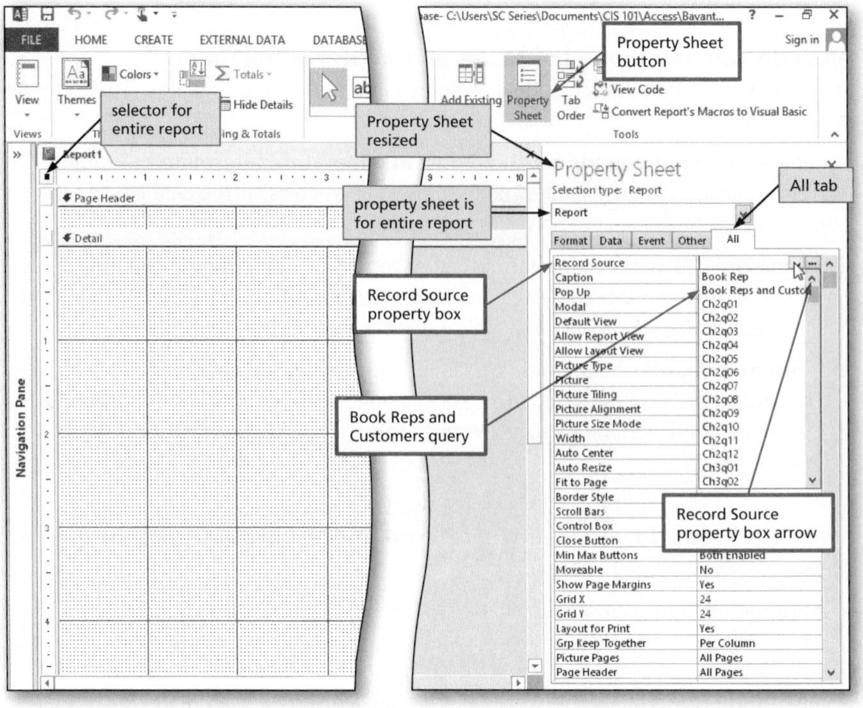

Figure 6–11

Other Ways

1. Press and hold or right-click report selector, tap or click Properties

To Group and Sort

1 CREATE TABLES | 2 CREATE QUERIES | 3 CREATE REPORT | 4 SPECIFY GROUPING & SORTING | 5 ADD FIELDS
6 ADD SUBREPORT | 7 ADD TITLE, PAGE NUMBER, & DATE | 8 CREATE SECOND REPORT

In Design view of the report, you can specify both grouping and sorting by using the Group & Sort button on the DESIGN tab, just as you did in Layout view. The following steps specify both grouping and sorting in the report. ***Why?*** *Bavant has determined that the records in the report should be grouped by book rep number. That is, all the customers of a given book rep should appear together. Within the customers of a given book rep, they have determined that customers are to be ordered by customer number.*

1

- Tap or click the Group & Sort button (REPORT DESIGN TOOLS DESIGN tab | Grouping & Totals group) to display the Group, Sort, and Total pane (Figure 6–12).

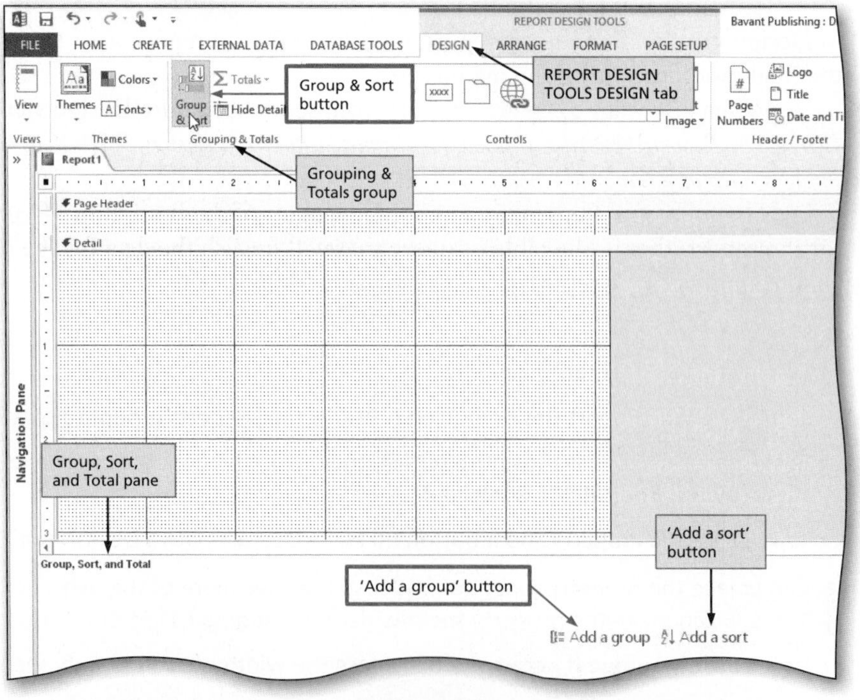

Figure 6–12

2

- Tap or click the 'Add a group' button to display the list of available fields for grouping (Figure 6–13).

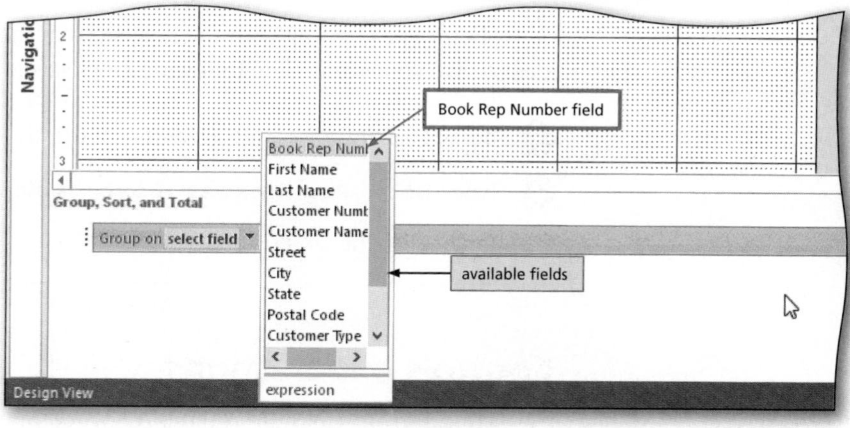

Figure 6–13

3

- Tap or click the Book Rep Number field to group by book rep number (Figure 6–14).

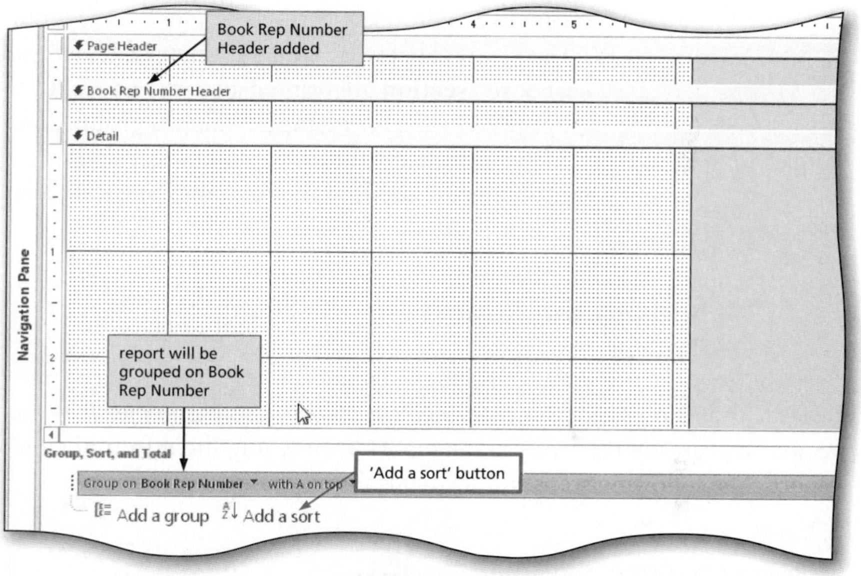

Figure 6–14

4

- Tap or click the 'Add a sort' button to display the list of available fields for sorting (Figure 6–15).

5

- Tap or click the Customer Number field to sort by customer number.

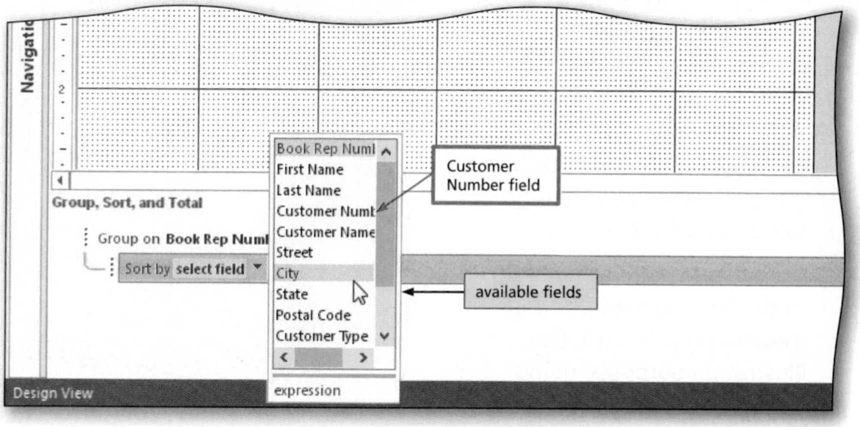

Figure 6–15

Other Ways

1. Press and hold or right-click any open area in the report, tap or click Sorting & Grouping

To Save the Report

Before proceeding with the next steps in the modification of the report, it is a good idea to save your work. The following steps save the report as Book Rep Master List.

1. Tap or click the Save button on the Quick Access Toolbar.
2. Type `Book Rep Master List` as the report name.
3. Tap or click the OK button.

Controls and Sections

Recall from Chapter 4 that a report contains three types of controls: bound controls, unbound controls, and calculated controls. As you learned previously, reports contain standard sections, including the Report Header, Report Footer, Page Header, Page Footer, and Detail sections. When the data in a report is grouped, there are two additional possible sections. The contents of the **Group Header section** are printed before the records in a particular group, and the contents of the **Group Footer section** are printed after the group. In the Discount Report (Figure 6–1b on page AC 332), for example, which is grouped by book rep number, the Group Header section contains the book rep number and name, and the Group Footer section contains subtotals of the Amount Paid and Current Due fields.

To Add Fields to the Report in Design View

1 CREATE TABLES | 2 CREATE QUERIES | 3 CREATE REPORT | 4 SPECIFY GROUPING & SORTING | **5 ADD FIELDS**
6 ADD SUBREPORT | 7 ADD TITLE, PAGE NUMBER, & DATE | 8 CREATE SECOND REPORT

Why? *Once you have determined the fields that are necessary for the report, you need to add them to the report design.* You can add the fields to the report by dragging them from the field list to the appropriate position on the report. The following steps add the fields to the report.

1

- Remove the Group, Sort, and Total pane by tapping or clicking the Group & Sort button, which is shown in Figure 6–12 on page AC 344 (REPORT DESIGN TOOLS DESIGN tab | Grouping & Totals group).
- Tap or click the 'Add Existing Fields' button (REPORT DESIGN TOOLS DESIGN tab | Tools group) to display a field list.
- Drag the Book Rep Number field to the approximate position shown in Figure 6–16. (For illustration purposes, do not release your finger or the mouse button yet.)

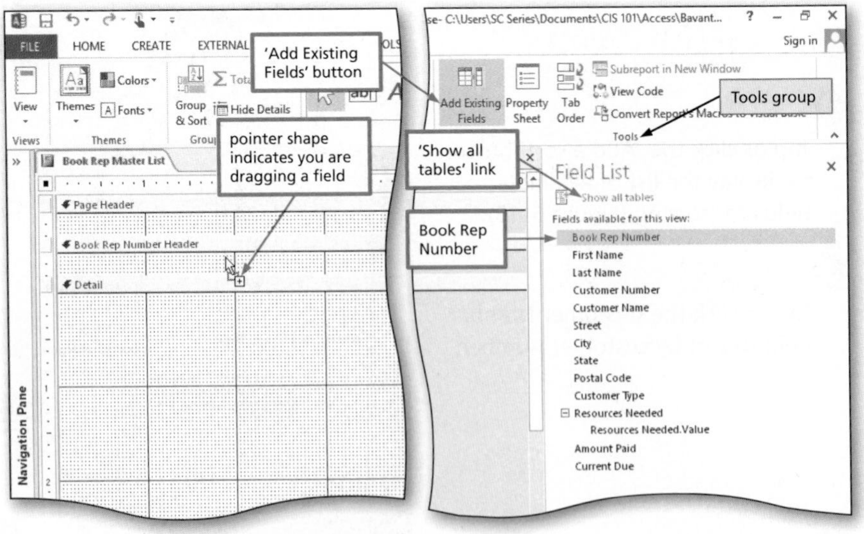

Figure 6–16

Q&A My field list does not look like the one in the figure. It has several tables listed, and at the top it has Show only fields in the current record source. Yours has Show all tables. What should I do?

Tap or click the 'Show only fields in the current record source' link. Your field list then should match the one in the figure.

2

- Release your finger or the mouse button to place the field (Figure 6–17).

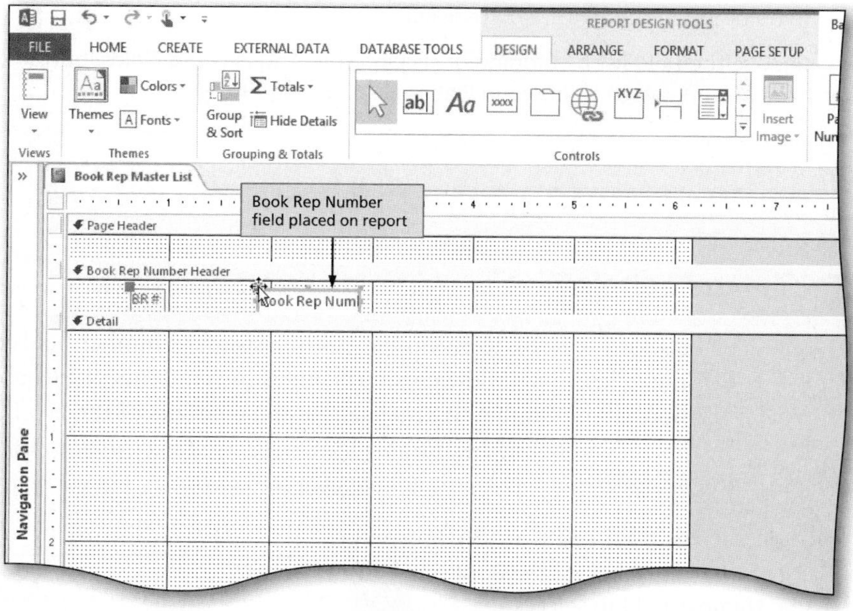

Figure 6–17

3

- Place the remaining fields in the positions shown in Figure 6–18.
- Adjust the positions of the labels to those shown in the figure. If any field is not in the correct position, drag it to its correct location. To move the control or the attached label separately, drag the large handle in the upper-left corner of the control or label. You can align controls using the Align button (REPORT DESIGN TOOLS ARRANGE tab | Sizing & Ordering group) or adjust spacing by using the Size/Space button (REPORT DESIGN TOOLS ARRANGE tab | Sizing & Ordering group).

Q&A Sometimes I find it hard to move a control a very small amount. Is there a simpler way to do this other than dragging it with my finger or with a mouse?

Yes. Once you have selected the control, you can use the arrow keys to move the control a very small amount in the desired direction.

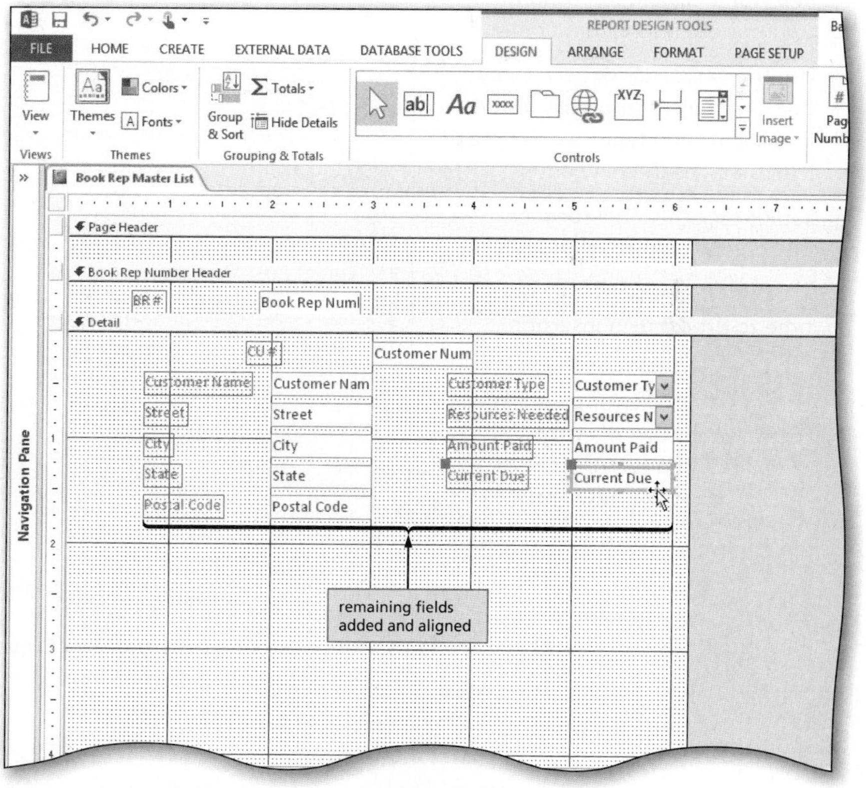

Figure 6–18

Experiment

- Select more than one control and then experiment with the Size/Space and the Align buttons (REPORT DESIGN TOOLS ARRANGE tab | Sizing & Ordering group) to see their effects. After trying each one, tap or click the Undo button to undo the change.

4

- If you used the ARRANGE tab, redisplay the DESIGN tab.
- Remove the field list by tapping or clicking the 'Add Existing Fields' button (REPORT DESIGN TOOLS DESIGN tab | Tools group), which is shown in Figure 6–16 on page AC 346.

To Change Labels

1 CREATE TABLES | 2 CREATE QUERIES | 3 CREATE REPORT | 4 SPECIFY GROUPING & SORTING | 5 ADD FIELDS
6 ADD SUBREPORT | 7 ADD TITLE, PAGE NUMBER, & DATE | 8 CREATE SECOND REPORT

The labels for the Book Rep Number and Customer Number fields currently contain the captions BR # and CU # for the fields. The following step changes the contents of the label for the Book Rep Number field from BR # to Book Rep Number. It also changes the contents of the label for the Customer Number field from CU # to Customer Number. ***Why?*** *Because there is plenty of room on the report to display longer names for both fields, you can make the report more descriptive by changing the labels.*

1

- Tap or click the label for the Book Rep Number field to select the label.
- Tap or click the label for the Book Rep Number field a second time to produce an insertion point.
- Use the BACKSPACE or DELETE key to erase the current entry in the label, and then type `Book Rep Number` as the new entry.
- Tap or click the label for the Customer Number field to select it.
- Tap or click the label a second time to produce an insertion point.
- Use the BACKSPACE or DELETE key to erase the current entry in the label and then type `Customer Number` as the new entry (Figure 6–19).

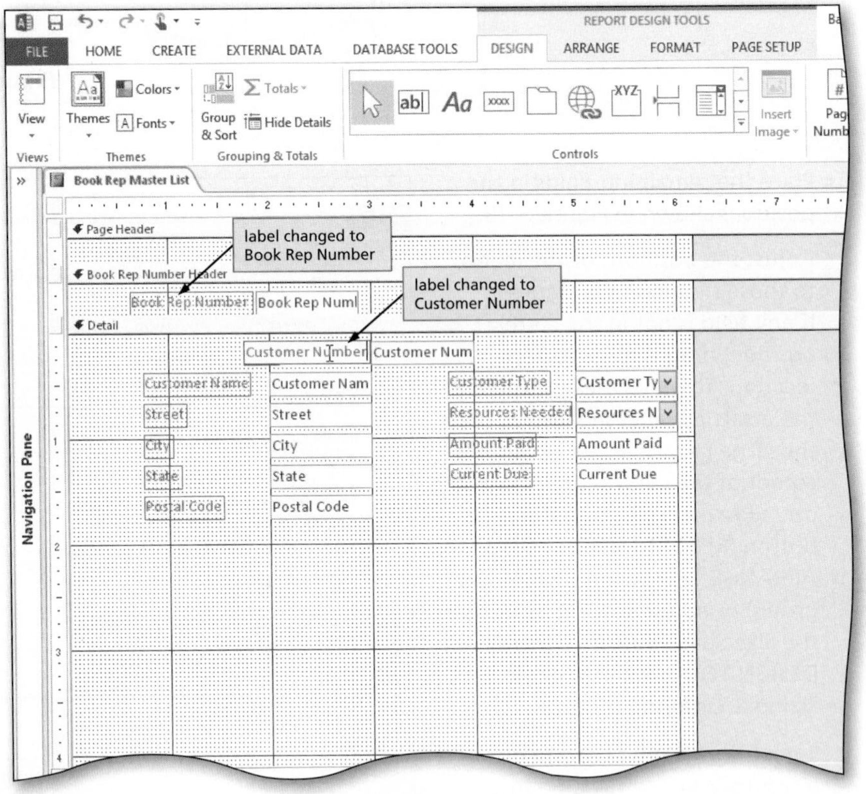

Figure 6–19

Using Other Tools in the Controls Group

Previously, you used the Subform/Subreport tool within the Controls group on the DESIGN tab to place special controls on a form. The Controls group has additional tools available that can be used with forms and reports. A description of the additional tools appears in Table 6–3.

Table 6–3 Additional Tools in the Controls Group

Tool	Description
Select	Select to be able to size, move, or edit existing controls. If you tap or click another tool and want to cancel the effect of the tool before using it, you can tap or click the Select tool.
Text Box	Create a text box for entering, editing, and displaying data. You also can bind the text box to a field in the underlying table or query.
Label	Create a label, which is a box containing text that cannot be edited and is independent of other controls, such as a title.
Button	Create a command button.
Tab Control	Create a tab control, which contains a series of tabbed pages. Each tabbed page can contain its own controls.
Hyperlink	Insert a hyperlink to an existing file, Web page, database object, or email address.
Option Group	Create an option group, which is a rectangle containing a collection of option buttons. To select an option, you tap or click the corresponding option button.
Insert or Remove Page Break	Insert or remove a physical page break (typically in a report).
Combo Box	Create a combo box, which is a combination of a text box and a list box.
Chart	Create a chart.
Line	Draw a line on a form or report.
Toggle Button	Add a toggle button. With a toggle button, a user can make a Yes/No selection by tapping or clicking the button. The button either appears to be pressed (for Yes) or not pressed (for No).
List Box	Create a list box, which is a box that allows the user to select from a list of options.
Rectangle	Create a rectangle.
Check Box	Insert a check box. With a check box a user can make multiple Yes/No selections.
Unbound Object Frame	Insert an OLE object (for example, a graph, picture, sound file, or video) that is not contained in a field in a table within the database.
Attachment	Insert an Attachment field.
Option Button	Insert an option button. With an option button, a user can make a single Yes/No selection from among a collection of at least two choices.
Subform/Subreport	Create a subform (a form contained within another form) or a subreport (a report contained within another report).
Bound Object Frame	Insert an OLE object (for example, a graph, picture, sound file, or video) that is contained in a field in a table within the database.
Image	Insert a frame into which you can insert a graphic. The graphic will be the same for all records.

To Add Text Boxes

1 CREATE TABLES | 2 CREATE QUERIES | 3 CREATE REPORT | 4 SPECIFY GROUPING & SORTING | 5 ADD FIELDS
6 ADD SUBREPORT | 7 ADD TITLE, PAGE NUMBER, & DATE | 8 CREATE SECOND REPORT

You can place a text box on a report or form by using the Text Box tool in the Controls group on the DESIGN tab. The text box consists of a control that is initially unbound and an attached label. The next step is to update the **control source,** which is the source of data for the control. You can do so by entering the appropriate expression in the text box or by updating the Control Source property in the property sheet with the expression.

Once you have updated the control source property with the expression, the control becomes a **calculated control**. If the expression is just a single field (for example, =[Amount Paid]), the control would be a **bound control**. *Why? The control is bound (tied) to the corresponding field.* The process of converting an unbound control to a bound control is called **binding**. Expressions also can be arithmetic operations: for example, calculating the sum of amount paid and current due. Many times, you need to **concatenate**, or combine, two or more text data items into a single expression; the process is called **concatenation**. To concatenate text data, you use the **ampersand (&)** operator. For example, [First Name]&' '&[Last Name] indicates the concatenation of a first name, a single blank space, and a last name.

The steps on the next page add text boxes and create calculated controls.

1

- Tap or click the Text Box tool (REPORT DESIGN TOOLS DESIGN tab | Controls group) and move the pointer to the approximate position shown in Figure 6–20.

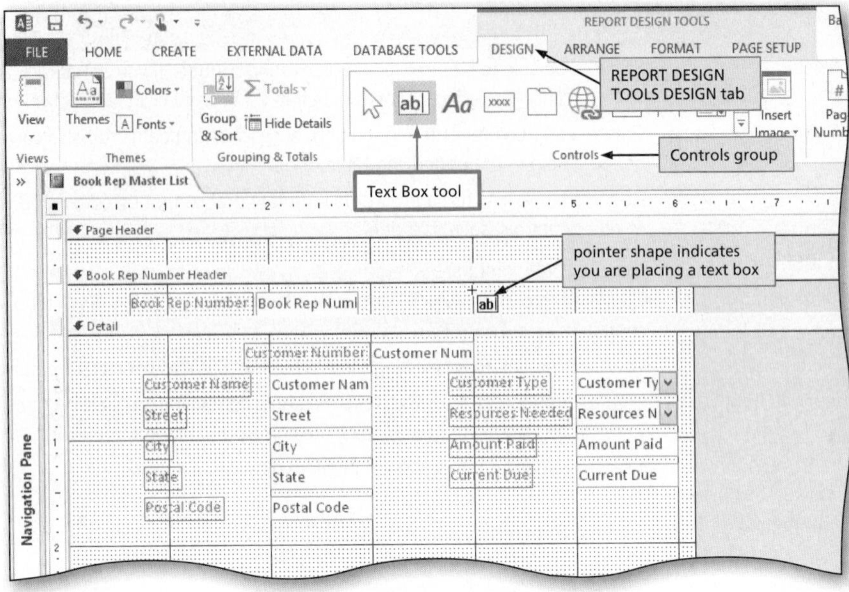

Figure 6–20

2

- Tap or click the position shown in Figure 6–20 to place a text box on the report (Figure 6–21).

Q&A My text box overlapped an object already on the screen. Is that a problem?

No. You can always move and/or resize your text box to the desired location and size later.

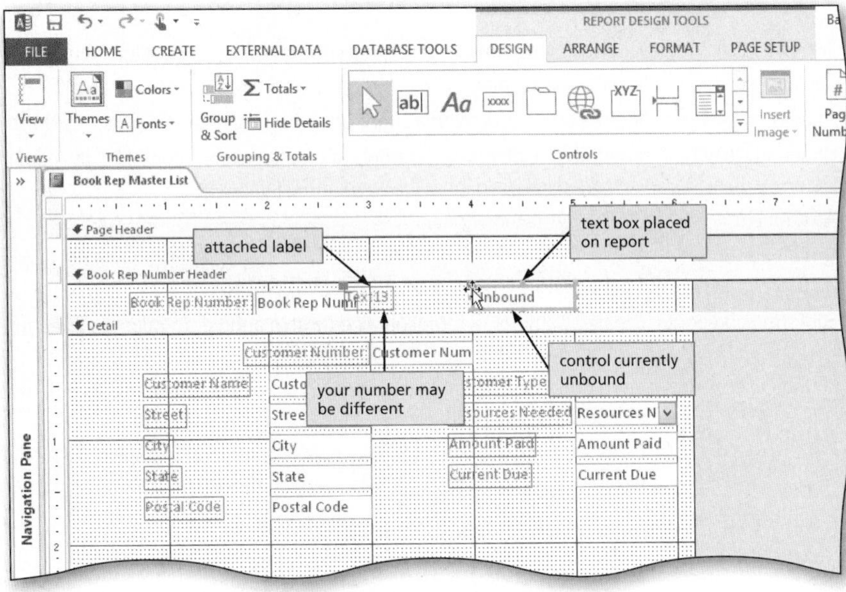

Figure 6–21

3

- Tap or click in the text box to produce an insertion point (Figure 6–22).

Q&A I inadvertently tapped or clicked somewhere else, so the text box was no longer selected. When I tapped or clicked the text box a second time, it was selected, but there was no insertion point. What should I do?

Simply tap or click another time.

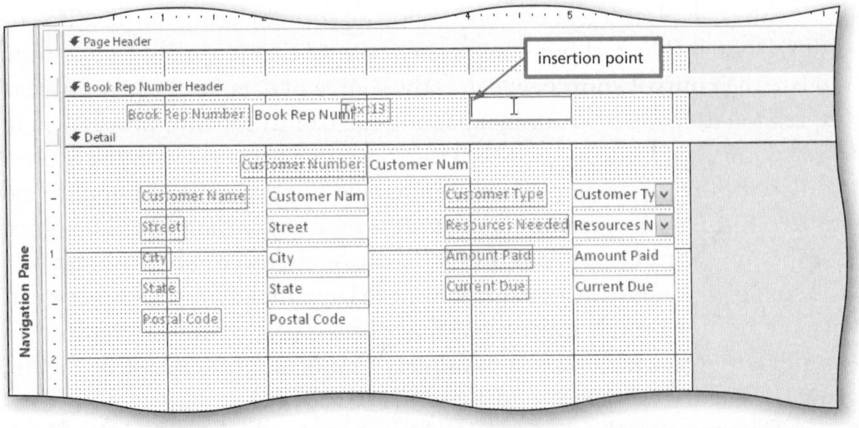

Figure 6–22

4

- In the text box, type **=[First Name]&' '&[Last Name]** to display the first name of the book rep, followed by a space, and then the last name of the book rep.

Q&A Could I use the Expression Builder instead of typing the expression?
Yes. Tap or click the Property Sheet button and then tap or click the Build button, which contains three dots, next to the Control Source property.

Do I need to use single quotes (')?
No. You also could use double quotes (").

- Tap or click in the text box label to select the label and then tap or click the label a second time to produce an insertion point (Figure 6–23).

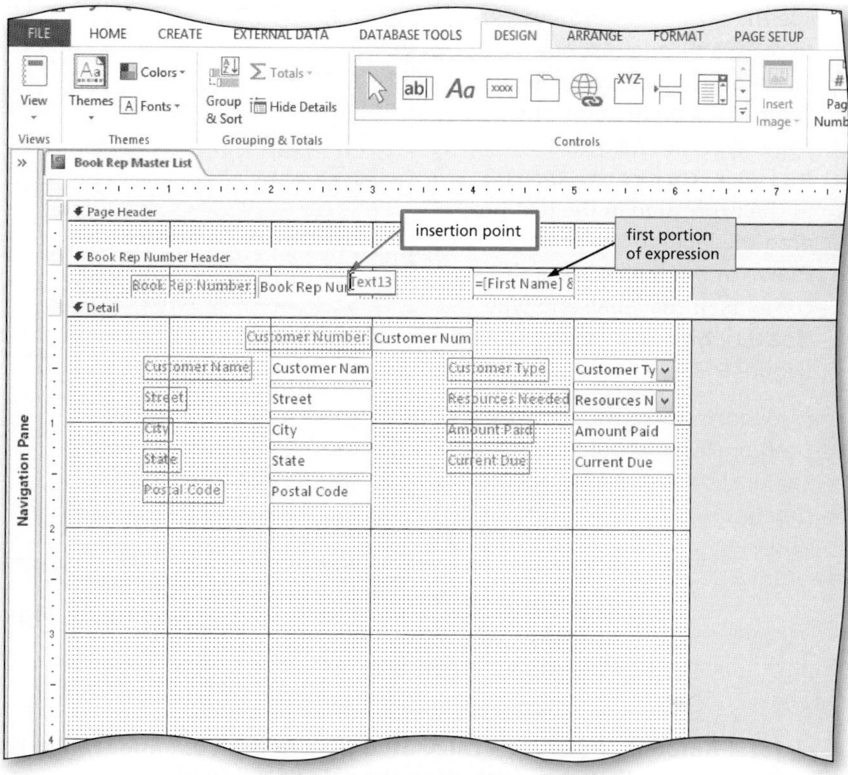

Figure 6–23

5

- Use the BACKSPACE or DELETE key to erase the current entry in the label and then type **Name** as the new entry.
- Tap or click outside the label to deselect it and then drag the label to the position shown in the figure by dragging the Move handle in the upper-left corner of the label (Figure 6–24).

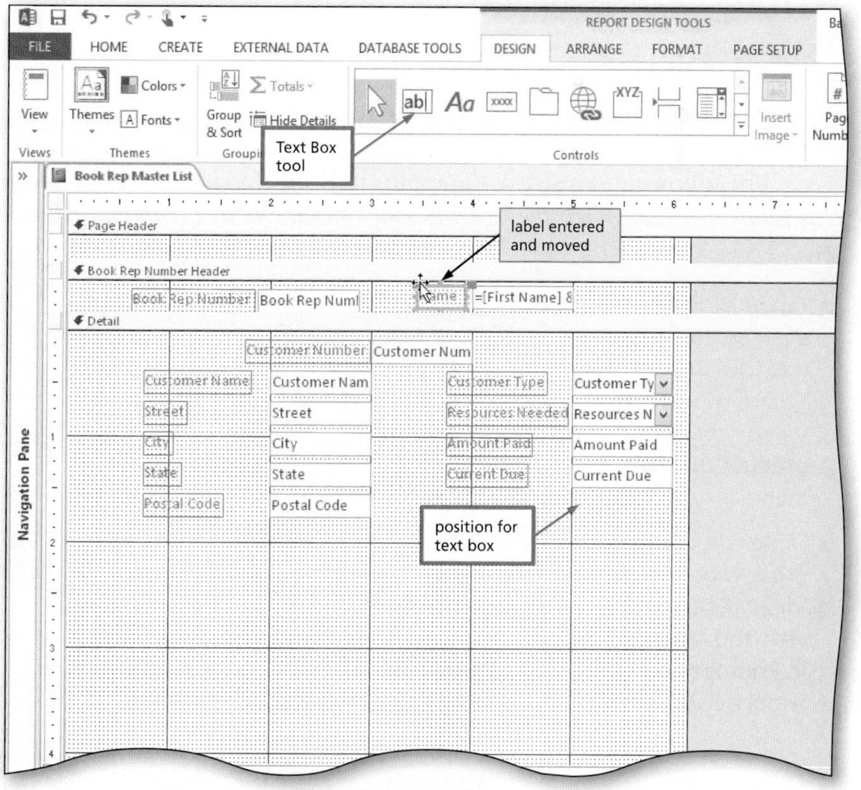

Figure 6–24

6

- Use the techniques in Steps 1 to 5 to place a second text box in the position indicated in Figure 6–24 on the previous page. Type `= [Amount Paid] + [Current Due]` as the expression in the text box, drag the label to the position shown in the figure, erase the contents of the label, and type `Total Amount` in the label (Figure 6–25).

Q&A My label is not in the correct position. What should I do?
Tap or click outside the label to deselect it, tap or click the label, and then drag it to the desired position.

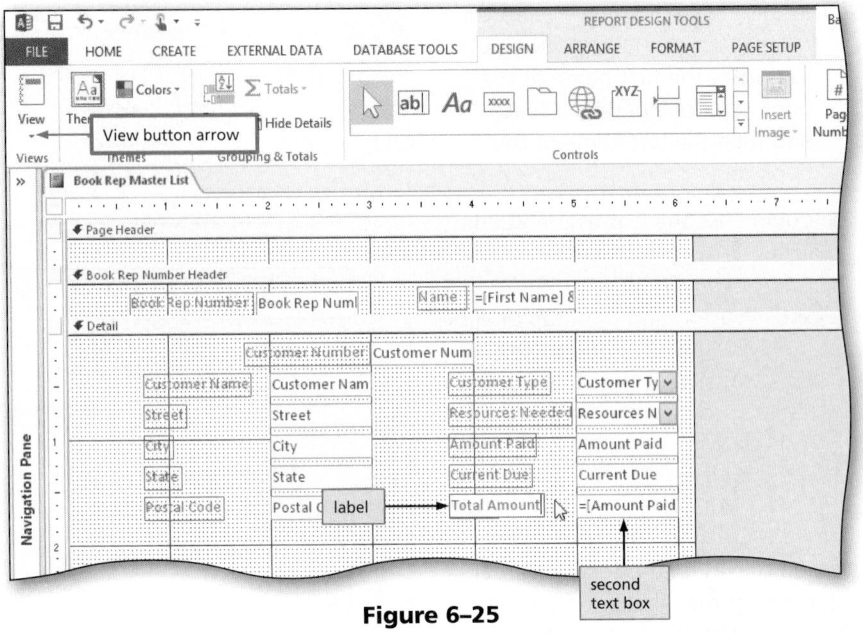

Figure 6–25

CONSIDER THIS

Total Amount already is a calculated field in the Customer table. Why would you add the calculation to the report rather than just using the calculated field?
One reason is that if you later decide to move this database to another database management system, such as SQL Server, the new DBMS may not allow calculated fields.

To View the Report in Print Preview

1 CREATE TABLES | 2 CREATE QUERIES | 3 CREATE REPORT | 4 SPECIFY GROUPING & SORTING | **5 ADD FIELDS**
6 ADD SUBREPORT | 7 ADD TITLE, PAGE NUMBER, & DATE | 8 CREATE SECOND REPORT

The following steps view the report in Print Preview. ***Why?*** *As you are working on a report in Design view, it is useful to periodically view the report to gauge how it will look containing data. One way to do so is to use Print Preview.*

1

- Tap or click the View button arrow (REPORT DESIGN TOOLS DESIGN tab | Views group) to produce the View menu.
- Tap or click Print Preview on the View menu to view the report in Print Preview (Figure 6–26).

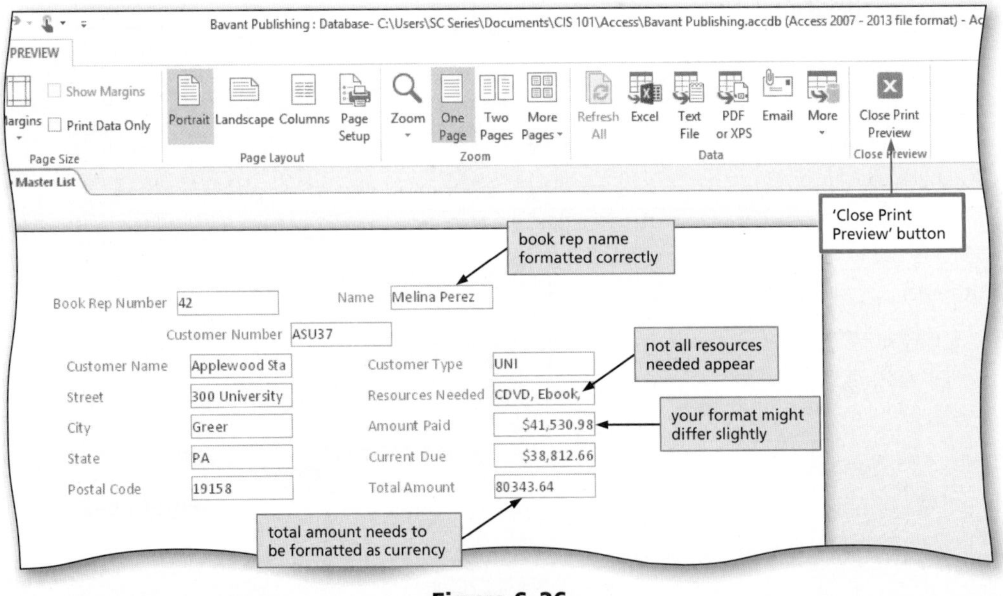

Figure 6–26

Q&A What would happen if I tapped or clicked the View button instead of the View button arrow?

The icon on the View button is the icon for Report View, so you would view the results in Report view. This is another useful way to view a report, but compared with Print Preview, Report View does not give as accurate a picture of how the final printed report will look.

The total amount does not appear as currency, and the Customer Name, Street, and Resources Needed fields do not display the entire value. How can I fix these issues?

You will fix these issues in the next sections.

2

- Tap or click the 'Close Print Preview' button (PRINT PREVIEW tab | Close Preview group) to return to Design view.

Other Ways

1. Tap or click Print Preview button on status bar

To Format a Control

1 CREATE TABLES | 2 CREATE QUERIES | 3 CREATE REPORT | 4 SPECIFY GROUPING & SORTING | **5 ADD FIELDS**
6 ADD SUBREPORT | 7 ADD TITLE, PAGE NUMBER, & DATE | 8 CREATE SECOND REPORT

Why? *When you add a calculated control to a report, you often need to format the control, for example, to display a currency value with a dollar sign, decimal point, and two decimal places.* You can use a control's property sheet to change the value in the appropriate property. If a property does not appear on the screen, you have two choices. You can tap or click the tab on which the property is located. For example, if it were a control related to data, you would tap or click the Data tab to only show data-related properties. Many people, however, prefer to tap or click the All tab, which shows all properties, and then simply scroll through the properties, if necessary, until locating the appropriate property. The following steps change the format of the Total Amount control to Currency by changing the value of the Format property and the Decimal Places property.

1

- Tap or click the control containing the expression for Total Amount to select it, and then tap or click the Property Sheet button (REPORT DESIGN TOOLS DESIGN tab | Tools group) to display the property sheet.
- If necessary, tap or click the All tab (Figure 6–27).

Experiment

- Tap or click the other tabs in the property sheet to see the types of properties on each tab. When finished, once again tap or click the All tab.

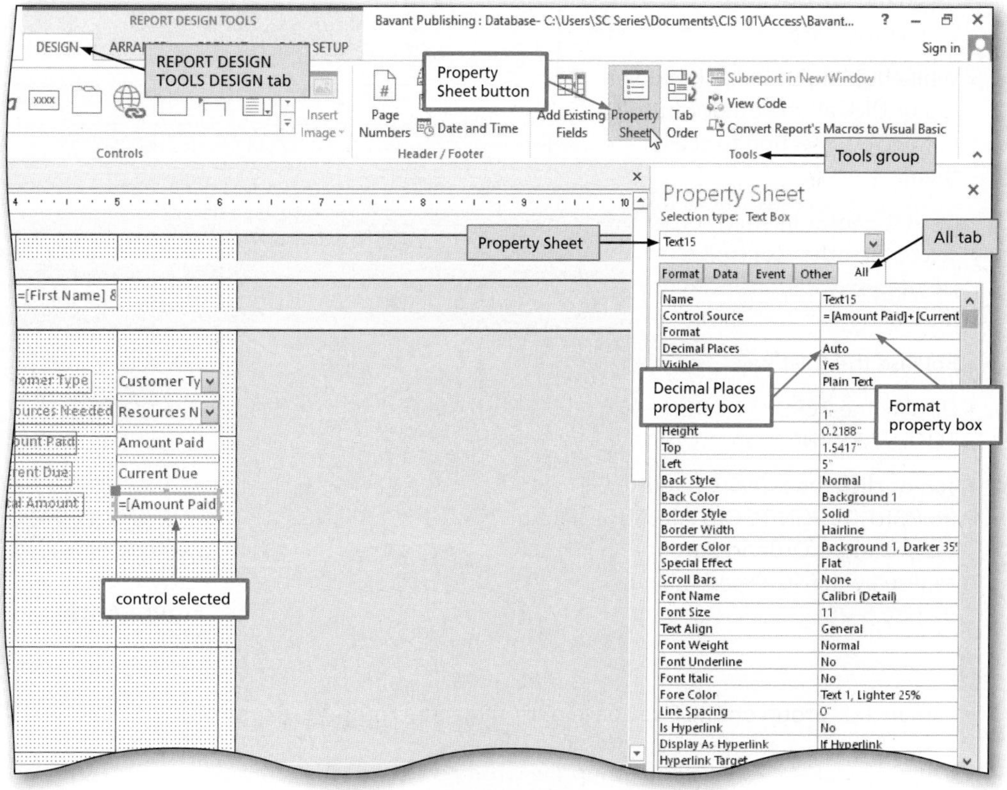

Figure 6–27

2

- Tap or click the Format property box, tap or click the arrow that appears, and then tap or click Currency to select Currency as the format.
- Tap or click the Decimal Places property box, tap or click the arrow that appears, and then tap or click 2 to select two decimal places.
- Remove the property sheet by tapping or clicking the Property Sheet button (REPORT DESIGN TOOLS DESIGN tab | Tools group) a second time.
- Preview the report using Print Preview to see the effect of the property changes.
- Tap or click the 'Close Print Preview' button (PRINT PREVIEW tab | Close Preview group) to return to Design view.

Other Ways

1. Press and hold or right-click control, tap or click Properties

To Group Controls

1 CREATE TABLES | 2 CREATE QUERIES | 3 CREATE REPORT | 4 SPECIFY GROUPING & SORTING | **5 ADD FIELDS**
6 ADD SUBREPORT | 7 ADD TITLE, PAGE NUMBER, & DATE | 8 CREATE SECOND REPORT

The following steps group the controls within the Detail section. ***Why?*** *If your report contains a collection of controls that you frequently will want to modify in the same way, you can simplify the process of selecting all the controls by grouping them. Once they are grouped, selecting any control in the group automatically selects all of the controls in the group. You then can apply the desired change to all the controls.*

1

- Tap or click the Customer Number control to select it.

Q&A Do I tap or click the white space or the label?
The white space.

- While holding the SHIFT key down, tap or click all the other controls in the Detail section to select them.

Q&A Does it matter in which order I select the other controls?
No. It is only important that you ultimately select all the controls.

- Release the SHIFT key.
- Display the REPORT DESIGN TOOLS ARRANGE tab.
- Tap or click the Size/Space button (REPORT DESIGN TOOLS ARRANGE tab | Sizing & Ordering group) to display the Size/Space menu (Figure 6–28).

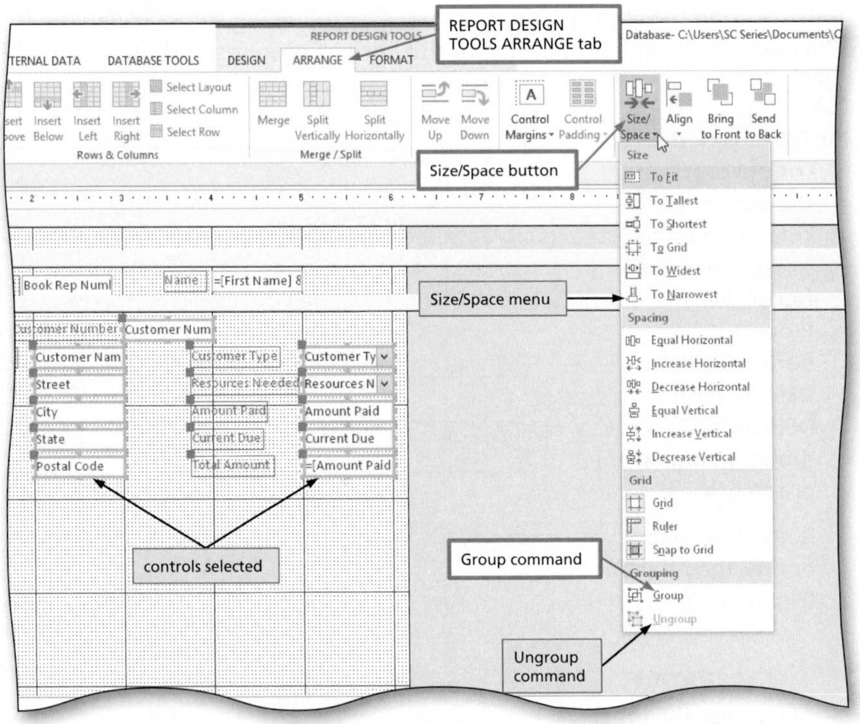

Figure 6–28

2

- Tap or click Group on the Size/Space button menu to group the controls.

Q&A What if I make a mistake and group the wrong collection of controls?
Ungroup the controls using the steps shown in the next section, and then group the correct collection of controls.

To Ungroup Controls

If you no longer need to simultaneously modify all the controls you have placed in a group, you can ungroup the controls. To do so, you would use the following steps.

1. Tap or click any of the controls in a group to select the entire group.
2. Display the REPORT DESIGN TOOLS ARRANGE tab.
3. Tap or click the Size/Space button (REPORT DESIGN TOOLS ARRANGE tab | Sizing & Ordering group) to display the Size/Space button menu.
4. Tap or click the Ungroup button on the Size/Space button menu to ungroup the controls.

BTW

Arguments
An argument is a piece of data on which a function operates. For example, in the expression =SUM ([Amount Paid]), Amount Paid is the argument because the SUM function will calculate the total of Amount Paid.

CONSIDER THIS

Can you group controls in forms?
Yes. The process is identical to the process of grouping controls in reports.

To Modify Grouped Controls

1 CREATE TABLES | 2 CREATE QUERIES | 3 CREATE REPORT | 4 SPECIFY GROUPING & SORTING | 5 ADD FIELDS
6 ADD SUBREPORT | 7 ADD TITLE, PAGE NUMBER, & DATE | 8 CREATE SECOND REPORT

To modify grouped controls, tap or click any control in the group to select the entire group. ***Why?*** *Any change you then make affects all controls in the group.* The following steps bold the controls in the group, resize them, and then change the border style.

1

- If necessary, tap or click any one of the grouped controls to select the group.
- Display the REPORT DESIGN TOOLS FORMAT tab.
- Tap or click the Bold button (REPORT DESIGN TOOLS FORMAT tab | Font group) to bold all the controls in the group (Figure 6–29).

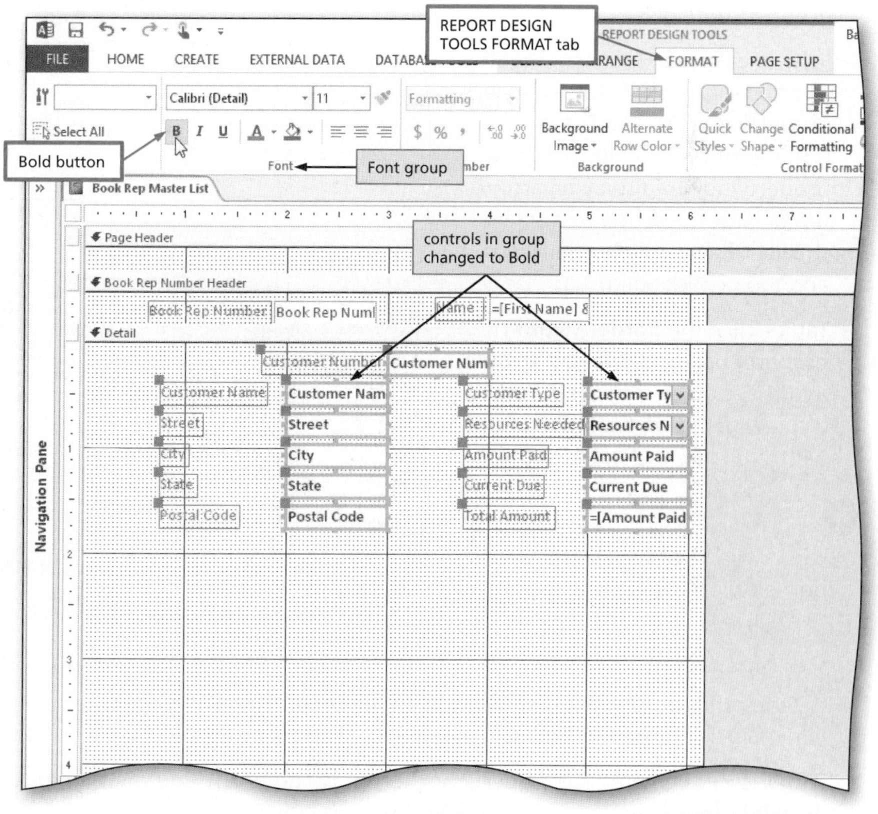

Figure 6–29

2

- Display the REPORT DESIGN TOOLS DESIGN tab.
- Drag the right sizing handle of the Resources Needed field to the approximate position shown in Figure 6–30 to resize all the controls in the group.

Q&A Do I need to use the Resources Needed field or could I use another field?

Any field in the group will work.

How do I change only one control in the group?

Double-tap or double-click the control to select just the one control and not the entire group. You then can make any change you want to that control.

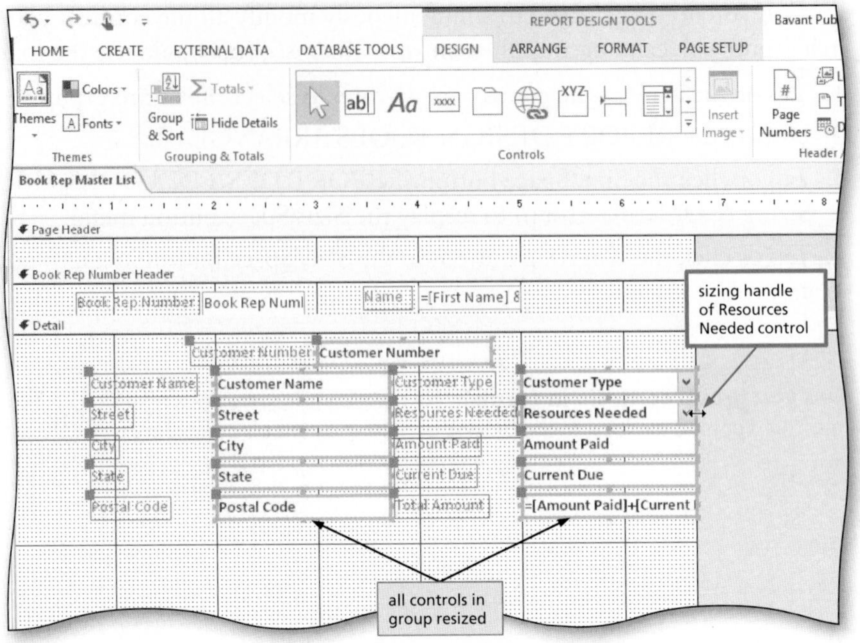

Figure 6–30

3

- Tap or click the Property Sheet button (REPORT DESIGN TOOLS DESIGN tab | Tools group) to display the property sheet for the grouped controls.
- With the All tab (Property Sheet) selected, ensure the Border Style property is set to Solid. If it is not, tap or click the Border Style property box to display an arrow, tap or click the arrow to display the list of available border styles, and tap or click Solid.
- Tap or click the Border Width property box to display an arrow and then tap or click the arrow to display the list of available border widths (Figure 6–31).

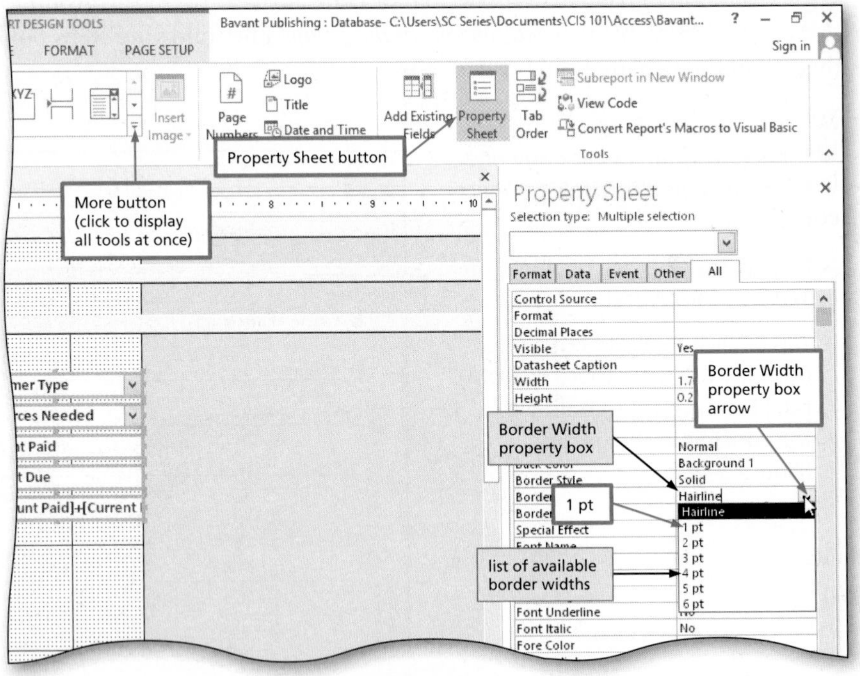

Figure 6–31

4

- Tap or click 1 pt to select the border width.

Experiment

- Try the other border styles and widths to see their effects. In each case, view the report and then return to Design view. When finished, once again select Solid as the border style and 1 pt as the border width.
- Tap or click the Font Size property box to display an arrow and then tap or click the arrow to display the list of available font sizes.
- Tap or click 10 to change the font size to 10.
- Close the property sheet.

5

- Double-tap or double-click the Resources Needed control to select the control without selecting the entire group.
- Resize the Resources Needed control to approximately the size shown in Figure 6–32.
- If necessary, drag the right boundary of your report so that it matches the one shown in Figure 6–32.

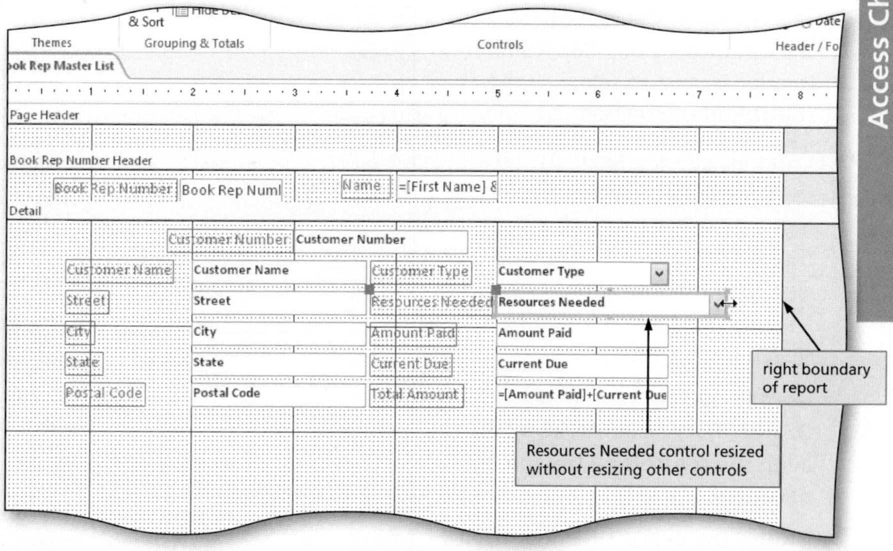

Figure 6–32

To Modify Multiple Controls That Are Not Grouped

1 CREATE TABLES | 2 CREATE QUERIES | 3 CREATE REPORT | 4 SPECIFY GROUPING & SORTING | **5 ADD FIELDS**
6 ADD SUBREPORT | 7 ADD TITLE, PAGE NUMBER, & DATE | 8 CREATE SECOND REPORT

To modify multiple controls that are not grouped together, you simultaneously must select all the controls you want to modify. To do so, tap or click one of the controls and then hold the SHIFT key down while selecting the others. The following steps italicize all the labels in the Detail section and then bold all the controls and labels in the Book Rep Number Header section. Finally, the steps increase the size of the Book Rep Name control. ***Why?*** *With the current size, some names are not displayed completely.*

1

- Tap or click the label for the Customer Number control to select it.
- While holding the SHIFT key down, tap or click the labels for all the other controls in the Detail section to select them.
- Release the SHIFT key.
- Display the REPORT DESIGN TOOLS FORMAT tab.
- Tap or click the Italic button (REPORT DESIGN TOOLS FORMAT tab | Font group) to italicize the labels (Figure 6–33).

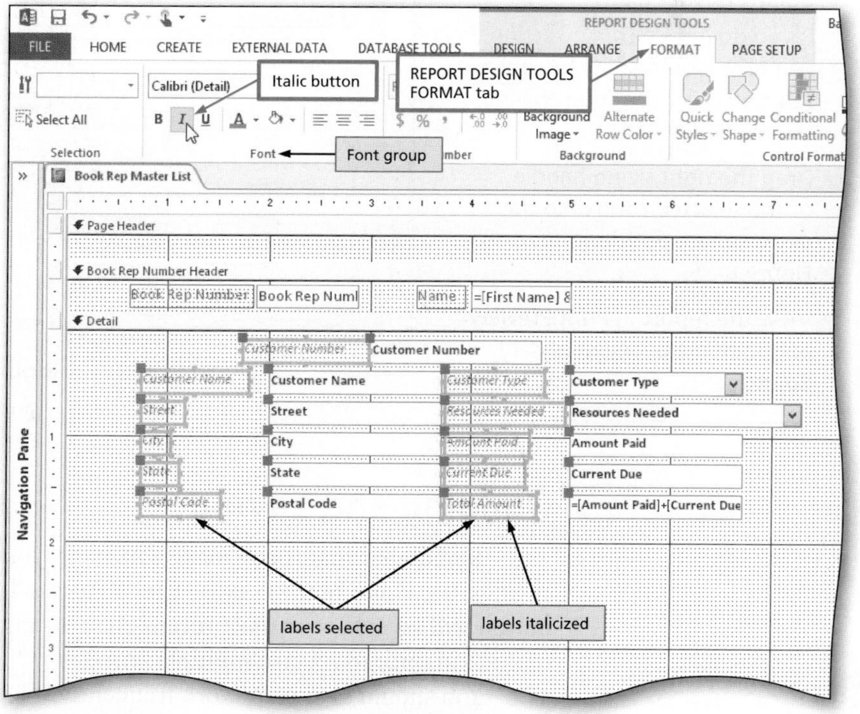

Figure 6–33

2

- Tap or click in the vertical ruler to the left of the Book Rep Number Header section to select all the controls in the section.

Q&A What exactly is selected when I tap or click in the vertical ruler?
If you picture a horizontal line through the point you tapped or clicked, any control that intersects that horizontal line would be selected.

- Use the buttons on the REPORT DESIGN TOOLS ARRANGE tab to align the controls on the top, if necessary.
- Display the REPORT DESIGN TOOLS FORMAT tab, if necessary, and then tap or click the Bold button (REPORT DESIGN TOOLS FORMAT tab | Font group) to bold all the selected controls (Figure 6–34).

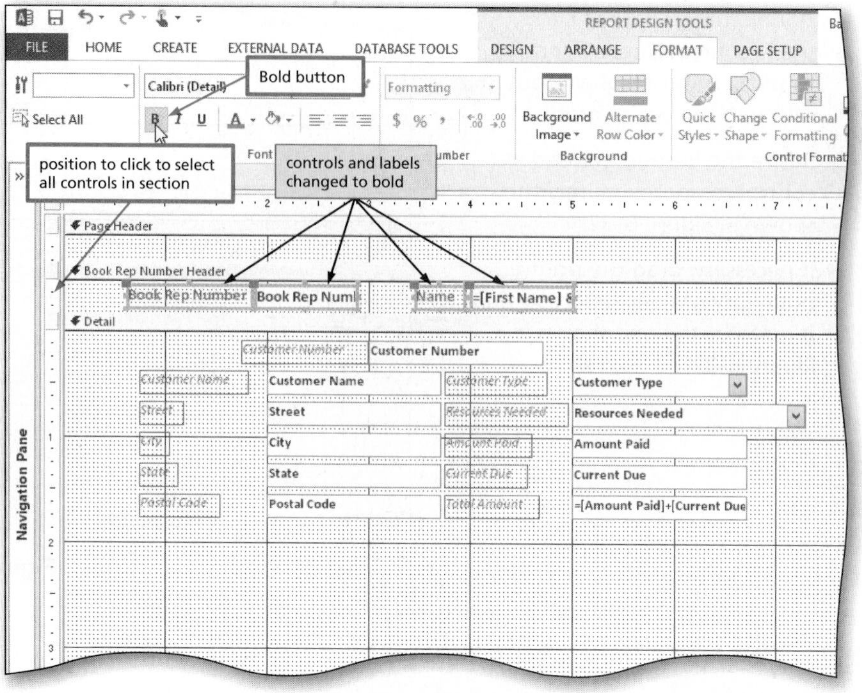

Figure 6–34

3

- Tap or click outside the selected controls to deselect them. Tap or click the control containing the expression for the book rep's name to select it.

Q&A Why do I have to deselect the controls and then select one of them a second time?
If you do not do so, any action you take would apply to all the selected controls rather than just the one you want.

- Drag the right sizing handle of the selected control to the approximate position shown in Figure 6–35.
- View the report in Print Preview and then make any necessary adjustments.

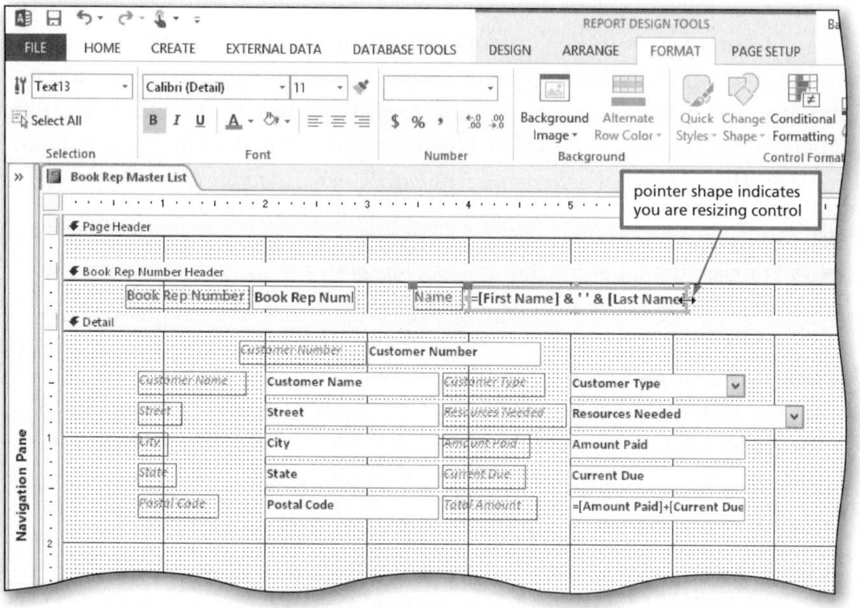

Figure 6–35

Undoing and Saving

Remember that if you make a mistake, you often can correct it by tapping or clicking the Undo button on the Quick Access Toolbar. Tapping or clicking the Undo button will reverse your most recent change. You also can tap or click the Undo button more than once to reverse multiple changes.

You should save your work frequently. That way, if you have problems that the Undo button will not fix, you can close the report without saving it and open it again. The report will be in exactly the state it was in the last time you saved it.

To Add a Subreport

1 CREATE TABLES | 2 CREATE QUERIES | 3 CREATE REPORT | 4 SPECIFY GROUPING & SORTING | 5 ADD FIELDS
6 ADD SUBREPORT | **7 ADD TITLE, PAGE NUMBER, & DATE** | **8 CREATE SECOND REPORT**

To add a subreport to a report, you use the Subform/Subreport tool on the DESIGN tab. The following steps add a subreport to display the seminar data, after first ensuring the 'Use Control Wizards' button is selected. ***Why?*** *Provided the 'Use Control Wizards' button is selected, a wizard will guide you through the process of adding the subreport.*

1

- Display the REPORT DESIGN TOOLS DESIGN tab.
- Tap or click the More button, which is shown below in Figure 6–37 (REPORT DESIGN TOOLS DESIGN tab | Controls group), to display a menu of available tools (Figure 6–36).

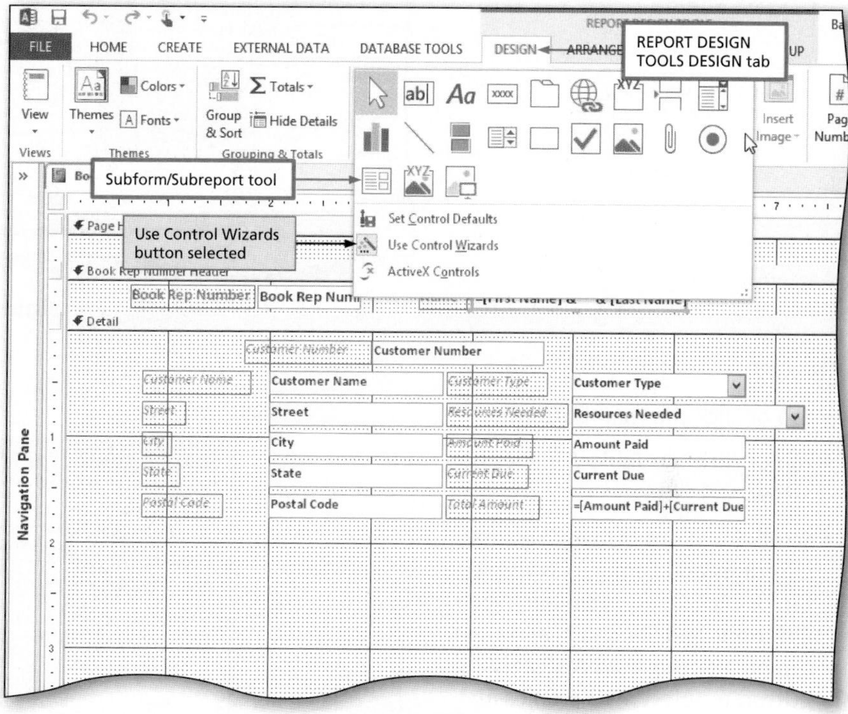

Figure 6–36

2

- Be sure the 'Use Control Wizards' button is selected, tap or click the Subform/Subreport tool, and then move the pointer, which has changed to a plus sign with a subreport, to the approximate position shown in Figure 6–37.

Q&A I do not see a pointer. Did I do something wrong?

If you are using your finger you will not see the pointer shape as indicated in the figure. Tapping with your finger in the indicated location, however, should still produce the desired action. If you prefer to see a pointer, then you should use a stylus or a mouse.

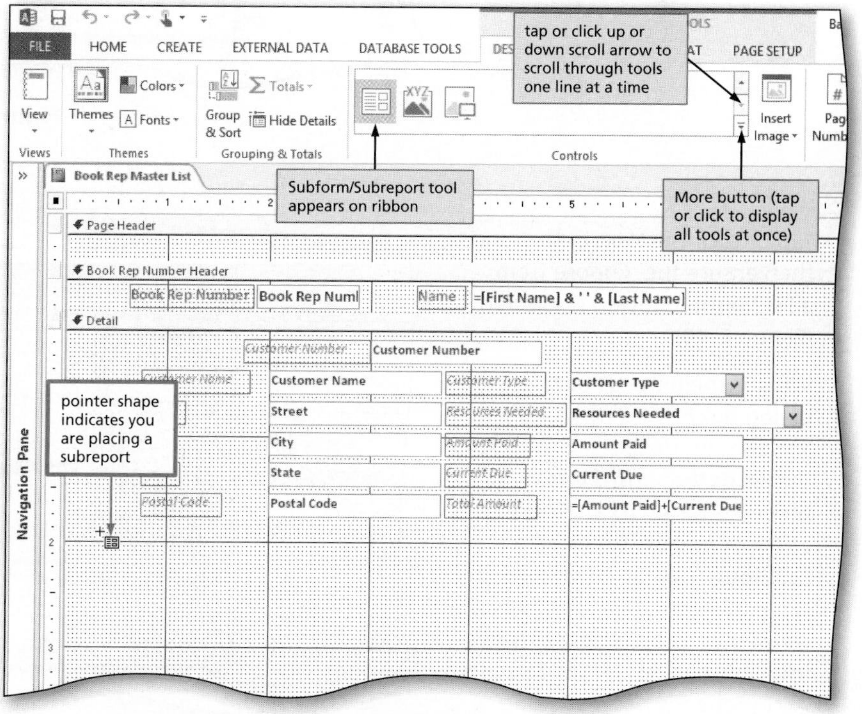

Figure 6–37

3

- Tap or click the position shown in Figure 6–37 on the previous page to place the subreport and display the SubReport Wizard dialog box. Be sure the 'Use existing Tables and Queries' option button is selected (Figure 6–38).

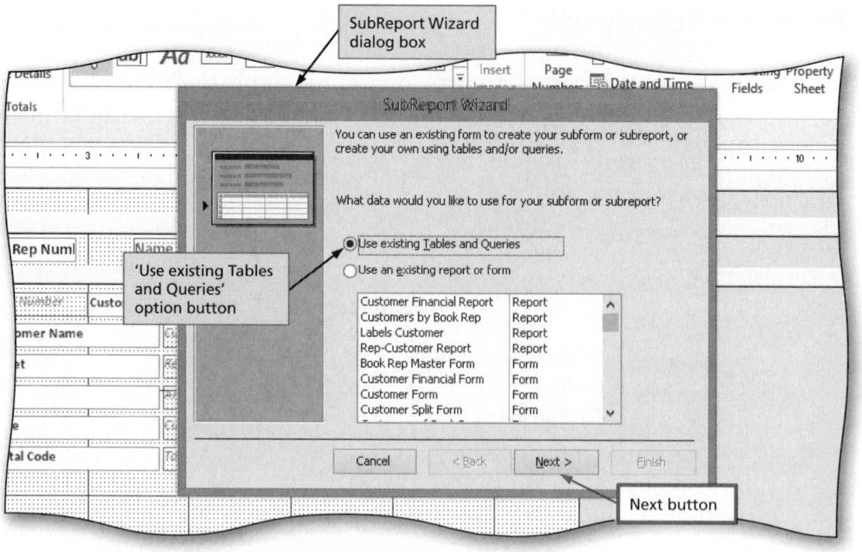

Figure 6–38

4

- Tap or click the Next button.
- Tap or click the Tables/Queries box arrow.
- Scroll down until Query: Seminar Offerings and Seminars is visible, tap or click Query: Seminar Offerings and Seminars, and then tap or click the 'Add All Fields' button to select all the fields in the query (Figure 6–39).

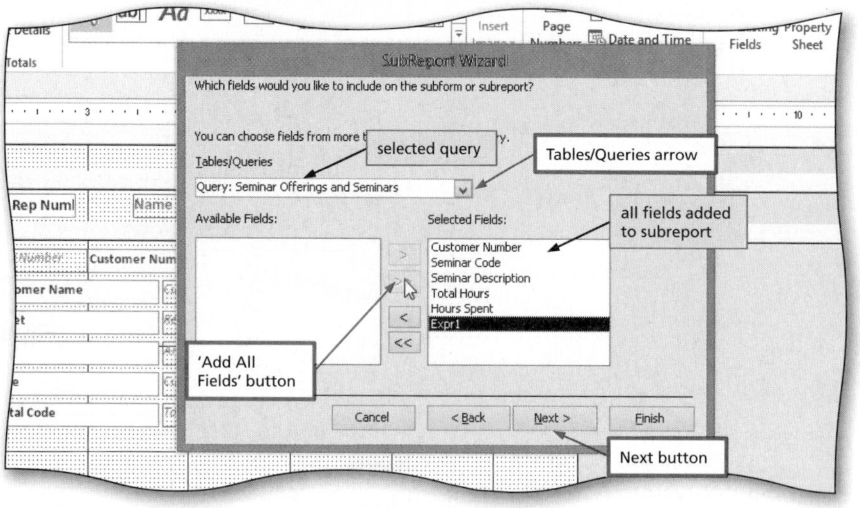

Figure 6–39

5

- Tap or click the Next button and then ensure the 'Choose from a list.' option button is selected (Figure 6–40).

Q&A What is the purpose of this dialog box?
You use this dialog box to indicate the fields that link the main report (referred to as "form") to the subreport (referred to as "subform"). If the fields have the same name, as they often will, you can simply select 'Choose from a list' and then accept the selection Access already has made.

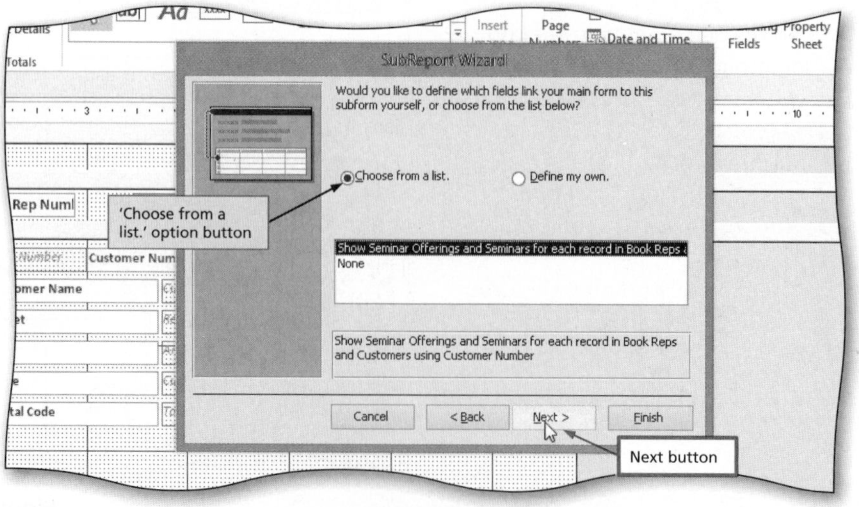

Figure 6–40

6

- Tap or click the Next button, type **Seminar Offerings by Customer** as the name of the subreport, and then tap or click the Finish button to add the subreport to the Book Rep Master List report (Figure 6–41).

7

- Tap or click outside the subreport to deselect the subreport.
- Tap or click the Save button on the Quick Access Toolbar to save your changes.
- Close the Book Rep Master List report.

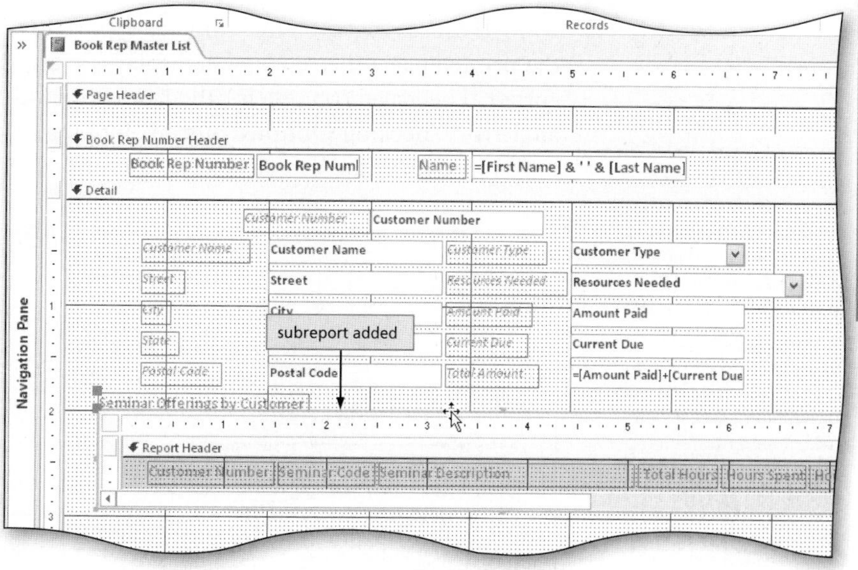

Figure 6–41

Break Point: If you wish to stop working through the chapter at this point, you can resume the project at a later time by starting Access, opening the database called Bavant Publishing, and continuing to follow the steps from this location forward.

To Open the Subreport in Design View

1 CREATE TABLES | 2 CREATE QUERIES | 3 CREATE REPORT | 4 SPECIFY GROUPING & SORTING | 5 ADD FIELDS
6 ADD SUBREPORT | 7 ADD TITLE, PAGE NUMBER, & DATE | 8 CREATE SECOND REPORT

The following step opens the subreport in Design view so it can be modified. ***Why?*** *The subreport appears as a separate report in the Navigation Pane. You can modify it just as you modify any other report.*

1

- Open the Navigation Pane, scroll down so that the Seminar Offerings by Customer report appears, and then press and hold or right-click the Seminar Offerings by Customer report to produce a shortcut menu.
- Tap or click Design View on the shortcut menu to open the subreport in Design view (Figure 6–42).

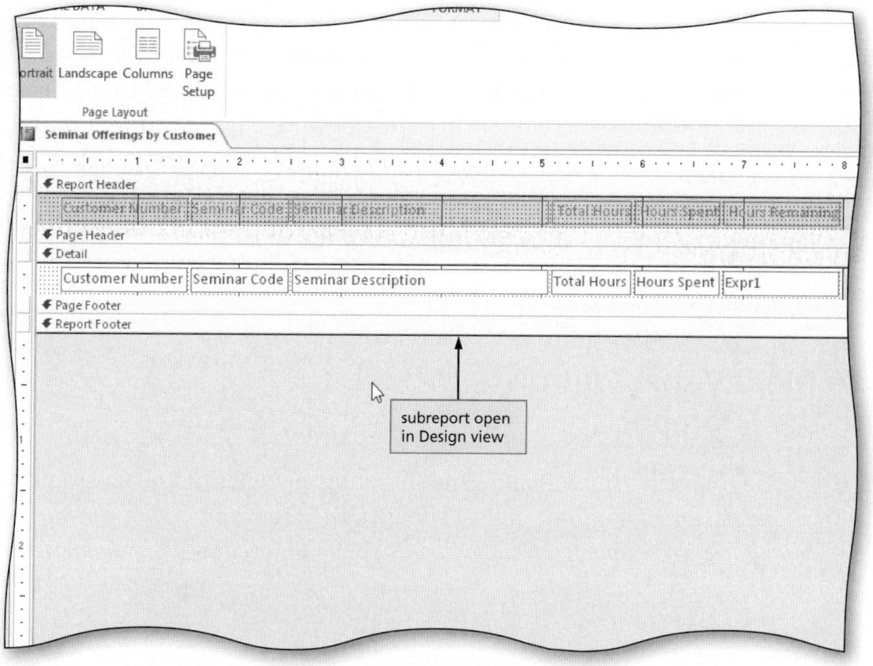

Figure 6–42

Print Layout Issues

BTW
Default Names for Controls
Because each control has properties associated with it, Access assigns a default name to each new control. The default name includes a control identifier and a number. For example, if you create a text box on a report, the default name may be Text32. You should change the default name to something meaningful to make it easier to remember the purpose of the control.

If there is a problem with your report, for example, a report that is too wide for the printed page, the report will display a green triangular symbol in the upper-left corner. The green triangle is called an **error indicator**. Tapping or clicking it displays an 'Error Checking Options' button. Tapping or clicking the 'Error Checking Options' button produces the 'Error Checking Options menu,' as shown in Figure 6–43.

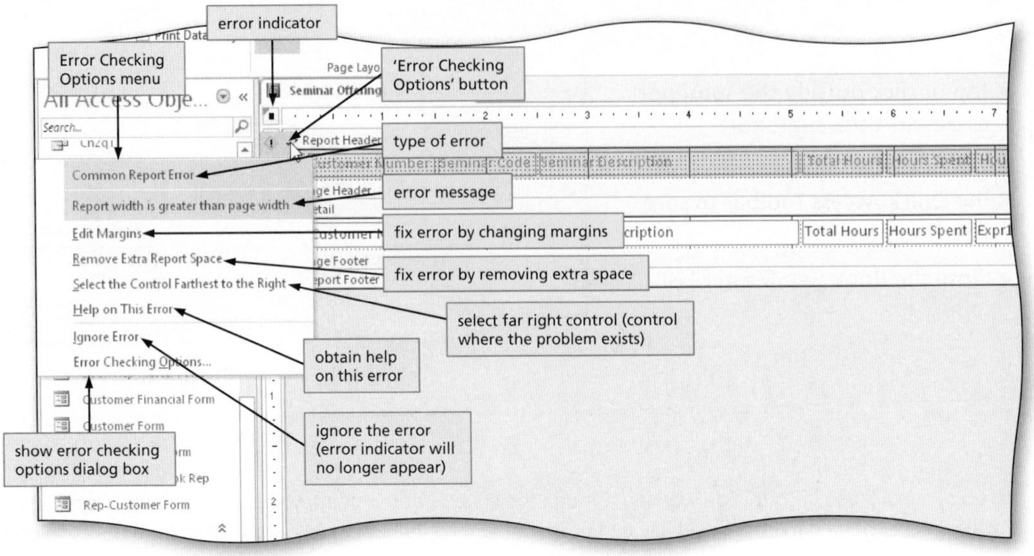

Figure 6–43

BTW
Subreports
Subreports provide more control in presenting data effectively than multiple levels of grouping can. Because grouping places headers in columns, it often can be difficult to determine the relationship between the group header and the detail. Also, you might want to present subreports side by side. You cannot do that with grouping.

The first line in the menu is simply a statement of the type of error that occurred. The second is a description of the specific error, in this case, the fact that the report width is greater than the page width. This situation could lead to data not appearing where you expect it to, as well as the printing of some blank pages.

The next three lines provide potential solutions to the error. You could change the margins to allow more space for the report. You could remove some extra space. You could select the control farthest to the right and move it. The fourth line gives more detailed help on the error. The Ignore Error command instructs Access to not consider this situation an error. Selecting Ignore Error would cause the error indicator to disappear without making any changes. The final line displays the Error Checking Options dialog box, where you can make other changes.

Later in this chapter, you will fix the problem by changing the width of the report, so you do not need to take any action at this time.

To Modify the Controls in the Subreport

1 CREATE TABLES | 2 CREATE QUERIES | 3 CREATE REPORT | 4 SPECIFY GROUPING & SORTING | 5 ADD FIELDS
6 ADD SUBREPORT | **7 ADD TITLE, PAGE NUMBER, & DATE** | **8 CREATE SECOND REPORT**

The following step modifies the subreport by deleting the Customer Number control and revising the appearance of the column headings. ***Why?*** *Because the customer number appears in the main report, it does not need to be duplicated in the subreport. In addition, the column headers in the subreport should extend over two lines, as shown in Figure 6–1a on page AC 331.*

1

- Close the Navigation Pane.
- Tap or click the Customer Number control in the Detail section to select the control. Hold the SHIFT key down and tap or click the Customer Number control in the Report Header section to select both controls.
- With both controls selected, press the DELETE key to delete the controls.
- Adjust the labels in the Report Header section to match those shown in Figure 6–44. To extend a heading over two lines, tap or click in front of the second word to produce an insertion point and then press SHIFT+ENTER to move the second word to a second line.
- Change the sizes and positions of the controls to match those in the figure by selecting the controls and dragging the sizing handles.

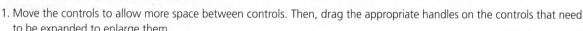

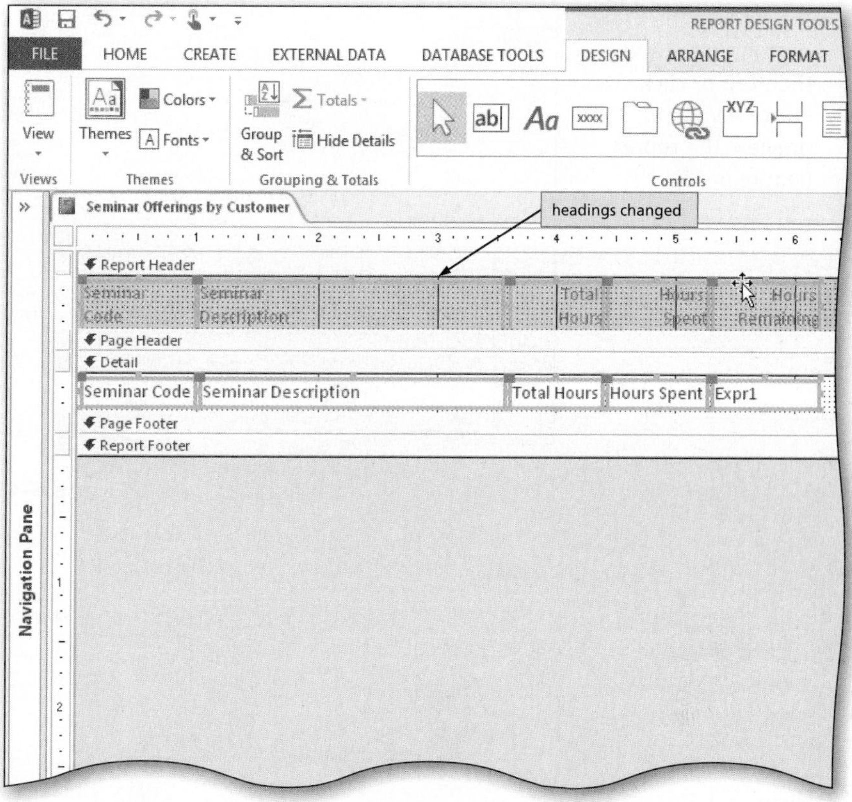

Figure 6–44

Q&A Why does Expr1 appear in the Detail section under the Hours Remaining label?

Expr1 indicates that Hours Remaining is a calculated control.

Experiment

- There is currently a space between the two words in the Report Header labels. To delete the space, tap or click immediately after the first word to produce an insertion point and then press the DELETE key. Try the various alignments (left, right, and center) before removing the space. Remove the space and try the various alignments again to see if the removal of the space makes any difference. When finished, make sure your labels look like the one in the figure.

CONSIDER THIS

How can you adjust fields where some of the entries are too long to fit in the available space?

This problem can be addressed in several ways.

1. Move the controls to allow more space between controls. Then, drag the appropriate handles on the controls that need to be expanded to enlarge them.
2. Use the Font Size property to select a smaller font size. This will allow more data to fit in the same space.
3. Use the Can Grow property. By changing the value of this property from No to Yes, the data can be spread over two lines, thus allowing all the data to print. Access will split data at natural break points, such as commas, spaces, and hyphens.

To Change the Can Grow Property

1 CREATE TABLES | 2 CREATE QUERIES | 3 CREATE REPORT | 4 SPECIFY GROUPING & SORTING | 5 ADD FIELDS
6 ADD SUBREPORT | 7 ADD TITLE, PAGE NUMBER, & DATE | 8 CREATE SECOND REPORT

The third approach to handling entries that are too long is the easiest to use and also produces a very readable report. The steps on the next page change the Can Grow property for the Seminar Description field. ***Why?*** *Some of the seminar descriptions are too long for the available space.*

1

- Tap or click the View button arrow and then tap or click Print Preview to preview the report (Figure 6–45).

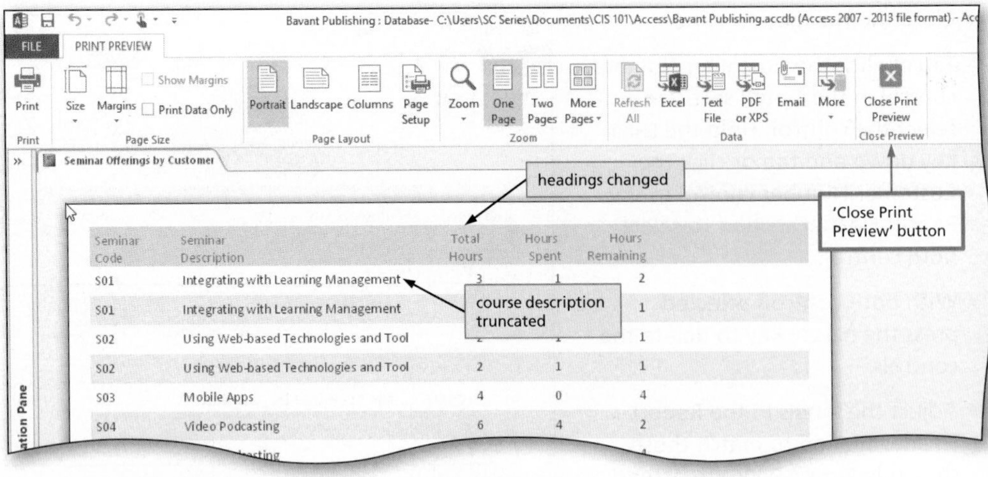

Figure 6–45

2

- Tap or click the 'Close Print Preview' button (PRINT PREVIEW tab | Close Preview group) to return to Design view.
- Click outside all of the selected controls to deselect the controls.
- Tap or click the Seminar Description control in the Detail section to select it.
- Tap or click the Property Sheet button (REPORT DESIGN TOOLS DESIGN tab | Tools group) to display the property sheet.
- With the All tab selected, scroll down until the Can Grow property appears, and then tap or click the Can Grow property box arrow to display the list of possible values for the Can Grow property (Figure 6–46).

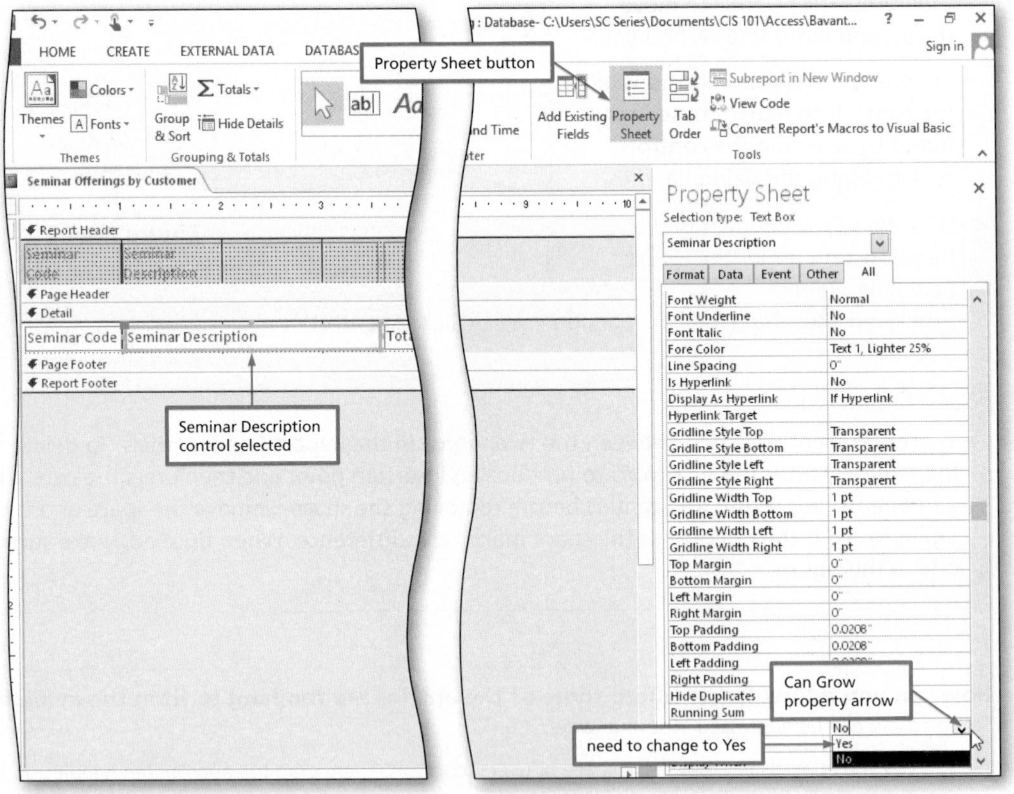

Figure 6–46

Q&A
What is the effect of the Can Shrink property?
If the value of the Can Shrink property is set to Yes, Access will remove blank lines that occur when the field is empty.

3

- Tap or click Yes in the list to allow the Seminar Description control to grow as needed.
- Close the property sheet.

To Change the Appearance of the Controls in the Subreport

1 CREATE TABLES | 2 CREATE QUERIES | 3 CREATE REPORT | 4 SPECIFY GROUPING & SORTING | 5 ADD FIELDS
6 ADD SUBREPORT | 7 ADD TITLE, PAGE NUMBER, & DATE | 8 CREATE SECOND REPORT

***Why?** Any changes you make to the appearance of the controls in the subreport will be reflected when you view the main report.* The following steps change the controls in the Detail section to bold and the controls in the Report Header section to italic. They also change the background color in the Report Header section to white.

1

- Drag the right boundary of the subreport to the approximate position shown in Figure 6–47.

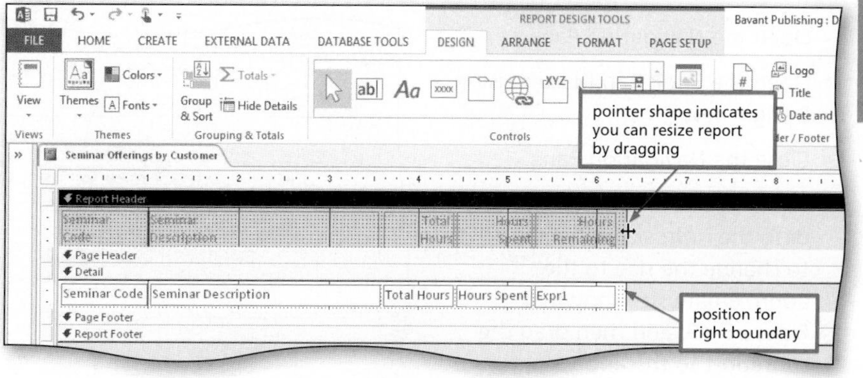

Figure 6–47

2

- Display the REPORT DESIGN TOOLS FORMAT tab.
- Tap or click the ruler to the left of the controls in the Detail section to select the controls, and then tap or click the Bold button (REPORT DESIGN TOOLS FORMAT tab | Font group) to bold the controls.
- Tap or click the ruler to the left of the controls in the Report Header section to select the controls, and then tap or click the Italic button (REPORT DESIGN TOOLS FORMAT tab | Font group) to italicize the controls.

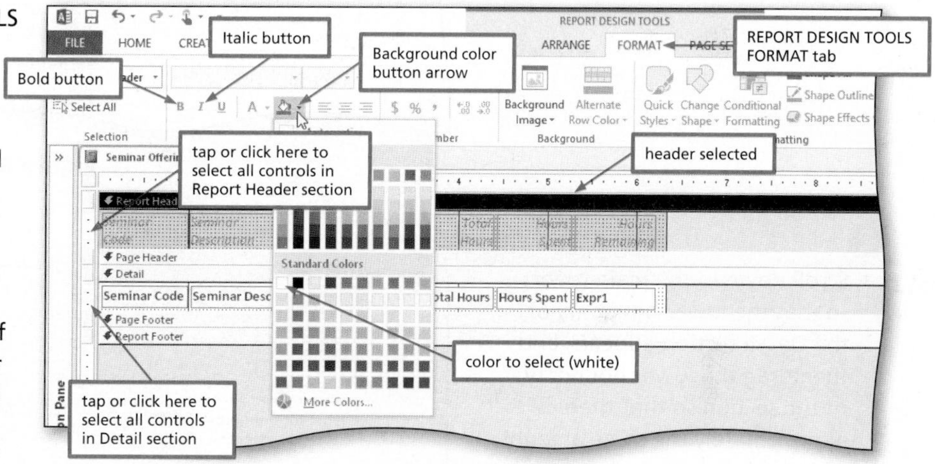

Figure 6–48

- Tap or click the title bar for the Report Header to select the header without selecting any of the controls in the header.
- Tap or click the Background Color button arrow (REPORT DESIGN TOOLS FORMAT tab | Font group) to display a color palette (Figure 6–48).

3

- Tap or click White in the first row, first column of the Standard Colors to change the background color to white.

Q&A What is the difference between tapping or clicking a color in the Theme colors and tapping or clicking a color in the Standard Colors?

The theme colors are specific to the currently selected theme. The first column, for example, represents "background 1," one of the selected background colors in the theme. The various entries in the column represent different intensities of the color at the top of the column. The colors would be different if a different theme were selected. If you select one of the theme colors and a different theme is selected in the future, the color you selected would change to the color in the same location. On the other hand, if you select a standard color, a change of theme would have no effect on the color.

- Tap or click the Save button on the Quick Access Toolbar to save the changes.
- Close the Seminar Offerings by Customer subreport.

To Resize the Subreport and the Report in Design View

1 CREATE TABLES | 2 CREATE QUERIES | 3 CREATE REPORT | 4 SPECIFY GROUPING & SORTING | 5 ADD FIELDS
6 ADD SUBREPORT | 7 ADD TITLE, PAGE NUMBER, & DATE | 8 CREATE SECOND REPORT

The following steps resize the subreport control in the main report. They then reduce the height of the detail section. ***Why?*** *Any additional white space at the bottom of the detail section appears as extra space at the end of each detail line in the final report.* Finally, the steps reduce the width of the main report.

1

- Open the Navigation Pane.
- Open the Book Rep Master List in Design view.
- Close the Navigation Pane.
- Tap or click the subreport and drag the right sizing handle to change the size to the approximate size shown in Figure 6–49, and then drag the subreport to the approximate position shown in the figure.

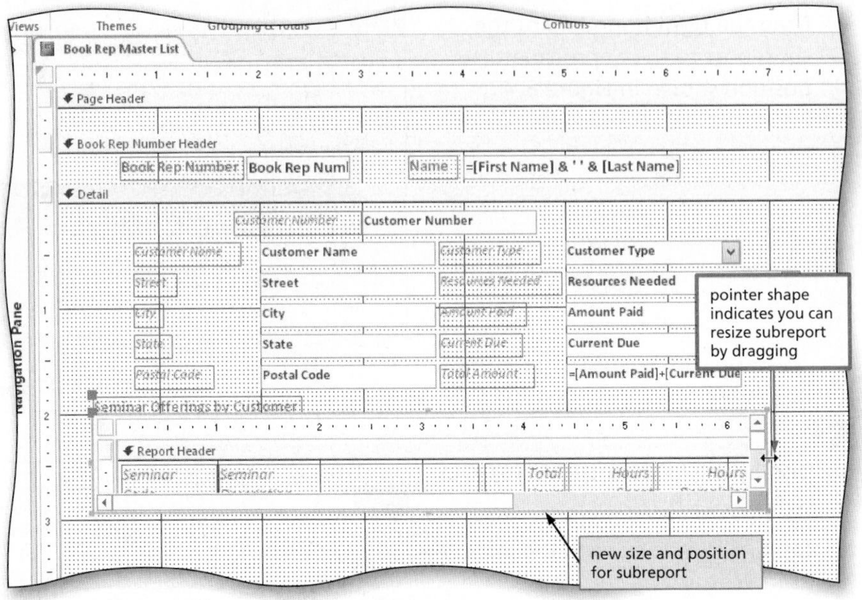

Figure 6–49

2

- Scroll down in the main report so that the lower boundary of the Detail section appears, and then drag the lower boundary of the section so that there is approximately the same amount of space below the subreport as that shown in Figure 6–50.

Q&A I scrolled down to see the lower boundary of the Detail section, and the controls are no longer on the screen. What is the easiest way to drag the boundary when the position to which I want to drag it is not visible?

You do not need to see the location to drag to it. As you get close to the top of the visible portion of the screen, Access automatically will scroll. You might find it easier, however, to drag the boundary near the top of the visible portion of the report, use the scroll bar to scroll up, and then drag some more. You might have to scroll a couple of times.

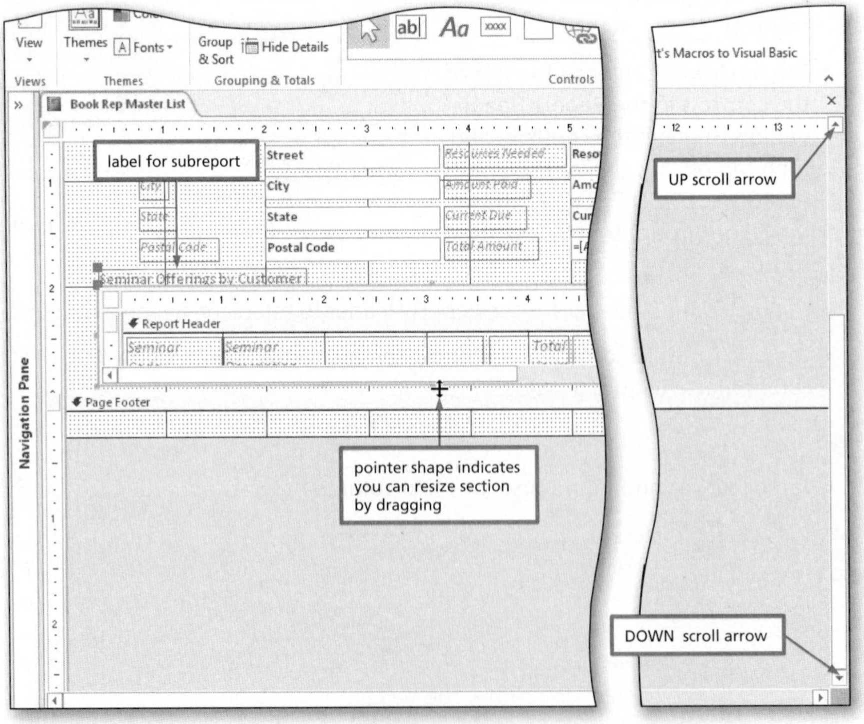

Figure 6–50

3

- If necessary, scroll back up to the top of the report, tap or click the label for the subreport (the label that reads Seminar Offerings by Customer), and then press the DELETE key to delete the label.
- Resize the report by dragging its right-hand border to the location shown in Figure 6–51.

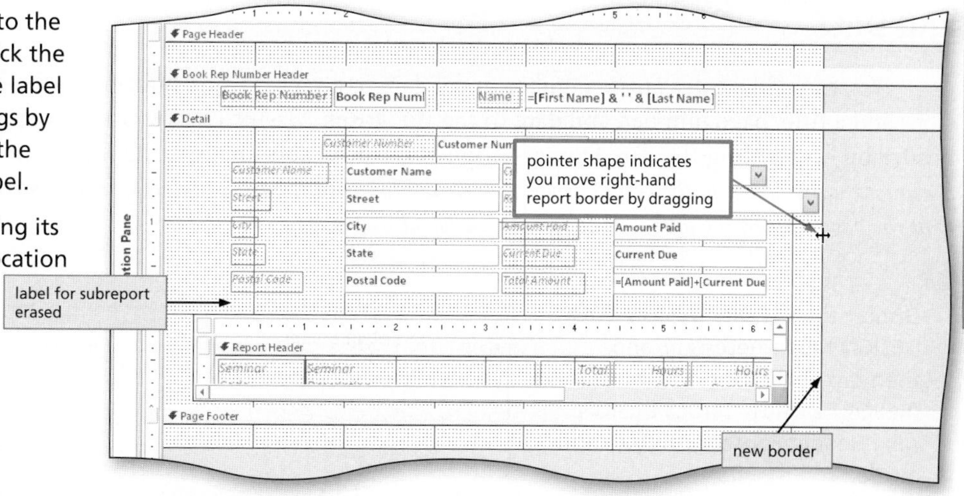

Figure 6–51

To Modify Section Properties

1 CREATE TABLES | 2 CREATE QUERIES | 3 CREATE REPORT | 4 SPECIFY GROUPING & SORTING | 5 ADD FIELDS
6 ADD SUBREPORT | 7 ADD TITLE, PAGE NUMBER, & DATE | 8 CREATE SECOND REPORT

The following step first deletes the label for the subreport and then makes two modifications to the Book Rep Number Header section. The first modification, which causes the contents of the Group Header section to appear at the top of each page, changes the Repeat Section property to Yes. ***Why?*** *Without this change, the book rep number and name only would appear at the beginning of the group of customers of that book rep. If the list of customers occupies more than one page, it would not be apparent on subsequent pages which book rep is associated with those customers.* The second modification changes the Force New Page property to Before Section, causing each section to begin at the top of a page.

1

- Tap or click the Book Rep Number Header bar to select the header, and then tap or click the Property Sheet button (REPORT DESIGN TOOLS DESIGN tab | Tools group) to display the property sheet.
- With the All tab selected, tap or click the Repeat Section property box, tap or click the arrow that appears, and then tap or click Yes to cause the contents of the group header to appear at the top of each page of the report.
- Tap or click the Force New Page property box, and then tap or click the arrow that appears to display the menu of possible values (Figure 6–52).

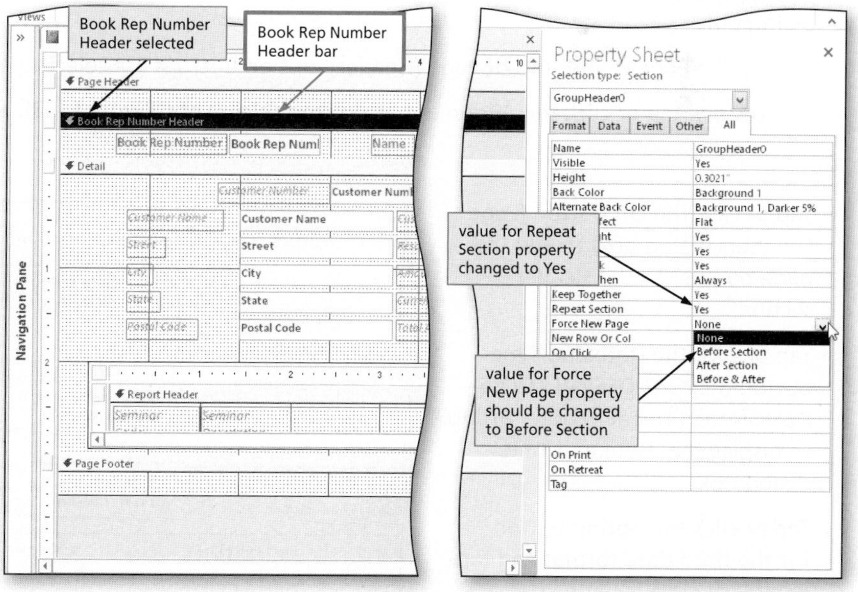

Figure 6–52

2

- Tap or click Before Section to cause a new group to begin at the top of the next page.
- Close the property sheet.

To Add a Title, Page Number, and Date

1 CREATE TABLES | 2 CREATE QUERIES | 3 CREATE REPORT | 4 SPECIFY GROUPING & SORTING | 5 ADD FIELDS
6 ADD SUBREPORT | 7 ADD TITLE, PAGE NUMBER, & DATE | 8 CREATE SECOND REPORT

You can add a title, a page number, and a date to a report using buttons on the DESIGN tab. The following steps add a title, page number, and date to the Book Rep Master List report. The steps move the date to the page header by first cutting the date from its original position and then pasting it into the page header. ***Why?*** *The date is automatically added to the report header, which would mean it only would appear once at the beginning of the report. If it is in the page header, the date will appear at the top of each page.*

1

- Display the REPORT DESIGN TOOLS DESIGN tab, if necessary, and then tap or click the Title button (REPORT DESIGN TOOLS DESIGN tab | Header/Footer group) to add a title.

Q&A The title is the same as the name of the report object. Can I change the report title without changing the name of the report object in the database?

Yes. The report title is a label, and you can change it using any of the techniques that you used for changing column headings and other labels.

- Tap or click the Page Numbers button (REPORT DESIGN TOOLS DESIGN tab | Header/Footer group) to display the Page Numbers dialog box.
- Be sure the Page N and 'Top of Page [Header]' option buttons are selected.
- If necessary, tap or click the Alignment arrow and select Left (Figure 6–53).

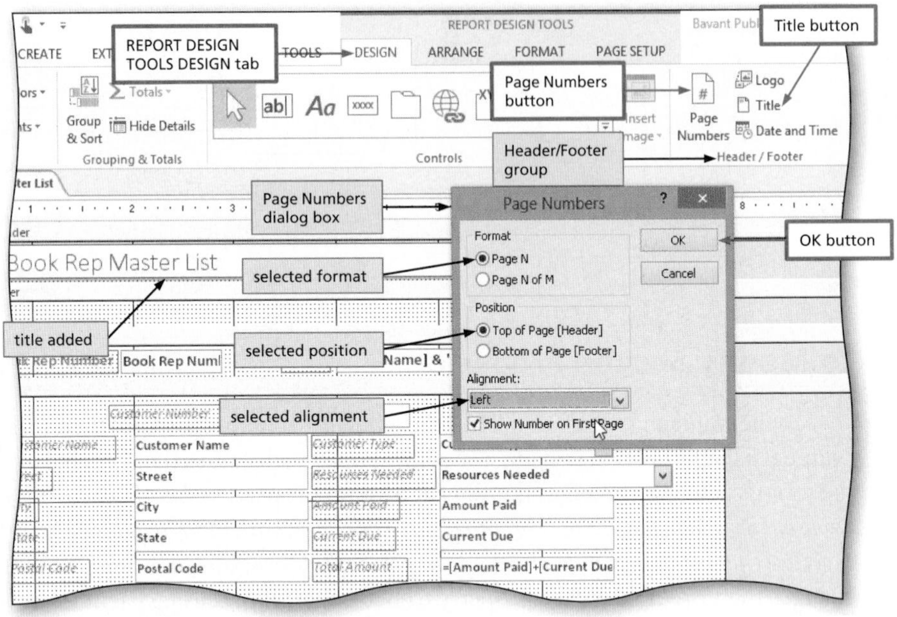

Figure 6–53

2

- Tap or click the OK button (Page Numbers dialog box) to add the page number to the Header section.
- Tap or click the Date and Time button (REPORT DESIGN TOOLS DESIGN tab | Header/Footer group) to display the 'Date and Time' dialog box.
- Tap or click the option button for the third date format and tap or click the Include Time check box to remove the check mark (Figure 6–54).

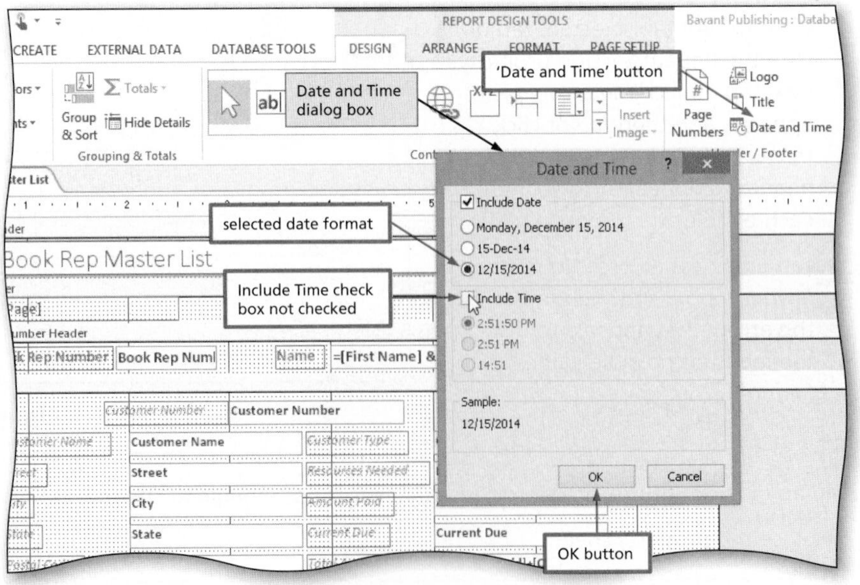

Figure 6–54

3

- Tap or click the OK button (Date and Time dialog box) to add the date to the Report Header.
- Display the HOME tab (Figure 6–55).

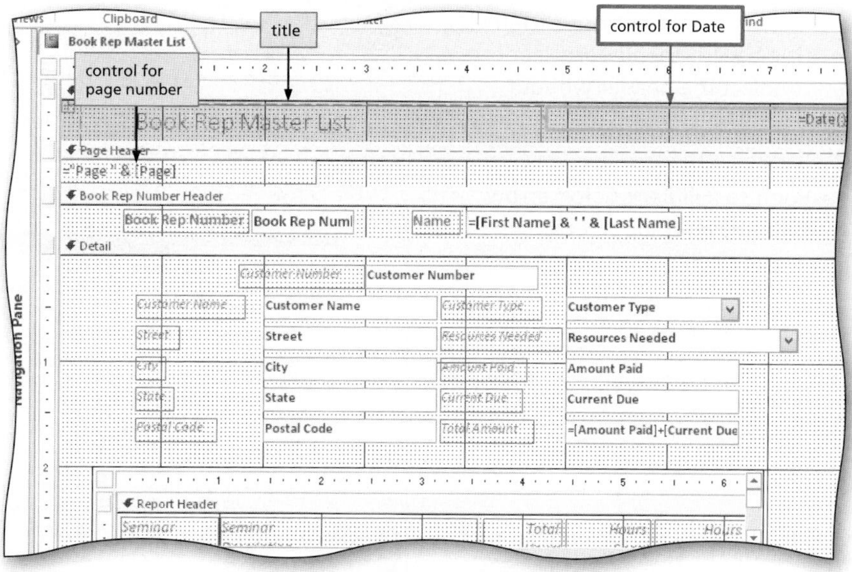

Figure 6–55

4

- With the control containing the date selected, tap or click the Cut button (HOME tab | Clipboard group) to cut the date, tap or click the title bar for the page header to select the page header, and then tap or click the Paste button (HOME tab | Clipboard group) to paste the Date control at the beginning of the page header.
- Drag the Date control, which is currently sitting on top of the Page Number control, to the position shown in Figure 6–56.

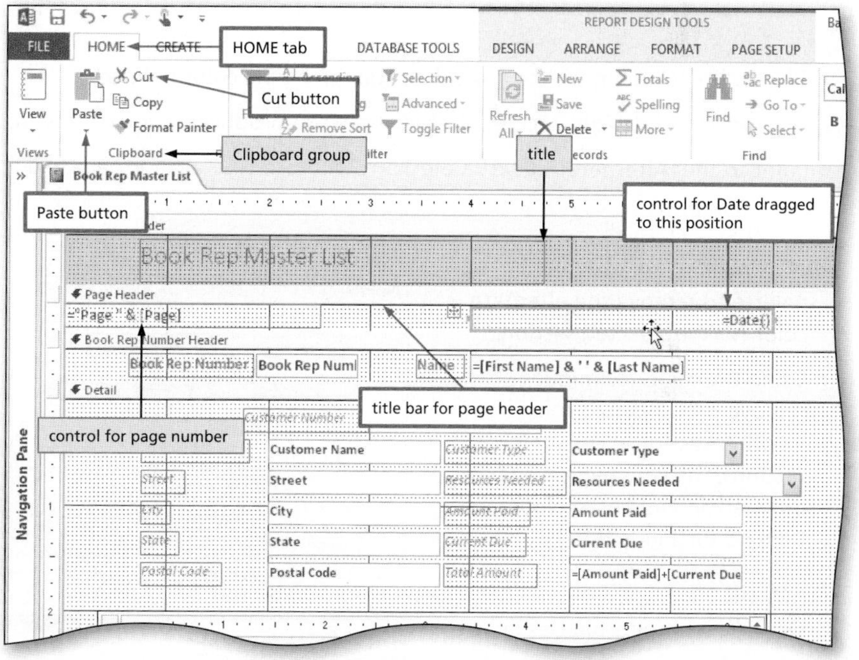

Figure 6–56

To Remove the Header Background Color and the Alternate Color

1 CREATE TABLES | 2 CREATE QUERIES | 3 CREATE REPORT | 4 SPECIFY GROUPING & SORTING | 5 ADD FIELDS
6 ADD SUBREPORT | 7 ADD TITLE, PAGE NUMBER, & DATE | **8 CREATE SECOND REPORT**

The report header currently has a blue background, whereas the desired report does not have such a background. In addition, the report has alternate colors. An **alternate color** is a color different from the main color that appears on every other line in a datasheet or report. Using alternate colors can sometimes make a datasheet or report more readable.

The steps on the next page first remove the color from the report header. They then remove the alternate colors from the various sections in the report, starting with the Detail section. ***Why?*** *Access automatically assigns alternate colors within the report. In reports with multiple sections, the alternate colors can be confusing. If you do not want these alternate colors, you must remove them.*

1

- Press and hold or right-click the title bar for the Report Header to select the header without selecting any of the controls in the header.
- Point to 'Fill/Back Color' arrow to display a color palette (Figure 6–57).

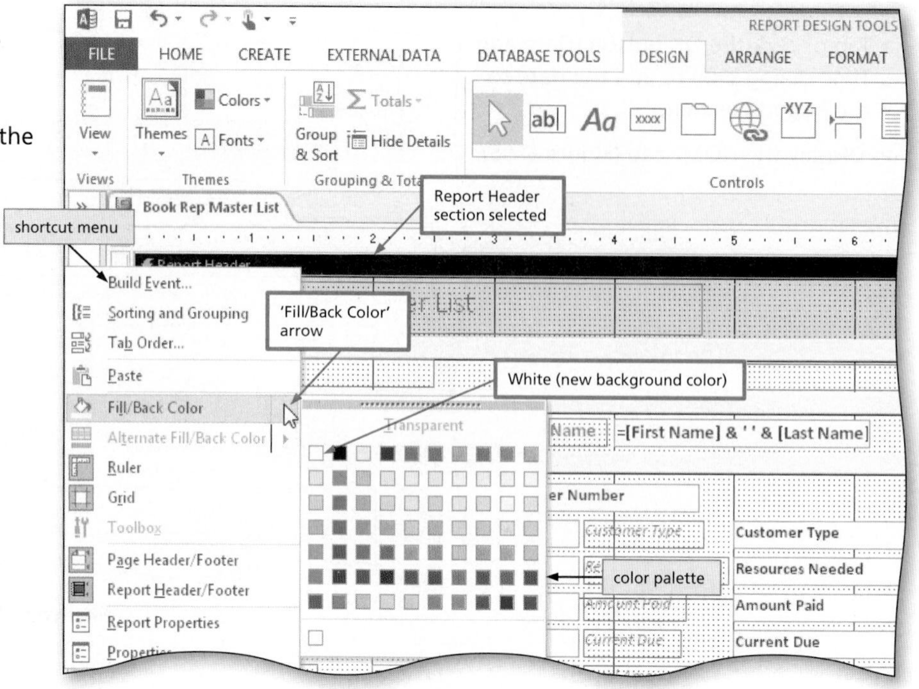

Figure 6–57

2

- Tap or click White in the first row, first column of the color palette.
- Press and hold or right-click the Detail section to produce a shortcut menu.
- Point to the 'Alternate Fill/Back Color' arrow to produce a color palette (Figure 6–58).

3

- Tap or click None on the color palette to remove the alternate color for the selected section.
- Using the same techniques, remove the alternate color from all other sections. (For some sections, the command may be dimmed, in which case you need take no further action.)
- Save and then close the report.
- Open the subreport in Design view.
- Remove the header background color and the alternate color from the subreport, just as you removed them from the main report.
- Save and then close the subreport.
- Open the main report in Design view.

Q&A How can I be sure I removed all the background colors?
Open the report in Print Preview to check that all color has been removed from the report.

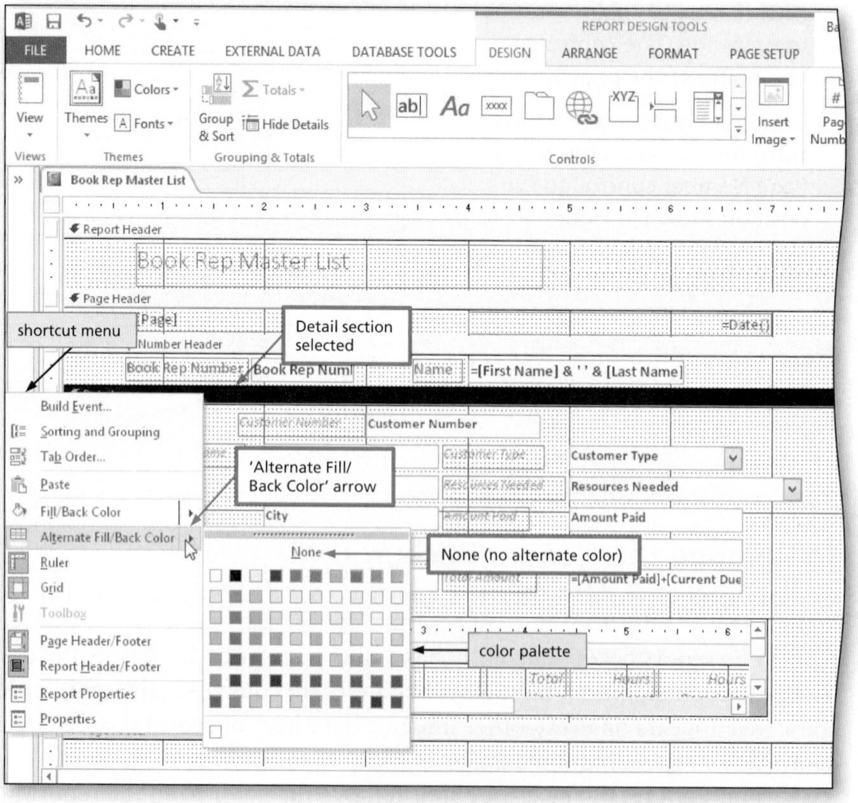

Figure 6–58

Headers and Footers

Access gives you some options for including or omitting headers and footers in your reports. They go together, so if you have a report header, you will also have a report footer. If you do not want one of them to appear you can shrink its size so there is no room for any content, or you can also remove them from your report altogether. If you later decide you want to include them, you once again can add them. You have similar options with page headers and page footers.

To Remove a Report Header and Footer

To remove a report header and footer, you would use the following steps.

1. With the report open in Design view, press and hold or right-click any open area of the report to produce a shortcut menu.
2. Tap or click the 'Report Header/Footer' command on the shortcut menu to remove the report header and footer.
3. If the Microsoft Access dialog box appears, asking if it is acceptable to delete any controls in the section, tap or click the Yes button.

BTW

Hyperlink Controls
You can add a hyperlink to tables, forms, and reports. To add a hyperlink, which provides single-click access to webpages, tap or click the Hyperlink tool, enter the hyperlink in the Address text box (Insert Hyperlink dialog box) and tap or click the OK button. If necessary, move the hyperlink control to the desired location on the report.

To Remove a Page Header and Footer

To remove a page header and footer, you would use the following steps.

1. With the report open in Design view, press and hold or right-click any open area of the report to produce a shortcut menu.
2. Tap or click the 'Page Header/Footer' command on the shortcut menu to remove the page header and footer.
3. If the Microsoft Access dialog box appears, asking if it is acceptable to delete any controls in the section, tap or click the Yes button.

To Insert a Report Header and Footer

To insert a report header and footer, you would use the following steps.

1. With the report open in Design view, press and hold or right-click any open area of the report to produce a shortcut menu.
2. Tap or click the 'Report Header/Footer' command on the shortcut menu to insert a report header and footer.

BTW

Drop Down Controls
Drop down boxes can be combo boxes or list boxes. To add a combo box to a report, tap or click the Combo Box tool, move the pointer to the desired location, and tap or click the position to place the combo box. Follow the directions in the Combo Box Wizard dialog box to specify the options and values for the combo box. To add a list box to a report, tap or click the List Box tool and follow the steps listed above for a combo box.

To Insert a Page Header and Footer

To insert a page header and footer, you would use the following steps.

1. With the report open in Design view, press and hold or right-click any open area of the report to produce a shortcut menu.
2. Tap or click the 'Page Header/Footer' command on the shortcut menu to insert a page header and footer.

To Include an Image in a Report

You can include a picture (image) in a report. You can also use a picture (image) as the background on a report. To include an image in a report, you would use the following steps.

1. Open the report in Design view or Layout view.
2. Tap or click the Insert Image button (REPORT DESIGN TOOLS DESIGN tab | Controls group), and then tap or click the Browse command.

BTW
Graphs
You can add graphs (charts) to a report using the Chart tool. To add a graph (chart) to a report, tap or click the Chart tool, move the pointer to the desired location, and tap or click the position to place the graph. Follow the directions in the Chart Wizard dialog box to specify the data source for the chart, the values for the chart, and the chart type.

3. Select the desired image.
4. Tap or click the desired location to add the image to the report.

To Use an Image as Background for a Report

To include an image as a background for a report, you would use the following steps.

1. Open the report in Design view or Layout view.
2. Tap or click anywhere in the report, tap or click the Background Image button (REPORT DESIGN TOOLS FORMAT tab | Background group), and then tap or click the Browse command.
3. Select the desired image for the background.

BTW
Page Breaks
You can force a page break to occur at a particular position in a report by adding a page break to the report. To do so, tap or click the Insert Page Break tool, move the pointer to the desired position, and tap or click the position to place the page break.

To Save and Close the Report

The following steps save the final report and then close the report.

1. Tap or click the Save button on the Quick Access Toolbar to save the report.
2. Close the report by tapping or clicking its Close button.

To Print the Report

The following steps print the Book Rep Master List report.

1. With the Book Rep Master List selected in the Navigation Pane, tap or click FILE on the ribbon to open the Backstage view.
2. Tap or click the Print tab in the Backstage view to display the Print gallery.
3. Tap or click the Quick Print button to print the report.

Q&A
Do I need to preview the report before I print it?
It is not necessary but previewing a report before you print it, especially if you have made changes since the last time you printed, prevents wasting paper if the report needs to be modified.

To Publish a Report

You can make a report available through email by publishing the report as either a PDF or XPS file. If you wanted to do so, you would use the following steps.

1. Select the report to be published in the Navigation Pane.
2. Display the EXTERNAL DATA tab.
3. Tap or click the PDF or XPS button (EXTERNAL DATA tab | Export group) to display the Publish as PDF or XPS dialog box.
4. Select the appropriate Save as type (either PDF or XPS).
5. Select either 'Standard (publishing online and printing)' or 'Minimum size (publishing online).'
6. If you want to publish only a range of pages, tap or click the Options button and select the desired range.

7. Tap or click the Publish button to publish the report in the desired format.
8. If you want to save the export steps, tap or click the 'Save export steps' check box, then tap or click the Save Export button. If not, tap or click the Close button.

Break Point: If you wish to stop working through the chapter at this point, you can resume the project at a later time by starting Access, opening the database called Bavant Publishing, and continuing to follow the steps from this location forward.

Creating a Second Report

Bavant Publishing also would like a report that groups customers by book rep. The report should include subtotals and grand totals. Finally, it should show the discount amount for each customer. The discount amount is based on the current due amount. Customers who owe more than $20,000 will receive a 4 percent discount, and customers who owe $20,000 or less will receive a 2 percent discount.

To Create a Second Report

The following steps create the Discount Report, select the record source, and specify grouping and sorting options.

1. Close the Navigation Pane.
2. Display the CREATE tab and then tap or click the Report Design button (CREATE tab | Reports group) to create a report in Design view.
3. Ensure the selector for the entire report, which is the box in the upper-left corner of the report, contains a small black square indicating it is selected, and then tap or click the Property Sheet button (REPORT DESIGN TOOLS DESIGN tab | Tools group) to display a property sheet.
4. With the All tab selected, tap or click the Record Source property box arrow, and then tap or click the Book Reps and Customers query to select the query as the record source for the report.
5. Close the property sheet.
6. Tap or click the Group & Sort button (REPORT DESIGN TOOLS DESIGN tab | Grouping & Totals group) to display the Group, Sort, and Total pane.
7. Tap or click the 'Add a group' button to display the list of available fields for grouping, and then tap or click the Book Rep Number field to group by book rep number.
8. Tap or click the 'Add a sort' button to display the list of available fields for sorting, and then tap or click the Customer Number field to sort by customer number.
9. Remove the Group, Sort, and Total pane by tapping or clicking the Group & Sort button (REPORT DESIGN TOOLS DESIGN tab | Grouping & Totals group).
10. Tap or click the Save button on the Quick Access Toolbar, type `Discount Report` as the report name, and tap or click the OK button to save the report.

Q&A Why save it at this point?
You do not have to save it at this point. It is a good idea to save it often, however. Doing so will give you a convenient point from which to restart if you have problems. If you have problems, you could close the report without saving it. When you reopen the report, it will be in the state it was in when you last saved it.

To Add and Move Fields in a Report

1 CREATE TABLES | 2 CREATE QUERIES | 3 CREATE REPORT | 4 SPECIFY GROUPING & SORTING | 5 ADD FIELDS
6 ADD SUBREPORT | 7 ADD TITLE, PAGE NUMBER, & DATE | 8 CREATE SECOND REPORT

As with the previous report, you can add a field to the report by dragging the field from the field list. You can drag an attached label separately from the control to which it is attached by dragging the move handle in its upper-left corner. This technique does not work, however, if you want to drag the attached label to a section different from the control's section. If you want the label to be in a different section, you must select the label, cut the label, select the section to which you want to move the label, and then paste the label. You then can move the label to the desired location.

The following steps add the Book Rep Number field to the Book Rep Number Header section and then move the label to the Page Header section. ***Why?*** *The label should appear at the top of each page, rather than in the group header.*

1

- Tap or click the 'Add Existing Fields' button (REPORT DESIGN TOOLS DESIGN tab | Tools group) to display a field list. (Figure 6–59).

Q&A My field list displays 'Show only fields in the current record source,' not 'Show all tables,' as in the figure. What should I do?
Tap or click the 'Show only fields in the current record source' link at the top of the field list to display only those fields in the Book Reps and Customers query.

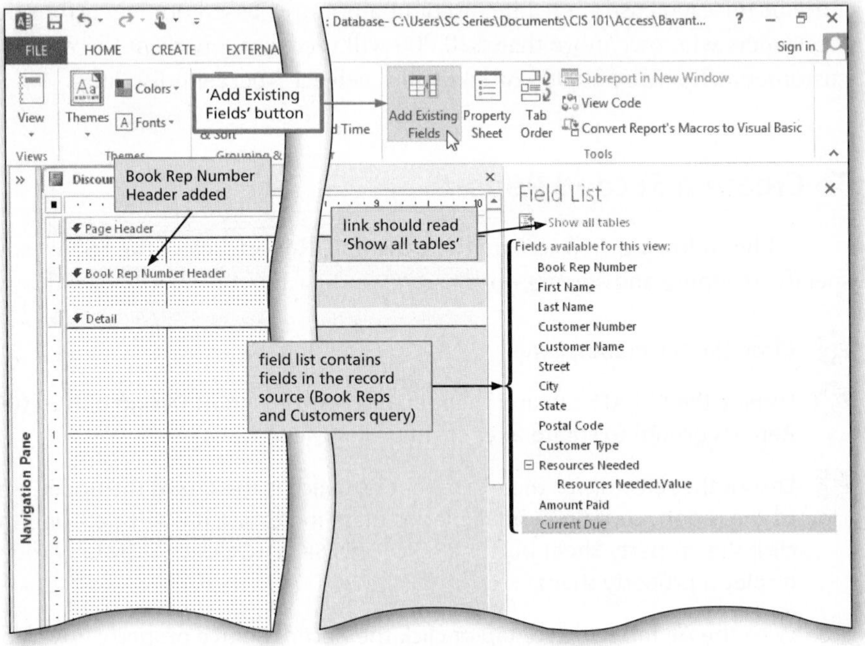

Figure 6–59

2

- Drag the Book Rep Number field to the approximate position shown in Figure 6–60.

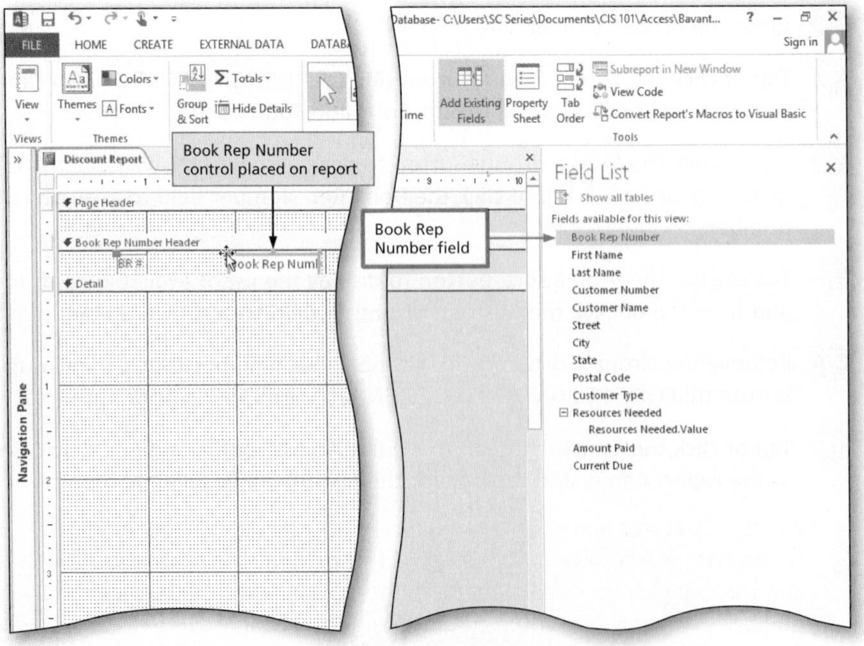

Figure 6–60

3

- Tap or click the label for the Book Rep Number control to select it (Figure 6–61).

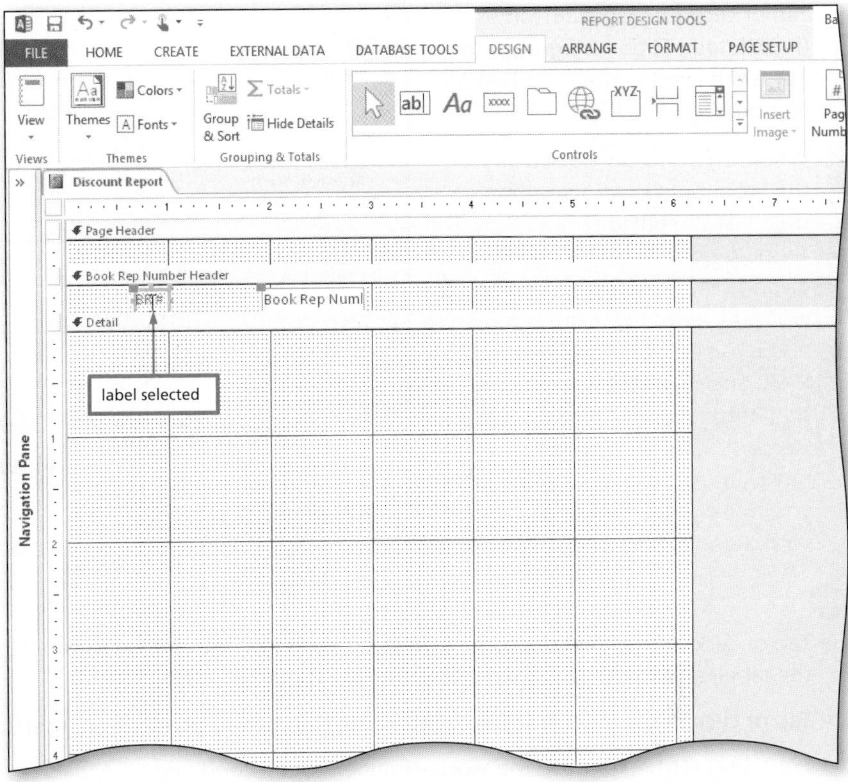

Figure 6–61

4

- Display the HOME tab.
- Tap or click the Cut button (HOME tab | Clipboard group) to cut the label.
- Tap or click the Page Header bar to select the page header (Figure 6–62).

Q&A Do I have to tap or click the bar, or could I tap or click somewhere else within the section?

You also could tap or click within the section. Tapping or clicking the bar usually is safer, however. If you tap or click in a section intending to select the section, but tap or click within one of the controls in the section, you will select the control rather than the section. Tapping or clicking the bar always selects the section.

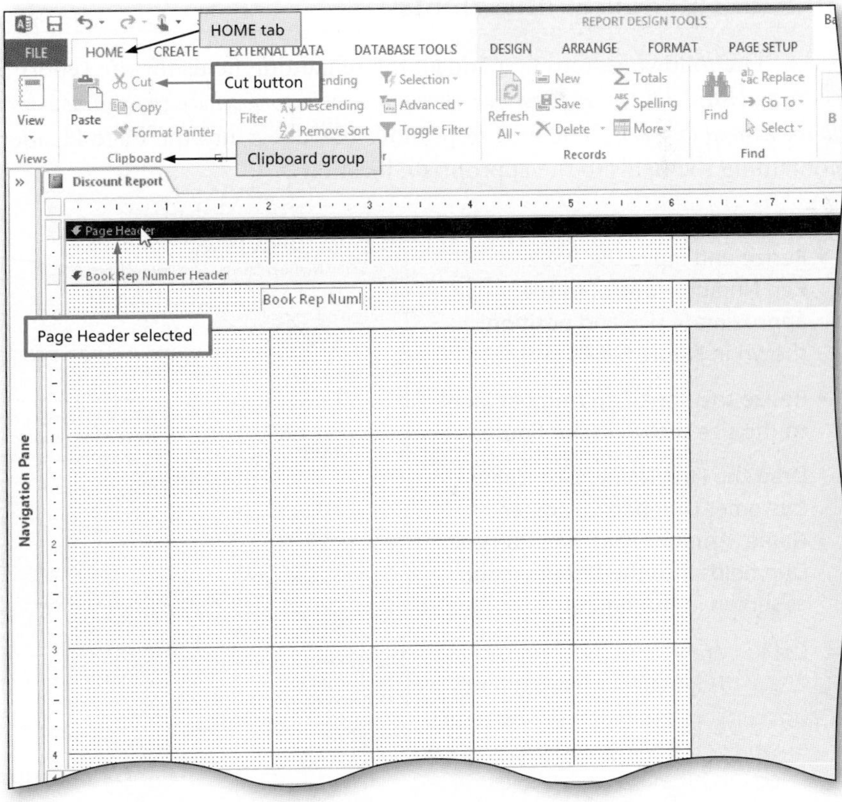

Figure 6–62

5

- Tap or click the Paste button (HOME tab | Clipboard group) to paste the label in the Page Header section (Figure 6–63).

Q&A When would I want to tap or click the Paste button arrow rather than just the button?
Tapping or clicking the arrow displays the Paste button menu, which includes the Paste command and two additional commands. Paste Special allows you to paste data into different formats. Paste Append, which is available if you have cut or copied a record, allows you to paste the record to a table with a similar structure. If you want the simple Paste command, you can just tap or click the button.

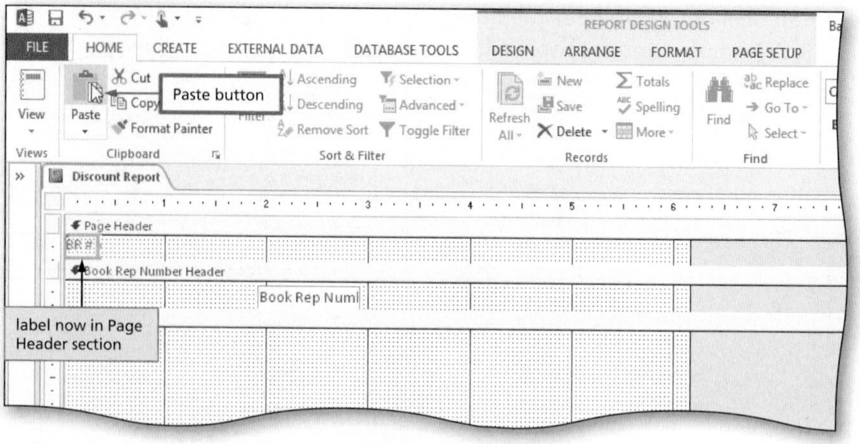

Figure 6–63

6

- Tap or click in the label to produce an insertion point, use the BACKSPACE or DELETE key to erase the current entry in the label, and then type `Rep Number` as the new entry.
- Tap or click in the label in front of the word, Number, to produce an insertion point.
- Press SHIFT+ENTER to move the word, Number, to a second line.

To Add the Remaining Fields

1 CREATE TABLES | 2 CREATE QUERIES | 3 CREATE REPORT | 4 SPECIFY GROUPING & SORTING | 5 ADD FIELDS
6 ADD SUBREPORT | 7 ADD TITLE, PAGE NUMBER, & DATE | 8 CREATE SECOND REPORT

The following steps first add all the remaining fields for the report by dragging them into the Detail section. ***Why?*** *Dragging them gets them onto the report, where you can now move the controls and labels individually to the desired locations.* The next steps move the labels into the Page Header section, and move the controls containing the fields to the appropriate locations.

1

- Resize and move the Book Rep Number control to the approximate size and position shown in Figure 6–64.
- Resize the Book Rep Number label to the size shown in the figure.
- Drag the First Name, Last Name, Customer Number, Customer Name, Amount Paid, and Current Due fields into the Detail section, as shown in the figure.

Q&A Could I drag them all at once?
Yes. You can select multiple fields by selecting the first field, holding down the SHIFT key, and then selecting other adjacent fields. To select fields that are not adjacent to each other, hold down the CTRL key and select the additional fields. Once you have selected multiple fields, you can drag them all at once. How you choose to select fields and drag them onto the report is a matter of personal preference.

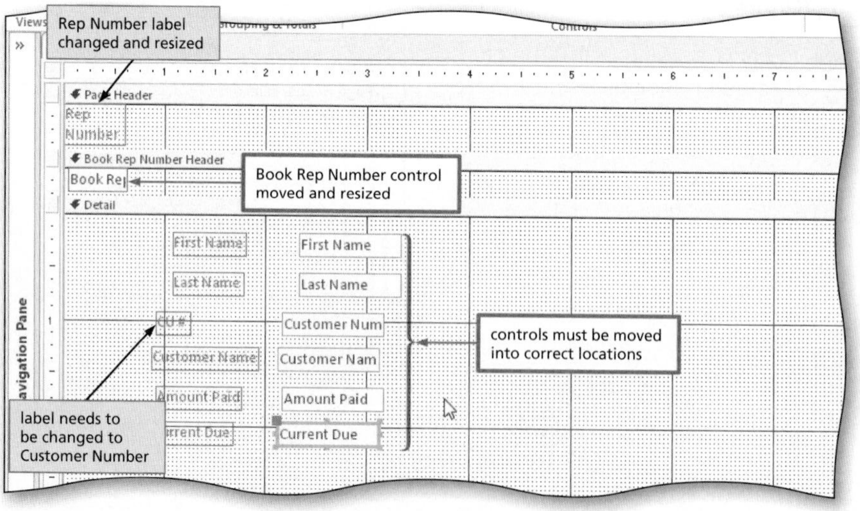

Figure 6–64

2

- Close the field list.
- One at a time, cut each of the labels, paste the label into the Page Header section, and then resize, reformat, and move the labels to the approximate positions shown in Figure 6–65.

Q&A When I paste the label, it is always placed at the left edge, superimposing the Book Rep Number control. Can I change where Access places it?
Unfortunately, when you paste to a different section, Access places the control at the left edge. You will need to drag each control to its proper location after pasting it into the Page Header section.

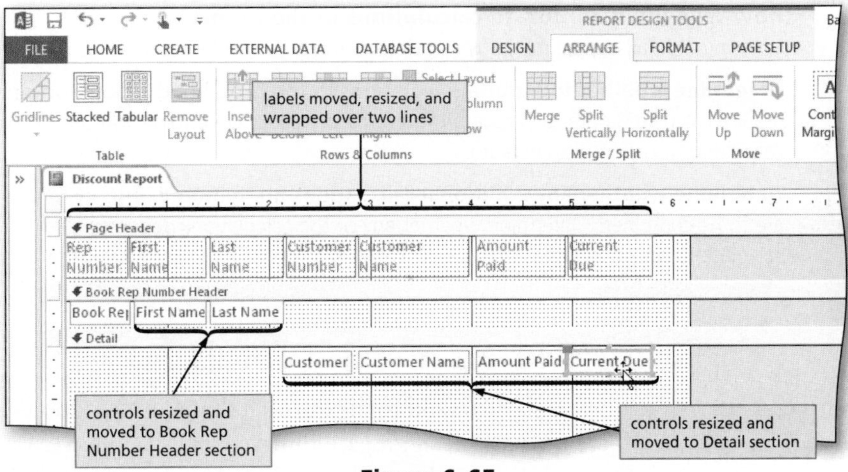

Figure 6–65

- One at a time, resize and move the First Name and Last Name controls to the approximate positions in the Book Rep Number Header section shown in the figure.
- One at a time, resize and move the Customer Number, Customer Name, Amount Paid, and Current Due controls to the approximate positions in the Detail section shown in the figure.
- Display the REPORT DESIGN TOOLS ARRANGE tab.
- Use the Align button (REPORT DESIGN TOOLS ARRANGE tab | Sizing & Ordering group) as necessary to align all the controls as shown in Figure 6–65.

To Change the Can Grow Property

The following steps change the Can Grow property for the Customer Name control so that names that are too long to fit in the available space will extend to additional lines.

1. Select the Customer Name control.
2. Display the property sheet and scroll down until the Can Grow property appears.
3. Tap or click the Can Grow property box and then tap or click the Can Grow property box arrow to display the menu of available values for the Can Grow property.
4. Tap or click Yes to change the value for the Can Grow property.
5. Close the property sheet.

To Resize the Detail Section

1 CREATE TABLES | 2 CREATE QUERIES | 3 CREATE REPORT | 4 SPECIFY GROUPING & SORTING | 5 ADD FIELDS
6 ADD SUBREPORT | 7 ADD TITLE, PAGE NUMBER, & DATE | 8 CREATE SECOND REPORT

The following step resizes the Detail section of the Discount Report to remove most of the extra space below the controls in the section. ***Why?*** *The extra space would appear after each detail line in the report, which adds unnecessary length to the report. The desired report (Figure 6–1b on page AC 332) does not include such space.*

1

- Scroll down so that the lower boundary of the Detail section appears, and then drag the lower boundary of the section to a position just slightly below the controls in the section.

CONSIDER THIS

How will you incorporate calculations in the report?
Determine details concerning any calculations required for the report.

Determine whether to include calculations in the group and report footers. The group footers or report footers might require calculated data such as subtotals or grand totals. Determine whether the report needs other statistics that must be calculated (for example, average).

Determine whether any additional calculations are required. If so, determine the fields that are involved and how they are to be combined. Determine whether any of the calculations depend on a true or false state for a criterion, in which case the calculations are conditional.

Totals and Subtotals

To add totals or other statistics to a footer, add a text box control. You can use any of the aggregate functions: COUNT, SUM, AVG (average), MAX (largest value), MIN (smallest value), STDEV (standard deviation), VAR (variance), FIRST, and LAST. To use a function, type an equal (=) sign, followed by the function name. You then include a set of parentheses containing the item for which you want to perform the calculation. If the item name contains spaces, such as Amount Paid, you must enclose it in square brackets. For example, to calculate the sum of the amount paid values, the expression would be =SUM([Amount Paid]).

Access will perform the calculation for the appropriate collection of records. If you enter this expression in the Book Rep Number Footer section, Access only will calculate the total for customers with the given book rep; that is, it will calculate the appropriate subtotal. If you enter the expression in the Report Footer section, Access will calculate the total for all customers.

Grouping and Sorting Options

As you learned in Chapter 4, tapping or clicking the More button in the Group, Sort, and Total pane allows you to specify additional options for grouping and sorting. The additional options are: Value, which lets you choose the amount of the value on which to group; Totals, which lets you choose the values to be totaled; Title, which lets you customize the group title; Header section, which lets you include or omit a header section for the group; Footer section, which lets you include or omit a footer section for the group; and Keep together, which lets you specify whether Access is to attempt to keep portions of a group together on a page.

To Add Totals and Subtotals

1 CREATE TABLES | 2 CREATE QUERIES | 3 CREATE REPORT | 4 SPECIFY GROUPING & SORTING | 5 ADD FIELDS
6 ADD SUBREPORT | 7 ADD TITLE, PAGE NUMBER, & DATE | **8 CREATE SECOND REPORT**

The following steps first display the Book Rep Number Footer section and then add the total of amount paid and current due to both the Book Rep Number Footer section and the Report Footer section. The steps label the totals in the Book Rep Number Footer section as subtotals and the totals in the Report Footer section as grand totals. The steps change the format of the new controls to currency and the number of decimal places to 2. ***Why?*** *The requirements at Bavant indicate that the Discount Report should contain subtotals and grand totals of amounts paid and current due.*

1

- If necessary, display the REPORT DESIGN TOOLS DESIGN tab.
- Tap or click the Group & Sort button (REPORT DESIGN TOOLS DESIGN tab | Grouping & Totals group) to display the Group, Sort, and Total pane.
- Tap or click 'Group on Book Rep Number' to select Group on Book Rep Number (Figure 6–66).

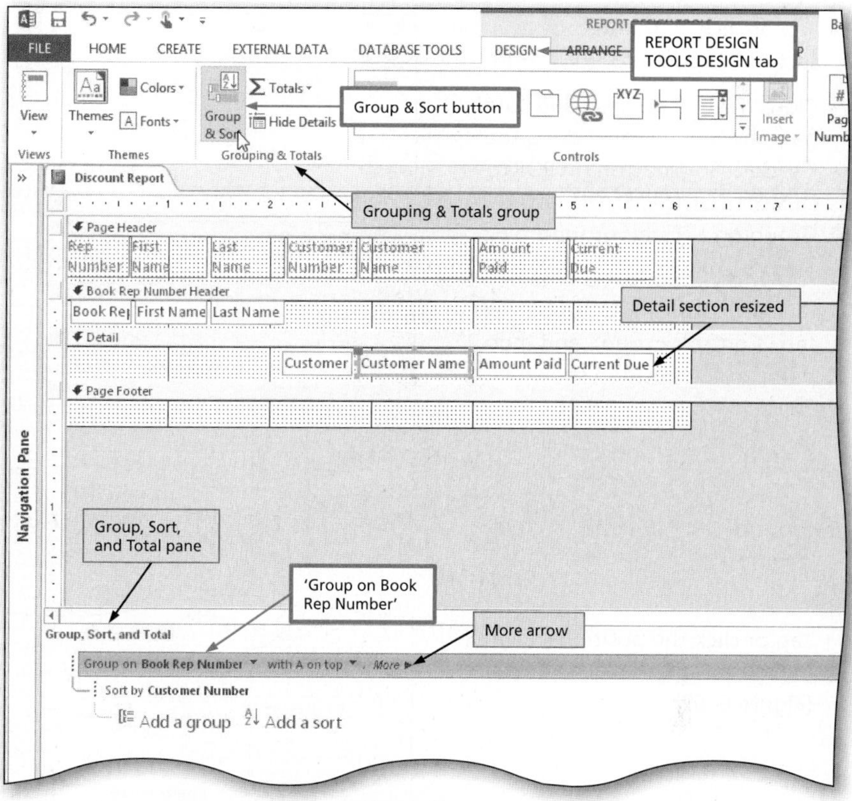

Figure 6–66

2

- Tap or click the More arrow to display additional options for grouping.
- Tap or click the 'without a footer section' arrow to display the available options (Figure 6–67).

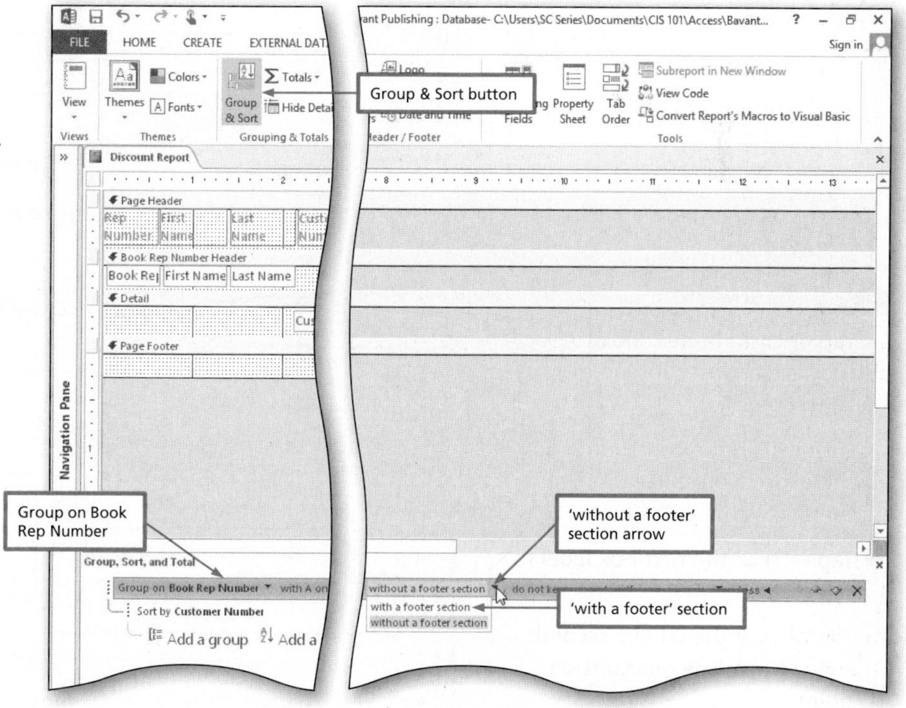

Figure 6–67

3

- Tap or click 'with a footer section' to add a footer.
- Close the Group, Sort, and Total pane by tapping or clicking the Group & Sort button (REPORT DESIGN TOOLS DESIGN tab | Grouping & Totals group).
- Tap or click the Text Box tool (REPORT DESIGN TOOLS DESIGN tab | Controls group), and then point to the position shown in Figure 6–68.

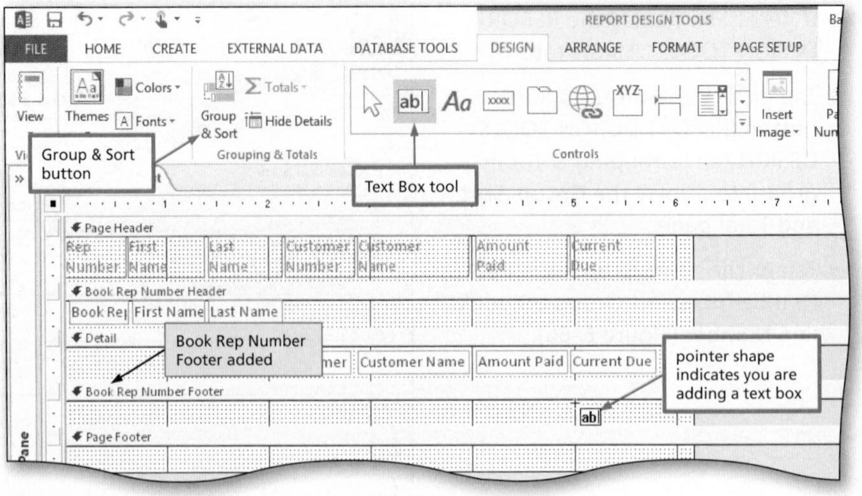

Figure 6–68

4

- Tap or click the position shown in Figure 6–68 to place a text box (Figure 6–69).

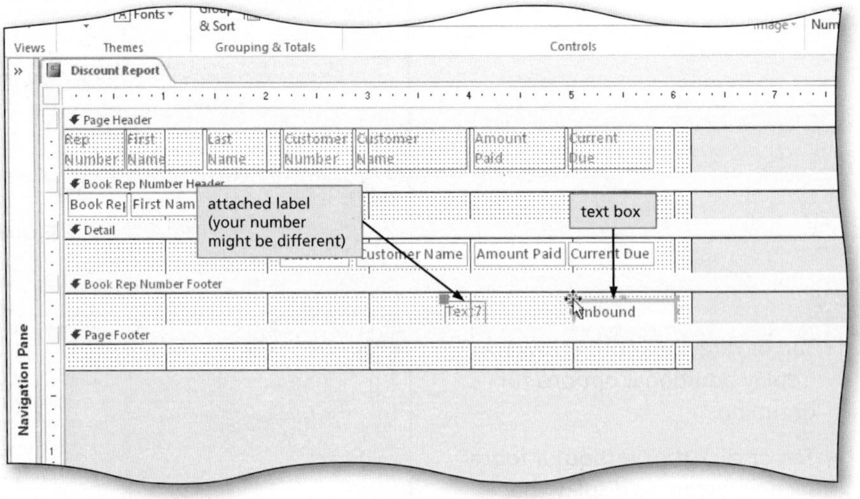

Figure 6–69

5

- Tap or click the text box to produce an insertion point.
- Type **=Sum([Current Due])** in the control to enter the expression calculation, and then press the ENTER key.
- Tap or click the text box label to select it.
- Tap or click the label a second time to produce an insertion point.
- Use the DELETE or BACKSPACE key to delete the Text7 label (your number might be different).
- Type **Subtotals** as the label.

If necessary, move the label to the position shown in Figure 6–70.

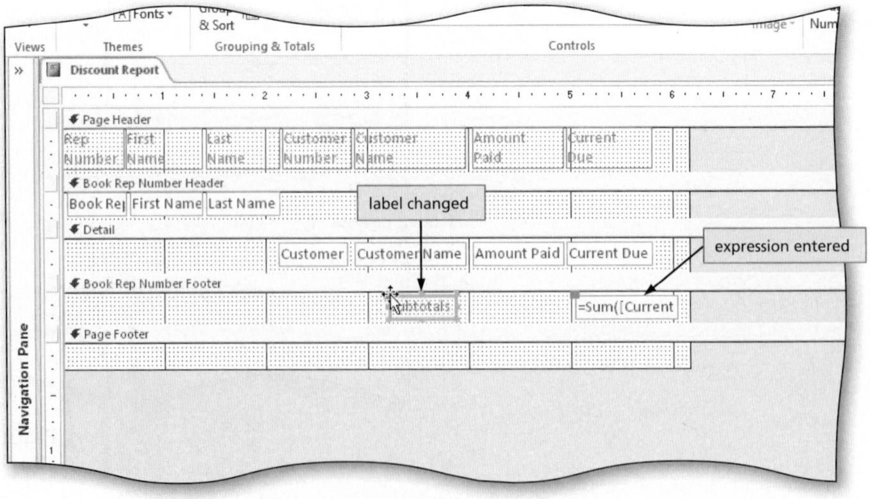

Figure 6–70

6

- Tap or click the Text Box tool (REPORT DESIGN TOOLS DESIGN tab | Controls group), and then tap or click in the Book Rep Number Footer section just to the left of the control for the sum of Current Due to place another text box.
- Tap or click the text box to produce an insertion point, type **=Sum([Amount Paid])** in the control, and then press the ENTER key to enter the expression (Figure 6–71).

Q&A Could I add the controls in the other order?

Yes. The only problem is that the label of the second control overlaps the first control. Adding the controls in the order shown in the steps reduces the overlap. It is not a major difference, however.

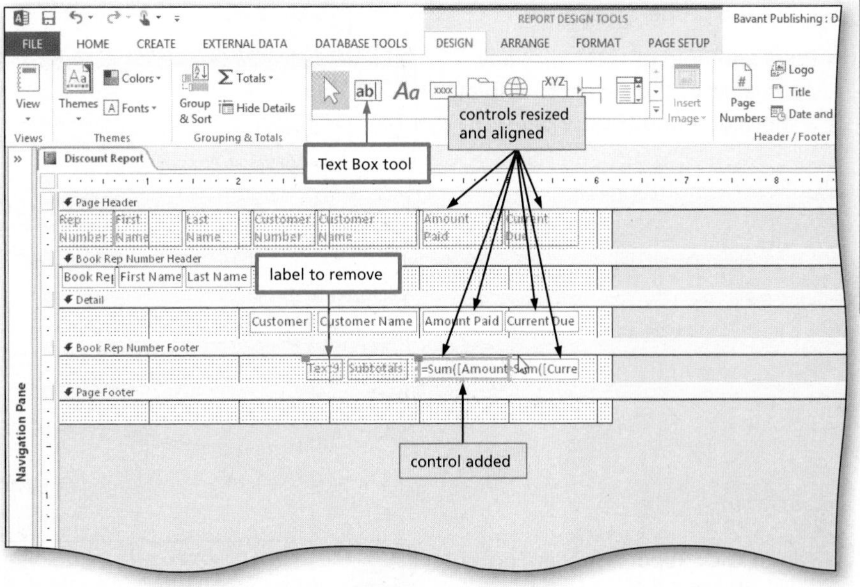

Figure 6–71

7

- Tap or click the label to select it, and then press the DELETE key to delete the label.

Q&A I inadvertently deleted the other control rather than the label. What should I do?

First, tap or click the Undo button on the Quick Access Toolbar to reverse your deletion. You then can delete the correct control. If that does not work, you can simply delete the remaining control or controls in the section and start these steps over.

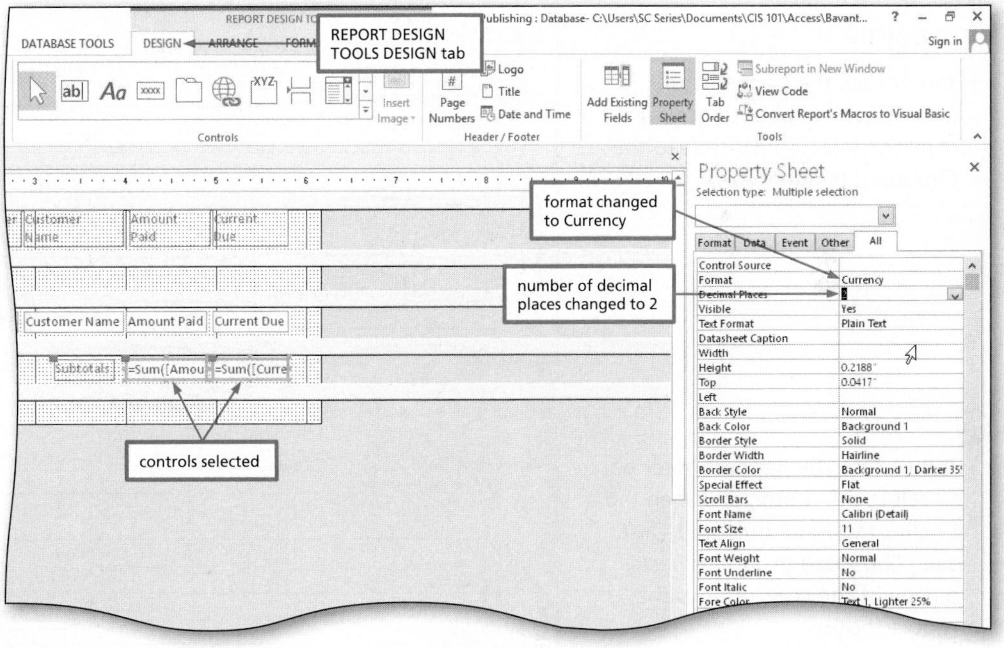

Figure 6–72

- Resize and align the Amount Paid and Current Due controls in the Detail section and the Book Rep Number Footer section to the positions shown in Figure 6–72.
- Tap or click the control for the sum of Amount Paid to select it, and then hold down the SHIFT key and tap or click the control for the sum of Current Due to select both controls.
- Tap or click the Property Sheet button (REPORT DESIGN TOOLS DESIGN tab | Tools group) to display the property sheet.
- Change the format to Currency and the number of decimal places to 2 as shown in the figure.

8

- Close the property sheet.
- Press and hold or right-click any open area of the report to display a shortcut menu (Figure 6–73).

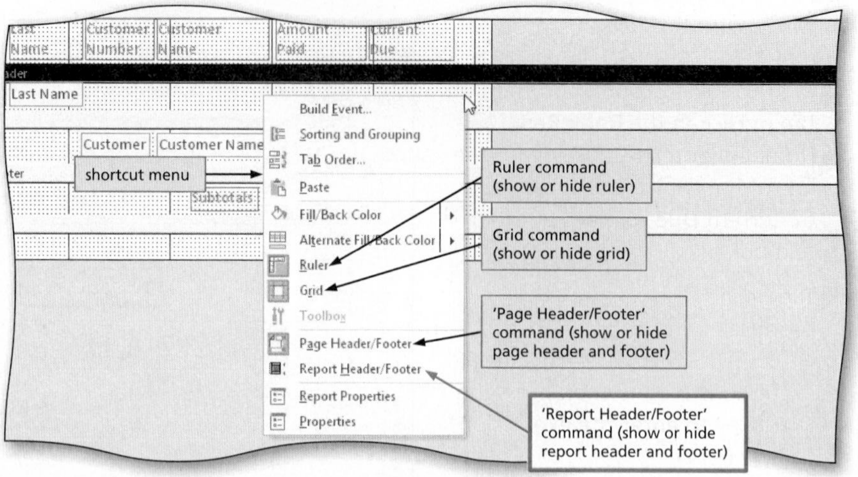

Figure 6–73

9

- Tap or click Report Header/Footer to display the Report Header and Footer sections.
- Tap or click the ruler in the Book Rep Number Footer to the left of the controls in the section to select the controls.
- Display the HOME tab.
- Tap or click the Copy button (HOME tab | Clipboard group) to copy the selected controls to the Clipboard (Figure 6–74).

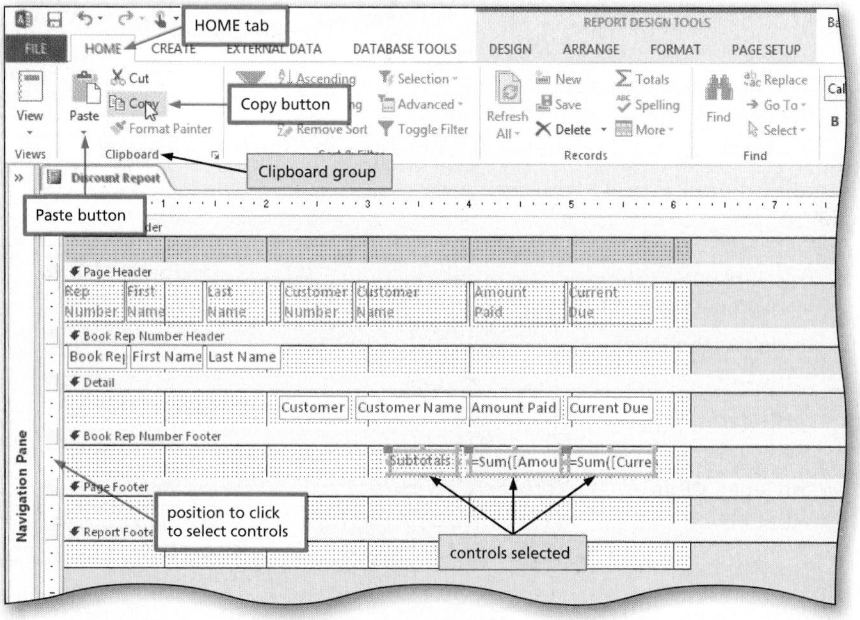

Figure 6–74

10

- Tap or click the Report Footer bar to select the footer, and then tap or click the Paste button (HOME tab | Clipboard group) to paste a copy of the controls into the report footer.
- Move the controls to the positions shown in Figure 6–75.
- Tap or click the label in the Report Footer section to select the label, and then tap or click a second time to produce an insertion point.

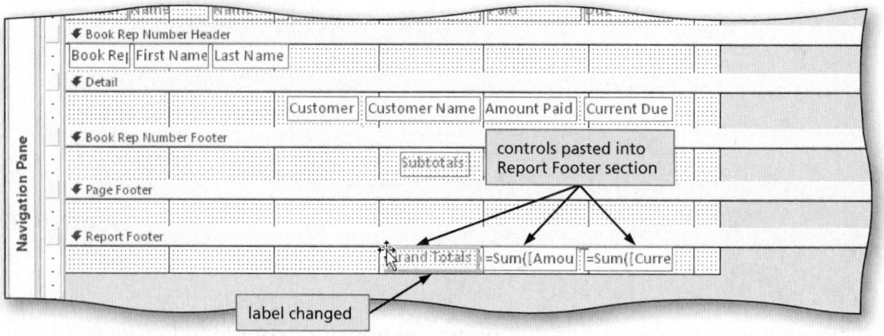

Figure 6–75

- Use the BACKSPACE or DELETE key to erase the current contents, and then type `Grand Totals` to change the label (Figure 6–75).

Q&A Could I enter the controls just as I did earlier, rather than copying and pasting?
Yes. Copying and pasting is a little simpler, but it is a matter of personal preference.

To View the Report

The following steps view the report in Report view, which is sometimes more convenient when you want to view the lower portion of the report.

1. Tap or click the View button arrow on the HOME tab to display the View button menu.
2. Tap or click Report View on the View button menu to view the report in Report view.
3. Scroll down to the bottom of the report so that the grand totals appear on the screen (Figure 6–76).

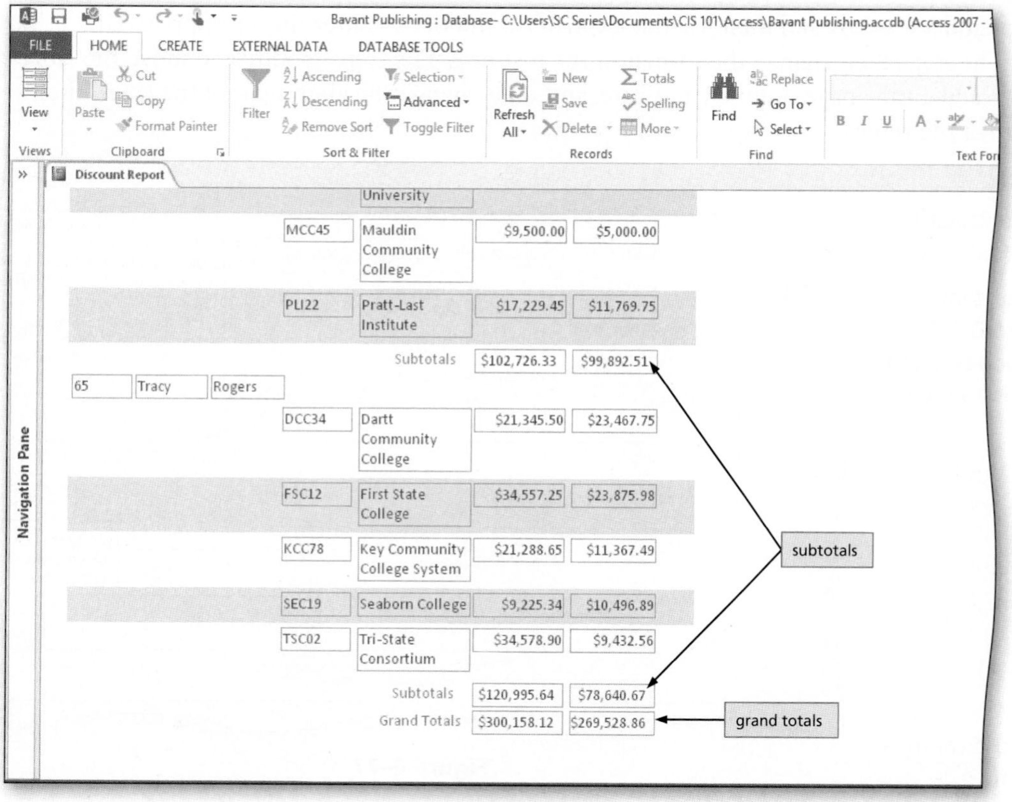

Figure 6–76

To Remove the Color from the Report Header

The following steps remove the color from the Report Header section by changing the background color for the header to white.

1. Tap or click the View button arrow and then tap or click Design View to return to Design view.
2. Press and hold or right-click the report header to produce a shortcut menu.
3. Point to the 'Fill/Back Color' arrow on the shortcut menu to display a color palette.
4. Tap or click White in the first row, first column to change the background color to white.

To Assign a Conditional Value

1 CREATE TABLES | 2 CREATE QUERIES | 3 CREATE REPORT | 4 SPECIFY GROUPING & SORTING | 5 ADD FIELDS
6 ADD SUBREPORT | 7 ADD TITLE, PAGE NUMBER, & DATE | **8 CREATE SECOND REPORT**

The Bavant requirements for this report also involved a conditional value related to the amount of a customer's discount. ***Why?*** *Bavant has determined that the amount of the discount depends on the amount paid. If the amount paid is greater than $20,000, the discount on the current due amount is 4 percent. If not, the discount is 2 percent.*

To assign a conditional value, you will use the IIf function. The IIf function consists of the letters IIf followed by three items, called **arguments**, in parentheses. The first argument is a criterion; the second and third arguments are expressions. If the criterion is true, the function assigns the value of the expression in the second argument. If the criterion is false, the function assigns the value of the expression in the third argument. The IIf function you will use is IIf([Amount Paid]>20000, .04*[Current Due], .02*[Current Due]). This function applies the following rules: If the amount paid is greater than $20,000, the value assigned is .04*[Current Due], that is, 4 percent of the current due amount. If the amount paid is not greater than $20,000, the value assigned is .02*[Current Due], that is, 2 percent of the current due amount.

The following steps add a text box and then use the Expression Builder to enter the appropriate IIf function in the text box. The steps then change the format of the text box. The steps modify and move the label for the text box. They also add a title, page number, and date, and then change the alignment of the title. The steps then change the size of the report.

1

- If necessary, display the REPORT DESIGN TOOLS DESIGN tab.
- Tap or click the Text Box tool (REPORT DESIGN TOOLS DESIGN tab | Controls group) and point to the approximate position shown in Figure 6–77.

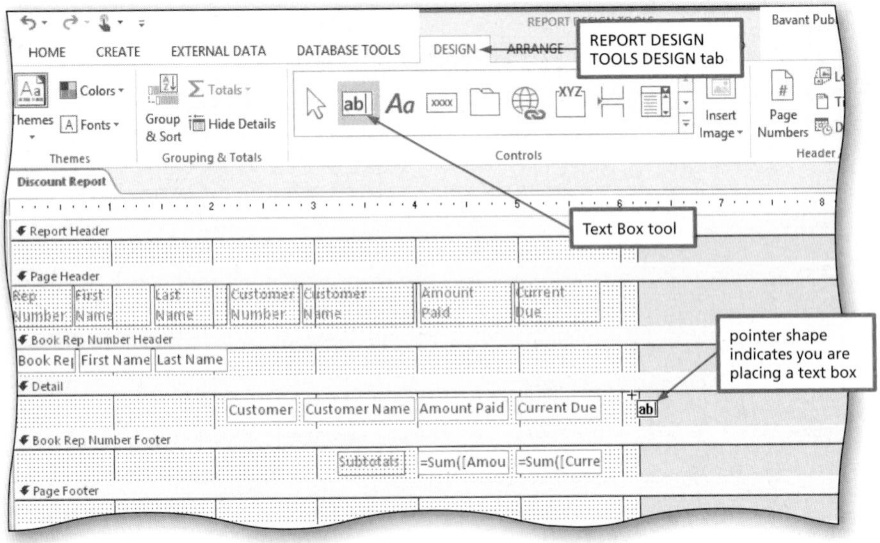

Figure 6–77

Q&A

How can I place the control accurately when there are no gridlines?
When you tap or click the position for the control, Access automatically will expand the grid. You then can adjust the control using the grid.

Can I automatically cause controls to be aligned to the grid?
Yes. Tap or click the Size/Space button (REPORT DESIGN TOOLS ARRANGE tab | Sizing & Ordering group) and then tap or click Snap to Grid on the Size/Space menu. From that point on, any controls you add will be automatically aligned to the grid.

2

- Tap or click the position shown in Figure 6–77 to place a text box.
- Tap or click the attached label to select it, and then press the DELETE key to delete the attached label.
- Tap or click the text box to select it, and then tap or click the Property Sheet button (REPORT DESIGN TOOLS DESIGN tab | Tools group) to display a property sheet.
- Tap or click the Control Source property to select it (Figure 6–78).

Q&A Why did I choose Control Source, not Record Source?

You use Record Source to select the source of the records in a report, usually a table or a query. You use the Control Source property to specify the source of data for the control. This allows you to bind an expression or field to a control.

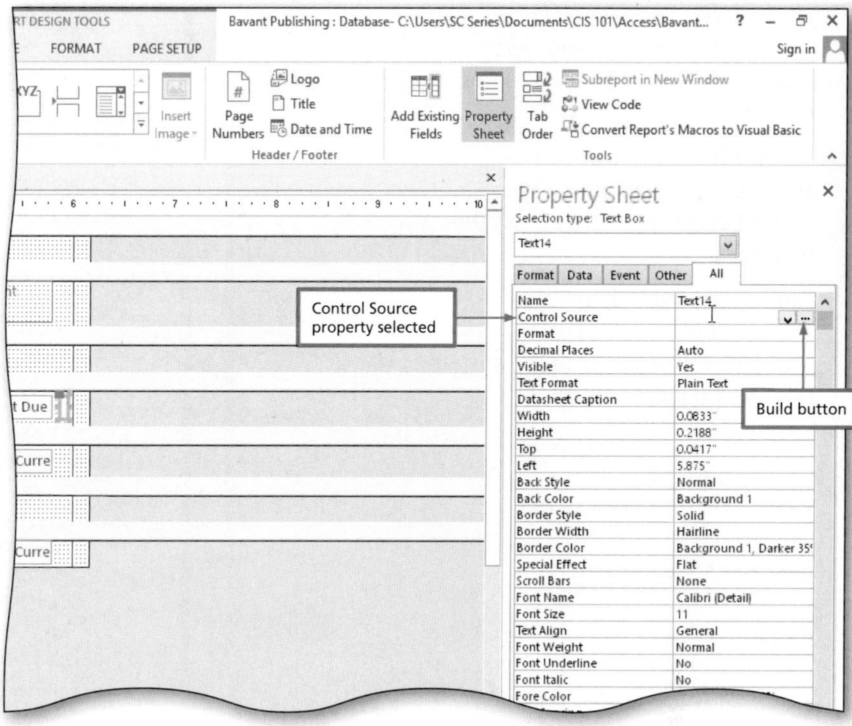

Figure 6–78

3

- Tap or click the Build button to display the Expression Builder dialog box.
- Double-tap or double-click Functions in the first column to display the function subfolders.
- Tap or click Built-In Functions in the first column to display the various function categories in the second column.
- Scroll down in the second column so that Program Flow appears, and then tap or click Program Flow to display the available program flow functions in the third column.
- Double-tap or double-click IIf in the third column to select the IIf function (Figure 6–79).

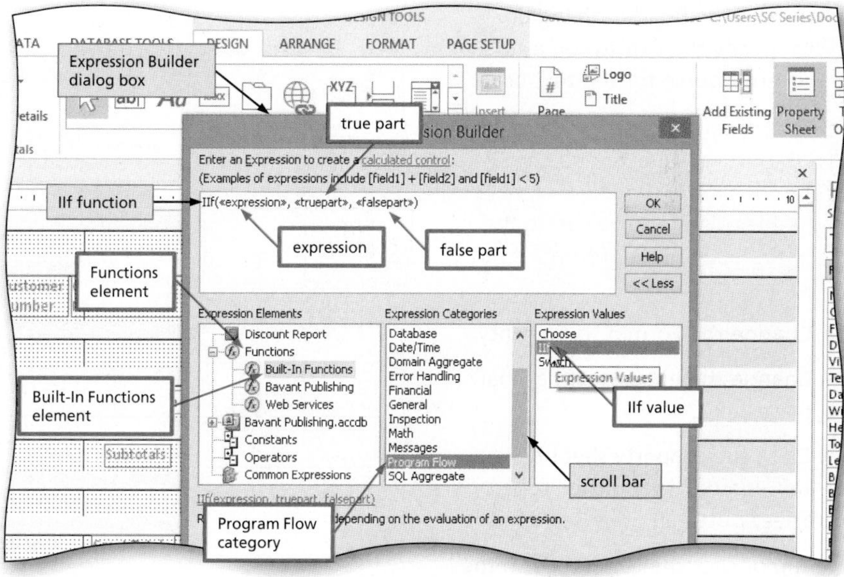

Figure 6–79

Q&A Do I have to select Program Flow? Could I not just scroll down to IIf?

You do not have to select Program Flow. You indeed could scroll down to IIf. You will have to scroll through a large number of functions in order to get to IIf, however.

4

- Tap or click the <<expression>> argument to select it and type `[Amount Paid]>20000` as the expression.
- Tap or click the <<truepart>> argument to select it and type `.04*[Current Due]` as the true part.
- Tap or click the <<falsepart>> argument to select it and type `.02*[Current Due]` as the false part (Figure 6–80).

Q&A Are there other ways I could enter the expression?

Yes. You could just type the whole expression. On the other hand, you could select the function just as in these steps, and, when entering each argument, you could select the fields from the list of fields and tap or click the desired operators.

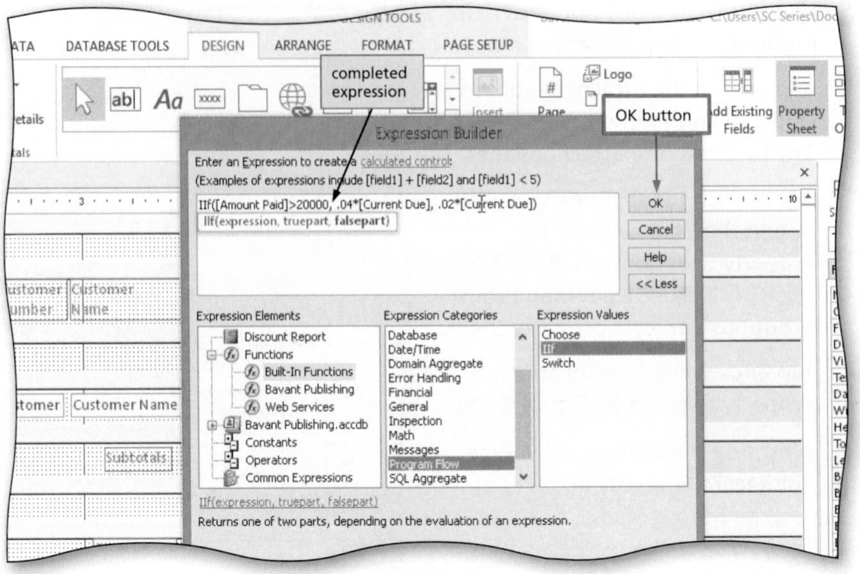

Figure 6–80

5

- Tap or click the OK button (Expression Builder dialog box) to specify the expression as the control source for the text box.

Q&A My property sheet is covering my OK button. What should I do?

Tap or click in the Expression Builder dialog box to bring the entire dialog box in front of the property sheet.

- Change the Format to Currency.
- Change the number of decimal places to 2.
- Close the property sheet by tapping or clicking the Property Sheet button.
- Tap or click the Label tool on the REPORT DESIGN TOOLS DESIGN tab and point to the approximate position shown in Figure 6–81.

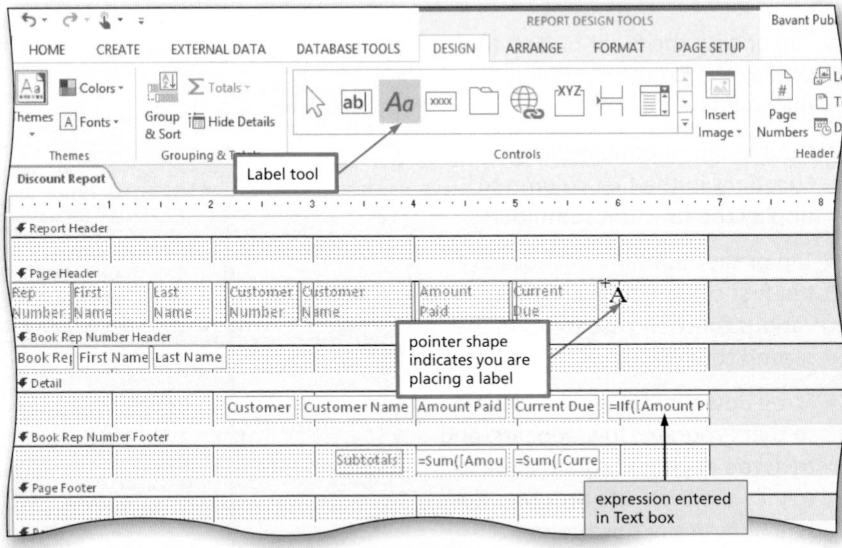

Figure 6–81

6

- Press and hold the left mouse button, drag the pointer to the approximate position at the lower-right corner of the label shown in Figure 6–82, and then release your finger or the mouse button to place the label.

Q&A I made the label the wrong size. What should I do?

With the label selected, drag the sizing handles to resize the label as needed. Drag the control in a position away from the sizing handles if you need to move the label.

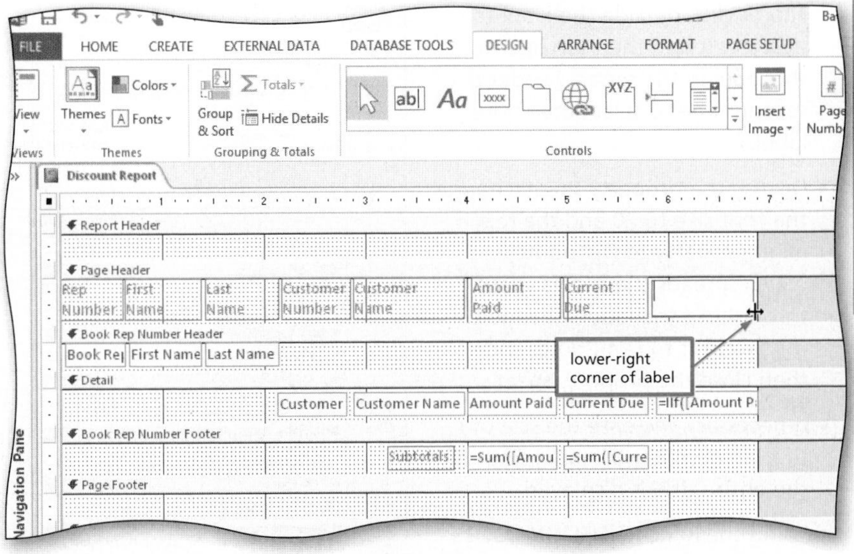

Figure 6–82

7

- Type `Discount` to enter the name of the label.
- Tap or click outside the label to deselect the label and then select the Amount Paid, Current Due, and Discount labels.
- With the labels selected, display the REPORT DESIGN TOOLS FORMAT tab and then tap or click the Align Right button (REPORT DESIGN TOOLS FORMAT tab | Font group) to right-align the text within the labels.
- Move or resize the Discount label as necessary so that it aligns with the text box containing the IIf and with the other controls in the Page Header section.

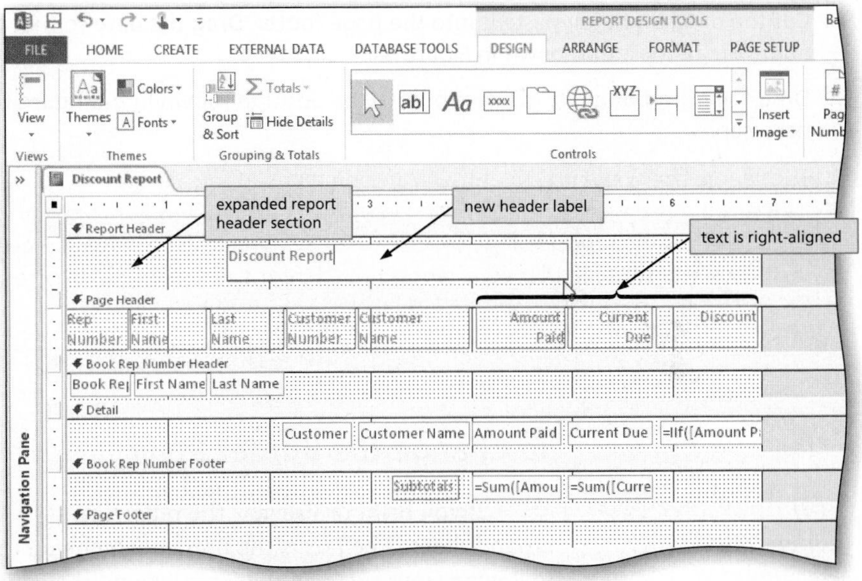

Figure 6–83

- Expand the Report Header section to the approximate size shown in Figure 6–83, place a label in the approximate position shown in the figure, and then type `Discount Report` in the label.

8

- Tap or click outside the label to deselect it and then tap or click the label in the report header a second time to select the entire label.
- Display the property sheet, change the font size to 20 and the text align property to Distribute, which spreads the letters evenly throughout the label. Change the font weight to Semi-bold, and then close the property sheet.
- If necessary, increase the size of the Discount Report label so that the entire title is displayed.
- Using the REPORT DESIGN TOOLS DESIGN tab and the techniques on pages AC 368 and AC 369, add a page number to the page footer, and add a date (use the same format you have used previously in this chapter).
- Cut the date, and then paste it into the page footer. Drag the date so that the date is positioned in the approximate position shown in Figure 6–84.
- Drag the right boundary of the report to the position shown in the figure to reduce the width of the report, if necessary.

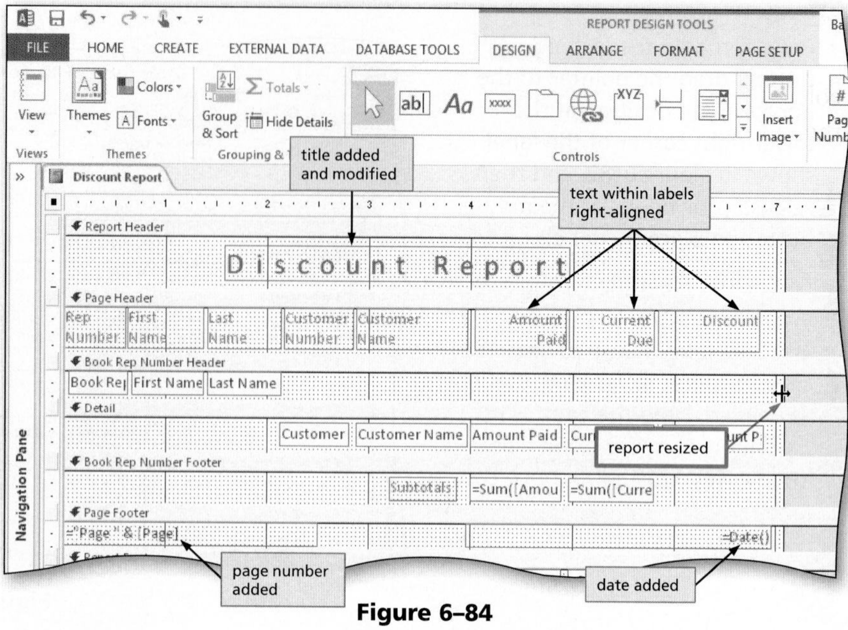

Figure 6–84

Q&A The report size was correct before. Why would I need to resize it?
When you move a control and a portion of the control extends into the area to the right of the right boundary of the report, the report will be resized. The new larger size will remain even if you move the control back to the left. Thus, it is possible that your report has a larger size than it did before. In this case, you need to drag the right boundary to resize the report.

To Change the Border Style

BTW
Report Title Placement
You also can place a report title in a page header. One advantage of doing so is that the title will then print on each page of the report.

If you print or preview the report, you will notice that all the controls have boxes around them. The box is the border, which you can select and modify if desired. The following steps remove the boxes around the controls by changing the border style to transparent.

1. Select all controls in the report. You can tap or click the first one, and then hold the SHIFT key down while tapping or clicking all the others. Alternatively, you can tap or click in the ruler to the left of the Report Header section and then hold the SHIFT key down while tapping or clicking to the left of all the other sections.
2. Display the REPORT DESIGN TOOLS DESIGN tab.
3. Tap or click the Property Sheet button (REPORT DESIGN TOOLS DESIGN tab | Tools group) to display the property sheet.
4. Tap or click the Border Style property box and then tap or click the Border Style property box arrow to display the menu of available border styles.
5. Tap or click Transparent to change the border style. Close the property sheet.

To Remove the Alternate Color

Just as with the Book Rep Master List, the Discount Report also has alternate colors that need to be removed. The following steps remove the alternate colors from the various sections in the report, starting with the Detail section.

1. Press and hold or right-click the Detail section to produce a shortcut menu.
2. Point to the Alternate Fill/Back Color arrow to produce a color palette.
3. Tap or click None on the color palette to specify that there is to be no alternate color for the selected section.
4. Using the same techniques, remove the alternate color from all other sections. (For some sections, the command may be dimmed.)

Obtaining Help on Functions

There are many functions included in Access that are available for a variety of purposes. To see the list of functions, display the Expression Builder. (See Figure 6–78 on page AC 385 for one way to display the Expression Builder.) Double-tap or double-click Functions in the first column and then tap or click Built-In Functions. You then can scroll through the entire list of functions in the third column. Alternatively, you can tap or click a function category in the second column, in which case the third column only will contain the functions in that category. To obtain detailed help on a function, highlight the function in the third column and tap or click the Help button. The Help presented will show the syntax of the function, that is, the specific rule for how you must type the function and any arguments. It will give you general comments on the function as well as examples illustrating the use of the function.

REPORT DESIGN TOOLS PAGE SETUP Tab

You can use the buttons on the REPORT DESIGN TOOLS PAGE SETUP tab to change margins, orientation, and other page setup characteristics of the report (Figure 6–85a). If you tap or click the Margins button, you can choose from among some predefined margins or set your own custom margins (Figure 6–85b on the next page). If you tap or click the Columns button, you will see the Page Setup dialog box with the Columns tab selected (Figure 6–85c on the next page). You can use this tab to specify multiple columns in a report as well as the column spacing. If you tap or click the Page Setup button, you will see the Page Setup dialog box with the Print Options tab selected (Figure 6–85d on the next page). You can use this tab to specify custom margins. You can specify orientation by tapping or clicking the Page tab (Figure 6–85e on the next page). You also can select paper size, paper source, and printer using this tab.

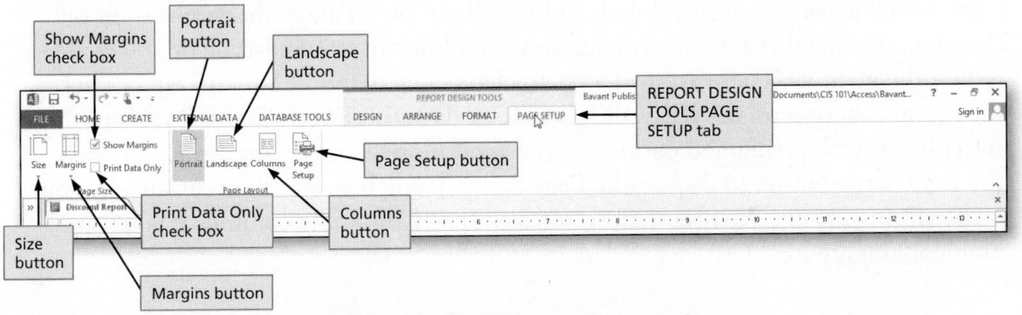

Figure 6–85 (a) Page Setup tab

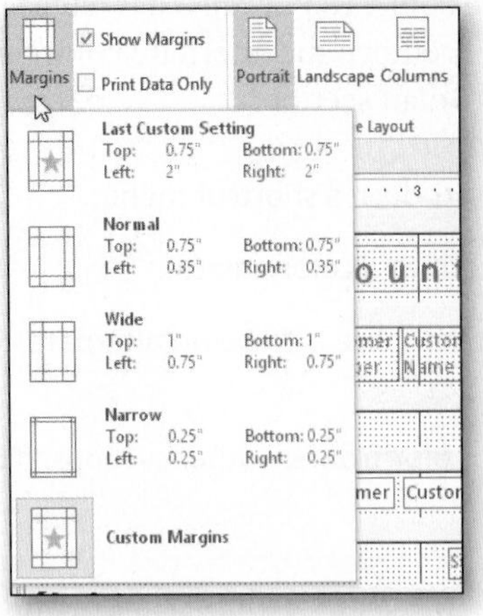

Figure 6–85 (b) Margins Button Menu

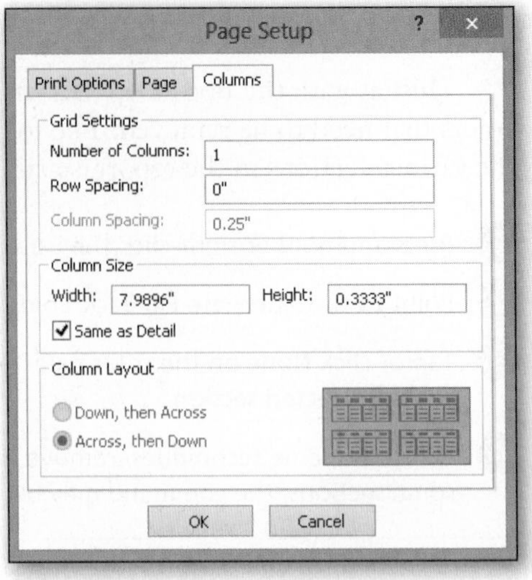

Figure 6–85 (c) Columns Tab

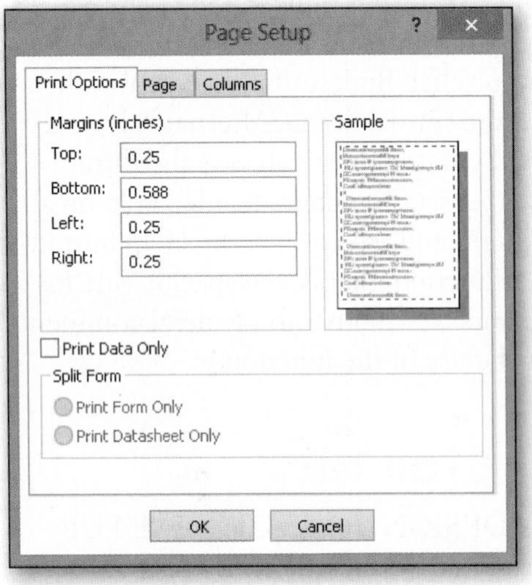

Figure 6–85 (d) Print Options Tab

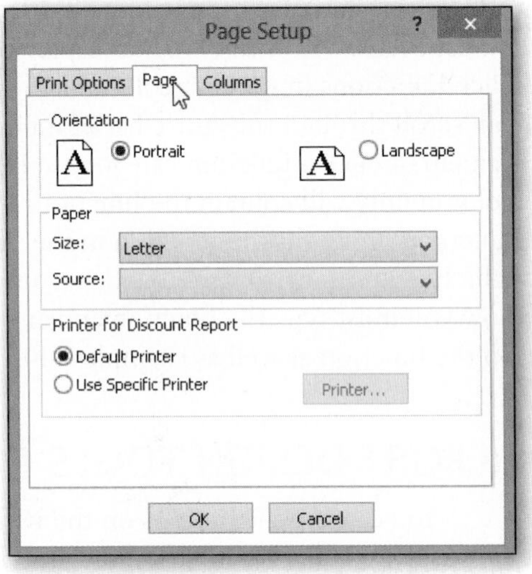

Figure 6–85 (e) Page Tab

To Change the Report Margins

If you look at the horizontal ruler in Figure 6–84 on page AC 388, you will notice that the report width is slightly over 7 inches. Because the report probably will print on standard 8½" × 11" paper, a 7-inch report with 1-inch margins on the left and right, which would result in a 9-inch width, will not fit. To allow the report to fit on the page, you could change the orientation from Portrait to Landscape or you could reduce the margins. There are two ways to change the margins. You can tap or click the Margins button on the REPORT DESIGN TOOLS PAGE SETUP tab and then select from some predefined options. If you want more control, you can tap or click the Page Setup button to display the Page Setup dialog box. You then can specify your own margins, change the orientation, and also specify multiple columns if you want a multicolumn report.

The following steps use the Margins button to select Narrow margins.

1. Display the REPORT DESIGN TOOLS PAGE SETUP tab.
2. Tap or click the Margins button (REPORT DESIGN TOOLS PAGE SETUP tab | Page Size group).
3. If necessary, tap or click Narrow to specify the Narrow margin option.

Fine-Tuning a Report

When you have finished a report, you should review several of its pages in Print Preview to make sure the layout is precisely what you want. You may find that you need to increase the size of a control, which you can do by selecting the control and dragging the appropriate sizing handle. You may decide to add a control, which you could do by using the appropriate tool in the Controls group or by dragging a field from the field list.

In both cases, if the control is between other controls, you have a potential problem. You may not have enough space between the other controls to increase the size or to add an additional control. If the control is part of a control layout that you had when you modified earlier reports in Layout view, you can resize controls or add new fields, and the remaining fields automatically adjust for the change. In Design view with individual controls, you must make any necessary adjustments manually.

To Make Room for Resizing or Adding Controls

To make room for resizing a control or for adding controls, you would use the following steps.

1. Select all controls to the right of the control you want to resize, or to the right of the position where you want to add another control.
2. Drag any of the selected controls to the right to make room for the change.

To Save and Close a Report

Now that you have completed your work on your report, you should save the report and close it. The following steps first save your work on the report and then close the report.

1. If instructed to do so by your instructor, change the title of the Discount Report to LastName Report where LastName is your last name.
2. Tap or click the Save button on the Quick Access Toolbar to save your work.
3. Close the Discount Report.

BTW
Distributing a Document
Instead of printing and distributing a hard copy of a document, you can distribute the document electronically. Options include sending the document via email; posting it on cloud storage (such as SkyDrive) and sharing the file with others; posting it on a social networking site, blog, or other website; and sharing a link associated with an online location of the document. You also can create and share a PDF or XPS image of the document, so that users can view the file in Acrobat Reader or XPS Viewer instead of in Access.

To Print a Report

The following steps print the report.

1. With the Discount Report selected in the Navigation Pane, tap or click File on the ribbon to open the Backstage view.
2. Tap or click the Print tab in the Backstage view to display the Print gallery.
3. Tap or click the Quick Print button to print the report and compare your results to Figure 6–1b on page AC 332.

BTW
Quick Reference
For a table that lists how to complete the tasks covered in this book using touch gestures, the mouse, ribbon, shortcut menu, and keyboard, see the Quick Reference Summary at the back of this book, or visit the Quick Reference resource on the Student Companion Site located on www.cengagebrain.com. For detailed instructions about accessing available resources, visit www.cengage.com/ct/studentdownload or contact your instructor for information about accessing the required files.

To Sign Out of a Microsoft Account

If you are signed in to a Microsoft account and are using a public computer or otherwise wish to sign out of your Microsoft account, you should sign out of the account from the Account gallery in the Backstage view before exiting Access. Signing out of the account is the safest way to make sure that nobody else can access SkyDrive files or settings stored in your Microsoft account. The following steps sign out of a Microsoft account from Access. For a detailed example of the procedure summarized below, refer to the Office and Windows chapter at the beginning of this book.

1. If you wish to sign out of your Microsoft account, tap or click FILE on the ribbon to open the Backstage view and then tap or click the Account tab to display the Account gallery.
2. Tap or click the Sign out link, which displays the Remove Account dialog box. If a Can't remove Windows accounts dialog box appears instead of the Remove Account dialog box, click the OK button and skip the remaining steps.

Q&A Why does a Can't remove Windows accounts dialog box appear?
If you signed in to Windows using your Microsoft account, then you also must sign out from Windows, rather than signing out from within Access. When you are finished using Windows, be sure to sign out at that time.

3. Tap or click the Yes button (Remove Account dialog box) to sign out of your Microsoft account on this computer.

Q&A Should I sign out of Windows after signing out of my Microsoft account?
When you are finished using the computer, you should sign out of your account for maximum security.

4. Tap or click the Back button in the upper-left corner of the Backstage view to return to the database.

BTW
Certification
The Microsoft Office Specialist (MOS) program provides an opportunity for you to obtain a valuable industry credential — proof that you have the Access 2013 skills required by employers. For more information, visit the Certification resource on the Student Companion Site located on www.cengagebrain.com. For detailed instructions about accessing available resources, visit www.cengage.com/ct/studentdownload or contact your instructor for information about accessing the required files.

To Exit Access

The following steps exit Access.

1. Tap or click the Close button on the right side of the title bar to exit Access.
2. If a Microsoft Access dialog box appears, tap or click the Yes button to save any changes made to the object since the last save.

Chapter Summary

In this chapter you have learned to create and relate additional tables; create queries for a report; create reports in Design view; add fields and text boxes to a report; format controls; group and ungroup controls; modify multiple controls; add and modify a subreport; modify section properties; add a title, page number, and date; add totals and subtotals; use a function in a text box; and publish a report. The items listed below include all the new Access skills you have learned in this chapter.

CONSIDER THIS

What decisions will you need to make when creating your own reports?

Use these guidelines as you complete the assignments in this chapter and create your own reports outside of this class.

1. Determine the intended audience and purpose of the report.
   a. Identify the user or users of the report and determine how they will use it.
   b. Specify the necessary data and level of detail to include in the report.
2. Determine the source of data for the report.
   a. Determine whether all the data is in a single table or whether it comes from multiple related tables.
3. Determine whether the data is stored in a query.
   a. You might need to create multiple reports for a query where the criterion for a field changes, in which case, you would use a parameter query and enter the criterion when you run the report.
   b. If the data comes from multiple related tables, you might want to create a query and use the query as a source of data.
4. Determine the fields that belong on the report.
   a. Identify the data items that are needed by the user of the report.
5. Determine the organization of the report.
   a. The report might be enhanced by displaying the fields in a particular order and arranged in a certain way.
   b. Should the records in the report be grouped in some way?
   c. Should the report contain any subreports?
6. Determine any calculations required for the report.
   a. Should the report contain totals or subtotals?
   b. Are there any special calculations?
   c. Are there any calculations that involve criteria?
7. Determine the format and style of the report.
   a. What information should be in the report heading?
   b. Do you want a title and date?
   c. Do you want special background colors or alternate colors?
   d. What should be in the body of the report?

CONSIDER THIS

How should you submit solutions to questions in the assignments identified with a ✲ symbol?

Every assignment in this book contains one or more questions identified with a ✲ symbol. These questions require you to think beyond the assigned database. Present your solutions to the questions in the format required by your instructor. Possible formats may include one or more of these options: write the answer; create a document that contains the answer; present your answer to the class; discuss your answer in a group; record the answer as audio or video using a webcam, smartphone, or portable media player; or post answers on a blog, wiki, or website.

Apply Your Knowledge

Reinforce the skills and apply the concepts you learned in this chapter.

Adding a Table and Creating a Report with a Subreport

Note: To complete this assignment, you will be required to use the Data Files for Students. Visit www.cengage.com/ct/studentdownload for detailed instructions or contact your instructor for information about accessing the required files.

Instructions: Start Access. Open the Apply Beauty Organically database that you modified in Chapter 5. If you did not use this database, contact your instructor for information on accessing the database required for this exercise.

Perform the following tasks:

1. Create a table in which to store data about orders for customers. These are orders that have not yet been delivered. Use Customer Orders as the name of the table. The Customer Orders table has the structure shown in Table 6–4.

Table 6–4 Structure of Customer Orders Table

Field Name	Data Type	Field Size	Comments
Order Number	Short Text	4	Primary Key
Amount	Currency (format with 2 decimal places)		
Customer Number	Short Text	4	Foreign Key; matches primary key of Customer table

2. Import the Customer Orders.txt file into the Customer Orders table. The file is delimited by tabs and the first row contains the field names. Do not save the import steps.
3. Create a one-to-many relationship between the Customer table and the Customer Orders table.
4. Create a query that joins the Sales Rep and Customer tables. Include the Sales Rep Number, First Name, and Last Name fields from the Sales Rep table. Include all fields except Total Amount and Sales Rep Number from the Customer table. Save the query as Sales Reps and Customers.
5. Create the report shown in Figure 6–86 on the next page. The report uses the Sales Reps and Customers query as the basis for the main report and the Customer Orders table as the basis for the subreport. Use the name Sales Rep Master List for the report. The report title has a Text Align property value of Center. The Border Width property for the detail controls is 1 pt and the subreport name is Orders by Customer. The report is similar in style to the Book Rep Master List shown in Figure 6–1a on page AC 331.
6. If requested to do so by your instructor, change the title for the report to First Name Last Name Master List where First Name and Last Name are your first and last names.
7. Submit the revised database in the format specified by your instructor.
8. How would you change the font weight of the report title to semi-bold?

Continued >

Apply Your Knowledge *continued*

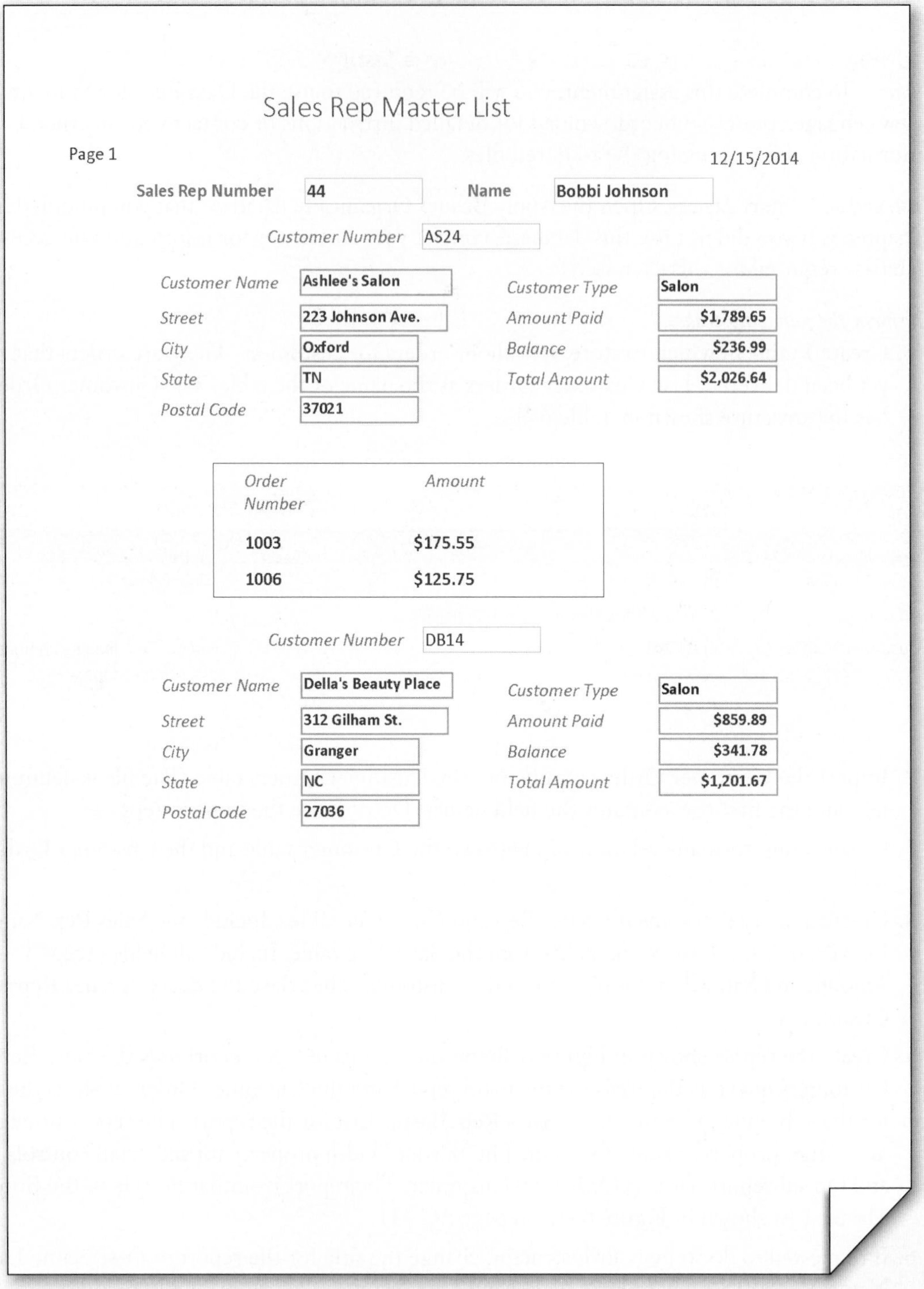

Sales Rep Master List

Page 1 12/15/2014

Sales Rep Number 44 Name Bobbi Johnson

Customer Number AS24

Customer Name	Ashlee's Salon	Customer Type	Salon
Street	223 Johnson Ave.	Amount Paid	$1,789.65
City	Oxford	Balance	$236.99
State	TN	Total Amount	$2,026.64
Postal Code	37021		

Order Number	Amount
1003	$175.55
1006	$125.75

Customer Number DB14

Customer Name	Della's Beauty Place	Customer Type	Salon
Street	312 Gilham St.	Amount Paid	$859.89
City	Granger	Balance	$341.78
State	NC	Total Amount	$1,201.67
Postal Code	27036		

Figure 6–86

Extend Your Knowledge

Extend the skills you learned in this chapter and experiment with new skills. You may need to use Help to complete the assignment.

Modifying Reports

Note: To complete this assignment, you will be required to use the Data Files for Students. Visit www.cengage.com/ct/studentdownload for detailed instructions or contact your instructor for information about accessing the required files.

Instructions: Start Access. Open the Extend Bookkeeping Services database. Extend Bookkeeping Services is an accounting firm that provides bookkeeping services to small businesses.

Perform the following tasks:

1. Open the Bookkeeper Master List in Design view. Change the date format to Long Date. Move the Date control to the page footer section.
2. Change the report title to Bookkeeper/Services Master List. Change the report header background to white. Change the font of the title text to Bookman Old Style with a font weight of semi-bold. Make sure the entire title is visible and the title is centered across the report.
3. Add a label to the report footer section. The label should contain text to indicate the end of the report, for example, End of Report or similar text.
4. Delete the Postal Code label and field. Remove any extra white space in the report.
5. Add a calculated control, Total Amount. The control should contain the sum of Amount Paid and Balance Due. Place this new control under the Balance Due field. The control should have the same format as the Balance Due field.
6. Use conditional formatting to format the total amount value in a bold red font for all records where the value is equal to or greater than $1,000.00.
7. If requested to do so by your instructor, open the Bookkeeper table and change the name of bookkeeper 22 to your name.
8. Submit the revised database in the format specified by your instructor.
9. Do you think the borders surrounding the controls enhance or detract from the appearance of the report? How would you remove the borders on all controls except the subreport?

Analyze, Correct, Improve

Analyze a database, correct all errors, and improve the design.

Correcting Report Design Errors and Improving a Report

Note: To complete this assignment, you will be required to use the Data Files for Students. Visit www.cengage.com/ct/studentdownload for detailed instructions or contact your instructor for information about accessing the required files.

Instructions: Start Access and open the Analyze Recruiters database from the Data Files for Students. Analyze Recruiters is a database for a professional recruiting company. One of the managers at the company has asked you to make some changes to the Discount Report she created.

Perform the following tasks:

1. Correct The report shown in Figure 6–87 on the next page is supposed to give all clients whose amount paid amount is greater than $20,000.00 a 4 percent discount. Clients with an amount paid amount of $20,000.00 or less should get a 2 percent discount. The IIf expression is not working correctly. Organizations such as Ferb Dentistry, which has an amount paid of less than $20,000.00,

Continued >

Analyze, Correct, Improve *continued*

Discount Report

Recruiter Number	First Name	Last Name	Client Number	Client Name	Amount Paid	Current Due	Discount
21	Alyssa	Kerry					
			AC34	Alys Clinic	$0.00	$17,500.00	$350.00
			FD89	Ferb Dentistry	$17,000.00	$12,500.00	$500.00
			PR11	Peel Radiology	$31,750.00	$0.00	$0.00
					$48,750.00	$30,000.00	
24	Camden	Reeves					
			BH72	Berls Hospital	$29,200.00	$0.00	$0.00
			FH22	Family Health	$0.00	$0.00	$0.00
			MH56	Munn Hospital	$0.00	$43,025.00	$860.50
			WL56	West Labs	$14,000.00	$100.00	$4.00
					$43,200.00	$43,125.00	
27	Jaime	Fernandez					
			RM32	Roz Medical	$0.00	$0.00	$0.00
			TC37	Tarleton Clinic	$18,750.00	$31,500.00	$1,260.00
					$18,750.00	$31,500.00	
					$110,700.00	$104,625.00	

Figure 6–87

shows a 4 percent discount. Analyze the problem and correct the IIf expression. Also, there are no labels for the subtotals and grand totals. Anyone reading the report has no way of knowing what the amounts mean.

2. Improve The report would be improved by adding page numbers and the current date to the page footer section. Also, the labels for Amount Paid, Current Due, and Discount could align better with the amounts if the labels were right-aligned. If instructed to do so by your instructor, change the title for the report to First Name Last Name Report where First Name and Last Name are your first and last name.

3. What was the error in the IIf expression? Why did the error indicator appear when you added the labels to the report?

In the Labs

Design, create, modify, and/or use a database following the guidelines, concepts, and skills presented in this chapter. Labs are listed in order of increasing difficulty. Labs 1 and 2, which increase in difficulty, require you to create solutions based on what you learned in the chapter; Lab 3 requires you to create a solution, which uses cloud and web technologies, by learning and investigating on your own from general guidance.

Lab 1: Adding Tables and Creating Reports for the Backup Services Database

Problem: The management of Backup Services needs to maintain data on service requests for clients. These service requests can be to install new hardware, update software, and other similar activities. To track service requests, the company needs two additional tables. The Service table describes services available to clients and the Service Requests table identifies the client needing the service. More than one client can require the same service.

Note: Use the database modified in the Lab 1 of Chapter 5 for this assignment. If you did not use the database, contact your instructor for information on accessing the database required for this exercise.

Instructions: Perform the following tasks:

1. Create two tables in which to store the data concerning services and service requests. The Service table contains data about the services that Backup Services offers. The Service Requests table contains data about services currently being performed for clients. The structure of the Service table is shown in Table 6–5 and the structure of the Service Requests table is shown in Table 6–6.

Table 6–5 Structure of Service Table

Field Name	Data Type	Field Size	Comments
Service Code	Short Text	3	Primary Key
Service Description	Short Text	50	
Hours	Number	Integer	
Increments	Number	Integer	

Table 6–6 Structure of Service Requests Table

Field Name	Data Type	Field Size	Comments
Client Number	Short Text	5	Part of Primary Key
Service Code	Short Text	3	Part of Primary Key
Total Hours	Number	Integer	
Hours Spent	Number	Integer	

Continued >

In the Labs *continued*

2. Import the data from the Service.txt file to the Service table. Import the data from the Service Requests.csv file to the Service Requests table.
3. Update the relationships for the Backup Services database.
4. Create a query that joins the Service Rep table and the Client table. Include the Service Rep Number, First Name, and Last Name from the Service Rep table. Include all fields except Total Amount and Service Rep Number from the Client table. Save the query as Service Reps and Clients.
5. Create a query that joins the Service table and the Service Requests table. Include the Client Number and Service Code fields from the Service Requests table, the Service Description field from the Service table, and the Total Hours and Hours Spent fields from the Service Requests

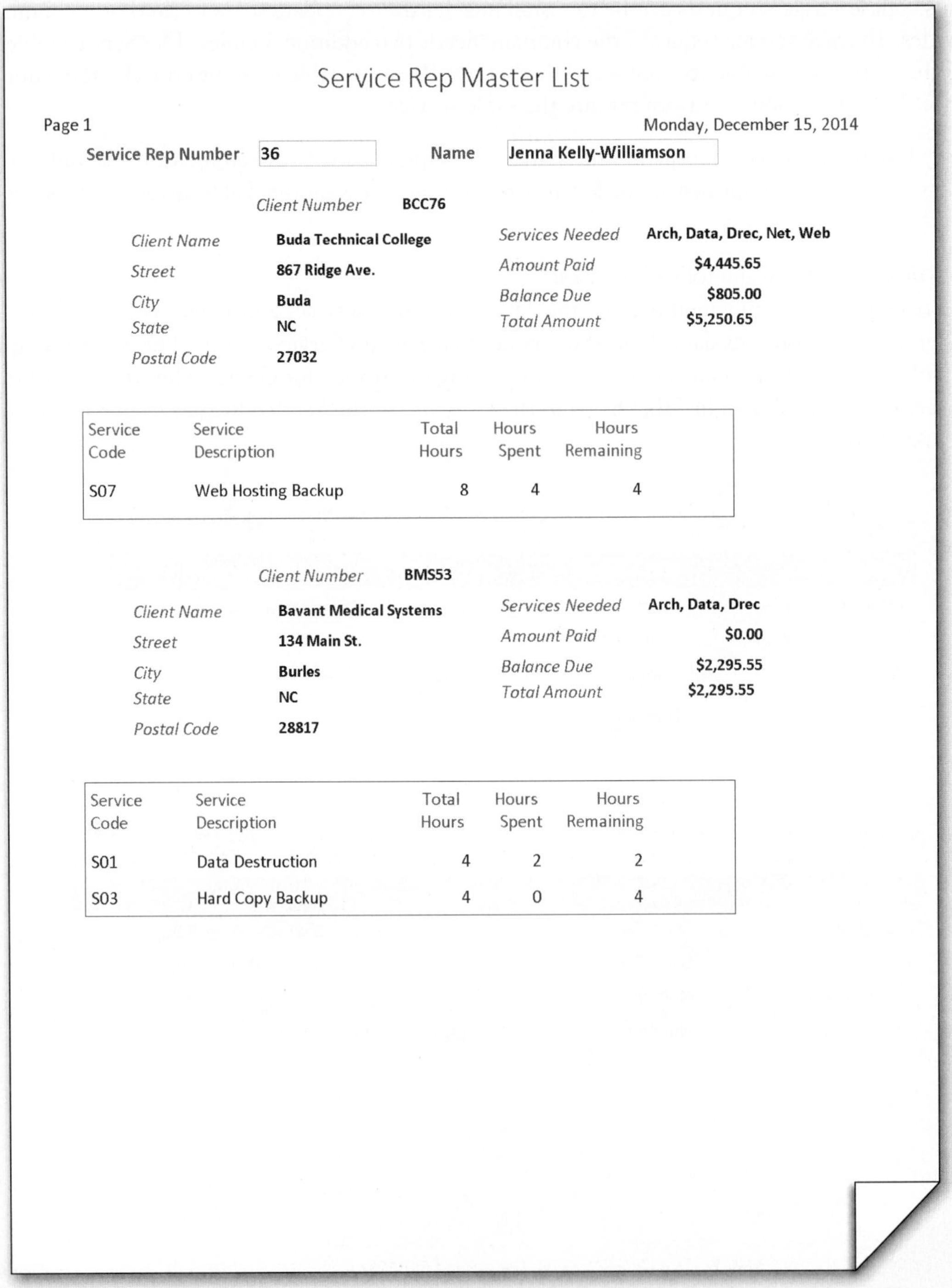

Service Rep Master List

Page 1 Monday, December 15, 2014

Service Rep Number 36 **Name** Jenna Kelly-Williamson

Client Number **BCC76**

Client Name	**Buda Technical College**	*Services Needed*	**Arch, Data, Drec, Net, Web**
Street	**867 Ridge Ave.**	*Amount Paid*	**$4,445.65**
City	**Buda**	*Balance Due*	**$805.00**
State	**NC**	*Total Amount*	**$5,250.65**
Postal Code	**27032**		

Service Code	Service Description	Total Hours	Hours Spent	Hours Remaining
S07	Web Hosting Backup	8	4	4

Client Number **BMS53**

Client Name	**Bavant Medical Systems**	*Services Needed*	**Arch, Data, Drec**
Street	**134 Main St.**	*Amount Paid*	**$0.00**
City	**Burles**	*Balance Due*	**$2,295.55**
State	**NC**	*Total Amount*	**$2,295.55**
Postal Code	**28817**		

Service Code	Service Description	Total Hours	Hours Spent	Hours Remaining
S01	Data Destruction	4	2	2
S03	Hard Copy Backup	4	0	4

Figure 6–88

table. Add a calculated field, Hours Remaining, that contains the difference between Total Hours and Hours Spent. Save the query as Service Requests and Services.

6. Create the report shown in Figure 6–88. The report is based on the two queries you created in Steps 4 and 5. The Date control uses the Long Date format, the title uses Center as the Text Align property, and there are no borders around the controls in the Detail section. The report is similar to the Book Rep Master List shown in Figure 6–1a on page AC 331.
7. Create the Client Discount Report shown in Figure 6–89. The report uses the Service Reps and Clients query. Clients who have paid $3,000.00 or more will receive a 3 percent discount on the remaining balance, and clients who have paid less than $3,000.00 will receive a 1 percent discount on the remaining balance. The report includes subtotals and grand totals for the Amount Paid and Balance Due fields and is similar in style to the Discount Report shown in Figure 6–1b on page AC 332.

Client Discount Report

Service Rep Number	First Name	Last Name	Client Number	Client Name	Amount Paid	Balance Due	Discount
36	Jenna	Kelly-Williamson					
			BCC76	Buda Technical	$4,445.65	$805.00	$24.15
			BMS53	Bavant Medical Systems	$0.00	$2,295.55	$22.96
			GCF56	Granger County Foundation	$200.00	$6,500.00	$65.00
			SLA77	Smarter Law Associates	$3,800.00	$0.00	$0.00
				Subtotals	$8,445.65	$9,600.55	
39	Melina	Liu					
			BBF32	Babbage CPA Associates	$3,524.00	$580.85	$17.43
			GAD74	Grant Antique Dealers	$2,435.65	$1,345.75	$13.46
			KDS21	KAL Art & Design Studio	$1,225.45	$895.95	$8.96
			WEC05	Walburg Energy Company	$1,567.45	$1,100.50	$11.01
			WSC01	Wood Sports Complex	$2,250.00	$1,600.00	$16.00
				Subtotals	$11,002.55	$5,523.05	
52	Matt	Martinez					
			CDS29	Carr Dental Services	$3,000.00	$1,150.50	$34.52
			HCH10	Hendley County Hospital	$3,209.25	$1,210.87	$36.33

Figure 6–89

Continued >

In the Labs *continued*

8. If instructed to do so by your instructor, change the title for the report to First Name Last Name Report where First Name and Last Name are your first and last name.
9. Submit the revised database in the format specified by your instructor.
10. How could you concatenate the Street, City, State, and Postal Code fields to display the complete address on one line?

Lab 2: Adding Tables and Creating Reports for the Sports Logo Database

Problem: The production manager of Sports Logo needs to track items that are being reordered from suppliers. The manager must know when an item was ordered and how many were ordered. He also needs a report that displays supplier information as well as information about items and the order status of items. Sports Logo is considering an in-store sale of items that do not yet have logo imprints. The marketing manager would like a report that shows the base cost as well as the sales price of all items.

Note: Use the database you used in Lab 2 of Chapter 5 on page AC 322 for this assignment. If you did not use this database, contact your instructor for information on accessing the database required for this exercise.

Instructions: Perform the following tasks:

1. Create a table in which to store the item reorder information using the structure shown in Table 6–7. Use Reorder as the name of the table.

Table 6–7 Structure of Reorder Table

Field Name	Data Type	Field Size	Comments
Item Number	Short Text	4	Part of Primary Key
Date Ordered	Date/Time (Use Short Date format)		Part of Primary Key
Number Ordered	Number	Integer	

2. Import the data from the Reorder.xlsx workbook to the Reorder table.
3. Add the Reorder table to the Relationships window and establish a one-to-many relationship between the Item table and the Reorder table.
4. Create a query that joins the Supplier table and the Item table. Include the Supplier Code and Supplier Name from the Supplier table. Include all fields except the Supplier Code from the Item table. Save the query as Suppliers and Items.
5. Create the report shown in Figure 6–90. The report uses the Suppliers and Items query as the basis for the main report and the Reorder table as the basis for the subreport. Use the name Supplier Master List as the name for the report. The report uses the same style as that demonstrated in the chapter project. Use conditional formatting to display the on-hand value in bold red font color for all items with fewer than 75 items on hand. Change the Border Style property to Transparent. Change the Text Align property for the title to Distribute.

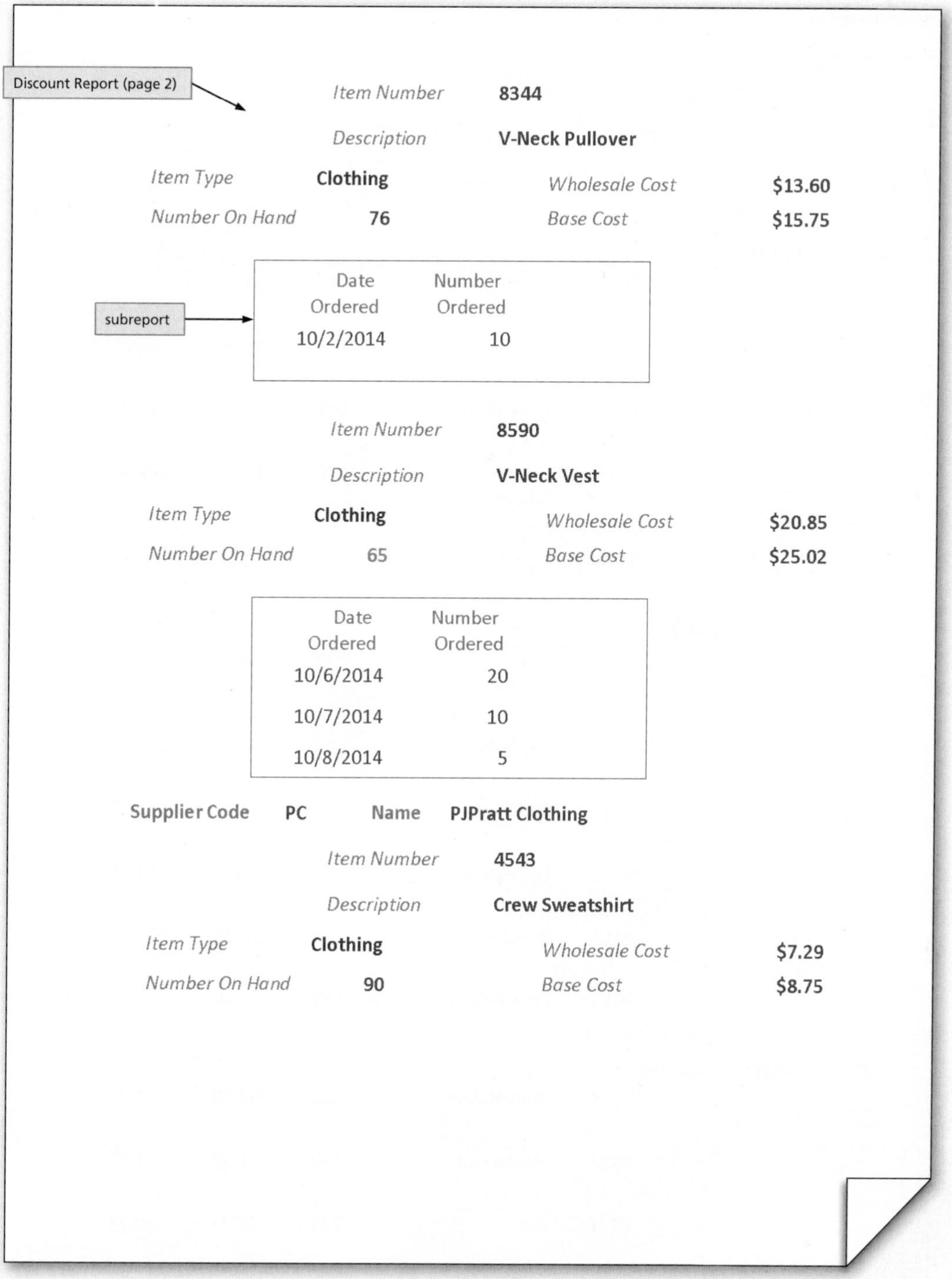

Figure 6–90

6. Create the Item Discount Report shown in Figure 6–91 on the next page. The report uses the Suppliers and Items Query and calculates the sale price for each item. Items with a base cost of more than $10 have a 2 percent discount; otherwise, the discount is 1 percent. Note that the report shows the sale price, not the discount. The report is similar to the Discount Report shown in Figure 6–1b on page AC 332. However, there are no group subtotals or report grand totals. The page number and current date appear in the page footer section. Change the Can Grow property for the Description field to Yes.

Continued >

In the Labs *continued*

Item Discount Report

Supplier Code	Supplier Name	Item Number	Description	On Hand	Base Cost	Sale Price
LM	Last Merchants					
		3673	Cotton Visor	145	$5.78	$5.72
		6234	Foam Visor	225	$1.00	$0.99
		7363	Baseball Cap	105	$6.15	$6.09
		8344	V-Neck Pullover	76	$15.75	$15.44
		8590	V-Neck Vest	65	$25.02	$24.52
PC	PJPratt Clothing					
		4543	Crew Sweatshirt	90	$8.75	$8.66
		6185	Fleece Vest	45	$34.50	$33.81
		6345	Golf Shirt	125	$12.35	$12.10
		8206	Turtleneck	55	$11.59	$11.36
		9458	Windbreaker	54	$18.20	$17.84
		9583	Crew T-Shirt	125	$3.40	$3.37
SD	Scrypt Distributors					
		5923	Drink Holder	80	$1.10	$1.09
		6523	Mouse Pad	150	$1.59	$1.57
		6974	Pen	225	$0.79	$0.78
		7123	Sports Bottle	150	$1.35	$1.34
		7934	Tote Bag	225	$1.75	$1.73
		8136	Travel Mug	80	$3.50	$3.47

Figure 6–91

7. If instructed to do so by your instructor, add a label to the page footer with your first and last name.
8. Submit the revised database in the format specified by your instructor.
9. What expression did you use to create the Sale Price calculated field?

Lab 3: Expand Your World: Cloud and Web Technologies

Adding a Logo, Background Images, and a Hyperlink to a Report

Problem: You work as an intern for a company that provides computer training to small businesses. The company has two reports, a Client Status Report and Trainer Master List, that need to be more clearly identified with the company. Management has asked for your help in designing a report style that they can use.

Note: To complete this assignment, you will be required to use the Data Files for Students. Visit www.cengage.com/ct/studentdownload for detailed instructions or contact your instructor for information about accessing the required files.

Instructions: Perform the following tasks:

1. Open the Lab 3 Training database from the Data Files for Students.
2. Search the web to find a suitable background image the company can use for its reports, or create your own background image.
3. Open the Client Status Report in Design view and delete any alternate background color in the report. Add the background image to the report.
4. Search the web to find a suitable logo or image the company can use for its reports, or create your own logo or image.
5. Add the logo or image to the Trainer Master List.
6. Add a hyperlink to the Trainer Master List that takes the user to a website that explains the Microsoft Office Specialist certification program.
7. Submit the revised database in the format specified by your instructor.
8. What did you select as a background image and as a logo? Justify your selection.

Consider This: Your Turn

Apply your creative thinking and problem solving skills to design and implement a solution.

Note: To complete this assignment, you will be required to use the Data Files for Students. Visit www.cengage.com/ct/studentdownload for detailed instructions or contact your instructor for information about accessing the required files.

1: Linking a Worksheet and Creating a Report for the Artisans Craft Database

Personal/Academic

Part 1: The university is considering a one-time sale of student-made handcrafts. Your instructor has asked you to prepare a report that would list the sale price of each available item. Because students often have trouble pricing their work, he has created a worksheet with prices charged by local artisans. He would like you to link the worksheet to the database. Open the Your Turn 1 Artisan Crafts database that you modified in Chapter 5 on page AC 325. If you did not modify this database, contact your instructor for information about accessing the required database. Then, use the concepts and techniques presented in this chapter to perform each of the following tasks:

a. Create a query that joins the Student table and the Item table. Include the Student Code, First Name, and Last Name fields from the Student table. Include the Item Number, Description, Price, and On Hand fields from the Item table. Save the query as Students and Items.

Continued >

Consider This: Your Turn *continued*

b. Create a report that is similar in style to the Discount Report shown in Figure 6–1b on page AC 332. Group the report by student code and include the student's first and last name. The Detail section should include the item number, description, price, and number on hand. Create a calculated control, Sale Price, that displays the sale price (not the discount) for all items. Items that have a price of $50 or more will have a 5 percent discount. Items that have a price of less than $50 will have a 3 percent discount. Do not include any subtotals or grand totals. Name the report Item Sale Report. Select your own fonts for the report.

c. Link the Items worksheet in the Prices workbook to the database and use the name Prices as the table name. Rename the linked table as Comparative Prices. Use the Linked Table Manager to update the link between the Excel worksheet and the Access table.

Submit your assignment in the format specified by your instructor.

Part 2: You made several decisions while creating the report and linking the worksheet. What was the rationale behind your decisions? If you changed the price for an item in the Prices workbook, would the changed price show in the Access table? Why?

2: Adding Tables and Creating Reports for the Carel Landscaping Database

Note: To complete this assignment, you will be required to use the Data Files for Students. Visit www.cengage.com/ct/studentdownload for detailed instructions or contact your instructor for information about accessing the required files.

Professional

Part 1: The owner of Carel Landscaping needs to maintain data on customer service requests. These requests can be for installing or repairing irrigation systems, fertilizing shrubs and trees, pruning, and so on. He also needs a report that will list supervisors as well as the customers they serve. Open the Your Turn 2 Carel Landscaping database that you modified in Chapter 5 on page AC 325. If you did not modify this database, contact your instructor for information about accessing the required database. Then, use the concepts and techniques presented in this chapter to perform each of the following tasks:

a. Create two tables in which to store data about the services requested by customers. The Service table contains data about the services that Carel offers. The structure of the table is similar to the Service table shown in Table 6–5 on page AC 399 except that there are only two fields in the table: Service Code and Service Description. Name the table Service and import the Carel Services.txt file. The Customer Requests table has the same structure as the Service Requests table shown in Table 6–6 on page AC 399 except that the Client Number field is Customer Number with a field size of 3. Create the Customer Requests table and import the Customer Requests.csv file. Update the relationships for the database.

b. Create a query that joins the Supervisor and the Customer tables. Include the Supervisor Number, First Name, and Last Name fields from the Supervisor table. Include all fields from the Customer table except Total Amount and Supervisor Number. Save the query.

c. Create a query that joins the Service and Customer Requests tables. Include the Customer Number and Service Code fields from the Customer Request table, the Service Description from the Service table, and the Total Hours and Hours Spent fields from the Customer Requests table. Add a calculated field that contains the difference between Total Hours and Hours Spent. Save the query.

d. Create a Supervisor Master Report that uses the query from Step b above as the basis for the main report and the query from Step c above as the basis for the subreport. The report should be similar in style to that shown in Figure 6–1a on page AC 331. Add a total amount field to the main report that sums the Amount Paid and Balance fields for each record.

Submit your assignment in the format specified by your instructor.

Part 2: You made several decisions while adding these tables and creating the report. What was the rationale behind your decisions? How could you add a logo to the report?

3: Understanding Reports

Research and Collaboration

Part 1: Copy the Bavant Publishing database and rename the database to your team name. For example, if your team is FabFour, then name the database FabFour Publishing. As a team, design an appropriate company letterhead for the Book Rep Master List and Discount Report. Try different themes, theme colors, and fonts. Incorporate a picture or clip art. Modify the report header sections in both reports to accommodate the letterhead. Add a label to the page footer section that includes the names of the team members.

Submit your assignment in the format specified by your instructor.

Part 2: You made several decisions while completing this assignment. What was the rationale behind your decisions? How could you save the letterhead to use in other reports?

Learn Online

Reinforce what you learned in this chapter with games, exercises, training, and many other online activities and resources.

Student Companion Site Reinforcement activities and resources are available at no additional cost on www.cengagebrain.com. Visit www.cengage.com/ct/studentdownload for detailed instructions about accessing the resources available at the Student Companion Site.

SAM Put your skills into practice with SAM! If you have a SAM account, go to www.cengage.com/sam2013 to access SAM assignments for this chapter.

7 Advanced Form Techniques

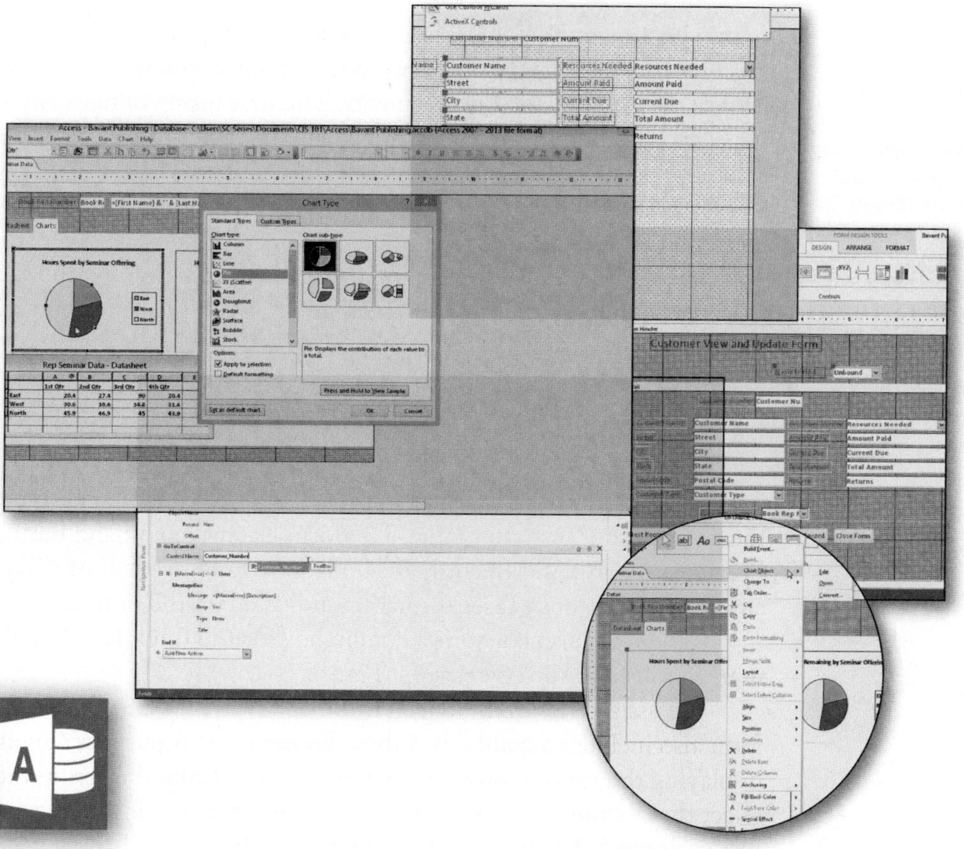

Objectives

You will have mastered the material in this project when you can:

- Add combo boxes that include selection lists
- Add combo boxes for searching
- Format and resize controls
- Apply formatting characteristics with the Format Painter
- Add command buttons
- Modify buttons and combo boxes
- Add a calculated field
- Use tab controls to create a multipage form
- Add and modify a subform
- Insert charts
- Modify a chart type
- Format a chart

7 | Advanced Form Techniques

Introduction

In previous chapters, you created basic forms using the wizard and you created more complex forms using Design view. In this chapter, you will create two new forms that feature more advanced form elements. The first form contains two combo boxes, one for selecting data from a related table and one for finding a record on the form. It also contains command buttons to accomplish various tasks.

The second form you will create is a **multipage form**, a form that contains more than one page of information. The form contains a tab control that allows you to access two different pages. Tapping or clicking the first tab displays a page containing a subform. Tapping or clicking the second tab displays a page containing two charts.

BTW
Q&As
For a complete list of the Q&As found in many of the step-by-step sequences in this book, visit the Q&A resource on the Student Companion Site located on www.cengagebrain.com. For detailed instructions about accessing available resources, visit www.cengage.com/ct/studentdownload or contact your instructor for information about accessing the required files.

Project — Advanced Form Techniques

Bavant Publishing wants two additional forms to use with its Customer and Book Rep tables. The first form, Customer View and Update Form (Figure 7–1a), contains the fields in the Customer table. The form has five command buttons: Next Record, Previous Record, Add Record, Delete Record, and Close Form. Tapping or clicking any of these buttons causes the action indicated on the button to occur.

The form also contains a combo box for the Book Rep Number field that assists users in selecting the correct rep (Figure 7–1b).

To assist users in finding a customer when they know the customer's name, the form also includes a combo box they can use for this purpose (Figure 7–1c). After displaying the list of customers by tapping or clicking the arrow, the user can simply select the customer they want to find; Access then will locate the customer and display that customer's data in the form (Figure 7–1d).

For the second new form, Bavant Publishing needs a multipage form that lists the numbers and names of reps. Each of the two pages that make up the form is displayed in its own tab page. Selecting the first tab, the one labeled Datasheet, displays a subform listing information about the seminar offerings for customers of the selected rep (Figure 7–2a on page AC 412).

BTW
BTWs
For a complete list of the BTWs found in the margins of this book, visit the BTW resource on the Student Companion Site located on www.cengagebrain.com. For detailed instructions about accessing available resources, visit www.cengage.com/ct/studentdownload or contact your instructor for information about accessing the required files.

Selecting the other tab, the one labeled Charts, displays two charts that illustrate the total hours spent and hours remaining by the rep for the various seminars (Figure 7–2b). In both charts, the slices of the pie represent the various seminars. They are color-coded and the legend at the bottom indicates the meaning of the various colors. The size of the pie slice gives a visual representation of the portion of the hours spent or hours remaining by the rep for that particular seminar. The chart also includes specific percentages. If you look at the yellow slice in the Hours Spent by Seminar Offering chart, for example, you see that the color represents seminar S05. It signifies 29 percent of the total. Thus, for all the hours already spent on the various seminar offerings by rep 65, 29 percent have been spent on seminar S05.

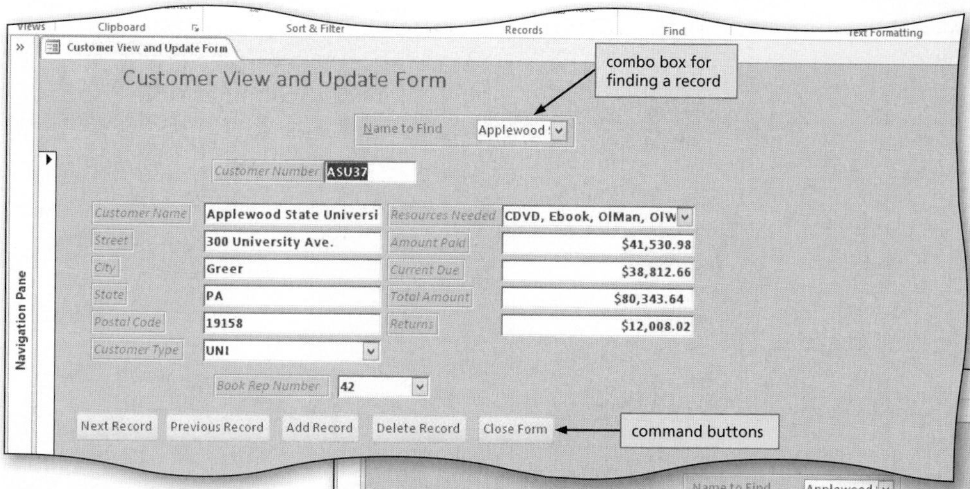

Figure 7–1 (a) Customer View and Update Form

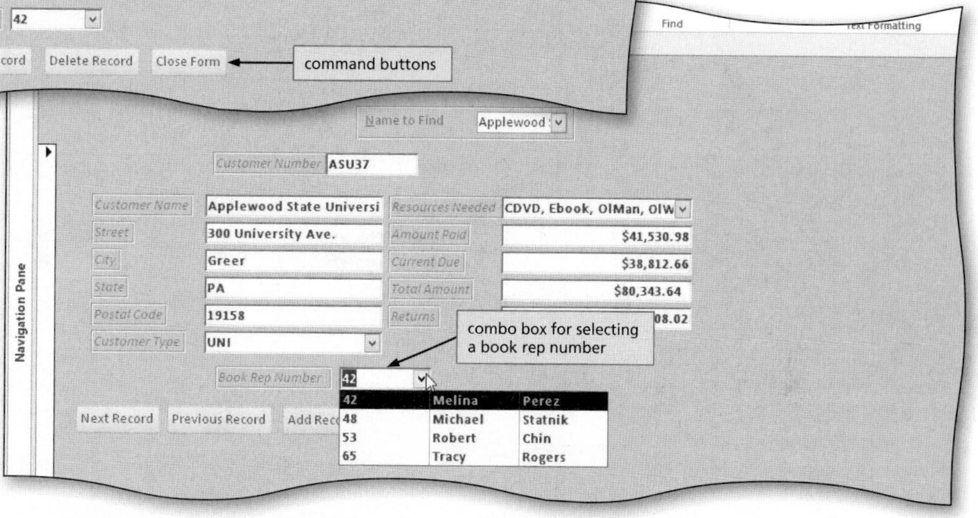

Figure 7–1 (b) Finding a Book Rep Number

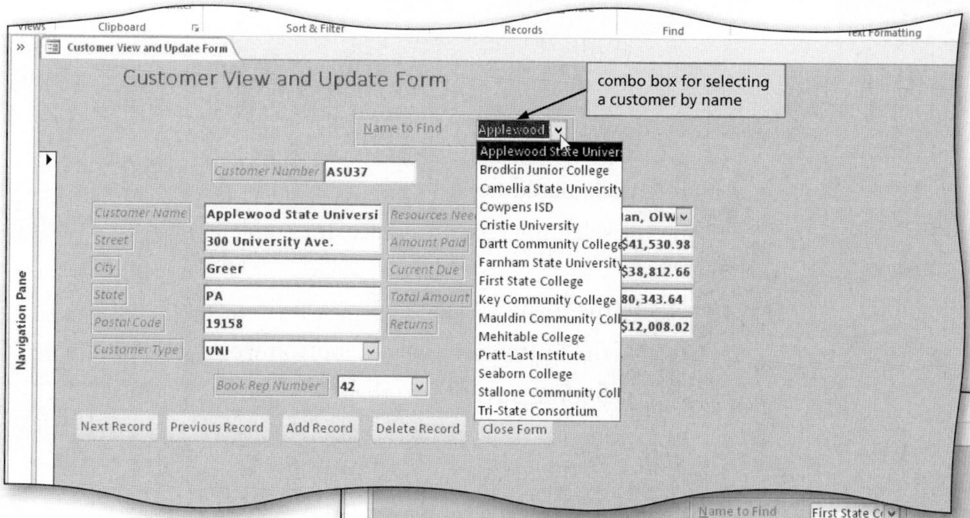

Figure 7–1 (c) Searching for a Customer by Name

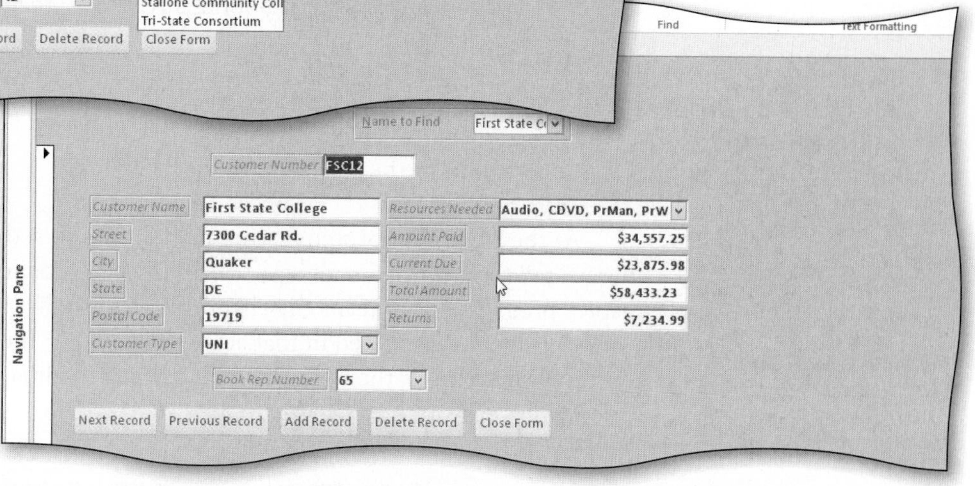

Figure 7–1 (d) Customer Data Returned by Search

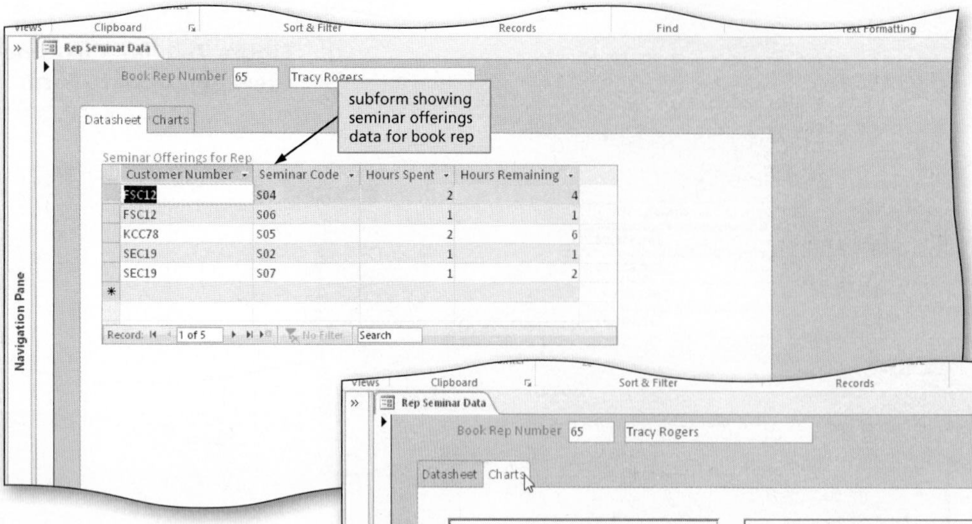

Figure 7–2 (a) Rep Seminar Data Form with Datasheet Tab Selected

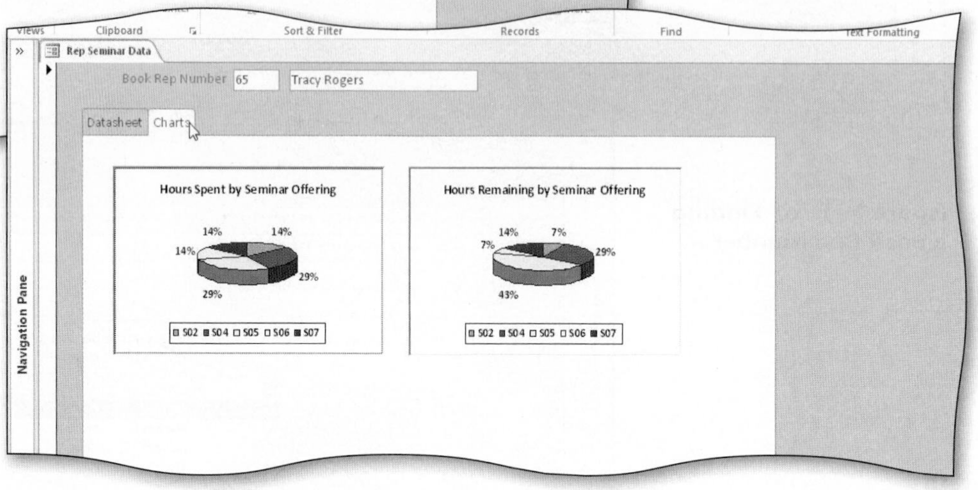

Figure 7–2 (b) Rep Seminar Data Form with Charts Tab Selected

Roadmap

In this chapter, you will learn how to create the forms shown in Figures 7–1 on the previous page and 7–2. The following roadmap identifies general activities you will perform as you progress through this chapter:

1. CREATE FORM containing a calculated field.
2. ADD COMBO BOXES, one for selecting data from a related table and one for finding a record on the form.
3. Add COMMAND BUTTONS to the form.
4. MODIFY a MACRO for one of the buttons so that the button works correctly.
5. MODIFY the COMBO BOX for finding a record so that the combo box works correctly.
6. CREATE a SECOND FORM, one that contains a tab control.
7. ADD a SUBFORM to one of the tabbed pages.
8. ADD a CHART to the other tabbed page.

At the beginning of step instructions throughout the chapter, you will see an abbreviated form of this roadmap. The abbreviated roadmap uses colors to indicate chapter progress: gray means the chapter is beyond that activity; blue means the task being shown is covered in that activity; and black means that activity is yet to be covered. For example, the following abbreviated roadmap indicates the chapter would be showing a task in the 3 COMMAND BUTTONS activity.

1 CREATE FORM | 2 ADD COMBO BOXES | 3 COMMAND BUTTONS | 4 MODIFY MACRO
5 MODIFY COMBO BOX | 6 CREATE SECOND FORM | 7 ADD SUBFORM | 8 ADD CHART

Use the abbreviated roadmap as a progress guide while you read or step through the instructions in this chapter.

To Run Access

If you are using a computer to step through the project in this chapter and you want your screens to match the figures in this book, you should change your screen's resolution to 1366 × 768. For information about how to change a computer's resolution, refer to the Office and Windows chapter at the beginning of this book.

The following steps, which assume Windows is running, use the Start screen or the search box to run Access based on a typical installation. You may need to ask your instructor how to run Access on your computer. For a detailed example of the procedure summarized below, refer to the Office and Windows chapter.

1. Scroll the Start screen for an Access 2013 tile. If your Start screen contains an Access 2013 tile, tap or click it to run Access; if the Start screen does not contain the Access 2013 tile, proceed to the next step to search for the Access app.
2. Swipe in from the right edge of the screen or point to the upper-right corner of the screen to display the Charms bar and then tap or click the Search charm on the Charms bar to display the Search menu.
3. Type `Access` as the search text in the Search text box and watch the search results appear in the Apps list.
4. Tap or click Access 2013 in the search results to run Access.

BTW

The Ribbon and Screen Resolution

Access may change how the groups and buttons within the groups appear on the ribbon, depending on the computer's screen resolution. Thus, your ribbon may look different from the ones in this book if you are using a screen resolution other than 1366 × 768.

To Open a Database from Access

The following steps open the Bavant Publishing database from the location you specified when you first created it (for example, the Access folder in the CIS 101 folder). For a detailed example of the procedure summarized below, refer to the Office and Windows chapter at the beginning of this book.

1. Tap or click FILE on the ribbon to open the Backstage view, if necessary.
2. If the database you want to open is displayed in the Recent list, tap or click the file name to open the database and display the opened database in the Access window; then skip to Step 7. If the database you want to open is not displayed in the Recent list or if the Recent list does not appear, tap or click Open Other Files to display the Open Gallery.
3. If the database you want to open is displayed in the Recent list in the Open gallery, tap or click the file name to open the database and display the opened database in the Access window; then skip to Step 7.
4. Tap or click Computer, SkyDrive, or another location in the left pane and then navigate to the location of the database to be opened (for example, the Access folder in the CIS 101 folder).
5. Tap or click Bavant Publishing to select the database to be opened.
6. Tap or click the Open button (Open dialog box) to open the selected file and display the opened database in the Access window.
7. If a Security Warning appears, tap or click the Enable Content button.

BTW

Touch Screen Differences

The Office and Windows interfaces may vary if you are using a touch screen. For this reason, you might notice that the function or appearance of your touch screen differs slightly from this chapter's presentation.

Creating a Form with Combo Boxes and Command Buttons

After planning a form, you may decide that including features such as combo boxes and command buttons will make the form easier to use. You can include such items while modifying the form in Design view.

To Create a Form in Design View

1 CREATE FORM | 2 ADD COMBO BOXES | 3 COMMAND BUTTONS | 4 MODIFY MACRO
5 MODIFY COMBO BOX | 6 CREATE SECOND FORM | 7 ADD SUBFORM | 8 ADD CHART

You can create a form using several different form tools, such as the Form Wizard and the Form button. The following steps create a form in Design view. ***Why?*** *Creating a form in Design view gives you the most flexibility in laying out the form. You will be presented with a blank design on which to place objects.*

1

- Display the CREATE tab.
- Tap or click the Form Design button (CREATE tab | Forms group) to create a new form in Design view.
- If necessary, close the Navigation Pane.
- Ensure the form selector for the entire form, the box in the upper-left corner of the form, is selected.
- If necessary, tap or click the Property Sheet button (FORM DESIGN TOOLS DESIGN tab | Tools group) to display a property sheet.
- With the All tab selected, tap or click the Record Source arrow, and then tap or click the Customer table to select the Customer table as the record source.
- Tap or click the Save button on the Quick Access Toolbar, then type `Customer Master Form` as the form name (Figure 7–3).

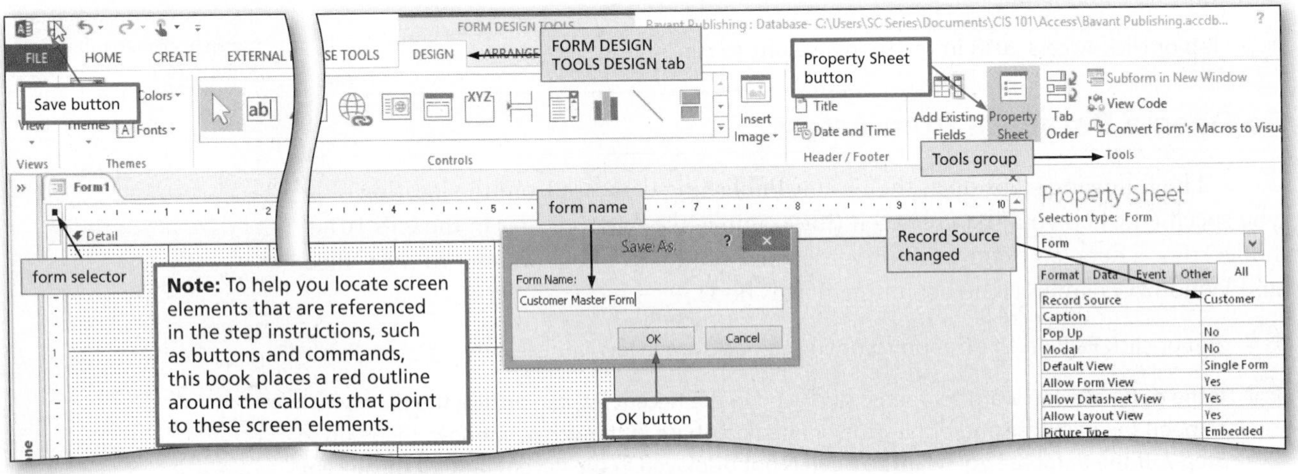

Figure 7–3

2

- Tap or click the OK button (Save As dialog box) to save the form.
- Tap or click the Caption property in the property sheet, and then type `Customer View and Update Form` as the new caption.
- Close the property sheet by tapping or clicking the Property Sheet button on the FORM DESIGN TOOLS DESIGN tab.
- Tap or click the 'Add Existing Fields' button (FORM DESIGN TOOLS DESIGN tab | Tools group) to display the field list (Figure 7–4).

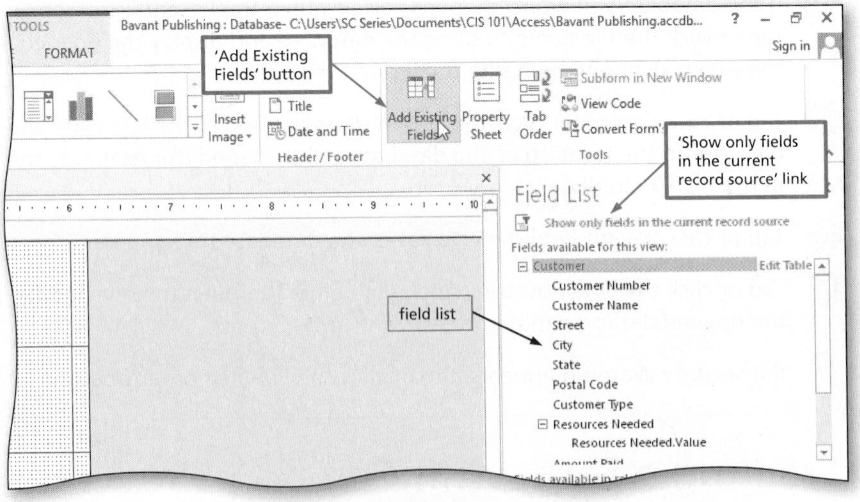

Figure 7–4

Q&A Why does the name on the tab not change to the new caption, Customer View and Update Form?
The name on the tab will change to the new caption in Form view. In Design view, you still see the name of the form object.

To Add Fields to the Form Design

1 CREATE FORM | 2 ADD COMBO BOXES | 3 COMMAND BUTTONS | 4 MODIFY MACRO
5 MODIFY COMBO BOX | 6 CREATE SECOND FORM | 7 ADD SUBFORM | 8 ADD CHART

After deciding which fields to add to the Customer View and Update Form, you can place them on the form by dragging the fields from the field list to the desired position. The following steps first display only the fields in the Customer table in the field list. ***Why?*** *If you are only including fields from a specific table or query, it is often convenient to simplify the field list so that it only includes fields from that source.* The steps then place the appropriate fields on the form.

1

- If necessary, tap or click the 'Show only fields in the current record source' link at the top of the field list to change the link to 'Show all tables' and display only the fields in the Customer table.
- Drag the Customer Number field from the field list to the approximate position shown in Figure 7–5.
- Tap or click the label once to select it and then tap or click it a second time to produce an insertion point.
- Use the BACKSPACE or DELETE key as necessary to erase the current entry (CU #) and then type `Customer Number` as the new label.
- Tap or click outside the label to deselect it, tap or click the label to select it a second time, and then drag the sizing handle in the upper-left corner of the label to move it to the approximate position shown in the figure.

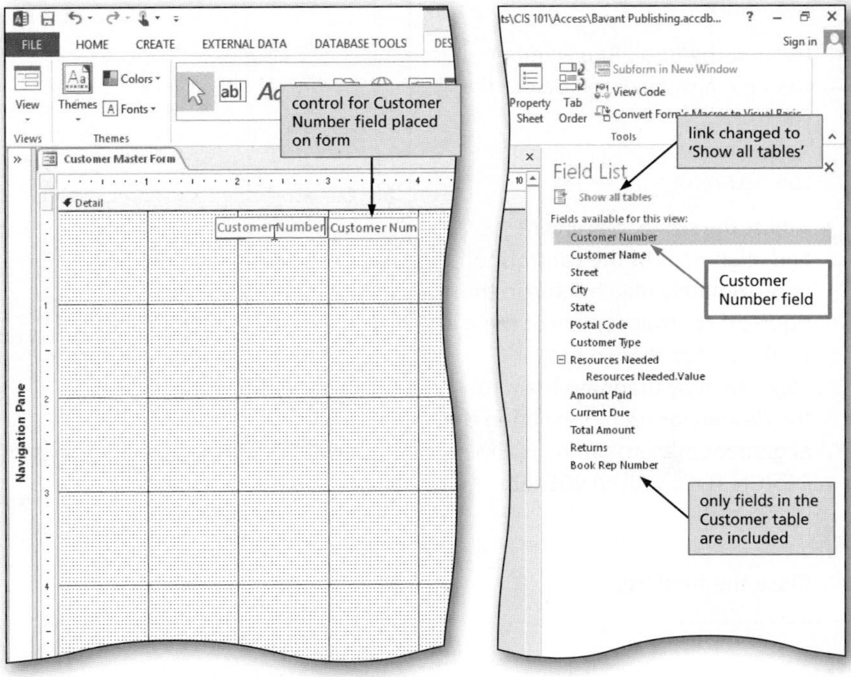

Figure 7–5

Q&A I thought the caption for Customer Number was changed to CU # so that this short caption would appear in datasheets, on forms, and on reports. Why am I now changing it back?

In these forms, there is plenty of room for the entire field name. Thus, there is no need for the short captions.

2

- Tap or click the Customer Name field in the field list.
- While holding the SHIFT key down, tap or click the Customer Type field in the field list to select multiple fields (Figure 7–6).

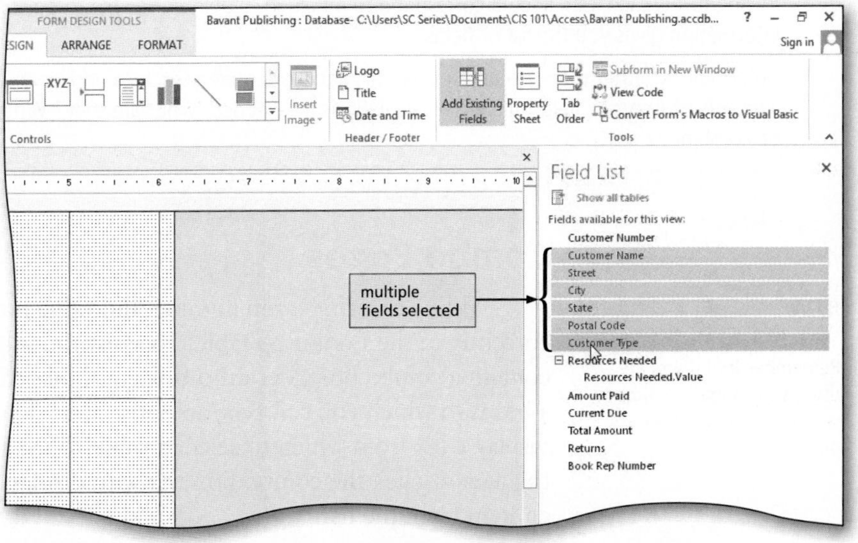

Figure 7–6

3

- Drag the selected fields to the approximate position shown in Figure 7–7.
- Select the Resources Needed through Returns fields and then drag the selected fields to the approximate position shown in the figure.

Q&A I added the Book Rep Number field by mistake. Can I delete the control?
Yes, select the control and press the DELETE key.

- Adjust the sizing, placement, and alignment of the controls to approximately match those in the figure. If controls for any of the fields are not aligned properly, align them by dragging them to the desired location or by using the alignment buttons on the FORM DESIGN TOOLS ARRANGE tab.

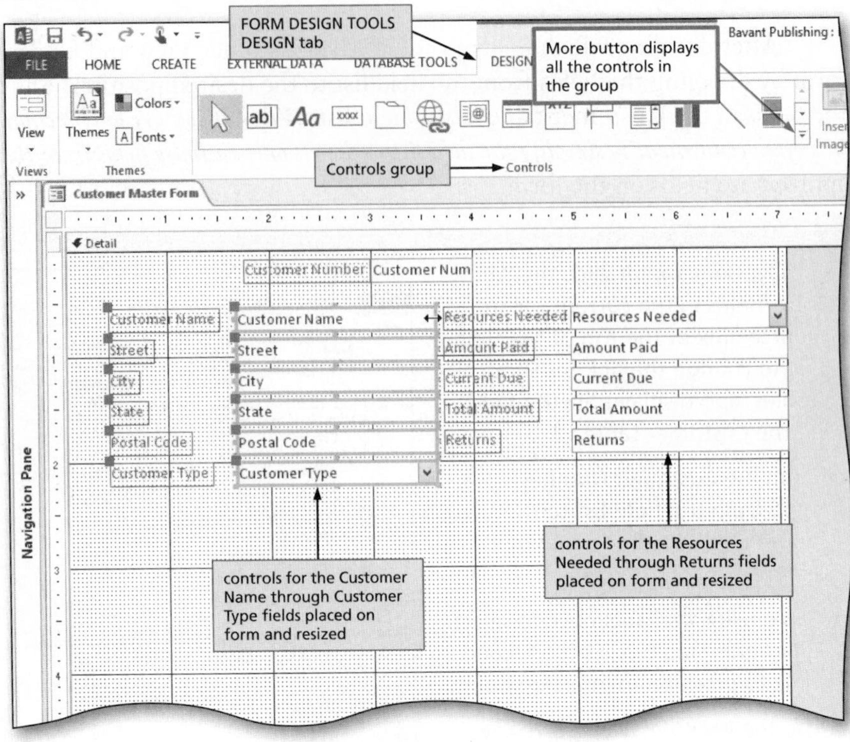

Figure 7–7

4

- Close the field list.

CONSIDER THIS

How do you decide on the contents of a form?

To design and create forms, follow these general guidelines:

Determine the fields that belong on the form. If you determine that data should be presented as a form, you then need to determine what tables and fields contain the data for the form.

Examine the requirements for the form in general to determine the tables. Do the requirements only relate to data in a single table, or does the data come from multiple tables? How are the tables related?

Examine the specific requirements for the form to determine the fields necessary. Look for all the data items that are specified for the form. Each item should correspond to a field in a table or be able to be computed from a field in a table. This information gives you the list of fields.

Determine whether there are any special calculations required, such as adding the values in two fields or combining the contents of two text fields. If special calculations are needed, what are they? What fields are involved and how are they to be combined?

Combo Boxes

BTW
Touch and Pointers
Remember that if you are using your finger on a touch screen, you will not see the pointer.

When entering a rep number, the value must match the number of a rep currently in the Book Rep table. To assist the users in entering this data, the form will contain a combo box. A **combo box** combines the properties of a **text box**, which is a box into which you can type an entry, and a **list box**, which is a box you can use to display a list from which to select a value. With a combo box, the user can either type the data or click the combo box arrow to display a list of possible values and then select an item from the list.

To Add a Combo Box that Selects Values

If you have determined that a combo box displaying values from a related table would be useful on your form, you can add the combo box to a form using the Combo Box tool in the Controls group on the FORM DESIGN TOOLS DESIGN tab. Before doing so, you should make sure the 'Use Control Wizards' button is selected. ***Why?*** *If the 'Use Control Wizards' button in the Controls group on the FORM DESIGN TOOLS DESIGN tab is selected, a wizard will guide you through the process of creating the combo box.* The following steps place on the form a combo box that displays values from a related table for the Book Rep Number field.

1

- Tap or click the FORM DESIGN TOOLS DESIGN tab and then tap or click the More button (FORM DESIGN TOOLS DESIGN tab | Controls group) (see Figure 7–7) to display all the available tools in the Controls group (Figure 7–8).

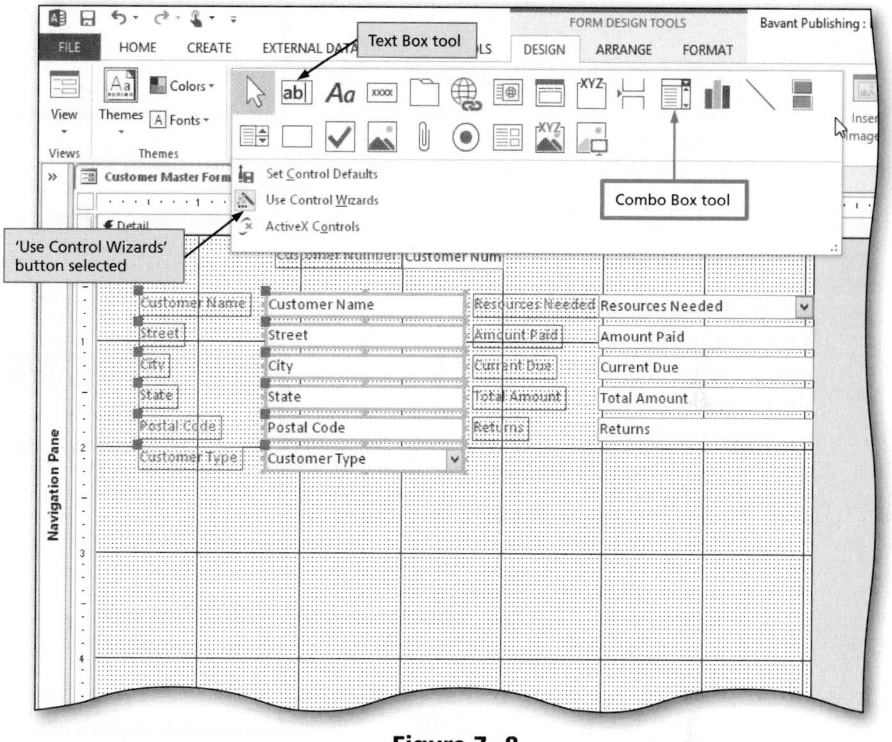

Figure 7–8

2

- With the 'Use Control Wizards' button in the Controls group on the FORM DESIGN TOOLS DESIGN tab selected, tap or click the Combo Box tool (FORM DESIGN TOOLS DESIGN tab | Controls group), and then move the pointer, whose shape has changed to a small plus symbol accompanied by a combo box, to the position shown in Figure 7–9.

Q&A I do not see a pointer. Did I do something wrong?

If you are using your finger you will not see the pointer shape as indicated in the figure. Tapping with your finger in the indicated location, however, should still produce the desired action. If you prefer to see a pointer, then you should use a stylus or a mouse.

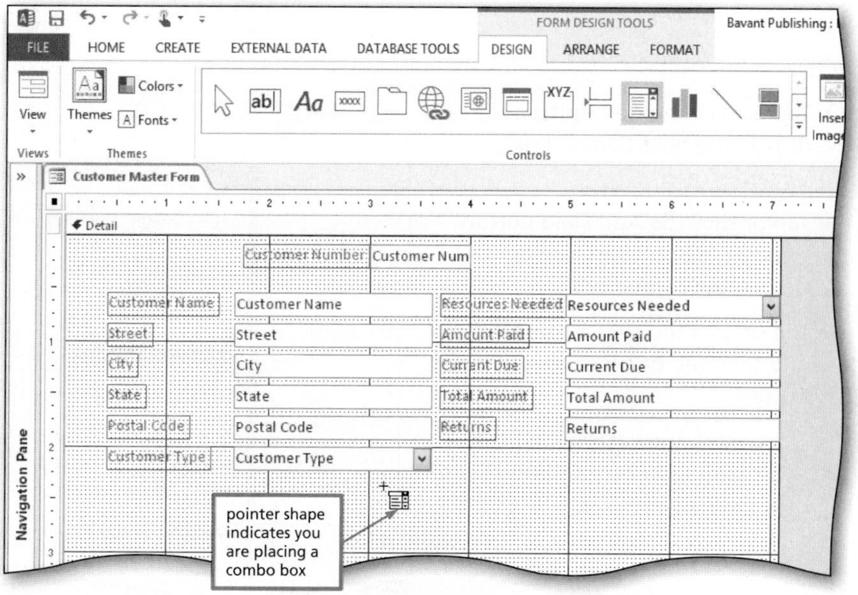

Figure 7–9

3

- Tap or click the position shown in Figure 7–9 on the previous page to place a combo box.
- If necessary, in the Combo Box Wizard dialog box, tap or click the 'I want the combo box to get the values from another table or query.' option button (Figure 7–10).

Q&A What is the purpose of the other options?
Use the second option if you want to type a list from which the user will choose. Use the third option if you want to use the combo box to search for a record.

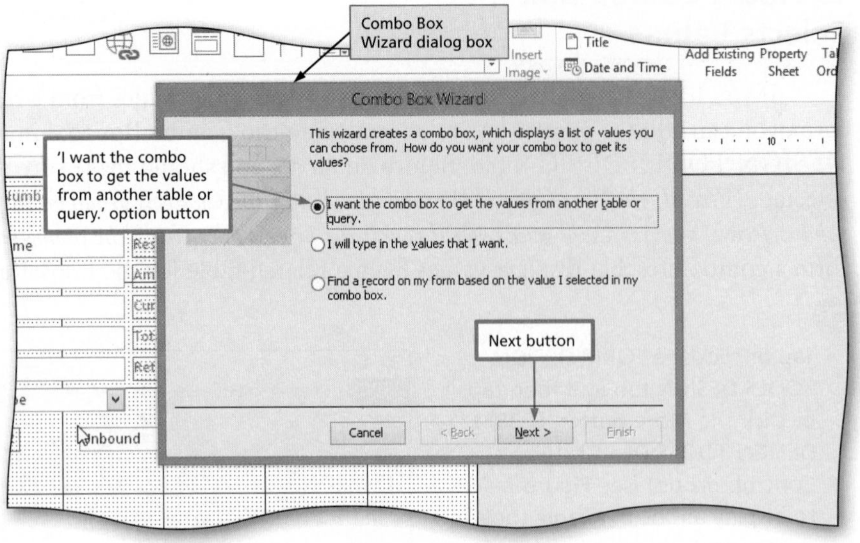

Figure 7–10

4

- Tap or click the Next button, and then, with the Tables option button selected, tap or click Table: Book Rep (Figure 7–11), if necessary, to specify that the combo box values will come from the Book Rep table.

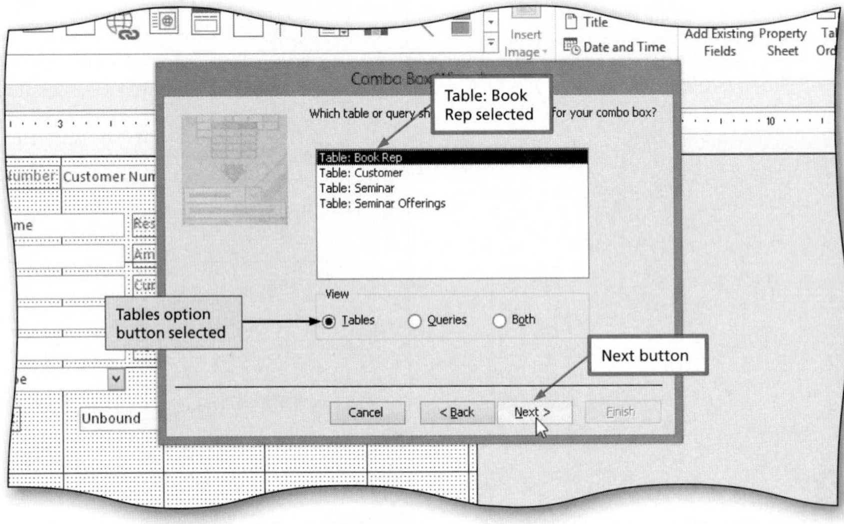

Figure 7–11

5

- Tap or click the Next button to display the next Combo Box Wizard screen.
- Tap or click the Add Field button to add the Book Rep Number as a field in the combo box.
- Tap or click the First Name field and then tap or click the Add Field button.
- Tap or click the Last Name field and then tap or click the Add Field button (Figure 7–12).

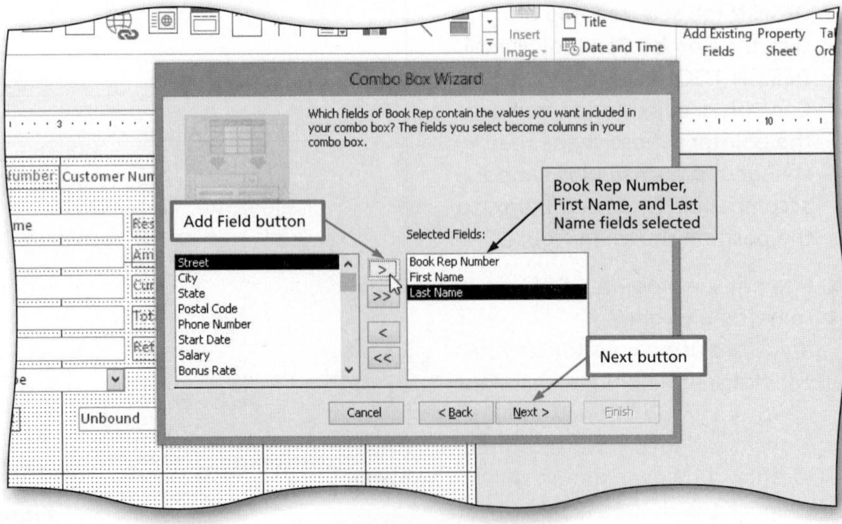

Figure 7–12

6

- Tap or click the Next button to display the next Combo Box Wizard screen.
- Tap or click the arrow in the first text box, and then select the Book Rep Number field to sort the data by book rep number. (Figure 7–13).

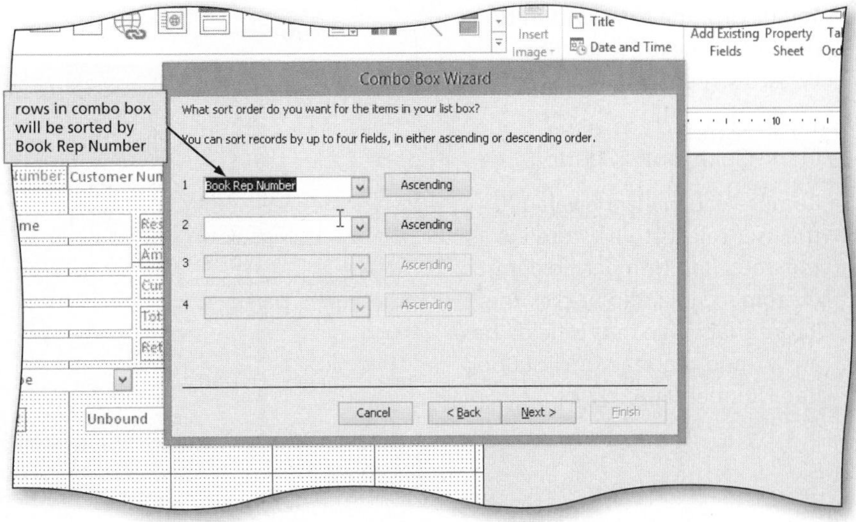

Figure 7–13

7

- Tap or click the Next button to display the next Combo Box Wizard screen (Figure 7–14).

Q&A What is the key column? Do I want to hide it?
The key column would be the Book Rep Number, the column that identifies both a first name and a last name. Because the purpose of this combo box is to update rep numbers, you want the book rep numbers to be visible.

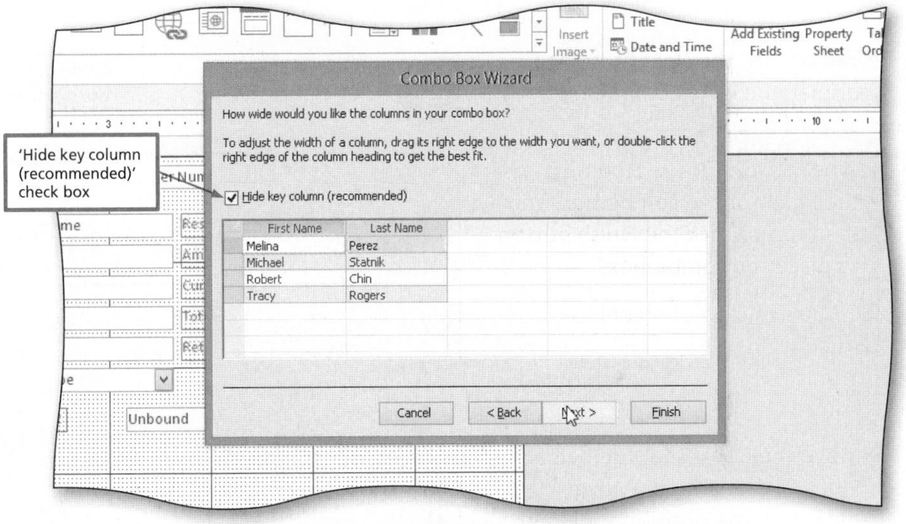

Figure 7–14

8

- Tap or click the 'Hide key column (recommended)' check box to remove the check mark so that the Book Rep Number field will appear along with the First Name and Last Name fields.
- Tap or click the Next button to display the next Combo Box Wizard screen (Figure 7–15).

Q&A Do I need to make any changes here?
No. The Book Rep Number field, which is the field you want to store, already is selected.

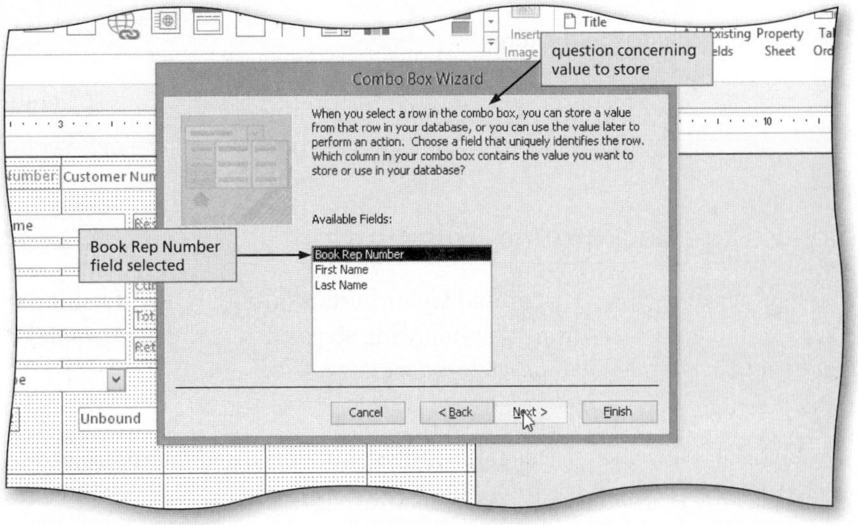

Figure 7–15

9

- Tap or click the Next button to display the next Combo Box Wizard screen.
- Tap or click the 'Store that value in this field:' option button.
- Because you want the value the user selects to be stored in the Book Rep Number field in the Customer table, tap or click the 'Store that value in this field:' box arrow, and then tap or click Book Rep Number (Figure 7–16).

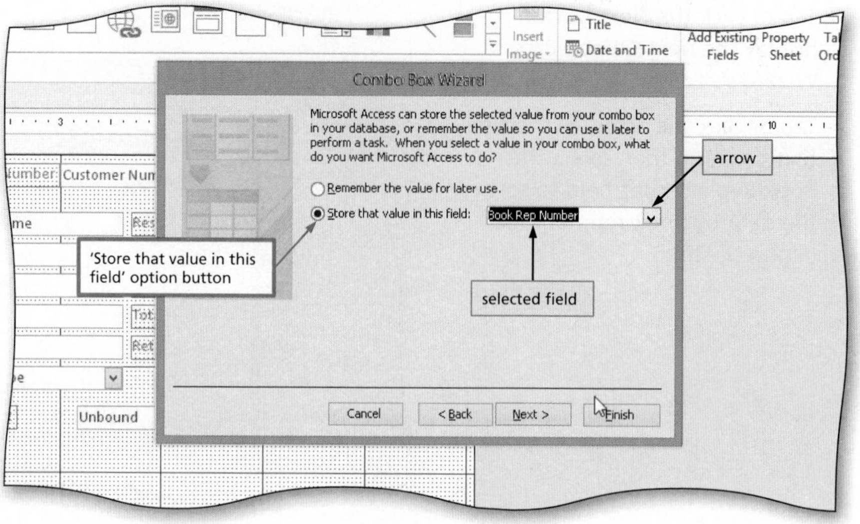

Figure 7–16

10

- Tap or click the Next button to display the next Combo Box Wizard screen.
- Type `Book Rep Number` as the label for the combo box, and then tap or click the Finish button to place the combo box.

Q&A Could I change the label to something else?

Yes. If you prefer a different label, you could change it.

- Move the Book Rep Number label by dragging its Move handle to the position shown in Figure 7–17.

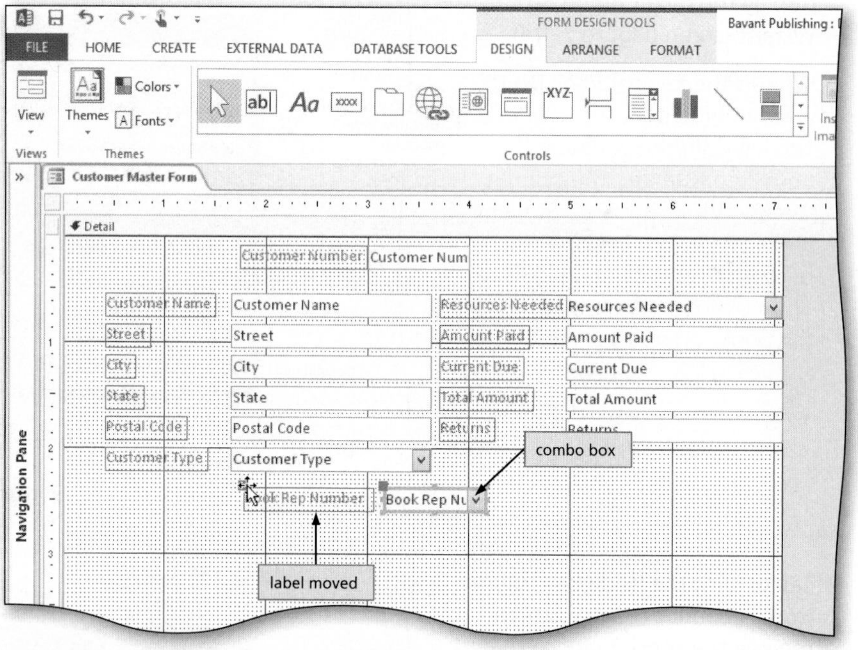

Figure 7–17

11

- Save your changes to the form.

To Use the Background Color Button

1 CREATE FORM | 2 ADD COMBO BOXES | 3 COMMAND BUTTONS | 4 MODIFY MACRO
5 MODIFY COMBO BOX | 6 CREATE SECOND FORM | 7 ADD SUBFORM | 8 ADD CHART

You can use the Background Color button on the FORM DESIGN TOOLS FORMAT tab to change the background color of a form. The following steps change the background color of the form to a light gray. ***Why?*** *Light gray is consistent with the form you created earlier.*

1

- Tap or click anywhere in the Detail section but outside all the controls to select the section.
- Display the FORM DESIGN TOOLS FORMAT tab.

- Tap or click the Background Color arrow (FORM DESIGN TOOLS FORMAT tab | Font group) to display a color palette (Figure 7–18).

2

- Tap or click the Light Gray 2 color, the first color in the third row under Standard Colors, to change the background color.

Experiment

- Try other colors to see their effect. When finished, once again select the Light Gray 2 color.

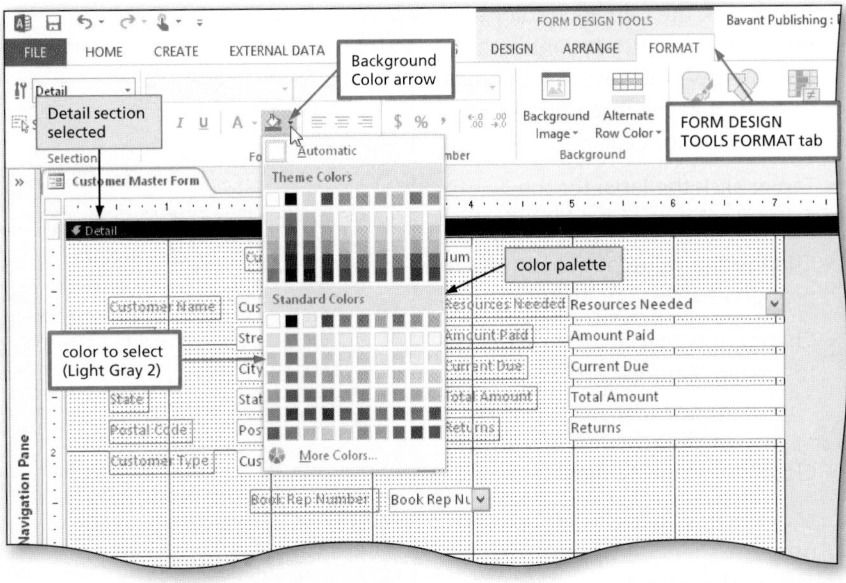

Figure 7–18

To Format a Control

1 CREATE FORM | 2 ADD COMBO BOXES | 3 COMMAND BUTTONS | 4 MODIFY MACRO
5 MODIFY COMBO BOX | 6 CREATE SECOND FORM | 7 ADD SUBFORM | 8 ADD CHART

You can use buttons on the FORM DESIGN TOOLS DESIGN tab to format a control in a variety of ways. The following steps use a property sheet, however, to make a variety of changes to the format of the Customer Number control. ***Why?*** *Using the property sheet gives you more choices over the types of changes you can make to the form controls than you have with simply using the buttons.*

1

- Display the FORM DESIGN TOOLS DESIGN tab.
- Tap or click the Customer Number control (the white space, not the label) to select it.
- Tap or click the Property Sheet button (FORM DESIGN TOOLS DESIGN tab | Tools group) to display the property sheet.
- Change the value of the Font Weight property to Semi-bold.
- Change the value of the Special Effect property to Sunken.

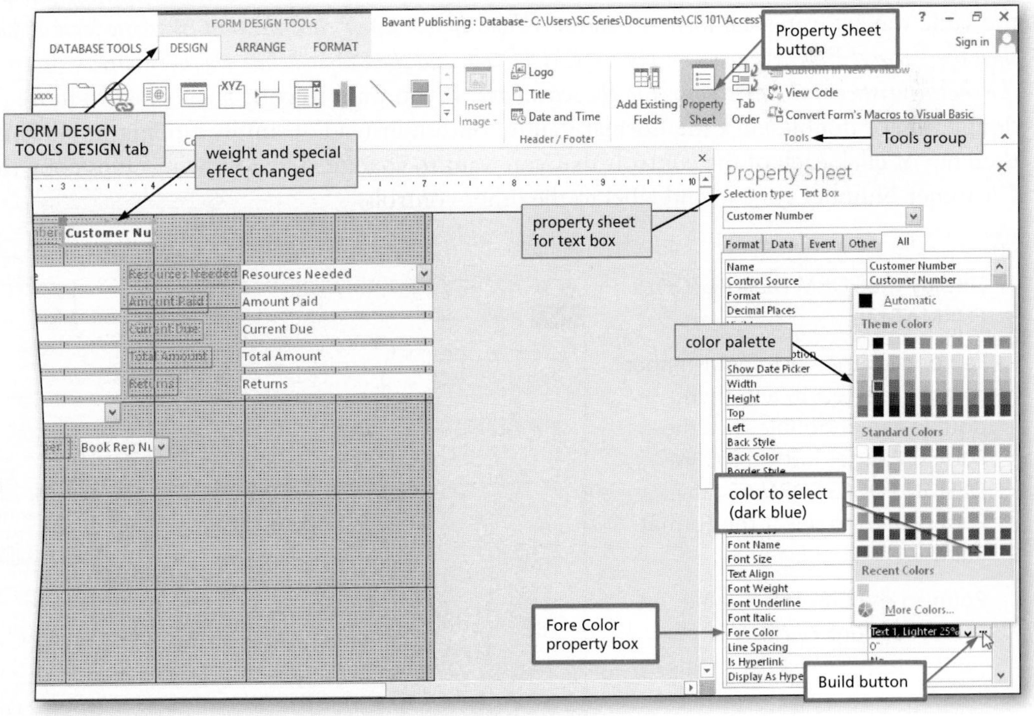

Figure 7–19

- Tap or click the Fore Color property box to select it, and then tap or click the Build button (the three dots) to display a color palette (Figure 7–19).

2

- Tap or click the Dark Blue color (the second color from the right in the bottom row under Standard Colors) to select it as the foreground color, which is the font color.
- Tap or click the label for the Customer Number field to select it.
- Change the value of the Font Italic property to Yes.
- Change the Special Effect property to Etched (Figure 7–20).

3

- Close the property sheet.

Q&A Should I not have closed the property sheet before selecting a different control?

You could have, but it is not necessary. The property sheet displayed on the screen always applies to the currently selected controls.

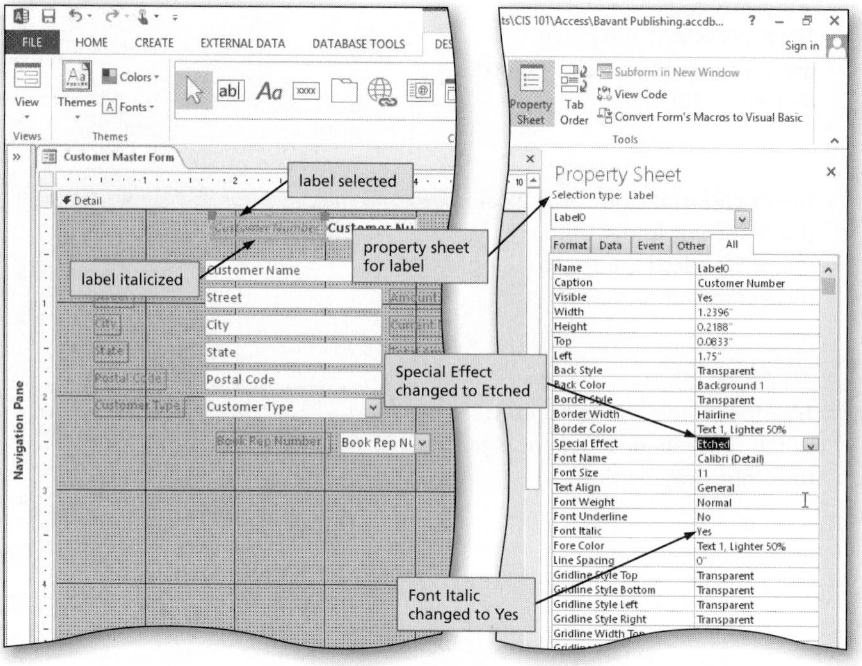

Figure 7–20

To Use the Format Painter

1 CREATE FORM | 2 ADD COMBO BOXES | 3 COMMAND BUTTONS | 4 MODIFY MACRO
5 MODIFY COMBO BOX | 6 CREATE SECOND FORM | 7 ADD SUBFORM | 8 ADD CHART

Once you have formatted a control and its label the way you want, you can format other controls in exactly the same way by using the format painter. ***Why?*** *If you tap or click the control whose format you want to copy, tap or click the Format Painter button on the FORMAT tab, and then tap or click another control, Access will automatically apply the characteristics of the first control to the second one.* If you want to copy the format to more than one other control, double-tap or double-click the Format Painter button instead of simply tapping or clicking the button, and then tap or click each of the controls that you want to change. The following steps copy the formatting of the Customer Number control and label to the other controls.

1

- Display the FORM DESIGN TOOLS FORMAT tab.
- Tap or click the Customer Number control to select it, and then double-tap or double-click the Format Painter button (FORM DESIGN TOOLS FORMAT tab | Font group) to select the Format Painter.
- Point to the Customer Name control (Figure 7–21).

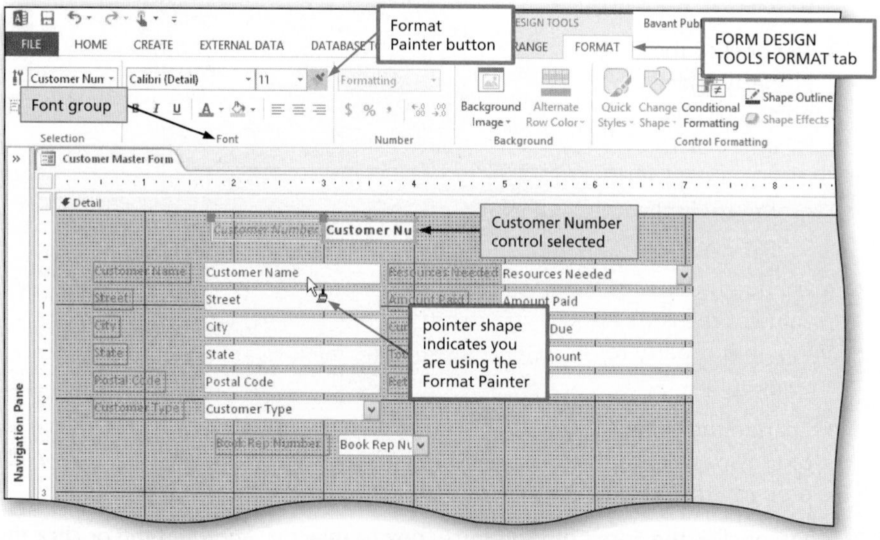

Figure 7–21

2

- Tap or click the Customer Name control to assign it the same formatting as the Customer Number control.
- Tap or click all the other controls on the form to assign them the same formatting.
- Tap or click the Format Painter button (FORM DESIGN TOOLS FORMAT tab | Font group) to deselect the Format Painter (Figure 7–22).

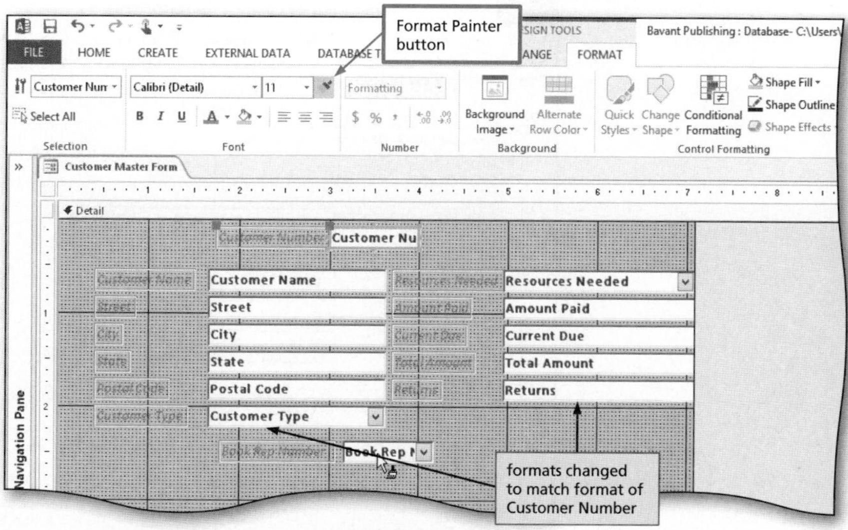

Figure 7–22

Q&A Do I always have to tap or click the Format Painter button when I have finished copying the formatting?

If you double-tapped or double-clicked the Format Painter button to enable you to copy the formatting to multiple controls, you need to tap or click the Format Painter button again to turn off the copying. If you simply tapped or clicked the Format Painter button to enable you to copy the formatting to a single control, you do not need to tap or click the button again. As soon as you copy the formatting to the single control, the copying will be turned off.

Does the order in which I tap or click the other controls matter?

No. The only thing that is important is that you ultimately tap or click all the controls whose formatting you want to assign.

3

- Save your changes to the form.

To View the Form

The following steps view the form in Form view and then return to Design view. ***Why?*** *As you are working on the design of a form, it is a good idea to periodically view the form in Form view to see the effects of your changes.*

1. Display the FORM DESIGN TOOLS DESIGN tab.
2. Tap or click the View button (FORM DESIGN TOOLS DESIGN tab | Views group) to view the form in Form view (Figure 7–23 on the next page).

Q&A Why did I have to change from the FORMAT tab to the DESIGN tab?

The FORMAT tab does not have a View button.

3. Tap or click the View button arrow (HOME tab | Views group) to produce the View button menu.
4. Tap or click Design View on the View menu to return to Design view.

Q&A Could I simply tap or click the View button?

No. The icon on the View button is the one for Layout view. Tapping or clicking the button would show you the form in Layout view, but you are working on the form in Design view.

BTW

On-Screen Keyboard

To display the on-screen touch keyboard, tap the Touch Keyboard button on the Windows taskbar. When finished using the touch keyboard, tap the X button on the touch keyboard to close the keyboard.

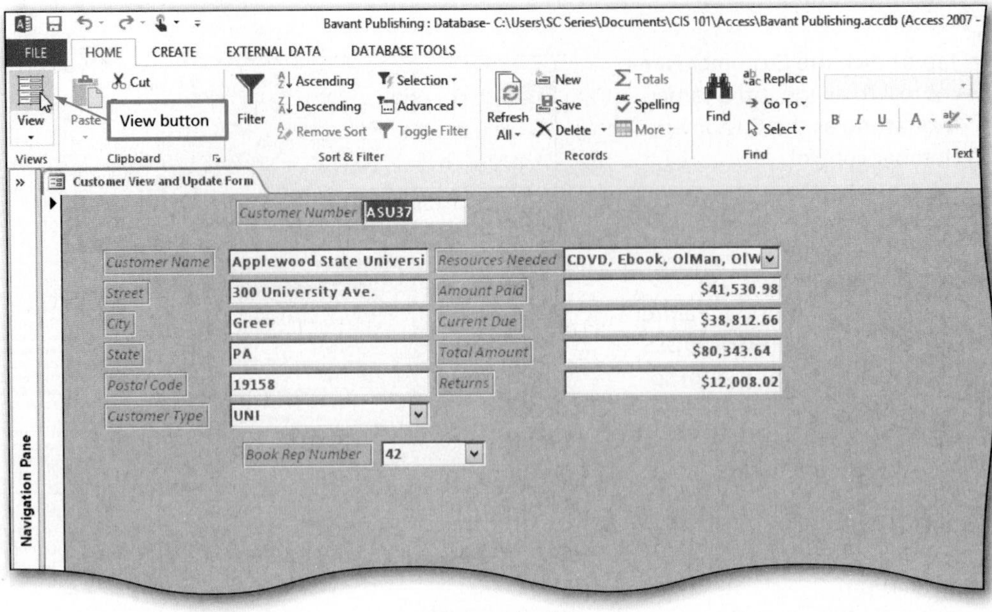

Figure 7–23

To Add a Title and Expand the Form Header Section

1 CREATE FORM | 2 ADD COMBO BOXES | 3 COMMAND BUTTONS | 4 MODIFY MACRO
5 MODIFY COMBO BOX | 6 CREATE SECOND FORM | 7 ADD SUBFORM | 8 ADD CHART

The form you are creating has a title, Customer View and Update Form. A form title appears in the Form Header section; however the Customer Master Form currently does not contain a Form Header section, which means that the title does not appear on the form. The following steps first insert the Form Header and Form Footer sections, and then add a title to the Form Header section. They also expand the Form Header section. ***Why?*** *You need sufficient room in the Form Header section to accommodate the combo box you will add later.*

1

- Tap or click the Title button (FORM DESIGN TOOLS DESIGN tab | Header/Footer group) to add a Form Header section and to add a control for the title to the Form Header section (Figure 7–24).

Q&A

Why is the title Customer View and Update Form rather than Customer Master Form?
If you have changed the caption, the title will use the new value of the Caption property.

Could I add the Form Header section before adding the title? If I do, what happens when I add the title?
Access will place the title in the Form Header section that you already added.

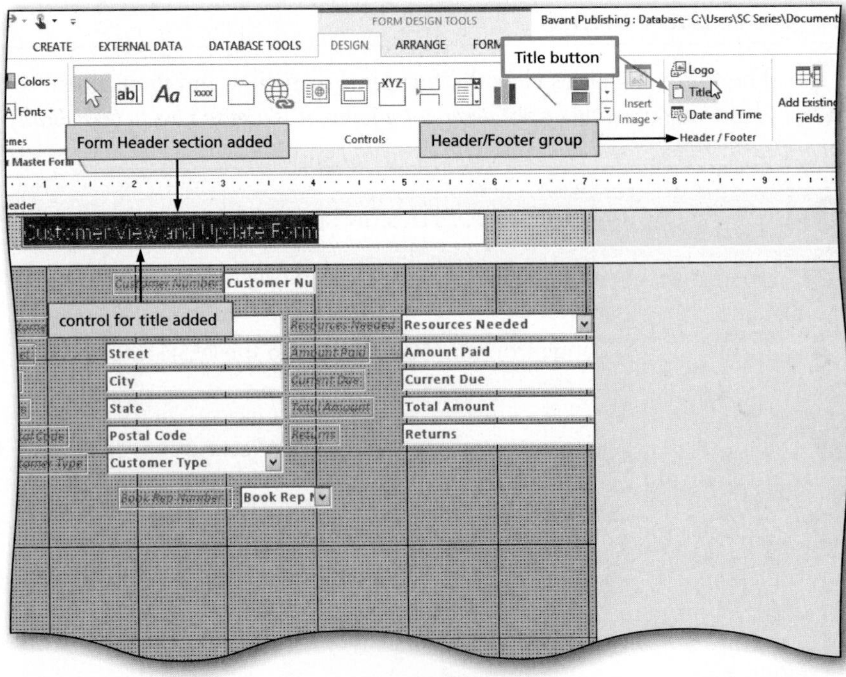

Figure 7–24

2

- Drag the lower boundary of the Form Header section down to the approximate position shown in Figure 7–25.

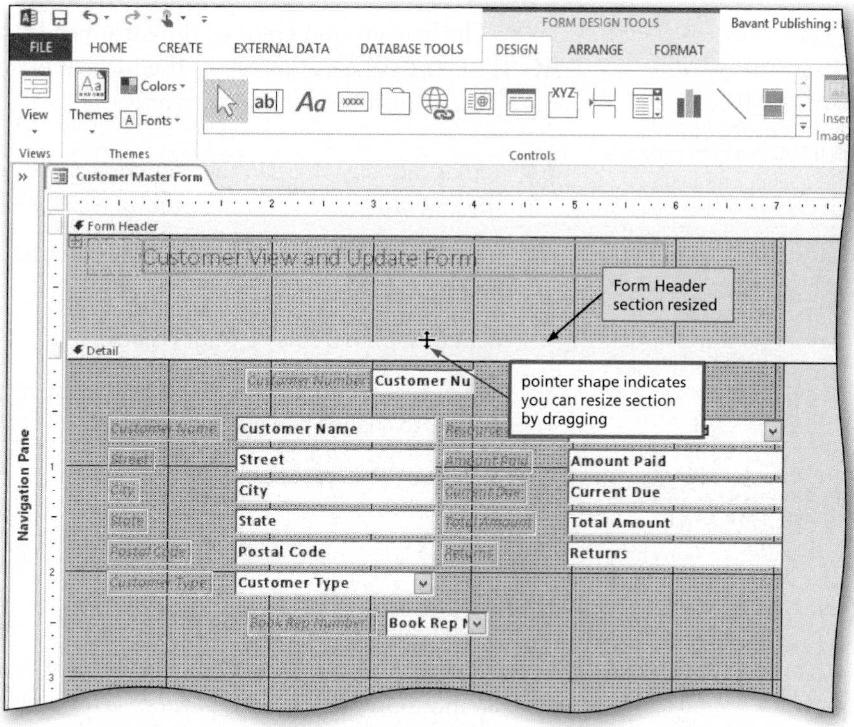

Figure 7–25

3

- Tap or click the control containing the title to select the control.
- Click the Bold button (FORM DESIGN TOOLS FORMAT tab | Font group) to make the title bold.
- Drag the right sizing handle to the approximate position shown in Figure 7–26 to resize the control to the appropriate size for the title.

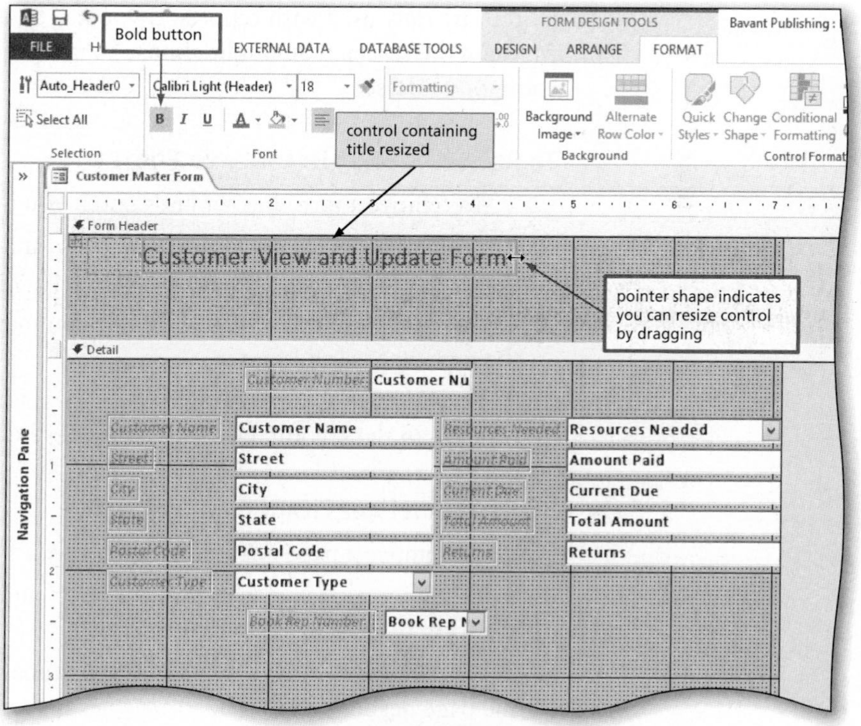

Figure 7–26

To Change the Background Color of the Form Header

The background color of the form header in the form in Figure 7–1 on page AC 411 is the same as the rest of the form. The following steps change the background color of the form header appropriately.

1. Tap or click anywhere in the Form Header section but outside all the controls to select the section.
2. If necessary, display the FORM DESIGN TOOLS FORMAT tab.
3. Tap or click the Background Color button arrow (FORM DESIGN TOOLS FORMAT tab | Font group) to display a color palette.
4. Tap or click the Light Gray 2 color, the first color in the third row under Standard Colors, to change the background color.
5. Save your changes to the form.

BTW
Distributing a Document
Instead of printing and distributing a hard copy of a document, you can distribute the document electronically. Options include sending the document via email; posting it on cloud storage (such as SkyDrive) and sharing the file with others; posting it on a social networking site, blog, or other website; and sharing a link associated with an online location of the document. You also can create and share a PDF or XPS image of the document, so that users can view the file in Acrobat Reader or XPS Viewer instead of in Access.

BTW
Combo Boxes
You also can create combo boxes for reports.

Headers and Footers

Just like with reports, you have control over whether your forms contain a form header and footer. They go together, so if you have a form header, you will also have a form footer. If you do not want them to appear you can shrink the size so there is no room for any content. You can also remove them from your form altogether. If you later decide you want to include them, you can once again add them. You have similar options with page headers and page footers, although typically page headers and page footers are only used with reports. If you had a very long form that spanned several pages on the screen, you might choose to use page headers and footers, but it is not common to do so.

To Remove a Form Header and Footer

To remove a form header and footer, you would use the following steps.

1. With the form open in Design view, press and hold or right-click any open area of the form to produce a shortcut menu.
2. Tap or click the Form Header/Footer command on the shortcut menu to remove the form header and footer.
3. If the Microsoft Access dialog box appears, asking if it is acceptable to delete any controls in the section, tap or click the Yes button.

BTW
Drop-Down Boxes
Combo boxes also are called drop-down boxes because a list drops down when you click the combo box arrow.

To Remove a Page Header and Footer

To remove a page header and footer, you would use the following steps.

1. With the form open in Design view, press and hold or right-click any open area of the form to produce a shortcut menu.
2. Tap or click the Page Header/Footer command on the shortcut menu to remove the page header and footer.
3. If the Microsoft Access dialog box appears, asking if it is acceptable to delete any controls in the section, tap or click the Yes button.

To Insert a Form Header and Footer

To insert a form header and footer, you would use the following steps.

1. With the form open in Design view, press and hold or right-click any open area of the form to produce a shortcut menu.
2. Tap or click the Form Header/Footer command on the shortcut menu to insert a form header and footer.

To Insert a Page Header and Footer

To insert a page header and footer, you would use the following steps.

1. With the form open in Design view, press and hold or right-click any open area of the form to produce a shortcut menu.
2. Tap or click the Page Header/Footer command on the shortcut menu to insert a page header and footer.

BTW
Font versus Foreground Color
The font color also is called the foreground color. When you change the font color using the ribbon, you tap or click the Font Color button. If you use the property sheet to change the color, you tap or click the Fore Color property, tap or click the Build button, and then tap or click the desired color.

Images

You can include a picture (image) in a form. You can also use a picture (image) as the background for a form.

To Include an Image in a Form

To include an image in a form, you would use the following steps.

1. Open the form in Design view or Layout view.
2. Tap or click the Insert Image button (FORM DESIGN TOOLS DESIGN tab | Controls group), and then tap or click the Browse command.
3. Select the desired image.
4. Tap or click the desired location to add the image to the form.

To Use an Image as Background for a Form

To include an image as background for a form, you would use the following steps.

1. Open the form in Design view or Layout view.
2. Tap or click anywhere in the form, tap or click the Background Image button (FORM DESIGN TOOLS FORMAT tab | Background group), and then tap or click the Browse command.
3. Select the desired image for the background.

BTW
Hyperlink Controls
You can add a hyperlink to forms. To add a hyperlink, tap or click the Hyperlink tool, enter the hyperlink in the Address text box (Insert Hyperlink dialog box) and tap or click the OK button. If necessary, move the hyperlink control to the desired location on the form.

Break Point: If you wish to stop working through the chapter at this point, you can quit Access now. You can resume the project later by starting Access, opening the database called Bavant Publishing, opening the Customer Master Form in Design view, and continuing to follow the steps from this location forward.

Command Buttons

Command buttons are buttons placed on a form that users can click to carry out specific actions. To add command buttons, you use the Button tool in the Controls group on the FORM DESIGN TOOLS DESIGN tab. When using the series of Command Button Wizard dialog boxes, you indicate the action that should be taken when the command button is tapped or clicked, for example, go to the next record. Access includes within wizards several categories of commonly used actions.

CONSIDER THIS

When would you include command buttons in your form?

You can make certain actions more convenient for users by including command buttons. Buttons can carry out record navigation actions (for example, go to the next record), record operation actions (for example, add a record), form operation actions (for example, close a form), report operation actions (for example, print a report), application actions (for example, quit application), and some miscellaneous actions (for example, run a macro).

To Add Command Buttons to a Form

1 CREATE FORM | 2 ADD COMBO BOXES | 3 COMMAND BUTTONS | 4 MODIFY MACRO
5 MODIFY COMBO BOX | 6 CREATE SECOND FORM | 7 ADD SUBFORM | 8 ADD CHART

You may find that you can improve the functionality of your form by adding command buttons. ***Why?*** *Command buttons enable users to accomplish tasks with a single click.* Before adding the buttons, you should make sure the 'Use Control Wizards' button is selected.

In the Record Navigation category, you will select the Go To Next Record action for one of the command buttons. From the same category, you will select the Go To Previous Record action for another. Other buttons will use the Add New Record and the Delete Record actions from the Record Operations category. The Close Form button will use the Close Form action from the Form Operations category.

The following steps add command buttons to move to the next record, move to the previous record, add a record, delete a record, and close the form.

1

- Display the FORM DESIGN TOOLS DESIGN tab, and then ensure the 'Use Control Wizards' button is selected.
- Tap or click the Button tool (FORM DESIGN TOOLS DESIGN tab | Controls group) and then move the pointer to the approximate position shown in Figure 7–27.

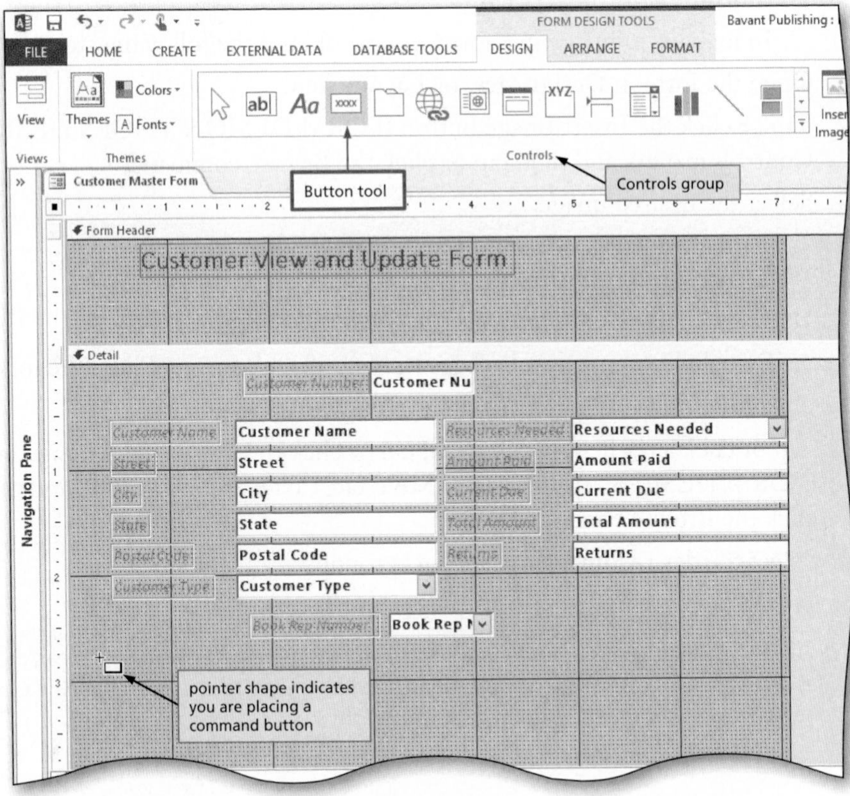

Figure 7–27

2

- Tap or click the position shown in Figure 7–27 to display the Command Button Wizard dialog box.
- With Record Navigation selected in the Categories box, click 'Go To Next Record' in the Actions box (Figure 7–28).

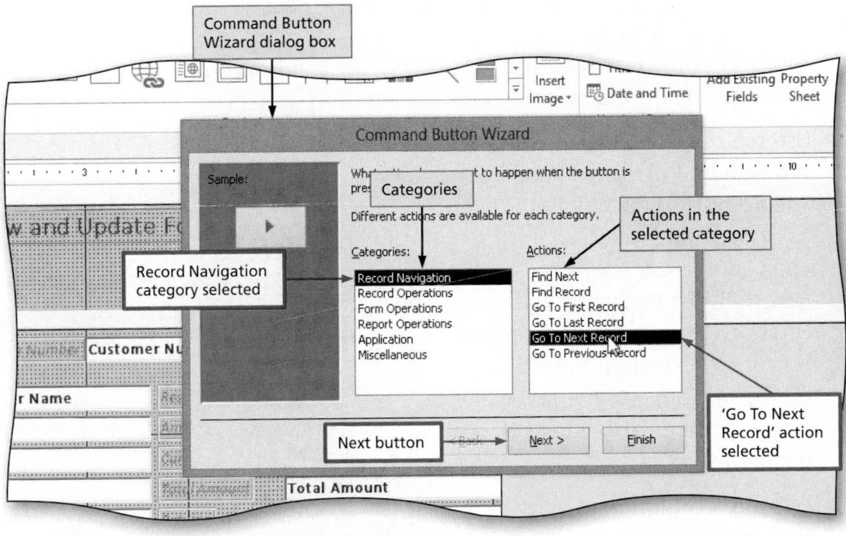

Figure 7–28

3

- Tap or click the Next button to display the next Command Button Wizard screen.
- Tap or click the Text option button (Figure 7–29).

Q&A What is the purpose of these option buttons?
Choose the first option button to place text on the button. You then can specify the text to be included or accept the default choice. Choose the second option button to place a picture on the button. You then can select a picture.

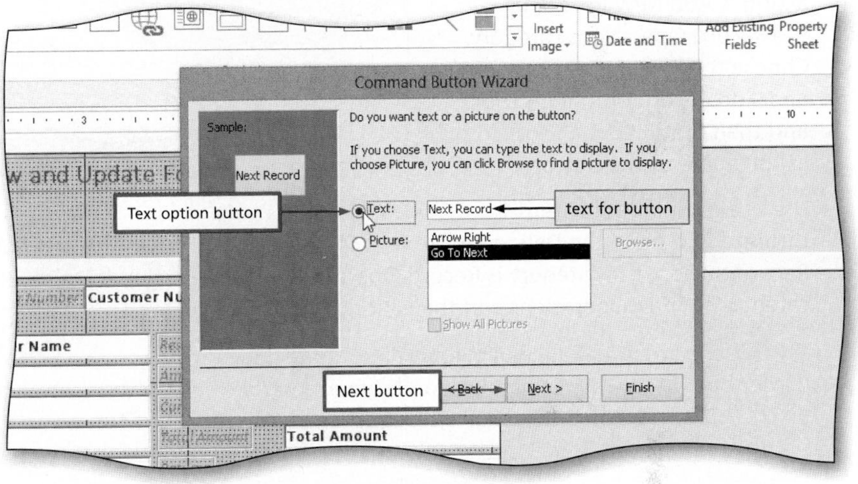

Figure 7–29

4

- Because Next Record is the desired text and does not need to be changed, tap or click the Next button.
- Type **Next Record** as the name of the button (Figure 7–30).

Q&A Does the name of the button have to be the same as the text that appears on the face of the button?
No. The text is what will appear on the screen. You use the name when you need to refer to the specific button. They can be different, but this can lead to confusion. Thus, many people will typically make them the same.

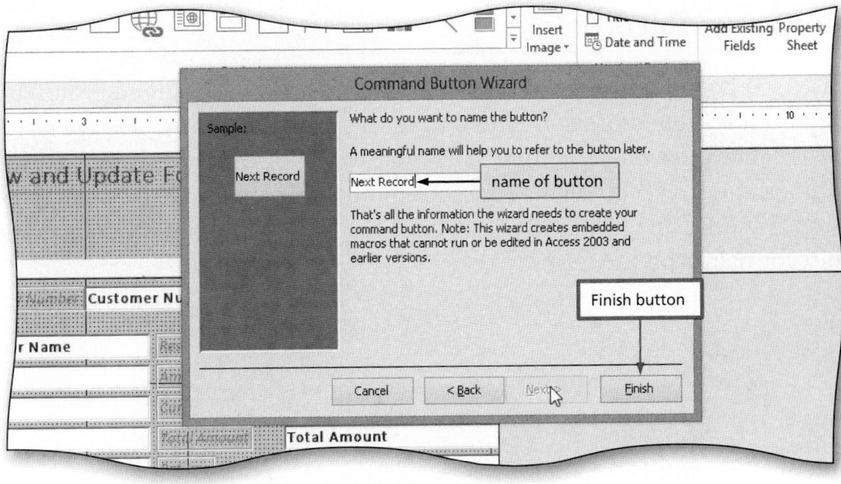

Figure 7–30

5

- Tap or click the Finish button to finish specifying the button.
- Use the techniques in Steps 1 through 5 to place the Previous Record button directly to the right of the Next Record button. The action is Go To Previous Record in the Record Navigation category. Choose the Text option button and Previous Record on the button, and then type **Previous Record** as the name of the button.
- Use the techniques in Steps 1 through 5 to place a button directly to the right of the Previous Record button. The action is Add New Record in the Record Operations category. Choose the Text option button and Add Record on the button, and then type **Add Record** as the name of the button.

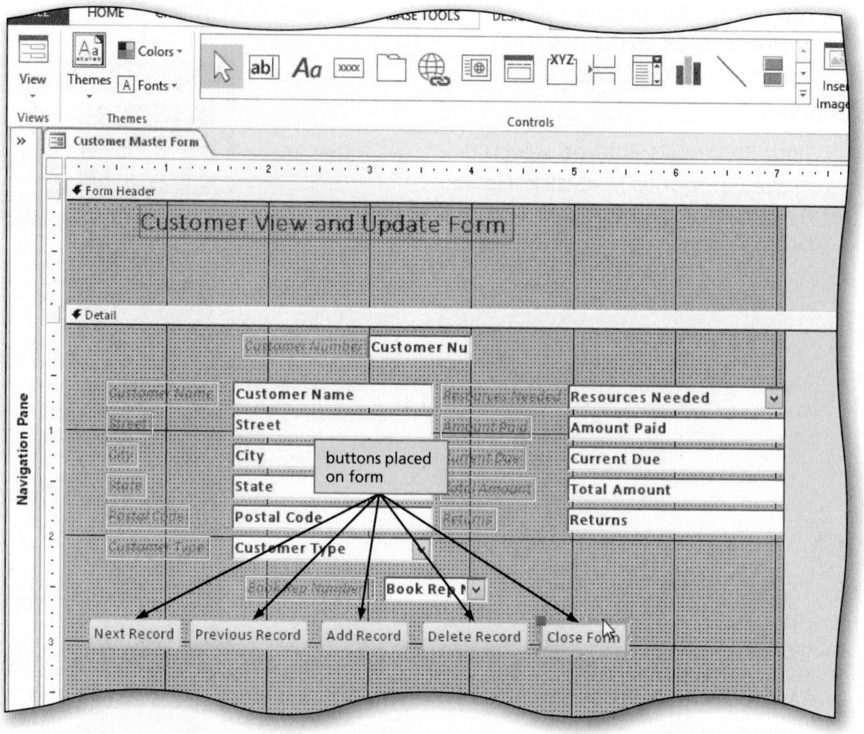

Figure 7–31

- Use the techniques in Steps 1 through 5 to place the Delete Record and Close Form buttons in the positions shown in Figure 7–31. For the Delete Record button, the category is Record Operations and the action is Delete Record. For the Close Form button, the category is Form Operations and the action is Close Form.

Q&A My buttons are not aligned like yours are. What should I do?
If your buttons are not aligned properly, you can drag them to the correct positions. You also can use the buttons on the FORM DESIGN TOOLS ARRANGE tab.

To Add a Combo Box for Finding a Record

1 CREATE FORM | 2 ADD COMBO BOXES | 3 COMMAND BUTTONS | **4 MODIFY MACRO**
5 MODIFY COMBO BOX | **6 CREATE SECOND FORM** | **7 ADD SUBFORM** | **8 ADD CHART**

Although you can use the Find button (HOME tab | Find group) to locate records on a form or a report, it is often more convenient to use a combo box. ***Why?*** *You can type the customer's name directly into the box. Alternatively, you can tap or click the combo box arrow to display a list and then select the desired entry from the list.*

To create a combo box, use the Combo Box tool in the Controls group on the DESIGN tab. The Combo Box Wizard then will guide you through the steps of adding the combo box. The following steps place a combo box for names on the form.

1

- Tap or click the More button (FORM DESIGN TOOLS DESIGN tab | Controls group) to display all the controls.
- With the 'Use Control Wizards' button selected, tap or click the Combo Box tool (FORM DESIGN TOOLS DESIGN tab | Controls group) and then move the pointer, whose shape has changed to a small plus sign with a combo box, to the position shown in Figure 7–32.

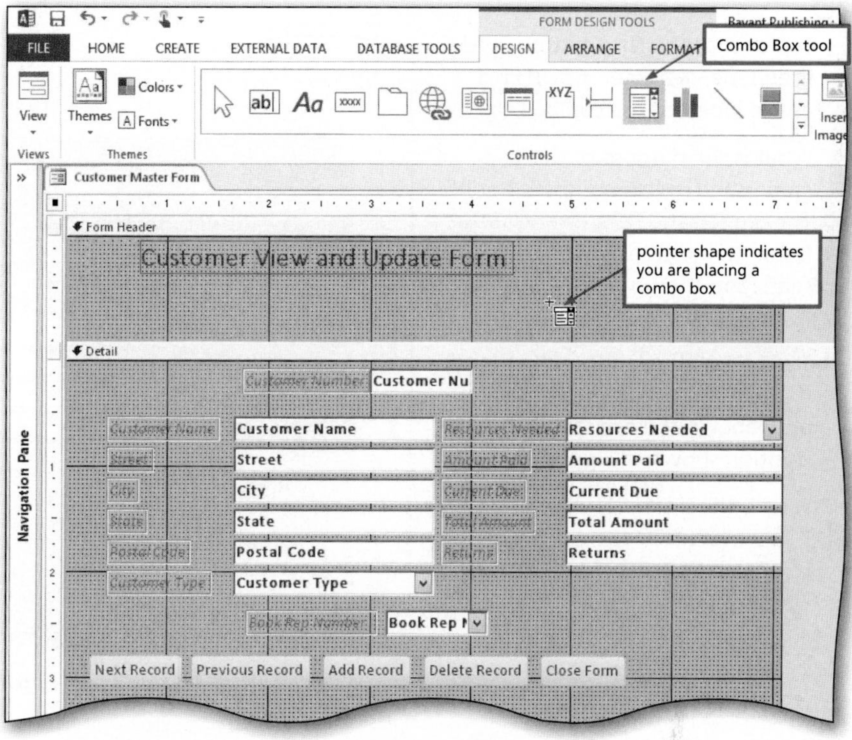

Figure 7–32

2

- Tap or click the position shown in Figure 7–32 to display the Combo Box Wizard.
- Tap or click the 'Find a record on my form based on the value I selected in my combo box.' option button to specify that the user will select from a list of values.
- Tap or click the Next button, tap or click the Customer Name field, and then tap or click the Add Field button to select the Customer Name field for the combo box (Figure 7–33).

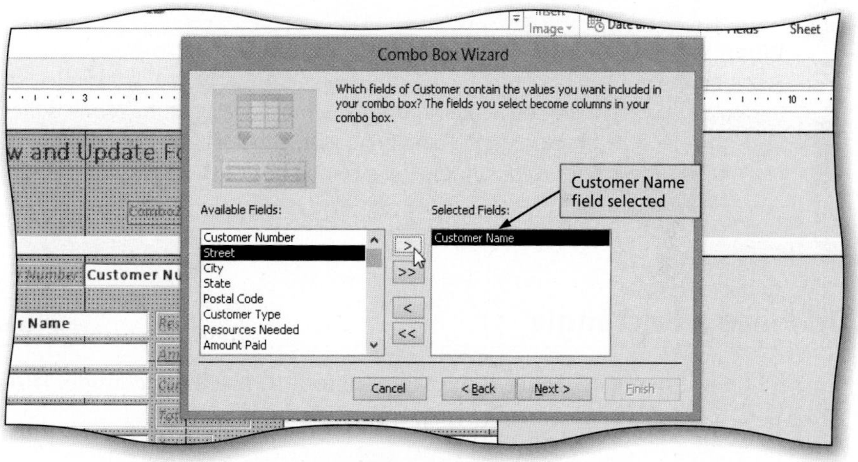

Figure 7–33

3

- Tap or click the Next button.
- Drag the right boundary of the column heading to the approximate size shown in Figure 7–34.

Q&A Can I also resize the column to best fit the data by double-tapping or double-clicking the right boundary of the column heading?

Yes.

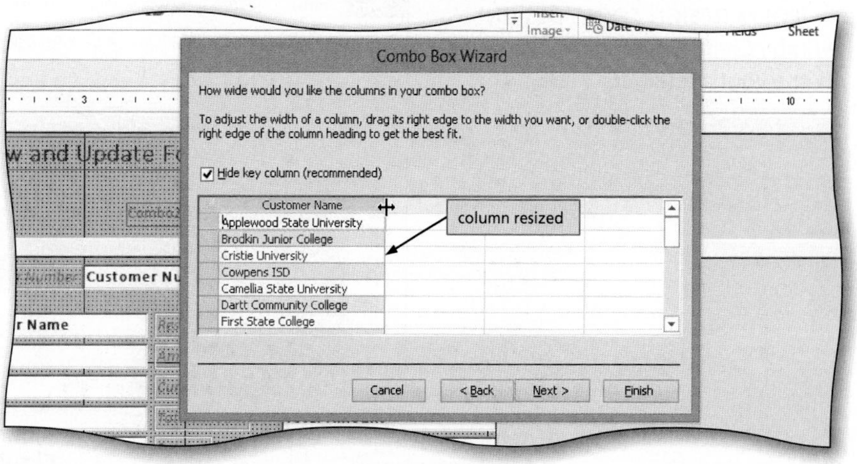

Figure 7–34

4

- Tap or click the Next button, and then type `&Name to Find` as the label for the combo box.

Q&A What is the purpose of the ampersand in front of the letter, N?
The ampersand (&) in front of the letter, N, indicates that users can select the combo box by pressing ALT+N.

- Tap or click the Finish button, and, if necessary, position the control and label in the approximate position shown in Figure 7–35.

Q&A Why is the letter, N, underlined?
The underlined letter, N, in the word, Name, indicates that you can press ALT+N to select the combo box. It is underlined because you preceded the letter, N, with the ampersand.

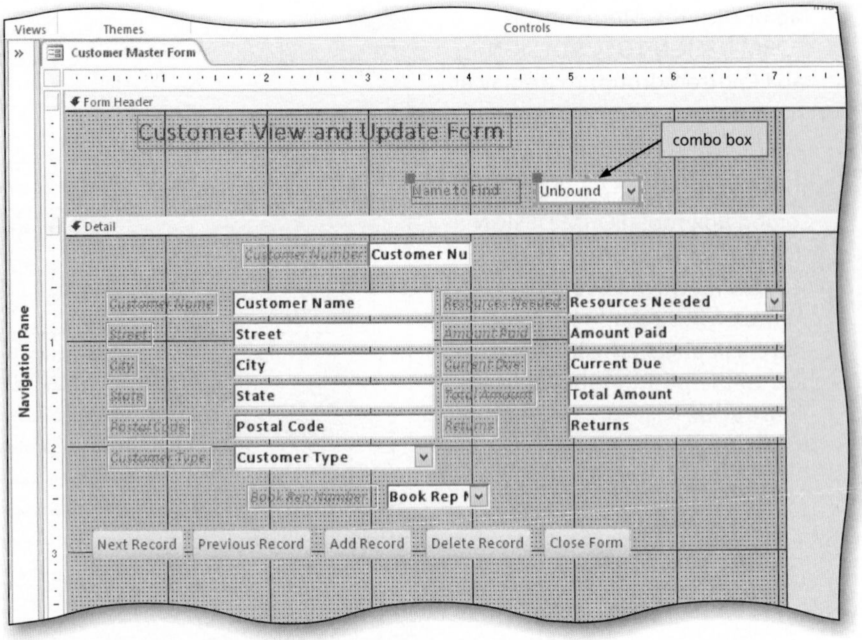

Figure 7–35

CONSIDER THIS

When would you include a combo box in your form?

A combo box is a combination of a text box, where users can type data, and a list box, where users can tap or click an arrow to display a list. Would a combo box improve the functionality of the form? Is there a place where it would be convenient for users to enter data by selecting the data from a list, either a list of predefined items or a list of values from a related table? If users need to search for records, including a combo box can assist in the process.

To Place a Rectangle

1 CREATE FORM | 2 ADD COMBO BOXES | 3 COMMAND BUTTONS | **4 MODIFY MACRO**
5 MODIFY COMBO BOX | 6 CREATE SECOND FORM | 7 ADD SUBFORM | 8 ADD CHART

The following steps use the Rectangle tool to place a rectangle. ***Why?*** *To emphasize an area of a form, you can place a rectangle around it as a visual cue.*

1

- Tap or click the More button (FORM DESIGN TOOLS DESIGN tab | Controls group) to display all the controls (Figure 7–36).

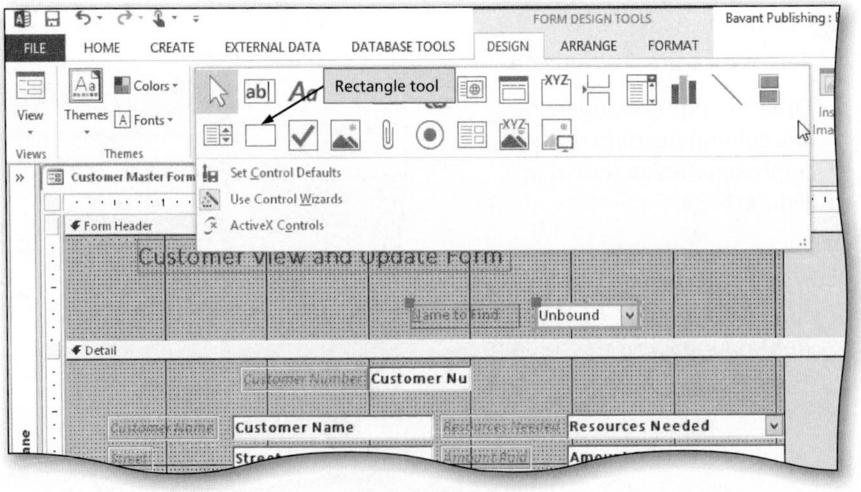

Figure 7–36

2

- Tap or click the Rectangle tool, which is the second tool in the second row, point to the position for the upper-left corner of the rectangle shown in Figure 7–37, and drag to the lower-right corner of the rectangle to place the rectangle.

3

- Tap or click the Property Sheet button (FORM DESIGN TOOLS DESIGN tab | Tools group) to display the property sheet for the rectangle.
- If necessary, change the value of the Special Effect property to Etched.
- Make sure the value of the Back Style property is Transparent, so the combo box will appear within the rectangle.

Q&A What if the value is not Transparent?
If the value is not Transparent, the rectangle would cover the combo box completely and the combo box would not be visible.

- Close the property sheet.
- Save and then close the form.

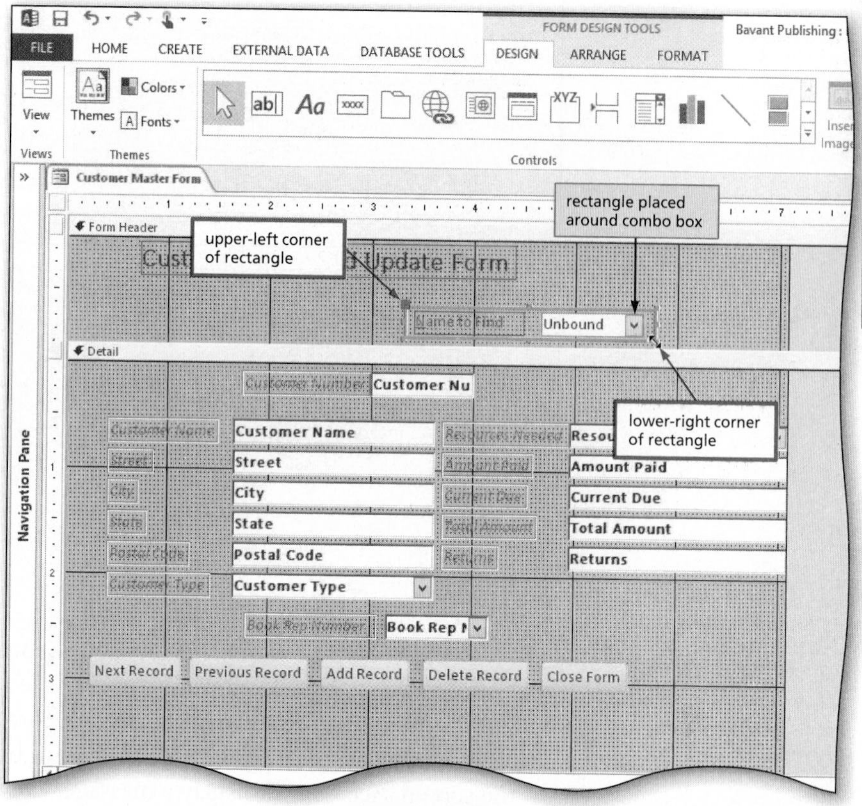

Figure 7–37

To Open the Customer Master Form

Once you have created the form, you can use it at any time by opening it. The following steps open the Customer Master Form.

1. Open the Navigation Pane, and then press and hold or right-click the Customer Master Form to display the shortcut menu.
2. Tap or click Open on the shortcut menu to open the form.
3. Close the Navigation Pane (Figure 7–38 on the next page).

BTW
Events
Events are actions that have happened or are happening at the present time. An event can result from a user action. For example, one of the events associated with a button on a form is tapping or clicking the button. The corresponding event property is On Click. If you associate VBA code or a macro with the On Click event property, the code or macro will execute any time you tap or click the button. Using properties associated with events, you can tell Access to run a macro, call a Visual Basic function, or run an event procedure in response to an event.

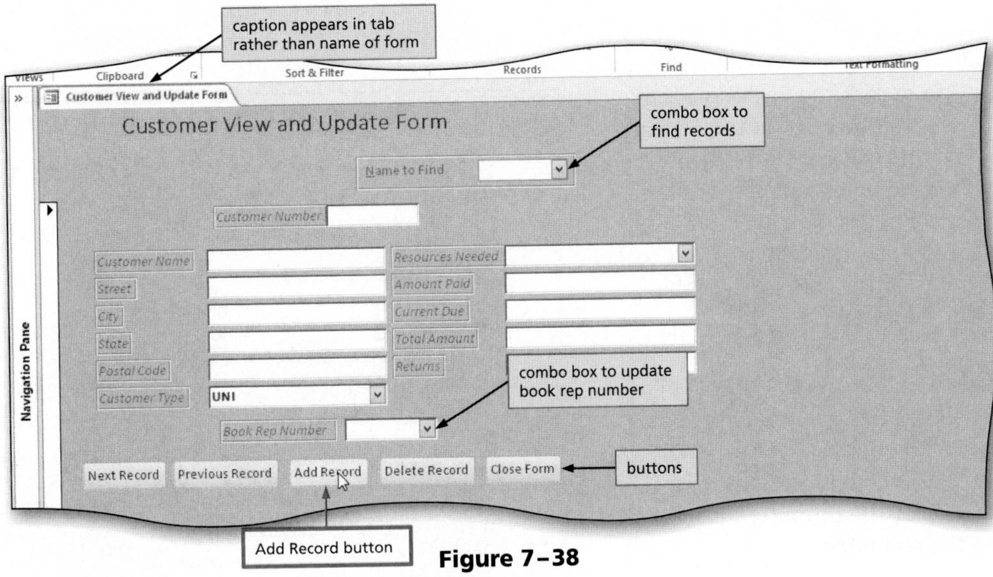

Figure 7–38

BTW
Comments in Macros
You can use the Comment action in the Action Catalog to place comments in macros.

Using the Buttons

To move from record to record on the form, you can use the buttons to perform the actions you specify. To move forward to the next record, tap or click the Next Record button. Tap or click the Previous Record button to move back to the previous record. Tapping or clicking the Delete Record button will delete the record currently on the screen. Access will display a message requesting that you verify the deletion before the record actually is deleted. Tapping or clicking the Close Form button will remove the form from the screen.

To Test the Add Record Button

1 CREATE FORM | 2 ADD COMBO BOXES | 3 COMMAND BUTTONS | 4 MODIFY MACRO
5 MODIFY COMBO BOX | 6 CREATE SECOND FORM | 7 ADD SUBFORM | 8 ADD CHART

The following step uses the Add Record button. ***Why?*** *Tapping or clicking the Add Record button will clear the contents of the form so you can add a new record.*

1

- Tap or click the Add Record button (Figure 7–39).

Q&A There is no insertion point in the Customer Number field. How would I begin entering a new record?
To begin entering a record, you would have to tap or click the Customer Number field before you can start typing.

Why does UNI appear in the Customer Type field?
The value UNI is the default value assigned to the Customer Type field.

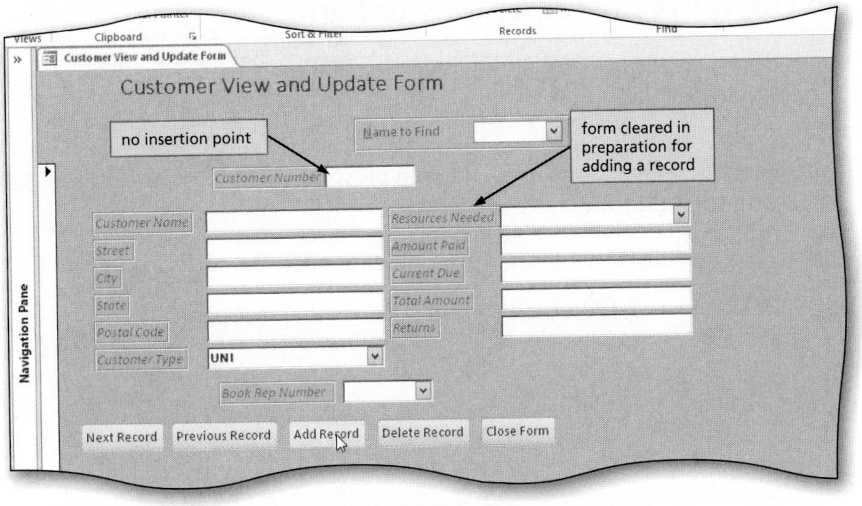

Figure 7–39

Experiment

- Try each of the other buttons to see their effects. Do not delete any records. After tapping or clicking the Close Form button, open the form once again and close the Navigation Pane.

To Use the Combo Box

Using the combo box, you can search for a customer in two ways. First, you can tap or click the combo box arrow to display a list of customer names, and then select the name from the list by tapping or clicking it. It is also easy to search by typing the name. ***Why?*** *As you type, Access will display automatically the name that begins with the letters you have typed. Once the correct name is displayed, select the name by pressing the tab key.* Regardless of the method you use, the data for the selected customer appears on the form once the selection is made.

The following steps first locate the customer whose name is First State College, and then use the Next Record button to move to the next customer.

1

- Tap or click the 'Name to Find' arrow to display a list of customer names (Figure 7–40).

Q&A Why does the list not appear in alphabetical order? It would be more useful and easier to use if it were alphabetized.
You will change the combo box later so that the names appear in alphabetical order.

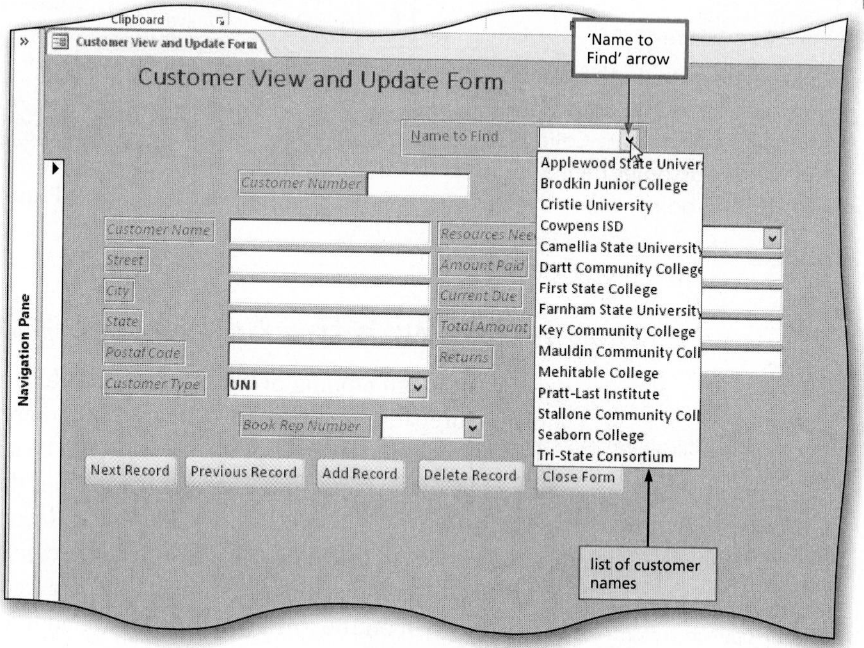

Figure 7–40

2

- Tap or click First State College to display the data for First State College in the form (Figure 7–41).

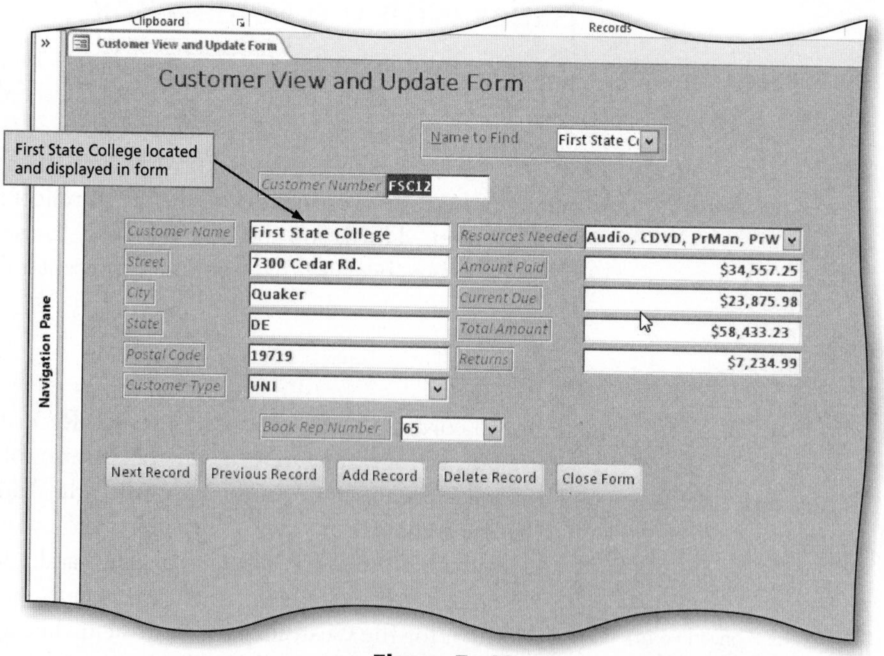

Figure 7–41

3

- Tap or click the Next Record button to display the next record (Figure 7–42).

Q&A Why does the combo box still contain First State College, rather than Farnham State University?
This is a problem with the combo box. You will address this issue later.

Experiment

- Select the entry in the combo box and enter the letter, k, to find Key Community College. Try other customer names in the combo box.

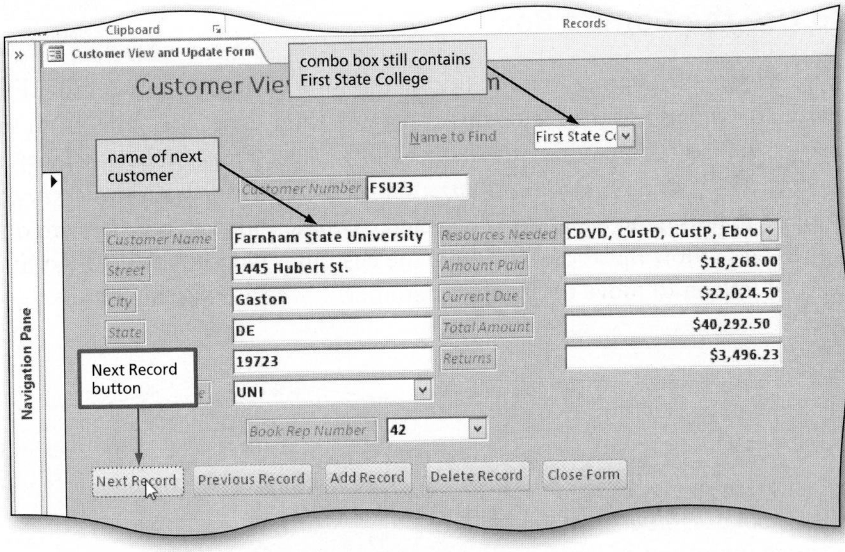

Figure 7–42

Issues with the Add Record Button

BTW
Focus
Sometimes it is difficult to determine which object on the screen has the focus. If a field has the focus, an insertion point appears in the field. If a button has the focus, a small rectangle appears inside the button.

Although tapping or clicking the Add Record button does erase the contents of the form in preparation for adding a new record, there is a problem with it. After tapping or clicking the Add Record button, there should be an insertion point in the control for the first field — the Customer Number field — but there is not. To display an insertion point automatically when you tap or click the Add Record button, you need to change the focus. A control is said to have the **focus** when it becomes active; that is, when it becomes able to receive user input through mouse, touch, or keyboard actions. At any point in time, only one item on the form has the focus. In addition to adding a new record, tapping or clicking the Add Record button needs to update the focus to the Customer Number field.

Issues with the Combo Box

The combo box has the following issues. First, if you examine the list of names in Figure 7–40 on the previous page, you will see that they are not in alphabetical order (Cristie University comes before Cowpens ISD). Second, when you move to a record without using the combo box, such as when navigating using the buttons, the name in the combo box does not change to reflect the name of the customer currently on the screen. Third, you should not be able to use the TAB key to change the focus to the combo box, because that does not represent a field to be updated.

Macros

BTW
Converting Macros to VBA Code
You can convert macros that are attached to forms to VBA (Visual Basic for Applications) code. To do so, open the form in Design view and tap or click the 'Convert Form's Macros to Visual Basic' button. You also can convert macros that are attached to reports.

To correct the problem with the Add Record button not displaying an insertion point, you will update a **macro**, which is a series of actions that Access performs when a particular event occurs, in this case when the Add Record button is tapped or clicked. (In the next chapter, you will create macros on your own. In this case, Access has already created the macro; you just need to add a single action to it.)

Specifically, you need to add an action to the macro that will move the focus to the control for the Customer Number field. The appropriate action is GoToControl. Like many actions, the GoToControl action requires additional information, called arguments. The argument for the GoToControl action is the name of the control, in this case, the Customer Number control.

To Modify the Macro for the Add Record Button

The following steps first change the name of the control to remove spaces. ***Why?*** *When creating or modifying macros in Access, control names cannot contain spaces.* You can use different methods of changing the names so that they do not contain spaces. One approach is to simply remove the space. This approach would change Customer Number to CustomerNumber, for example. The approach you will use is to insert an underscore (_) in place of the space. For example, you will change Customer Number to Customer_Number.

After changing the name of the control, the steps modify the macro that is associated with the tapping or clicking of the Add Record button by adding an action that will change the focus to the control for the Customer Number field.

1

- Tap or click the View button arrow and then tap or click Design View to return to Design view.
- Tap or click the control for the Customer Number field (the white space, not the label), and then tap or click the Property Sheet button (FORM DESIGN TOOLS DESIGN tab | Tools group) to display the property sheet.
- If necessary, tap or click the All tab. Ensure the Name property is selected, tap or click immediately following the word, Customer, press the DELETE key to delete the space, and then type an underscore (_) to change the name to Customer_Number (Figure 7–43).

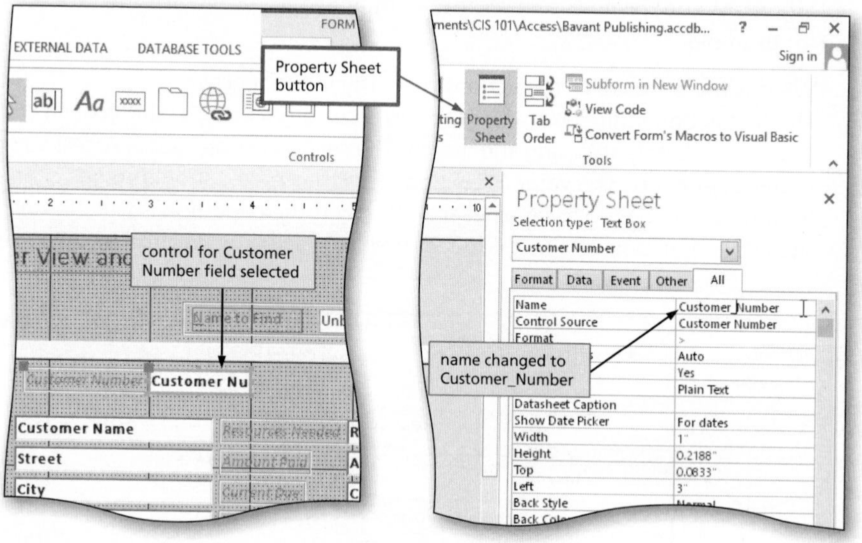

Figure 7–43

Q&A Could I just erase the old name and type Customer_Number?
Yes. Use whichever method you find most convenient.

2

- Close the property sheet and then press and hold or right-click the Add Record button to display a shortcut menu (Figure 7–44).

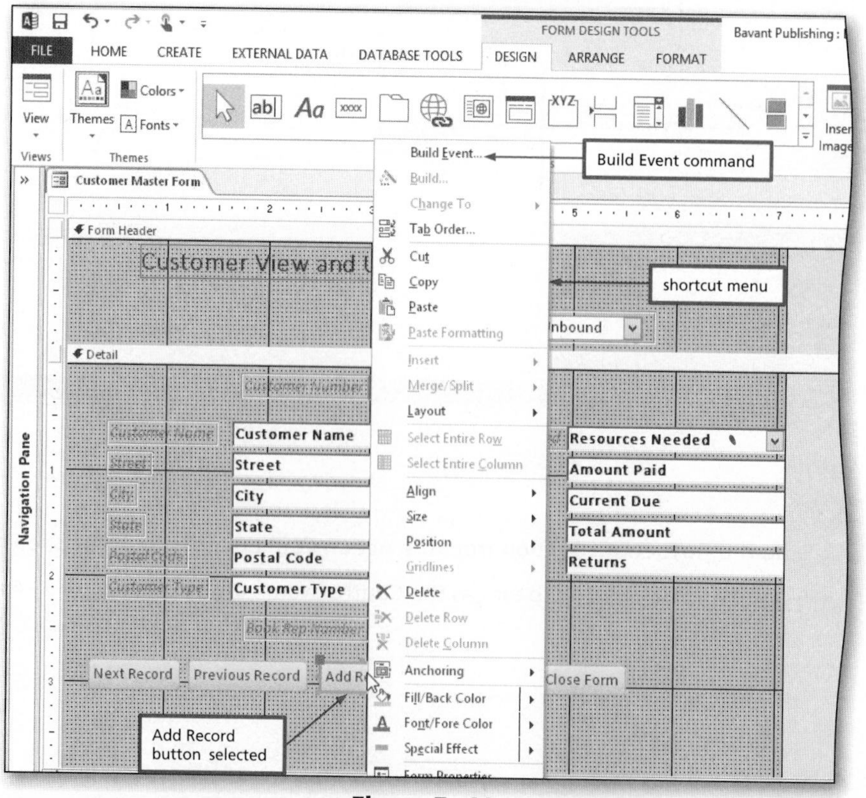

Figure 7–44

3

- Tap or click Build Event on the shortcut menu to display the macro associated with the On Click event that Access created automatically.
- If the Action Catalog, the catalog that lists all of the available actions, does not appear, tap or click the Action Catalog button (MACRO TOOLS DESIGN tab | Show/Hide group) to display the Action Catalog.
- In the Action Catalog, if the expand indicator is an open triangle in front of Actions, tap or click the triangle to display all actions.
- If the expand indicator in front of Database Objects is an open triangle, tap or click the expand indicator to display all actions associated with Database Objects (Figure 7–45).

Q&A

How can I recognize actions? How can I recognize the arguments of the actions?
The actions are in bold. The arguments for the action follow the action and are not bold. The value for an argument appears to the right of the argument. The value for the 'Go to' argument of the OnError action is Next, for example.

What is the purpose of the actions currently in the macro?
The first action indicates that, if there is an error, Access should proceed to the next action in the macro rather than immediately stopping the macro. The second action causes Access to go to the record indicated by the values in the arguments. The value, New, indicates that Access should to go to a new record. Because the final action has a condition, the action will be executed only if the condition is true, that is, the error code contains a value other than 0. In that case, the MsgBox action will display a description of the error.

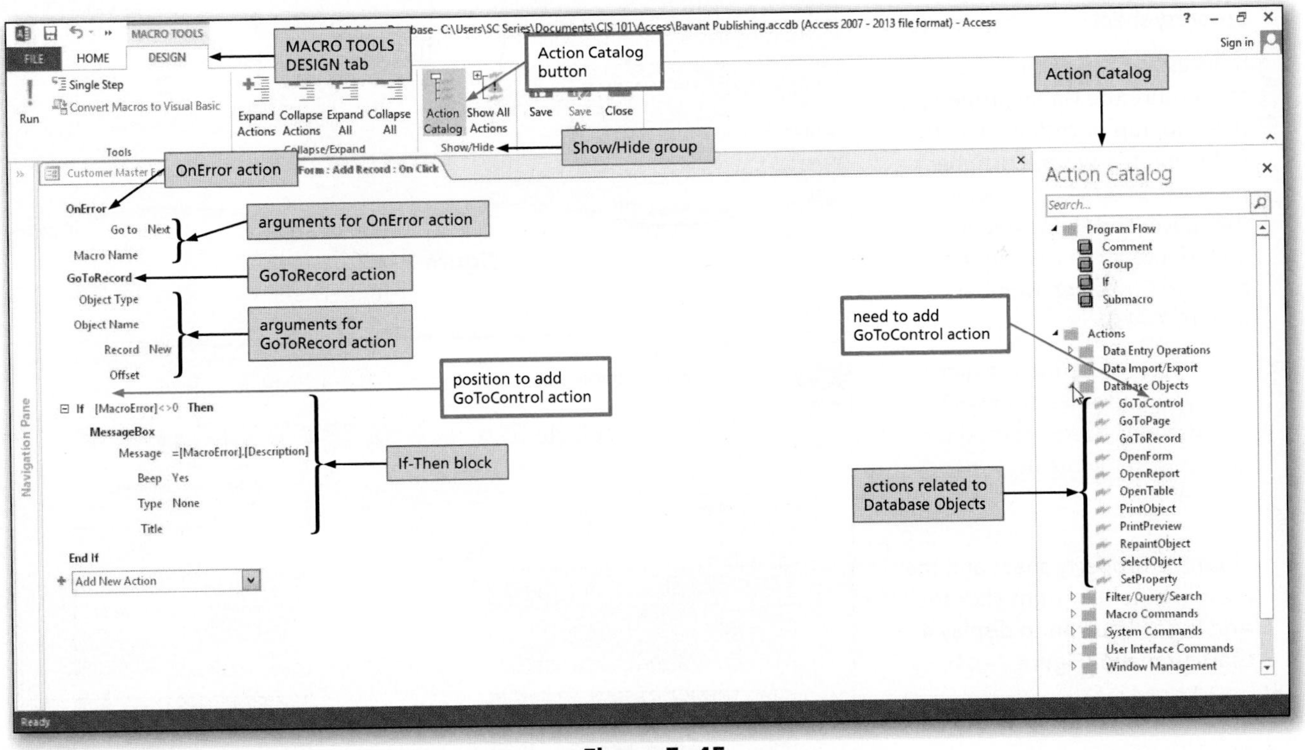

Figure 7–45

4

- Drag the GoToControl action from the Action Catalog to the position shown in Figure 7–46.
- Type **`Customer_Number`** as the Control Name argument (Figure 7–46).

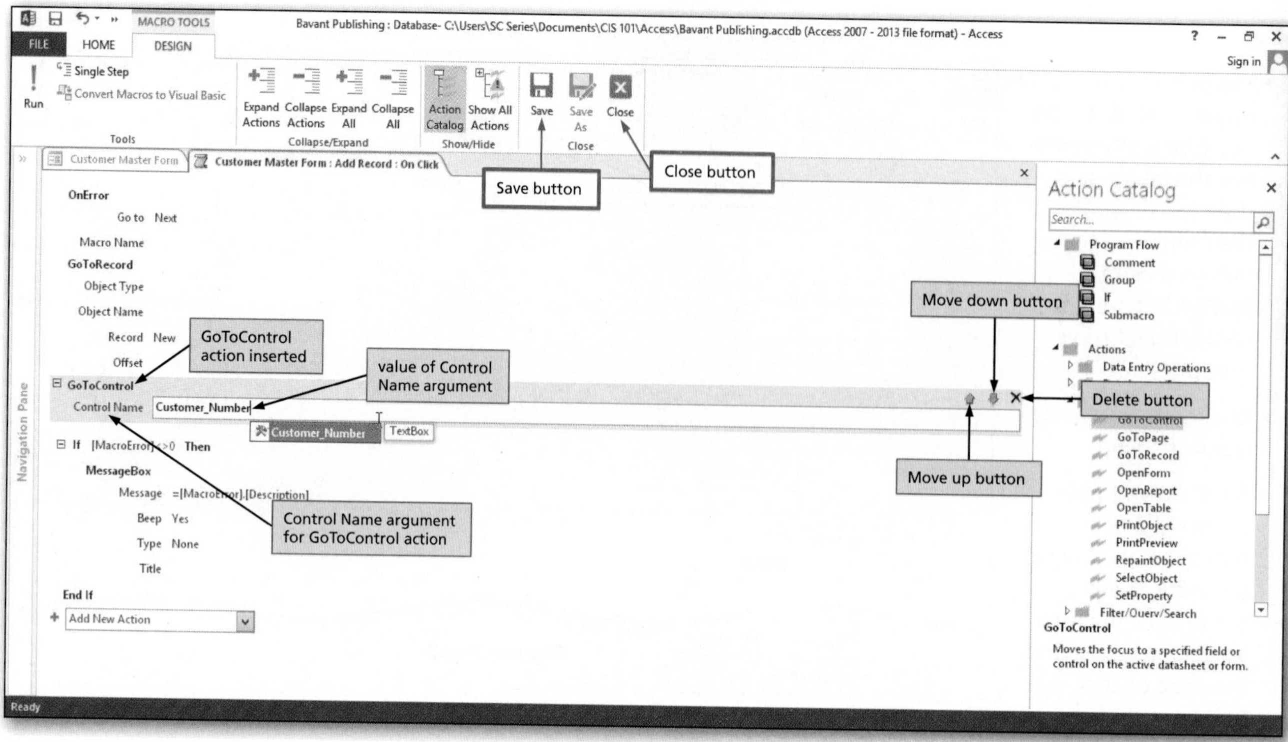

Figure 7–46

Q&A What is the effect of the GoToControl action?
When Access executes this action, the focus will move to the control indicated in the Control Name argument, in this case, the Customer_Number control.

I added the GoToControl action to the wrong place in the macro. How do I move it?
To move it up in the list, tap or click the Move up button. To move it down, tap or click the Move down button.

I added the wrong action. What should I do?
Tap or click the Delete button to delete the action you added, and then add the GoToControl action. If you decide you would rather start over instead, tap or click the Close button (MACRO TOOLS DESIGN tab | Close group) and then tap or click the No button when asked if you want to save your changes. You can then begin again from Step 3.

5

- Tap or click the Save button (MACRO TOOLS DESIGN tab | Close group) to save your changes.
- Tap or click the Close button (MACRO TOOLS DESIGN tab | Close group) to close the macro and return to the form design.

To Modify the Combo Box

1 CREATE FORM | 2 ADD COMBO BOXES | 3 COMMAND BUTTONS | 4 MODIFY MACRO
5 MODIFY COMBO BOX | **6 CREATE SECOND FORM** | **7 ADD SUBFORM** | **8 ADD CHART**

In a previous step, you discovered that the combo box does not display customer names in alphabetical order. To ensure the data is sorted in the correct order, you need to modify the query that Access has created for the combo box so the data is sorted by customer name. Also, the combo box does not update the name in the combo box to reflect the name of customers currently on the screen, which will require you to modify the VBA (Visual Basic for Applications) code associated with what is termed the On Current event property of the entire form. ***Why?*** *The modification to the On Current event property will ensure that the combo box remains current with the rest of the form; that is, it contains the name of the customer whose number currently appears in the Customer Number field.* The steps on the next page modify the query and then the code associated with the On Current event property appropriately. The final step changes the Tab Stop property for the combo box from Yes to No.

1

- Tap or click the Name to Find combo box (the white space, not the label), and then tap or click the Property Sheet button (FORM DESIGN TOOLS DESIGN tab | Tools group).
- Change the name to Name_to_Find.
- Scroll down in the property sheet so that the Row Source property appears, tap or click the Row Source property, and then tap or click the Build button (the three dots) to display the Query Builder.

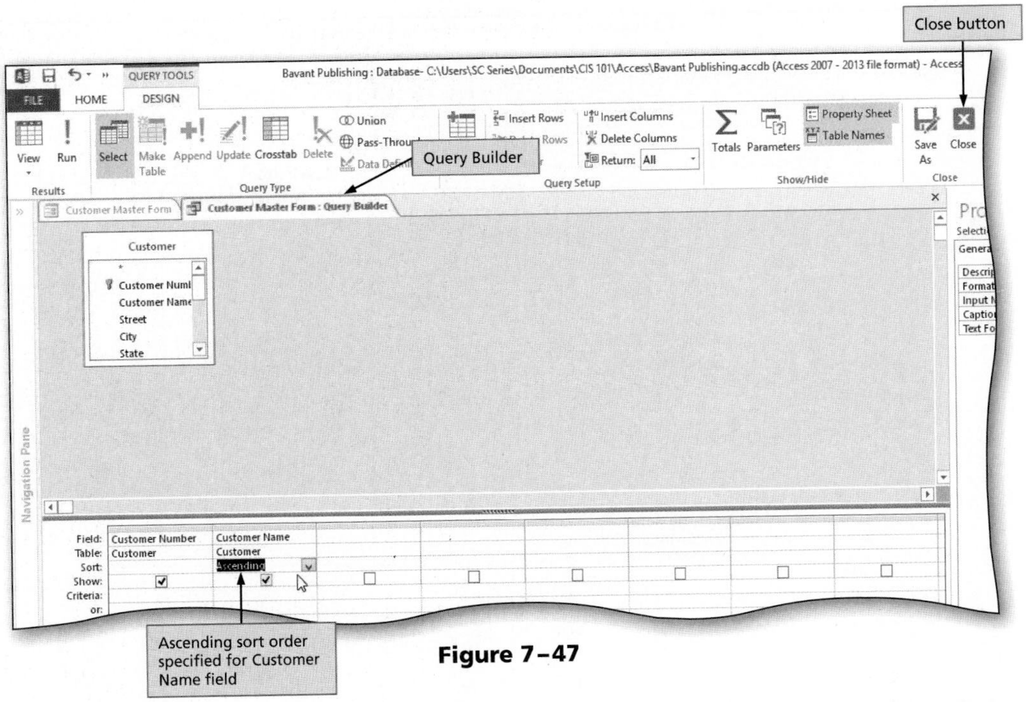

Figure 7–47

- Tap or click the Sort row in the Customer Name field, tap or click the arrow that appears, and then tap or click Ascending to change the order and display customer names in alphabetical order in the combo box (Figure 7–47).

2

- Tap or click the Save button on the Quick Access Toolbar to save your changes.
- Close the Query Builder window by tapping or clicking the Close button on the DESIGN tab.
- Close the property sheet.
- Tap or click the form selector (the box in the upper-left corner of the form) to select the form.
- If necessary, tap or click the Property Sheet button (FORM DESIGN TOOLS DESIGN tab | Tools group), scroll down until the On Current property appears, and then tap or click the On Current property.

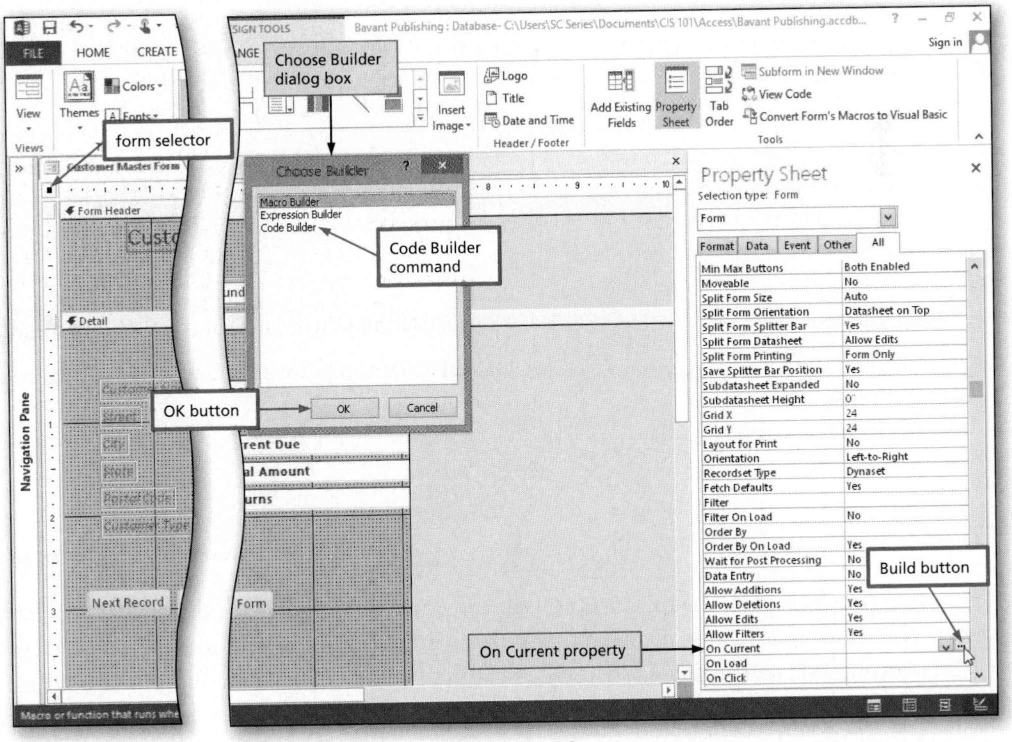

Figure 7–48

- Tap or click the Build button (the three dots) to display the Choose Builder dialog box (Figure 7–48).

3

- Tap or click Code Builder in the Choose Builder dialog box, and then tap or click the OK button to display the VBA code generated for the form (Figure 7–49).

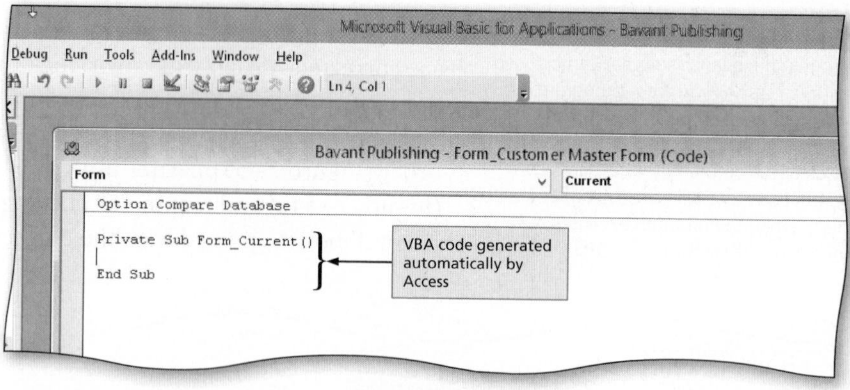

Figure 7–49

4

- Press the TAB key and then type `Name_to_Find = Customer_Number ' Update the combo box` as shown in Figure 7–50, to create the command and a comment that describes the effect of the command.

Q&A How would I construct a command like this in my own form?
Begin with the name you assigned to the combo box, followed by an equal sign, and then the name of the control containing the primary key of the table. The portion of the statement following the single quotation mark is a comment describing the purpose of the command. You could simply type the same thing that you see in this command.

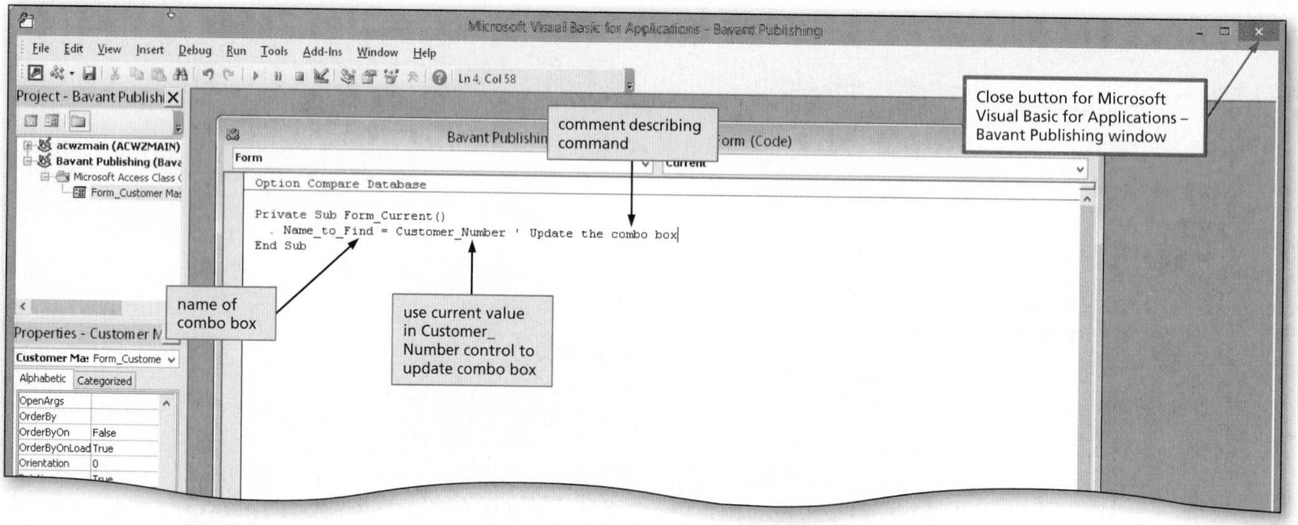

Figure 7–50

5

- Tap or click the Close button for the Microsoft Visual Basic for Applications - Bavant Publishing window, and then close the Form property sheet.
- Tap or click the Name to Find combo box and then tap or click the Property Sheet button (FORM DESIGN TOOLS DESIGN tab | Tools group).
- Scroll down until the Tab Stop property appears, tap or click the Tab Stop property, and then tap or click the Tab Stop property box arrow.
- Tap or click No to change the value of the Tab Stop property, which skips over the combo box in the tab sequence, and then close the property sheet.
- Save your changes and then close the form.

BTW
VBA
Visual Basic for Applications (VBA) is a programming language that can be used with Access. As with other programming languages, programs in VBA consist of code; that is, a collection of statements, also called commands, which are instructions that will cause actions to take place when the program executes. VBA is included with all Microsoft Office apps.

Using the Modified Form

The problems with the Add Record button and the combo box now are corrected. When you tap or click the Add Record button, an insertion point appears in the Customer Number field (Figure 7–51a). When you tap or click the 'Name to Find' box arrow, the list of names is in alphabetical order (Figure 7–51b). After using the 'Name to Find' box to find a customer (Figure 7–51c) and tapping or clicking the Next Record button, the 'Name to Find' box is updated with the correct customer name (Figure 7–51d).

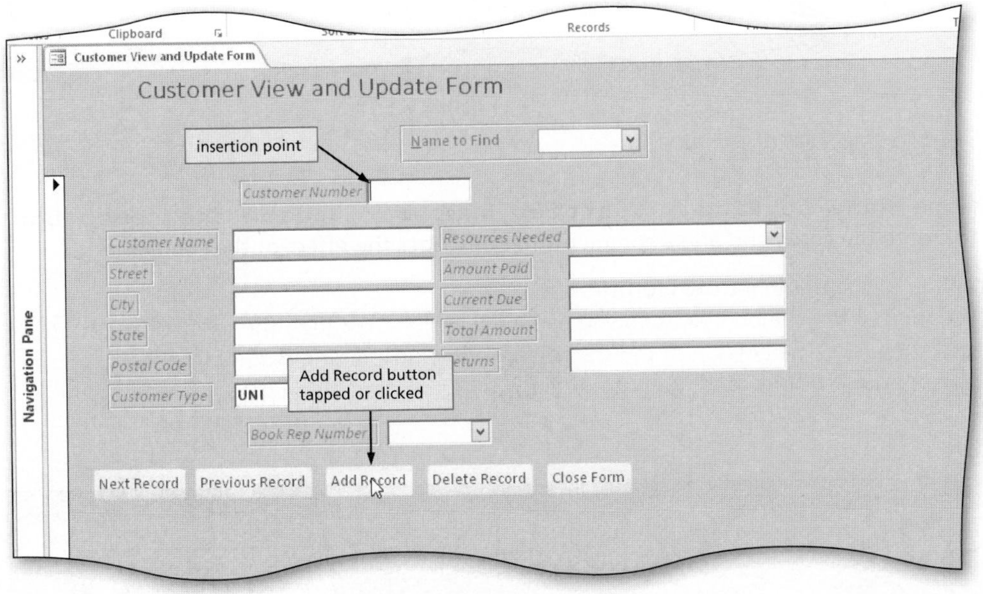

Figure 7–51 (a) Using the Add Record Button

Figure 7–51 (b) Using the 'Name to Find' Box

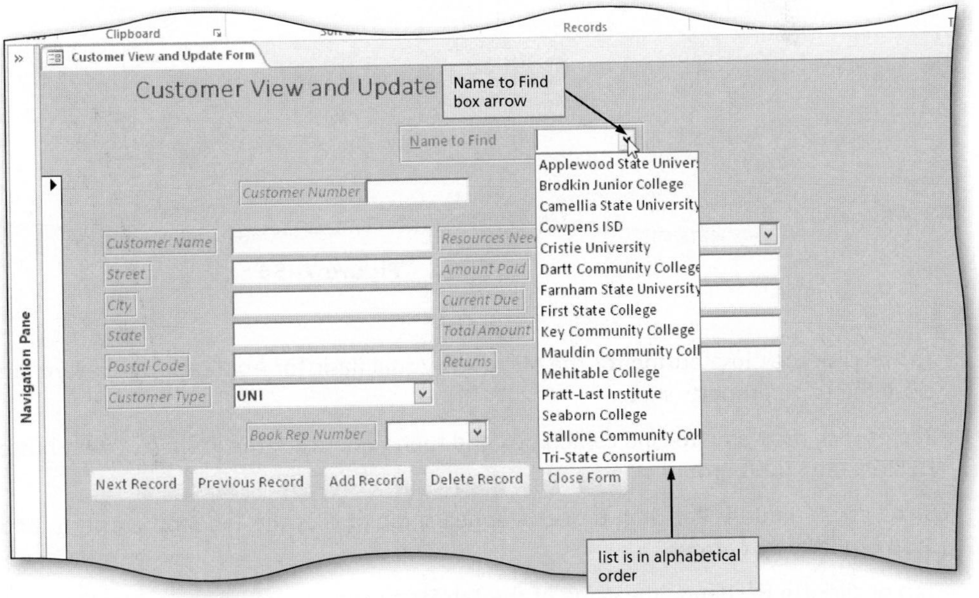

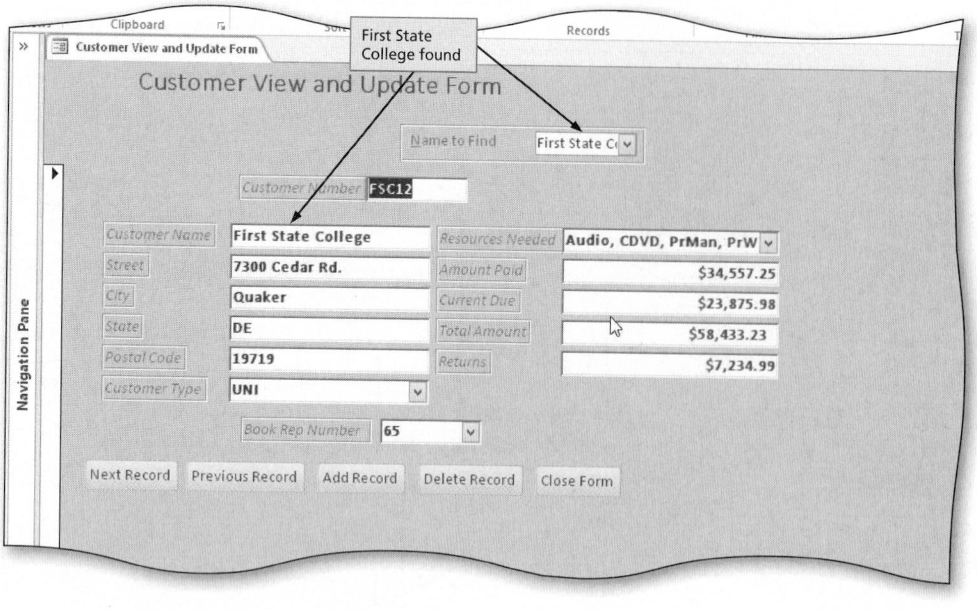

Figure 7–51 (c) Results of Using the Name to Find Box

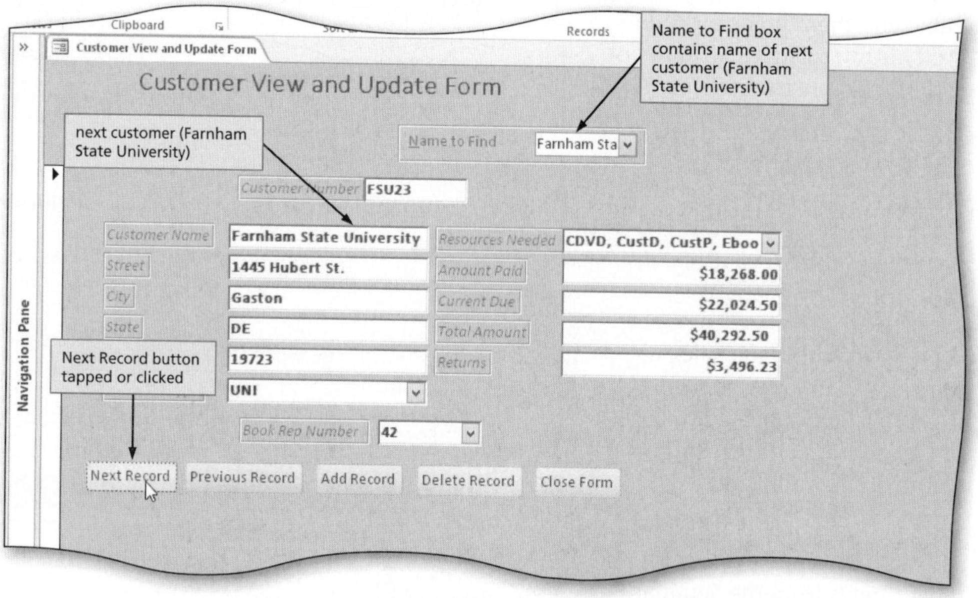

Figure 7–51 (d) Using the Next Record Button

BTW

Record Order

When you use the Next Record button to move through the records, recall that the records are in order by Customer Number, which is the primary key, and not alphabetical order.

Break Point: If you wish to stop working through the chapter at this point, you can quit Access now. You can resume the project later by starting Access, opening the database called Bavant Publishing, and continuing to follow the steps from this location forward.

Creating a Multipage Form

If you have determined that you have more data than will fit conveniently on one screen, you can create a **multipage form**, a form that includes more than a single page. There are two ways to create a multipage form. One way is to insert a page break at the desired location or locations. An alternative approach that produces a nice-looking and easy-to-use multipage form is to insert a tab control. The multiple pages, called tabbed pages, are all contained within the tab control. To move from one page in the tab control to another, a user simply taps or clicks the desired tab. The tab control shown in Figure 7–2 on page AC 412, for example, has a tab labeled Datasheet that contains a datasheet showing the relevant data. It has a second tab, labeled Charts, that displays the relevant data in two charts.

To Create a Query

Why? *The second form contains data from the Book Rep, Customer, and Seminar Offerings tables. The simplest way to incorporate this data is to create a query that joins all three tables.* The following steps create the necessary query.

1

- Display the CREATE tab, and then tap or click the Query Design button (CREATE tab | Queries group) to create a query.
- Tap or click the Book Rep table, if necessary, and then tap or click the Add button to add the Book Rep table to the query.
- Tap or click the Customer table and then tap or click the Add button to add the Customer table to the query.
- Tap or click the Seminar Offerings table and then tap or click the Add button to add the Seminar Offerings table to the query.
- Tap or click the Close button (Show Table dialog box).
- Resize the Book Rep and Customer field lists to display as many fields as possible (Figure 7–52).

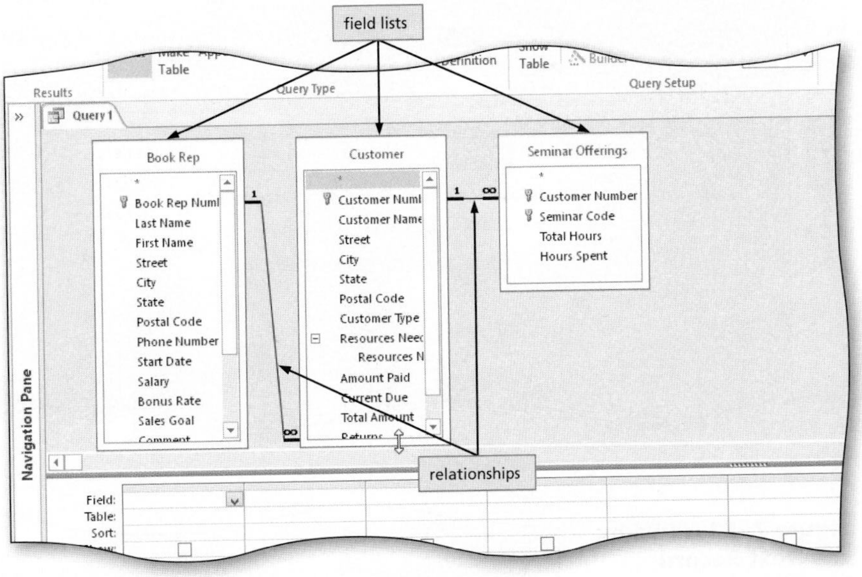

Figure 7–52

2

- Double-tap or double-click the Book Rep Number field from the Book Rep table and the Customer Number field from the Customer table.
- Double-tap or double-click the Seminar Code and Hours Spent fields from the Seminar Offerings table.
- Press and hold or right-click the Field row in the first open column of the design grid to produce a shortcut menu.
- Tap or click Zoom on the shortcut menu to display the Zoom dialog box and then type **`Hours Remaining:[Total Hours]-[Hours Spent]`** in the Zoom dialog box to enter the expression for the field (Figure 7–53).

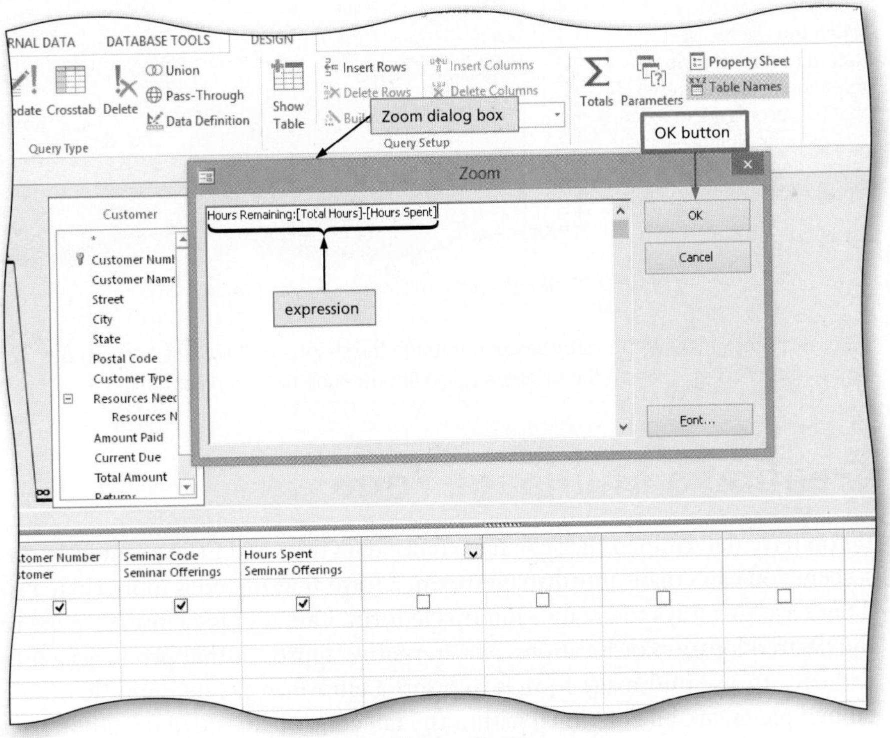

Figure 7–53

3

- Tap or click the OK button and then tap or click the View button (QUERY TOOLS DESIGN tab | Results group) to ensure your results are correct. The order of your records may differ.
- Tap or click the Save button on the Quick Access Toolbar and type `Reps and Seminar Offerings` as the name of the query (Figure 7–54).

4

- Tap or click the OK button to save the query.
- Close the query.

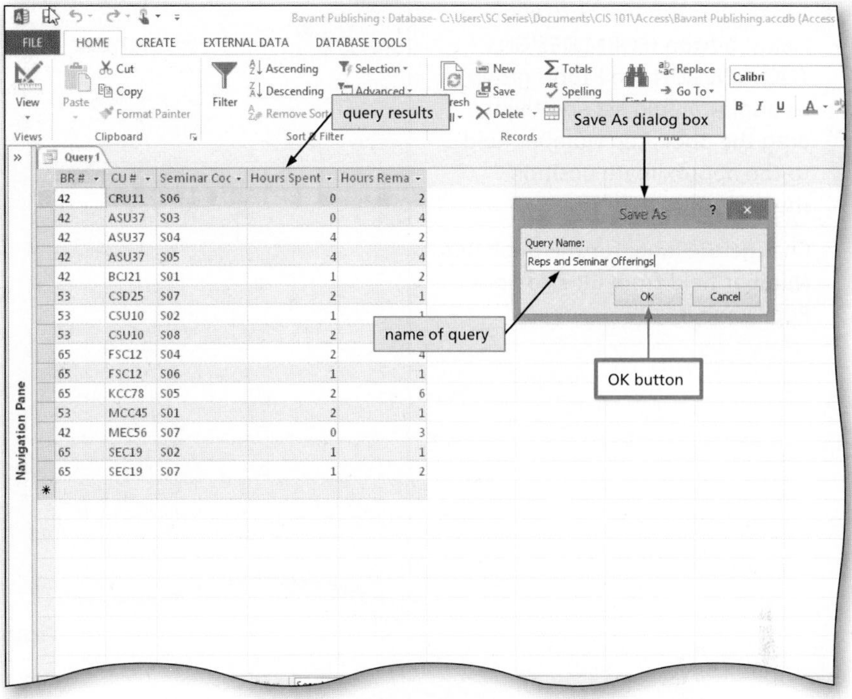

Figure 7–54

To Create a Second Form in Design View

1 CREATE FORM | 2 ADD COMBO BOXES | 3 COMMAND BUTTONS | 4 MODIFY MACRO
5 MODIFY COMBO BOX | 6 CREATE SECOND FORM | **7 ADD SUBFORM** | **8 ADD CHART**

Why? *The second form will contain the tab control including two tabs: one that displays a datasheet and another that displays two charts.* The following step begins the process by creating a form for the Book Rep table in Design view.

1

- If necessary, close the Navigation Pane.
- Display the CREATE tab.
- Tap or click the Form Design button (CREATE tab | Forms group) to create a new form in Design view.
- Ensure the selector for the entire form — the box in the upper-left corner of the form — is selected.
- If necessary, tap or click the Property Sheet button (FORM DESIGN TOOLS DESIGN tab | Tools group) to display a property sheet.
- With the All tab selected, tap or click the Record Source property, if necessary, to display an arrow, tap or click the arrow that appears, and then tap or click Book Rep to select the Book Rep table as the record source.

Q&A I see more than one choice that begins with the same letters as Book Rep. How do I know I am selecting the right one?

There are two ways to find out if you are selecting the right choice. You could tap or click one of them to produce an insertion point and then repeatedly press the RIGHT ARROW key to see the remainder of the name. If it is not the correct one, select another. The other way is to expand the width of the property sheet so that it is large enough for the entire name to appear. You do so by dragging the left border further to the left.

- Close the property sheet.
- Tap or click the 'Add Existing Fields' button (FORM DESIGN TOOLS DESIGN tab | Tools group) to display a field list and then drag the Book Rep Number field to the approximate position shown in Figure 7–55.
- Change the label for the Book Rep Number field from BR # to Book Rep Number.

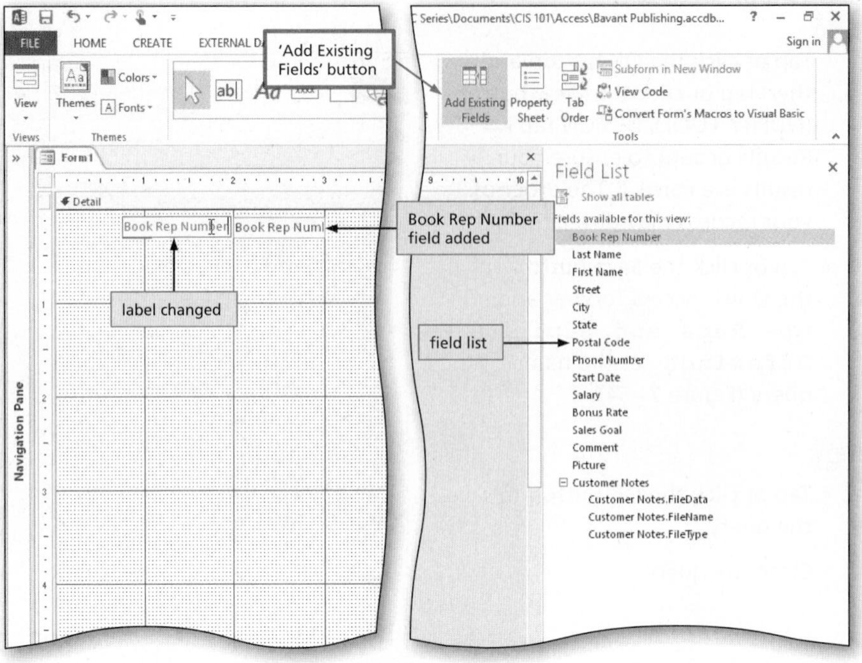

Figure 7–55

To Use the Text Box Tool with Concatenation

1 CREATE FORM | 2 ADD COMBO BOXES | 3 COMMAND BUTTONS | 4 MODIFY MACRO
5 MODIFY COMBO BOX | 6 CREATE SECOND FORM | 7 ADD SUBFORM | 8 ADD CHART

Why? If you have determined that ***concatenation****, which simply means combining objects together in a series, is appropriate for a form, you can create a concatenated field by using the Text Box tool in the Controls group on the DESIGN tab and then indicating the concatenation that is to be performed.* The following steps add a concatenated field, involving two text fields, First Name and Last Name. Specifically, you will concatenate the first name, a single space, and the last name.

1

- Tap or click the Text Box tool (FORM DESIGN TOOLS DESIGN tab | Controls group) and then move the pointer, whose shape has changed to a small plus symbol accompanied by a text box, to the position shown in Figure 7–56.

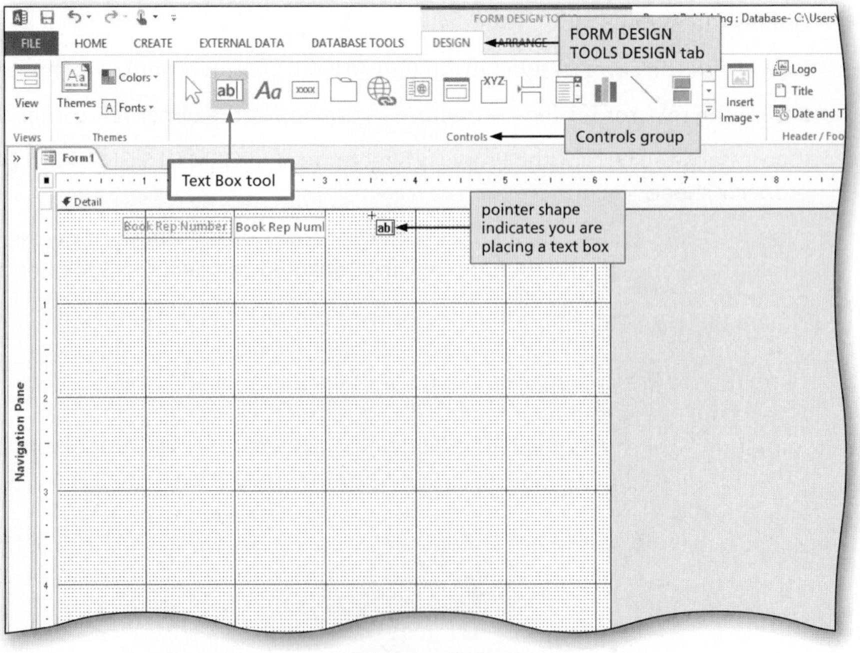

Figure 7–56

2

- Tap or click the position shown in Figure 7–56 to place a text box on the report.
- Tap or click in the text box to produce an insertion point.
- Type **=[First Name]&' '&[Last Name]** as the entry in the text box.
- Tap or click the attached label to select it (Figure 7–57).

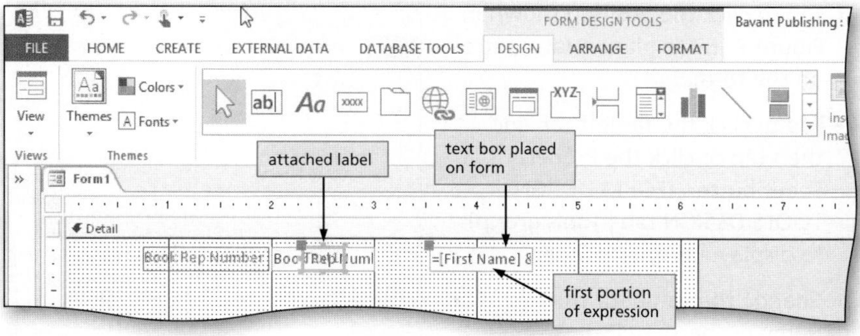

Figure 7–57

3

- Press the DELETE key to delete the attached label.
- Resize the Book Rep Number control to the approximate size shown in Figure 7–58.
- Tap or click the text box to select it, drag it to the position shown in Figure 7–58, and then drag the right sizing handle to the approximate position shown in the figure.

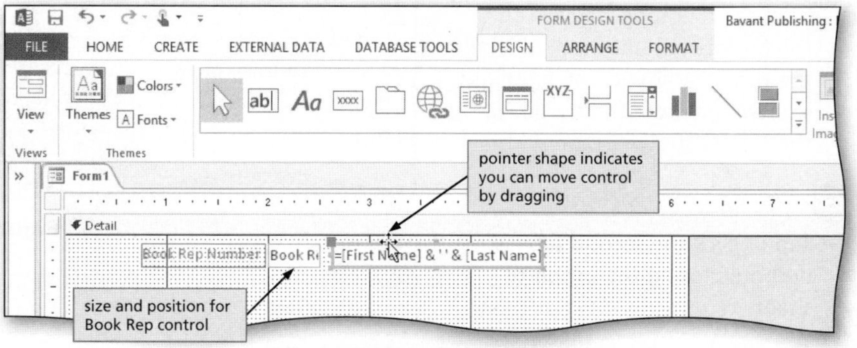

Figure 7–58

4

- Close the field list by tapping or clicking the 'Add Existing Fields' button (FORM DESIGN TOOLS DESIGN tab | Tools group).

To Use Tab Controls to Create a Multipage Form

1 CREATE FORM | 2 ADD COMBO BOXES | 3 COMMAND BUTTONS | 4 MODIFY MACRO
5 MODIFY COMBO BOX | 6 CREATE SECOND FORM | **7 ADD SUBFORM** | **8 ADD CHART**

Why? *To use tabs on a form, you need to insert a tab control.* The following steps insert a tab control with two tabs: Datasheet and Charts. Users will be able to tap or click the Datasheet tab in the completed form to view seminar offerings in Datasheet view. Tapping or clicking the Charts tab will display two charts representing the same seminar data as in the Datasheet tab.

1

- Tap or click the Tab Control tool (FORM DESIGN TOOLS DESIGN TAB | Controls group) and move the pointer to the approximate location shown in Figure 7–59.

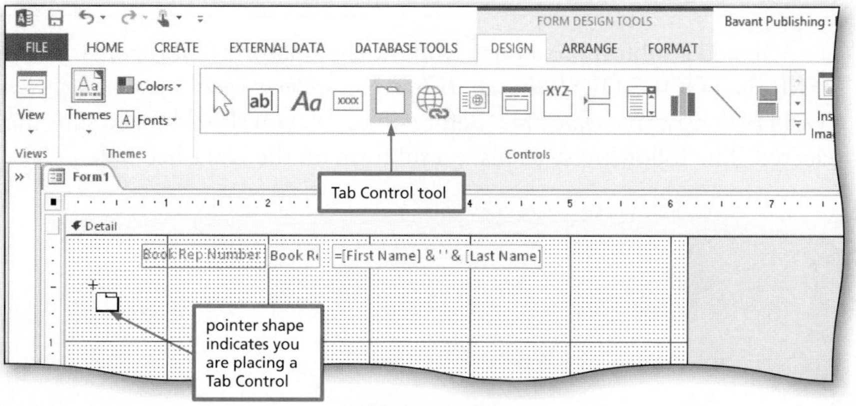

Figure 7–59

2

- Tap or click the position shown in Figure 7–59 to place a tab control on the form.
- Tap or click the far left tab and then tap or click the Property Sheet button (FORM DESIGN TOOLS DESIGN tab | Tools group) to display a property sheet.
- Change the value for the Name property to Datasheet (Figure 7–60).

Q&A My property sheet looks different. What should I do?
Be sure you tapped or clicked the far left tab before displaying the property sheet. The highlight should be within the border of the tab, as shown in the figure.

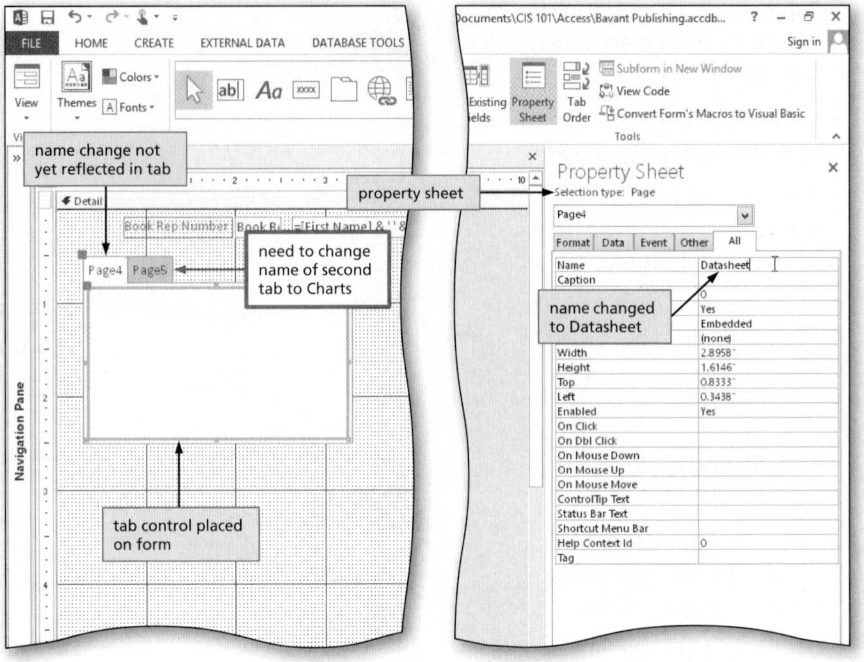

Figure 7–60

3

- Tap or click the second tab without closing the property sheet.
- Change the value for the Name property to Charts.
- Close the property sheet.
- Save the form using the name, Rep Seminar Data.

CONSIDER THIS

When would you include a tab control in your form?

If the form contains more information than conveniently will fit on the screen at a time, consider adding a tab control. With a tab control, you can organize the information within a collection of tabbed pages. To access any of the tabbed pages, users need only tap or click the corresponding tab.

To Add a Subform

1 CREATE FORM | 2 ADD COMBO BOXES | 3 COMMAND BUTTONS | 4 MODIFY MACRO
5 MODIFY COMBO BOX | 6 CREATE SECOND FORM | 7 ADD SUBFORM | 8 ADD CHART

To add a subform to a form, you use the Subform/Subreport tool in the Controls group on the FORM DESIGN TOOLS DESIGN tab. ***Why?** The subform enables you to show data for multiple seminar offerings for a given book rep at the same time.* Before doing so, you should make sure the 'Use Control Wizards' button is selected. The following steps place a subform on the Datasheet tab.

1

- Tap or click the Datasheet tab.
- Resize the tab control to the approximate size shown in Figure 7–61 by dragging the appropriate sizing handles.

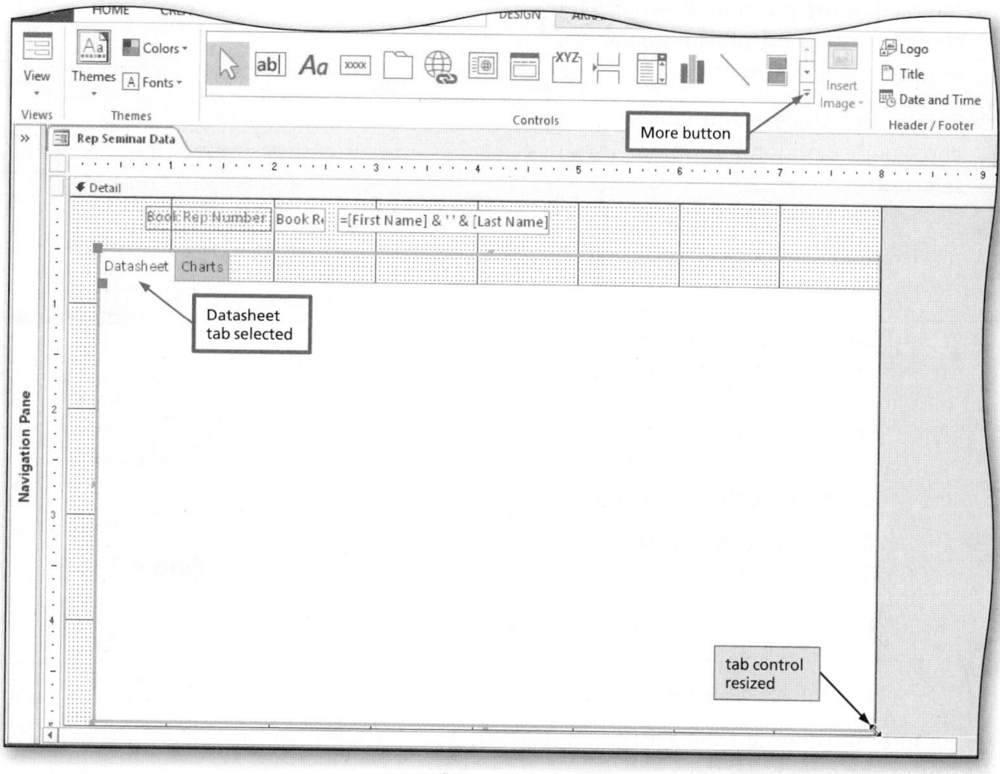

Figure 7–61

2

- Tap or click the More button (FORM DESIGN TOOLS DESIGN tab | Controls group).
- With the 'Use Control Wizards' button selected, tap or click the Subform/Subreport tool (FORM DESIGN TOOLS DESIGN tab | Controls group) and then move the pointer to the approximate position shown in Figure 7–62.

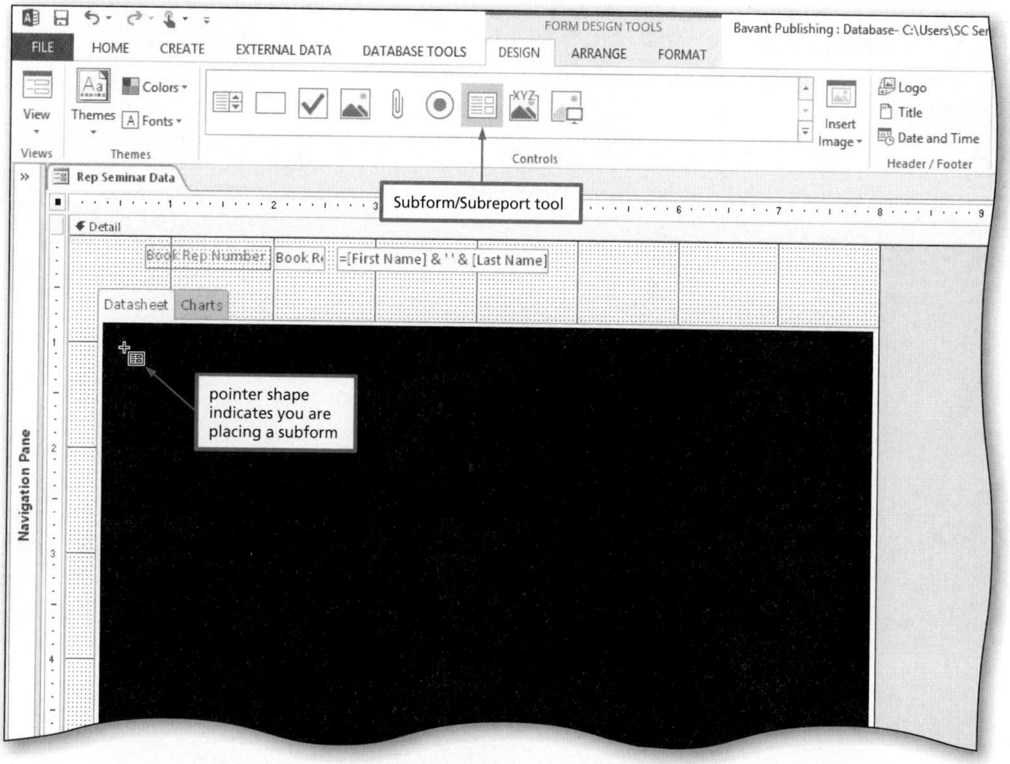

Figure 7–62

3

- Tap or click the position shown in Figure 7–62 on the previous page to open the SubForm Wizard.
- Be sure the 'Use existing Tables and Queries' option button is selected.
- Tap or click the Next button to display the next SubForm Wizard screen.
- Tap or click the Tables/Queries arrow and then tap or click the Reps and Seminar Offerings query to indicate that the fields for the subform will be selected from the Reps and Seminar Offerings query.
- Tap or click the 'Add All Fields' button (Figure 7–63).

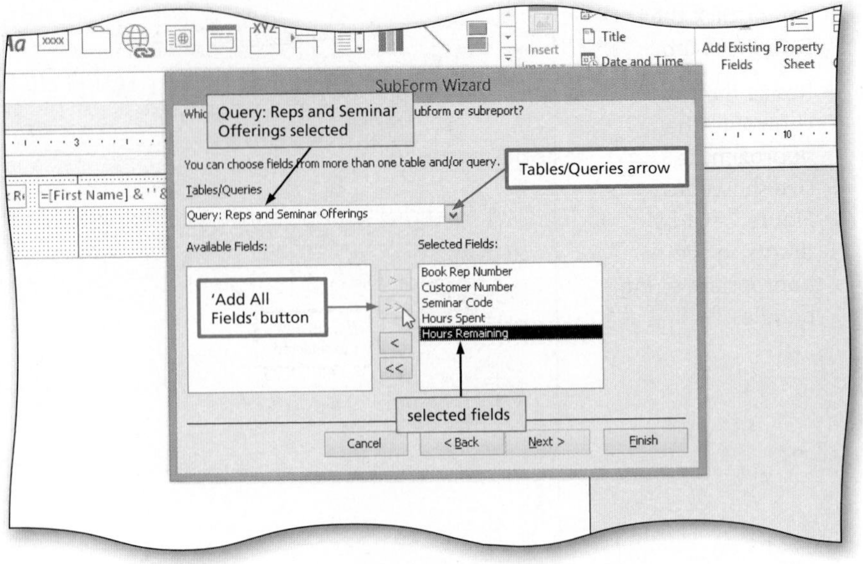

Figure 7–63

4

- Tap or click the Next button.
- Be sure the 'Choose from a list' option button is selected.
- Tap or click the Next button.
- Type `Seminar Offerings for Rep` as the name of the subform and then tap or click the Finish button to complete the creation of the subform (Figure 7–64).

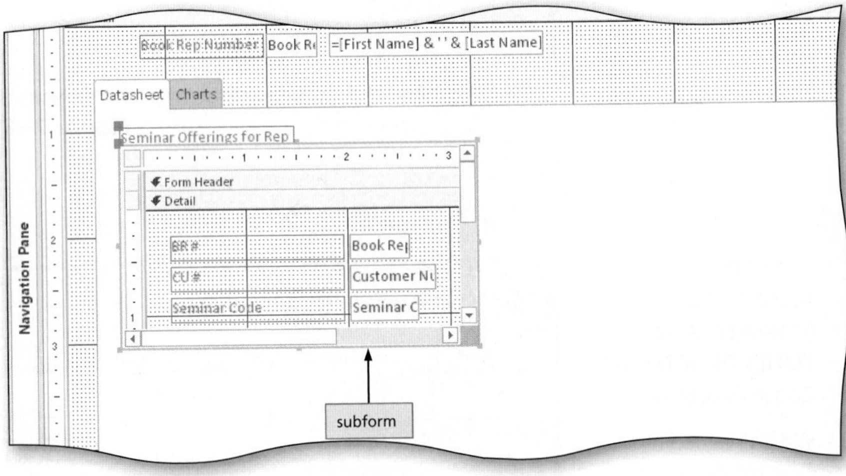

Figure 7–64

5

- Save and then close the Rep Seminar Data form.

To Modify a Subform

The next task is to modify the subform. The first step is to remove the Book Rep Number field from the subform. ***Why?*** *The Book Rep Number field needed to be included initially in the subform because it is the field that is used to link the data in the subform to the data in the main form. It is not supposed to appear in the form, however.* In addition, the remaining columns need to be resized to appropriate sizes. The following step first removes the Book Rep Number field. The step then switches to Datasheet view to resize the remaining columns.

1

- Open the Navigation Pane, press and hold or right-click the Seminar Offerings for Rep form, and then tap or click Design View on the shortcut menu.
- Tap or click the Book Rep Number control, and then press the DELETE key to delete the control.
- Change the label for the Customer Number control from CU # to Customer Number.
- Save the subform and close it.
- Press and hold or right-click the subform in the Navigation Pane and tap or click Open on the shortcut menu.
- Resize each column to best fit the data by double-tapping or double-clicking the right boundary of the column's field selector (Figure 7–65).
- Save the subform and then close it.

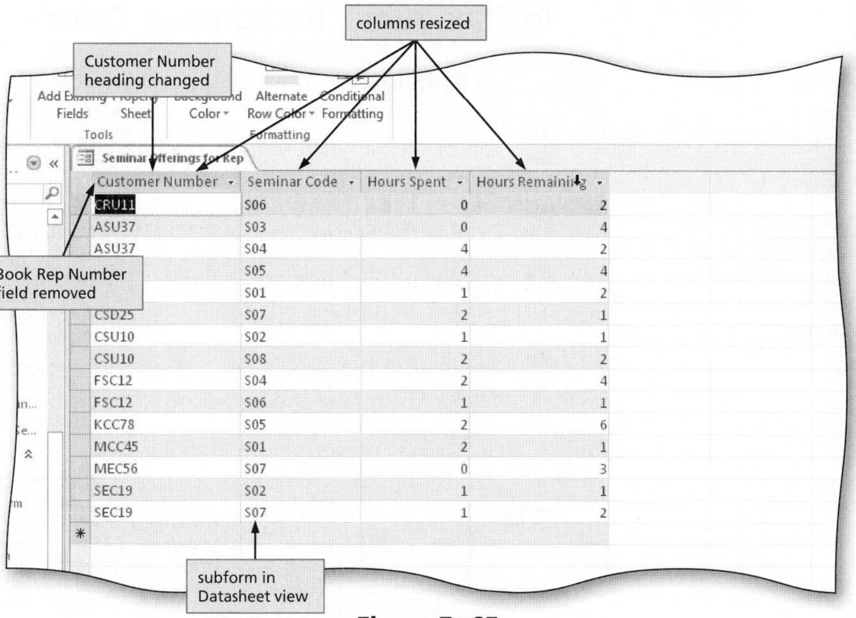

Figure 7–65

To Resize the Subform

1 CREATE FORM | 2 ADD COMBO BOXES | 3 COMMAND BUTTONS | 4 MODIFY MACRO
5 MODIFY COMBO BOX | 6 CREATE SECOND FORM | 7 ADD SUBFORM | 8 ADD CHART

The following step resizes the subform. ***Why?*** *The size should match the size shown in Figure 7–2a on page AC 412.*

1

- If necessary, open the Navigation Pane, press and hold or right-click Rep Seminar Data and then tap or click Design View on the shortcut menu.
- Close the Navigation Pane.
- Resize the subform to the size shown in Figure 7–66 by dragging the right sizing handle.

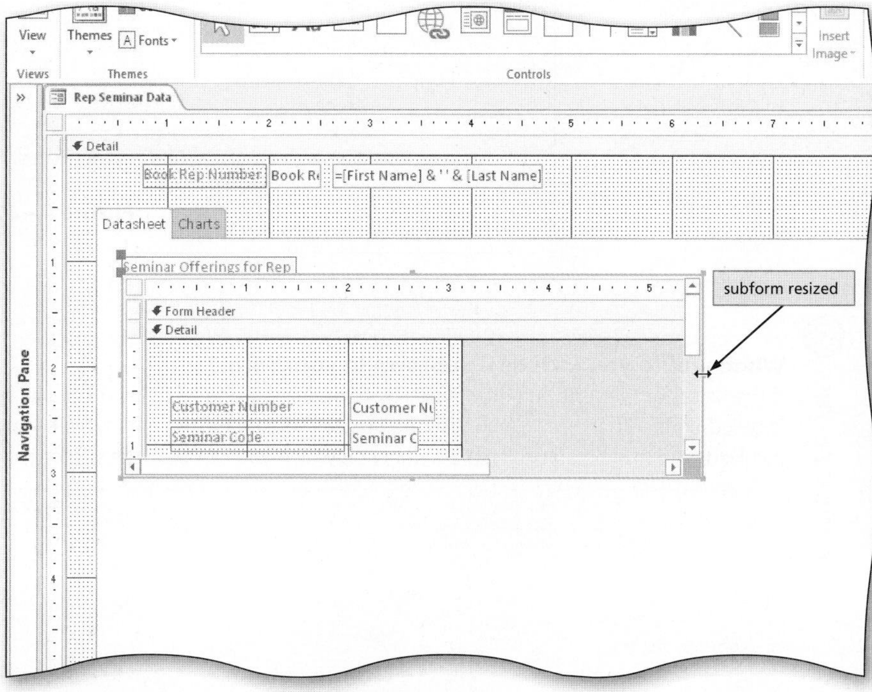

Figure 7–66

To Change the Background Color

BTW

Tab Controls

You can change the order of tab controls. To do so, press and hold or right-click any tab control and tap or click Page Order on the shortcut menu. Use the Move Up and Move Down buttons to change to the desired order.

The following steps change the background color of the form to a light gray.

1. Tap or click anywhere in the Detail section but outside all the controls to select the section.
2. Display the FORM DESIGN TOOLS FORMAT tab.
3. Tap or click the Background Color button arrow (FORM DESIGN TOOLS FORMAT tab | Font group) to display a color palette (Figure 7–67).
4. Tap or click the Light Gray 2 color, the first color in the third row under Standard Colors, to change the background color.

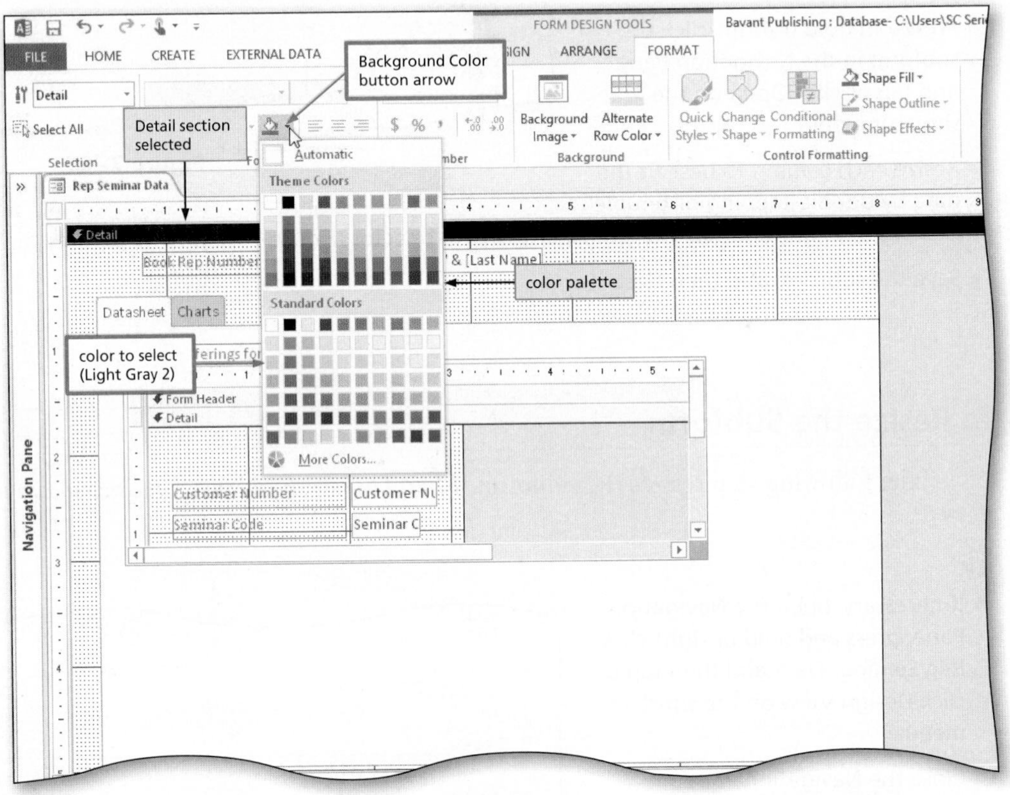

Figure 7–67

CONSIDER THIS

When would you include a subform in your form?

If the fields for the form come from exactly two tables, a one-to-many relationship exists between the two tables, and the form is based on the "one" table, you will often place the data for the "many" table in a subform. If there are more than two tables involved, you may be able to create a query on which you can base the subform.

To Insert Charts

Why? *To visually represent data in a table or query, you can create a chart.* To insert a chart, use the Chart tool on the FORM DESIGN TOOLS DESIGN tab. The Chart Wizard then will ask you to indicate the fields to be included on the chart and the type of chart you want to insert. The following steps insert a chart that visually represents the amount of time reps have spent in their various seminars.

1

- Display the FORM DESIGN TOOLS DESIGN tab.
- Tap or click the Charts tab on the tab control.
- Tap or click the More button (FORM DESIGN TOOLS DESIGN tab | Controls group).
- Tap or click the Chart tool.
- Move the pointer to the approximate position shown in Figure 7–68.

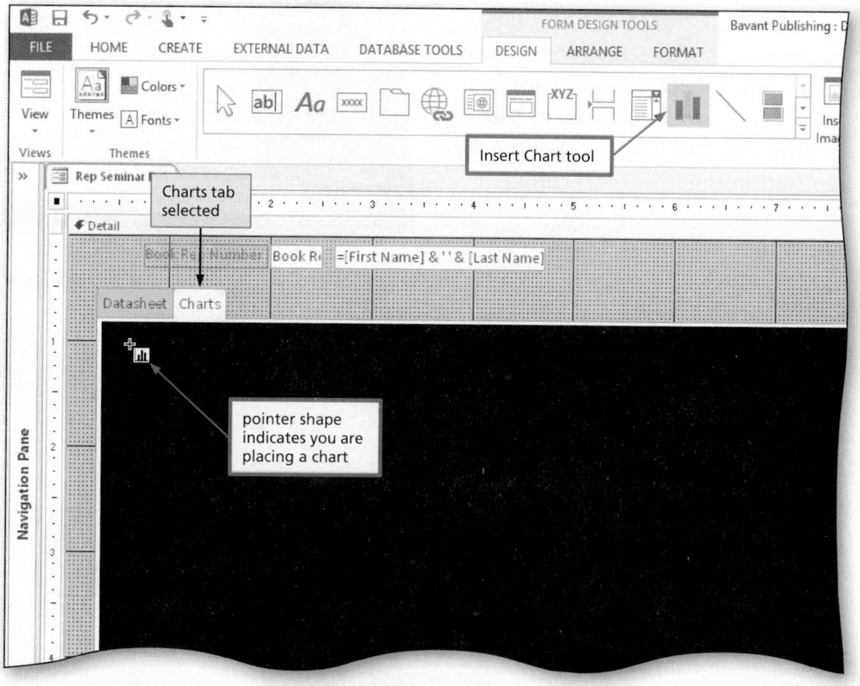

Figure 7–68

2

- Tap or click the position shown in Figure 7–68 to display the Chart Wizard dialog box.
- Tap or click the Queries option button in the Chart Wizard dialog box to indicate that the data will come from a query, tap or click the Reps and Seminar Offerings query to indicate the specific query containing the desired fields, and then tap or click the Next button.
- Select the Seminar Code and Hours Spent fields by tapping or clicking them and then tapping or clicking the Add Field button (Figure 7–69).

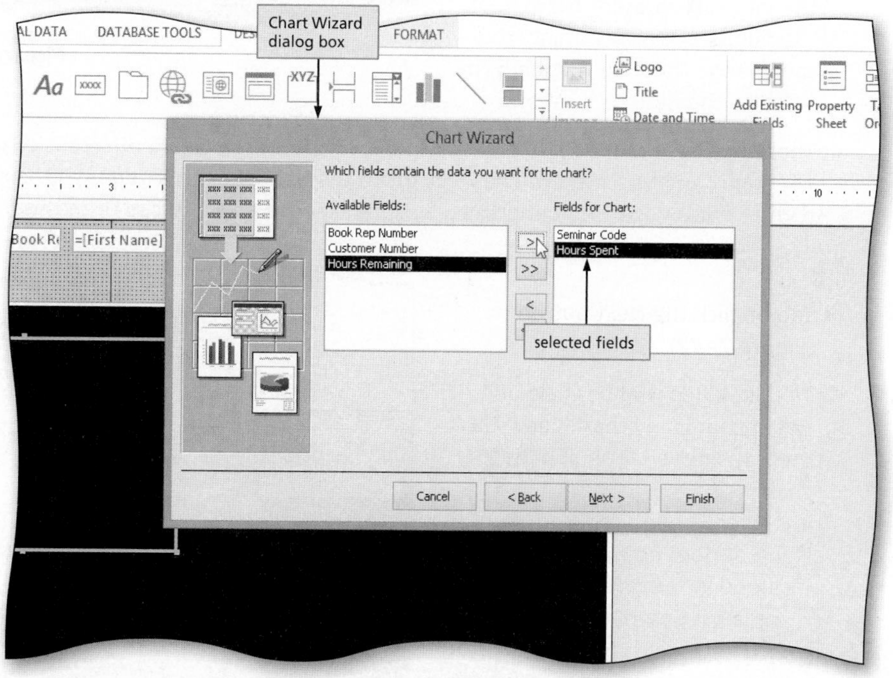

Figure 7–69

3

- Tap or click the Next button.
- Tap or click the Pie Chart, the chart in the lower-left corner (Figure 7–70).

Experiment

- Tap or click the other chart types and read the descriptions of chart types in the lower-right corner of the Chart Wizard dialog box. When finished, tap or click the Pie Chart in the lower-left corner.

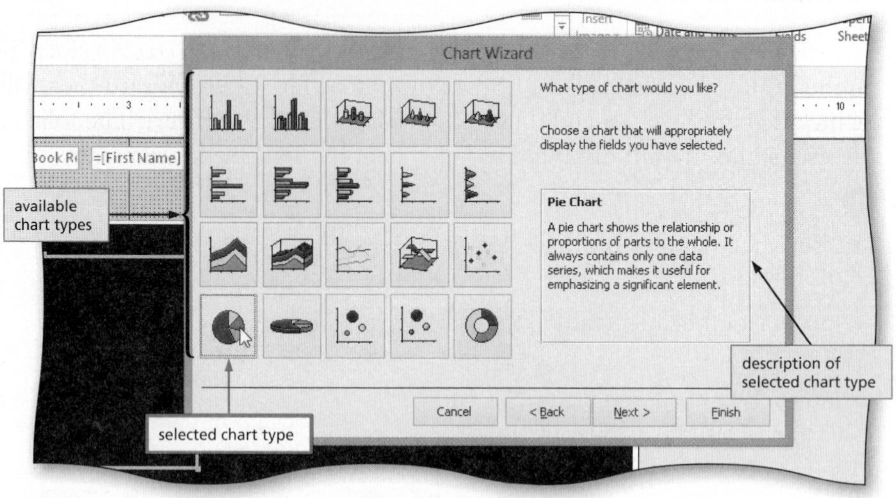

Figure 7–70

4

- Tap or click the Next button to create the chart (Figure 7–71). Your screen might take several seconds to refresh.

Q&A What do these positions represent? Can I change them?
The field under the chart represents the data that will be summarized by slices of the pie. The other field is used to indicate the series. In this example, the field for the series is the seminar code, and the sizes of the slices of the pie will represent the sum of the number of hours spent. You can change these by dragging the fields to the desired locations.

These positions make sense for a pie chart. What if I selected a different chart type?
The items on this screen will be relevant to the particular chart type you select. Just as with the pie chart, the correct fields will often be selected automatically. If not, you can drag the fields to the correct locations.

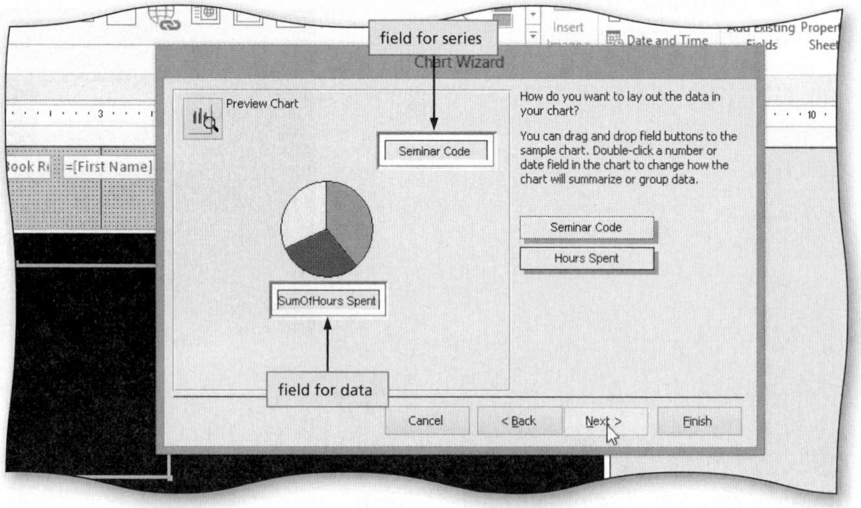

Figure 7–71

5

- Tap or click the Next button (Figure 7–72).

Q&A The Book Rep Number field does not appear in my chart. Can I still use it to link the form and the chart?
Yes. Even though the Book Rep Number does not appear, it is still included in the query on which the chart is based. In fact, it is essential that it is included so that you can link the document (that is, the form) and the chart. Linking the document and the chart ensures that the chart will reflect accurately the data for the correct rep, that is, the rep who currently appears in the form.

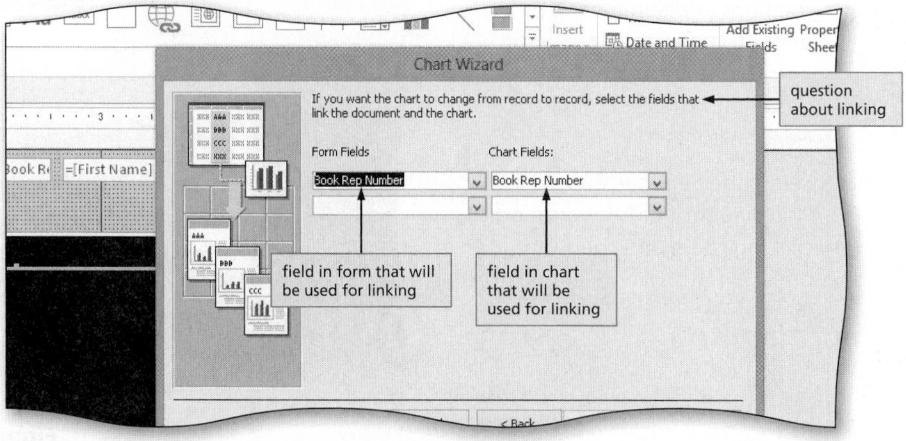

Figure 7–72

6

- Tap or click the Next button, type **Hours Spent by Seminar Offering** as the title, and then tap or click the Finish button (Figure 7–73).

Q&A The data does not look right. What is wrong and what do I need to do to fix it?
The data in your chart might be fictitious, as in Figure 7–73. In that case, the data simply represents the general way the chart will look. When you view the actual form, the data represented in the chart should be correct.

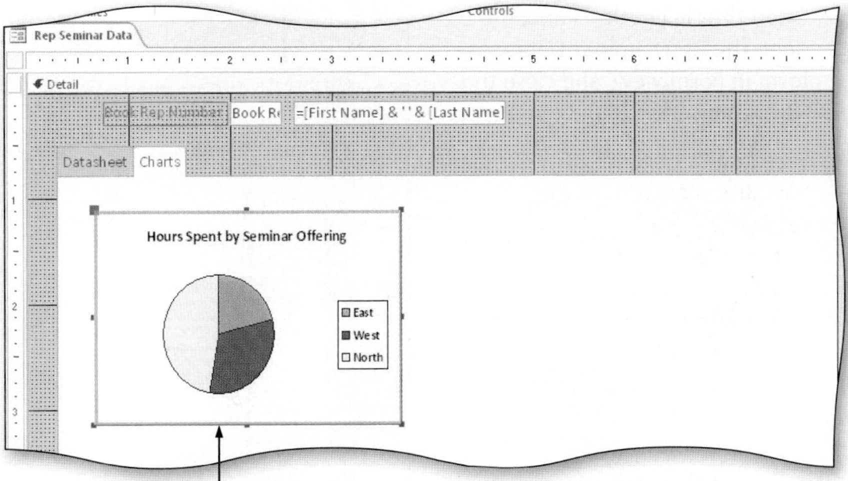

Figure 7–73

7

- Use the techniques shown in Steps 1 through 6 to add a second chart at the position shown in Figure 7–74. In this chart, select Hours Remaining instead of Hours Spent and type **Hours Remaining by Seminar Offering** as the title of the chart instead of Hours Spent by Seminar Offering.
- Resize the two charts to the size shown in the figure, if necessary, by tapping or clicking the chart and then dragging an appropriate sizing handle.

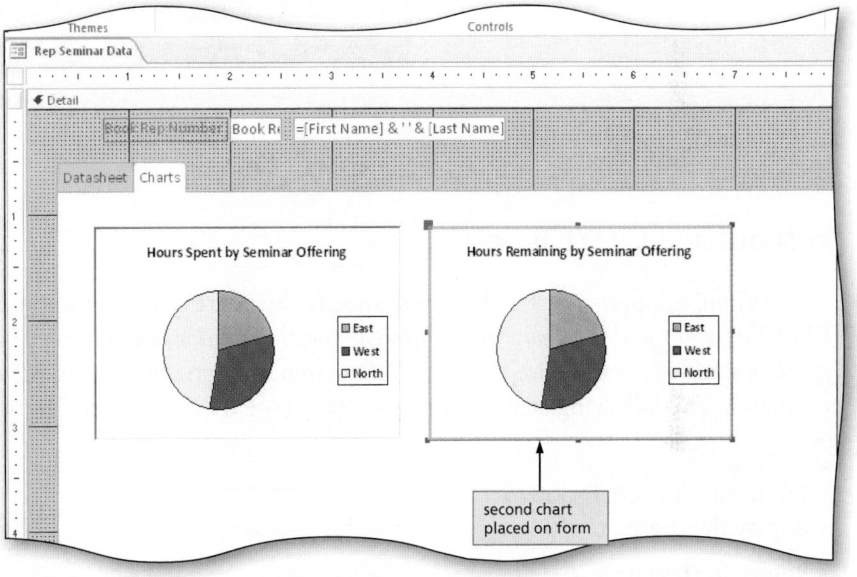

Figure 7–74

8

- If requested to do so by your instructor, add a title with your first and last name to the form.
- Save your changes.
- Close the form.

To Use the Form

1 CREATE FORM | 2 ADD COMBO BOXES | 3 COMMAND BUTTONS | 4 MODIFY MACRO
5 MODIFY COMBO BOX | 6 CREATE SECOND FORM | 7 ADD SUBFORM | 8 ADD CHART

You use this form just like the other forms you have created and used. When using the form, it is easy to move from one tabbed page to another. ***Why?*** *All you have to do is to tap or click the tab for the desired tabbed page.* The step on the next page uses the form to view the seminar data.

1

- Open the Navigation Pane, open the Rep Seminar Data form in Form view, and close the Navigation Pane (Figure 7–75).

Q&A What is the purpose of the navigation buttons in the subform?

These navigation buttons allow you to move within the records in the subform, that is, within the seminar offerings for the rep whose number and name appear at the top of the form.

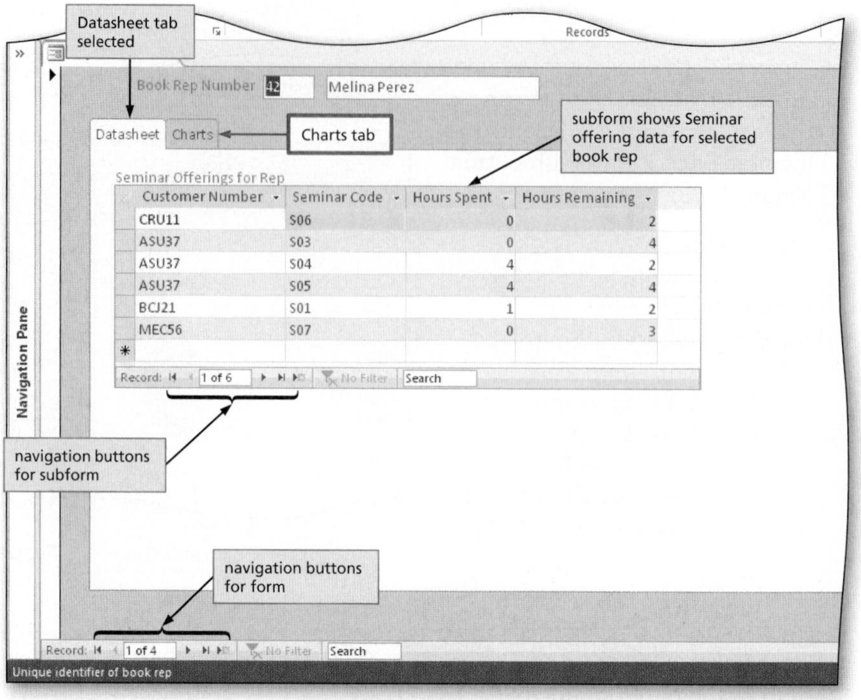

Figure 7–75

To Modify a Chart Type

1 CREATE FORM | 2 ADD COMBO BOXES | 3 COMMAND BUTTONS | 4 MODIFY MACRO
5 MODIFY COMBO BOX | 6 CREATE SECOND FORM | 7 ADD SUBFORM | **8 ADD CHART**

When you first create a chart, you specify the chart type. You sometimes will later want to change the type. ***Why?*** *You might find that you want a different type. In addition, you have more options when you later change the chart type than when you first created the chart.* You change the type by editing the chart and selecting the Chart Type command. The following steps change the chart type by selecting a different style of pie chart.

1

- Tap or click the Charts tab to display the charts.
- Return to Design view.
- Tap or click the Charts tab, if necessary, to display the charts in Design view (Figure 7–76).

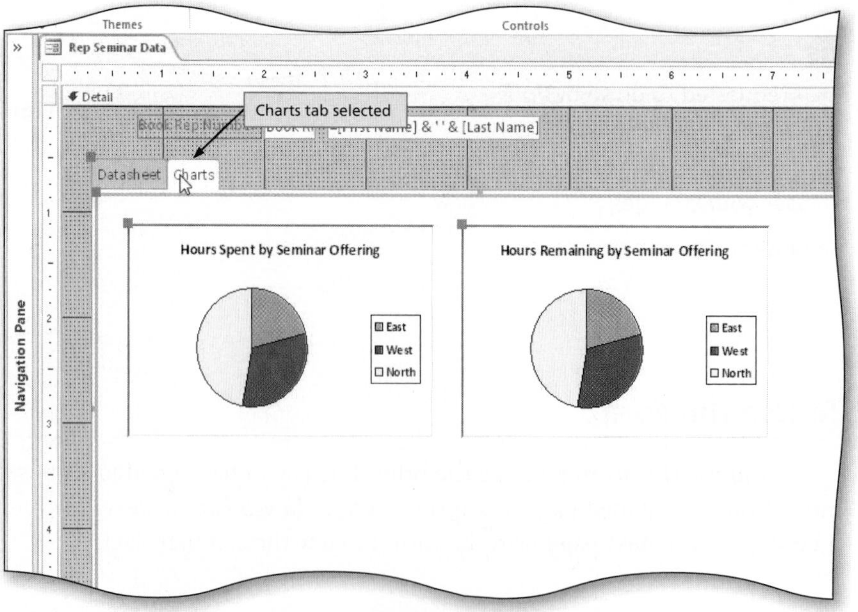

Figure 7–76

2

- Press and hold or right-click the Hours Spent by Seminar Offering chart to display a shortcut menu.

Q&A Does it matter where I press and hold or right-click?
You should press and hold or right-click within the rectangle but outside any of the items within the rectangle, in other words, in the white space.

My shortcut menu is very different. What should I do?
Tap or click the View button arrow, then tap or click Design View to ensure that you are viewing the form in Design view, and then try again.

- Point to Chart Object on the shortcut menu to display the Chart Object submenu (Figure 7–77).

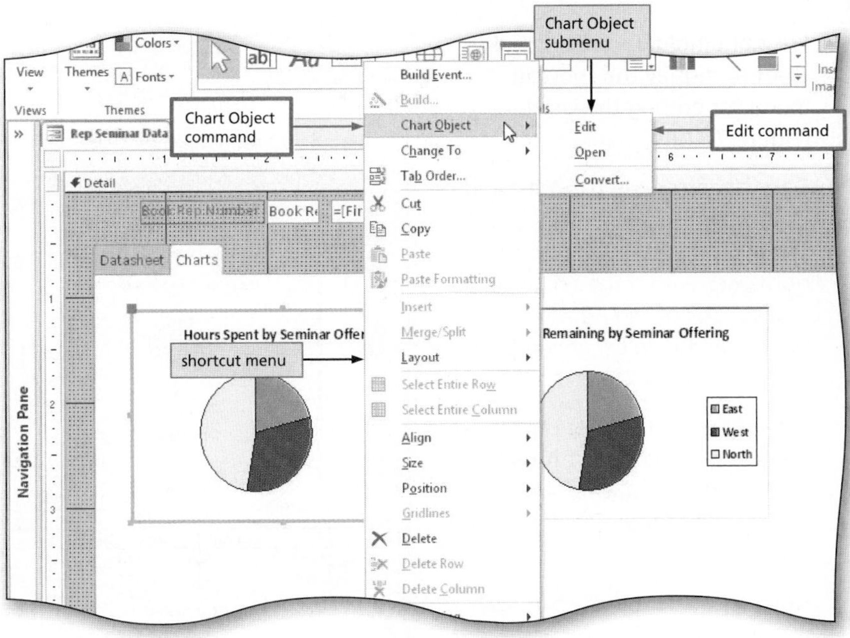

Figure 7–77

3

- Tap or click Edit on the Chart Object submenu to edit the chart. Access will automatically display the underlying chart data in Datasheet view (Figure 7–78).

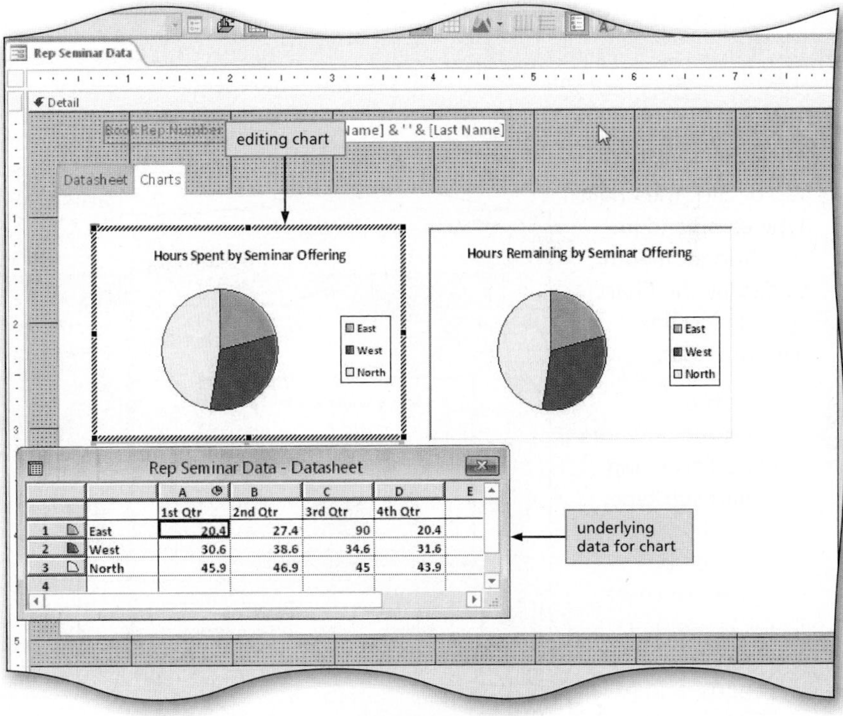

		A	B	C	D	E
		1st Qtr	2nd Qtr	3rd Qtr	4th Qtr	
1	East	20.4	27.4	90	20.4	
2	West	30.6	38.6	34.6	31.6	
3	North	45.9	46.9	45	43.9	
4						

Figure 7–78

4

- Press and hold or right-click the chart to display the shortcut menu for editing the chart (Figure 7–79).

Q&A Does it matter where I press and hold or right-click?
You should press and hold or right-click within the rectangle but outside any of the items within the rectangle, in other words, in the white space.

What types of changes can I make if I select Format Chart Area?
You can change such things as border style, color, fill effects, and fonts.

How do I make other changes?
By tapping or clicking Chart Options on the shortcut menu, you can change titles, legends, and labels. For 3-D charts, by tapping or clicking 3-D View on the shortcut menu, you can change the elevation and rotation of the chart. You also can format specific items on the chart, as you will see in the next section.

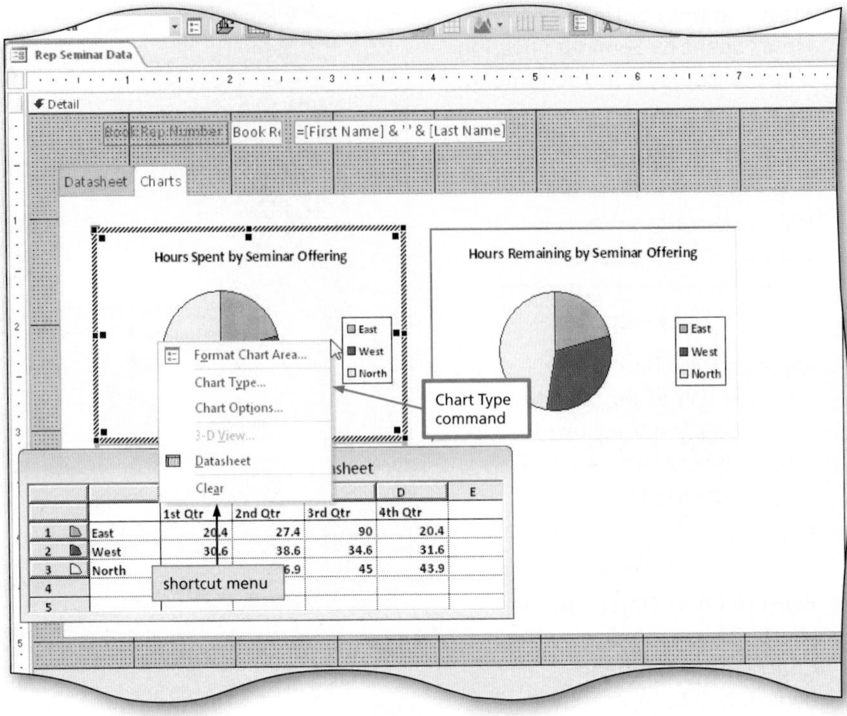

Figure 7–79

5

- Tap or click the Chart Type command on the shortcut menu to display the Chart Type dialog box (Figure 7–80).

Q&A What is the relationship between the Chart type and the Chart sub-type?
You can think of Chart types as categories of charts. There are column charts, bar charts, line charts, and so on. Once you have selected a category, the chart sub-types are those charts in that category. If you have selected the Pie chart category, for example, the charts within the category are the ones shown in the list of chart sub-types in Figure 7–80.

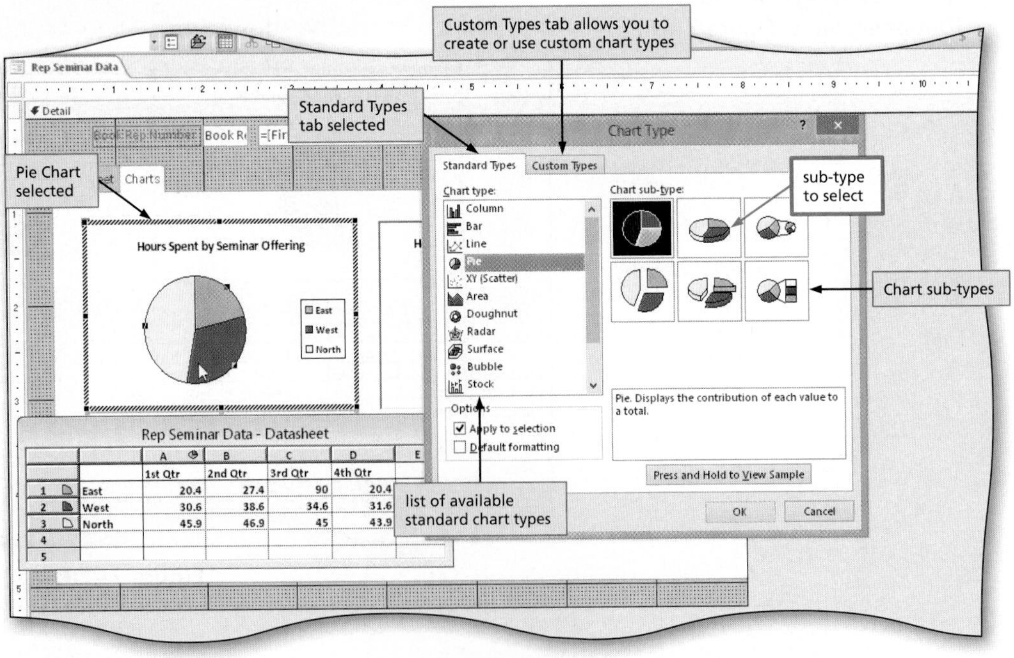

Figure 7–80

6

- Tap or click the chart sub-type in the middle of the first row of chart sub-types to select it as the chart sub-type.

Experiment

- Tap or click each of the chart types and examine the chart sub-types associated with that chart type. When finished, select Pie as the chart type and the sub-type in the middle of the first row as the chart sub-type.

- Tap or click the OK button to change the chart sub-type.
- Tap or click outside the chart and the datasheet to deselect the chart.
- Make the same change to the other chart (Figure 7–81).

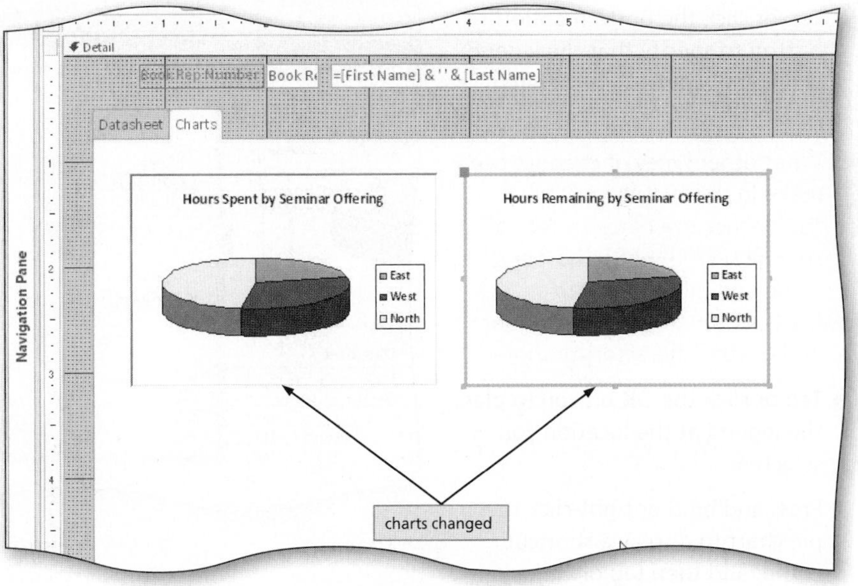

Figure 7–81

To Format a Chart

1 CREATE FORM | 2 ADD COMBO BOXES | 3 COMMAND BUTTONS | 4 MODIFY MACRO
5 MODIFY COMBO BOX | 6 CREATE SECOND FORM | 7 ADD SUBFORM | 8 ADD CHART

By pressing and holding or right-clicking a chart and then tapping or clicking Edit object, you have many formatting options available. You can change the border style, color, fill effects, and fonts by using the Format Chart Area command. You can change titles, legends, and labels by using the Chart Options command. You also can format specific portions of a chart by pressing and holding or right-clicking the portion you want to format and then tapping or clicking the appropriate command on the shortcut menu. The following steps use this technique to move the legend so that it is at the bottom of the chart. They also include percentages in the chart. ***Why?*** *Percentages provide valuable information in a pie chart.*

1

- Press and hold or right-click the Hours Spent by Seminar Offering chart to display a shortcut menu, point to Chart Object on the shortcut menu to display the Chart Object submenu, and then tap or click Edit on the Chart Object submenu.
- Press and hold or right-click the legend to display a shortcut menu, and then tap or click Format Legend on the shortcut menu to display the Format Legend dialog box.
- Tap or click the Placement tab (Figure 7–82).

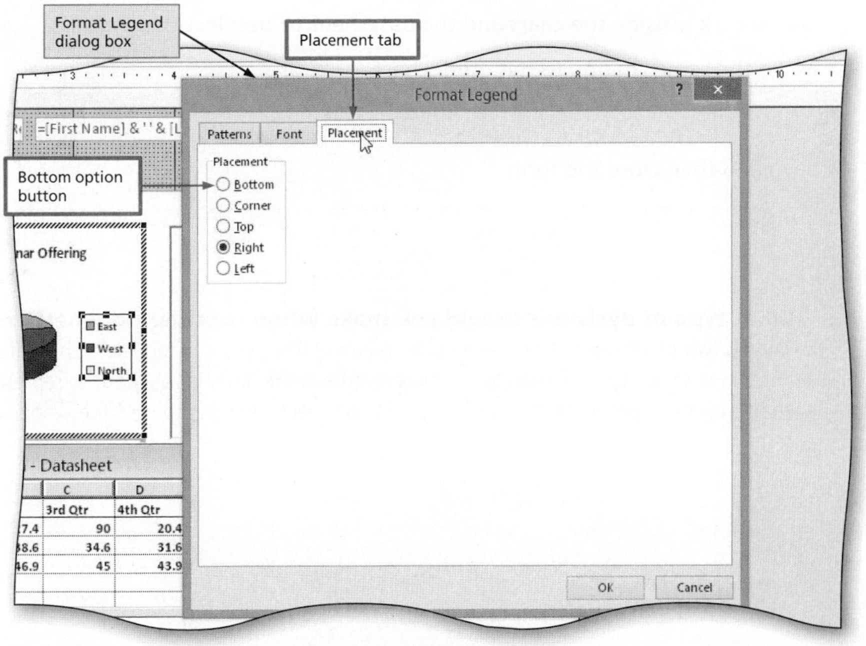

Figure 7–82

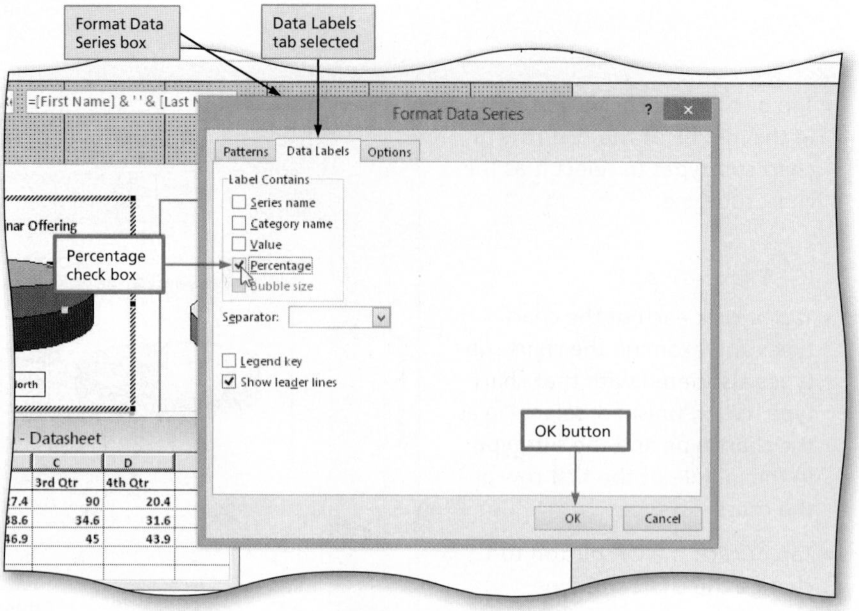

Figure 7–83

2

- Tap or click the Bottom option button to specify that the legend should appear at the bottom of the chart.

Q&A What other types of changes can I make in this dialog box?
Tap or click the Patterns tab to change such things as border style, color, and fill effects. Tap or click the Font tab to change the font and/or font characteristics.

- Tap or click the OK button to place the legend at the location you selected.
- Press and hold or right-click the pie chart to display a shortcut menu, and then tap or click Format Data Series on the shortcut menu to display the Format Data Series dialog box.
- Tap or click the Data Labels tab.
- Tap or click the Percentage check box to specify that percentages are to be included (Figure 7–83).

Q&A I see a Patterns tab just as with the legend, but how would I use the Options tab? Also, does the fact that these are check boxes rather than option buttons mean that I can select more than one?
Use the Options tab to indicate whether the color is to vary by slice and to specify the angle of the first slice in the pie. Because these are check boxes, you can select as many as you want. Selecting too many can clutter the chart, however.

These options make sense for a pie chart, but what about other chart types?
The options that you see will vary from one chart type to another. They will be relevant for the selected chart type.

3

- Tap or click the OK button to include percentages on the chart.
- Tap or click outside the chart and the datasheet to deselect the chart.
- Make the same change to the other chart.

4

- Save and then close the form.

CONSIDER THIS

What type of decisions should you make when considering whether to use a chart?
Do you want to represent data in a visual manner? If so, you can include a chart. If you decide to use a chart, you must determine which type of chart would best represent the data. If you want to represent total amounts, for example, a bar chart may be appropriate. If, instead, you want to represent portions of the whole, a pie chart may be better.

To Sign Out of a Microsoft Account

If you are signed in to a Microsoft account and are using a public computer or otherwise wish to sign out of your Microsoft account, you should sign out of the account from the Account gallery in the Backstage view before exiting Access. Signing out of the account is the safest way to make sure that nobody else can access SkyDrive files or settings stored in your Microsoft account. The following steps sign out of a Microsoft account from Access. For a detailed example of the procedure summarized below, refer to the Office and Windows chapter at the beginning of this book.

1. If you wish to sign out of your Microsoft account, tap or click FILE on the ribbon to open the Backstage view and then tap or click the Account tab to display the Account gallery.
2. Tap or click the Sign out link, which displays the Remove Account dialog box. If a Can't remove Windows accounts dialog box appears instead of the Remove Account dialog box, click the OK button and skip the remaining steps.

Q&A Why does a Can't remove Windows accounts dialog box appear?
If you signed in to Windows using your Microsoft account, then you also must sign out from Windows, rather than signing out from within Access. When you are finished using Windows, be sure to sign out at that time.

3. Tap or click the Yes button (Remove Account dialog box) to sign out of your Microsoft account on this computer.

Q&A Should I sign out of Windows after signing out of my Microsoft account?
When you are finished using the computer, you should sign out of your account for maximum security.

4. Tap or click the Back button in the upper-left corner of the Backstage view to return to the database.

To Exit Access

This project now is complete. The following steps exit Access.

1. Tap or click the Close button on the right side of the title bar to exit Access.
2. If a Microsoft Access dialog box appears, tap or click the Yes button to save any changes made to the object since the last save.

BTW
Certification
The Microsoft Office Specialist (MOS) program provides an opportunity for you to obtain a valuable industry credential — proof that you have the Access 2013 skills required by employers. For more information, visit the Certification resource on the Student Companion Site located on www.cengagebrain.com. For detailed instructions about accessing available resources, visit www.cengage.com/ct/studentdownload or contact your instructor for information about accessing the required files.

BTW
Quick Reference
For a table that lists how to complete the tasks covered in this book using touch gestures, the mouse, ribbon, shortcut menu, and keyboard, see the Quick Reference Summary at the back of this book, or visit the Quick Reference resource on the Student Companion Site located on www.cengagebrain.com. For detailed instructions about accessing available resources, visit www.cengage.com/ct/studentdownload or contact your instructor for information about accessing the required files.

Chapter Summary

In this chapter you have learned to create a form in Design view, add a combo box that displays information from a related table as well as a combo box that is used to find records on a form, format controls and use the Format Painter, add command buttons to a form, modify a button and a combo box, add a calculated field to a form, use a tab control to create a multipage form, add and modify a subform, insert charts, change chart types, and format charts. The items listed below include all the new Access skills you have learned in this chapter.

CONSIDER THIS: PLAN AHEAD

What decisions will you need to make when creating your own forms?

Use these guidelines as you complete the assignments in this chapter and create your own forms outside of this class.

1. Determine the intended audience and the purpose of the form.
   a. Who will use the form?
   b. How will they use it?
   c. What data do they need?
   d. What level of detail do they need?
2. Determine the source of data for the form.
   a. Determine whether data comes from a single table or from multiple related tables.
   b. Which table or tables contain the data?
3. Determine the fields that belong on the form.
   a. What data items are needed by the user of the form?
4. Determine any calculations required for the form.
   a. Decide whether the form should contain any special calculations, such as adding two fields.
   b. Determine whether the form should contain any calculations involving text fields, such as concatenating (combining) the fields.
5. Determine the organization of the form.
   a. In what order should the fields appear?
   b. How should they be arranged?
   c. Does the form need multiple pages?
6. Determine any additional controls that should be on the form.
   a. Should the form contain a subform?
   b. Should the form contain a chart?
   c. Should the form contain command buttons to assist the user in performing various functions?
   d. Should the form contain a combo box to assist the user in searching for a record?
7. Determine the format and style of the form.
   a. What should be in the form heading?
   b. Do you want a title?
   c. Do you want an image?
   d. What should be in the body of the form?
   e. What visual characteristics, such as background color and special effects, should the various portions of the form have?

CONSIDER THIS

How should you submit solutions to questions in the assignments identified with a ✻ symbol?

Every assignment in this book contains one or more questions identified with a ✻ symbol. These questions require you to think beyond the assigned database. Present your solutions to the questions in the format required by your instructor. Possible formats may include one or more of these options: write the answer; create a document that contains the answer; present your answer to the class; discuss your answer in a group; record the answer as audio or video using a webcam, smartphone, or portable media player; or post answers on a blog, wiki, or website.

Apply Your Knowledge

Reinforce the skills and apply the concepts you learned in this chapter.

Creating a Multipage Form for the Apply Beauty Organically Database

Instructions: Start Access. Open the Apply Beauty Organically database that you modified in Chapter 6. If you did not use this database, contact your instructor for information on accessing the database required for this exercise.

Perform the following tasks:

1. Create a query that joins the Sales Rep, Customer, and Customer Orders tables. Include the Sales Rep Number field from the Sales Rep table, the Customer Number from the Customer table, and the Order Number and Amount fields from the Customer Orders table. Sort the query in ascending order by Sales Rep Number, Customer Number, and Order Number. Save the query as Customers and Orders.
2. Create the Sales Rep Order Data form shown in Figure 7–84. Concatenate the first and last name of the sales rep and change the background color to Light Gray 1 (the first color in row 2 of the Standard Colors.) The Datasheet tab displays a subform listing information about orders for customers of the sales rep (Figure 7–84a). Data for the subform is based on the Customers and Orders query. Data for the Chart tab also is based on the Customers and Orders query and displays the total amount of orders for each customer (Figure 7–84b).
3. If requested to do so by your instructor, rename the Sales Rep Order Data form as LastName Order Data where LastName is your last name.
4. Submit the revised database in the format specified by your instructor.
5. How can you add a title to the Sales Rep Order Data form?

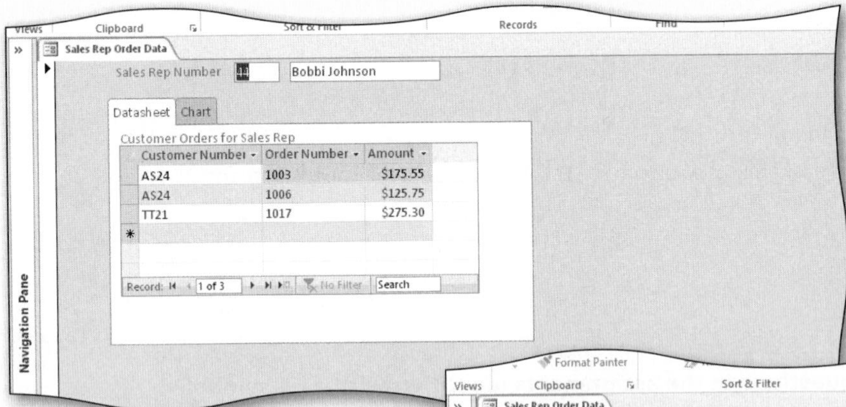

Figure 7–84 (a)

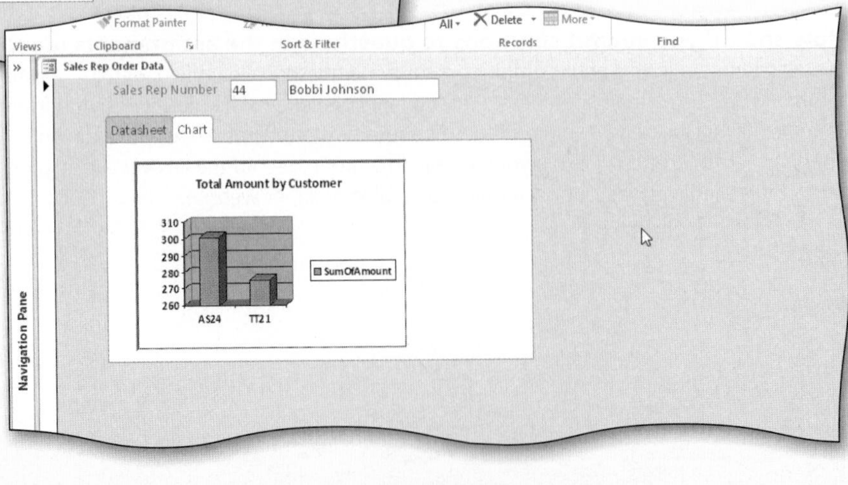

Figure 7–84 (b)

Extend Your Knowledge

Extend the skills you learned in this chapter and experiment with new skills. You may need to use Help to complete the assignment.

Modifying Forms

Note: To complete this assignment, you will be required to use the Data Files for Students. Visit www.cengage.com/ct/studentdownload for detailed instructions or contact your instructor for information about accessing the required files.

Instructions: Start Access. Open the Extend Training database. The Extend Training database contains information about a company that provides computer training to corporate clients.

Perform the following tasks:

1. Open the Trainer Class Data form in Design view. Add a title to the form and insert the current date in the form header. Bold the label for Trainer Number.
2. Add a third tab control to the form. Name the tab control, Clients.
3. Add a subform to the Clients tab control. The Client table is the basis of the subform. Display the Client Number, Client Name, and Client Type fields in a datasheet on the subform. Accept the default name for the subform and delete the label that appears above the datasheet. Change the label for the Client Number control from CL # to Client Number. Resize the datasheet so that all columns appear in the control.
4. Move the Clients tab control so that it appears after the Datasheet tab control. Rename the Datasheet tab control as Class Offerings. Save the changes to the form.
5. Open the Client Update Form in Design view. Add a command button to close the form and use a picture on the button. Place the button to the right of the Delete Record button and align to match the alignment of the other four buttons.
6. Change the font color of the title to Dark Red (Standard colors) and format the title as bold. Add a Shadowed special effect. Save the changes to the form.
7. If requested to do so by your instructor, open the Trainer table in Datasheet view and change the first and last name of trainer 42 to your first and last name.
8. Submit the revised database in the format specified by your instructor.
9. Which picture did you use for the Close Form button? Why?

Analyze, Correct, Improve

Analyze a database, correct all errors, and improve the design.

Correcting Form Design Errors and Improving a Form

Note: To complete this assignment, you will be required to use the Data Files for Students. Visit www.cengage.com/ct/studentdownload for detailed instructions or contact your instructor for information about accessing the required files.

Instructions: Start Access and open the Analyze Home Health database from the Data Files for Students. The Analyze Home Health database contains data about a health care company that provides nonmedical assistance to individuals in the home. The owner has asked you to correct some errors in the form she created and to improve the form design.

Perform the following tasks:

1. Correct The form shown in Figure 7–85 on the next page should have the caption and the title, Client View and Update Form. The name in the Name to Find combo box should change when

Continued >

Analyze, Correct, Improve *continued*

the Next record navigation button is tapped or clicked. Users should not be able to tab through the Name to Find combo box.

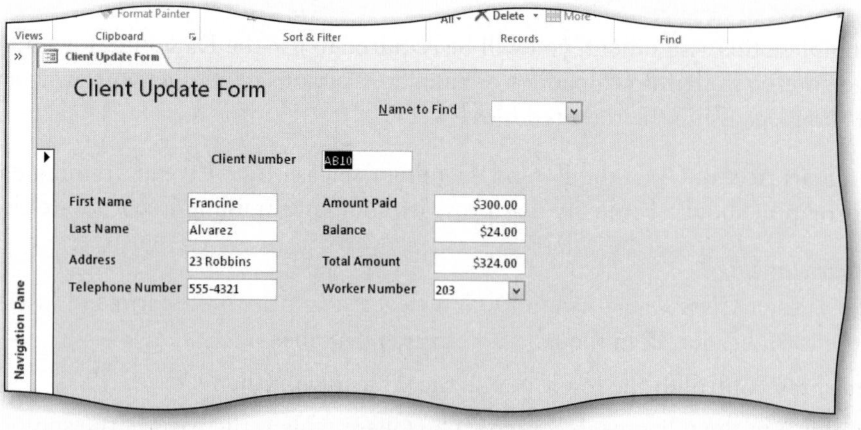

Figure 7–85

2. Improve The owner would like to improve the form's appearance by placing a rectangle around the Name to Find combo box. Both the title and the rectangle should have a raised special effect. She also would like the controls in the Detail section to have a sunken special effect and the labels to have a semi-bold font weight. (*Hint:* You might need to resize and adjust controls after making these changes.)

3. In this database, the client's last names were in alphabetical order. How can you ensure that the client names in the Name to Find combo box appear in alphabetical order?

In the Labs

Design, create, modify, and/or use a database following the guidelines, concepts, and skills presented in this chapter. Labs are listed in order of increasing difficulty. Labs 1 and 2, which increase in difficulty, require you to create solutions based on what you learned in the chapter; Lab 3 requires you to create a solution, which uses cloud and web technologies, by learning and investigating on your own from general guidance.

Lab 1: Applying Advanced Form Techniques to the Backup Services Database

Problem: The management of Backup Services needs a form for the Client table that allows users to update data in the table. Backup Services also needs a form to display open service request data for service reps.

Note: Use the database modified in the Lab 1 of Chapter 6 for this assignment. If you did not use the database, contact your instructor for information on accessing the database required for this exercise.

Instructions: Perform the following tasks:

1. Create the Client View and Update Form shown in Figure 7–86. Save the form with the name, Client Master Form. The form includes a title, command buttons, a combo box for the Service Rep Number field, and a combo box to search for clients by name. Be sure to sort the client names in alphabetical order, place a rectangle around the combo box, and update the combo

box. The user should not be able to tab to the combo box. When the Add Record button is tapped or clicked, the insertion point should be in the Client Number field. The background of the Detail section of the form is Light Gray 1 (Standard colors). The controls have a semi-bold font weight and a sunken special effect. The labels are italicized with a chiseled special effect. The form is similar in style to that shown in Figure 7–1 on page AC 411.

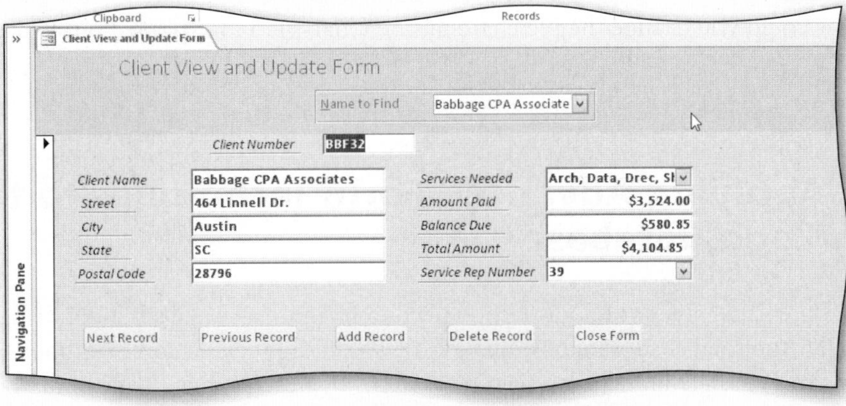

Figure 7–86

2. Create a query that includes the Service Rep Number from the Service Rep table, the Client Number from the Client table, and the Service Code and Hours Spent fields from the Service Requests table. Include a calculated field to calculate the Hours Remaining for each service request. Sort the query in ascending order by Service Rep Number, Client Number, and Service Code. Save the query as Reps and Service Requests.

3. Create the Service Rep Request Data form shown in Figure 7–87. The subform that appears in the Datasheet tab uses the Reps and Service Requests query (Figure 7–87a). The charts in the Charts tab use the same query (Figure 7–87b). Be sure to concatenate the first and last names of the service rep. Change the background color to Light Gray 2. The form is similar in style to that shown in Figure 7–2 on page AC 412.

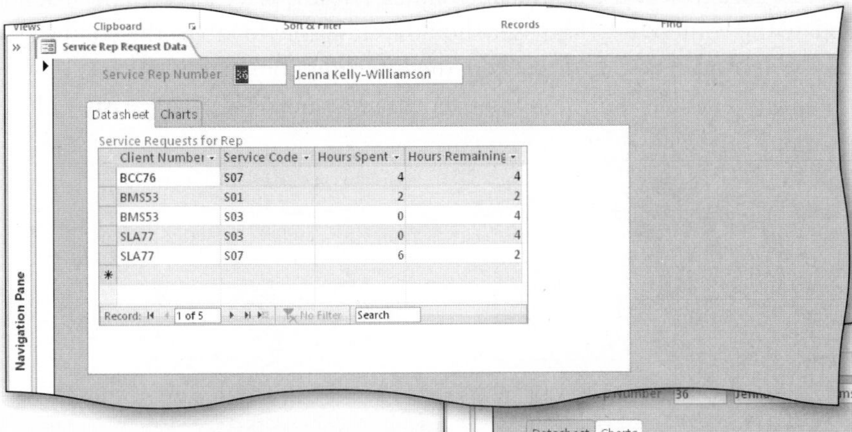

Figure 7–87 (a)

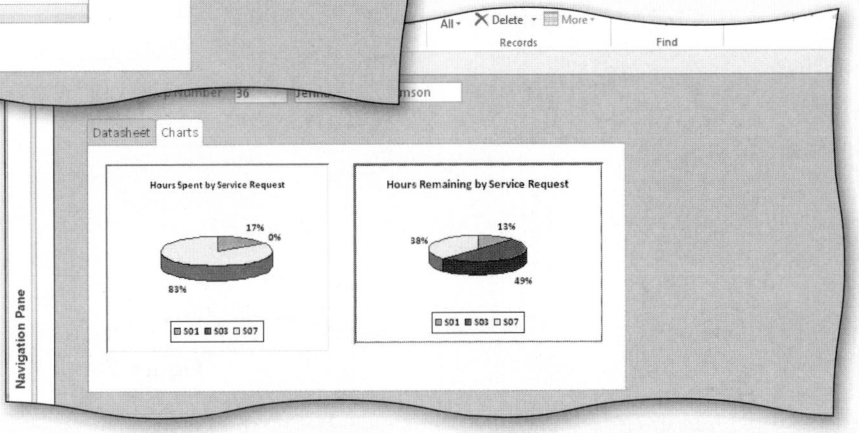

Figure 7–87 (b)

Continued >

In the Labs *continued*

4. If instructed to do so by your instructor, open the Service Rep table and change the first and last name of service rep 36 to your first and last name.
5. Submit the revised database in the format specified by your instructor.
6. How could you change the pie charts in the Charts tab to exploded pie charts with a 3-D visual effect?

Lab 2: Applying Advanced Form Techniques to the Sports Logo Database

Problem: The management of Sports Logo needs a form that displays item information. The form should display the total cost of items on hand. It also should include command buttons to perform common operations, a combo box to search for items by description, and a combo box for supplier code. Management also needs a form that displays supplier information as well as items on order and all items associated with a supplier.

Note: Use the database you used in Lab 2 of Chapter 6 on page AC 402 for this assignment. If you did not use this database, contact your instructor for information on accessing the database required for this exercise.

Instructions: Perform the following tasks:

1. Create the Item Master Form shown in Figure 7–88. Use the caption Item View and Update Form for the form. The form includes command buttons, a drop-down box (combo box) for the Supplier Code field, and combo box to search for items by name. Inventory Value is the result of multiplying On Hand by Wholesale Price. Format Inventory Value as currency with two decimal places. Change the tab order for the controls in the Detail section so that Supplier Code follows Item Type. Be sure to sort the item names alphabetically, place a rectangle around the combo box, and update the combo box. The user should not be able to tab to the combo box. When the Add Record button is tapped or clicked, the insertion point should be in the Item Number field. The form is similar in style to that shown in Figure 7–1 on page AC 411.

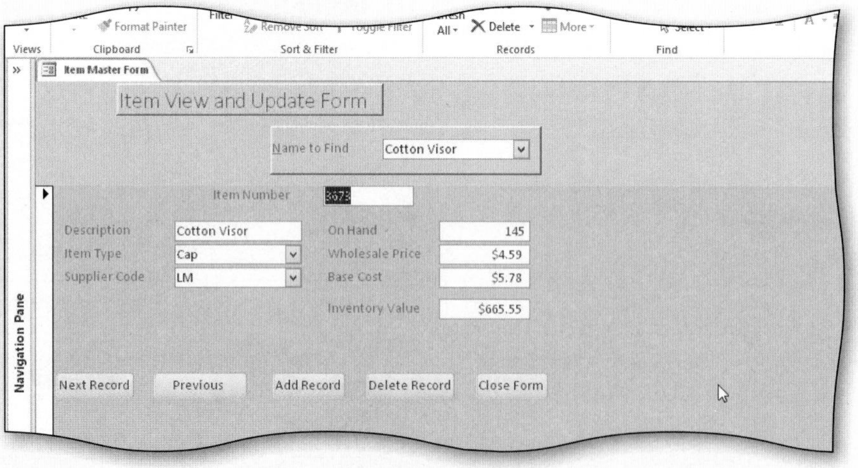

Figure 7–88

2. Create a query that includes the Supplier Code field from the Supplier table, the Item Number and Description fields from the Item table, and the Date Ordered and Number Ordered fields from the Reorder table. Sort the query in ascending order by Supplier Code, Item Number, and Date Ordered. Save the query as Suppliers and Orders.
3. Create the Supplier Orders Data form shown in Figure 7–89. The In Inventory tab uses the Item table for the subform (Figure 7–89a.) The On Order tab (Figure 7–89b) uses the Suppliers and Orders query for the subform. Note that the labels for Supplier Code and Supplier Name have been changed and that there is a title on the form. The title and the labels in the Detail section are bold and have the raised special effect. The controls have the sunken special effect. You can use the Format Painter to copy formatting for controls and labels.

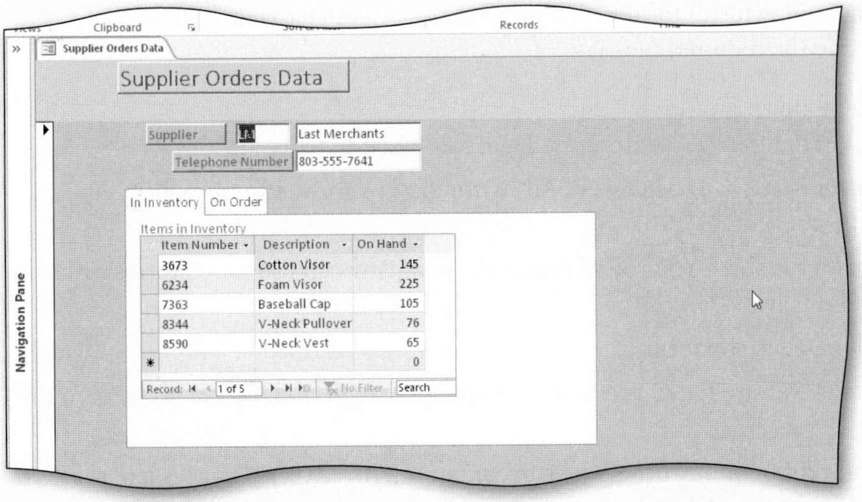

Figure 7–89 (a)

Figure 7–89 (b)

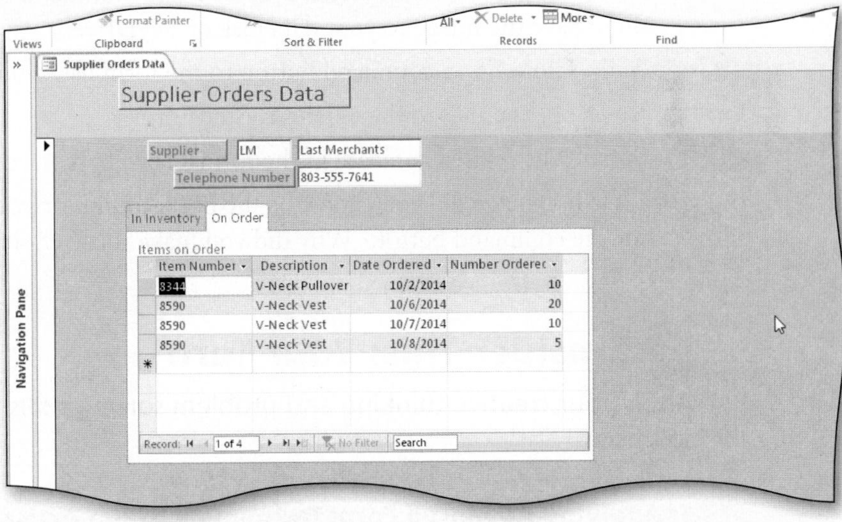

4. If instructed to do so by your instructor, change the phone number for supplier LM to your phone number.
5. Submit the revised database in the format specified by your instructor.
6. How could you rearrange the tab controls for the Supplier Orders Data form so that the On Order tab appears before the In Inventory tab?

Continued >

In the Labs *continued*

Lab 3: Expand Your World: Cloud and Web Technologies

Adding an Image, Background Image, and Hyperlink to a Form

Problem: Bookkeeping is a database maintained by an accounting firm that employs bookkeepers who maintain the books for those clients who need bookkeeping services. You will modify the Client Master Form to include a background image and a hyperlink. You also will add images to command buttons.

Note: To complete this assignment, you will be required to use the Data Files for Students. Visit www.cengage.com/ct/studentdownload for detailed instructions or contact your instructor for information about accessing the required files.

Instructions: Perform the following tasks:

1. Open the Lab 3 Bookkeeping database from the Data Files for Students.
2. Open the Client Master Form in Design view. Add a combo box for the Bookkeeper Number field.
3. Search the web to find a suitable background image the company can use for its forms or create your own background image.
4. Add the background image to the form.
5. Search the web to find a website for an accounting firm. Add a hyperlink for the website to the Form Header.
6. Access the office.com website or any other website containing royalty-free images and search for an image suitable to use on a Close Form command button: for example, a Stop sign or a door. Save the image to your data disk or SkyDrive.
7. Add a Close Form command button to the form using the image you downloaded.
8. Save your changes to the Client Master Form.
9. Submit the revised database in the format specified by your instructor.
10. What image did you choose as the background for your form? What image did you choose for the command button? Why did you make those choices?

Consider This: Your Turn

Apply your creative thinking and problem solving skills to design and implement a solution.

1: Applying Advanced Form Techniques to the Artisans Craft Database

Personal/Academic

Part 1: Your instructor has asked you to prepare an Item Master Form. He also would like you to modify the Student Master Form you created previously. Open the Your Turn 1 Artisan Crafts database that you modified in Chapter 6 on page AC 405. If you did not modify this database, contact your instructor for information about accessing the required database. Then, use the concepts and techniques presented in this chapter to perform each of the following tasks:

a. Create an Item Master Form that is similar in style to that shown in Figure 7-1 on page AC 411. The form should include a combo box to search for items by description and a combo box for the Student Code field. Include command buttons to add records, delete records, and close the form. Be sure to sort the description in ascending order and update the combo box. The user should not be able to tab to the combo box. When the Add Record button is tapped or clicked, the insertion point should be in the Item Number field. Customize the form by using special effects and formatting controls.

b. Modify the Student Master Form by adding command buttons to move to the next record, move to the previous record, and close the form.

Submit your assignment in the format specified by your instructor.

Part 2: You made several decisions while creating the Item Master Form. What was the rationale behind your decisions? Which option did you use, text or pictures on the command buttons? Why?

2: Applying Advanced Form Techniques to the Carel Landscaping Database

Professional

Part 1: The owner of Carel Landscaping needs a form to use to update customer data. He also needs a form to track customer requests by supervisor. Open the Your Turn 2 Carel Landscaping database that you modified in Chapter 6 on page AC 406. If you did not modify this database, contact your instructor for information about accessing the required database. Then, use the concepts and techniques presented in this chapter to perform each of the following tasks:

a. Create a Customer Master Form that is similar in style and appearance to the form shown in Figure 7–1 on page AC 411. The form should include a combo box to search for customers by name and a combo box for the Supervisor Number field. Include command buttons to go to the next record, go to the previous record, add records, delete records, and close the form. Be sure to sort the customer names in alphabetical order and update the combo box. The user should not be able to tab to the combo box. When the Add Record button is tapped or clicked, the focus should be the Customer Number field.

b. Create a query that joins the Supervisor, Customer, and Customer Requests tables. Include the Supervisor Number field from the Supervisor table, the Customer Number field from the Customer table, and the Service Code and Hours Spent fields from the Customer Requests table. Add a calculated field for Hours Remaining (Total Hours – Hours Spent). Sort the query in ascending order by Supervisor Number, Customer Number, and Service Code. Save the query.

c. Create a form for the Supervisor table that is similar to the form shown in Figure 7–2a on page AC 412. The form should have two tabs, a Datasheet tab and a Charts tab. The Datasheet tab displays a subform listing information about services for customers of the supervisor. Data for the subform is based on the query you created in Step b. The Charts tab includes two charts that are similar to the charts shown in Figure 7–2b on page AC 412. Data for the Charts tab also is based on the query created in Step b.

Submit your assignment in the format specified by your instructor.

Part 2: You made several decisions while creating these two forms. What was the rationale behind your decisions? What chart style did you choose for the two charts? Why? What other chart styles could you use to represent the data?

3: Understanding Forms

Research and Collaboration

Part 1: Copy the Bavant Publishing database and rename the database to your team name. For example, if your team is Terrific Threes, then name the database Terrific Threes Publishing. As a team, design an appropriate company image to add to the forms. Add the image to the Customer Master Form in the form header. Delete the combo box for the Book Rep Number and replace it with a list box. Design a background image and add it to the Rep Seminar Data form. Change the chart style of the two charts. Add a page header section to the Customer Master Form and then add a label to the page header section that includes the names of the team members. Create a new form

Continued >

Consider This: Your Turn *continued*

that includes the same data as the Rep Seminar data form but uses the Insert Page Break control instead of the Tab Control.

Submit your assignment in the format specified by your instructor.

Part 2: You made several decisions while completing this assignment including adding an image to the form header. What was the rationale behind your decisions? What is the difference between a combo box and a list box?

Learn Online

Reinforce what you learned in this chapter with games, exercises, training, and many other online activities and resources.

Student Companion Site Reinforcement activities and resources are available at no additional cost on www.cengagebrain.com. Visit www.cengage.com/ct/studentdownload for detailed instructions about accessing the resources available at the Student Companion Site.

SAM Put your skills into practice with SAM Projects! If you have a SAM account, go to www.cengage.com/sam2013 to access SAM assignments for this chapter.

8 Macros, Navigation Forms, and Control Layouts

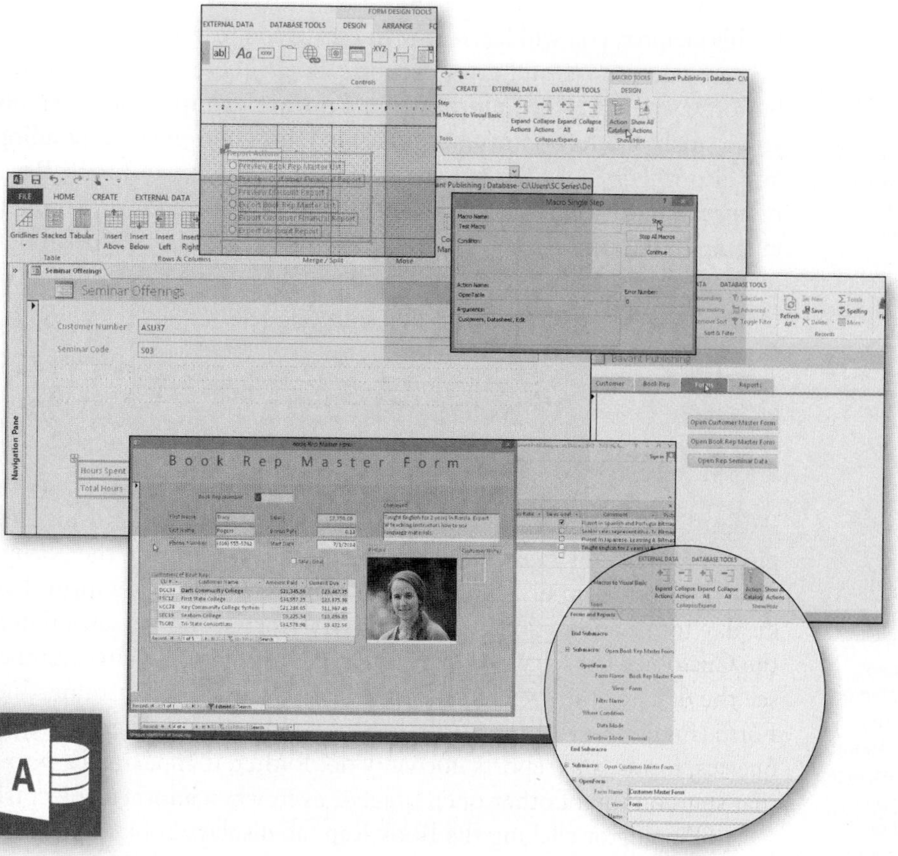

Objectives

You will have mastered the material in this project when you can:

- Create and modify macros and submacros
- Create a menu form with command buttons
- Create a menu form with an option group
- Create a macro for the option group
- Use an IF statement in a macro
- Create datasheet forms
- Create user interface (UI) macros
- Create navigation forms
- Add tabs to a navigation form
- Create data macros
- Create and remove control layouts
- Use the ARRANGE tab to modify control layouts on forms and reports

8 Macros, Navigation Forms, and Control Layouts

Introduction

In this chapter, you will learn how to create and test macros that open forms and that preview reports and export reports. You will create a menu form with command buttons as well as a menu form with an **option group**, which is an object that enables you to make a selection by choosing the option button corresponding to your choice. You also will create and use user interface (UI) macros in forms. Bavant Publishing requires a navigation form that will allow users to open forms and reports simply by tapping or clicking appropriate tabs and buttons. You will learn about the use of data macros for ensuring that updates to the database are valid. Finally, you will learn how to use control layouts on forms and reports.

BTW
Q&As
For a complete list of the Q&As found in many of the step-by-step sequences in this book, visit the Q&A resource on the Student Companion Site located on www.cengagebrain.com. For detailed instructions about accessing available resources, visit www.cengage.com/ct/studentdownload or contact your instructor for information about accessing the required files.

Project — Macros, Navigation Forms, and Control Layouts

Bavant Publishing would like its users to be able to access forms and reports by simply tapping or clicking tabs and buttons, rather than by using the Navigation Pane. A **navigation form** like the one shown in Figure 8–1a is a form that includes tabs to display forms and reports. This navigation form contains several useful features. With the Customer tab selected, you can tap or click the customer number on any row to see the data for the selected customer displayed in the Customer View and Update Form (Figure 8–1b). The form does not appear in a tabbed sheet, the way tables, queries, forms, and reports normally do. Rather, it appears as a **pop-up form**, a form that stays on top of other open objects, even when another object is active.

Tapping or clicking the Book Rep tab displays book rep data. As with customers, tapping or clicking the book rep number on any record displays data for that rep in a pop-up form.

Tapping or clicking the Forms tab in the Bavant Publishing navigation form displays buttons for each of the available forms (Figure 8–1c). You can open the desired form by tapping or clicking the appropriate button. Tapping or clicking the Reports tab displays an option group for displaying reports (Figure 8–1d). You can preview or export any of the reports one at a time by tapping or clicking the corresponding option button. Bavant plans to use the navigation form because they believe it will improve the user-friendliness of the database, thereby improving employee satisfaction and efficiency.

Before creating the navigation form, Bavant will create **macros**, which are collections of actions designed to carry out specific tasks. To perform the actions in a macro, you run the macro. When you run a macro, Access will execute the various steps, called **actions**, in the order indicated by the macro. You run the navigation form macros by tapping or clicking certain buttons in the form.

BTW
BTWs
For a complete list of the BTWs found in the margins of this book, visit the BTW resource on the Student Companion Site located on www.cengagebrain.com. For detailed instructions about accessing available resources, visit www.cengage.com/ct/studentdownload or contact your instructor for information about accessing the required files.

BTW
Macros
A macro is a series of commands used to automate repeated tasks. You can create macros in other Office apps, such as Word and Excel.

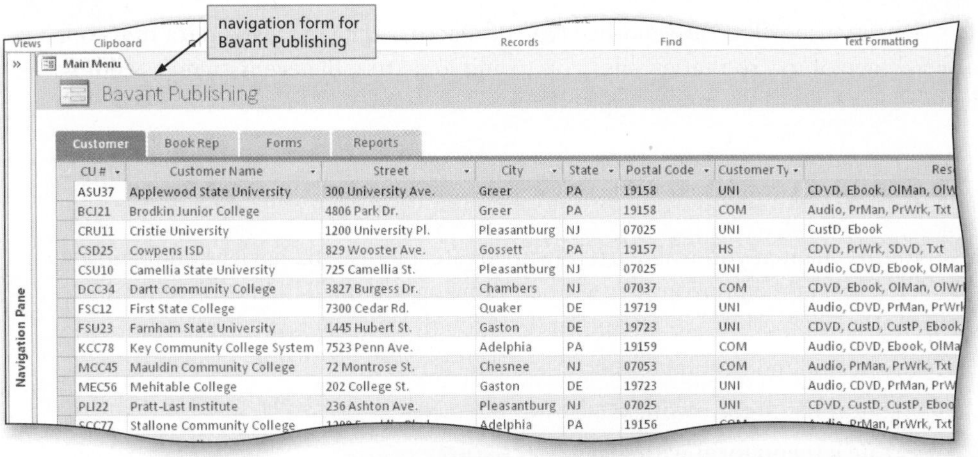

Figure 8–1 (a) Navigation Form

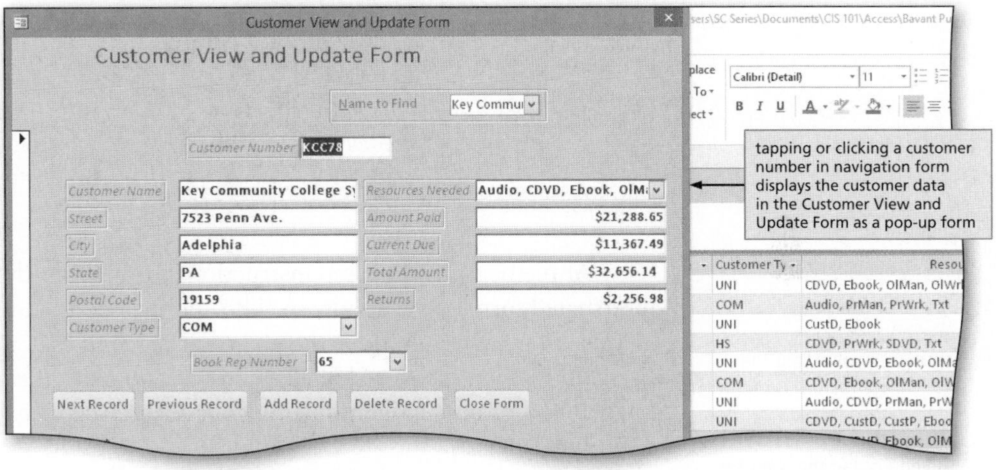

Figure 8–1 (b) Pop-Up Form Displaying Customer Data

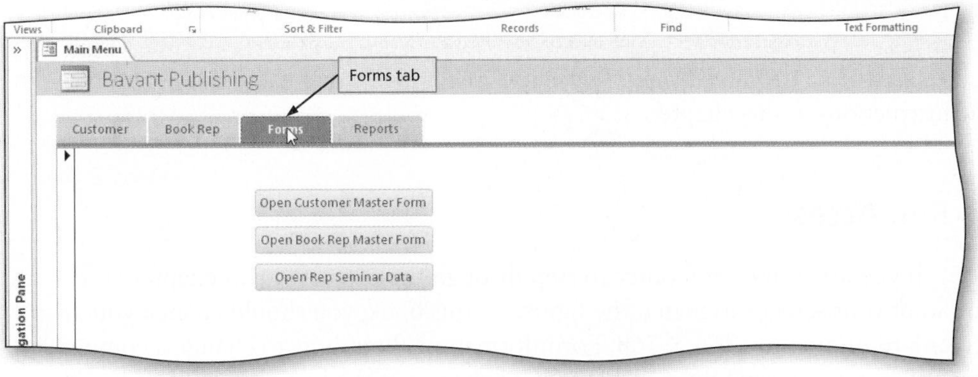

Figure 8–1 (c) Forms Tab

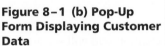

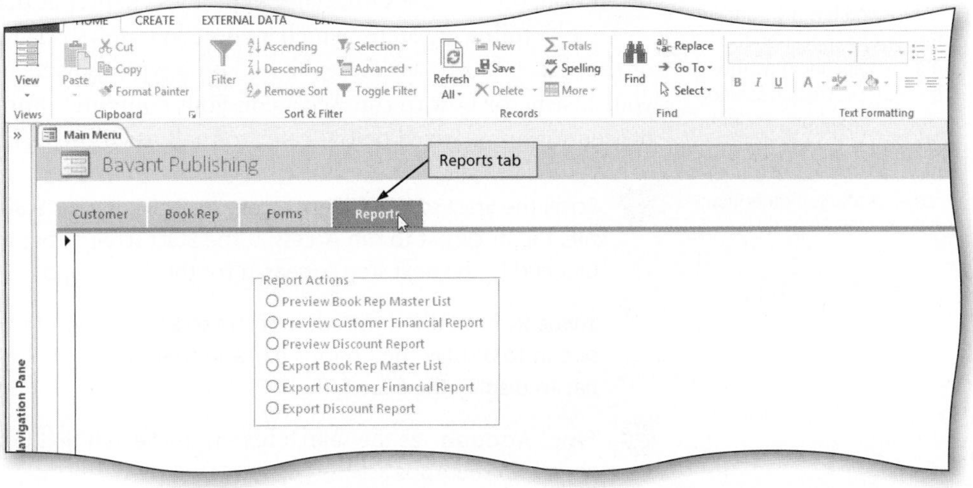

Figure 8–1 (d) Reports Tab

Bavant also will create another type of macro, a data macro. A **data macro** is a special type of macro that enables you to add logic to table events such as adding, changing, or deleting data. You typically use data macros to ensure data validity.

Roadmap

BTW
Touch and Pointers
Remember that if you are using your finger on a touch screen, you will not see the pointer.

In this chapter, you will learn how to create and use the navigation form shown in Figure 8–1 on the previous page. The following roadmap identifies general activities you will perform as you progress through this chapter:

1. Create and modify a MACRO WITH SUBMACROS
2. Create a menu form with COMMAND BUTTONS
3. Create a menu form with an OPTION GROUP
4. Create a MACRO FOR the OPTION GROUP
5. Create DATASHEET FORMS
6. Create USER INTERFACE (UI) MACROS
7. Create a NAVIGATION FORM
8. Create a DATA MACRO

BTW
On-Screen Keyboard
To display the on-screen touch keyboard, tap the Touch Keyboard button on the Windows taskbar. When finished using the touch keyboard, tap the X button on the touch keyboard to close the keyboard.

At the beginning of step instructions throughout the chapter, you will see an abbreviated form of this roadmap. The abbreviated roadmap uses colors to indicate chapter progress: gray means the chapter is beyond that activity; blue means the task being shown is covered in that activity, and black means that activity is yet to be covered. For example, the following abbreviated roadmap indicates the chapter would be showing a task in the 3 OPTION GROUP activity.

1 MACRO WITH SUBMACROS | 2 COMMAND BUTTONS | 3 OPTION GROUP | 4 MACRO FOR OPTION GROUP
5 DATASHEET FORMS | 6 USER INTERFACE MACROS | 7 NAVIGATION FORM | 8 DATA MACRO

Use the abbreviated roadmap as a progress guide while you read or step through the instructions in this chapter.

To Run Access

BTW
The Ribbon and Screen Resolution
Access may change how the groups and buttons within the groups appear on the ribbon, depending on the computer's screen resolution. Thus, your ribbon may look different from the ones in this book if you are using a screen resolution other than 1366 × 768.

If you are using a computer to step through the project in this chapter and you want your screens to match the figures in this book, you should change your screen's resolution to 1366 × 768. For information about how to change a computer's resolution, refer to the Office and Windows chapter at the beginning of this book.

The following steps, which assume Windows is running, use the Start screen or the search box to run Access based on a typical installation. You may need to ask your instructor how to run Access on your computer. For a detailed example of the procedure summarized below, refer to the Office and Windows chapter.

1. Scroll the Start screen for an Access 2013 tile. If your Start screen contains an Access 2013 tile, tap or click it to run Access; if the Start screen does not contain the Access 2013 tile, proceed to the next step to search for the Access app.
2. Swipe in from the right edge of the screen or point to the upper-right corner of the screen to display the Charms bar and then tap or click the Search charm on the Charms bar to display the Search menu.
3. Type `Access` as the search text in the Search text box and watch the search results appear in the Apps list.
4. Tap or click Access 2013 in the search results to run Access.

To Open a Database from Access

The following steps open the Bavant Publishing database from the location you specified when you first created it (for example, the Access folder in the CIS 101 folder). For a detailed example of the procedure summarized below, refer to the Office and Windows chapter at the beginning of this book.

1. Tap or click FILE on the ribbon to open the Backstage view, if necessary.
2. If the database you want to open is displayed in the Recent list, tap or click the file name to open the database and display the opened database in the Access window; then skip to Step 7. If the database you want to open is not displayed in the Recent list or if the Recent list does not appear, tap or click Open Other Files to display the Open Gallery.
3. If the database you want to open is displayed in the Recent list in the Open gallery, tap or click the file name to open the database and display the opened database in the Access window; then skip to Step 7.
4. Tap or click Computer, SkyDrive, or another location in the left pane and then navigate to the location of the database to be opened (for example, the Access folder in the CIS 101 folder).
5. Tap or click Bavant Publishing to select the database to be opened.
6. Tap or click the Open button (Open dialog box) to open the selected file and display the opened database in the Access window.
7. If a Security Warning appears, tap or click the Enable Content button.

BTW
Touch Screen Differences
The Office and Windows interfaces may vary if you are using a touch screen. For this reason, you might notice that the function or appearance of your touch screen differs slightly from this chapter's presentation.

Creating and Using Macros

Similar to other Office apps, Access allows you to create and use macros. A macro consists of a series of actions that Access performs when the macro is run. When you create a macro, you specify these actions. Once you have created a macro, you can simply run the macro, and Access will perform the various actions you specified. For example, the macro might open a form in read-only mode, a mode where changes to the data are prohibited. Another macro might export a report as a PDF file. You can group related macros into a single macro, with the individual macros existing as submacros within the main macro.

CONSIDER THIS

How do you create macros? How do you use them?

You create a macro by entering a specific series of actions in a window called the Macro Builder window. Once a macro is created, it exists as an object in the database, and you can run it from the Navigation Pane by pressing and holding or right-clicking the macro and then tapping or clicking Run on the shortcut menu. Macros also can be associated with buttons on forms. When you tap or click the corresponding button on the form, Access will run the macro. Whether a macro is run from the Navigation Pane or from a form, the effect is the same: Access will execute the actions in the order in which they occur in the macro.

In this chapter, you will create macros for a variety of purposes. As you enter actions, you will select them from a list presented to you by the Macro Builder. The names of the actions are self-explanatory. The action to open a form, for example, is OpenForm. Thus, it is not necessary to memorize the specific actions that are available.

To Begin Creating a Macro

1 MACRO WITH SUBMACROS | 2 COMMAND BUTTONS | 3 OPTION GROUP | 4 MACRO FOR OPTION GROUP
5 DATASHEET FORMS | 6 USER INTERFACE MACROS | 7 NAVIGATION FORM | 8 DATA MACRO

The following steps begin creating a macro. ***Why?*** *Once you have created the macro, you will be able to add the appropriate actions.*

1

- If necessary, close the Navigation Pane.
- Display the CREATE tab (Figure 8–2).

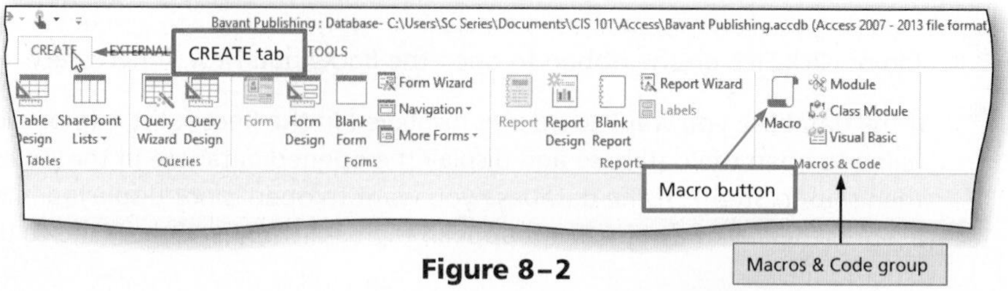

Figure 8–2

2

- Tap or click the Macro button (CREATE tab | Macros & Code group) to create a new macro.
- Tap or click the Action Catalog button (MACRO TOOLS DESIGN tab | Show/Hide group) if necessary to display the action catalog (Figure 8–3).

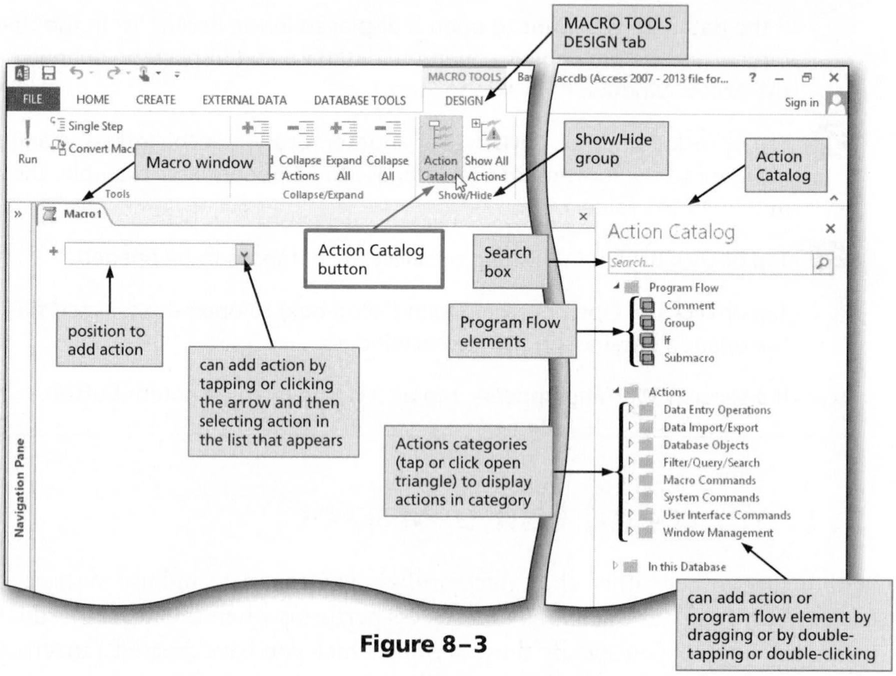

Figure 8–3

The Macro Builder Window

You create a macro by adding actions in the macro window, shown in Figure 8–3. You can add actions by tapping or clicking the Add New Action arrow and selecting the desired action from the list of possible actions. You can also use the Action Catalog, which is a list of macro actions organized by type. If the Action Catalog does not appear, tap or click the Action Catalog button (MACRO TOOLS DESIGN tab | Show/Hide group) to display it. You can add an action by double-tapping or double-clicking the action in the Action Catalog or by dragging it.

Access arranges the available actions in categories. To see the actions in a category, tap or click the **expand indicator** (the open triangle) in front of the category. The actions will appear and the expand indicator will change to a solid triangle. To hide the actions in a category, tap or click the solid triangle.

CONSIDER THIS

How can you find an action if you are not sure which category contains the action?

You can search the list by typing in the Search box. Access will then reduce the list of actions displayed to only those actions whose names or descriptions contain the text you have typed.

Many actions require additional information, called the **arguments** of the action. For example, if the action is OpenForm, Access needs to know which form is to be opened. You indicate the form to be opened by setting the value of the Form Name argument to the desired form. If the value for the Form Name argument for the OpenForm action is Rep Seminar Data, then Access will open the Rep Seminar Data form when it executes this action.

Actions can have more than one argument. For example, in addition to the Form Name argument, the OpenForm action also has a Data Mode argument. If the value of the Data Mode argument is Read Only, then the form will be opened in read-only mode, which indicates users will be able to view but not change data. When you select an action, the arguments will appear along with the action, and you can make any necessary changes to them.

In the forms you will create later in this chapter, you need macros for opening the Rep Seminar Data form as read-only (to prevent updates), opening the Book Rep Master Form, opening the Customer Master Form, previewing the Book Rep Master List, previewing the Customer Financial Report, previewing the Discount Report, exporting the Book Rep Master List as a PDF file, exporting the Customer Financial Report as a PDF file, and exporting the Discount Report as a PDF file. You could create nine separate macros to accomplish these tasks. A simpler way, however, is to make each of these a submacro within a single macro. You can run a submacro just as you can run a macro.

You will create a macro called Forms and Reports that contains these nine submacros. Table 8–1 shows the submacros. Submacros can contain many actions, but each one in this table includes only a single action. For each submacro, the table gives

BTW

Converting a Macro to VBA Code

If you want to use many of the resources provided by Windows or communicate with another Windows app, you will need to convert any macros to VBA (Visual Basic for Applications) code. To convert a macro to VBA code, open the macro in Design view and tap or click the 'Convert Macros to Visual Basic' button (MACRO TOOLS DESIGN tab | Tools group). When the Convert Macro dialog box appears, select the appropriate options, and then tap or click Convert.

Table 8–1 Forms and Reports Macro

Submacro	Action	Arguments to be Changed
Open Rep Seminar Data		
	OpenForm	Form Name: Rep Seminar Data Data Mode: Read Only
Open Book Rep Master Form		
	OpenForm	Form Name: Book Rep Master Form
Open Customer Master Form		
	OpenForm	Form Name: Customer Master Form
Preview Book Rep Master List		
	OpenReport	Report Name: Book Rep Master List View: Print Preview
Preview Customer Financial Report		
	OpenReport	Report Name: Customer Financial Report View: Print Preview
Preview Discount Report		
	OpenReport	Report Name: Discount Report View: Print Preview
Export Book Rep Master List		
	ExportWithFormatting	Object Type: Report Object Name: Book Rep Master List Output Format: PDF Format (*.pdf)
Export Customer Financial Report		
	ExportWithFormatting	Object Type: Report Object Name: Customer Financial Report Output Format: PDF Format (*.pdf)
Export Discount Report		
	ExportWithFormatting	Object Type: Report Object Name: Discount Report Output Format: PDF Format (*.pdf)

BTW

Saving a Macro as a VBA Module

You can save a macro as a VBA module using the Save Object As command in Backstage view. Open the macro in Design view, tap or click FILE on the ribbon to open Backstage view, and then tap or click Save As. When the Save As gallery appears, tap or click Save Object As in the File Types area, and then tap or click the Save As button. When the Save As dialog box appears, tap or click Module in the As text box and then tap or click the OK button.

the action, those arguments that need to be changed, and the values you need to assign to those arguments. If an argument is not listed, then you do not need to change the value from the default value that is assigned by Access.

To Add an Action to a Macro

1 MACRO WITH SUBMACROS | 2 COMMAND BUTTONS | 3 OPTION GROUP | 4 MACRO FOR OPTION GROUP
5 DATASHEET FORMS | 6 USER INTERFACE MACROS | 7 NAVIGATION FORM | 8 DATA MACRO

To continue creating the Forms and Reports macro, enter the actions in the Macro Builder. In these steps, you will enter actions by double-tapping or double-clicking the action in the Action Catalog. ***Why?*** *The actions in the Action Catalog are organized by function, making it easier to locate the action you want.* Access will add the action to the Add New Action box. If there is more than one Add New Action box, you need to ensure that the one where you want to add the action is selected before you double-tap or double-click.

The following steps add the first action. They also make the necessary changes to any arguments. Finally, the steps save the macro.

1

- Double-tap or double-click the Submacro element from the Program Flow section of the Action Catalog to add a second submacro and then type **`Open Rep Seminar Data`** as the name of the submacro (Figure 8–4).

Q&A How can I tell the purpose of the various actions?
If necessary, expand the category containing the action so that the action appears. Point to the action. An expanded ScreenTip will appear, giving you a description of the action.

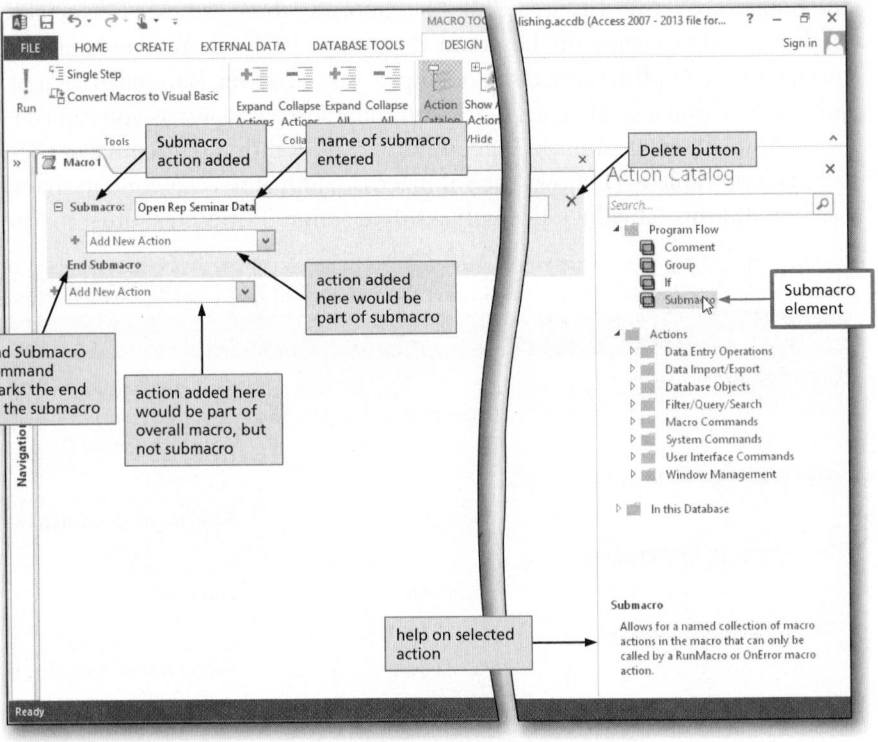

Figure 8–4

2

- Tap or click the expand indicator for the Database Objects category of actions to display the actions within the category.
- Double-tap or double-click the OpenForm action to add it to the submacro (Figure 8–5).

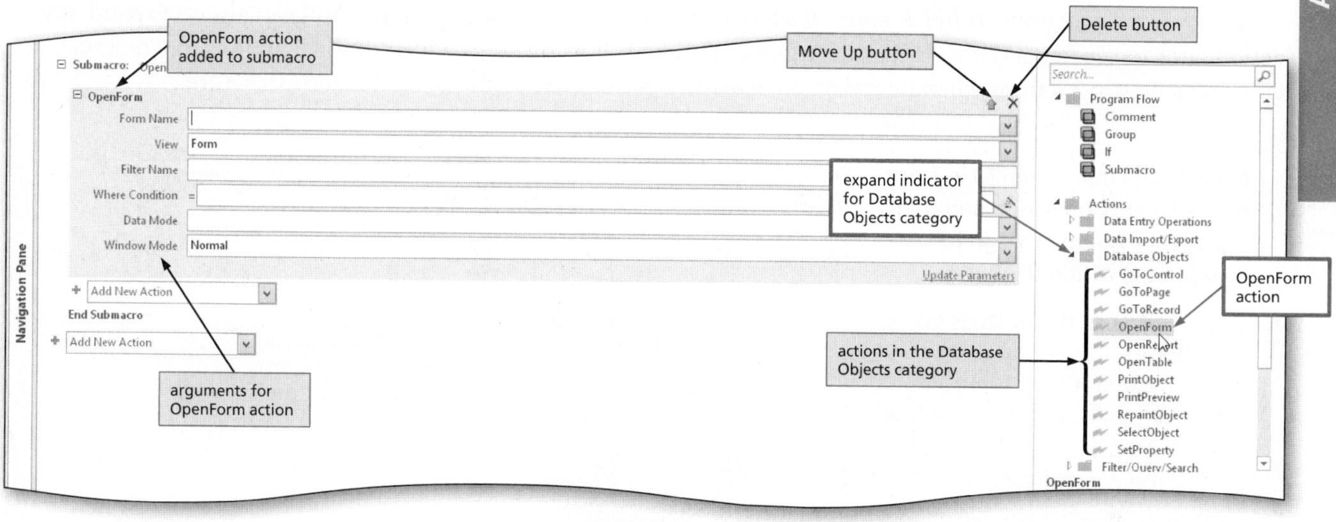

Figure 8–5

Q&A What should I do if I add an action in the wrong position? What should I do if I add the wrong action?
If you add an action in the wrong position, use the Move Up or Move Down buttons to move it to the correct position. If you added the wrong action, tap or click the Delete button to delete the action, and then fix the error by adding the correct action.

3

- Tap or click the drop-down arrow for the Form Name argument and then select Rep Seminar Data as the name of the form to be opened.
- Tap or click the drop-down arrow for the Data Mode argument and then select Read Only to specify that users cannot change the data in the form (Figure 8–6).

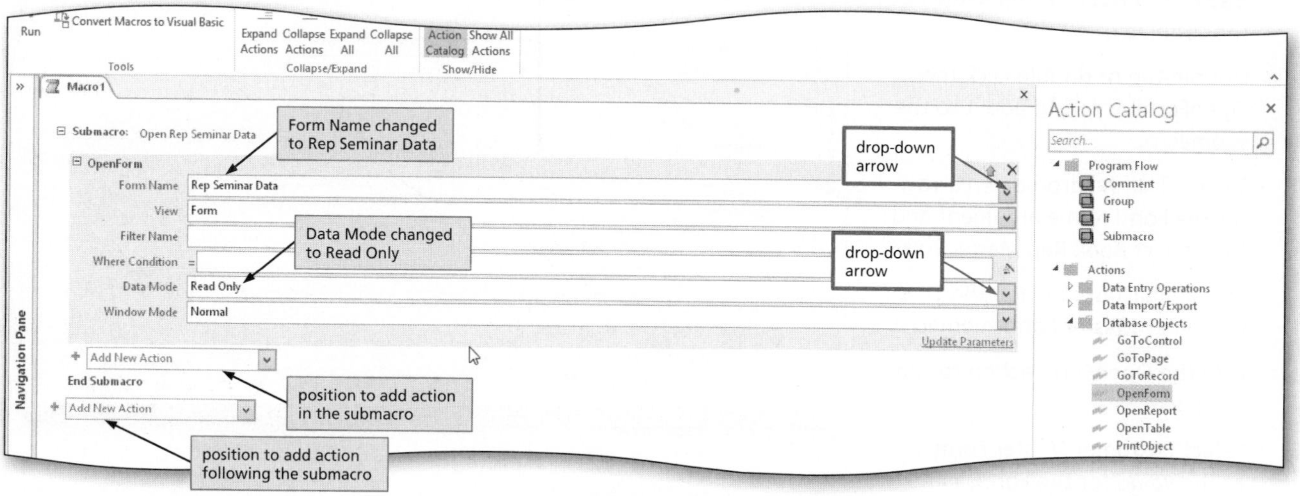

Figure 8–6

Q&A What is the effect of the other Data Mode options?
Add allows viewing records and adding new records, but not updating records. Edit allows viewing records, adding new records, and updating existing records.

4

- Tap or click the Save button on the Quick Access Toolbar, type `Forms and Reports` as the name of the macro, and then tap or click the OK button to save the macro.

To Add More Actions to a Macro

To complete the macro, you need to add the additional actions shown in Table 8–1 on page AC 479. You add the additional actions just as you added the first action. Initially, Access displays all the actions you have added with their arguments clearly visible. After you have added several actions, you might want to collapse some or all of the actions. ***Why?** It makes it easier to get an overall view of your macro.* You can always expand any action later to see details concerning the arguments. The following steps add additional actions to a macro, collapsing existing actions when necessary to provide a better view of the overall macro structure.

1

- Point to the minus sign (-) in front of the OpenForm action and then tap or click the minus sign to collapse the action (Figure 8–7).

Q&A Could I also use the buttons on the ribbon?

Yes, you can use the buttons in the Collapse/Expand group on the MACRO TOOLS DESIGN tab. Tap or click the Expand Actions button to expand the selected action, or tap or click the Collapse Actions button to collapse the selected action. You can expand all actions at once by tapping or clicking the Expand All button, or you can collapse all actions at once by tapping or clicking the Collapse All button.

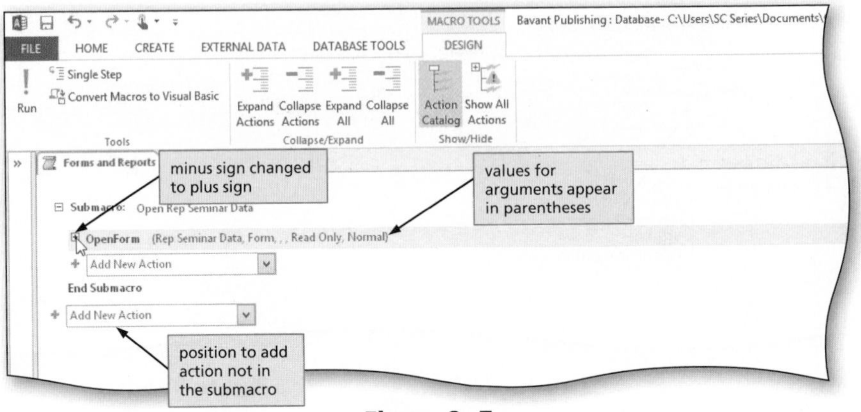

Figure 8–7

2

- Double-tap or double-click the Submacro element from the Program Flow section of the Action Catalog to add a submacro and then type `Open Book Rep Master Form` as the name of the submacro.
- Double-tap or double-click the OpenForm action to add it to the submacro.
- Tap or click the drop-down arrow for the Form Name argument and then select Book Rep Master Form.
- In a similar fashion, add the Open Customer Master Form submacro.
- Add the OpenForm action to the submacro.
- Select Customer Master Form as the value for the Form Name argument (Figure 8–8).

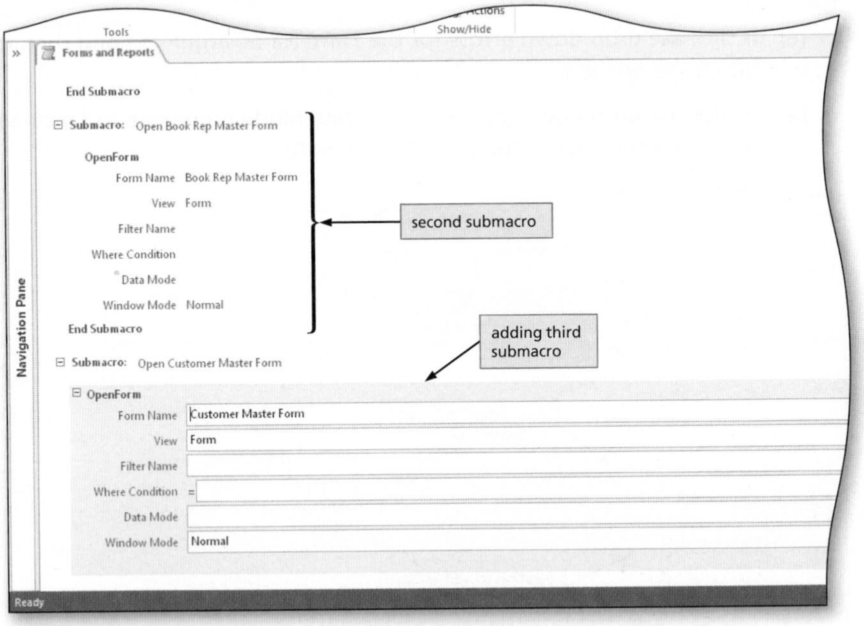

Figure 8–8

Q&A Do I have to change the values of any of the other arguments?

No. The default values that Access sets are appropriate.

3

- For each of the three submacros, point to the minus sign in front of the submacro and then tap or click the minus sign to collapse the submacro.
- Add a submacro named Preview Book Rep Master List.
- Add the OpenReport action to the macro.
- Select Book Rep Master List as the report name.
- Select Print Preview as the view (Figure 8–9).

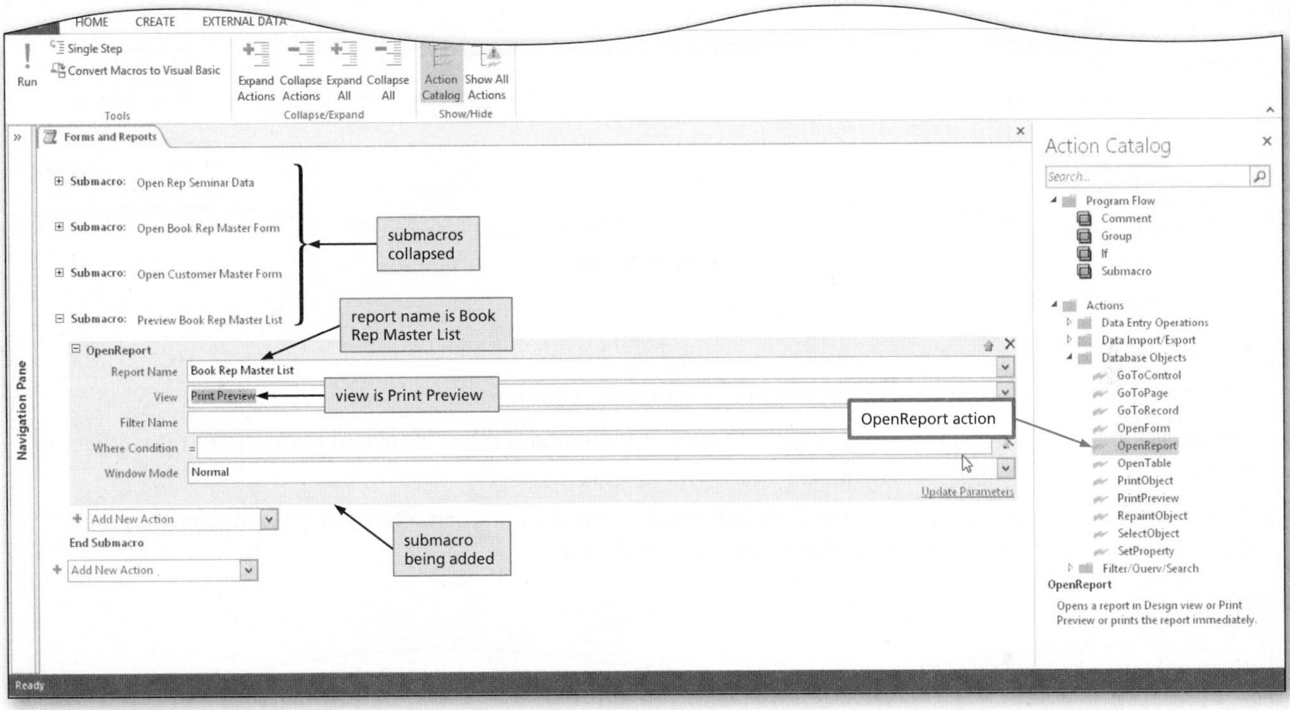

Figure 8–9

4

- Collapse the Preview Book Rep Master List submacro.
- Add the Preview Customer Financial Report submacro. Include the action described in Table 8–1 on page AC 479. The report name is Customer Financial Report and the view is Print Preview.
- Add the Preview Discount Report submacro. Include the action described in Table 8–1. The report name is Discount Report and the view is Print Preview.
- Collapse the Preview Customer Financial Report and Preview Discount Report submacros.
- Collapse the Database Objects category and then expand the Data Import/Export category.
- Add a submacro called Export Book Rep Master List.
- Add the ExportWithFormatting action, which will export and maintain any special formatting in the process.
- Tap or click the drop-down arrow for the Object Type argument to display a list of possible object types (Figure 8–10 on the next page).

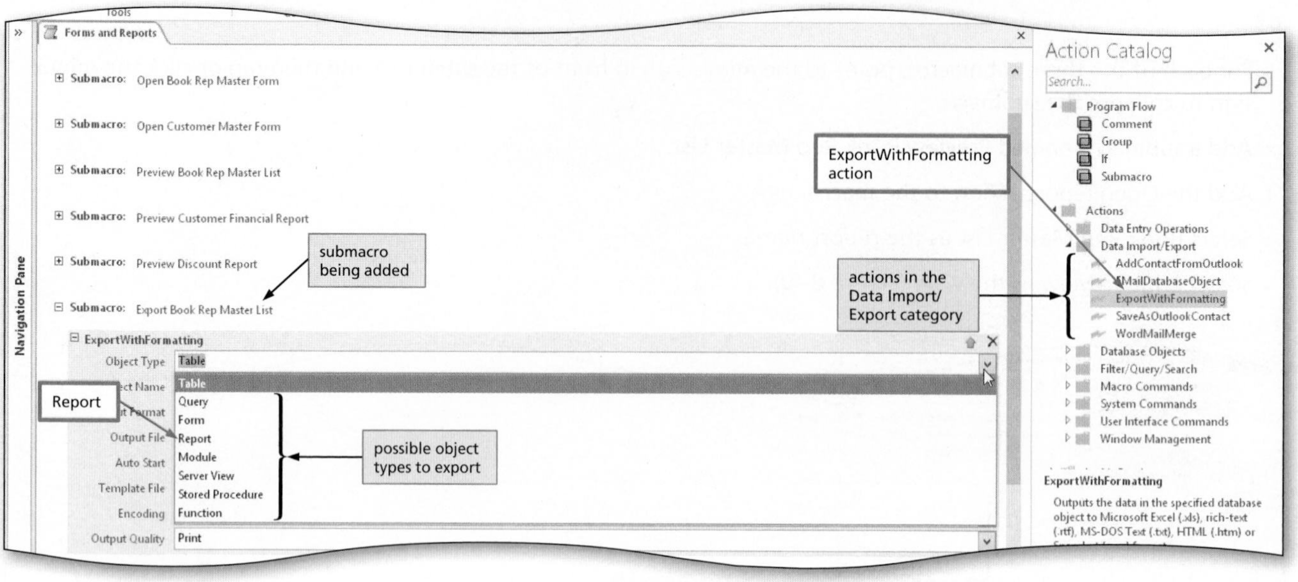

Figure 8–10

5

- Tap or click Report in the list to indicate that Access is to export a report.
- Tap or click the drop-down arrow for the Object Name argument and select Book Rep Master List as the object name.
- Tap or click the drop-down arrow for the Output Format argument and then select PDF Format (*.pdf) as the Output Format to export the report in PDF format (Figure 8–11).

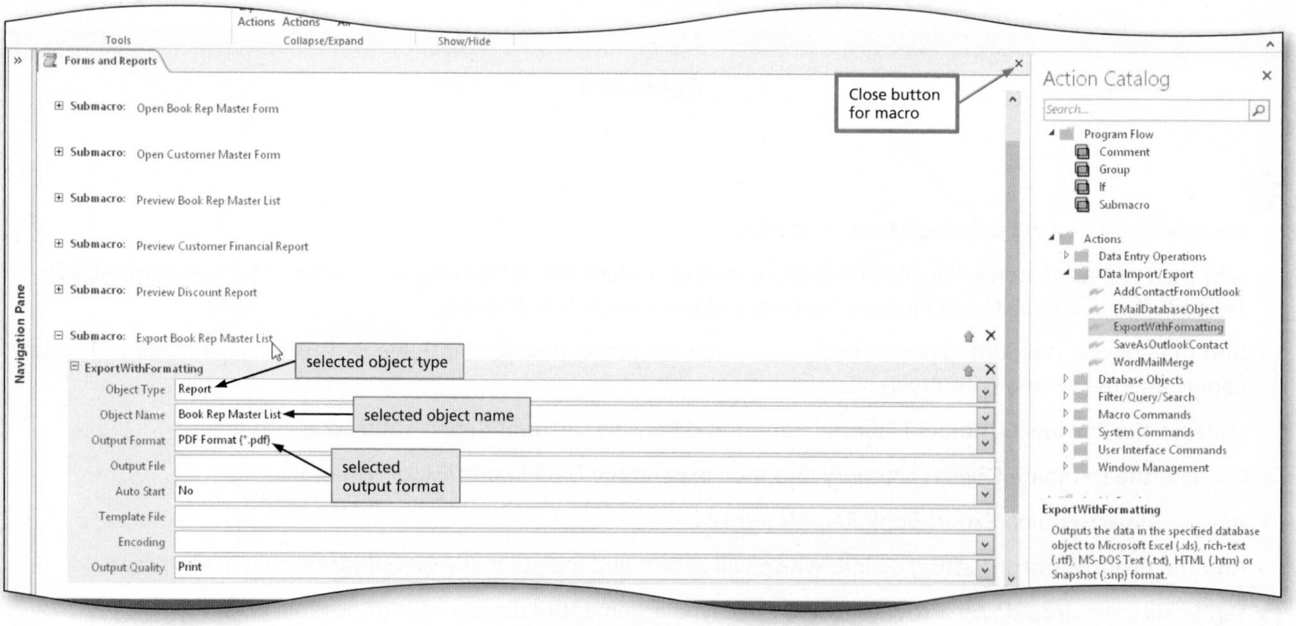

Figure 8–11

6

- Add the Export Customer Financial Report submacro and the action from Table 8–1 on page AC 479.
- Include the action described in Table 8–1 and select Customer Financial Report as the report name.

- Select PDF Format (*.pdf) as the Output Format to export the report in PDF format.
- Add the Export Discount Report submacro.
- Select Discount Report as the report name.
- Select PDF Format (*.pdf) as the Output Format to export the report in PDF format.
- Save the macro.
- Close the macro by tapping or clicking its Close button, shown in Figure 8–11.

Opening Databases Containing Macros

It is possible that a macro stored in a database can contain a computer virus. By default, Access disables macros when it opens a database and displays a Security Warning. If the database comes from a trusted source and you are sure that it does not contain any macro viruses, tap or click the Enable Content button. You can make adjustments to Access security settings by tapping or clicking FILE on the ribbon to open the Backstage view, and then tapping or clicking Options to display the Access Options dialog box, tapping or clicking Trust Center, tapping or clicking Trust Center Settings, and then tapping or clicking Macro Settings.

BTW

Viewing VBA Code

You can view VBA code that is attached to a form or report. To do so, open the form or report in Design view and tap or click the View Code button (REPORT DESIGN TOOLS DESIGN tab | Tools group) for reports or (FORM DESIGN TOOLS DESIGN tab | Tools group) for forms.

Errors in Macros

Macros can contain errors. The macro may abort. It might open the wrong table or produce a wrong message. If you have problems with a macro, you can **single-step the macro**, that is, proceed through a macro a step at a time in Design view.

Figure 8–12 shows a macro open in Design view. This macro first has an action to open the Customer table in Datasheet view in Read Only mode. It then changes the view to Print Preview. Next, it opens the Customer table in Datasheet view, this time in Edit mode. Finally, it opens the Rep-Customer Query in Datasheet view in Edit mode. The macro in the figure is a common type of macro that opens several objects at once. To open all these objects, the user only has to run the macro. Unfortunately, this macro contains an error. The name of the Customer table is written as "Customers" in the second OpenTable action.

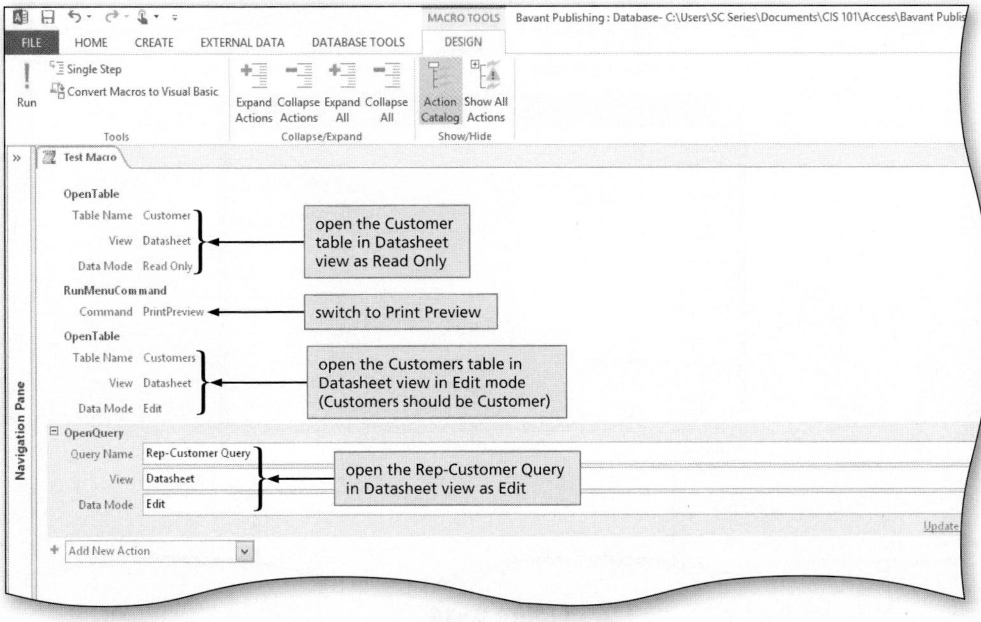

Figure 8–12

To run this macro in single-step mode, you first would tap or click the Single Step button (MACRO TOOLS DESIGN tab | Tools group). You next would tap or click the Run button (MACRO TOOLS DESIGN tab | Tools group) to run the macro. Because you tapped or clicked the Single Step button, Access would display the Macro Single Step dialog box (Figure 8–13). The dialog box shows the action to be executed and the values of the various arguments. You can tap or click the Step button to proceed to the next step.

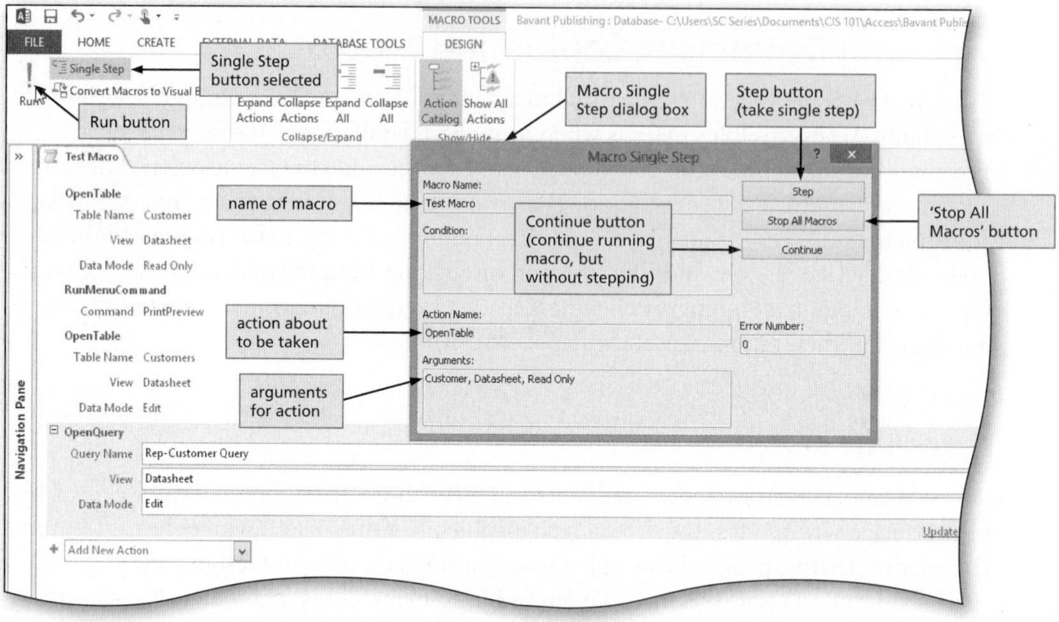

Figure 8–13

With this macro, after you tapped or clicked the Step button twice, you would arrive at the screen shown in Figure 8–14. Access is about to execute the OpenTable command. The arguments are Customers, Datasheet, and Edit. At this point, you might spot the fact that "Customers" is misspelled. It should be "Customer." If so, you could tap or click the 'Stop All Macros' button and then make the necessary changes.

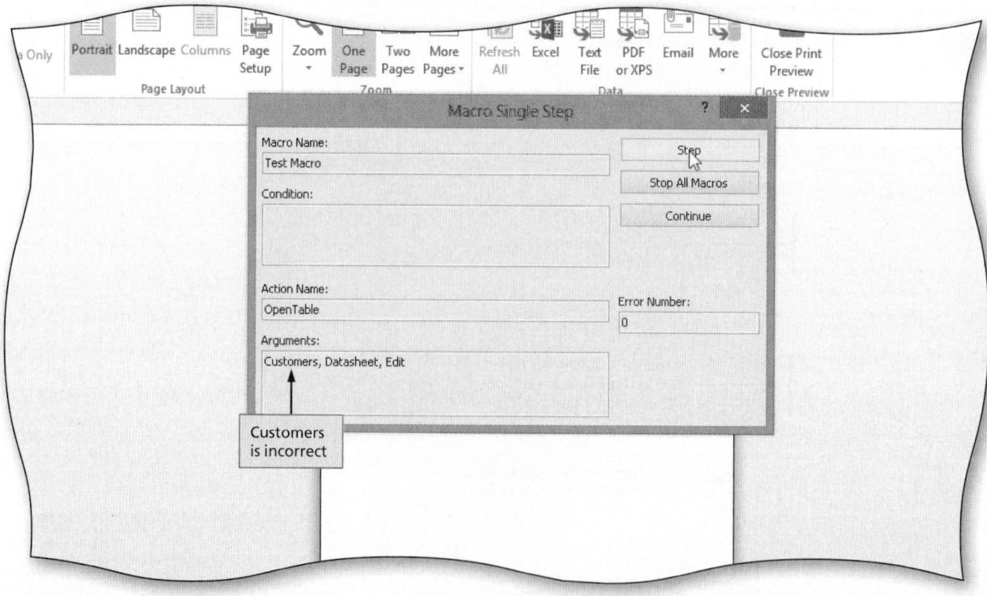

Figure 8–14

If you instead tap or click the Step button, the misspelled name will cause the macro to abort. Access would display the appropriate error message in the Microsoft Access dialog box (Figure 8–15). This error indicates that Access could not find the object named Customers. Armed with this knowledge, you can tap or click the OK button, stop the macro, and then make the necessary change.

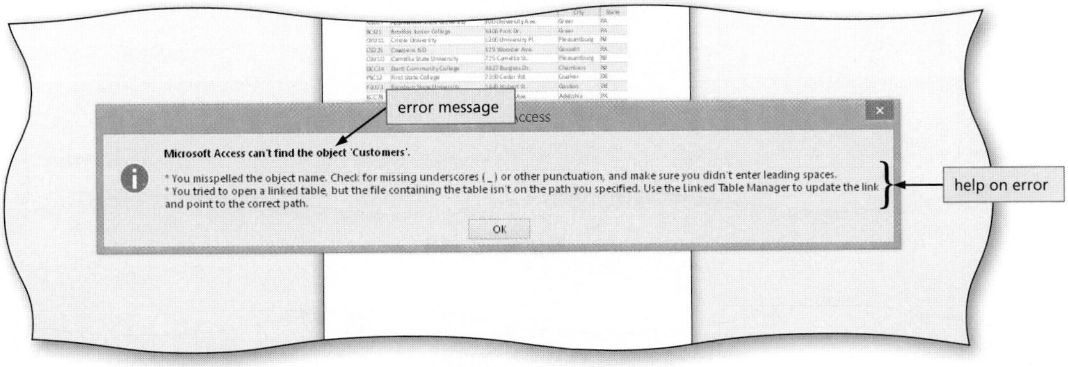

Figure 8–15

You do not need to step through a macro to discover the error. You can simply run the macro, either by tapping or clicking the Run button (MACRO TOOLS DESIGN tab | Tools group) with the macro open, or by pressing and holding or right-clicking the macro in the Navigation Pane and tapping or clicking Run. In either case, Access will run the macro until it encounters the error. When it does, it will display the same message shown in Figure 8–15. Just as with stepping through the macro, you would tap or click the OK button, stop the macro, and then make the necessary change.

Break Point: If you wish to stop working through the chapter at this point, you can resume the project later by starting Access, opening the database called Bavant Publishing, and continuing to follow the steps from this location forward.

Creating and Using a Navigation Form

Figure 8–1a on page AC 475 showed a navigation form for Bavant Publishing. A **navigation form** is a form that contains a **navigation control**, a control that can display a variety of forms and reports. Like the form in Figure 8–1, navigation controls contain tabs. Tapping or clicking the tab displays the corresponding form or report. The tabs can be arranged across the top and/or down the sides.

You only can include forms and reports on the tabs; you cannot include either tables or queries. The navigation form in Figure 8–1, however, appears to have a tab corresponding to the Customer table. There is a technique you can use to make it appear as though the navigation form contains tables or queries. You create a datasheet form based on the table or query. Figure 8–1 actually shows a datasheet form based on the Customer table and does not show the Customer table itself.

Before creating the navigation form, you have some other forms to create. For example, you might want the users to be able to tap or click a tab in the navigation form and then choose from a list of forms or reports. Figure 8–16 on the next page shows a list of forms presented as buttons; the user would tap or click the button for the desired form. Tapping or clicking the Open Customer Master Form button, for example, would display the Customer View and Update Form as shown in Figure 8–17 on the next page.

BTW
Navigation Forms
A navigation form often is used as a switchboard or main page for a database to reduce clutter and target the most commonly used database objects. A navigation form contains a navigation control and a subform control. After you create a navigation form, you can use the Navigation Where Clause property associated with a navigation control to automatically apply a filter.

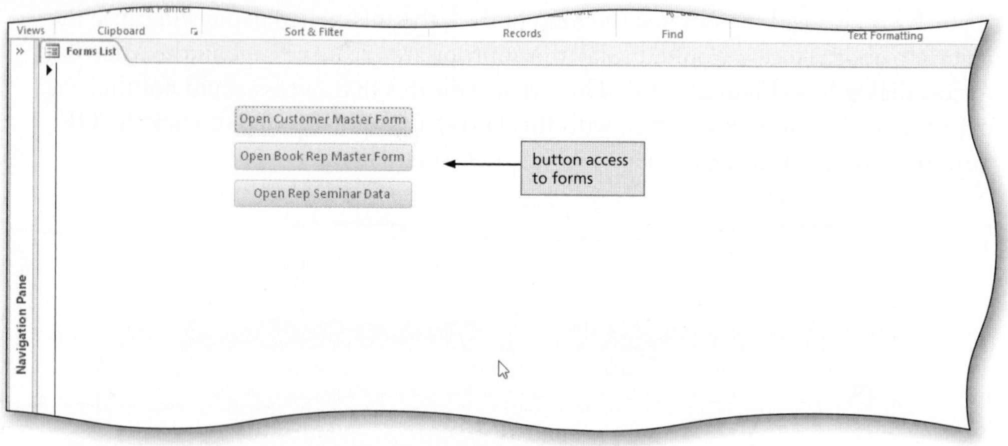

Figure 8–16

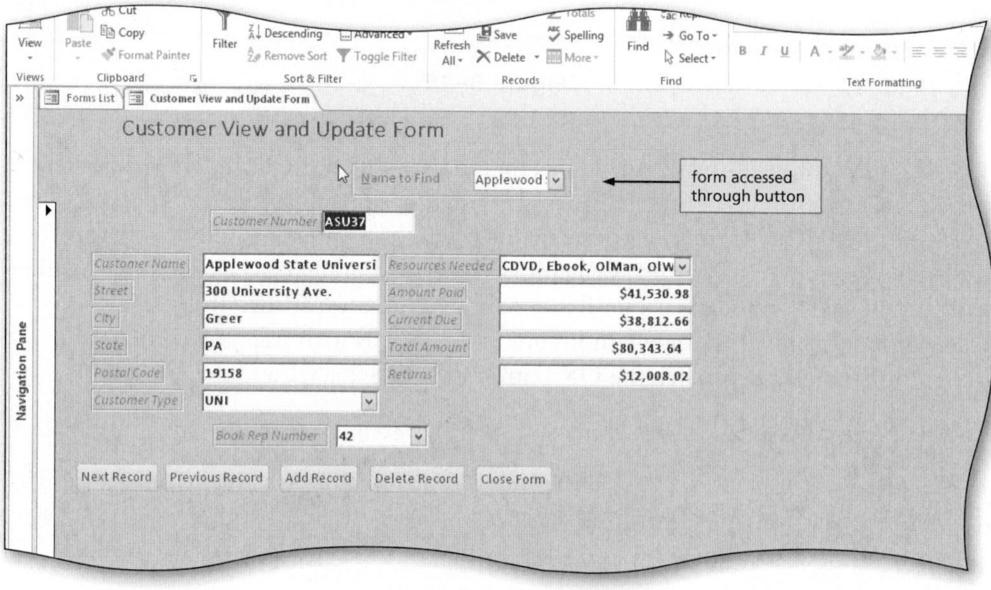

Figure 8–17

To implement options like these, you create blank forms and add either the command buttons or the option group. You then include the form you have created in the navigation form. When users tap or click the corresponding tab, Access displays the form and users can then tap or click the appropriate button.

To Create a Menu Form Containing Command Buttons

1 MACRO WITH SUBMACROS | 2 COMMAND BUTTONS | 3 OPTION GROUP | 4 MACRO FOR OPTION GROUP
5 DATASHEET FORMS | 6 USER INTERFACE MACROS | 7 NAVIGATION FORM | 8 DATA MACRO

Why? A menu form in which you make a selection by clicking the appropriate command button provides a convenient way to select a desired option. You can create a menu form by adding command buttons to the form, just as you added command buttons to the form in Chapter 7 on pages AC 428 through AC 430. The following steps use this technique to create a menu form with three buttons: Open Customer Master Form, Open Book Rep Master Form, and Open Rep Seminar Data. The actions assigned to each button will run a macro that causes the desired action to occur. For example, the action for the Open Customer Master Form button will run the Open Customer Master Form submacro, which in turn will open the Customer Master Form.

The following steps create a form in Design view and then add the necessary buttons.

1

- Display the CREATE tab.
- Tap or click the Form Design button (CREATE tab | Forms group) to create a blank form in Design view.
- If a field list appears, tap or click the 'Add Existing Fields' button (FORM DESIGN TOOLS DESIGN tab | Tools group) to remove the field list.
- If a property sheet appears, tap or click the Property Sheet button (FORM DESIGN TOOLS DESIGN tab | Tools group) to remove the property sheet (Figure 8–18).

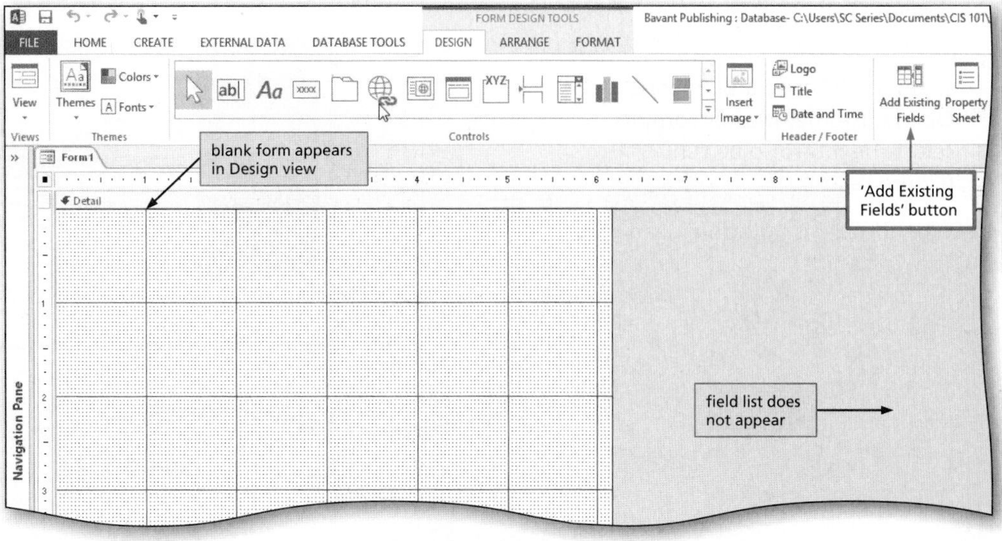

Figure 8–18

2

- Make sure the 'Use Control Wizards' button is selected.
- Tap or click the Button tool (FORM DESIGN TOOLS DESIGN tab | Controls group) and move the pointer to the approximate position shown in Figure 8–19.

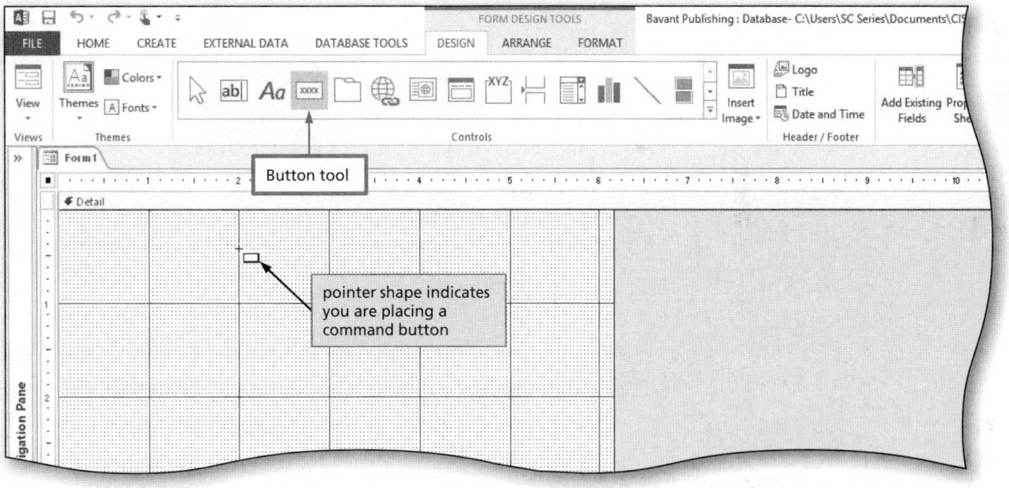

Figure 8–19

3

- Tap or click the position shown in Figure 8–19 to display the Command Button Wizard dialog box.
- Tap or click Miscellaneous in the Categories box, and then tap or click Run Macro in the Actions box (Figure 8–20).

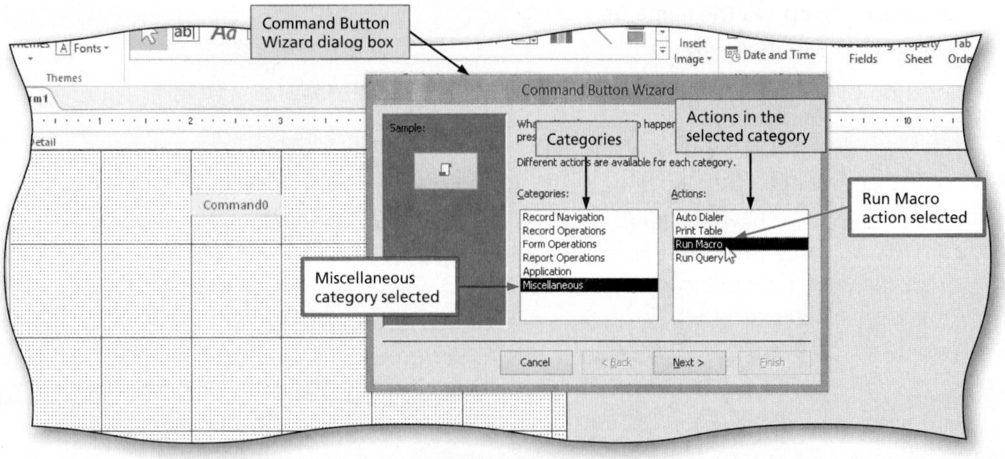

Figure 8–20

4

- Tap or click the Next button to display the next screen in the wizard.
- Tap or click Forms and Reports. Open Customer Master Form to select the macro to be run (Figure 8–21).

Q&A What does this notation mean?
The portion before the period is the macro and the portion after the period is the submacro. Thus, this notation means the Open Customer Master Form submacro within the Forms and Reports macro.

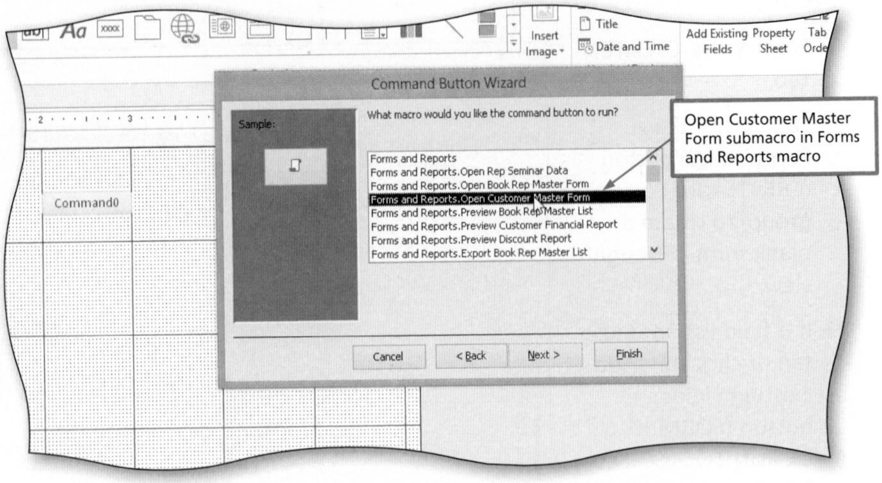

Figure 8–21

5

- Tap or click the Next button to display the next Command Button Wizard screen.
- Tap or click the Text option button.

Q&A What is the purpose of these option buttons?
Choose the first option button to place text on the button. You then can specify the text to be included or accept the default choice. Choose the second option button to place a picture on the button. You then can select a picture.

- If necessary, delete the default text and then type `Open Customer Master Form` as the text (Figure 8–22).

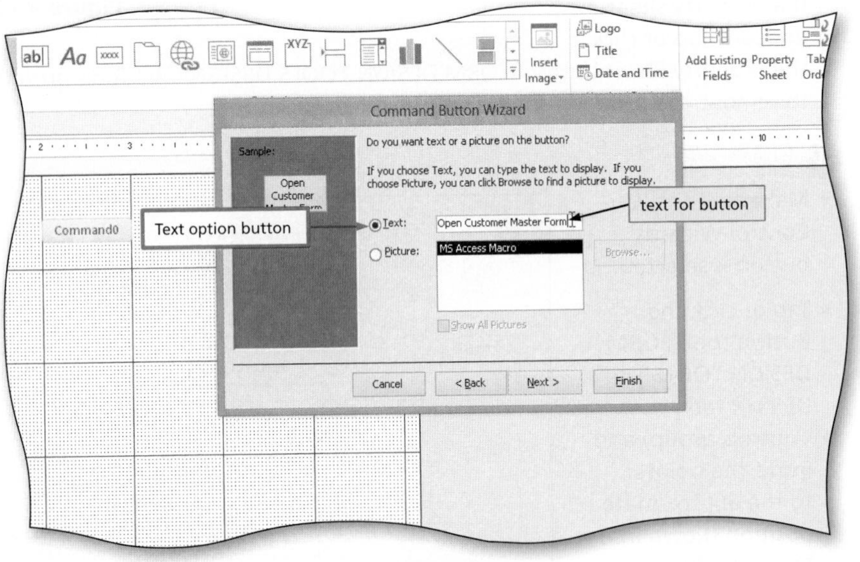

Figure 8–22

6

- Tap or click the Next button.
- Type `Open_Customer_Master_Form` as the name of the button (Figure 8–23).

Q&A Why do you include the underscores in the name of the button?
If you are working with macros or VBA, you cannot have spaces in names. One way to avoid spaces and still make readable names is to include underscores where you would normally have had spaces. Thus, Open Customer Master Form becomes Open_Customer_Master_Form.

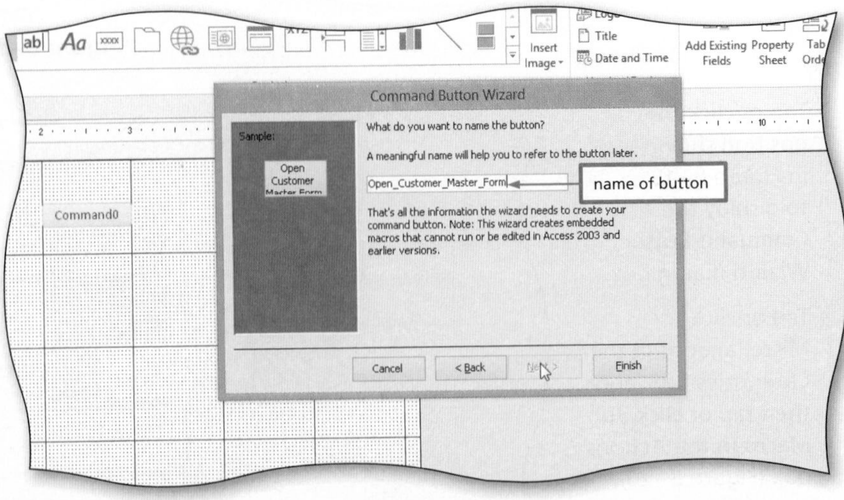

Figure 8–23

7

- Tap or click the Finish button to finish specifying the button.
- Use the techniques in Steps 2 through 6 to place the Open Book Rep Master Form button below the Open Customer Master Form button. The only difference is that the macro to be run is the Open Book Rep Master Form submacro, the text is Open Book Rep Master Form, and the name of the button is Open_Book_Rep_Master_Form.
- Use the techniques in Steps 2 through 6 to place the Open Rep Seminar Data button below the Open Book Rep Master Form button. The only difference is that the macro to be run is the Open Rep Seminar Data submacro, the text is Open Rep Seminar Data, and the name of the button is Open_Rep_Seminar_Data.

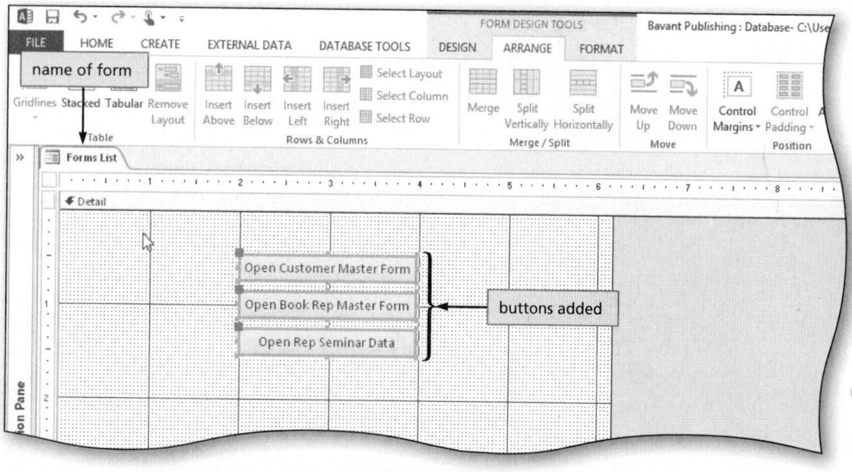

Figure 8–24

- Adjust the size and spacing of the buttons to approximately match those in Figure 8–24, using the ARRANGE tab, if necessary.
- Save the form using the name, Forms List.

Q&A How can I test the buttons to make sure the macros work?
Press and hold or right-click the Forms List form in the Navigation Pane and tap or click Open. Tap or click each of the buttons on the form. If there are errors in any of the macros, open the macro in the Macro Builder window and correct the errors.

Experiment

- Test each of the buttons on the form. Ensure that the correct form opens. If there are errors, correct the corresponding macro.

8

- Close the form.

Option Groups

You might find it useful to allow users to make a selection from some predefined options by including an option group. An **option group** is a rectangle containing a collection of option buttons. To select an option, you simply tap or click the corresponding option button. Figure 8–25 on the next page shows a list of reports presented in an option group where the user would tap or click the desired option button. Notice that the user could tap or click an option button to preview a report. The user could tap or click a different option button to export the report as a PDF file. Tapping or clicking the Preview Book Rep Master List option button, for example, would display a preview of the Book Rep Master List (Figure 8–26 on the next page). Tapping or clicking the Close Print Preview button would return you to the option group.

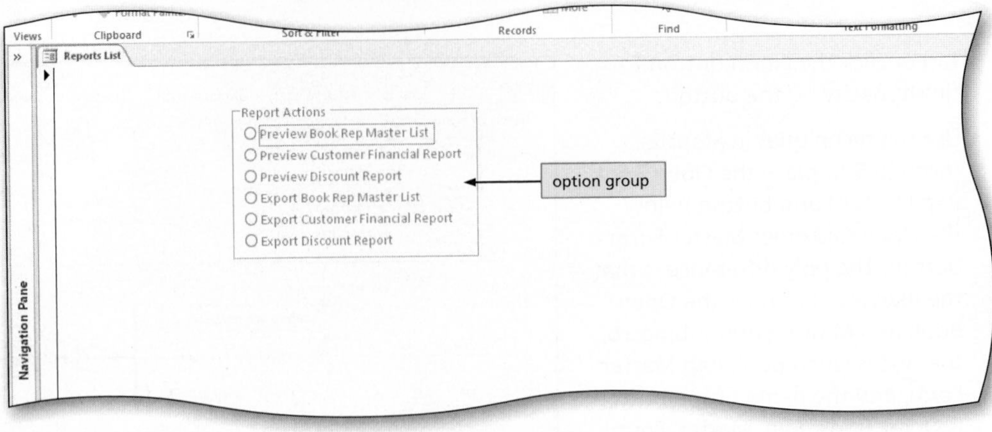

Figure 8–25

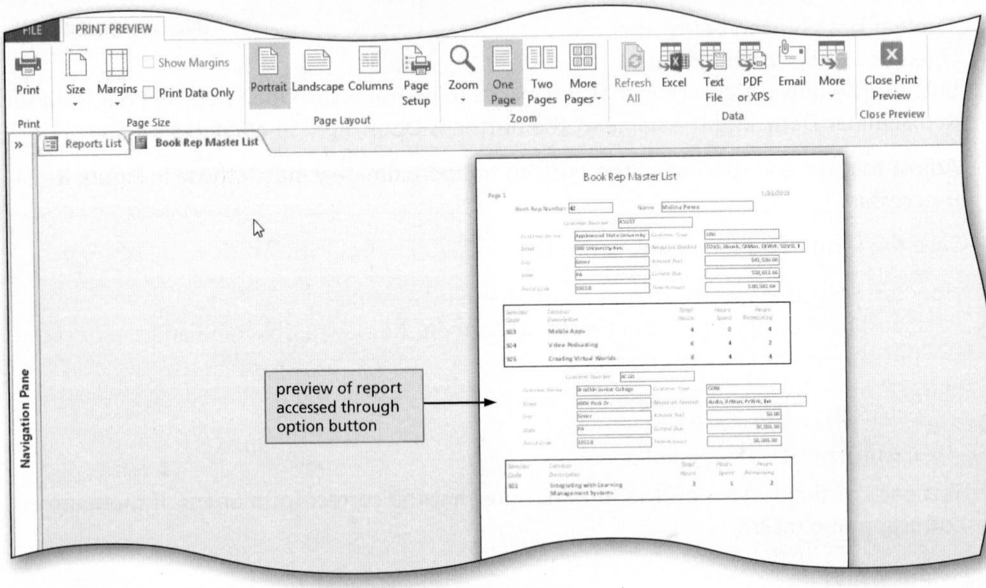

Figure 8–26

To Create a Menu Form Containing an Option Group

1 MACRO WITH SUBMACROS | 2 COMMAND BUTTONS | 3 OPTION GROUP | **4 MACRO FOR OPTION GROUP**
5 DATASHEET FORMS | 6 USER INTERFACE MACROS | 7 NAVIGATION FORM | 8 DATA MACRO

The form you are creating will contain an option group called Form Options. ***Why?*** *The option group allows users to select an option button to indicate either a report to preview or a report to export.*

The following steps use the Option Group tool to create the Form Options option group.

1

- Display the CREATE tab.
- Tap or click the Form Design button (CREATE tab | Forms group) to create a blank form in Design view.
- If a field list appears, tap or click the 'Add Existing Fields' button (FORM DESIGN TOOLS DESIGN tab | Tools group) to remove the field list (Figure 8–27).

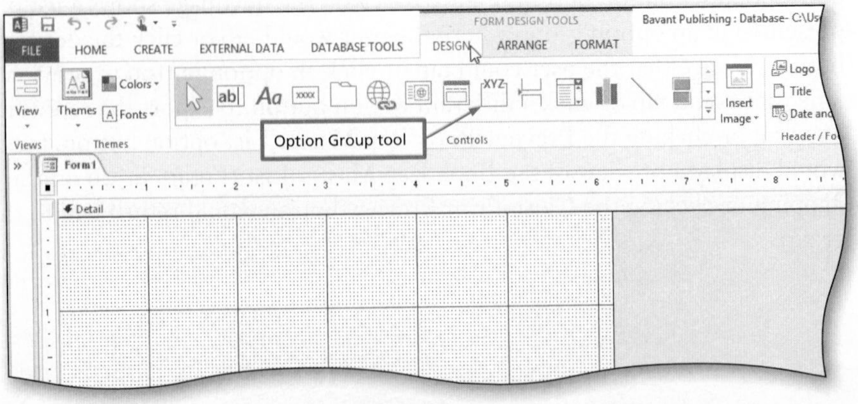

Figure 8–27

2

- Tap or click the Option Group tool (FORM DESIGN TOOLS DESIGN tab | Controls group) and then move the pointer to the approximate position shown in Figure 8–28.

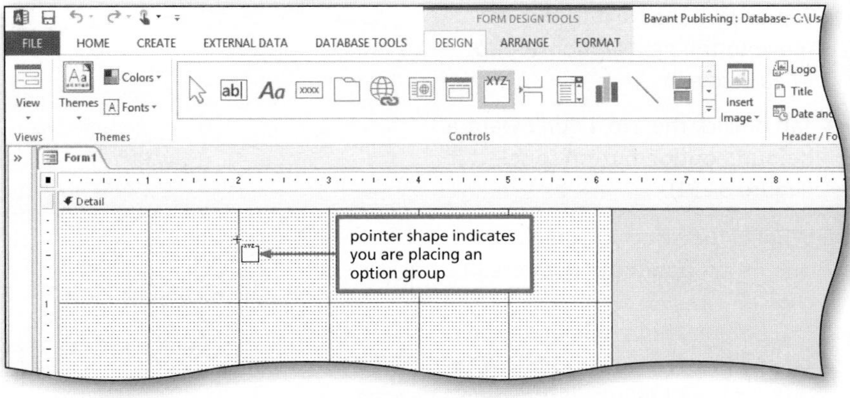

Figure 8–28

3

- Tap or click the position shown in Figure 8–28 to place an option group and start the Option Group Wizard (Figure 8–29).

Q&A The Option Group Wizard did not start for me. What should I do?

You must not have had the 'Use Control Wizards' button selected. With the option group selected, press the DELETE key to delete the option group. Select the 'Use Control Wizards' button, and then add the option group a second time.

- Type **`Preview Book Rep Master List`** in the first row of label names and press the DOWN ARROW key.
- Type **`Preview Customer Financial Report`** in the second row of label names and press the DOWN ARROW key.
- Type **`Preview Discount Report`** in the third row of label names and press the DOWN ARROW key.
- Type **`Export Book Rep Master List`** in the fourth row of label names and press the DOWN ARROW key.
- Type **`Export Customer Financial Report`** in the fifth row of label names and press the DOWN ARROW key.
- Type **`Export Discount Report`** in the sixth row of label names (Figure 8–30).

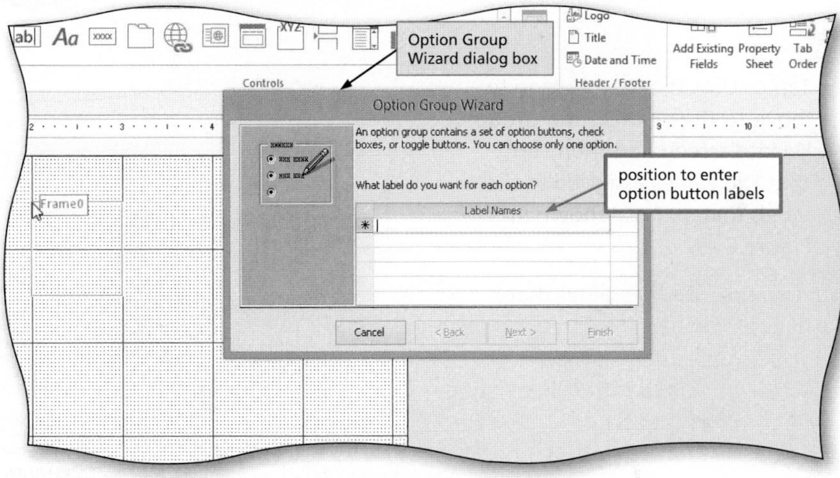

Figure 8–29

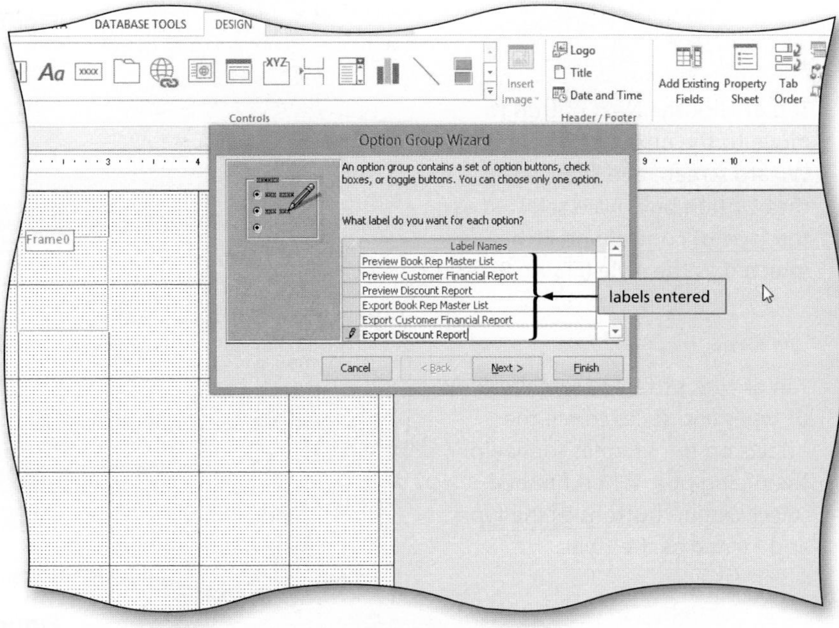

Figure 8–30

4

- Tap or click the Next button to move to the next Option Group Wizard screen.
- Tap or click the 'No, I don't want a default.' option button to select it (Figure 8–31).

Q&A What is the effect of specifying one of the options as the default choice?

The default choice will initially be selected when you open the form. If there is no default choice, no option will be selected.

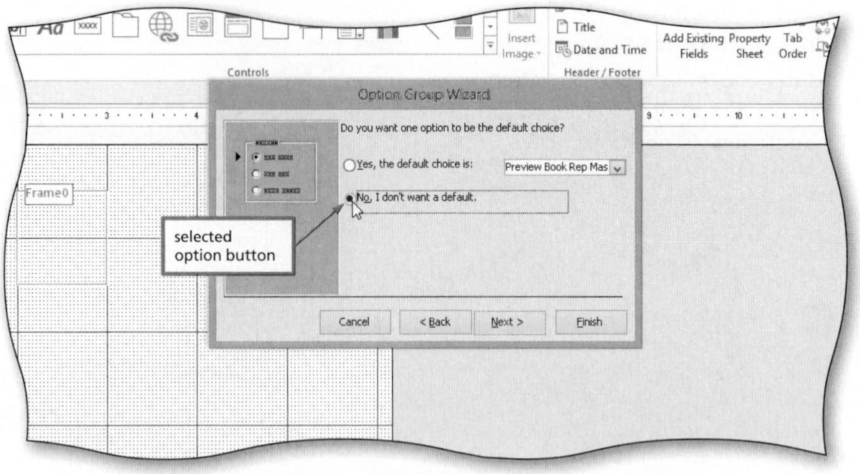

Figure 8–31

5

- Tap or click the Next button to move to the next Option Group Wizard screen and then verify that the values assigned to the labels match those shown in Figure 8–32.

Q&A How do I use the values that I have assigned?

You can use them in macros or VBA. You will use them in a macro later in this chapter.

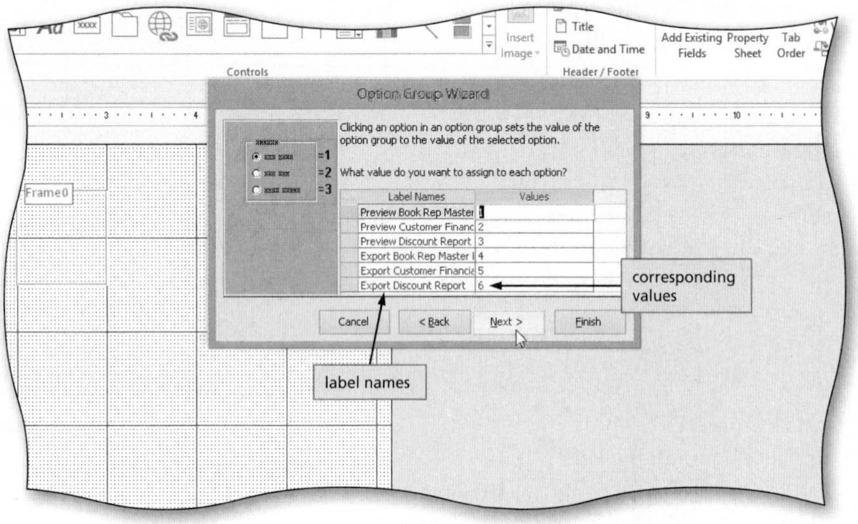

Figure 8–32

6

- Tap or click the Next button to move to the next Option Group Wizard screen, and then ensure that Option buttons is selected as the type of control and Etched is selected as the style (Figure 8–33).

Experiment

- Tap or click different combinations of types and styles to see the effects on the samples shown in the dialog box. When finished, select Option buttons as the type and Etched as the style.

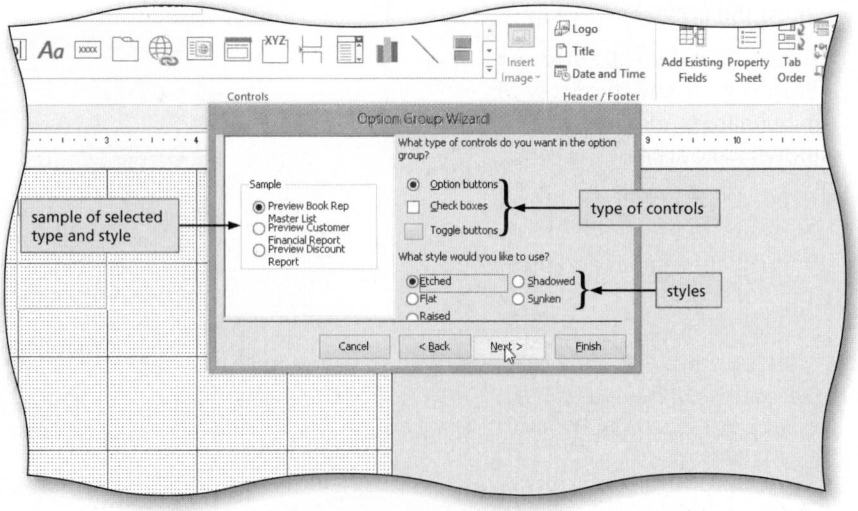

Figure 8–33

7

- Tap or click the Next button to move to the next Option Group Wizard screen and then type **`Report Actions`** as the caption.
- Tap or click the Finish button to complete the addition of the option group (Figure 8–34).

8

- Save the form using the name, Reports List.

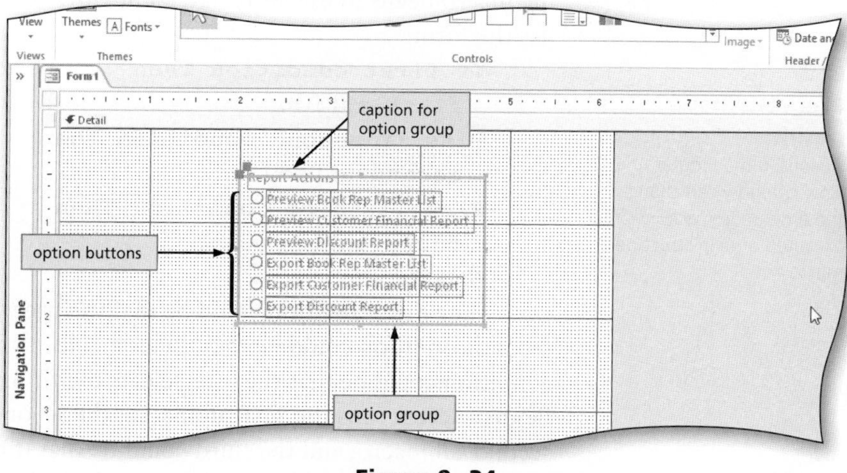

Figure 8–34

Using an If Statement

You will create a macro that will take appropriate action when the user updates the option group, that is, when the user taps or clicks an option button in the group. The macro will run the appropriate submacro, depending on which option the user has selected.

Because the specific actions that the macro will perform depend on the option button the user selects, the macro will contain conditions. The conditions will determine which action should be taken. If the user selects the first option button, Access should run the Preview Book Rep Master List submacro. If, on the other hand, the user selects the second option button, Access should instead run the Preview Customer Financial Report submacro. For each of the six possible option buttons a user can select, Access should run a different submacro.

To instruct Access to perform different actions based on certain conditions, the macro will contain an If statement. The simplest form of an If statement is:

```
If condition Then
  action
End If
```

If the condition is true, Access will take the indicated action. If the condition is false, no action will be taken. For example, the condition could be that the user selects the first option button, and the action could be to run the Book Rep Master List submacro. No action would be taken if the user selects any other button.

Another form of the If statement contains an Else clause. This form is:

```
If condition Then
  first action
Else
  second action
End If
```

If the condition is true, the first action is taken; if the condition is false, the second action is taken. For example, the condition could be that the user selects option button 1; the first action could be to run the Preview Book Rep Master List submacro, and the second action could be to run the Preview Customer Financial Report submacro. If the user selects option button 1, Access would run the Preview Book Rep Master list submacro. If the user selects any other option button, Access would run the

Preview Customer Financial Report submacro. Because there are six option buttons, the macro needs to use an If statement with multiple Else Ifs. This type of If statement has the form:

```
If first condition Then
  first action
Else If second condition Then
  second action
Else If third condition Then
  third action
End If
```

The first condition could be that the user selects the first option button; the second condition could be that the user selects the second option button; and the third condition could be that the user selects the third option button. The first action could be that Access runs the first submacro; the second action could be that it runs the second submacro; and the third could be that it runs the third submacro. This would work, except that in this case there are six option buttons and six submacros. For six conditions, as required in this macro, the If statement will contain five Else Ifs. The If statement along with the five Else Ifs will collectively contain six conditions: one to test if the user selected option 1, one for option 2, one for option 3, one for option 4, one for option 5, and one for option 6.

BTW
Program Flow Actions
Actions in the Program Flow category can change the order macro actions are executed or help structure a macro.

To Create a Macro with a Variable for the Option Group

1 MACRO WITH SUBMACROS | 2 COMMAND BUTTONS | 3 OPTION GROUP | 4 MACRO FOR OPTION GROUP
5 DATASHEET FORMS | 6 USER INTERFACE MACROS | 7 NAVIGATION FORM | 8 DATA MACRO

The following steps begin creating the macro and add an action to set a variable to the desired value. ***Why?*** *The expression that contains the option number is [Forms]![Customer Master Form]![Form_Options]. Because this expression is fairly lengthy, the macro will begin by setting a temporary variable to this expression.* A **variable** is a named location in computer memory. You can use a variable to store a value that you can use later in the macro. You will assign the name Optno (short for option number) as the variable name for the expression. This location can contain a value, in this case, the option number on the form. In each of the conditions, you can then use Optno rather than the full expression.

1

- With the option group selected, display a property sheet.
- If necessary, tap or click the All tab.
- Change the name of the option group to Form_Options (Figure 8–35).

Q&A Why this name?
The name Form_Options reflects the fact that these are options that control the action that will be taken on this form. The underscore keeps the name from containing a space.

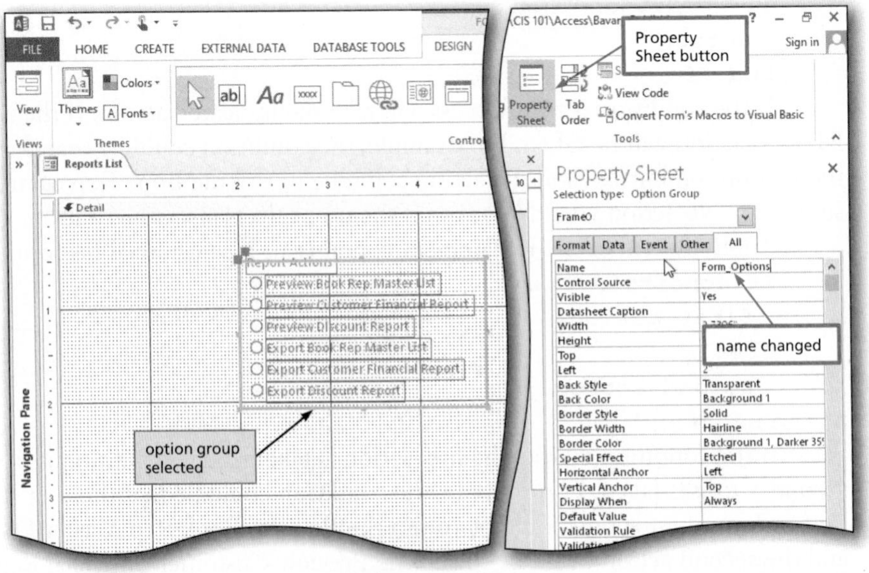

Figure 8–35

2

- Tap or click the After Update property.
- Tap or click the Build button to display the Choose Builder dialog box (Figure 8–36).

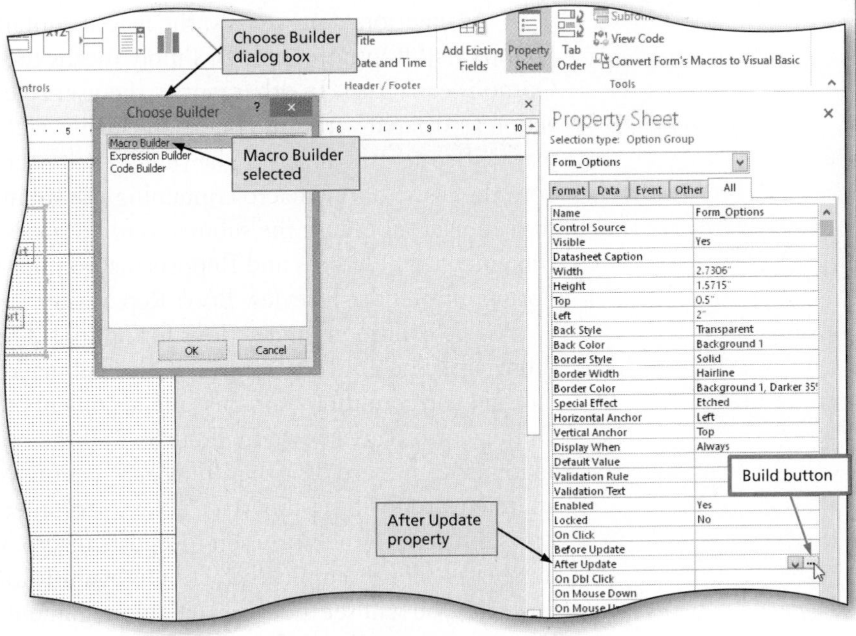

Figure 8–36

3

- With Macro Builder selected in the Choose Builder dialog box, tap or click the OK button to create a macro.
- If necessary, tap or click the Action Catalog button (MACRO TOOLS DESIGN tab | Show/Hide group) to display the Action Catalog.
- If necessary, collapse the Data Import/Export category.
- Expand the Macro Commands action category.
- Double-tap or double-click the SetTempVar action in the Action Catalog to add the SetTempVar action to the macro.
- Enter `Optno` as the value for the Name argument.
- Enter `[Form_Options]` as the value for the Expression argument (Figure 8–37).

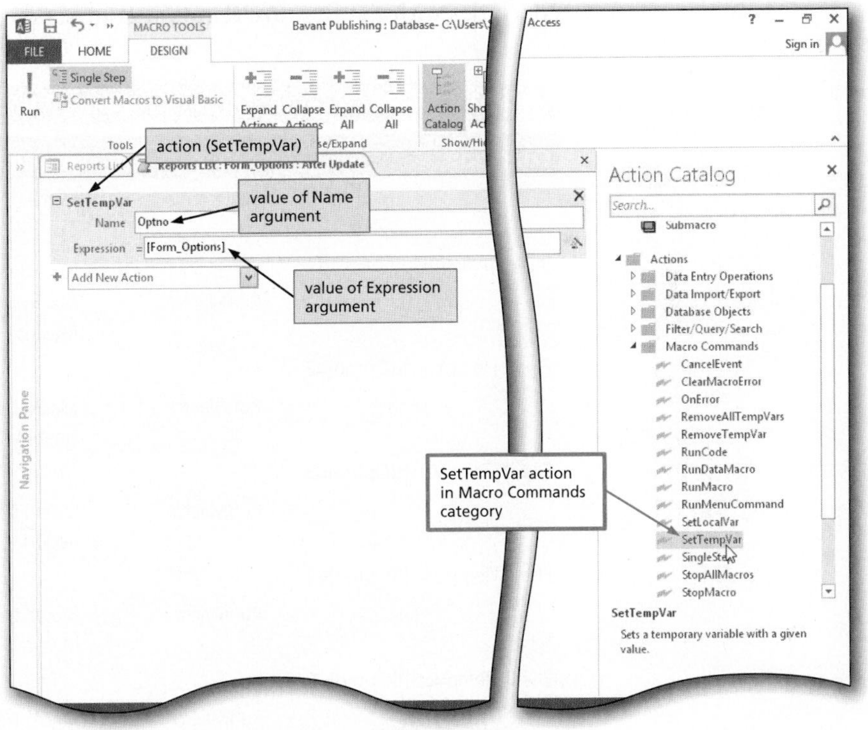

Figure 8–37

How can Access make it easier to enter values for arguments?

Access helps you in three ways. First, if you point to the argument, Access will display a description of the argument. Second, many arguments feature a drop-down list, where you can display the list and then select the desired value. Finally, if you begin typing an expression, a feature called IntelliSense will suggest possible values that start with the letters you have already typed and that are appropriate in the context of what you are typing. If you see the value you want in the list, you can simply tap or click it to select the value.

CONSIDER THIS

Macro for Option Group

As mentioned previously, the macro contains six conditions. The first is [TempVars]! [Optno]=1, which simply means the value in the temporary variable Optno is equal to 1. In other words, the user selected the first option button. The action associated with this condition is RunMacro. The argument is the name of the macro. Because the macro to be run is a submacro, the name of the macro includes both the name of the macro containing the submacro, a period, and then the name of the submacro. Because the submacro to be run is Preview Book Rep Master List and is contained in the Forms and Reports macro, the value of the Macro Name argument is Forms and Reports.Preview Book Rep Master List.

The conditions and actions for options 2 through 6 are similar to the first submacro. The only difference is which submacro is associated with each option button. The conditions, actions, and arguments that you will change for the Form_Options macro are shown in Table 8–2. If the option number is 1, for example, the action is RunMacro. For the RunMacro action, you will change the Macro Name argument. You will set the Macro Name argument to the Preview Book Rep Master List submacro in the Forms and Reports macro. On the other hand, if the option number is 2, for example, the action is again RunMacro. If the option number is 2, however, you will set the Macro Name argument to the Preview Customer Financial Report submacro in the Forms and Reports macro. Similar actions take place for the other possible values for the Optno variable, that is, for option buttons 3-6. Because the temporary variable, Optno, is no longer needed at the end of the macro, the macro concludes with the RemoveTempVar command to remove this variable.

Table 8–2 Macro for After Update Property of the Option Group

Condition	Action	Arguments to be Changed
	SetTempVar	Name: Optno Expression: [Form_Options]
If [TempVars]![Optno]=1		
	RunMacro	Macro Name: Forms and Reports.Preview Book Rep Master List
Else If [TempVars]![Optno]=2		
	RunMacro	Macro Name: Forms and Reports.Preview Customer Financial Report
Else If [TempVars]![Optno]=3		
	RunMacro	Macro Name: Forms and Reports.Preview Discount Report
Else If [TempVars]![Optno]=4		
	RunMacro	Macro Name: Forms and Reports.Export Book Rep Master List
Else If [TempVars]![Optno]=5		
	RunMacro	Macro Name: Forms and Reports.Export Customer Financial Report
Else If [TempVars]![Optno]=6		
	RunMacro	Macro Name: Forms and Reports.Export Discount Report
End If		
	RemoveTempVar	Name: Optno

To Add Actions to the Form Options Macro

The following steps add the conditions and actions to the Form_Options macro. ***Why?*** *The macro is not yet complete. Adding the conditions and actions will complete the macro.*

1

- Double-tap or double-click the If element from the Program Flow section of the Action Catalog to add an If statement to the submacro and then type **[TempVars]![Optno]=1** as the condition in the If statement.
- With the Macro Commands category expanded, double-tap or double-click RunMacro to add the RunMacro action.
- Tap or click the drop-down arrow for the Macro Name argument and select the Preview Book Rep Master List submacro within the Forms and Reports macro as the value for the argument (Figure 8–38).

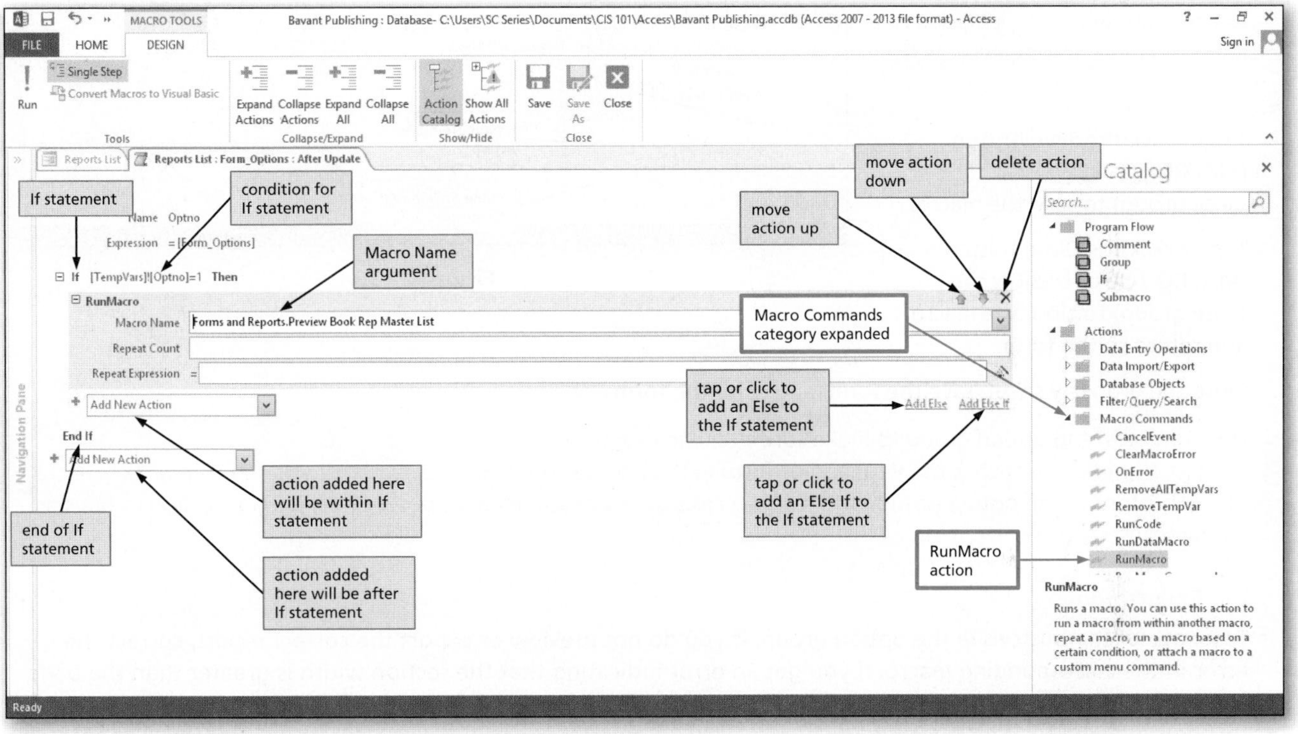

Figure 8–38

Q&A What should I do if I add an action in the wrong position? What should I do if I add the wrong action?
If you add an action in the wrong position, use the Move Up or Move Down buttons to move it to the correct position. If you added the wrong action, tap or click the Delete button to delete the action, and then fix the error by adding the correct action.

2

- Tap or click Add Else If to add an Else If clause to the If statement.
- Add the conditions and actions associated with options 2, 3, 4, 5, and 6 as described in Table 8–2, and specify the arguments for the actions. Tap or click Add Else If after adding each action except for the last one.

Q&A Do I have to enter all these actions? They seem to be very similar to the ones associated with option 1.
You can copy and paste the action for option 1. Press and hold or right-click the action to select it and display a shortcut menu. Tap or click Copy on the shortcut menu. Press and hold or right-click the action just above where you want to insert the selected action and then tap or click Paste. If the new action is not inserted in the correct position, select the new action and then tap or click either the Move Up or Move Down buttons to move it to the correct location. Once the action is in the correct location, you can make any necessary changes to the arguments.

- Add the RemoveTempVar action and argument after the end of the If statement, as shown in Figure 8–39.
- Enter **Optno** as the name of the TempVar to remove.

Q&A Do I need to remove the temporary variable?
Technically, no. In fact, if you plan to use this temporary variable in another macro and want it to retain the value you assigned in this macro, you would definitely not remove it. If you do not plan to use it elsewhere, it is a good idea to remove it, however.

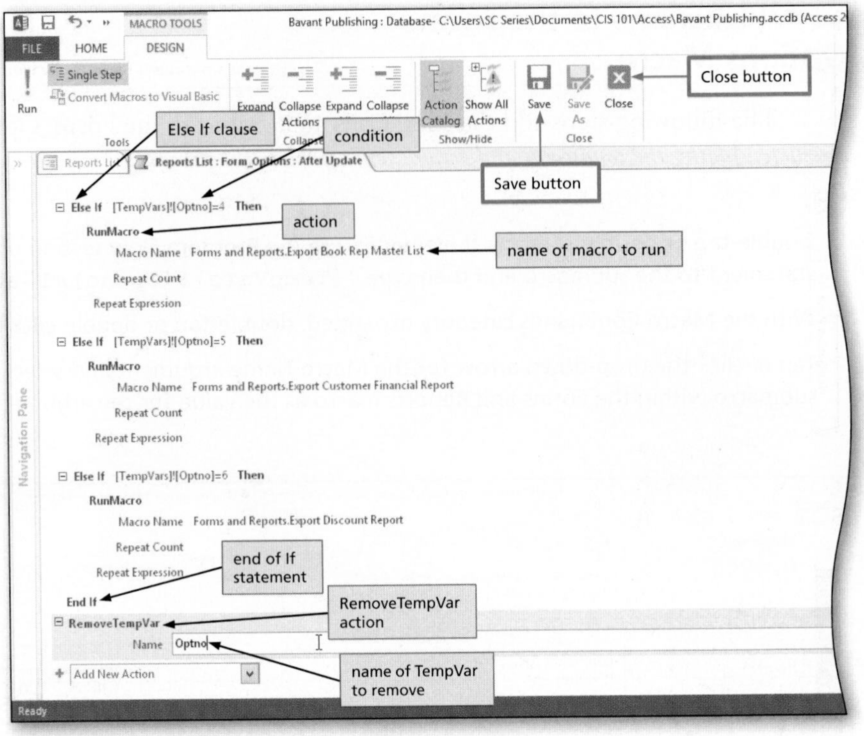

Figure 8–39

3

- Tap or click the Save button (MACRO TOOLS DESIGN tab | Close group) to save the macro.
- Tap or click the Close button (MACRO TOOLS DESIGN tab | Close group) to close the macro and return to the form.
- Close the property sheet, save the form, and close the form.

Q&A How can I test the option group to make sure the macros work?
Press and hold or right-click the Reports List form in the Navigation Pane and tap or click Open. Tap or click each of the buttons in the option group. If there are errors in any of the macros, open the macro in the Macro Builder window and correct the errors.

Experiment

- Test each of the buttons in the option group. If you do not preview or export the correct report, correct the error in the corresponding macro. If you get an error indicating that the section width is greater than the page width, you have an error in the corresponding report. Correct the error using the instructions on pages AC 485 through AC 487.

Break Point: If you wish to stop working through the chapter at this point, you can resume the project at a later time by starting Access, opening the database called Bavant Publishing, and continuing to follow the steps from this location forward.

User Interface (UI) Macros

A **user interface (UI) macro** is a macro that is attached to a user interface object, such as a command button, an option group, or a control on a form. The macro you just created for the option group is thus a UI macro, as were the macros you attached to command buttons. A common use for UI macros is to associate actions with the tapping or clicking of a control on a form. In the Customer form shown in Figure 8–40, for example, if you tap or click the customer number on the row in the datasheet where the customer number is CRU11, Access displays the data for that customer in a pop-up form (Figure 8–41), that is, a form that stays on top of other open objects, even when another object is active.

Figure 8–40

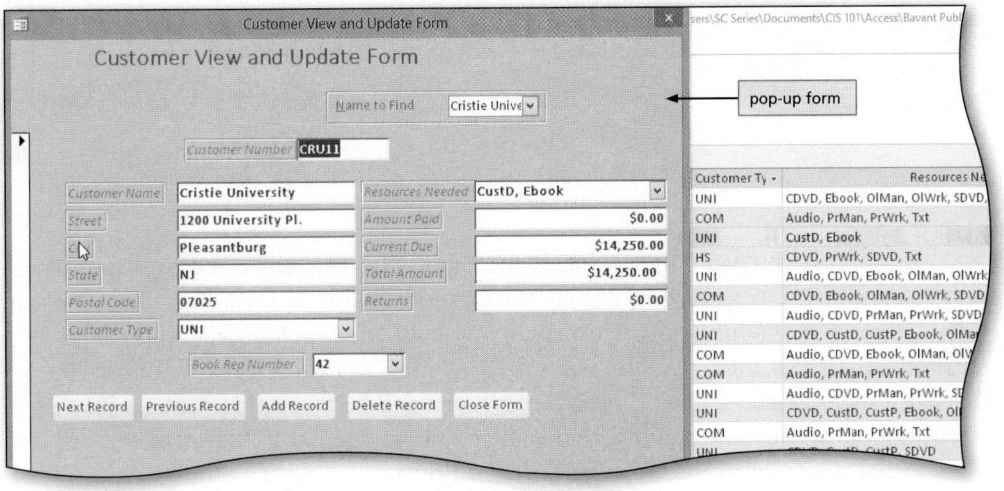

Figure 8–41

Similarly, in the Book Rep form shown in Figure 8–42, for example, if you tap or click the book rep number on the row in the datasheet where the book rep number is 65, Access displays the data for that book rep in a pop-up form (Figure 8–43 on the next page).

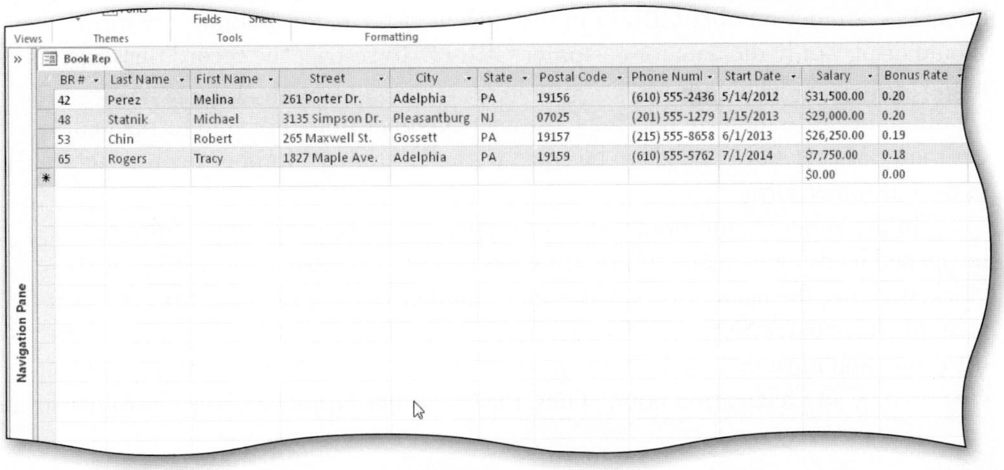

Figure 8–42

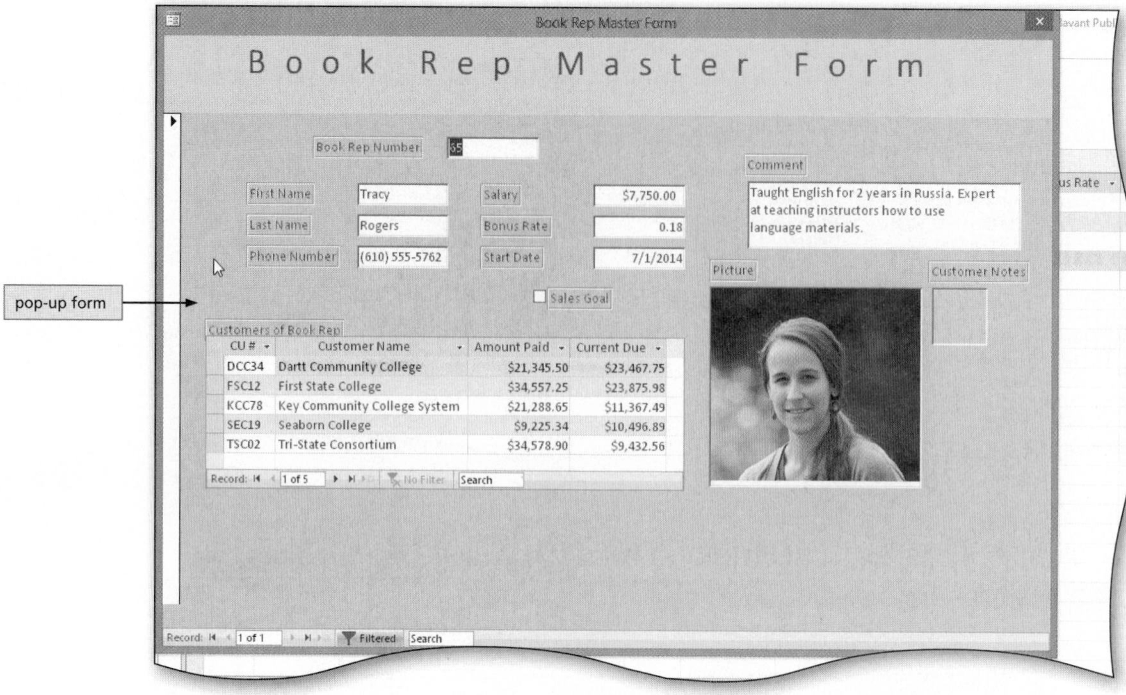

Figure 8–43

BTW
Distributing a Document
Instead of printing and distributing a hard copy of a document, you can distribute the document electronically. Options include sending the document by email; posting it on cloud storage (such as SkyDrive) and sharing the file with others; posting it on a social networking site, blog, or other website; and sharing a link associated with an online location of the document. You also can create and share a PDF or XPS image of the document, so that users can view the file in Acrobat Reader or XPS Viewer instead of in Access.

Recall that you can only use forms and reports for the tabs in a navigation form, yet the Customer tab appears to display the Customer table in Datasheet view. You can make it appear as though you are displaying the Customer table in Datasheet view by creating a datasheet form that you will call Customer. You will create a UI macro in this Customer datasheet form. The UI macro that will be associated with the tapping or clicking of the customer number on some record in the Customer form will display the selected customer in the Customer Master Form.

To display the Customer Master Form, the UI macro will use the OpenForm action. You must set the Form Name argument of the OpenForm action to the actual name of the form to be opened, Customer Master Form. (Customer View and Update Form is just the form caption.) Bavant wants to prevent the user from updating data using this form, so the Data Mode argument is set to Read Only. The form should appear as a pop-up, which you accomplish by setting the value of the Window Mode argument to Dialog.

The form should display only the record that the user selected. If the user taps or clicks customer number CRU11 in the Customer form, for example, the form should display only the data for customer CRU11. To restrict the record that appears in the form, you include the Where Condition argument in the UI macro. The condition needs to indicate that the Customer Number in the form to be opened, Customer Master Form, needs to be equal to the Customer Number the user selected in the Customer form.

In the Where Condition, you can simply refer to a control in the form to be opened by using its name. If the name has spaces, you must enclose it in square brackets. Thus, the name for the Customer Number in the Customer Master Form is simply [Customer Number]. To reference a control that is part of any other form, the expression must include both the name of the form and the name of the control, separated by an exclamation point. Thus, the Customer Number in the Customer form would be [Customer]![Customer Number]. This declaration works correctly when you are programming a macro that simply opens the Customer form. However, when you associate the Customer form with a tab in the navigation form, the Customer form becomes a subform, which requires modification to the expression. This means that a form that works correctly when you open the form may not work correctly when the form is assigned to a tab in a navigation form. A safer approach avoids these issues by using a temporary variable.

Table 8–3 shows the UI macro for the Customer form. It is associated with the On Click event for the Customer Number control. When a user taps or clicks a Customer Number, the UI macro will display the data for the selected customer in the Customer Master Form. The main function of the macro is to open the appropriate form using the OpenForm action.

Table 8–3 UI Macro Associated with On Tap or Click Event in the Customer Form

Condition	Action	Arguments to be Changed
	SetTempVar	Name: CN Expression: [Customer Number]
	OpenForm	Form Name: Customer Master Form Where Condition: [Customer Number]=[TempVars]![CN] Data Mode: Read Only Window Mode: Dialog
	RemoveTempVar	Name: CN

In the macro shown in Table 8–3, the first action, SetTempVar, assigns the temporary variable CN to the Customer Number. The two arguments are Name, which is set to CN, and Expression, which is set to [Customer Number]. The CN temporary variable refers to the Customer Number in the Customer form; recall that the completed macro will open the Customer form. You then can use that temporary variable in the Where Condition argument. The expression is thus [Customer Number]=[TempVars]![CN]. The [Customer Number] portion refers to the Customer Number in the Customer Master Form. The [TempVars]![CN] portion is the temporary variable that has been set equal to the Customer Number in the Customer form.

The macro ends by removing the temporary variable.

Table 8–4 shows the macro for the Book Rep form, which is very similar to the macro for the Customer form.

Table 8–4 UI Macro Associated with On Tap or Click Event in the Book Rep Form

Condition	Action	Arguments to be Changed
	SetTempVar	Name: BN Expression: [Book Rep Number]
	OpenForm	Form Name: Book Rep Master Form Where Condition: [Book Rep Number]=[TempVars]![BN] Data Mode: Read Only Window Mode: Dialog
	RemoveTempVar	Name: BN

To Create Datasheet Forms

1 MACRO WITH SUBMACROS | 2 COMMAND BUTTONS | 3 OPTION GROUP | 4 MACRO FOR OPTION GROUP
5 DATASHEET FORMS | 6 USER INTERFACE MACROS | 7 NAVIGATION FORM | 8 DATA MACRO

The following steps create two datasheet forms, one for the Customer table and one for the Book Rep table. ***Why?*** *The datasheet forms enable the Customer and Book Rep tables to appear to be displayed in Datasheet view, while satisfying the restriction that tables cannot be used on the tabs in a navigation form.*

1

- Open the Navigation Pane and select the Customer table.
- Display the CREATE tab and then tap or click the More Forms button (CREATE tab | Forms group) to display the More Forms gallery (Figure 8–44).

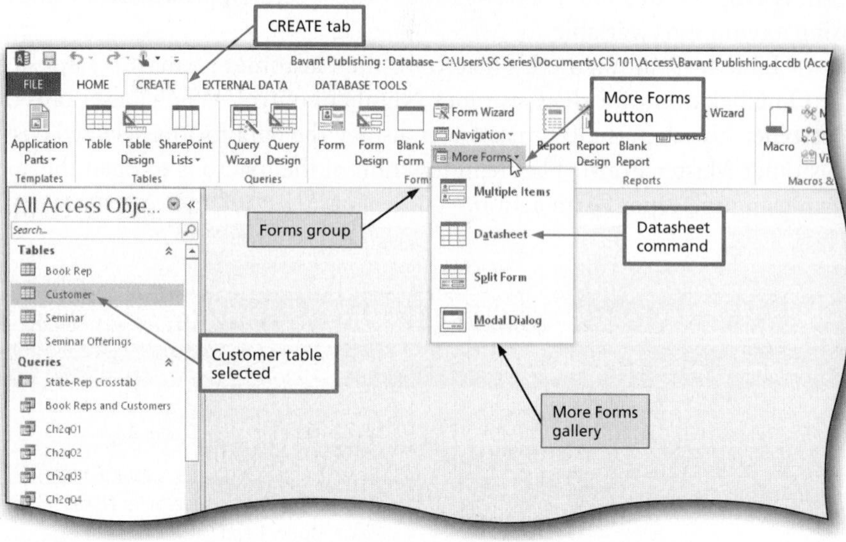

Figure 8–44

2

- Tap or click Datasheet to create a datasheet form.
- Save the form using the name, Customer.

Q&A Is it acceptable to use the same name for the form as for the table?
Yes. In this case, you want it to appear to the user that the Customer table is open in Datasheet view. One way to emphasize this fact is to use the same name as the table.

What is the difference between this form, Customer, and the form named Customer Form?
The Customer Form is a simple form that displays only one record at a time. The form you just created displays the data in a datasheet.

- Use the same technique to create a datasheet form named Book Rep for the Book Rep table.
- Close both forms.

To Create UI Macros for the Datasheet Forms

1 MACRO WITH SUBMACROS | 2 COMMAND BUTTONS | 3 OPTION GROUP | 4 MACRO FOR OPTION GROUP
5 DATASHEET FORMS | 6 USER INTERFACE MACROS | 7 NAVIGATION FORM | 8 DATA MACRO

The following steps create the UI macro for the Customer table shown in Table 8–3 on the previous page and the UI macro for the Book Rep table shown in Table 8–4 on the previous page. ***Why?*** *The UI macros will cause the appropriate pop-up forms to appear as a result of tapping or clicking the appropriate position on the forms.*

1

- Open the Customer form and then close the Navigation Pane.
- Tap or click the Customer Number (CU #) heading to select the Customer Number column in the datasheet.
- If necessary, tap or click the Property sheet button (FORM TOOLS DATASHEET tab | Tools group) to display a property sheet.
- Tap or click the Event tab to display only event properties.

Q&A Why tap or click the Event tab? Why not just use the All tab as we have before?
You can always use the All tab; however, if you know the category that contains the property in which you are interested, you can greatly reduce the number of properties that Access will display by tapping or clicking the tab for that category. That gives you fewer properties to search through to find the property you want. Whether you use the All tab or one of the other tabs is strictly a matter of personal preference.

- Tap or click the On Click event and then tap or click the Build button (the three dots) to display the Choose Builder dialog box (Figure 8–45).

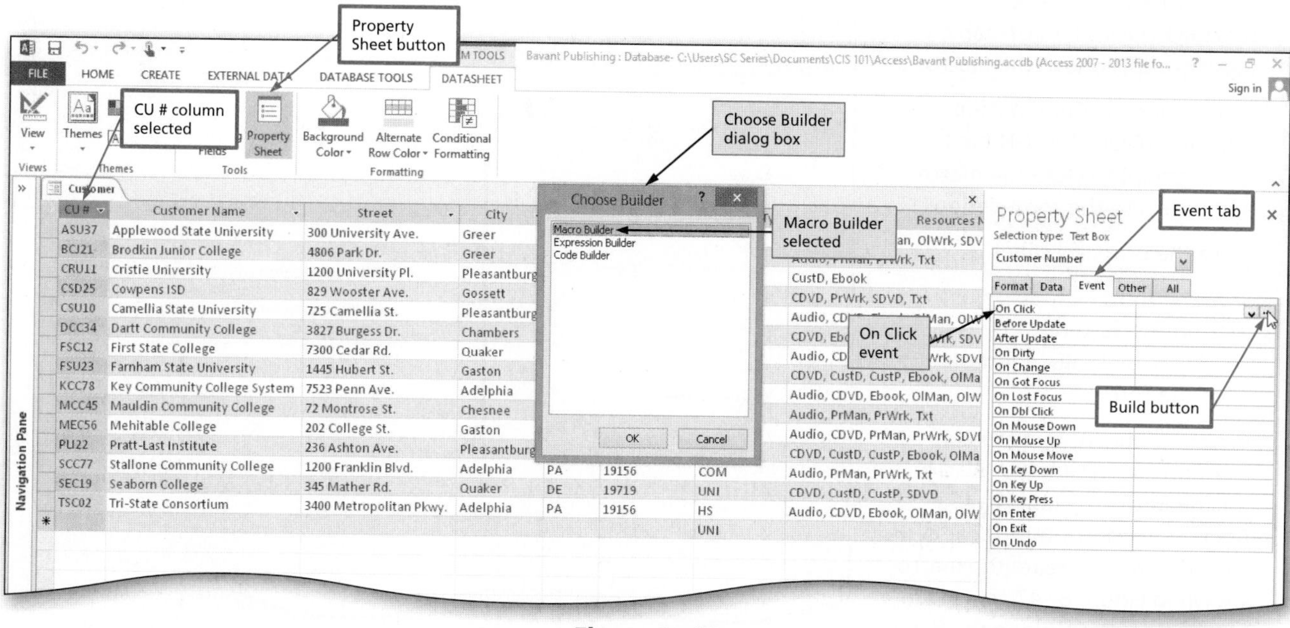

Figure 8–45

2

- Tap or click the OK button (Choose Builder dialog box) to display the Macro Builder window.
- Add the SetTempVar action to the macro, enter **CN** as the value for the Name argument, and enter **[Customer Number]** as the value for the Expression argument.
- Add the OpenForm action to the macro, select Customer Master Form as the value for the Form Name argument, leave the value of the View argument set to Form, enter **[Customer Number]=[TempVars]![CN]** as the value for the Where Condition argument, select Read Only as the value for the Data Mode argument, and select Dialog as the value for the Window Mode argument.

Q&A What does this expression mean?
The portion before the equal sign, [Customer Number], refers to the Customer Number in the form just opened, that is, in the Customer Master Form. The portion to the right of the equal sign, [TempVars]![CN], is the temporary variable that was set equal to the Customer Number on the selected record in the Customer form. This Where Condition guarantees that the record displayed in the Customer Master Form will be the record with the same Customer Number as the one selected in the Customer form.

- Add the RemoveTempVar action to the macro and enter **CN** as the value for the Name argument (Figure 8–46).

Q&A Why do you need to remove the temporary variable?
Technically, you do not. It has fulfilled its function, however, so it makes sense to remove it at this point.

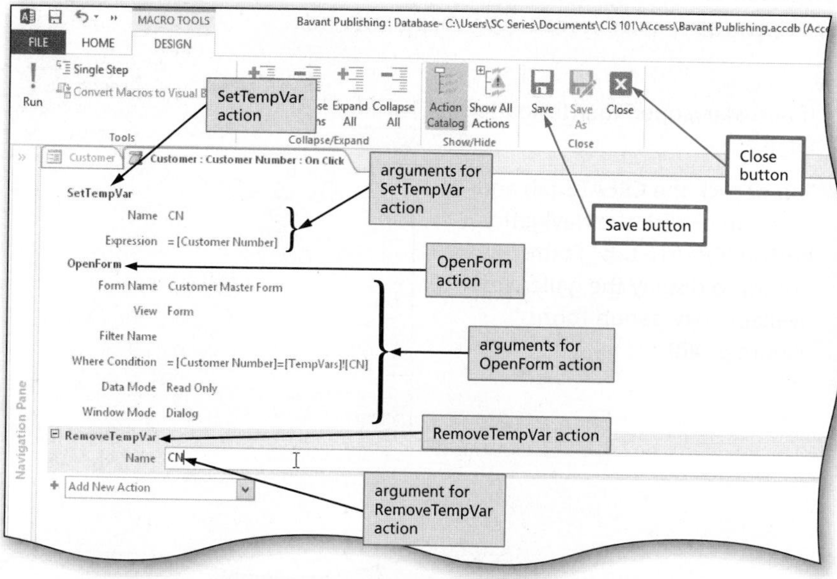

Figure 8–46

3

- Tap or click the Save button (MACRO TOOLS DESIGN tab | Close group) to save the macro.
- Tap or click the Close button (MACRO TOOLS DESIGN tab | Close group) to close the macro and return to the form design.
- Close the property sheet.
- Save the form by tapping or clicking the Save button on the Quick Access Toolbar and then close the form.
- Use the techniques in Steps 1 through 3 to create a UI macro for the Book Rep table called Book Rep, referring to Table 8–4 for the actions. Create the macro shown in Figure 8–47 associated with tapping or clicking the Book Rep Number (BR #) column.

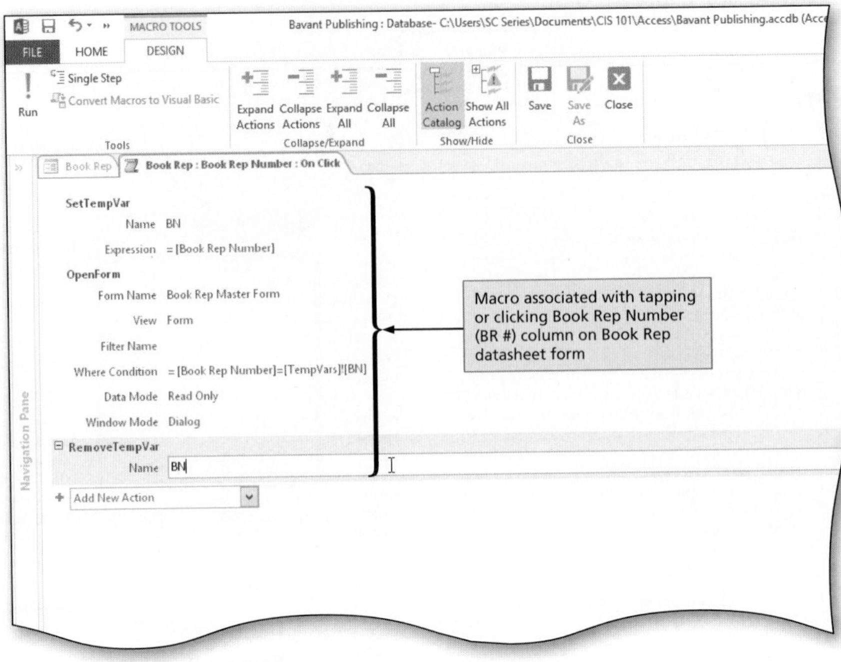

Figure 8–47

4

- Tap or click the Save button (MACRO TOOLS DESIGN tab | Close group) to save the macro.
- Tap or click the Close button (MACRO TOOLS DESIGN tab | Close group) to close the macro and return to the datasheet form.
- Close the property sheet.
- Save the form by tapping or clicking the Save button on the Quick Access Toolbar and then close the form.

To Create a Navigation Form

1 MACRO WITH SUBMACROS | 2 COMMAND BUTTONS | 3 OPTION GROUP | 4 MACRO FOR OPTION GROUP
5 DATASHEET FORMS | 6 USER INTERFACE MACROS | 7 NAVIGATION FORM | **8 DATA MACRO**

You now have all the forms you need to include in the navigation form. The following steps create the navigation form using horizontal tabs. ***Why?*** *Horizontal tabs are common on navigation forms and are easy to use.* The steps then save the form and change the title.

1

- If necessary, open the Navigation Pane.
- Tap or click the CREATE tab and then tap or click the Navigation button (CREATE tab | Forms group) to display the gallery of available navigation forms (Figure 8–48).

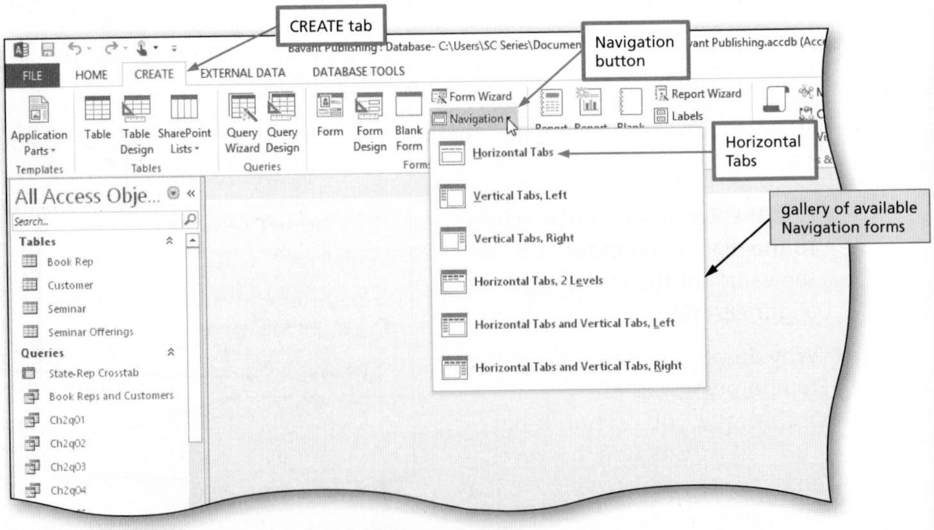

Figure 8–48

2

- Tap or click Horizontal Tabs in the gallery to create a form with a navigation control in which the tabs are arranged horizontally in a single row.
- If a field list appears, tap or click the 'Add Existing Fields' button (FORM LAYOUT TOOLS DESIGN tab | Tools group) to remove the field list (Figure 8–49).

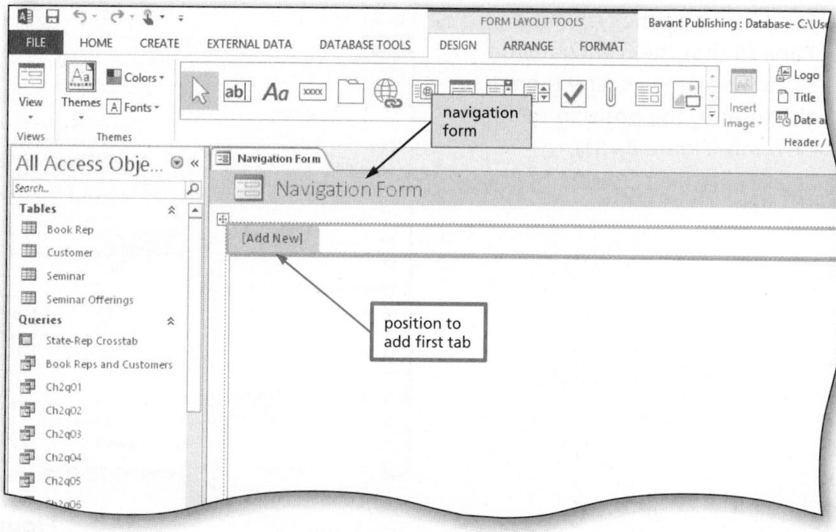

Figure 8–49

3

- Save the form using the name, Main Menu.
- Tap or click the form title twice: once to select it and the second time to produce an insertion point.
- Erase the current title and then type **`Bavant Publishing`** as the new title (Figure 8–50).

4

- Save the form.

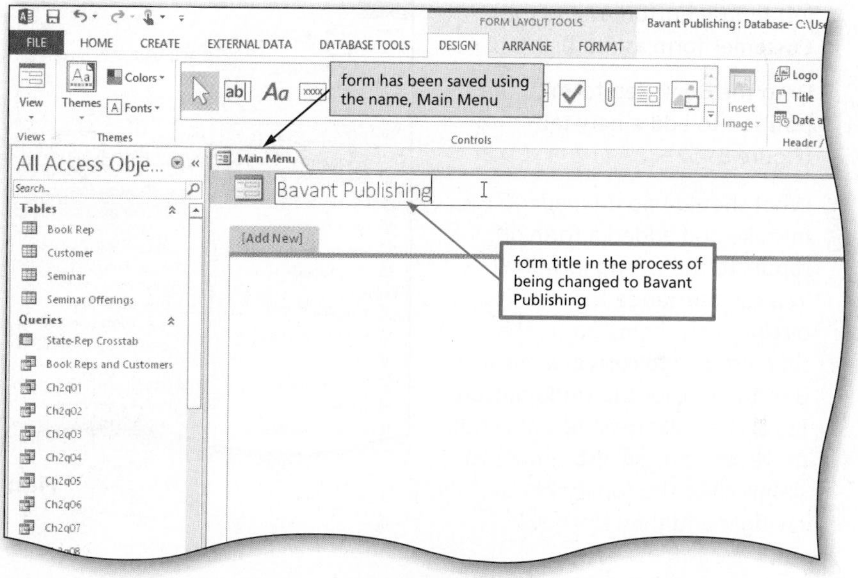

Figure 8–50

To Add Tabs to a Navigation Form

1 MACRO WITH SUBMACROS | 2 COMMAND BUTTONS | 3 OPTION GROUP | 4 MACRO FOR OPTION GROUP
5 DATASHEET FORMS | 6 USER INTERFACE MACROS | 7 NAVIGATION FORM | **8 DATA MACRO**

To add a form or report to a tab in a navigation form, be sure the Navigation Pane is open and then drag the form or report to the desired tab. As a result, users can display that form or report by tapping or clicking the tab. For the Bavant Publishing navigation form, you will drag four forms to the tabs. The Customer form is a datasheet form that appears to display the Customer table open in Datasheet view. Similarly, the Book Rep form is a datasheet form that appears to display the Book Rep table open in Datasheet view. The Forms List form contains three buttons users can tap or click to display the form of their choice. Finally, the Reports List form contains an option group users can use to select a report to preview or export. The steps on the next page add the tabs to the navigation form. They also change the name of the Forms List and Reports List tabs. ***Why?*** *The names of the tabs do not have to be the same as the name of the corresponding forms. By changing them, you can often make tabs more readable.*

1

- Scroll down in the Navigation Pane so that the form named Customer appears, and then drag the form to the position to add a new tab (Figure 8–51).

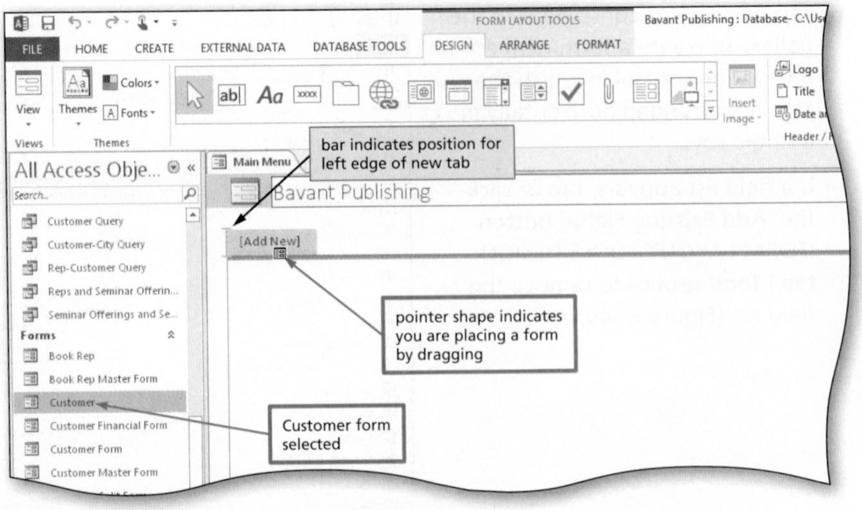

Figure 8–51

2

- Release your finger or the left mouse button to add the Customer form as the first tab.
- Drag the Book Rep form to the position to add a new tab (Figure 8–52).

Q&A What should I do if I made a mistake and added a form or report to the wrong location?
You can rearrange the tabs by dragging them. Often, the simplest way to correct a mistake is to tap or click the Undo button to reverse your most recent action, however. You can also choose to simply close the form without saving it and then start over.

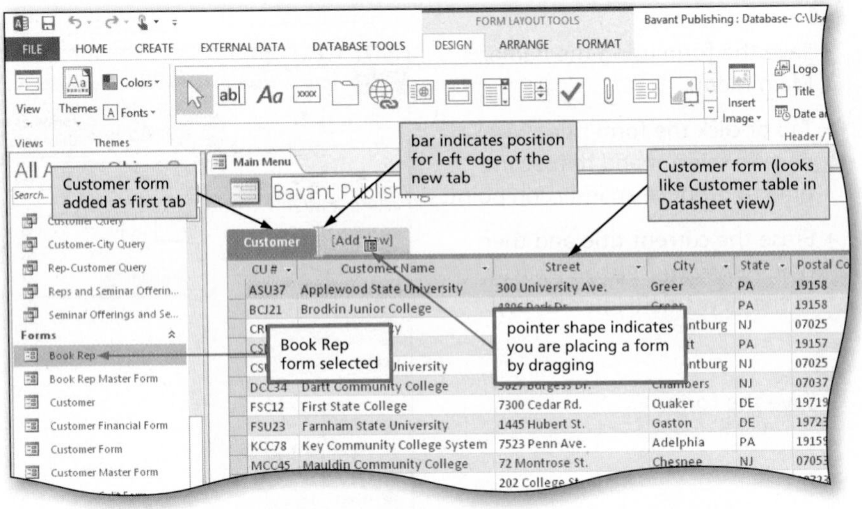

Figure 8–52

3

- Release your finger or the left mouse button to add the Book Rep form as the second tab.
- Using the techniques illustrated in Steps 1 and 2, add the Forms List form as the third tab and the Reports List form as the fourth tab (Figure 8–53).

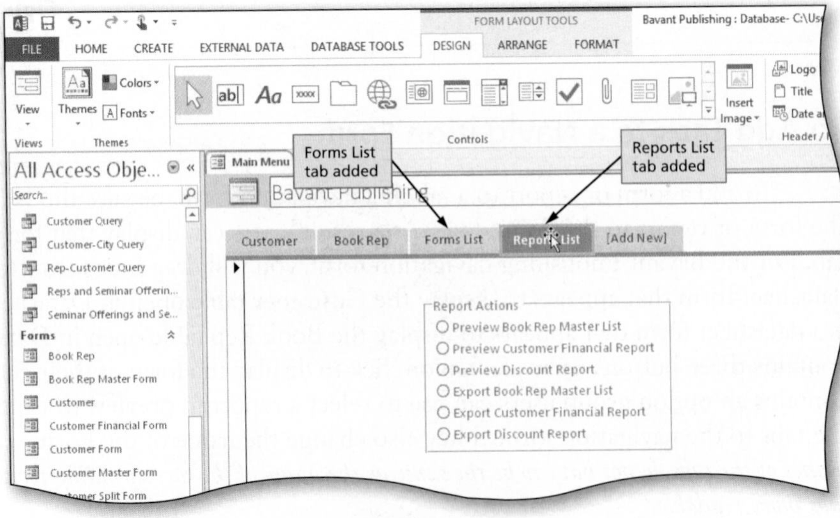

Figure 8–53

4

- Tap or click the Forms List tab twice: once to select it and the second time to produce an insertion point.
- Change the name from Forms List to Forms.
- In a similar fashion, change the name of the Reports List tab from Reports List to Reports (Figure 8–54).

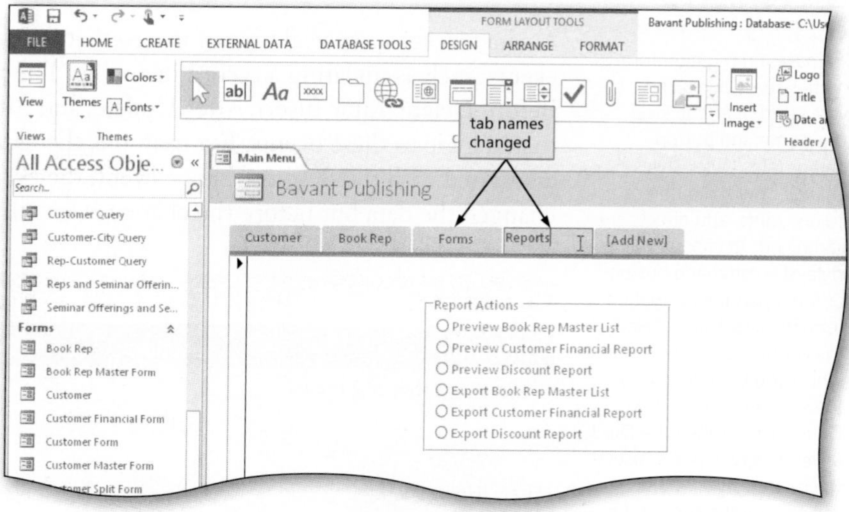

Figure 8–54

Q&A I created these two forms using the names Forms List and Reports List. Now I have changed the names to Forms and Reports. Why not call them Forms and Reports in the first place, so I would not have to rename the tabs?
Because the words, forms and reports, have specific meaning in Access, you cannot use these names. Thus, you needed to use some other names, like Forms List and Reports List. Because tabs are not database objects, you can rename them to be any name you want.

5

- Save the Main Menu form.
- Close the form.
- If requested to do so by your instructor, rename the Main Menu form as LastName Main Menu where LastName is your last name.

Using a Navigation Form

The Main Menu navigation form is complete and ready for use. To use the navigation form, press and hold or right-click the form in the Navigation Pane, and then tap or click Open on the shortcut menu. The Main Menu form then will appear with the first tabbed object (see Figure 8–1 on page AC 475). To display the other forms, simply tap or click the appropriate tab.

CONSIDER THIS

How do you determine the organization of the navigation form?
Once you decide you want a navigation form, you need to decide how to organize the form.

Determine which tasks should be accomplished by having the user tap or click tabs or buttons in the navigation form. Which forms should be opened? Which reports should be opened? Are there any tables or queries that you need to be able to open in the navigation form? If so, you must create forms for the tables or queries.

Determine any special requirements for the way the tasks are to be performed. When a form is opened, should a user be able to edit data, or should the form open as read-only? Should a report be exported or simply viewed on the screen?

Determine how to group the various tasks. Should forms or reports simply be assigned to the tabs in the navigation form? Should they be grouped as buttons on a menu form? Should they be placed as options within an option group? (For consistency, you would usually decide on one of these approaches and use it throughout. In this chapter, one menu form uses command buttons, and the other uses an option group simply to illustrate both approaches.) As far as the navigation form is concerned, is a single set of horizontal tabs sufficient, or would you also like vertical tabs? Would you like two rows of horizontal tabs?

Data Macros

A data macro is a special type of macro that is associated with specific table-related events, such as updating a record in a table. The possible events are Before Change, Before Delete, After Insert, After Update, and After Delete. Data macros allow you to add logic to these events. For example, the data macro shown in Table 8–5 is associated with the Before Change event, the event that occurs after the user has changed the data but before the change is actually made in the database.

Table 8–5 Data Macro for Before Change Event

Condition	Action	Arguments to Be Changed
If [Hours Spent]>[Total Hours]		
	SetField	Name: [Hours Spent] Value: [Total Hours]
Else If [Hours Spent]<0		
	SetField	Name: [Hours Spent] Value: 0
End If		

BTW

Quick Styles for Controls

To make a navigation form more visually appealing, you can change the style of a command button and/or tabs. Quick styles change how the different colors, fonts, and effects are combined. To change the style of a command button or tab, open the navigation form in Layout view. Select the controls or controls for which you want to change the style and tap or click Quick Styles. When the Quick Styles gallery appears, select the desired style. You also can change the style of a control in Design view.

This macro will examine the value in the Hours Spent field in the Seminar Offerings table. If the user's update would cause the value in the Hours Spent field to be greater than the value in the Total Hours field, the macro will change the value in the Hours Spent field so that it is equal to the value in the Total Hours field. Likewise, if the update would cause the value in the Hours Spent field to be less than zero, the macro will set the value in the Hours Spent field to 0. These changes take place after the user has made the change on the screen but before Access commits the change to the database, that is, before the data in the database is actually changed.

There are other events to which you can assign data macros. The actions in a data macro associated with the Before Delete event will take place after a user has indicated that he or she wants to delete a record, but before the record actually is removed from the database. The actions in a macro associated with the After Insert event will take place immediately after a record physically is added to the database. The actions in a macro associated with the After Update event will take place immediately after a record physically is changed in the database. The actions in a macro associated with the After Delete event will take place immediately after a record physically is removed from the database.

BTW

Data Macros

Data macros are similar to SQL triggers. You attach logic to record or table events and any forms and code that update those events inherit the logic. Data macros are stored with the table.

To Create a Data Macro

1 MACRO WITH SUBMACROS | 2 COMMAND BUTTONS | 3 OPTION GROUP | 4 MACRO FOR OPTION GROUP
5 DATASHEET FORMS | 6 USER INTERFACE MACROS | 7 NAVIGATION FORM | 8 DATA MACRO

The following steps create the data macro in Table 8–5, a macro that will be run after a user makes a change to a record in the Seminar Offerings table, but before the record is updated in the database. ***Why?*** *Bavant Publishing management wants to prevent users from entering invalid data into the database.*

1

- Open the Seminar Offerings table in Datasheet view and close the Navigation Pane.
- Display the TABLE TOOLS TABLE tab (Figure 8–55).

Q&A What is the meaning of the events in the Before Events and After Events groups?
Actions in macros associated with the Before events will occur after the user has taken action to change or delete a record, but before the change or deletion is made permanent in the database. Actions in macros associated with the After Events will occur after the corresponding update has been made permanent in the database.

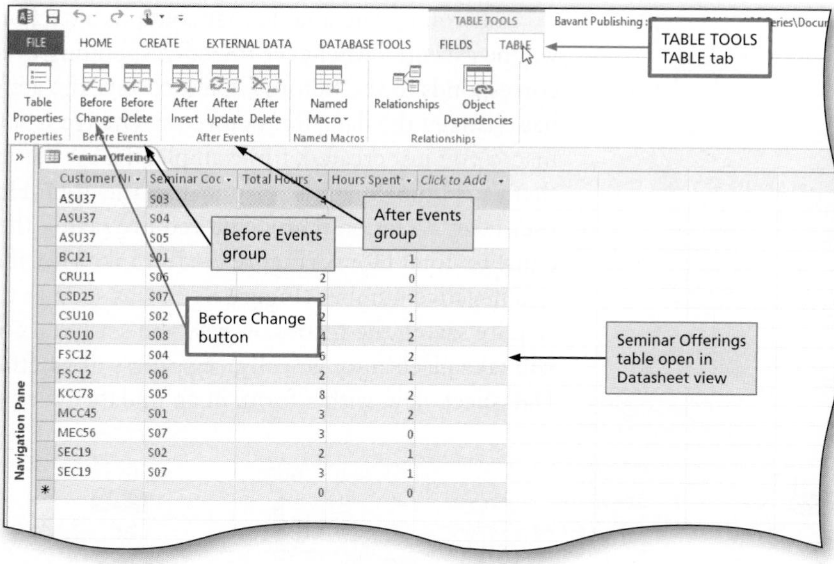

Figure 8–55

2

- Tap or click the Before Change button (TABLE TOOLS TABLE tab | Before Events group).
- Create the macro shown in Figure 8–56.

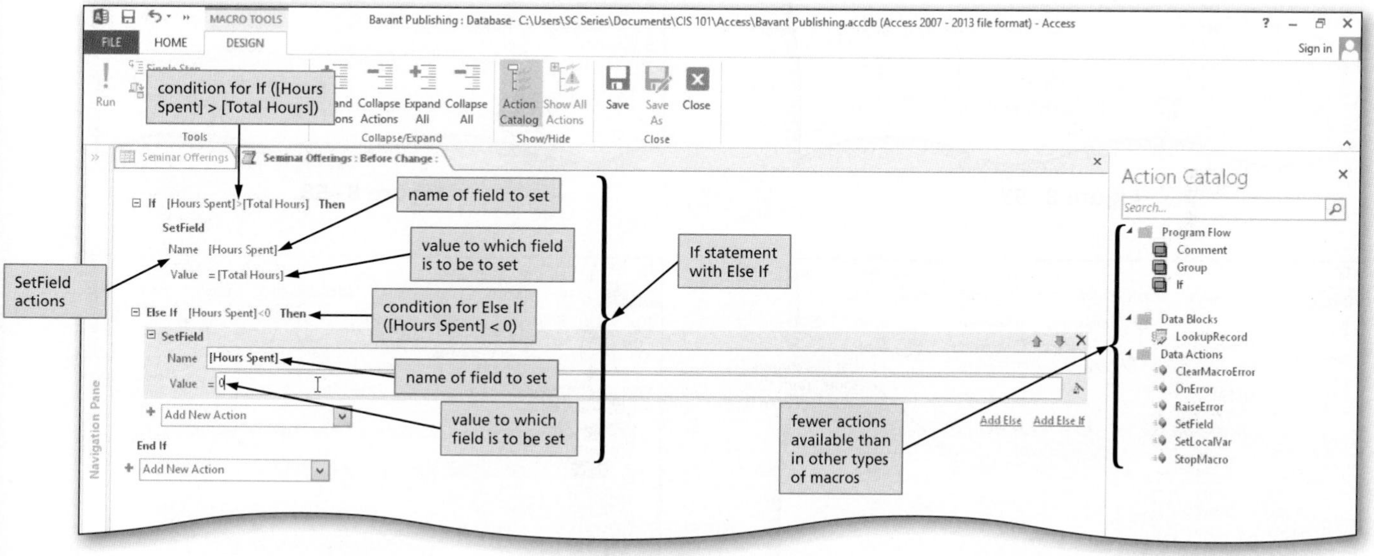

Figure 8–56

Q&A What happened to all the actions that were in the list? In the previous macros we created, there seemed to be many more actions available.
There are only certain actions that make sense in data macros. Only those actions appear. The list of actions that appear is much smaller in a data macro than in other macros.

3

- Save the macro.
- Close the macro.
- Save and close the Seminar Offerings table.

Using a Table that Contains a Data Macro

If you update a table that contains a data macro, the actions in the data macro will be executed whenever the corresponding event takes place. If the data macro corresponds to the Before Change event, the actions will be executed after the user has changed the data, but before the change is saved in the database. With the data macro you just created, for example, if a user attempts to change the data in such a way that the Hours Spent is greater than the Total Hours (Figure 8–57), as soon as the user takes an action that would require saving the record, Access makes Hours Spent equal to Total Hours (Figure 8–58). Likewise, if a user attempts to set Hours Spent to a negative number (Figure 8–59), as soon as the user takes an action that would require saving the record, Access will set Hours Spent to 0 (Figure 8–60). This change will take place automatically, regardless of whether the user changes the values in Datasheet view, with a form, in an update query, or in any other fashion.

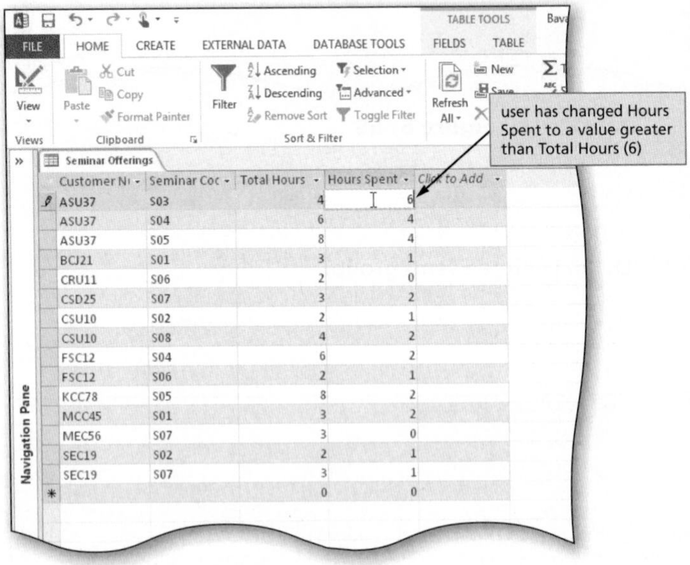

Figure 8–57

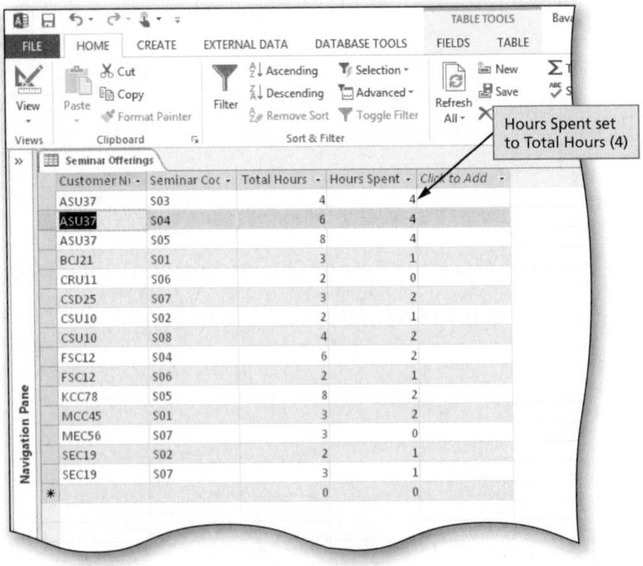

Figure 8–58

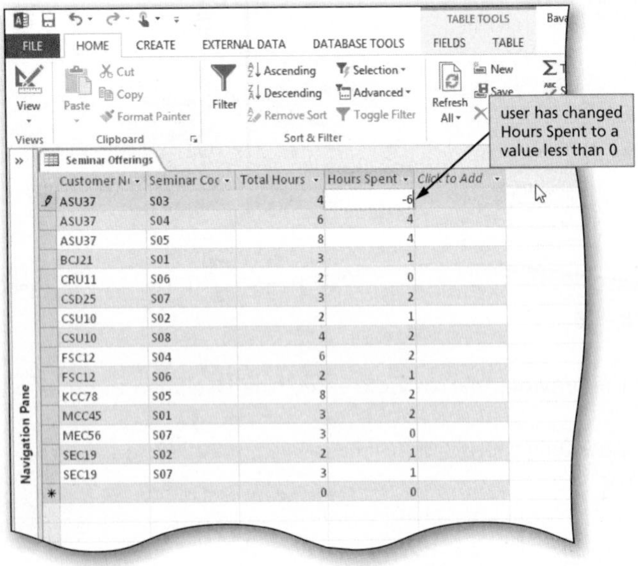

Figure 8–59

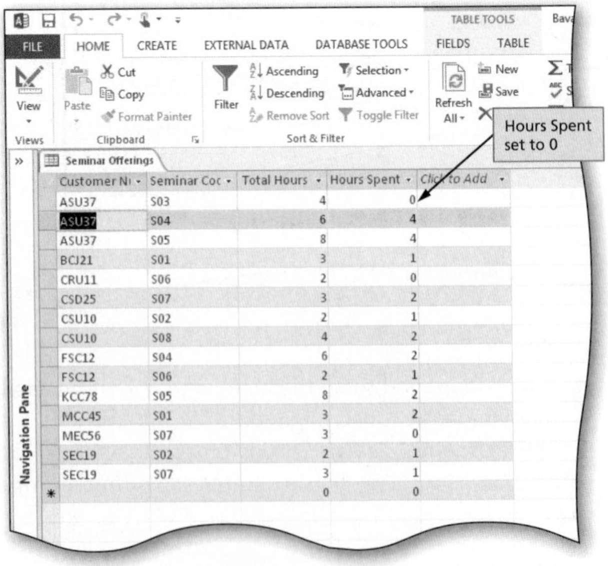

Figure 8–60

Break Point: If you wish to stop working through the chapter at this point, you can resume the project at a later time by starting Access, opening the database called Bavant Publishing, and continuing to follow the steps from this location forward.

Using Control Layouts on Forms and Reports

In earlier chapters, you worked with control layouts in forms and reports. In a control layout, the data is aligned either horizontally or vertically. The two types of layouts are stacked layouts, which are most commonly used in forms, and tabular layouts, which are most commonly used in reports (Figure 8–61).

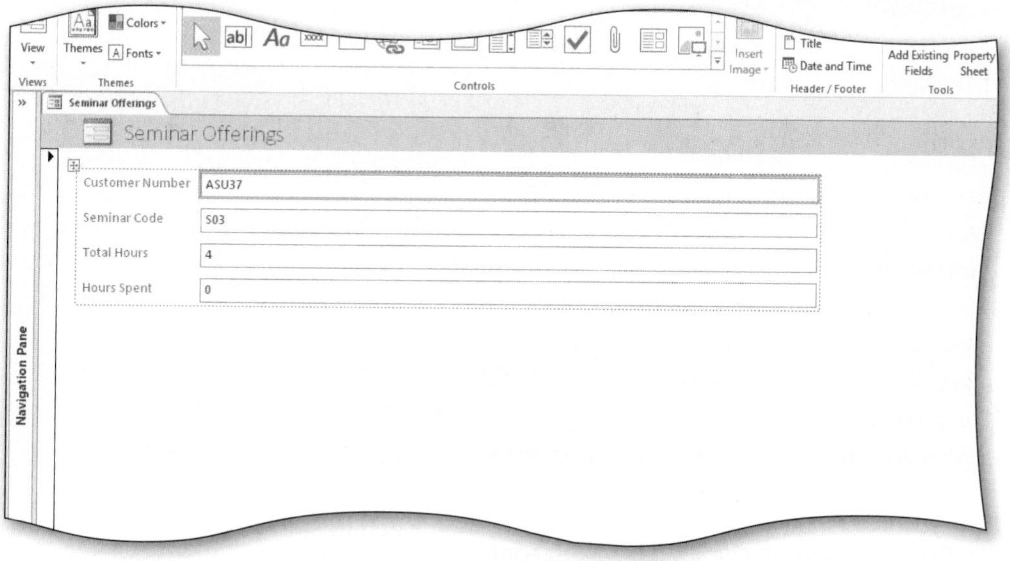

Figure 8–61 (a) Stacked Layout

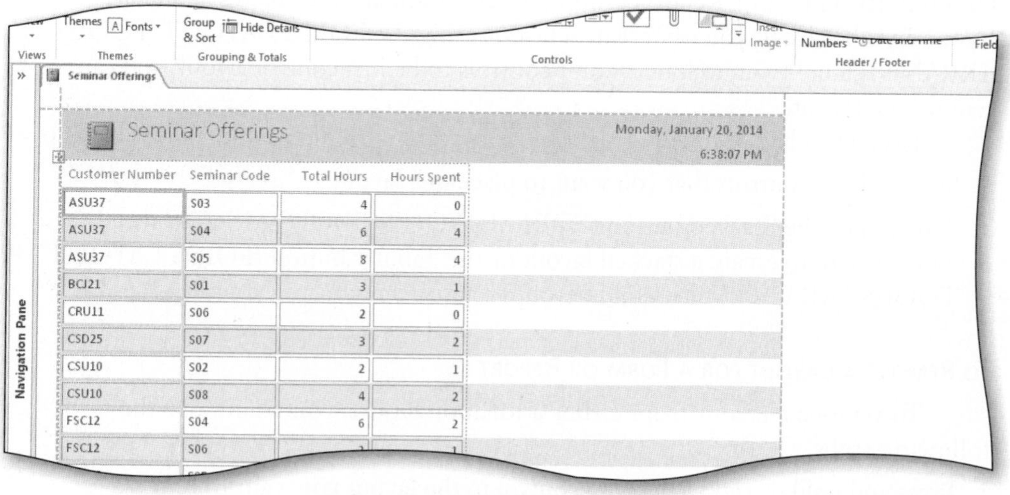

Figure 8–61 (b) Tabular Layout

In working with control layouts, there are many functions you can perform using the FORM LAYOUT TOOLS ARRANGE tab. You can insert rows and columns, delete rows and columns, split and merge cells, and move rows. You also can change margins, which affects spacing within cells, and padding, which affects spacing between rows and columns. You can split a layout into two layouts and move layouts. Finally, you can anchor controls so that they maintain the same distance between the control and the anchor position as the form or report is resized. Table 8–6 on the next page gives descriptions of the functions available on the FORM LAYOUT TOOLS ARRANGE tab.

Table 8–6 ARRANGE Tab

Button	Enhanced ScreenTip
Gridlines	Gridlines.
Stacked	Create a layout similar to a paper form with labels to the left of each field.
Tabular	Create a layout similar to a spreadsheet with labels across the top and data in columns below the labels.
Insert Above	Insert above.
Insert Below	Insert below.
Insert Left	Insert left.
Insert Right	Insert right.
Select Layout	Select layout.
Select Column	Select column.
Select Row	Select row.
Merge	Merge cells.
Split Vertically	Split the selected layout into two rows.
Split Horizontally	Split the selected layout into two columns.
Move Up	Move up.
Move Down	Move down.
Control Margins	Specify the location of information displayed within the control.
Control Padding	Set the amount of spacing between controls and the gridlines of a layout.

BTW
Change the Shape of a Control
Command buttons and tabs have a default shape. For example, both command buttons and tabs have a rounded rectangle shape as the default shape. You can change the shape of a button or tab control on a navigation form. To do so, open the navigation form in Layout view. Select the controls or controls for which you want to change the shape and tap or click Change Shape. When the Change Shape gallery appears, select the desired shape. You also can change the shape of a command button or tab in Design view.

To Create a Layout for a Form or Report

If you create a form using the Form button (CREATE tab | Forms group), Access automatically creates a stacked layout. If you create a report using the Report button (CREATE tab | Reports group), Access automatically creates a tabular layout. In other cases, you can create a layout using the FORM LAYOUT TOOLS ARRANGE tab. If you no longer want controls to be in a control layout, you can remove the layout.

To create a layout in either a form or report, you would use the following steps.

1. Select all the controls that you want to place in a layout.
2. Tap or click the Stacked button (FORM LAYOUT TOOLS ARRANGE tab | Table group) to create a stacked layout or the Tabular button (FORM LAYOUT TOOLS ARRANGE tab | Table group) to create a tabular layout.

To Remove a Layout for a Form or Report

To remove a layout from either a form or report, you would use the following steps.

1. Press and hold or right-click any control in the layout you want to remove to produce a shortcut menu.
2. Point to Layout on the shortcut menu and then tap or click Remove Layout on the submenu to remove the layout.

Using Undo

When making changes with the FORM LAYOUT TOOLS ARRANGE tab buttons, it is not uncommon to make a change that you did not intend. Sometimes taking appropriate action to reverse the change can prove difficult. If so, remember that you can undo the change by tapping or clicking the Undo button on the Quick

Access Toolbar. It is also a good idea to save your work frequently. That way, you can always close the form or report without saving. When you reopen the form or report, it will not have any of your most recent changes.

To Insert a Row

You can insert a blank row either above or below a selected row (Figure 8–62). You can then fill in the row by either typing a value or dragging a field from a field list. In a similar fashion, you can insert a blank column either to the left or right of a selected column.

You would use the following steps to insert a blank row.

1. Select any control in the row above or below where you want to insert a new row.
2. Tap or click the Select Row button (FORM LAYOUT TOOLS ARRANGE tab | Rows & Columns group) to select the row.
3. Tap or click the Insert Above button (FORM LAYOUT TOOLS ARRANGE tab | Rows & Columns group) to insert a blank row above the selected row or the Insert Below button (FORM LAYOUT TOOLS ARRANGE tab | Rows & Columns group) to insert a blank row below the selected row.

BTW
PivotTables and PivotCharts
PivotTable view and PivotChart view have been discontinued in Access 2013. To create a PivotChart or PivotTable, create a new workbook in the Microsoft Excel app, tap or click the From Access button (DATA tab | Get External Data group) and follow the directions in the Select Data Source dialog box to import an Access table. You then can use the PivotTable and PivotChart features of Excel.

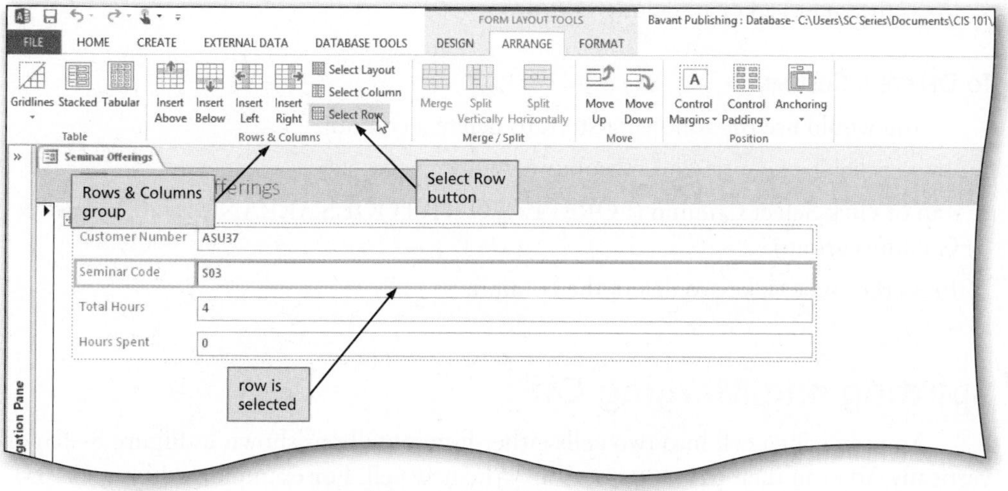

Figure 8–62 (a) Selecting a Row

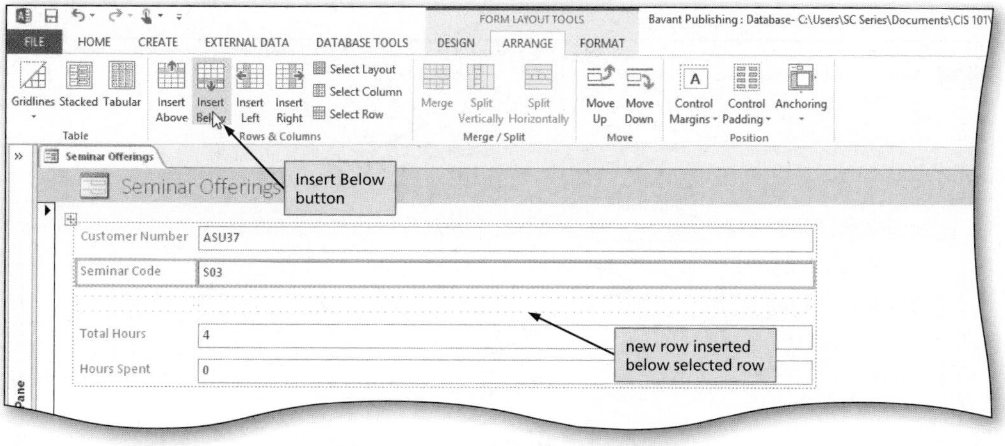

Figure 8–62 (b) Inserting a Row

As you have seen earlier in the text, you also can insert a row containing a field by simply dragging the field from the field list to the desired location.

To Insert a Column

You would use the following steps to insert a new column.

1. Select any control in the column to the right or left of where you want to insert a new column.
2. Tap or click the Select Column button (FORM LAYOUT TOOLS ARRANGE tab | Rows & Columns group) to select the column.
3. Tap or click the Insert Left button (FORM LAYOUT TOOLS ARRANGE tab | Rows & Columns group) to insert a blank column to the left of the selected column or the Insert Right button (FORM LAYOUT TOOLS ARRANGE tab | Rows & Columns group) to insert a blank column to the right of the selected column.

To Delete a Row

You can delete any unwanted row or column from a control layout. You would use the following steps to delete a row.

1. Tap or click any control in the row you want to delete.
2. Tap or click Select Row (FORM LAYOUT TOOLS ARRANGE tab | Rows & Columns group).
3. Press the DELETE key to delete the row.

To Delete a Column

You would use the following steps to delete a column.

1. Tap or click any control in the column you want to delete.
2. Tap or click Select Column (FORM LAYOUT TOOLS ARRANGE tab | Rows & Columns group).
3. Press the DELETE key to delete the column.

Splitting and Merging Cells

You can split a cell into two cells either horizontally, as shown in Figure 8–63, or vertically. You can then enter contents into the new cell. For example, in Figure 8–63, you could type text into the new cell that gives information about customer numbers. You can also merge two cells into one.

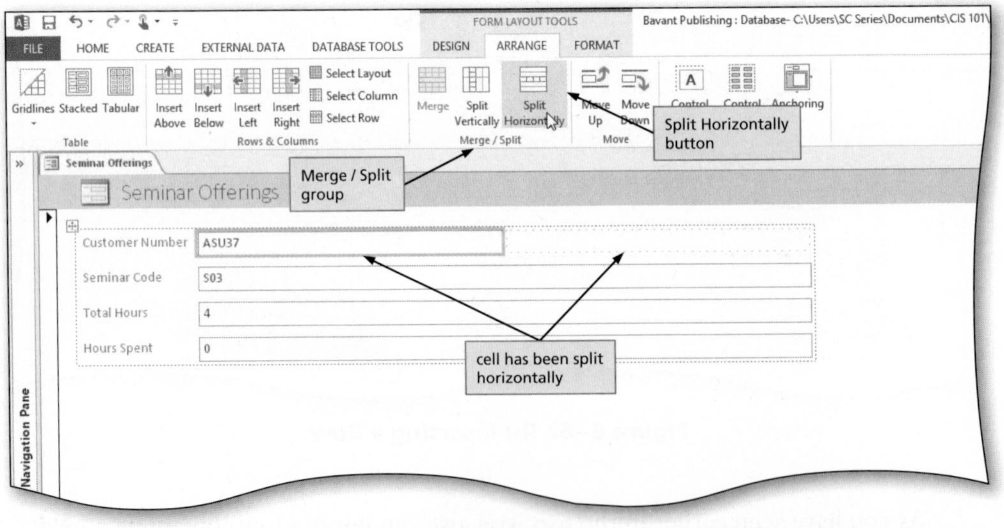

Figure 8–63

To Split a Cell

To split a cell, you would use the following steps.

1. Tap or click the cell to be split.
2. Tap or click the Split Vertically button (FORM LAYOUT TOOLS ARRANGE tab | Merge / Split group) to split the selected cell vertically or the Split Horizontally button (FORM LAYOUT TOOLS ARRANGE tab | Merge / Split group) to split the selected cell horizontally.

To Merge Cells

You would use the following steps to merge cells.

1. Select the first cell to be merged.
2. While holding down the CTRL key, tap or click all the other cells to be merged.
3. Tap or click the Merge button (FORM LAYOUT TOOLS ARRANGE tab | Merge / Split group) to merge the cells.

Moving Cells

You can move a cell in a layout by dragging it to its new position. Most often, however, you will not want to move individual cells, but rather whole rows (Figure 8–64). You can move a row by selecting the row and then dragging it to the new position or you can use the Move buttons on the FORM LAYOUT TOOLS ARRANGE tab.

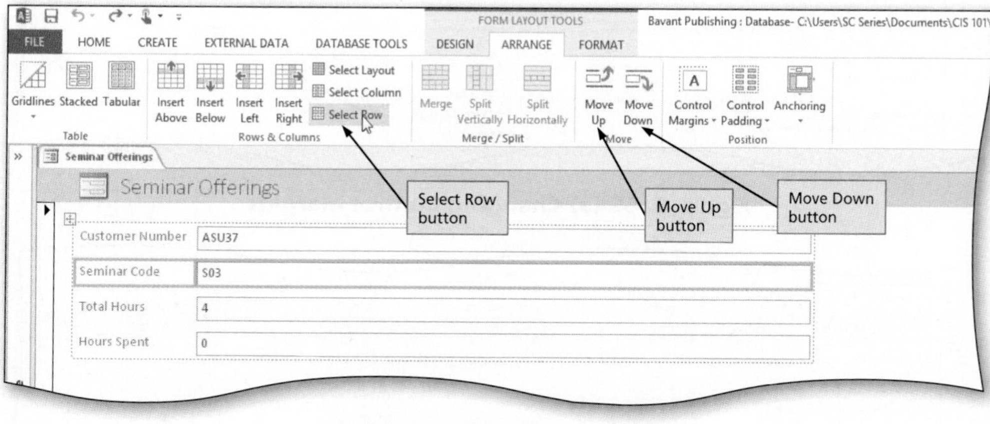

Figure 8–64 (a) Row Selected

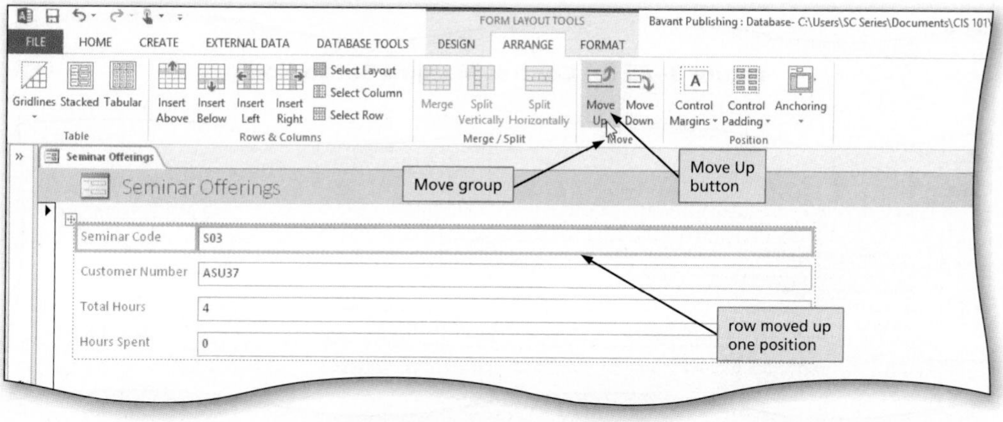

Figure 8–64 (b) Row Moved

To Move Rows Using the Move Buttons

You would use the following steps to move a row.

1. Select any cell in the row to be moved.
2. Tap or click the Select Row button (FORM LAYOUT TOOLS ARRANGE tab | Rows & Columns group) to select the entire row.
3. Tap or click the Move Up button (FORM LAYOUT TOOLS ARRANGE tab | Move group) to move the selected row up one row or the Move Down button (FORM LAYOUT TOOLS ARRANGE tab | Move group) to move the selected row down one row.

Margins and Padding

You can change the spacing within a layout by changing the control margins and the control padding. The control margins, which you change with the Control Margins button, affect the spacing around the text inside a control. Figure 8–65 shows the various options as well as samples of two of the options.

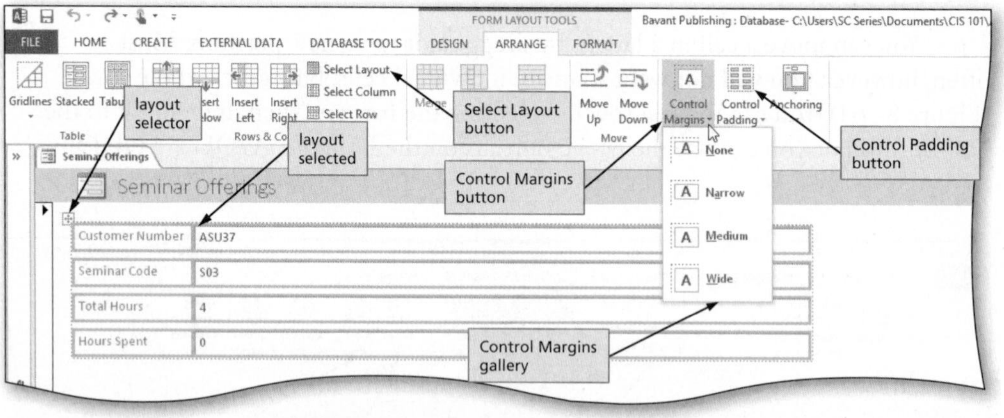

Figure 8–65 (a) Changing Control Margins

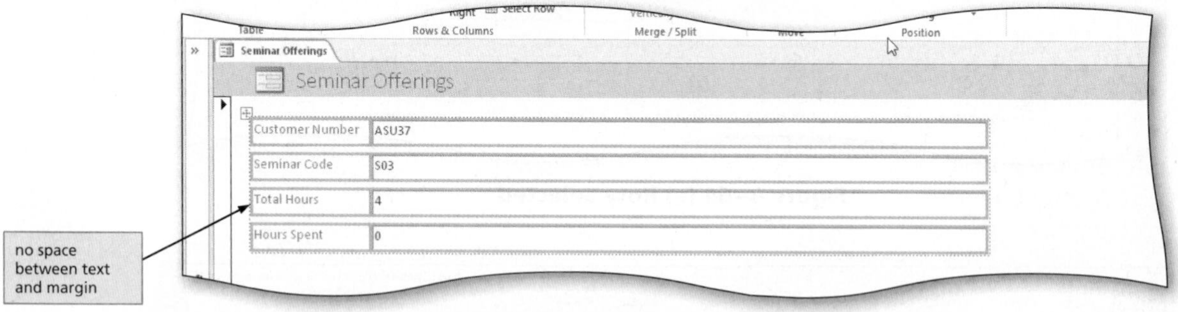

Figure 8–65 (b) Control Margins Set to None

Figure 8–65 (c) Control Margins Set to Medium

The control padding, which you change with the Control Padding button, affects the spacing around the outside of a control. The options are the same as those for control margins. Figure 8–66 shows samples of two of the options.

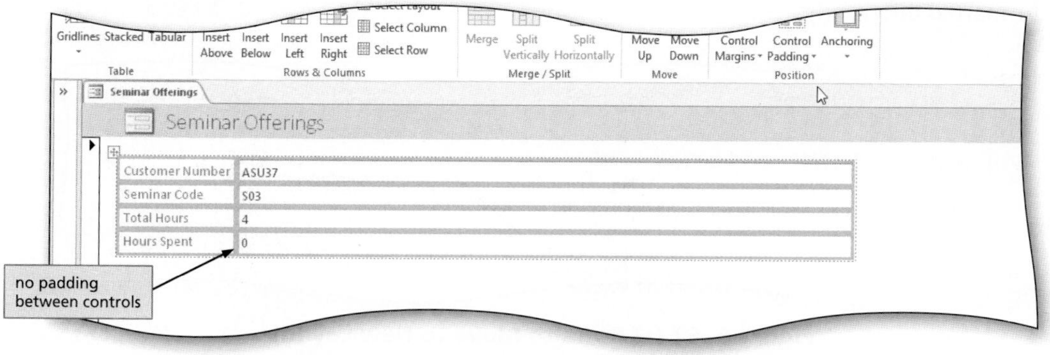

Figure 8–66 (a) Control Padding Set to None

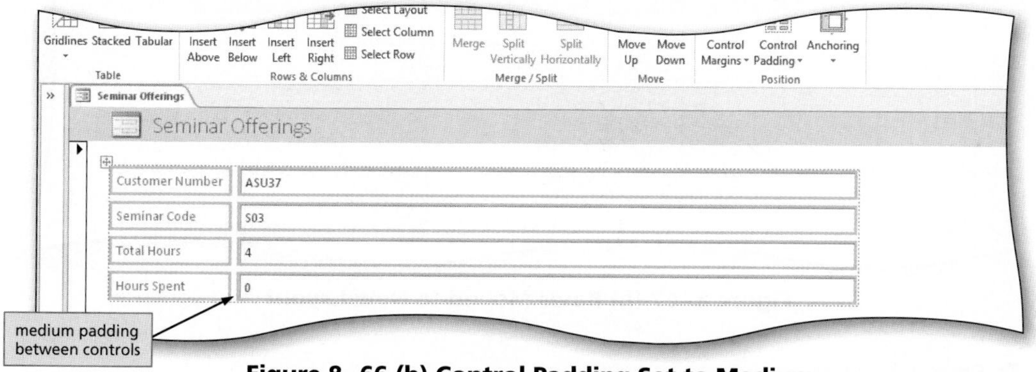

Figure 8–66 (b) Control Padding Set to Medium

To Change Control Margins

You would use the following steps to change a control's margins.

1. Select any cell in the layout.
2. Tap or click the Select Layout button (FORM LAYOUT TOOLS ARRANGE tab | Rows & Columns group) to select the entire layout. (You also can select the layout by tapping or clicking the layout selector.)
3. Tap or click the Control Margins button (FORM LAYOUT TOOLS ARRANGE tab | Position group) to display the available margin settings.
4. Tap or click the desired margin setting.

BTW

Control Padding

The term, padding, refers to the amount of space between a control's border and its contents. Effectively, you can increase or decrease the amount of white space in a control.

To Change Control Padding

You would use the following steps to change control padding.

1. Select the layout.
2. Tap or click the Control Padding button (FORM LAYOUT TOOLS ARRANGE tab | Position group) to display the available padding settings.
3. Tap or click the desired padding setting.

Although you can make the margin and padding changes for individual controls, it is much more common to do so for the entire layout. Doing so gives a uniform appearance to the layout.

BTW
Gridlines
You also can add gridlines to a form. To do so, select the control or controls for which you want to add gridlines, then tap or click the Gridlines button. When the Gridlines menu appears, select the desired option. You also can change the color, border, style, and width of gridlines using the Gridlines menu.

Splitting a Layout

You can split a single control layout into two separate layouts (Figure 8–67) and then modify each layout separately. They can be moved to different locations and formatted differently.

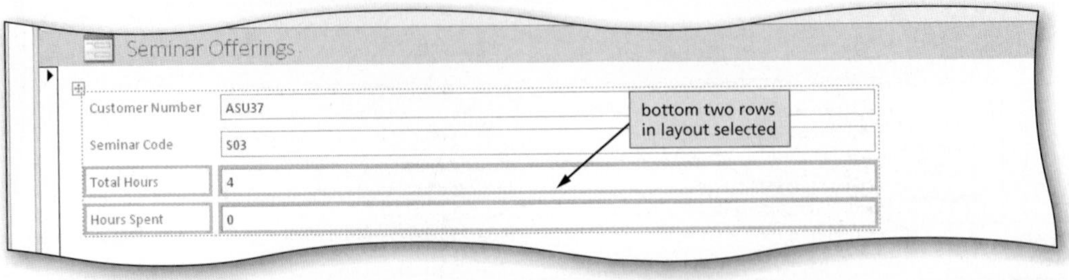

Figure 8–67 (a) Rows to Move to New Layout

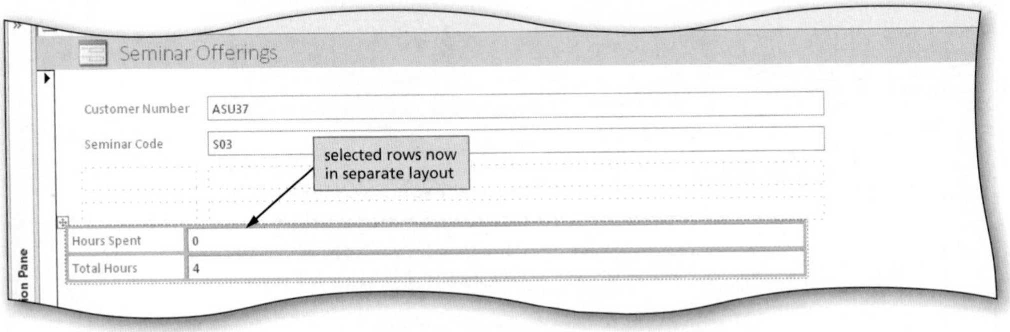

Figure 8–67 (b) Rows Moved to New Layout

To Split a Layout

To split a layout, you would use the following steps.

1. Select all the cells that you want to move to a new layout.
2. Tap or click the Stacked button (FORM LAYOUT TOOLS ARRANGE tab | Table group) to place the cells in a stacked layout or the Tabular button (FORM LAYOUT TOOLS ARRANGE tab | Table group) to place the cells in a tabular layout.

Moving a Layout

You can move a control layout to a different location on the form (Figure 8–68).

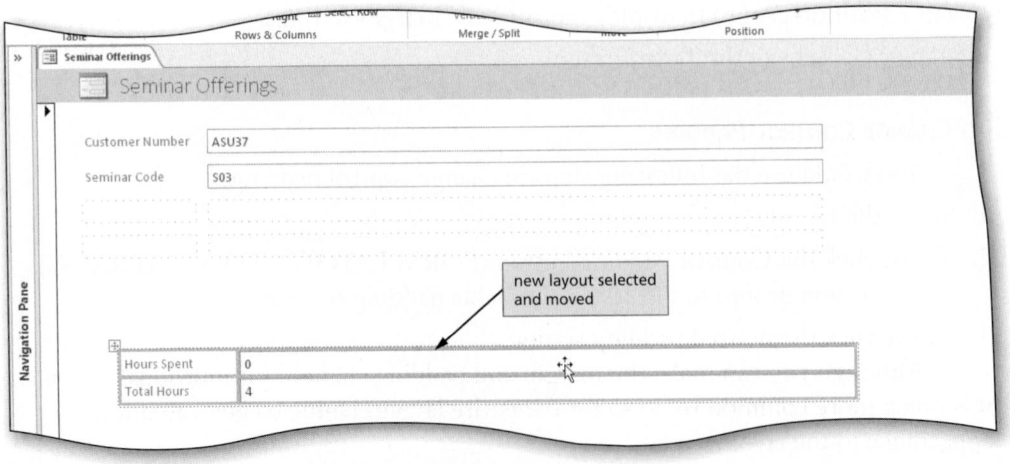

Figure 8–68

To Move a Layout

You would use the following steps to move a layout.

1. Tap or click any cell in the layout to be moved and then tap or click the Select Layout button (FORM LAYOUT TOOLS ARRANGE tab | Rows & Columns group) to select the layout.
2. Drag the layout to the new location.

Anchoring Controls

The Anchoring button allows you to tie (anchor) controls to a section or to other controls so that they maintain the same distance between the control and the anchor position as the form is resized. To anchor the controls you have selected, you use the Anchoring gallery (Figure 8–69).

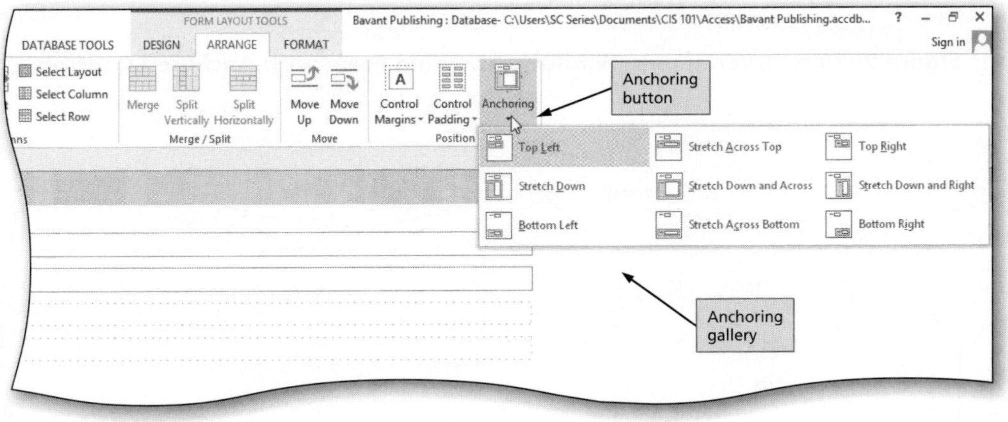

Figure 8–69

The Top Left, Top Right, Bottom Left, and Bottom Right options anchor the control in the indicated position on the form. The other five operations also stretch the controls in the indicated direction.

To Anchor Controls

You would use the following steps to anchor controls.

1. Select the control or controls to be anchored.
2. Tap or click the Anchoring button (FORM LAYOUT TOOLS ARRANGE tab | Position group) to produce the Anchoring gallery.
3. Select the desired Anchoring option from the Anchoring gallery.

The best way to see the effect of anchoring is to display objects in overlapping windows rather than tabbed documents. With overlapping windows, you can resize the object by dragging the border of the object. Anchored objects keep their same relative position (Figure 8–70 on the next page).

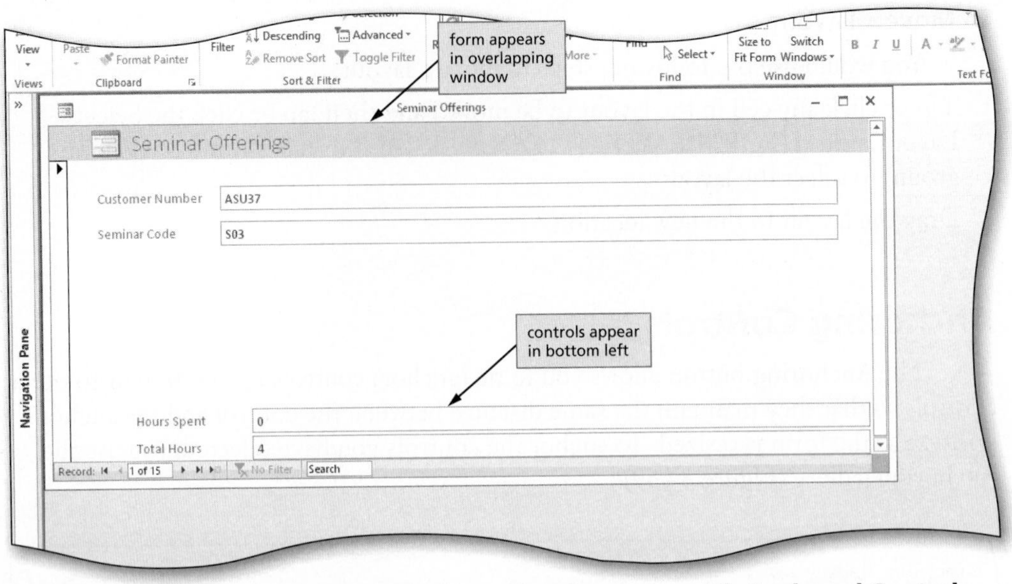

Figure 8–70 (a) Overlapping Windows Showing Form with Anchored Controls

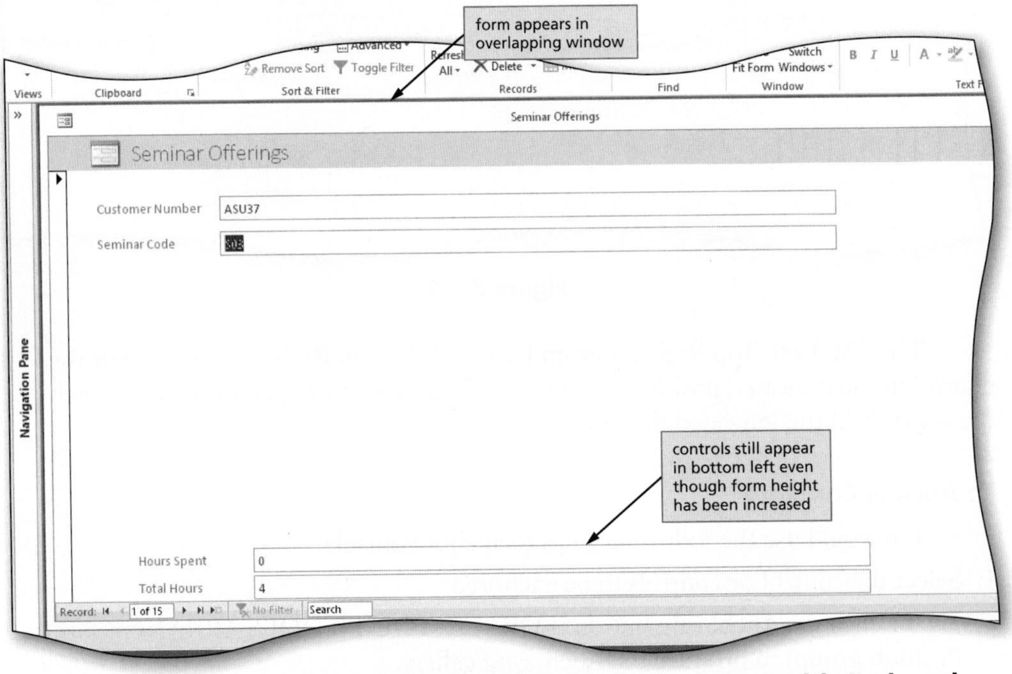

Figure 8–70 (b) Overlapping Window Showing Resized Form with Anchored Controls

If you want to display objects in overlapping windows, you have to modify the appropriate Access option.

BTW
Overlapping Windows
When you display objects in overlapping windows, each database object appears in its own windows. When multiple objects are open, these windows overlap each other. By default, Access 2013 displays database objects in a single pane separated by tabs.

To Display Objects in Overlapping Windows

You would use the following steps to overlap windows.

1. Tap or click FILE on the ribbon to open the Backstage view.
2. Tap or click Options to display the Access Options dialog box.
3. Tap or click Current Database to display the Current Database options.
4. In the Application Options area, tap or click the Overlapping Windows option button.

5. Tap or click the OK button to close the Access Options dialog box.
6. For the changes to take effect, you will need to close and then reopen the database.

You use a similar process to return to displaying objects in tabbed documents.

To Display Objects in Tabbed Documents

You would use the following steps to display tabbed documents.

1. Tap or click FILE on the ribbon to open the Backstage view.
2. Tap or click Options to display the Access Options dialog box.
3. Tap or click Current Database to display the Current Database options.
4. In the Application Options area, tap or click the Tabbed Documents option button.
5. Tap or click the OK button to close the Access Options dialog box.
6. For the changes to take effect, you will need to close and then reopen the database.

BTW

Certification

The Microsoft Office Specialist (MOS) program provides an opportunity for you to obtain a valuable industry credential — proof that you have the Access 2013 skills required by employers. For more information, visit the Certification resource on the Student Companion Site located on www.cengagebrain.com. For detailed instructions about accessing available resources, visit www.cengage.com/ct/studentdownload or contact your instructor for information about accessing the required files.

To Sign Out of a Microsoft Account

If you are signed in to a Microsoft account and are using a public computer or otherwise wish to sign out of your Microsoft account, you should sign out of the account from the Account gallery in the Backstage view before exiting Access. Signing out of the account is the safest way to make sure that nobody else can access SkyDrive files or settings stored in your Microsoft account. The following steps sign out of a Microsoft account from Access. For a detailed example of the procedure summarized below, refer to the Office and Windows chapter at the beginning of this book.

1. If you wish to sign out of your Microsoft account, tap or click FILE on the ribbon to open the Backstage view and then tap or click the Account tab to display the Account gallery.
2. Tap or click the Sign out link, which displays the Remove Account dialog box. If a Can't remove Windows accounts dialog box appears instead of the Remove Account dialog box, click the OK button and skip the remaining steps.

Q&A Why does a Can't remove Windows accounts dialog box appear?
If you signed in to Windows using your Microsoft account, then you also must sign out from Windows, rather than signing out from within Access. When you are finished using Windows, be sure to sign out at that time.

3. Tap or click the Yes button (Remove Account dialog box) to sign out of your Microsoft account on this computer.

Q&A Should I sign out of Windows after signing out of my Microsoft account?
When you are finished using the computer, you should sign out of your account for maximum security.

4. Tap or click the Back button in the upper-left corner of the Backstage view to return to the database.

BTW

Quick Reference

For a table that lists how to complete the tasks covered in this book using touch gestures, the mouse, ribbon, shortcut menu, and keyboard, see the Quick Reference Summary at the back of this book, or visit the Quick Reference resource on the Student Companion Site located on www.cengagebrain.com. For detailed instructions about accessing available resources, visit www.cengage.com/ct/studentdownload or contact your instructor for information about accessing the required files.

To Exit Access

The following steps exit Access.

1. Tap or click the Close button on the right side of the title bar to exit Access.
2. If a Microsoft Access dialog box appears, tap or click the Yes button to save any changes made to the object since the last save.

Chapter Summary

In this chapter you have learned to create and use macros; create a menu form that uses command buttons for the choices; create a menu form that uses an option group for the choices; create a macro that implements the choices in the option group; create datasheet forms that utilize user interface macros; create a navigation form; add tabs to a navigation form; and create data macros. You also learned to use control layouts.

CONSIDER THIS: PLAN AHEAD

What decisions will you need to make when creating your own macros and navigation forms?

Use these guidelines as you complete the assignments in this chapter and create your own macros and navigation forms outside of this class.

1. Determine when it would be beneficial to automate tasks in a macro.
   a. Are there tasks involving multiple steps that would be more conveniently accomplished by running a macro than by carrying out all the individual steps? For example, opening a form in read-only mode could be accomplished conveniently through a macro.
   b. Are there tasks that are to be performed when the user taps or clicks buttons on a menu form?
   c. Are there tasks to be performed when a user taps or clicks a control on a form?
   d. Are there tasks to be performed when a user updates a table? These tasks can be placed in a macro that can be run when the button is tapped or clicked.
2. Determine whether it is appropriate to create a navigation form.
   a. If you want to make it easy and convenient for users to perform a variety of tasks just by tapping or clicking tabs and buttons, consider creating a navigation form.
   b. You can associate the performance of the various tasks with the tabs and buttons in the navigation form.
3. Determine the organization of the navigation form.
   a. Determine the various tasks that need to be performed by tapping or clicking tabs and buttons.
   b. Decide the logical grouping of the tabs and buttons.

CONSIDER THIS

How should you submit solutions to questions in the assignments identified with a ✱ symbol?

Every assignment in this book contains one or more questions identified with a ✱ symbol. These questions require you to think beyond the assigned database. Present your solutions to the questions in the format required by your instructor. Possible formats may include one or more of these options: write the answer; create a document that contains the answer; present your answer to the class; discuss your answer in a group; record the answer as audio or video using a webcam, smartphone, or portable media player; or post answers on a blog, wiki, or website.

Apply Your Knowledge

Reinforce the skills and apply the concepts you learned in this chapter.

Creating UI Macros and a Navigation Form

Note: To complete this assignment, you will be required to use the Data Files for Students. Visit www.cengage.com/ct/studentdownload for detailed instructions or contact your instructor for information about accessing the required files.

Instructions: Start Access. Open the Apply Natural Products database. Natural Products is a company that distributes cleaning supplies, hand lotions, soaps, and other items that are eco-friendly. The company markets to retail stores, fitness centers, salons, and spas.

Perform the following tasks:

1. Create a datasheet form for the Customer table and name the form Customer. Create a UI macro for the Customer form. When a user taps or clicks a customer number on a row in the datasheet form, the Customer Master Form should appear in a pop-up form.
2. Create a datasheet form for the Sales Rep table and name the form Sales Rep. Create a UI macro for the Sales Rep form. When a user taps or clicks a sales rep number on a row in the datasheet form, the Sales Rep Master Form should appear in a pop-up form.
3. Create the navigation form shown in Figure 8–71. The purpose of the form is to display the two datasheet forms in the database as horizontal tabs. Name the form Datasheet Forms Menu and change the title to Natural Products Navigation Form.

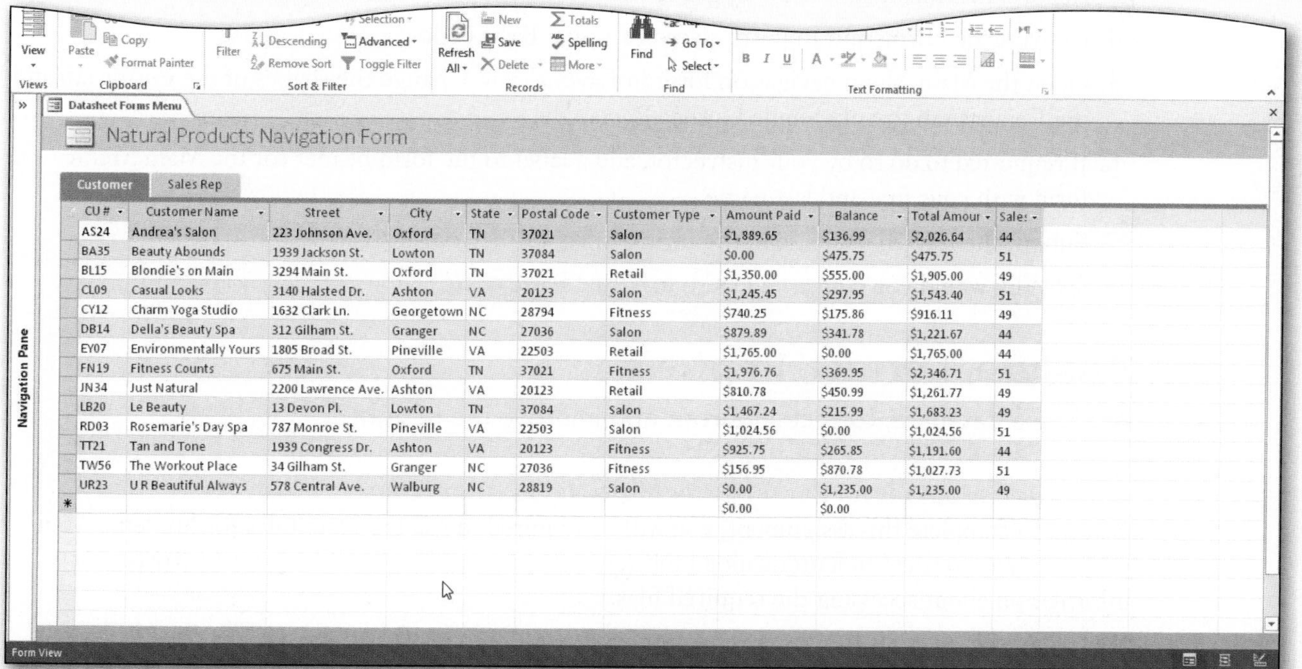

Figure 8–71

Continued >

Apply Your Knowledge *continued*

4. If requested to do so by your instructor, open the Sales Rep datasheet form and change the first and last names of sales rep 44 to your first and last name.
5. Submit the revised database in the format specified by your instructor.
6. How could you add the Sales Rep Order Data form to the navigation form?

Extend Your Knowledge

Extend the skills you learned in this chapter and experiment with new skills. You may need to use Help to complete the assignment.

Modifying Navigation Forms

Note: To complete this assignment, you will be required to use the Data Files for Students. Visit www.cengage.com/ct/studentdownload for detailed instructions or contact your instructor for information about accessing the required files.

Instructions: Start Access. Open the Extend Corporate Training database. Corporate Training provides training on Microsoft Office apps to commercial businesses.

Perform the following tasks:

1. Open the Main Menu form in Design view and change the theme for this object only to Organic. Expand the size of the form header and add the current date to the form header. Add a command button to the form header that closes the form. Save the changes and close the form.
2. Open the Reports List form in Design view. Select the Report Actions label, and change the font weight to semi-bold and the special effect to raised. You may need to enlarge the label slightly. Select all the option buttons and use the Size/Space menu to adjust the labels to be the same width as the widest label. Select the option group and change the special effect to Shadowed. Change the theme colors to Green. Change the background color of the form to White, Background 1, Darker 5%. Save the changes to the form.
3. Open the Forms List form in Design view and make the same changes that you made to the Reports List form. Save the changes to the form.
4. Convert the Forms and Reports macro to Visual Basic code.
5. Open the Main Menu navigation form in Layout view. Change the shapes of the Forms tab and the Reports tab to Snip Single Corner Rectangle.
6. If requested to do so by your instructor, add a label to the form header for the Main Menu form with your first and last name.
7. Submit the revised database in the format specified by your instructor.
8. Why would you convert a macro to Visual Basic code?

Analyze, Correct, Improve

Analyze a database, correct all errors, and improve the design.

Correcting Macro Errors and Improving a Navigation Form

Note: To complete this assignment, you will be required to use the Data Files for Students. Visit www.cengage.com/ct/studentdownload for detailed instructions or contact your instructor for information about accessing the required files.

Instructions: Start Access and open the Analyze Consignment database from the Data Files for Students. Analyze Consignment is a database maintained by the Friends group of the local animal shelter. The Friends group manages a consignment store and uses the monies raised to help the animal shelter. The store manager has asked you to correct some errors in macros and to improve the navigation form.

Perform the following tasks:

1. Correct The store manager created a datasheet form for the Seller table and a UI macro that should open the Seller Master Form when a seller code is selected. When she tries to run the macro, she receives the error message shown in Figure 8–72.

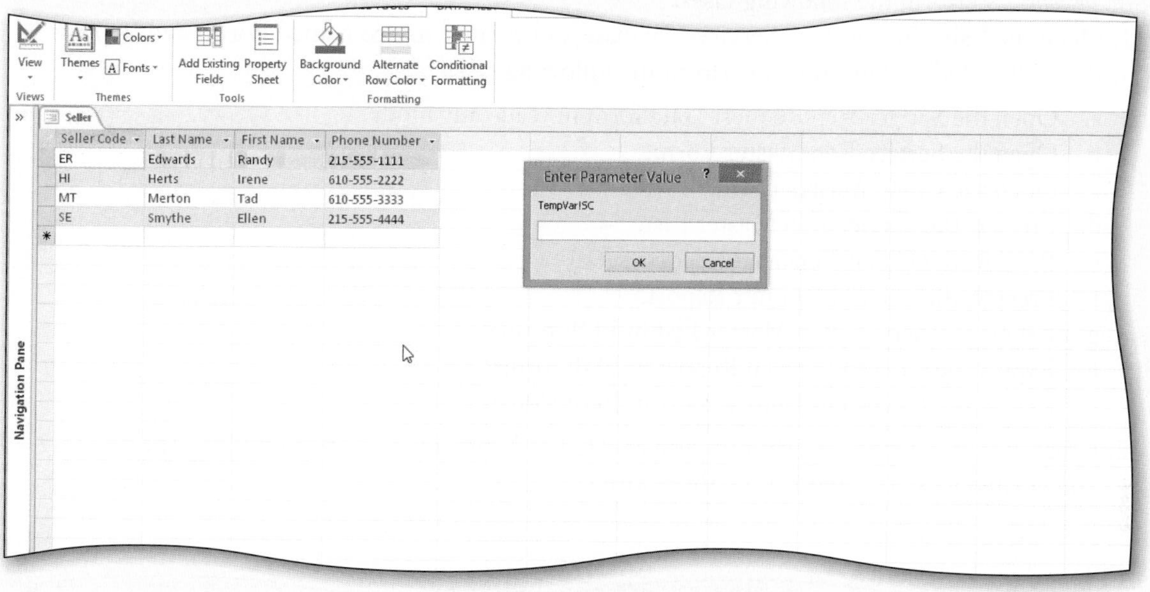

Figure 8–72

Also, she inadvertently selected the XPS exporting format instead of PDF in the two export report submacros that she created.

2. Improve The Forms and Reports form has an option group for forms and an option group for reports that appear side by side. The manager prefers these option groups to appear vertically, one above the other, with the Forms option group appearing at the top. The title on the navigation form could be improved by changing it from Main Menu to Friends Consignment.

3. Why do you think the name of the navigation form is Main Menu? Is there another name that would more accurately describe the purpose of the navigation form?

In the Labs

Design, create, modify, and/or use a database following the guidelines, concepts, and skills presented in this chapter. Labs are listed in order of increasing difficulty. Labs 1 and 2, which increase in difficulty, require you to create solutions based on what you learned in the chapter; Lab 3 requires you to create a solution, which uses cloud and web technologies, by learning and investigating on your own from general guidance.

Lab 1: Creating Macros and a Navigation Form for the Technology Services Database

Note: To complete this assignment, you will be required to use the Data Files for Students. Visit www.cengage.com/ct/studentdownload for detailed instructions or contact your instructor for information about accessing the required files.

Continued >

In the Labs *continued*

Problem: Technology Services provides information technology services to local businesses and service organizations. The services include backup and recovery, troubleshooting, software and hardware upgrades, and web hosting. The company would like an easy way to access the various tables, forms, and reports included in the database. This would make the database easier to maintain and update.

Instructions: Perform the following tasks:

1. Open the Lab 1 Technology Services database and create a macro named Forms and Reports that will include submacros to perform the following tasks:
   a. Open the Service Rep Request Data form in read-only mode.
   b. Open the Service Rep Master Form.
   c. Open the Client Master Form.
   d. Preview the Service Rep Master List.
   e. Preview the Client Financial Report.
   f. Preview the Client Discount Report.
   g. Export the Service Rep Master List in PDF format.
   h. Export the Client Financial Report in PDF format.
   i. Export the Client Discount Report in PDF format.
2. Create the menu form shown in Figure 8–73. The command buttons should use the macros you created in Step 1 to open the three forms.

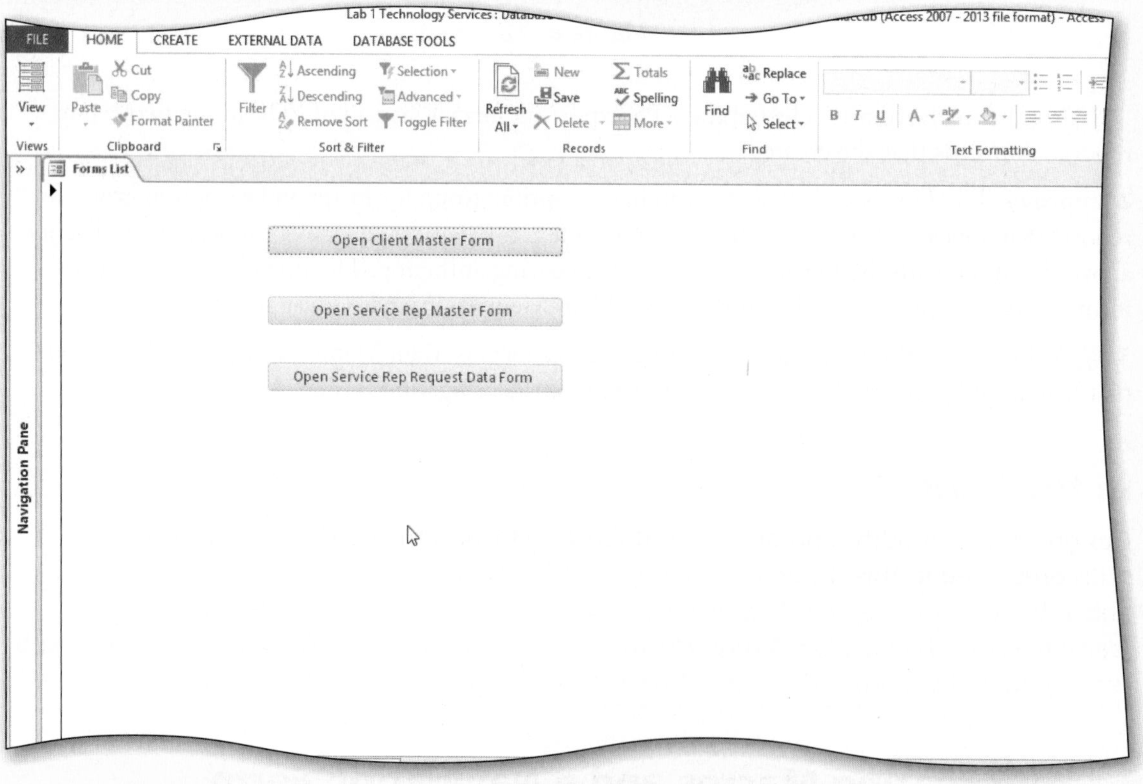

Figure 8–73

3. Create the menu form shown in Figure 8–74. The option group should use the macros you created in Step 1 to preview and export the three reports.

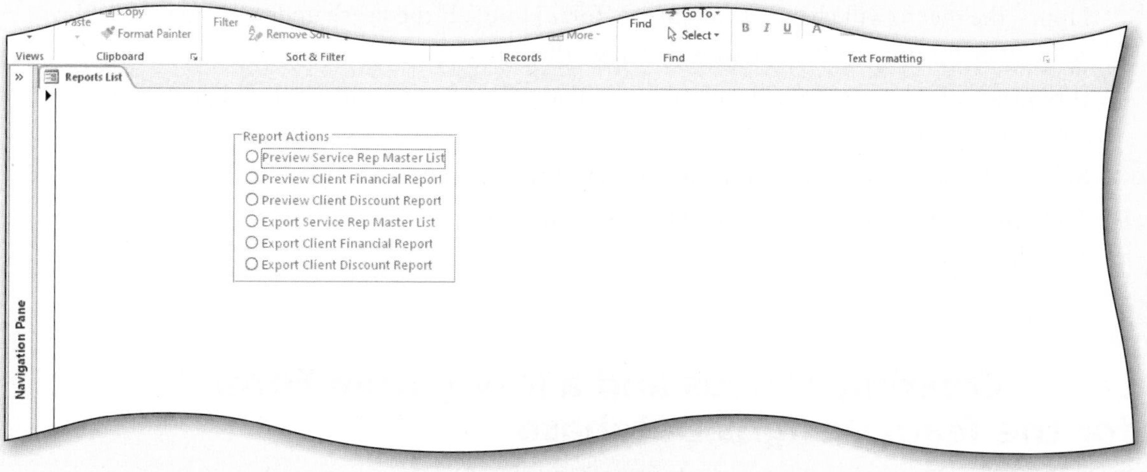

Figure 8–74

4. Create a datasheet form for the Client table and name the form Client. Create a UI macro for the Client form. When a user taps or clicks a client number on a row in the datasheet, the Client Master Form should appear in a pop-up form.
5. Create a datasheet form for the Service Rep table and name the form Service Rep. Create a UI macro for the Service Rep form. When a user taps or clicks a service rep number on a row in the datasheet, the Service Rep Master Form should appear in a pop-up form.
6. Create the navigation form shown in Figure 8–75 for the Technology Services database. Use the same design for your navigation form as the one illustrated in this chapter. For example, the Client tab should display the Client form you created in Step 4, and the Service Rep tab should display the Service Rep form you created in Step 5. The Forms tab should display the Forms List form you created in Step 2, and the Reports tab should display the Reports List form you created in Step 3.

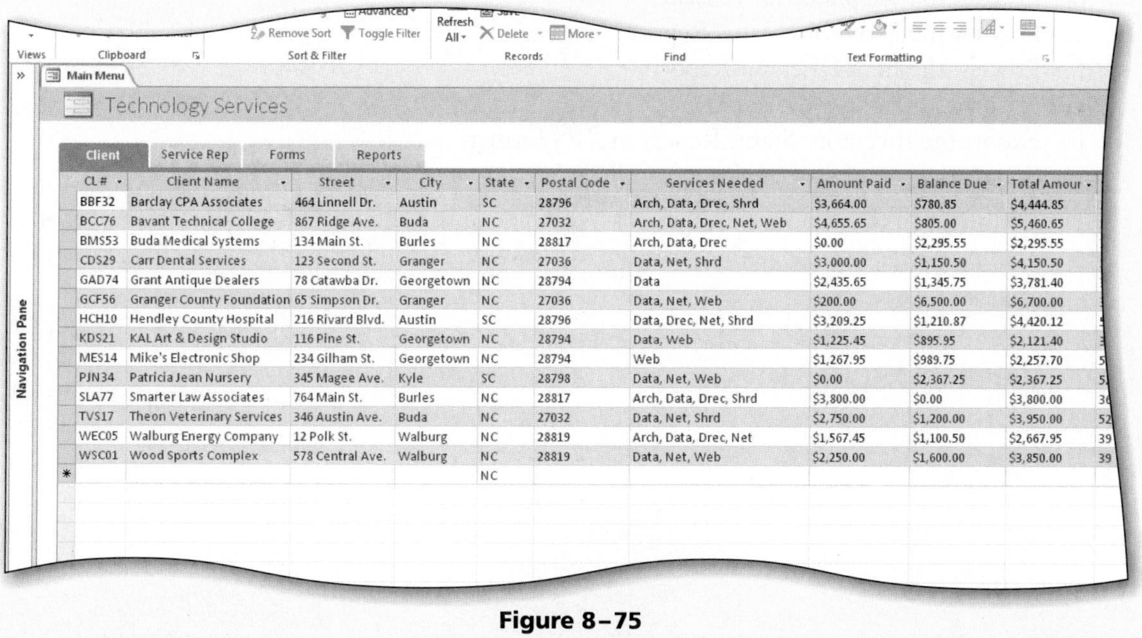

Figure 8–75

Continued >

In the Labs *continued*

7. Create a data macro for the Service Requests table. The macro will examine the value in the Hours Spent field. If the user's update would cause the value to be greater than the Total Hours, the macro will change the value to Total Hours. If the user's update would cause the value to be less than 0, the macro will change the value to 0.
8. If requested to do so by your instructor, add your name to the title for the Main Menu navigation form.
9. Submit the revised database in the format specified by your instructor.
10. In this exercise, you have created both command buttons and option groups to run macros. Which do you prefer? Why?

Lab 2: Creating Macros and a Navigation Form for the Team Designs Database

Problem: Team Designs is a company that supplies customized clothing and accessories to sports teams. The company purchases these items from suppliers at wholesale prices and adds the team's design. The final item price is determined by marking up the wholesale price and adding a fee that is based on the complexity of the design. The company would like an easy way to access the various tables, forms, and reports included in the database. This would make the database easier to maintain and update.

Note: To complete this assignment, you will be required to use the Data Files for Students. Visit www.cengage.com/ct/studentdownload for detailed instructions or contact your instructor for information about accessing the required files.

Instructions: Perform the following tasks:

1. Open the Lab 2 Team Designs database and create a macro named Forms and Reports that will include submacros to perform the following tasks:
   a. Open the Supplier Orders Data form in read-only mode.
   b. Open the Supplier Master Form.
   c. Open the Item Master Form.
   d. Preview the Supplier Master List.
   e. Preview the Inventory Status Report.
   f. Preview the Item Discount Report.
   g. Export the Supplier Master List in XPS format.
   h. Export the Inventory Status Report in XPS format.
   i. Export the Item Discount Report in XPS format.
2. Create the menu form shown in Figure 8–76. The command buttons should use the macros you created in Step 1 to open the three forms. Be sure to include the title on the form.

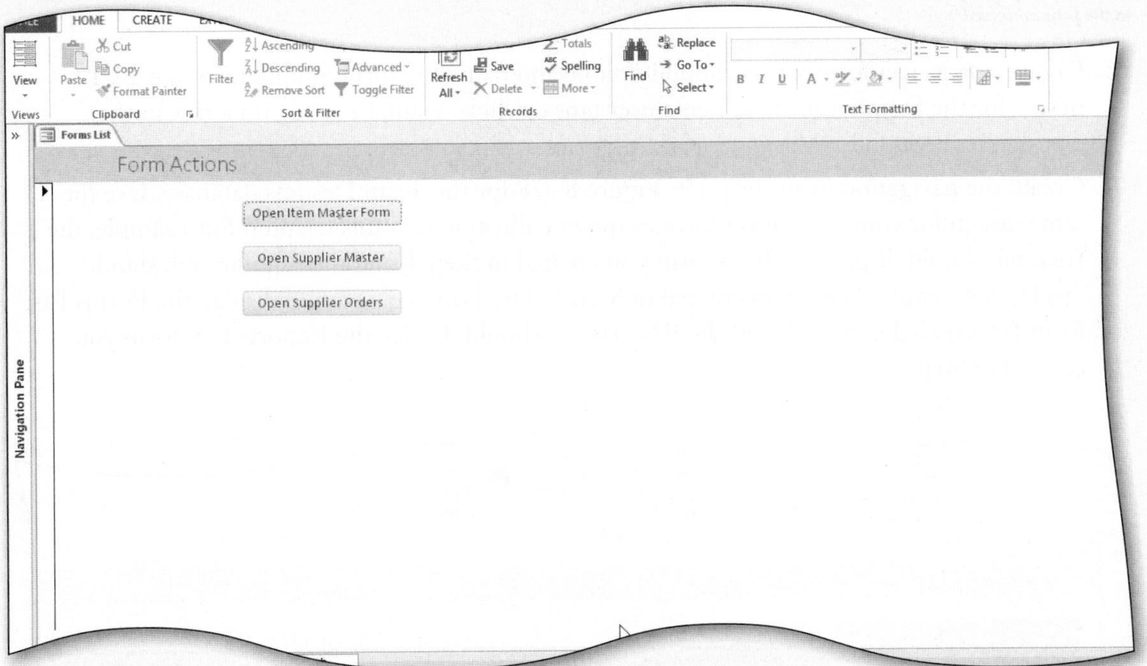

Figure 8–76

3. Create the menu form shown in Figure 8–77. The command buttons should use the macros you created in Step 1 to preview and export the three reports. Be sure to include the title on the form.

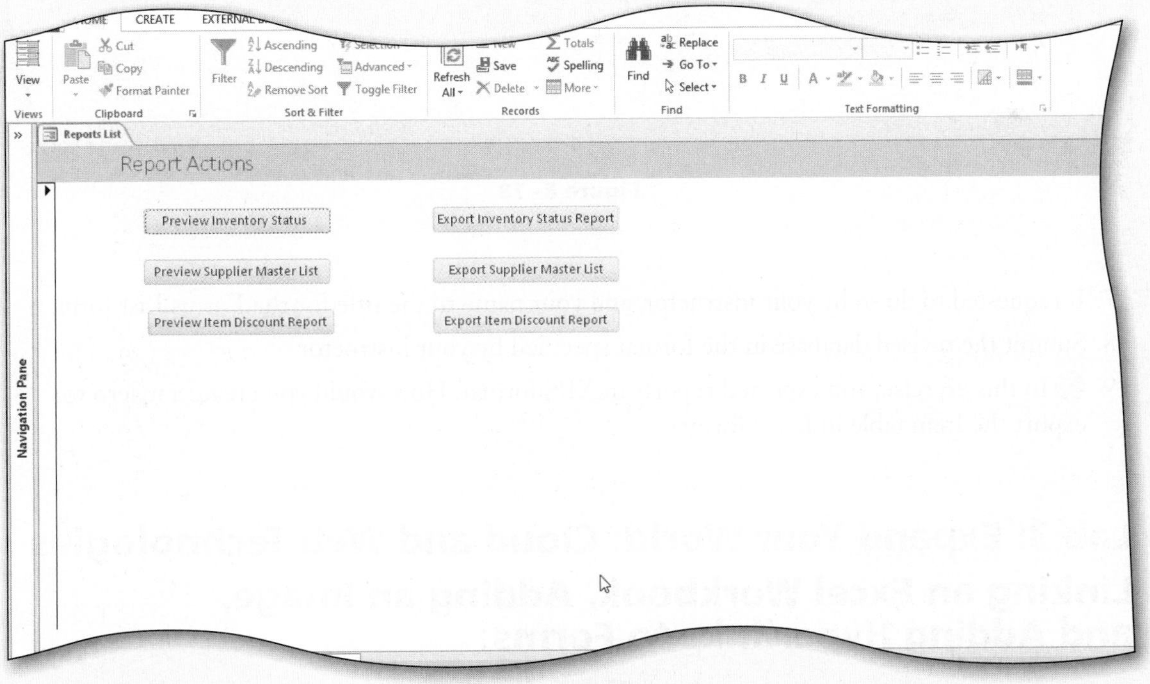

Figure 8–77

4. Create a datasheet form for the Item table and name the form Item. Create a UI macro for the Item form. When a user taps or clicks an item number on a row in the datasheet, the Item Master Form should appear in a pop-up form.

Continued >

In the Labs *continued*

5. Create a datasheet form for the Supplier table and name the form Supplier. Create a UI macro for the Supplier form. When a user taps or clicks a supplier code on a row in the datasheet, the Supplier Master Form should appear in a pop-up form.
6. Create the navigation form shown in Figure 8–78 for the Team Designs database. Use the same design for your navigation form as the one illustrated in this chapter. For example, the Item tab should display the Item form you created in Step 4, and the Supplier tab should display the Supplier form you created in Step 5. The Forms tab should display the Forms List form you created in Step 2, and the Reports tab should display the Reports List form you created in Step 3.

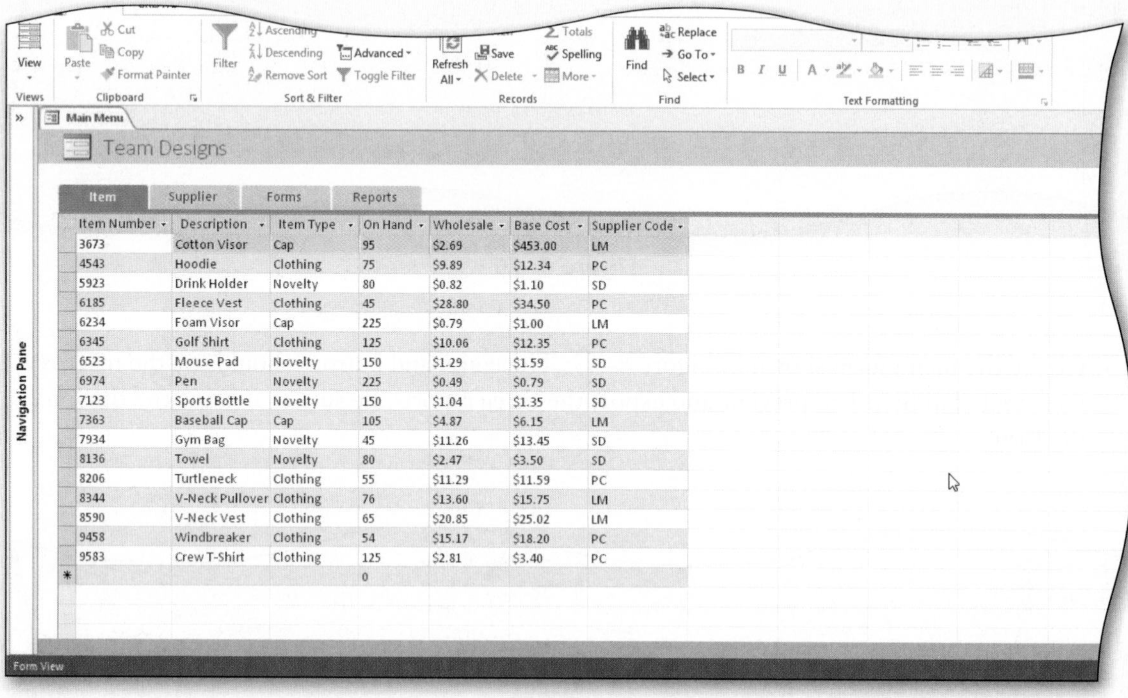

Figure 8–78

7. If requested to do so by your instructor, add your name to the title for the Forms List form.
8. Submit the revised database in the format specified by your instructor.
9. In this exercise, you exported reports in XPS format. How would you create a macro to export the Item table in Excel format?

Lab 3: Expand Your World: Cloud and Web Technologies

Linking an Excel Workbook, Adding an Image, and Adding Hyperlinks to Forms

Problem: Energy Savings is an organization that provides energy saving devices. The organization has created macros and a navigation form but would like to link a workbook containing residential energy statistics and add a hyperlink to a form.

Note: To complete this assignment, you will be required to use the Data Files for Students. Visit www.cengage.com/ct/studentdownload for detailed instructions or contact your instructor for information about accessing the required files.

Instructions: Perform the following tasks:

1. Open your browser and navigate to the U. S. Energy Information Administration website, www.eia.gov/consumption/residential/data/2009/. Select the Consumption & Expenditures tab, and then select By End Uses. Download the expenditure workbook for the region of the country where you live. If you do not live in one of those regions, download the workbook for the United States.
2. Open the Lab 3 Energy Savings database from the Data Files for Students and link the workbook you downloaded to the database.
3. Access the office.com website or any other website containing royalty-free images and search for an energy-related image suitable for a navigation form.
4. Open the navigation form in Design view and add the image to the form header. Add a hyperlink to the main U.S. Energy Information Administration website to the form header.
5. Save your changes.
6. Submit the revised database in the format specified by your instructor.
7. Which workbook did you download and link? What image did you choose for the navigation form? Why did you make those choices?

Consider This: Your Turn

Apply your creative thinking and problem solving skills to design and implement a solution.

1: Creating Macros and a Navigation Form for the Fine Crafts Database

Personal/Academic

Note: To complete this assignment, you will be required to use the Data Files for Students. Visit www.cengage.com/ct/studentdownload for detailed instructions or contact your instructor for information about accessing the required files.

Part 1: You attend a university that is renowned for its school of arts and crafts. Students who major in arts and crafts can sell their work through an agreement with the university bookstore. For your senior capstone project, you have created a database in which to store data about the craft items for sale and the students who created the items. You now need to add macros and a navigation form to make the database easier to use.

Open the Your Turn 1 Fine Crafts database from the Data Files for Students. Then, use the concepts and techniques presented in this chapter to perform each of the following tasks:

a. Create a macro that includes submacros to open the two forms: Item Master Form and Student Master Form in Read-Only mode. The macro also should include submacros to preview and export three reports in PDF format: Crafts for Sale, Item Sale Report, and Items by Student.

b. Create a menu form for the two forms and a menu form for the three reports. Use an option group for each form and include a descriptive title on each form.

c. Create a datasheet form for the Item table and name the form Item. Create a UI macro for the Item form. When a user taps or clicks an item number on a row in the datasheet form, the Item Master Form should appear in a pop-up form in Edit mode.

d. Create a datasheet form for the Student table and name the form Student. Create a UI macro for the Student form. When a user taps or clicks a student code on a row in the datasheet form, the Student Master Form should appear in a pop-up form in Edit mode.

e. Create a navigation form for the Fine Crafts database. Use the same design for your navigation form as that shown in Figure 8–1a on page AC 475. Include the Item form, the Student form, the menu form for the forms, and the menu form for the reports.

Submit your assignment in the format specified by your instructor.

Continued >

Consider This: Your Turn *continued*

Part 2: You made several decisions while in this assignment, including creating option groups. What was the rationale behind your decisions? Do you think it is necessary to have a title on the option group menu forms? Why or why not?

2: Creating Macros and a Navigation Form for the Landscaping Services Database

Professional

Note: To complete this assignment, you will be required to use the Data Files for Students. Visit www.cengage.com/ct/studentdownload for detailed instructions or contact your instructor for information about accessing the required files.

Part 1: Landscaping Services is a local company that provides landscaping and lawn maintenance services to commercial customers, such as businesses, homeowner's associations, and schools. You work part-time for the company while attending college. The owner, Carol Williams has asked you to create macros and a navigation form to make the database easier to use.

Open the Your Turn 2 Landscaping Services database from the Data Files for Students. Then, use the concepts and techniques presented in this chapter to perform the following tasks:

a. Create a macro that includes submacros to open the Customer Master Form, the Supervisor Master Form, and the Supervisor Request Data form. The macro should also include submacros to preview and export in XPS format the Customer Financial Report, the Supervisor Master Report, and the Customers by Supervisor report.
b. Create a menu form for the forms and a menu form for the reports. Use command buttons for each form and include a descriptive title on each form.
c. Create a datasheet form for the Customer table and name the form Customer. Create a user interface macro for the Customer form. When a user taps or clicks a customer number on a row in the datasheet form, the Customer Master Form should appear in a pop-up form.
d. Create a datasheet form for the Supervisor table and name the form Supervisor. Create a UI macro for the Supervisor form. When a user taps or clicks a supervisor number on a row in the datasheet form, the Supervisor Master Form should appear in a pop-up form.
e. Create a data macro for the Customer Requests table. The macro will examine the value in the Hours Spent field. If the user's update would cause the value to be greater than the Total Hours, the macro will change the value to Total Hours. If the user's update would cause the value to be less than 0, the macro will change the value to 0.
f. Create a navigation form for the Landscaping Services database. Use the same design for your navigation form as that shown in Figure 8–1a on page AC 475. Include the Customer form, the Supervisor form, and the menu forms you created in Step b.

Submit your assignment in the format specified by your instructor.

Part 2: You made several decisions while completing this assignment, including creating a macro to open a pop-up form. What was the rationale behind your decisions? The window mode to open a form as a pop-up form is Dialog. What would be the effect if the form opened in Normal mode?

3: Understanding Navigation Forms and Control Layouts

Research and Collaboration

Part 1: Before you begin this assignment, save the Bavant Publishing database as your team name database. For example, if your team is the Fab Four, then name the database Fab Four. Use the database for this assignment. Create a blog, a Google document, or a Word document on the SkyDrive on which to store the team's research findings and observations for this assignment.

a. In this project, you created a navigation form with horizontal tabs. Create additional navigation forms using a different tab arrangement. Compare the arrangements and as a team vote on which navigation form arrangement you prefer. Record your vote and your reason in your blog or other shared document.
b. Open the Customer Form in Layout view. Use the ARRANGE tab to create a form that has the City, State, and Postal Code on one row. Record which features on the ARRANGE tab you used in your blog or other shared document.
c. Create a new workbook in Microsoft Excel. Import the Customer table in Excel and use the recommended PivotTable feature to create a PivotTable for the Customer table. Create a PivotChart from the same data.

Submit your assignment in the format specified by your instructor.

Part 2: You made several decisions while completing this assignment, including changing the arrangement of a navigation form. What was the rationale behind your decisions? Which navigation form best suits the database and why?

Learn Online

Reinforce what you learned in this chapter with games, exercises, training, and many other online activities and resources.

Student Companion Site Reinforcement activities and resources are available at no additional cost on www.cengagebrain.com. Visit www.cengage.com/ct/studentdownload for detailed instructions about accessing the resources available at the Student Companion Site.

SAM Put your skills into practice with SAM Projects! SAM Projects for this chapter can be found online. If you have a SAM account, go to www.cengage.com/sam2013 to access SAM assignments for this chapter.

9 Administering a Database System

Objectives

You will have mastered the material in this project when you can:

- Convert a database to and from earlier versions of Access
- Use the Table Analyzer, Performance Analyzer, and Documenter
- Create custom categories and groups in the Navigation Pane
- Use table, database, and field properties
- Create indexes
- Enable and use automatic error checking
- Create custom data type parts
- Create a database for a template
- Create a custom template
- Encrypt a database and set a password
- Lock a database and split a database
- Create a custom web app
- Create custom views for a web app

9 Administering a Database System

Introduction

Administering a database system is an important activity that has many facets. Going far beyond the simple updating of a database, administration activities improve the usability, accessibility, security, and efficiency of the database.

BTW
Q&As
For a complete list of the Q&As found in many of the step-by-step sequences in this book, visit the Q&A resource on the Student Companion Site located on www.cengagebrain.com. For detailed instructions about accessing available resources, visit www.cengage.com/ct/studentdownload or contact your instructor for information about accessing the required files.

Project — Administering a Database System

Bavant Publishing realizes the importance of database administration, that is, the importance of administering its database system properly. Making a database available on the web using a web app (Figure 9–1) is part of this activity. The Clients and Recruiters database shown in Figure 9–1 is a database that contains information about a recruiting agency that specializes in placing health science professionals. The recruiting agency is a division in a company in which Bavant recently acquired a controlling interest. Figure 9–1a shows the Recruiter table selected in List view. Not only does the data about the recruiter appear on the screen, but data concerning the clients of the selected recruiter does as well. Figure 9–1b shows the Client table selected in By City view, which has grouped the clients by City. Clients in the selected city, Berridge in this case, appear on the screen. Tapping or clicking an individual client causes all the data for the client to appear as shown in Figure 9–1c.

BTW
BTWs
For a complete list of the BTWs found in the margins of this book, visit the BTW resource on the Student Companion Site located on www.cengagebrain.com. For detailed instructions about accessing available resources, visit www.cengage.com/ct/studentdownload or contact your instructor for information about accessing the required files.

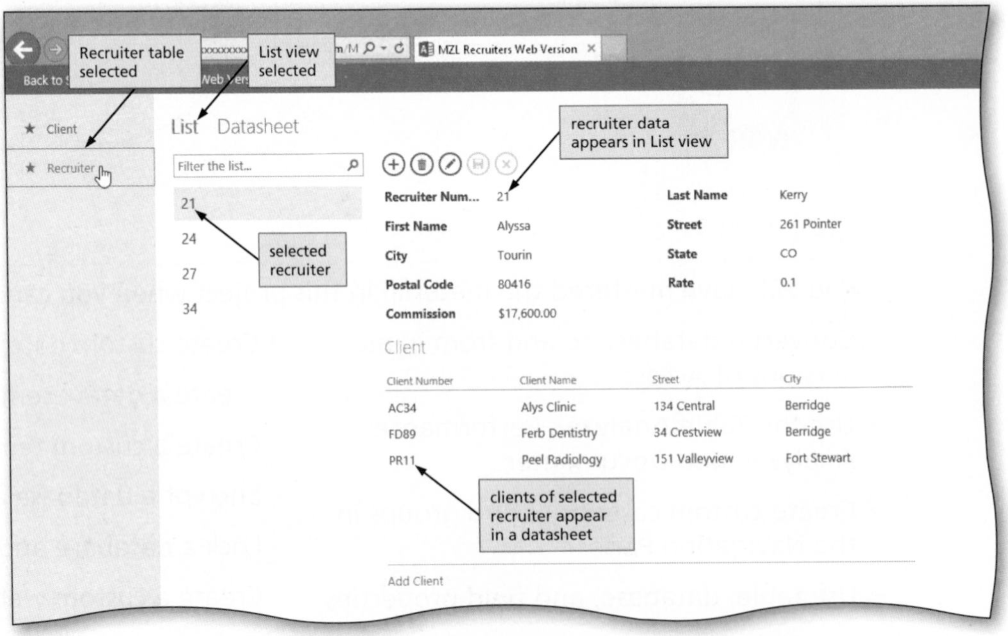

Figure 9–1 (a) Recruiter Table Shown in Web App

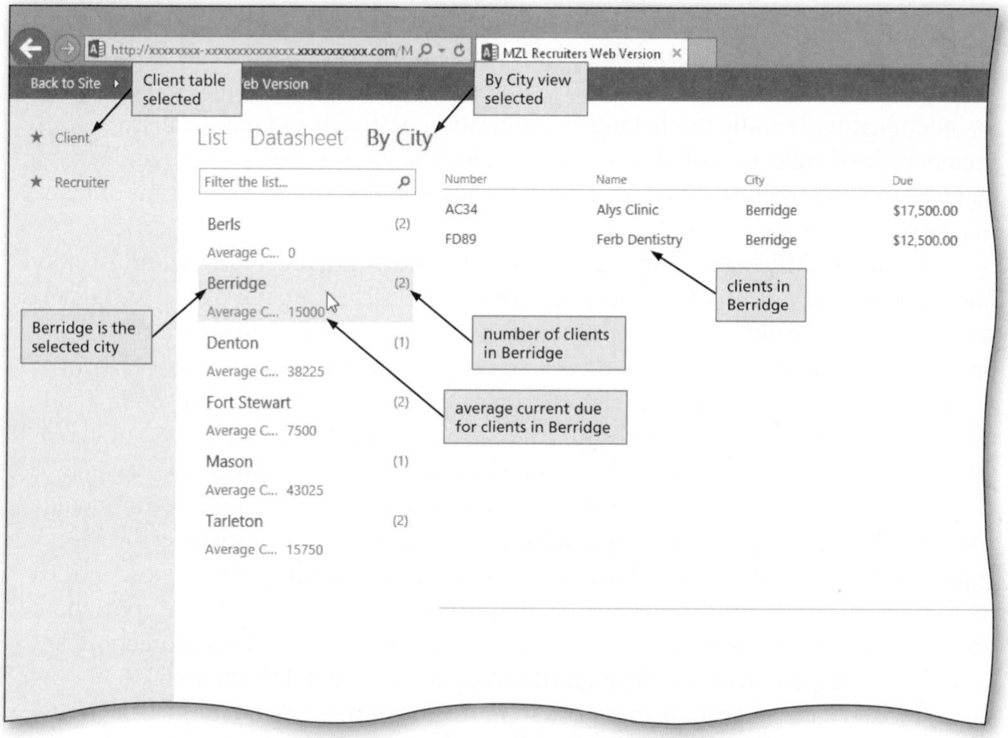

Figure 9–1 (b) Client Table Shown in Web App

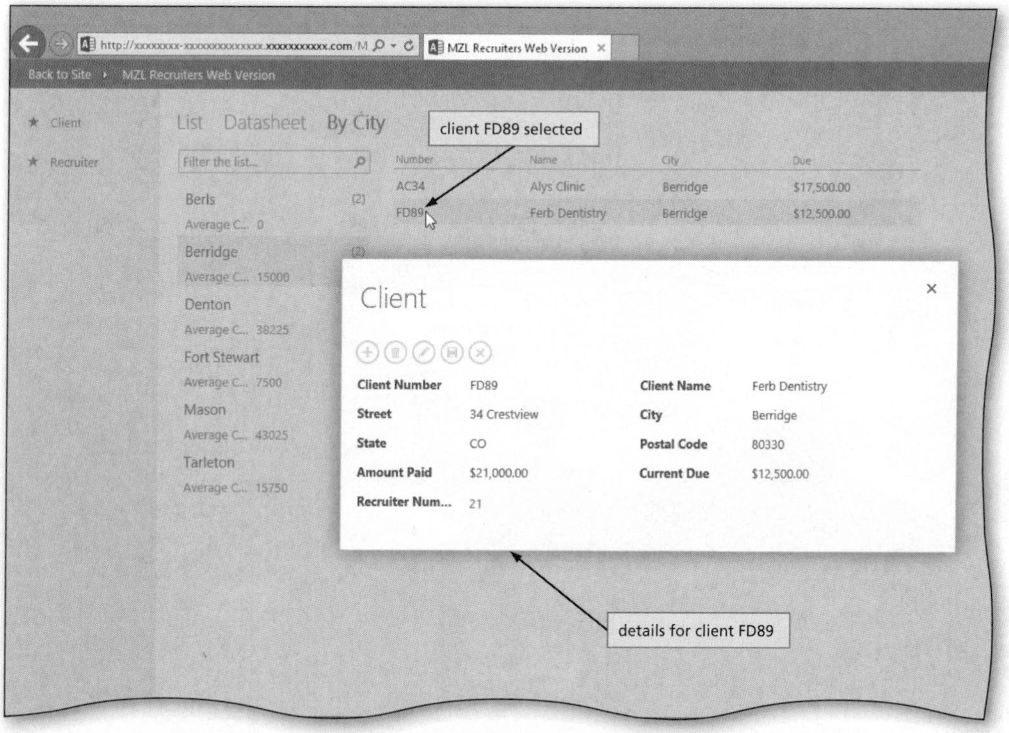

Figure 9–1 (c) Client Details Shown in Web App

Another important activity in administering databases is the creation of custom templates, application parts, and data type parts. **Application parts** and **data type parts** are templates included in Access that you can add to your database to extend its functionality. Tapping or clicking an application part adds to your database a predetermined collection of objects such as tables, queries, forms, reports, and/or macros. Tapping or clicking a data type part adds a predetermined collection of fields to a table.

Figure 9–2 illustrates the range of activities involved in database administration, including the conversion of an Access database to an earlier version of Access. Database administration usually includes such activities as analyzing tables for potential problems, analyzing performance to see if changes could make the system perform more efficiently, and documenting the various objects in the database. It can include creating custom categories and groups in the Navigation Pane as well as changing table and database properties. It also can include the use of field properties in such tasks as creating a custom input mask and allowing zero-length strings. It can include the creation of indexes to speed up retrieval. The inclusion of automatic error checking is part of the administration of a database system. Understanding the purpose of the Trust Center is critical to the database administration function. Another important area of database administration is the protection of the database. This protection includes locking the database through the creation of an ACCDE file to prevent unauthorized changes from being made to the VBA source code or to the design of forms and reports. Splitting the database into a front-end and a back-end database is another way to protect the functionality and efficiency of a database.

Figure 9–2

Roadmap

In this chapter, you will learn how to perform a variety of database administration tasks. The following roadmap identifies general activities you will perform as you progress through this chapter:

1. Learn how to CONVERT a DATABASE
2. Use tools to ANALYZE AND DOCUMENT a database
3. Customize the NAVIGATION PANE
4. Use CUSTOM PROPERTIES AND create INDEXES
5. Create a CUSTOM DATA PART
6. Create a CUSTOM TEMPLATE
7. ENCRYPT, LOCK, AND SPLIT a database
8. Learn how to create a CUSTOM WEB APP
9. Learn how to create CUSTOM VIEW in a web app

At the beginning of step instructions throughout the chapter, you will see an abbreviated form of this roadmap. The abbreviated roadmap uses colors to indicate chapter progress: gray means the chapter is beyond that activity; blue means the task being shown is covered in that activity, and black means that activity is yet to be covered. For example, the following abbreviated roadmap indicates the chapter would be showing a task in the 3 NAVIGATION PANE activity.

1 CONVERT DATABASE | 2 ANALYZE & DOCUMENT | 3 NAVIGATION PANE | 4 CUSTOM PROPERTIES & INDEXES
5 CUSTOM DATA PART | 6 CUSTOM TEMPLATE | 7 ENCRYPT LOCK & SPLIT | 8 CUSTOM WEB APP | 9 CUSTOM VIEW

Use the abbreviated roadmap as a progress guide while you read or step through the instructions in this chapter.

BTW
Touch Screen Differences
The Office and Windows interfaces may vary if you are using a touch screen. For this reason, you might notice that the function or appearance of your touch screen differs slightly from this chapter's presentation.

To Run Access

If you are using a computer to step through the project in this chapter and you want your screens to match the figures in this book, you should change your screen's resolution to 1366 × 768. For information about how to change a computer's resolution, refer to the Office and Windows chapter at the beginning of this book.

The following steps, which assume Windows is running, use the Start screen or the search box to run Access based on a typical installation. You may need to ask your instructor how to run Access on your computer. For a detailed example of the procedure summarized below, refer to the Office and Windows chapter.

1. Scroll the Start screen for an Access 2013 tile. If your Start screen contains an Access 2013 tile, tap or click it to run Access; if the Start screen does not contain the Access 2013 tile, proceed to the next step to search for the Access app.
2. Swipe in from the right edge of the screen or point to the upper-right corner of the screen to display the Charms bar, and then tap or click the Search charm on the Charms bar to display the Search menu.
3. Type `Access` as the search text in the Search text box and watch the search results appear in the Apps list.
4. Tap or click Access 2013 in the search results to run Access.

BTW
The Ribbon and Screen Resolution
Access may change how the groups and buttons within the groups appear on the ribbon, depending on the computer's screen resolution. Thus, your ribbon may look different from the ones in this book if you are using a screen resolution other than 1366 x 768.

To Open a Database from Access

BTW
Distributing a Document
Instead of printing and distributing a hard copy of a document, you can distribute the document electronically. Options include sending the document via email; posting it on cloud storage (such as SkyDrive) and sharing the file with others; posting it on a social networking site, blog, or other website; and sharing a link associated with an online location of the document. You also can create and share a PDF or XPS image of the document, so that users can view the file in Acrobat Reader or XPS Viewer instead of in Access.

The following steps open the Bavant Publishing database from the location you specified when you first created it (for example, the Access folder in the CIS 101 folder). For a detailed example of the procedure summarized below, refer to the Office and Windows chapter at the beginning of this book.

1. Tap or click FILE on the ribbon to open the Backstage view, if necessary.
2. If the database you want to open is displayed in the Recent list, tap or click the file name to open the database and display the opened database in the Access window; then skip to Step 7. If the database you want to open is not displayed in the Recent list or if the Recent list does not appear, tap or click Open Other Files to display the Open Gallery.
3. If the database you want to open is displayed in the Recent list in the Open gallery, tap or click the file name to open the database and display the opened database in the Access window; then skip to Step 7.
4. Tap or click Computer, SkyDrive, or another location in the left pane and then navigate to the location of the database to be opened (for example, the Access folder in the CIS 101 folder).
5. Tap or click Bavant Publishing to select the database to be opened.
6. Tap or click the Open button (Open dialog box) to open the selected file and display the opened database in the Access window.
7. If a Security Warning appears, tap or click the Enable Content button.

Converting Databases

BTW
Maintaining Backward Compatibility
If you plan to share your database with users who may have an earlier version of Access, be sure to maintain backward compatibility. Do not include multivalued fields, attachment fields, or calculated fields in your database design. For example, if there is a calculation that is used frequently, create a query with the calculated field and use the query as the basis for forms and reports rather than adding the field to the table design.

Access 2007, Access 2010, and Access 2013 all use the same file format, the .accdb format. The format is usually referred to as the Access 2007 file format. Thus, in Access 2013, you can use any database created in Access 2007. You should be aware of the following changes in Access 2013:

1. Unlike previous versions, Access 2013 does not support PivotTables or PivotCharts.
2. The Text data type is now Short Text and the Memo data type is now Long Text.
3. Smart Tags are no longer supported.
4. Replication is no longer available.

To convert an Access 2007 database to an earlier version, the database cannot contain any features that are specific to Access 2007, 2010, or 2013. These include attachments, multivalued fields, offline data, or links to external files not supported in earlier versions of Access. They also include objects published to the web, data macros, and calculated columns. Provided the database does not contain such features, you can convert the database by tapping or clicking the Save As tab in the Backstage view (Figure 9–3). You then can choose the appropriate format.

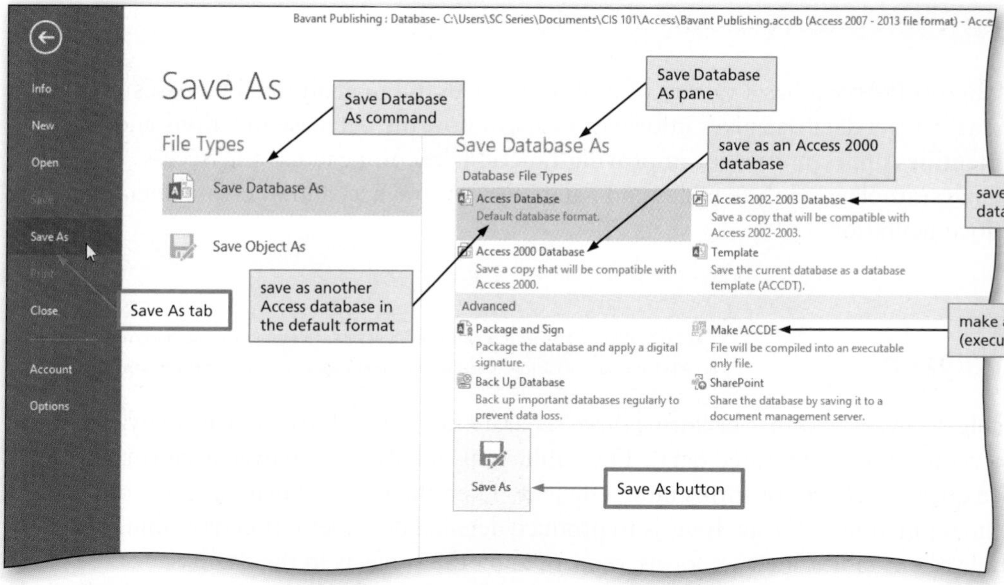

Figure 9–3

1 CONVERT DATABASE | 2 ANALYZE & DOCUMENT | 3 NAVIGATION PANE | 4 CUSTOM PROPERTIES & INDEXES
5 CUSTOM DATA PART | 6 CUSTOM TEMPLATE | 7 ENCRYPT LOCK & SPLIT | 8 CUSTOM WEB APP | 9 CUSTOM VIEW

To Convert an Access 2007–2013 Database to an Earlier Version

Specifically, to convert an Access 2007–2013 database to an earlier version, you would use the following steps.

1. With the database to be converted open, tap or click FILE on the ribbon to open the Backstage view.
2. Tap or click the Save As tab.
3. With the Save Database As command selected, tap or click the desired format, and then tap or click the Save As button.
4. Type the name you want for the converted database, select a location in which to save the converted database, and tap or click the Save button.

BTW
Saving Databases to External Locations
You also can save a database to an external location such as SkyDrive, and to any portable storage device, such as a USB flash drive. To do so, select the desired external location or portable storage device when you browse to specify a location for your database.

1 CONVERT DATABASE | 2 ANALYZE & DOCUMENT | 3 NAVIGATION PANE | 4 CUSTOM PROPERTIES & INDEXES
5 CUSTOM DATA PART | 6 CUSTOM TEMPLATE | 7 ENCRYPT LOCK & SPLIT | 8 CUSTOM WEB APP | 9 CUSTOM VIEW

To Convert an Access 2000 or 2002–2003 Database to an Access 2013 Database

To convert an Access 2000 or Access 2002–2003 database to the default database format for Access 2013, you open the database in Access 2013. Initially, the database is open in compatibility mode, where features that are new to Access 2013 and that cannot easily be displayed or converted are disabled. In this mode, the database remains in its original format. If you want to convert it so that you can use it in Access 2013, you use the Access Database command on the Backstage view. Once the database is converted, the disabled features will be enabled. You will no longer be able to share the database with users of Access 2000 or Access 2002–2003, however.

Specifically, to convert an Access 2000 or 2002–2003 database to the default database format for Access 2013, you would use the following steps.

1. With the database to be converted open, tap or click FILE on the ribbon to open the Backstage view.
2. Tap or click the Save As tab.
3. With the Save Database As command selected, tap or click Access Database and then tap or click the Save As button.
4. Type the name you want for the converted database, select a location, and tap or click the Save button.

BTW
Exporting XML Data
Database administration also may include responsibility for exchanging data between dissimilar systems or apps. Extensible Markup Language (XML) is a data interchange standard for describing and delivering data on the web. With XML, you can describe both the data and the structure (schema) of the data. You can export tables queries, forms, or reports. To export a database object, select the object and tap or click the XML File button (EXTERNAL DATA tab | Export group). Select the appropriate options in the Export XML dialog box.

BTW
Creating Databases in Older Formats
To create a database in an older format, create a database and browse to select a location for the database, then tap or click the Save As Type arrow in the File New Database dialog box, and select either 2002–2003 format or 2000 format.

Microsoft Access Analysis Tools

Microsoft Access has a variety of tools that are useful in analyzing databases. Analyzing a database gives information about how the database functions and identifies opportunities for improving functionality. You can use the Access analysis tools to analyze tables and database performance, and to create detailed documentation.

To Use the Table Analyzer

1 CONVERT DATABASE | 2 ANALYZE & DOCUMENT | 3 NAVIGATION PANE | 4 CUSTOM PROPERTIES & INDEXES
5 CUSTOM DATA PART | 6 CUSTOM TEMPLATE | 7 ENCRYPT LOCK & SPLIT | 8 CUSTOM WEB APP | 9 CUSTOM VIEW

Access contains a Table Analyzer tool that performs three separate functions. This tool can analyze tables while looking for potential redundancy (duplicated data). The Table Analyzer also can analyze performance and check for ways to make queries, reports, or forms more efficient. Then the tool will make suggestions for possible changes. The final function of the analyzer is to produce detailed documentation describing the structure and content of the various tables, queries, forms, reports, and other objects in the database.

The following steps use the Table Analyzer to examine the Customer table for **redundancy**, or duplicated data. ***Why?*** *Redundancy is one of the biggest potential sources of problems in a database.* If redundancy is found, the Table Analyzer will suggest ways to split the table in order to eliminate the redundancy.

1

- Open the Bavant Publishing database.
- If necessary, close the Navigation Pane.
- Display the DATABASE TOOLS tab (Figure 9–4).

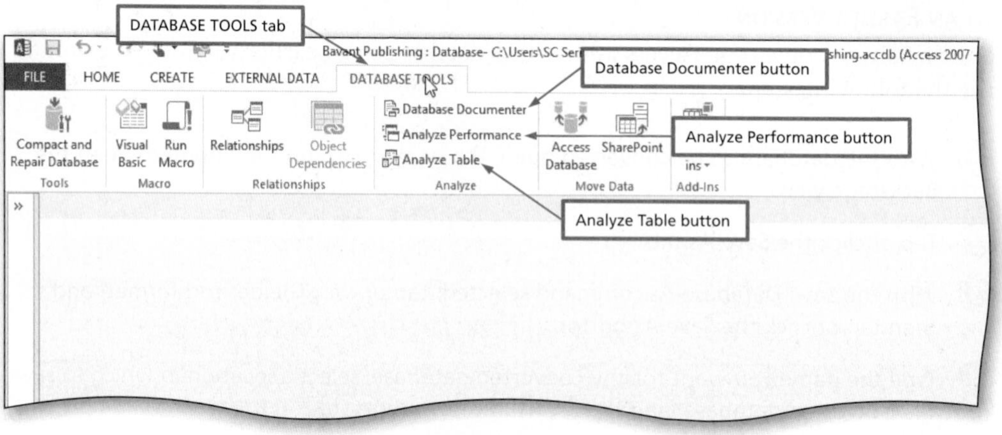

Figure 9–4

2

- Tap or click the Analyze Table button (DATABASE TOOLS tab | Analyze group) to display the Table Analyzer Wizard dialog box (Figure 9–5).

Q&A Where did the data in the figure come from? It does not look like my data.
The data is fictitious. It is just intended to give you an idea of what the data might look like.

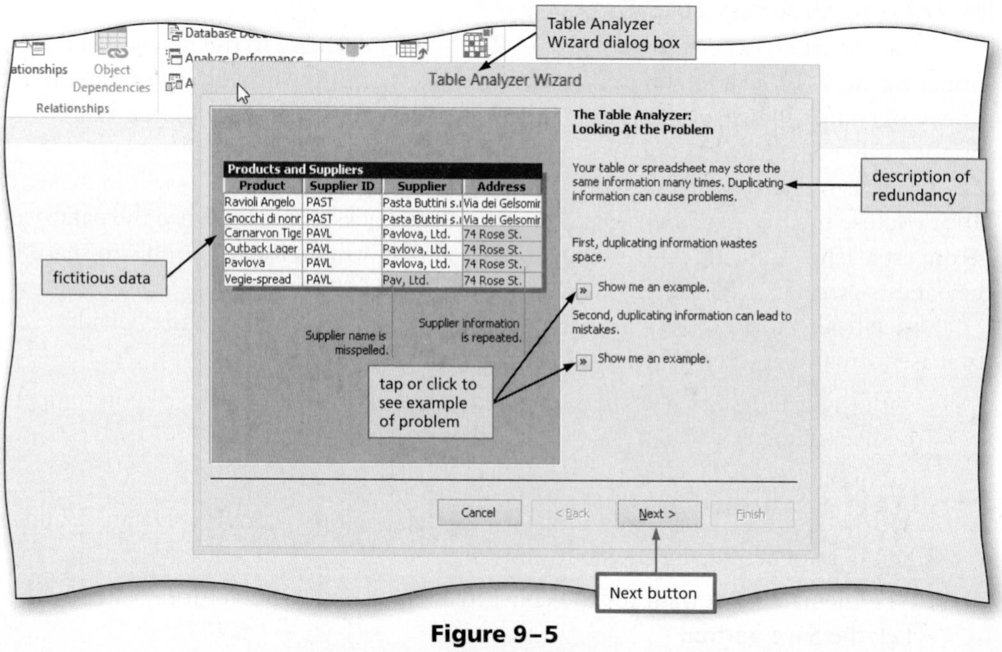

Figure 9–5

3

- Tap or click the Next button to display the next Table Analyzer Wizard screen (Figure 9–6).

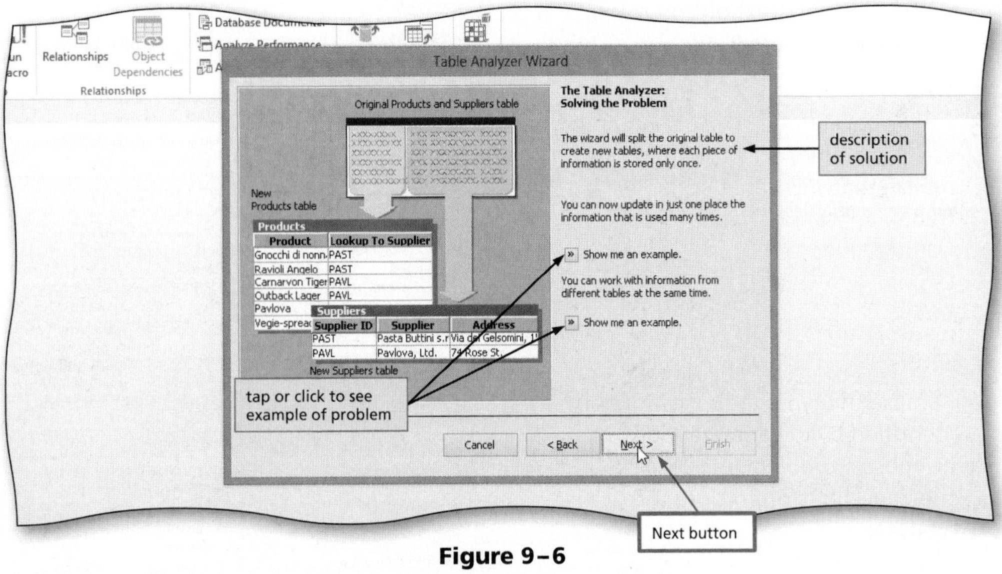

Figure 9–6

4

- Tap or click the Next button to display the next Table Analyzer Wizard screen.
- Select the Customer table (Figure 9–7).

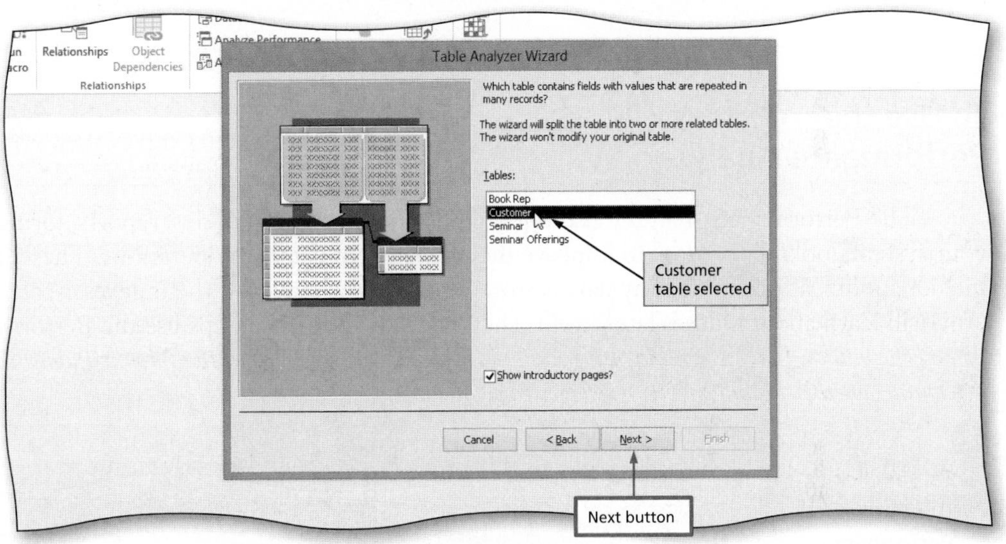

Figure 9–7

5

- Tap or click the Next button.
- Be sure the 'Yes, let the wizard decide.' option button is selected (Figure 9–8) to let the wizard determine what action to take.

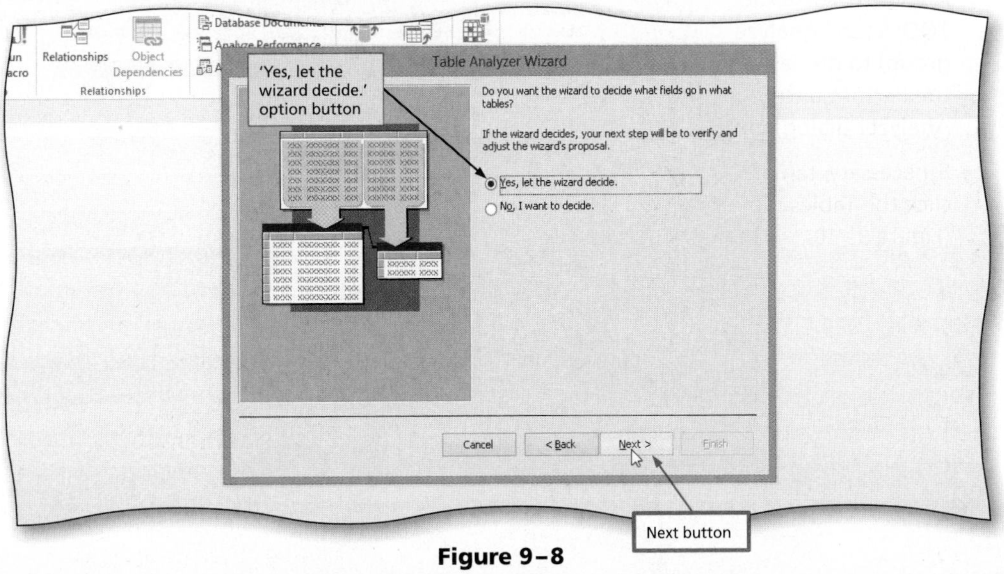

Figure 9–8

6

- Tap or click the Next button to run the analysis (Figure 9–9).

Q&A I do not really want to put the city, state, and postal code in a different table, even though I realize that this data does appear to be duplicated. Do I have to follow this advice?

Certainly not. This is only a suggestion.

7

- Because the type of duplication identified by the analyzer does not pose a problem, tap or click the Cancel button to close the analyzer.

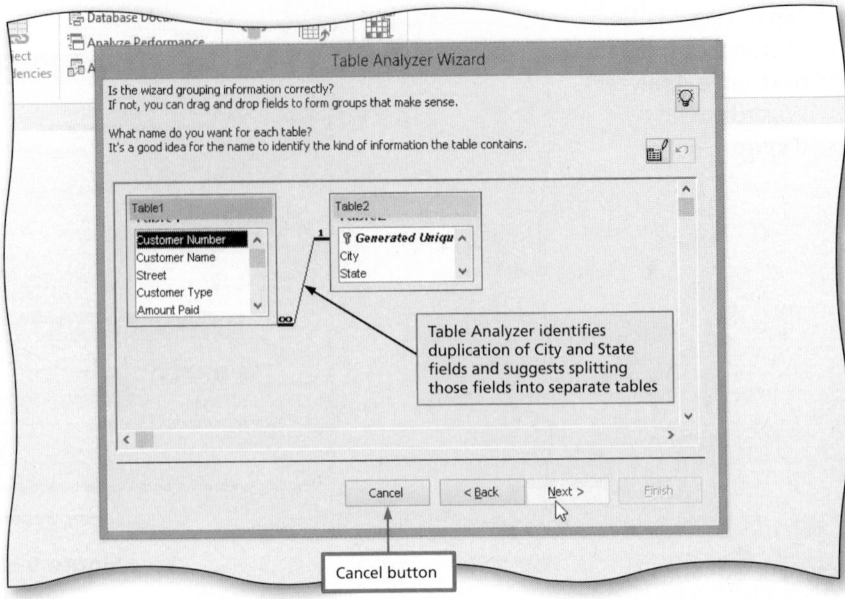

Figure 9–9

To Use the Performance Analyzer

1 CONVERT DATABASE | 2 ANALYZE & DOCUMENT | 3 NAVIGATION PANE | 4 CUSTOM PROPERTIES & INDEXES
5 CUSTOM DATA PART | 6 CUSTOM TEMPLATE | 7 ENCRYPT LOCK & SPLIT | 8 CUSTOM WEB APP | 9 CUSTOM VIEW

The Performance Analyzer examines the database's tables, queries, reports, forms, and other objects in your system, looking for ways to improve the efficiency of database operations. These improvements could include modifications to the way data is stored, as well as changes to the indexes created for the system. (You will learn about indexes later in this chapter.) The following steps use the Performance Analyzer. ***Why?*** *The Performance Analyzer will identify possible areas for improvement in the Bavant Publishing database. Users then can determine whether to implement the suggested changes.*

1

- Tap or click the Analyze Performance button, shown in Figure 9–4 on page AC 544, (DATABASE TOOLS tab | Analyze group) to display the Performance Analyzer dialog box.
- If necessary, tap or click the Tables tab (Figure 9–10).

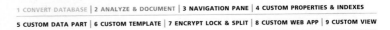

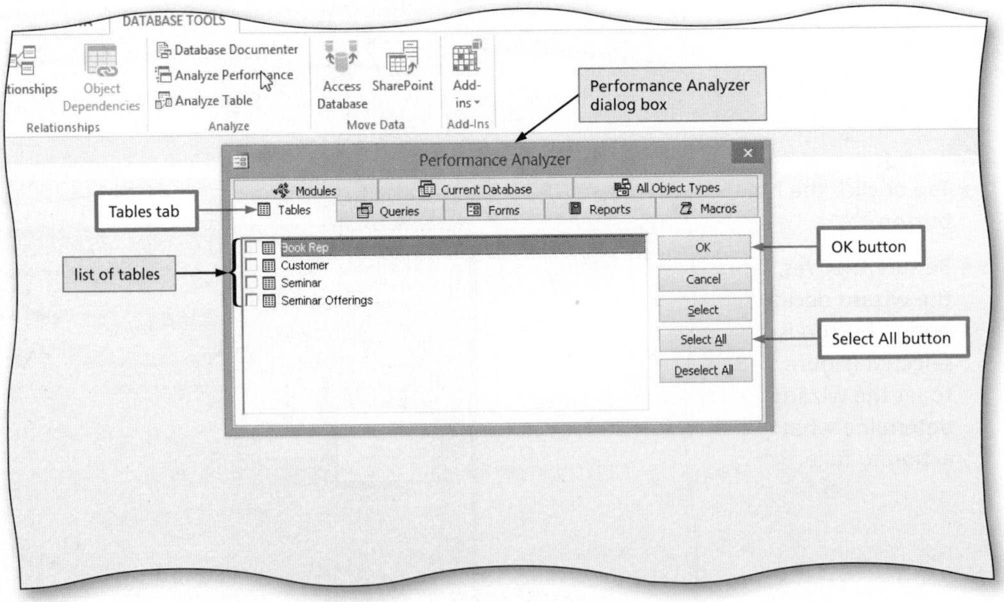

Figure 9–10

2

- Tap or click the Select All button to select all tables.
- Tap or click the OK button to display the results (Figure 9–11).

Q&A What do the results mean?

Because both fields contain only numbers, Access is suggesting that you might improve the efficiency of the table by changing the data types of the fields to Long Integer. As the icon in front of the suggestions indicates, this is simply an idea — something to consider. For these particular fields, Short Text is a better type, however, so you should ignore this suggestion.

3

- Tap or click the Close button to finish working with the Performance Analyzer.

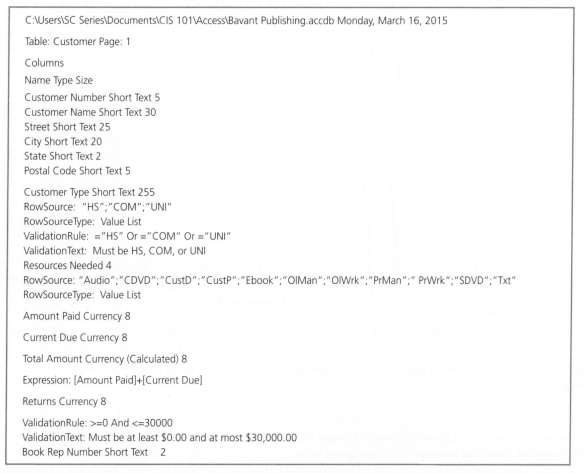

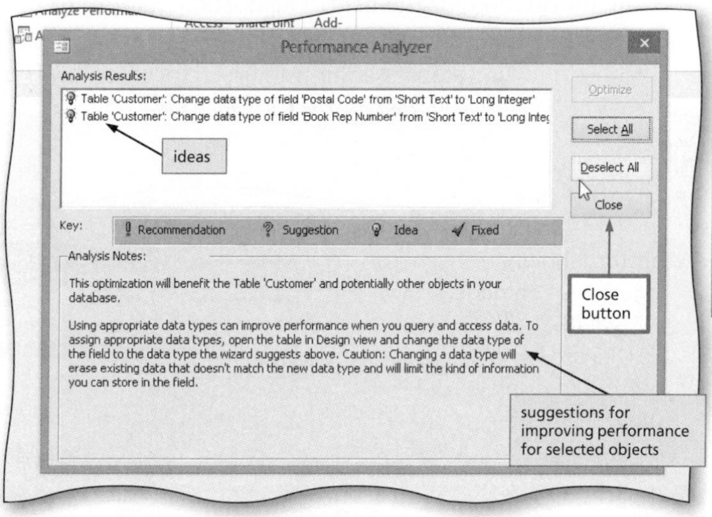

Figure 9–11

To Use the Database Documenter

The Database Documenter allows you to produce detailed documentation of the various tables, queries, forms, reports, and other objects in your database. Documentation is required by many organizations. It is used for backup, disaster recovery, and planning for database enhancements. Figure 9–12 shows a portion of the documentation for the Customer table. The complete documentation is much lengthier than the one shown in the figure.

C:\Users\SC Series\Documents\CIS 101\Access\Bavant Publishing.accdb Monday, March 16, 2015

Table: Customer Page: 1

Columns

Name Type Size

Customer Number Short Text 5
Customer Name Short Text 30
Street Short Text 25
City Short Text 20
State Short Text 2
Postal Code Short Text 5

Customer Type Short Text 255
RowSource: "HS";"COM";"UNI"
RowSourceType: Value List
ValidationRule: ="HS" Or ="COM" Or ="UNI"
ValidationText: Must be HS, COM, or UNI
Resources Needed 4
RowSource: "Audio";"CDVD";"CustD";"CustP";"Ebook";"OlMan";"OlWrk";"PrMan";" PrWrk";"SDVD";"Txt"
RowSourceType: Value List

Amount Paid Currency 8

Current Due Currency 8

Total Amount Currency (Calculated) 8

Expression: [Amount Paid]+[Current Due]

Returns Currency 8

ValidationRule: >=0 And <=30000
ValidationText: Must be at least $0.00 and at most $30,000.00
Book Rep Number Short Text 2

Figure 9–12

Notice that the documentation of the Customer Type field contains the row source associated with the Lookup information for the field. The documentation for both the Customer Type and Returns fields contains validation rules and validation text.

The following steps use the Database Documenter. ***Why?*** *The Database Documenter is the easiest way to produce detailed documentation for the Customer table.*

1

- Tap or click the Database Documenter button, shown in Figure 9–4 on page AC 544 (DATABASE TOOLS tab | Analyze group), to display the Documenter dialog box.
- If necessary, tap or click the Tables tab and then tap or click the Customer check box to specify documentation for the Customer table (Figure 9–13).

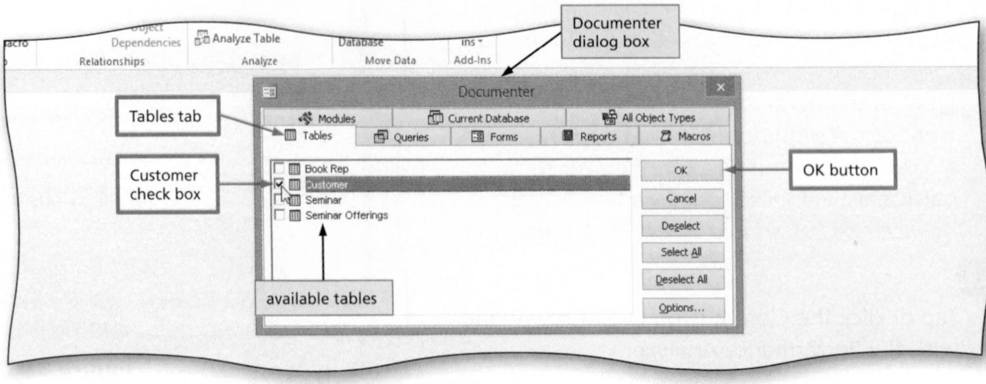

Figure 9–13

2

- Tap or click the OK button to produce a preview of the documentation (Figure 9–14).

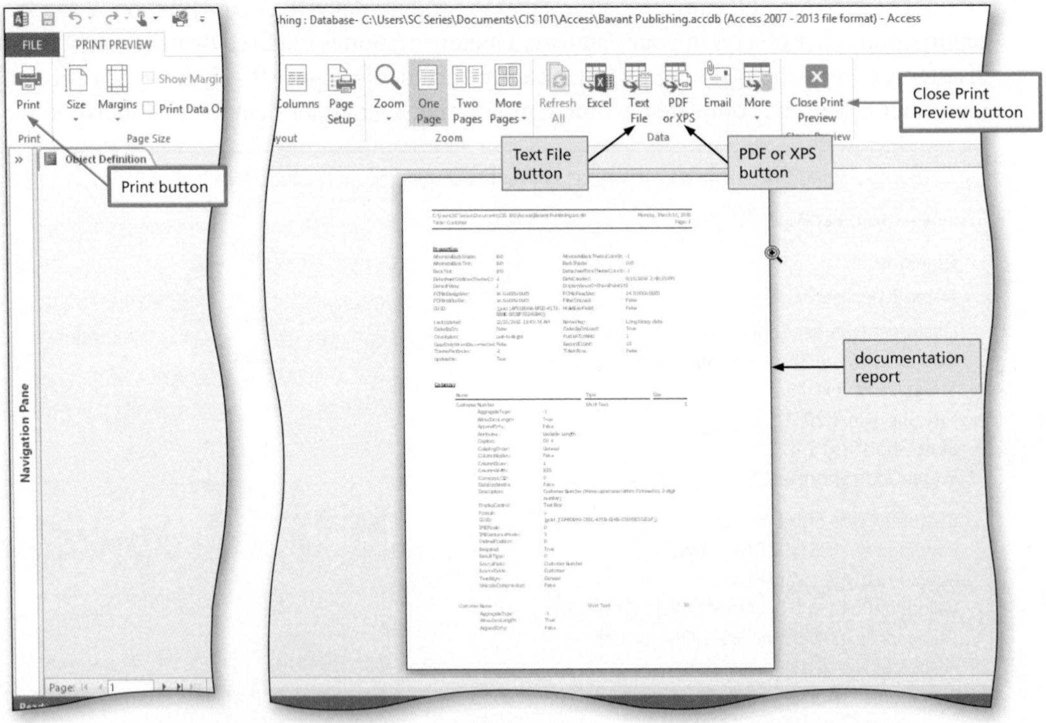

Figure 9–14

Q&A What can I do with this documentation?
You could print it by tapping or clicking the Print button (PRINT PREVIEW tab | Print group). You could create a PDF or XPS file containing the documentation by tapping or clicking the PDF or XPS button (PRINT PREVIEW tab | Data group) and following the directions. You could create a Word (RTF) file by tapping or clicking the More button (PRINT PREVIEW tab | Data group), and then tapping or clicking Word and following the directions. Whatever option you choose, you may need to use this documentation later if you make changes to the database design.

- Tap or click the Close Print Preview button (PRINT PREVIEW tab | Close Preview group) to close the preview of the documentation.

Experiment

- Try other options within the Database Documenter to see the effect of your choice on the documentation produced. Each time, close the preview of the documentation.

Navigation Pane Customization

You already have learned how to customize the Navigation Pane by selecting the category and the filter as well as how to use the Search Bar to restrict the items that appear in the Navigation Pane. You also can create custom categories and groups that you can use to categorize the items in the database in ways that are most useful to you.

To Create Custom Categories and Groups

1 CONVERT DATABASE | 2 ANALYZE & DOCUMENT | 3 NAVIGATION PANE | 4 CUSTOM PROPERTIES & INDEXES
5 CUSTOM DATA PART | 6 CUSTOM TEMPLATE | 7 ENCRYPT LOCK & SPLIT | 8 CUSTOM WEB APP | 9 CUSTOM VIEW

You can create custom categories in the Navigation Pane. You can further refine the objects you place in a category by adding custom groups to the categories. ***Why?*** *Custom groups allow you to tailor the Navigation Pane for your own specific needs.* The following steps create a custom category called Financial Items. They then add two custom groups, Detailed and Summary, to the Financial Items category.

1

- If necessary, display the Navigation Pane.
- Press and hold or right-click the Navigation Pane title bar to display a shortcut menu (Figure 9–15).

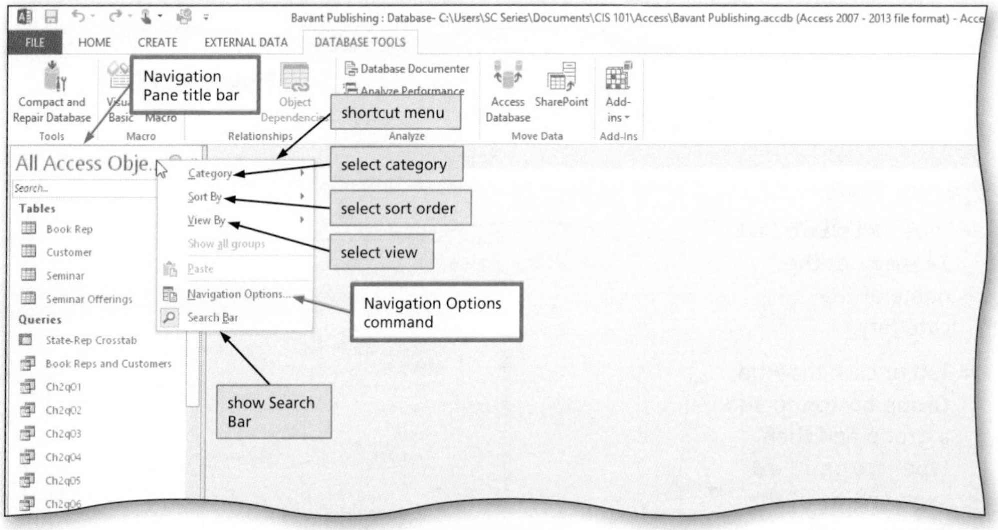

Figure 9–15

2

- Tap or click the Navigation Options command on the shortcut menu to display the Navigation Options dialog box (Figure 9–16).

Q&A What else could I do with the shortcut menu?
You could select a category, select a sort order, or select how to view the items within the Navigation Pane.

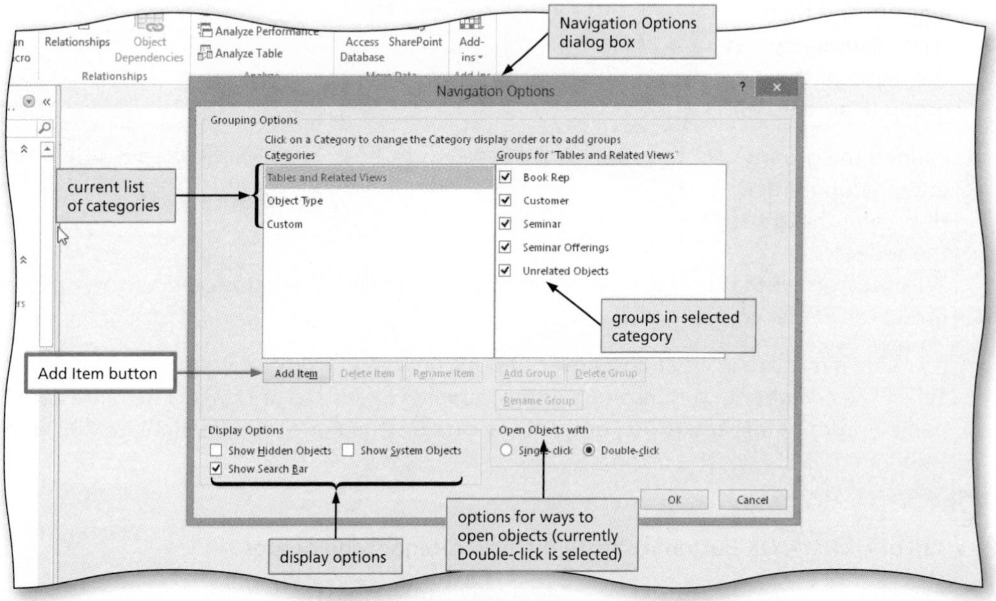

Figure 9–16

3

- Tap or click the Add Item button to add a new category (Figure 9–17).

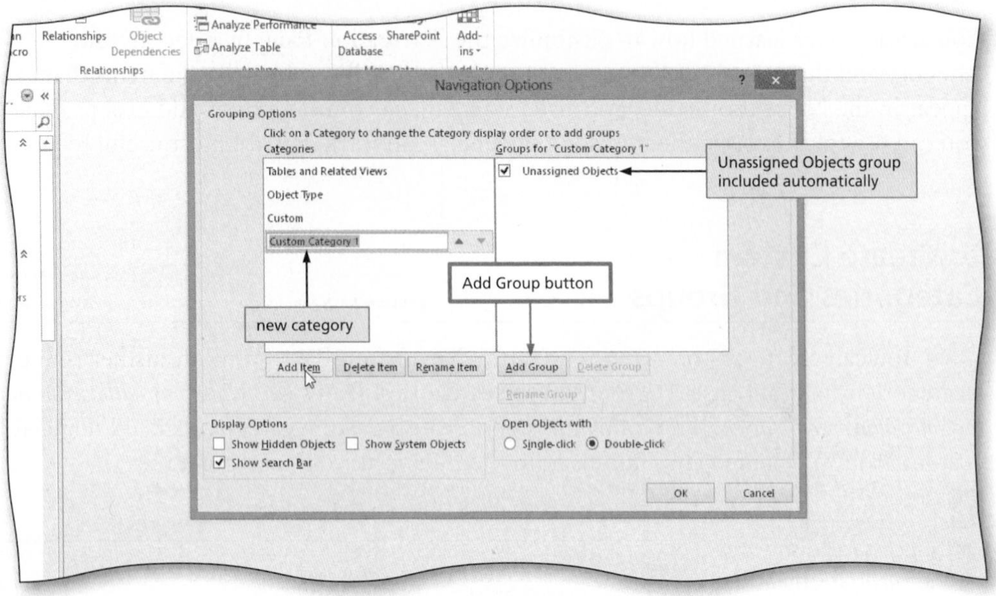

Figure 9–17

4

- Type **Financial Items** as the name of the category.
- Tap or click the Add Group button to add a group and then type **Detailed** as the name of the group.
- Tap or click the Add Group button to add a group and then type **Summary** as the name of the group (Figure 9–18).

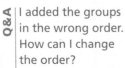

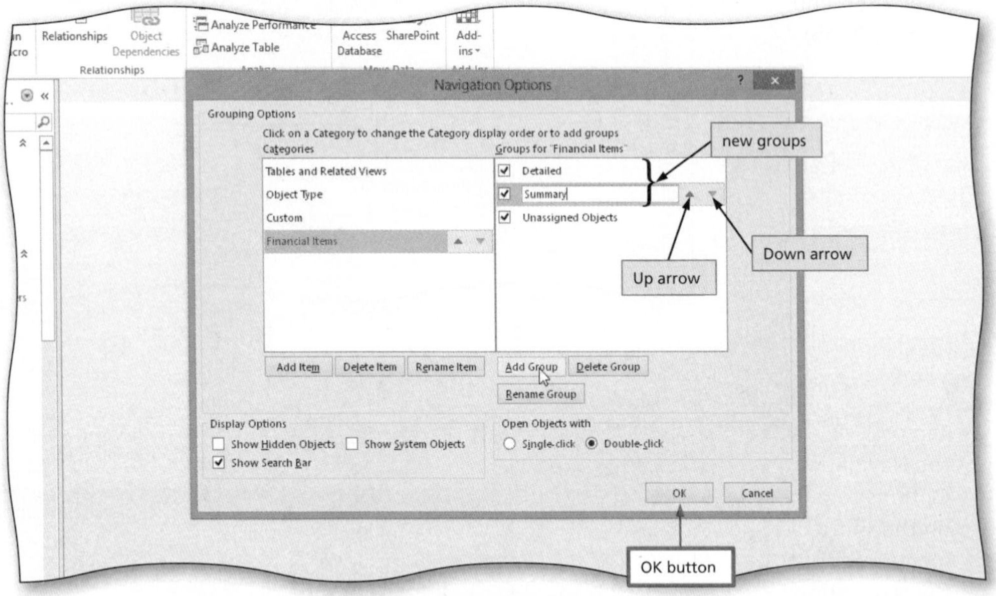

Figure 9–18

Q&A

I added the groups in the wrong order. How can I change the order?

Select the group that is in the wrong position. Tap or click the Up or Down arrows to move the group to the correct location.

If I made a mistake in creating a new category, how can I fix it?

Select the category that is incorrect. If the name is wrong, tap or click the Rename Item button and change the name appropriately. If you do not want the category, tap or click the Delete Item button to delete the category and then tap or click the OK button.

5

- Tap or click the OK button to create the new category and groups.

To Add Items to Groups

Once you have created new groups, you can add existing items to the new groups. The following steps add items to the Summary and Detailed groups in the Financial Items category. ***Why?*** *These items are all financial in nature.*

1

- Tap or click the Navigation Pane arrow to produce the Navigation Pane menu (Figure 9–19).

Q&A Do I have to tap or click the arrow?

No. If you prefer, you can tap or click anywhere in the title bar for the Navigation Pane. Tapping or clicking arrows is a good habit, however, because there are many situations where you must tap or click the arrow.

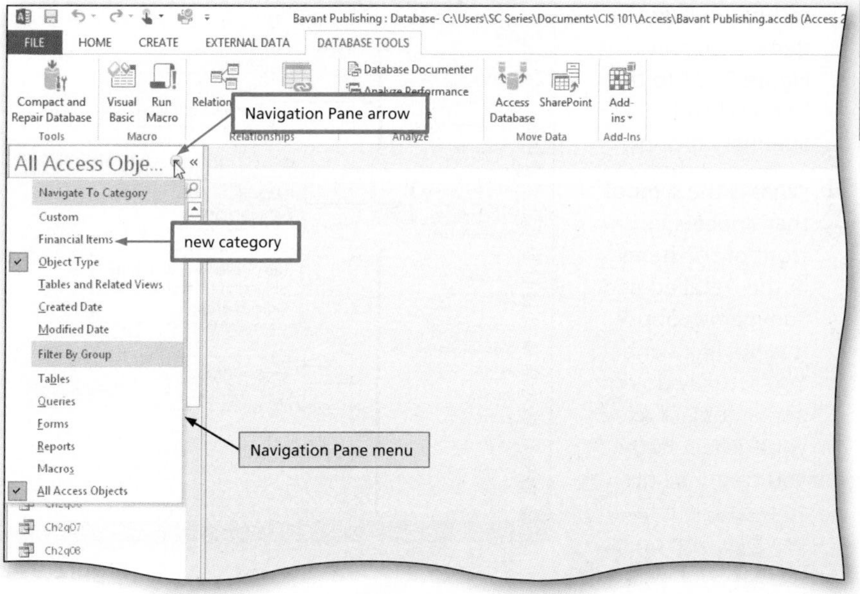

Figure 9–19

2

- Tap or click the Financial Items category to display the groups within the category. Because you created the Detailed and Summary groups but did not assign items, the table objects all appear in the Unassigned Objects area of the Navigation Pane.
- Press and hold or right-click State-Rep Crosstab to display the shortcut menu.
- Point to the 'Add to group' command on the shortcut menu to display the list of available groups (Figure 9–20).

Q&A I did not create an Unassigned Objects group. Where did it come from?

Access creates the Unassigned Objects group automatically. Until you add an object to one of the groups you created, it will be in the Unassigned Objects group.

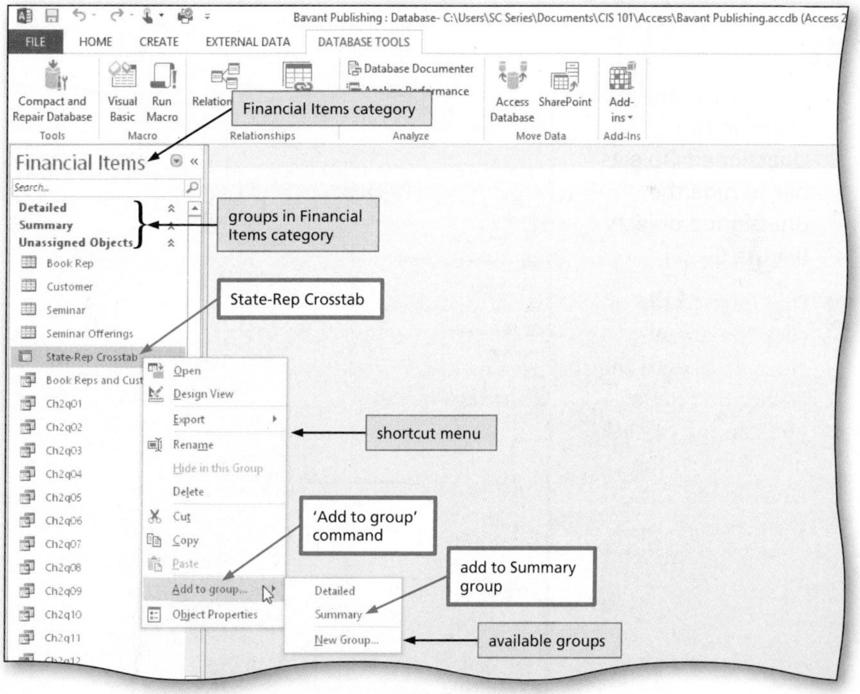

Figure 9–20

What is the purpose of the New Group on the submenu?

You can create a new group using this submenu. This is an alternative to using the Navigation Options dialog box. Use whichever approach you find most convenient.

3

- Tap or click Summary to add the State-Rep Crosstab to the Summary group.
- Using the same technique, add the items shown in Figure 9–21 to the Detailed and Summary groups.

Q&A What is the symbol that appears in front of the items in the Detailed and Summary groups?
It is the link symbol. You actually do not add an object to your group. Rather, you create a link to the object. In practice, you do not have to worry about this. The process for opening an object in one of your custom groups remains the same.

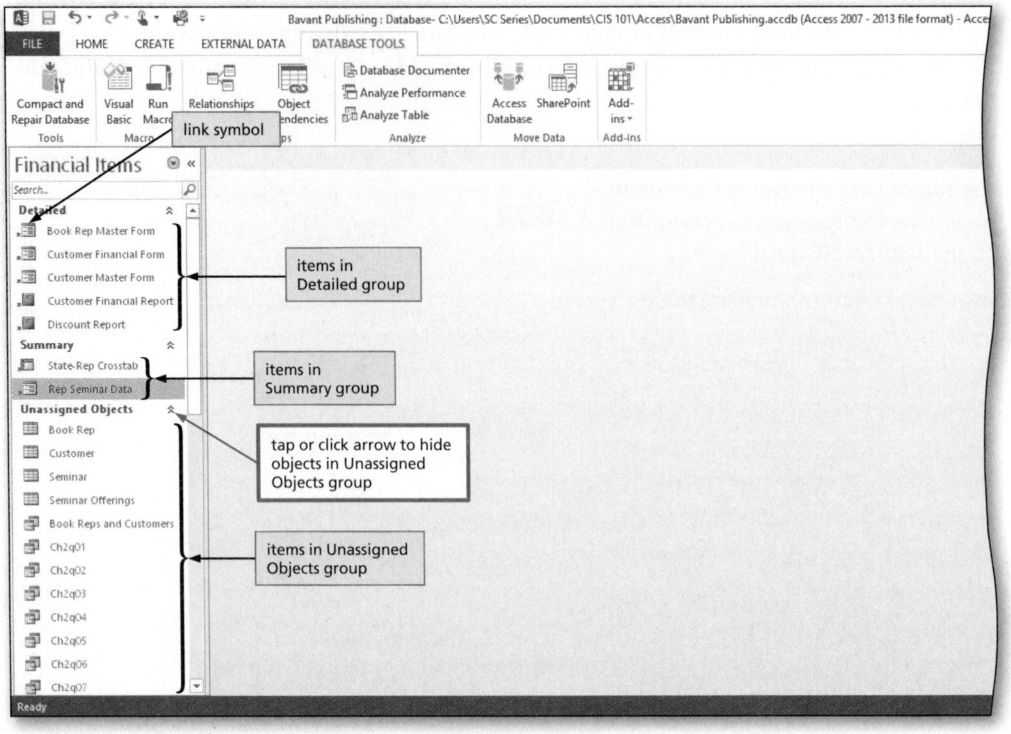

Figure 9–21

4

- Tap or click the arrow in the Unassigned Objects bar to hide the unassigned objects (Figure 9–22).

Q&A Do I have to tap or click the arrow?
No. Just as with the Navigation Pane, you can tap or click anywhere in the Unassigned Objects bar.

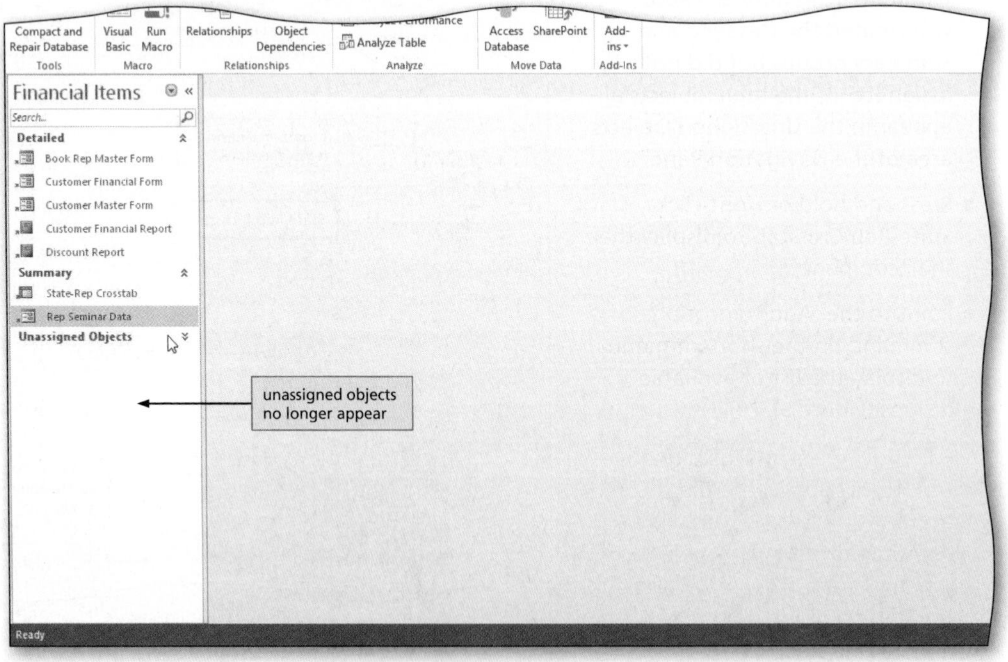

Figure 9–22

Break Point: If you wish to stop working through the chapter at this point, you can close Access now. You can resume the project at a later time by starting Access, opening the Bavant Publishing database, and continuing to follow the steps from this location forward.

CONSIDER THIS

What issues do you consider in determining the customization of the Navigation Pane?

The types of issues to consider are the following:

- Would a new category be useful?
- If so, are there new groups that would be useful to include in the new category?
- If you have created a new category and new groups, which items should be included in the new groups, and which should be left uncategorized?

Table and Database Properties

You can assign properties to tables. For example, you could assign a validation rule and validation text to an entire table. You also can assign properties to the database, typically for documentation purposes.

To Create a Validation Rule for a Table

1 CONVERT DATABASE | 2 ANALYZE & DOCUMENT | 3 NAVIGATION PANE | 4 CUSTOM PROPERTIES & INDEXES
5 CUSTOM DATA PART | 6 CUSTOM TEMPLATE | 7 ENCRYPT LOCK & SPLIT | 8 CUSTOM WEB APP | 9 CUSTOM VIEW

Previously, you created validation rules that applied to individual fields within a table. Some, however, apply to more than one field. In the Seminar Offerings table, you created a macro that would change the value of the Hours Spent field in such a way that it could never be greater than the Total Hours field. You also can create a validation rule that ensures this will never be the case; that is, the validation rule would require that the hours spent must be less than or equal to the total hours. To create a validation rule that involves two or more fields, you need to create the rule for the table using the table's Validation Rule property. The following steps create a table validation rule. ***Why?*** *This rule involves two fields, Hours Spent and Total Hours.*

1

- If necessary, tap or click the arrow for Unassigned Objects to display those objects in the Navigation Pane.
- Open the Seminar Offerings table in Design view and close the Navigation Pane.
- Tap or click the Property Sheet button (TABLE TOOLS DESIGN tab | Show/Hide group) to display the table's property sheet.
- Tap or click the Validation Rule property and type `[Hours Spent]<=[Total Hours]` as the validation rule.
- Tap or click the Validation Text property and type `Hours spent cannot exceed total hours` as the validation text (Figure 9–23).

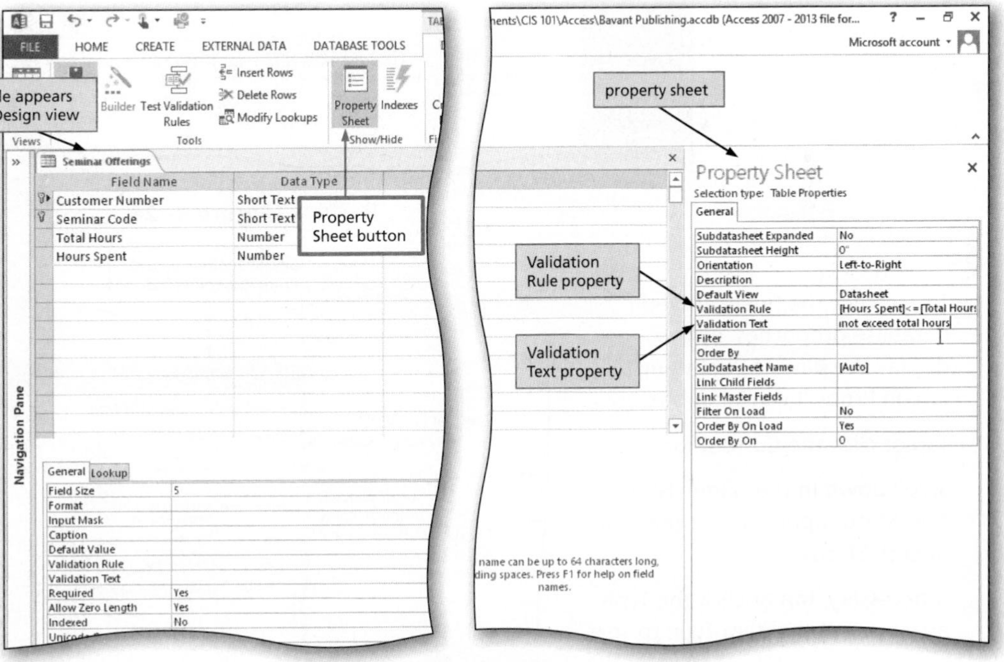

Figure 9–23

Q&A Could I use the Expression Builder to create the validation rule?
Yes. Use whichever method you find the most convenient.

2

- Close the property sheet.
- Tap or click the Save button on the Quick Access Toolbar to save the validation rule and the validation text.
- When asked if you want to test existing data, tap or click the No button.
- Close the Seminar Offerings table.

To Create Custom Properties

1 CONVERT DATABASE | 2 ANALYZE & DOCUMENT | 3 NAVIGATION PANE | 4 CUSTOM PROPERTIES & INDEXES
5 CUSTOM DATA PART | 6 CUSTOM TEMPLATE | 7 ENCRYPT LOCK & SPLIT | 8 CUSTOM WEB APP | 9 CUSTOM VIEW

In addition to the general database property categories, you also can use custom properties. ***Why?*** *You can use custom properties to further document your database in a variety of ways. If you have needs that go beyond the custom properties, you can create your own original or unique properties.* The following steps **populate** the Status custom property; that is, they set a value for the property. In this case, they set the Status property to Live Version, indicating this is the live version of the database. If the database were still in a test environment, the property would be set to Test Version. The steps also create and populate a new property, Production, that represents the date the database was placed into production.

1

- Tap or click FILE on the ribbon to open the Backstage view.
- Ensure the Info tab is selected (Figure 9–24).

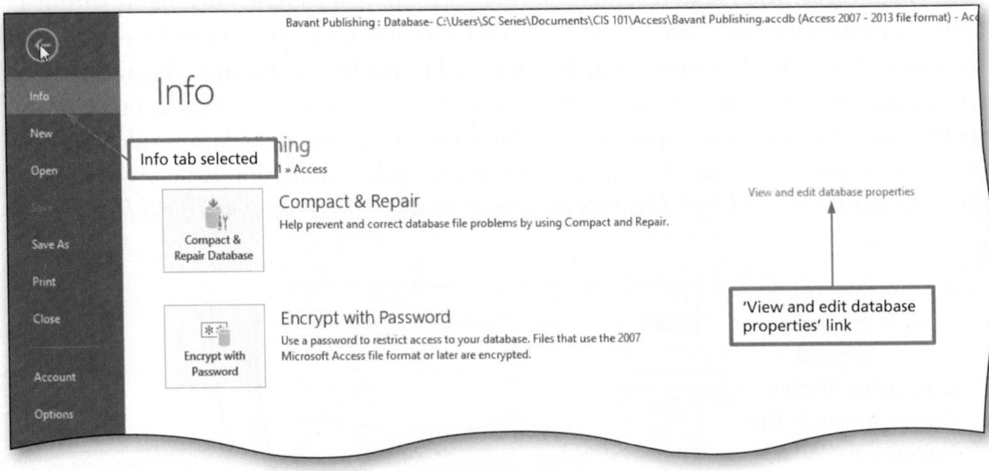

Figure 9–24

2

- Tap or click the 'View and edit database properties' link to display the Bavant Publishing .accdb Properties dialog box.
- Tap or click the Custom tab.
- Scroll down in the Name list so that Status appears, and then tap or click Status.
- If necessary, tap or click the Type arrow to set the data Type to Text.
- Tap or click the Value box and type `Live Version` as the value to create the custom category (Figure 9–25).

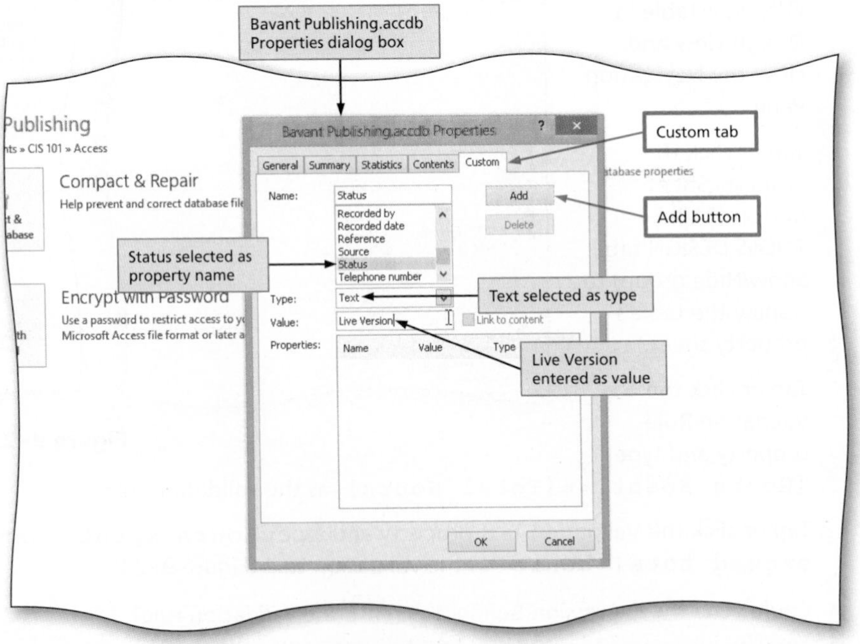

Figure 9–25

3

- Tap or click the Add button to add the property.
- Type **Production** in the Name box.
- If requested to do so by your instructor, type your first and last name in the Name box.
- Select Date as the Type.
- Type **03/03/2015** as the value (Figure 9–26) to indicate that the database went into production on March 3, 2015.

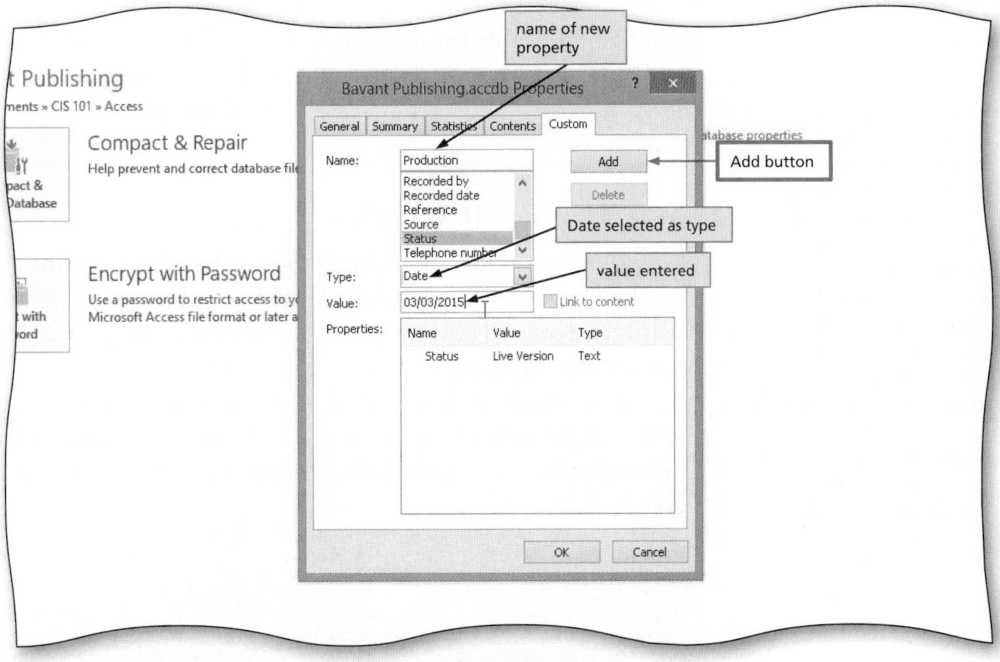

Figure 9–26

4

- Tap or click the Add button to add the property (Figure 9–27).

Q&A What if I add a property that I decide I do not want?
You can delete it. To do so, tap or click the property you no longer want and then tap or click the Delete button.

5

- Tap or click the OK button to close the Bavant Publishing .accdb Properties dialog box.

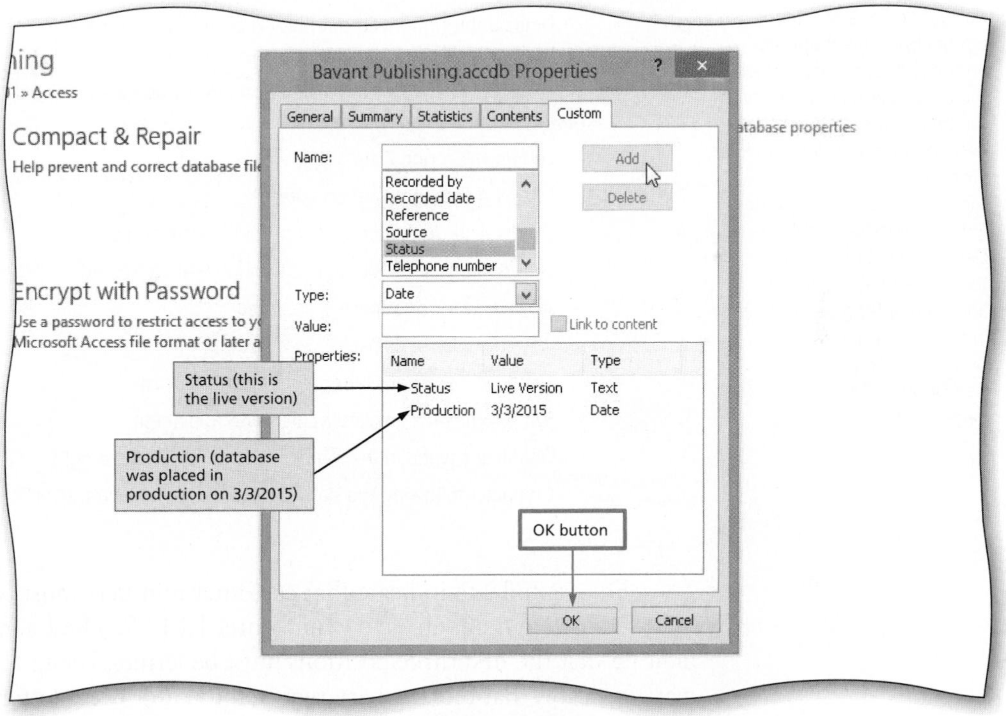

Figure 9–27

Q&A How do I view these properties in the future?
The same way you created them. Tap or click FILE on the ribbon, tap or click the Info tab, and then tap or click the 'View and edit database properties' link. Tap or click the desired tab to see the properties you want.

Special Field Properties

BTW
Changing Data Formats
To create custom data formats, enter various characters in the Format property of a table field. The characters can be placeholders (such as 0 and #), separators (such as periods and commas), literal characters, and colors. You can create custom formats for short text, date, number, and currency fields. Date, number, and currency fields also include a number of standard data formats.

Each field in a table has a variety of field properties available. Recall that field properties are characteristics of a field. Two special field properties, the Custom Input Mask property and the Allow Zero Length property, are described in this section.

Custom Input Masks

One way to help users enter data using a certain format is to use an input mask. You already have used the Input Mask Wizard to create an input mask. Using the wizard, you can select the input mask that meets your needs. This often is the best way to create the input mask.

If the input mask you need to create is not similar to any in the list provided by the wizard, you can create a custom input mask by entering the appropriate characters as the value for the Input Mask property. In doing so, you use the symbols from Table 9–1.

BTW
Table Descriptions
To add a description for a table, press and hold or right-click the table in the Navigation Pane and then tap or click Table Properties on the shortcut menu. When the Properties dialog box for the table appears, enter the description in the Description property and then tap or click the OK button. To enter a description for a table in Design view, tap or click the Property Sheet button, and then enter a description in the Description property on the property sheet (see Figure 9-23 on page AC 553).

Table 9–1 Input Mask Symbols

Symbol	Type of Data Accepted	Data Entry Optional
0	Digits 0 through 9 without plus (+) or minus (-) sign are accepted. Positions left blank appear as zeros.	No
9	Digits 0 through 9 without plus (+) or minus (-) sign are accepted. Positions left blank appear as spaces.	Yes
#	Digits 0 through 9 with plus (+) or minus (-) sign are accepted. Positions left blank appear as spaces.	Yes
L	Letters A through Z are accepted.	No
?	Letters A through Z are accepted.	Yes
A	Letters A through Z or digits 0 through 9 are accepted.	No
a	Letters A through Z or digits 0 through 9 are accepted.	Yes
&	Any character or a space is accepted.	No
C	Any character or a space is accepted.	Yes
<	Symbol converts any letter entered to lowercase.	Does not apply
>	Symbol converts any letter entered to uppercase.	Does not apply
!	Characters typed in the input mask fill it from left to right.	Does not apply
\	Character following the slash is treated as a literal in the input mask.	Does not apply

For example, to indicate that customer numbers must consist of three letters followed by two numbers, you would enter LLL99. The Ls in the first three positions indicate that the first three positions must be letters. Using L instead of a question mark indicates that the users are required to enter these letters. If you had used the question mark, they could leave these positions blank. The 9s in the last two positions indicate that the users can enter only digits 0 through 9. Using 9 instead of 0 indicates that they could leave these positions blank; that is, they are optional. Finally, to ensure that any letters entered are displayed as uppercase, you would use the > symbol at the beginning of the input mask. The complete mask would be >LLL99.

To Create a Custom Input Mask

The following step creates a custom input mask for the Customer Number field. ***Why?*** *None of the input masks in the list meet the specific needs for the Customer Number field.*

1

- Open the Navigation Pane, open the Customer table in Design view, and then close the Navigation Pane.
- With the Customer Number field selected, tap or click the Input Mask property, and then type **>LLL99** as the value (Figure 9–28).

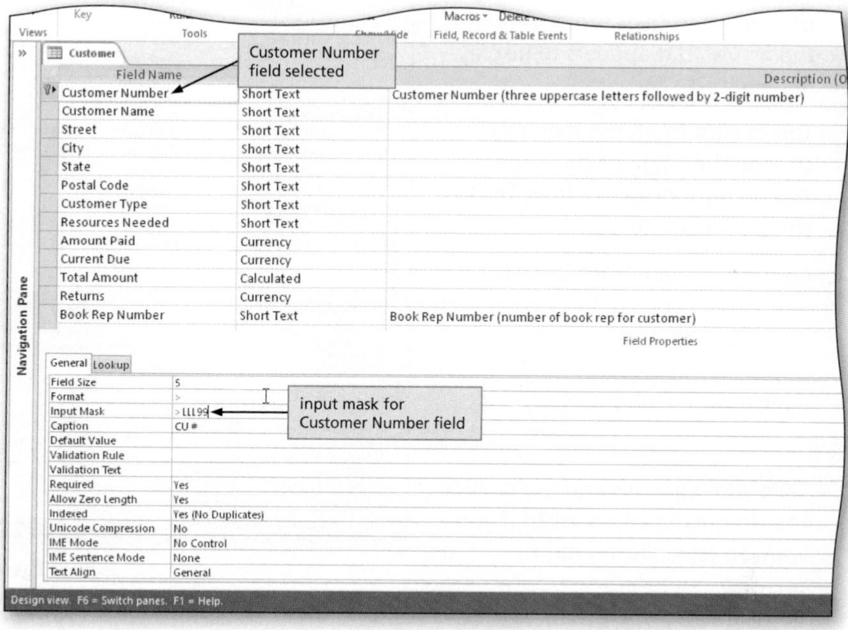

Figure 9–28

Q&A

What is the difference between the Format property and the Input Mask property?
The Format property ensures that data is displayed consistently, for example, always in uppercase. The Input Mask property controls how data is entered.

What is the effect of this input mask?
From this point on, anyone entering a customer number will be restricted to letters in the first three positions and numeric digits in the last two. Further, any letters entered in the first three positions will be displayed as uppercase.

In Figure 9–28, the Customer Number field has both a custom input mask and a format. Is this a problem?
Technically, you do not need both. When the same field has both an input mask and a format, the format takes precedence. Because the format specified for the Customer Number field is the same as the input mask (uppercase), it will not affect the data.

To Allow Zero Length

You can use zero-length strings to distinguish data that does not exist from data that is unknown. ***Why?*** *Entering a zero-length string is not the same as leaving the field blank.* For example, in the Book Rep table, you may want to set the Required property for the Comment field to Yes, so that users do not forget to enter a comment. If the user forgets to enter a comment, Access will display an error message and not add the record until the user enters a comment. If, on the other hand, there are certain reps for whom no comment is appropriate, users can enter a **zero-length string** — a string that contains no characters — and Access will accept the record without generating an error message. To enter a zero-length string, you type two quotation marks with no space in between (""). If you enter a zero-length string into a Short Text or Long Text field whose Required property is set to Yes, Access will not report an error.

If you want to ensure that data is entered in the field and a zero-length string is not appropriate, you can set the Required property to Yes and the Allow Zero Length property to No. The steps on the next page set the Allow Zero Length property for the Customer Name field to No. (The Required property already has been set to Yes.)

1

- Tap or click the row selector for the Customer Name field to select the field.
- Tap or click the Allow Zero Length property and then tap or click the arrow that appears to display a menu.
- Tap or click No in the menu to change the value of the Allow Zero Length property from Yes to No (Figure 9–29).

Q&A Could I just type the word, No?
Yes. In fact, you could type the letter, N, and Access would complete the word, No. Use whichever technique you prefer.

2

- Save your changes and tap or click the No button when asked if you want to test existing data.
- Close the table.

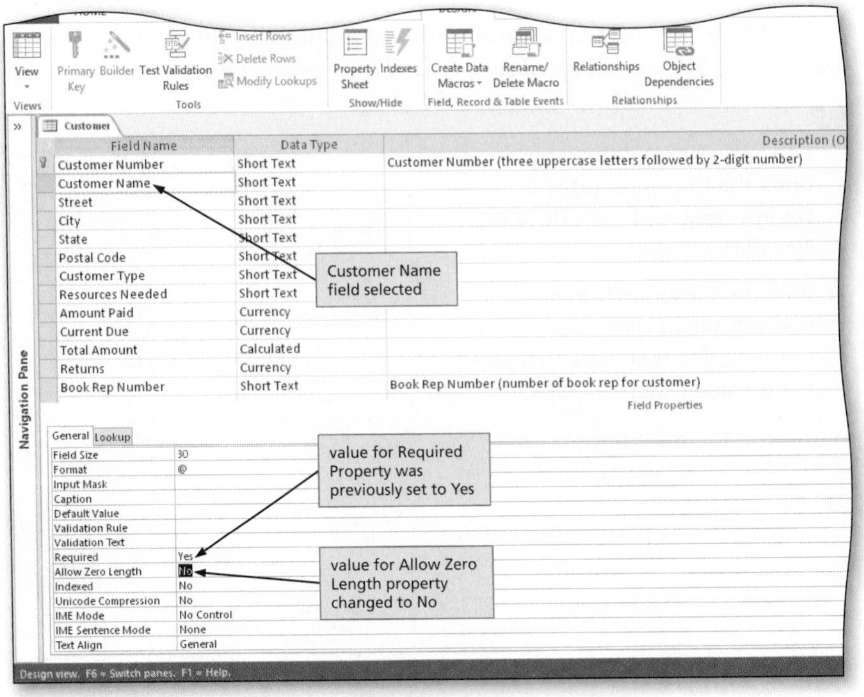

Figure 9–29

Q&A What is the effect of this change?
If the value for the Allow Zero Length property is set to No, an attempt to enter a zero-length string ("") will result in an error message.

Creating and Using Indexes

BTW
Indexes
The most common structure for high-performance indexes is called a B-tree. It is a highly efficient structure that supports very rapid access to records in the database as well as a rapid alternative to sorting records. Virtually all systems use some version of the B-tree structure.

You already are familiar with the concept of an index. The index in the back of a book contains important words or phrases along with a list of pages on which the given words or phrases can be found. An **index** for a table is similar. An index is a database object that is created based on a field or combination of fields. An index on the Customer Name field, for example, would enable Access to rapidly locate a record that contains a particular customer name. In this case, the items of interest are customer names instead of keywords or phrases, as is the case in the back of this book. The field or fields on which the index is built is called the **index key**. Thus, in the index on customer names, the Customer Name field is the index key.

Each name occurs in the index along with the number of the record on which the corresponding customer is located. Further, the names appear in the index in alphabetical order, so Access can use this index to rapidly produce a list of customers alphabetized by customer name.

Another benefit of indexes is that they provide an efficient way to order records. That is, if the records are to appear in a certain order in a database object, Access can use an index instead of physically having to rearrange the records in the database. Physically rearranging the records in a different order can be a very time-consuming process.

To gain the benefits of an index, you first must create one. Access automatically creates an index on some special fields. If, for example, a table contains a field called Postal Code, Access would create an index for this field automatically. You must create any other indexes you determine would improve database performance, indicating the field or fields on which the index is to be built.

Although the index key usually will be a single field, it can be a combination of fields. For example, you might want to sort records by amount paid within customer type. In other words, the records are ordered by a combination of fields: Customer Type and Amount Paid. An index can be used for this purpose by using a combination of fields for the index key. In this case, you must assign a name to the index. It is a good idea to assign a name that represents the combination of fields. For example, an index whose key is the combination of the Customer Type and Amount Paid fields might be called TypePaid.

BTW

Changing Default Sort Order

To display the records in a table in an order other than the primary key (the default sort order), use the Order By property on the table's property sheet (see Figure 9-23 on page AC 553).

How Access Uses Indexes

You can create indexes in Access automatically. If you request that data be sorted in a particular order and Access determines that an index is available that it can use to make the process efficient, it will do so automatically. If no index is available, it still will sort the data in the order you requested; it will just take longer than with the index.

Similarly, if you request that Access locate a particular record that has a certain value in a particular field, Access will use an index if an appropriate one exists. If not, it will have to examine each record until it finds the one you want.

To Create a Single-Field Index

1 CONVERT DATABASE | 2 ANALYZE & DOCUMENT | 3 NAVIGATION PANE | 4 CUSTOM PROPERTIES & INDEXES
5 CUSTOM DATA PART | 6 CUSTOM TEMPLATE | 7 ENCRYPT LOCK & SPLIT | 8 CUSTOM WEB APP | 9 CUSTOM VIEW

The following steps create a single-field index on the Customer Name field. ***Why?*** *This index will make finding customers based on their name more efficient than it would be without the index. It also will improve the efficiency of sorting by customer name.*

1

- Open the Navigation Pane, open the Customer table in Design view, and then close the Navigation Pane.
- Select the Customer Name field.
- Tap or click the Indexed property box in the Field Properties pane to select the property.
- Tap or click the down arrow that appears to display the Indexed list (Figure 9–30).

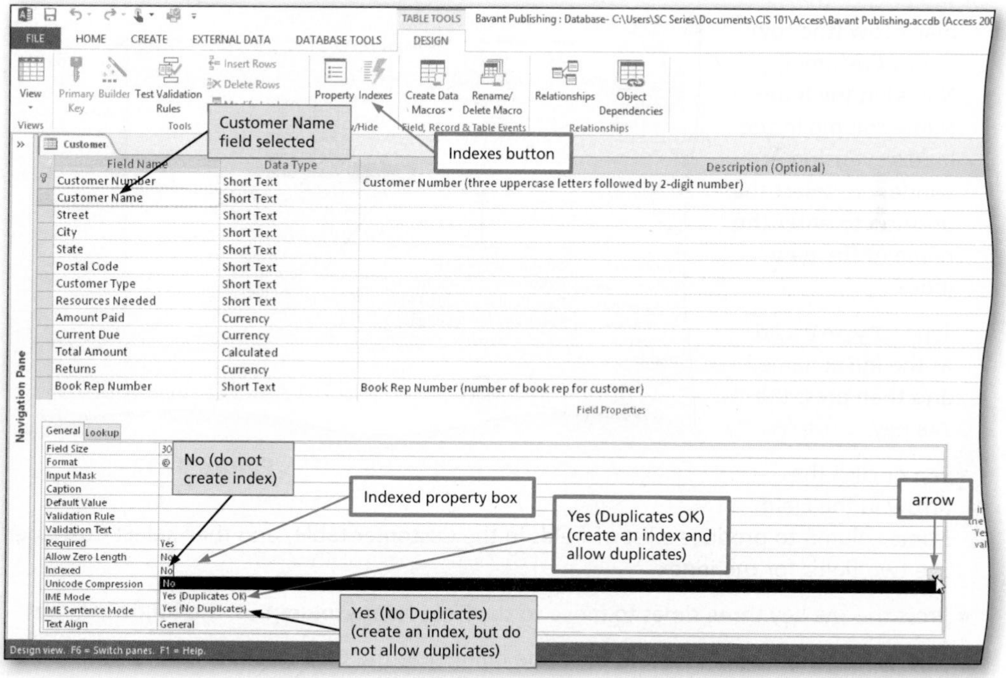

Figure 9–30

2

- Tap or click Yes (Duplicates OK) in the list to specify that duplicates are to be allowed.

To Create a Multiple-Field Index

Creating **multiple-field indexes** — that is, indexes whose key is a combination of fields — involves a different process than creating single-field indexes. To create multiple-field indexes, you will use the Indexes button, enter a name for the index, and then enter the combination of fields that make up the index key. The following steps create a multiple-field index on the combination of Customer Type and Amount Paid. ***Why?*** *Bavant needs to sort records on the combination of Customer Type and Amount Paid and wants to improve the efficiency of this sort.* The steps assign this index the name TypePaid.

1

- Tap or click the Indexes button, shown in Figure 9–30 on the previous page, (TABLE TOOLS DESIGN tab | Show/Hide group) to display the Indexes: Customer window (Figure 9–31).

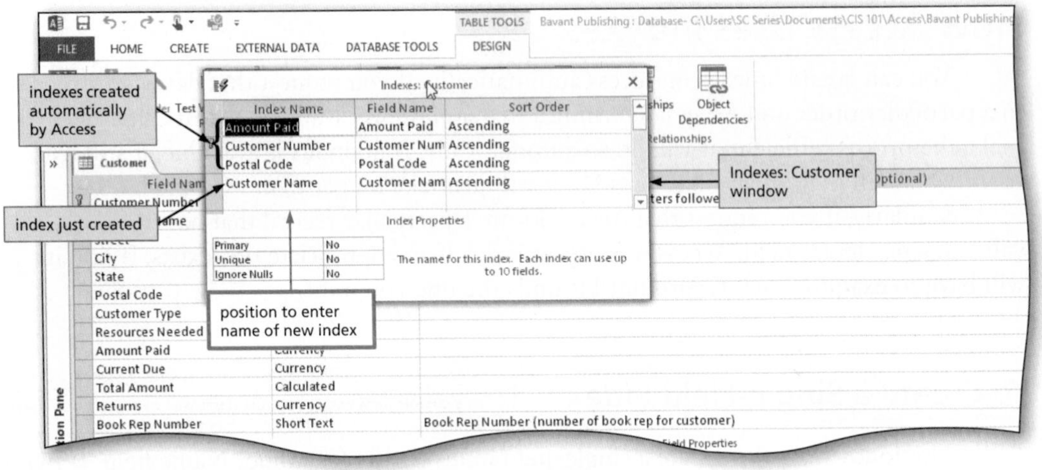

Figure 9–31

2

- Tap or click the blank row (the row below Customer Name) in the Index Name column in the Indexes: Customer window to select the position to enter the name of the new index.
- Type **TypePaid** as the index name, and then press the TAB key.
- Tap or click the arrow in the Field Name column to produce a list of fields in the Customer table, and then select Customer Type to enter the first of the two fields for the index.
- Press the TAB key three times to move to the Field Name column on the following row.
- Select the Amount Paid field in the same manner as the Customer Type field (Figure 9–32).

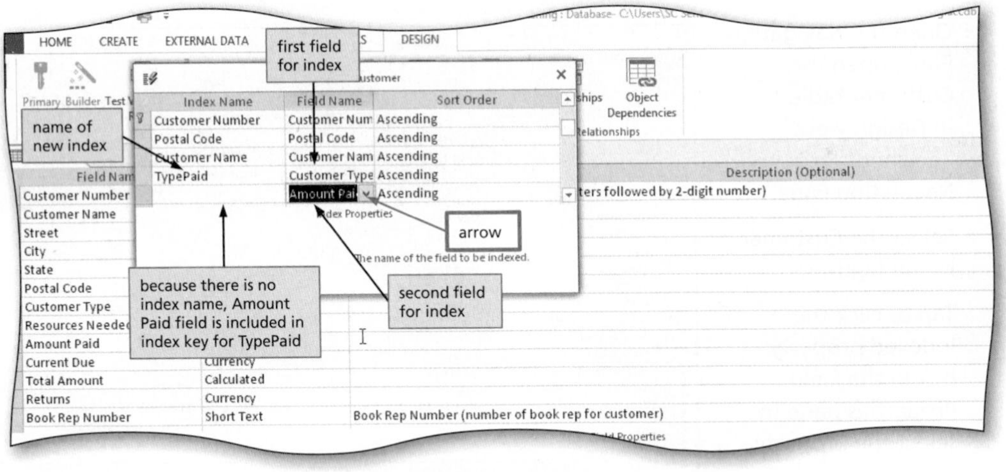

Figure 9–32

3

- Close the Indexes: Customer window by tapping or clicking its Close button.
- Tap or click the Save button on the Quick Access Toolbar to save your changes.
- Close the Customer table.

CONSIDER THIS

How do you determine when to use an index?

An index improves efficiency for sorting and finding records. On the other hand, indexes occupy space on your disk. They also require Access to do extra work. Access must keep current all the indexes that have been created. The following guidelines help determine how and when to use indexes to their fullest advantage.

Create an index on a field (or combination of fields) if one or more of the following conditions are present:

1. The field is the primary key of the table. (Access creates this index automatically.)
2. The field is the foreign key in a relationship you have created.
3. You frequently will need your data to be sorted on the field.
4. You frequently will need to locate a record based on a value in this field.

Because Access handles condition 1 automatically, you only need to concern yourself about conditions 2, 3, and 4. If you think you will need to see customer data arranged in order of current due amounts, for example, you should create an index on the Current Due field. If you think you will need to see the data arranged by amount paid within customer type, you should create an index on the combination of the Customer Type field and the Amount Paid field. Similarly, if you think you will need to find a customer given the customer's name, you should create an index on the Customer Name field.

Automatic Error Checking

Access can automatically check for several types of errors in forms and reports. When Access detects an error, it warns you about the existence of the error and provides you with options for correcting it. The types of errors that Access can detect and correct are shown in Table 9–2.

BTW

Touch and Pointers
Remember that if you are using your finger on a touch screen, you will not see the pointer.

BTW

On-Screen Keyboard
To display the on-screen touch keyboard, tap the Touch Keyboard button on the Windows taskbar. When finished using the touch keyboard, tap the X button on the touch keyboard to close the keyboard.

Table 9–2 Types of Errors

Error Type	Description
Unassociated label and control	A label and control are selected and are not associated with each other.
New unassociated labels	A newly added label is not associated with any other control.
Keyboard shortcut errors	A shortcut key is invalid. This can happen because an unassociated label has a shortcut key, there are duplicate shortcut keys assigned, or a blank space is assigned as a shortcut key.
Invalid control properties	A control property is invalid. For example, the property contains invalid characters.
Common report errors	The report has invalid sorting or grouping specifications, or the report is wider than the page size.

To Enable Error Checking

1 CONVERT DATABASE | 2 ANALYZE & DOCUMENT | 3 NAVIGATION PANE | 4 CUSTOM PROPERTIES & INDEXES
5 CUSTOM DATA PART | 6 CUSTOM TEMPLATE | 7 ENCRYPT LOCK & SPLIT | 8 CUSTOM WEB APP | 9 CUSTOM VIEW

Why? *For automatic error checking to take place, it must be enabled.* The steps on the next page ensure that error checking is enabled and that errors are found and reported.

1

- Tap or click FILE on the ribbon and then tap or click the Options tab to display the Access Options dialog box.
- Tap or click Object Designers to display the options for creating and modifying objects.
- Scroll down so that the Error checking area appears.
- Ensure the 'Enable error checking' check box is checked (Figure 9–33).

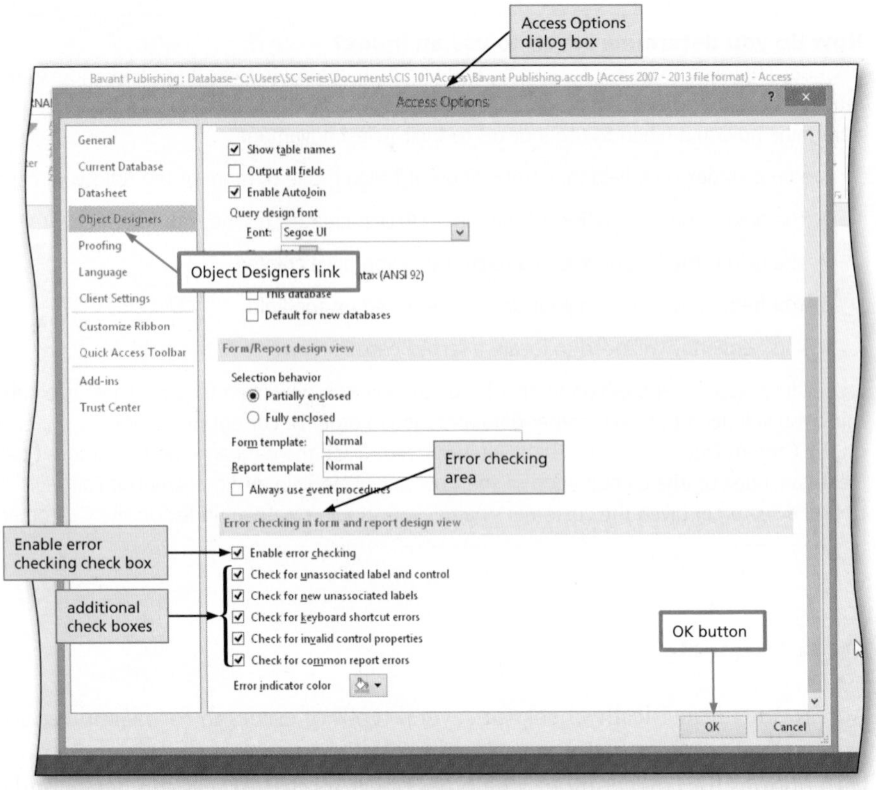

Figure 9–33

Q&A What is the purpose of the other check boxes in the section?

All the other check boxes are checked, indicating that Access will perform all the various types of automatic error checking that are possible. If there were a particular type of error checking that you would prefer to skip, you would remove its check mark before tapping or clicking the OK button.

2

- Tap or click the OK button to close the Access Options dialog box.

Error Indication

With error checking enabled, if an error occurs, a small triangle called an **error indicator** appears in the appropriate field or control. For example, you could change the label for Book Rep Number in the Customer View and Update Form to include an ampersand (&) before the letter, N, making it a keyboard shortcut for this control. This would be a problem because N is already a shortcut for Name to Find. If this happens, an error indicator appears in both controls in which N is the keyboard shortcut, as shown in Figure 9–34.

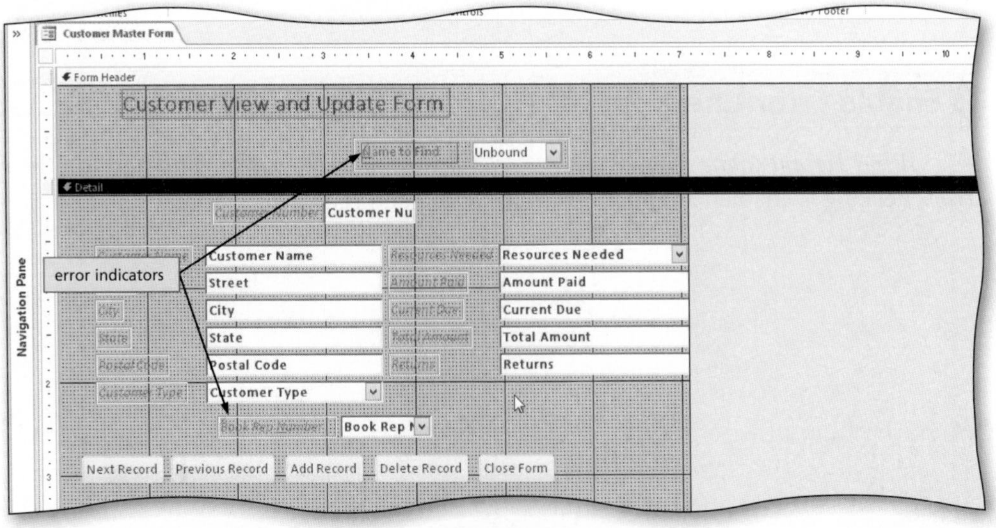

Figure 9–34

Selecting a control containing an error indicator displays an 'Error Checking Options' button. Tapping or clicking the 'Error Checking Options' button produces the 'Error Checking Options' menu, as shown in Figure 9–35. The first line in the menu is simply a statement of the type of error that occurred, and the second is a description of the specific error. The Change Caption command gives a submenu of the captions that can be changed. The 'Edit Caption Property' command allows you to change the caption directly and is the simplest way to correct this error. The 'Help on This Error' command gives help on the specific error that occurred. You can choose to ignore the error by using the Ignore Error command. The final command, 'Error Checking Options', allows you to change the same error checking options shown in Figure 9–33.

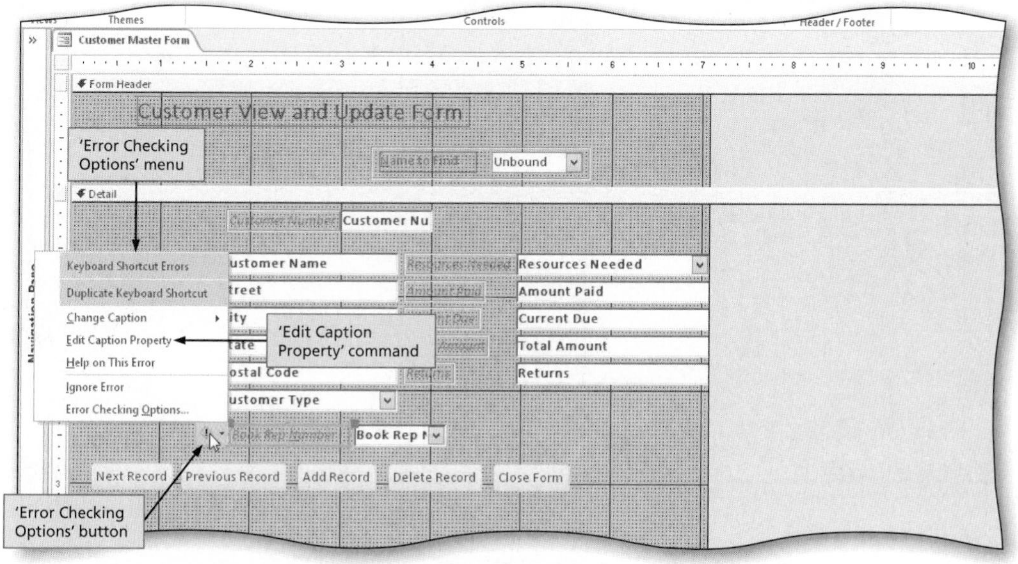

Figure 9–35

BTW

Freezing Fields

The Freeze Fields command allows you to place a column or columns in a table on the left side of the table. As you scroll to the right, the column or columns remain visible. To freeze a column or columns, select the column(s) in Datasheet view, press and hold or right-click and tap or click Freeze Fields on the shortcut menu. To unfreeze fields, tap or click the 'Unfreeze All Fields' command on the shortcut menu. When you freeze a column, Access considers it a change to the layout of the table. When you close the table, Access will ask you if you want to save the changes.

The simplest way to fix this error is to edit the caption property. Tapping or clicking the 'Edit Caption Property' command produces a property sheet with the Caption property highlighted. You then could change the Caption property to make another letter the shortcut key. For example, you could make the letter, B, the shortcut key by typing `&Book Rep Number` as the entry.

Data Type Parts

Access contains data type parts that are available on the More Fields gallery. Some data type parts, such as the Category part, consist of a single field. Others, such as the Address part, consist of multiple fields. To insert all the fields in the part into your table, all you need to do is tap or click the part. In addition to the parts provided by Access, you can create your own parts.

To Create Custom Data Parts

1 CONVERT DATABASE | 2 ANALYZE & DOCUMENT | 3 NAVIGATION PANE | 4 CUSTOM PROPERTIES & INDEXES
5 CUSTOM DATA PART | 6 CUSTOM TEMPLATE | 7 ENCRYPT LOCK & SPLIT | 8 CUSTOM WEB APP | 9 CUSTOM VIEW

To create data parts in the Quick Start category from existing fields, you select the desired field or fields and then select the Save Selection as New Data Type command in the More Fields gallery. If you select multiple fields, the fields must be adjacent.

Bavant has decided that combining several address-related fields into a single data part would make future database updates easier. The following steps create a Quick Start field consisting of the Last Name, First Name, Street, City, State, and Postal Code fields in the Book Rep table. ***Why?*** *Once you have created this Quick Start field, users can add this collection of fields to a table by simply tapping or clicking the Quick Start field.*

1

- Open the Navigation Pane, open the Book Rep table in Datasheet view, and then close the Navigation Pane.
- Tap or click the column heading for the Last Name field to select the field.
- Hold the SHIFT key down and tap or click the column heading for the Postal Code field to select all the fields from the Last Name field to the Postal Code field.
- Display the TABLE TOOLS FIELDS tab.
- Tap or click the More Fields button (TABLE TOOLS FIELDS tab | Add & Delete group) to display the More Fields gallery (Figure 9–36).

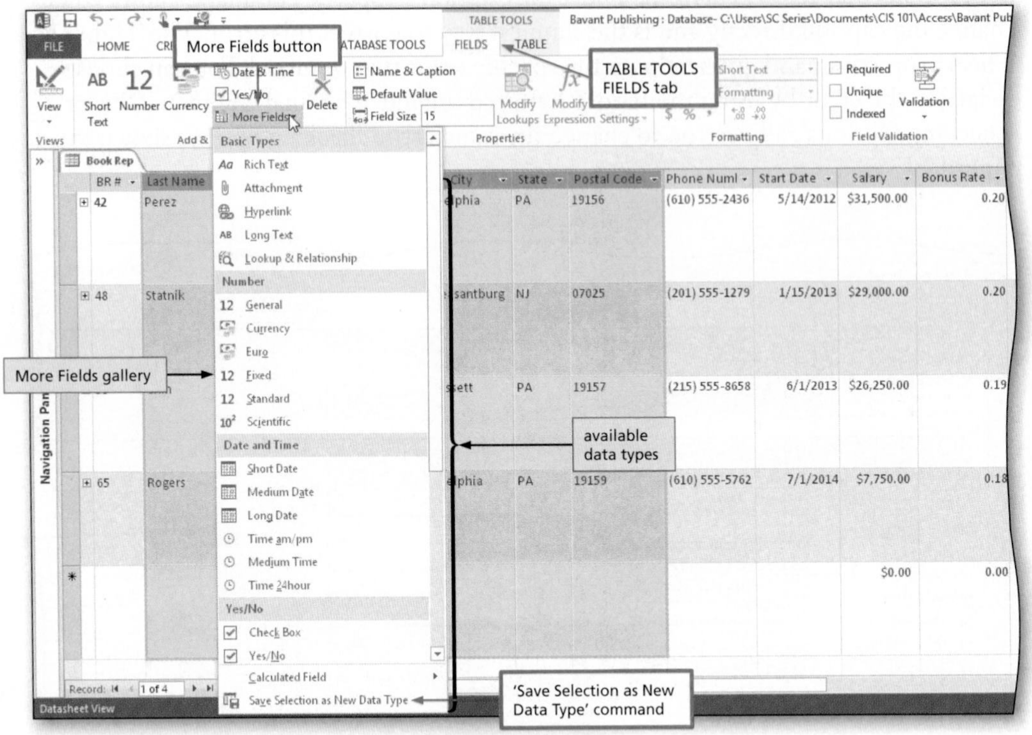

Figure 9–36

2

- Tap or click 'Save Selection as New Data Type' to display the Create New Data Type from Fields dialog box.
- Enter `Name-Address` as the name.
- Enter `Last Name, First Name, Street, City, State, and Postal Code` as the description.

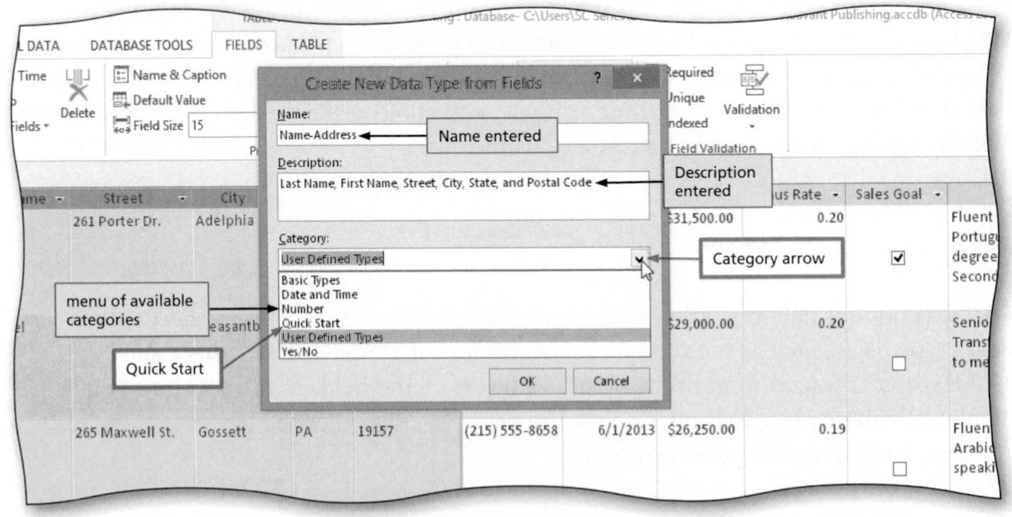

Figure 9–37

Q&A What is the purpose of the description?

When a user points to the Quick Start field you created, a ScreenTip will appear containing the description you entered.

- Tap or click the Category arrow to display a list of available categories (Figure 9–37).

3

- Tap or click Quick Start to indicate the new data type will be added to the Quick Start category.

Q&A What is the difference between the Quick Start and User Defined Types category?
If you select the Quick Start category, the data type you create will be listed among the Quick Start data types that are part of Access. If you select the User Defined Types category, the data type you create will be in a separate category containing only those data types you create. In either case, however, tapping or clicking the data type will produce the same result.

- Tap or click the OK button (Create New Data Type from Fields dialog box) to save the data type.
- When Access indicates that your template (that is, your Quick Start field) has been saved, tap or click the OK button (Microsoft Access dialog box).
- Close the table.
- If necessary, tap or click No when asked if you want to save the changes to the layout of the table.

CONSIDER THIS

How do you rearrange fields that are not adjacent?

You can hide the fields that keep your fields from being adjacent. To hide a field, press and hold or right-click the field to display a shortcut menu, and then tap or click Hide Fields on the shortcut menu. To later unhide a field you have hidden, press and hold or right-click any column heading and then tap or click Unhide Fields on the shortcut menu. You will see a list of fields with a check box for each field. The hidden field will not have a check mark in the check box. To unhide the field, tap or click the check box for the field.

Templates

You have worked with Access templates in previous chapters. You can use a template to create a complete database application containing tables, forms, queries, and other objects. There are many templates available for Access.

You can create your own template from an existing database. To do so, you must first ensure that you have created a database with all the characteristics you want in your template. In this chapter, the database you create will have two tables, a query, two single-item forms, two datasheet forms that use macros, and a navigation form that will serve as the main menu. In addition, the navigation form will be set to appear automatically whenever you open the database. Once you have incorporated all these features, you will save the database as a template. From that point on, anyone can use your template to create a new database. The database that is created will incorporate all the same features as your original database.

Later in this chapter, you will create a web app, which is a database that anyone can use through a browser. The easiest way to create the tables for the web app is to import them from an existing database. You will use your template to create such a database. While the queries and forms that are part of the template will not be included in the web app, the tables will.

Access enforces some restrictions to tables used in web apps, so the tables in your template should adhere to these restrictions, as follows:

- While you can change the name of the default autonumber primary key, you cannot change its data type. If you have a text field that you want to be the primary key, the best you can do is to specify that the field must be both required and unique.
- You cannot create relationships as you can do with a typical database. Rather, any relationships must be specified through lookup fields.

To Create a Desktop Database

The following steps create the Clients and Recruiters **desktop database**, that is, a database designed to run on a personal computer. ***Why?*** *This database will become the basis for a template.*

1

- Tap or click FILE on the ribbon to open the Backstage view.
- Tap or click the New tab.
- Tap or click the 'Blank desktop database' button.
- Type `Clients and Recruiters` as the name of the database file.
- Tap or click the Browse button to display the File New Database dialog box, navigate to the desired save location (for example, the Access folder in the CIS 101 folder), and then tap or click the OK button to return to the Backstage view (Figure 9–38).

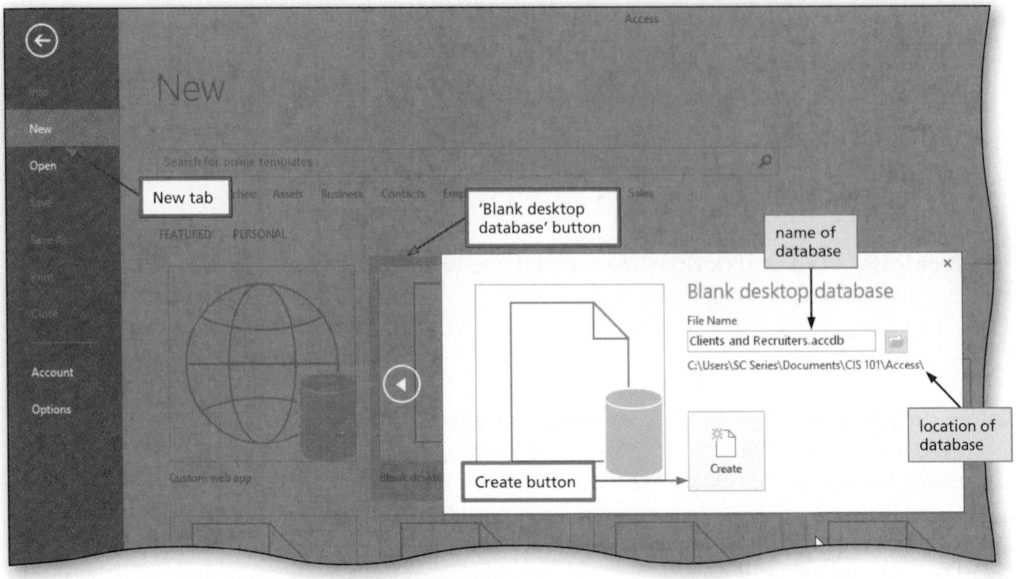

Figure 9–38

2

- Tap or click the Create button to create the database (Figure 9–39).

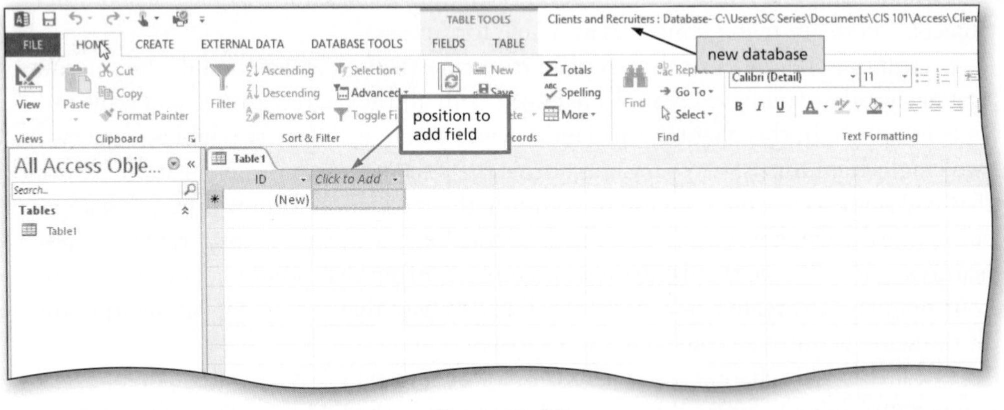

Figure 9–39

To Add Fields to the Table

The tables will have an autonumber ID field as the primary key. ***Why?*** *You will later import the tables in this database to a web app, and tables in a web app must have an autonumber field as a primary key.* In addition, the field that normally would be the primary key will be designated both required and unique, two characteristics of the primary key.

The following steps add the Recruiter Number, Last Name, First Name, Street, City, State, Postal Code, Rate, and Commission to a table. The Rate field is a Number field and the Commission field is a Currency field.

The steps designate the Recruiter Number field as both required and unique. They add the Last Name, First Name, Street, City, State, and Postal Code as a single operation by using the Quick Start field created earlier. After adding the fields, they save the table using the name, Recruiter. They also change the field size for the Rate field, a Number field, to Single so that the field can contain decimal places.

1

- Tap or click the Click to Add column heading and select Short Text as the data type.
- Type **Recruiter Number** as the field name.
- Tap or click the white space below the field name to complete the change of the name. Tap or click the white space a second time to select the field.
- Change the field size to 2.
- Tap or click the Required check box (TABLE TOOLS FIELDS tab | Field Validation group) to make the field a required field.
- Tap or click the Unique check box (TABLE TOOLS FIELDS tab | Field Validation group) so that Access will ensure that values in the field are unique (Figure 9–40).

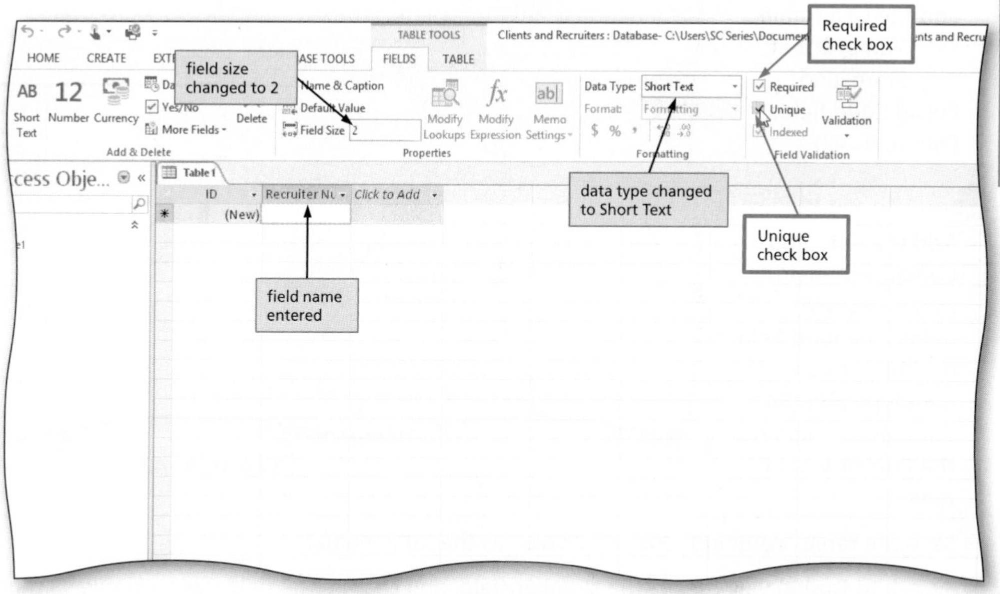

Figure 9–40

2

- Tap or click under the Click to Add column heading to produce an insertion point in the next field.
- Tap or click the More Fields button (TABLE TOOLS FIELDS tab | Add & Delete group) to display the More Fields menu (Figure 9–41).

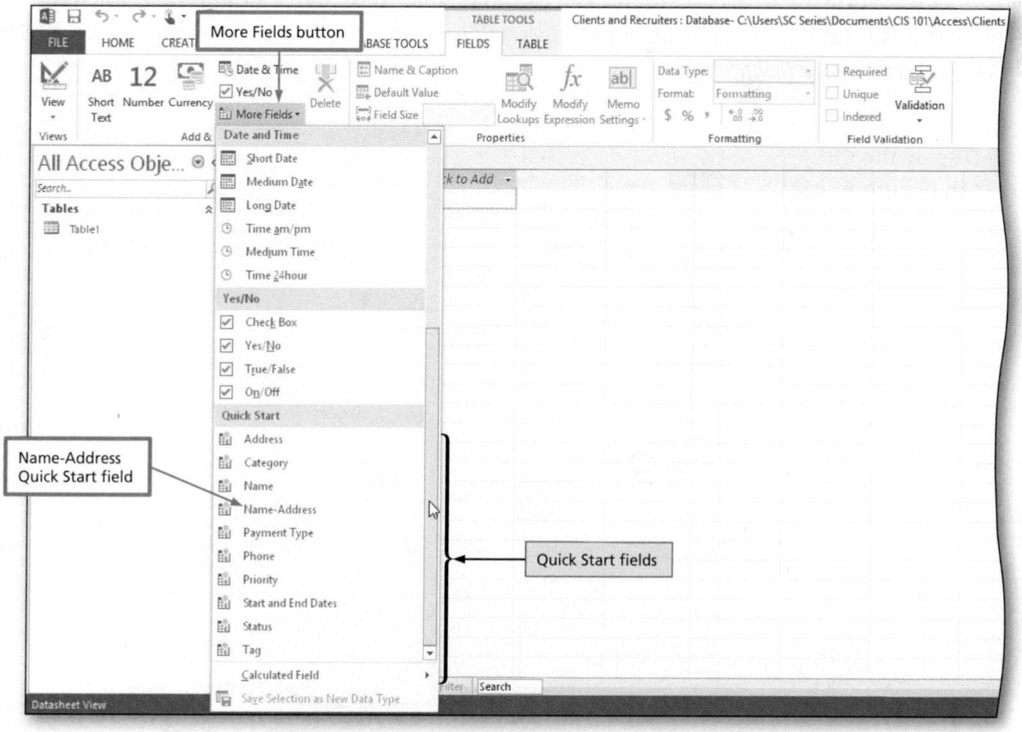

Figure 9–41

3

- Tap or click the Name-Address Quick Start field that you created earlier to add the Last Name, First Name, Street, City, State, and Postal Code fields (Figure 9–42).

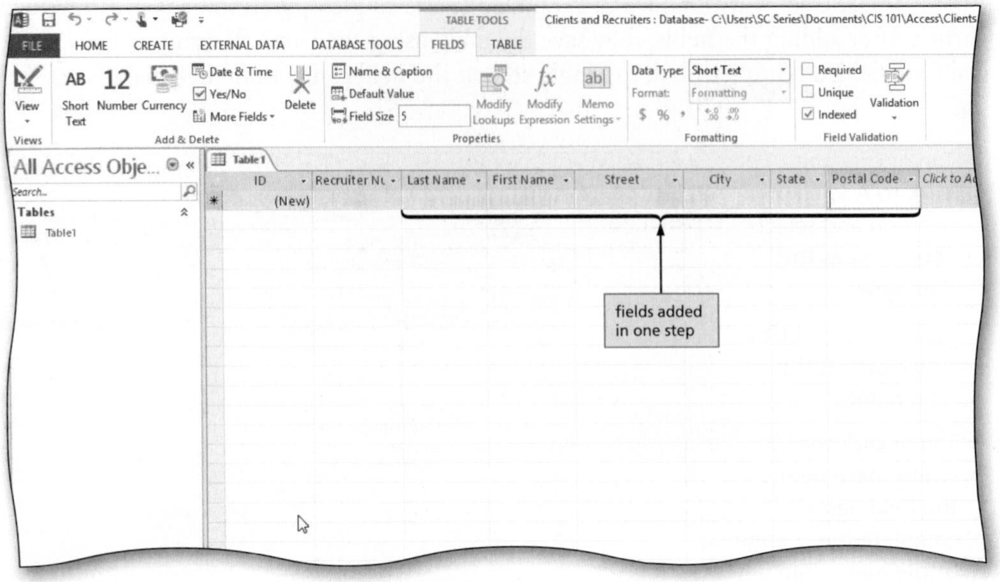

Figure 9–42

4

- Add the Rate and Commission fields as the last two fields. The Rate field has the Number data type and the Commission field has the Currency data type.
- Save the table, assigning `Recruiter` as the table name.
- Switch to Design view, select the Number field, and change the field size to Single so that the Rate field can include decimal places.
- Save and close the table.

To Create a Second Table

1 CONVERT DATABASE | 2 ANALYZE & DOCUMENT | 3 NAVIGATION PANE | 4 CUSTOM PROPERTIES & INDEXES
5 CUSTOM DATA PART | 6 CUSTOM TEMPLATE | 7 ENCRYPT LOCK & SPLIT | 8 CUSTOM WEB APP | 9 CUSTOM VIEW

The following steps create the Client table. The steps add a lookup field for Recruiter Number to relate the two tables. ***Why?*** *Because the tables will be used in a web app, the relationship between the tables needs to be implemented using a lookup field.*

1

- Display the CREATE tab (Figure 9–43).

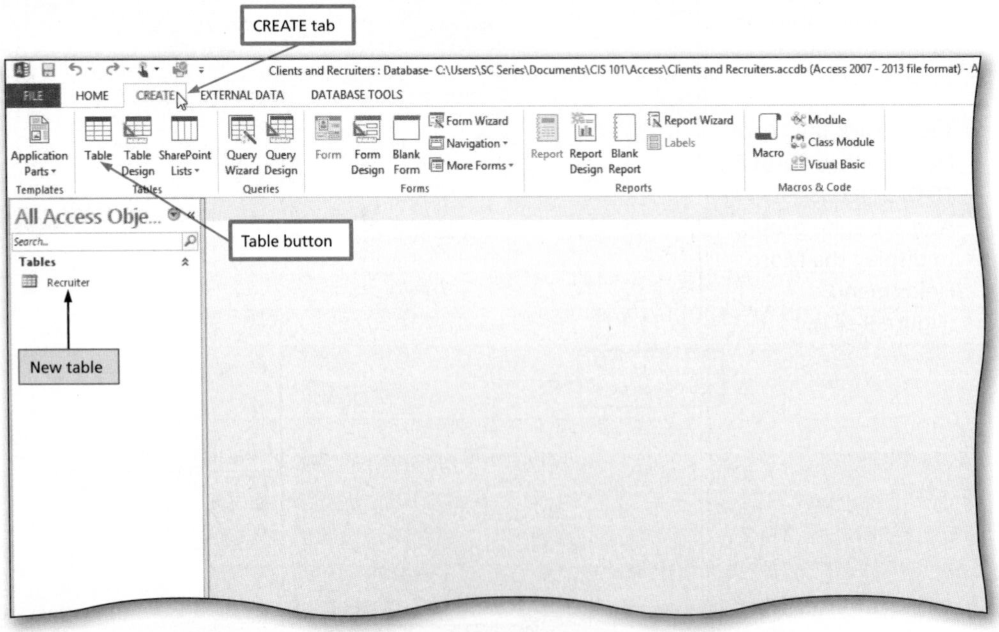

Figure 9–43

2

- Tap or click the Table button (CREATE tab | Tables group) to create a new table.
- Tap or click the 'Click to Add' column heading and select Short Text as the data type.
- Type `Client Number` as the field name.
- Tap or click the white space below the field name to complete the change of the name. Tap or click the white space a second time to select the field.

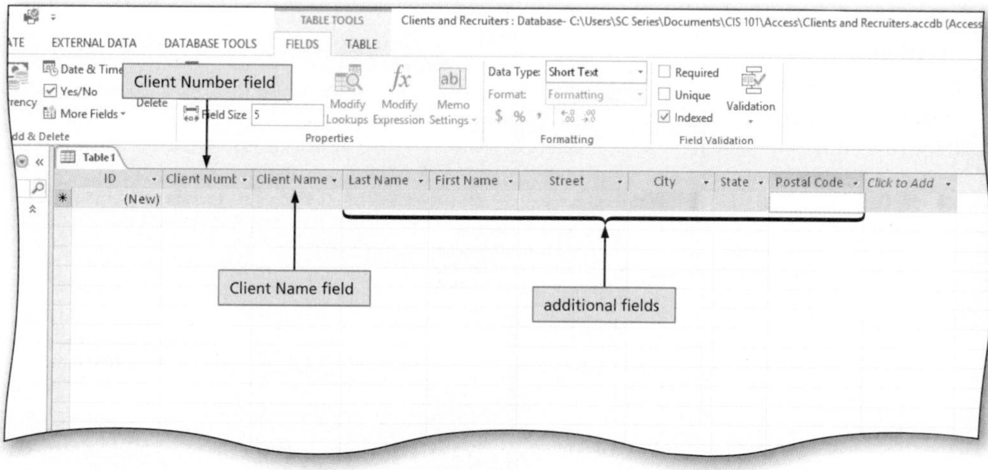

Figure 9–44

- Change the field size to 5.
- Tap or click the Required check box (TABLE TOOLS FIELDS tab | Field Validation group) to make the field a required field.
- Tap or click the Unique check box (TABLE TOOLS FIELDS tab | Field Validation group) so that Access will ensure that values in the field are unique.
- In a similar fashion, add the Client Name field and change the field size to 30. Do not check the Required or Unique check boxes.
- Tap or click under the 'Click to Add' column heading to produce an insertion point in the next field.
- Tap or click the More Fields button (TABLE TOOLS FIELDS tab | Add & Delete group) to display the More Fields menu (see Figure 9–41 on page AC 567).
- Tap or click the Name-Address Quick Start field that you added earlier to add the Last Name, First Name, Street, City, State, and Postal Code fields (Figure 9–44).

3

- Press and hold or right-click the Last Name field to produce a shortcut menu, and then tap or click Delete Field to delete the field.
- Press and hold or right-click the First Name field to produce a shortcut menu, and then tap or click Delete Field to delete the field.
- Add the Amount Paid and Current Due fields. Both fields have the Currency data type.
- Save the table, assigning Client as the table name.
- Scroll, if necessary, so that the 'Click to Add' column appears on your screen.
- Tap or click the 'Click to Add' column heading to display a menu of available data types (Figure 9–45).

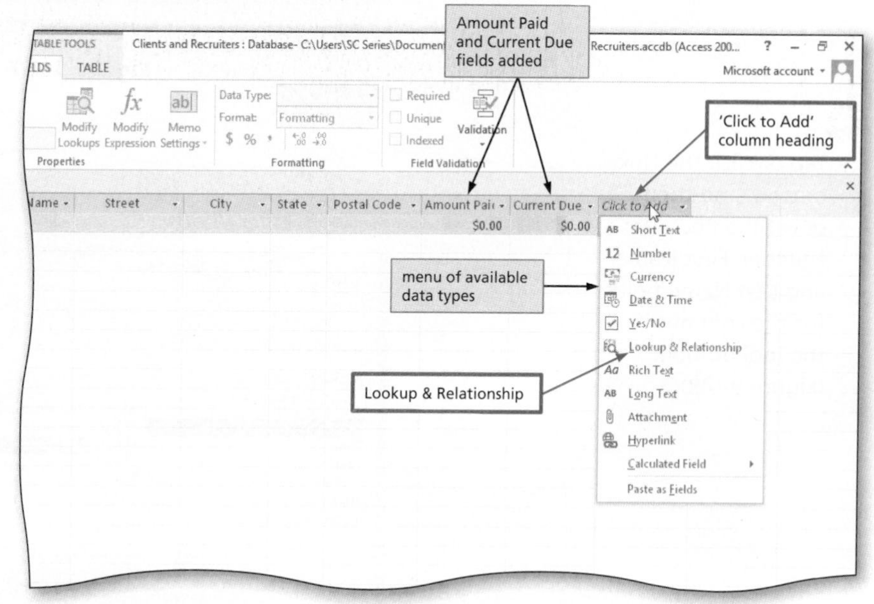

Figure 9–45

4

- Tap or click Lookup & Relationship to display the Lookup Wizard dialog box (Figure 9–46).

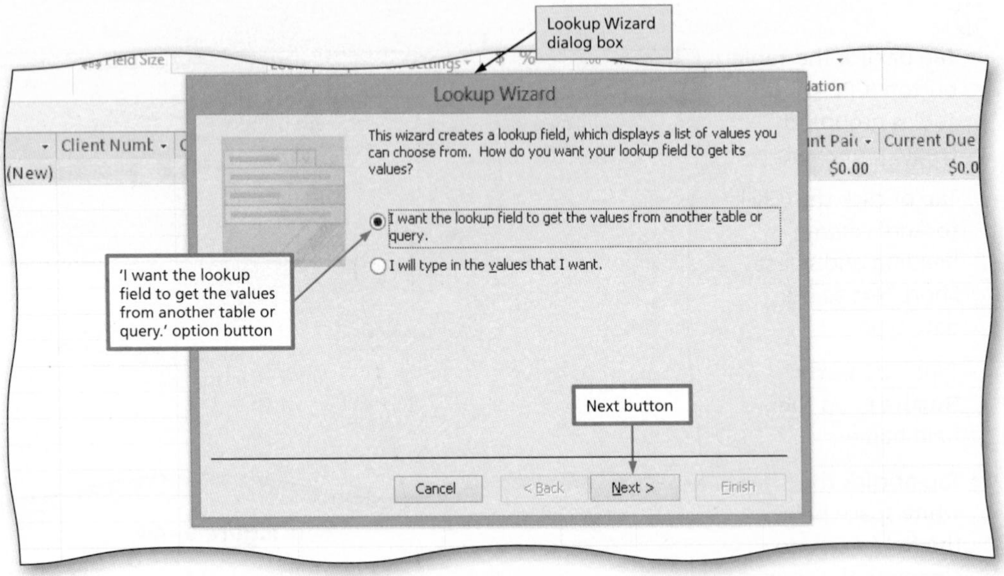

Figure 9–46

5

- Tap or click the Next button to display the next Lookup Wizard screen, and then tap or click the Recruiter table to select it so that you can add a lookup field for the Recruiter Number to the Client table (Figure 9–47).

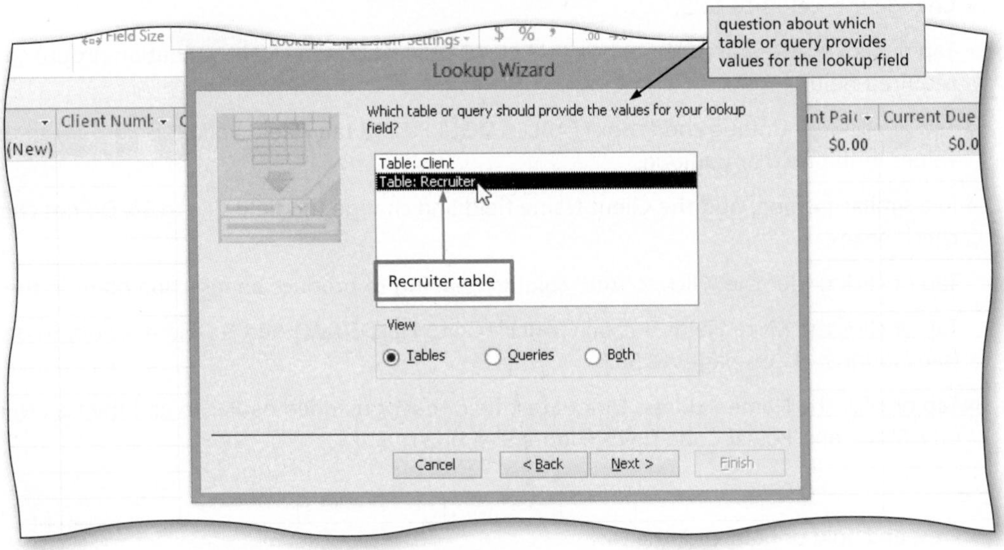

Figure 9–47

6

- Tap or click the Next button, and then select the Recruiter Number, First Name, and Last Name fields for the columns in the lookup field (Figure 9–48).

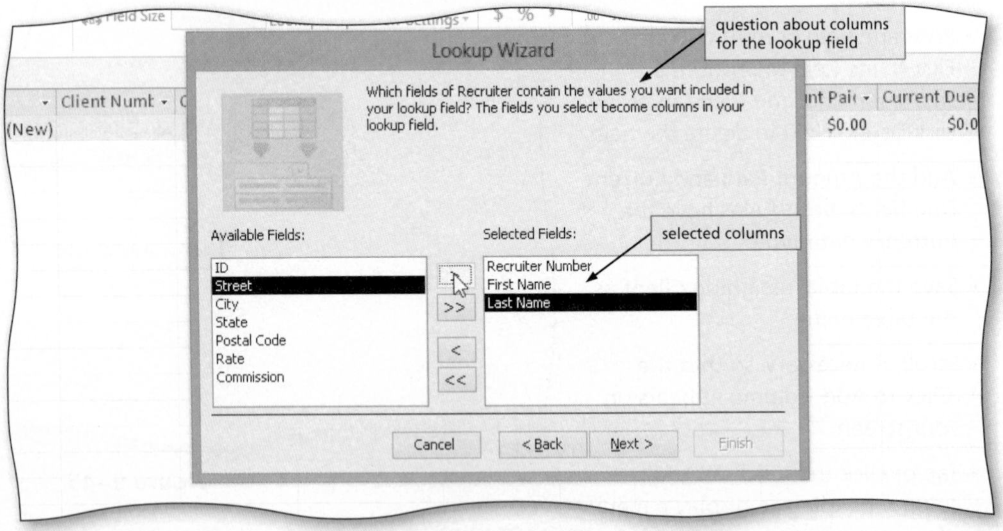

Figure 9–48

7

- Tap or click the Next button, select the Recruiter Number field for the sort order, and then tap or click the Next button again. (Figure 9–49).

Q&A I see the ID field listed when I am selecting the Recruiter Number field for the sort order. Did I do something wrong?
No. Access automatically included the ID field.

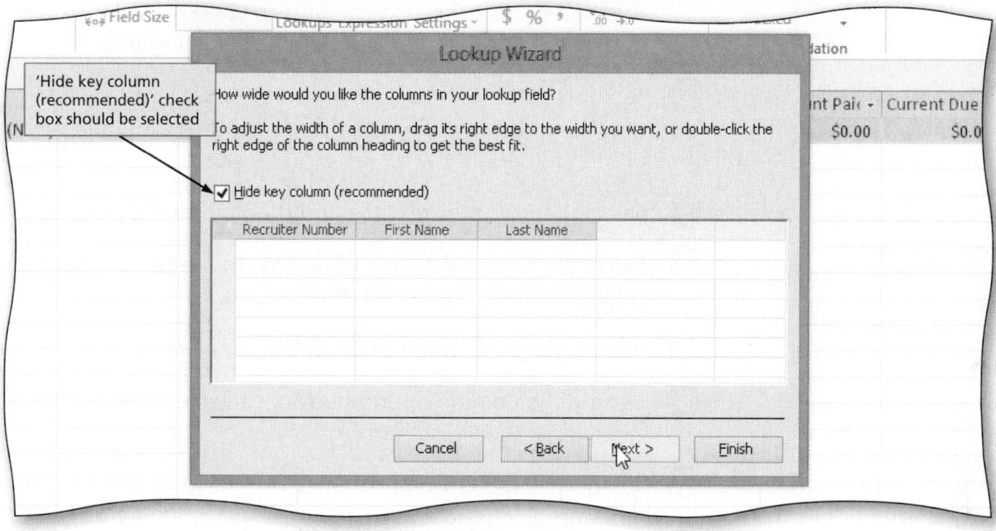

Figure 9–49

8

- Ensure the 'Hide key column (recommended)' check box is selected, and then tap or click the Next button.
- Type **Recruiter Number** as the label for the lookup field.
- Tap or click the 'Enable Data Integrity' check box to select it (Figure 9–50).

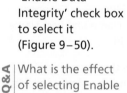

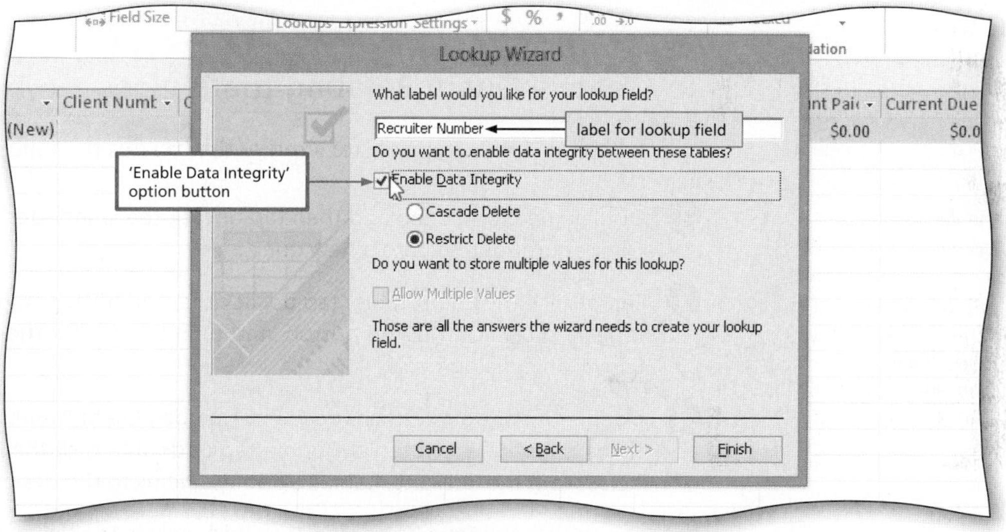

Figure 9–50

Q&A What is the effect of selecting Enable Data Integrity?
Access will enforce referential integrity for the Recruiter Number. That is, Access will not allow a recruiter number in a client record that does not match the number of a recruiter in the Recruiter table.

9

- Tap or click the Finish button to add the lookup field.
- Save the table.
- Close the table.

To Import the Data

Now that the tables have been created, you need to add data to them. You could enter the data, or if the data is already in electronic form, you could import the data. The data for the Recruiter and Client tables are included in the Data Files for Students as text files. The steps on the next page import the data.

BTW
Importing Tables from Other Databases
You can import tables from other Access databases. To do so, tap or click the Access button (EXTERNAL DATA tab | Import & Link group) then navigate to the location containing the database and select the database. Tap or click the Open button. Ensure that the 'Import tables, queries, forms, reports, macros, and modules into the current database' option button is selected and tap or click OK. When the Import Object dialog box appears, select the table or tables you want to import and then tap or click OK. You also can import other objects by tapping or clicking the appropriate object tabs.

1. With the Clients and Recruiters database open, display the EXTERNAL DATA tab, and then tap or click the Text File button (EXTERNAL DATA tab | Import & Link group) to display the Get External Data - Text File dialog box.
2. Tap or click the Browse button (Get External Data - Text File dialog box) and select the location of the files to be imported (for example, the Access folder in the CIS 101 folder).
3. Select the Recruiter text file and then tap or click the Open button.
4. Select the 'Append a copy of records to the table' option button, select the Recruiter table, and then tap or click the OK button.
5. Be sure the Delimited option button is selected, and then tap or click the Next button.
6. Be sure the Comma option button is selected, tap or click the Next button, and then tap or click the Finish button.
7. Tap or click the Close button to close the Get External Data – Text File dialog box without saving the import steps.
8. Use the technique shown in Steps 1 through 7 to import the Client text file into the Client table.

To Create a Query Relating the Tables

The following steps create a query that relates the Client and Recruiter tables.

BTW
Rearranging Fields in a Query
If you add fields to a query in the wrong order, you can select the field in the design grid, and drag it to the appropriate location.

1. Display the CREATE tab and then tap or click the Query Design button (CREATE tab | Queries group) to create a new query.
2. Tap or click the Client table, tap or click the Add button, tap or click the Recruiter table, tap or click the Add button, and then tap or click the Close button to close the Show Table dialog box.
3. Double-tap or double-click the Client Number, Client Name, and Recruiter Number fields from the Client table. Double-tap or double-click the First Name and Last Name fields from the Recruiter table to add the fields to the design grid.
4. Tap or click the Save button on the Quick Access Toolbar to save the query, type `Client-Recruiter Query` as the name of the query, and then tap or click the OK button.
5. Close the query.

Creating Forms

There are several types of forms that need to be created for this database. The Client and Recruiter detail forms show a single record at a time. The Client, Recruiter, and Client-Recruiter Query forms are intended to look like the corresponding table or query in Datasheet view. Finally, the main menu is a navigation form.

To Create Single-Item Forms

The following steps create two single-item forms, that is, forms that display a single record at a time. The first form, called Client Details, is for the Client table. The second form is for the Recruiter table and is called Recruiter Details.

1. Select the Client table in the Navigation Pane and then display the CREATE tab.
2. Tap or click the Form button (CREATE tab | Forms group) to create a single-item form for the Client table.
3. Tap or click the Save button on the Quick Access Toolbar and then type `Client Details` as the name of the form, click the OK button (Save As dialog box) to save the form, and then close the form.
4. Select the Recruiter table, display the CREATE tab, and then tap or click the Form button (CREATE tab | Forms group) to create a single-item form for the Recruiter table.
5. Save the form, using `Recruiter Details` as the form name.
6. Close the form.

To Create Datasheet Forms

1 CONVERT DATABASE | 2 ANALYZE & DOCUMENT | 3 NAVIGATION PANE | 4 CUSTOM PROPERTIES & INDEXES
5 CUSTOM DATA PART | 6 CUSTOM TEMPLATE | **7 ENCRYPT LOCK & SPLIT** | **8 CUSTOM WEB APP** | **9 CUSTOM VIEW**

The following steps create two datasheet forms, that is, forms that display the data in the form of a datasheet. ***Why?*** *These forms enable you to make it appear that you are displaying datasheets in a navigation form; recall that navigation forms can display only forms.* The first form is for the Client table and is also called Client. The second is for the Recruiter table and is also called Recruiter. The steps also create macros that will display the data for a selected record in a single-item form, as you did in Chapter 8 on pages AC 504 through AC 507.

1

- Select the Client table and then display the CREATE tab.
- Tap or click the More Forms button (CREATE tab | Forms group) to display the More Forms menu (Figure 9–51).

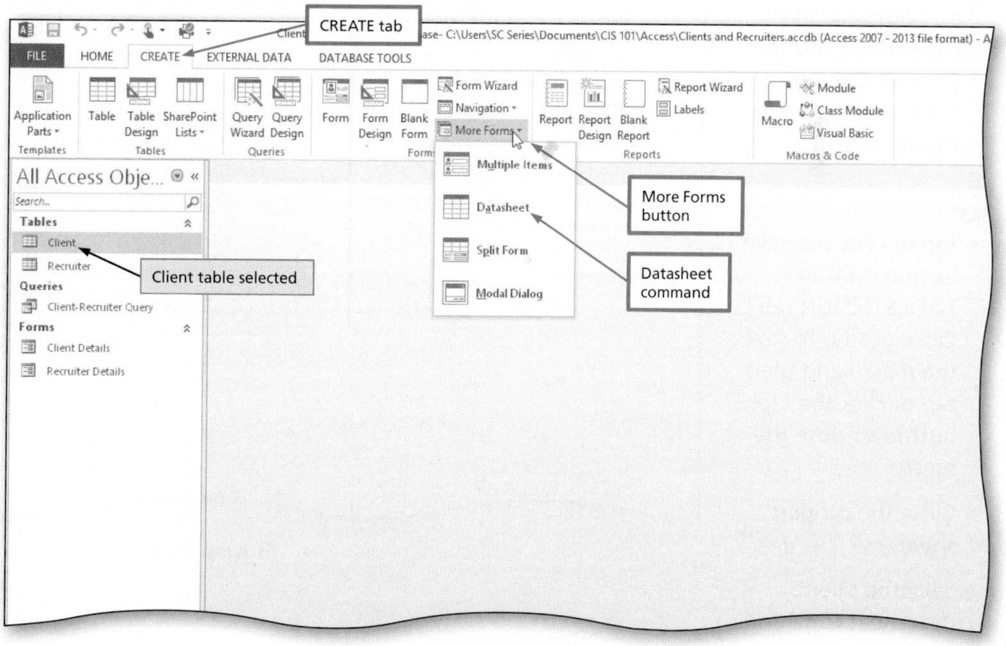

Figure 9–51

2

- Tap or click Datasheet to create a datasheet form for the Client table.
- Tap or click the Save button on the Quick Access Toolbar and then accept Client as the default name of the form.
- Tap or click the column heading for the ID field to select the field.
- Display the property sheet and tap or click the Event tab to display only the event properties (Figure 9–52).

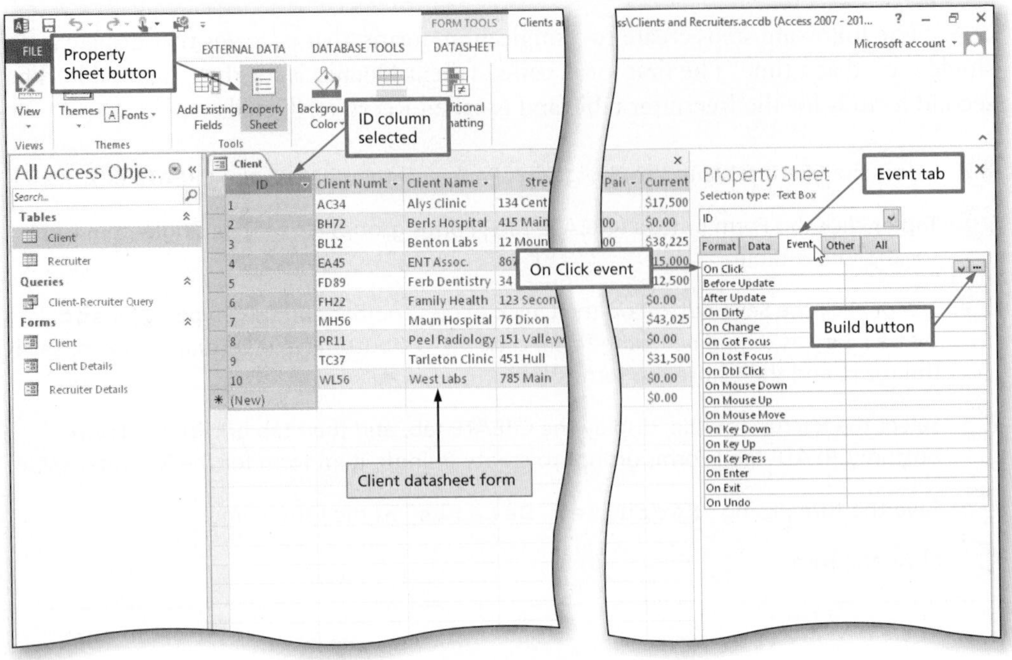

Figure 9–52

3

- Tap or click the Build button (the three dots) for the On Click event and then use the techniques on pages AC 504 through AC 507 in Chapter 8 to enter the macro shown in Figure 9–53.

4

- Tap or click the Save button (MACRO TOOLS DESIGN tab | Close group) to save the macro and then tap or click the Close button to close the macro.
- Close the property sheet.
- Save the Client datasheet form and then close the form.

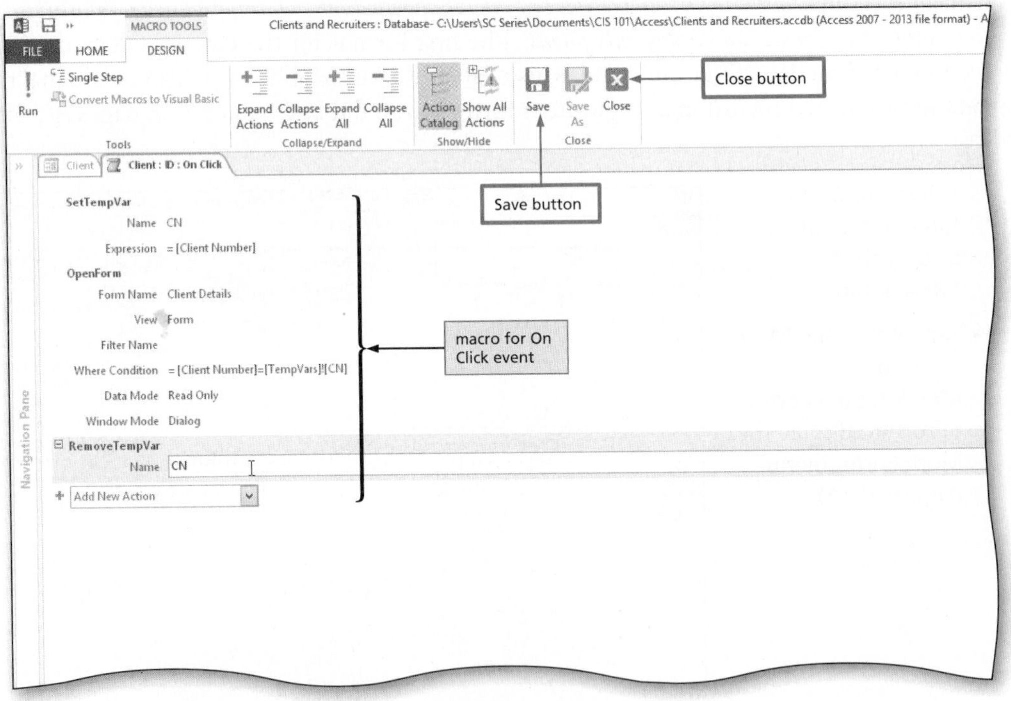

Figure 9–53

5

- Use the techniques in Steps 1 and 2 to create a datasheet form for the Recruiter table. Use `Recruiter` as the name for the form. The macro for the On Click event for the ID field is shown in Figure 9–54.

6

- Save and close the macro.
- Close the property sheet.
- Save and close the form.

7

- Select the Client-Recruiter Query.
- Create a datasheet form for the Client-Recruiter Query. Save the form, using `Client-Recruiter Query` as the form name.
- Close the Client-Recruiter Query form.

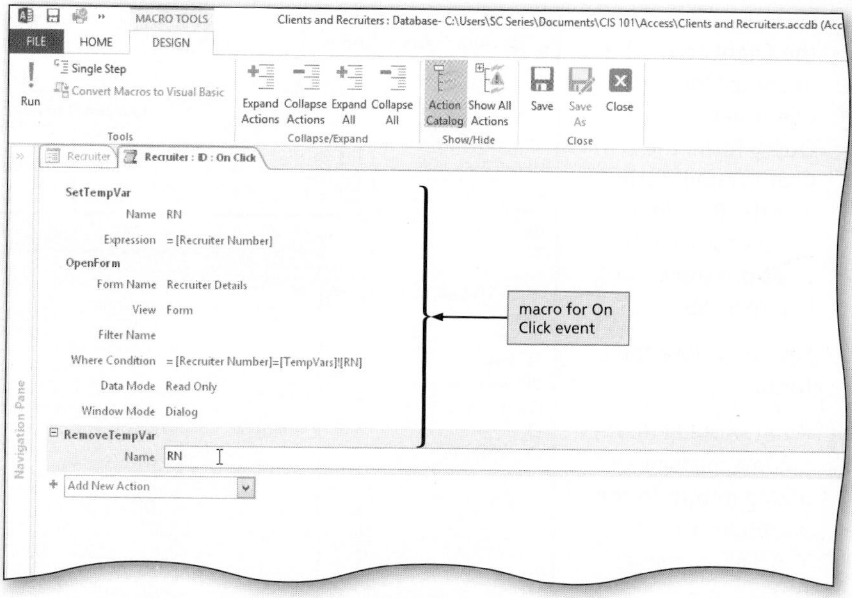

Figure 9–54

Experiment

- Test each of the macros by tapping or clicking the client number in the Client form or the recruiter number in the Recruiter form. Ensure that the correct form opens. If there are errors, correct the corresponding macro. When finished, close any form you have opened.

To Create a Navigation Form

1 CONVERT DATABASE | 2 ANALYZE & DOCUMENT | 3 NAVIGATION PANE | 4 CUSTOM PROPERTIES & INDEXES
5 CUSTOM DATA PART | 6 CUSTOM TEMPLATE | **7 ENCRYPT LOCK & SPLIT | 8 CUSTOM WEB APP | 9 CUSTOM VIEW**

The following steps create a navigation form containing a single row of horizontal tabs. The steps save the form using the name, Main Menu. ***Why?*** *This form is intended to function as a menu.* The steps change the form title and add the appropriate tabs.

1

- Display the CREATE tab and then tap or click the Navigation button (CREATE tab | Forms group) to show the menu of available navigation forms.
- Tap or click Horizontal Tabs in the menu to create a form with a navigation control in which the tabs are arranged in a single row, horizontally.
- If a field list appears, tap or click the 'Add Existing Fields' button (FORM LAYOUT TOOLS DESIGN tab | Tools group) to remove the field list.

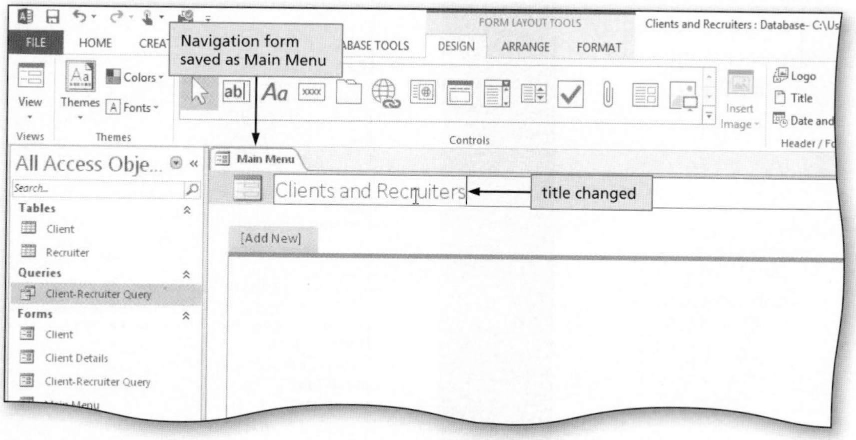

Figure 9–55

- Save the navigation form, using Main Menu as the form name.
- Tap or click the form title twice, once to select it and the second time to produce an insertion point.
- Erase the current title and then type `Clients and Recruiters` as the new title (Figure 9–55).

2

- One at a time, drag the Client form, the Recruiter form, the Client-Recruiter Query form, the Client Details form, and the Recruiter Details form to the positions shown in Figure 9–56.
- Save and close the form.

Q&A What should I do if I made a mistake and added a form to the wrong location?
You can rearrange the tabs by dragging. Often, the simplest way to correct a mistake is to tap or click the Undo button to reverse your most recent action, however. You also can choose to simply close the form without saving it and then start over.

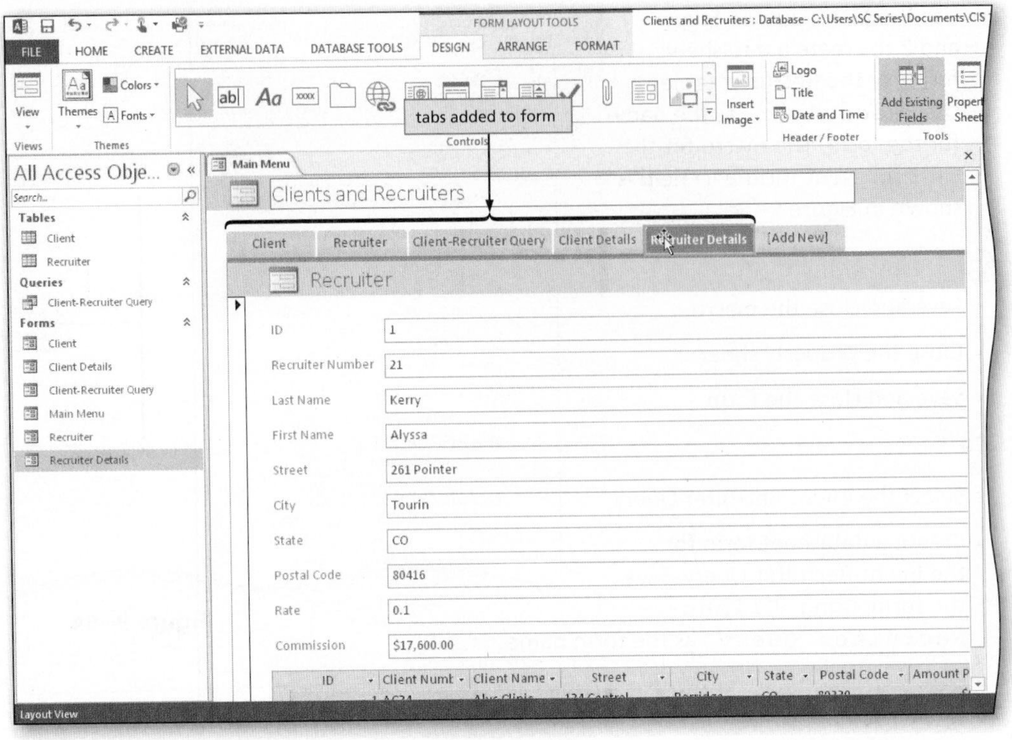

Figure 9–56

To Select a Startup Form

1 CONVERT DATABASE | 2 ANALYZE & DOCUMENT | 3 NAVIGATION PANE | 4 CUSTOM PROPERTIES & INDEXES
5 CUSTOM DATA PART | 6 CUSTOM TEMPLATE | 7 ENCRYPT LOCK & SPLIT | 8 CUSTOM WEB APP | 9 CUSTOM VIEW

If the database includes a navigation form, it is common to select the navigation form as a **startup form,** which launches when the user opens the database. ***Why?*** *Designating the navigation form as a startup form ensures that the form will appear automatically when a user opens the database.* The following steps designate the navigation form as a startup form.

1

- Tap or click FILE on the ribbon to display the Backstage view (Figure 9–57).

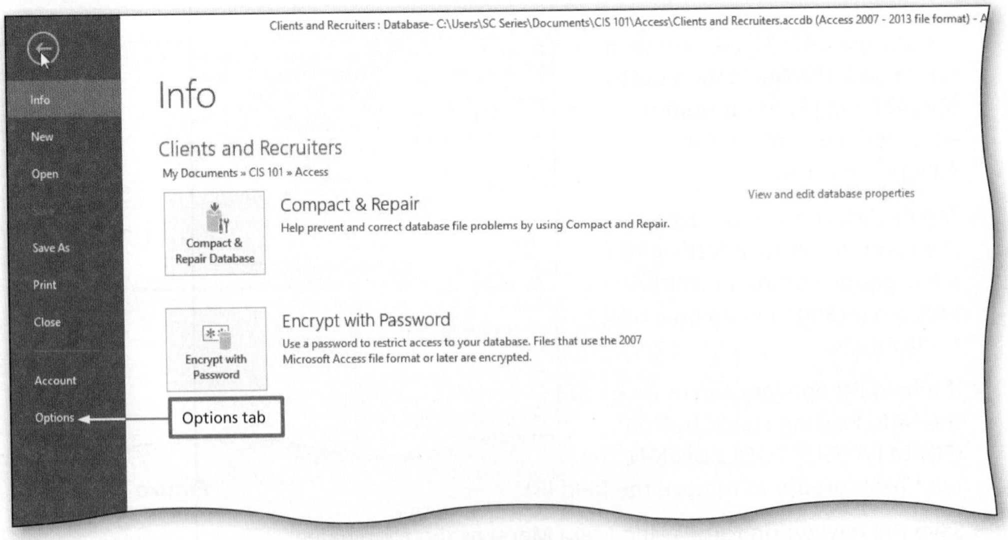

Figure 9–57

2

- Tap or click the Options tab.
- Tap or click Current Database (Access Options dialog box) to select the options for the current database.
- Tap or click the Display Form arrow to display the list of available forms.
- Tap or click Main Menu to select it as the form that will automatically be displayed whenever the database is opened (Figure 9–58).

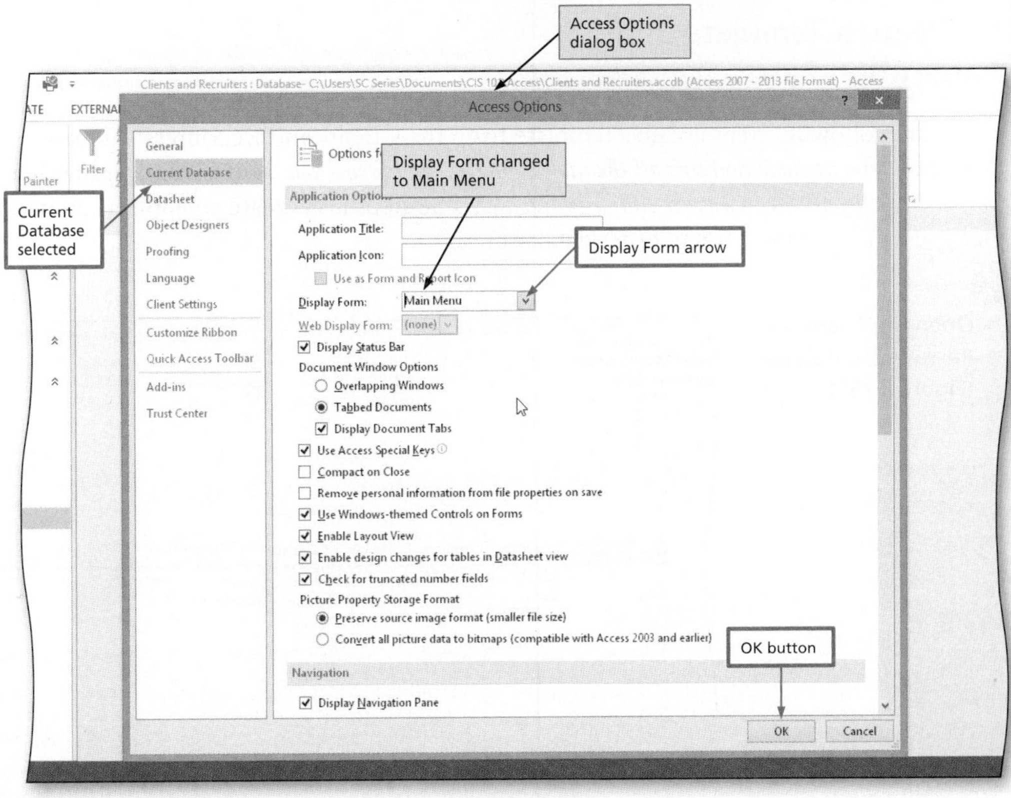

Figure 9–58

3

- Tap or click the OK button (Access Options dialog box) to save your changes.
- Tap or click the OK button (Microsoft Access dialog box) when Access displays a message indicating that you must close and reopen the database for the change to take effect.
- Close the database.

Break Point: If you wish to stop working through the chapter at this point, you can close Access now. You can resume the project at a later time by starting Access, and continuing to follow the steps from this location forward.

Templates

An Access **template** is a file that contains the elements needed to produce a specific type of complete database. You can select a template when you create a database. The resulting database will contain all the tables, queries, forms, reports, and/or macros included in the template. In addition, with some templates, the resulting database also might contain data.

Some templates are also available as **application parts**. Application parts are very similar to templates in that selecting a single application part can create tables, queries, forms, reports, and macros. The difference is you select a template when you first create a database, whereas you select an application part after you have already created a database. The objects (tables, queries, forms, reports, and macros) in the application part will be added to any objects you already have created.

Access provides a number of templates representing a variety of types of databases. You also can create your own template from an existing database. When you create a template, you can choose to create an application part as well. When creating templates and application parts, you can also include data if desired.

BTW
Templates and Application Parts
By default, user-created templates and application parts are stored in the C:\Users*user name*\AppData\Roaming\Microsoft\Templates\Access folder.

To Create a Template and Application Part

The following steps create a template from the Clients and Recruiters database. ***Why?*** *The Clients and Recruiters database now contains all the tables, queries, and forms you want in the template. You then will be able to use the template when you want to create similar databases.* The steps also create an application part from the database so that you can reuse the parts in other databases.

1

- Open the Clients and Recruiters database (Figure 9–59).

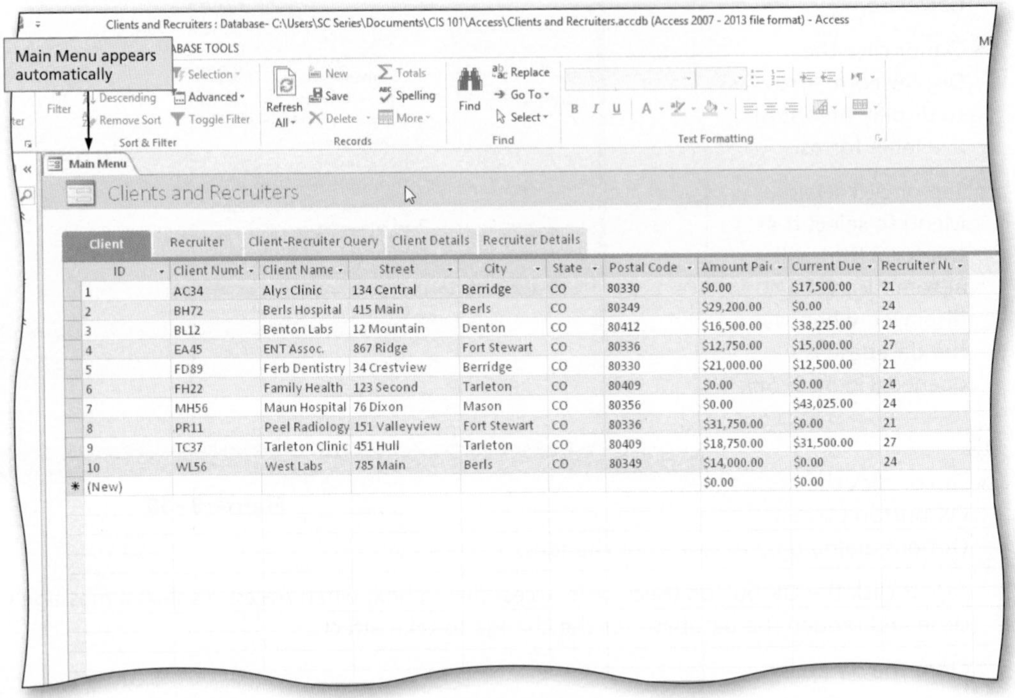

Figure 9–59

2

- Close the Main Menu form.
- Open the Backstage view.
- Tap or click the Save As tab.
- Tap or click the Template button in the Save Database As area to indicate you are creating a template (Figure 9–60).

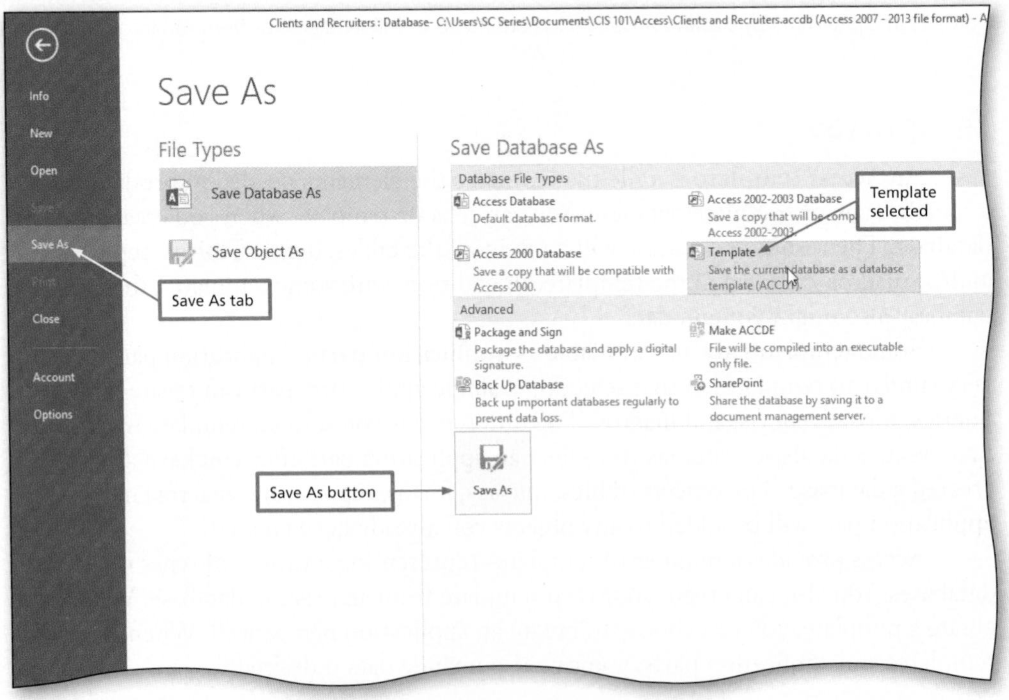

Figure 9–60

3

- Tap or click the Save As button to display the Create New Template from This Database dialog box.
- Type `Clients and Recruiters` as the name for the new template.
- Type `Database of clients and recruiters with navigation form menu.` as the description.
- Tap or click the Application Part check box to indicate that you also want to create an application part.

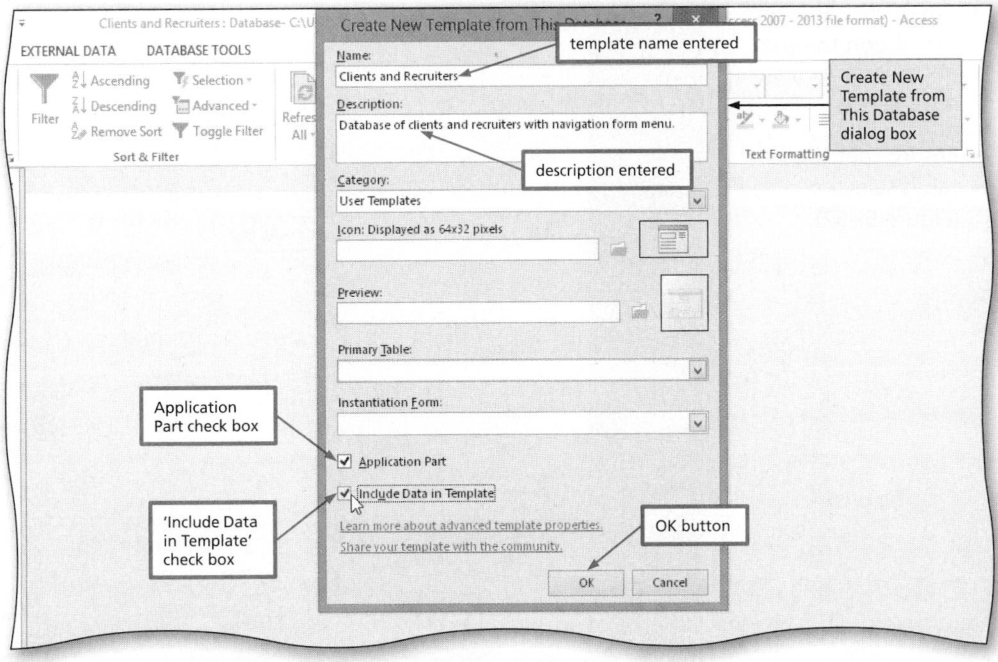

Figure 9–61

- Tap or click the 'Include Data in Template' check box to indicate you want to include the data in the database as part of the template (Figure 9–61).

Q&A Why include data?
Anytime a user creates a database using the template, the database automatically will include data. This enables the users to see what any reports, forms, or queries look like with data in them. Once the users have the reports, forms, and queries the way they want them, they can delete all this data. At that point, they can begin adding the real data to the database.

4

- Tap or click the OK button (Create New Template from This Database dialog box) to create the template.
- When Access indicates that the template has been successfully saved, tap or click the OK button (Microsoft Access dialog box).

To Use the Template

1 CONVERT DATABASE | 2 ANALYZE & DOCUMENT | 3 NAVIGATION PANE | 4 CUSTOM PROPERTIES & INDEXES
5 CUSTOM DATA PART | 6 CUSTOM TEMPLATE | 7 ENCRYPT LOCK & SPLIT | 8 CUSTOM WEB APP | 9 CUSTOM VIEW

You can use the Clients and Recruiters template just as you would use any other template, such as the Blank database template you previously used. The only difference is that, after tapping or clicking the New tab in the Backstage view, you need to tap or click the PERSONAL link. ***Why?*** *The PERSONAL link displays any templates you created and lets you select the template you want.*

The steps on the next page use the template created earlier to create the MZL Recruiters database. Later in the chapter, you will learn how to use this database to import tables to a web app.

1

- Tap or click FILE on the ribbon to open the Backstage view, if necessary.
- Ensure that the New tab is selected (Figure 9–62).

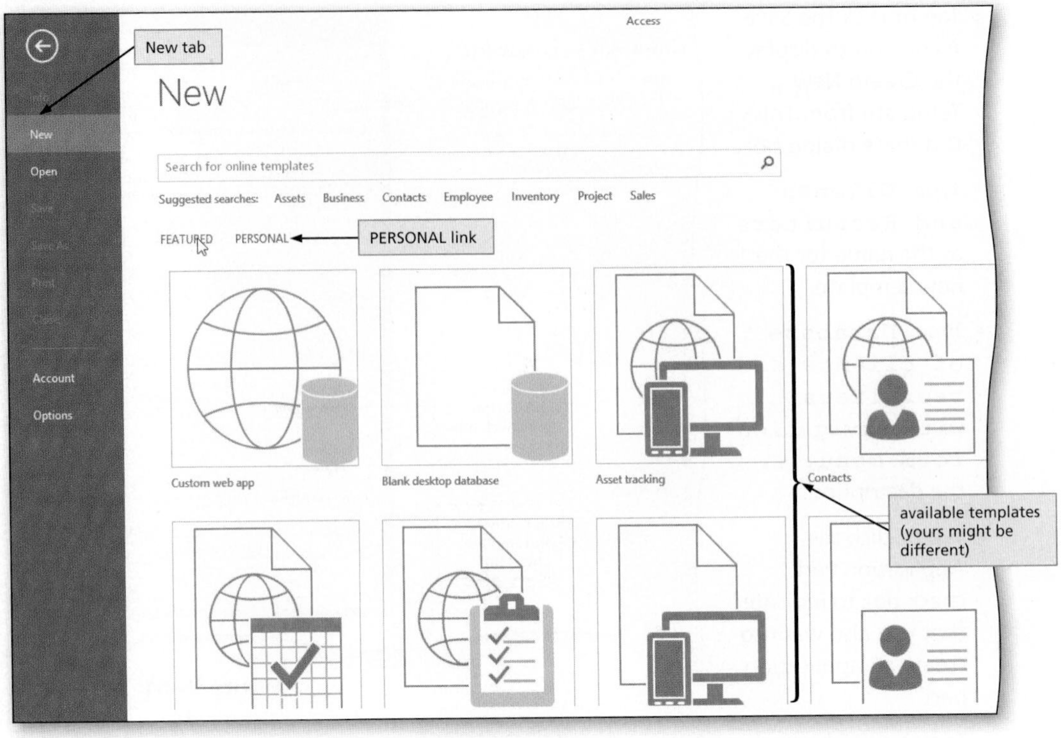

Figure 9–62

2

- Tap or click the PERSONAL link to display the templates you have created (Figure 9–63).

3

- Tap or click the 'Clients and Recruiters' template that you created earlier.
- Type **`MZL Recruiters`** as the name of the database and then navigate to the location of the database to be opened (for example, the Access folder in the CIS 101 folder).

Figure 9–63

- Tap or click the Create button to create the database from the template.
- Close the database.

Note: Unless your instructor indicates otherwise, you are strongly encouraged to simply read the material in this chapter from this point on without carrying out any operations. If you decide to try it for yourself, it is important to make a backup copy of your database and store it in a secure location before performing the operation. That way, if something damages your database or you can no longer access your database, you still can use the backup copy. In addition, for the material on web apps, you must have access to a SharePoint 2013 site.

Using an Application Part

To use the application part you created, you first need to create a database. After doing so, you tap or click the Application Parts button (CREATE tab | Templates group) to display the Application Parts menu (Figure 9–64).

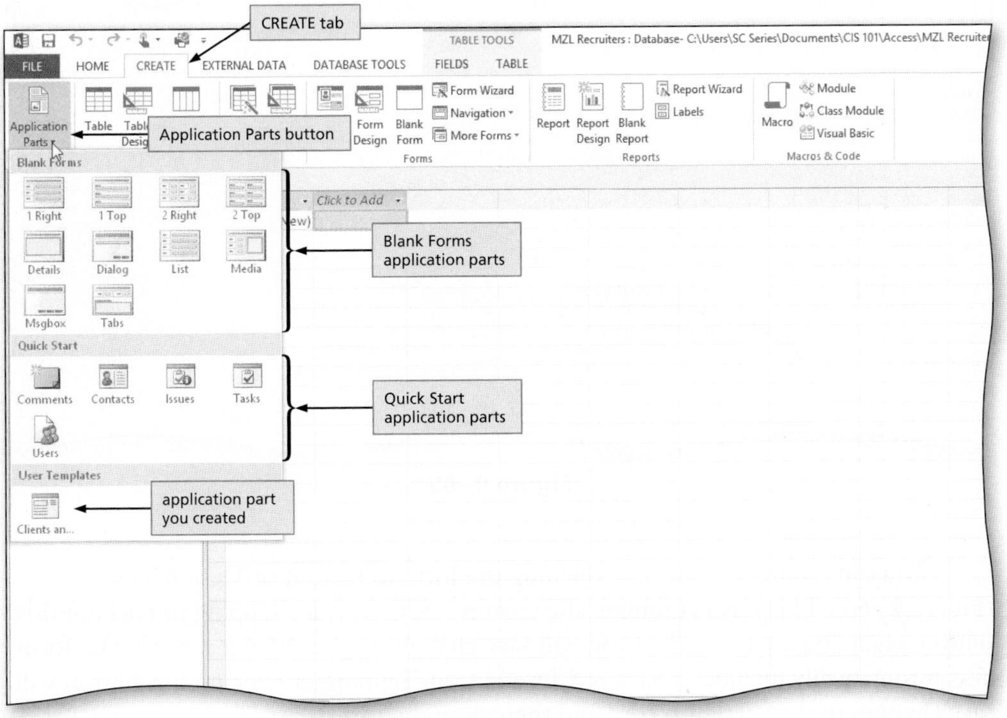

Figure 9–64

You then can tap or click the application part you created, which will be located in the User Templates section of the Application Parts menu. If you have any open objects, Access will indicate that "all open objects must be closed before instantiating this application part" and ask if you want Access to close all open objects. After you tap or click the Yes button, Access will add all the objects in the Application part to the database. If you already had created other objects in the database, they still would be included.

1 CONVERT DATABASE | 2 ANALYZE & DOCUMENT | 3 NAVIGATION PANE | 4 CUSTOM PROPERTIES & INDEXES
5 CUSTOM DATA PART | 6 CUSTOM TEMPLATE | 7 ENCRYPT LOCK & SPLIT | 8 CUSTOM WEB APP | 9 CUSTOM VIEW

To Use the Application Part

Specifically, to use the application part created earlier, you would use the following steps.

1. Create or open the database for which you want to use the application part.
2. Display the CREATE tab and then tap or click the Application Parts button (CREATE tab | Templates group).
3. Tap or click the application part to be added.
4. If Access indicates that open objects must be closed, tap or click the Yes button.

Blank Forms Application Parts

Blank Forms application parts (see Figure 9–64 on the previous page) represent a way to create certain types of forms (Figure 9–64). To do so, you click the Application Parts button to display the gallery of application part styles, and then tap or click the desired type of form, for example, 1 Right. Access then creates a form with the desired characteristics and assigns it a name. It does not open the form, but you can see the form in the Navigation Pane (Figure 9–65).

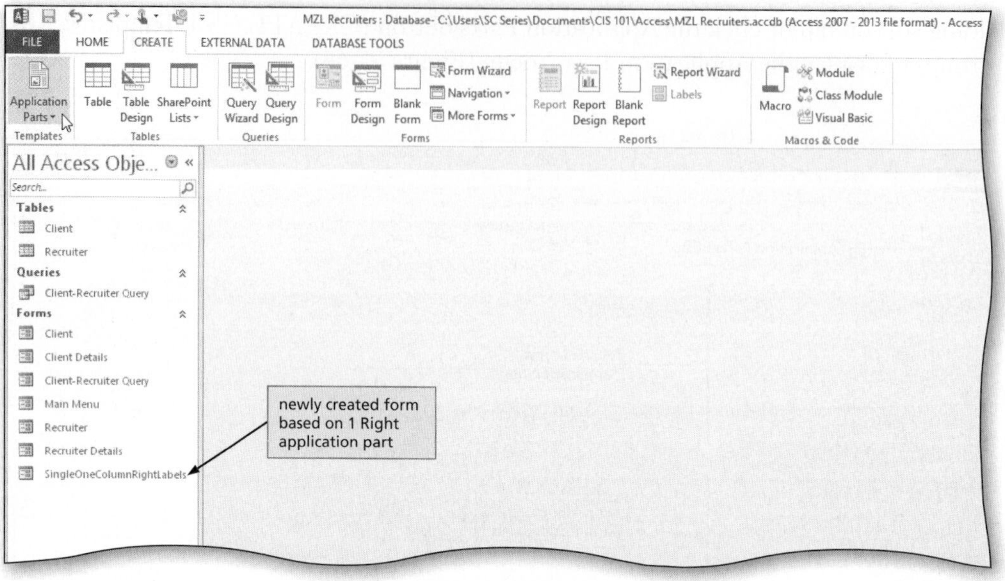

Figure 9–65

You can modify the form by opening the form in Layout or Design view (Figure 9–66). This form automatically creates a Save button. Tapping or clicking this button when you are using the form will save changes to the current record. The form also automatically includes a Save & Close button. Tapping or clicking this button will save changes to the current record and then close the form.

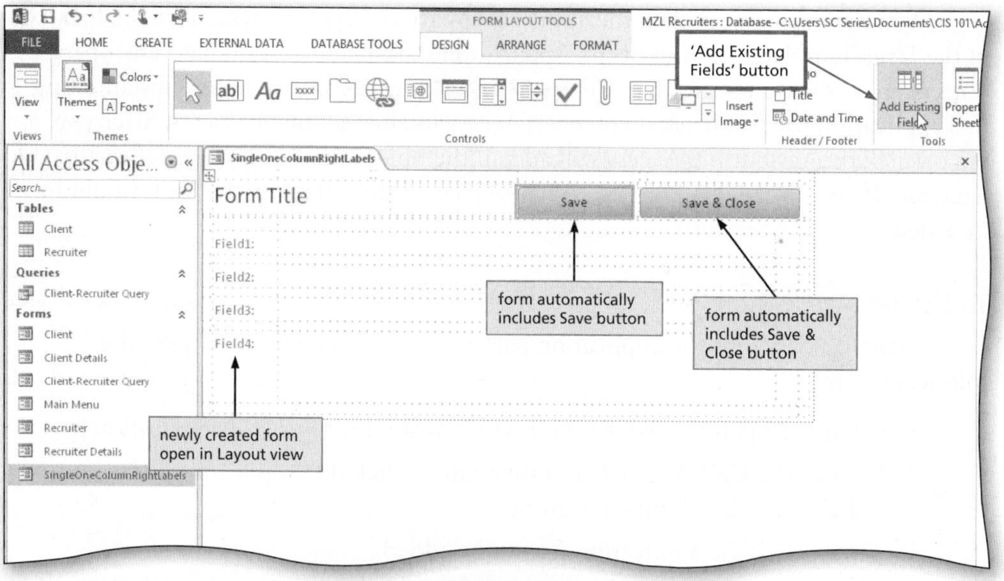

Figure 9–66

To add the specific fields you want to the form, display a field list. You then can drag a field onto the form while holding down the CTRL key (Figure 9–67). Once you have added the field, you can change the corresponding label by tapping or clicking the label to select it, tapping or clicking the label a second time to produce an insertion point, and then making the desired change.

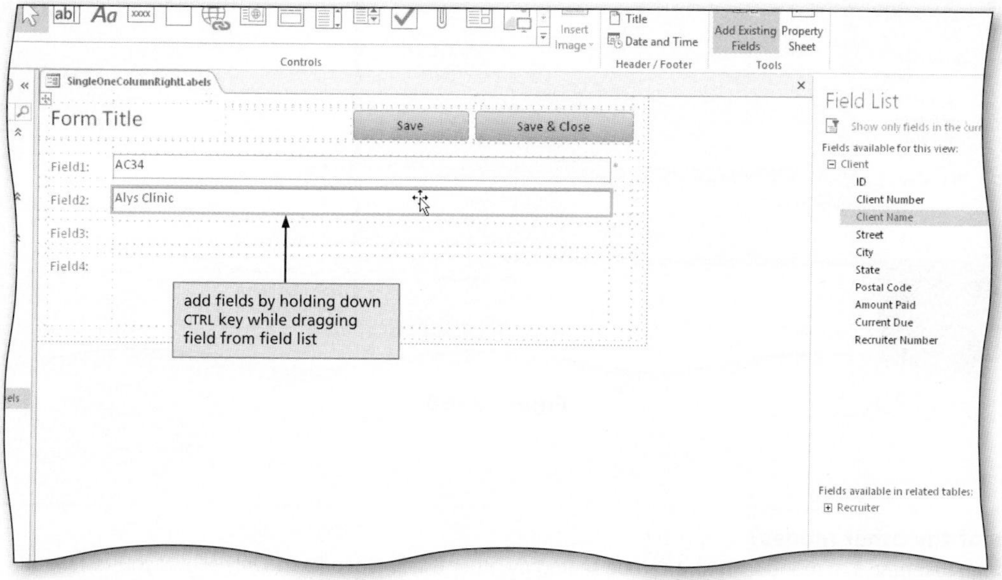

Figure 9–67

> BTW
> **Encryption and Passwords**
> Encryption helps prevent unauthorized use of an Access database. Consider using encryption when the database contains sensitive data, such as medical records or employee records. Passwords should be eight or more characters in length. The longer the length of the password and the more random the characters, the more difficult it is for someone to determine. Use a combination of uppercase and lowercase letters as well as numbers and special symbols when you create a password. Make sure that you remember your password. If you forget it, there is no method for retrieving it. You will be unable to open the encrypted database.

Encrypting a Database

Encrypting refers to the storing of data in the database in an encoded, or encrypted, format. Anytime a user stores or modifies data in the encrypted database, the database management system (DBMS) will encode the data before actually updating the database. Before a legitimate user retrieves the data using the DBMS, the data will be decoded. The whole encrypting process is transparent to a legitimate user; that is, he or she is not even aware it is happening. If an unauthorized user attempts to bypass all the controls of the DBMS and get to the database through a utility program or a word processor, however, he or she will be able to see only the encoded, and unreadable, version of the data. In Access, you encrypt a database and set a password as part of the same operation.

1 CONVERT DATABASE | 2 ANALYZE & DOCUMENT | 3 NAVIGATION PANE | 4 CUSTOM PROPERTIES & INDEXES
5 CUSTOM DATA PART | 6 CUSTOM TEMPLATE | 7 ENCRYPT LOCK & SPLIT | 8 CUSTOM WEB APP | 9 CUSTOM VIEW

To Open a Database in Exclusive Mode

To encrypt a database and set a password, the database must be open in exclusive mode; that is, no other user can access the database in any way. To open a database in exclusive mode, you use the Open arrow (Figure 9–68 on the next page) rather than simply tapping or clicking the Open button.

To open a database in exclusive mode, you would use the following steps.

1. If necessary, close any open databases.
2. Tap or click Open in the Backstage view to display the Open dialog box.
3. Tap or click Computer, then tap or click Browse.
4. Navigate to the location of the database to be opened.
5. Tap or click the name of the database to be opened.
6. Tap or click the Open arrow to display the Open button menu.
7. Tap or click Open Exclusive to open the database in exclusive mode.

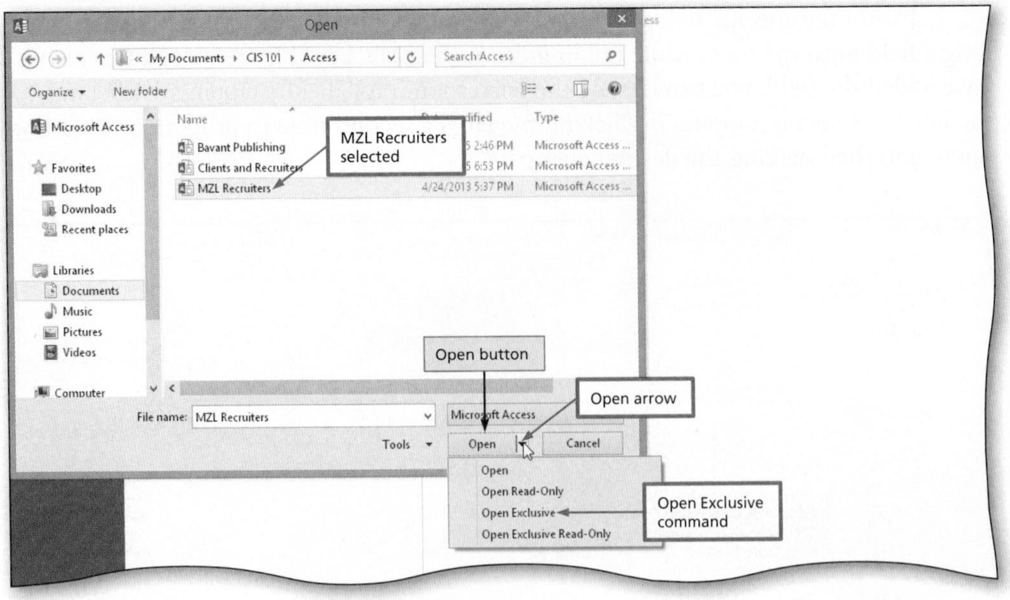

Figure 9–68

CONSIDER THIS

What is the purpose of the other modes?

The Open option opens the database in a mode so that it can be shared by other users. Open Read-Only allows you to read the data in the database, but not update the database.

Encrypting a Database with a Password

If you wanted to encrypt the database with a password, you would open the Backstage view (Figure 9–69).

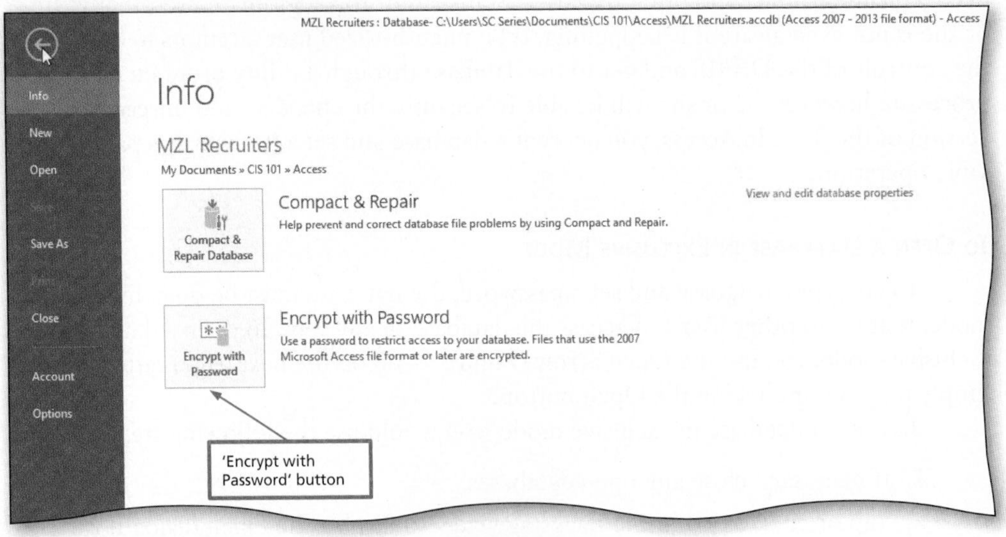

Figure 9–69

You then would select 'Encrypt with Password' and enter the password you have chosen in both the Password text box and Verify text box (Figure 9–70).

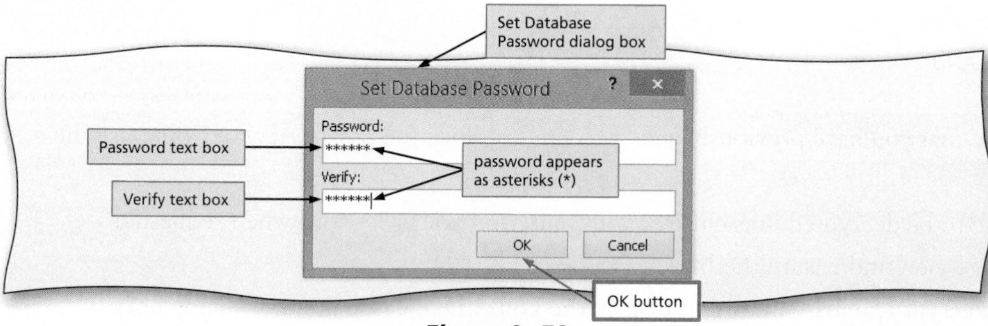

Figure 9–70

To Encrypt a Database with a Password

With the database open in exclusive mode, you would use the following steps to encrypt the database with a password.

1. Tap or click FILE on the ribbon to open the Backstage view and ensure the Info tab is selected.
2. Tap or click the 'Encrypt with Password' button to display the Set Database Password dialog box.
3. Type the desired password in the Password text box in the Set Database Password dialog box.
4. Press the TAB key and then type the password again in the Verify text box.
5. Tap or click the OK button to encrypt the database and set the password.
6. If you get a message indicating that row level locking will be ignored, tap or click the OK button.
7. Close the database.

Is the password case sensitive?
Yes, you must enter the password using the same case you used when you created it.

CONSIDER THIS

Opening a Database with a Password

When you open a database that has a password, you will be prompted to enter your password in the Password Required dialog box. Once you have done so, tap or click the OK button. Assuming you have entered your password correctly, Access then will open the database.

Decrypting a Database and Removing a Password

If the encryption and the password no longer are necessary, you can decrypt the database and remove the password. The button to encrypt a database with a password has changed to Decrypt Database (Figure 9–71).

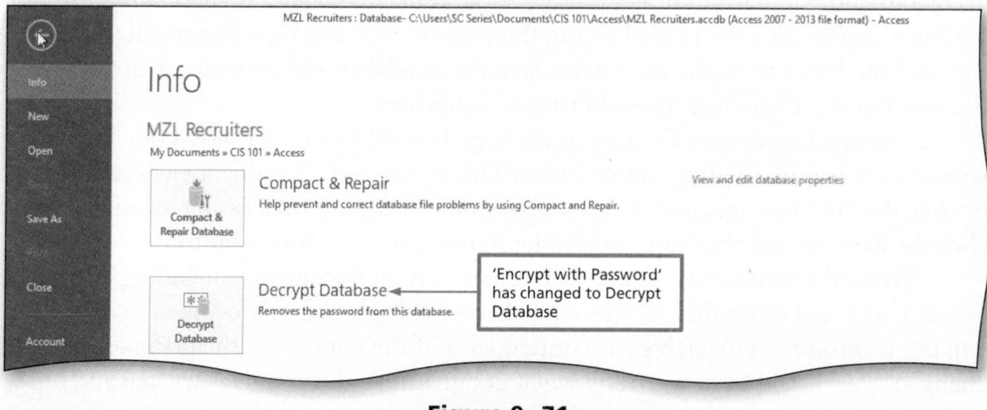

Figure 9–71

To Decrypt the Database and Remove the Password

To decrypt a database that you have previously encrypted and remove the password, you would use the following steps.

1. Open the database to be decrypted in exclusive mode, entering your password when requested.
2. Open the Backstage view and ensure the Info tab is selected.
3. Tap or click the Decrypt Database button to display the Unset Database Password dialog box.
4. Type the password in the Password dialog box.
5. Tap or click the OK button to remove the password and decrypt the database.
6. Close the database.

The Trust Center

The Trust Center is a feature within Access where you can set security options and also find the latest information on technology related to privacy, safety, and security. To use the Trust Center, you tap or click FILE on the ribbon and then tap or click the Options tab to display the Access Options dialog box. You then tap or click Trust Center to display the Trust Center content (Figure 9–72). You then would tap or click the 'Trust Center Settings' button to display the Trust Center dialog box in which you can make changes in the following categories.

BTW
Security
Security is the prevention of unauthorized access to a database. Within an organization, the database administrator determines the types to access individual users can have to the database. Various government rules and regulations, such as the Sarbannes-Oxley Act (SOX) and the Health Insurance Portability and Accountability Act (HIPPA), require database administrators to have strict security procedures in place to protect data from unauthorized users.

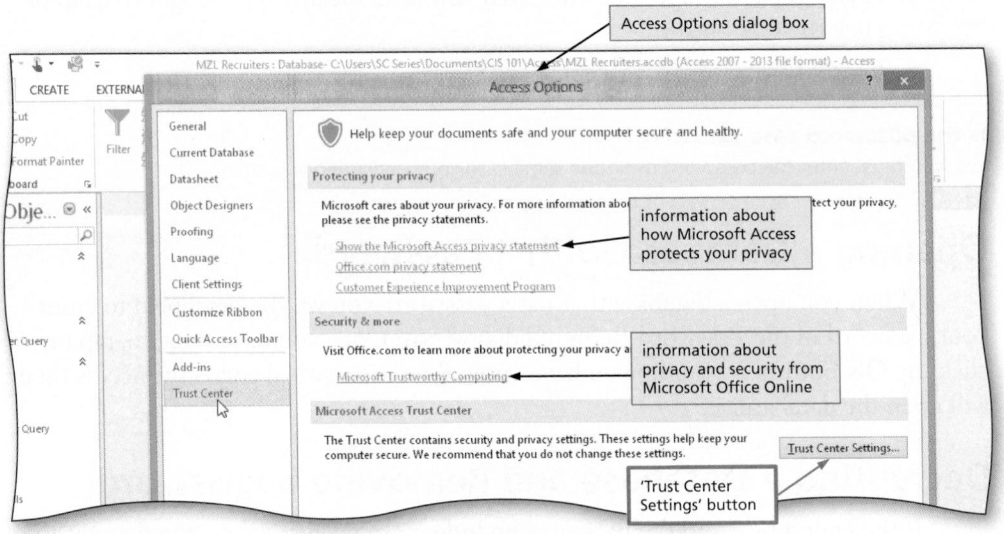

Figure 9–72

Trusted Publishers. Tapping or clicking Trusted Publishers in the Trust Center dialog box shows the list of trusted software publishers. To view details about a trusted publisher, tap or click the publisher and then tap or click the View button. To remove a trusted publisher from the list, tap or click the publisher and then tap or click the Remove button. Users may also add trusted publishers.

Trusted Locations. Tapping or clicking Trusted Locations shows the list of trusted locations on the Internet or within a user's network. To add a new location, tap or click the 'Add new location' button. To remove or modify an existing location, tap or click the location and then tap or click the Remove or the Modify button.

Trusted Documents. You can designate certain documents, including database, Word, Excel, and other files, as trusted. When opening a trusted document, you will not be prompted to enable the content, even if the content of the document has changed. You should be very careful when designating a document as trusted and only do so when you are absolutely sure the document is from a trusted source.

Add-ins. Add-ins are additional programs that you can install and use within Access. Some come with Access and are typically installed using the Access Setup program. Others can be purchased from other vendors. Tapping or clicking Add-ins gives you the opportunity to specify restrictions concerning Add-ins.

ActiveX Settings. When you use ActiveX controls within an Office app, Office prompts you to accept the controls. The ActiveX settings allow you to determine the level of prompting from Office.

Macro Settings. Macros written by other users have the potential to harm your computer; for example, a macro could spread a virus. The Trust Center uses special criteria, including valid digital signatures, reputable certificates, and trusted publishers, to ensure a macro is safe. If the Trust Center discovers a macro that is potentially unsafe, it will take appropriate action. The action the Trust Center takes depends on the Macro Setting you have selected. Tapping or clicking Macro Settings enables you to select or change this setting.

Message Bar. Tapping or clicking Message Bar lets you choose whether the message bar should appear when content has been blocked.

Privacy Options. Tapping or clicking Privacy Options lets you set security settings to protect your personal privacy.

Managing Add-ins. You can manage add-ins by opening the Backstage view, tapping or clicking Options, and then tapping or clicking Add-ins. You can view details concerning existing add-ins. You also can manage existing add-ins or add new ones by selecting the add-in category in the Manage box and then tapping or clicking the Go button to start the Add-in Manager. You also can start the Add-in Manager by tapping or clicking DATABASE TOOLS on the ribbon to display the DATABASE TOOLS tab and then tapping or clicking the Add-ins button.

Locking a Database

By **locking** a database, you can prevent users from viewing or modifying VBA code in your database or from making changes to the design of forms or reports while still allowing them to update records. When you lock the database, Access changes the file name extension from .accdb to .accde. To do so, you would use the Make ACCDE command shown in Figure 9–3 on page AC 543.

To Create a Locked Database (ACCDE File)

1 CONVERT DATABASE | 2 ANALYZE & DOCUMENT | 3 NAVIGATION PANE | 4 CUSTOM PROPERTIES & INDEXES
5 CUSTOM DATA PART | 6 CUSTOM TEMPLATE | 7 ENCRYPT LOCK & SPLIT | 8 CUSTOM WEB APP | 9 CUSTOM VIEW

To lock a database, you would use the following steps.

1. With the database open, tap or click FILE on the ribbon to open the Backstage view.
2. Tap or click the Save As tab.
3. Tap or click Make ACCDE in the Advanced area.
4. Tap or click the Save As button.
5. In the Save As dialog box, indicate a location and name for the ACCDE file.
6. Tap or click the Save button in the Save As dialog box to create the file.

Using the Locked Database

You use an ACCDE file just as you use the databases with which you now are familiar, with two exceptions. First, you must select ACCDE files in the 'Files of type' box when opening the file. Second, you will not be able to modify any source code or change the design of any forms or reports. If you pressed and held or right-clicked the Client Form, for example, you would find that the Design View command on the shortcut menu is dimmed, as are many other commands (Figure 9–73).

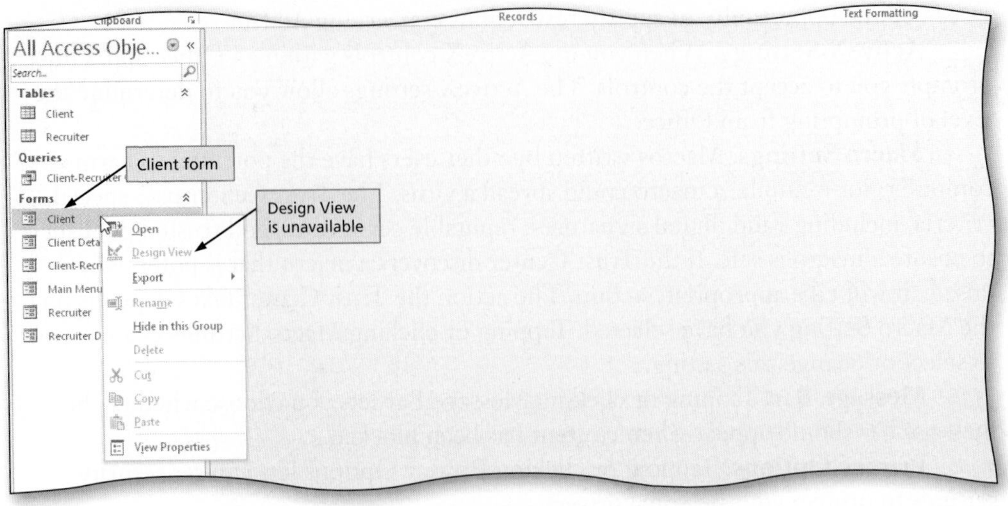

Figure 9–73

It is very important that you save your original database in case you ever need to make changes to VBA code or to the design of a form or report. You cannot use the ACCDE file to make such changes, nor can you convert the ACCDE file back to the ACCDB file format.

Record Locking

You can indicate how records are to be locked when multiple users are using a database at the same time. To do so, tap or click FILE on the ribbon, tap or click the Options tab, and then tap or click Client Settings. Scroll down so that the Advanced area appears on the screen (Figure 9–74).

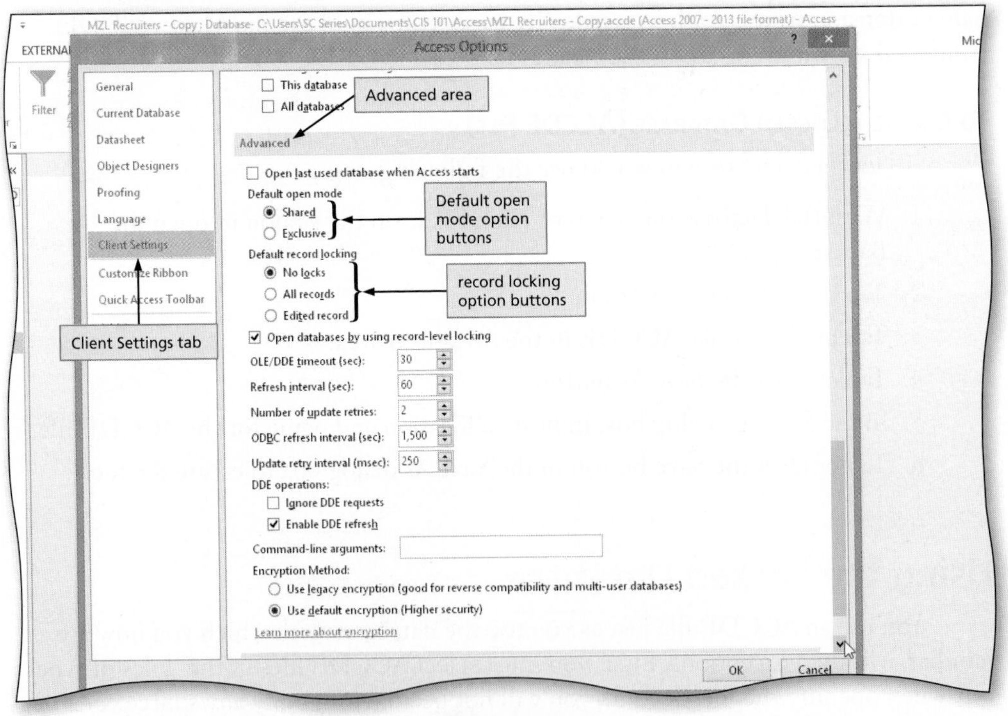

Figure 9–74

If you wanted the default open mode to be exclusive (only one user can use the database at a time) rather than shared (multiple users can simultaneously use the database), you could tap or click the Exclusive option button. You also can select the approach you want for record locking by tapping or clicking the appropriate record locking option button. The possible approaches to record locking are shown in Table 9–3.

Table 9–3 Record Locking Approaches

Locking Type	Description
No locks	When you edit a record, Access will not lock the record. Thus, other users also could edit the same record at the same time. When you have finished your changes and attempt to save the record, Access will give you the option of overwriting the other user's changes (not recommended), copying your changes to the clipboard, or canceling your changes.
All records	All records will be locked as long as you have the database open. No other user can edit or lock the records during this time.
Edited record	When you edit a record, Access will lock the record. When other users attempt to edit the same record, they will not be able to do so. Instead, they will see the locked record indicator.

Database Splitting

You can **split** a database into two databases, one called the **back-end database** containing only the table data, and another database called the **front-end database** containing the other objects. Only a single copy of the back-end database can exist, but each user could have his or her own copy of the front-end database. Each user would create the desired custom reports, forms, and other objects in his or her own front-end database, thereby not interfering with any other user.

Splitting a Database

When splitting a database, the database to be split must be open. In the process, you will identify a name and location for the back-end database that will be created by the Access splitter. In the process, you would display the Database Splitter dialog box (Figure 9–75).

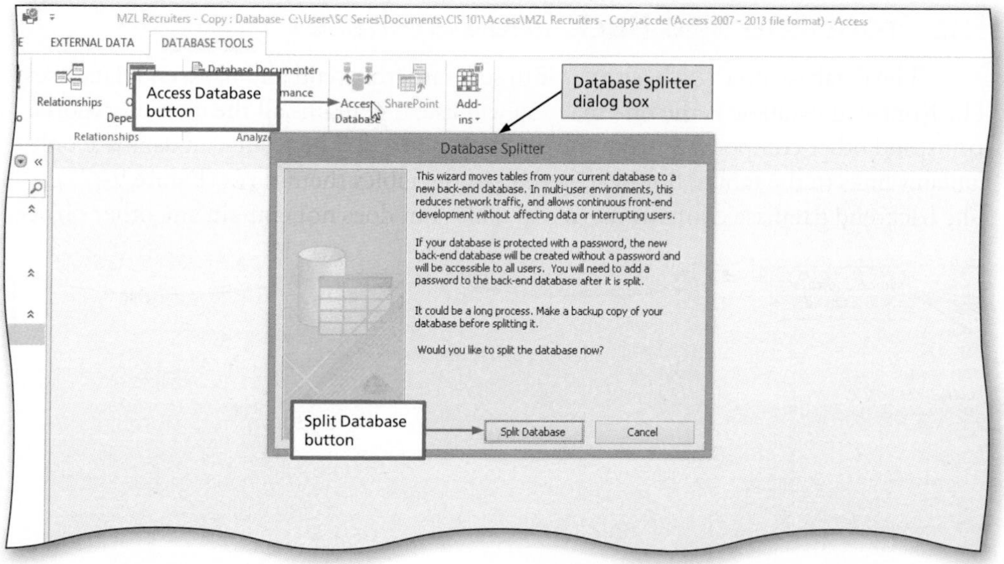

Figure 9–75

You also would have to select a location for the back-end database (Figure 9–76 on the next page). Access assigns a name to the back-end database that ends with an underscore and the letters, be. You can override this name if you prefer.

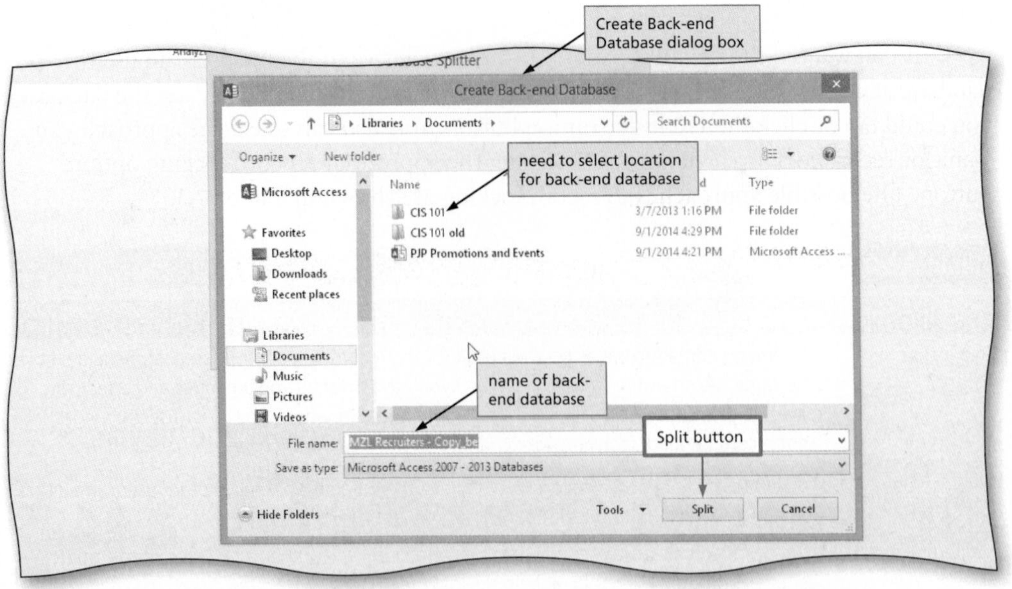

Figure 9–76

1 CONVERT DATABASE | 2 ANALYZE & DOCUMENT | 3 NAVIGATION PANE | 4 CUSTOM PROPERTIES & INDEXES
5 CUSTOM DATA PART | 6 CUSTOM TEMPLATE | 7 ENCRYPT LOCK & SPLIT | 8 CUSTOM WEB APP | 9 CUSTOM VIEW

To Split the Database

To split a database, you would use the following steps.

1. Open the database to be split.
2. Display the DATABASE TOOLS tab.
3. Tap or click the Access Database button (DATABASE TOOLS tab | Move Data group) to display the Database Splitter dialog box.
4. Tap or click the Split Database button to display the Create Back-end Database dialog box.
5. Either accept the file name Access suggests or change it to the one you want.
6. Select a location for the back-end database.
7. Tap or click the Split button to split the database.
8. Tap or click the OK button to close the dialog box reporting that the split was successful.

The Front-End and Back-End Databases

The database now has been split into separate front-end and back-end databases. The front-end database is the one that you will use; it contains all the queries, reports, forms, and other components from the original database. The front-end database only contains links to the tables, however, instead of the tables themselves (Figure 9–77). The back-end database contains the actual tables but does not contain any other objects.

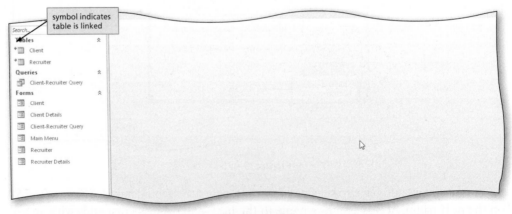

Figure 9–77

Web Apps

A **web app** is a database that you use in a web browser. You do not need to have Access installed to use the web app. You design and modify the web app using Access 2013, but users do not need Access 2013 to use the web app. To create or use a web app, you need a SharePoint server to host the web app. There are three typical ways of getting access to a SharePoint server. If your company has a SharePoint server using the full version of SharePoint 2013, you could use that. You also could purchase an Office 365 subscription plan that includes SharePoint. Finally, you could get SharePoint 2013 hosting from some other company.

Access provides a specific interface for creating web apps. When you create web apps, Access restricts some of the available database features. Tables in web apps must have AutoNumber fields as the primary key. Relationships between tables must be accomplished through lookup fields. Web apps viewed in a browser consist solely of a collection of related tables and various views of those tables. List view, which is similar to Form view, and Datasheet view are automatically included. You can define additional summary views that group data on selected fields.

BTW
Web Apps
Wep apps replace Access web databases, which were a feature of Access 2010. In Access 2013, you create web apps where the data and database objects are stored in SQL Server or a Windows Azure SQL Database.

Creating Web Apps

You can create custom web apps, in which you will indicate the specific tables and fields you want to include. Alternatively, you can select one of the web app templates. In either case, you must enter a name for your app as well as a web location for the app (Figure 9–78).

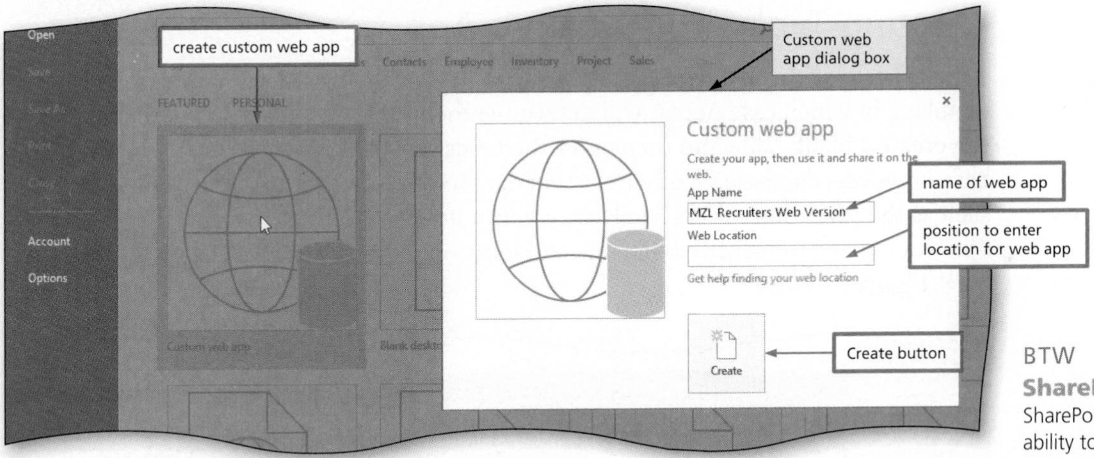

Figure 9–78

BTW
SharePoint 2013
SharePoint offers users the ability to store data on the web so that access to that data can be shared across a network. It is essentially a storage location that can be accessed collaboratively. No special software is required on the client side. SharePoint 2013 allows users to share calendars, blogs, wikis, surveys, document libraries and task lists.

To Create a Web App

1 CONVERT DATABASE | 2 ANALYZE & DOCUMENT | 3 NAVIGATION PANE | 4 CUSTOM PROPERTIES & INDEXES
5 CUSTOM DATA PART | 6 CUSTOM TEMPLATE | 7 ENCRYPT LOCK & SPLIT | 8 CUSTOM WEB APP | 9 CUSTOM VIEW

To create a web app, you would use the following steps.

1. Tap or click either 'Custom web app' to create a web app of your own design or one of the web app templates to create a web app matching the template.
2. Enter a descriptive name for the web app.
3. If you see a list of available locations for the web app, you can select one of the locations. If not, or if none of the available locations is appropriate, enter the URL that points to your SharePoint site.
4. Tap or click the Create button to create the web app.
5. If requested, enter the User ID and password for your SharePoint site and click the Sign In button to finish creating the web app on your SharePoint site.

Figure 9–79 shows the result of creating a custom web app called MZL Recruiters Web Version.

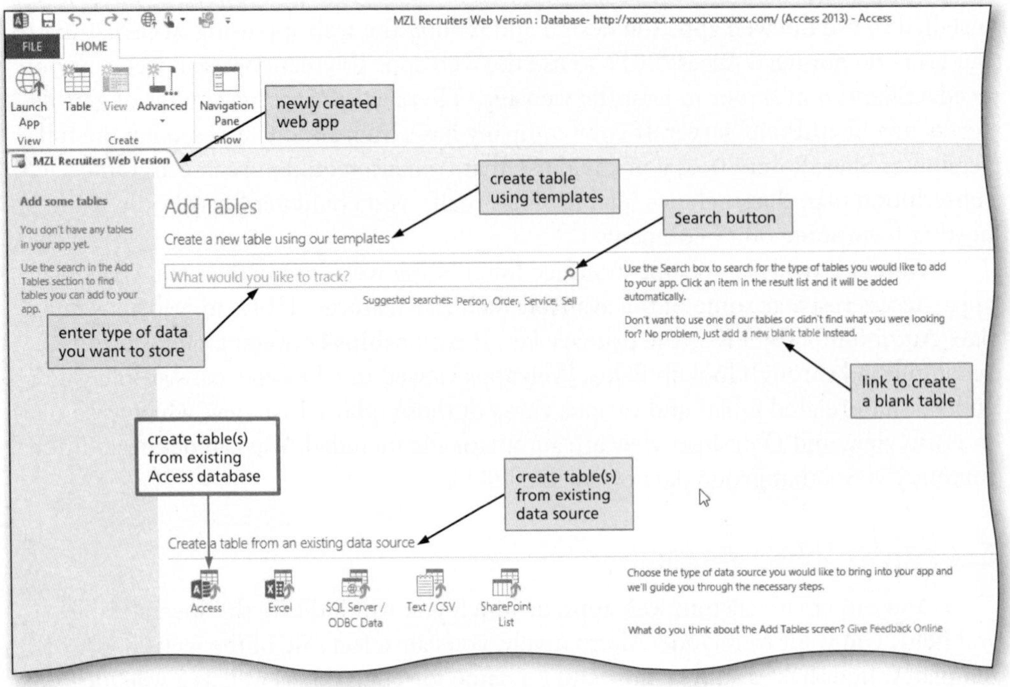

Figure 9–79

Creating Tables for the Web App

There are three ways of creating the tables for the web app. You can use a template, in which case Access will determine the fields to be included in the table. You can create a blank table and then enter the fields and data types yourself. Finally, if you have an Access database or other existing data source that contains the desired tables, such as the MZL Recruiters database, you can import the data. In importing the data, you would need to identify the name and location of the file that contains the desired data (Figure 9–80).

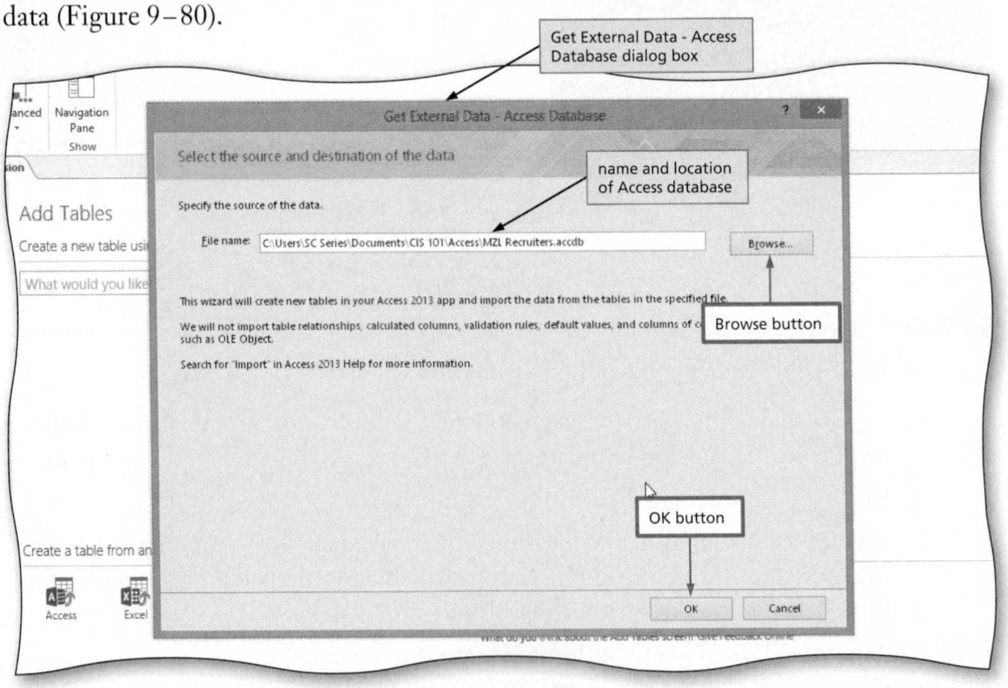

Figure 9–80

After identifying the file containing the tables, you would be presented with a list of tables in that file (Figure 9–81). You could select individual tables in the list or select all the tables by tapping or clicking the Select All button. Once you have made your selection, you would tap or click the OK button to import the data.

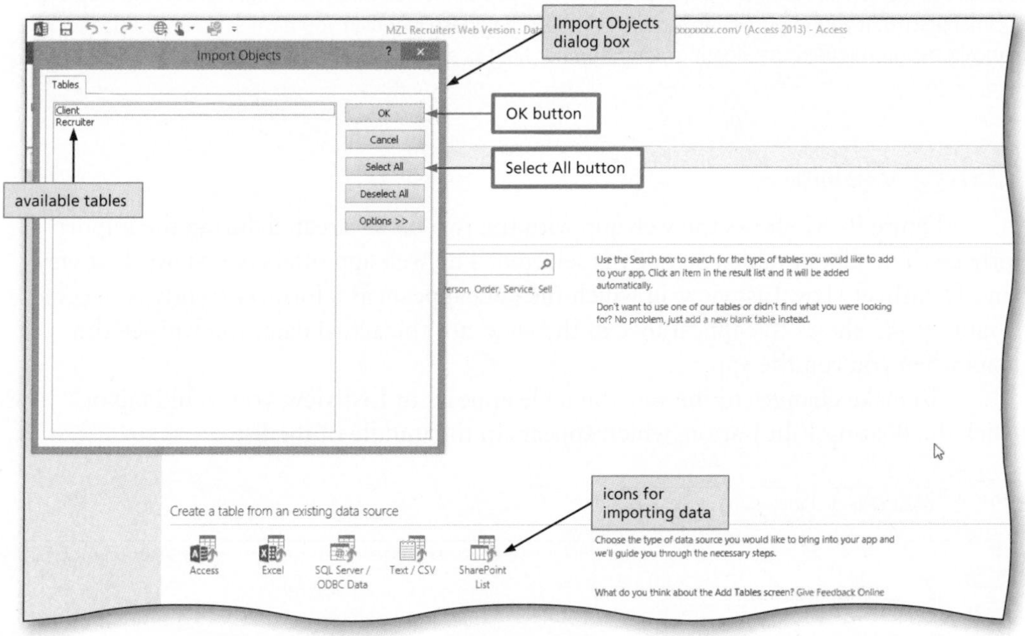

Figure 9–81

1 CONVERT DATABASE | 2 ANALYZE & DOCUMENT | 3 NAVIGATION PANE | 4 CUSTOM PROPERTIES & INDEXES
5 CUSTOM DATA PART | 6 CUSTOM TEMPLATE | 7 ENCRYPT LOCK & SPLIT | 8 CUSTOM WEB APP | 9 CUSTOM VIEW

To Create Tables by Importing Data

To import data from an existing source such as an Access database, you would use the following steps.

1. Tap or click the icon for the type of data to import.
2. Browse to the location of the data to import and select the file to import.
3. Tap or click the OK button.
4. Select the tables to import. If you want to import all the tables in the data source, tap or click the Select All button.
5. Tap or click the OK button to import the data.

To Create Tables from Templates

Access provides templates to assist in the creation of tables. To create a table for a web app from a template, you would use the following steps.

1. Enter the type of object for which you will be storing data (for example, Customers), and tap or click the Search button.
2. When Access presents a list of options, tap or click the option that best fits your needs.

To Create Blank Tables

You can create a blank table for the web app and then enter the names, data types, and other characteristics of the fields in Design view just as you have created other tables. To create a blank table, you would use the following step.

1. Tap or click the 'add a new blank table' link to create the table and display the table in Design view.

CONSIDER THIS

The Rate field has a special field size, Single, which is necessary to display decimal places. If you create the Recruiter table as a blank table in a web app, do you still have the option to change the field size to Single?

Not exactly. The possible field sizes for Number fields are slightly different when you create a web app than when you create a desktop database. The possibilities are Whole Number (no decimal places), Fixed-point number (6 decimal places), and Floating-point number (variable decimal places). If you import a table from a desktop database in which you have set the field size to Single, Access will automatically assign the field the Floating-point number field size, which is appropriate.

Using Views

Figure 9–82 shows the web app with the two tables created during the import process. The Client table currently is selected. The web app offers two views, List view and Datasheet view. List view, in which the data appears as a form, currently is selected. Figure 9–82 shows the appearance of the view, not the actual data. You will see the data when you run the app.

To make changes to the way the table appears in List view, you would tap or click the floating Edit button, which appears in the middle of the list.

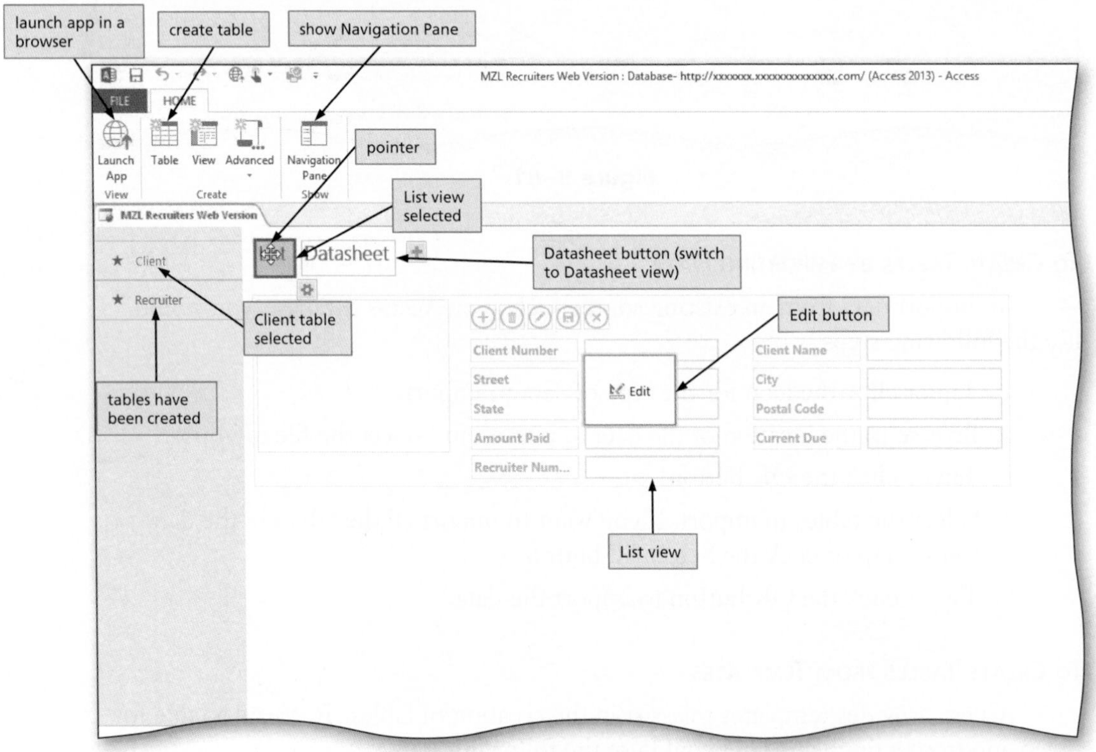

Figure 9–82

If you tap or click the Edit button, you will be able to edit the view (Figure 9–83). Editing the view allows you to change the appearance of the view, not the underlying data. The process is similar to modifying the layout of a form in either Layout or Design view. You can display a field list as shown in the figure by tapping or clicking the 'Add Existing Fields' button. You can add a field by dragging it from the field list into the desired location in the view. You can delete an existing field by tapping or clicking the field, and then pressing the DELETE key. You can move fields within the list by dragging them to the desired location. You also can tap or click a field and then tap or click the Formatting button to display the FORMATTING menu. Using that menu, you can display a tooltip for the field, choose whether the field is visible, or choose whether the field is enabled.

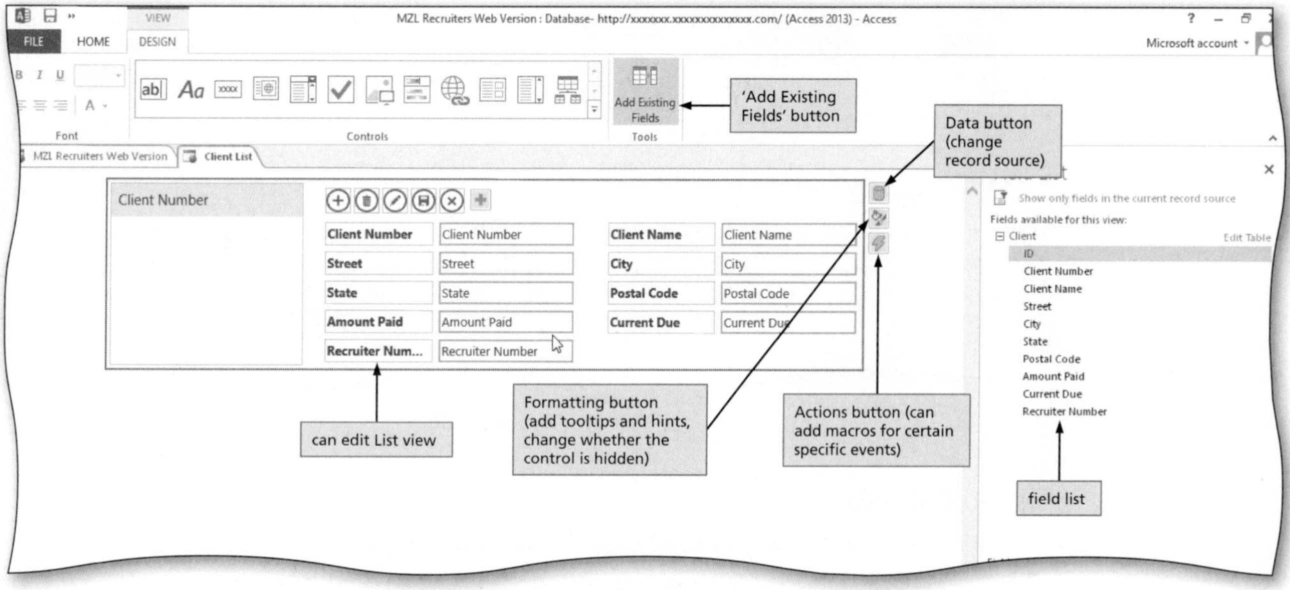

Figure 9–83

If you tap or click the Datasheet view button for the same table, you will see the Datasheet view for the table, which is similar to viewing the normal Datasheet view you see when working with a desktop database (Figure 9–84).

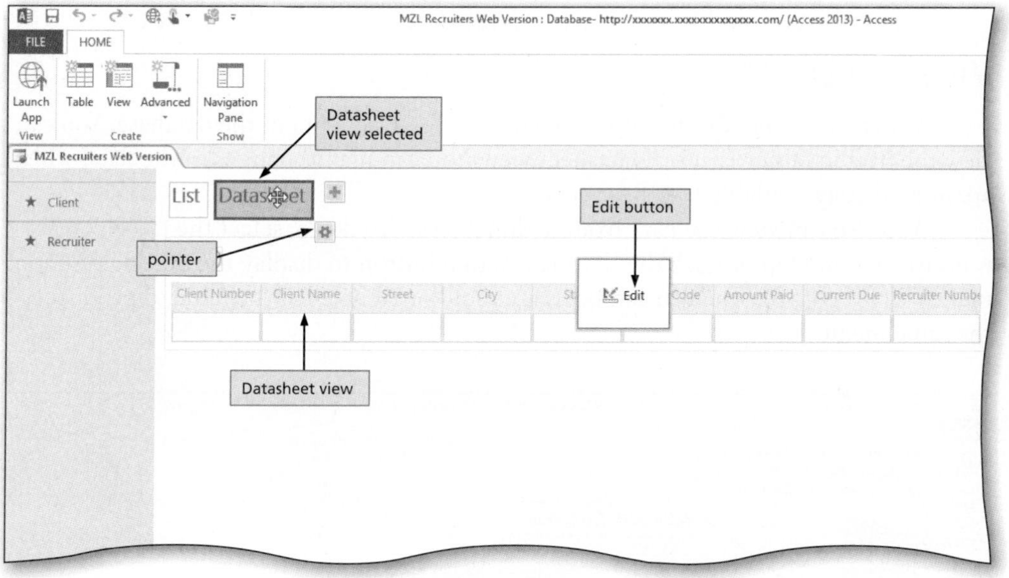

Figure 9–84

Just as with List view, you can tap or click the floating Edit button to be able to edit the view (Figure 9–85 on the next page). You can then use the same techniques as when editing List view to make any desired changes.

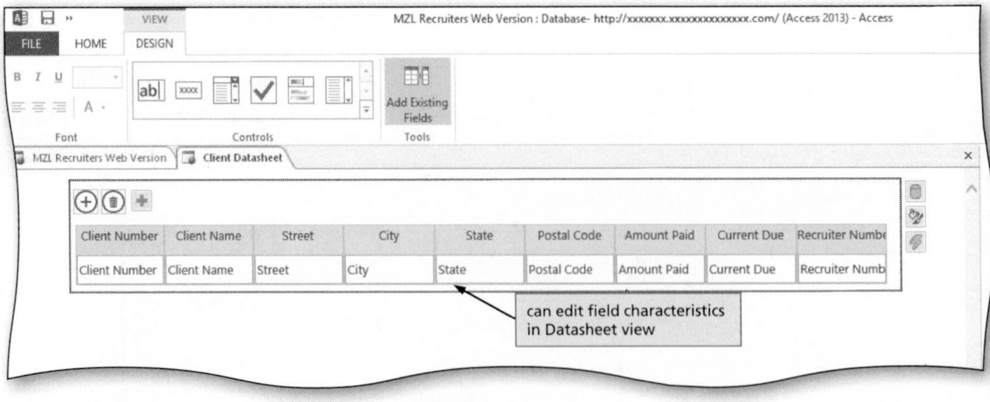

Figure 9–85

To Edit Views

To edit a view, you would use the following steps.

1. Tap or click the table whose view you want to edit.
2. Tap or click the view to edit.
3. Tap or click the Edit button.
4. When finished editing, tap or click the Close button for the view you are editing.
5. Tap or click the Yes button to save your changes. Tap or click the No button if you do not want to save your changes.

Viewing Data

When you later run the app, you will see the actual data in the database. You can view the data in either List or Datasheet view. You can make changes to the data, which are immediately available to other users.

You also can view the data from within Access. To do so, select the table you want to view and tap or click the Settings/Action button to display the Settings/Action menu (Figure 9–86). You also can press and hold or right-click the table to produce the same menu.

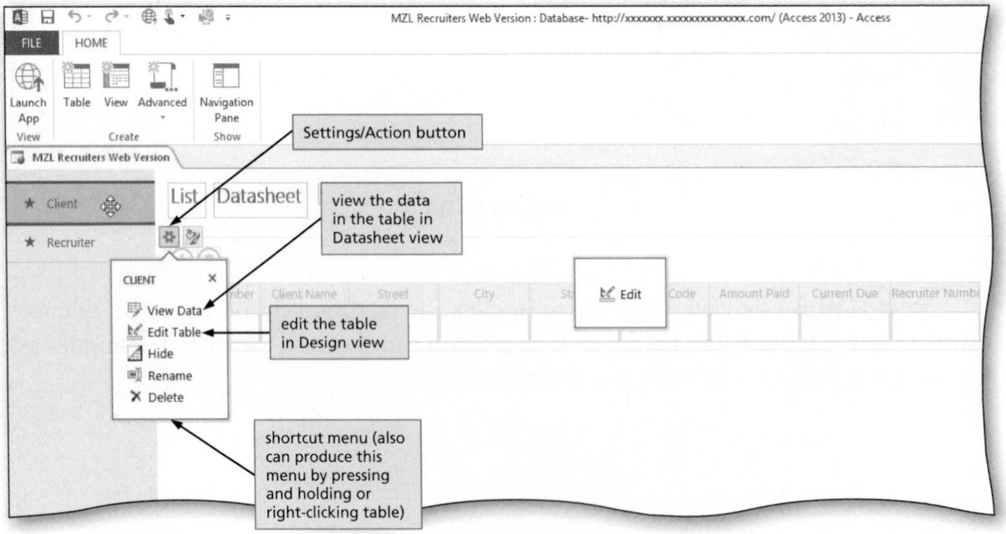

Figure 9–86

If you tap or click View Data on the Settings/Action menu, you will see the data in Datasheet view (Figure 9–87). You can both view and change the data.

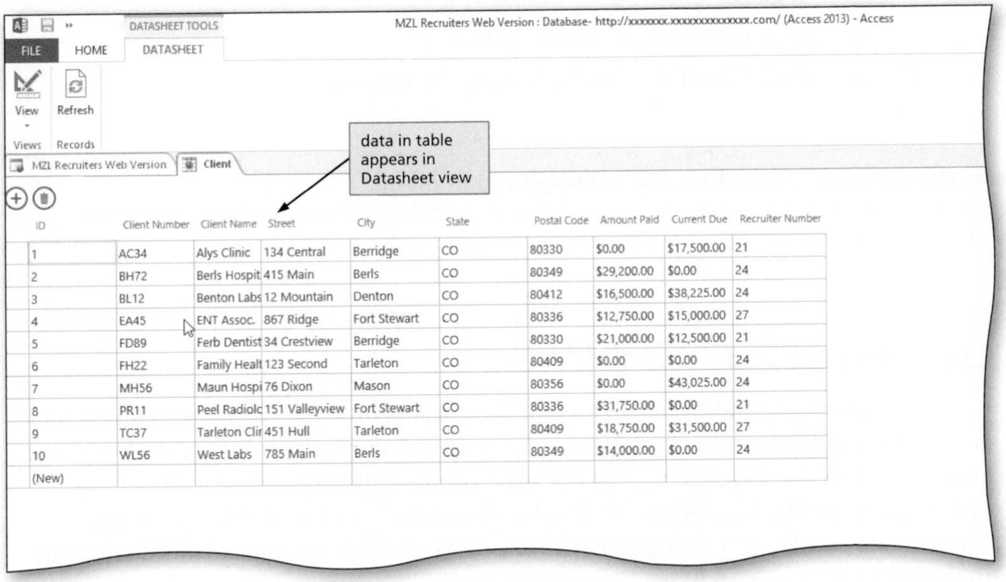

Figure 9–87

To View Data

To view or update the data in a table from Access, you would use the following steps.

1. Tap or click the table containing the data you want to view or update.
2. Tap or click the Settings/Action button.
3. Tap or click View Data on the Settings/Action menu.

You also can modify the design of a table using the Settings/Action button. To do so, you would tap or click Edit Table rather than View Data. You then would see the table displayed in Design view (Figure 9–88). You can make changes to the table design similar to how you updated other tables in Design view.

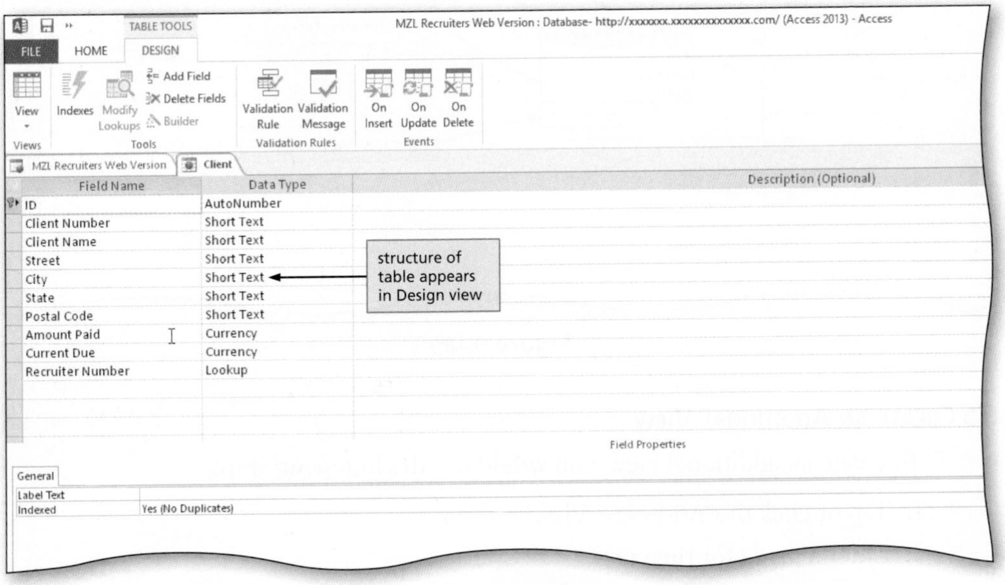

Figure 9–88

To Change the Design of a Table

To view or modify the design of a table, you would use the following steps.

1. Tap or click the table whose design you want to view or update.
2. Tap or click the Settings/Action button.
3. Tap or click Edit Table on the Settings/Action menu.

CONSIDER THIS

What is the purpose of the other commands on the Settings/Action menu?
If you select Hide, the selected table will not appear when you run the app. If you hide a table, you can later select Unhide, in which case it will once again appear. You can rename a table by selecting Rename and delete the table by selecting Delete.

Creating an Additional View

You can create additional views that then are included in the app. To do so, tap or click the 'Add New View' button (Figure 9–89) to display the ADD NEW VIEW dialog box. You also can tap or click the View button (HOME tab | Create group) to display the dialog box. Figure 9–89 also shows the list of available view types. The available types are List Details (List view), Datasheet, Summary, and Blank. You already have seen List and Datasheet views. You will see how to create a Summary view later in this chapter. A Blank view allows you to create a view from scratch, similar to using a blank form.

In the ADD NEW VIEW dialog box, you enter a name for the view, select the View Type, and then select the record source. The record source can be either a table or a query.

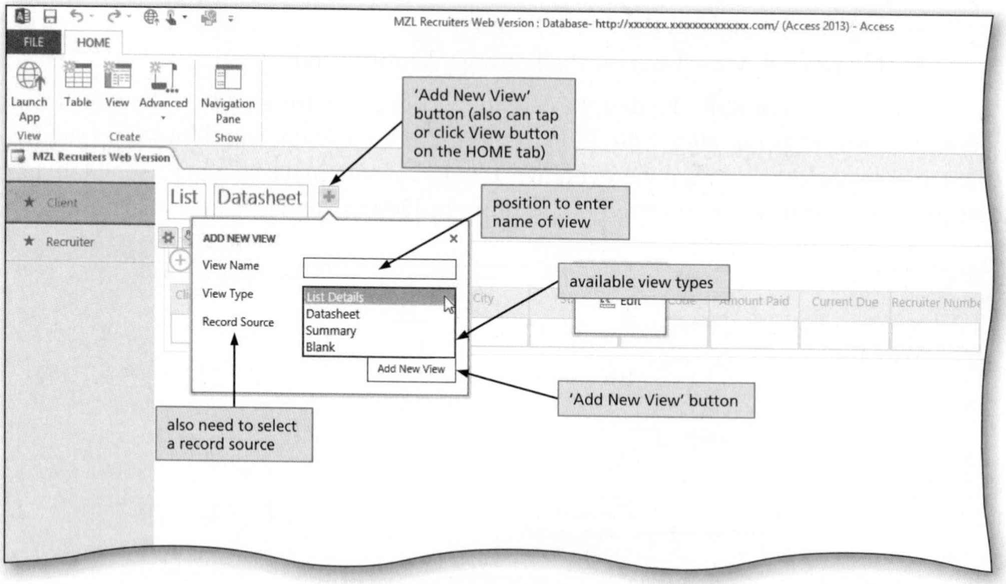

Figure 9–89

To Create an Additional View

To create an additional view, you would use the following steps.

1. Tap or click the 'Add New View' button.
2. Enter a name for the view.
3. Tap or click the View Type arrow to display the menu of available view types.

4. Tap or click the desired view type.
5. Tap or click the Record Source arrow to display a list of the available tables and queries.
6. Tap or click the desired table or query.
7. Tap or click the 'Add New View' button to create the new view.

CONSIDER THIS

How can you delete a view you do not want?
Tap or click the view to select the view. Tap or click the Settings/Action button that will appear near the view to display a shortcut menu. Tap or click Delete on the shortcut menu. Tap or click the OK button to confirm the deletion.

Creating Additional Objects

You can create tables by tapping or clicking the Table button (HOME tab | Create group). You then will see the same screen you saw earlier (Figure 9–79 on page AC 592). You then have the same three options for creating tables: You can create the table using a template, create a blank table, or import a table from an existing data source.

You can create other objects, such as queries, by tapping or clicking the Advanced button (HOME tab | Create group) to produce the Advanced menu (Figure 9–90). The Advanced menu gives you options for creating queries, blank views, blank List views, blank Datasheet views, and various types of macros.

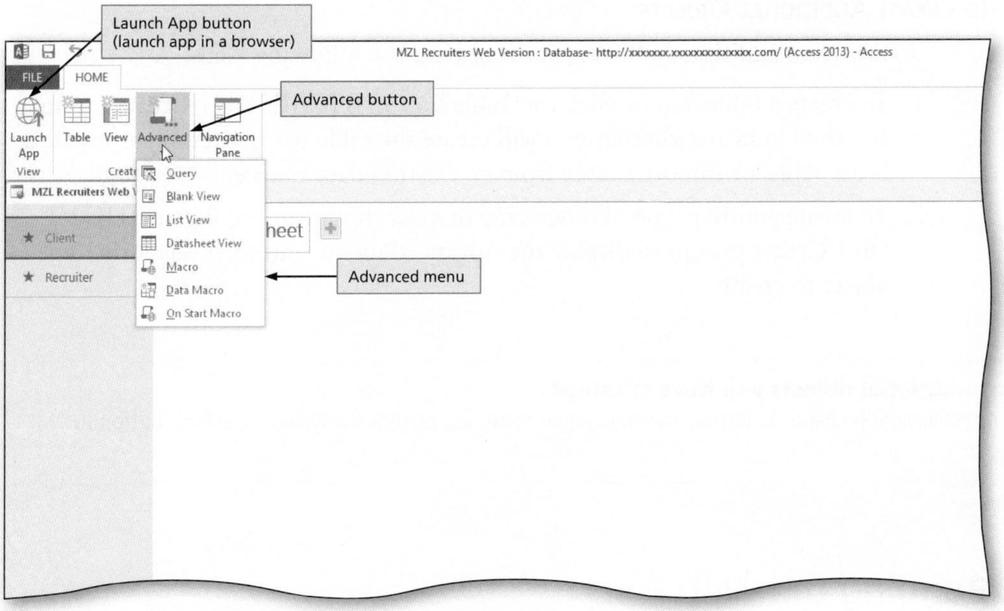

Figure 9–90

To use any of the blank views, you can place fields in the view by dragging the field from a field list, just as you have done in previous chapters with forms and reports. Creating macros uses the same process you have seen earlier. However, creating macros in the web app does limit some of the available options. Creating a query in the web app also is similar to the process you used to create queries earlier; the design grid used in the web app is similar to that used in Access (Figure 9–91 on the next page). As with macros, creating queries in the web app limits some of the options, but the options that are present function in the manner you expect. Once you have created a query, you can use it as the record source for a view.

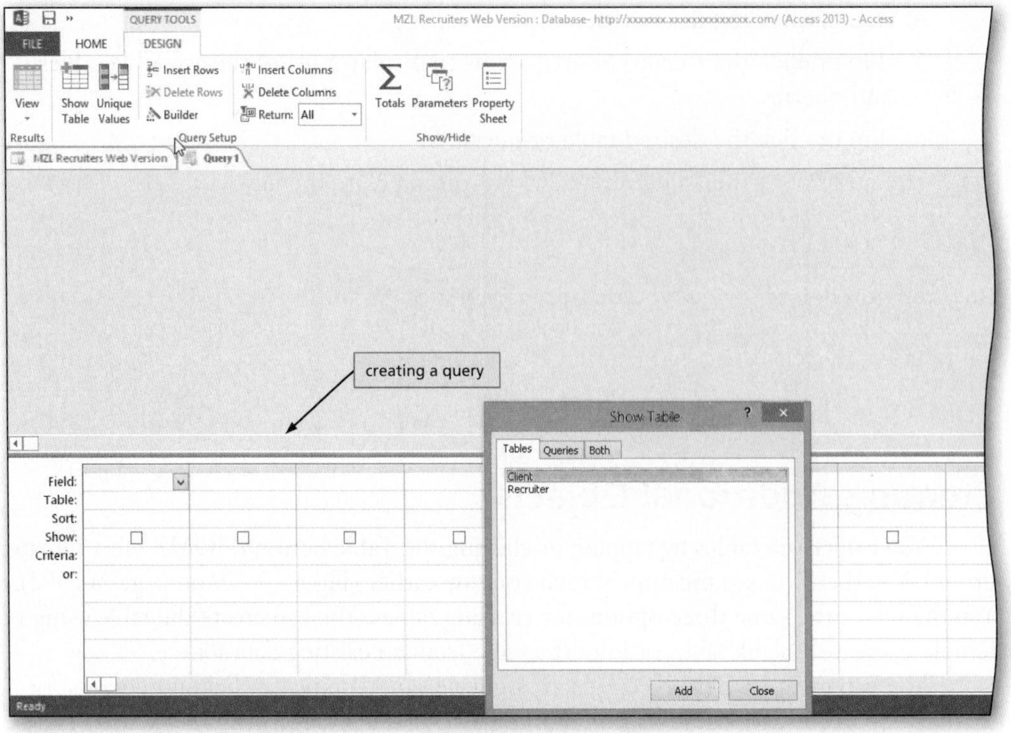

Figure 9–91

To Create Additional Objects

To create an additional object, you would use the following steps.

1. To create a table, tap or click the Table button (HOME tab | Create group), and then indicate whether you will create the table using a template, create a blank table, or import a table from an existing data source.
2. To create another type of object, tap or click the Advanced button (HOME tab | Create group) to display the Advanced menu, and then select the type of object to create.

CONSIDER THIS

How can you see the additional objects you have created?

You can only see them in the Navigation Pane. To display the Navigation Pane, tap or click the Navigation Pane button (HOME tab | Show group).

Running the Web App

You run the web app in a browser. You can do so from Access by tapping or clicking the Launch App button (HOME tab | View group). You then will see the web app in your browser (Figure 9–92). On the left side of the screen, you see the list of tables in the app. At anytime, one of the tables will be selected. In the figure, the Client table is currently selected.

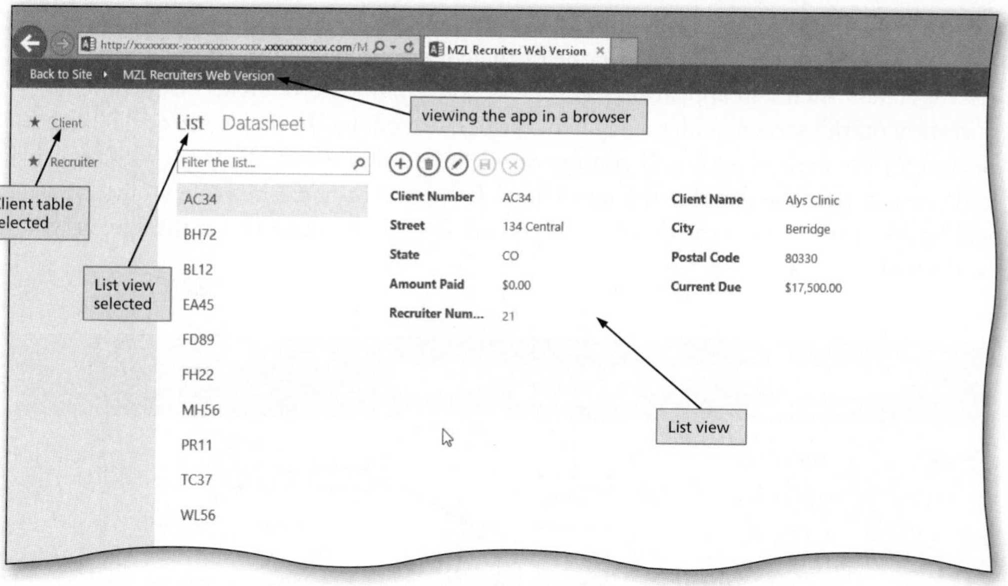

Figure 9–92

Is Launch the same as Run?
Yes. They are different words for the same operation.

CONSIDER THIS

The available views for the selected table are displayed at the top of the screen. There are currently two views, List view and Datasheet view. List view is currently selected. The list view for the table as well as a list of key values, in this case, client numbers, are displayed in the center area of the screen.

To Run an App from Access

1 CONVERT DATABASE | 2 ANALYZE & DOCUMENT | 3 NAVIGATION PANE | 4 CUSTOM PROPERTIES & INDEXES
5 CUSTOM DATA PART | 6 CUSTOM TEMPLATE | 7 ENCRYPT LOCK & SPLIT | 8 CUSTOM WEB APP | 9 CUSTOM VIEW

To run an app from Access, the app must be open. Assuming it is, you would use the following step to run the app.

1. Click the Launch App button (HOME tab | View group) to run the app.

To display a table in Datasheet view, first be sure the desired table is selected. Next, tap or click the Datasheet link. The table will appear in Datasheet view (Figure 9–93).

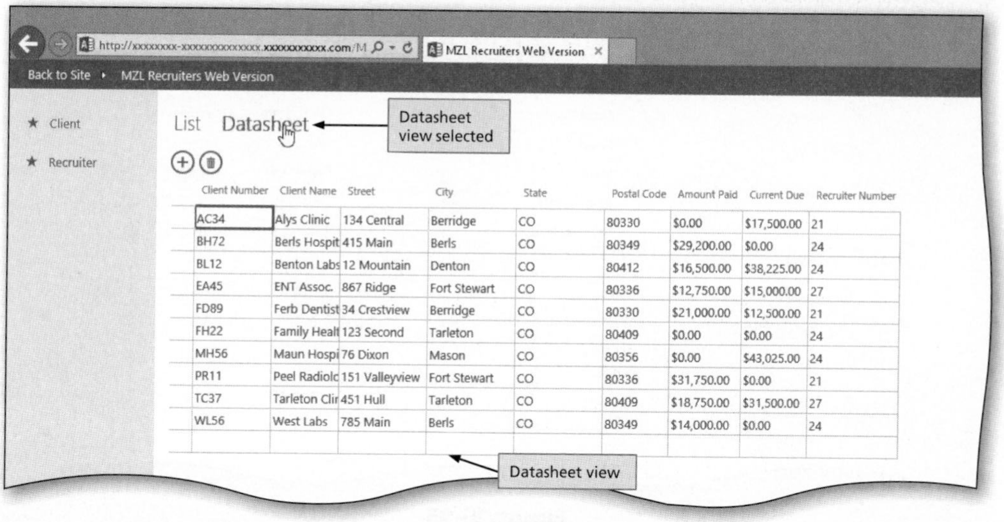

Figure 9–93

If you tap or click the List link, the table again will appear in List view (Figure 9–94). You can tap or click one of the client numbers on the left and the data for that client then will appear on the screen. You can update the data for the client currently on the screen, add a new client, or delete a client. To do so, tap or click the button for the desired action. If you tap or click the Add button, the form will be blank and you can type the data for the new client. If you tap or click the Delete button, you will be asked to confirm the deletion. If you do, the client currently on the screen will be deleted.

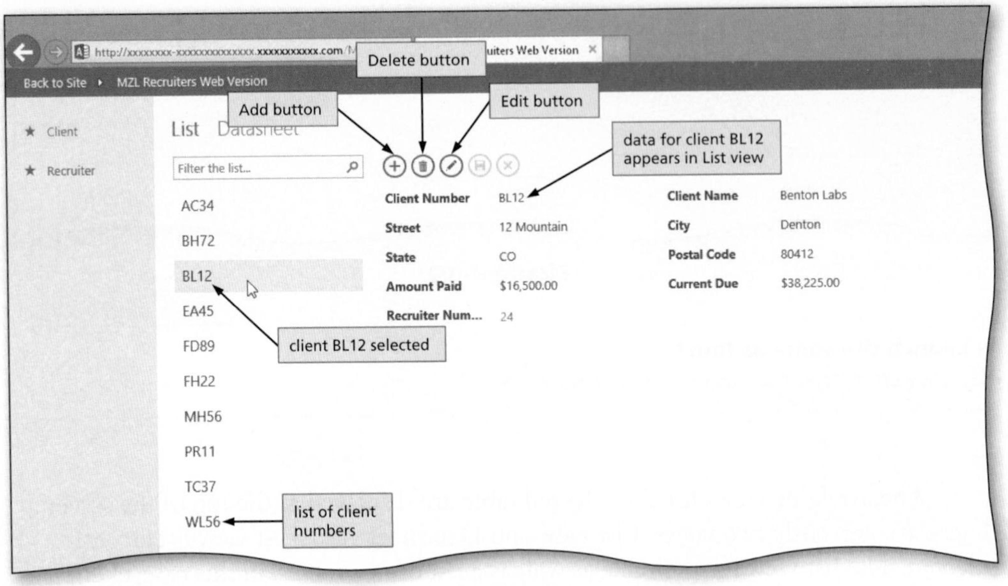

Figure 9–94

If you tap or click the Edit button, the buttons change slightly (Figure 9–95). The Add, Delete, and Edit buttons are dimmed whereas the Save and Cancel buttons are not. After making a change, such as the change of the state as shown in the figure, you can tap or click the Save button to save the change or the Cancel button to cancel the change.

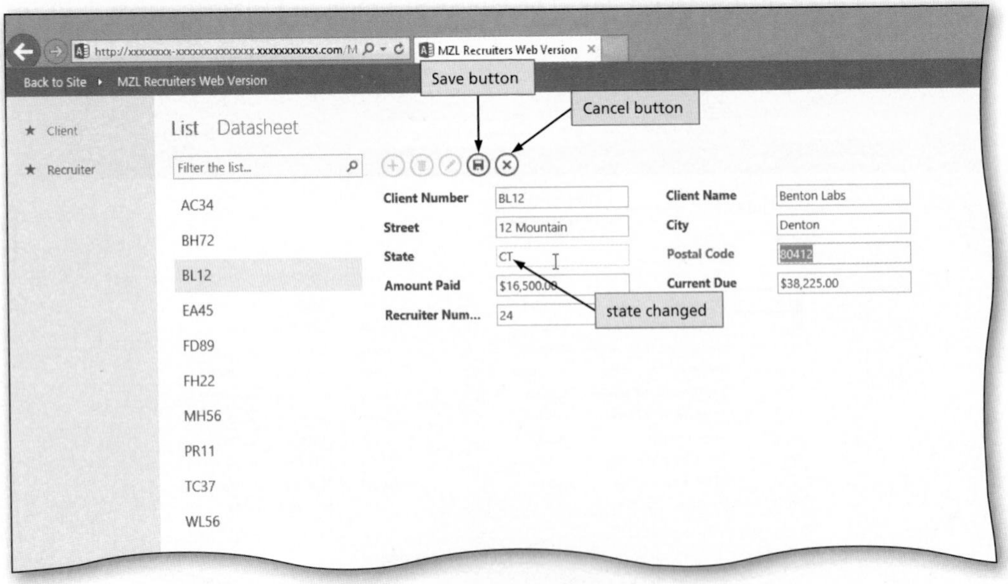

Figure 9–95

You also can update data in Datasheet view. To add a record, tap or click the Add button and type the contents of the new record. To delete a record, tap or click anywhere in the record, tap or click the Delete button, and then confirm the deletion. To edit a record, tap or click in the field to be changed and make the desired change.

To Update Data Using a Web App

To update data using a web app, you would use the following steps after running the app.

1. Tap or click the table to be updated.
2. Tap or click either the List link to select List view or the Datasheet link to select Datasheet view.
3. To add a record in Datasheet view, tap or click the Add button, enter the contents of the record, and press the TAB key after entering the final field. To add in List view, tap or click the Add button, enter the contents of the record, and tap or click the Save button.
4. To delete a record in either view, select the record to be deleted, click the Delete button, and then confirm the deletion.
5. To edit a record in Datasheet view, tap or click the field to be changed and make the necessary change. As soon as you leave the record, the change will automatically be saved. To edit a record in List view, select the record to be edited, tap or click the Edit button, make the change, and then tap or click the Save button.

Showing a Relationship in List View

If you view the "one" table in a one-to-many relationship in List view, you will see the corresponding records in the "many" table appear in a datasheet. Figure 9–96 shows the Recruiter table appearing in List view. The data for the selected recruiter appears in List view. The clients of the selected recruiter appear in a datasheet just below the data for the recruiter. Note that this is the only way to see the relationship. Viewing the "one" table in Datasheet view will not show the relationship, nor will viewing the "many" table in either view.

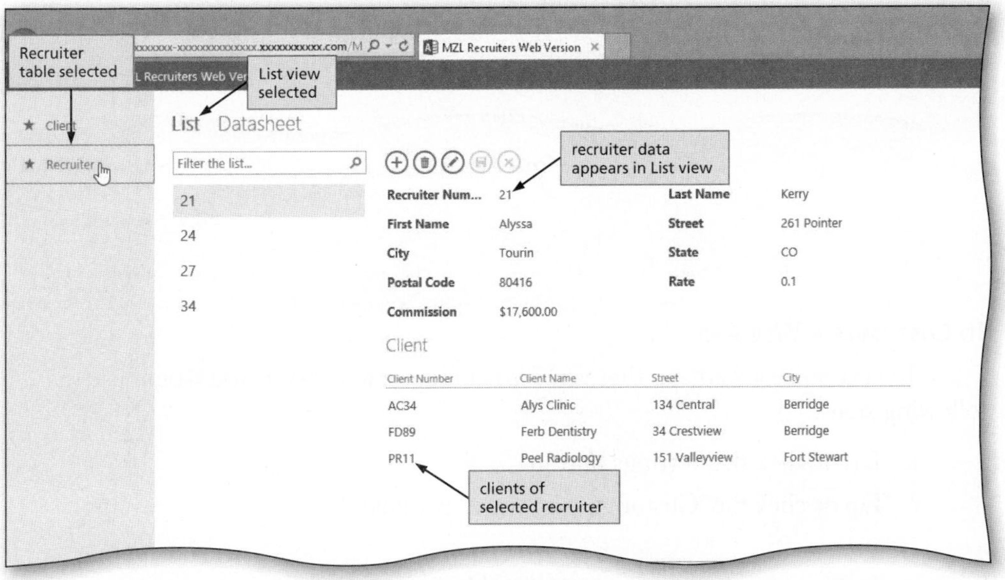

Figure 9–96

Running a Web App from a Browser

To run a web app, you navigate to your SharePoint site and simply run the app. You do not have to run Access, open the app, and then run the app. It is not even necessary to have Access on your computer. You can run the app directly from your browser.

1 CONVERT DATABASE | 2 ANALYZE & DOCUMENT | 3 NAVIGATION PANE | 4 CUSTOM PROPERTIES & INDEXES
5 CUSTOM DATA PART | 6 CUSTOM TEMPLATE | 7 ENCRYPT LOCK & SPLIT | 8 CUSTOM WEB APP | 9 CUSTOM VIEW

To Run a Web App from a Browser

To run a web app from a browser, you would use the following steps.

1. Type the URL for your SharePoint site and press ENTER.
2. When requested, type your user name and password.
3. Tap or click the OK button to display the contents of your SharePoint site.
4. Tap or click the desired web app to run the app.

Customizing a Web App

You can customize a web app from within Access. If you are running the app in a browser, you launch Access by tapping or clicking the Settings button to display the 'Customize in Access' command (Figure 9–97) and then tapping or clicking the 'Customize in Access' command.

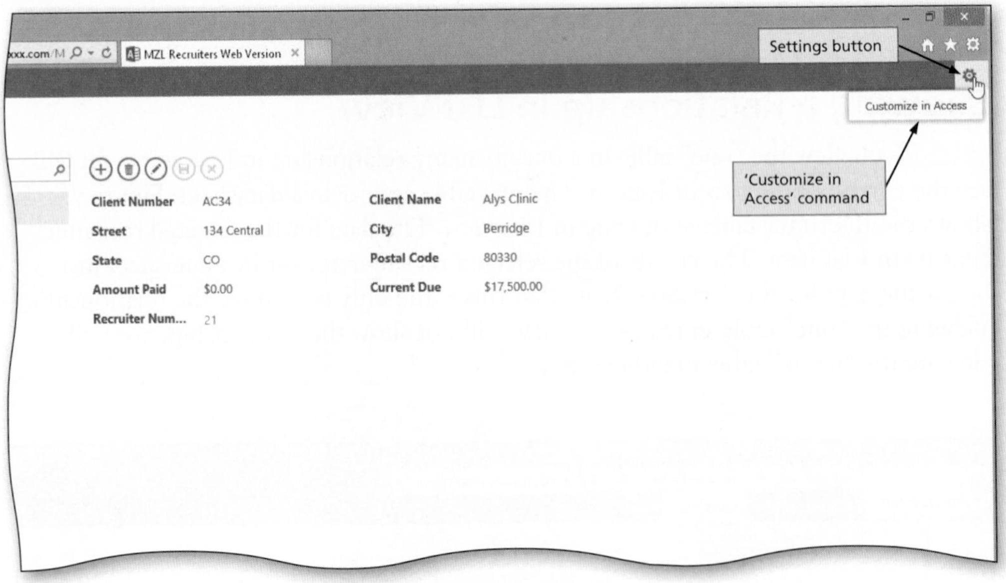

Figure 9–97

1 CONVERT DATABASE | 2 ANALYZE & DOCUMENT | 3 NAVIGATION PANE | 4 CUSTOM PROPERTIES & INDEXES
5 CUSTOM DATA PART | 6 CUSTOM TEMPLATE | 7 ENCRYPT LOCK & SPLIT | 8 CUSTOM WEB APP | 9 CUSTOM VIEW

To Customize a Web App

To customize a web app that you are running in a browser, you would use the following steps.

1. Tap or click the Settings button.
2. Tap or click the 'Customize in Access' command.

Adding a Summary View

One of the ways you can customize a web app is to add an additional view, such as a Summary view. After selecting the table for which you want to add the view, you use the 'Add New View' button to select Summary as the view type and select the record source table (Figure 9–98).

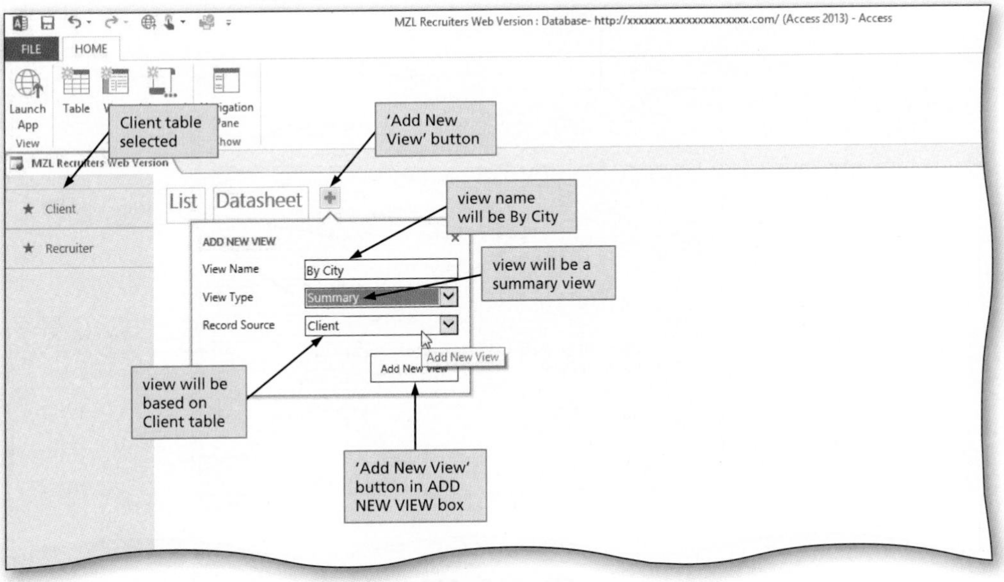

Figure 9–98

Tapping or clicking the 'Add New View' button in the ADD NEW VIEW dialog box again creates the view. You can edit the view using the EDIT button. Then, you can use the Data button to display the DATA box, where you indicate Group By field, Sort Order, Calculation Field, and Calculation Type (Figure 9–99).

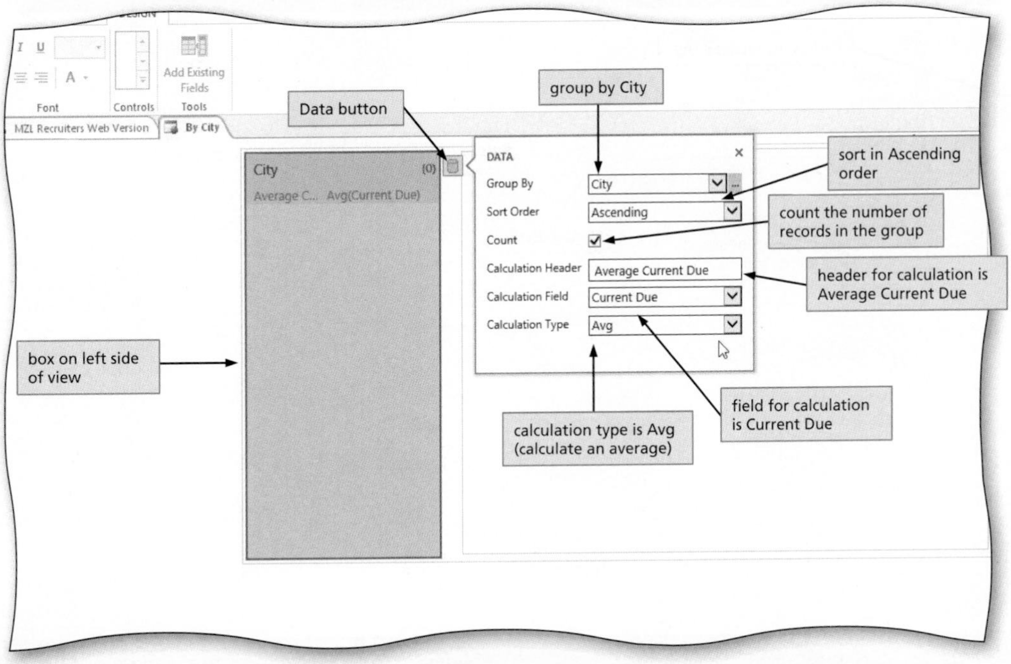

Figure 9–99

By tapping or clicking the box on the right and then tapping or clicking the Data button, you can enter up to four fields to be displayed and optionally display captions for the fields. Specifying the popup view determines the view that will appear as a popup when the user taps or clicks a specific record and will give additional information about that record. The final step is to enter the sort order (Figure 9–100).

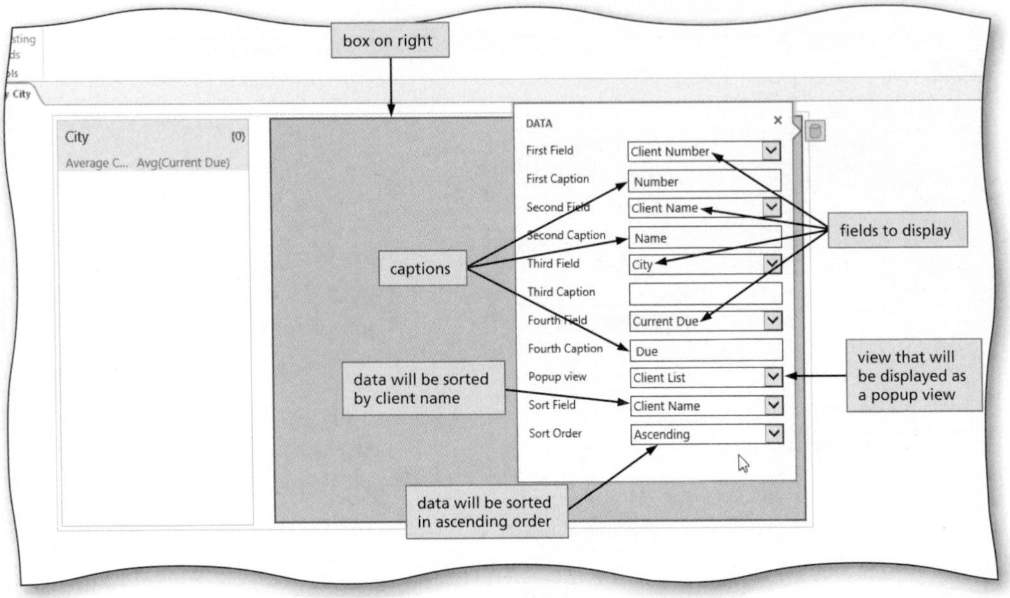

Figure 9–100

After closing the view and saving the changes, you can run the app by tapping or clicking the Launch App button, being sure the appropriate table is selected. You tap or click the new view to test the view, and then close the view (Figure 9–101).

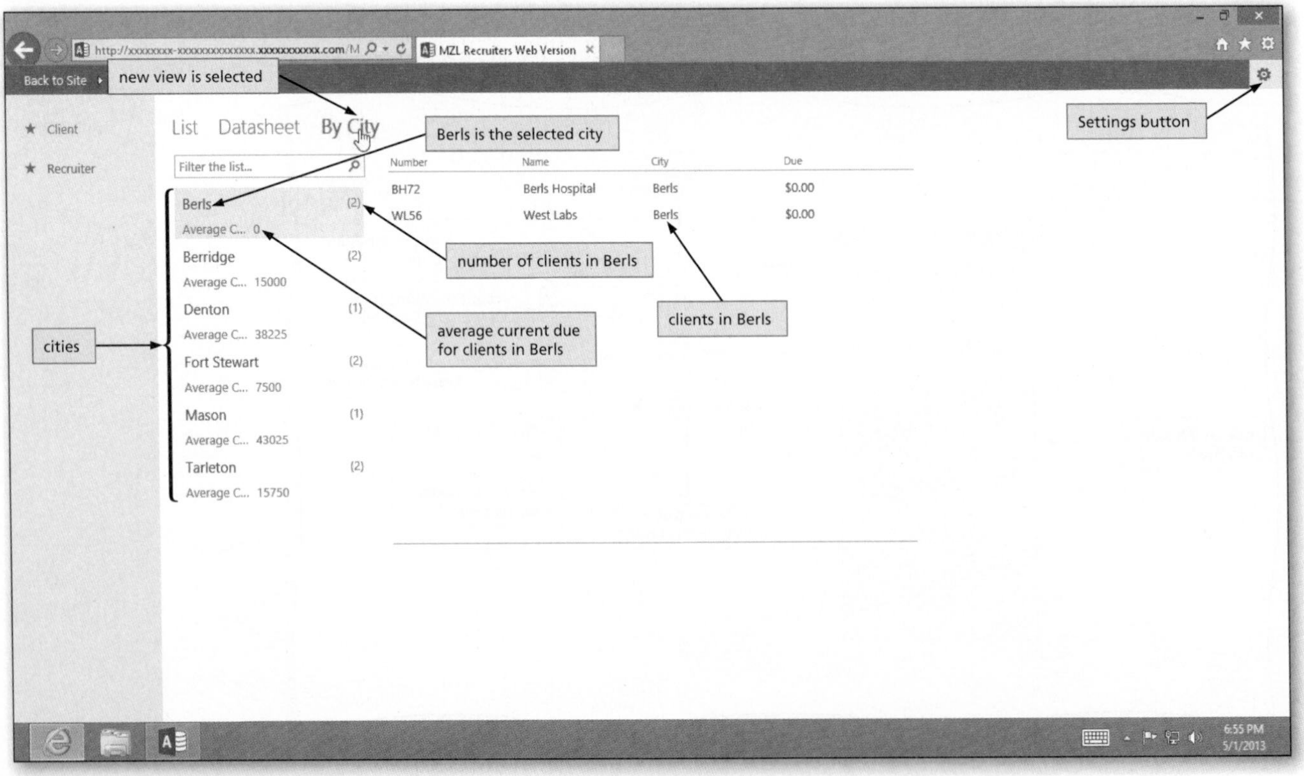

Figure 9–101

If you select another value in the left-hand column, all the corresponding records will now appear in the right column (Figure 9–102).

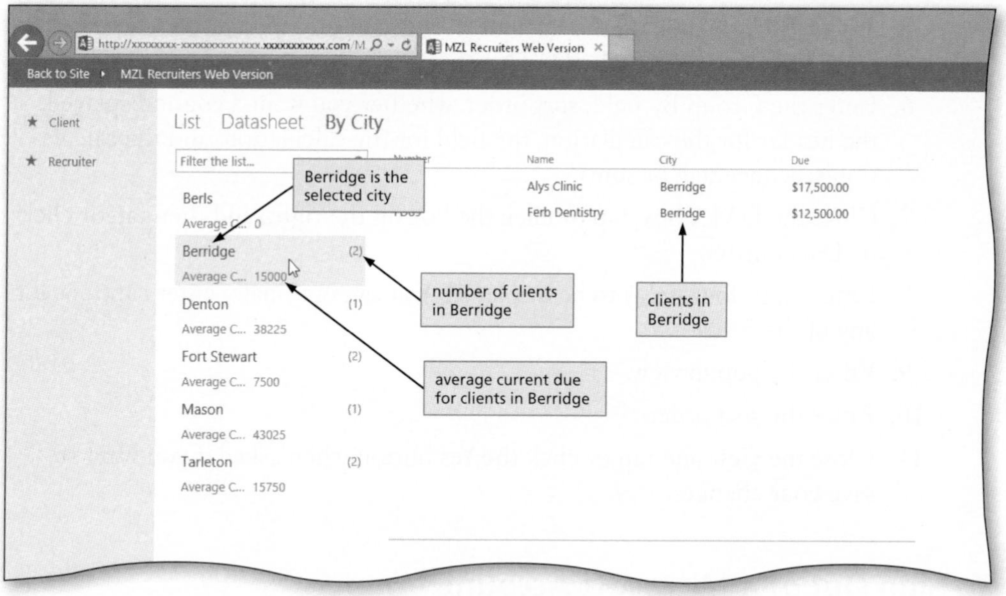

Figure 9–102

Select one of the records in the group to display details concerning that record in a popup view (Figure 9–103).

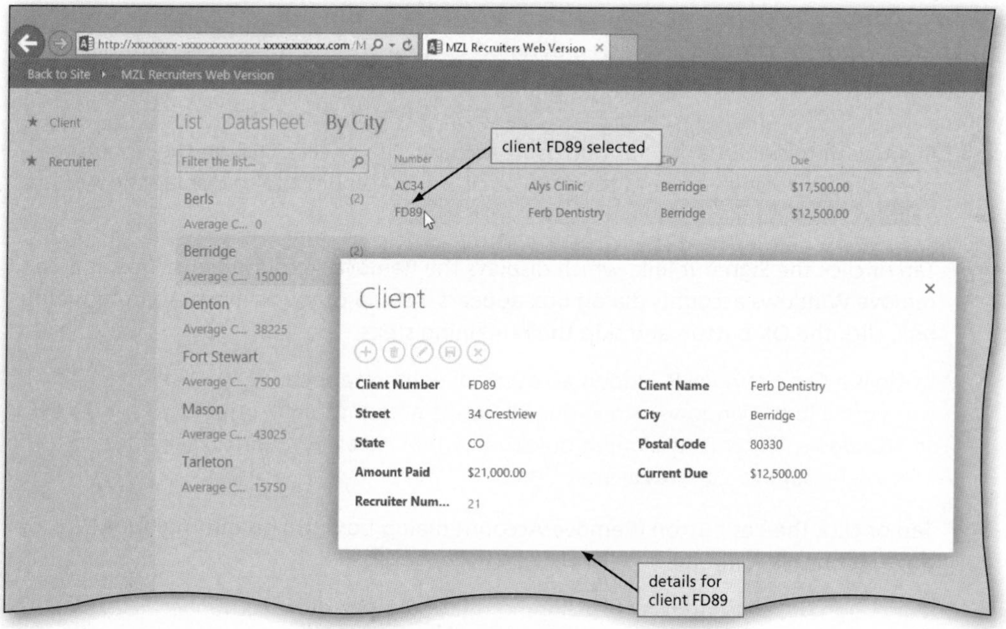

Figure 9–103

1 CONVERT DATABASE | 2 ANALYZE & DOCUMENT | 3 NAVIGATION PANE | 4 CUSTOM PROPERTIES & INDEXES
5 CUSTOM DATA PART | 6 CUSTOM TEMPLATE | 7 ENCRYPT LOCK & SPLIT | 8 CUSTOM WEB APP | 9 CUSTOM VIEW

To Create a Summary View

To create a Summary view, you would use the following steps.

1. Tap or click the table for which you want to add the view and then tap or click the 'Add New View' button to display the ADD NEW VIEW box.
2. Enter a name for the view, select Summary as the view type, and select the table that will be the record source.

BTW
Certification
The Microsoft Office Specialist (MOS) program provides an opportunity for you to obtain a valuable industry credential — proof that you have the Access 2013 skills required by employers. For more information, visit the Certification resource on the Student Companion Site located on www.cengagebrain.com. For detailed instructions about accessing available resources, visit www.cengage.com/ct/studentdownload or contact your instructor for information about accessing the required files.

3. Tap or click the 'Add New View' button (ADD NEW VIEW dialog box) to create the view.
4. Tap or click the Edit button to edit the view.
5. Tap or click the box on the left side of the view and then tap or click the Data button to display the DATA box.
6. Enter the Group By field, sort order, whether you want a count displayed, the header for the calculation, the field for the calculation, and the calculation type (average or sum).
7. Close the DATA box, tap or click the box on the right, and then tap or click its Data button.
8. Enter up to four fields to be displayed. You can optionally enter captions for any of the fields.
9. Enter the popup view.
10. Enter the sort order.
11. Close the view and tap or click the Yes button when asked if you want to save your changes.

To Sign Out of a Microsoft Account

BTW
Quick Reference
For a table that lists how to complete the tasks covered in this book using touch gestures, the mouse, ribbon, shortcut menu, and keyboard, see the Quick Reference Summary at the back of this book, or visit the Quick Reference resource on the Student Companion Site located on www.cengagebrain.com. For detailed instructions about accessing available resources, visit www.cengage.com/ct/studentdownload or contact your instructor for information about accessing the required files.

If you are signed in to a Microsoft account and are using a public computer or otherwise wish to sign out of your Microsoft account, you should sign out of the account from the Account gallery in the Backstage view before exiting Access. Signing out of the account is the safest way to make sure that nobody else can access SkyDrive files or settings stored in your Microsoft account. The following steps sign out of a Microsoft account from Access. For a detailed example of the procedure summarized below, refer to the Office and Windows chapter at the beginning of this book.

1. If you wish to sign out of your Microsoft account, tap or click FILE on the ribbon to open the Backstage view and then tap or click the Account tab to display the Account gallery.

2. Tap or click the Sign out link, which displays the Remove Account dialog box. If a Can't remove Windows accounts dialog box appears instead of the Remove Account dialog box, click the OK button and skip the remaining steps.

Q&A Why does a Can't remove Windows accounts dialog box appear?
If you signed in to Windows using your Microsoft account, then you also must sign out from Windows, rather than signing out from within Access. When you are finished using Windows, be sure to sign out at that time.

3. Tap or click the Yes button (Remove Account dialog box) to sign out of your Microsoft account on this computer.

Q&A Should I sign out of Windows after signing out of my Microsoft account?
When you are finished using the computer, you should sign out of your account for maximum security.

4. Tap or click the Back button in the upper-left corner of the Backstage view to return to the database.

To Exit Access

The following steps exit Access.

1. Tap or click the Close button on the right side of the title bar to exit Access.
2. If a Microsoft Access dialog box appears, tap or click the Yes button to save any changes made to the object since the last save.

Chapter Summary

In this chapter you have learned to convert Access databases to and from earlier versions; use Microsoft Access tools to analyze and document an Access database; add custom categories and groups to the Navigation Pane; use table and database properties; use field properties to create a custom input mask; allow zero-length strings; create indexes; use automatic error checking; create custom data parts; create and use templates and application parts; encrypt a database and set a password; understand the Trust Center; lock a database; split a database; create and run a web app; customize a web app. The following list includes all the new Access skills you have learned in this chapter.

Data Parts
Create Custom Data Parts (AC 563)

Database, Creation for Template
Create a Desktop Database (AC 566)
Add Fields to the Table (AC 566)
Create a Second Table (AC 568)
Create Datasheet Forms (AC 573)
Create a Navigation Form (AC 575)
Select a Startup Form (AC 576)

Database Conversion
Convert an Access 2007-2013 Database to an Earlier Version (AC 543)
Convert an Access 2000 or 2002-2003 Database to an Access 2013 Database (AC 543)

Database Tools
Use the Table Analyzer (AC 544)
Use the Performance Analyzer (AC 546)
Use the Database Documenter (AC 547)

Encryption
Open a Database in Exclusive Mode (AC 583)
Encrypt a Database with a Password (AC 585)
Decrypt the Database and Remove the Password (AC 586)

Groups
Create Custom Categories and Groups (AC 549)
Add Items to Groups (AC 551)

Indexes
Create a Single-Field Index (AC 559)
Create a Multiple-Field Index (AC 560)

Objects in Web Apps
Edit Views (AC 596)
View Data (AC 597)
Change the Design of a Table (AC 598)
Create an Additional View (AC 598)
Create Additional Objects (AC 600)
Create a Summary View (AC 607)

Properties
Create Custom Properties (AC 554)
Create a Custom Input Mask (AC 557)
Allow Zero Length (AC 557)
Enable Error Checking (AC 561)

Special Database Operations
Create a Locked Database (ACCDE File) (AC 587)
Split the Database (AC 590)

Templates
Create a Template and Application Part (AC 578)
Use the Template (AC 579)
Use the Application Part (AC 581)

Validation
Create a Validation Rule for a Table (AC 553)

Web Apps
Create a Web App (AC 591)
Create Tables by Importing Data (AC 593)
Create Tables from Templates (AC 593)
Create Blank Tables (AC 593)
Run an App from Access (AC 601)
Update Data Using a Web App (AC 603)
Run a Web App from a Browser (AC 604)
Customize a Web App (AC 604)

CONSIDER THIS: PLAN AHEAD

What decisions will you need to make when administering your own databases?

Use these guidelines as you complete the assignments in this chapter and administer your own databases outside of this class.

1. Determine whether a database needs to able to be shared over the web.

a. Do you have users who would profit from being able to access a database over the web? If so, you will need to create a web app, which requires you to have access to a SharePoint server.

b. Determine the tables that should be in the web app.

c. Determine the views of the tables that should be included in the web app.

2. Determine whether you should create any templates, application parts, or data type parts.

a. Is there a particular combination of tables, queries, forms, reports, and/or macros that you would like to enable users to easily include in their databases? If so, you could create a template and an application part containing the specific objects you want them to be able to include.

b. Is there a particular collection of fields that you would like to enable users to include in a table with a single click? If so, you could create a data type part containing those fields.

3. Determine whether a database needs to be converted to or from an earlier version.

a. Do users of a previous version of Access need to be able to use the database? If so, you will need to be sure the database does not contain any features that would prevent it from being converted.

b. Do you use a database that was created in an earlier version of Access that you would like to use in Access 2013? If so, you can convert the database for use in Access 2013.

4. Determine when to analyze and/or document the database.

a. Once you create a database, you should use the table and performance analyzers to determine if any changes to the structure are warranted.

b. You also should document the database.

5. Determine the most useful way to customize the Navigation Pane.

a. Would it be helpful to have custom categories and groups?

b. What objects should be in the groups?

c. Would it be helpful to restrict the objects that appear to only those whose names contain certain characters?

6. Determine any table-wide validation rules.

a. Are there any validation rules that involve more than a single field?

7. Determine any custom database properties.

a. Are there properties that would be helpful in documenting the database and are not included in the list of database properties you can use?

8. Determine indexes.

a. Examine retrieval and sorting requirements to determine possible indexes. Indexes can make both retrieval and sorting more efficient.

9. Determine whether the database should be encrypted.

a. If you need to protect the security of the database's contents, you strongly should consider encryption.

b. As part of the process, you also will set a password.

10. Determine whether the database should be locked.

a. Should users be able to change the design of forms, reports, and/or macros?

11. Determine whether the database should be split.

a. It is often more efficient to split the database into a back-end database, which contains only the table data, and a front-end database, which contains other objects, such as queries, forms, and reports.

CONSIDER THIS

How should you submit solutions to questions in the assignments identified with a symbol?

Every assignment in this book contains one or more questions identified with a symbol. These questions require you to think beyond the assigned database. Present your solutions to the questions in the format required by your instructor. Possible formats may include one or more of these options: write the answer; create a document that contains the answer; present your answer to the class; discuss your answer in a group; record the answer as audio or video using a webcam, smartphone, or portable media player; or post answers on a blog, wiki, or website.

Apply Your Knowledge

Reinforce the skills and apply the concepts you learned in this chapter.

Administering the Natural Products Database

Note: To complete this assignment, you will be required to use the Data Files for Students. Visit www.cengage.com/ct/student download for detailed instructions or contact your instructor for information about accessing the required files.

Instructions: Start Access. Open the Apply Natural Products database that you modified in Chapter 8. If you did not use this database, contact your instructor for information about accessing the required database.

Perform the following tasks:

1. Open the Customer table in Design view and create an index that allows duplicates on the Customer Name field. Zero-length strings should not be allowed in the Customer Name field.
2. Create a custom input mask for the Customer Number field. The first two characters of the customer number must be uppercase letters and the last two characters must be numerical digits.
3. Create an index on the combination of Customer Type and Amount Paid. Name the index TypePaid.
4. Save the changes to the Customer table.
5. Use the Database Documenter to produce detailed documentation for the Customer Orders table. Export the documentation to a Word RTF file. (*Hint*: See the Q&A on page AC 548.) Change the name of the file to LastName_Documentation.rtf where LastName is your last name.
6. Use the Table Analyzer to analyze the table structure of the Customer table. Open the rtf file that you created in Step 5 and record the results of the analysis at the end of the file.
7. Use the Performance Analyzer to analyze all the tables in the database. Report the results of your analysis in your rtf file.
8. Populate the Status property for the database with the value Apply Natural Products.
9. If requested to do so by your instructor, populate the Status property with your first and last name.
10. Create a custom property with the name, Due Date. Use Date as the type and enter the current date as the value.
11. Submit the revised Apply Natural Products database and the rtf file in the format specified by your instructor.
12. Can you convert the Apply Natural Products to an Access 2002-2003 database? Why or Why not?

Extend Your Knowledge

Extend the skills you learned in this chapter and experiment with new skills. You may need to use Help to complete the assignment.

Note: To complete this assignment, you will be required to use the Data Files for Students. Visit www.cengage.com/ct/studentdownload for detailed instructions or contact your instructor for information about accessing the required files.

Instructions: Start Access. Open the Extend Reuse Restore database. The Extend Reuse Restore database contains information about a used furnishings store owned and operated by college students.

Continued >

Extend Your Knowledge *continued*

Perform the following tasks:

1. Change the Current Database options to ensure that the Main Menu opens automatically.
2. Currently, when you open the Items table in Datasheet view, the table is ordered by Item Number. Change the property for the table so the table is in order by Description. (*Hint*: See the BTW on page AC 559).
3. Customize the Navigation Pane by adding a custom category called Reuse Store. Then add two custom groups, Current and Reduced, to the Reuse Store category.
4. Add the Item Master Form and Available Items Report to the Current group. Add the Item Sale Report, the Reduced Price Report, and the Seller and Items Query to the Reduced group.
5. Add the Address Quick Start field to the Seller table. Move the Phone Number field so that it follows the Country Region field. Save the changes to the table.
6. If requested to do so by your instructor, add a table description to the Seller table that includes your first and last name.
7. Submit the revised database in the format specified by your instructor.
8. What advantages are there to listing items by Description rather than by Item Number?

Analyze, Correct, Improve

Analyze a database, correct all errors, and improve the design.

Correcting Table Design Errors

Note: To complete this assignment, you will be required to use the Data Files for Students. Visit www.cengage.com/ct/studentdownload for detailed instructions or contact your instructor for information about accessing the required files.

Instructions: Start Access and open the Analyze Maintenance database. The database contains data about a local business that provides maintenance and repairs.

Perform the following tasks:

1. Correct The owner created an input mask for the Customer Number, which is shown in Figure 9–104. The input mask does not work correctly. It allows a user to input a customer number that does not include letters. The customer number must be two uppercase letters followed by two numbers. (*Hint*: There are two reasons that the input mask does not work.) The owner also added the index shown in Figure 9–104 but she gets an error message when she tries to save the table. Create the input mask and the index correctly. If requested to do so by your instructor, change the first and last name for the worker with Worker Number 102 to your first and last name.

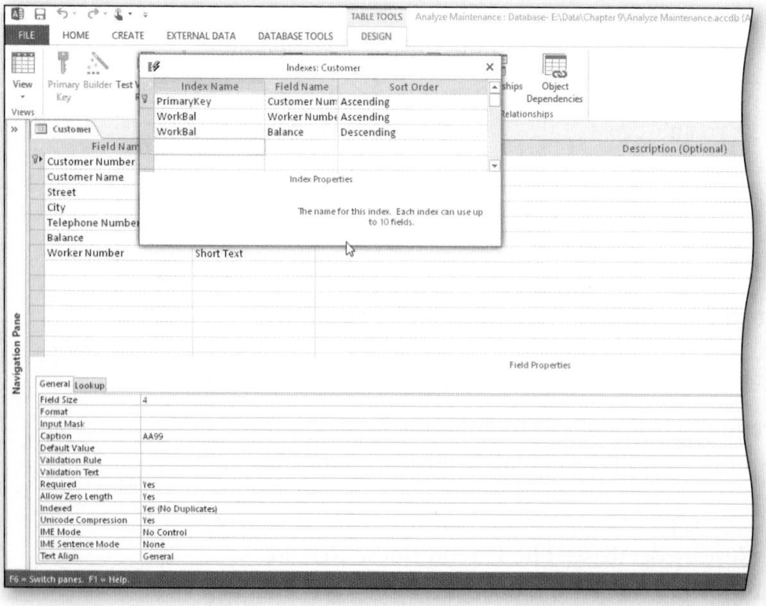

Figure 9–104

2. Improve One of the employees for the company has agreed to help maintain the database on his own time, but he only has Access 2003. Save the database in the 2002-2003 format as Analyze Maintenance_02_03 so the employee can use it.

3. What were the two input mask errors in this database?

In the Labs

Design, create, modify, and/or use a database following the guidelines, concepts, and skills presented in this chapter. Labs are listed in order of increasing difficulty. Labs 1 and 2, which increase in difficulty, require you to create solutions based on what you learned in the chapter; Lab 3 requires you to create a solution, which uses cloud and web technologies, by learning and investigating on your own from general guidance.

Lab 1: Administering the Technology Services Database

Note: To complete this assignment, you will be required to use the Data Files for Students. Visit www.cengage.com/ct/studentdownload for detailed instructions or contact your instructor for information about accessing the required files.

Problem: Technology Services has determined a number of database administration tasks that need to be done. These include creating indexes and custom input masks, adding table and database properties, creating a template, and splitting a database.

Instructions: Perform the following tasks:

1. Start Access and open the Lab 1 Technology Services database you modified in Chapter 8. If you did not use this database, contact your instructor for information about accessing the required database.
2. Open the Service Requests table in Datasheet view and add the Quick Start Status field to the end of the table. In Datasheet view, assign the value Not Started to all requests where the Hours Spent is 0. Assign the value In Progress to all other requests. You do not need to use a query.
3. Open the Service Requests table in Design view and create a validation rule that ensures that the value in the Hours Spent field is less than or equal to the value in the Total Hours field.
4. Open the Client table in Design view and create custom input masks for the following fields: Client Number, State, Postal Code, and Service Rep Number. The Client Number field should consist of three uppercase letters followed by two numbers. The State field should contain two uppercase letters. Both the Postal Code and Service Rep Number fields only can contain numbers.
5. Create an index on the Client Name field that allows duplicates.
6. Change the options to ensure that the Main Menu form is displayed automatically when a user opens the database.
7. Save the Lab 1 Technology Services database as a template with data but not as an application part. Create a new database from the Lab 1 Technology Services template. Name the database Lab 1 Technology New. Split the Lab 1 Technology New database.
8. If requested to do so by your instructor, open the front-end database, open the Forms List in Layout view, and add a title with your first and last name.
9. Submit the revised databases in the format specified by your instructor.
10. In this exercise, you split a database into a front-end and a back-end. Why would you split a database?

Lab 2: Administering the Team Designs Database

Problem: Team Designs has determined a number of database administration tasks that need to be done. These include creating indexes and custom input masks, adding table and database properties, and creating a locked database.

Note: To complete this assignment, you will be required to use the Data Files for Students. Visit www.cengage.com/ct/studentdownload for detailed instructions or contact your instructor for information about accessing the required files.

Continued >

In the Labs *continued*

Instructions: Perform the following tasks:

1. Start Access and open the Lab 2 Team Designs database you modified in Chapter 8. If you did not use this database, contact your instructor for information about accessing the required database.
2. Open the Item table in Design view and add a validation rule that ensures that the wholesale price always is less than the base cost of an item. Include validation text.
3. Create an index on the combination of item type and description. Name the index TypeDesc.
4. Do not allow zero-length strings for the Description field.
5. Create custom input masks for the Item Number and the Supplier Code fields.
6. Save the changes to the table design.
7. In Datasheet view, add the Address Quick Start field to the Supplier table following the Supplier Name field. Delete the Attachments field.
8. If requested to do so by your instructor, change the Supplier Name for Supplier Code LM to your last name and change the phone to your phone number.
9. Rename the Main Menu form object in the Navigation Pane as Team Designs Menu.
10. Change the Current Database options to ensure that the Team Designs Menu opens automatically.
11. Create a locked database.
12. Submit the revised database and the locked database in the format specified by your instructor.
13. Why would you lock a database?

Lab 3: Expand Your World: Cloud and Web Technologies
Sharing Access Databases

Problem: There are many ways to share an Access database. Some ways require each user to have Microsoft Access installed on their computer, while others do not. The method you select depends on factors such as need and available resources.

Instructions: Perform the following tasks:

1. Create a blog, a Google document, or a Word document on the SkyDrive on which to store your findings.
2. Use the web to search for different ways to share an Access database, such as Bavant Publishing, with others. Be sure to note any specific resources needed, such as an Access database or a SharePoint server, and provide examples of different reasons for sharing a database such as Bavant Publishing. Record your findings in your blog, Google document, or Word document, being sure to appropriately reference your sources.
3. Save your Bavant Publishing database to the SkyDrive. What happens when you open your database on the SkyDrive?
4. Submit the assignment in the format specified by your instructor.
5. Based on your research, what method would you choose to share your Access databases?

Consider This: Your Turn

Apply your creative thinking and problem solving skills to design and implement a solution.

1: Creating a Template for the Fine Crafts Database

Personal/Academic

Note: To complete this assignment, you will be required to use the Data Files for Students. Visit www.cengage.com/ct/studentdownload for detailed instructions or contact your instructor for information about accessing the required files.

Part 1: Your instructor has asked you to create a template from your database and then create a database that could be used as the basis for a web app. Open the Your Turn 1 Fine Crafts database you used in Chapter 8. If you did not use this database, contact your instructor for information about accessing the required database. Use the concepts and techniques presented in this chapter to perform each of the following tasks:

a. Create a Quick Start data type that includes all fields in the Item table except Total Value and Student Code. Save the data type as Basic Item Data.
b. Create a Quick Start data type that includes all fields in the Student table except the Picture and Biography fields. Save the data type as Basic Student Data.
c. Create a new desktop database named Students and Crafts.
d. Create a Student table using the Basic Student Data Quick Start data type. Student Code should be both required and unique. ID is the first field in the table.
e. Create an Item table using the Basic Item Data Quick Start data type. Item Number should be both required and unique. ID is the first field in the table. Add the Student Code field to the Item table as a Lookup & Relationship data type. Be sure to enable data integrity.
f. Import the Student.txt file into the Student table and the Item.txt table into the Item table. Because there is a relationship between the Student table and the Item table; be sure to import the Student table first.
g. Create a query that joins the Student and Item tables. Include the Student Code, First Name, Last Name, Item Number, Description, Price, and On Hand fields. Save the query as Students and Items.
h. Create single-item forms for the Student and Item tables. Name these forms Student Details and Item Details.
i. Create datasheet forms for the Student and Item tables. Include an On Click macro in each form that opens the respective Details form.
j. Create a datasheet form for the Students and Items query.
k. Create a navigation form similar to the one shown in Figure 9–59 on page AC 578. Include the datasheet forms and the detail forms.
l. Create a template and an application part for this database. Name the template Students and Crafts and include data in the template.
m. Create a new database named First Name Last Name Crafts where First Name and Last Name are your first and last name using the template you created in Step l.
n. If you have access to SharePoint and you have your instructor's permission, create a web app using the database you created in Step m.

Submit your assignment in the format specified by your instructor.

Part 2: You made several decisions while completing this assignment. What was the rationale behind your decisions?

2: Administering the Landscaping Services Database

Professional

Note: To complete this assignment, you will be required to use the Data Files for Students. Visit www.cengage.com/ct/studentdownload for detailed instructions or contact your instructor for information about accessing the required files.

Part 1: The owner of the landscaping company has asked you to perform a number of administration tasks. Open the Your Turn 2 Landscaping Services database you used in Chapter 8. If you did not use this database, contact your instructor for information about accessing the required database. Use the concepts and techniques presented in this chapter to perform each of the following tasks.

a. Change the Current Database options to ensure that the Main Menu opens automatically.
b. Open the Customer table in Design view and add custom input masks for the Customer Number and Postal Code fields. Create an index for the Customer Name field that allows duplicates. Do not allow zero-length strings for the Customer Name field.

Continued >

Consider This: Your Turn *continued*

c. Open the Supervisor table in Design view and create an index named LastFirst on the last name and the first name.
d. Open the Customer Requests table in Design view and create a validation rule to ensure that Hours Spent are less than or equal to Total Hours.
e. Open the Customer Requests table in Datasheet view and add the Quick Start Priority field to the table. Assign a High priority to requests for customers B10 and S11. Assign a Low priority to the request for customer T16. All other requests have a Normal priority.
f. Populate the Editor custom database property with your first and last name.
g. Use the 1 Right Blank Forms application part to create a form for the Service Requests table. Include all fields except Priority on the form. Change the title and the name of the form to Service Requests.

Submit your assignment in the format specified by your instructor.

Part 2: You made several decisions while completing this project, including using an application part to create a form. What was the rationale behind your decisions? Would you use an application part to create another form? Why or why not?

3: Understanding Database Administration Tasks

Research and Collaboration

Part 1: Before you begin this assignment, save the Bavant Publishing database as your team name database. For example, if your team is the Fab Four, then name the database Fab Four. Use the re-named database for this assignment. For each of the tasks listed below, perform the task and record the outcome. Create a blog, a Google document, or a Word document on the SkyDrive on which to store the team's results and observations for this assignment.

a. Create an earlier version of the database (Access 2003 or previous version).
b. Use the Table Analyzer on every table in the database.
c. Use the Performance Analyzer on all database objects.
d. Encrypt the database and set a password.
e. Decrypt the database.
f. Change macro settings.
g. Change privacy options.
h. Determine which add-ins are available for Access.
i. Change error checking options.

Submit your assignment in the format specified by your instructor.

Part 2: You made several decisions while completing this assignment. What was the rationale behind your decisions? Were you able to create an earlier version of the database? Why or why not?

Learn Online

Reinforce what you learned in this chapter with games, exercises, training, and many other online activities and resources.

Student Companion Site Reinforcement activities and resources are available at no additional cost on www.cengagebrain.com. Visit www.cengage.com/ct/studentdownload for detailed instructions about accessing the resources available at the Student Companion Site.

SAM Put your skills into practice with SAM Projects! SAM Projects for this chapter can be found online. If you have a SAM account, go to www.cengage.com/sam2013 to access SAM assignments for this chapter.

10 Using SQL

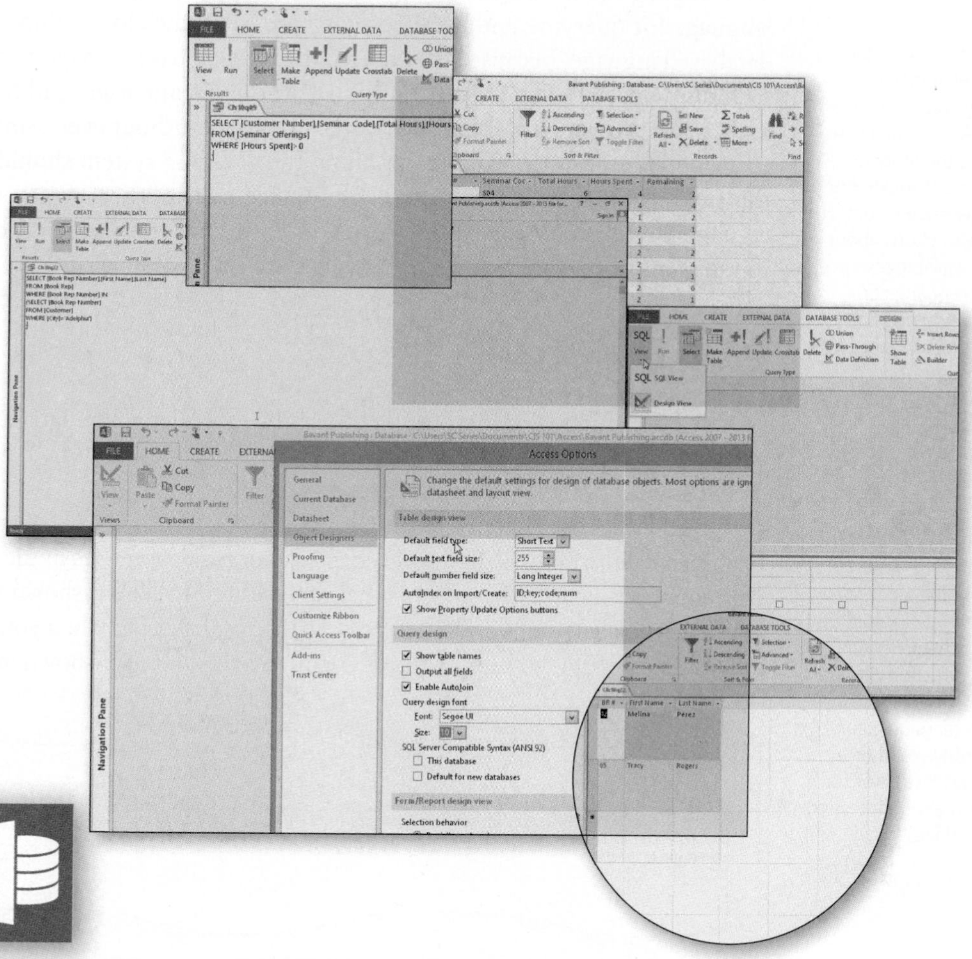

Objectives

You will have mastered the material in this project when you can:

- Understand the SQL language and how to use it
- Change the font or font size for queries
- Create SQL queries
- Include fields in SQL queries
- Include simple and compound criteria in SQL queries
- Use computed fields and built-in functions in SQL queries
- Sort the results in SQL queries
- Use aggregate functions in SQL queries
- Group the results in SQL queries
- Join tables in SQL queries
- Use subqueries
- Compare SQL queries with Access-generated SQL
- Use INSERT, UPDATE, and DELETE queries to update a database

10 | Using SQL

Introduction

BTW
Q&As
For a complete list of the Q&As found in many of the step-by-step sequences in this book, visit the Q&A resource on the Student Companion Site located on www.cengagebrain.com. For detailed instructions about accessing available resources, visit www.cengage.com/ct/studentdownload or contact your instructor for information about accessing the required files.

The language called **SQL (Structured Query Language)** is a very important language for querying and updating databases. It is the closest thing to a universal database language, because the vast majority of database management systems, including Access, use it in some fashion. Although some users will be able to do all their queries through the query features of Access without ever using SQL, those in charge of administering and maintaining the database system should be familiar with this important language. You also can use Access as an interface to other database management systems, such as SQL Server. Using or interfacing with SQL Server requires knowledge of SQL. Virtually every DBMS supports SQL.

Project — Using SQL

BTW
BTWs
For a complete list of the BTWs found in the margins of this book, visit the BTW resource on the Student Companion Site located on www.cengagebrain.com. For detailed instructions about accessing available resources, visit www.cengage.com/ct/studentdownload or contact your instructor for information about accessing the required files.

Bavant Publishing wants to be able to use the extended data management capabilities available through SQL. As part of becoming familiar with SQL, Bavant would like to create a wide variety of SQL queries.

Similar to creating queries in Design view, SQL provides a way of querying relational databases. In SQL, however, instead of making entries in the design grid, you type commands into SQL view to obtain the desired results, as shown in Figure 10–1a. You then can click the View button to view the results just as when you are creating queries in Design view. The results for the query in Figure 10–1a are shown in Figure 10–1b.

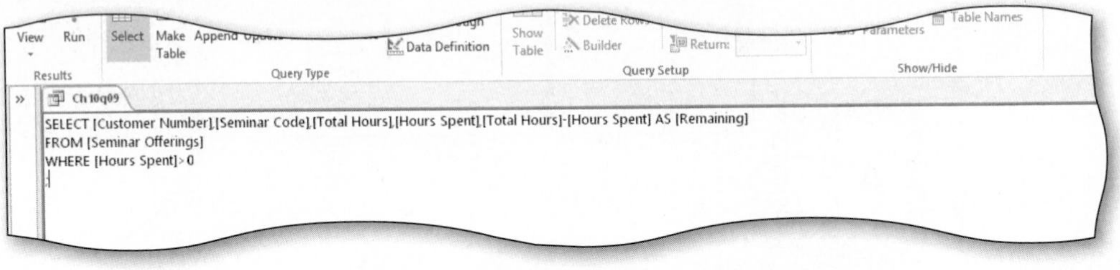

Figure 10–1 (a) Query in SQL

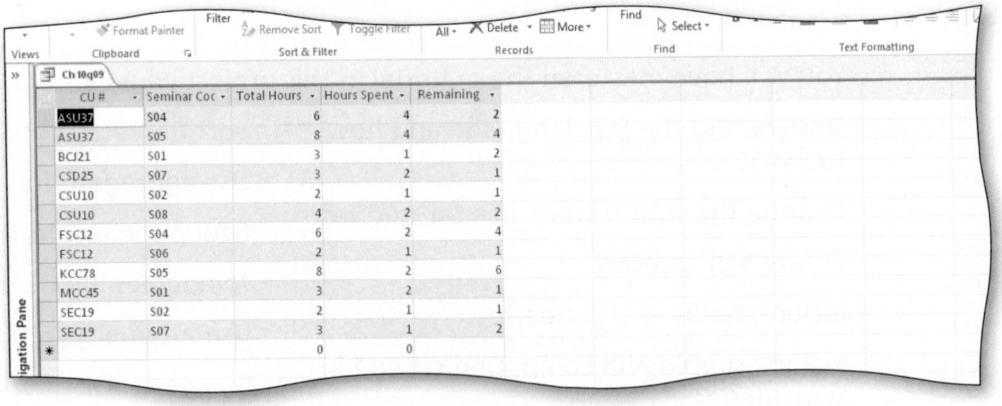

Figure 10–1 (b) Results

Roadmap

In this chapter, you will learn how to create and use SQL queries like the one shown in Figure 10–1. The following roadmap identifies general activities you will perform as you progress through this chapter:

1. Create a query in SQL VIEW
2. Use SIMPLE CRITERIA in a query
3. Use COMPOUND CRITERIA in a query
4. SORT RESULTS of a query
5. GROUP RESULTS of a query
6. JOIN TABLES in a query
7. USE a SUBQUERY in a query
8. UPDATE DATA with a query

At the beginning of step instructions throughout the chapter, you will see an abbreviated form of this roadmap. The abbreviated roadmap uses colors to indicate chapter progress: gray means the chapter is beyond that activity; blue means the task being shown is covered in that activity, and black means that activity is yet to be covered. For example, the following abbreviated roadmap indicates the chapter would be showing a task in the 3 COMPOUND CRITERIA activity.

1 SQL VIEW | 2 SIMPLE CRITERIA | 3 COMPOUND CRITERIA | 4 SORT RESULTS
5 GROUP RESULTS | 6 JOIN TABLES | 7 USE SUBQUERY | 8 UPDATE DATA

Use the abbreviated roadmap as a progress guide while you read or step through the instructions in this chapter.

BTW
Distributing a Document
Instead of printing and distributing a hard copy of a document, you can distribute the document electronically. Options include sending the document via email; posting it on cloud storage (such as SkyDrive) and sharing the file with others; posting it on a social networking site, blog, or other website; and sharing a link associated with an online location of the document. You also can create and share a PDF or XPS image of the document, so that users can view the file in Acrobat Reader or XPS Viewer instead of in Access.

To Run Access

If you are using a computer to step through the project in this chapter and you want your screens to match the figures in this book, you should change your screen's resolution to 1366 × 768. For information about how to change a computer's resolution, refer to the Office and Windows chapter at the beginning of this book.

The following steps, which assume Windows is running, use the Start screen or the search box to run Access based on a typical installation. You may need to ask your instructor how to run Access on your computer. For a detailed example of the procedure summarized below, refer to the Office and Windows chapter.

1. Scroll the Start screen for an Access 2013 tile. If your Start screen contains an Access 2013 tile, tap or click it to run Access; if the Start screen does not contain the Access 2013 tile, proceed to the next step to search for the Access app.
2. Swipe in from the right edge of the screen or point to the upper-right corner of the screen to display the Charms bar and then tap or click the Search charm on the Charms bar to display the Search menu.
3. Type `Access` as the search text in the Search text box and watch the search results appear in the Apps list.
4. Tap or click Access 2013 in the search results to run Access.

BTW
The Ribbon and Screen Resolution
Access may change how the groups and buttons within the groups appear on the ribbon, depending on the computer's screen resolution. Thus, your ribbon may look different from the ones in this book if you are using a screen resolution other than 1366 × 768.

To Open a Database from Access

BTW
Touch Screen Differences
The Office and Windows interfaces may vary if you are using a touch screen. For this reason, you might notice that the function or appearance of your touch screen differs slightly from this chapter's presentation.

The following steps open the Bavant Publishing database from the location you specified when you first created it (for example, the Access folder in the CIS 101 folder). For a detailed example of the procedure summarized below, refer to the Office and Windows chapter at the beginning of this book.

1. Tap or click FILE on the ribbon to open the Backstage view, if necessary.
2. If the database you want to open is displayed in the Recent list, tap or click the file name to open the database and display the opened database in the Access window; then skip to Step 7. If the database you want to open is not displayed in the Recent list or if the Recent list does not appear, tap or click Open Other Files to display the Open Gallery.
3. If the database you want to open is displayed in the Recent list in the Open gallery, tap or click the file name to open the database and display the opened database in the Access window; then skip to Step 7.
4. Tap or click Computer, SkyDrive, or another location in the left pane and then navigate to the location of the database to be opened (for example, the Access folder in the CIS 101 folder).
5. Tap or click Bavant Publishing to select the database to be opened.
6. Tap or click the Open button (Open dialog box) to open the selected file and display the opened database in the Access window.
7. If a Security Warning appears, tap or click the 'Enable Content' button.

BTW
On-Screen Keyboard
To display the on-screen touch keyboard, tap the Touch Keyboard button on the Windows taskbar. When finished using the touch keyboard, tap the X button on the touch keyboard to close the keyboard.

SQL Background

In this chapter, you query and update a database using the language called **SQL (Structured Query Language)**. Similar to using the design grid in the Access Query window, SQL provides users with the capability of querying a relational database. Because SQL is a language, however, you must enter **commands** to obtain the desired results, rather than completing entries in the design grid. SQL uses commands to update tables and to retrieve data from tables. The commands that are used to retrieve data are usually called **queries**.

SQL was developed under the name SEQUEL at the IBM San Jose research facilities as the data manipulation language for IBM's prototype relational model DBMS, System R, in the mid-1970s. In 1980, it was renamed SQL to avoid confusion with an unrelated hardware product called SEQUEL. Most relational DBMSs, including Microsoft Access and Microsoft SQL Server, use a version of SQL as a data manipulation language.

Some people pronounce SQL by pronouncing the three letters, that is, "ess-que-ell." It is very common, however to pronounce it as the name under which it was developed originally, that is, "sequel."

BTW
Datasheet Font Size
You also can use the Access Options dialog box to change the default font and font size for datasheets. To do so, tap or click Datasheet in the Access Options dialog box and make the desired changes in the Default font area.

To Change the Font Size

You can change the font and/or the font size for queries using the Options button in the Backstage view and then Object Designers in the list of options in the Access Options dialog box. There usually is not a compelling reason to change the font, unless there is a strong preference for some other font. It often is worthwhile to change the font size, however. ***Why?*** *With the default size of 8, the queries can be hard to read. Increasing the font size to 10 can make a big difference.* The following steps change the font size for queries to 10.

1

- Tap or click FILE on the ribbon to open the Backstage view.
- Tap or click Options to display the Access Options dialog box.
- Tap or click Object Designers to display the Object Designer options.
- In the Query design area, tap or click the Size box arrow, and then tap or click 10 in the list to change the size to 10 (Figure 10–2).

2

- Tap or click the OK button to close the Access Options dialog box.

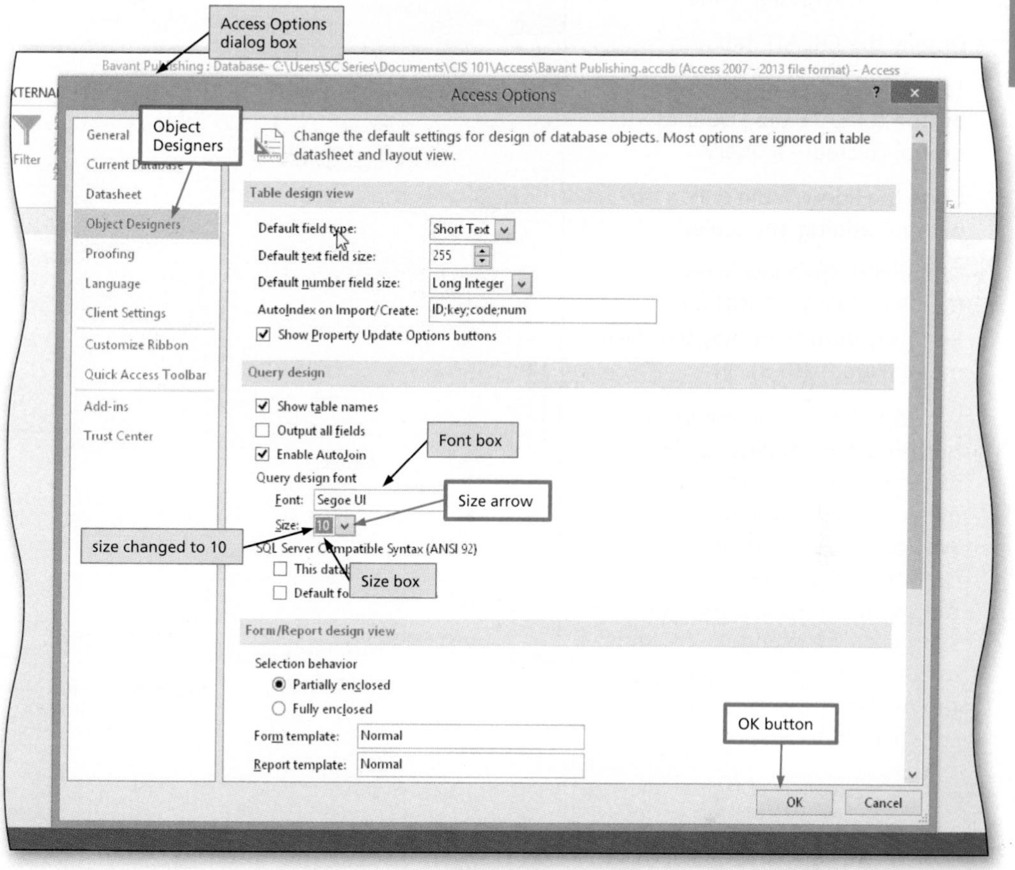

Figure 10–2

SQL Queries

When you query a database using SQL, you type commands in a blank window rather than filling in the design grid. When the command is complete, you can view your results just as you do with queries you create using the design grid.

BTW

Touch and Pointers

Remember that if you are using your finger on a touch screen, you will not see the pointer.

To Create a New SQL Query

You begin the creation of a new **SQL query**, which is a query expressed using the SQL language, just as you begin the creation of any other query in Access. The only difference is that you will use SQL view instead of Design view. ***Why?*** *SQL view enables you to type SQL commands rather than making entries in the design grid.* The following steps create a new SQL query.

1

- Close the Navigation Pane.
- Display the CREATE tab.
- Tap or click the Query Design button (CREATE tab | Queries group) to create a query.
- Close the Show Table dialog box without adding any tables.
- Tap or click the View arrow (QUERY TOOLS DESIGN tab | Results group) to display the View menu (Figure 10–3).

Q&A Why did the icon on the View button change to SQL, and why are there only two items on the menu instead of the usual five?
Without any tables selected, you cannot view any results. You only can use the normal Design view or SQL view. The change in the icon indicates that you could simply tap or click the button to transfer to SQL view.

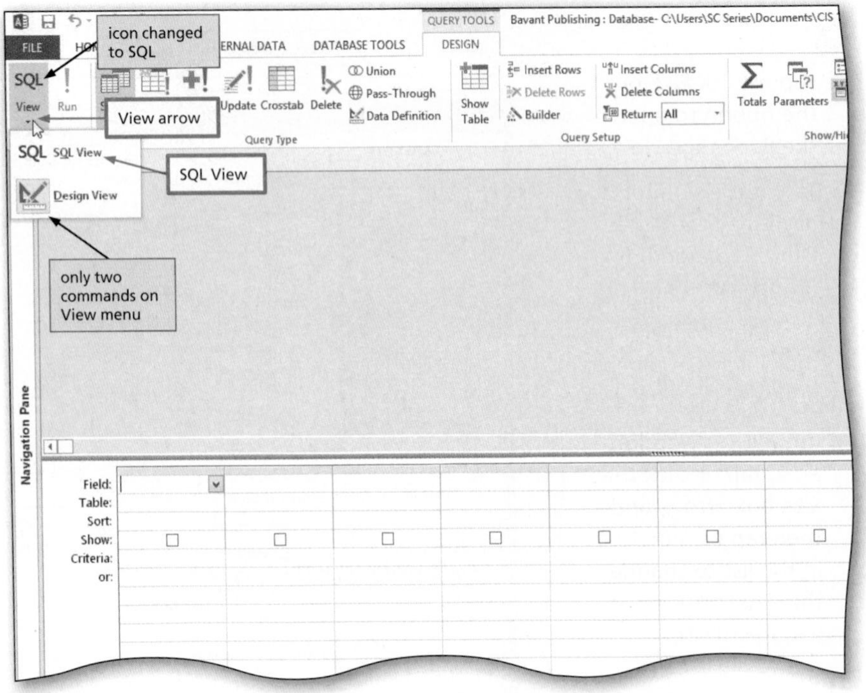

Figure 10–3

2

- Tap or click SQL View on the View menu to view the query in SQL view (Figure 10–4).

Q&A What happened to the design grid?
In SQL view, you specify the queries by typing SQL commands rather than making entries in the design grid.

Figure 10–4

SQL Commands

The basic form of SQL expressions is quite simple: SELECT-FROM-WHERE. The command begins with a **SELECT clause**, which consists of the word, SELECT, followed by a list of those fields you want to include. The fields will appear in the results in the order in which they are listed in the expression. Next, the command contains a **FROM clause**, which consists of the word, FROM, followed by a list of the table or tables involved in the query. Finally, there is an optional **WHERE clause**, which consists of the word, WHERE, followed by any criteria that the data you want to retrieve must satisfy. The command ends with a semicolon (;), which in this text will appear on a separate line.

SQL has no special format rules for placement of terms, capitalization, and so on. One common style is to place the word FROM on a new line, and then place the word WHERE, when it is used, on the next line. This style makes the commands easier to read. It also is common to show words that are part of the SQL language in uppercase and others in a combination of uppercase and lowercase. Because it is a common convention, and necessary in some versions of SQL, you will place a semicolon (;) at the end of each command.

Microsoft Access has its own version of SQL that, unlike some other versions of SQL, allows spaces within field names and table names. There is a restriction, however, to the way such names are used in SQL queries. When a name containing a space appears in SQL, it must be enclosed in square brackets. For example, Customer Number must appear as [Customer Number] because the name includes a space. On the other hand, City does not need to be enclosed in square brackets because its name does not include a space. For consistency, all names in this text are enclosed in square brackets. Thus, the City field would appear as [City] even though the brackets technically are not required by SQL.

BTW

Context-Sensitive Help in SQL

When you are working in SQL view, you can obtain context-sensitive help on any of the keywords in your query. To do so, tap or click anywhere in the word about which you wish to obtain help and press F1.

BTW

Entering Field Names

Be sure to enclose field names in square brackets. If you accidentally use parentheses or curly braces, Access will display a syntax error (missing operator) message.

To Include Only Certain Fields

1 SQL VIEW | 2 SIMPLE CRITERIA | 3 COMPOUND CRITERIA | 4 SORT RESULTS
5 GROUP RESULTS | 6 JOIN TABLES | 7 USE SUBQUERY | 8 UPDATE DATA

To include only certain fields in a query, list them after the word, SELECT. If you want to list all rows in the table, you do not include the word, WHERE. ***Why?*** *If there is no WHERE clause, there is no criterion restricting which rows appear in the results. In that case, all rows will appear.* The steps on the next page create a query for Bavant Publishing that will list the number, name, amount paid, and current due amount of all customers.

1

- Type **SELECT [Customer Number],[Customer Name],[Amount Paid],[Current Due]** as the first line of the command, and then press the ENTER key.

Q&A What is the purpose of the SELECT clause?
The SELECT clause indicates the fields that are to be included in the query results. This SELECT clause, for example, indicates that the Customer Number, Customer Name, Amount Paid, and Current Due fields are to be included.

- Type **FROM [Customer]** as the second line to specify the source table, press the ENTER key, and then type a semicolon (**;**) on the third line.

Q&A What is the purpose of the FROM clause?
The FROM clause indicates the table or tables that contain the fields used in the query. This FROM clause indicates that all the fields in this query come from the Customer table.

- Tap or click the View button (QUERY TOOLS DESIGN tab | Results group) to view the results (Figure 10–5).

Q&A My screen displays a dialog box that asks me to enter a parameter value. What did I do wrong?
You typed a field name incorrectly. Tap or click Cancel to close the dialog box and then correct your SQL statement.

Why does CU # appear as the column heading for the Customer Number field?
This is the caption for the field. If the field has a special caption defined, Access will use the caption rather than the field name. You will learn how to change this later in this chapter.

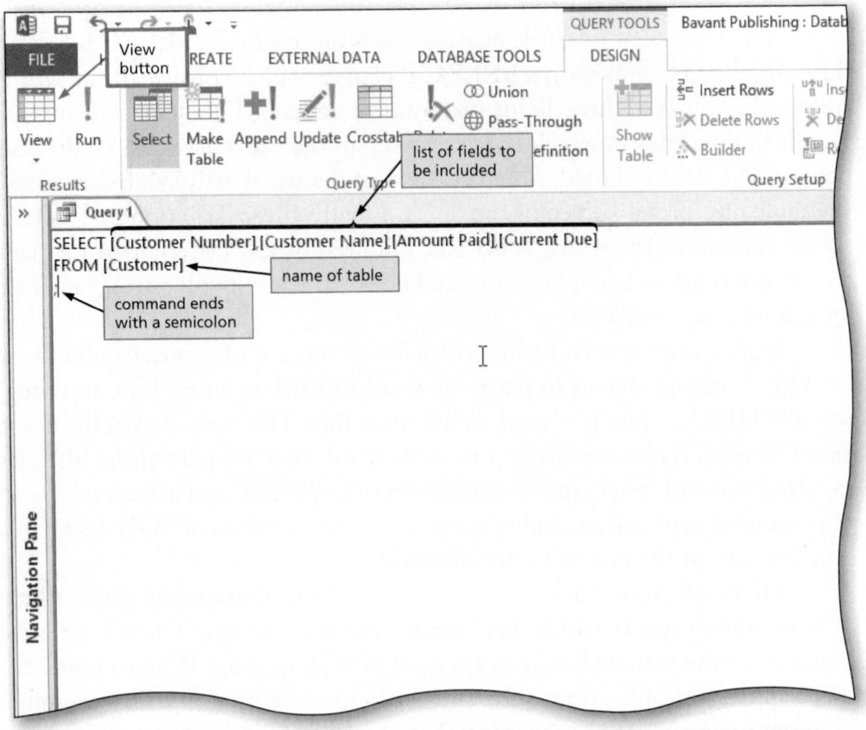

Figure 10–5 (a) Query to List the Customer Number, Customer Name, Amount Paid, and Current Due for All Customers

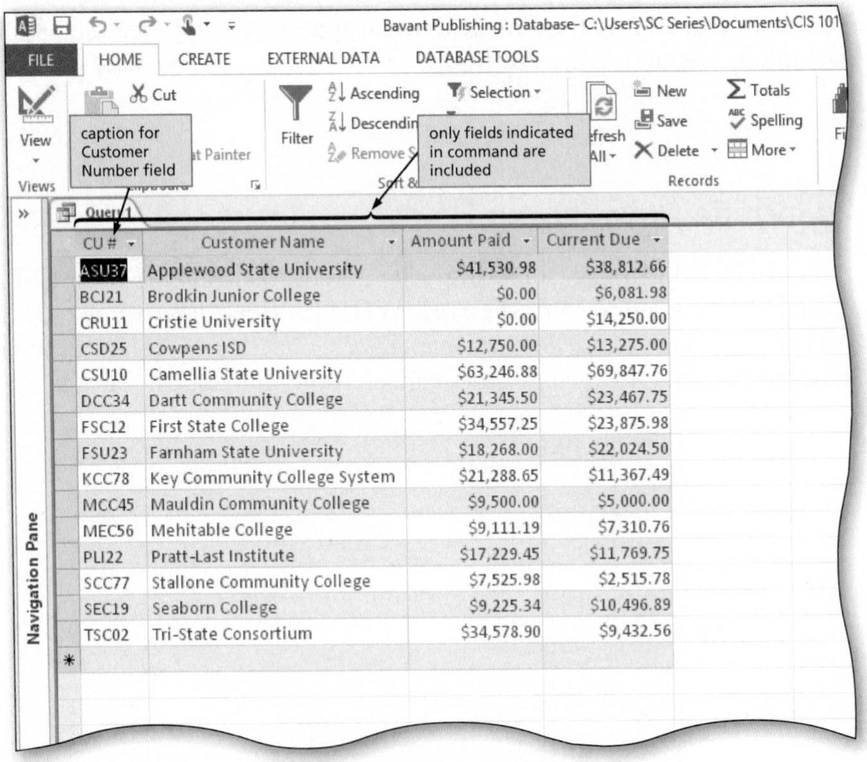

CU #	Customer Name	Amount Paid	Current Due
ASU37	Applewood State University	$41,530.98	$38,812.66
BCJ21	Brodkin Junior College	$0.00	$6,081.98
CRU11	Cristie University	$0.00	$14,250.00
CSD25	Cowpens ISD	$12,750.00	$13,275.00
CSU10	Camellia State University	$63,246.88	$69,847.76
DCC34	Dartt Community College	$21,345.50	$23,467.75
FSC12	First State College	$34,557.25	$23,875.98
FSU23	Farnham State University	$18,268.00	$22,024.50
KCC78	Key Community College System	$21,288.65	$11,367.49
MCC45	Mauldin Community College	$9,500.00	$5,000.00
MEC56	Mehitable College	$9,111.19	$7,310.76
PLI22	Pratt-Last Institute	$17,229.45	$11,769.75
SCC77	Stallone Community College	$7,525.98	$2,515.78
SEC19	Seaborn College	$9,225.34	$10,496.89
TSC02	Tri-State Consortium	$34,578.90	$9,432.56

Figure 10–5 (b) Results

2

- Tap or click the Save button on the Quick Access Toolbar, type **Ch10q01** as the name in the Save As dialog box, and tap or click the OK button to save the query as Ch10q01.

To Prepare to Enter a New SQL Query

1 SQL VIEW | 2 SIMPLE CRITERIA | 3 COMPOUND CRITERIA | 4 SORT RESULTS
5 GROUP RESULTS | 6 JOIN TABLES | 7 USE SUBQUERY | 8 UPDATE DATA

To enter a new SQL query, you could close the window, tap or click the No button when asked if you want to save your changes, and then begin the process from scratch. A quicker alternative is to use the View menu and then select SQL View. ***Why?*** *You will be returned to SQL view with the current command appearing. At that point, you could erase the current command and then enter a new one. If the next command is similar to the previous one, however, it often is simpler to modify the current command instead of erasing it and starting over.* The following step shows how to prepare to enter a new SQL query.

1

- Tap or click the View arrow (HOME tab | Views group) to display the View menu (Figure 10–6).
- Tap or click SQL View to return to SQL view.

Q&A Could I just tap or click the View button, or do I have to tap or click the arrow?
Because the icon on the button is not the icon for SQL view, you must tap or click the arrow.

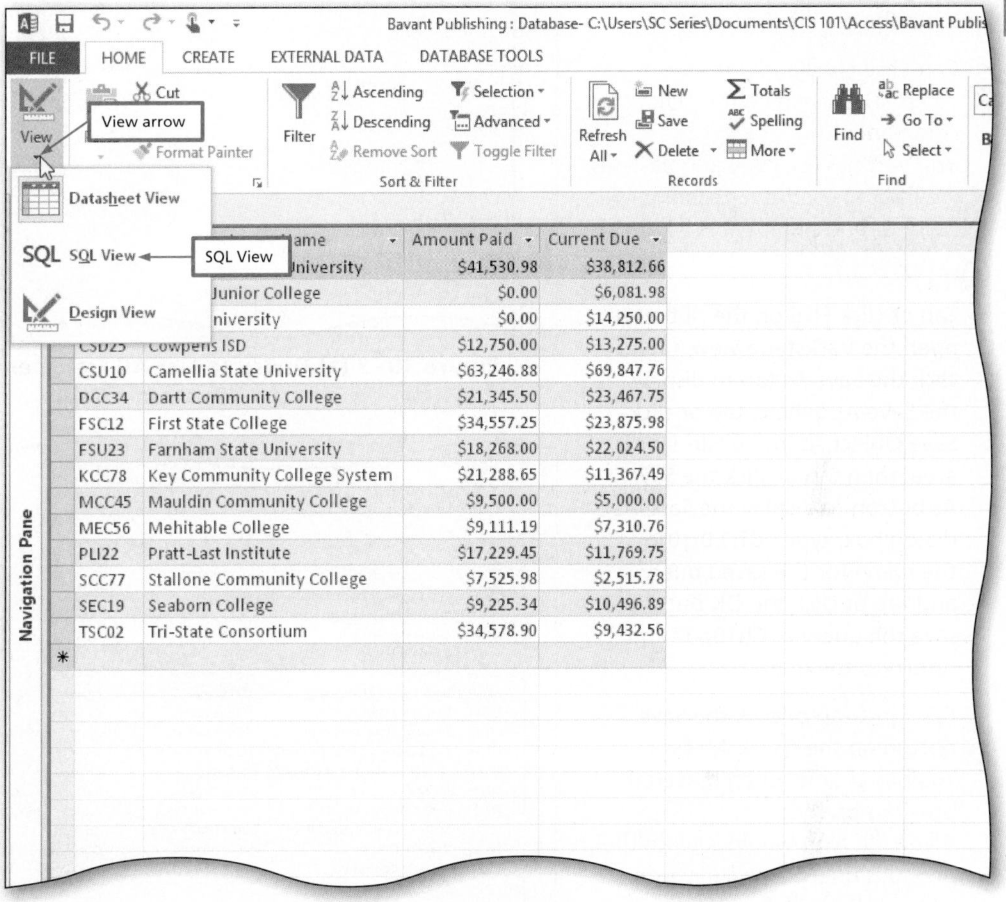

Figure 10–6

To Include All Fields

1 SQL VIEW | 2 SIMPLE CRITERIA | 3 COMPOUND CRITERIA | 4 SORT RESULTS
5 GROUP RESULTS | 6 JOIN TABLES | 7 USE SUBQUERY | 8 UPDATE DATA

To include all fields, you could use the same approach as in the previous steps, that is, list each field in the Customer table after the word, SELECT. There is a shortcut, however. Instead of listing all the field names after SELECT, you can use the asterisk (*) symbol. ***Why?*** *Just as when working in the design grid, the asterisk symbol represents all fields.* This indicates that you want all fields listed in the order in which you described them to the system during data definition. The steps on the next page list all fields and all records in the Customer table.

1

- Delete the current command, type `SELECT *` as the first line of the command, and then press the ENTER key.
- Type `FROM [Customer]` as the second line, press the ENTER key, and type a semicolon (`;`) on the third line.
- View the results (Figure 10–7).

Q&A Can I use copy and paste commands when I enter SQL commands?

Yes, you can use copy and paste as well as other editing techniques, such as replacing text.

2

- Tap or click FILE on the ribbon to open the Backstage view, tap or click the Save As tab to display the Save As gallery, tap or click Save Object As in the File Types area, then tap or click the Save As button to display the Save As dialog box, type `Ch10q02` as the name for the saved query, and tap or click the OK button to save the query as Ch10q02 and return to the query.

Q&A Can I just tap or click the Save button on the Quick Access Toolbar as I did when I saved the previous query?

If you did, you would replace the previous query with the version you just created. Because you want to save both the previous query and the new one, you need to save the new version with a different name. To do so, you must use Save Object As, which is available through the Backstage view.

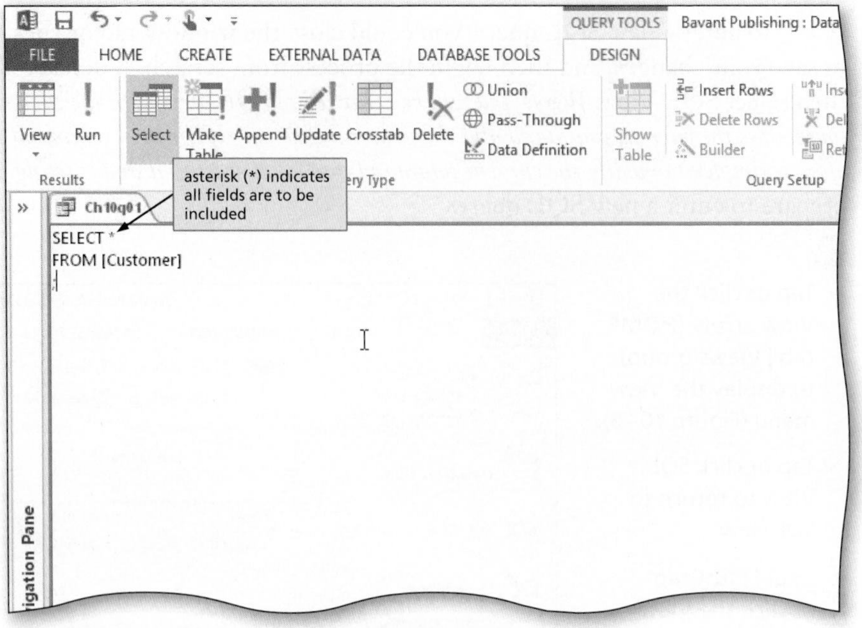

Figure 10–7 (a) Query to List All Fields and All Records in the Customer Table

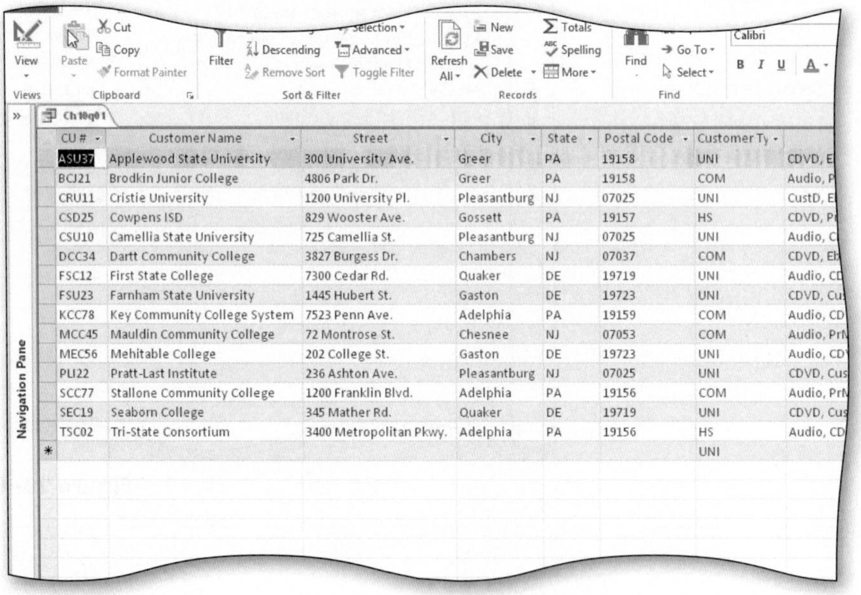

Figure 10–7 (b) Results

To Use a Criterion Involving a Numeric Field

To restrict the records to be displayed, include the word WHERE followed by a criterion as part of the command. If the field involved is a numeric field, you simply type the value. In typing the number, you do not type commas or dollar signs. ***Why?*** *If you enter a dollar sign, Access assumes you are entering text. If you enter a comma, Access considers the criterion invalid.* The following steps create a query to list the customer number and name of all customers whose returns amount is $0.00.

1

- Return to SQL view and delete the current command.
- Type **`SELECT [Customer Number],[Customer Name]`** as the first line of the command.
- Type **`FROM [Customer]`** as the second line.
- Type **`WHERE [Returns]=0`** as the third line, and then type a semicolon (**;**) on the fourth line.

Q&A What is the purpose of the WHERE clause?
The WHERE clause restricts the rows to be included in the results to only those that satisfy the criteria included in the clause. With this WHERE clause, for example, only those rows on which Returns is equal to 0 will be included.

- View the results (Figure 10–8).

Q&A On my screen, the customers are listed in a different order. Did I do something wrong?
No. The order in which records appear in a query result is random unless you specifically order the records. You will see how to order records later in this chapter.

2

- Save the query as Ch10q03.

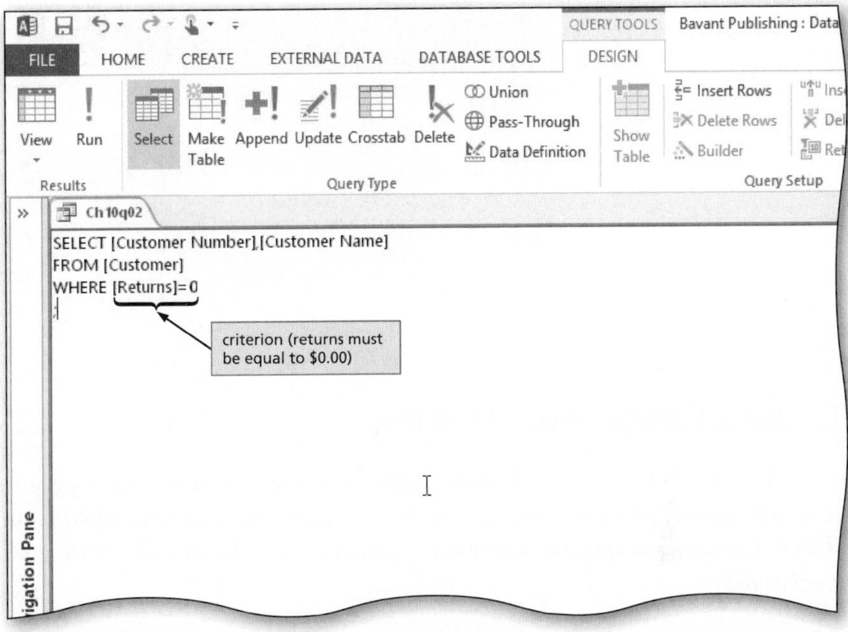

Figure 10–8 (a) Query to List the Customer Number and Customer Name for Those Customers Where Returns is Equal to 0

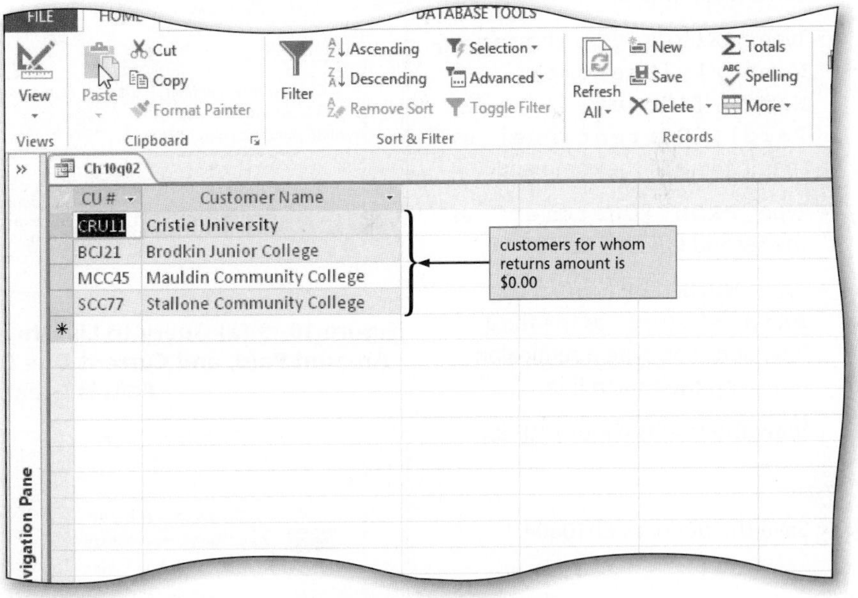

Figure 10–8 (b) Results

BTW
SQL Standards
The International Standards Organization (ISO) and the American National Standards Institute (ANSI) recognize SQL as a standardized language. Different relational database management systems may support the entire set of standardized SQL commands or only a subset.

Simple Criteria

The criterion following the word WHERE in the preceding query is called a simple criterion. A **simple criterion** has the form: field name, comparison operator, then either another field name or a value. The possible comparison operators are shown in Table 10–1.

Table 10–1 Comparison Operators

Comparison Operator	Meaning
=	equal to
<	less than
>	greater than
<=	less than or equal to
>=	greater than or equal to
<>	not equal to

To Use a Comparison Operator

1 SQL VIEW | 2 SIMPLE CRITERIA | 3 COMPOUND CRITERIA | 4 SORT RESULTS
5 GROUP RESULTS | 6 JOIN TABLES | 7 USE SUBQUERY | 8 UPDATE DATA

In the following steps, Bavant Publishing uses a comparison operator to list the customer number, customer name, amount paid, and current due for all customers whose amount paid is greater than $20,000. ***Why?*** *A comparison operator allows you to compare the value in a field with a specific value or with the value in another field.*

1

- Return to SQL view and delete the current command.
- Type `SELECT [Customer Number],[Customer Name],[Amount Paid],[Current Due]` as the first line of the command.
- Type `FROM [Customer]` as the second line.
- Type `WHERE [Amount Paid]>20000` as the third line, and then type a semicolon (`;`) on the fourth line.
- View the results (Figure 10–9).

2

- Save the query as Ch10q04.

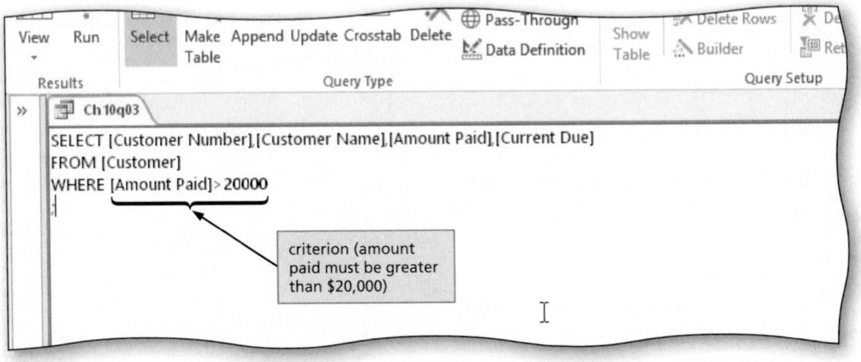

Figure 10–9 (a) Query to List the Customer Number, Customer Name, Amount Paid, and Current Due for Those Customers Where Amount Paid is Greater than $20,000

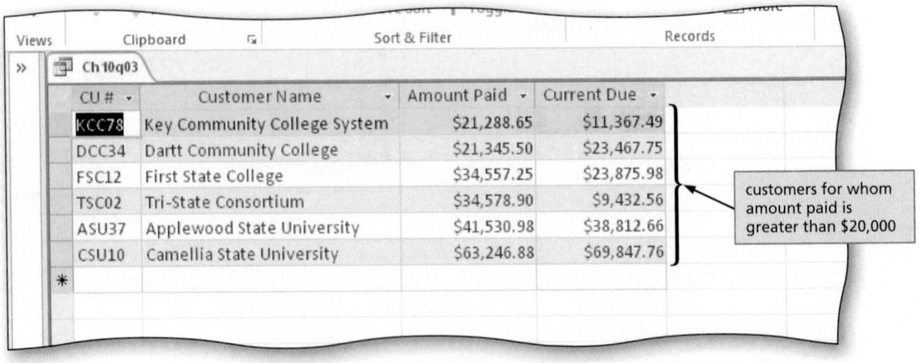

Figure 10–9 (b) Results

To Use a Criterion Involving a Text Field

1 SQL VIEW | 2 SIMPLE CRITERIA | 3 COMPOUND CRITERIA | 4 SORT RESULTS
5 GROUP RESULTS | 6 JOIN TABLES | 7 USE SUBQUERY | 8 UPDATE DATA

If the criterion involves a text field, the value must be enclosed in quotation marks. ***Why?*** *Unlike when you work in the design grid, Access will not insert the quotation marks around text data for you in SQL view. You need to include them.* The following example lists the customer number and name of all of Bavant Publishing's customers located in Adelphia, that is, all customers for whom the value in the City field is Adelphia.

1

- Return to SQL view, delete the current command, and type **SELECT [Customer Number],[Customer Name]** as the first line of the command.
- Type **FROM [Customer]** as the second line.
- Type **WHERE [City]='Adelphia'** as the third line and type a semicolon (**;**) on the fourth line.
- View the results (Figure 10–10).

Q&A Could I enclose the text field value in double quotation marks instead of single quotation marks?

Yes. It is usually easier, however, to use single quotes when entering SQL commands.

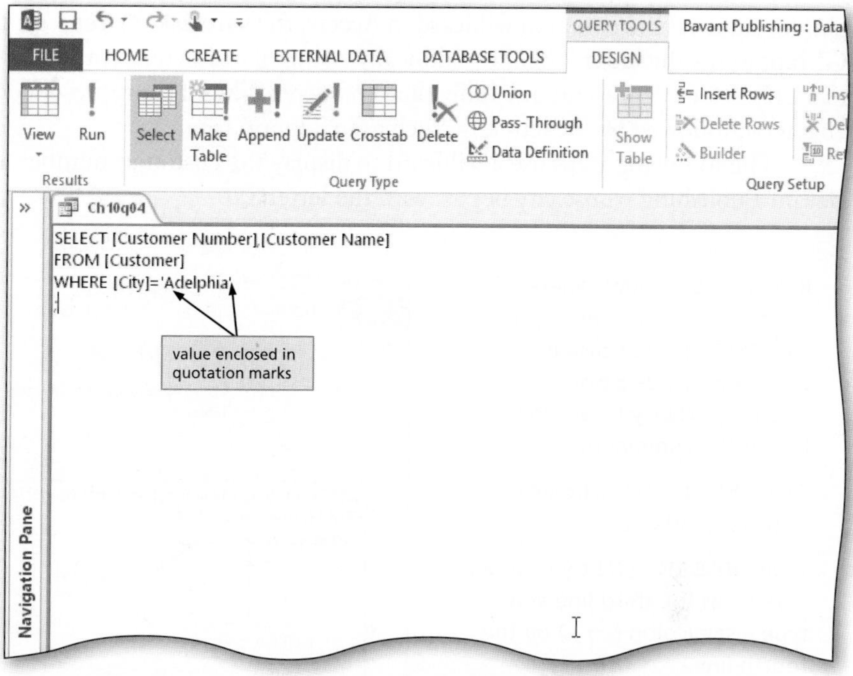

Figure 10–10 (a) Query to List the Customer Number and Customer Name for Those Customers Whose City is Adelphia

2

- Save the query as Ch10q05.

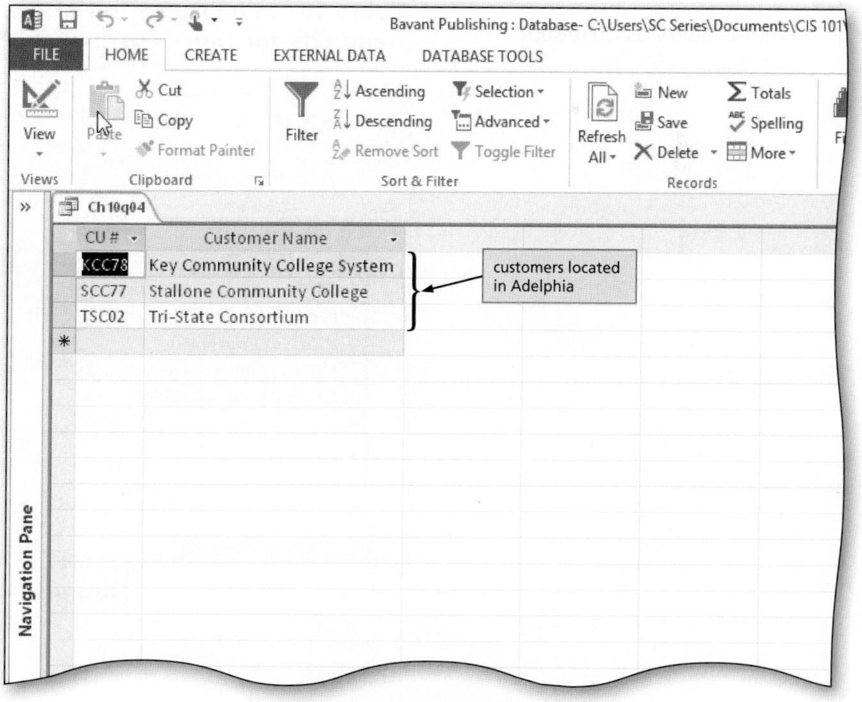

Figure 10–10 (b) Results

To Use a Wildcard

In most cases, the conditions in WHERE clauses involve exact matches, such as retrieving rows for each customer located in the city of Adelphia. In some cases, however, exact matches do not work. ***Why?*** *You might only know that the desired value contains a certain collection of characters.* In such cases, you use the LIKE operator with a wildcard symbol.

Rather than testing for equality, the LIKE operator uses one or more wildcard characters to test for a pattern match. One common wildcard in Access, the **asterisk** (*), represents any collection of characters. Thus, G* represents the letter, G, followed by any string of characters. Another wildcard symbol is the question mark (?), which represents any individual character. Thus T?m represents the letter, T, followed by any single character, followed by the letter, m, such as in Tim or Tom.

The following steps use a wildcard to display the customer number and name for every customer of Bavant Publishing whose city begins with the letter, G.

1

- Return to SQL view, delete the previous query, and type `SELECT [Customer Number], [Customer Name], [City]` as the first line of the command.
- Type `FROM [Customer]` as the second line.
- Type `WHERE [City] LIKE 'G*'` as the third line and type a semicolon (`;`) on the fourth line.
- View the results (Figure 10–11).

2

- Save the query as Ch10q06.

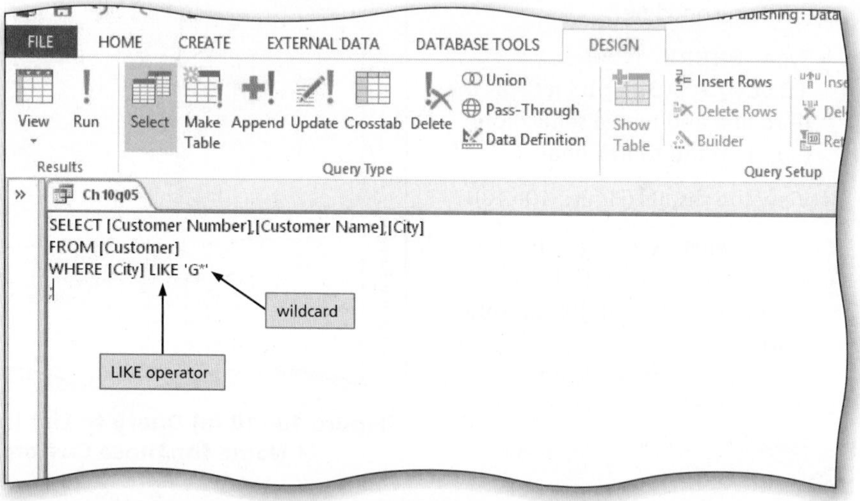

Figure 10–11 (a) Query to List the Customer Number, Customer Name, and City for Those Customers Whose City Begins with the Letter G

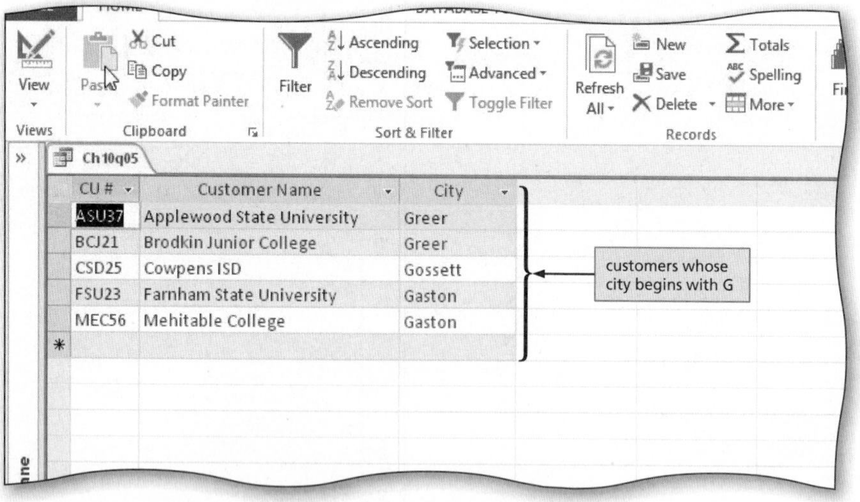

Figure 10–11 (b) Results

Break Point: If you wish to stop working through the chapter at this point, you can close Access now. You can resume the project later by starting Access, opening the database called Bavant Publishing, creating a new query in SQL view, and continuing to follow the steps from this location forward.

Compound Criteria

You are not limited to simple criteria in SQL. You also can use compound criteria. **Compound criteria** are formed by connecting two or more simple criteria using AND, OR, and NOT. When simple criteria are connected by the word AND, all the simple criteria must be true in order for the compound criterion to be true. When simple criteria are connected by the word OR, the compound criterion will be true whenever any of the simple criteria are true. Preceding a criterion by the word NOT reverses the truth or falsity of the original criterion. That is, if the original criterion is true, the new criterion will be false; if the original criterion is false, the new one will be true.

BTW
Wildcards
Other implementations of SQL do not use the asterisk (*) and question mark (?) wildcards. In SQL for Oracle and for SQL Server, the percent sign (%) is used as a wildcard to represent any collection of characters. In Oracle and SQL Server, the WHERE clause shown in Figure 10–11 on page AC 630 would be WHERE [City] LIKE 'G%'.

To Use a Compound Criterion Involving AND

1 SQL VIEW | 2 SIMPLE CRITERIA | **3 COMPOUND CRITERIA** | **4 SORT RESULTS**
5 GROUP RESULTS | **6 JOIN TABLES** | **7 USE SUBQUERY** | **8 UPDATE DATA**

The following steps use a compound criterion. ***Why?*** *A compound criterion allows you to impose multiple conditions.* In particular, the steps enable Bavant to display the number and name of those customers located in Greer who have a returns amount of $0.00.

1

- Return to SQL view, delete the previous query, and type **SELECT [Customer Number],[Customer Name]** as the first line of the command.
- Type **FROM [Customer]** as the second line.
- Type **WHERE [City]='Greer'** as the third line.
- Type **AND [Returns]=0** as the fourth line and type a semicolon (**;**) on the fifth line.

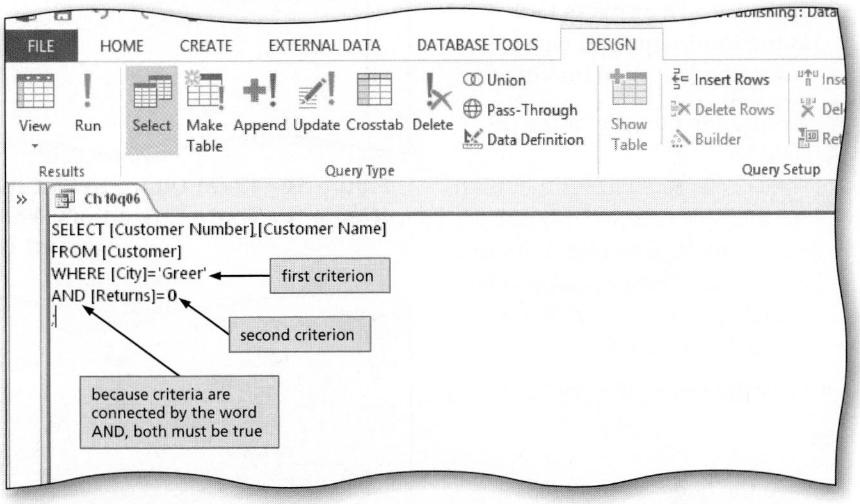

Figure 10–12 (a) Query to List the Customer Number and Customer Name for Those Customers Whose City is Greer and Whose Returns Amount is Equal to $0

Q&A What is the purpose of the AND clause?
The AND clause indicates that there are multiple criteria, all of which must be true. With this AND clause, only rows on which BOTH City is Greer AND Returns is 0 will be included.

- View the results (Figure 10–12).

2

- Save the query as Ch10q07.

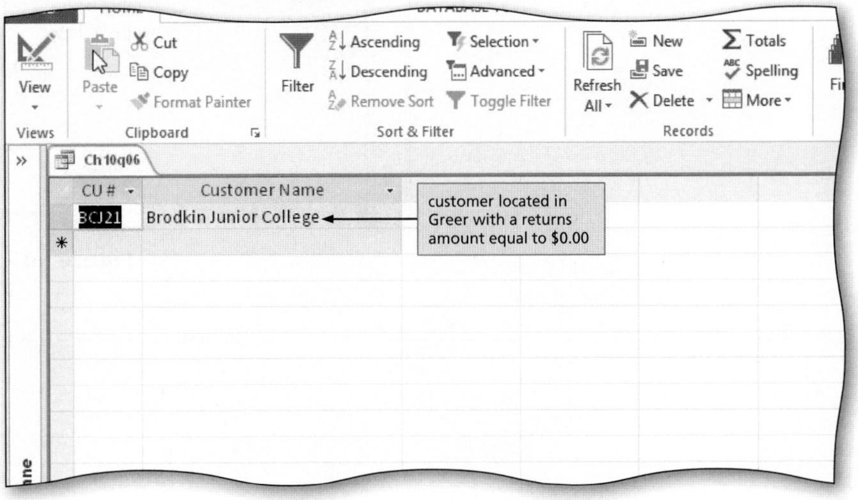

Figure 10–12 (b) Results

To Use a Compound Criterion Involving OR

1 SQL VIEW | 2 SIMPLE CRITERIA | 3 COMPOUND CRITERIA | 4 SORT RESULTS
5 GROUP RESULTS | 6 JOIN TABLES | 7 USE SUBQUERY | 8 UPDATE DATA

The following steps use a compound criterion involving OR to enable Bavant Publishing to display the customer number and name of those customers located in Greer or for whom the returns amount is $0.00. ***Why?*** *In an OR criterion only one of the individual criteria needs to be true in order for the record to be included in the results.*

1

- Return to SQL view, delete the previous query, and type `SELECT [Customer Number], [Customer Name]` as the first line of the command.
- Type `FROM [Customer]` as the second line.
- Type `WHERE [City]='Greer'` as the third line.
- Type `OR [Returns]=0` as the fourth line and type a semicolon (`;`) on the fifth line.

Q&A What is the purpose of the OR clause?

The OR clause indicates that there are multiple criteria, only one of which needs to be true. With this AND clause, those rows on which EITHER City is Greer OR Returns is 0 (or both) will be included.

- View the results (Figure 10–13).

2

- Save the query as Ch10q08.

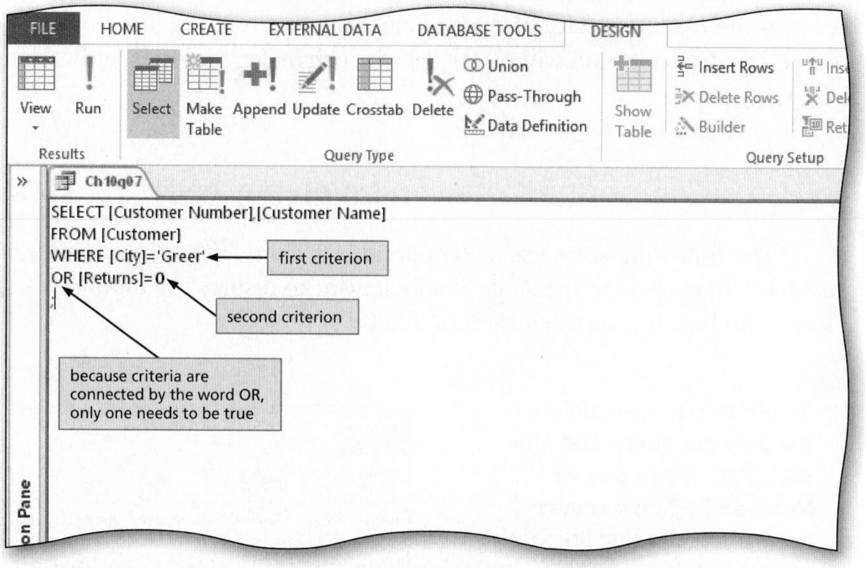

Figure 10–13 (a) Query to List the Customer Number and Customer Name for Those Customers Whose City is Greer or Whose Returns Amount is Equal to $0

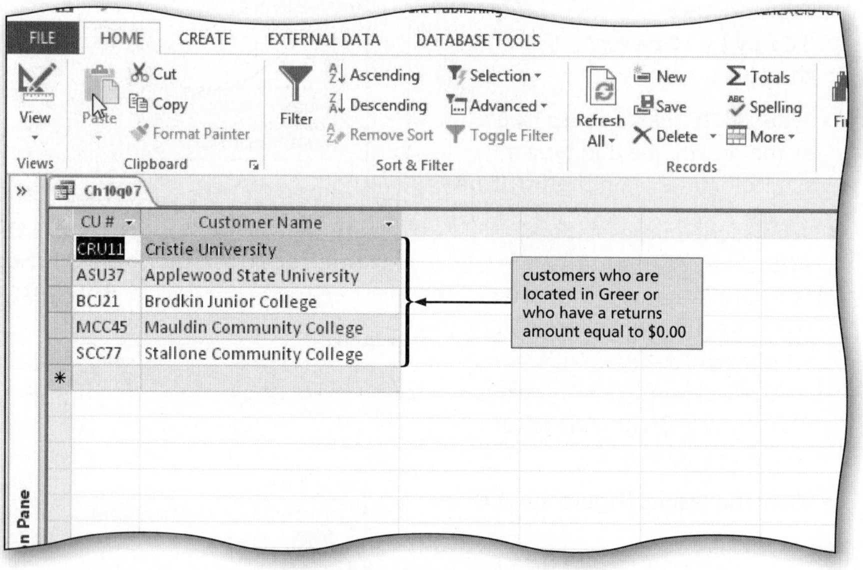

Figure 10–13 (b) Results

To Use NOT in a Criterion

Why? You can negate any criterion by preceding the criterion with the word NOT. The following steps use NOT in a criterion to list the numbers and names of the customers of Bavant Publishing not located in Greer.

1

- Return to SQL view and delete the previous query.
- Type `SELECT [Customer Number],[Customer Name],[City]` as the first line of the command.
- Type `FROM [Customer]` as the second line.
- Type `WHERE NOT [City]='Greer'` as the third line and type a semicolon (`;`) on the fourth line.
- View the results (Figure 10–14).

2

- Save the query as Ch10q09.

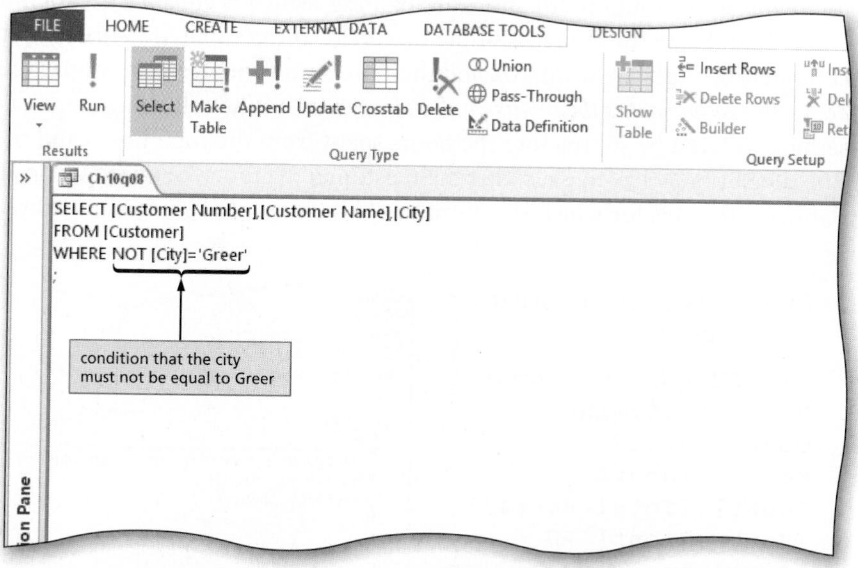

Figure 10–14 (a) Query to List the Customer Number, Customer Name, and City for Those Customers Whose City is not Greer

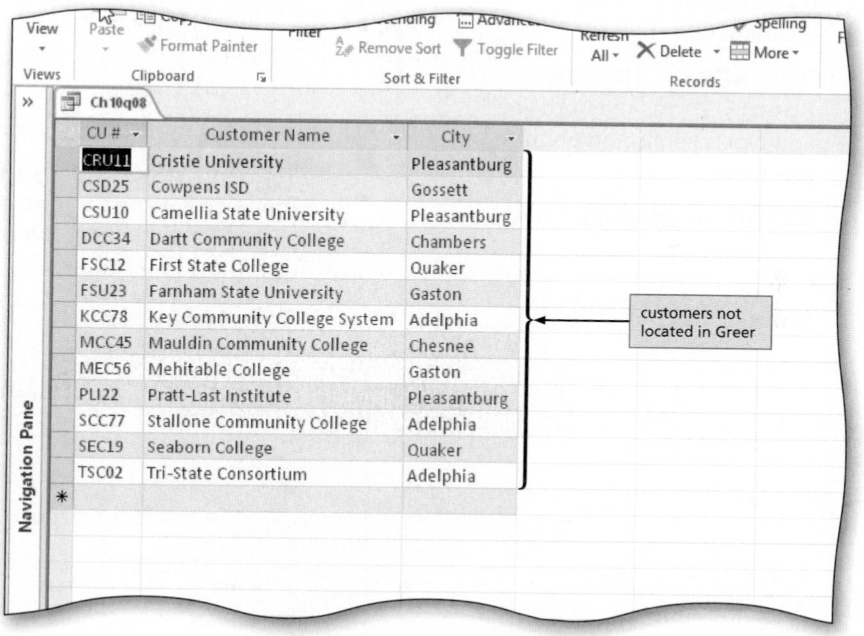

CU #	Customer Name	City
CRU11	Cristie University	Pleasantburg
CSD25	Cowpens ISD	Gossett
CSU10	Camellia State University	Pleasantburg
DCC34	Dartt Community College	Chambers
FSC12	First State College	Quaker
FSU23	Farnham State University	Gaston
KCC78	Key Community College System	Adelphia
MCC45	Mauldin Community College	Chesnee
MEC56	Mehitable College	Gaston
PLI22	Pratt-Last Institute	Pleasantburg
SCC77	Stallone Community College	Adelphia
SEC19	Seaborn College	Quaker
TSC02	Tri-State Consortium	Adelphia

Figure 10–14 (b) Results

To Use a Computed Field

Just as with queries created in Design view, you can include fields in queries that are not in the database, but that can be computed from fields that are. Such a field is called a **computed** or **calculated field**. Computations can involve addition (+), subtraction (-), multiplication (*), or division (/). The query in the following steps computes the hours remaining, which is equal to the total hours minus the hours spent.

To indicate the contents of the new field (the computed field), you can name the field by following the computation with the word, AS, and then the name you want to assign the field. ***Why?*** *Assigning the field a descriptive name makes the results much more readable.* The following steps calculate the hours remaining for each seminar offered by subtracting the hours spent from the total hours and then assigning the name Remaining to the calculation. The steps also list the Customer Number, Seminar Code, Total Hours, and Hours Spent for all seminar offerings for which the number of hours spent is greater than 0.

1

- Return to SQL view and delete the previous query.
- Type `SELECT [Customer Number],[Seminar Code],[Total Hours],[Hours Spent],[Total Hours]-[Hours Spent] AS [Remaining]` as the first line of the command.
- Type `FROM [Seminar Offerings]` as the second line.
- Type `WHERE [Hours Spent]>0` as the third line and type a semicolon on the fourth line.
- View the results (Figure 10–15).

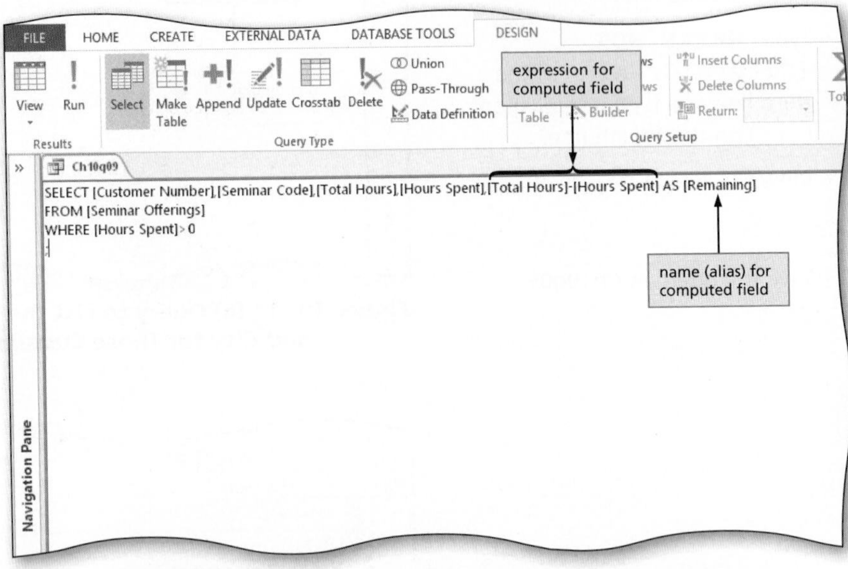

Figure 10–15 (a) Query to list the Customer Number, Seminar Code, Hours Spent, and Hours Remaining for Those Seminar Offerings on Which Hours Spent is Greater than 0

2

- Save the query as Ch10q10.

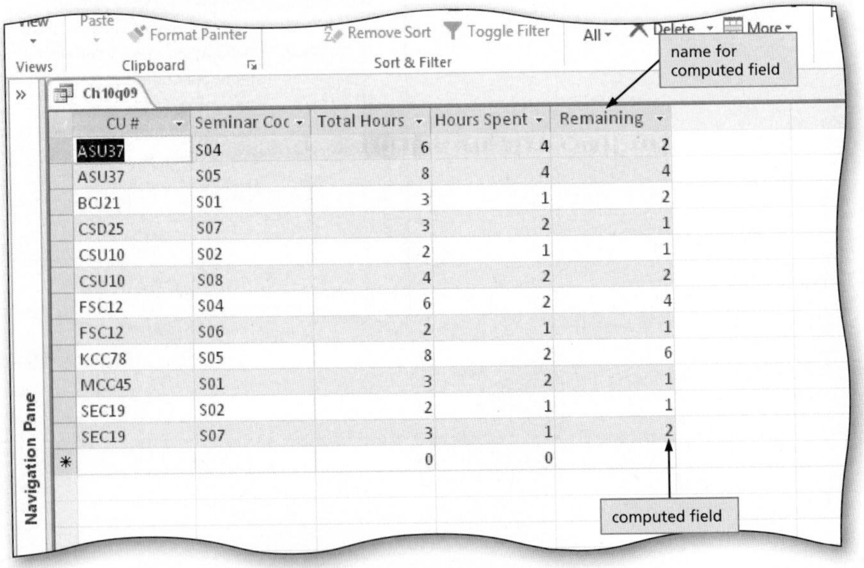

CU #	Seminar Coc	Total Hours	Hours Spent	Remaining
ASU37	S04	6	4	2
ASU37	S05	8	4	4
BCJ21	S01	3	1	2
CSD25	S07	3	2	1
CSU10	S02	2	1	1
CSU10	S08	4	2	2
FSC12	S04	6	2	4
FSC12	S06	2	1	1
KCC78	S05	8	2	6
MCC45	S01	3	2	1
SEC19	S02	2	1	1
SEC19	S07	3	1	2
*		0	0	

Figure 10–15 (b) Results

Sorting

Sorting in SQL follows the same principles as when using Design view to specify sorted query results, employing a sort key as the field on which data is to be sorted. SQL uses major and minor sort keys when sorting on multiple fields. By following a sort key with the word DESC with no comma in between, you can specify descending sort order. If you do not specify DESC, the data will be sorted in ascending order.

To sort the output, you include an **ORDER BY clause**, which consists of the words ORDER BY followed by the sort key. If there are two sort keys, the major sort key is listed first. Queries that you construct in Design view require that the major sort key is to the left of the minor sort key in the list of fields to be included. In SQL, there is no such restriction. The fields to be included in the query are in the SELECT clause, and the fields to be used for sorting are in the ORDER BY clause. The two clauses are totally independent.

BTW
SELECT clause
When you enter field names in a SELECT clause, you do not need to enter a space after the comma. Access inserts a space after the comma when you save the query and close it. When you re-open the query in SQL view, a space will appear after each comma that separates fields in the SELECT clause.

To Sort the Results on a Single Field

1 SQL VIEW | 2 SIMPLE CRITERIA | 3 COMPOUND CRITERIA | **4 SORT RESULTS**
5 GROUP RESULTS | 6 JOIN TABLES | 7 USE SUBQUERY | 8 UPDATE DATA

The following steps list the customer number, name, amount paid, current due, and book rep number for all customers sorted by customer name. ***Why?*** *Bavant Publishing wants this data to appear in alphabetical order by customer name.*

1

- Return to SQL view and delete the previous query.
- Type `SELECT [Customer Number], [Customer Name], [Amount Paid], [Current Due], [Book Rep Number]` as the first line of the command.
- Type `FROM [Customer]` as the second line.
- Type `ORDER BY [Customer Name]` as the third line and type a semicolon (`;`) on the fourth line.

Q&A What is the purpose of the ORDER BY clause?
The ORDER BY clause indicates that the results of the query are to be sorted by the indicated field or fields. This ORDER BY clause, for example, would cause the results to be sorted by Customer Name.

- View the results (Figure 10–16).

2

- Save the query as Ch10q11.

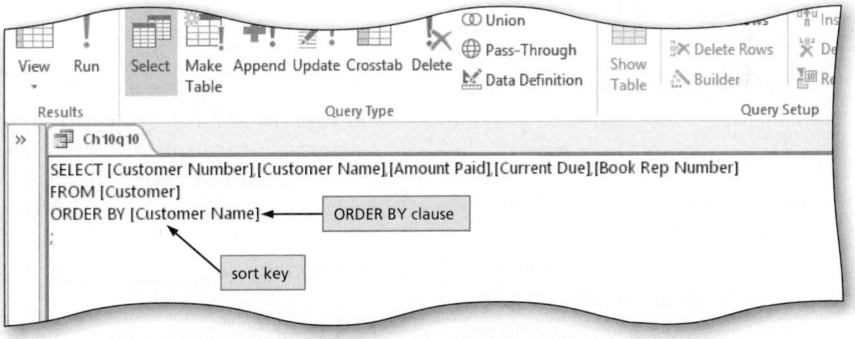

Figure 10–16 (a) Query to List the Customer Number, Customer Name, Amount Paid, Current Due, and Book Rep Number for All Customers with the Results Sorted by Customer Name

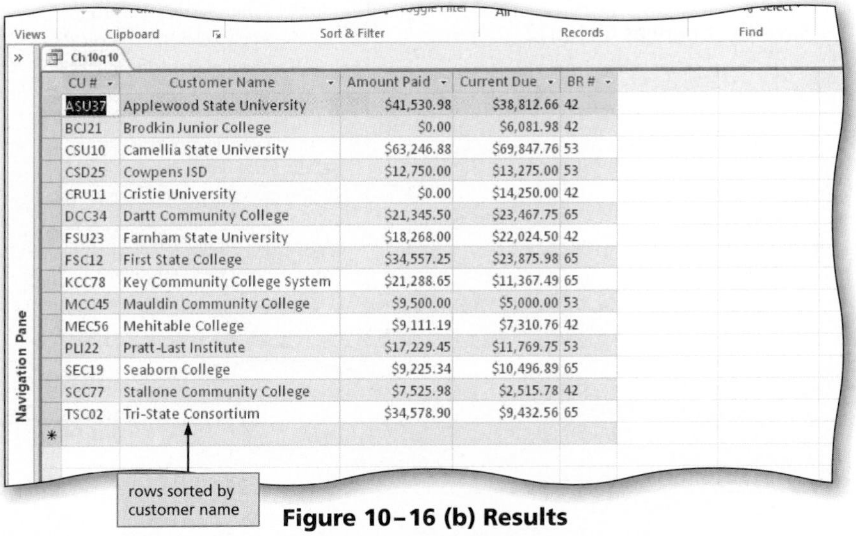

Views
Clipboard
Sort & Filter
Records
Find
Ch10q10
Navigation Pane
CU # | Customer Name | Amount Paid | Current Due | BR #
ASU37 | Applewood State University | $41,530.98 | $38,812.66 | 42
BCJ21 | Brodkin Junior College | $0.00 | $6,081.98 | 42
CSU10 | Camellia State University | $63,246.88 | $69,847.76 | 53
CSD25 | Cowpens ISD | $12,750.00 | $13,275.00 | 53
CRU11 | Cristie University | $0.00 | $14,250.00 | 42
DCC34 | Dartt Community College | $21,345.50 | $23,467.75 | 65
FSU23 | Farnham State University | $18,268.00 | $22,024.50 | 42
FSC12 | First State College | $34,557.25 | $23,875.98 | 65
KCC78 | Key Community College System | $21,288.65 | $11,367.49 | 65
MCC45 | Mauldin Community College | $9,500.00 | $5,000.00 | 53
MEC56 | Mehitable College | $9,111.19 | $7,310.76 | 42
PLI22 | Pratt-Last Institute | $17,229.45 | $11,769.75 | 53
SEC19 | Seaborn College | $9,225.34 | $10,496.89 | 65
SCC77 | Stallone Community College | $7,525.98 | $2,515.78 | 42
TSC02 | Tri-State Consortium | $34,578.90 | $9,432.56 | 65
rows sorted by customer name

Figure 10–16 (b) Results

To Sort the Results on Multiple Fields

1 SQL VIEW | 2 SIMPLE CRITERIA | 3 COMPOUND CRITERIA | 4 SORT RESULTS
5 GROUP RESULTS | 6 JOIN TABLES | 7 USE SUBQUERY | 8 UPDATE DATA

The following steps list the customer number, name, amount paid, current due, and book rep number for all customers. The data is to be sorted on multiple fields. ***Why?*** *Bavant wants the data to be sorted by amount paid within book rep number. That is, the data is to be sorted by book rep number. In addition, within the group of customers that have the same rep number, the data is to be sorted further by amount paid.* To accomplish this sort, the Book Rep Number field is the major (primary) sort key and the Amount Paid field is the minor (secondary) sort key.

1

- Return to SQL view and delete the previous query.
- Type `SELECT [Customer Number],[Customer Name],[Amount Paid],[Current Due],[Book Rep Number]` as the first line of the command.
- Type `FROM [Customer]` as the second line.
- Type `ORDER BY [Book Rep Number],[Amount Paid]` as the third line and type a semicolon (`;`) on the fourth line.
- View the results (Figure 10–17).

Experiment

- Try reversing the order of the sort keys to see the effect. Also, try to specify descending order for one or both of the sort keys. In each case, view the results to see the effect of your choice. When finished, return to the original sorting order for both fields.

2

- Save the query as Ch10q12.

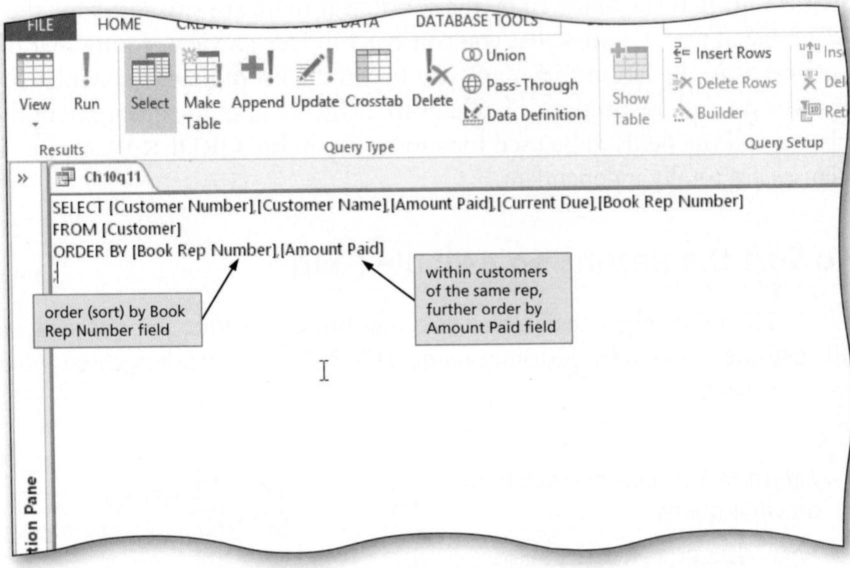

Figure 10–17 (a) Query to List the Customer Number, Customer Name, Amount Paid, Current Due, and Book Rep Number for All Customers with Results Sorted by Book Rep Number and Amount Paid

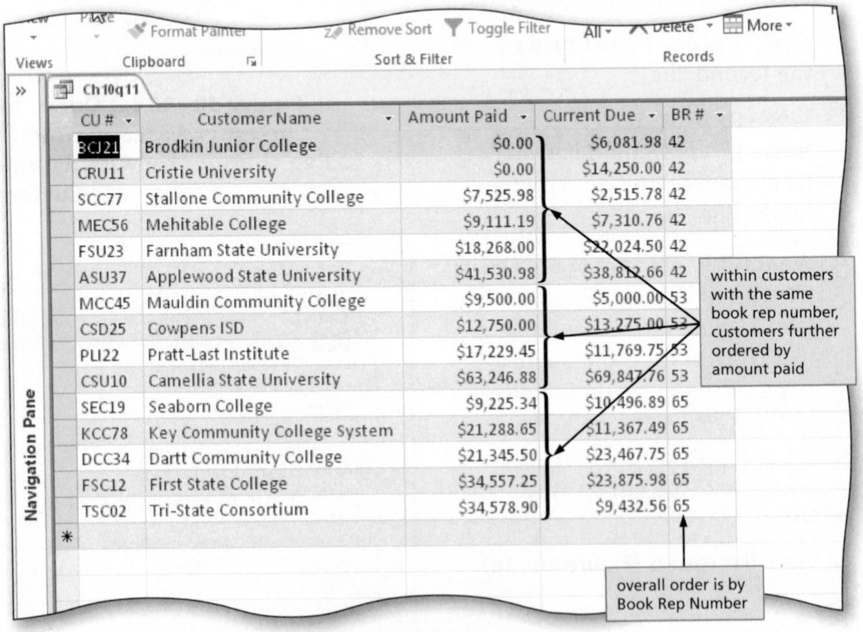

Figure 10–17 (b) Results

To Sort the Results in Descending Order

Why? *To show the results in high-to-low rather than low-to-high order, you sort in descending order.* To sort in descending order, you follow the name of the sort key with the DESC operator. The following steps list the customer number, name, amount paid, current due, and book rep number for all customers. Bavant wants the data to be sorted by descending current due within book rep number. That is, within the customers having the same rep number, the data is to be sorted further by current due in descending order.

1

- Return to SQL view and delete the previous query.
- Type **`SELECT [Customer Number],[Customer Name],[Amount Paid],[Current Due],[Book Rep Number]`** as the first line of the command.
- Type **`FROM [Customer]`** as the second line.
- Type **`ORDER BY [Book Rep Number],[Current Due] DESC`** as the third line and type a semicolon (**;**) on the fourth line.

Q&A Do I need a comma between [Current Due] and DESC?

No. In fact, you must not use a comma. If you did, SQL would assume that you want a field called DESC. Without the comma, SQL knows that the DESC indicates that the sort on the [Current Due] field is to be in descending order.

- View the results (Figure 10–18).

2

- Save the query as Ch10q13.

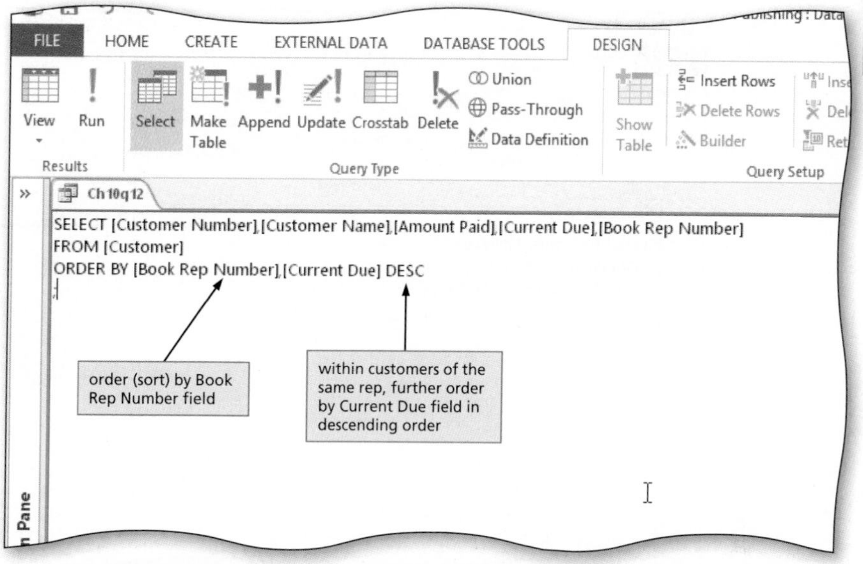

Figure 10–18 (a) Query to List the Customer Number, Customer Name, Amount Paid, Current Due, and Book Rep Number for All Customers with Results Sorted by Book Rep Number and Descending Current Due

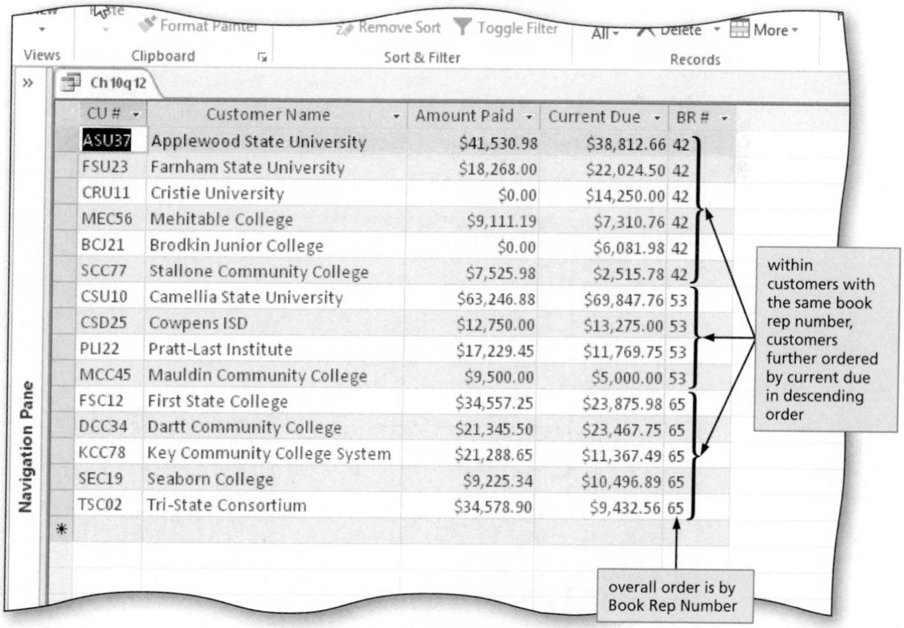

Figure 10–18 (b) Results

To Omit Duplicates When Sorting

When you sort data, duplicates normally are included. For example, the query in Figure 10–19 sorts the customer numbers in the Seminar Offerings table. Because any customer can be offered many seminars at a time, customer numbers can be included more than once. Bavant does not find this useful and would like to eliminate these duplicate customer numbers. To do so, use the DISTINCT operator in the query. ***Why?*** *The DISTINCT operator eliminates duplicate values in the results of a query.* To use the operator, you follow the word DISTINCT with the field name in parentheses.

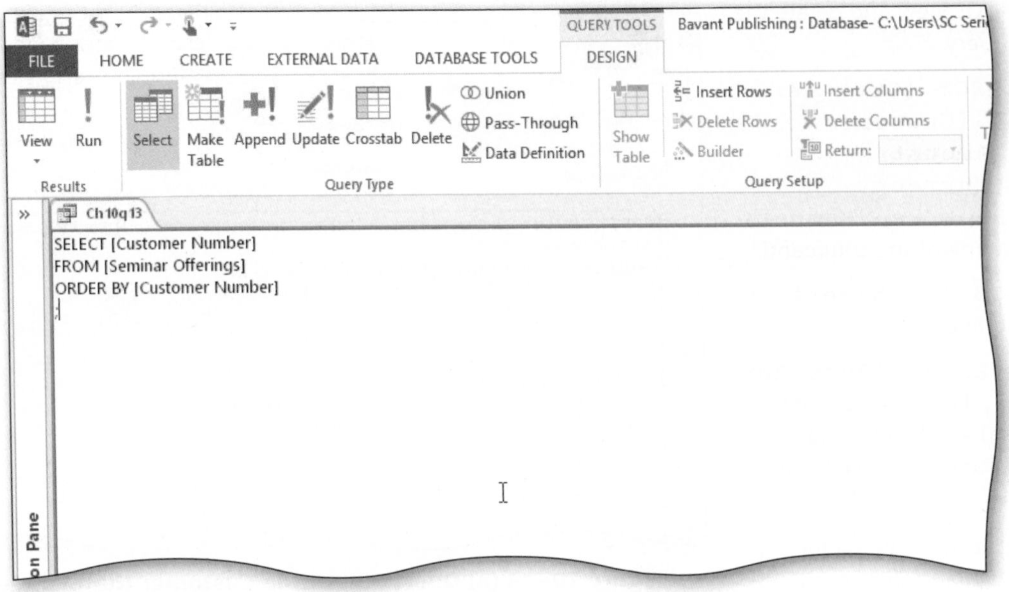

Figure 10–19 (a) Query to List the Customer Numbers in the Seminar Offerings Table Sorted by Customer Number

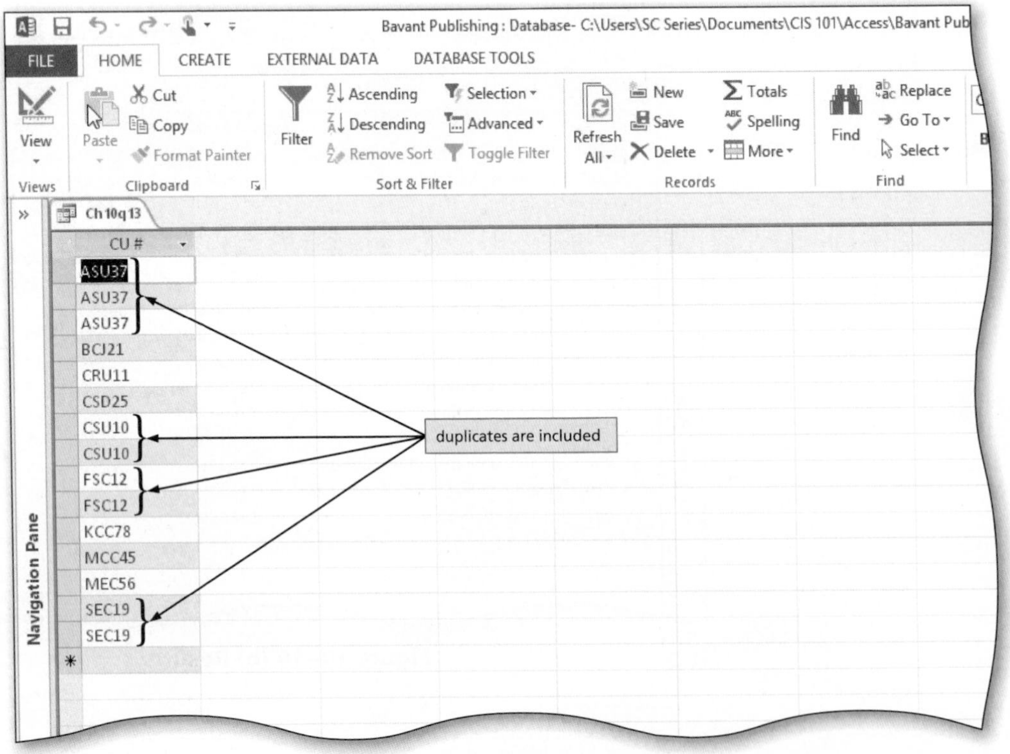

Figure 10–19 (b) Results

The following steps display the customer numbers in the Seminar Offerings table in customer number order, but with any duplicates removed.

1

- Return to SQL view and delete the previous query.
- Type `SELECT DISTINCT([Customer Number])` as the first line of the command.
- Type `FROM [Seminar Offerings]` as the second line.
- Type `ORDER BY [Customer Number]` as the third line and type a semicolon (`;`) on the fourth line.
- View the results (Figure 10–20).

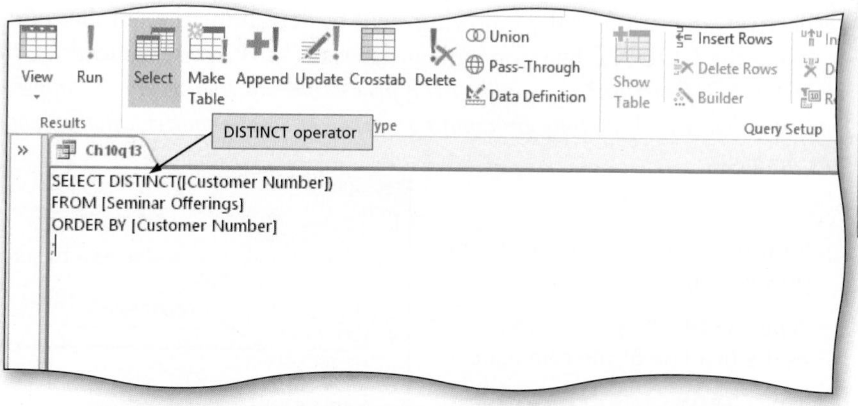

Figure 10–20 (a) Query to List the Customer Numbers in the Seminar Offerings Table Sorted by Customer Number Ensuring That No Customer Number is Listed More Than Once

2

- Save the query as Ch10q14. Return to the query.

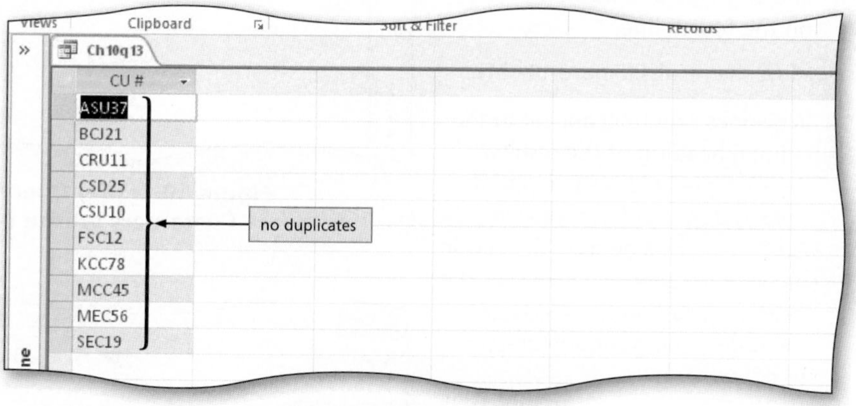

Figure 10–20 (b) Results

CONSIDER THIS

How do you determine sorting when creating a query?

Examine the query or request to see if it contains words such as *order* or *sort* that would imply that the order of the query results is important. If so, you need to sort the query.

Determine whether data is to be sorted. Examine the requirements for the query looking for words like *sorted by*, *ordered by*, *arranged by*, and so on.

Determine sort keys. Look for the fields that follow sorted by, ordered by, or any other words that signify sorting. If the requirements for the query include the phrase, ordered by customer name, then Customer Name is a sort key.

If there is more than one sort key, determine which one will be the major sort key and which will be the minor sort key. Look for words that indicate which field is more important. For example, if the requirements indicate that the results are to be ordered by amount paid within book rep number, Book Rep Number is the more important sort key.

Break Point: If you wish to stop working through the chapter at this point, you can close Access now. You can resume the project later by starting Access, opening the database called Bavant Publishing, creating a new query in SQL view, and continuing to follow the steps from this location forward.

To Use a Built-In Function

SQL has built-in functions, also called aggregate functions, to perform various calculations. Similar to the functions you learned about in Chapter 2, these functions in SQL are COUNT, SUM, AVG, MAX, and MIN, respectively. Bavant uses the following steps to determine the number of customers assigned to rep number 42 by using the COUNT function with an asterisk (*). ***Why use an asterisk rather than a field name when using the COUNT function?*** *You could select a field name, but that would be cumbersome and imply that you were just counting that field. You really are counting records. It doesn't matter whether you are counting names or street addresses or anything else.*

1

- Return to SQL view and delete the previous query.
- Type `SELECT COUNT(*)` as the first line of the command.
- Type `FROM [Customer]` as the second line.
- Type `WHERE [Book Rep Number]='42'` as the third line and type a semicolon (`;`) on the fourth line.
- View the results (Figure 10–21).

Q&A Why does Expr1000 appear in the column heading of the results?
Because the field is a computed field, it does not have a name. Access assigns a generic expression name. You can add a name for the field by including the AS clause in the query, and it is good practice to do so.

2

- Save the query as Ch10q15.

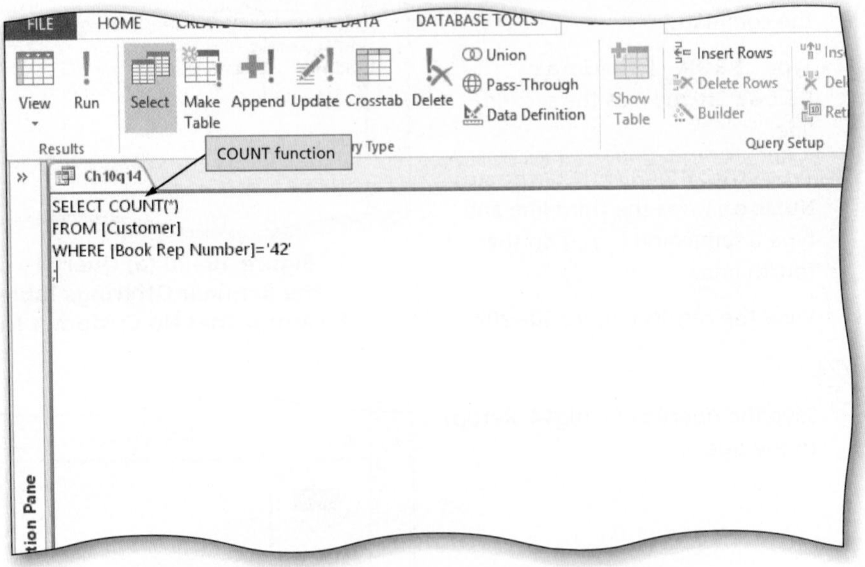

Figure 10–21 (a) Query to Count the Number of Customers Whose Book Rep Number is 42

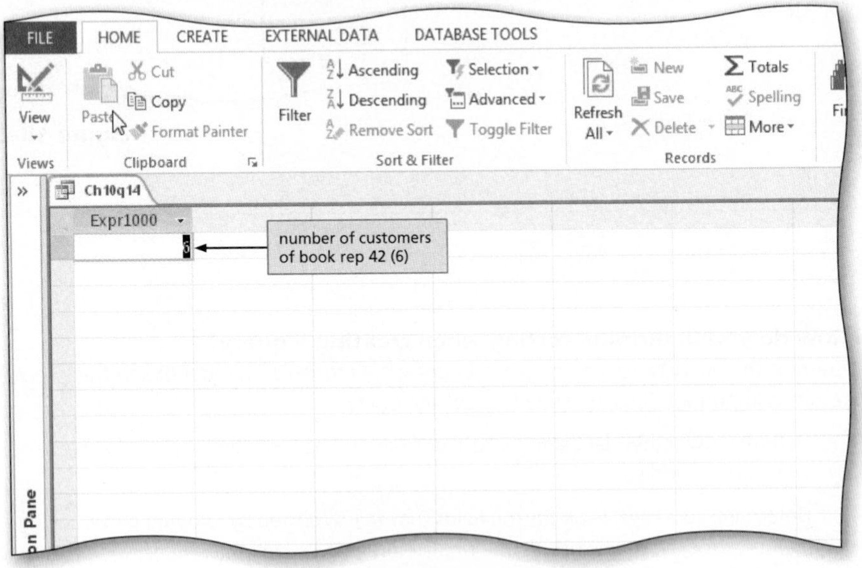

Figure 10–21 (b) Results

To Assign a Name to the Results of a Function

Bavant Publishing would prefer to have a more meaningful name than Expr1000 for the results of counting customer numbers. ***Why?*** *The default name of Expr1000 does not describe the meaning of the calculation.* Fortunately, just as you can assign a name to a calculation that includes two fields, you can assign a name to the results of a function. To do so, follow the expression for the function with the word AS and then the name to be assigned to the result. The following steps assign the name, Customer Count, to the expression in the previous query.

1

- Return to SQL view and delete the previous query.
- Type `SELECT COUNT(*) AS [Customer Count]` as the first line of the command.
- Type `FROM [Customer]` as the second line.
- Type `WHERE [Book Rep Number]='42'` as the third line and type a semicolon (`;`) on the fourth line.
- View the results (Figure 10–22).

2

- Save the query as Ch10q16.

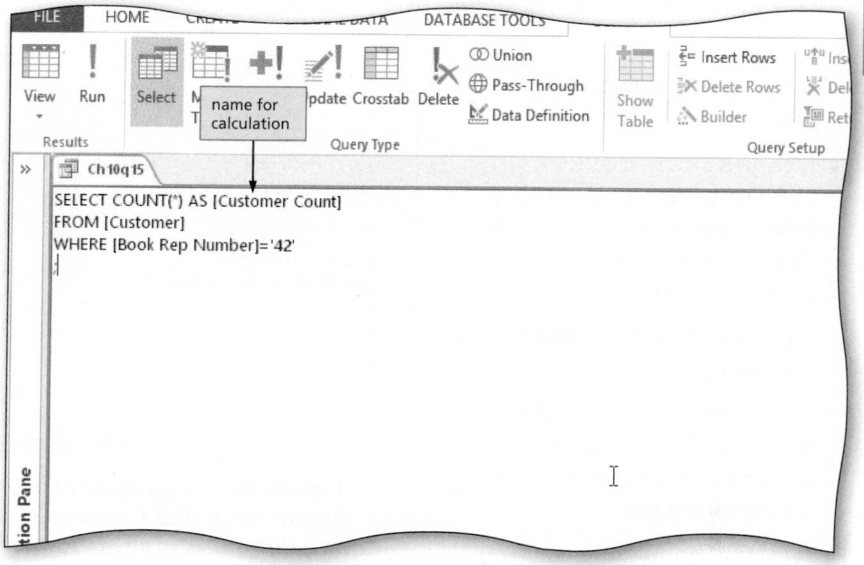

Figure 10–22 (a) Query to Count the Number of Customers Whose Book Rep Number is 42 With Results Called Customer Count

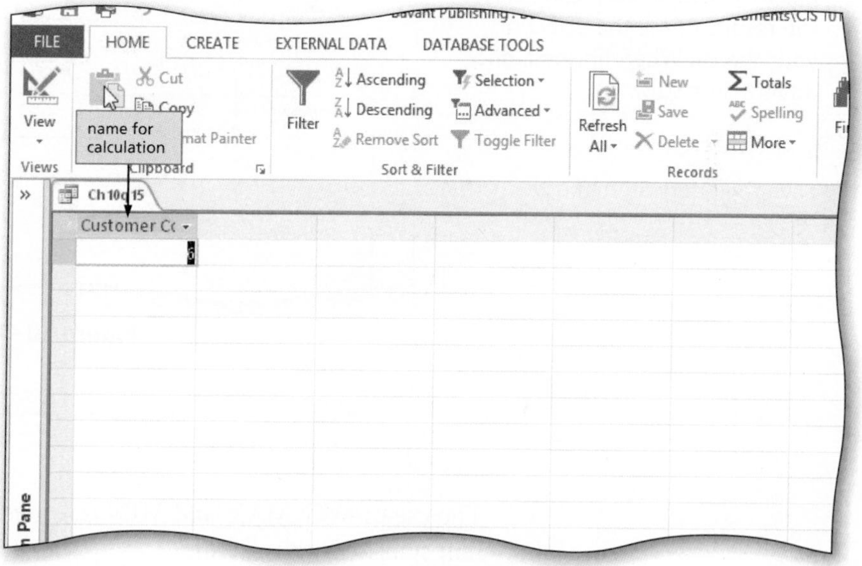

Figure 10–22 (b) Results

To Use Multiple Functions in the Same Command

There are two differences between COUNT and SUM, other than the obvious fact that they are computing different statistics. First, in the case of SUM, you must specify the field for which you want a total, instead of an asterisk (*); second, the field must be numeric. ***Why?*** *If the field is not numeric, it does not make sense to calculate a sum. You could not calculate a sum of names or addresses, for example.* The following steps use both the COUNT and SUM functions to count the number of customers whose book rep number is 42 and calculate the sum (total) of their amounts paid. The steps use the word AS to name COUNT(*) as Customer Count and to name SUM([Amount Paid]) as Sum Paid.

1

- Return to SQL view and delete the previous query.
- Type `SELECT COUNT(*) AS [Customer Count], SUM([Amount Paid]) AS [Sum Paid]` as the first line of the command.
- Type `FROM [Customer]` as the second line.
- Type `WHERE [Book Rep Number]='42'` as the third line and type a semicolon (`;`) on the fourth line.
- View the results (Figure 10–23).

Experiment

- Try using the other functions in place of SUM. In each case, view the results to see the effect of your choice. When finished, once again select SUM.

2

- Save the query as Ch10q17.

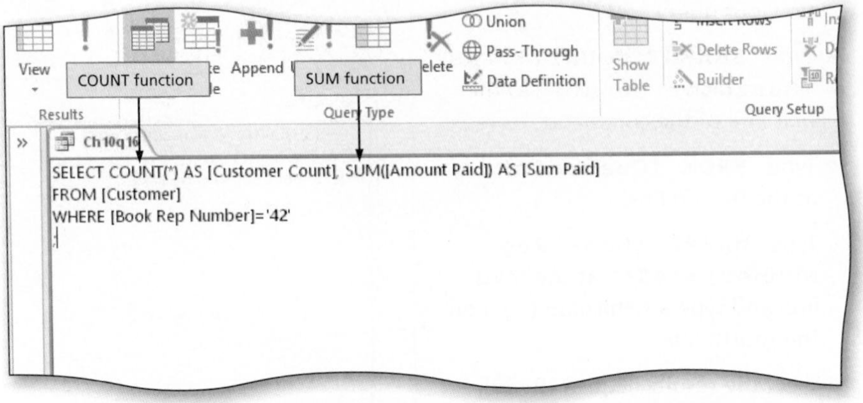

Figure 10–23 (a) Query to Count the Number of Customers Whose Book Rep Number is 42 With Results Called Customer Count and Calculate the Sum of Amount Paid With Results Called Sum Paid

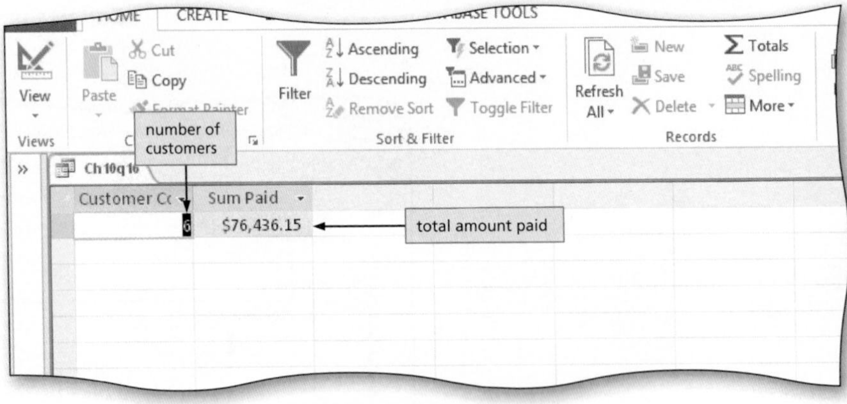

Figure 10–23 (b) Results

The use of AVG, MAX, and MIN is similar to SUM. The only difference is that a different statistic is calculated.

Grouping

Recall that grouping means creating groups of records that share some common characteristic. When you group rows, any calculations indicated in the SELECT command are performed for the entire group.

To Use Grouping

1 SQL VIEW | 2 SIMPLE CRITERIA | 3 COMPOUND CRITERIA | 4 SORT RESULTS
5 GROUP RESULTS | 6 JOIN TABLES | 7 USE SUBQUERY | 8 UPDATE DATA

Bavant Publishing wants to calculate the totals of the Amount Paid field, called Sum Paid, and the Current Due field, called Sum Due, for the customers of each rep. To calculate the totals, the command will include the calculations, SUM([Amount Paid]) and SUM([Current Due]). To get totals for the customers of each rep, the command also will include a **GROUP BY clause**, which consists of the words, GROUP BY, followed by the field used for grouping, in this case, Book Rep Number. ***Why?*** *Including GROUP BY Book Rep Number will cause the customers for each rep to be grouped together; that is, all customers with the same book rep number will form a group. Any statistics, such as totals, appearing after the word SELECT will be calculated for each of these groups.* Using GROUP BY does not mean that the information will be sorted.

The following steps use the GROUP BY clause to produce the results Bavant wants. The steps also rename the total amount paid as Sum Paid and the total current due as Sum Due by including appropriate AS clauses; finally, the steps sort the records by book rep number.

1

- Return to SQL view and delete the previous query.
- Type `SELECT [Book Rep Number], SUM([Amount Paid]) AS [Sum Paid], SUM([Current Due]) AS [Sum Due]` as the first line of the command.
- Type `FROM [Customer]` as the second line.
- Type `GROUP BY [Book Rep Number]` as the third line.

Q&A What is the purpose of the GROUP BY clause?
The GROUP BY clause causes the rows to be grouped by the indicate field. With this GROUP BY clause, the rows will be grouped by Book Rep Number.

- Type `ORDER BY [Book Rep Number]` as the fourth line and type a semicolon (`;`) on the fifth line.
- View the results (Figure 10–24).

2

- Save the query as Ch10q18.

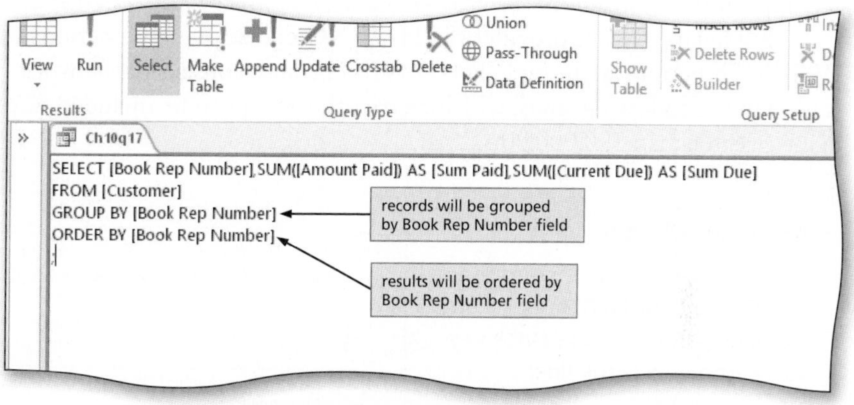

Figure 10–24 (a) Query to Group Records by Book Rep Number and List the Book Rep Number, the Sum of Amount Paid, and the Sum of Current Due

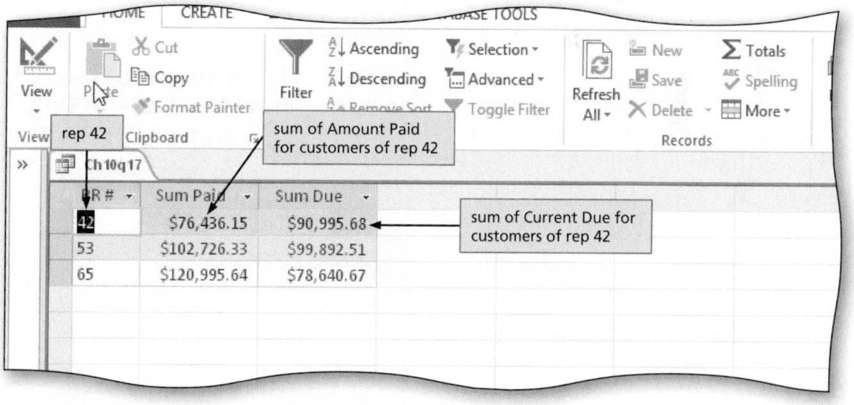

Figure 10–24 (b) Results

Grouping Requirements

When rows are grouped, one line of output is produced for each group. The only output that SQL can display is statistics that are calculated for the group or fields whose values are the same for all rows in a group. For example, when grouping rows by book rep number as in the previous query, it is appropriate to display the book rep number, because the number in one row in a group must be the same as the number in any other row in the group. It is appropriate to display the sum of the Amount Paid and Current Due fields because they are statistics calculated for the group. It would not be appropriate to display a customer number, however, because the customer number varies on the rows in a group; the rep is associated with many customers. SQL would not be able to determine which customer number to display for the group. SQL will display an error message if you attempt to display a field that is not appropriate, such as the customer number.

To Restrict the Groups that Appear

1 SQL VIEW | 2 SIMPLE CRITERIA | 3 COMPOUND CRITERIA | 4 SORT RESULTS
5 GROUP RESULTS | 6 JOIN TABLES | 7 USE SUBQUERY | 8 UPDATE DATA

In some cases, Bavant Publishing may want to display only certain groups. For example, management may want to display only those reps for whom the sum of the current due amounts are greater than $90,000.00. This restriction does not apply to individual rows, but instead to groups. You cannot use a WHERE clause to accomplish this restriction. ***Why?*** *WHERE applies only to rows, not groups.*

Fortunately, SQL provides the **HAVING clause**, which functions with groups similarly to the way WHERE functions with rows. The HAVING clause consists of the word HAVING followed by a criterion. It is used in the following steps, which restrict the groups to be included to those on which the sum of the current due is greater than $90,000.00.

1

- Return to SQL view.
- Tap or click the beginning of the fourth line (ORDER BY [Book Rep Number]) and press the ENTER key to insert a new blank line.
- Tap or click the beginning of the new blank line, and then type `HAVING SUM([Current Due])>90000` as the new fourth line.

Q&A What is the purpose of the HAVING clause?
The HAVING clause restricts the groups that will be included to only those satisfying the indicated criteria. With this clause, only groups on which the sum of the current due amount is greater than 90000 will be included.

- View the results (Figure 10–25).

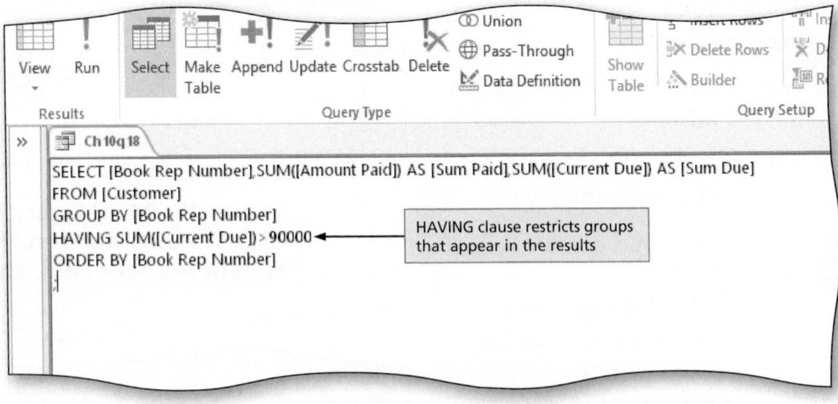

Figure 10–25 (a) Query to Restrict the Results of The Previous Query to Only Those Groups For Which the Sum of Current Due is More Than $90,000

2

- Save the query as Ch10q19.

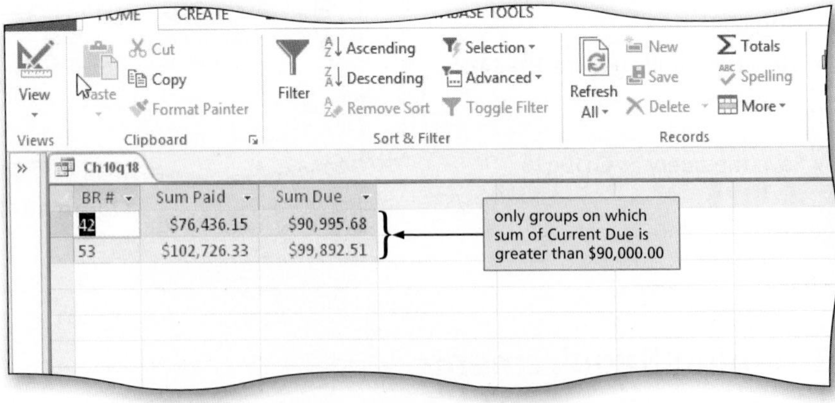

Figure 10–25 (b) Results

CONSIDER THIS

How do you determine grouping when creating a query?

Examine the query or request to determine whether records should be organized by some common characteristic.

Determine whether data is to be grouped in some fashion. Examine the requirements for the query to see if they contain individual rows or information about groups of rows.

Determine the field or fields on which grouping is to take place. By which field is the data to be grouped? Look to see if the requirements indicate a field along with several group calculations.

Determine which fields or calculations are appropriate to display. When rows are grouped, one line of output is produced for each group. The only output that can appear are statistics that are calculated for the group or fields whose values are the same for all rows in a group. For example, it would make sense to display the rep number, because all the customers in the group have the same rep number. It would not make sense to display the customer number, because the customer number will vary from one row in a group to another. SQL could not determine which customer number to display for the group.

Break Point: If you wish to stop working through the chapter at this point, you can close Access now. You can resume the project later by starting Access, opening the database called Bavant Publishing, creating a new query in SQL view, and continuing to follow the steps from this location forward.

Joining Tables

Many queries require data from more than one table. Just as with creating queries in Design view, SQL should provide a way to **join** tables, that is, to find rows in two tables that have identical values in matching fields. In SQL, this is accomplished through appropriate criteria following the word WHERE.

If you want to list the customer number, name, book rep number, first name of the rep, and last name of the rep for all customers, you need data from both the Customer and Book Rep tables. The Book Rep Number field is in both tables, the Customer Number field is only in the Customer table, and the First Name and Last Name fields are only in the Book Rep Table. You need to access both tables in your SQL query, as follows:

1. In the SELECT clause, you indicate all fields you want to appear.
2. In the FROM clause, you list all tables involved in the query.
3. In the WHERE clause, you give the criterion that will restrict the data to be retrieved to only those rows included in both of the two tables, that is, to the rows that have common values in matching fields.

BTW

Inner Joins

A join that compares the tables in the FROM clause and lists only those rows that satisfy the condition in the WHERE clause is called an inner join. SQL has an INNER JOIN clause. You could replace the query shown in Figure 10–26a on page AC 646 with FROM [Customer] INNER JOIN [Book Rep] ON [Customer].[Book Rep Number]=[Book Rep].[Book Rep Number] to get the same results as shown in Figure 10–26b.

Qualifying Fields

There is a problem in indicating the matching fields. The matching fields are both called Book Rep Number. There is a field in the Customer table called Book Rep Number, as well as a field in the Book Rep Table called Book Rep Number. In this case, if you only enter Book Rep Number, it will not be clear which table you mean. It is necessary to **qualify** Book Rep Number, that is, to specify to which field in which table you are referring. You do this by preceding the name of the field with the name of the table, followed by a period. The Book Rep Number field in the Customer table, for example, is [Customer].[Book Rep Number].

Whenever a query is potentially ambiguous, you must qualify the fields involved. It is permissible to qualify other fields as well, even if there is no confusion. For example, instead of [Customer Name], you could have typed [Customer].[Customer Name] to indicate the Customer Name field in the Customer table. Some people prefer to qualify all fields, and this is not a bad approach. In this text, you only will qualify fields when it is necessary to do so.

BTW

Qualifying Fields

There is no space on either side of the period that is used to separate the table name from the field name. Adding a space will result in an error message.

To Join Tables

1 SQL VIEW | 2 SIMPLE CRITERIA | 3 COMPOUND CRITERIA | 4 SORT RESULTS
5 GROUP RESULTS | 6 JOIN TABLES | 7 USE SUBQUERY | 8 UPDATE DATA

Bavant Publishing wants to list the customer number, customer name, book rep number, first name of the rep, and last name of the rep for all customers. The following steps create a query to join the tables. ***Why?** The data comes from two tables.* The steps also order the results by customer number.

1

- Return to SQL view and delete the previous query.
- Type `SELECT [Customer Number],[Customer Name],[Customer].[Book Rep Number],[First Name],[Last Name]` as the first line of the command.
- Type `FROM [Customer], [Book Rep]` as the second line.

Q&A Why does the FROM clause contain more than one table?
The query involves fields from both tables.

- Type `WHERE [Customer].[Book Rep Number]=[Book Rep].[Book Rep Number]` as the third line.

Q&A What is the purpose of the WHERE clause?
The WHERE clause specifies that only rows on which the rep numbers match are to be included. In this case, the rep number in the Customer table ([Customer].[Book Rep Number]) must be equal to the rep number in the Book Rep table ([Book Rep].[Book Rep Number]).

- Type `ORDER BY [Customer Number]` as the fourth line and type a semicolon (`;`) on the fifth line.
- View the results (Figure 10–26).

2

- Save the query as Ch10q20.

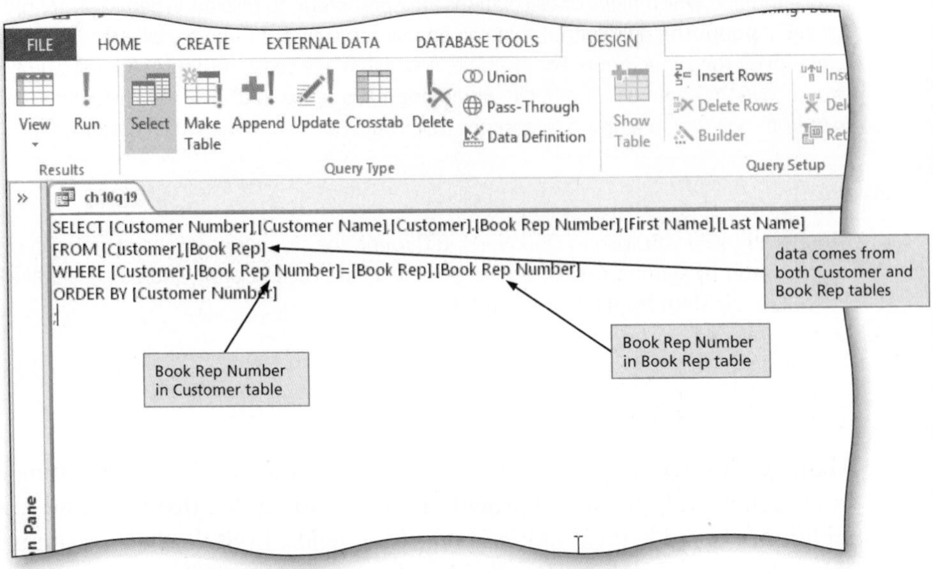

Figure 10–26 (a) Query to List the Customer Number, Customer Name, Book Rep Number, First Name, and Last Name for All Customers

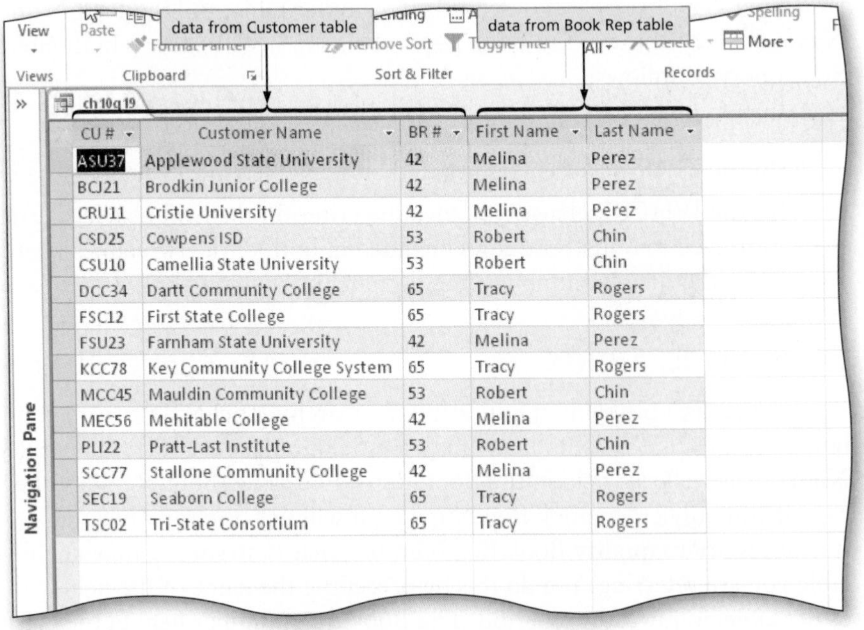

Figure 10–26 (b) Results

To Restrict the Records in a Join

You can restrict the records to be included in a join by creating a compound criterion. The compound criterion will include the criterion necessary to join the tables along with a criterion to restrict the records. The criteria will be connected with AND. ***Why?*** *Both the criterion that determines the records to be joined and the criterion to restrict the records must be true.*

Bavant would like to modify the previous query so that only reps whose start date is prior to May 1, 2014, are included. The following steps modify the previous query appropriately. The date is enclosed between number signs (#), which is the date format used in the Access version of SQL.

1

- Return to SQL view.
- Tap or click the end of line 1.
- Type `, [Start Date]` to add the Start Date field to the SELECT clause.
- Tap or click immediately prior to the ORDER BY clause.
- Type `AND [Start Date]<#5/1/2014#` and press the ENTER key.

Q&A Could I use other formats for the date in the criterion?
Yes. You could type #May 1, 2014# or #1-May-2014#.

- View the results (Figure 10–27).

2

- Save the query as Ch10q21.

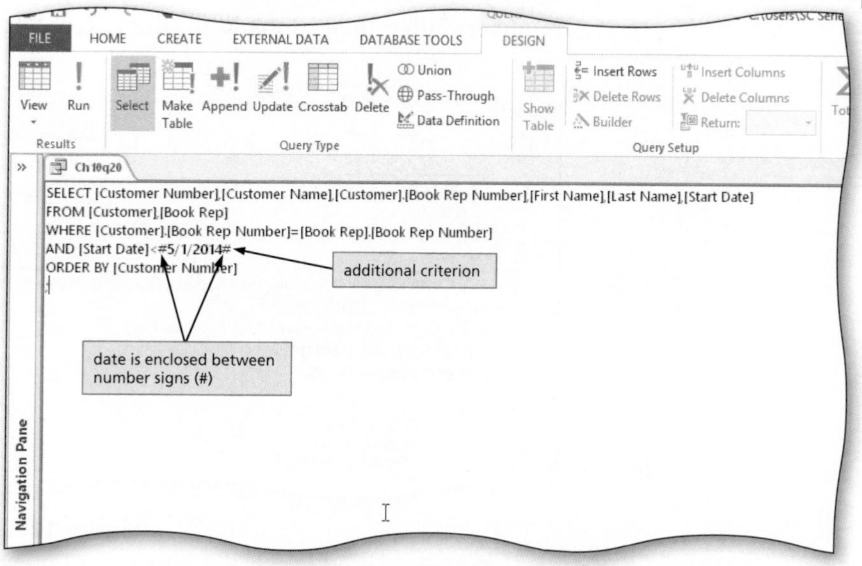

Figure 10–27 (a) Query to Restrict the Results of Previous Query to Only Those Customers Whose Start Date is Before 5/1/2014

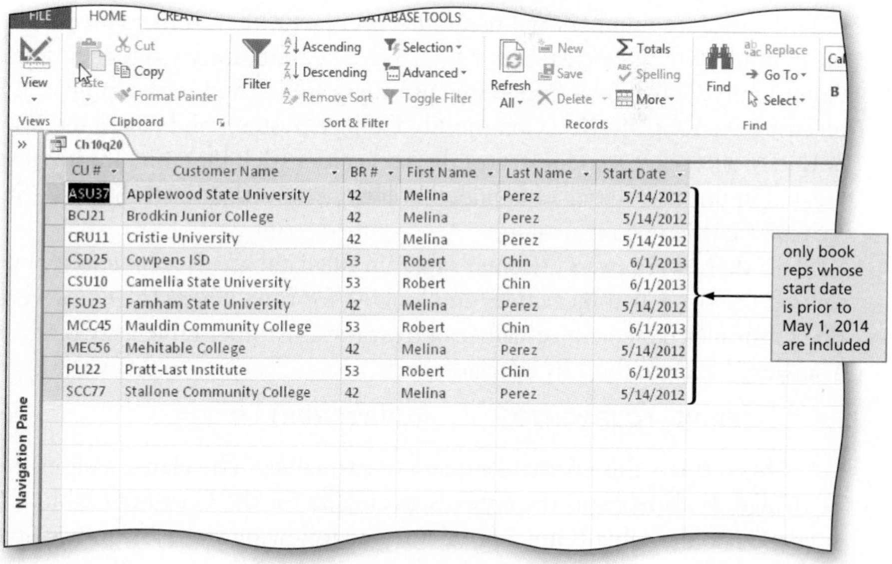

CU #	Customer Name	BR #	First Name	Last Name	Start Date
ASU37	Applewood State University	42	Melina	Perez	5/14/2012
BCJ21	Brodkin Junior College	42	Melina	Perez	5/14/2012
CRU11	Cristie University	42	Melina	Perez	5/14/2012
CSD25	Cowpens ISD	53	Robert	Chin	6/1/2013
CSU10	Camellia State University	53	Robert	Chin	6/1/2013
FSU23	Farnham State University	42	Melina	Perez	5/14/2012
MCC45	Mauldin Community College	53	Robert	Chin	6/1/2013
MEC56	Mehitable College	42	Melina	Perez	5/14/2012
PLI22	Pratt-Last Institute	53	Robert	Chin	6/1/2013
SCC77	Stallone Community College	42	Melina	Perez	5/14/2012

Figure 10–27 (b) Results

Aliases

When tables appear in the FROM clause, you can give each table an **alias**, or an alternative name, that you can use in the rest of the statement. You create an alias by typing the name of the table, pressing the SPACEBAR, and then typing the name of the alias. No commas or periods are necessary to separate the two names.

You can use an alias for two basic reasons: for simplicity or to join a table to itself. Figure 10–28 shows the same query as in Figure 10–27 on the previous page, but with the Customer table assigned the letter, C, as an alias and the Book Rep table assigned the letter, B. The query in Figure 10–28 is less complex. Whenever you need to qualify a field name, you can use the alias. Thus, you only need to type B.[Book Rep Number] rather than [Book Rep].[Book Rep Number].

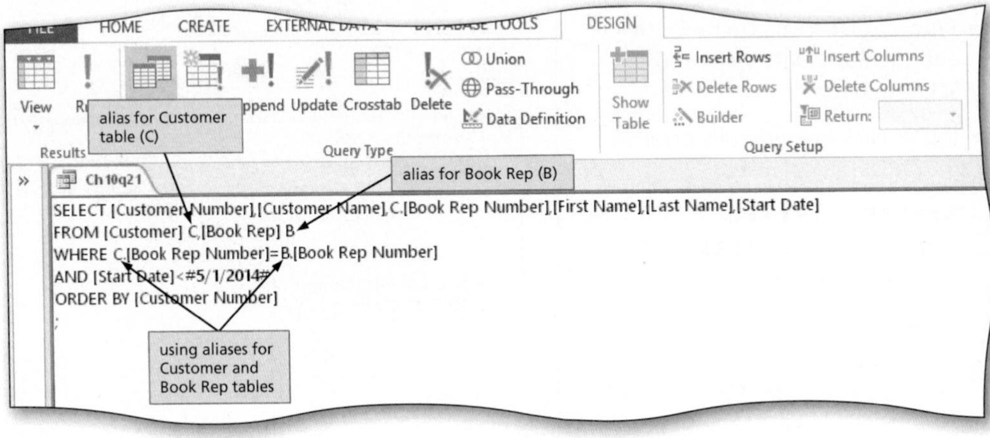

Figure 10–28

To Join a Table to Itself

1 SQL VIEW | 2 SIMPLE CRITERIA | 3 COMPOUND CRITERIA | 4 SORT RESULTS
5 GROUP RESULTS | 6 JOIN TABLES | 7 USE SUBQUERY | 8 UPDATE DATA

The other use of aliases is in joining a table to itself. An example of this type of join would enable Bavant to find customer numbers and names for every pair of customers located in the same city. One such pair, for example, would be customer KCC78 (Key Community College System) and customer SCC77 (Stallone Community College) because both customers are located in the same city (Adelphia). Another example would be customer KCC78 (Key Community College System) and customer TSC02 (Tri-State Consortium) because both customers are also located in the same city (Adelphia). Finally, because both SCC77 and TSC02 are located in the same city (Adelphia), there would be a third pair: SCC77 (Stallone Community College) and TSC02 (Tri-State Consortium).

If there were two Customer tables in the database, Bavant could obtain the results they want by simply joining the two Customer tables and looking for rows where the cities were the same. Even though there is only one Customer table, you actually can treat the Customer table as two tables in the query by creating two aliases. You would change the FROM clause to:

```
FROM [CUSTOMER] F, [CUSTOMER] S
```

SQL treats this clause as a query of two tables. The clause assigns the first Customer table the letter, F, as an alias. It also assigns the letter, S, as an alias for the Customer table. The fact that both tables are really the single Customer table is not a problem. The following steps assign two aliases (F and S) to the Customer table and list the customer number and customer name of both customers as well as the city in which both are located. The steps also include a criterion to ensure F.[Customer Number] < S.[Customer Number]. ***Why?*** *If you did not include this criterion, the query would contain four times as many results. On the first row in the results, for example, the first customer number is ASU37 and the second is BCJ21. Without this criterion, there would be a row on which both the first and second customer numbers are ASU37, a row on which both are BCJ21, and a row on which the first is BCJ21 and the second is ASU37. This criterion only selects the one row on which the first customer number (ASU37) is less than the second customer number (BCJ21).*

1

- Return to SQL view and delete the previous query.
- Type **SELECT F.[Customer Number],F.[Customer Name],S.[Customer Number],S.[Customer Name],F.[City]** as the first line of the command to select the fields to display in the query result.
- Type **FROM [Customer] F,[Customer] S** as the second line to create the aliases for the first and second Customer tables.
- Type **WHERE F.[City]=S.[City]** as the third line to indicate that the cities in each table must match.
- Type **AND F.[Customer Number]<S.[Customer Number]** as the fourth line to indicate that the customer number from the first table must be less than the customer number from the second table, and then type a semicolon (**;**) on the fifth line.
- View the results (Figure 10–29).

2

- Save the query as Ch10q22.

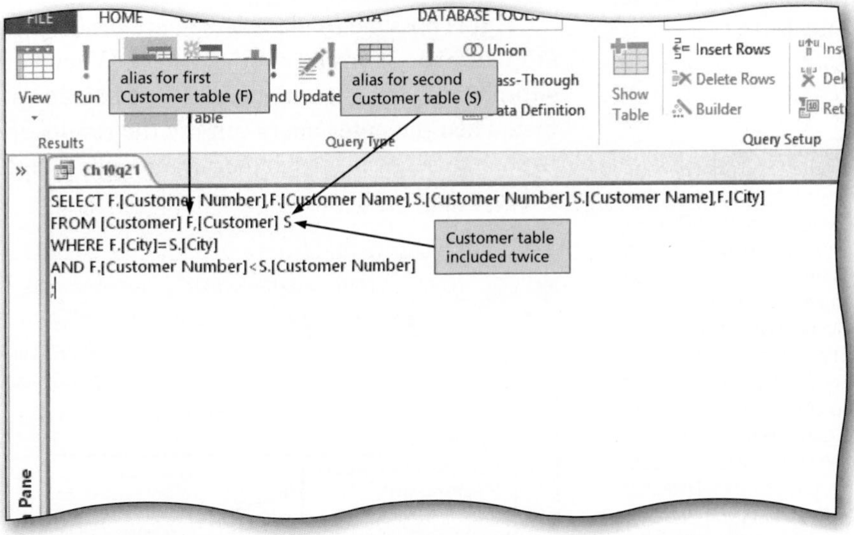

Figure 10–29 (a) Query to List the Customer Name and Customer Number For Pairs of Customers Located in the Same City

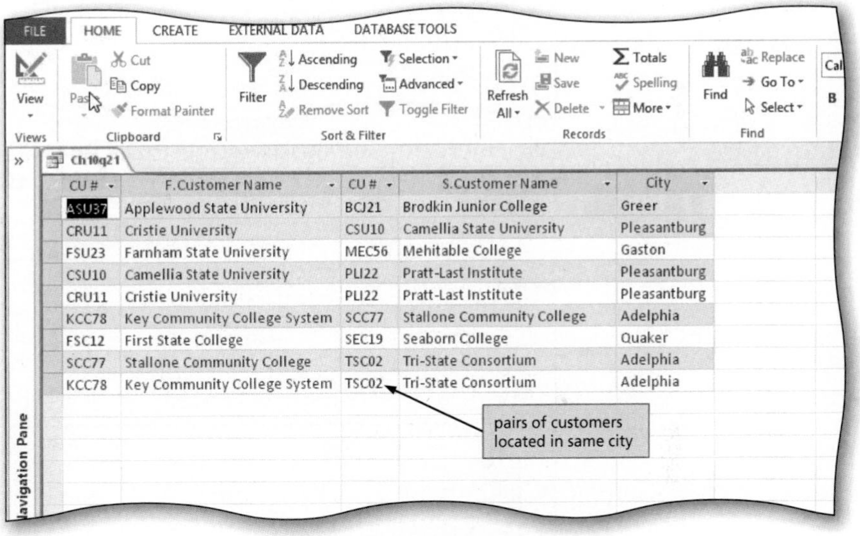

CU #	F.Customer Name	CU #	S.Customer Name	City
ASU37	Applewood State University	BCJ21	Brodkin Junior College	Greer
CRU11	Cristie University	CSU10	Camellia State University	Pleasantburg
FSU23	Farnham State University	MEC56	Mehitable College	Gaston
CSU10	Camellia State University	PLI22	Pratt-Last Institute	Pleasantburg
CRU11	Cristie University	PLI22	Pratt-Last Institute	Pleasantburg
KCC78	Key Community College System	SCC77	Stallone Community College	Adelphia
FSC12	First State College	SEC19	Seaborn College	Quaker
SCC77	Stallone Community College	TSC02	Tri-State Consortium	Adelphia
KCC78	Key Community College System	TSC02	Tri-State Consortium	Adelphia

Figure 10–29 (b) Results

CONSIDER THIS

How do you determine criteria when creating a query?

Examine the query or request to determine any restrictions or conditions that records must satisfy to be included in the results.

Determine the fields involved in the criteria. For any criterion, determine the fields that are included. Determine the data types for these fields. If the criterion uses a value that corresponds to a Text field, enclose the value in single quotation marks. If the criterion uses a date, enclose the value between number signs (for example, #4/15/2014#).

Determine comparison operators. When fields are being compared to other fields or to specific values, determine the appropriate comparison operator (equals, less than, greater than, and so on). If a wildcard is involved, then the query will use the LIKE operator.

Determine join criteria. If tables are being joined, determine the fields that must match.

Determine compound criteria. If more than one criterion is involved, determine whether all individual criteria are to be true, in which case you will use the AND operator, or whether only one individual criterion needs to be true, in which case you will use the OR operator.

BTW
Union, Pass-Through, and Data Definition Queries
There are three queries that cannot be created in Design view. When you tap or click the button on the ribbon for any of these three queries in Design view, the SQL view window opens. The Union query combines fields from more than one table into one query result set. The Pass-Through query enables you to send SQL commands directly to ODBC (Open Database Connectivity) databases using the ODBC database's SQL syntax. The Data Definition query allows you to create or alter database tables or create indexes in Access directly.

Subqueries

It is possible to place one query inside another. You will place the query shown in Figure 10–30 inside another query. When you have done so, it will be called a **subquery**, which is an inner query, contained within parentheses, that is evaluated first. Then the outer query can use the results of the subquery to find its results. In some cases, using a subquery can be the simplest way to produce the desired results, as illustrated in the next set of steps.

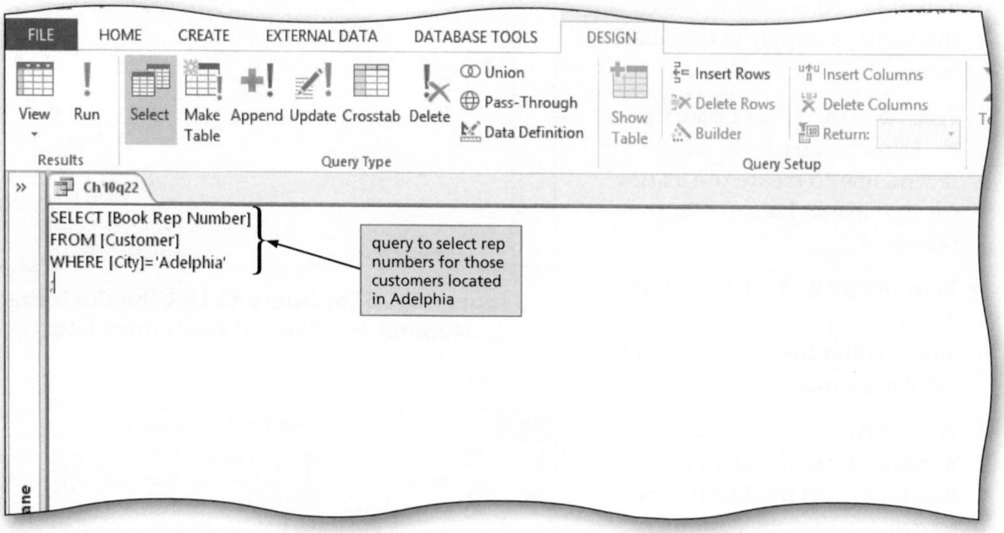

Figure 10–30 (a) Query to List the Book Rep Number For All Records In The Customer Table on Which the City is Adelphia

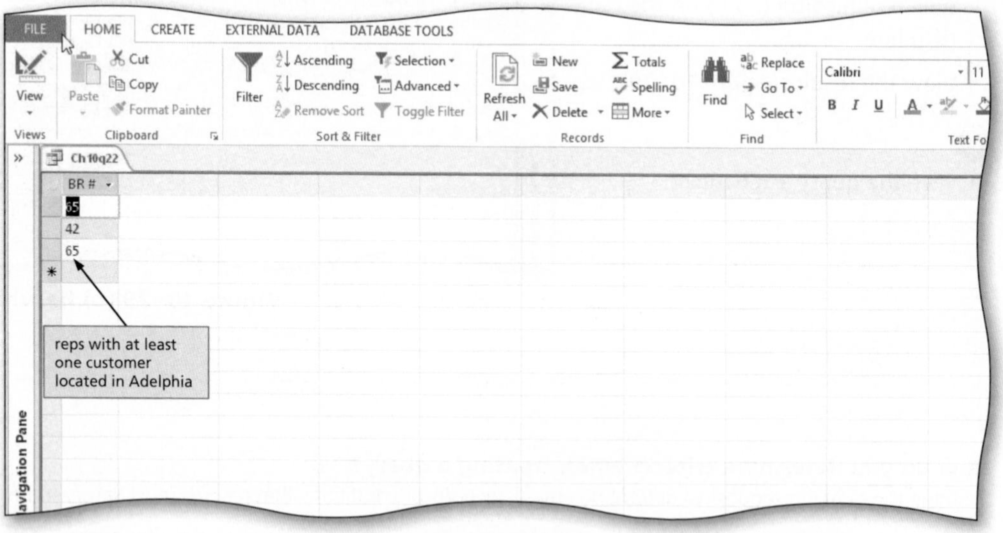

Figure 10–30 (b) Results

CONSIDER THIS

Why does book rep 65 appear twice?
The Bavant Publishing database includes two customers whose city is Adelphia and whose book rep number is 65. This is not a problem because in the next query it is only important what numbers are included, not how many times they appear. If you wanted the numbers only to appear once, you would use the order the results by Book Rep Number and use the DISTINCT operator.

To Use a Subquery

The following steps use the query shown in Figure 10–30 as a subquery. ***Why?*** *Bavant Publishing can use this query to select rep numbers for those reps who have at least one customer located in Adelphia.* After the subquery is evaluated, the outer query will select the rep number, first name, and last name for those reps whose rep number is in the list produced by the subquery.

1

- Return to SQL view and delete the previous query.
- Type `SELECT [Book Rep Number],[First Name],[Last Name]` as the first line of the command.
- Type `FROM [Book Rep]` as the second line.
- Type `WHERE [Book Rep Number] IN` as the third line.
- Type `(SELECT [Book Rep Number]` as the fourth line.
- Type `FROM [Customer]` as the fifth line.
- Type `WHERE [City]='Adelphia')` as the sixth line and type a semicolon (`;`) on the seventh line.
- View the results (Figure 10–31).

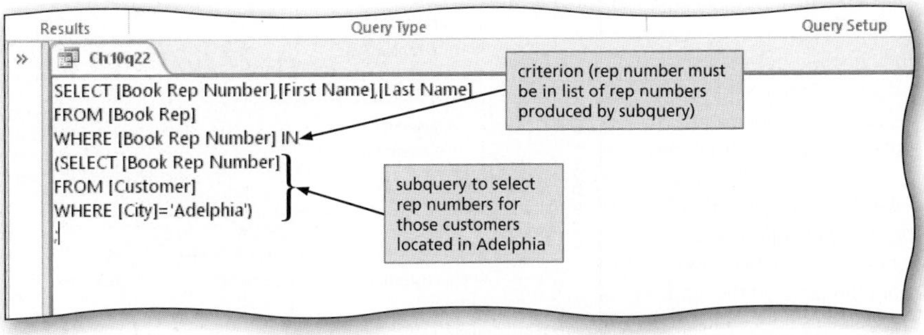

Figure 10–31 (a) Query to List Book Rep Number, First Name, and Last Name for All Book Reps Who Represent At Least One Customer Located in Adelphia

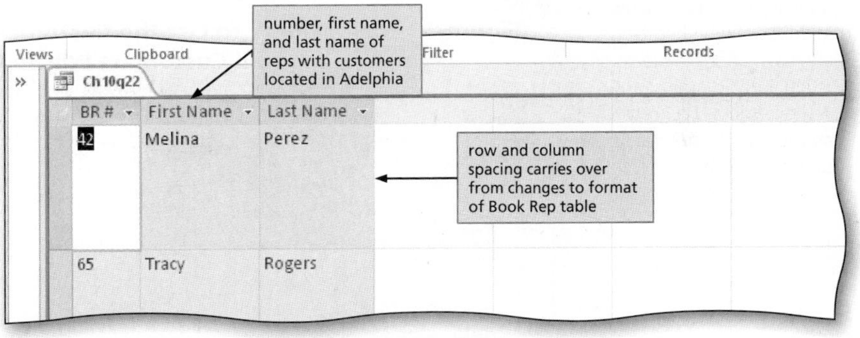

Figure 10–31 (b) Results

2

- Save the query as Ch10q23.

Using an IN Clause

The query in Figure 10–31 uses an IN clause with a subquery. You also can use an IN clause with a list as an alternative to an OR criterion when the OR criterion involves a single field. For example, to find customers whose city is Adelphia, Gaston, or Greer, the criterion using IN would be City IN ('Adelphia', 'Gaston', 'Greer'). The corresponding OR criterion would be City='Adelphia' OR City= 'Gaston' OR City= 'Greer'. The choice of which one to use is a matter of personal preference.

You also can use this type of IN clause when creating queries in Design view. To use the criterion in the previous paragraph, for example, include the City field in the design grid and enter the criterion in the Criteria row.

BTW

BETWEEN Operator
The BETWEEN operator allows you to search for a range of values in one field. For example, to find all customers whose amount paid is between $20,000.00 and $30,000.00, the WHERE clause would be WHERE [Amount Paid] BETWEEN 20000 AND 30000.

Comparison with Access-Generated SQL

When you create a query in Design view, Access automatically creates a corresponding SQL query that is similar to the queries you have created in this chapter. The Access query shown in Figure 10–32 on the next page, for example, was created in Design view and includes the Customer Number and Customer Name fields. The City field has a criterion (Greer), but the City field will not appear in the results.

BTW

Outer Joins

Sometimes you need to list all the rows from one of the tables in a join, regardless of whether they match any rows in the other table. For example, you can perform a join on the Customer and Seminar Offerings table but display all customers — even the ones without seminar offerings. This type of join is called an outer join. In a left outer join, all rows from the table on the left (the table listed first in the query) will be included regardless of whether they match rows from the table on the right (the table listed second in the query). Rows from the right will be included only if they match. In a right outer join, all rows from the table on the right will be included regardless of whether they match rows from the table on the left. The SQL clause for a left outer join is LEFT JOIN and the SQL clause for a right outer join is RIGHT JOIN.

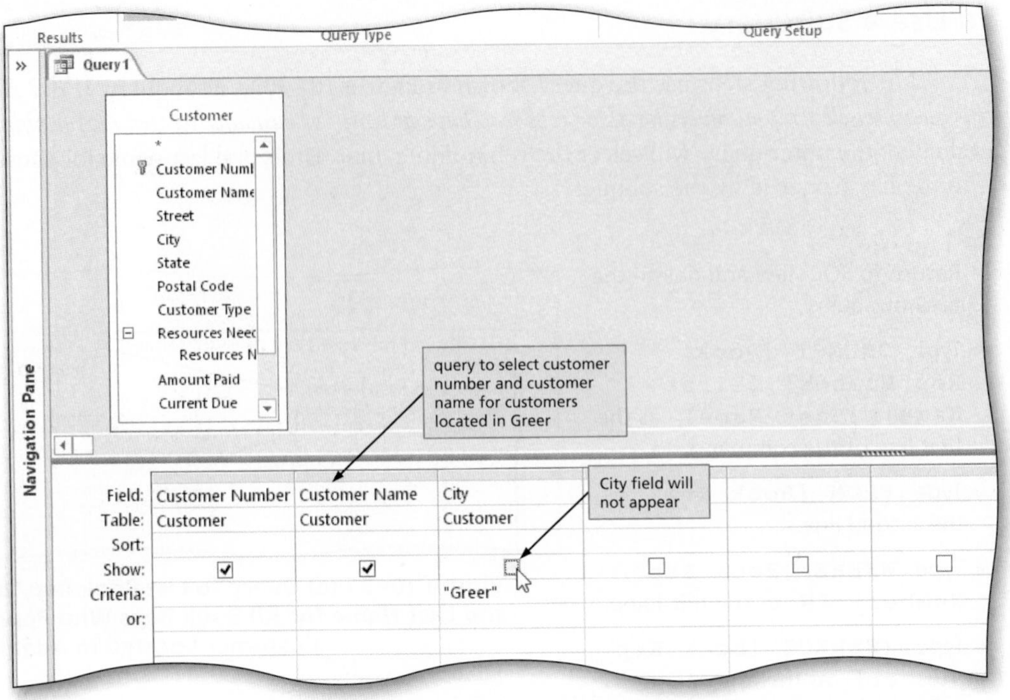

Figure 10–32 (a) Query to List the Customer Number and Customer Name for all Customers Whose City is Greer

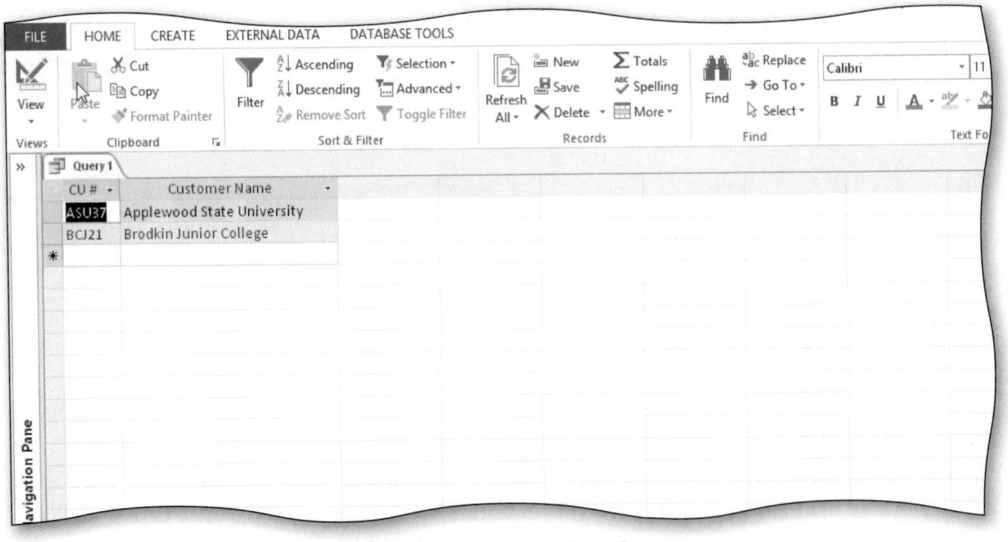

Figure 10–32 (b) Results

The SQL query that Access generates in correspondence to the Design view query is shown in Figure 10–33. The query is very similar to the queries you have entered, but there are three slight differences. First, the Customer.[Customer Number] and Customer.[Customer Name] fields are qualified, even though they do not need to be; only one table is involved in the query, so no qualification is necessary. Second, the City field is not enclosed in square brackets. The field legitimately is not enclosed in square brackets because there are no spaces or other special characters in the field name. Finally, there are extra parentheses in the criteria.

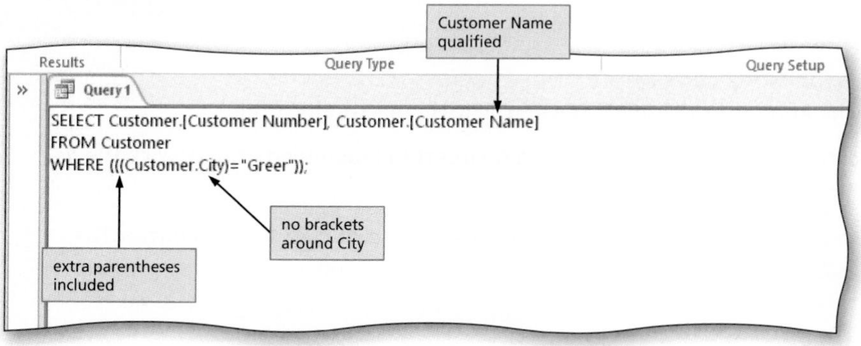

Figure 10–33

Both the style used by Access and the style you have been using are legitimate. The choice of style is a personal preference.

Updating Data through SQL

Although SQL is often regarded as a language for querying databases, it also contains commands to update databases. You can add new records, update existing records, and delete records.

To Use an INSERT Command

1 SQL VIEW | 2 SIMPLE CRITERIA | 3 COMPOUND CRITERIA | 4 SORT RESULTS
5 GROUP RESULTS | 6 JOIN TABLES | 7 USE SUBQUERY | 8 UPDATE DATA

You can add records to a table using the SQL INSERT command. The command consists of the words INSERT INTO followed by the name of the table into which the record is to be inserted. Next is the word VALUE, followed by the values for the fields in the record. Values for Text fields must be enclosed within quotation marks. Why? *Just as you needed to type the quotation marks when you used text data in a criterion, you need to do the same when you use text values in an INSERT INTO command.* The following steps add a record that Bavant Publishing wants to add to the Seminar Offerings table. The record is for customer BCJ21 and Seminar S06, and indicates that the seminar will be offered for a total of 2 hours, of which 0 hours already have been spent.

1

- If necessary, return to SQL view and delete the existing query.
- Type **INSERT INTO [Seminar Offerings]** as the first line of the command.

Q&A What is the purpose of the INSERT INTO clause?
The clause indicates the table into which data is to be inserted.

- Type **VALUES** as the second line.
- Type **('BCJ21','S06',2,0)** as the third line and type a semicolon (**;**) on the fourth line (Figure 10–34).

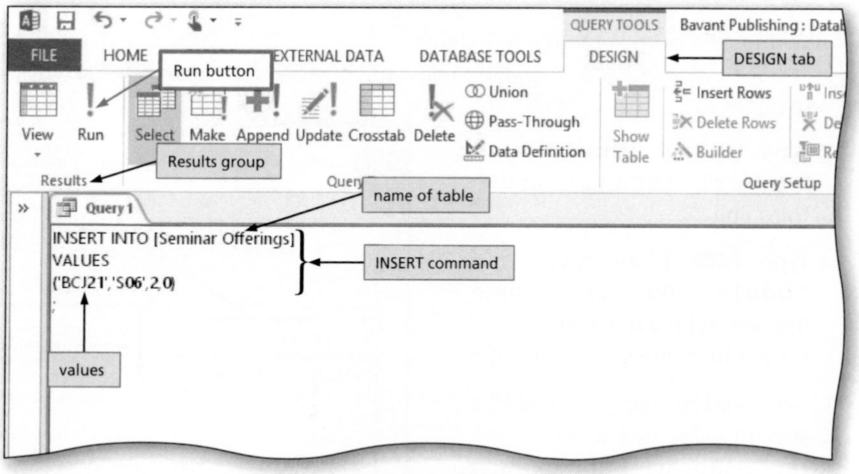

Figure 10–34

Q&A What is the purpose of the VALUES clause?
The VALUES clause, which typically extends over two lines, indicates the values that are to be inserted into a new record in the table. For readability, it is common to place the word VALUES on one line and the actual values on a separate line.

2

- Run the query by tapping or clicking the Run button (QUERY TOOLS DESIGN tab | Results group).
- When Access displays a message indicating the number of records to be inserted (appended), tap or click the Yes button to insert the records.

Q&A I tapped or clicked the View button and did not get the message. Do I need to tap or click the Run button?
Yes. You are making a change to the database, so you must tap or click the Run button, or the change will not be made.

How can I see if the record was actually inserted?
Use a SELECT query to view the records in the Seminar Offerings table.

3

- Save the query as Ch10q24.

To Use an UPDATE Command

You can update records in SQL by using the UPDATE command. The command consists of UPDATE, followed by the name of the table in which records are to be updated. Next, the command contains one or more SET clauses, which consist of the word SET, followed by a field to be updated, an equal sign, and the new value. The SET clause indicates the change to be made. Finally, the query includes a WHERE clause. ***Why?*** *When you execute the command, all records in the indicated table that satisfy the criterion will be updated.* The following steps use the SQL UPDATE command to perform an update requested by Bavant Publishing. Specifically, they change the Hours Spent to 1 on all records in the Seminar Offerings table on which the customer number is BCJ21 and the seminar code is S06. Because the combination of the Customer Number and Seminar Code fields is the primary key, only one record will be updated.

1

- Delete the existing query.
- Type **UPDATE [Seminar Offerings]** as the first line of the command.

Q&A What is the purpose of the UPDATE clause?
The UPDATE clause indicates the table to be updated. This clause indicates that the update is to the Seminar Offerings table.

- Type **SET [Hours Spent]=1** as the second line.

Q&A What is the purpose of the SET clause?
The SET clause indicates the field to be changed as well as the new value. This SET clause indicates that the hours spent is to be set to 1.

- Type **WHERE [Customer Number]='BCJ21'** as the third line.
- Type **AND [Seminar Code]='S06'** as the fourth line and type a semicolon (**;**) on the fifth line (Figure 10–35).

Q&A Do I need to change a field to a specific value such as 1?
No. You could use an expression. For example, to add $100 to the Current Due amount, the SET clause would be SET [Current Due]=[Current Due]+100.

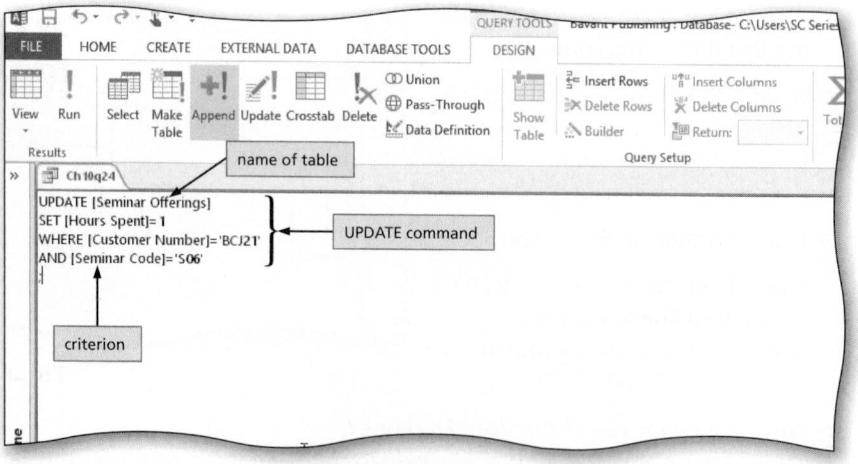

Figure 10–35

2

- Run the query.
- When Access displays a message indicating the number of records to be updated, tap or click the Yes button to update the records.

Q&A How can I see if the update actually occurred?
Use a SELECT query to view the records in the Seminar Offerings table.

3

- Save the query as Ch10q25.

To Use a DELETE Command

1 SQL VIEW | 2 SIMPLE CRITERIA | 3 COMPOUND CRITERIA | 4 SORT RESULTS
5 GROUP RESULTS | 6 JOIN TABLES | 7 USE SUBQUERY | 8 UPDATE DATA

You can delete records in SQL using the DELETE command. The command consists of DELETE FROM, followed by the name of the table from which records are to be deleted. Finally, you include a WHERE clause to specify the criteria. ***Why?** When you execute the command, all records in the indicated table that satisfy the criterion will be deleted.* The following steps use the SQL DELETE command to delete all records in the Seminar Offerings table on which the customer number is BCJ21 and the seminar code is S06, as Bavant Publishing has requested. Because the combination of the Customer Number and Seminar Code fields is the primary key, only one record will be deleted.

1

- Delete the existing query.
- Type `DELETE FROM [Seminar Offerings]` as the first line of the command.

Q&A What is the purpose of the DELETE clause?
The DELETE clause indicates the table from which records will be deleted. This DELETE clause indicates that records will be deleted from the Seminar Offerings table.

- Type `WHERE [Customer Number]='BCJ21'` as the second line.
- Type `AND [Seminar Code]='S06'` as the third line and type a semicolon (`;`) on the fourth line (Figure 10–36).

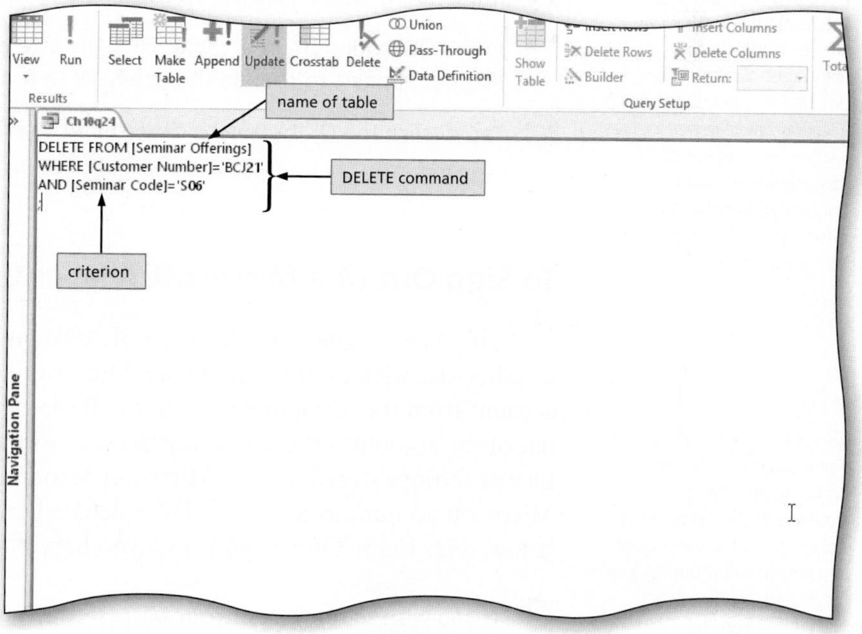

Figure 10–36

2

- Run the query.
- When Access displays a message indicating the number of records to be deleted, tap or click the Yes button to delete the records.

Q&A How can I see if the deletion actually occurred?
Use a SELECT query to view the records in the Seminar Offerings table.

3

- Save the query as Ch10q26.
- Close the query.

CONSIDER THIS

How do you determine any update operations to be performed?

Examine the database to determine if records must be added, updated, and/or deleted.

Determine INSERT operations. Determine whether new records need to be added. Determine to which table they should be added.

Determine UPDATE operations. Determine changes that need to be made to existing records. Which fields need to be changed? Which tables contain these fields? What criteria identify the rows that need to be changed?

Determine DELETE operations. Determine which tables contain records that are to be deleted. What criteria identify the rows that need to be deleted?

To Restore the Font Size

Earlier you changed the font size from its default setting of 8 to 10 so the SQL queries would be easier to read. Unless you prefer to retain this new setting, you should change the setting back to the default. The following steps restore the font size to its default setting.

1. Tap or click FILE on the ribbon to open the Backstage view.
2. Tap or click Options to display the Access Options dialog box.
3. If necessary, tap or click Object Designers to display the Object Designer options.
4. In the Query design area, tap or click the Size box arrow, and then tap or click 8 in the list that appears to change the size back to 8.
5. Tap or click the OK button to close the Access Options dialog box.

BTW

Certification

The Microsoft Office Specialist (MOS) program provides an opportunity for you to obtain a valuable industry credential — proof that you have the Access 2013 skills required by employers. For more information, visit the Certification resource on the Student Companion Site located on www.cengagebrain.com. For detailed instructions about accessing available resources, visit www.cengage.com/ct/studentdownload or contact your instructor for information about accessing the required files.

To Sign Out of a Microsoft Account

If you are signed in to a Microsoft account and are using a public computer or otherwise wish to sign out of your Microsoft account, you should sign out of the account from the Account gallery in the Backstage view before exiting Access. Signing out of the account is the safest way to make sure that nobody else can access SkyDrive files or settings stored in your Microsoft account. The following steps sign out of a Microsoft account from Access. For a detailed example of the procedure summarized below, refer to the Office and Windows chapter at the beginning of this book.

1. If you wish to sign out of your Microsoft account, tap or click FILE on the ribbon to open the Backstage view and then tap or click the Account tab to display the Account gallery.
2. Tap or click the Sign out link, which displays the Remove Account dialog box. If a Can't remove Windows accounts dialog box appears instead of the Remove Account dialog box, click the OK button and skip the remaining steps.

Q&A

Why does a Can't remove Windows accounts dialog box appear?

If you signed in to Windows using your Microsoft account, then you also must sign out from Windows, rather than signing out from within Access. When you are finished using Windows, be sure to sign out at that time.

BTW

Quick Reference

For a table that lists how to complete the tasks covered in this book using touch gestures, the mouse, ribbon, shortcut menu, and keyboard, see the Quick Reference Summary at the back of this book, or visit the Quick Reference resource on the Student Companion Site located on www.cengagebrain.com. For detailed instructions about accessing available resources, visit www.cengage.com/ct/studentdownload or contact your instructor for information about accessing the required files.

3. Tap or click the Yes button (Remove Account dialog box) to sign out of your Microsoft account on this computer.

Q&A Should I sign out of Windows after signing out of my Microsoft account?
When you are finished using the computer, you should sign out of your account for maximum security.

4. Tap or click the Back button in the upper-left corner of the Backstage view to return to the database.

To Exit Access

The following steps exit Access.

1. Tap or click the Close button on the right side of the title bar to exit Access.
2. If a Microsoft Access dialog box appears, tap or click the Yes button to save any changes made to the object since the last save.

Chapter Summary

In this chapter you have learned to create SQL queries; include fields in a query; use criteria involving both numeric and text fields as well as use compound criteria; use computed fields and rename the computation; sort the results of a query; use the built-in functions; group records in a query and also restrict the groups that appear in the results; join tables and restrict the records in a join; and use subqueries. You looked at the SQL that is generated automatically by Access. Finally, you used the INSERT, UPDATE, and DELETE commands to update data. The items listed below include all the new Access skills you have learned in this chapter.

Compound Criteria
Use a Compound Criterion Involving AND (AC 631)
Use a Compound Criterion Involving OR (AC 632)
Use NOT in a Criterion (AC 633)

Display Change
Change the Font Size (AC 621)

Field Selection
Include Only Certain Fields (AC 623)
Include All Fields (AC 625)
Use a Computed Field (AC 634)

Functions
Use a Built-In Function (AC 640)
Assign a Name to the Results of a Function (AC 641)
Use Multiple Functions in the Same Command (AC 642)

Grouping
Use Grouping (AC 643)
Restrict the Groups that Appear (AC 644)

Joining Tables
Join Tables (AC 646)
Restrict the Records in a Join (AC 647)
Join a Table to Itself (AC 648)

Query Creation
Create a New SQL Query (AC 622)
Prepare to Enter a New SQL Query (AC 625)

Simple Criteria
Use a Criterion Involving a Numeric Field (AC 627)
Use a Comparison Operator (AC 628)
Use a Criterion Involving a Text Field (AC 629)
Use a Wildcard (AC 630)

Sort Results
Sort the Results on a Single Field (AC 635)
Sort the Results on Multiple Fields (AC 636)
Sort the Results in Descending Order (AC 637)
Omit Duplicates When Sorting (AC 638)

Subqueries
Use a Subquery (AC 651)

Updates
Use an INSERT Command (AC 653)
Use an UPDATE Command (AC 654)
Use a DELETE Command (AC 655)

STUDENT ASSIGNMENTS

CONSIDER THIS: PLAN AHEAD

What decisions will you need to make when creating your own SQL queries?
Use these guidelines as you complete the assignments in this chapter and create your own queries outside of this class.

1. **Select the fields for the query.**
   a. Examine the requirements for the query you are constructing to determine which fields are to be included.
2. **Determine which table or tables contain these fields.**
   a. For each field, determine the table in which it is located.
3. **Determine criteria.**
   a. Determine any criteria that data must satisfy to be included in the results.
   b. If there are more than two tables in the query, determine the criteria to be used to ensure the data matches correctly.
4. **Determine sort order.**
   a. Is the data to be sorted in some way?
   b. If so, by what field or fields is it to be sorted?
5. **Determine grouping.**
   a. Is the data to be grouped in some way?
   b. If so, by what field is it to be grouped?
   c. Identify any calculations to be made for the group.
6. **Determine any update operations to be performed.**
   a. Determine whether rows need to be inserted, changed, or deleted.
   b. Determine the tables involved.

CONSIDER THIS

How should you submit solutions to questions in the assignments identified with a symbol?
Every assignment in this book contains one or more questions identified with a symbol. These questions require you to think beyond the assigned database. Present your solutions to the questions in the format required by your instructor. Possible formats may include one or more of these options: write the answer; create a document that contains the answer; present your answer to the class; discuss your answer in a group; record the answer as audio or video using a webcam, smartphone, or portable media player; or post answers on a blog, wiki, or website.

Apply Your Knowledge

Reinforce the skills and apply the concepts you learned in this chapter.

Using Criteria, Joining Tables, and Sorting in SQL Queries

Note: To complete this assignment, you will be required to use the Data Files for Students. Visit www.cengage.com/ct/studentdownload for detailed instructions or contact your instructor for information about accessing the required files.

Instructions: Start Access. Open the Apply Natural Products database that you used in Apply Your Knowledge in Chapter 9 on page AC 611. (If you did not complete the exercise, see your instructor for a copy of the database.) Use SQL to query the Apply Natural Products database.

Perform the following tasks:

1. Find all customers whose customer type is Salon. Display all fields in the query result. Save the query as AYK Step 1 Query.
2. Find all customers whose amount paid amount or balance amount is $0.00. Display the Customer Number, Customer Name, Amount Paid, and Balance fields in the query result. Save the query as AYK Step 2 Query.
3. Find all customers in the Customer table who are not located in TN. Display the Customer Number, Customer Name, and State in the query result. Save the query as AYK Step 3 Query.

4. Display the Customer Number, Customer Name, Sales Rep Number, First Name, and Last Name for all customers. Sort the records in ascending order by sales rep number and customer number. Save the query as AYK Step 4 Query.
5. Display the Sales Rep Number, First Name, Last Name, and Salary YTD for all sales reps whose Salary YTD amount is greater than $15,000. Save the query as AYK Step 5 Query.
6. If requested to do so by your instructor, rename the AYK Step 5 Query as Last Name Query where Last Name is your last name.
7. Submit the revised database in the format specified by your instructor.
8. What WHERE clause would you use if you wanted to find all customers who lived in cities beginning with the letter G?

Extend Your Knowledge

Extend the skills you learned in this chapter and experiment with new skills. You may need to use Help to complete the assignment.

Using Wildcards, Special Operators, and Subqueries

Note: To complete this assignment, you will be required to use the Data Files for Students. Visit www.cengage.com/ct/studentdownload for detailed instructions or contact your instructor for information about accessing the required files.

Instructions: Start Access. Open the Extend Personal Training database. Personal Training is a small company that offers personal fitness training and customized workouts. Use SQL to answer the following queries.

Perform the following tasks:

1. Find all clients where the client's first name is either Alex or Alec. Display the Client Number, First Name, Last Name, and Address fields in the query result. Save the query as EYK Step 1 Query.
2. Find all clients who live in Fort Mill or Indian Land. Use the IN operator. Display the Client Number, First Name, Last Name, and City fields in the query result. Save the query as EYK Step 2 Query.
3. Find all clients whose amount paid amount is greater than or equal to $400.00 and less than or equal to $500.00. Use the BETWEEN operator. Display the Client Number, First Name, Last Name, and Amount Paid fields in the query result. Save the query as EYK Step 3 Query.
4. Use a subquery to find all trainers whose clients are located in Ballantyne. Display the Trainer Number, First Name, and Last Name fields in the query result. Save the query as EYK Step 4 Query.
5. If requested to do so by your instructor, rename the EYK Step 4 Query as First Name City Query where First Name is your first name and City is the city where you currently reside.
6. Submit the revised database in the format specified by your instructor.
7. What WHERE clause would you use to find the answer to Step 2 without using the IN operator?

Analyze, Correct, Improve

Analyze a database, correct all errors, and improve the design.

Correcting SQL Errors and Improving a Query Result

Note: To complete this assignment, you will be required to use the Data Files for Students. Visit www.cengage.com/ct/studentdownload for detailed instructions or contact your instructor for information about accessing the required files.

Instructions: Start Access and open the Analyze Metro Couriers database. Metro Couriers is a local company that provides courier services to business organizations in the metro area of a large city.

Continued >

Analyze, Correct, Improve *continued*

Perform the following tasks:

1. Correct The owner created the SQL query shown in Figure 10–37 but when he viewed the query results, there were 36 records and he knows that is not correct. Also, the query results did not sort correctly. The results should be sorted by ascending courier number and then by descending balance. Open the Analyze Courier Query in SQL view, correct the errors, and then save the query with the same name.

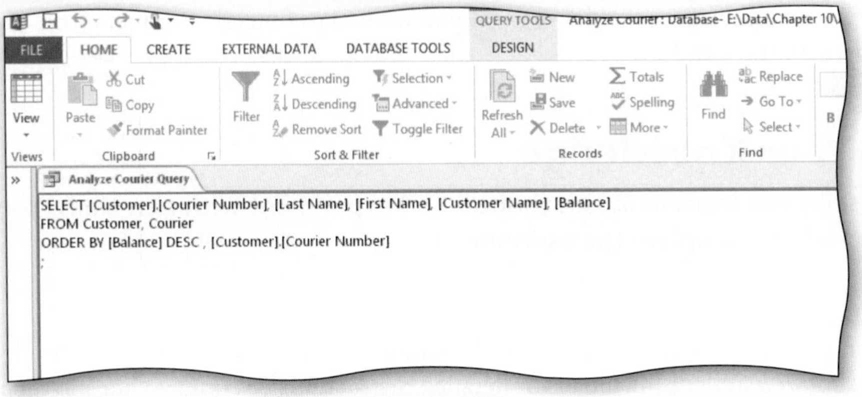

Figure 10–37

2. Improve The owner also created a SQL query to total customer balances for each courier. The query results are shown in Figure 10–38. The owner does not understand why Expr1001 is displayed as the column heading for the total balances. He has asked you to add a more meaningful name for the calculation. Open the Analyze Grouping Query in SQL view, improve the query, and then save the query with the same name. If requested to do so by your instructor, rename the query as Analyze Last Name Query where Last Name is your last name. Submit the revised database in the format specified by your instructor.

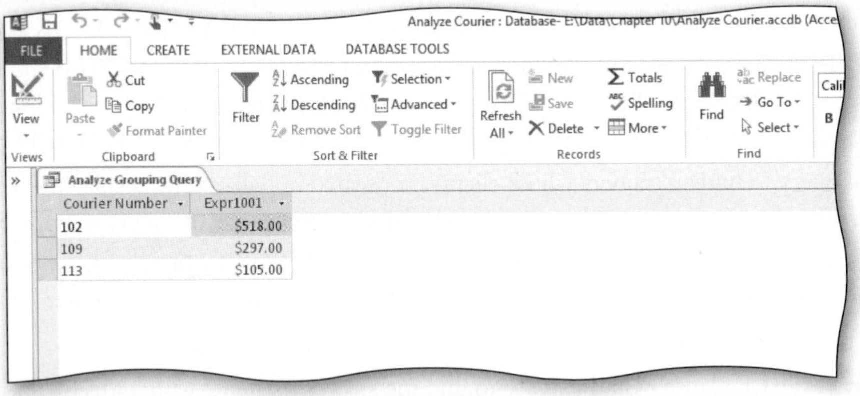

Figure 10–38

3. Why does the query shown in Figure 10–37 return 36 results?

In the Labs

Design, create, modify, and/or use a database following the guidelines, concepts, and skills presented in this chapter. Labs are listed in order of increasing difficulty. Labs 1 and 2, which increase in difficulty, require you to create solutions based on what you learned in the chapter; Lab 3 requires you to create a solution, which uses cloud and web technologies, by learning and investigating on your own from general guidance.

Lab 1: Querying the Technology Services Database Using SQL

Note: Use the database modified in Lab 1 of Chapter 9 on page AC 613 for this assignment, or see your instructor for information on accessing the required files.

Problem: Technology Services wants to learn more about SQL and has determined a number of questions it wants SQL to answer. You must obtain answers to the questions using SQL.

Instructions: Perform the following tasks:

1. Start Access. Open the Lab 1 Technology Services database and create a new query in SQL view. Find all clients who are located in the city of Austin. Include the Client Number, Client Name, and City in the query results. Save the query as ITL 1 Step 1 Query.
2. Find all clients located in North Carolina (NC) with an amount paid amount greater than $3,000.00. Include the Client Number, Client Name, and Amount Paid fields in the query results. Save the query as ITL 1 Step 2 Query.
3. Find all clients whose names begin with the letter W. Include the Client Number, Client Name, and City fields in the query result. Save the query as ITL 1 Step 3 Query.
4. List all cities in descending order. Each city should appear only once. Save the query as ITL 1 Step 4 Query.
5. Display the client number, client name, service rep number, first name, and last name for all clients. Sort the results in ascending order by service rep number and client number. Save the query as ITL 1 Step 5 Query.
6. List the average balance due amount grouped by service rep number. Name the average balance as Average Balance. Save the query as ITL 1 Step 6 Query.
7. Find the client number, name, and city for every pair of clients who are located in the same city. Save the query as ITL 1 Step 7 Query.
8. Find the client numbers, names, and service rep numbers for all clients that have service requests. Use the alias S for the Service Requests table and C for the Client table. Each client should appear only once in the results. Save the query as ITL 1 Step 8 Query.
9. Use a subquery to find all service reps whose clients are located in Georgetown. Save the query as ITL 1 Step 9 Query.
10. Find the average balance due amount for service rep 52. Save the query as ITL 1 Step 10 Query.
11. If requested to do so by your instructor, open the Service Rep table and change the first and last name for service rep 52 to your first and last name.
12. Submit the revised database in the format specified by your instructor.
13. What WHERE clause would you use to find all records where one of the resources needed was DATA?

Lab 2: Querying the Team Designs Database Using SQL

Problem: Team Designs wants to learn more about SQL and has determined a number of questions it wants SQL to answer. You must obtain answers to the questions using SQL.

Note: Use the database modified in Lab 2 of Chapter 9 on page AC 613 for this assignment, or see your instructor for information on accessing the required files.

Instructions: Perform the following tasks.

1. Start Access and open the Lab 2 Team Designs database. Using SQL, find all records in the Item table where the difference between the base cost of an item and the wholesale price is

Continued >

In the Labs *continued*

greater than $2.00. Display the item number, description, wholesale price, and base cost in the query result. Save the query as ITL 2 Step 1 Query.

2. Display the item number, description, and difference (base cost – wholesale cost) for all items. Name the computed field Markup. Save the query as ITL 2 Step 2 Query.
3. Find all items where the description begins with the letter, F. Include the item number and description in the query result. Save the query as ITL 2 Step 3 Query.
4. Display the supplier name, item number, description, and base cost for all items where the number on hand is greater than 100. Sort the results in ascending order by supplier name and description. Save the query as ITL 2 Step 4 Query.
5. Find the average wholesale price by supplier. Name the computed field Avg Wholesale. Include the supplier code in the result. Save the query as ITL 2 Step 5 Query.
6. Find the total number of reordered items in the Reorder table. Name the computed field Total Ordered. Include the item number in the result. Save the query as ITL 2 Step 6 Query.
7. Add the following record to the Reorder table.

Item Number	Date Ordered	Number Ordered
6345	10/9/2014	8

Save the query to add the record as ITL 2 Step 7 Query.

8. If requested to do so by your instructor, rename the ITL 2 Step 7 Query as LastName Reorder Query where LastName is your last name.
9. Update the Number Ordered field to 12 for those records where the Item Number is 6345. Save the query to update the records as ITL 2 Step 9 Query.
10. Delete all records from the Reorder table where the Item Number is 6345. Save the query to delete the records as ITL 2 Step 10 Query.
11. Submit the revised database in the format specified by your instructor.
12. How would you write a SQL query for Step 9 if the instructions were to increment the number ordered by 4?

Lab 3: Expand Your World: Cloud and Web Technologies
Using SQL on the Web

Problem: Many SQL tutorials are available on the web. One site, www.w3schools.com/sql/, has an online SQL editor that allows you to edit SQL commands and then run the commands. You will use this editor to create and run queries.

Note: For each SQL statement that you create and run, use the * to select all fields in the table. Copy the SQL statement and the number of results retrieved to your blog, Google document, or Word document.

Instructions: Perform the following tasks:

1. Create a blog, a Google document, or a Word document on the SkyDrive on which to store your SQL statements and the number of results obtained from the query.
2. Access the www.w3schools.com/sql/ website and spend some time becoming familiar with the tutorial and how it works.
3. Create a query to find all records in the OrderDetails table where the ProductID is 14 and the Quantity is less than 15.
4. Create a query to find all records in the Customers table where the City begins with the letter M. (*Hint*: Use the percent symbol (%), not the asterisk, in this query.)

5. Create a query to find all records in the Employees table where the birth date of the employee is before January 1, 1960. (*Hint*: View all the records in the table first to determine how dates are stored.)
6. Submit the document containing your statements and results in the format specified by your instructor.
7. What differences did you notice between the online SQL editor and Access SQL? Which one would you prefer to use? Why?

Consider This: Your Turn

Apply your creative thinking and problem solving skills to design and implement a solution.

1: Querying the Fine Crafts Database Using SQL

Personal/Academic

Instructions: Open the Fine Crafts database you modified in Chapter 9 on page AC 614. If you did not modify this database, contact your instructor for information about accessing the required files.

Part 1: Use the concepts and techniques presented in this chapter to create queries using SQL for the following. Save each query using the format CT 1 Step x Query where x is the step letter.

a. Find the item number and description of all items that contain the word, Stool.
b. Find the item number, description, price, and number on hand for all items where the price is less than $50.00 and the number on hand is less than 5.
c. Calculate the total price (price * on hand) of each item available for sale. Show the item number, description, and total price.
d. Find the students who made each item. Show the student's first name and last name as well as the item number, description, price, and on hand.
e. Modify the query you created in Step d to restrict retrieval to those items with a price less than $20.00.
f. Find the average price amount grouped by student code.

Submit your assignment in the format specified by your instructor.

Part 2: You made several decisions while creating the queries in this assignment. What was the rationale behind your decisions? How could you modify the query in Step e to find items with a price between $20.00 and $40.00?

2: Creating Queries for the Landscaping Services Database Using SQL

Professional

Instructions: Open the Landscaping Services database you modified in Chapter 9 on page AC 615. If you did not modify this database, contact your instructor for information about accessing the required files.

Part 1: Use the concepts and techniques presented in this chapter to create queries using SQL for the following. Save each query using the format CT 2 Step x Query where x is the step letter.

a. Find the names of all customers who have the letters, comm, in their customer name.
b. Find the totals of the amount paid and the balance amounts for all customers.
c. Find all supervisors who started before 1/1/2013. Show the supervisor first name, last name, and start date.
d. Find the supervisor for each customer. List the supervisor number, first name, last name, customer number, and customer name. Assign aliases to the Customer and Supervisor tables. Sort the results in ascending order by supervisor number and customer number.
e. Restrict the records retrieved in Step d above to only those records where the balance is greater than $800.00.

Continued >

Consider This: Your Turn *continued*

f. Find the average balance amount grouped by supervisor number.
g. Restrict the records retrieved in Step f to only those groups where the average balance amount is greater than $700.00.
h. List the customer number, customer name, service code, service description, and hours spent for all service requests. Sort the results by customer number and service code.

Submit your assignment in the format specified by your instructor.

Part 2: You made several decisions while doing this assignment. What was the rationale behind your decisions? How could you modify the query in Step h to find only those customers where hours spent is equal to zero?

3: Understanding Advanced SQL Commands

Research and Collaboration

Note: To complete this assignment, you will be required to use the Data Files for Students. Visit www.cengage.com/ct/studentdownload for detailed instructions or contact your instructor for information about accessing the required files.

Part 1: Before you begin this assignment, download the Your Turn 3 Courier Services database from the Data Files for students and rename the database as your team name database. For example, if your team is the Fab Four, then name the database Fab Four. Use the database for this assignment. For this assignment you will create several SQL queries for the Courier Services database. Your team may need to use Help or research SQL commands on the web to complete the assignment. Create the following queries:

a. List the courier number, customer number, service code, and service fee for all weekly services provided to customers.
b. Find the number and name of all customers who had a service performed at 10:00 a.m. on any day of the week.
c. Add a new service to the Services Offered table. The service is Food Delivery, the charge is $8.00, and the service code is 06.
d. Update the fees for all services by adding $1.50 to the current service fees.
e. Find the five customers with the highest balances. (*Hint*: You will need to add a new clause to your SQL command.)

Submit your assignment in the format specified by your instructor.

Part 2: You made several decisions while doing this assignment. What was the rationale behind your decisions? What resources did you use to help you create the SQL commands for this assignment?

Learn Online

Reinforce what you learned in this chapter with games, exercises, training, and many other online activities and resources.

Student Companion Site Reinforcement activities and resources are available at no additional cost on www.cengagebrain.com. Visit www.cengage.com/ct/studentdownload for detailed instructions about accessing the resources available at the Student Companion Site.

SAM Put your skills into practice with SAM Projects! SAM Projects for this chapter can be found online. If you have a SAM account, go to www.cengage.com/sam2013 to access SAM assignments for this chapter.

1 Database Design

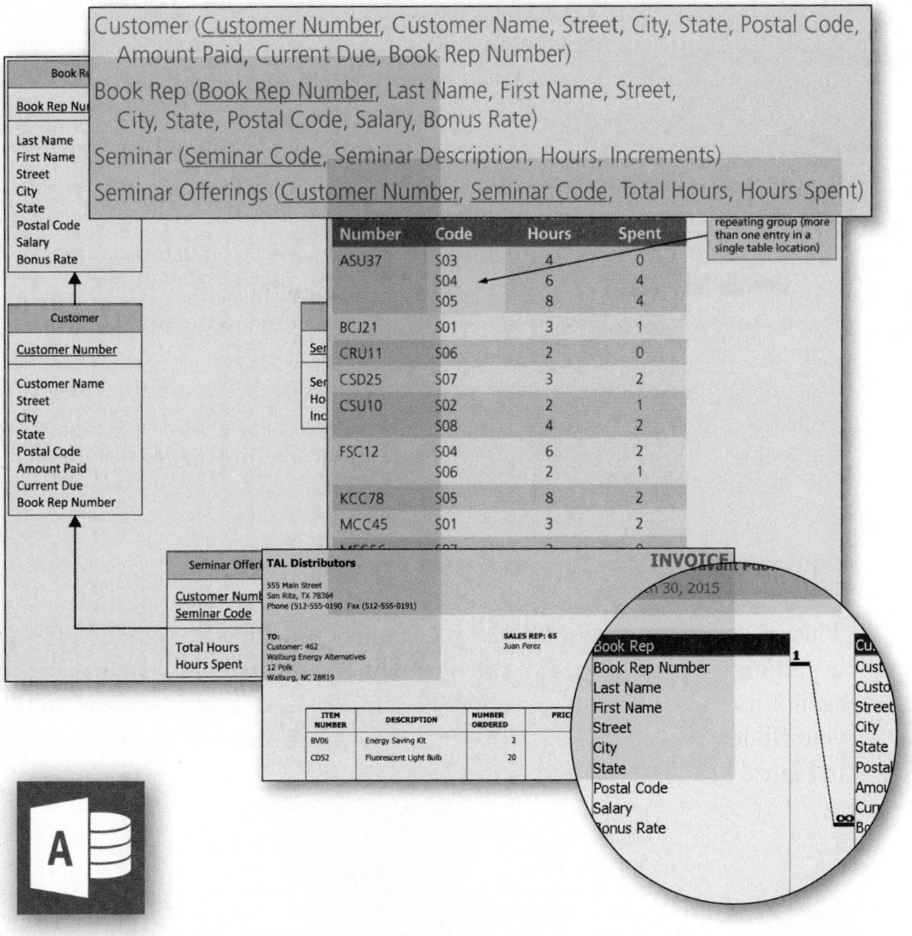

Objectives

You will have mastered the material in this chapter when you can:

- Understand the terms entity, attribute, and relationship
- Understand the terms relation and relational database
- Understand functional dependence and identify when one column is functionally dependent on another
- Understand the term primary key and identify primary keys in tables
- Design a database to satisfy a set of requirements
- Convert an unnormalized relation to first normal form
- Convert tables from first normal form to second normal form
- Convert tables from second normal form to third normal form
- Understand how to represent the design of a database using diagrams

11 | Database Design

Introduction

BTW
BTWs
For a complete list of the BTWs found in the margins of this book, visit the BTW resource on the Student Companion Site located on www.cengagebrain.com. For detailed instructions about accessing available resources, visit www.cengage.com/ct/studentdownload or contact your instructor for information about accessing the required files.

This chapter presents a method for determining the tables and fields necessary to satisfy a set of requirements. **Database design** is the process of determining the particular tables and fields that will comprise a database. In designing a database, you must identify the tables in the database, the fields in the tables, the primary keys of the tables, and the relationships between the tables.

The chapter begins by examining some important concepts concerning relational databases and then presents the design method. To illustrate the process, the chapter presents the requirements for the Bavant Publishing database. It then applies the design method to those requirements to produce the database design. The chapter applies the design method to a second set of requirements, which are requirements for a company called TAL Distributors. It next examines normalization, which is a process that you can use to identify and fix potential problems in database designs. The chapter concludes by explaining how to use a company's policies and objectives — which are typically addressed in existing documentation — to plan and design a database. Finally, you will learn how to represent a database design with a diagram.

Project — Design a database

This chapter expands on the database design guidelines presented in Chapter 1 beginning on page AC 58. Without a good understanding of database design, you cannot use a database management system such as Access effectively. In this chapter, you will learn how to design two databases by using the database design process shown in Figure 11–1.

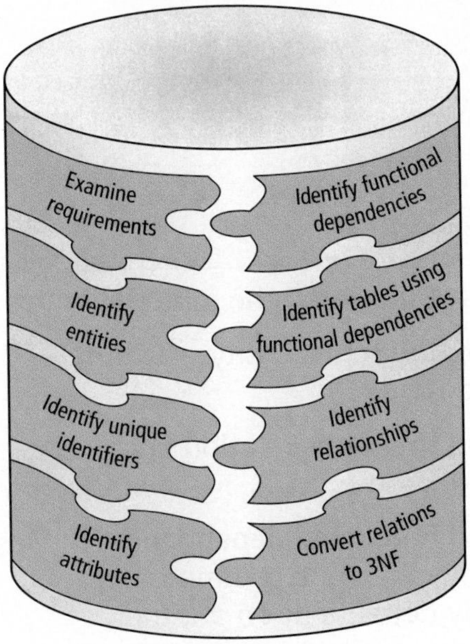

Database Design Process

Figure 11–1

You will design a database for Bavant Publishing that is similar to the database you have used in the previous chapters. You also will design a database for TAL Distributors, a distributor of energy-saving and water-conservation devices.

Entities, Attributes, and Relationships

Working in the database environment requires that you be familiar with some specific terms and concepts. The terms *entity*, *attribute*, and *relationship* are fundamental when discussing databases. An **entity** is like a noun: it is a person, place, thing, or event. The entities of interest to Bavant Publishing, for example, are such things as book reps, customers, and seminars. The entities that are of interest to a college include students, faculty, and classes; a real estate agency is interested in buyers, sellers, properties, and agents; and a used car dealer is interested in vehicles, customers, salespeople, and manufacturers. When creating a database, an entity is represented as a table.

An **attribute** is a property of an entity. The term is used here exactly as it is used in everyday English. For the entity *person*, for example, the list of attributes might include such things as eye color and height. For Bavant Publishing, the attributes of interest for the entity *customer* are such things as name, address, city, and so on. For the entity *faculty* at a school, the attributes would be such things as faculty number, name, office number, phone, and so on. For the entity *vehicle* at a car dealership, the attributes are such things as the vehicle identification number, model, price, year, and so on. In databases, attributes are represented as the fields in a table or tables.

A **relationship** is an association between entities. There is an association between book reps and customers, for example, at Bavant Publishing. A book rep is associated with all of his or her customers, and a customer is associated with the one book rep to whom the customer is assigned. Technically, you say that a book rep is *related* to all of his or her customers, and a customer is *related* to his or her book rep.

The relationship between book reps and customers is an example of a one-to-many relationship because one book rep is associated with many customers, but each customer is associated with only one book rep. In this type of relationship, the word *many* is used in a way that is different from everyday English; it might not always mean a large number. In this context, for example, the term *many* means that a book rep might be associated with *any* number of customers. That is, one book rep can be associated with zero, one, or more customers.

There also is a relationship between customers and seminars. Each customer can be offered many seminars, and each seminar can be offered to many customers. This is an example of a many-to-many relationship.

How does a relational database handle entities, attributes of entities, and relationships between entities? Entities and attributes are fairly simple. Each entity has its own table; in the Bavant Publishing database, there is one table for book reps, one table for customers, and so on. The attributes of an entity become the columns in the table. In the table for customers, for example, there is a column for the customer number, a column for the customer name, and so on.

What about relationships? Relationships are implemented through matching fields. One-to-many relationships, for example, are implemented by including matching fields in the related tables. Book reps and customers are related, for example, by including the Book Rep Number field in both the Book Rep table and the Customer table.

Many-to-many relationships are implemented through an additional table that contains matching fields for both of the related tables. Customers and Seminars are related, for example, through the Seminar Offerings table. Both the Customer table and the Seminar Offerings table contain Customer Number fields. In addition, both the Seminar and the Seminar Offerings table contain Seminar Code fields.

BTW

Systems Analysis

The determination of database requirements is part of a process known as systems analysis. A systems analyst interviews users, examines existing and proposed documents, investigates current procedures, and reviews organizational policies to determine exactly the type of data needs the database must support.

BTW

Entities

Bavant Publishing could include many other entities in a database, such as entities for employees, textbooks, and authors. The decisions on which entities to include are part of the process of determining database requirements based on user needs.

Relational Databases

A relational database is a collection of tables similar to the tables for Bavant Publishing that appear in Figure 11–2. In the Bavant Publishing database, the Customer table contains information about the customers to which Bavant Publishing provides foreign language textbooks (Figure 11–2a). Note that, for simplification purposes, the tables in the figure do not include all the fields of the final Bavant database in Chapter 10.

Customer

Customer Number	Customer Name	Street	City	State	Postal Code	Amount Paid	Current Due	Book Rep Number
ASU37	Applewood State University	300 University Ave.	Greer	PA	19158	$41,530.98	$38,812.66	42
BCJ21	Brodkin Junior College	4806 Park Dr.	Greer	PA	19158	$0.00	$6,081.98	42
CRU11	Cristie University	1200 University Pl.	Pleasantburg	NJ	07025	$0.00	$14,250.00	42
CSD25	Cowpens ISD	829 Wooster Ave.	Gossett	PA	19157	$12,750.00	$13,275.00	53
CSU10	Camellia State University	725 Camellia St.	Pleasantburg	NJ	07025	$63,246.88	$69,847.76	53
DCC34	Dartt Community College	3827 Burgess Dr.	Chambers	NJ	07037	$21,345.50	$23,467.75	65
FSC12	First State College	7300 Cedar Rd.	Quaker	DE	19719	$34,557.25	$23,875.98	65
FSU23	Farnham State University	1445 Hubert St.	Gaston	DE	19723	$18,268.00	$22,024.50	42
KCC78	Key Community College System	7523 Penn Ave.	Adelphia	PA	19159	$21,288.65	$11,367.49	65
MCC45	Mauldin Community College	72 Montrose St.	Chesnee	NJ	07053	$9,500.00	$5,000.00	53
MEC56	Mehitable College	202 College St.	Gaston	DE	19723	$9,111.19	$7,310.76	42
PLI22	Pratt-Last Institute	236 Ashton Ave.	Pleasantburg	NJ	07025	$17,229.45	$11,769.75	53
SCC77	Stallone Community College	1200 Franklin Blvd.	Adelphia	PA	19156	$7,525.98	$2,515.78	42
SEC19	Seaborn College	345 Mather Rd.	Quaker	DE	19719	$9,225.34	$10,496.89	65
TSC02	Tri-State Consortium	3400 Metropolitan Pkwy.	Adelphia	PA	19156	$34,578.90	$9,432.56	65

Figure 11–2 (a) Customer Table

Bavant assigns each customer to a specific book rep. The Book Rep table contains information about the reps to whom these customers are assigned (Figure 11–2b).

Book Rep

Book Rep Number	Last Name	First Name	Street	City	State	Postal Code	Salary	Bonus Rate
42	Perez	Melina	261 Porter Dr.	Adelphia	PA	19156	$31,500.00	0.20
48	Statnik	Michael	3135 Simpson Dr.	Pleasantburg	NJ	07025	$29,000.00	0.20
53	Chin	Robert	265 Maxwell St.	Gossett	PA	19157	$26,250.00	0.19
65	Rogers	Tracy	1827 Maple Ave.	Adelphia	PA	19159	$7,750.00	0.18

Figure 11–2 (b) Book Rep Table

The Seminar table lists the specific seminars that the reps at Bavant Publishing offer to their customers (Figure 11–2c). Each seminar has a code and a description. The table also includes the number of hours for which the seminar usually is offered and the seminar's increments, that is, the standard time blocks, in which the seminar usually is offered. The first row, for example, indicates that seminar S01 is Integrating with Learning Management Systems. The seminar typically is offered in 1-hour increments for a total of 3 hours.

Seminar			
Seminar Code	**Seminar Description**	**Hours**	**Increments**
S01	Integrating with Learning Management Systems	3	1
S02	Using Web-based Technologies and Tools	2	1
S03	Mobile Apps	4	2
S04	Video Podcasting	6	2
S05	Creating Virtual Worlds	8	2
S06	Clickers in the Classroom	2	1
S07	Online Seminar Strategies	3	1
S08	Using Social Networking	4	2

Figure 11–2 (c) Seminar Table

BTW
Relationships
One-to-one relationships also can occur but they are not common. To implement a one-to-one relationship, treat it as a one-to-many relationship. You must determine which table will be the one table and which table will be the many table. To do so, consider what may happen in the future. In the case of one project that has one employee assigned to it, more employees could be added. Therefore, the project table would be the one table and the employee table would be the many table.

The Seminar Offerings table contains a customer number, a seminar code, the total number of hours for which the seminar is scheduled, and the number of hours the customer has already spent in the seminar (Figure 11–2d). The first record shows that customer number ASU37 currently has scheduled seminar S03. The seminar is scheduled for 4 hours, of which no hours have currently been spent. The total hours is usually the same as the number of hours indicated for the seminar in the Seminar table, but it can differ.

Seminar Offerings			
Customer Number	**Seminar Code**	**Total Hours**	**Hours Spent**
ASU37	S03	4	0
ASU37	S04	6	4
ASU37	S05	8	4
BCJ21	S01	3	1
CRU11	S06	2	0
CSD25	S07	3	2
CSU10	S02	2	1
CSU10	S08	4	2
FSC12	S04	6	2
FSC12	S06	2	1
KCC78	S05	8	2
MCC45	S01	3	2
MEC56	S07	3	0
SEC19	S02	2	1
SEC19	S07	3	1

Figure 11–2 (d) Seminar Offerings Table

The formal term for a table is relation. If you study the tables shown in Figure 11–2 on the previous page, you might see that there are certain restrictions you should place on relations. Each column in a table should have a unique name, and entries in each column should match this column name. For example, in the Postal Code column, all entries should in fact *be* postal codes. In addition, each row should be unique. After all, if two rows in a table contain identical data, the second row does not provide any information that you do not already have. In addition, for maximum flexibility, the order in which columns and rows appear in a table should be immaterial. Finally, a table's design is less complex if you restrict each position in the table to a single entry, that is, you do not permit multiple entries, often called **repeating groups,** in the table. These restrictions lead to the following definition:

A **relation** is a two-dimensional table in which:

1. The entries in the table are single-valued; that is, each location in the table contains a single entry.
2. Each column has a distinct name, technically called the *attribute name.*
3. All values in a column are values of the same attribute; that is, all entries must correspond to the column name.
4. Each row is distinct; that is, no two rows are identical.

Figure 11–3a shows a table with repeating groups, which violates Rule 1. Figure 11–3b shows a table in which two columns have the same name, which violates Rule 2. Figure 11–3c shows a table in which one of the entries in the Seminar Description column is not a seminar description, which violates Rule 3. Figure 11–3d shows a table with two identical rows, which violates Rule 4.

Seminar Offerings

Customer Number	Seminar Code	Total Hours	Hours Spent
ASU37	S03 S04 S05	4 6 8	0 4 4
BCJ21	S01	3	1
CRU11	S06	2	0
CSD25	S07	3	2
CSU10	S02 S08	2 4	1 2
FSC12	S04 S06	6 2	2 1
KCC78	S05	8	2
MCC45	S01	3	2
MEC56	S07	3	0
SEC19	S02 S07	2 3	1 1

repeating group (more than one entry in a single table location)

Figure 11–3 (a) Seminar Offerings Table Violation of Rule 1 – Table Contains Repeating Groups

two columns with the same name

Seminar

Seminar Code	Seminar Description	Hours	Hours	Increments
S01	Integrating with Learning Management Systems	3	2	1
S02	Using Web-based Technologies and Tools	2	1	1
S03	Mobile Apps	4	2	2
S04	Video Podcasting	6	5	2
S05	Creating Virtual Worlds	8	4	2
S06	Clickers in the Classroom	2	2	1
S07	Online Seminar Strategies	3	3	1
S08	Using Social Networking	4	4	2

Figure 11–3 (b) Seminar Table Violation of Rule 2 – Each Column has a Distinct Name

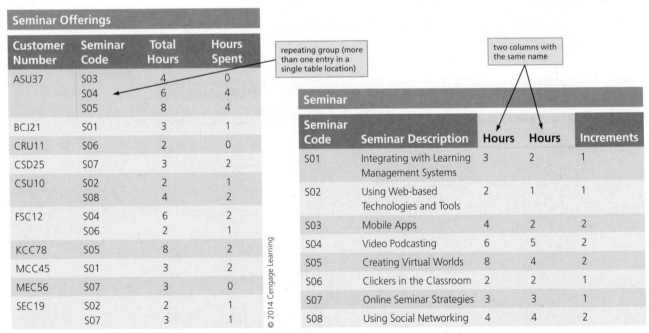

Seminar			
Seminar Code	**Seminar Description**	**Hours**	**Increments**
S01	Integrating with Learning Management Systems	3	1
S02	Using Web-based Technologies and Tools	2	1
S03	7@!	4	2
S04	Video Podcasting	6	2
S05	Creating Virtual Worlds	8	2
S06	Clickers in the Classroom	2	1
S07	Online Seminar Strategies	3	1
S08	Using Social Networking	4	2

value does not correspond to column name; that is, it is not a seminar description

Figure 11–3 (c) Seminar Table Violation of Rule 3 – All Entries in a Column Must Correspond to the Column Name

Seminar			
Seminar Code	**Seminar Description**	**Hours**	**Increments**
S01	Integrating with Learning Management Systems	3	1
S02	Using Web-based Technologies and Tools	2	1
S03	Mobile Apps	4	2
S03	Mobile Apps	4	2
S04	Video Podcasting	6	2
S05	Creating Virtual Worlds	8	2
S06	Clickers in the Classroom	2	1
S07	Online Seminar Strategies	3	1
S08	Using Social Networking	4	2

identical rows

Figure 11–3 (d) Seminar Table Violation of Rule 4 – Each Row is Distinct

In addition, in a relation, the order of columns is immaterial. You can view the columns in any order you want. The order of rows is also immaterial. You can view the rows in any order you want.

A **relational database** is a collection of relations. Rows in a table (relation) often are called **records** or **tuples**. Columns in a table (relation) often are called **fields** or **attributes**. Typically, the terms *record* and *field* are used in Access.

To depict the structure of a relational database, you can use a commonly accepted shorthand representation: you write the name of the table and then within parentheses list all of the fields in the table. Each table should begin on a new line. If the entries in the table occupy more than one line, the entries that appear on the next line should be indented so it is clear that they do not constitute another table. Using this method, you would represent the Bavant Publishing database as in Figure 11–4.

Customer (Customer Number, Customer Name, Street, City, State, Postal Code,
  Amount Paid, Current Due, Book Rep Number)

Book Rep (Book Rep Number, Last Name, First Name, Street,
  City, State, Postal Code, Salary, Bonus Rate)

Seminar (Seminar Code, Seminar Description, Hours, Increments)

Seminar Offerings (Customer Number, Seminar Code, Total Hours, Hours Spent)

Figure 11–4

The Bavant Publishing database contains some duplicate field names. For example, the Book Rep Number field appears in *both* the Book Rep table *and* the Customer table. This duplication of names can lead to possible confusion. If you write Book Rep Number, it is not clear to which Book Rep Number field you are referring.

When duplicate field names exist in a database, you need to indicate the field to which you are referring. You do so by writing both the table name and the field name, separated by a period. You would write the Book Rep Number field in the Customer table as Customer.Book Rep Number and the Book Rep Number field in the Book Rep table as Book Rep.Book Rep Number. Technically, when you combine a field name with a table name, you say that you **qualify** the field names. It is *always* acceptable to qualify field names, even if there is no possibility of confusion. If confusion may arise, however, it is *essential* to qualify field names.

Functional Dependence

BTW

Functional Dependence

To help identify functional dependencies, ask yourself the following question. If you know a unique value for an attribute, do you know the unique values for another attribute? For example, when you have three attributes — Book Rep Number, Last Name, and First Name — and you know a unique value for Book Rep Number, do you also know a unique value for Last Name and First Name? If so, then Last Name and First Name are functionally dependent on Book Rep Number.

In the Bavant Publishing database (Figure 11–2 on page AC 668), a given customer number in the database will correspond to a single customer because customer numbers are unique. Thus, if you are given a customer number in the database, you could find a single name that corresponds to it. No ambiguity exists. The database terminology for this relationship between customer numbers and names is that Customer Number determines Customer Name, or, equivalently, that Customer Name is functionally dependent on Customer Number. Specifically, if you know that whenever you are given a value for one field, you will be able to determine a single value for a second field, the first field is said to **determine** the second field. In addition, the second field is said to be **functionally dependent** on the first.

There is a shorthand notation that represents functional dependencies using an arrow. To indicate that Customer Number determines Customer Name, or, equivalently, that Customer Name is functionally dependent on Customer Number, you would write Customer Number → Customer Name. The field that precedes the arrow determines the field that follows the arrow.

If you were given a city and asked to find a single customer's name, you could not do it. Given Greer as the city, for example, you would find two customer names, Applewood State University and Brodkin Junior College (Figure 11–5). Formally, you would say the City does *not* determine Customer Name, or that Customer Name is *not* functionally dependent on City.

CONSIDER THIS

In the Book Rep table, is Last Name functionally dependent on Book Rep Number?

Yes. If you are given a value for Book Rep Number, for example 42, you will always find a *single* last name, in this case Perez, associated with it.

In the Customer table, is Customer Name functionally dependent on Book Rep Number?

No. A given Book Rep Number occurs on multiple rows. Book Rep Number 42, for example, occurs on a row on which the Customer Name is Applewood State University. It also occurs on a row on which the Customer Name is Brodkin Junior College. Thus, rep number 42 is associated with more than one customer name.

city is Greer; name is Applewood State University

city is also Greer, but name is Brodkin Junior College (same city, but different customer name)

Customer

Customer Number	Customer Name	Street	City	State	Postal Code	Amount Paid	Current Due	Book Rep Number
ASU37	Applewood State University	300 University Ave.	Greer	PA	19158	$41,530.98	$38,812.66	42
BCJ21	Brodkin Junior College	4806 Park Dr.	Greer	PA	19158	$0.00	$6,081.98	42
CRU11	Cristie University	1200 University Pl.	Pleasantburg	NJ	07025	$0.00	$14,250.00	42
CSD25	Cowpens ISD	829 Wooster Ave.	Gossett	PA	19157	$12,750.00	$13,275.00	53
CSU10	Camellia State University	725 Camellia St.	Pleasantburg	NJ	07025	$63,246.88	$69,847.76	53
DCC34	Dartt Community College	[illegible]	Chambers	NJ	07037	$21,345.50	$23,467.75	65
FSC12	First State College	7300 Cedar Rd.	Quaker	DE	19719	$34,557.25	$23,875.98	65
FSU23	Farnham State University	1445 Hubert St.	Gaston	DE	19723	$18,268.00	$22,024.50	42
KCC78	Key Community College System	7523 Penn Ave.	Adelphia	PA	19159	$21,288.65	$11,367.49	65
MCC45	Mauldin Community College	72 Montrose St.	Chesnee	NJ	07053	$9,500.00	$5,000.00	53
MEC56	Mehitable College	202 College St.	Gaston	DE	19723	$9,111.19	$7,310.76	42
PLI22	Pratt-Last Institute	236 Ashton Ave.	Pleasantburg	NJ	07025	$17,229.45	$11,769.75	53
SCC77	Stallone Community College	1200 Franklin Blvd.	Adelphia	PA	19156	$7,525.98	$2,515.78	42
SEC19	Seaborn College	345 Mather Rd.	Quaker	DE	19719	$9,225.34	$10,496.89	65
TSC02	Tri-State Consortium	3400 Metropolitan Pkwy.	Adelphia	PA	19156	$34,578.90	$9,432.56	65

Figure 11–5

CONSIDER THIS

In the Seminar Offerings table, is Hours Spent functionally dependent on Customer Number?
No. There is a row, for example, on which the Customer Number is ASU37 and the Hours Spent is 0. There is another row on which the Customer Number is ASU37 but the Hours Spent is 4, a different number.

In the Seminar Offerings table, is Hours Spent functionally dependent on Seminar Code?
No. There is a row, for example, on which the Seminar Code is S04 and the Hours Spent is 4. There is another row on which the Seminar Code is S04 but the Hours Spent is 2, a different number.

On which fields is the Hours Spent functionally dependent?
To determine a value for Hours Spent, you need both a Customer Number and a Seminar Code. In other words, Hours Spent is functionally dependent on the combination, formally called the **concatenation**, of Customer Number and Seminar Code. That is, given a Customer Number ***and*** a Seminar Code, you can find a single value for Hours Spent.

On which fields is the Total Hours functionally dependent?
Because the Total Hours for a given seminar can vary from one customer to another, Total Hours is also functionally dependent on the combination of Customer Number and Seminar Code.

On which fields would the Total Hours be functionally dependent if every time a seminar was scheduled, the Total Hours had to be the same as the number of hours given in the Seminar table?
In that case, to determine Total Hours, you would only need to know the Seminar Code. Thus, Total Hours would be functionally dependent on Seminar Code.

Primary Key

The **primary key** of a table is the field or minimum collection of fields — the fewest number of fields possible — that uniquely identifies a given row in that table. In the Book Rep table, the rep's number uniquely identifies a given row. Any rep number appears on only one row of the table. Thus, Book Rep Number is the primary key. Similarly, Customer Number is the primary key of the Customer table, and Seminar Code is the primary key of the Seminar table.

CONSIDER THIS

Is the Customer Number field the primary key for the Seminar Offerings table?
No, because it does not functionally determine either Total Hours or Hours Spent.

Is the Seminar Code field the primary key for the Seminar Offerings table?
No, because, like Customer Number, it does not functionally determine either Total Hours or Hours Spent.

What is the primary key of the Seminar Offerings table?
The primary key is the combination of the Customer Number and Seminar Code fields. You can determine all other fields from this combination. Further, neither the Customer Number nor the Seminar Code alone has this property.

Is the combination of the Seminar Code and Seminar Description fields the primary key for the Seminar table?
No. Although it is true that you can determine all fields in the Seminar table by this combination, Seminar Code alone also has this property. The Seminar Code field is the primary key.

The primary key provides an important way of distinguishing one row in a table from another. In the shorthand representation, you underline the field or collection of fields that comprise the primary key for each table in the database. Thus, the complete shorthand representation for the Bavant Publishing database is shown in Figure 11–6.

Customer (<u>Customer Number</u>, Customer Name, Street, City, State, Postal Code, Amount Paid, Current Due, Book Rep Number)
Book Rep (<u>Book Rep Number</u>, Last Name, First Name, Street, City, State, Postal Code, Salary, Bonus Rate)
Seminar (<u>Seminar Code</u>, Seminar Description, Hours, Increments)
Seminar Offerings (<u>Customer Number</u>, <u>Seminar Code</u>, Total Hours, Hours Spent)

Figure 11–6

BTW
Candidate Keys
According to the definition of a candidate key, a Social Security number is a legitimate primary key. Many databases use a person's Social Security number as a primary key. However, many institutions and organizations are moving away from using Social Security numbers because of privacy issues. Instead, many institutions and organizations use unique student numbers or employee numbers as primary keys.

Occasionally, but not often, there might be more than one possibility for the primary key. For example, if the Bavant Publishing database included the rep's Social Security number in the Book Rep table, either the rep number or the Social Security number could serve as the primary key. In this case, both fields are referred to as candidate keys. Similar to a primary key, a **candidate key** is a field or combination of fields on which all fields in the table are functionally dependent. Thus, the definition for primary key really defines candidate key as well. There can be many candidate keys, although having more than one is very rare. By contrast, there is only one primary key. The remaining candidate keys are called **alternate keys**.

Database Design

This section presents a specific database design method, based on a set of requirements that the database must support. The section then presents a sample of such requirements and illustrates the design method by designing a database to satisfy these requirements.

Design Process

The following is a method for designing a database for a set of requirements.

1. Examine the requirements and identify the entities, or objects, involved. Assign names to the entities. The entities will become tables. If, for example, the design involves the entities departments and employees, you could assign the names, Department and Employee. If the design involves the entities customers, orders, and parts, you could assign the names, Customer, Orders, and Part.

NOTE: The word, Order, has special meaning in SQL. If you use it for the name of a table, you will not be able to use SQL to query that table. A common approach to avoid this problem is to make the name plural. That is the reason for choosing Orders rather than Order as the name of the table.

2. Identify a unique identifier for each entity. For example, if one of the entities is parts, you would determine what it takes to uniquely identify each individual part. In other words, what enables the organization to distinguish one part from another? For a part entity, it may be Item Number. For a customer entity, it may be Customer Number. If there is no such unique identifier, it is a good idea to add one. Perhaps the previous system was a manual one where customers were not assigned numbers, in which case this would be a good time to add Customer Numbers to the system. If there is no natural candidate for a primary key, you can add an AutoNumber field, which is similar to the ID field that Access adds automatically when you create a new table.
3. Identify the attributes for all the entities. These attributes will become the fields in the tables. It is possible that more than one entity has the same attribute. At Bavant Publishing, for example, customers and reps both have the attributes of street address, city, state, and postal code. To address this duplication, you can follow the name of the attribute with the corresponding entity in parentheses. Thus, Street (Customer) would be the street address of a customer, whereas Street (Book Rep) would be the street address of a rep.
4. Identify the functional dependencies that exist among the attributes.
5. Use the functional dependencies to identify the tables. You do this by placing each attribute with the attribute or minimum combination of attributes on which it is functionally dependent. The attribute or attributes on which all other attributes in the table are dependent will be the primary key of the table. The remaining attributes will be the other fields in the table. Once you have determined all the fields in the table, you can assign an appropriate name to the table.

6. Determine and implement relationships among the entities. The basic relationships are one-to-many and many-to-many.

   One-to-many. You implement a one-to-many relationship by including the primary key of the "one" table as a foreign key in the "many" table. A **foreign key** is a field in one table whose values are required to match the primary key of another table. In the one-to-many relationship between book reps and customers, for example, you include the primary key of the Book Rep Table, Book Rep Number, as a foreign key in the Customer table. You may already have included this field in the earlier steps. If so, you simply would designate it to be a foreign key. If you had not added it already, you would need to add it at this point, designating it as a foreign key.

   Many-to-many. A many-to-many relationship is implemented by creating a new table whose primary key is the combination of the keys of the original tables. To implement the many-to-many relationship between customers and seminars, for example, you would create a table whose primary key is the combination of Customer Number and Seminar Code, which are the primary keys of the original tables. Both of the fields that make up the primary key of the new table will be foreign keys also. The Customer Number field, for example, will be a foreign key required to match the primary key of the Customer table. Similarly, the Seminar Code field will be a foreign key required to match the primary key of the Seminar table.

You already may have identified such a table in the earlier steps, in which case, all you need to do is to be sure you have designated each portion of the primary key as a foreign key that is required to match the primary key of the appropriate table. If you have not, you would add the table at this point. The primary key will consist of the primary keys from each of the tables to be related. If there are any attributes that depend on the combination of fields that make up the primary key, you need to include them in this table. (*Note:* There may not be any other fields that are dependent on this combination. In that case, there will be no fields besides the fields that make up the primary key.)

The following sections illustrate the design process by designing the database for Bavant Publishing. The next section gives the requirements that this database must support, and the last section creates a database design based on those requirements.

Requirements for the Bavant Publishing Database

Systems analysts have examined the needs and organizational policies at Bavant Publishing and have determined that the Bavant Publishing database must support the following requirements:

1. For a customer, Bavant needs to maintain the customer number, name, street address, city, state, postal code, amount paid, and the amount that is currently due. They also need the total amount, which is the sum of the amount already paid and the current amount due.
2. For a book rep, store the rep number, last name, first name, street address, city, state, postal code, salary paid, and bonus rate.

3. For a seminar, store the seminar code, seminar description, hours, and increments. In addition, for each offering of the seminar, store the number of the customer for whom the seminar is offered, the total number of hours planned for the offering of the seminar, and the number of hours already spent in the seminar. The total hours may be the same as the normal number of hours for the seminar, but it need not be. This gives Bavant the flexibility of tailoring the offering of the seminar to the specific needs of the customer.
4. Each customer has a single rep to which the customer is assigned. Each rep may be assigned many customers.
5. A customer may be offered many seminars and a seminar may be offered to many customers.

Design of the Bavant Publishing Database

The following represents the application of the design method for the Bavant Publishing requirements.

1. There appear to be three entities: customers, reps, and seminars. Reasonable names for the corresponding tables are Customer, Book Rep, and Seminar, respectively.
2. The unique identifier for customers is the customer number. The unique identifier for reps is the rep number. The unique identifier for seminars is the seminar code. Reasonable names for the unique identifiers are Customer Number, Book Rep Number, and Seminar Code, respectively.
3. The attributes are:

   Customer Number
   Customer Name
   Street (Customer)
   City (Customer)
   State (Customer)
   Postal Code (Customer)
   Amount Paid
   Current Due
   Book Rep Number
   Last Name
   First Name
   Street (Book Rep)
   City (Book Rep)
   State (Book Rep)
   Postal Code (Book Rep)
   Salary
   Bonus Rate
   Seminar Code

Seminar Description
Hours
Increments
Total Hours
Hours Spent

Remember that parentheses after an attribute indicate the entity to which the attribute corresponds. Thus, Street (Customer) represents the street address of a customer in a way that distinguishes it from Street (Book Rep), which represents the street address of a rep.

CONSIDER THIS

Why is Total Amount not included?

Total Amount, which is Amount Paid plus Current Due, can be calculated from other fields. You can perform this calculation in queries, forms, and reports. Thus, there is no need to include it as a field in the Customer table. Further, by including it, you introduce the possibility of errors in the database. For example, if Amount Paid is $5,000, Current Due is $2,000, yet you set Total Amount equal to $8,000, you have an error. You also need to be sure to change Total Amount appropriately whenever you change either Amount Paid or Current Due. If it is not stored, but rather calculated when needed, you avoid all these problems.

If including the Total Amount field is not appropriate, why did we include the Total Amount field in the Customer table in Chapter 3?

Access allows calculated fields. Rather than storing a value, you simply indicate the calculation. Access will calculate the value when needed. This approach avoids the above problems, so you actually could include the field. Often, however, you still will decide not to include it. If you plan to use another database management system, for example, an earlier version of Access, you should not include it. In addition, if you are using Access but plan to use the database with SQL Server, you should not include it.

4. The functional dependencies among the attributes are:

   Customer Number → Customer Name, Street (Customer), City (Customer), State (Customer), Postal Code (Customer), Amount Paid, Current Due, Book Rep Number

   Book Rep Number → Last Name, First Name, Street (Book Rep), City (Book Rep), State (Book Rep), Postal Code (Book Rep), Salary, Bonus Rate

   Seminar Code → Seminar Description, Hours, Increments

   Customer Number, Seminar Code → Total Hours, Hours Spent

CONSIDER THIS

Why is Total Hours listed with Customer Number and Seminar Code rather than just with Seminar Code?

If the total hours were required to be the same as the number of hours for the seminar, then it indeed would be listed with Seminar Code because it would not vary from one customer to another. Because Bavant wants the flexibility of tailoring the number of hours for which a particular seminar is offered to the specific needs of the customer, Total Hours also is dependent on Customer Number.

The customer's name, street address, city, state, postal code, amount paid, and current due are dependent only on customer number. Because a customer has a single rep, the rep number is dependent on customer number as well. The rep's last name, first name, street address, city, state, postal code, salary, and bonus rate are dependent only on Book Rep Number. A seminar description, the number of hours for the seminar, and the increments in which the seminar is offered are dependent only on seminar code. The total hours for a particular seminar offering as well as the hours already spent are dependent on the combination of customer number and seminar code.

5. The shorthand representation for the tables is shown in Figure 11–7.

Customer (<u>Customer Number</u>, Customer Name, Street, City, State, Postal Code, Amount Paid, Current Due, Book Rep Number)

Book Rep (<u>Book Rep Number</u>, Last Name, First Name, Street, City, State, Postal Code, Salary, Bonus Rate)

Seminar (<u>Seminar Code</u>, Seminar Description, Hours, Increments)

Seminar Offerings (<u>Customer Number</u>, <u>Seminar Code</u>, Total Hours, Hours Spent)

Figure 11–7

6. The following are the relationships between the tables:
   a. The Customer and Book Rep tables are related using the Book Rep Number fields, which is the primary key of the Book Rep table. The Book Rep Number field in the Customer table is a foreign key.
   b. The Customer and Seminar Offerings tables are related using the Customer Number fields, which is the primary key of the Customer table. The Customer Number field in the Seminar Offerings table is a foreign key.
   c. The Seminar and Seminar Offerings tables are related using the Seminar Code fields, which is the primary key of the Seminar table. The Seminar Code field in the Seminar Offerings table is a foreign key.

CONSIDER THIS

Does a many-to-many relationship exist between customers and seminars?
Yes. The Seminar Offerings table is precisely the table that will implement a many-to-many relationship between customers and seminars. You identified this table as part of the database design process. If you had not, you would need to add it at this point.

In the Seminar Offerings table, the primary key consists of two fields, Customer Number and Seminar Code. There are two additional fields, Total Hours and Hours Spent. What if the design requirements did not require these additional fields? Would we still need the Seminar Offerings table?
Yes, because this table implements the many-to-many relationship between customers and seminars. It is perfectly legitimate for the table that implements a many-to-many relationship to contain no columns except the two columns that constitute the primary key.

In the Seminar Offerings table, the primary key consists of two fields, Customer Number and Seminar Code. Does the Customer Number field have to come first?
No. The Seminar Code could have come first just as well.

NOTE: In the shorthand representation for the table containing the primary key, represent the foreign key by using the letters FK, followed by an arrow, followed by the name of the table containing the primary key. For example, to indicate that the Book Rep Number in the Customer table is a foreign key that must match the primary key of the Book Rep table, you would write FK Book Rep Number → Book Rep.

The shorthand representation for the tables and foreign keys is shown in Figure 11–8. It is common to list a table containing a foreign key after the table that contains the corresponding primary key, when possible. Thus, in the figure, the Book Rep table has been moved so that it comes before the Customer table.

Book Rep (<u>Book Rep Number</u>, Last Name, First Name, Street, City, State, Postal Code, Salary, Bonus Rate)

Customer (<u>Customer Number</u>, Customer Name, Street, City, State, Postal Code, Amount Paid, Current Due, Book Rep Number)
FK Book Rep Number → Book Rep

Seminar (<u>Seminar Code</u>, Seminar Description, Hours, Increments)

Seminar Offerings (<u>Customer Number</u>, <u>Seminar Code</u>, Total Hours, Hours Spent)
FK Customer Number → Customer
FK Seminar Code → Seminar

Figure 11–8

TAL Distributors

The management of TAL Distributors, a distributor of energy-saving and water-conservation items, has determined that the company's rapid growth requires a database to maintain customer, order, and inventory data. With the data stored in a database, management will be able to ensure that the data is current and more accurate. In addition, managers will be able to obtain answers to their questions concerning the data in the database easily and quickly, with the option of producing a variety of reports.

Requirements for the TAL Distributors Database

A system analyst has interviewed users and examined documents at TAL Distributors, and has determined that the company needs a database that will support the following requirements:

1. For a sales rep, store the rep's number, last name, first name, street address, city, state, postal code, total commission, and commission rate.
2. For a customer, store the customer's number, name, street address, city, state, postal code, balance owed, and credit limit. These customers are businesses, so it is appropriate to store a single name, rather than first name and last name as you would if the customers were individuals. Additional fields you need to store are the number, last name, and first name of the sales rep representing this customer. The analyst also has determined that a sales rep can represent many customers, but a customer must have exactly one sales rep. In other words, one sales rep must represent each customer; a customer cannot be represented by zero or more than one sales rep.
3. For a part, store the part's number, description, units on hand, the category the part is in, and the price.

4. For an order, store the order number, order date, the number and name of the customer placing the order, and the number of the sales rep representing that customer. For each line item within an order, store the part's number and description, the number ordered, and the quoted price. The analyst also obtained the following information concerning orders:
   a. There is only one customer per order.
   b. On a given order, each part is listed only as a single line item. For example, part DR93 cannot appear on multiple lines within the same order.
   c. The quoted price might differ from the actual price in cases in which the sales rep offers a discount for a certain part on a specific order.

Design of the TAL Distributors Database

The following steps apply the design process to the requirements for TAL Distributors to produce the appropriate database design:

1. Assign entity names. There appear to be four entities: reps, customers, parts, and orders. The names assigned to these entities are Rep, Customer, Part, and Orders, respectively.
2. Determine unique identifiers. From the collection of entities, review the data and determine the unique identifier for each entity. For the Rep, Customer, Part, and Orders entities, the unique identifiers are the rep number, the customer number, the item number, and the order number, respectively. These unique identifiers are named Rep Number, Customer Number, Item Number, and Order Number, respectively.
3. Assign attribute names. The attributes mentioned in the first requirement all refer to sales reps. The specific attributes mentioned in the requirement are the sales rep's number, last name, first name, street address, city, state, postal code, total commission, and commission rate. Assigning appropriate names to these attributes produces the following list:

   Rep Number
   Last Name
   First Name
   Street
   City
   State
   Postal Code
   Commission
   Rate

BTW
Line Items
A line item is a unit of information that appears on its own line. For example, when you purchase groceries, each grocery item appears on its own line. Line items also can be referred to as order line items or item detail lines.

The attributes mentioned in the second requirement refer to customers. The specific attributes are the customer's number, name, street address, city, state, postal code, balance, and credit limit. The requirement also mentions the number, first name, and last name of the sales rep representing this customer. Assigning appropriate names to these attributes produces the following list:

Customer Number
Customer Name
Street
City
State

Postal Code
Balance
Credit Limit
Rep Number
Last Name
First Name

CONSIDER THIS

Do you need to include the last name and first name of a sales rep in the list of attributes for the second requirement?

There is no need to include them in this list, because they both can be determined from the sales rep number and already are included in the list of attributes determined by Rep Number. They will be removed in a later step.

There are attributes named Street, City, State, and Postal Code for sales reps as well as attributes named Street, City, State, and Postal Code for customers. To distinguish these attributes in the final collection, the name of the attribute is followed by the name of the corresponding entity. For example, the street for a sales rep is Street (Rep) and the street for a customer is Street (Customer).

The attributes mentioned in the third requirement refer to parts. The specific attributes are the part's number, description, units on hand, category, and price. Assigning appropriate names to these attributes produces the following list:

Item Number
Description
On Hand
Category
Price

The attributes mentioned in the fourth requirement refer to orders. The specific attributes include the order number, order date, the number and name of the customer placing the order, and the number of the sales rep representing the customer. Assigning appropriate names to these attributes produces the following list:

Order Number
Order Date
Customer Number
Customer Name
Rep Number

The statement concerning orders indicates that there are specific attributes to be stored for each line item within the order. These attributes are the item number, description, the number ordered, and the quoted price. If the quoted price must be the same as the price, you simply could call it Price. According to requirement 4c, however, the quoted price might differ from the price. Thus, you must add the quoted price to the list. Assigning appropriate names to these attributes produces the following list:

Item Number
Description
Number Ordered
Quoted Price

The complete list grouped by entity is as follows:

Rep

- **Rep Number**
- **Last Name**
- **First Name**
- **Street (Rep)**
- **City (Rep)**
- **State (Rep)**
- **Postal Code (Rep)**
- **Commission**
- **Rate**

Customer

- **Customer Number**
- **Customer Name**
- **Street (Customer)**
- **City (Customer)**
- **State (Customer)**
- **Postal Code (Customer)**
- **Balance**
- **Credit Limit**
- **Rep Number**
- **Last Name**
- **First Name**

Part

- **Item Number**
- **Description**
- **On Hand**
- **Category**
- **Price**

Orders

- **Order Number**
- **Order Date**
- **Customer Number**
- **Customer Name**
- **Rep Number**

For line items within an order:

- **Order Number**
- **Item Number**
- **Description**
- **Number Ordered**
- **Quoted Price**

4. Identify functional dependencies. The fact that the unique identifier for sales reps is the Rep Number gives the following functional dependencies:

   Rep Number → Last Name, First Name, Street (Rep), City (Rep), State (Rep), Postal Code (Rep), Commission, Rate

   The fact that the unique identifier for customers is the Customer Number gives the following preliminary list of functional dependencies:

   Customer Number → Customer Name, Street (Customer), City (Customer), State (Customer), Postal Code (Customer), Balance, Credit Limit, Rep Number, Last Name, First Name

   The fact that the unique identifier for parts is the Item Number gives the following functional dependencies:

   Item Number → Description, On Hand, Category, Price

   The fact that the unique identifier for orders is the Order Number gives the following functional dependencies:

   Order Number → Order Date, Customer Number, Customer Name, Rep Number

CONSIDER THIS

Do you need to include the name of a customer and the number of the customer's rep in the list of attributes determined by the order number?

There is no need to include the customer name and the rep number in this list because you can determine them from the customer number, and they already are included in the list of attributes determined by customer number. They will be removed in the next step.

The final attributes to be examined are those associated with the line items within the order: Item Number, Description, Number Ordered, and Quoted Price.

CONSIDER THIS

Why are Number Ordered and Quoted Price not included in the list of attributes determined by the Order Number?

To uniquely identify a particular value for Number Ordered or Quoted Price, Order Number alone is not sufficient. It requires the combination of Order Number and Item Number.

The following shorthand representation indicates that the combination of Order Number and Item Number functionally determines Number Ordered and Quoted Price:

Order Number, Item Number → Number Ordered, Quoted Price

CONSIDER THIS

Does Description need to be included in this list?

No, because Description can be determined by the Item Number alone, and it already appears in the list of attributes dependent on the Item Number.

The complete list of functional dependencies with appropriate revisions is as follows:

Rep Number → Last Name, First Name, Street (Rep), City (Rep), State (Rep), Postal Code (Rep), Commission, Rate

Customer Number → Customer Name, Street (Customer), City (Customer), State (Customer), Postal Code (Customer), Balance, Credit Limit, Rep Number

Item Number → Description, On Hand, Category, Price

Order Number → Order Date, Customer Number

Order Number, Item Number → Number Ordered, Quoted Price

5. Create the tables. Using the functional dependencies, you can create tables with the attribute(s) to the left of the arrow being the primary key and the items to the right of the arrow being the other fields. For tables corresponding to those entities identified in Step 1, you simply can use the name you already determined. Because you did not identify any entity that had a unique identifier that was the combination of Order Number and Item Number, you need to assign a name to the table whose primary key consists of these two fields. Because this table represents the individual line items within an order, the name Line Item is a good choice. The final collection of tables is shown in Figure 11–9.

Rep (<u>Rep Number</u>, Last Name, First Name, Street, City, State, Postal Code, Commission, Rate)

Customer (<u>Customer Number</u>, Customer Name, Street, City, State, Postal Code, Balance, Credit Limit, Rep Number)

Part (<u>Item Number</u>, Description, On Hand, Category, Price)

Orders (<u>Order Number</u>, Order Date, Customer Number)

Line Item (<u>Order Number</u>, <u>Item Number</u>, Number Ordered, Quoted Price)

Figure 11–9

6. Identify relationships.
   a. The Customer and Rep tables are related using the Rep Number fields. The Rep Number field in the Rep table is the primary key. The Rep Number field in the Customer table is a foreign key.
   b. The Orders and Customer tables are related using the Customer Number fields. The Customer Number field in the Customer table is the primary key. The Customer Number field in the Orders table is a foreign key.
   c. The Line Item and Orders tables are related using the Order Number fields. The Order Number field in the Orders table is the primary key. The Order Number field in the Line Item table is a foreign key.
   d. The Line Item and Part tables are related using the Item Number fields. The Item Number field in the Part table is the primary key. The Item Number field in the Line Item table is a foreign key.

CONSIDER THIS

Does a many-to-many relationship exist between orders and parts?

Yes. The Line Item table is precisely the table that will implement a many-to-many relationship between orders and parts. You identified this table as part of the database design process. If you had not, you would need to add it at this point.

CONSIDER THIS

In the Line Item table, the primary key consists of two fields, Order Number and Item Number. There are two additional fields, Number Ordered and Quoted Price. What if the design requirements did not require these additional fields? Would we still need the Line Item table?

Yes, because this table implements the many-to-many relationship between orders and parts. It is perfectly legitimate for the table that implements a many-to-many relationship to contain only the two columns that constitute the primary key.

The shorthand representation for the tables and foreign keys is shown in Figure 11–10.

Rep (<u>Rep Number</u>, Last Name, First Name, Street,
City, State, Postal Code, Commission, Rate)

Customer (<u>Customer Number</u>, Customer Name, Street,
City, State, Postal Code, Balance, Credit Limit,
Rep Number)
FK Rep Number → Rep

Part (<u>Item Number</u>, Description, On Hand, Category, Price)

Orders (<u>Order Number</u>, Order Date, Customer Number)
FK Customer Number → Customer

Line Item (<u>Order Number</u>, <u>Item Number</u>, Number Ordered,
Quoted Price)
FK Order Number → Orders
FK Item Number → Part

Figure 11–10

Sample data for the TAL Distributors database is shown in Figure 11–11.

Rep Table

Rep Number	Last Name	First Name	Street	City	State	Postal Code	Commission	Rate
20	Kaiser	Valerie	624 Randall	Georgetown	NC	28794	$2,542.50	0.05
35	Hull	Richard	532 Jackson	Kyle	SC	28797	$3,216.00	0.07
65	Perez	Juan	1626 Taylor	Byron	SC	28795	$2,487.00	0.05

Customer Table

Customer Number	Customer Name	Street	City	State	Postal Code	Balance	Credit Limit	Rep Number
148	Al's Hardware Store	2837 Greenway	Oxford	TN	37021	$2,550.00	$7,500.00	20
282	Brookings Direct	3827 Devon	Ashton	VA	20123	$431.50	$2,500.00	35
356	Ferguson's	382 Wildwood	Georgetown	NC	28794	$2,785.00	$7,500.00	65
408	The Energy Shop	1828 Raven	Granger	NC	27036	$1,285.25	$5,000.00	35
462	Walburg Energy Alternatives	12 Polk	Walburg	NC	28819	$1,412.00	$2,500.00	65
524	Kline's	838 Ridgeland	Oxford	TN	37021	$3,762.00	$7,500.00	20
608	Conservation Foundation	372 Oxford	Ashton	VA	20123	$106.00	$5,000.00	65
687	CleanPlanet	282 Evergreen	Lowton	TN	37084	$2,851.00	$5,000.00	35
725	Patricia Jean's Home Center	282 Columbia	Walburg	NC	28819	$248.00	$7,500.00	35
842	The Efficient Home	28 Lakeview	Pineville	VA	22503	$4,221.00	$7,500.00	20

Figure 11–11

Orders Table

Order Number	Order Date	Customer Number
12608	4/5/2015	148
12610	4/5/2015	356
12613	4/6/2015	408
12614	4/6/2015	282
12617	4/8/2015	608
12619	4/8/2015	148
12623	4/8/2015	608

Item Table

Item Number	Description	On Hand	Category	Price
AT94	Air Deflector	50	General	$5.45
BV06	Energy Saving Kit	45	Energy	$42.75
CD52	Fluorescent Light Bulb	65	Energy	$4.75
DL71	Low Flow Shower Head	21	Water	$8.75
DR93	Smoke Detector	38	General	$6.10
DW11	Retractable Clothesline	12	General	$13.25
FD21	Water Conservation Kit	22	Water	$13.45
KL62	Toilet Tank Water Saver	32	Water	$3.35
KT03	Programmable Thermostat	8	Energy	$34.25
KV29	Windows Insulator Kit	19	Energy	$4.95

Line Item Table

Order Number	Item Number	Number Ordered	Quoted Price
12608	AT94	11	$5.45
12610	DR93	5	$6.10
12610	DW11	3	$12.50
12613	KL62	10	$3.35
12614	KT03	6	$33.00
12617	BV06	2	$40.25
12617	CD52	20	$4.25
12619	DR93	12	$6.00
12623	KV29	8	$4.95

Figure 11–11 (continued)

Normalization

After you create your database design, you should analyze it using a process called **normalization** to make sure the design is free of potential update, redundancy, and consistency problems. This process also supplies methods for correcting these problems.

The normalization process involves converting tables into various types of **normal forms**. A table in a particular normal form possesses a certain desirable set of properties. Several normal forms exist, the most common being first normal form (1NF), second normal form (2NF), and third normal form (3NF). The forms create a progression in which a table that is in 1NF is better than a table that is not in 1NF;

a table that is in 2NF is better than one that is in 1NF; and so on. The goal of normalization is to take a table or collection of tables and produce a new collection of tables that represents the same information but is free of problems.

First Normal Form

A table that contains a **repeating group**, or multiple entries for a single row, is called an **unnormalized table**. Recall from the definition of relation that an unnormalized table actually violates the definition of relation.

Removal of repeating groups is the starting point in the goal of having tables that are as free of problems as possible. In fact, in most database management systems, tables cannot contain repeating groups. A table (relation) is in **first normal form (1NF)** if it does not contain repeating groups.

In designing a database, you may have created a table with a repeating group. For example, you might have created a Seminar Offerings table in which the primary key is the Customer Number and there is a repeating group consisting of Seminar Code, Total Hours, and Hours Spent. In the example, each customer appears on a single row and Seminar Code, Total Hours, and Hours Spent are repeated as many times as necessary for each customer (Figure 11–12).

Seminar Offerings

Customer Number	Seminar Code	Total Hours	Hours Spent
ASU37	S03 S04 S05	4 6 8	0 4 4
BCJ21	S01	3	1
CRU11	S06	2	0
CSD25	S07	3	2
CSU10	S02 S08	2 4	1 2
FSC12	S04 S06	6 2	2 1
KCC78	S05	8	2
MCC45	S01	3	2
MEC56	S07	3	0
SEC19	S02 S07	2 3	1 1

repeating group (more than one entry in a single table location)

fifth row indicates that Customer CSU10 is being offered both seminar S02 and seminar S08

Figure 11–12

In the shorthand representation, you represent a repeating group by enclosing the repeating group within parentheses. The shorthand representation for the Seminar Offerings table from Figure 11–12 is shown in Figure 11–13.

Seminar Offerings (<u>Customer Number</u>, (Seminar Code, Total Hours, Hours Spent))

Figure 11–13

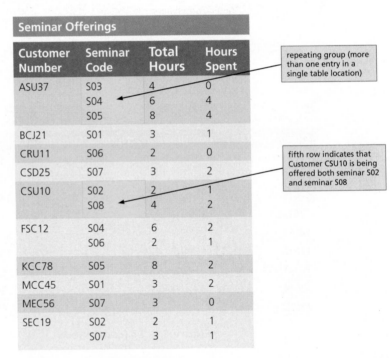

Conversion to First Normal Form

Figure 11 – 14 shows the normalized version of the table. Note that the fifth row of the unnormalized table (Figure 11 – 12) indicates that customer CSU10 currently is being offered both seminar S02 and seminar S08. In the normalized table, this information is represented by *two* rows, the seventh and the eighth. The primary key for the unnormalized Seminar Offerings table was the Customer Number only. The primary key for the normalized table now is the combination of Customer Number and Seminar Code.

Seminar Offerings

Customer Number	Seminar Code	Total Hours	Hours Spent
ASU37	S03	4	0
ASU37	S04	6	4
ASU37	S05	8	4
BCJ21	S01	3	1
CRU11	S06	2	0
CSD25	S07	3	2
CSU10	S02	2	1
CSU10	S08	4	2
FSC12	S04	6	2
FSC12	S06	2	1
KCC78	S05	8	2
MCC45	S01	3	2
MEC56	S07	3	0
SEC19	S02	2	1
SEC19	S07	3	1

seventh row indicates that Customer CSU10 is being offered seminar S02

eighth row indicates that Customer CSU10 is being offered seminar S08

Figure 11 – 14

In general, when converting a non-1NF table to 1NF, the primary key typically will include the original primary key concatenated with the key of the repeating group, that is, the field that distinguishes one occurrence of the repeating group from another within a given row in the table. In this case, Seminar Code is the key to the repeating group and thus becomes part of the primary key of the 1NF table.

To convert the table to 1NF, remove the parentheses enclosing the repeating group and expand the primary key to include the key to the repeating group. The shorthand representation for the resulting table is shown in Figure 11 – 15. Notice that the primary key is now the combination of the Customer Number field and the Seminar Code field.

Seminar Offerings (Customer Number, Seminar Code, Total Hours, Hours Spent)

Figure 11 – 15

Second Normal Form

Even though the following table is in 1NF, problems may exist that will cause you to want to restructure the table. In the database design process, for example, you might have created the Seminar Offerings table shown in Figure 11–16.

Seminar Offerings (<u>Customer Number</u>, Customer Name, <u>Seminar Code</u>, Seminar Description, Total Hours, Hours Spent)

Figure 11–16

This table contains the following functional dependencies:

Customer Number → Customer Name

Seminar Code → Seminar Description

Customer Number, Seminar Code → Total Hours, Hours Spent

This notation indicates that Customer Number alone determines Customer Name; Seminar Code alone determines Seminar Description, but it requires *both* a Customer Number *and* a Seminar Code to determine either Total Hours or Hours Spent. Figure 11–17 shows a sample of this table.

description of seminar S05 occurs more than once

Seminar

Customer Number	Customer Name	Seminar Code	Seminar Description	Total Hours	Hours Spent
ASU37	Applewood State University	S03	Mobile Apps	4	0
ASU37	Applewood State University	S04	Video Podcasting	6	4
ASU37	Applewood State University	S05	Creating Virtual Worlds	8	4
BCJ21	Brodkin Junior College	S01	Integrating with Learning Management Systems	3	1
CRU11	Cristie University	S06	Clickers in the Classroom	2	0
CSD25	Cowpens ISD	S07	Online Course Strategies	3	2
CSU10	Camellia State University	S02	Using Web-based Technologies and Tools	2	1
CSU10	Camellia State University	S08	Using Social Networking	4	2
FSC12	First State College	S04	Video Podcasting	6	2
FSC12	First State College	S06	Clickers in the Classroom	2	1
KCC78	Key Community College System	S05	Creating Virtual Worlds	8	2
MCC45	Mauldin Community College	S01	Integrating with Learning Management Systems	3	2
MEC56	Mehitable College	S07	Online Course Strategies	3	0
SEC19	Seaborn College	S02	Using Web-based Technologies and Tools	2	1
SEC19	Seaborn College	S07	Online Course Strategies	3	1

name of customer FSC12 occurs more than once

Figure 11–17

The name of a specific customer, FSC12 for example, occurs multiple times in the table, as does the description of a seminar. This redundancy causes several problems. It is certainly wasteful of space, but that is not nearly as serious as some of the other problems. These other problems are called **update anomalies**, and they fall into four categories:

1. **Update.** A change to the name of customer FSC12 requires not one change to the table, but several: you must change each row in which FSC12 appears. This certainly makes the update process much more cumbersome; it is more complicated logically and takes longer to update.

2. **Inconsistent data.** There is nothing about the design that would prohibit customer FSC12 from having two or more different names in the database. The first row, for example, might have First State College as the name, whereas the second row might have First Statewide College.
3. **Additions.** There is a real problem when you try to add a new seminar and its description to the database. Because the primary key for the table consists of both Customer Number and Seminar Code, you need values for both of these to add a new row. If you have a customer to add but there are so far no seminars scheduled for it, what do you use for a Seminar Code? The only solution would be to make up a placeholder Seminar Code and then replace it with a real Seminar Code once the customer requests a seminar. Certainly this is not an acceptable solution.
4. **Deletions.** In Figure 11–17, if you delete seminar S01 from the database, you would need to delete all rows on which the Seminar Code is S01. In the process, you will delete the only row on which customer MCC45 appears, so you also would *lose* all the information about customer MCC45. You no longer would know that the name of customer MCC45 is Mauldin Community College.

These problems occur because there is a field, Customer Name, that is dependent on only a Customer Number, which is just a portion of the primary key. There is a similar problem with Seminar Description, which depends only on the Seminar Code, not the complete primary key. This leads to the definition of second normal form. Second normal form represents an improvement over first normal form because it eliminates update anomalies in these situations. In order to understand second normal form, you need to understand the term, nonkey field.

A field is a **nonkey field**, also called a **nonkey attribute**, if it is not a part of the primary key. A table (relation) is in **second normal form (2NF)** if it is in first normal form and no nonkey field is dependent on only a portion of the primary key.

Note that if the primary key of a table contains only a single field, the table is automatically in second normal form. In that case, there could not be any field dependent on only a portion of the primary key.

Conversion to Second Normal Form

To correct the problems, convert the table to a collection of tables in second normal form. Then name the new tables. The following is a method for performing this conversion.

1. Take each subset of the set of fields that make up the primary key and begin a new table with this subset as its primary key. The result of applying this step to the Seminar Offerings table is shown in Figure 11–18.

(<u>Customer Number</u>,
(<u>Seminar Code</u>,
(<u>Customer Number</u>, <u>Seminar Code</u>,

Figure 11–18

2. Place each of the other fields with the appropriate primary key; that is, place each one with the minimal collection of fields on which it depends. The result of applying this step to the Seminar Offerings table is shown in Figure 11–19 on the next page.

(Customer Number, Customer Name)
(Seminar Code, Seminar Description)
(Customer Number, Seminar Code, Total Hours, Hours Spent)

Figure 11–19

3. Give each of these new tables a name that is descriptive of the meaning of the table, such as Customer, Seminar, and Seminar Offerings.

   Figure 11–20 shows samples of the tables.

Customer

Customer Number	Customer Name
ASU37	Applewood State University
BCJ21	Brodkin Junior College
CRU11	Cristie University
CSD25	Cowpens ISD
CSU10	Camellia State University
DCC34	Dartt Community College
FSC12	First State College
FSU23	Farnham State University
KCC78	Key Community College System
MCC45	Mauldin Community College
MEC56	Mehitable College
PLI22	Pratt-Last Institute
SCC77	Stallone Community College
SEC19	Seaborn College
TSC02	Tri-State Consortium

name of Customer FSC12 occurs only once

Seminar

Seminar Code	Seminar Description
S01	Integrating with Learning Management Systems
S02	Using Web-based Technologies and Tools
S03	Mobile Apps
S04	Video Podcasting
S05	Creating Virtual Worlds
S06	Clickers in the Classroom
S07	Online Course Strategies
S08	Using Social Networking

description of seminar S05 occurs only once

Figure 11–20

Seminar Offerings			
Customer Number	Seminar Code	Total Hours	Hours Spent
ASU37	S03	4	0
ASU37	S04	6	4
ASU37	S05	8	4
BCJ21	S01	3	1
CRU11	S06	2	0
CSD25	S07	3	2
CSU10	S02	2	1
CSU10	S08	4	2
FSC12	S04	6	2
FSC12	S06	2	1
KCC78	S05	8	2
MCC45	S01	3	2
MEC56	S07	3	0
SEC19	S02	2	1
SEC19	S07	3	1

Figure 11–20 (continued)

The new design eliminates the update anomalies. A customer name occurs only once for each customer, so you do not have the redundancy that you did in the earlier design. Changing the name of a customer is now a simple process involving a single change. Because the name of a customer occurs in a single place, it is not possible to have multiple names for the same customer in the database at the same time.

To add a new customer, you create a new row in the Customer table, and thus there is no need to have a seminar offering already scheduled for that customer. In addition, deleting seminar S01 has nothing to do with the Customer table and, consequently, does not cause customer MCC45 to be deleted. Thus, you still have its name, Mauldin Community College, in the database. Finally, you have not lost any information in the process.

CONSIDER THIS

Can I reconstruct the data in the original design from the data in the new design?

Yes. The following SQL query would produce the data in the form shown in Figure 11–17 on page AC 690:

```
SELECT [Customer].[Customer Number], [Customer Name],
  [Seminar].[Seminar Code], [Seminar Description],
  [Total Hours], [Hours Spent]
FROM [Customer],[Seminar],[Seminar Offerings]
WHERE [Customer].[Customer Number]=
  [Seminar Offerings].[Customer Number]
AND [Seminar].[Seminar Code]=
  [Seminar Offerings].[Seminar Code];
```

Third Normal Form

BTW

3NF

The definition given for third normal form is not the original definition. This more recent definition, which is preferable to the original, is often referred to as Boyce-Codd normal form (BCNF) when it is important to make a distinction between this definition and the original definition. This text does not make such a distinction but will take this to be the definition of third normal form.

Problems still can exist with tables that are in 2NF, as illustrated in the Customer table whose shorthand representation is shown in Figure 11–21.

Customer (<u>Customer Number</u>, Customer Name, Street, City, State, Postal Code, Amount Paid, Current Due, Book Rep Number, Last Name, First Name)

Figure 11–21

The functional dependencies in this table are:

Customer Number → Customer Name, Street, City, State, Postal Code, Amount Paid, Current Due, Book Rep Number

Book Rep Number → Last Name, First Name

As these dependencies indicate, Customer Number determines all the other fields. In addition, Book Rep Number determines Last Name and First Name.

Because the primary key of the table is a single field, the table is automatically in second normal form. As the sample of the table shown in Figure 11–22 demonstrates, however, this table has problems similar to those encountered earlier, even though it is in 2NF. In this case, it is the last name and first name of a rep that can occur many times in the table; see rep 42, Melina Perez, for example. (Note that the three dots represent fields that do not appear due to space considerations.)

Customer

Customer Number	Customer Name	...	Amount Paid	Current Due	Book Rep Number	Last Name	First Name
ASU37	Applewood State University	...	$41,530.98	$38,812.66	42	Perez	Melina
BCJ21	Brodkin Junior College	...	$0.00	$6,081.98	42	Perez	Melina
CRU11	Cristie University	...	$0.00	$14,250.00	42	Perez	Melina
CSD25	Cowpens ISD	...	$12,750.00	$13,275.00	53	Chin	Robert
CSU10	Camellia State University	...	$63,246.88	$69,847.76	53	Chin	Robert
DCC34	Dartt Community College	...	$21,345.50	$23,467.75	65	Rogers	Tracy
FSC12	First State College	...	$34,557.25	$23,875.98	65	Rogers	Tracy
FSU23	Farnham State University	...	$18,268.00	$22,024.50	42	Perez	Melina
KCC78	Key Community College System	...	$21,288.65	$11,367.49	65	Rogers	Tracy
MCC45	Mauldin Community College	...	$9,500.00	$5,000.00	53	Chin	Robert
MEC56	Mehitable College	...	$9,111.19	$7,310.76	42	Perez	Melina
PLI22	Pratt-Last Institute	...	$17,229.45	$11,769.75	53	Chin	Robert
SCC77	Stallone Community College	...	$7,525.98	$2,515.78	42	Perez	Melina
SEC19	Seaborn College	...	$9,225.34	$10,496.89	65	Rogers	Tracy
TSC02	Tri-State Consortium	...	$34,578.90	$9,432.56	65	Rogers	Tracy

name of rep 42 occurs more than once

Figure 11–22

This redundancy results in the same set of problems described previously with the Seminar Offerings table. In addition to the problem of wasted space, you have similar update anomalies, as follows:

1. **Updates.** A change to the name of a rep requires not one change to the table, but several changes. Again the update process becomes very cumbersome.
2. **Inconsistent data.** There is nothing about the design that would prohibit a rep from having two different names in the database. On the first row, for example, the name for rep 42 might read Melina Perez, whereas on the third row (another row on which the rep number is 42), the name might be Melina Gomez.
3. **Additions.** In order to add rep 59, whose name is Mary Simpson, to the database, she must have at least one customer. If she has not yet been assigned any customers, either you cannot record the fact that her name is Mary Simpson, or you have to create a fictitious customer for her to represent. Again, this is not a desirable solution to the problem.
4. **Deletions.** If you were to delete all the customers of rep 42 from the database, then you also would lose all information concerning rep 42.

These update anomalies are due to the fact that Book Rep Number determines Last Name and First Name, but Book Rep Number is not the primary key. As a result, the same Book Rep Number and consequently the same Last Name and First Name can appear on many different rows.

You have seen that 2NF is an improvement over 1NF, but to eliminate 2NF problems, you need an even better strategy for creating tables in the database. Third normal form provides that strategy.

Before looking at third normal form, you need to become familiar with the special name that is given to any field that determines another field, like Book Rep Number in the Customer table. Any field or collection of fields that determines another field is called a **determinant**. Certainly the primary key in a table is a determinant. Any candidate key is a determinant as well. (Remember that a candidate key is a field or collection of fields that could function as the primary key.) In this case, Book Rep Number is a determinant, but it certainly is not a candidate key for the Customer table shown in Figure 11–22, and that is the problem.

A table is in **third normal form** (3NF) if it is in second normal form and if the only determinants it contains are candidate keys.

Conversion to Third Normal Form

You now have identified the problem with the Customer table: it is not in 3NF. You need a way to correct the deficiency in the Customer table and in all tables having similar deficiencies. Such a method follows.

First, for each determinant that is not a candidate key, remove from the table the fields that depend on this determinant, but do not remove the determinant. Next, create a new table containing all the fields from the original table that depend on this determinant. Finally, make the determinant the primary key of this new table.

In the Customer table, for example, Last Name and First Name are removed because they depend on the determinant Book Rep Number, which is not a candidate key. A new table is formed, consisting of Book Rep Number as the primary key, Last Name, and First Name. Specifically, you would replace the Customer table in Figure 11–22 with the two tables shown in Figure 11–23 on the next page.

Customer (<u>Customer Number</u>, Customer Name, Street, City, State, Postal Code, Amount Paid, Current Due, Book Rep Number)

Book Rep (<u>Book Rep Number</u>, Last Name, First Name)

Figure 11–23

Figure 11–24 shows samples of the tables.

Customer

Customer Number	Customer Name	...	Amount Paid	Current Due	Book Rep Number
ASU37	Applewood State University	...	$41,530.98	$38,812.66	42
BCJ21	Brodkin Junior College	...	$0.00	$6,081.98	42
CRU11	Cristie University	...	$0.00	$14,250.00	42
CSD25	Cowpens ISD	...	$12,750.00	$13,275.00	53
CSU10	Camellia State University	...	$63,246.88	$69,847.76	53
DCC34	Dartt Community College	...	$21,345.50	$23,467.75	65
FSC12	First State College	...	$34,557.25	$23,875.98	65
FSU23	Farnham State University	...	$18,268.00	$22,024.50	42
KCC78	Key Community College System	...	$21,288.65	$11,367.49	65
MCC45	Mauldin Community College	...	$9,500.00	$5,000.00	53
MEC56	Mehitable College	...	$9,111.19	$7,310.76	42
PLI22	Pratt-Last Institute	...	$17,229.45	$11,769.75	53
SCC77	Stallone Community College	...	$7,525.98	$2,515.78	42
SEC19	Seaborn College	...	$9,225.34	$10,496.89	65
TSC02	Tri-State Consortium	...	$34,578.90	$9,432.56	65

name of rep 42 occurs only once

Book Rep

Book Rep Number	Last Name	First Name
42	Perez	Melina
48	Statnik	Michael
53	Chin	Robert
65	Rogers	Tracy

Figure 11–24

This design corrects the previously identified problems. A rep's name appears only once, thus avoiding redundancy and making the process of changing a rep's name a very simple one. With this design, it is not possible for a rep to have two different names in the database. To add a new rep to the database, you add a row in the Book Rep table; it is not necessary to have a pre-existing customer for the rep. Finally, deleting all the customers of a given rep will not remove the rep's record from the Book Rep table, so you retain the rep's name; all the data in the original table can be reconstructed from the data in the new collection of tables. All previously mentioned problems indeed have been solved.

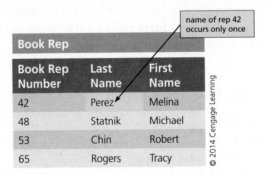

CONSIDER THIS

Can I reconstruct the data in the original design from the data in the new design?

Yes. The following SQL query would produce the data in the form shown in Figure 11–22 on page AC 694:

```
SELECT [Customer Number], [Customer Name], [Street],
  [City], [State], [Postal Code], [Amount Paid],
  [Current Due], [Customer].[Book Rep Number],
  [Last Name], [First Name]
FROM [Customer],[Book Rep]
WHERE [Customer].[Book Rep Number]=
  [Book Rep].[Book Rep Number];
```

Special Topics

In addition to knowing how to design a database and how to normalize tables, there are two other topics with which you should be familiar. First, you may be given a requirement for a database in the form of a document the database must be capable of producing, for example, an invoice. In addition, you should know how to represent your design with a diagram.

BTW
Existing Documents
Other examples of existing documents would be purchase orders, procedure manuals, organizational policy manuals, inventory lists, and so on.

Obtaining Information from Existing Documents

Existing documents often can furnish helpful information concerning the database design. You need to know how to obtain information from the document that you then will use in the design process. An existing document, like the invoice for the company named TAL Distributors shown in Figure 11–25 on the next page, often will provide the details that determine the tables and fields required to produce the document.

The first step in obtaining information from an existing document is to identify and list all fields and give them appropriate names. You also need to understand the business policies of the organization. For example, in the order shown in Figure 11–25, the information on TAL Distributors is preprinted on the form, and it is not necessary to describe the company. The following is a list of the fields you can determine from the invoice shown in Figure 11–25.

Order Number
Order Date
Customer Number
Customer Name
Street (Customer)
City (Customer)
State (Customer)
Postal Code (Customer)
Rep Number
Last Name (Rep)
First Name (Rep)
Item Number
Description
Number Ordered
Price
Total
Order Total

TAL Distributors

INVOICE

555 Main Street
San Rita, TX 78364
Phone (512-555-0190 Fax (512-555-0191)

ORDER: 12617
DATE: APRIL 15, 2015

TO:
Customer: 462
Walburg Energy Alternatives
12 Polk
Walburg, NC 28819

SALES REP: 65
Juan Perez

ITEM NUMBER	DESCRIPTION	NUMBER ORDERED	PRICE	TOTAL
BV06	Energy Saving Kit	2	40.25	80.50
CD52	Fluorescent Light Bulb	20	4.25	85.00
		TOTAL		165.50

Make all checks payable to TAL Distributors
Total due in 15 days. Overdue accounts subject to a service charge of 1% per month.

Thank you for your business!

Figure 11–25

Next, you need to identify functional dependencies. If the document you are examining is unfamiliar to you, you may have difficulty determining the dependencies and may need to get all the information directly from the user. On the other hand, you often can make intelligent guesses based on your general knowledge of the type of document you are studying. You may make mistakes, of course, and these should be corrected when you interact with the user. After initially determining the functional dependencies, you may discover additional information. The following are possible initial functional dependencies:

Customer Number → Customer Name, Street (Customer), City (Customer), State (Customer), Postal Code (Customer), Rep Number, Last Name (Rep), First Name (Rep)

Item Number → Description, Price

Order Number → Order Date, Customer Number, Order Total

Order Number, Item Number → Number Ordered, Price, Total

You may find, for example, that the price for a particular item on an order need not be the same as the standard price for the item. If that is the case, Price and Total are functionally dependent on the combination of Order Number and Item Number, not just Item Number alone. You also may decide to change the field name to Quoted Price to indicate the fact that it can vary from one order to another.

For the same reasons that you did not include Total Amount in the Bavant Publishing database, you probably would not want to include either Total or Order Total. Both can be computed from other data. The other correction that you should make to the functional dependencies is to realize that the last name and first name of a rep depend on the data in the Rep Number field.

Given these corrections, a revised list of functional dependencies might look like the following:

Rep Number → Last Name, First Name

Customer Number → Customer Name, Street (Customer), City (Customer), State (Customer), Postal Code (Customer), Rep Number

Item Number → Description, Price

Order Number → Order Date, Customer Number

Order Number, Item Number → Number Ordered, Quoted Price

After you have determined the preliminary functional dependencies, you can begin determining the tables and assigning fields. You could create tables with the determinant — the field or fields to the left of the arrow — as the primary key and with the fields to the right of the arrow as the remaining fields. This would lead to the following initial collection of tables shown in Figure 11–26.

Rep (<u>Rep Number</u>, Last Name, First Name)

Customer (<u>Customer Number</u>, Customer Name, Street, City, State, Postal Code, Rep Number)

Part (<u>Item Number</u>, Description)

Orders (<u>Order Number</u>, Order Date, Customer Number)

OrderLine (<u>Order Number</u>, <u>Item Number</u>, Number Ordered, Quoted Price)

Figure 11–26

Adding the foreign key information produces the shorthand representation shown in Figure 11–27.

Rep (<u>Rep Number</u>, Last Name, First Name)
Customer (<u>Customer Number</u>, Customer Name, Street, City, State, Postal Code, Rep Number)
FK Rep Number → Rep
Part (<u>Item Number</u>, Description)
Orders (<u>Order Number</u>, Order Date, Customer Number)
FK Customer Number → Customer
OrderLine (<u>Order Number</u>, <u>Item Number</u>, Number Ordered, Quoted Price)
FK Order Number → Orders
FK Item Number → Part

Figure 11–27

BTW
Merging Entities
When you merge entities, do not assume that the merged entities will be in 3NF. Apply normalization techniques to convert all entities to 3NF.

BTW
Certification
The Microsoft Office Specialist (MOS) program provides an opportunity for you to obtain a valuable industry credential — proof that you have the Access 2013 skills required by employers. For more information, visit the Certification resource on the Student Companion Site located on www.cengagebrain.com. For detailed instructions about accessing available resources, visit www.cengage.com/ct/studentdownload or contact your instructor for information about accessing the required files.

At this point, you would need to verify that all the tables are in third normal form. If any are not in 3NF, you need to convert them. If you had not determined the functional dependency of Last Name and First Name on Rep Number earlier, for example, you would have had Last Name and First Name as fields in the Customer table. These fields were dependent on Rep Number, making Rep Number a determinant that is not a primary key, violating third normal form. Once you converted that table to 3NF, you would have the tables shown in Figure 11–27.

You already may have created some tables in your database design. For example, you may have obtained financial data on customers from the Accounting department. If so, you would need to merge the tables in Figure 11–27 with those tables you already created. To merge tables, you combine tables that have the same primary key. The new table contains all the fields in either individual table and does not repeat fields that are present in both tables. Figure 11–28, for example, illustrates the merging of two tables that both have the Customer Number field as the primary key. In addition to the primary key, the result contains the Customer Name and Rep Number fields, which are included in both of the original tables; the Street, City, State, and Postal Code fields, which are only in the first table; and the Balance and Credit Limit fields, which are only in the second table. The order in which you decide to list the fields is immaterial.

Merging
Customer (<u>Customer Number</u>, Customer Name, Street, City, State, Postal Code, Rep Number)
and
Customer (<u>Customer Number</u>, Customer Name, Balance, Credit Limit, Rep Number)
gives
Customer (<u>Customer Number</u>, Customer Name, Street, City, State, Postal Code, Balance, Credit Limit, Rep Number)

Figure 11–28

Diagrams for Database Design

You now have seen how to represent a database design as a list of tables, fields, primary keys, and foreign keys. It is often helpful to also be able to represent a database design with a diagram. If you already have created the database and relationships in Access, the Relationships window and Relationships report provide a helpful diagram of the design. Figure 11–29 shows the Access Relationship diagram and report for the Bavant Publishing database. In these diagrams, rectangles represent tables. The fields in the table are listed in the corresponding rectangle with a key symbol appearing in front of the primary key. Relationships are represented by lines with the "one" end of the relationship represented by the number, 1, and the "many" end represented by the infinity symbol (∞).

BTW

Quick Reference

For a table that lists how to complete the tasks covered in this book using touch gestures, the mouse, ribbon, shortcut menu, and keyboard, see the Quick Reference Summary at the back of this book, or visit the Quick Reference resource on the Student Companion Site located on www.cengagebrain.com. For detailed instructions about accessing available resources, visit www.cengage.com/ct/studentdownload or contact your instructor for information about accessing the required files.

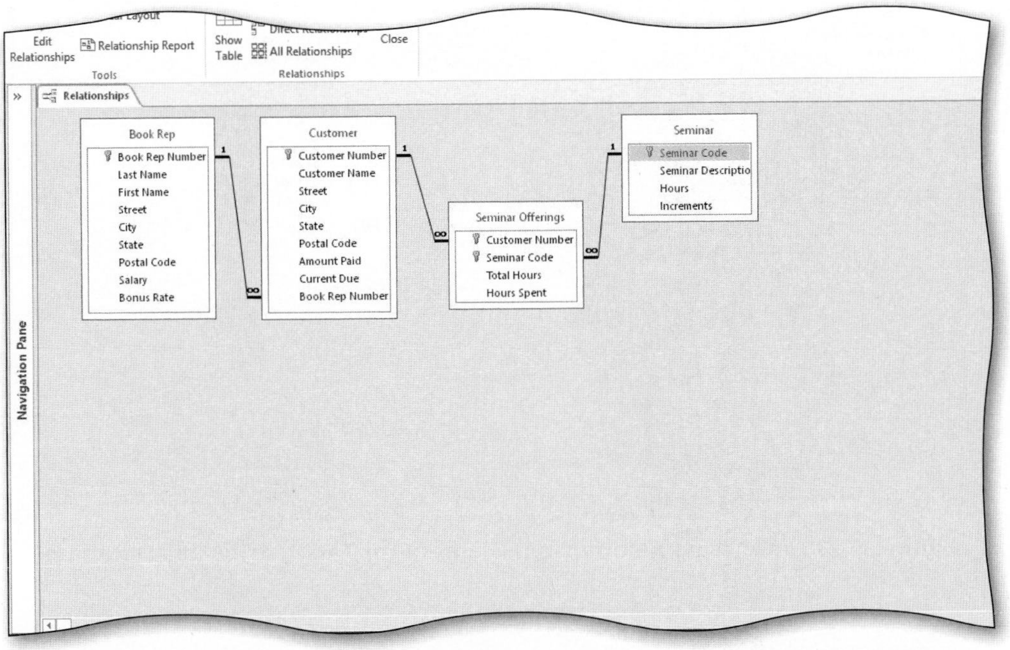

Figure 11–29 (a) Access Relationship Diagram for Bavant Publishing Database

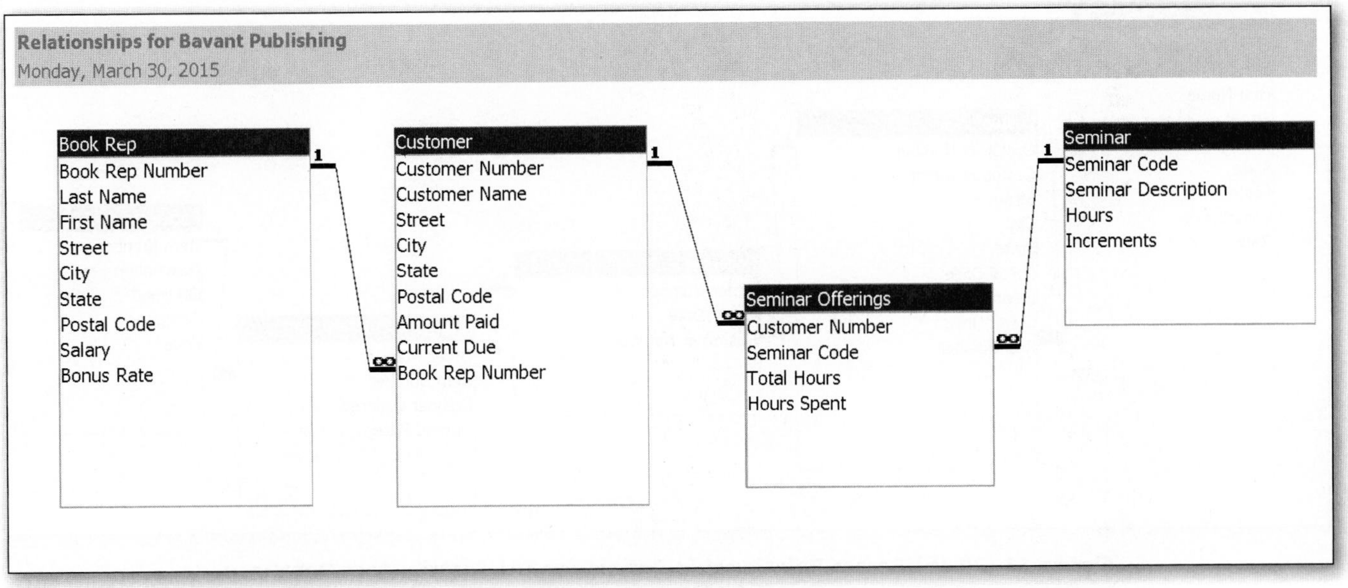

Figure 11–29 (b) Access Relationship Report for Bavant Publishing Database

Figure 11–30 shows the Access Relationship diagram and report for the TAL Distributors database.

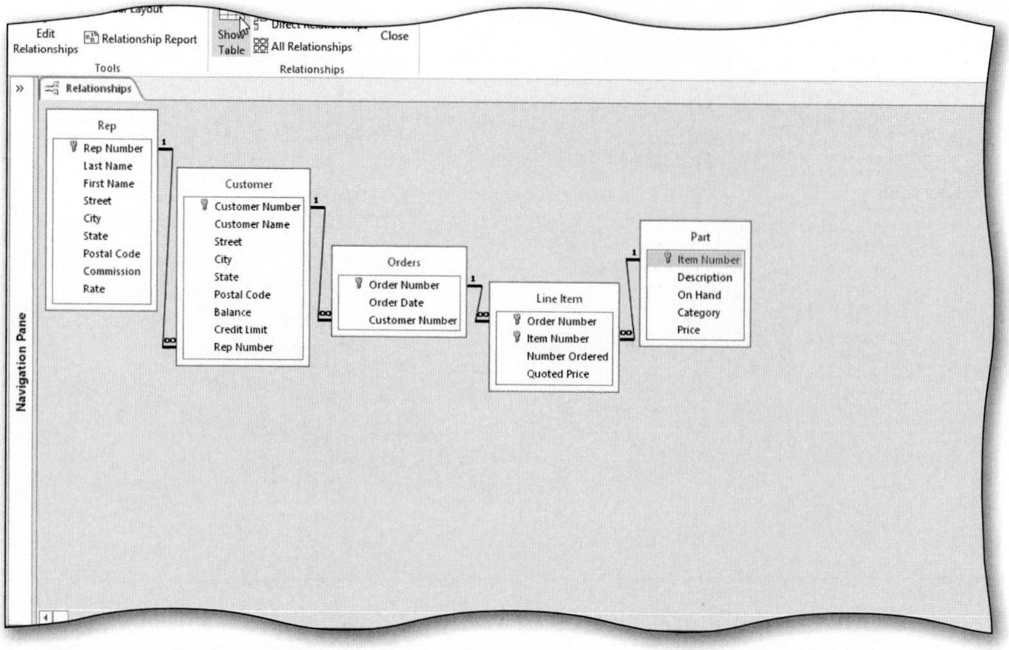

Figure 11–30 (a) Access Relationship Diagram for TAL Distributors Database

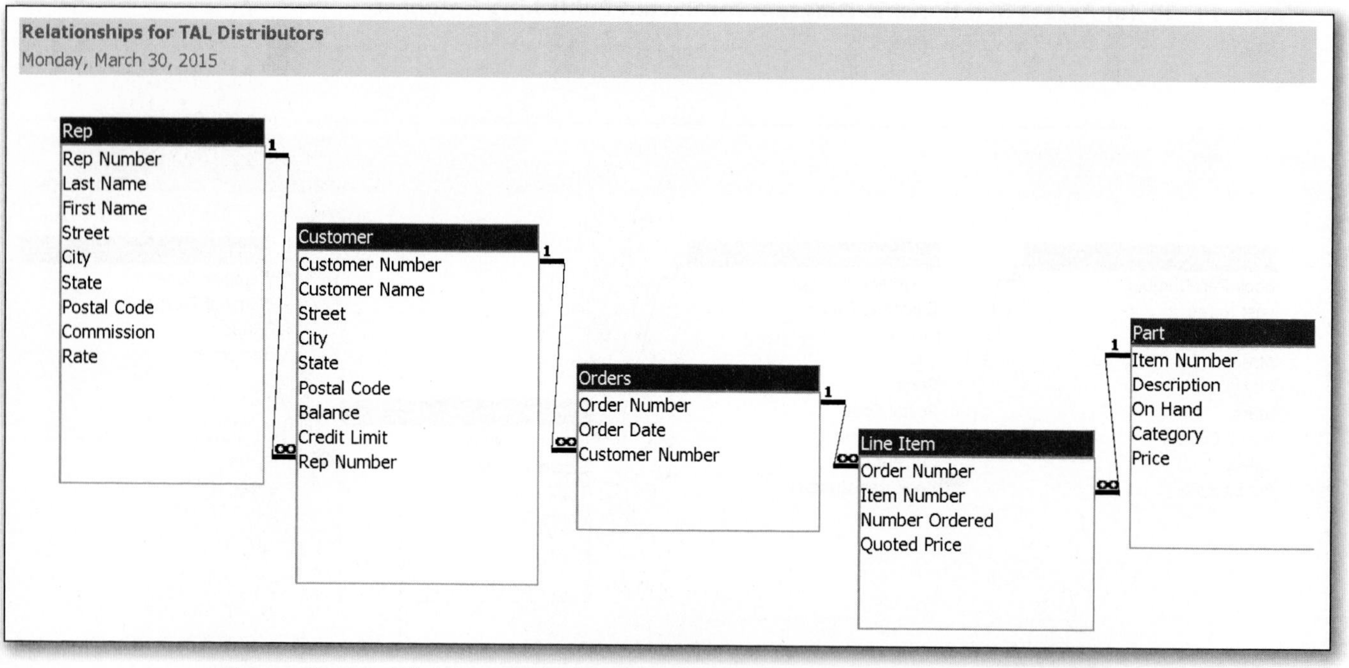

Figure 11–30 (b) Access Relationship Report for TAL Distributors Database

Another popular option for diagramming a database design is the **entity-relationship diagram (ERD)**. Figure 11–31 shows a sample ERD for the Bavant Publishing database. In this type of diagram, rectangles represent the tables. The primary key is listed within the table above a line. Below the line are the other fields in the table. The arrow goes from the rectangle that represents the many part of the relationship to the one part of the relationship.

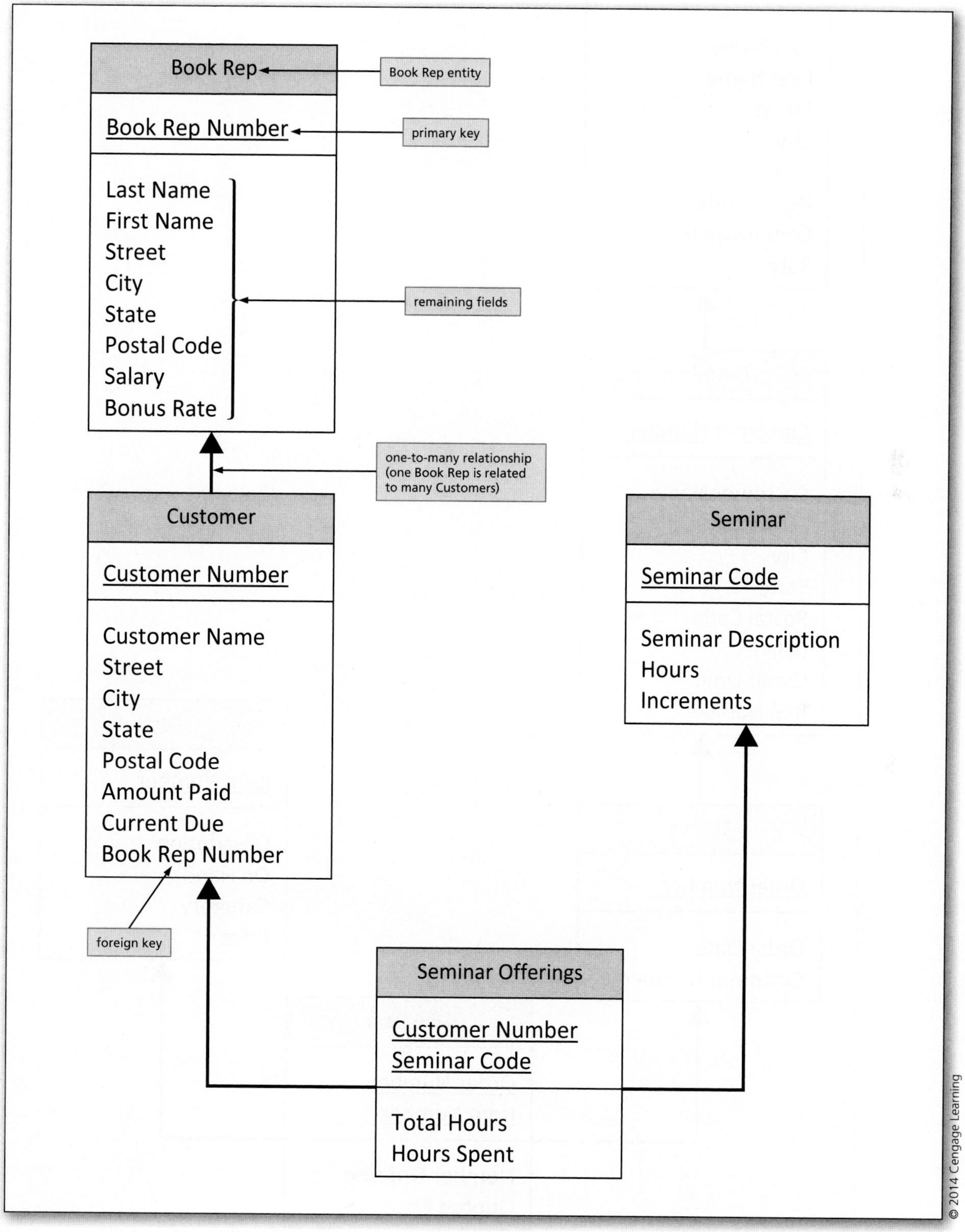

Figure 11–31

Figure 11–32 shows a similar diagram for the TAL Distributors database.

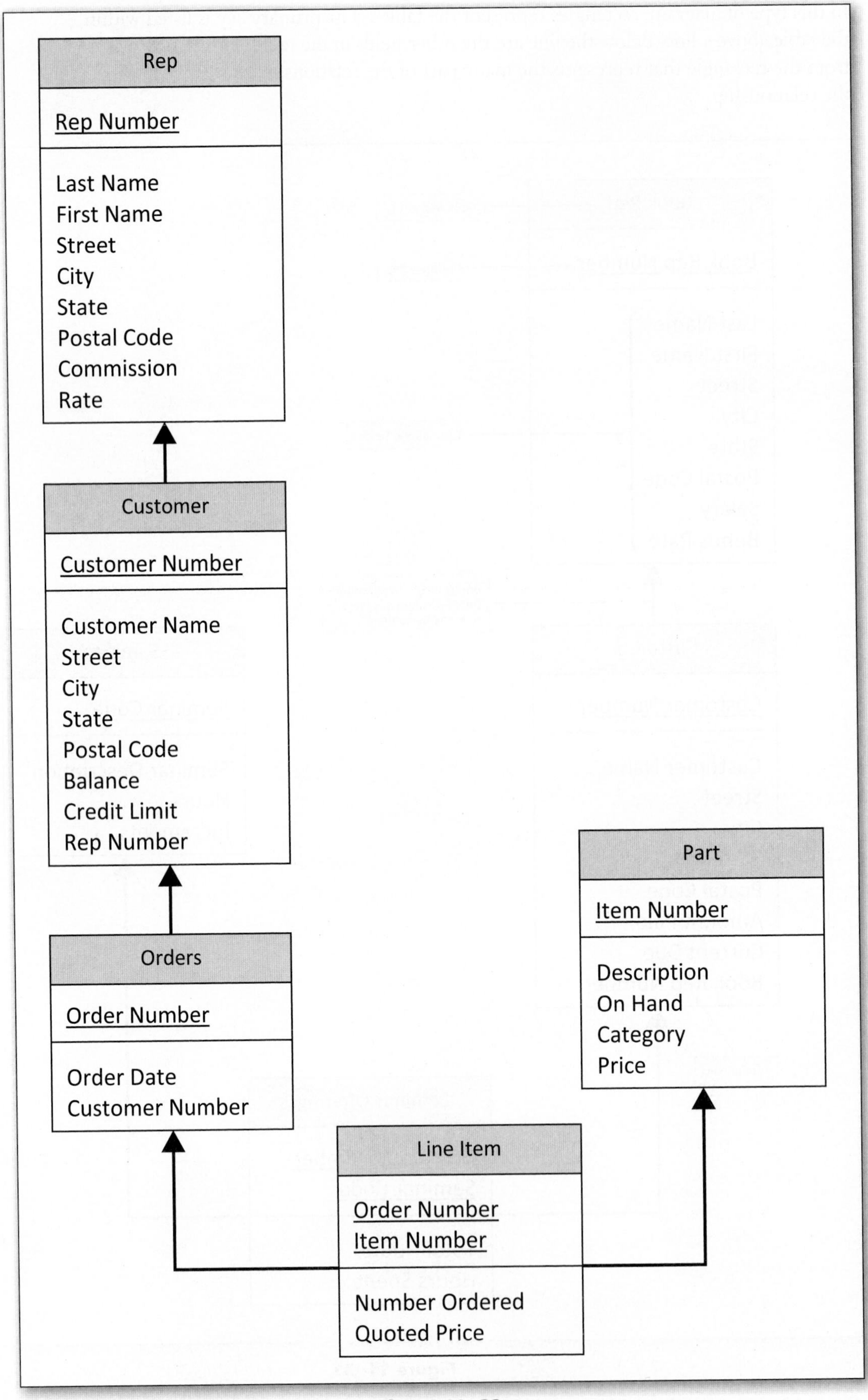

Figure 11–32

There are many options for such diagrams. Some options include more detail than shown in the figure. You can include, for example, such details as data types and indexes. Other options have less detail, showing only the name of the table in the rectangle, for example. There are also other options for the appearance of the lines representing relationships.

Chapter Summary

In this chapter, you have learned the following concepts.

1. An entity is a person, place, thing, or event. An attribute is a property of an entity. A relationship is an association between entities.
2. A relation is a two-dimensional table in which the entries in the table are single-valued, each column has a distinct name, all values in a column are values of the same attribute (that is, all entries must correspond to the column name), and each row is distinct.
3. In a relation, the order of columns is immaterial. You can view the columns in any order you want. The order of rows is also immaterial. You can view the rows in any order you want.
4. A relational database is a collection of relations.
5. Rows in a table (relation) often are called records or tuples. Columns in a table (relation) often are called fields or attributes. Typically, the terms *record* and *field* are used in Access.
6. If you know that whenever you are given a value for one field, you will be able to determine a single value for a second field, then the first field is said to determine the second field. In addition, the second field is said to be functionally dependent on the first.
7. The primary key of a table is the field or minimum collection of fields that uniquely identifies a given row in that table.
8. The following is a method for designing a database for a set of requirements.
    a. Examine the requirements and identify the entities (objects) involved. Assign names to the entities.
    b. Identify a unique identifier for each entity.
    c. Identify the attributes for all the entities. These attributes will become the fields in the tables.
    d. Identify the functional dependencies that exist among the attributes.
    e. Use the functional dependencies to identify the tables.
    f. Identify any relationships between tables by looking for matching fields where one of the fields is a primary key. The other field then will be a foreign key. In the shorthand representation for the table containing the primary key, represent the foreign key by using the letters FK, followed by an arrow, followed by the name of the table containing the primary key.
9. A table (relation) is in first normal form (1NF) if it does not contain repeating groups.
10. To convert a table to 1NF, remove the parentheses enclosing the repeating group and expand the primary key to include the key to the repeating group.
11. A field is a nonkey field (also called a nonkey attribute) if it is not a part of the primary key. A table (relation) is in second normal form (2NF) if it is in first normal form and no nonkey field is dependent on only a portion of the primary key.
12. To convert a table to 2NF, take each subset of the set of fields that make up the primary key and begin a new table with this subset as its primary key. Place each of the other fields with the appropriate primary key; that is, place each one with the minimal collection of fields on which it depends. Give each of these new tables a name that is descriptive of the meaning of the table.
13. Any field (or collection of fields) that determines another field is called a determinant. A table is in third normal form (3NF) if it is in second normal form and if the only determinants it contains are candidate keys.

14. To convert a table to 3NF, for each determinant that is not a candidate key, remove from the table the fields that depend on this determinant, but do not remove the determinant. Create a new table containing all the fields from the original table that depend on this determinant and make the determinant the primary key of this new table.
15. An entity-relationship diagram (ERD) is a diagram used to represent database designs. In ERDs, rectangles represent tables and lines between rectangles represent one-to-many relationships between the corresponding tables. You also can diagram a database design by using the Access relationship window.

CONSIDER THIS

How should you submit solutions to questions in the assignments identified with a symbol?
Every assignment in this book contains one or more questions identified with a symbol. These questions require you to think beyond the assigned database. Present your solutions to the questions in the format required by your instructor. Possible formats may include one or more of these options: write the answer; create a document that contains the answer; present your answer to the class; discuss your answer in a group; record the answer as audio or video using a webcam, smartphone, or portable media player; or post answers on a blog, wiki, or website.

Apply Your Knowledge

Reinforce the skills and apply the concepts you learned in this chapter.

Understanding Keys and Normalization

Instructions: Answer the following questions in the format specified by your instructor.

1. Figure 11–33 contains sample data for a Book table. Use this figure to answer the following:
   a. Is the table in first normal form (1NF)? Why or why not?
   b. Is the table in second normal form (2NF)? Why or why not?
   c. Is the table in third normal form (3NF)? Why or why not?
   d. Identify candidate keys for the table.

Book

ISBN	Book Code	Title	Publisher Code	Publisher Name
0-7895-1344-7	0180	The Stranger	BP	Bavant Publishing
0-8967-1544-8	079X	Second Sight	SB	Science Books
1-1234-2334-5	1351	Travel Mysteries	MP	Mysterious Press
1-4188-3635-4	3350	Dawn	BP	Bavant Publishing

Figure 11–33

2. Figure 11–34 contains sample data for books and stores. In discussing the data with users, you find that book codes — but not titles — uniquely identify books and that location names uniquely identify store location. Multiple book stores can stock the same book.
   a. Convert the data in Figure 11–34 into a relation in first normal form (1NF) using the shorthand representation used in this chapter.
   b. Identify all functional dependencies using the notation demonstrated in this chapter.
3. Using only the data in Figure 11–33, how could you identify the entities and attributes that would be the starting point for a database design?

Book

Book Code	Title	Location Name	Address	Number of Copies
0180	The Stranger	Phil Downtown	Georgetown	2
		Phil Brentwood	Brentwood	1
079X	Second Sight	Phil Downtown	Georgetown	4
		Phil Brentwood	Brentwood	3
		Phil Eastshore	Georgetown	5

Figure 11–34

Extend Your Knowledge

Extend the skills you learned in this chapter and experiment with new skills. You may need to use Help to complete the assignment.

Modifying a Database Design and Understanding Diagrams

Instructions: Answer the following questions in the format specified by your instructor.

1. Using the shorthand representation illustrated in this chapter, indicate the changes you would need to make to the Bavant Publishing database design shown in Figure 11–8 on page AC 680 in order to support the following requirements:
   a. A customer does not necessarily work with one book rep but can work with several book reps.
   b. Hours and Total Hours do not vary based on customer.
2. Using the shorthand representation illustrated in this chapter, indicate the changes you would need to make to the TAL Distributors database design shown in Figure 11–10 on page AC 686 to support the following requirements.
   a. The price for a part does not change but is the same for all customers.
   b. TAL also needs to keep track of the wholesale cost of a part.
3. Use the Access Relationship Report for the JMS TechWizards database shown in Figure 11–35 to answer the following:
   a. Identify the foreign keys in the Work Orders table.
   b. What is the purpose of the Work Orders table?
   c. What is the primary key of the Work Orders table?

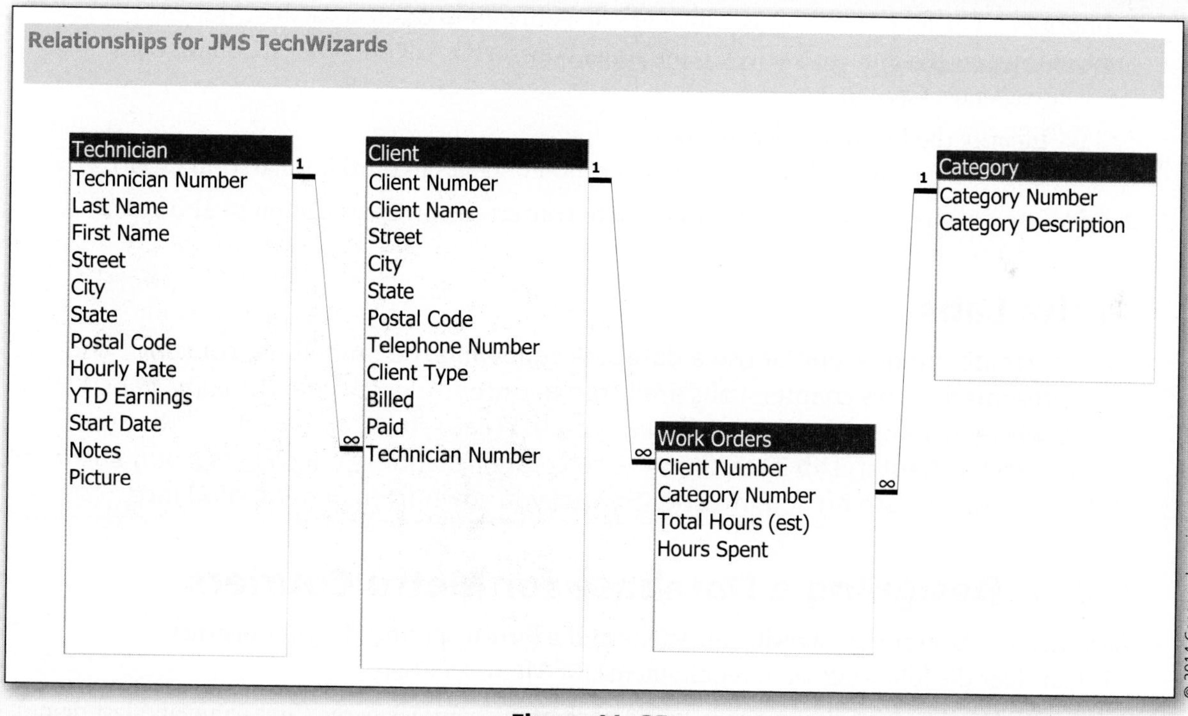

Figure 11–35

4. TAL Distributors has decided to add its suppliers to the database. One supplier can supply many items but an item has only one supplier. What changes would you need to make to the database design for TAL Distributors?

Analyze, Correct, Improve

Analyze a database, correct all errors, and improve the design.

Correcting a Database Design

Instructions: Answer the following questions in the format specified by your instructor.

1. Correct List four relational characteristics that are violated in the Book table shown in Figure 11–36.

Book			
Date	**Book Code**	**Number Ordered**	**Date**
04/06/2015	0180	11	04/01/2015
04/06/2015	0189 0378	1 1	04/09/2015 Friday
04/07/2015	0808	3	04/13/2015
04/07/2015	1382 2226	4 2	04/12/2015 $23.95
04/07/2015	0808	3	04/13/2015
04/08/2015	7559	2	04/15/2015
04/09/2015	9883	5	04/15/2015

Figure 11–36

2. Improve The following table is a student's first attempt to create a database design:
Student (<u>StudentID</u>, StudentName, CreditHours, AdvisorID, AdvisorName, (CourseID, CourseName, Grade))

a. Identify the functional dependencies.
b. Convert this table to an equivalent collection of tables in third normal form (3NF).

3. What assumptions did you need to make to convert the Student relation to 3NF?

In the Labs

Design, create, modify, and/or use a database following the guidelines, concepts, and skills presented in this chapter. Labs are listed in order of increasing difficulty. Labs 1 and 2, which increase in difficulty, require you to create solutions based on what you learned in the chapter; Lab 3 requires you to create a solution, which uses cloud and web technologies, by learning and investigating on your own from general guidance.

Lab 1: Designing a Database for Metro Couriers

Instructions: Answer the following questions in the format specified by your instructor.

1. Consider the following set of requirements for Metro Couriers:
   a. For each courier, the company keeps track of the courier's name (first name and last name), courier's address (street, city, state, postal code), courier's driver license number, and mobile telephone number.
   b. For each motorbike, the company keeps track of a unique motorbike ID number, motorbike license number, and motorbike model.
   c. A courier can be assigned to more than one motorbike. A motorbike will have multiple couriers but only one courier at a time.

2. Based on these requirements, do the following:
   a. Identify and list the entities and attributes of those entities.
   b. Identify and list the functional dependencies.
   c. Create a set of 3NF relations using the shorthand notation given in the chapter. Be sure to identify all primary and foreign keys appropriately.
3. Submit your database design in the format specified by your instructor.
4. Metro Couriers wants to add the customers it serves to the database. One customer can be serviced by many couriers and one courier can service many customers. What entities would you need to add to the database design?

Lab 2: Normalizing a Patient Relation

Instructions: Answer the following questions in the format specified by your instructor.

Consider the following relation:

Patient (Patient#, PatientName, BalanceDue, DentistID, DentistName, ServiceCode, ServiceDesc, ServiceFee, ServiceDate)

This is a relation concerning data about patients of dentists at a dental clinic and the services the dentists perform for their patients. The following dependencies exist in Patient:

Patient# → PatientName, BalanceDue, DentistID, DentistName
DentistID → DentistName
ServiceCode → ServiceDesc, ServiceFee
Patient#, DentistID, ServiceCode → ServiceDate

1. Convert Patient to 1NF based on the functional dependencies given.
2. Convert to a set of relations in 3NF.
3. The database design needs to include an attribute for the date of the patient's last visit. In what table would you place this attribute?

Lab 3: Expand Your World: Cloud and Web Technologies Database Models

Instructions: There are several websites that provide examples of database models, such as www.databaseanswers.org/data_models/index.htm. These models provide a good starting point for creating your own database design.

1. Create a blog, a Google document, or a Word document on the SkyDrive on which to store your assignment.
2. Open your browser and access www.databaseanswers.org/data_models/index.htm or another website of your choice.
3. Browse the different database models and select one in which you have an interest.
4. In your own words, create a scenario for which the database model would work. Study the model to see if you would need to modify it to make it applicable to your scenario. If changes are necessary, document the required modifications.
5. Why did you select the model that you did? How easy was it to understand the entities, attributes, and relationships? Were the relations in 3NF?

Consider This: Your Turn

Apply your creative thinking and problem solving skills to design and implement a solution.

1: Designing a Community Center Sports Program Database

Personal/Academic

Instructions: You have been hired as an intern at the local community center. The center has a number of sports programs for youth. You have been asked to create a database to keep track of the programs and the youths who participate in these sports activities. Use the concepts and techniques presented in this chapter to design a database to meet the following requirements:

Part 1: The Community Center database must support the following requirements:

1. For an activity, store its number and name, for example, 013, Track. Each activity has a cost associated with it.
   a. For a participant, store his or her number, first name, and last name as well as the name, home telephone number, and cell telephone number of the parent or guardian primarily responsible for the participant.
   b. One participant can enroll in many activities, and one activity can include many participants. One parent/guardian can have many participants.

   Based on these requirements:
   a. Identify and list the entities and attributes of those entities.
   b. Identify and list the functional dependencies.
   c. Create a set of 3NF relations using the shorthand notation given in the chapter. Be sure to identify all primary keys and foreign keys appropriately.

Submit your database design in the format specified by your instructor.

Part 2: You made several decisions while designing this database. What was the rationale behind your decisions? Are there other requirements that would have been helpful to you in the design process?

2: Designing a Mobile Dog Groomers Database

Professional

Part 1: You have just started a mobile dog grooming business. You want to create a database to keep track of your customers and their dogs. Use the concepts and techniques presented in this chapter to design a database to meet the following requirements:

1. The Mobile Dog Groomers database must support the following requirements:
   a. For each dog, list the dog ID, dog name, breed name (for example, Standard Poodle, mixed breed, Collie, and so on), size (large, medium, small), gender, frequency of grooming (monthly, weekly, quarterly), owner's first name and last name, home telephone number, mobile telephone number.
   b. For each owner/customer, list the customer ID, the customer's first and last name, address (street, city, state, postal code), home telephone number, mobile telephone number, and amount paid.
   c. The database also must store the grooming cost of each dog. The grooming cost depends on both the dog and the customer.

A dog belongs to only one breed, but a breed can have many dogs. An owner/customer also can have many dogs.

2. Based on these requirements:
   a. Identify and list the entities and the attributes of those entities.
   b. Identify and list the functional dependencies.
   c. Create a set of 3NF relations using the shorthand notation given in this chapter. Be sure to identify all primary keys and foreign keys appropriately.

Submit your database design in the format specified by your instructor.

Part 2: You made several decisions while designing this database. What was the rationale behind your decisions? Are there other requirements that would have been helpful to you in the design process?

3: Understanding Normalization

Research and Collaboration

Part 1: Create a blog, a Google document, or a Word document on the SkyDrive on which to store your research findings and results for this assignment.

This chapter discussed the concept of normalization and applied the normalization process to a database. Three normal forms were identified. Many database designers also recognize a fourth normal form (4NF). Use the web to research 4NF, and then apply the normalization techniques for 4NF to the databases used in this chapter. Decide whether all relations are in 4NF. If a relation is not in 4NF, convert the database to 4NF.

Submit your assignment in the format specified by your instructor.

Part 2: You made several decisions while designing this database. What was the rationale behind your decisions? How important do you think it is to ensure that all relations in a database are in 4NF?

Learn Online

Reinforce what you learned in this chapter with games, exercises, training, and many other online activities and resources.

Student Companion Site Reinforcement activities and resources are available at no additional cost on www.cengagebrain.com. Visit www.cengage.com/ct/studentdownload for detailed instructions about accessing the resources available at the Student Companion Site.

SAM Put your skills into practice with SAM Projects! SAM Projects for this chapter can be found online. If you have a SAM account, go to www.cengage.com/sam2013 to access SAM assignments for this chapter.

Appendix A

SAM Projects

Introduction

With SAM Projects—SAM's hands-on, live-in-the-application projects—students master Microsoft Office skills that are essential to academic and career success. SAM Projects engage students in applying the latest Microsoft Office 2013 skills to real-world scenarios. Immediate grading and feedback allow students to fix errors and understand where they may need more practice.

This appendix provides the printed instructions for one SAM Project that corresponds to this text. This project was created by an instructor currently teaching an Introduction to Computing course:

- Access Project: created by Emily H. Shepard, Instructor, Central Carolina Community College

To complete the project in this appendix, you must log into your SAM account. Go to sam .cengage.com for more information or contact your instructor.

Access 2013: Student Engagement Project 1a

Zombie Apocalypse

Creating Queries for Quick Access to Data

Project Description

Created by Emily H. Shepard, Instructor, Central Carolina Community College

The only place you used to be able to find zombies was in horror movies or on television. Since the Zombie Apocalypse began in Boston, Massachusetts, finding a zombie is the least of the world's problems. You are a member of the Shepards (named after the group's founder, Emily Shepard), a group of survivors attempting to end the zombie plague. Your group combats the zombies by finding zombie herds before they become major threats and by administering the experimental zombie vaccine (as it becomes available) in neighboring towns.

You are responsible for tracking your team's efforts in an Access database. You've already generated a few tables of records regarding medics, missions, zombie herds, and cities that your group supports. Because time is of the essence, you've decided to create queries to allow you to more rapidly access and update table data.

Getting Started

- Download the following file from the SAM website:
  - **SAM_Access2013_SE_P1a_*FirstLastName*_1.accdb**
- Open the file you just downloaded and save it with the name:
  - **SAM_Access2013_SE_P1a_*FirstLastName*_2.accdb**
  - *Hint*: If you do not see the **.accdb** file extension in the Save file dialog box, do not type it. Access will add the file extension for you automatically.
- Open the **_GradingInfoTable** table and ensure that your first and last name is displayed as the first record in the table. If the table does not contain your name, delete the file and download a new copy from the SAM website.

Project Steps

1. Create a new query in Query Design View based on the *KnownHerds* table as described below:
   a. Add the fields **HerdID**, **HerdSize**, **Active**, **FirstEncounterDate**, **FirstEncounterLocation**, and **HerdNotes** to the query in that order.
   b. Add a **descending** sort order on the *FirstEncounterLocation* field.
   c. Save the query with the name **Known Herds Query**.

   Run the *Known Herds Query* query to confirm it works, and then close the query.
2. Create a new query in Query Design View based on the *City* table as described below:
   a. Add the **City**, **State**, **Population**, **VaccinatedPopulation**, **LastReview**, and **MissionSecurityCost** fields (from the *City* table) to the query in that order.
   b. Add a **descending** sort order on the *State* field.
   c. Save the query with the name **City Query**.

   Run the *City Query* query to confirm it works, and then close the query.
3. Create a new parameter query in Design View based on the *VaccinationMissions* and *Medics* tables as described below:
   a. Add the **VMissionID** field from the *VaccinationMissions* table to the query.
   b. After the *VMissionID* field, add the **MedicFirstName** and **MedicLastName** fields (in that order) from the *Medics* table to the query.
   c. After the *MedicLastName* field, add the **VMTeamSize**, **VMCasualties**, **VMCasualtyNumber**, and **VMLocation** fields (in that order) from the *VaccinationMissions* table to the query.
   d. Add the criterion **[Enter Vaccination Mission Location]** (including brackets) to the *VMLocation* field.
   e. Save the query with the name **Vaccination Parameter Query**.

   Run the *Vaccination Parameter Query* query to confirm it works, and then close the query. (*Hint*: If you enter **NCRAL** as the parameter value, the query should return 6 records.)

4. Create a new query in Query Design View based on the *ReconMissions* table with the following options:
   a. Add the fields **RMissionID**, **RMLocation**, **RMEndDate**, and **NewHerd** from the *ReconMissions* table to the query in that order.
   b. Add an **ascending** sort order on the *RMLocation* field.
   c. Add a criterion to select only those records where the *RMEndDate* field is **greater than 5/8/2014**.
   d. Save the query with the name **Recent Recon Query**.

   Run the *Recent Recon Query* query to confirm it works, and then close the query. (*Hint*: If you entered the criterion correctly, the query should display 9 records.)
5. Create a copy of the *Medic Query* query, using the name **Living Medic Query**. In Query Design View, modify the *Living Medic Query* query as described below:
   a. Modify the query to show only records where the *Deceased* field is equal to **False**.
   b. Save the query.

   Run the *Living Medic Query* query to confirm it works, and then close the query. (*Hint*: If you modified the criterion correctly, the query should return 9 records.)
6. Create a copy of the *Medic Query* query and name it **Expert Deceased Query**. In Query Design View, modify the *Expert Deceased Query* query as described below:
   a. Modify the query to show only records where the *DateDeceased* is **greater than or equal to 4/20/2014** and the *SecurityLevel* is **equal to Expert**.
   b. Save the query.

   Run the *Expert Deceased Query* query to confirm it works, and then close the query. (*Hint*: If you modified the criterion correctly, the query should return 2 records.)
7. Create a copy of the *Recon Query* query and name it **New or Large Recon Query**. In Query Design View, modify the *New or Large Recon Query* query as described below:
   a. Add criteria to the query so that it will return records with an *RTeamSize* value **greater than 10** or a *NewHerd* field value of **True**.
   b. Save the query.

   Run the *New or Large Recon Query* query to confirm that it works, and then close the query. (*Hint*: If you entered the criteria correctly, the query should return 9 records.)
8. Create a copy of the *Recon Query* query and name it **Recon N Location Query**. In Query Design View, modify the *Recon N Location Query* query as described below:
   a. Using a wildcard criterion, modify the query so that it only returns records with *RMLocation* field values that begin with the letter **N**.
   b. Save the query.

   Run the *Recon N Location Query* query to confirm that it works, and then close the query. (*Hint*: If you entered the criterion correctly, the query should return 6 records.)
9. Create a copy of the *Vaccination Query* query and name it **Containment Vac Query**. In Query Design View, modify the *Containment Vac Query* query as described below:
   a. Modify the query to show only records where the *Specialty* field value is equal to **Containment**.
   b. Hide the **Specialty** field, so that it does not appear in the query results.
   c. Save the query.

Run the *Containment Vac Query* query to confirm it works, and then close the query. (*Hint*: Your query should return 3 records when run and, if you switch back to Query Design View, the *Specialty* field should still be available in the query.)

10. Create a copy of the *Vaccination Query* query and name it **Vaccination Sort Query**. In Query Design View, modify the *Vaccination Sort Query* query as described below:
    a. Modify the query to sort records first in **ascending** order by the values of the *Specialty* field and then in **descending** order by the values of the *TotalVaccinations* field.
    b. Save the query.

    Run the *Vaccination Sort Query* query to confirm it works, and then close your query.
11. Create a copy of the *Vaccination Query* query and name it **High Vaccination Query**. In Query Design View, modify the *High Vaccination Query* query as described below:
    a. Add a criterion to select only those records where the value in the *AdministeredVaccinations* field is **greater than or equal to 20**.
    b. Sort the query in **descending** order by the *AdministeredVaccinations* field values.
    c. Save the query.

    Run the *High Vaccination Query* query to confirm it works, and then close the query. (*Hint*: If you entered the criterion correctly, the query should return 8 results.)
12. Open the *Vaccination Mission Query* query in Design View, and then hide the **VMTeamSize** and **VMCasualties** fields in the query. Save the query, and then run it to confirm the query works as expected before closing it. (*Hint*: The *VMTeamSize* and *VMCasualties* fields should not appear in the query results, but they should still be available when viewing the query in Design View.)
13. Open the *City Resource Query* query in Design View and update it as described below:
    a. Delete the criterion associated with the *Security* field.
    b. Move the **VaccinatedPopulation** field so that it is the last field in the query (after the *WaterAccess* field).
    c. Add an **ascending** sort order on the *MedicalFacilities* and *WaterAccess* fields.
    d. Save the query.

    Run the *City Resource Query* query to confirm that it matches Figure, and then close the query.

City Resource Query

	City	State	Population	Security	MedicalFacil	WaterAcces:	VaccinatedP
	Seattle	WA	125,000	Medium	☑	☑	7,000
	Boston	MA	353,000	High	☑	☑	75,000
	Los Angeles	CA	250,000	High	☑	☑	10,000
	Dallas	TX	300,000	Medium	☑	☐	23,000
	New York	NY	450,000	High	☐	☑	53,000
	Sioux Falls	SD	27,000	Low	☐	☐	3,000
	Las Vegas	NV	200,000	Low	☐	☐	17,000
	Raleigh	NC	100,000	Medium	☐	☐	25,000
*			0		☐	☐	0

Figure 1 City Resource Query

14. Use the **Form** button to create a simple form based on the *Medic Query* query, and then save the form as **Medic Form** and close the form.
15. Using the Report Wizard, create a new report based on the *Recon Query* query with the following options:
    a. Include the **RMissionID**, **RTeamSize**, **RMLocation**, **RMEndDate**, **HerdEncountered**, **NewHerd**, and **HerdID** fields (in that order) from the *Recon Query* query in the report.
    b. Group the report by the default **HerdID** field, but use no additional grouping in the report.
    c. Use no additional sorting in the report.
    d. Use a **Stepped** layout and **Landscape** orientation for the report.
    e. Name the report **Recon Report**, and then preview the report to confirm it matches Figure 2.

    Save and close the report.

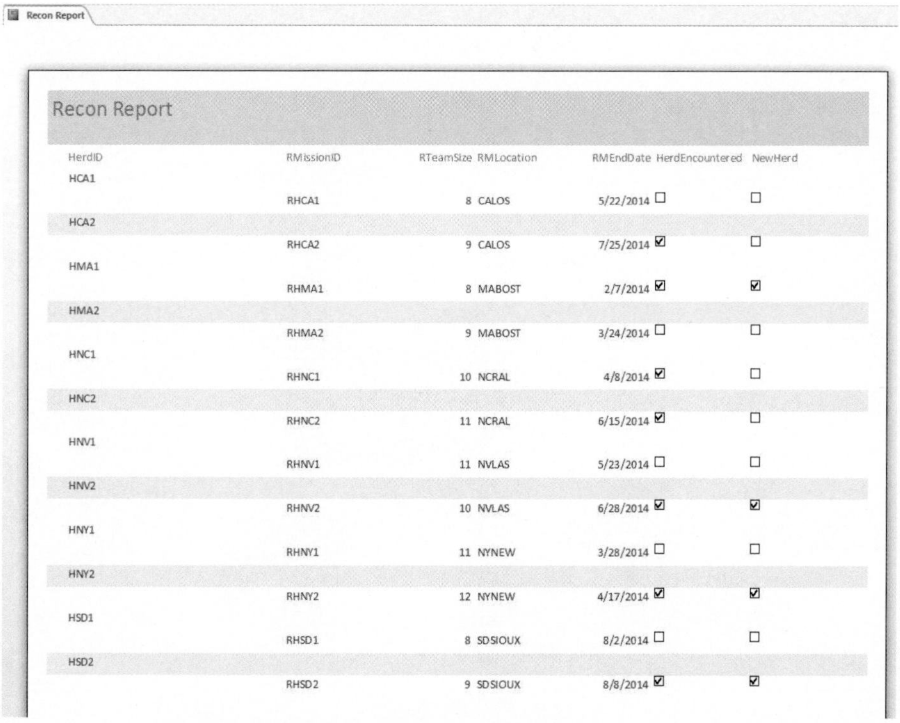

Recon Report

Recon Report

HerdID	RMissionID	RTeamSize	RMLocation	RMEndDate	HerdEncountered	NewHerd
HCA1						
	RHCA1	8	CALOS	5/22/2014	☐	☐
HCA2						
	RHCA2	9	CALOS	7/25/2014	☑	☐
HMA1						
	RHMA1	8	MABOST	2/7/2014	☑	☑
HMA2						
	RHMA2	9	MABOST	3/24/2014	☐	☐
HNC1						
	RHNC1	10	NCRAL	4/8/2014	☑	☐
HNC2						
	RHNC2	11	NCRAL	6/15/2014	☑	☐
HNV1						
	RHNV1	11	NVLAS	5/23/2014	☐	☐
HNV2						
	RHNV2	10	NVLAS	6/28/2014	☑	☑
HNY1						
	RHNY1	11	NYNEW	3/28/2014	☐	☐
HNY2						
	RHNY2	12	NYNEW	4/17/2014	☑	☑
HSD1						
	RHSD1	8	SDSIOUX	8/2/2014	☐	☐
HSD2						
	RHSD2	9	SDSIOUX	8/8/2014	☑	☑

Figure 2 Recon Report in Print Preview View

Save and close any open database objects. Compact and repair your database, and then exit Access. Follow the directions on the SAM website to submit your completed project.

Appendix B

Capstone Projects

Capstone Project 1

Problem: You are working with the organizers of the Solar Convention to be held in San Diego, California, in April 2016. The conference will bring together delegates from companies around the world that specialize in developing solar energy solutions. A database for the conference has already been developed. This database includes tables listing data about workshops, delegates and the companies they represent, and conference staff. You are working on the database and will be editing some of the tables and other components as part of ongoing efforts to ensure the database is as up-to-date and useful as possible.

Note: To complete this assignment, you will be required to use the Data Files for Students. Visit www.cengage.com/ct/studentdownload for detailed instructions or contact your instructor for information about accessing the required files.

Instructions: Run Access. Open the database SC_Access2013_Capstone_1-1.accdb and save it with the name SC_Access2013_Capstone_1-2.accdb. Enable content if necessary. You will also need the following support file from the student data files:

SC_Access2013_Capstone_Company.xlsx

Perform the following tasks:

1. Create a new table in Datasheet view with the following options:
2. Rename the default primary key ID field to PackageID and change the Data Type to Short Text. (*Hint:* PackageID should remain the primary key.)
3. Change the Field Size of the PackageID field to 4.
4. Add a new field with the name PackageName and change the Data Type to Short Text.
5. Add another field to the table with the name Price and change the Data Type to Currency.
6. Save the table with the name Conference Packages.
7. With the Conference Packages table open in Datasheet view, change the font in the table to Tahoma and the font size of the table to 12 point.
8. With the Conference Packages table still open, add the records shown in bold in Table 1–1 to the Conference Packages table. As necessary, widen the columns to make all text visible for each record. Save and close the table.

Table 1–1 Conference Packages

PackageID	PackageName	Price
FC16	Full Conference Package	$200.00
WO16	Workshop Package	$125.00
SV16	Site Visit Package	$100.00
KO16	Keynote Package	$80.00

9. Open the Relationships window and add the Delegates and Conference Packages table to the Relationships window. Create a one-to-many relationship between the PackageID field in the Conference Packages table and the PackageID field in the Delegates table. Select Enforce Referential Integrity and Cascade Update Related Fields. Do not make the relationship cascade delete related records. Save and close the Relationships window.
10. Open the Delegates table in Design view and make the following changes to the Deposit field: Change the Data Type from Short Text to Currency. Change the Default Value property to 50. With the Delegates table still open in Design view, specify PackageID field as a required field.
11. Add a field to the end of the Delegates table with the following options: Set SpecAccommodations for the field name. Set the Data Type property of the field to Long Text. Set the Description property to Special Accommodations required for Workshop or Site Visit participation. Set the Caption property of the field to Special Accommodations. Change the Field Size property of the ReservationID field to 6. Save the changes to the Delegates table. (*Note:* Because there was a change to a field size, the "Some data may be lost" warning message will appear. The data fits within the valid ranges, so ignore this error and continue saving the table.)
12. View the Delegates table in Datasheet view and then find or navigate to the record with the ReservationID value of LO001. Update the Special Accommodations field value to Wheel Chair accessibility.
13. With the Delegates table still in Datasheet view, apply a filter by selection to locate all records where the CompanyID value is equal to DSNM01. Update the PackageID field value for Luana Botelho's record (who has a ReservationID of LB001) to FC16. Also update the Workshop field value to SCF01. Clear all filters applied to the table. Save and close the Delegates table.
14. Open the Workshops table in Design view. Use the Lookup Wizard to change the Category field to a Lookup field. Type in the following three values (in the order shown) as the list of possible values for the field: Presentation, Panel Discussion, and Hands-On Training. Limit the field values to only the items in the list and do not allow multiple values for the field.
15. With the Workshops table still open in Design view, delete the Confirmed field from the Workshops table. Save the Workshops table.
16. Switch the Workshops table to Datasheet view and change the Category field value to Panel Discussion for the Efficiency Levels for Solar Power workshop (which has the WorkshopID field value ESP01). Close the table.
17. The Solar Energy Conference organizers offer priority registration for Platinum-level corporate sponsors, but are planning to open the registration to companies at other support levels. To identify the companies in the Company table as Platinum-level corporate sponsors, create an Update query to update the SponsorLevel field value to "Platinum" for all records currently in the Company table. Run the query and save it as Platinum Update Query. Close the query.
18. Import the data from the Excel file SC_Access2013_Capstone_Company.xlsx from the student data files. Append the records into the Company table. Do not create a new table and do not save the import steps.
19. Create a simple query using the Query Wizard based on the Sites table with the following options: Include the SiteName, ContactName, and ContactNumber fields (in that order).
20. Save the query with the title Sites Contact Query.

21. Run and close the query.
22. Create a new query in Design view based on the Company and Delegates tables with the following options: Include the Company field from the Company table. Include the LastName, FirstName, and Phone fields (in that order) from the Delegates table.
23. Sort the records in ascending order based on the Company field and then by the LastName field.
24. Save the query with the name Company Contact Query.
25. Run and close the query.
26. Create a crosstab query based on the Delegates table with the following options: Use only data from the Delegates table in the query. Use the PackageID field as the row heading. Use the CompanyID field as the column heading. Use a Count of the ReservationID field as the calculated value for each row and column intersection in the crosstab query.
27. Save the query with the name Package-Company Crosstab.
28. View the query and then close it.
29. Create a query based on the Conference Packages and Delegates tables with the following options: Select the FirstName, LastName, and Deposit fields from the Delegates table. Select the PackageName and Price fields from the Conference Packages table. Move the Deposit field to the right of the Price field. Add a calculated field after the Deposit field with the alias TotalDue that calculates the difference between the Price field and the Deposit field.
30. Save the query with the name Outstanding Payments Query.
31. View the query, confirm that it matches Figure 1–1 and then close it.

Outstanding Payments Query

FirstName	LastName	PackageName	Price	Deposit	TotalDue
Alice	Banks	Full Conference Package	$200.00	$50.00	$150.00
Bethany	Clark	Full Conference Package	$200.00	$100.00	$100.00
Cynthia	Brown	Full Conference Package	$200.00	$100.00	$100.00
Clyde	Donswerk	Full Conference Package	$200.00	$75.00	$125.00
Dow-Lin	Hsu	Full Conference Package	$200.00	$175.00	$25.00
Faroh	Jacobs	Full Conference Package	$200.00	$100.00	$100.00
Flora	Padilla	Full Conference Package	$200.00	$100.00	$100.00
Igor	Yashenkov	Full Conference Package	$200.00	$75.00	$125.00
Juliana	Perez	Full Conference Package	$200.00	$100.00	$100.00
Kevin	Staszowski	Full Conference Package	$200.00	$175.00	$25.00
Luana	Botelho	Full Conference Package	$200.00	$100.00	$100.00
Lauren	Katz	Full Conference Package	$200.00	$175.00	$25.00
Martha	Potts	Full Conference Package	$200.00	$100.00	$100.00
Marika	Underberg	Full Conference Package	$200.00	$100.00	$100.00
Nashota	Castillo	Full Conference Package	$200.00	$100.00	$100.00
Raul	Flores	Full Conference Package	$200.00	$175.00	$25.00
Ernie	Vergada	Full Conference Package	$200.00	$175.00	$25.00
Rebecca	Staszowski	Full Conference Package	$200.00	$175.00	$25.00
Stephan	Lukac	Full Conference Package	$200.00	$175.00	$25.00
Sarah	Vargas	Full Conference Package	$200.00	$100.00	$100.00

Figure 1–1 Outstanding Payments Query

32. Open the Keynote Attendance Query and add the criteria to select only those records with a PackageID field value of FC16 or KO16. Save and run the query and then close it.
33. Open the Sunworks Small Deposit Query and add the criteria to select only those records with a CompanyID field value of SWWA01 AND a Deposit field value less than 100. Hide the CompanyID field. Save and run the query and then close it.

34. Open the Site Visits Total Query in Design view and modify it by adding totals to the query. For the SiteName field, set the total row to Group By. For the ReservationID field, set the total row to Count. Save and run the query and then close it.
35. Create a Split Form based on the Delegates table. Save the form as Delegates Entry Form.
36. Use the Delegates Entry Form to add a new record to the Delegates table, using the values shown in Figure 1–2.

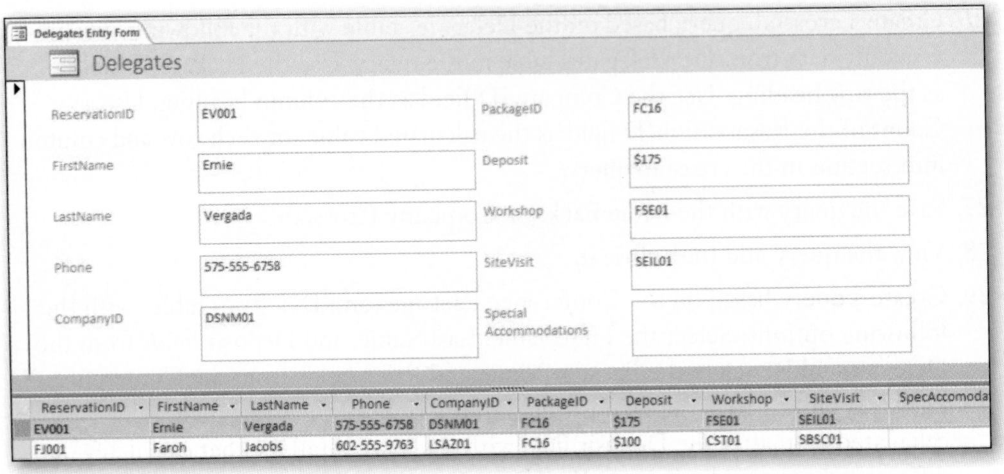

Figure 1–2 Delegates Entry Form

37. Create the simple report shown in Figure 1–3 for the Workshops table. Save the report with the name Workshops Report and close the report. (*Hint:* The time and date values in your report header may not match those shown in Figure 1–3.)

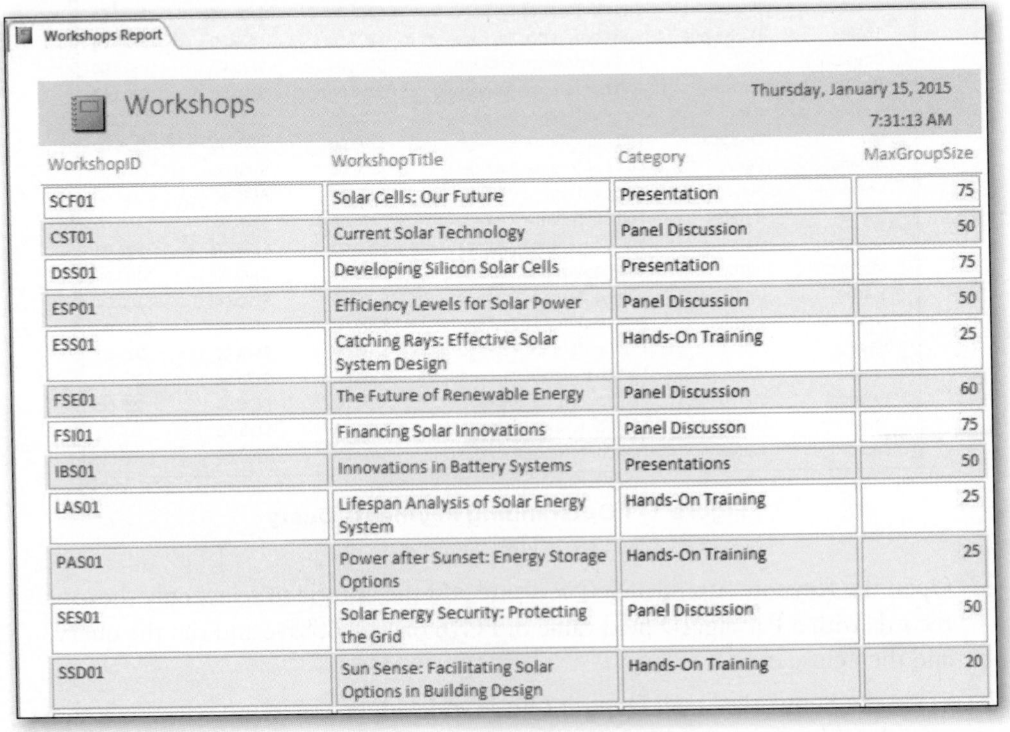

WorkshopID	WorkshopTitle	Category	MaxGroupSize
SCF01	Solar Cells: Our Future	Presentation	75
CST01	Current Solar Technology	Panel Discussion	50
DSS01	Developing Silicon Solar Cells	Presentation	75
ESP01	Efficiency Levels for Solar Power	Panel Discussion	50
ESS01	Catching Rays: Effective Solar System Design	Hands-On Training	25
FSE01	The Future of Renewable Energy	Panel Discussion	60
FSI01	Financing Solar Innovations	Panel Discusson	75
IBS01	Innovations in Battery Systems	Presentations	50
LAS01	Lifespan Analysis of Solar Energy System	Hands-On Training	25
PAS01	Power after Sunset: Energy Storage Options	Hands-On Training	25
SES01	Solar Energy Security: Protecting the Grid	Panel Discussion	50
SSD01	Sun Sense: Facilitating Solar Options in Building Design	Hands-On Training	20

Figure 1–3 Workshops Report

38. Create a new report using the Report Wizard based on the Company Payment Query with the following options: Include all fields from the Company Payment Query. Use no additional grouping in the report. Sort the report in ascending order by the Company field values. Use the Tabular layout and the Portrait orientation for the report. Set the title of the report to Company Payment Report. Preview the report and then save it. The report should match the one shown in Figure 1–4.

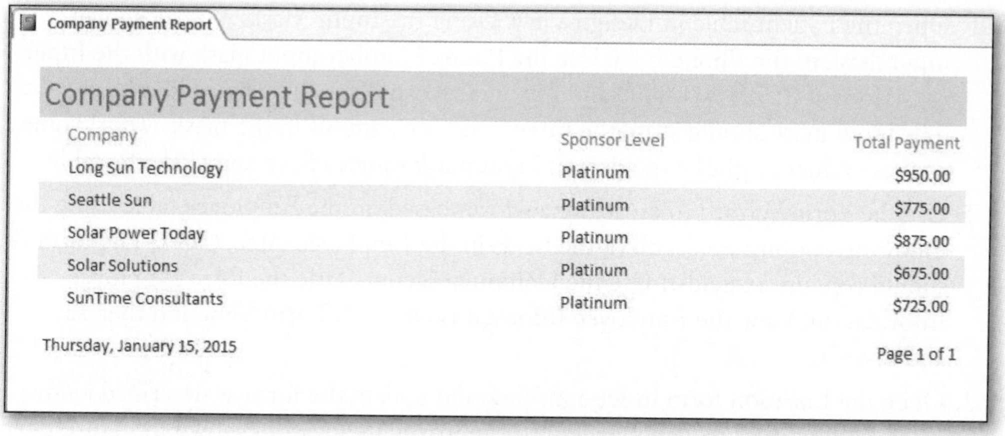
Company Payment Report

Company Payment Report

Company	Sponsor Level	Total Payment
Long Sun Technology	Platinum	$950.00
Seattle Sun	Platinum	$775.00
Solar Power Today	Platinum	$875.00
Solar Solutions	Platinum	$675.00
SunTime Consultants	Platinum	$725.00

Thursday, January 15, 2015 Page 1 of 1

Figure 1–4 Company Payment Report

39. Open the Company report in Layout view and make the following updates to the report so that it matches Figure 1–5: Change the title of the report to Company Representation. Remove the Address and Postal Code columns from the report. Add a Total row to the Company report that calculates the sum of the values in the Number of Delegates column. If necessary, expand the size of the total control so that it appears completely. View the Company report in Report view, confirm that it matches Figure 1–5, and then save and close the report.

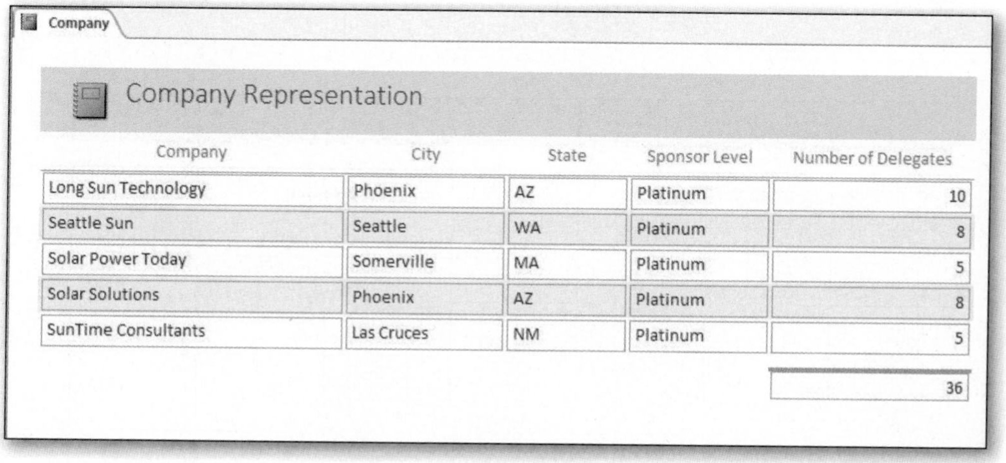
Company

Company Representation

Company	City	State	Sponsor Level	Number of Delegates
Long Sun Technology	Phoenix	AZ	Platinum	10
Seattle Sun	Seattle	WA	Platinum	8
Solar Power Today	Somerville	MA	Platinum	5
Solar Solutions	Phoenix	AZ	Platinum	8
SunTime Consultants	Las Cruces	NM	Platinum	5
				36

Figure 1–5 Company Report

40. Save and close any open objects in your database. Compact and repair your database, close it, and exit Access. Submit the assignment as specified by your instructor.

Capstone Project 2

Problem: You work in the business office of a network of podiatry offices. You manage employees, locations, doctors, patients, and patient visits in an Access relational database. In this project, you will enhance several forms and reports to work more effectively.

Note: To complete this assignment, you will be required to use the Data Files for Students. Visit www.cengage.com/ct/studentdownload for detailed instructions or contact your instructor for information about accessing the required files.

Instructions: Run Access. Open the database SC_Access2013_Capstone_2-1.accdb and save it with the name SC_Access2013_Capstone_2-2.accdb. Enable content if necessary.

Perform the following tasks:

1. Open the Patient table in Design View. Using the Input Mask Wizard, add an input mask to the Phone field. Use the Phone Number input mask with the Input Mask format !(999) 000-0000 and the underscore (_) as the placeholder character. The input mask should store the values without symbols in the mask. (*Hint:* Some of these values might be the default input mask values.) Save and close the table.
2. Use the Form Wizard to create a new form based on the Employee table using the following options: Select all of the fields in the Employee table. (*Hint:* The form should contain six fields.) Use the Columnar layout. Title the form Employee Information. View the Employee Information form in Form View and then save and close it.
3. Open the Location form in Design View and update the form as described below: Add the Phone control and label in the approximate location shown in Figure 2–1.
4. Select the Phone and ZipCode controls and their associated labels and then align them using the Top option.
5. Select the Phone and LocationName controls and align them using the Left option.
6. Select the Phone and Location Name labels and align them using the Left option.
7. Change the Tab Order so that users tab to the Phone control directly after the LocationName control.
8. Save but do not close the form.

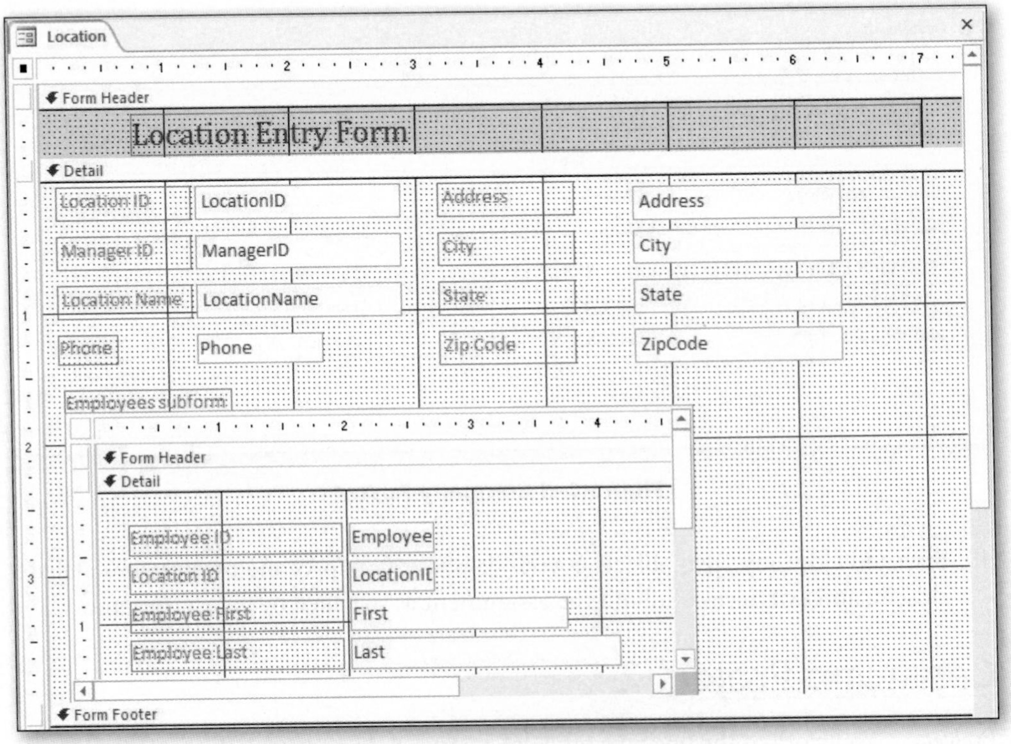

Figure 2–1 Location Form in Design View

9. With the Location form still open in Design View, ensure that the Use Control Wizards button is selected. Use the Subform/Subreport Wizard to add a subform with the following options: Use the Employee table for the subform and Select the EmployeeID, LocationID, First, Last, Title, and MonthlySalary fields (in that order) from the Employee table to add to the subform. Accept the default link (Show Employee for each record in Location using LocationID) to link the main form to the subform.
10. Save the subform as Employees subform.
11. If necessary, reposition the subform to match the approximate location shown in Figure 2–1.
12. Save the Location form but do not close it.
13. With the Location form still open in Design View, add a title to the form. Change the default title text to read Location Entry Form. Save and close the form.
14. Open the Podiatrist Entry form in Design View and ensure that the Use Control Wizards button is selected. Add a combo box to the right side of the Form Header section as described below: The combo box should find a record in the form. The PodiatristID, First, and Last fields (in that order) should be selected for the combo box. The key column should be hidden. The combo box label should be Go to Podiatrist. (*Hint:* Do not include the period.)
15. Resize and reposition the combo box control and label to be in the approximate location shown in Figure 2–2.
16. Save the Podiatrist Entry form, but do not close it. (*Hint:* You can switch to Form View to test whether the new combo box is working properly.)
17. With the Podiatrist Entry form still open in Design View, add a command button to the right side of the Form Footer section with these options: The command button action should be used to close the form (using the Close Form action). The button should display the text Close and no picture. The meaningful name for the command button should be Close Button.
18. Save the Podiatrist Entry form, but do not close it.
19. With the Podiatrist Entry form still open in Design View, add a rectangle control to enclose the Specialty, Certification, and Accepts Minors labels and controls.
20. The upper-left corner of the rectangle should be located at approximately the 0.5" mark on the horizontal ruler.
21. The lower-right corner of the rectangle should be located at approximately the 4.5" mark on the horizontal ruler.
22. Save the Podiatrist Entry form, but do not close it.

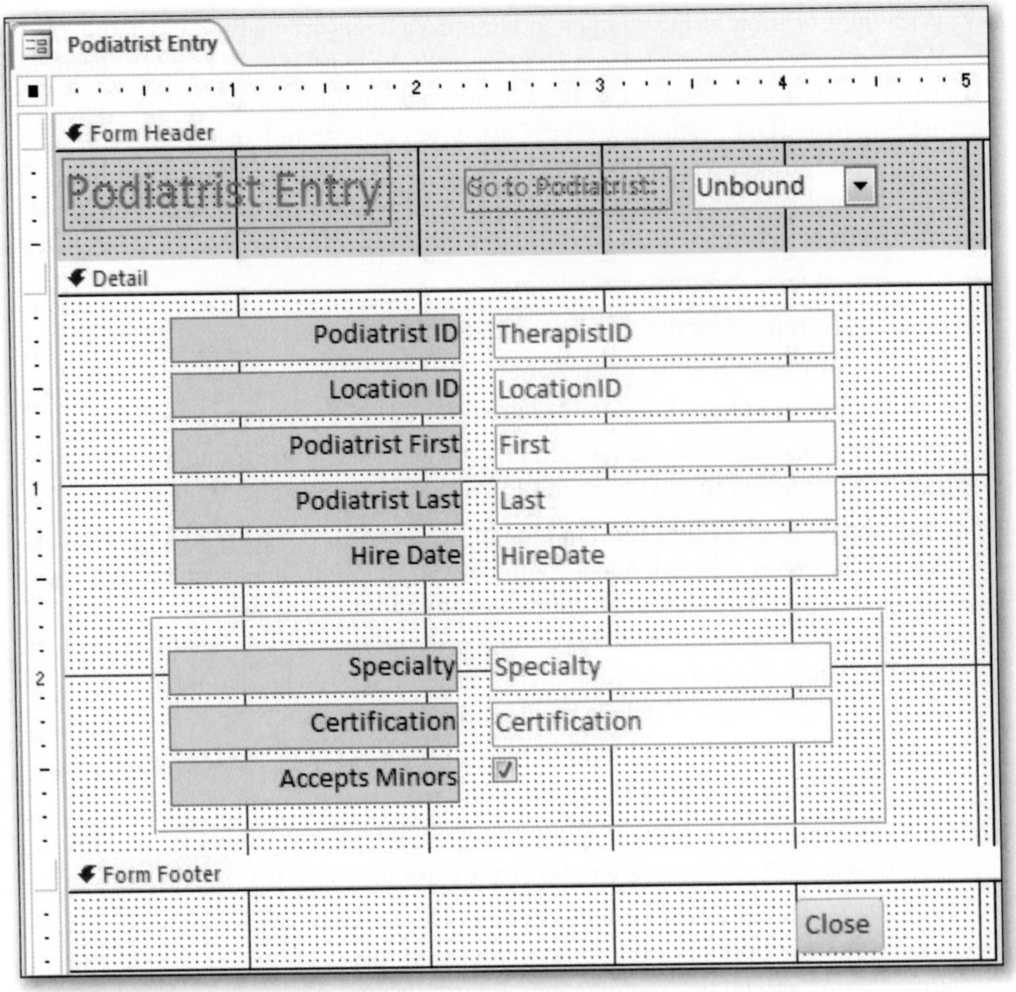

Figure 2–2 Podiatrist Entry Form in Design View

23. With the Podiatrist Entry form still open in Design View, make the following formatting updates: Use the Format Painter to copy the formatting from the PodiatristID label to the other seven labels in the Detail section of the form.
24. In the Detail section of the form, change the fore color of the PodiatristID, LocationID, First, Last, HireDate, Specialty, and Certification fields to Dark Blue, Text 2 (1st row, 4th column in the Theme Colors palette).
25. Save the Podiatrist Entry form, compare the form to Figure 2–2, and then close the form.
26. Open the Location Charts form in Design View. In the Tab control, make the following updates: Change the name of the first tab control to Billing. Change the name of the second tab control to Sessions. Save but do not close the Location Charts form.
27. With the Location Charts form still open in Design View, switch to viewing the Pie chart in the first tab control. Modify the chart type so that it appears as a Clustered Bar chart. Compare the chart on the first tab control to the chart in Figure 2–3. Save but do not close the Location Charts form.

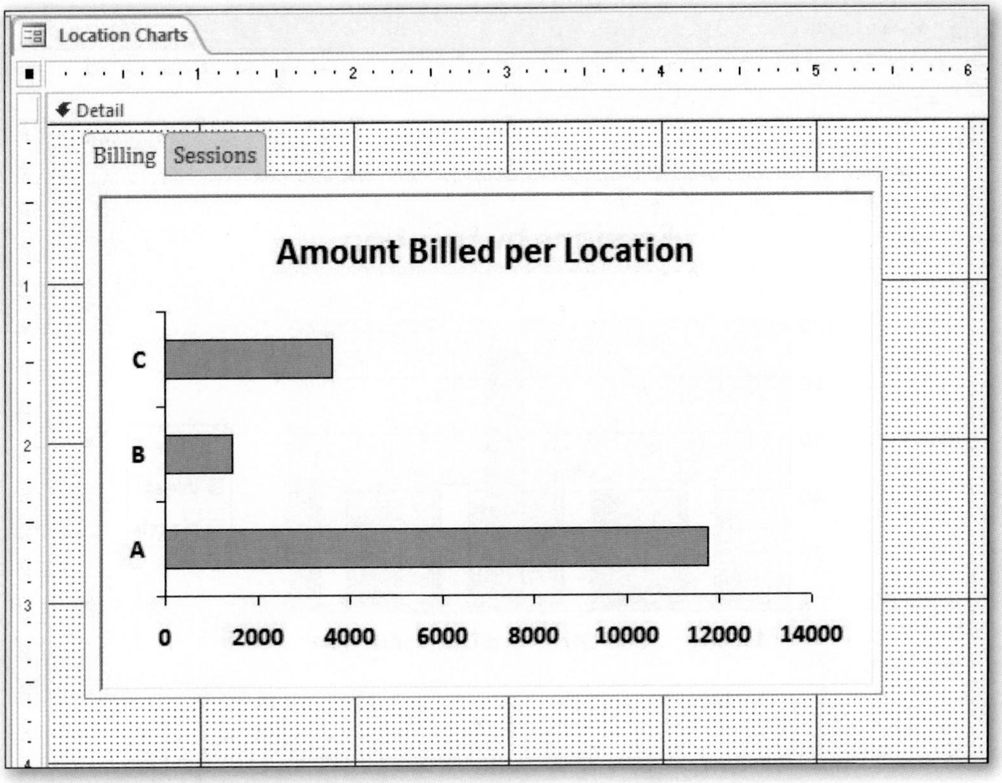

Figure 2–3 Location Charts Form – Billing Tab in Design View

28. With the Location Charts form still open in Design View, switch to viewing the second tab control. Insert a chart into the second tab control with the following options: Base the chart on the Locations and Billing query. Use the LocationID and SumOfSessions fields (in that order) in your chart. Use 3-D Colum Chart as the chart type for your chart.
29. The LocationID field should be the field for series and the SumOfSessions (which will be renamed SumOfSumOfSessions) field should be the field for data in the graph. (*Hint:* These fields should automatically be assigned to the correct areas in the Chart wizard.)
30. Use the LocationID field as the link between the form and the chart.
31. Use Sessions by Location as the name of your chart.
32. Display a legend in the chart.
33. Save the form, compare it to Figure 2–4, and then close the form.

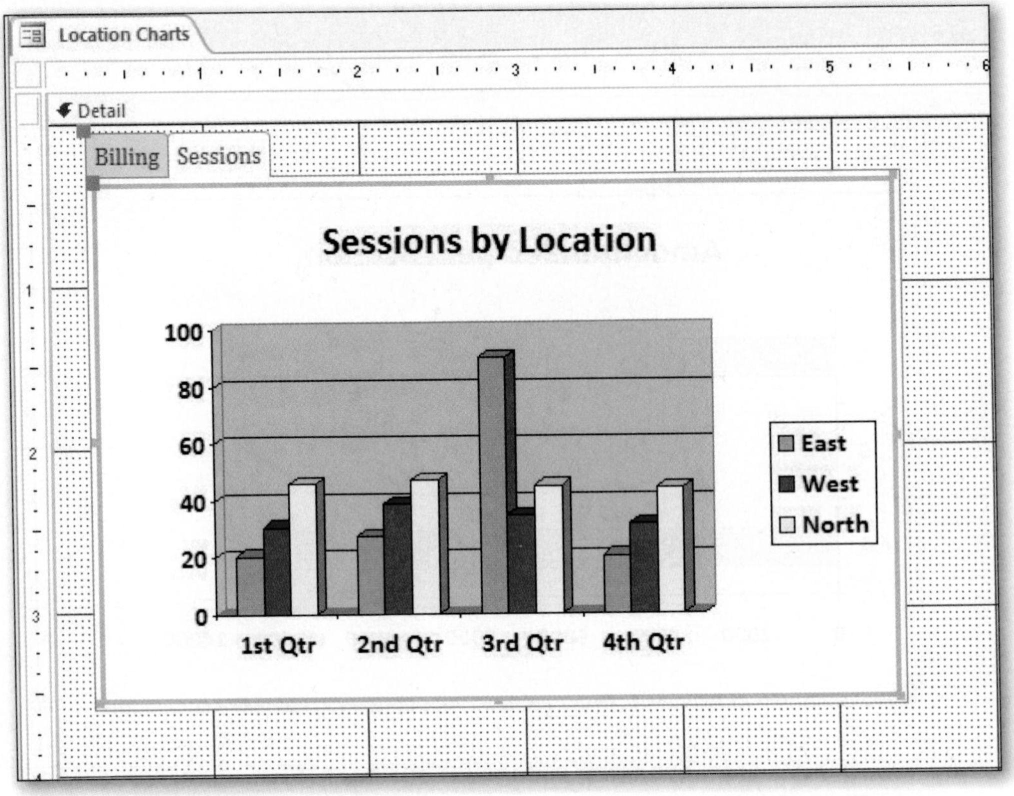

Figure 2-4 Location Charts Form – Sessions Tab in Design View

34. Use the Report Wizard to create a multi-table report with the following options: Add the PatientFirst and PatientLast fields (in that order) from the Patient table to the report. Add the PodiatristID, StartDate, EndDate, Sessions, and Amount fields (in that order) from the Billing table to the form. The data should be viewed by Patient with no additional grouping levels. Sort the report in ascending order by StartDate. Use the Stepped layout and Landscape orientation for the report. Use Patient Billing as the report title.
35. Compare your report to Figure 2–5 and then save and close the report.

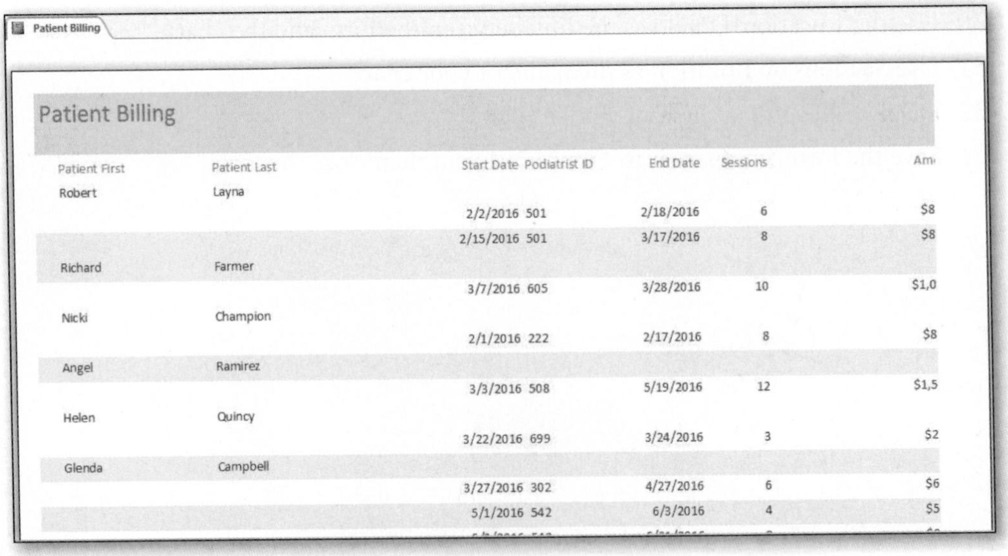

Patient Billing
Patient Billing
Patient First
Patient Last
Start Date
Podiatrist ID
End Date
Sessions
Robert
Layna
2/2/2016 501
2/18/2016
6
2/15/2016 501
3/17/2016
8
Richard
Farmer
3/7/2016 605
3/28/2016
10
Nicki
Champion
2/1/2016 222
2/17/2016
8
Angel
Ramirez
3/3/2016 508
5/19/2016
12
Helen
Quincy
3/22/2016 699
3/24/2016
3
Glenda
Campbell
3/27/2016 302
4/27/2016
6
5/1/2016 542
6/3/2016
4

Figure 2-5 Patient Billing Report in Print Preview View

36. Use the Label Wizard to create mailing labels for the Patient table using the following options: Use the Avery 5160 label size. Use Arial font, 12-point font size, Normal font weight, and Black font color with no special font styles for the labels. (*Hint:* These formatting options may be the default settings for your label.)
37. On the first line of the label, include the PatientFirst field, a space, and the PatientLast field.
38. On the second line of the label, include the Address field.
39. On the third line of the label, include the City field, a comma (,), a space, the State field, a space, and then the Zip field. Your label should match the label in Figure 2–6.

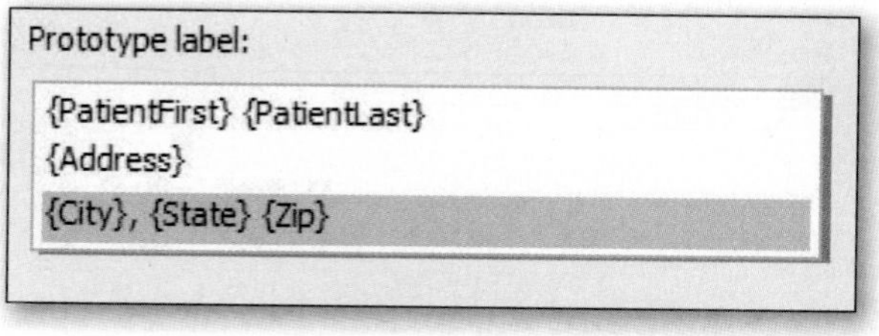

Figure 2–6 Patient Prototype Label

40. Sort the labels by the PatientLast field and then the PatientFirst field.
41. Name the report Patient Mailing Labels. (*Hint:* If you receive a message indicating that all information may not be displayed, click OK.)
42. Preview the mailing labels, confirming they match Figure 2–7. Save and close the Patient Mailing Labels report.

Kelly Balarbar
568 Hwy 5
Canton, OH 44709
Glenda Campbell
3 River Road
Dueber, OH 44706
Nicki Champion
34 Duck Lake
Dueber, OH 44706
Richard Farmer
550 Riverside Dr
McKinley, OH 44704
Louise Francis
235 Hwy 5
Cincinnati, OH 44213
Lexie Garcia
4 Lakeside Dr
Hyde Park, OH 45208
Mary Gibbs
1876 Champion
Cincinnati, OH 45221
Maria Green
12 Malabar
Cincinnati, OH 45209
Robert Layna
48 Mettle Cove
Canton, OH 44702
Al Pandola
45 South Main St
Canton, OH 44701
Helen Quincy
1907 Montalba Rd
Richville, OH 44706
Michael Quincy
1907 Montalba Rd
Richville, OH 44706
Simone Quinn
98 South Hwy 8
Waco, OH 44707
Angel Ramirez
583 South 1st St
Richville, OH 44706
Anna Rodriguez
48652 Hwy 49
Clifton, OH 45220
Marty Spencer
Montgomery Stewart
Monica Tellus

Figure 2–7 Patient Mailing Labels in Print Preview View

43. Open the Billing by Podiatrist report in Layout View. Open the Group, Sort, and Total pane and then add an ascending sort order to the PatientLast field within the PodiatristID group. Save but do not close the report.
44. With the Billing by Podiatrist report still open in Layout View, select the Amount column and then add subtotals and a grand total to the column using the Sum function. Save but do not close the report.
45. With the Billing by Podiatrist report still open in Layout View, apply conditional formatting to the values in the Amount field so that if the field value is greater than or equal to 1,000, the field's font color is set to red and the font is bold. Compare the report to Figure 2–8 and then save and close the Billing by Podiatrist report.

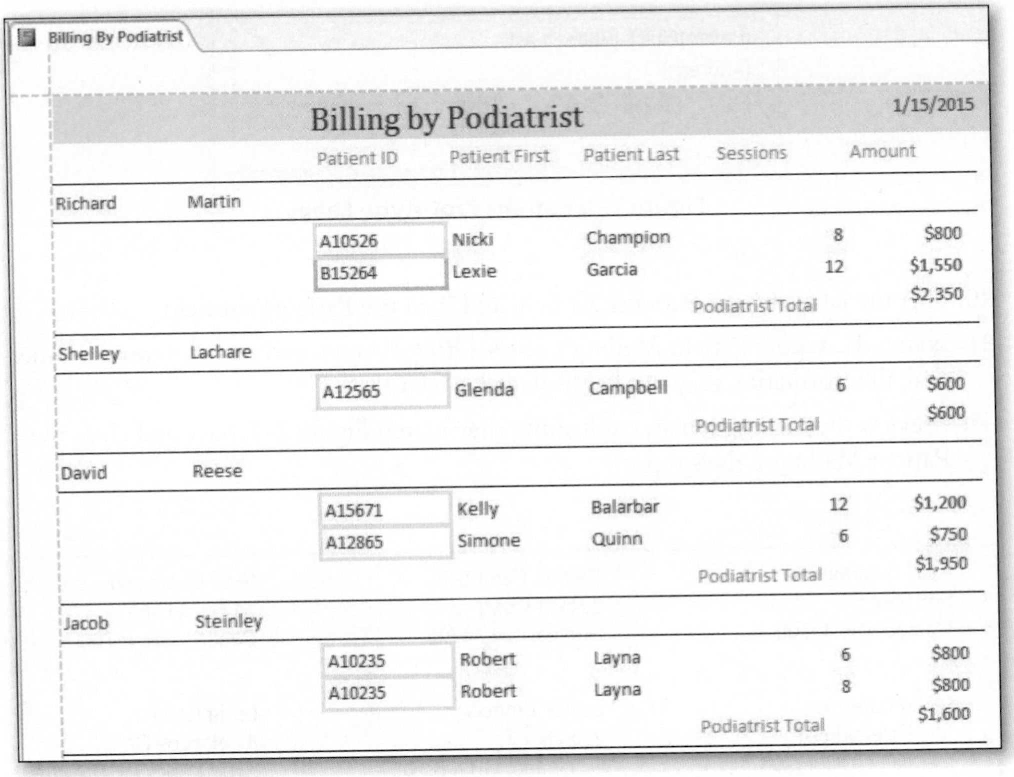

Figure 2–8 Billing by Podiatrist Report in Layout View

46. Open the Podiatrists by Location report in Design View and set the Record Source property to the Locations and Podiatrists query. Save the Podiatrist by Location report without closing it.
47. With the Podiatrists by Location report still open in Design View, add a grouping field to the report with the following options: Open the Group, Sort, and Total pane and then add the LocationName field as a grouping field. Select the LocationName header and change the Repeat Section property value to Yes. With the LocationName header still selected, modify the Force New Page property so that a new page should be created after each section (using the After Section option). Save the Podiatrists by Location report, but do not close it.

48. With the Podiatrists by Location report still open in Design View, add a field to the LocationName header with the following options: Add the LocationName field to the LocationName header in the approximate location shown in Figure 2–9. (Hint: Use the Add Existing Fields button to open the Field List.) Delete the label associated with the LocationName control. Select the LocationName control and modify it to display with a font size of 16 point and a font weight of Bold.
49. Move the control so that the left edge of the LocationName control is touching the left edge of the report.
50. Resize the LocationName control so that the right edge of the control is at the 2" mark on the horizontal ruler.
51. Save but do not close the Podiatrists by Location report.
52. With the Podiatrists by Location report still open in Design View, add page numbers and dates to the report with the following options: Add the Date to the report, using the Short Date (e.g., 12/12/2017) format. Do not include the time in the report. Add Page Numbers to the report, using the Page N of M format, at the Bottom of the Page, with the Right alignment option.
53. Save the report and compare it to Figure 2–9. Close the Podiatrists by Location report.

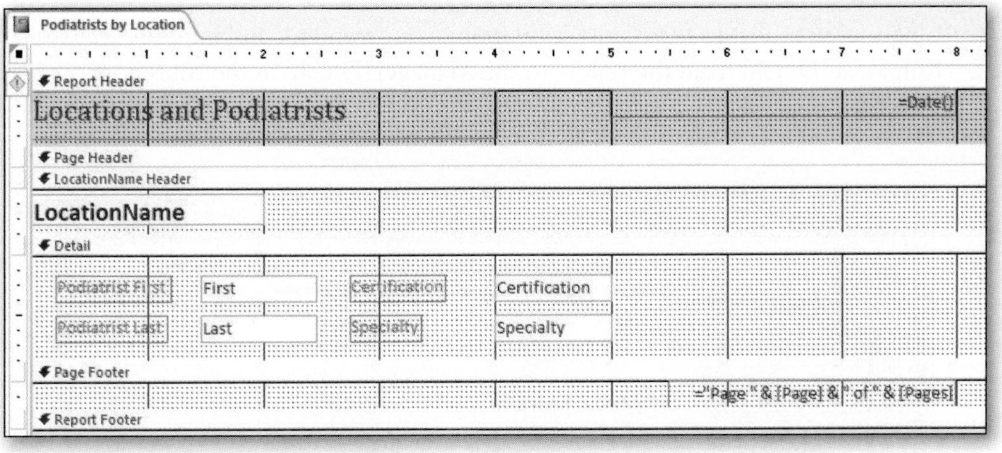

Figure 2–9 Podiatrists by Location Report in Design View

54. Open the Employees and Managers report in Design View. Remove the Page Header and Footer from the report. Save but do not close the report.
55. With the Employees and Managers report still open in Design View, add a text box control to the LocationName header with the following options:

56. Add the text box control to the LocationName header in the approximate location shown in Figure 2–11. (*Hint:* The left edge of the text box control should line up with the left edge of the ManagerID control.) Enter the following expression into the text box control: =[First] & " " & [Last]
57. Reposition and resize the text box control so that it is approximately as long as the ManagerID control above it and it appears in the approximate location shown in Figure 2–11.
58. Set the border style property of the text box control to Transparent.
59. Change the label associated with the text box to Manager Name.
60. Reposition and resize the label so that all text in the label is visible and the label appears in the approximate location shown in Figure 2–11.
61. Save but do not close the Employees and Managers report.
62. With the Employees and Managers report still open in Design View, ensure that the Use Control Wizards button is selected. Insert a subreport into the Detail section of the report with the following options: Add the subreport to the Detail section of the report at approximately the 0.5" mark on the horizontal ruler and the 0.5" mark on the vertical ruler.
63. Base your subreport on the existing query Employees and Managers.
64. Include the ManagerID, First, Last, and Title fields (in that order) in the subreport.
65. Link the subreport to the report by defining your own link, linking the EmployeeID field from the report to the ManagerID field in the subreport, as shown in Figure 2–10.

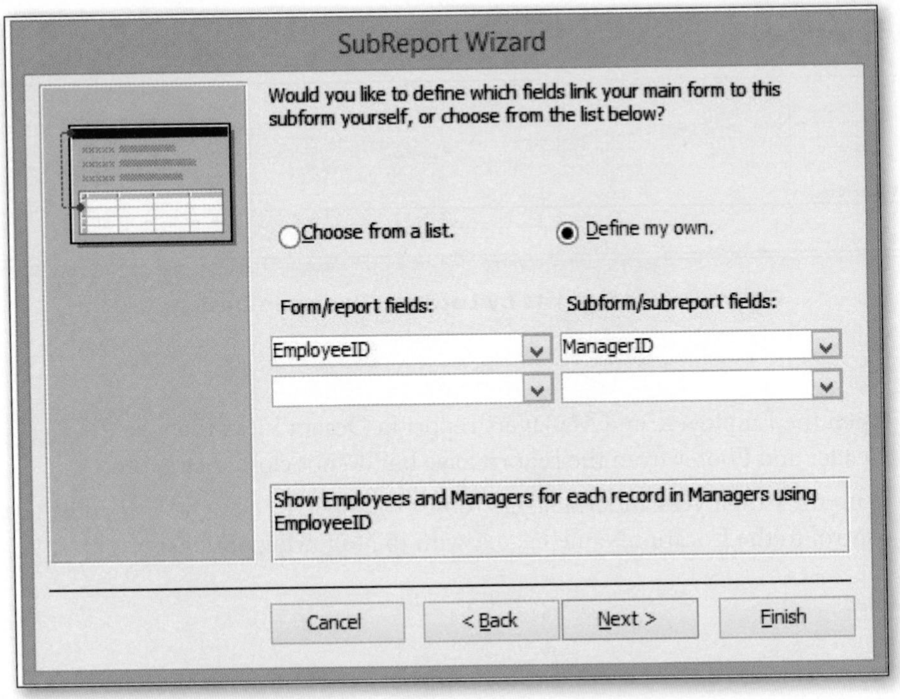

Figure 2–10 Linking Fields in the SubReport Wizard

66. Use the default name Employees and Managers subreport as the name of the subreport.
67. In Design View, delete the label associated with the subreport.
68. Reposition the subreport to the approximate location shown in Figure 2–11.

69. Save the report and compare it to Figure 2–11. Close the Employees and Managers report.

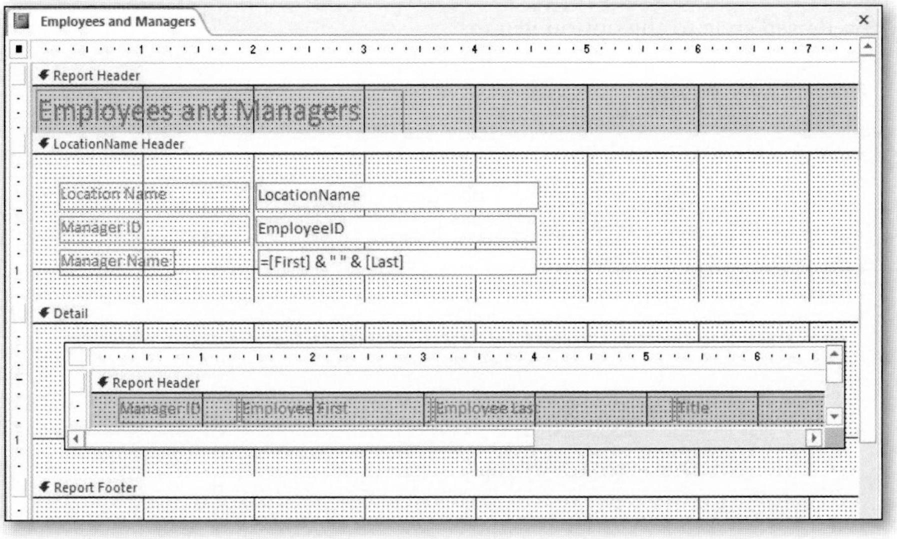

Figure 2–11 Employees and Managers Report in Design View

70. Save and close any open objects in your database. Compact and repair your database, close it, and exit Access. Submit the assignment as specified by your instructor.

Capstone Project 3

Problem: Essence Salon is a full-service day spa that offers a range of beauty and wellness treatments. Spa manager Anne Marie Taylor would like a better way of keeping track of the salon's various aestheticians and the services each provides. The business is growing, and Anne Marie would also like to be able to easily access information about clients. You will create reports and forms that Anne Marie can use to keep track of the business.

Note: To complete this assignment, you will be required to use the Data Files for Students. Visit www.cengage.com/ct/studentdownload for detailed instructions or contact your instructor for information about accessing the required files.

Instructions, Part 1: Start Access and open the Essence Salon database from the Data Files for Students. Anne Marie needs forms that will help streamline her work. Create a macro named Forms and Reports that includes submacros to perform the following tasks:

a. Open the Client Name Form and allow editing
b. Open the Employee Phone Numbers Form in Read Only mode
c. Preview the Employee Services Report
d. Export the Client Name Form in PDF format
e. Export the Employee Services Report in PDF format
f. Export the Clients Report in PDF format

Create the menu forms shown in Figures 3–1 and 3–2. The command buttons on the Open Forms should use the macros you created to open the two forms. The option group on the Export Actions Form should use the macros you created to export the reports. For the form actions, use option buttons, do not specify a default value, and apply the Raised style to the option group.

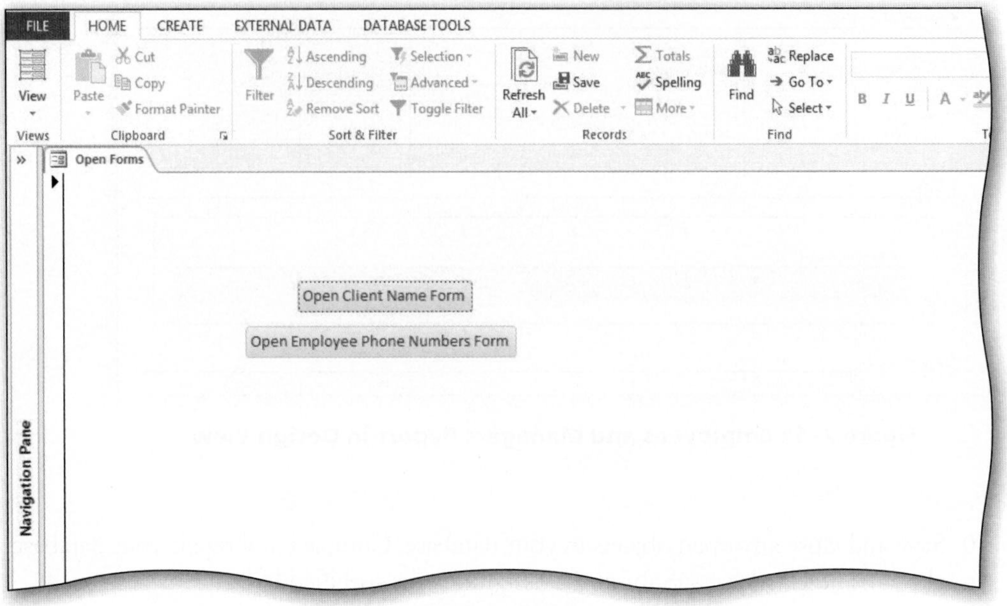

Figure 3–1

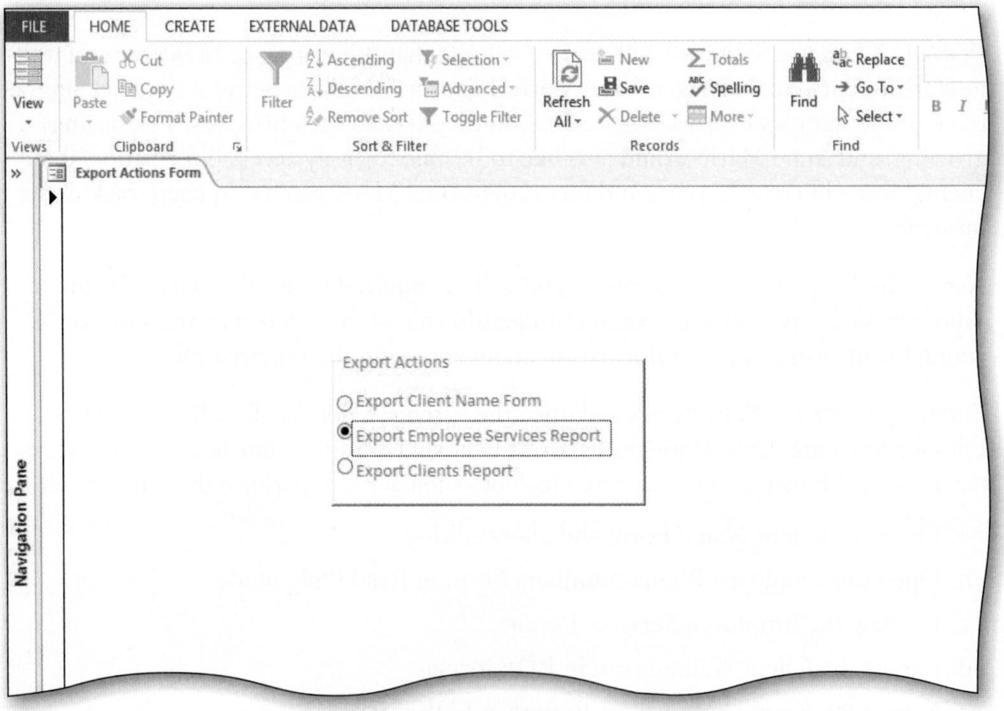

Figure 3–2

Instructions, Part 2: Create the datasheet forms shown in Figure 3–3 and Figure 3–4.

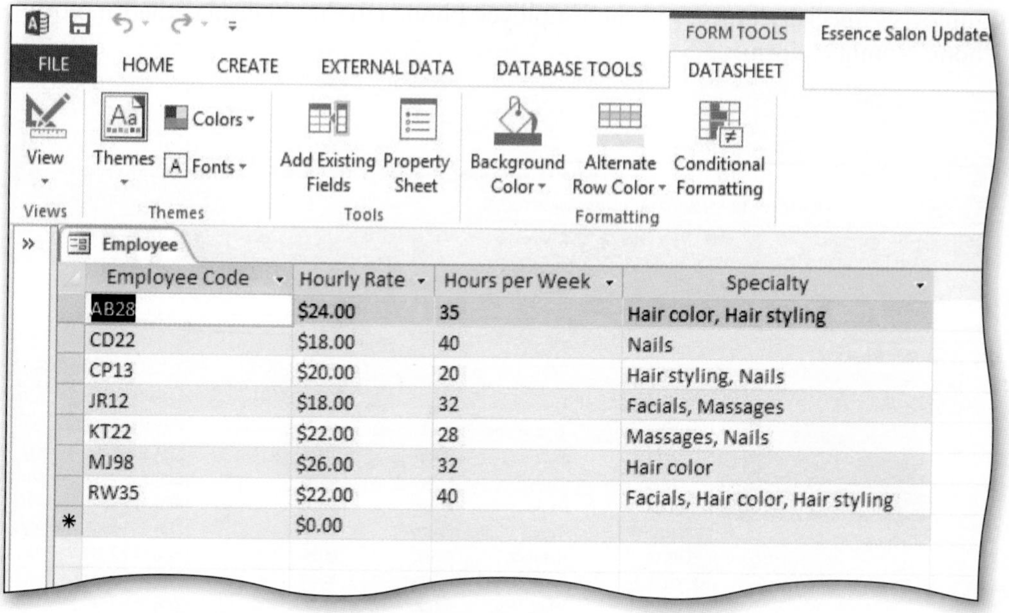

Figure 3–3

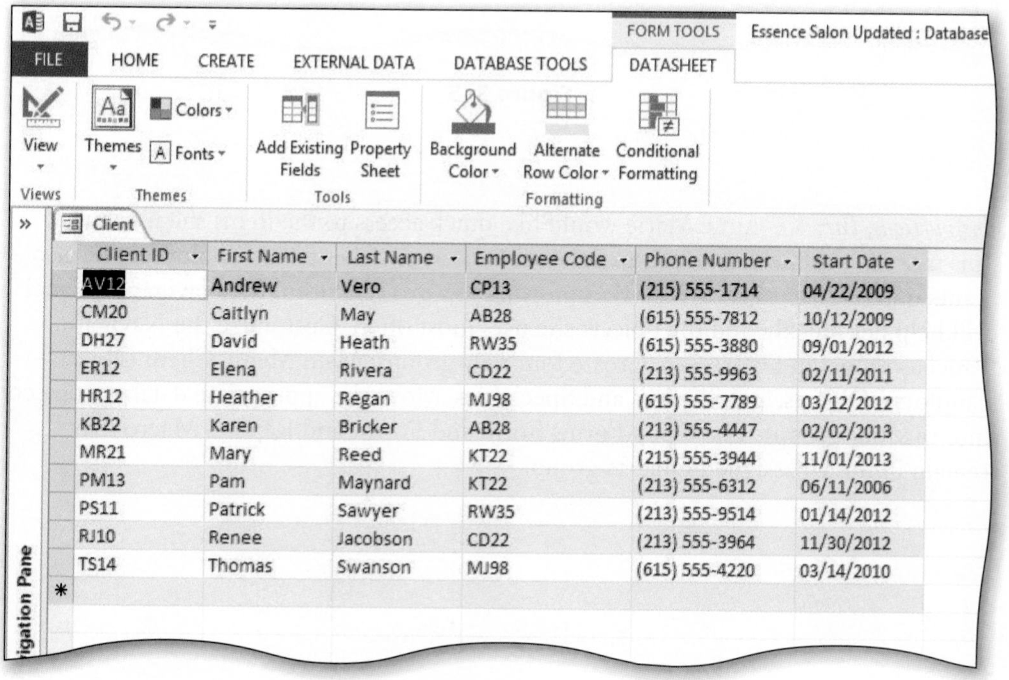

Figure 3–4

Create the navigation form shown in Figure 3–5. Using a Vertical Tabs Layout, name the form Main Menu. The title of the form is Essence Salon Form. The Client tab should display the Client Name Form, the Specialties tab should display the Employees Specialty Form, and the Employee Phone tab should display the Employee Phone Numbers Form.

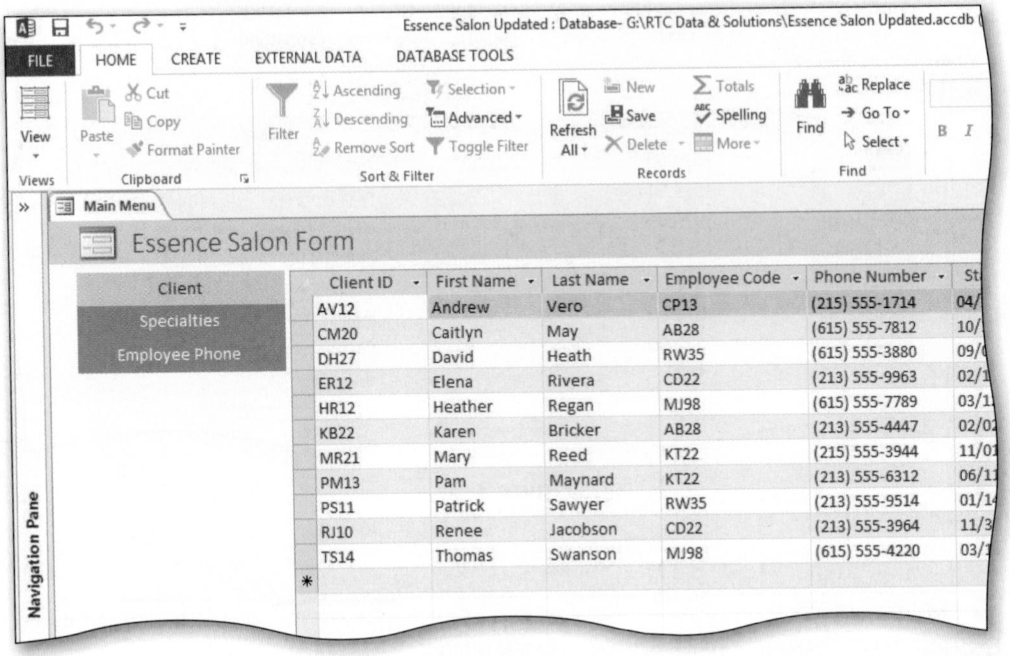

Figure 3–5

Instructions, Part 3: Anne Marie would like quick access to the items she uses most. It is more logical for her to group database objects by Client and Employee. She also wants quick access to the Main Menu form. New groups within the Navigation Panel will help her quickly find the objects she uses most often. Customize the Navigation Panel as shown in Figure 3–6. Create four new groups: Main Menu, Client Objects, Employee Objects, and Services and Specialties. Move the appropriate database objects into the four groups. The Open Forms Form and Forms and Reports Macro may remain in the Unassigned Objects group.

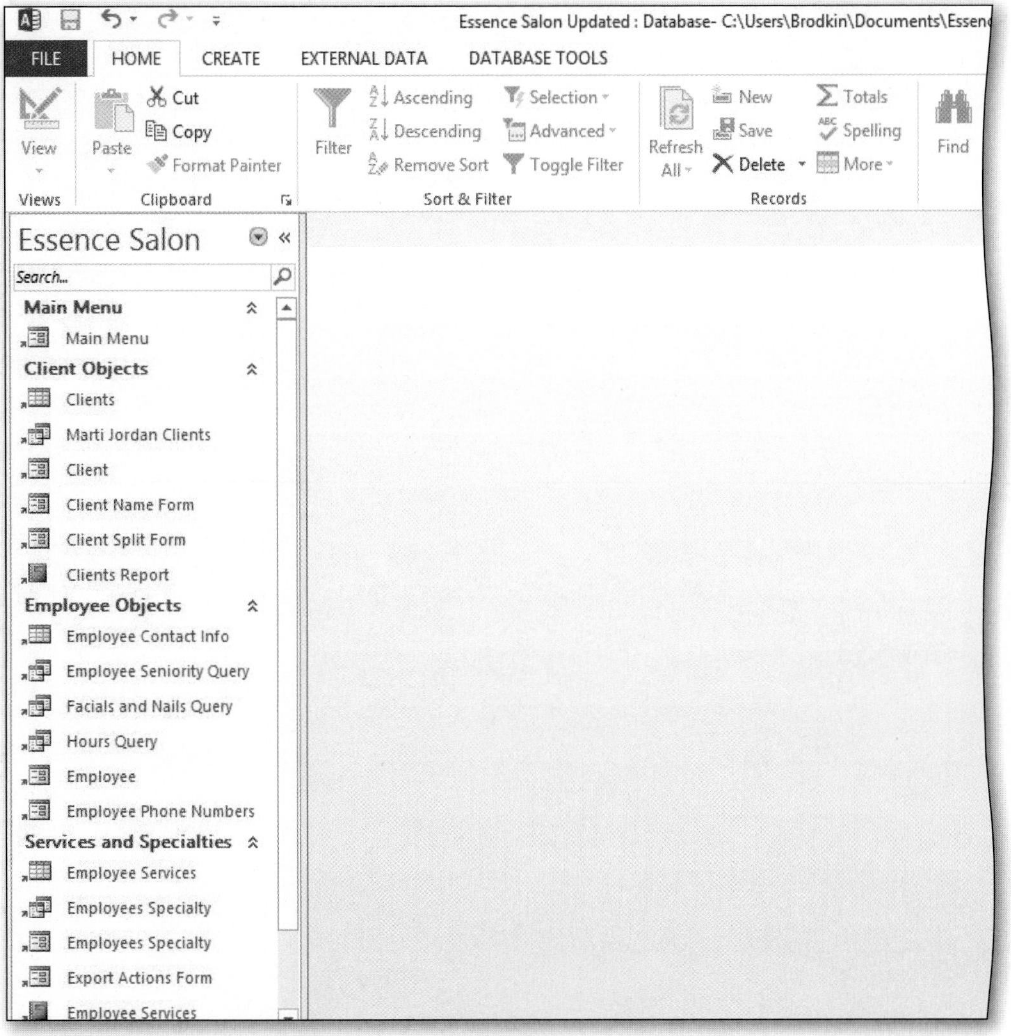

Figure 3–6

Create an input mask for the Client ID field of the Clients table. The Client ID field must consist of two uppercase letters followed by two digits. Create and apply the same input mask to the Employee Code field of the Employee Contact Info table.

Exit Access and submit the database in the format specified by your instructor.

Appendix C

Microsoft Office 2013 Specialist and Expert Certifications

What Are Microsoft Office Specialist and Expert Certifications?

Microsoft Corporation has developed a set of standardized, performance-based examinations that you can take to demonstrate your overall expertise with Microsoft Office 2013 programs, including Microsoft Word 2013, Microsoft PowerPoint 2013, Microsoft Excel 2013, Microsoft Access 2013, and Microsoft Outlook 2013. When you successfully complete an examination for one of these Office programs, you will have earned the designation as a specialist or as an expert in that particular Office program. These examinations collectively are called the Microsoft Office 2013 Specialist and Microsoft Office 2013 Expert certification exams.

Why Should You Be Certified?

Microsoft Office 2013 certification provides a number of benefits for both you and your potential employer. The benefits for you include the following:

- You can differentiate yourself in the employment marketplace from those who are not Microsoft Office Specialist or Expert certified.
- You have proved your skills and expertise when using Microsoft Office 2013.
- You will be able to perform at a higher skill level in your job.
- You will be working at a higher professional level than those who are not certified.
- You will broaden your employment opportunities and advance your career more rapidly.

For employers, Microsoft Office 2013 certification offers the following advantages:

- When hiring or promoting employees, employers have immediate verification of employees' skills.
- Companies can maximize their productivity and efficiency by employing Microsoft Office 2013 certified individuals.

Skills Mapping

The following mapping information shows where each skill in the Access 2013 certification exam is covered in this text.

Table C–1 Specialist-Level Skill Sets and Locations in Book for Microsoft Access 2013

Skill Set	Page Number
1.0 Create and Manage a Database	
1.1 Create a New Database	
creating new databases	OFF 23–26, AC 6–7
creating databases using templates	AC 7, AC 579–580
creating databases in older formats	AC 542–543, AC 544
creating databases using wizards	AC 40–42 (Simple Query wizard), AC 103–104 (Report wizard), AC 155–156 (Lookup wizard), AC 233–235 (Form wizard)
1.2 Manage Relationships and Keys	
editing references between tables	AC 111 (BTW), AC 184 (CT)
creating and modifying relationships	AC 181–185
setting primary key fields	AC 11–13, AC 336
enforcing referential integrity	AC 181–185, AC 338–339
setting foreign keys	AC 181–185
viewing relationships	AC 184 (Q&A), AC 338
1.3 Navigate through a Database	
navigating to specific records	AC 142 (Experimental Step using Navigation buttons), AC 143–145 (searching for a record), AC 307 (BTW)
setting a form as the startup option	AC 576–577
using navigation forms	AC 506–509 (create navigation form), AC 509 (use navigation form), AC 575–576
setting navigation options	AC 549–553
changing views	AC 17 (Datasheet view of a table to Design view), AC 44 (Design view of a query to Datasheet view), AC 83 (Datasheet view of a query to Design view), AC 295 (Design view to Form view)
1.4 Protect and Maintain a Database	
compacting databases	AC 57
repairing databases	AC 57
backing up databases	AC 56
splitting databases	AC 589–590
encrypting databases with a password	AC 583–585
merging databases	AC 160, AC 162
recovering data from backups	AC 57
1.5 Print and Export a Database	
printing reports	AC 54, AC 221
printing records	AC 244–245
maintaining backward compatibility	AC 542 (BTW)
saving databases as templates	AC 578–579
saving databases to external locations	AC 543 (BTW)
exporting to alternate formats	AC 107–111, AC 543 (BTW)

Table C–1 Specialist-Level Skill Sets and Locations in Book for Microsoft Access 2013 *(continued)*

Skill Set	Page Number
2.0 Build Tables	
2.1 Create a Table	
creating new tables	AC 10–15, AC 335–336
importing external data into tables	AC 32–38, AC 337, AC 571–572
creating linked tables from external sources	AC 337
importing tables from other databases	AC 572 (BTW)
creating tables from templates and application parts	AC 578–579 (create templates and application parts), AC 579–581 (use templates and application parts)
2.2 Format a Table	
hiding fields in tables	AC 565 (CT)
changing data formats	AC 159 (BTW), AC 165 (BTW), AC 556 (BTW)
adding total rows	AC 175–176
adding table descriptions	AC 197 (Step 10), AC 556 (BTW)
renaming tables	AC 58
2.3 Manage Records	
updating records	AC 145, AC 160–161, AC 168–171
adding new records	AC 20–23, AC 26–27, AC 143
deleting records	AC 23, AC 145–146
appending records from external data	AC 337
finding and replacing data	AC 143–145 (finding), AC 143 (CT) (replacing)
sorting records	AC 151–152, AC 187–189
filtering records	AC 146–153
grouping records	AC 118–119 (for queries), AC 208–211 (for reports), AC 344–345
2.4 Create and Modify Fields	
adding fields to tables	AC 153–159
adding a validation rules to fields	AC 162–166
changing field captions	AC 13
changing field sizes	AC 13, AC 163
changing field data types	AC 13, AC 153 (BTW)
configuring fields to auto-increment	AC 9 (BTW)
setting default values	AC 164
using input masks	AC 270–272, AC 556–557
deleting fields	AC 15
3.0 Create Queries	
3.1 Create a Query	
running queries	AC 80–82
creating crosstab queries	AC 118–121
creating parameter queries	AC 86–88
creating action queries	AC 160–162
creating multi-table queries	AC 99–102
saving queries	AC 82, AC 84–85 (saving a query with a new name)
deleting queries	AC 58 (deleting any objects)
3.2 Modify a Query	
renaming queries	AC 58 (renaming any object), AC 84–85 (saving a query with a new name)

Table C–1 Specialist-Level Skill Sets and Locations in Book for Microsoft Access 2013 *(continued)*	
Skill Set	**Page Number**
adding new fields	AC 79–80
removing fields	AC 80 (Q&A)
hiding fields	AC 85–86
sorting data within queries	AC 93–97
formatting fields within queries	AC 114, AC 312 (BTW)
3.3 Utilize Calculated Fields and Grouping within a Query	
adding calculated fields	AC 112–113 (enter expression) and AC 340–342 (use Expression Builder)
adding conditional logic	AC 89–92
grouping and summarizing data	AC 115–121
using comparison operators	AC 89–90
using basic operators	AC 92
4.0 Create Forms	
4.1 Create a Form	
creating new forms	AC 45–47, AC 233–235, and AC 283–307
creating forms with application parts	AC 582–583
saving forms	AC 47, AC 244, and AC 285
deleting forms	AC 58 (deleting any object)
4.2 Set Form Controls	
moving form controls	AC 239–241 (Layout view), AC 284–290 (Design view), and AC 415–416 (Design view)
adding form controls	AC 284–285, AC 415–420, AC 424–425, AC 428–433
modifying data sources	AC 415
removing form controls	AC 285 (Q&A), AC 416 (Q&A)
setting form control properties	AC 298–303, AC 420–423
managing labels	AC 240–241, AC 298–302, and AC 420–423
4.3 Format a Form	
modifying Tab order in forms	AC 304–305
formatting print layouts	AC 227 (BTW), AC 389–391
sorting records	AC 208–210, AC 344–345, AC 378
applying themes	AC 230–232
changing margins	AC 389–391
inserting backgrounds	AC 427
auto-ordering forms	AC 304 (BTW)
inserting headers and footers	AC 426–427
inserting images	AC 427
modifying existing forms	AC 296–304, AC 437–441, AC 451–455
5.0 Create Reports	
5.1 Create a Report	
creating new reports	AC 48–53 (Layout view), AC 103–104 (Report wizard), AC 222–226 (Report wizard), AC 227–229 (Layout view), AC 343–370 (Design view)
creating reports with application parts	*Functionality not found in Access 2013
deleting reports	AC 58 (deleting any objects)
5.2 Set Report Controls	
grouping data by fields	AC 208–210, AC 344–346
sorting data	AC 208–210, AC 344–346

Table C–1 Specialist-Level Skill Sets and Locations in Book for Microsoft Access 2013 *(continued)*

Skill Set	Page Number
adding sub-forms	AC 359–366 (This is really adding sub-reports.)
modifying data sources	AC 343–344
adding report controls	AC 210–213 (Layout view), AC 227–229 (Layout view), AC 346–352 (Design view), and AC 376–382 (Design view)
managing labels	AC 353–358
5.3 Format a Report	
formatting reports into multiple columns	AC 227 (BTW)
adding calculated fields	AC 349–352, AC 384–386
setting margins	AC 220–221, AC 389–391
adding backgrounds	AC 372
changing report orientation	AC 390
changing sort order	AC 208–210, AC 344–346
inserting headers and footers	AC 371
inserting images	AC 371
inserting page numbers	AC 368–369
applying themes	AC 230–232
modifying existing reports	AC 208–218, AC 361–365, AC 366–370

D

J

K

L

M

N

O

P

R

Index

U

V

W

X

Y

Z

Quick Reference Summary

Microsoft Office 2013 Access Comprehensive Quick Reference

Task	Page Number	Ribbon	Other On-Screen Areas	Shortcut Menu	Keyboard Shortcut
Advanced Filter/ Sort, Use	AC 151	Advanced button (HOME tab | Sort & Filter group), Advanced Filter/Sort			
Append Query, Use	AC 162	Append button (QUERY TOOLS DESIGN Tab | Query Type group)			
Ascending Button, Use to Order Records	AC 187	Select field, Ascending button (HOME tab | Sort & Filter group)	Sort A to Z (for ascending) or Sort Z to A (for descending)		
Back up Database	AC 56	FILE tab, Save As tab, 'Back Up Database', Save As button			
Background Color Button, Use	AC 420	Background Color arrow (FORM DESIGN TOOLS FORMAT tab | Font group), select color from palette			
Border Style, Change	AC 356	Select controls, Property Sheet button (REPORT DESIGN TOOLS DESIGN tab | Tools group), tap or click Border Style property box, select style			
Calculated Field in Query, Create using Expression Builder	AC 340	Builder button (QUERY TOOLS DESIGN tab | Query Setup group)		Press and hold or right-click field row, Build command	
Calculated Field in Query, Use	AC 112			Press and hold or right-click field row, Zoom	
Calculated Field, Create	AC 158		In Design view, create new field, tap or click Data Type arrow, tap or click Calculated		
Can Grow Property, Change	AC 363	Select control, Property Sheet button (REPORT DESIGN TOOLS DESIGN tab | Tools group), change Can Grow property to Yes		Press and hold or right-click control, tap or click Properties, change Can Grow property to Yes	

Microsoft Office 2013 Access Comprehensive Quick Reference *(continued)*

Task	Page Number	Ribbon	Other On-Screen Areas	Shortcut Menu	Keyboard Shortcut
Caption, Change	AC 114	Property Sheet button (DESIGN tab | Show/Hide group), Caption box	Select field in design grid, tap or click Properties on shortcut menu	Press and hold or right-click field in design grid, tap or click Properties on shortcut menu	
Chart Type, Modify	AC 456		In Design view, press and hold or right-click chart, Chart Object command, Edit command, Chart Type command		
Chart, Format	AC 459		Press and hold or right-click chart, Chart Object command, Edit command		
Chart, Insert	AC 453	More button (FORM DESIGN TOOLS DESIGN tab | Controls group), Chart tool			
Close Object	AC 20		Close button for object	Close	
Collection of Legal Values, Specify	AC 165		In Design view, enter values in Validation Rule property box in Field Properties pane		
Colors and Font, Change in Datasheet	AC 177	Font Color arrow (HOME tab | Text Formatting group)			
Column, Resize	AC 28		Double-click or double-tap right boundary of field selector in datasheet	Press and hold or right-click field name, Field Width	
Combo Box, Add	AC 417		More button (FORM DESIGN TOOLS DESIGN tab | Controls group), Combo Box tool		
Combo Box, Modify	AC 439	Select combo box, Property Sheet button (FORM DESIGN TOOLS DESIGN tab | Tools group), change properties			
Combo Box, Use	AC 435		Tap or click combo box arrow, select item to find		
Command Buttons, Add to a Form	AC 428	Button tool (FORM DESIGN TOOLS DESIGN tab | Controls group), position control			
Common Filter, Use	AC 148			Arrow for field, point to Text Filters	
Compact Database	AC 57	FILE tab, Info tab in Backstage view, 'Compact & Repair Database' button			
Comparison Operator, Use	AC 90		Create query, enter comparison operator on Criteria row		
Compound Criterion Involving AND, Use	AC 91				Place criteria on same line

Microsoft Office 2013 Access Comprehensive Quick Reference *(continued)*

Task	Page Number	Ribbon	Other On-Screen Areas	Shortcut Menu	Keyboard Shortcut
Compound Criterion Involving OR, USE	AC 92				Place criteria on separate lines
Conditional Value, Assign	AC 384	Text Box tool (REPORT DESIGN TOOLS DESIGN tab | Controls group), select text box, click Property Sheet button (REPORT DESIGN TOOLS DESIGN tab | Tools group), tap or click Control Source property, tap or click Build button, assign condition using Expression Builder dialog box			
Control for a Field, Add to Form Design	AC 284		Drag field from field list to form		
Control Margins, Change in Layout	AC 519	Select any cell, Select Layout button (FORM LAYOUT TOOLS ARRANGE tab | Rows & Columns group), Control Margins button, select desired margin setting			
Control Padding, Change in Layout	AC 519	Select layout, Control Padding button (FORM LAYOUT TOOLS ARRANGE tab | Position group), select desired padding setting			
Control, Change Format	AC 238	Select control, FORM LAYOUT TOOLS tab, select formatting option from Font group			
Control, Move	AC 239		Point to control, drag with four-headed mouse pointer		
Controls, Align	AC 286-287		Select controls, Align button (FORM DESIGN TOOLS ARRANGE tab | Sizing & Ordering group), select alignment style	Press and hold or right-click controls, tap or click Align	
Controls, Anchor	AC 521	Select controls to anchor, Anchoring button (FORM LAYOUT TOOLS ARRANGE tab | Position group), select desired option			
Controls, Conditionally Format	AC 215	Conditional Formatting button (REPORT LAYOUT TOOLS FORMAT tab | Control Formatting group), Conditional Formatting Rules Manager dialog box, specify rule			
Controls, Move in Control Layout	AC 240		Select labels and controls for fields, drag to desired location		
Controls, Place in Control Layout	AC 236	Open form in Layout view, FORM LAYOUT TOOLS ARRANGE tab, select form controls, select control style from Table group			

Microsoft Office 2013 Access Comprehensive Quick Reference *(continued)*

Task	Page Number	Ribbon	Other On-Screen Areas	Shortcut Menu	Keyboard Shortcut
Convert Earlier Access Database to Access 2013	AC 543		With database to be converted open, tap or click FILE for backstage view, Save As tab, select Save Database As command, tap or click Access Database		
Criteria, Use in Calculating Statistics	AC 117	Totals button (QUERY TOOLS DESIGN tab | Show/Hide group), Total arrow, tap or click calculation			
Criterion, Use in a Query	AC 43		In Design View, tap or click Criteria row, enter criterion		
Crosstab Query, Create	AC 119	Query Wizard button (CREATE tab | Queries group), Crosstab Query Wizard			
Custom Categories and Groups, Create	AC 549			Press and hold or right-click Navigation Pane title bar, Navigation Options command, Add Item button, specify category and group names, OK button	
Custom Input Mask, Create	AC 557		In Design view, select field for mask, select Input Mask property, enter mask		
Custom Properties, Create	AC 554		In Backstage view, select Info tab, tap or click 'View and edit database properties'		
Data Macro, Create	AC 510	TABLE TOOLS TABLE tab, Before Change button, enter macro code			
Data Parts, Create	AC 563	Select fields to include, tap or click More Fields button (TABLE TOOLS FIELDS tab | Add & Delete group), tap or click 'Save Selection as New Data Type'			
Data, Enter in Attachment Field	AC 280			Press and hold or right-click field for attachment, Manage Attachments command, Add button	
Data, Enter in Hyperlink Field	AC 282			Press and hold or right-click hyperlink field, Hyperlink command, Edit Hyperlink command, enter web address	

Microsoft Office 2013 Access Comprehensive Quick Reference *(continued)*

Task	Page Number	Ribbon	Other On-Screen Areas	Shortcut Menu	Keyboard Shortcut
Data, Enter in Long Text Fields	AC 269		In Datasheet view, select field, type data		
Data, Enter in OLE Object Field	AC 278			Press and hold or right-click object field, Insert Object command, navigate to file to insert	
Data, Enter in Yes/No fields	AC 275		In Datasheet view, enter check in check box to indicate Yes value		
Data, Enter Using an Input Mask	AC 274		In Datasheet view, type data into field		
Data, Export to Excel	AC 107	Excel button (EXTERNAL DATA tab | Export group)		Press and hold or right-click object in Navigation Pane, tap or click Export	
Data, Import	AC 33	Button for imported data format (EXTERNAL DATA tab | Import & Link group)			
Data, Sort in Query	AC 94	Select field in design grid, tap or click Sort row, tap or click Sort arrow, select order			
Database Documenter, Use	AC 548	Database Documenter button (DATABASE TOOLS tab | Analyze group)			
Database Properties, Change	AC 55	View and edit database properties link (FILE tab | Info tab)			
Database, Convert to Earlier Version of Access	AC 543		With database to be converted open, tap or click FILE for Backstage view, Save As tab, select desired format, with Save Database As selected, tap or click Save As button		
Database, Create	AC 6	Blank desktop database thumbnail (FILE tab | New tab)			
Database, Create using Template	AC 7		FILE tab, New tab, select template		
Datasheet Forms, Create	AC 504, AC 573	More Forms button (CREATE tab | Forms group), tap or click Datasheet			
Date, Add	AC 237	In form, 'Date and Time' button (FORM LAYOUT TOOLS DESIGN tab | Header/Footer group), select date format, OK button			

Microsoft Office 2013 Access Comprehensive Quick Reference *(continued)*

Task	Page Number	Ribbon	Other On-Screen Areas	Shortcut Menu	Keyboard Shortcut
Decrypt a Database	AC 58?		Open database in exclusive mode, open Backstage view, select Info tab, tap or click Decrypt Database		
Default Value, Specify	AC 164		In Design view, select field in upper pane, enter value in Default Value property box in Field Properties pane		
Delete Object	AC 58			Delete	
Delete Query, Use	AC 161		Create query, Delete button (QUERY TOOLS DESIGN tab | Results group)	Press and hold or right-click any open area in upper pane, point to Query Type, tap or click Delete Query	
Design Grid, Clear	AC 93		In Design view, select all columns, tap or click DELETE		
Desktop Database, Create	AC 566		In Backstage view, tap or click New tab, 'Blank desktop database' button, enter name for database, Browse button, navigate to storage location, OK button		
Duplicate Records, Find	AC 187	Query Wizard button (CREATE tab | Queries group), 'Find Duplicates Query Wizard'			
Duplicates, Omit	AC 94	In Design view, Property Sheet button (QUERY TOOLS DESIGN tab | Show/Hide group), tap or click Unique Values property, tap or click Yes			
Encrypt a Database with Password	AC 584		In Backstage view, select Info tab, tap or click 'Encrypt with Password' button		
Error Checking, Enable	AC 561		In Backstage view, tap or click Options tab, tap or click Object Designers, select 'Enable error checking' check box		
Exit Access	AC 24		Close button on right side of title bar		
Field Contents, Change	AC 168		In Datasheet view, tap or click in field, enter data		
Field in Query, Add to Design Grid	AC 79		Double-click or double-tap field in field list		
Field List, Move	AC 288		Drag field list title bar		
Field, Add New	AC 154	In Design view, Insert Rows button (TABLE TOOLS DESIGN tab | Tools group)			Design View, INSERT
Field, Add to Form	AC 241	'Add Existing Fields' button (FORM LAYOUT TOOLS DESIGN tab | Tools group), drag fields from field list to form			
Field, Delete	AC 158		In Design view, tap or click row selector for field, DELETE		

Microsoft Office 2013 Access Comprehensive Quick Reference *(continued)*

Task	Page Number	Ribbon	Other On-Screen Areas	Shortcut Menu	Keyboard Shortcut
Field, Move	AC 154		In Design view, tap or click row selector for field to move, drag to new position		
Filter and Sort in Form	AC 243	Advanced button (HOME tab | Sort & Filter group), add field names to design grid, select sort order and specify criteria in design grid, Toggle Filter button			
Filter By Form, Use	AC 150	Advanced button (HOME tab | Sort & Filter group), 'Clear All Filters', Advanced button, 'Filter By Form'			
Filter By Selection, Use	AC 157	Selection button (HOME tab | Sort & Filter group), select criterion			
Filter, Clear	AC 148	Advanced button (HOME tab | Sort & Filter group), 'Clear All Filters'			
Filter, Toggle	AC 148	Toggle Filter button (HOME tab | Sort & Filter group)			
Form Fill/Back Color, Change	AC 290			Press and hold or right-click form, 'Fill/Back Color' arrow, select color	
Form for Query, Create	AC 105	Select query, Form button (CREATE tab | Forms group)			
Form Header and Footer, Insert	AC 427		In Design view, press and hold or right-click in form, Form Header/Footer command		
Form Header and Footer, Remove	AC 426		In Design view, press and hold or right-click in form, Form Header/Footer command		
Form Header Section, Add Section and Add Title	AC 424		Tap or click Title button (FORM DESIGN TOOLS DESIGN tab | Header/Footer group)		
Form Label Text, Change	AC 298		In Design view, tap or click label twice to produce insertion point, edit text		
Form Title, Modify Appearance	AC 302	In Design view, select control, Property Sheet button (FORM DESIGN TOOLS DESIGN tab | Tools group)			
Form with a Datasheet, Create in Layout view	AC 314	Blank Form button (CREATE tab | Forms group), display field list, tap or click Show all tables, expand "one" table and drag fields to desired locations, expand "many" table and drag first field onto form, drag remaining fields			
Form, Create	AC 45	Form button (CREATE tab | Forms group)			
Form, Create in Design View	AC 305, AC 414	Select table, Form Design button (CREATE tab | Forms group)			

Microsoft Office 2013 Access Comprehensive Quick Reference *(continued)*

Task	Page Number	Ribbon	Other On-Screen Areas	Shortcut Menu	Keyboard Shortcut
Form, Create using Form Wizard	AC 233	Select table, Form Wizard button (CREATE tab | Forms group)			
Form, Use	AC 283, AC 456		Open Form in Form view, scroll forms using navigation buttons		
Form, View in Form View	AC 295	View button (HOME tab | Views group)			
Format Painter, Use	AC 422	Select format to copy, Format Painter button (FORM DESIGN TOOLS FORMAT tab | Font group), tap or click object to format			
Format, Specify	AC 165		In Design view, select field, tap or click Format property box in field grid, enter format		
Gridlines, Change in Datasheet	AC 176	Gridlines button (HOME tab | Text Formatting group)			
Group and Sort in Report	AC 208	Open report in Layout view, Group & Sort button (REPORT LAYOUT TOOLS DESIGN tab | Grouping and Totals group), 'Add a group' or 'Add a sort' button			
Group, Sort and Total Pane, Remove	AC 214	Group & Sort button (REPORT LAYOUT TOOLS DESIGN tab | Grouping & Totals group)	'Close Grouping Dialog Box' button		
Grouping, Use	AC 118		Create query, select Group By in Total row, select field to group by		
Image, Add to Form	AC 427	Insert Image button (FORM DESIGN TOOLS DESIGN tab | Controls group), Browse command, select image to add			
Image, Use as Form Background	AC 427	Background Image button (FORM DESIGN TOOLS FORMAT tab | Background group), Browse command, select image to add			
Input Mask Wizard, Use	AC 270		In Design view, tap or click Input Mask property box in Field Properties pane, Build button, select desired mask		
Items, Add to Groups	AC 551		Navigation Pane arrow, tap or click category, press and hold or right-click object, point to 'Add to Group,' select desired group		
Join Properties, Change	AC 101			In Design view, press and hold or right-click join line, click Join Properties	
Labels, Create	AC 245	Labels button (CREATE tab | Reports group)			

Microsoft Office 2013 Access Comprehensive Quick Reference *(continued)*

Task	Page Number	Ribbon	Other On-Screen Areas	Shortcut Menu	Keyboard Shortcut
Layout, Create	AC 514	Select all controls to include in layout, FORM LAYOUT TOOLS ARRANGE tab, Stacked button or Tabular button			
Layout, Delete Column	AC 516	Select column, Select Column button (FORM LAYOUT TOOLS ARRANGE tab | Rows & Columns group), DELETE key			
Layout, Delete Row	AC 516	Select row (FORM LAYOUT TOOLS ARRANGE tab | Rows & Columns group), Select Row button, DELETE key			
Layout, Insert Column	AC 516	Select column (FORM LAYOUT TOOLS ARRANGE tab | Rows & Columns group), Select Column button, tap or click Insert Left or Insert Right button			
Layout, Insert Row	AC 515	Select row (FORM LAYOUT TOOLS ARRANGE tab | Rows & Columns group), Select Row button, tap or click Insert Above or Insert Below button			
Layout, Merge Cells	AC 517	Select cells to merge, Merge button (FORM LAYOUT TOOLS ARRANGE tab | Merge/Split group)			
Layout, Move	AC 521	Select any cell in layout, Select Layout button (FORM LAYOUT TOOLS ARRANGE tab | Rows & Columns group), drag layout to new position			
Layout, Remove	AC 514		Press and hold or right-click control in layout, point to Layout, tap or click Remove Layout		
Layout, Split	AC 520	Select cells to move to new layout, Stacked button (FORM LAYOUT TOOLS ARRANGE tab | Table group)			
Layout, Split Cell	AC 517	Select cell, Split Vertically button (FORM LAYOUT TOOLS ARRANGE tab | Merge/Split group) or Split Horizontally button (FORM LAYOUT TOOLS ARRANGE tab | Merge/Split group)			
Lock Database	AC 587		With database to lock open, tap or click FILE tab to switch to Backstage view, tap or click Save As tab, tap or click Make ACCDE, tap or click Save As button		
Lookup Field, Create	AC 154		In Design view, select Data Type column for field, Data Type arrow, Lookup Wizard		
Macro, Add Action	AC 480		Double-tap or double-click Submacro element in Action Catalog, enter actions in Macro Builder		
Macro, Create	AC 478	Macro button (CREATE tab | Macros & Code group), Action Catalog button			

Microsoft Office 2013 Access Comprehensive Quick Reference *(continued)*

Task	Page Number	Ribbon	Other On-Screen Areas	Shortcut Menu	Keyboard Shortcut
Make-Table Query, Use	AC 162	Create query, Make Table button (QUERY TOOLS DESIGN tab | Query Type group)			
Menu Form with Command Buttons, Create	AC 488	Form Design button (CREATE tab | Forms group), remove field list and property sheet if necessary, with 'Use Control Wizards' button selected, tap or click Button tool (FORM DESIGN TOOLS DESIGN tab | Controls group), tap or click form to display Command Button Wizard dialog box			
Menu Form with Option Group, Create	AC 492	Form Design button (CREATE tab | Forms group), remove field list and property sheet if necessary, with 'Use Control Wizards' button selected, tap or click Option Group tool (FORM DESIGN TOOLS DESIGN tab | Controls group), tap or click form to display Option Group Wizard dialog box			
Multipage Form, Create Using Tab Controls	AC 447		Tab Control tool (FORM DESIGN TOOLS DESIGN tab | Controls group), place tab control on form		
Multiple Keys, Sort on	AC 96		Assign two sort keys in design grid		
Multiple Table Form Based on Many Table, Create	AC 315	Blank Form button (CREATE tab | Forms group), 'Add Existing Fields' button			
Multiple-Field Index, Create	AC 560		Indexes button (TABLE TOOLS DESIGN tab | Show/ Hide group), click blank row in Indexes: (*Table*) window		
Multitable Report, Create	AC 222	Select table, Report Wizard button (CREATE tab | Reports group), add fields for first table in Report Wizard, select second table, add fields for second table			
Multivalued Field, Query Showing Multiple Values on a Single Row	AC 179		Create query with specified fields		
Multivalued Lookup Field, Use	AC 170		In Datasheet view, tap or click field, tap or click check boxes, OK		
Navigation Form, Create	AC 506, AC 575	Navigation button (CREATE tab | Forms group), tap or click Horizontal Tabs			
Navigation Pane, Customize	AC 122		Navigation Pane arrow		

Microsoft Office 2013 Access Comprehensive Quick Reference *(continued)*

Task	Page Number	Ribbon	Other On-Screen Areas	Shortcut Menu	Keyboard Shortcut
Number Criterion, Use	AC 89		Create query, select table, enter number as criterion in field grid		
Object Dependencies, View	AC 308	Select table, Object Dependencies button (DATABASE TOOLS tab | Relationships group), 'Objects that depend on me' option button			
Objects, Display in Overlapping Windows	AC 522		In Backstage view, Options, Current Database, Overlapping Windows option button		
Objects, Display in Tabbed Documents	AC 523		In Backstage view, Options, Current Database, Tabbed Documents option button		
Open Database	AC 25	Open button (FILE tab)			
Open Table	AC 21		Double-click or double-tap table in Navigation Pane	Press and hold or right-click table in Navigation Pane, tap or click Open	
Page Header and Footer, Insert	AC 427		In Design view, press and hold or right-click open area of form, Page Header/Footer command		
Page Header and Footer, Remove	AC 426		In Design view, press and hold or right-click open area of form, Page Header/Footer command		
Parameter Query, Create	AC 87		In Design view, type parameter in square brackets in criterion row of field grid, Run button (QUERY TOOLS DESIGN tab | Results group)		
Parameter Query, Use	AC 87			Right-click or press and hold query in Navigation Pane, tap or click Open	
Performance Analyzer, Use	AC 546	Analyze Performance button (DATABASE TOOLs tab | Analyze group)			
Preview or Print Object	AC 30	Print or Print Preview button (FILE tab | Print tab)			CTRL+P, ENTER
Primary Key, Modify	AC 11	Select field, Data Type arrow (TABLE TOOLS FIELDS tab | Formatting group), select data type			
Query, Create in Design View	AC 78	Query Design button (CREATE tab | Queries group)			

Microsoft Office 2013 Access Comprehensive Quick Reference *(continued)*					
Task	**Page Number**	**Ribbon**	**Other On-Screen Areas**	**Shortcut Menu**	**Keyboard Shortcut**
Query, Create using Simple Query Wizard	AC 40	Query Wizard button (CREATE tab | Queries group)			
Query, Export	AC 107		Select query in Navigation Pane, application button (EXTERNAL DATA tab | Export group)	Press and hold or right-click query in Navigation Pane, Export	
Range, Specify	AC 164		In Design view, select field, enter rule in Validation Rule property box in Field Properties pane		
Record, Add using a Form	AC 143	New button (HOME tab | Records Group)	'New (blank) record' button in Navigation buttons	Open, tap or click in field	CTRL+PLUS SIGN (+)
Record, Delete	AC 145	Delete arrow (HOME tab | Records group), Delete Record	In Datasheet view, tap or click record selector, DELETE		DELETE
Record, Search for	AC 143	Find button (HOME tab | Find group)			CTRL+F
Record, Update	AC 143		In Form view, change desired data		In Datasheet, select field and edit
Records in a Join, Restrict	AC 111		In Design view, enter criterion for query		
Records, Filter in Report	AC 218	Selection button (HOME tab | Sort & Filter group)		Right-click field, select filter	
Rectangle, Place on Form	AC 432		More button (FORM DESIGN TOOLS DESIGN tab | Controls group), Rectangle tool, drag on form		
Referential Integrity, Specify	AC 182	Relationships button (DATABASE TOOLS tab | Relationships group)			
Rename Object	AC 58			Press and hold or right-click object in Navigation Pane, Rename, enter new name, press ENTER	
Report Column Headings, Modify	AC 50			Press and hold or right-click field name, Rename Field	
Report Filter, Clear	AC 219		Advanced button (HOME tab | Sort & Filter group), 'Clear All Filters' command on Advanced menu	Press and hold or right-click field, clear filter from menu option	
Report Margins, Change	AC 390	Margins button (REPORT DESIGN TOOLS PAGE SETUP tab | Page Size group)			

Microsoft Office 2013 Access Comprehensive Quick Reference *(continued)*

Task	Page Number	Ribbon	Other On-Screen Areas	Shortcut Menu	Keyboard Shortcut
Report, Add a Date	AC 368	'Date and Time' button (REPORT DESIGN TOOLS DESIGN tab | Header/Footer group)			
Report, Add a Group	AC 344	Group & Sort button (REPORT DESIGN TOOLS DESIGN tab | Grouping & Totals group), 'Add a Group' button			
Report, Add a Page Number	AC 368	Page Numbers button (REPORT DESIGN TOOLS DESIGN tab | Header/Footer group)			
Report, Add a Sort	AC 345	Group & Sort button (REPORT DESIGN TOOLS DESIGN tab | Grouping & Totals group), 'Add a Sort' button			
Report, Add a Subreport	AC 349	More button (REPORT DESIGN TOOLS DESIGN tab | Controls group), Subform/Subreport tool			
Report, Add a Text Box	AC 384	Text Box tool (REPORT DESIGN TOOLS DESIGN tab | Controls group)			
Report, Add a Title	AC 368	Title button (REPORT DESIGN TOOLS DESIGN tab | Header/Footer group)			
Report, Add Fields	AC 346, AC 374, AC 376	'Add Existing Fields' button (REPORT DESIGN TOOLS DESIGN tab |Tools group)			
Report, Add Totals or Subtotals	AC 53, AC 211, AC 378	Select control, Group & Sort button or Totals button (REPORT DESIGN TOOLS DESIGN tab | Grouping & Totals group), Sum command			
Report, Create	AC 48	Report button (CREATE tab | Reports group)			
Report, Create in Design View	AC 343	Report Design button (CREATE tab | Reports group)			
Report, Create in Layout View by Creating a Blank Report	AC 229	Blank Report button (CREATE tab | Reports group)			
Report, Group Controls	AC 354	Select controls, Size/Space button (REPORT DESIGN TOOLS ARRANGE tab | Sizing & Ordering group), click Group			
Report, Publish	AC 372	PDF or XPS button (EXTERNAL DATA tab | Export group)			
Required Field, Specify	AC 163		In Design view, select field, Required property box in Field Properties pane, down arrow, Yes		
Row and Column Size, Change	AC 276		In Datasheet view, drag field selector edge		
Rows, Move using Move Buttons	AC 581	Select cell in row to move, Select Row button (FORM LAYOUT TOOLS ARRANGE tab | Rows & Columns group), Move Up or Move Down buttons			

Microsoft Office 2013 Access Comprehensive Quick Reference *(continued)*

Task	Page Number	Ribbon	Other On-Screen Areas	Shortcut Menu	Keyboard Shortcut
Run Access	AC 5		Access 2013 tile on Windows Start screen or display Charms bar, tap or click Search charm, type Access, tap or click Access 2013		
Save Object	AC 16	FILE tab, Save	Save button on Quick Access Toolbar		CTRL+S
Save Object As	AC 45	FILE tab, Save As tab, 'Save Object As', Save As button			
Simple Form with a Datasheet, Create	AC 312		Select "one" table, Form button (CREATE tab | Forms group)		
Single-Field Index, Create	AC 559		In Design view, select field, change Indexed field property to Yes		
Size Mode, Change	AC 299		Select control, Property Sheet button (FORM DESIGN TOOLS DESIGN tab | Tools group), Size Mode property		
Split a Database	AC 590	With database to split open, tap or click Access Database button (DATABASE TOOLS tab | Move Data group), tap or click Split Database button			
Split Form, Create	AC 141	Select table in Navigation Pane, More Forms button (CREATE tab | Forms group), Split Form button			
Startup Form, Select	AC 576		In Backstage view, tap or click Options tab, Current Database, Display Form arrow, Main Menu		
Statistics, Calculate	AC 115	Create query, Totals button (QUERY TOOLS DESIGN tab | Show/Hide group), tap or click Total row, tap or click Total arrow, select calculation			
Subdatasheet, Use	AC 185		In Datasheet view, plus sign in front of row		
Subform, Add	AC 292, AC 448	More button (FORM DESIGN TOOLS DESIGN Tab | Controls group), Subform/Subreport tool, tap or click in form to launch SubForm Wizard			
Subform, Resize	AC 450		Drag subform sizing handles		
Summary Report, Create	AC 232	Open report in Layout view, Hide Details button (REPORT LAYOUT TOOLS DESIGN tab | Grouping & Totals group)			
Summary View, Create in Web Apps	AC 607		Select table, 'Add New View' button		

Microsoft Office 2013 Access Comprehensive Quick Reference *(continued)*

Task	Page Number	Ribbon	Other On-Screen Areas	Shortcut Menu	Keyboard Shortcut
Tab Stop, Change	AC 304		In Design view, select control, Property Sheet button Property Sheet button (FORM DESIGN TOOLS DESIGN tab | Tools group), on All tab, change Tab Stop property to No		
Table Analyzer, Use	AC 544		Analyze Table button (DATABASE TOOLS tab | Analyze group)		
Table, Create by Importing Data	AC 593		Select icon for type of data to import, select file to import, tap or click OK button, select tables to import, tap or click OK button		
Table, Create from Template	AC 593		Enter type of data that will be stored, tap or click Search button, select template from search results		
Table, Modify in Design View	AC 37	Table Design button (CREATE tab | Tables group)			
Table, View in Design View	AC 17	View arrow (TABLE TOOLS FIELDS tab | Views group), Design View	Design View button on status bar		
Tables, Join	AC 100	Query Design button (CREATE tab | Queries group), add field lists for tables to join, add desired fields to design grid, run query			
Template and Application Part, Create	AC 578		In Backstage view, tap or click Save As tab, tap or click Template button, tap or click Save As button		
Template, Use	AC 579		In Backstage view, select New tab, tap or click PERSONAL link, tap or click template from which to create database, enter name for new database, tap or click Create button		
Text Box, Use with Concatenation	AC 446		Tap or click in text box, type = (equal sign), enter formula for concatenation		
Text Data Criterion, Use	AC 81		Create query, select table, enter text as criterion in field grid		
Theme, Assign to a Single Object	AC 232	Open object in Layout view, Themes button (REPORT LAYOUT TOOLS DESIGN tab | Themes group), right-click theme in Theme picker, 'Apply Theme to This Object Only' command			

Microsoft Office 2013 Access Comprehensive Quick Reference *(continued)*

Task	Page Number	Ribbon	Other On-Screen Areas	Shortcut Menu	Keyboard Shortcut
Theme, Assign to All Objects	AC 231	Open object in Layout view, Themes button (REPORT LAYOUT TOOLS DESIGN tab | Themes group), select theme from Theme picker			
Title, Add to a Form	AC 291	Title button (FORM DESIGN TOOLS DESIGN tab | Header/Footer group)			
Top-Values Query, Create	AC 98	In Design view, Return arrow (QUERY TOOLS DESIGN tab | Query Setup group)			
Totals or Subtotals, Add to Report	AC 53, AC 211, AC 378	Select control, Group & Sort button or Totals button (REPORT DESIGN TOOLS DESIGN tab | Grouping & Totals group), Sum command		Press and hold or right-click column header, tap or click Total	
Totals, Include in a Datasheet	AC 175	In Datasheet view, Totals button (HOME tab | Records group), tap or click Total row, tap or click arrow			
Totals, Remove from a Datasheet	AC 176	Totals button (HOME tab | Records group)			
Unmatched Records, Find	AC 187	Query Wizard button (CREATE tab | Queries group), 'Find Unmatched Query Wizard'			
Update Data using Web App	AC 603		With app running, select table to update, select desired view, tap or click Add button, enter data for record, tap or click Save button		
Update Query, Use	AC 160	Create query, Update button (QUERY TOOLS DESIGN tab | Query Type group), select field, click Update To row, enter new value, run query		Press and hold or right-click any open area in upper pane, point to Query Type, tap or click Update Query	
User Interface Macros, Create	AC 504		Select object, display property sheet, Event tab, On Click event, Build button, OK button, add SetTempVar action to macro, enter Name and Expression argument values		
Validation Rule for Table, Create	AC 553		In Design view, tap or click Property Sheet button (TABLE TOOLS DESIGN tab | Show/Hide group), tap or click Validation Rule property, enter rule		
View Data in Web Apps	AC 597		Select table, tap or click Settings/Action button, tap or click View Data		

Microsoft Office 2013 Access Comprehensive Quick Reference *(continued)*

Task	Page Number	Ribbon	Other On-Screen Areas	Shortcut Menu	Keyboard Shortcut
Views, Edit in Web Apps	AC 596		Select table, select view to edit, tap or click Edit button		
Web App, Create	AC 591		In Backstage view, click 'Custom web app,' enter app name, select a storage location, tap or click Create button		
Web App, Customize	AC 604	Tap or click Settings button, tap or click 'Customize in Access' command			
Web App, Run from Access	AC 601	With app open, click Launch App button (HOME tab | View group)			
Wildcard, Use	AC 83		In Design view, tap or click Criteria row in design grid, type wildcard and text		
Zero Length, Allow	AC 557		Select field, tap or click Zero Length property, change Allow Zero Length field property value to yes		